Year	Price Level			Population (millions)	Labor Force* (millions)	Civilian Unemployment Rate (percent)	Money Supply M1 M2 (in December) (billions of dollars)		Interest Rates Treasury Corporate Bills Bonds† (percent)		Exchange Value of U.S. Dollar (March 1973=100)	Federal Budget Surplus(+) or Deficit(-) (billions of dollars)
	GNP Deflator (1982=100)	Consumer Price Index (1967=100)	Real Average Hourly Earnings (1977=100)				M1	M2	Bills	Bonds†		
1929	14.6	51.3	—	121.9	49.2	3.2	—	—	—	4.73	—	+1.2
1933	11.2	38.8	—	125.7	51.6	24.9	—	—	0.52	4.49	—	−1.3
1939	12.7	41.6	—	131.0	55.2	17.2	—	—	0.02	3.01	—	−2.2
1945	15.7	53.9	—	139.9	53.9	1.9	—	—	0.38	2.62	—	−42.1
1950	23.9	72.1	64.0	151.7	62.2	5.3	—	—	1.22	2.62	—	+9.2
1955	27.2	80.2	73.3	165.3	65.0	4.4	—	—	1.75	3.06	—	+4.4
1956	28.1	81.4	75.9	168.2	66.5	4.1	—	—	2.66	3.36	—	+6.1
1957	29.1	84.3	76.9	171.3	66.9	4.3	—	—	3.27	3.89	—	+2.3
1958	29.7	86.6	78.0	174.1	67.6	6.8	—	—	1.84	3.79	—	−10.3
1959	30.4	87.3	80.0	177.1	68.4	5.5	141.0	297.8	3.41	4.38	—	−1.1
1960	30.9	88.7	81.4	180.8	69.6	5.5	141.8	312.3	2.93	4.41	—	+3.0
1961	31.2	89.6	83.0	183.7	70.5	6.7	146.5	335.5	2.38	4.35	—	−3.9
1962	31.9	90.6	85.0	186.6	70.6	5.5	149.2	362.7	2.78	4.33	—	−4.2
1963	32.4	91.7	86.3	189.3	71.8	5.7	154.7	393.2	3.16	4.26	—	+0.3
1964	32.9	92.9	87.5	191.9	73.1	5.2	161.9	424.8	3.55	4.40	—	−3.3
1965	33.8	94.5	89.0	194.3	74.4	4.5	169.5	459.4	3.95	4.49	—	+0.5
1966	35.0	97.2	90.3	196.6	75.7	3.8	173.7	480.0	4.88	5.13	—	−1.8
1967	35.9	100.0	92.2	198.7	77.3	3.8	185.1	524.3	4.32	5.51	120.0	−13.2
1968	37.7	104.2	94.0	200.7	78.7	3.6	199.4	566.3	5.34	6.18	122.1	−6.0
1969	39.8	109.8	95.0	202.7	80.7	3.5	205.8	589.5	6.68	7.03	122.4	+8.4
1970	42.0	116.3	95.7	205.1	82.8	4.9	216.6	628.2	6.46	8.04	121.1	−12.4
1971	44.4	121.3	98.3	207.7	84.4	5.9	230.8	712.7	4.35	7.39	117.8	−22.0
1972	46.5	125.3	101.2	209.9	87.0	5.6	252.0	805.1	4.07	7.21	109.1	−16.8
1973	49.5	133.1	101.1	211.9	89.4	4.9	265.9	861.0	7.04	7.44	99.1	−5.6
1974	54.0	147.7	98.3	213.9	92.0	5.6	277.5	908.5	7.89	8.57	101.4	−11.6
1975	59.3	161.2	97.6	216.0	93.8	8.5	291.1	1023.2	5.84	8.83	98.5	−69.4
1976	63.1	170.5	99.0	218.1	96.2	7.7	310.4	1163.7	4.99	8.43	105.6	−53.5
1977	67.3	181.5	100.0	220.3	99.0	7.1	335.3	1286.8	5.27	8.02	103.3	−46.0
1978	72.2	195.4	100.5	222.6	102.2	6.1	363.0	1389.2	7.22	8.73	92.4	−29.3
1979	78.6	217.4	97.4	225.1	105.0	5.8	391.1	1500.3	10.04	9.63	88.1	−16.1
1980	85.7	246.8	93.5	227.8	107.0	7.1	416.6	1633.1	11.51	11.94	87.4	−61.3
1981	94.0	272.4	92.6	230.2	109.0	7.6	443.2	1795.5	14.03	14.17	102.9	−63.8
1982	100.0	289.1	93.4	232.5	110.2	9.7	481.3	1953.8	10.69	13.79	116.6	−145.9
1983	103.9	298.4	94.9	234.8	111.6	9.6	526.9	2184.6	8.63	12.04	125.3	−176.0
1984	107.7	311.1	94.6	237.1	113.5	7.5	557.5	2369.1	9.58	12.71	138.3	−169.6
1985	111.2	322.2	94.1	239.3	115.5	7.2	627.0	2569.6	7.48	11.37	143.2	−196.0
1986	114.1	328.4	95.0	241.6	117.8	7.0	730.5	2798.4	5.98	9.02	112.0	−204.7

* Counts persons 14 years and older 1929–1946, 16 years and older 1947–present.
† Moody's Aaa rating.
a Multilateral trade-weighted average. Federal Reserve series.

ECONOMICS
PRINCIPLES AND POLICY
FOURTH EDITION

WILLIAM J. BAUMOL

New York University
and
Princeton University

ALAN S. BLINDER

Princeton University

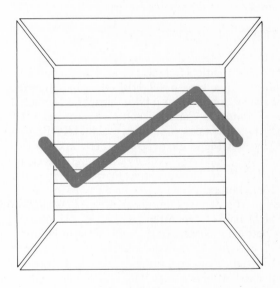

Harcourt Brace Jovanovich, Publishers
and its subsidiary, Academic Press

San Diego   New York   Chicago   Austin   Washington, D.C.
London   Sydney   Tokyo   Toronto

To my four children,
Ellen, Daniel,
and now Sabrina and Jim
W.J.B.

For Scott, now of age to read this book,
and William, who prefers Garfield
A.S.B.

ISBN: 0-15-518851-8

Library of Congress Catalog Card Number: 87–81151

Printed in the United States of America

ILLUSTRATION CREDITS

Page 12: © 1971, General Drafting Co.; Gousha-Chek Chart; p. 14: London School of Economics and Political Science; p. 47: National Portrait Gallery, London; p. 51: The Bettmann Archive, Inc.; p. 69: HBJ Photo; p. 84: Reproduced from the collections of the Library of Congress; p. 87: UPI/Bettmann Newsphotos; p. 101: From *The Wall Street Journal*—Permission, Cartoon Features Syndicate; p. 110: Camera Press-Photo Trends; p. 178: British Information Service; p. 240: UPI/Bettmann Newsphotos; p. 242: Drawing by Alex Mendoza; p. 252: By permission of Johnny Hart and Creators Syndicate, Inc.; p. 253: University Museum, University of Pennsylvania; p. 313: HBJ photo; p. 337: From *The Wall Street Journal*—Permission, Cartoon Features Syndicate; p. 340: HBJ photo; p. 387: Culver Pictures; p. 393: George H. Harrison from Grant Heilman; p. 397: Zephyr Pictures; p. 401: AP/Wide World; p. 402: Culver Pictures; p. 413: McDonald's Corporation; p. 452: © 1987 Peter Menzel/Stock, Boston; p. 454: Reuters/Bettmann Newsphotos; p. 467: Harvard University; p. 494: Du Pont Company; p. 520: Photothyne, Canadian National Film Board; p. 585: Krokodil/Sovfoto; p. 628: Douglas Aircraft Company; p. 647: © Bryce Flynn/Stock, Boston; p. 671: Courtesy of San Francisco Forty-Niners; p. 685: UPI/Bettmann Newsphotos; p. 693: Photo: © Houston Chronicle; p. 696: Courtesy of Union Electric Company; p. 700: Courtesy of AT&T Phone Service; p. 730: AP/Wide World; p. 736: UPI/Bettmann Newsphotos; p. 739: THE FAR SIDE, © 1985, Universal Press Syndicate, reprinted with permission. All rights reserved.; p. 754: Courtesy of John Palmisano, President, AER*X Division of RMT; p. 764: UPI/Bettmann Newsphotos; p. 795: © Bob Englehart. The Hartford Courant.; p. 807: UPI/Bettmann Newsphotos; p. 813: UPI/Bettmann Newsphotos; p. 826: Public Information Office, NY Urban Development Corp.; p. 842: UPI/Bettmann Newsphotos; p. 862: United Nations; p. 873: UPI/Bettmann Newsphotos; p. 888: UPI/Bettmann Newsphotos; p. 901: Sovfoto; p. 914: UPI/Bettmann Newsphotos; p. 915: UPI/Bettmann Newsphotos.

Preface

For decades, the "principles of economics" book has been expected to codify the entire discipline of economics. In recent years, this has become at once more difficult and more imperative. The explosion of economic knowledge has made it impossible to put all of economics between two covers. But at the same time, more and more public policy issues either are basically economic in nature or involve important economic considerations. Intelligent citizens can no longer afford to be innocent of economics.

The preparation of this Fourth Edition continued to be guided by this dilemma. We have studiously avoided the encyclopedic approach and abandoned the fiction, so popular among textbook writers, that literally everything is of the utmost importance. Since students are sufficiently intelligent to see through this ruse in any event, we have tried to highlight those important ideas that are likely to be of lasting significance—principles that you will want to remember long after the course is over because they offer insights that are far from obvious, because they are of practical importance, and because they are widely misunderstood by intelligent laymen. A dozen of the most important of these ideas have been selected as **12 Ideas for Beyond the Final Exam** and are called to your attention when they occur through the use of the book's logo.

All modern economics textbooks abound with "real world" examples, but we have tried to go beyond this, to elevate the examples to preeminence. For in our view, the policy issue or everyday economic problem ought to lead the student naturally to the economic principle, not the other way around. For this reason, many chapters start with a real policy issue or a practical problem that may seem puzzling or paradoxical to noneconomists, and then proceed to describe the economic analysis required to remove the mystery. In doing this, we have tried to utilize technical jargon and diagrams only where there is a clear need for them, never for their own sake.

Still, economics is a somewhat technical subject and, except for a few rather light chapters, this is a book for the desk, not for the bed. We have, however, made strenuous efforts to simplify the technical level of the discussion as much as we could without sacrificing content. Fortunately, almost every important idea in economics can be explained in plain English, and this, in general, is how we have tried to explain them. Yet, even while reducing the technical difficulty of the book, we have incorporated some elements of economic analysis that have traditionally been left out of introductory books but that are really too important to omit.

Foremost among these is our extensive treatment of prices and inflation in Parts 2 through 5. For years, textbooks devoted many chapters to unrealistic but simpler economic models in which prices never rose. Ours was the first introductory text to put inflation into the story from the very beginning, rather than as an afterthought—a practice we maintain and expand in the Fourth Edition.

Another example is our treatment of how the market mechanism is able, under ideal circumstances, to allocate society's resources in the most efficient manner possible. Many introductory textbooks, thinking the topic too difficult for beginning students, give little more than some general hints about this important result. We offer a genuine proof and an extensive discussion of precisely what the result does—and does not—imply about the efficiency of real-world market economies.

Changes from the Third Edition

Macroeconomics

The most notable change in the Fourth Edition is the greater "internationalization" of the book, reflected especially in two new chapters and considerable reorganization of Part 4. *Economics: Principles and Policy* now places much more emphasis on the world economy and America's place in it. Recent events necessitate this reorientation. Students simply cannot understand the major economic controversies of the day—over large budget and trade deficits, dramatic swings in exchange rates, and international coordination of economic policy, for example—without a deeper understanding of international economics. Such issues are in the newspapers every day and promise to play a role in the 1988 presidential campaign and beyond.

The decision to emphasize international economics is reflected, most obviously, in the placement of Part 5 ("The United States in the World Economy") early in the book (Chapters 18–20). But the change is much more than cosmetic. While Chapters 18 and 19 are extensive updates and revisions of Chapters 36 and 37 of the Third Edition, Chapter 20 ("Macroeconomics in a World Economy") is entirely new. We think it is by far the most extensive treatment of open-economy macroeconomics to be found in any major principles textbook.

Although open-economy macroeconomics has long been standard fare in Europe and Canada, it has traditionally been considered too difficult for the principles course in the United States. However, we have concluded that the subject is far too important to omit and have therefore prepared an elementary treatment geared to the needs of the contemporary American student. Specifically, we avoid the traditional taxanomic approach by concentrating on the case that is most relevant to the contemporary United States: a large economy with a floating exchange rate and high (but not perfect) capital mobility.

The other new chapter is Chapter 7 on productivity ("Productivity, Progress, and Prosperity"), which represents a complete revision of Chapter 38 of the Third Edition. Not only does it come much earlier in the book, but it now has a much more international and historical flavor; it is intended to help students place our economy in a broader perspective. Finally, references to open-economy aspects of macroeconomics are sprinkled throughout Parts 3 and 4.

To make room for the new Chapter 20, we have consolidated materials that formerly took up six chapters into five (current Chapters 13–17). This required considerable reorganization, a little pruning, and some longer chapters. The ordering of certain topics differs from the Third Edition's but, in many ways, is more logical. For example, everything pertaining to the Keynesian–monetarist controversy now appears in a single chapter (Chapter 15), rather than being scattered over three chapters.

Most of the other macroeconomic chapters will look familiar to users of previous editions, although few paragraphs survived untouched. Some changes are worth noting, however. There is, of course, extensive revision and updating of the materials on Reaganomics and the events of the 1980s, especially in Chapters 5, 11, 12, and 16. Both Chapter 11's explanation of the aggregate supply curve and Chapter 13's explanation of deposit creation have been rewritten, based on helpful suggestions from readers. Chapter 14 has a new section explaining the relationship between bond prices and interest rates, and Chapter 17 has one on Martin Weitzman's "share economy" proposal.

Microeconomics

In microeconomics, the discussion continues to be organized around a central theme that we believe deals with the most significant lessons to be learned in an introductory economics course: what a market system does well, and what it does poorly.

Thus Part 1 introduces the central theme and some of the fundamental ideas of economics (such as scarcity, opportunity cost, markets, and prices). Then Part 6 acquaints students with the central analytical tools of microeconomics and uses them to explain how both consumers (Chapters 21 and 22) and producers (Chapters 23 and 24) make decisions that best serve their own interests. Part 7 examines how these decisions interact in the marketplace and provides an extensive examination of the virtues and vices of free markets. The early chapters of Part 7 (Chapters 25 and 26) extol the remarkable accomplishments of an idealized system of markets, while the later chapters (Chapters 27–29) discuss some of the market system's principal failings. In this way, Part 7 sets the stage for Parts 8 and 9, in which we discuss where, why, and how the government intervenes in the economy.

Much of this material has been rewritten and/or reorganized since the Third Edition, partly in response to many extremely useful suggestions we have had from readers. Difficult points are explained more patiently, and there are more examples and graphs than in the Third Edition. Much in the "core" microeconomic chapters (Chapters 21–24) has been extensively revised. In particular, at the suggestion of a number of commentators, the discussion of the technicalities of the elasticity formula in Chapter 22 has been simplified, and we have introduced the important distinction between fixed and sunk costs in Chapters 23 and 24. A misleading association between scale economies and declining average costs that occurred in the previous edition has also been avoided.

The policy-oriented chapters have been updated to reflect new developments in regulatory (Chapter 31), antitrust (Chapter 32), and environmental (Chapter 34) policy. The tax revision of 1986 is, of course, incorporated into Chapter 33 and elsewhere. Finally, we introduce a new feature: "At the Frontier," offering students a taste of newer areas of economic analysis. Under this heading we include boxed inserts on principal-agent and asymmetric information problems, strategic-entry deterrence models in game theory, and the theory of contestable markets.

Studying Principles of Economics

Most courses will begin with Part 1, where we have touched most of the traditional bases while keeping the introductory materials briefer than in most textbooks. Courses concentrating on macroeconomic theory and policy will proceed next to Parts 2 through 5, while courses specializing in microeconomics will skip to Part 6. Either sort of course may make use of some of the chapters in Part 10.

Whatever the nature of your course, we would like to offer one suggestion. Unlike some of the other courses you may be taking, principles of economics is cumulative—each week's lesson builds on what you have learned before. You will save yourself a lot of frustration (and also a lot of work) if you keep up on a week-to-week basis. To help you do this, there is a chapter summary, a list of important terms and concepts, and a selection of discussion questions to help you review at the end of each chapter. In addition to these aids, many students will find the *Study Guide*, designed specifically to accompany this text by Professor Craig Swan, helpful as a self-testing and diagnostic device. When you encounter difficulties in the *Study Guide*, you will know which sections of the text you need to review.

Note to the Instructor

The ordering of chapters in the book is based on courses that treat macroeconomics before microeconomics. The macroeconomic analysis is found in Parts 2 through 5. The core micro materials occupy Parts 6 through 9, in an order chosen to emphasize the central theme: the working of markets. Part 10 contains an assortment of miscellaneous topics that you will use or omit at your discretion. There seems to us no obvious "order" in which to treat these chapters. Similarly, some instructors may prefer to take up international trade (Chapter 18) in a course on microeconomics.

In trying to improve the book from one edition to the next, we rely heavily on our own experiences as teachers. But our experience using the book is minuscule compared with that of the hundreds of instructors who use it nationwide. If you encounter problems, or have suggestions for improving the book, we urge you to let us know by writing to either one of us in care of Harcourt Brace Jovanovich, College Department, 1250 Sixth Avenue, San Diego, California 92101. Such letters are invaluable, and we are glad to receive them, even if they are critical.

What follows is a set of suggested course outlines predicated on the assumptions that a one-semester course will be able to cover about half the book, and a one-quarter course will be able to cover about one-third of the book.

OUTLINE FOR A ONE-SEMESTER COURSE EMPHASIZING MACROECONOMICS

Chapter Number	Title
1	What Is Economics?
2	The Use and Misuse of Graphs
3	Scarcity and Choice: *The* Economic Problem
4	Supply and Demand: An Initial Look
5	Macroeconomics and Microeconomics
6	Macroeconomic Maladies: Unemployment and Inflation
7	Productivity, Progress, and Prosperity
8	Income and Spending: The Powerful Consumer
9	Demand-Side Equilibrium: Unemployment or Inflation?
10	Changes on the Demand Side: Multiplier Analysis
11	Supply-Side Equilibrium: Unemployment *and* Inflation?
12	Fiscal Policy and Supply-Side Economics
13	Money and the Banking System
14	Monetary Policy and the National Economy
15	The Keynesian–Monetarist Debate
16	Budget Deficits and the National Debt: Fact and Fiction
17	The Trade-Off Between Inflation and Unemployment
18	International Trade and Comparative Advantage
19	The International Monetary System: Order or Disorder?
20	Macroeconomics in a World Economy
38	Growth in Developed and Developing Countries

OUTLINE FOR A ONE-SEMESTER COURSE EMPHASIZING MICROECONOMICS

OUTLINE FOR A ONE-SEMESTER COURSE COVERING BOTH MACRO AND MICRO

OUTLINE FOR A ONE-QUARTER COURSE IN MACROECONOMICS

OUTLINE FOR A ONE-QUARTER COURSE IN MICROECONOMICS

OUTLINE FOR A ONE-QUARTER COURSE ON APPLICATIONS OF BOTH MACRO AND MICRO

With Thanks

Finally, and with great pleasure we turn to the customary acknowledgments of indebtedness. Ours have been accumulating now through four editions. In these days of specialization, not even a pair of authors can master every subject that an introductory text must cover. Our friends and colleagues Charles Berry, Rebecca Blank, William Branson, Lester Chandler, Gregory Chow, Avinash Dixit, Robert Eisner, Stephen Goldfeld, Claudia Goldin, Ronald Grieson, Daniel Hamermesh, Peter Kenen, Melvin Krauss, Arthur Lewis, Burton Malkiel, Edwin Mills, Janusz Ordover, Uwe Reinhardt, Harvey Rosen, Carl Shapiro, Hans Soderstrom, Laura Tyson, and Martin Weitzman have all given generously of their knowledge in particular areas over the course of four editions. We have learned much from them, and only wish we had learned more.

Many economists at other colleges and universities offered useful suggestions for improvements, many of which we have incorporated into the Fourth Edition. We wish to thank J. David Bowman of State University of New York—Oswego, Gerald Breger of University of South Carolina, Hsin Chang of University of Michigan, Carol Clark of Guilford College, Elizabeth Crowell of University of Michigan, Elizabeth Dickhaus of University of Missouri—Columbia, Patricia

Euznet of University of Central Florida, Marianne Felton of Indiana University, Richard Fritz of University of Central Florida, Phillip Gilbert of Mira Costa College, Jonathan Goldstein of Bowdin College, Joseph Guerin of Saint Joseph's University, Thomas Hamer of Glassboro State College, James Hanson of Willamette University, Richard Harmstone of Pennsylvania State University, Benjamin Hitchner of Glassboro State College, John Isbister of University of California—Santa Cruz, Hassan Khademian of University of Missouri—St. Louis, Wolfgang Mayer of University of Cincinnati, John Mogab of Southwest Texas State University, David Ramsey of Illinois State University, Neil Reznik of Community College of Philadelphia, Steven Rock of Illinois Institute of Technology, Gary Sellers of University of Akron, Scott Sumner of Bentley College, Robert Thomas of Iowa State University, Roger Trenary of Kansas State University, Wayne Wangsness of Luther College, Walter Wessels of North Carolina State University, Travis Wilson of DeKalb Community College, and Anthony Zambelli of Cuyamaca College.

We also wish to thank the many economists who responded to our questionnaire; their responses were invaluable in planning this revision: Nick Adnett of California State University—Sacramento, Lori Alden of California State University—Sacramento, Polly Allen of University of Connecticut, Sandra Alvis of North Carolina State University, Kenneth Arakelian of University of Rhode Island, Robert Baade of Lake Forest College, Moshen Bahmani of University of Wisconsin, Barbara Bladwin of Diablo Valley College, Douglas Barnett of Biola University, Nancy Barry of Baldwin-Wallace College, Klaus Becker of Ohio University, Dwight M. Blood of Brigham Young University, Ronald Braeutigan of Northwestern University, Philip Bryson of University of Arizona, Judy Butler of Baylor University, David Butz of Northwestern University, Wendy A. Campione of Northern Arizona University, Thomas M. Carroll of Central Oregon Community College, Paula Cech of University of Arizona, Darrel Christy of University of Wisconsin, Carolyn Clark of Washington State University, Paul Coomes of University of Louisville, Granger Coudle of University of Colorado at Boulder, Dan Dabney of Southwest Texas State University, Rosalee Danielson of Illinois State University, Gary Dymski of University of Southern California, James Eaton of Bridgewater College, David Emery of St. Olaf College, Carol Engle of Auburn University—Montgomery, Homer Erekson of Miami University, Paul Farnham of Georgia State University, Ellen Foster of State University of New York—Albany, Jack Fulcher of University of Nebraska—Omaha, Albert Gray, Jr., of Baldwin-Wallace College, John Green of University of Northern Colorado, W. Clayton Hall of Illinois Institute of Technology, Thomas Hatcher of Fordham University, Charles Hegji of Auburn University—Montgomery, Bruce Herrick of Washington and Lee University, Harold H. Hiskey of Southern Utah State College, Paul Huszar of Colorado State University, Robert Jensen of Pacific Lutheran University, William Kammrath of Concordia College, Bruce Kanago of Miami University, Robert Walter Kerr of College of Lake County, Kusum Ketkar of Seton Hall University, Jong Seok Kim of Dartmouth College, Lori Kletzer of Williams College, L. Emil Kreider of Beloit College, Dale Kuntz of Bentley College, Thomas Leary of University of North Carolina—Greensboro, Michael Leonesio of University of Missouri, Dennis Leyden of University of North Carolina—Greensboro, John Wakeman-Linn of Williams College, R.F. Litro of Mattatuck Community College, John Lyons of Miami University, Bruce Mann of University of Puget Sound, Barbara Marcus of Davenport College of Business, Rebecca Marton of Nicholls State University, Lester McAllister of Beloit College, Peter McKay of Bakersfield College, Richard Megna of Kansas State University, Ruby Pandey of Southwest Texas State University, Theodore Paulos of Eastern Montana College, Rosemary Peavler of Morehead State University, Charles Revier of Colorado State University, Bruce Roberts of College of William and Mary, Robert Robertson of Indiana State University, Steve Russell of Arizona State University, Stephen Sacks of University of Connecticut, John Shaw of California State University—Fresno, John Shieh of California State Polytechnic University, William Sloan of North Carolina State University, John Ewing-Smith of Burlington County College, Steven Smith of Bakersfield College, Shane Stevens of Bridgewater College, Mary Stevenson of University of Massachusetts—Boston, Gabriel Talmain of State University of New York—Albany, Kenneth Taylor of Villanova University, Nita Thacker of State University of New York—Albany, Carolyn Tuttle of Lake Forest College, Terry Von Ende of Ohio University, Dale Warnke of College of Lake County, Chris Weber of University of North Carolina—Greensboro, Mark Weglarski of Macomb County Community College, Cathleen Whiting of Willamette University, John Wolfe of Michigan State University, William Wood of Bridgewater College, and William P. Yohe of Duke University.

We were, of course, most gratified by a number of spontaneous and kind letters from student readers. Since it is for such readers that the book is primarily intended, no other comments have meant as much to us.

The book you hold in your hand was not done by us alone. The fine people at Harcourt Brace Jovanovich, including Mimi Egan, Margie Rogers, Bruce Daniels, Lynn Edwards, Rebecca Lytle, and Diane Pella, worked hard and well to turn our manuscript into the book you see. We appreciate their efforts.

Our sanity and survival during the preparation of the Fourth Edition were assured by the intelligence, ability, and pleasantness of our secretaries, Phyllis Durepos and Karen Garner-Lipman, who did so many things and did them all so well. Sue Anne Batey Blackman, who seems to know our thoughts on the subject better than we do ourselves, besides catching a number of mistakes, brought up to date the chapter on the environment and the economics of natural resources. She and, more recently, Vacharee Devakula have both provided superb assistance.

And finally there are our wives, Hilda Baumol and Madeline Blinder. They have now participated in this project a dozen years, and with each successive revision they help in more and more ways. Their patience, good judgment, and love have made everything go more smoothly than we had any right to expect. This we appreciate deeply.

William J. Baumol
Alan S. Blinder

Brief Contents

Contents

PART 3   Aggregate Supply and Demand Analysis

19 THE INTERNATIONAL MONETARY SYSTEM: ORDER OR DISORDER? 407

20 MACROECONOMICS IN A WORLD ECONOMY 431

PART 6 Essentials of Microeconomics: Consumers and Firms

PART 7 The Market System: Virtues and Vices — 555

PART 8   The Government and the Economy   675

31   LIMITING MARKET POWER: REGULATION OF INDUSTRY   676

32   LIMITING MARKET POWER: ANTITRUST POLICY   699

PART 1

Getting Acquainted with Economics

1

What Is Economics?

Why does public discussion of economic policy so often show the abysmal ignorance of the participants? Why do I so often want to cry at what public figures, the press, and television commentators say about economic affairs?

ROBERT M. SOLOW

Economics is a broad-ranging discipline, both in the questions it asks and the methods it uses to seek answers. Many definitions of economics have been proposed, but we prefer to avoid any attempt to define the discipline in a single sentence or paragraph. Instead, this chapter will introduce you to economics by letting the subject matter speak for itself.

The first part of the chapter is intended to give you some idea of the types of problems that can be approached through economic analysis and the kinds of solutions that economic principles suggest. Many of the world's most pressing problems are economic in nature. So a little knowledge of basic economics is essential to anyone who wants to understand the world in which we live.

The second part briefly introduces the methods of economic inquiry and the tools that economists use. These are tools you may find useful in your life as a citizen, consumer, and worker long after the course is over.

Ideas for Beyond the Final Exam

As college professors, we realize it is inevitable that you will forget much of what you learn in this course—perhaps with a sense of relief—soon after the final exam. There is not much point bemoaning this fact; elephants may never forget, but people do.

Nevertheless, some economic ideas are so important that you will want to remember them well beyond the final exam. If you do not, you will have shortchanged your own education. To help you pick out a few of the most crucial concepts, we have selected 12 from among the many ideas contained in this book. Some offer critical and enduring insights into the workings of the economy. Others bear on important policy issues that often appear in the newspapers and that may have relevance to your own future decisions. Others point out common misunderstandings that occur among even the most thoughtful lay observers. As the opening quotation of this chapter suggests, many learned judges, politicians, business leaders, and university administrators who failed to understand or misused these economic principles could have made far wiser decisions than they did.

Each of the **12 Ideas for Beyond the Final Exam** will be discussed in depth as it occurs in the course of the book, so you should not expect to understand them fully after reading this first chapter. Nonetheless, we think it useful to sketch them briefly here both to introduce you to economics and to provide a selective preview of what is to come.

We have organized our 12 Ideas into two groups, corresponding to the way economics is normally taught. The first six are likely to be encountered in courses that specialize in *macroeconomics* (the study of the national economy). The last six are likely to be covered in courses that specialize in *microeconomics* (the study of the price system). Some will appear in both types of courses.

The Trade-off Between Inflation and Unemployment   IDEA 1

At the start of the 1980s, U.S. policy makers declared all-out war on inflation. Some people, including some partisans of Reaganomics, claimed that this war could be waged without heavy casualties in the form of high unemployment. As things turned out, however, the battle against inflation proved to be costly. Inflation was reduced dramatically. But the national unemployment rate, which averaged 6.1 percent during the 1970s, averaged 8.1 percent during 1981–1986 and exceeded 9.5 percent in both 1982 and 1983.

Economists maintain that this conjunction of events was no coincidence. Owing to features of our economy that we will study in Parts 2 and 3, there is an agonizing *trade-off between inflation and unemployment,* meaning that most policies that bring down inflation also cause unemployment to rise.

Since this trade-off poses the fundamental dilemma of national economic policy, we will devote all of Chapter 17 to examining it in detail. And we shall also consider some suggestions for escaping from the trade-off, such as supply-side economics (Chapter 12) and wage-price controls (Chapter 17).

The Illusion of High Interest Rates   IDEA 2

Is it more costly to borrow money at 10 percent interest or at 14 percent interest? That would seem an easy question to answer, even without a course in economics. But, in fact, it is not. An example will show why.

In 1987, banks were lending money to home buyers at annual interest rates of 10 percent or less. Just seven years earlier, these rates had been 14 percent or more. Yet economists maintain that it was actually cheaper to borrow in 1980 than in 1987. Why? Because inflation in 1980 was running at about 12 percent per year while it was only about 4 percent in 1987.

But why is information on inflation relevant for deciding how costly it is to borrow? Consider the position of a person who borrows $100 for one year at a 14 percent rate of interest when the inflation rate is 10 percent. At the end of the year the borrower pays back his $100 plus $14 interest. But over that same year, because of inflation, his indebtedness declines by $10 *in terms of what that money will buy*. Thus, in terms of *purchasing power*, the borrower really pays only $4 in interest on his $100 loan, or 4 percent.

Now consider someone who borrows $100 at 10 percent interest when prices are rising only 4 percent a year. This borrower pays back the original $100 plus $10 in interest and sees the purchasing power of his debt decline by $4 due to inflation — for a net payment in purchasing-power terms of $6, or 6 percent. Thus, in the economically relevant sense, the 10 percent loan is actually more expensive than the 14 percent loan.

As we will learn in Chapter 6, the failure to understand this principle has caused troubles for our tax laws, for the financial system, and for the housing and public utility industries. And in Chapter 16 we will see that it has even led to misunderstanding of the size and nature of the government budget deficit.

IDEA 3

The Consequences of Budget Deficits

Large federal budget deficits have been much in the news in recent years. Congress has struggled continually to cut the deficit and has failed to comply with a deficit-reduction law (the Gramm-Rudman-Hollings Act of 1985) that it set for itself. President Reagan, while defending the policies that led to large deficits, has advocated a constitutional amendment to require a balanced budget.

The conflicting claims and counterclaims that have marked this debate are bound to confuse the layman. Some critics claim that deficits hold dire consequences—including higher interest rates, more inflation, a stagnant economy, and an irksome burden on future generations of Americans. Others deny these charges.

Who is right? Are deficits really malign or benign influences on our economy? The answers, economists insist, are so complicated that the only correct short answer is: It all depends. The precise factors on which the answers depend, and the reasons why, are sufficiently important that they merit an entire chapter of this book (Chapter 16). There we will learn that a budget deficit may be sound or unsound policy, depending on its size and on the reasons for its existence.

IDEA 4

Mutual Gains from Voluntary Exchange

One of the most fundamental ideas of economics is that in a voluntary exchange both parties must gain something, or at least expect to gain something. Otherwise why would they both agree to the exchange? This principle may seem self-evident, and it probably is. Yet it is amazing how often it is ignored in practice.

For example, it was widely believed for centuries that governments should interfere with international trade because one country's gain from a swap must be the other country's loss. (See Chapter 18.) Analogously, some people feel instinctively that if Mr. A profits handsomely from a deal with Mr. B, then Mr. B must have been exploited. Laws sometimes prohibit mutually beneficial exchanges between buyers and sellers—as when a loan transaction is banned because the interest rate is "too high" (Chapter 6), or when a willing worker cannot be hired because the wage rate is "too low" (Chapter 36), or when the resale of tickets to sporting events ("ticket scalping") is outlawed even though the buyer is happy to pay the high price (Chapter 4).

In every one of these cases, and many more, well-intentioned but misguided reasoning blocks the mutual gains that arise from voluntary exchange—and thereby interferes with one of the most basic functions of an economic system (see Chapter 3).

IDEA 5

The Surprising Principle of Comparative Advantage

The Japanese economy produces many products that Americans buy in huge quantities—including cars, TV sets, cameras, and electronic equipment. American manufacturers have complained about the competition and demanded protection against the flood of imports that, in their view, threatens American standards of living. Is this view justified?

Economists think not. But what if a combination of higher productivity and lower wages were to permit Japan to produce *everything* more cheaply than we could? Would it not then be true that Americans would have no work and that our nation would be impoverished?

A remarkable result, called the law of **comparative advantage,** shows that even in this extreme case the two nations should still trade and that each can gain as a result! We will explain this principle fully in Chapter 18, where we will also note some potentially valid arguments in favor of protecting particular domestic industries. But for now a simple parable will make the reason clear.

Suppose Sam grows up on a farm and is a whiz at plowing, but is also a successful country singer who earns $2000 a performance at hotels and nightclubs. Should Sam refuse some singing engagements to leave time for plowing? Of course not. Instead he should hire Alfie, a much less efficient farmer, to plow for him. Sam is the better farmer, but he earns so much more by specializing in singing that it pays him to leave the farming to Alfie. Alfie, though a poorer farmer than Sam, is an even worse singer. Thus Alfie earns a living by specializing in the job at which he at least has a *comparative* advantage (his farming is not quite as bad as his singing), and both Alfie and Sam gain. The same is true of two countries. Even if one of them is more efficient at everything, both countries can gain by producing the things they do best *comparatively*.

The Overwhelming Importance of Productivity Growth in the Long Run   IDEA 6

In Geneva a worker in a watch factory now turns out roughly one hundred times as many mechanical watches per year as his ancestor did three centuries earlier. The **productivity** of labor (output per worker hour) in cotton production has probably gone up more than a thousandfold in two hundred years. It is estimated that production per hour of labor in manufacturing in the United States has gone up about seven times in the past century. This means the average American can enjoy about seven times as much clothing, housewares, and luxury goods as were available to a typical inhabitant of the United States one hundred years before.

Economic issues such as inflation, unemployment, and monopoly are important to us all, and will receive great attention in this book. But in the long run nothing has as great an effect on our material well-being and the amounts society can afford to spend on hospitals, schools, and social amenities as the rate of growth of productivity. Chapter 7 points out that what appears to be a small increase in productivity growth can have a huge effect on a country's standard of living over a long period of time because productivity compounds like the interest on savings in a bank. Since 1870, for example, U. S. productivity is estimated to have grown only about 2 percent a year on the average. But that was enough to increase the volume of goods and services available to each person about twelve times — a truly incredible amount.

Attempts to Repeal the Laws of Supply and Demand: The Market Strikes Back   IDEA 7

When a commodity is in short supply, its price naturally tends to rise. Sometimes disgruntled consumers badger politicians into "solving" the problem by imposing a legal ceiling on the price. Similarly, when supplies are abundant — say, when fine weather produces extraordinarily abundant crops — prices tend to fall. This naturally dismays producers, who often succeed in getting legislation prohibiting low prices by imposing price floors. But such attempts to repeal the laws of supply and demand usually backfire and sometimes produce results virtually the opposite of those that were intended.

Where rent controls are adopted to protect tenants, housing grows scarce because the law makes it unprofitable to build and maintain apartments. When minimum wages are enacted to protect low-wage workers, low-wage jobs disappear. Price floors are placed under agricultural products and surpluses pile up. History provides spectacular examples of the way in which free markets strike back at attempts to interfere with the way they would otherwise work. In Chapter 4, we will see that price controls played a role in causing the oft-recounted hardships of Washington's army at Valley Forge. Two centuries earlier, when the armies of Spain surrounded Antwerp in 1584, hoping to starve the city into submission, profiteers kept Antwerp going by smuggling food and supplies through enemy lines. However, when the city fathers adopted price controls to end these "unconscionable" prices, supplies suddenly dried up and the city soon surrendered.

As we will see in Chapter 4 and elsewhere in this book, such consequences of interference with the price mechanism are no accident. They follow inevitably from the way free markets work.

Externalities: A Shortcoming of the Market Cured by Market Methods

IDEA 8

Markets are very efficient in producing the goods that consumers want in the quantities in which they are desired. They do so by offering large financial rewards to those who respond to what consumers want to buy and who produce these products economically. Similarly, the market mechanism minimizes waste and inefficiency by causing inefficient producers to lose money.

This works out well as long as an exchange between a seller and a buyer affects only those two parties. But often an economic transaction affects uninvolved third parties. Examples abound. A cigarette smoker blows smoke in your face. The utility which supplies electricity to your home also produces soot that discolors your curtains and pollutants that despoil the air and even affect your health. After a farmer sprays his crops with toxic pesticides, the poison may seep into the ground water and affect the health of neighboring communities.

Such social costs—called **externalities** because they affect parties *external* to the economic transaction that causes them—escape the control of the market mechanism, as we will learn in Chapter 29. There is no financial incentive that motivates polluters to minimize the damages they do. As a consequence, it pays firms to make their products as cheaply as possible, disregarding externalities that may damage the quality of life.

Yet, as we will learn in Chapters 29 and 34, there is a way for the government to use the market mechanism to control undesirable externalities. If the public utility and the farmer are charged for the harm they cause the public, just as they are charged when they use tangible resources such as coal and fertilizer, then they will have an incentive to reduce the amount of pollution they generate. Thus, in this case, economists believe that market methods are often the best way to cure one of the market's most important shortcomings.

Rational Choice and True Economic Costs

IDEA 9

Despite dramatic improvements in our standard of living since the industrial revolution, we have not come anywhere near a state of unlimited abundance, and so we must constantly make choices. If you purchase a new home, you may not be able to afford to eat at expensive restaurants as often as you used to. If a firm decides to retool its factories, it may have to postpone plans for new executive offices. If a government expands its defense program, it may be forced to reduce its outlays on roads or school buildings.

Economists say that the true costs of such decisions are not the number of dollars spent on the house, the new equipment, or the military establishment, but rather *the value of what must be given up in order to acquire the item* — the restaurant meals, the new executive offices, the improved roads and new schools. These are called **opportunity costs** because they represent the *opportunities* the individual, firm, or government must forego to make the desired expenditure. Economists maintain that opportunity costs must be considered in the decision-making process, if rational choices are to be made (see Chapter 3).

The cost of a college education provides a vivid example that is probably close to the hearts of all students reading this book. How much do you think it *costs* to go to college? Most likely you would answer this question by adding together your expenditures on tuition, room and board, books, and the like, and then deducting any scholarship funds you may receive. Economists would not. They would first want to know how much you could be earning if you were not attending college. This may sound like an irrelevant question; but because you give up these earnings by attending college, they must be added to your tuition bill as a cost of your education. Nor would economists accept the university's bill for room and board as a measure of your living costs. They would want to know by how much this exceeds what it would have cost you to live at home, and only this extra cost would be counted as an expense. On balance, a college education probably costs more than you think.

The Importance of Marginal Analysis   IDEA 10

Many pages in this book will be spent explaining, and extolling the virtues of, a type of decision-making process called **marginal analysis** (see especially Chapters 21–24), which can best be illustrated by an example.

Suppose that an airline is told by its accountants that the full cost of transporting one passenger from Los Angeles to New York is $180. Can the airline profit by offering a reduced rate of $100 to students who fly on a standby basis? The surprising answer is: probably yes. The reason is that most of the $180 cost per passenger must be paid whether the plane carries 20 passengers or 120 passengers. Marginal analysis points out that full costs—which include costs of maintenance, landing rights, ground crews, and so on—are irrelevant to an airline interested in making as much profit as possible. The only costs that are relevant in deciding whether to carry standby passengers for reduced rates are the *extra* costs of writing and processing additional tickets, the food and beverages these passengers consume, the additional fuel required, and so on. These costs are called **marginal costs,** and they are probably quite small in this instance. Any passenger who pays the airline more than its marginal cost will add something to the company's profit, so it probably is more profitable to let the students ride for the reduced fare than to fly the plane with empty seats.

There are many real cases in which decisionmakers, not understanding marginal analysis, have rejected advantageous possibilities like the reduced fare in our hypothetical example. These people were misled by calculating in terms of *average* rather than *marginal* cost figures—an error that can be quite costly.

IDEA 11 — The Cost Disease of the Service Sector

There is a distressing phenomenon occurring throughout the industrialized world. Many community services have apparently been growing poorer — fewer postal deliveries, larger classes in public schools, less reliable garbage pickups — while the public is paying more and more for them. Indeed, the costs of providing public services have risen consistently faster than the rate of inflation. A natural response is to attribute the problem to political corruption and government inefficiency. But this is certainly not the whole story, because private services have also grown more costly.

As we shall see in Chapter 29, one of the major causes of the problem is economic. And it has nothing to do with corruption or inefficiency of public employees; rather, it has to do with the dazzling growth in efficiency of private manufacturing industries! Because technological improvements make workers more productive in manufacturing, wages rise. And they rise not only for the manufacturing workers but also for postal workers, teachers, and other public employees, because workers can leave industries with low-paying jobs and compete for jobs in high-paying industries. But in personal services technology is not easily changed. Since it still takes one person to drive a postal truck and one teacher to teach a class, the cost of these services is forced to rise. The same sort of cost disease affects other services like medical care, university teaching, restaurant cooking, retailing, and automobile repairs.

This is important to understand not because it excuses the financial record of our governments, but because an understanding of the problem suggests what we should expect the future to bring and, perhaps, indicates what policies should be advocated to correct it.

IDEA 12 — Increasing Output May Require Sacrificing Equality

"Supply-side" economics was one of the cornerstones of President Reagan's economic policy. The basic idea behind supply-side tax cuts (which are discussed in detail in Chapter 12) is to spur productivity and efficiency by providing greater incentives for working, saving, and investing. Those were, for example, among the major goals of the large tax cuts of 1981.

Yet there is at least one problem with supply-side economics — a problem that has figured prominently in the debate over Reaganomics. In order to provide stronger incentives for success in the economic game, the gaps between the "winners" and the "losers" must necessarily be widened. For it is these gaps that, after all, provide the incentives to work harder, to save more, and to invest productively.

However, some observers feel that the unequal distribution of income in our society is unjust; that it is inequitable for the super rich to sail yachts and give expensive parties while poor people live in slums and eat inadequate diets. People who hold this view are disturbed by the fact that supply-side tax cuts are likely to make the distribution of income even more unequal than it already is.

This example illustrates a genuine and pervasive dilemma. There is often a *trade-off* between the *size* of a nation's output and the degree of *equality* with which that output is distributed. As illustrated by the example of supply-side tax cuts, programs that increase production often breed inequality. And, as we will see in Chapter 37, many policies designed to divide the proverbial economic pie more equally inadvertently cause the size of the pie to shrink.

Epilogue

These, then, are a dozen of the more fundamental concepts to be found in this book — ideas that we hope you will retain **Beyond the Final Exam.** Do not try to learn them perfectly right now, for you will hear much more about each as the book progresses. Instead, keep them in mind as you read — we will point them out to you as they occur by the use of the book's logo ☑ — and look back over this list at the end of the course. You may be amazed to see how natural, or even obvious, they will seem then.

Inside the Economist's Tool Kit

Now that you have some idea of the kinds of issues economists deal with, you should know something about the way they grapple with these problems.

Economics as a Discipline

Economics has something of a split personality. Clearly the most rigorous of the social sciences, it nevertheless looks decidedly more "social" than "scientific" when compared with physics. Economists strive to be humanists and scientists simultaneously. An economist is, by necessity, a jack of several trades. Economists borrow modes of investigation from numerous fields, adjusting each to fit the particular problems posed by economic events. Usefulness, not methodological purity, is the criterion for inclusion in the economist's tool kit.

Mathematical reasoning is used extensively in economics, but so is historical study. And neither looks quite the same as when practiced by a mathematician or a historian. Statistical inference, too, plays an important role in economic inquiry; but economists have had to modify standard statistical procedures to fit the kinds of data they deal with. In 1926, John Maynard Keynes, the great British economist, summed up the many faces of economic inquiry in a statement that still rings true today.

The master-economist . . . must understand symbols and speak in words. He must contemplate the particular in terms of the general, and touch abstract and concrete in the same flight of thought. He must study the present in the light of the past for the purposes of the future. No part of man's nature or his institutions must lie entirely outside his regard. He must be purposeful and disinterested in a simultaneous mood; as aloof and incorruptible as an artist, yet sometimes as near the earth as a politician. [1]

Economics is distinguished both by the types of *problems* it addresses and by the investigative *techniques* it employs to study them. An introductory course in economics cannot make you an economist, but it should help you approach social problems from a pragmatic and dispassionate point of view. Answers to all society's problems will not be found in this book. But you should learn how to pose questions in ways that will help produce answers that are both useful and illuminating.

The Need for Abstraction

Some students find economics unduly abstract and "unrealistic." The stylized world envisioned by economic theory seems only a distant cousin to the world

[1] See his *Essays in Biography* (New York: Norton, 1951), pages 140–141.

they see around them. There is an old joke about three people—a chemist, a physicist, and an economist—stranded on an isolated island with an ample supply of canned food but no implements to open the cans. In debating what to do, the chemist suggested lighting a fire under the cans, thus expanding their contents and causing the cans to burst. The physicist doubted that this would work. He advocated building a catapult with which they could smash the cans against some nearby boulders. Then they turned to the economist for his suggestion. After a moment's thought, he announced his solution: "Let's assume we have a can opener."

Economists *do* make unrealistic assumptions; you will encounter many of them in the pages that follow. But this propensity to abstract from reality results from the incredible complexity of the real world, not from any fondness economists have for sounding absurd.

Compare the chemist's simple task of explaining the interactions of compounds in a chemical reaction with the economist's complex task of explaining the interactions of people in an economy. Are molecules motivated by greed or altruism, by envy or ambition? Do they ever emulate other molecules? Do forecasts about them influence their behavior? People, of course, do all these things, and many, many more. It is therefore immeasurably more difficult to predict human behavior than it is to predict chemical reactions. If economists tried to keep track of every aspect of human behavior, they could surely never hope to understand the nature of the economy. Thus:

Abstraction from unimportant details is necessary to understand the functioning of anything as complex as the economy.

Abstraction means ignoring many details in order to focus on the most important factors in a problem.

To appreciate why the economist **abstracts** from details, put yourself in the following hypothetical situation. You have just arrived, for the first time in your life, in Los Angeles. You are now at the Los Angeles Convention Center. This is the point marked A in Figures 1–1 and 1–2, which are alternative maps of part of Los Angeles. You want to drive to the famous La Brea tar pits, marked B on each map. Which map would you find more useful? You will notice that Map 1 (Figure 1–1) has the full details of the Los Angeles road system. Consequently, it requires a major effort to read it. In contrast, Map 2 (Figure 1–2) omits many minor roads so that the freeways and major arteries stand out more clearly.

Most strangers to the city would prefer Map 2. With its guidance they are likely to find the tar pits in a reasonable amount of time, even though a slightly shorter route might have been found by careful calculation and planning using Map 1. Map 2 seems to *abstract* successfully from a lot of confusing details while retaining the essential aspects of the city's geography. Economic theories strive to do the same thing.

Map 3 (Figure 1–3), which shows little more than the major interstate routes that pass through the greater Los Angeles area, illustrates a danger of which all theorists must beware. Armed only with the information provided on this map, you might never find the La Brea tar pits. Instead of a useful idealization of the Los Angeles road network, the map makers have produced a map that is oversimplified for our purpose. Too much has been assumed away. Of course, this map was never intended to be used as a guide to the La Brea tar pits, which brings us to a very important point:

There is no such thing as one "right" degree of abstraction for all analytic purposes. The optimal degree of abstraction depends on the objective of the

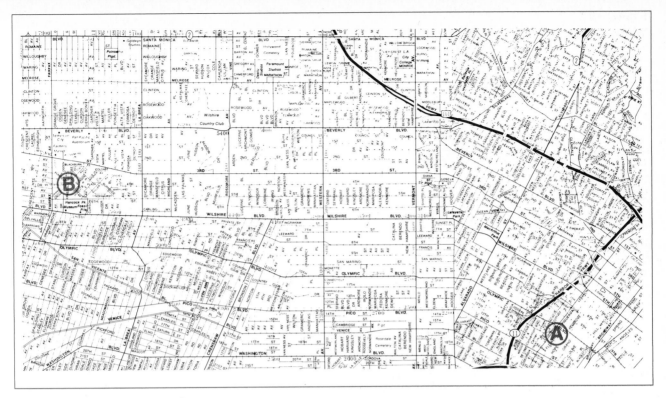

analysis. A model that is a gross oversimplification for one purpose may be needlessly complicated for another.

Economists are constantly treading the thin line between Map 2 and Map 3, between useful generalization about complex issues and gross distortions of the pertinent facts. How can they tell when they have abstracted from reality just enough? There is no objective answer to this question, which is why applied economics is as much art as science. One of the factors distinguishing good economics from bad economics is the degree to which analysts are able to find the factors that constitute the equivalent of Map 2 (rather than Maps 1 or 3) for the problem at hand. It is not always easy to do, as the following examples illustrate.

Example: The Distribution of Income

Suppose you are interested in learning why different people have different incomes, why some are fabulously rich while others are pathetically poor. People differ in many ways, too many to enumerate, much less to study. The economist ignores most of these details in order to focus on a few important facts. The color of a person's hair or eyes probably is not important to the problem at hand, but the color of his skin certainly is. Height and weight may not matter, but education probably does. Proceeding in this way, we pare Map 1 down to the manageable dimensions of Map 2. But there is a danger of going too far. To make it easy to analyze a problem, we can end up stripping away some of its most crucial features.

Example: The Determination of National Income

Suppose we want to know what factors determine the size of the output of the whole economy. Since the volume of goods and services turned out by the whole economy is affected by literally millions of decisions by investors,

Figure 1-1
MAP 1
Map 1 gives complete details of the road system of Los Angeles. If you are like most people, you will find it hard to read and not very useful for figuring out how to get from the Convention Center (point A) to the La Brea tar pits (point B). For this purpose, the map carries far too much detail, though for some other purposes (for example, locating some small street in Hollywood), it may be the best map available.
© MCMLXXV by North American Maps, P.O. Box 5850, San Francisco, CA 94101.

Figure 1–2

MAP 2

Map 2 shows a different perspective of Los Angeles. Minor roads are eliminated — we might say, *assumed away* — in order to present a clearer picture of where the major arteries and freeways go. As a result of this simplification, several ways of getting from the Convention Center (point *A*) to the La Brea tar pits (point *B*) stand out clearly. For example, we can take the Harbor Freeway north to Wilshire Boulevard, and then follow Wilshire west to the tar pits. While we might find a shorter route by poring over the details of Map 1, most of us will feel more comfortable with Map 2.

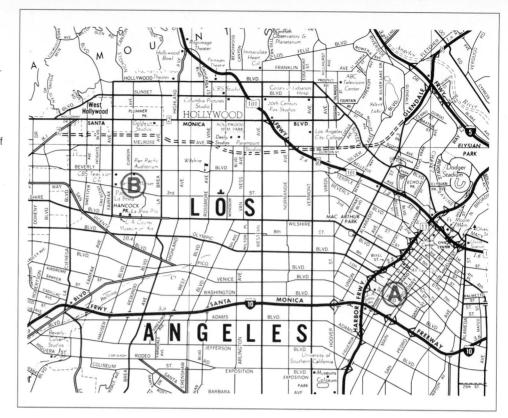

Figure 1–3

MAP 3

Map 3 strips away still more details of the Los Angeles road system. In fact, only major trunk roads and freeways remain. This map may be useful for passing through the city or getting around it, but it will not help the tourist who wants to see the sights of Los Angeles. For this purpose, too many details are missing.

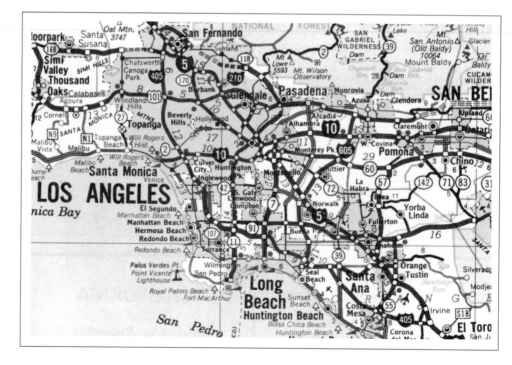

business managers, employees, government officials, and others, a complete enumeration of all the factors determining the nation's output clearly makes analysis unworkable (Map 1). Abstraction is necessary. We must prune the list to manageable size. Parts 3 and 4 of this book explain how economists do this;

that is, how they draw up a Map 2 of the nation's output. Several shortcuts to this process have been proposed, but in the opinion of their critics, they have proved on inspection to be like Map 3.

The Role of Economic Theory

A person "can stare stupidly at phenomena; but in the absence of imagination they will not connect themselves together in any rational way." These words of the renowned American philosopher-scientist C. S. Peirce succinctly express the crucial role of theory in scientific inquiry and help explain why economists are so enamored of it. To the economist or the natural scientist, the word *theory* does not mean what it does in common parlance. In scientific usage, a theory is *not* an untested assertion of alleged fact. The statement that saccharine causes cancer is not a theory, it is a *hypothesis*, which will either prove to be true or false after the right sorts of experiments have been completed.

Instead, a **theory** is a deliberate simplification (abstraction) of factual relationships that attempts to explain how those relationships work. In other words, it is an *explanation* of the mechanism behind observed phenomena. For example, astronomers' data describe the paths of the planets, and gravity forms the basis of theories that are intended to explain these data. Similarly, economists have data suggesting that government policies can affect the degree of a country's prosperity. Keynesian theory (which will be discussed in Parts 3 and 4) seeks to describe and explain these relationships.

A **theory** is a deliberate simplification of relationships whose purpose is to explain how those relationships work.

Economic theory has acquired an unsavory public image in recent years — partly because of inaccurate predictions by some economists, partly because doctrinal disputes have spilled over into the news media, and partly because some politicians have found it expedient to scoff at economists. This bad image is unfortunate because theorizing is not a luxury but a necessity. Economic theory provides a logical structure for organizing and analyzing economic data. It proceeds deductively from assumptions to conclusions — which can later be tested against data. Without theory, economists could only "stare stupidly" at the world. With theory, they can attempt to understand it.

People who have never studied economics often draw a false distinction between *theory* and *practical policy*. Politicians and business people, in particular, often reject abstract economic theory as something that is best ignored by "practical" policymakers. The irony of these statements is that:

It is precisely the concern for policy that makes economic theory so necessary and important.

If there were no possibility of changing the economy through public policy, economics might be a historical and descriptive discipline, asking, for example, what happened in the United States during the Great Depression of the 1930s or how is it that industrial pollution got to be so serious in the 1960s.

But deep concern about public policy forces economists to go beyond historical and descriptive questions. To analyze policy options, they are forced to deal with possibilities that have not actually occurred. For example, to learn how to prevent depressions, they must investigate whether the Great Depression could have been avoided by more astute government policies. Or to determine what environmental programs will be most effective, they must understand how and why a market economy produces pollution and what might happen if government placed taxes on industrial waste discharges and automobile emissions. As Peirce pointed out, not even a lifetime of ogling at real-world data will answer such questions.

Figure 1–4
THE PHILLIPS MACHINE
The late Professor A. W. Phillips, while teaching at the London School of Economics in the early 1950s, built this machine to illustrate Keynesian theory. This is the same theory that we will explain with words and diagrams later in the book; but Phillips's background as an engineer enabled him to depict the theory with the help of tubes, valves, and pumps. Because economists are not very good plumbers, few of them try to build models of this sort; most rely on paper and pencil instead. But the two sorts of models fulfill precisely the same role. They simplify reality in order to make it understandable

Indeed, the facts can sometimes be highly misleading. Statistics often indicate that two variables behave very similarly: Whenever one rises so does the other, and they also both go down simultaneously. But this **correlation** in the data does not prove that either of these variables *causes* the other. For example, in rainy weather, people tend to drive their cars more slowly, and there are also more traffic accidents. But this correlation does not mean that slow driving causes accidents. Rather, both phenomena can be attributed to a common underlying factor (more rain) which leads both to more accidents and to slower driving. Thus, just looking at the degree of correlation (the degree of similarity) between the behavior of two sets of statistics (like accidents and driving speeds) may not tell us much about cause and effect. We need to use theory as part of the analysis.

Because most economic issues hinge on some question of cause and effect, only a combination of theoretical reasoning and data analysis can hope to provide solutions. Simply observing correlations in data is not enough. We must understand how, if at all, different government policies will lead to a lower unemployment rate or how a tax on emissions will reduce pollution.

What Is an Economic "Model"?

An **economic model** is a representation of a theory or a part of a theory, often for the purpose of illuminating cause-and-effect relationships. The notion of a "model" is familiar enough to children, and economists (in common with other scientists) use the term in much the same way that children do.

A child's model automobile or airplane looks and operates much like the real thing, but it is much smaller and much simpler, and so it is easier to manipulate and understand. Engineers for General Motors and Boeing also build models of cars and planes. While their models are far bigger and much more elaborate than a child's toy, they use them for much the same purposes: to observe the workings of these vehicles "up close," to experiment with them in order to see how they might behave under different circumstances ("What happens if I do this?"). From these experiments, they make educated guesses as to how the real-life version will perform. Often these guesses prove uncannily accurate, as exemplified by the success of the Boeing 747. But sometimes they are wide of the mark: The chronic mechanical problems of General Motors' Corvair prompted Ralph Nader's acclaimed book *Unsafe at Any Speed*, which helped launch the consumer movement.

Economists use models for similar purposes and with similarly mixed results. A. W. Phillips, the famous engineer-turned-economist who discovered the "Phillips curve" (discussed in Chapter 17), was talented enough to construct a working model of the determination of national income in a simple economy, using colored water flowing through pipes. For years this contraption, depicted in Figure 1–4, graced the basement of the London School of Economics. However, most economists lack Phillips's manual dexterity, so economic models are generally built with paper and pencil rather than with hammer and nails.

Because many of the models used in this book are depicted in diagrams, we explain the construction and use of various types of graphs in the next chapter. But sometimes economic models are expressed only in words. The statement "Business people produce the level of output that maximizes their profits," is the basis for a behavioral model whose consequences are explored in some detail in Parts 6 through 9. Don't be put off by seemingly abstract models. Think of them as useful road maps, and remember how hard it would be to find your way around Los Angeles without one.

Reasons for Disagreements:
Imperfect Information and Value Judgments

"If all the earth's economists were laid end to end, they could not reach an agreement," or so the saying goes. And President Reagan once quipped that the special version of the game *Trivial Pursuit* for economists has 100 questions, but 3000 answers. If economics is a scientific discipline, why do economists quarrel so much? Politicians and reporters are fond of pointing out that economists can generally be found on both sides of every issue of public policy. Physicists, on the other hand, do not debate whether the earth revolves around the sun or vice versa.

The question reflects a misunderstanding of the nature of science. As a matter of fact, physicists formerly did argue over whether the earth revolves around the sun, often with rather grim results for themselves. (Economists, fortunately, are not often burned at the stake!) Nowadays, physicists argue about "black holes," the existence of certain subatomic particles, and other esoterica. These arguments often go unnoticed by the public because few of us understand what they are talking about. In contrast, everyone is eager to join economic debates over inflation, unemployment, pollution, and almost everything else. Because economics is a *social* science, its disputes are aired in public, and almost everyone is personally concerned with the subject matter. Anyone who has ever bought or sold anything, it seems, fancies himself an amateur economist.

Furthermore, the fact is that economists agree much more than is commonly supposed. Virtually all economists, regardless of their politics, agree that taxing polluters is one of the best ways to protect the environment (see Chapters 29 and 34), that rent controls can ruin a city (Chapter 4), and that free trade among nations is preferable to the erection of barriers through tariffs and quotas (see Chapter 18). The list could go on and on. It is probably true that the issues about which economists agree *far* exceed the subjects on which they disagree.

Finally, many disputes among economists are not scientific disputes at all. Economists, like everyone else, come in all political stripes: conservative, middle-of-the-road, liberal, radical. Each may have different values and hold a different view of what is best for society. So each may have a different opinion on what is the "right" solution to any problem of public policy. In addition, some of the pertinent facts might not be known.

While economists can contribute the best theoretical and factual knowledge there is on a particular issue, the final decision on policy questions often rests either on information that is not currently available or on tastes and ethical opinions about which people differ (the things we call "value judgments"), or on both.

Some examples will illustrate why pure scientific analysis often does not lead to a policy conclusion.

Taxing Industrial Wastes

As you will learn in Chapter 34, the proper tax to levy on industrial wastes depends on quantitative estimates of the harm done by the pollutant. For most waste products, these numbers are not yet known, although knowledge is accumulating rapidly. So a lack of complete information makes it difficult to formulate a concrete policy proposal.

Inflation and Unemployment

Government policies that succeed in shortening a recession are virtually certain to cause higher inflation for a while. Using tools that we will describe in Parts 2 through 5, many economists believe they can even measure how much more inflation the economy will suffer as the price of fighting a recession. Is it worth it? An economist cannot answer this any more than a nuclear physicist could have determined whether dropping the atomic bomb on Hiroshima was a good idea. The decision rests on value judgments about the moral trade-off between inflation and unemployment, judgments that can be made only by the citizenry through its elected officials.

These examples underscore something we said earlier in this chapter: Economics cannot provide all the *answers*, but it can teach you how to ask the right *questions*. By the time you finish studying this book, you should have a good understanding of when the right course of action turns on disputed facts, on value judgments, and on some combination of the two.

The Economist's Odd Vocabulary

George Bernard Shaw once remarked that America and England are two nations separated by a common language. Much the same might be said of economists and other people, for economists often assign peculiar meanings to familiar words. Here are two examples; you will find many others later on.

The **opportunity cost** of some decision is the value of the next best alternative which you have to give up because of that decision (for example, working instead of going to school).

1. *Cost.* We have already mentioned that when economists speak of "costs" they are normally referring to *opportunity costs*. Accountants, on the other hand, almost always measure costs as only the direct monetary expenses involved in any activity. Thus, in calculating the costs of the same activity, the accountant and the economist may arrive at two very different results, as the example of the costs of going to college illustrated. Accountants and economists are indeed divided by a common language.

2. *Money.* Most people work for money, or so they think. Again, the economist disagrees. He will insist that people work to earn *income*, which often happens to be paid—for reasons of convenience—in the form of *money*. What is the difference? To the economist *money* refers to the amount of cash and bank-account balances you own at any particular moment. Your holdings of money change frequently, often several times in a single day. But *income* refers to the rate at which you earn money over time. A worker would answer the question "What is your income?" by saying "$10,000 a year," or "$200 a week," or something like that. Income probably changes much less frequently than holdings of money, perhaps only once a year. The distinction between money and income is important, and it will occupy our attention in Part 4.

The economist, it would appear, is much like Humpty Dumpty in *Alice in Wonderland* who said imperiously, "When I use a word it means just what I choose it to mean—neither more nor less." Why such obstinacy? Because economists need a *scientific jargon*, just as other scientists do. Any dictionary will testify to the fact that most words in any language have a multiplicity of meanings. Scientists must be more precise than that. And, rather than conjure up entirely new words, as natural scientists frequently do, economists take ordinary words and give them slightly special meanings.

One wag once pointed out that Canada has a radical group called *separatists* whose members steadfastly refuse to speak English, and that America also has such a group—but calls them *economists*. Who, though, would prefer that we say "phlogiston" instead of "cost" or "nutches" instead of "money"?

Summary

1. To help you get the most out of your first course in economics, we have devised a list of *12 Important Ideas* that you will want to remember *Beyond the Final Exam*. Here we list them, very briefly, indicating where each idea occurs in the book.

   (1) Most government policies that reduce inflation are likely to intensify the unemployment problem, and vice versa. (Chapter 17)

   (2) Interest rates that appear very high may actually be very low if they are accompanied by rapid inflation. (Chapter 6)

   (3) Budget deficits may or may not be advisable, depending on the circumstances. (Chapter 16)

   (4) In a voluntary exchange, both parties must expect to benefit. (Chapters 3 and 18)

   (5) Two nations can gain from international trade, even if one is more efficient at making everything. (Chapter 18)

   (6) In the long run, productivity is almost the only thing that matters for a nation's material well-being. (Chapter 7)

   (7) Lawmakers who try to repeal the "law" of supply and demand are liable to open a Pandora's box of troubles they never expected. (Chapter 4)

   (8) Externalities cause the market mechanism to misfire, but this defect of the market can be remedied by market-oriented policies. (Chapters 29 and 34)

   (9) To make a rational decision, the opportunity cost of an action must be measured, because only this calculation will tell the decision-maker what he has given up. (Chapter 3)

   (10) Decisionmaking often requires the use of marginal analysis to isolate the costs and benefits of that particular decision. (Chapter 24)

   (11) The operation of free markets is likely to lead to rising prices for public and private services. (Chapter 29)

   (12) Most policies that equalize income will exact a cost by reducing the nation's output. (Chapter 37)

2. Economics is a discipline that uses a variety of approaches, some of them scientific and others humanistic, to address important social questions.

3. Because of the great complexity of human behavior, the economist is forced to abstract from many details, make generalizations that he knows are not quite true, and organize what knowledge he has according to some theoretical structure.

4. Correlation need not imply causation.

5. Economists use simplified models to understand the real world and predict its behavior, much as a child uses a model railroad to learn how trains work.

6. While these models, if skillfully constructed, can illuminate important economic problems, they rarely can answer the questions that policymakers are confronted with. For this purpose, value judgments are needed, and the economist is no better equipped to make them than is anyone else.

7. A course in economics seeks to teach the student how to formulate the right questions, questions that point to the value judgments or unknown pieces of data that must be obtained in order to make an intelligent decision. It does not try to provide all the answers.

Concepts for Review

Voluntary exchange
Comparative advantage
Productivity
Externalities

Marginal analysis
Marginal costs
Abstraction and generalization
Theory

Correlation versus causation
Model
Opportunity cost

Questions for Discussion

1. Think about how you would construct a "model" of how your college is governed. Which officers and administrators would you include and exclude from your model if the objective were
   a. to explain how decisions on tuition payments are made?
   b. to explain the quality of the football team?
   Relate this to the map example in the chapter.

2. Relate the process of "abstraction" to the way you take notes in a lecture. Why do you not try to transcribe every word the lecturer utters? Why do you not just write down the title of the lecture and stop there? How do you decide, roughly speaking, on the correct amount of detail?

3. Explain why a government policymaker cannot afford to ignore economic theory.

2

The Use and Misuse of Graphs

Everything should be made as simple as possible, but not more so.

ALBERT EINSTEIN

Chapter 1 noted that economic models are frequently analyzed and explained with the help of graphs. This book is full of them. But that is not the only reason for you to study how they work. Most of you will deal with graphs in the future, perhaps frequently. They appear in newspapers. Doctors use graphs to keep track of patients' progress. Business firms use them to check their profit and sales performance. Persons concerned with social issues use them to examine trends in ethnic composition of cities and the relation of felonies to family income.

Graphs are invaluable because of the large quantity of data they can display and the way they facilitate interpretation and analysis of the data. They enable the eye to take in at a glance important statistical relationships that would be far less apparent from prose descriptions or long lists of numbers. But badly constructed graphs can confuse and mislead.

In this chapter we show, first, how to read a graph that depicts a relationship between two variables. Second, we define the term *slope* and describe how it is measured and interpreted. Third, we explain how the behavior of three variables can be shown on a two-dimensional graph. Fourth, we discuss how misinterpretation is avoided by adjusting economic graphs to take account of changes in the purchasing power of the dollar, in the population of the nation, and in other pertinent developments. And finally, we examine several other common ways in which graphs can be misleading if not drawn and interpreted with care.

Graphs Used in Economic Analysis*

Two-Variable Diagrams

A **variable** is an object, such as price, whose magnitude is measured by a number; it is used to analyze what happens to other things when the size of that number changes (varies).

Much of the economic analysis to be found in this and other books requires that we keep track of two **variables** simultaneously. For example, in studying the

*Students who have a nodding acquaintance with geometry and feel quite comfortable with graphs can safely skip the first sections of this chapter and proceed directly to the second part, which begins on page 25.

operation of markets, we will want to keep one eye on the price of a commodity and the other on the quantity that is bought and sold.

For this reason, economists frequently find it useful to display real or imaginary figures in a *two-dimensional graph*, which simultaneously represents the behavior of two economic variables. The numerical value of one variable is measured along the bottom of the graph (called the *horizontal axis*), starting from the **origin** (the point labeled "0"), and the numerical value of the other is measured up the side of the graph (called the *vertical axis*), also starting from the origin.

Figures 2–1(a) and 2–1(b) are typical graphs of economic analysis. They depict an (imaginary) *demand curve*, represented by the blue dots in Figure 2–1(a) and the heavy blue line in Figure 2–1(b). The graphs show the price of natural gas on their vertical axes and the quantity of gas people want to buy at each such price on the horizontal axes. The dots in Figure 2–1(a) are connected by the continuous blue curve labeled DD.

Economic diagrams are generally read as one reads latitudes and longitudes on a map. On the demand curve in Figure 2–1, the point marked *a* represents a hypothetical combination of price and quantity demanded in St. Louis. By drawing a horizontal line leftward from that point to the vertical axis, we learn that the average price for gas in St. Louis is $3 per thousand cubic feet. By dropping a line straight down to the horizontal axis, we find that 80 billion cubic feet are wanted by consumers at this price, just as the statistics in Table 2–1 show. The other points on the graph give similar information. For example, point *b* indicates that if natural gas in St. Louis cost only $2 per thousand cubic feet, quantity demanded would be higher—it would reach 120 billion cubic feet.

Notice that information about price and quantity is *all* we can learn from the diagram. The demand curve will not tell us about the kinds of people who

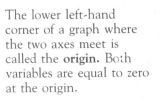

The lower left-hand corner of a graph where the two axes meet is called the **origin.** Both variables are equal to zero at the origin.

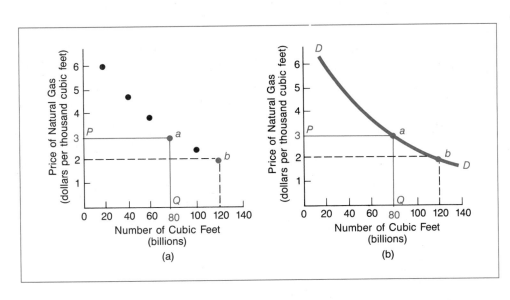

Figure 2–1
A DEMAND CURVE FOR NATURAL GAS IN ST. LOUIS
This demand curve shows the relationship between the price of natural gas and the quantity of it that will be demanded. For example, the point labeled *a* indicates that at a price of $3 per thousand cubic feet (point *P*), the quantity demanded will be 80 billion cubic feet (point *Q*).

Table 2–1
QUANTITIES OF NATURAL GAS DEMANDED AT VARIOUS PRICES

Price ($ per thousand cubic ft.)	$2	3	4	5	6
Quantity Demanded (billions of cubic feet)	120	80	56	38	20

live in St. Louis, the size of their homes, or the condition of their furnaces. It tells us about the price and the quantity demanded at that price; no more, no less. Specifically, it does tell us that when price declines there is an increase in the amount of gas consumers are willing and able to buy.

A diagram abstracts from many details, some of which may be quite interesting, in order to focus on the two variables of primary interest — in this case, the price of natural gas and the amount of gas that is demanded at each price. All the diagrams used in this book share this basic feature. They cannot tell the reader the "whole story" any more than a map's latitude and longitude figures for a particular city can make someone an authority on that city.

The Definition and Measurement of Slope

One of the most important features of the diagrams used by economists is the pace with which the line, or curve, being sketched runs uphill or downhill as we move to the right. The demand curve in Figure 2–1 clearly slopes downhill (the price falls) as we follow it to the right (that is, as more gas is demanded). In such instances we say that *the curve has a negative slope, or is negatively sloped, because one variable falls as the other one rises*.

The **slope of a straight line** is the ratio of the vertical change to the corresponding horizontal change as we move to the right along the line, or as it is often said, the ratio of the "rise" over the "run."

The four panels of Figure 2–2 show all the possible slopes for a straight-line relationship between two unnamed variables called Y (measured along the vertical axis) and X (measured along the horizontal axis). Figure 2–2(a) shows a negative slope, much like our demand curve. Figure 2–2(b) shows a positive slope, because variable Y rises (we go uphill) as variable X rises (as we move to the right). Figure 2–2(c) shows a *zero* slope, where the value of Y is the same irrespective of the value of X. Figure 2–2(d) shows an *infinite* slope, meaning that the value of X is the same irrespective of the value of Y.

Slope is a numerical concept, not just a qualitative one. The two panels of Figure 2–3 show two positively sloped straight lines with different slopes. The line in Figure 2–3(b) is clearly steeper. But by how much? The labels should help you compute the answer. In Figure 2–3(a) a horizontal movement, AB, of 10 units (13–3) corresponds to a vertical movement, BC, of 1 unit (9 − 8). So the slope is $BC/AB = \frac{1}{10}$. In Figure 2–3(b), the same horizontal movement of

Figure 2–2

DIFFERENT TYPES OF SLOPE OF A STRAIGHT-LINE GRAPH

In Figure 2–2(a), the curve goes downward as we read from left to right, so we say it has a negative slope. The slopes in the other figures can be interpreted similarly.

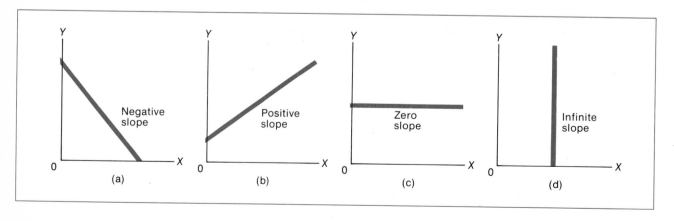

| (a) Negative slope | (b) Positive slope | (c) Zero slope | (d) Infinite slope |

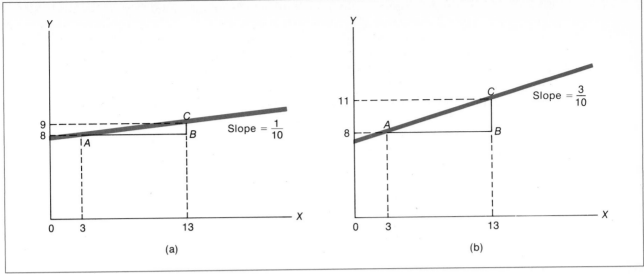

(a)

(b)

10 units corresponds to a vertical movement of 3 units $(11 - 8)$. So the slope is $\frac{3}{10}$, which is larger.

By definition, the slope of any particular straight line is the same no matter where on that line we choose to measure it. That is why we can pick any horizontal distance, AB, and the corresponding slope triangle, ABC, to measure slope. But this is not true of lines that are curved.

Curved lines also have slopes, but the numerical value of the slope is different at every point.

The four panels of Figure 2–4 provide some examples of **slopes of curved lines.** The curve in Figure 2–4(a) has a negative slope everywhere, while the curve in Figure 2–4(b) has a positive slope everywhere. But these are not the only possibilities. In Figure 2–4(c) we encounter a curve that has a positive slope at first but a negative slope later on. Figure 2–4(d) shows the opposite case: a negative slope followed by a positive slope.

It is possible to measure the slope of a smooth curved line numerically *at any particular point*. This is done by drawing a *straight* line that *touches*, but does not *cut*, the curve at the point in question. Such a line is called a **tangent to the curve.**

Figure 2–3
HOW TO MEASURE SLOPE
Slope indicates how much the graph rises per unit move from left to right. Thus, in Figure 2–3(b), as we go from point A to point B, we go $13 - 3 = 10$ units to the right. But in that interval, the graph rises from the height of point B to the height of point C, that is, it rises 3 units. Consequently, the slope of the line is $BC/AB = 3/10$.

Figure 2–4
BEHAVIOR OF SLOPES IN CURVED GRAPHS
As Figures 2–4(c) and 2–4(d) indicate, where a graph is not a straight line it may have a slope that starts off as positive but that becomes negative farther to the right, or vice versa.

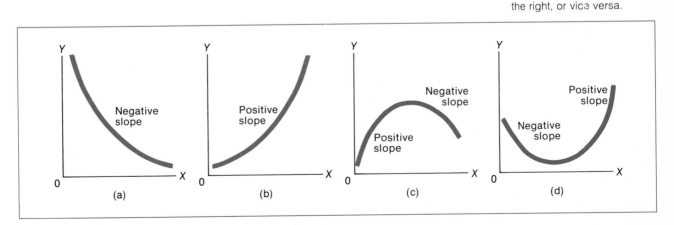

(a)

(b)

(c)

(d)

The slope of a curved line at a particular point is the slope of the straight line that is tangent to the curve at that point.

In Figure 2–5 we have constructed tangents to a curve at two points. Line tt is tangent at point C, and line TT is tangent at point F. We can measure the slope of the curve at these two points by applying the definition. The calculation for point C, then, is the following:

$$\text{Slope at point } C = \text{Slope of line } tt = \frac{\text{Distance } BC}{\text{Distance } AB}$$

$$= \frac{6 - 2}{10 - 0} = \frac{4}{10} = +0.4.$$

A similar calculation yields the slope of the curve at point F, which, as we can see from Figure 2–5, must be smaller:

$$\text{Slope at Point } F = \text{Slope of line } TT = \frac{14 - 9}{50 - 0} = \frac{5}{50} = +0.1.$$

EXERCISE
Show that the slope of the curve at point D is between $+0.1$ and $+0.4$.

What would happen if we tried to apply this graphical technique to the high point in Figure 2–4(c) or to the low point in Figure 2–4(d)? Take a ruler and try it. The tangents that you construct should be horizontal, meaning that they should have a slope of exactly zero. It is always true that where the slope of a smooth curve changes from positive to negative, or vice versa, there will be at least a single point with a zero slope.

Figure 2–5
HOW TO MEASURE SLOPE AT A POINT ON A CURVED GRAPH
To find the slope at point F, draw the line TT, which is tangent to the curve at point F; then measure the slope of the straight-line tangent TT as in Figure 2–3. The slope of the tangent is the same as the slope of the curve at point F.

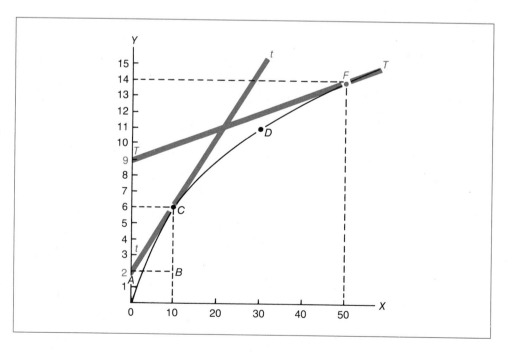

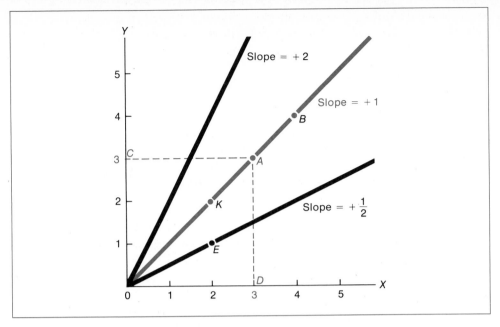

Figure 2–6
RAYS THROUGH THE ORIGIN

Rays are straight lines drawn through the zero point on the graph (*the origin*). Three rays with different slopes are shown. The middle ray, the one with slope = +1, has two properties that make it particularly useful in economics: (1) it makes a 45° angle with either axis, and (2) any point on that ray (for example, point *A*) is exactly equal in distance from the horizontal and vertical axes (length *DA* = length *CA*). So if the items measured on the two axes are in equal units, then at any point on that ray, such as *A*, the number on the *X*-axis (the abscissa) will be the same as the number on the *Y*-axis (the ordinate).

Curves that have the shape of a hill, such as Figure 2–4(c), have a zero slope at their *highest* point. Curves that have the shape of a valley, such as Figure 2–4(d), have a zero slope at their *lowest* point.

Rays Through the Origin and 45° Lines

The point at which a straight line cuts the vertical (Y) axis is called the *Y-intercept*. For example, the Y-intercept of line *tt* in Figure 2–5 is 2, while the Y-intercept of line *TT* is 9. Lines whose Y-intercept is zero have so many special uses that they have been given a special name, a **ray through the origin,** or a **ray.**

Figure 2–6 contains three rays through the origin, and the slope of each is indicated in the diagram. The ray in the center—whose slope is 1—is particularly useful in many economic applications because it marks off points where X and Y are equal (as long as X and Y are measured in the same units). For example, at point A we have X = 3 and Y = 3, at point B, X = 4 and Y = 4, and a similar relation holds at any other point on that ray.

How do we know that this is always true for a ray whose slope is 1? If we start from the origin (where both X and Y are zero) and the slope of the ray is 1, we know from the definition of slope that:

$$\text{Slope} = \frac{\text{Vertical change}}{\text{Horizontal change}} = 1.$$

This implies that the vertical change and the horizontal change are always equal, so the two variables must always remain equal.

Rays through the origin with a slope of 1 are called **45° lines** because they form an angle of 45° with the horizontal axis. If a point representing some data

The point on the graph where both variables are zero is called **the origin.**

A straight line emanating from the origin, or zero point on a graph, is called a **ray through the origin** or, sometimes, just a **ray.**

A **45° line** is a ray through the origin with a slope of + 1. It marks off points where the variables measured on each axis have equal values.[1]

[1]The definition assumes that both variables are measured in the same units.

is above the 45° line, we know that the value of Y exceeds the value of X. Conversely, whenever we find a point below the 45° line, we know that X is larger than Y.

Squeezing Three Dimensions into Two: Contour Maps

Sometimes, because a problem involves more than two variables, two dimensions just are not enough, which is unfortunate since paper is only two dimensional. When we study the decision making process of a business firm, for example, we may want to keep track simultaneously of three variables: how much labor it employs, how much machinery it uses, and how much output it creates.

Luckily, there is a well-known device for collapsing three dimensions into two, namely a *contour map*. Figure 2–7 is a contour map of Mount Rainier, the highest peak in the state of Washington. On several of the irregularly shaped "rings" we find a number indicating the height above sea level at that particular spot on the mountain. Thus, unlike the more usual sort of map, which gives only latitudes and longitudes, this contour map exhibits three pieces of information about each point: latitude, longitude, and altitude.

Figure 2–8 looks more like the contour maps encountered in economics. It shows how some third variable, called Z (think of it as a firm's output, for example), varies as we change either variable X (think of it as a firm's employment) or variable Y (think of it as the use of a firm's machines). Just like the map of Mount Rainier, any point on the diagram conveys three pieces of data. At point A, we can read off the values of X and Y in the conventional way (X is 30 and Y is 40), and we can also note the value of Z by checking to see on which contour line point A falls. (It is on the $Z = 20$ contour.) So point A is able to tell us that 30 hours of labor and 40 hours of machine time produce 20 units of output.

While most of the analyses presented in this book will be based on the simpler two-variable diagrams, contour maps will find their applications, especially in the appendixes to Chapters 21 and 23.

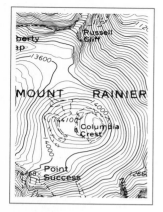

Figure 2–7
A GEOGRAPHIC CONTOUR MAP
All points on any particular contour line represent geographic locations that are at the same height above sea level.
SOURCE: U.S. Geological Survey.

Figure 2–8
AN ECONOMIC CONTOUR MAP
In this contour map, all points on a given contour line represent different combinations of labor and capital capable of producing a given output. For example, all points on the curve $Z = 20$ represent input combinations that can produce 20 units of output. Point A on that line means that the 20 units of output can be produced using 30 labor hours and 40 machine hours. Economists call such maps *production indifference maps*.

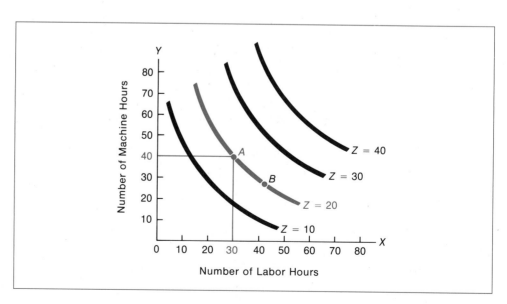

Perils in the Interpretation of Graphs

The preceding materials contain just about all you will need in order to understand the simple graphics used in economic models. We turn now to the second objective of this chapter: to show how statistical data are portrayed on graphs and some of the pitfalls to watch out for.

The Interpretation of Growth Trends

Probably the most common form of graph in empirical economics is a year-by-year (or perhaps a month-by-month) depiction of the behavior of some economic variable — the profits of a particular corporation, or its annual sales, or the number of persons unemployed in the U.S. economy, or some measure of consumer prices. For example, Figure 2–9 is this sort of **time series graph** showing year by year the total amount of money borrowed by U.S. corporations. It shows that the amount of money acquired increased almost constantly over the quarter century 1960–1986, although in the last few years it has declined. Time series graphs are a type of two-variable diagram in which time is always the variable measured along the horizontal axis.

Such graphs can be quite illuminating, offering an instant visual grasp of the course of the relevant events. *However, if misused, such graphs are very dangerous.* They can easily mislead persons who are not experienced in dealing with them.[2] Perhaps even more dangerous are the lies perpetrated accidentally and unintentionally by people who draw graphs without sufficient care and who may innocently mislead themselves as well as others.

A fine example of this latter occurrence is illustrated in Figure 2–10. Many people felt that there was a "cultural boom" underway in the period after World

A **time series graph** depicts how a variable changes over time.

[2]An interesting and informative book on the subject is called *How to Lie with Statistics*, by Darrell Huff and Irving Geis (New York: Norton, 1954).

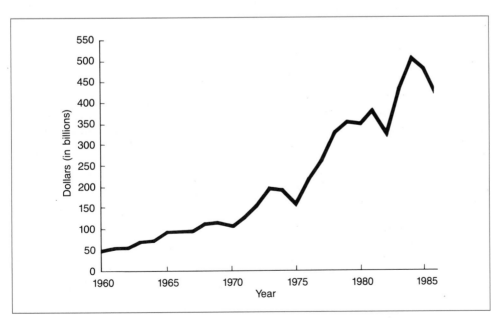

Figure 2–9
TIME SERIES GRAPH: FUNDS ACQUIRED BY U.S. CORPORATIONS, 1960–1986
This graph shows the amount of money acquired by U.S. non-farm corporations in each year from 1960 through 1986.
SOURCE: *Economic Report of the President*, Washington, D.C.: U.S. Government Printing Office, 1987, p. 348.

Figure 2–10

INDEX OF EXPENDITURES ON ADMISSIONS TO ARTISTIC PERFORMANCES

This graph, showing expenditures on admissions to artistic performances, seems to indicate that since about 1932 Americans have become much more interested in attending the performing arts.

SOURCE: *Survey of Current Business*, July issues, various years; and *Economic Report of the President*, Washington D.C.: U.S. Government Printing Office, various years.

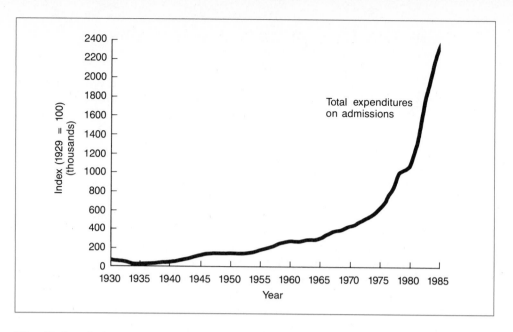

War II that led to an explosion in the demand for tickets to all sorts of artistic performances. This boom, it was thought, accounted for the rapidly rising prices of theater tickets. Figure 2–10 shows the time series graph that formed the basis for this allegation. The growth in spending for theater tickets certainly looks impressive; expenditures rose about 2300 percent from 1929 to 1985.

But there is less to this graph than meets the eye — much less. Most of the spectacular growth in spending on theater admissions was a reflection of three rather banal facts. First, there were many more Americans alive in 1982 than in 1929, so spending *per person* rose by much less than Figure 2–10 suggests. Second, the price of almost everything, not just theater tickets, was higher in 1985 than in 1929. In fact, average prices were more than five times their 1929 levels. Third, the average American was richer in 1985 than in 1929, and consequently was more inclined to spend money on everything — not just on cultural activities.

All three of these factors can be accounted for by expressing spending on theater admissions as a *fraction* of total consumer income. The results of this "correction" are shown in Figure 2–11. The explosive growth suggested by the uncorrected data really amounts to a decline in the share of income that the average American spent on theater tickets — from about 15 cents out of each $100 in 1929 to only 8 cents in 1985! How misleading it can be simply to "look at the facts." There is a general lesson to be learned from this example:

The facts, as portrayed in a time series graph, most assuredly do not "speak for themselves." Because almost everything grows in a growing economy, one must use judgment in interpreting growth trends. Depending on what kind of data are being analyzed, it may be essential to correct for population growth, for rising prices, for rising incomes, or for all three.[3]

Distorting Trends by Choice of the Time Period

In addition to possible misinterpretations of growth trends, users of statistical data must be on guard for distortions of trends caused by unskillfully or un-

[3]For a full discussion of how to use a "price index" to correct for rising prices, see the appendix to Chapter 6.

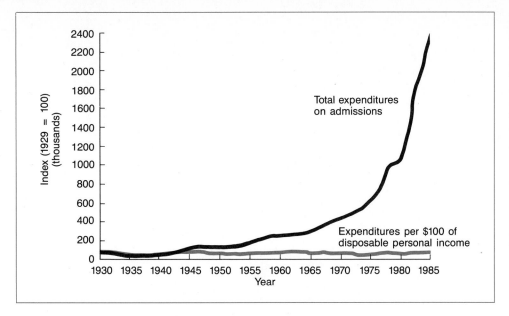

Figure 2–11
APPEARANCE AND
REALITY IN ARTS
EXPENDITURE
The curve in black shows
correctly that the number of
dollars spent on the arts by
Americans rose dramatically
after 1932. But because of
inflation, a dollar in 1985 was
worth much less than in
1929, and there were many
more Americans in the latter
year, who were also wealthier
on the average. After
correction for inflation,
population changes, and so
on, the black line is
transformed into the blue line,
showing that in 1985 an
average American actually
spent less of his purchasing
power on the arts than in
1929.
SOURCE: *Survey of Current
Business*, July issues, various
years; and *Economic Report of
the President*, Washington, D.C.:
U.S. Government Printing Office,
various years.

scrupulously chosen first and last periods for the graph. This is best explained by an example.

Figures 2–12 and 2–13 on the next page show the behavior of average stock market prices over the periods 1929–1932 and 1973–1975. They both display a clear downhill movement and would suggest to anyone who does not have other information that stocks are a terrible investment.

However, an unscrupulous seller of stocks could use the same set of stock market statistics to tell exactly the opposite story by carefully selecting another group of years. Figure 2–14 shows the behavior of average stock prices from 1940 through 1965. The persistence and size of the increase is quite dramatic. Stocks now look like a rather good investment.

An even longer and less biased period gives a less distorted picture (Figure 2–15). It indicates that investments in stocks are sometimes profitable and other times unprofitable.

The deliberate or inadvertent distortion resulting from an unfortunate or unscrupulous choice of time period for a graph must constantly be watched for.

There are no rules that can give absolute protection from this difficulty, but several precautions can be helpful.

1. Make sure the first date shown on the graph is not an exceptionally high or low point. In comparison with 1929, a year of unusually high stock market prices, the years immediately following are bound to give the impression of a downward trend.

2. For the same reason, make sure the graph does not end in a year that is extraordinarily high or low (although this may be unavoidable if the graph simply ends with figures that are as up-to-date as possible).

3. Make sure that (in the absence of some special justification) the graph does not depict only a very brief period, which can easily be atypical.

Figure 2–12
STOCK PRICES,
1929–1932
This graph seems to show
that stock market prices
generally go down.

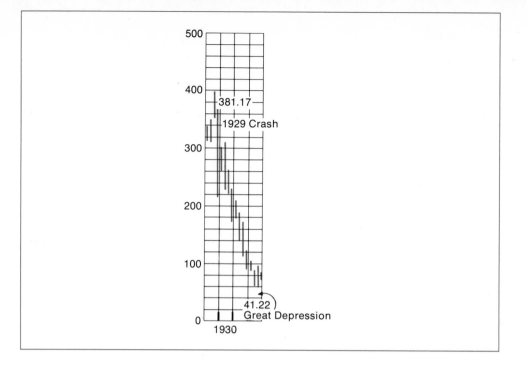

Figure 2–13
STOCK PRICES,
1973–1975
This figure also seems to
show that stock prices
generally fall.

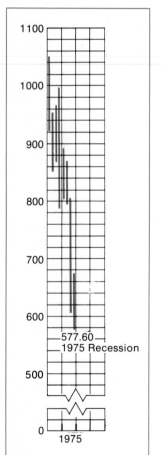

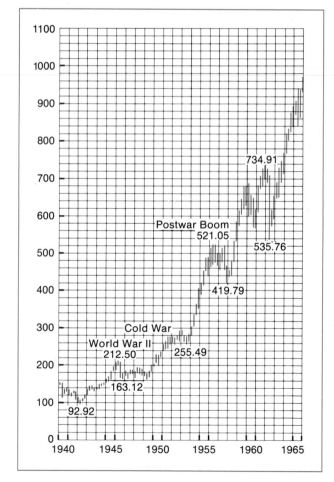

Figure 2–14
STOCK PRICES,
1940–1965
This graph seems to indicate
that the value of stocks is on
a never-ending climb.

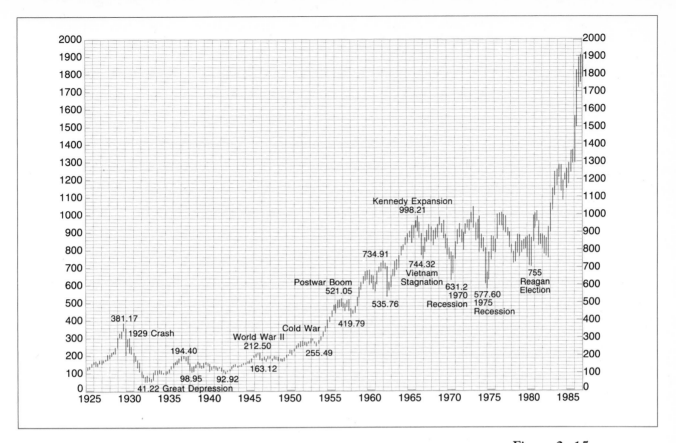

Figure 2–15
THE FULL HISTORY OF STOCK PRICES, 1925–1987
Here we see that stock prices have lots of ups and downs, though they have risen quite a bit on the average.

Dangers of Omitting the Origin

Frequently, the value of an economic variable described on a graph does not fall anywhere near zero during the period under consideration. For example, as Figure 2–16 shows, toward the end of 1983 the interest rate on three-month Treasury securities never rose as high as 9.5 percent and never fell as low as 8 percent. This means that a graph representing the behavior of interest rates in

Figure 2–16
A GRAPH SHOWING OMISSION OF THE ORIGIN
A hasty glance at this figure seems to show that, from the end of August to December 1983, the interest rate collapsed almost to zero, and then shot up again almost as fast.
SOURCE: *The New York Times*, December 6, 1983.

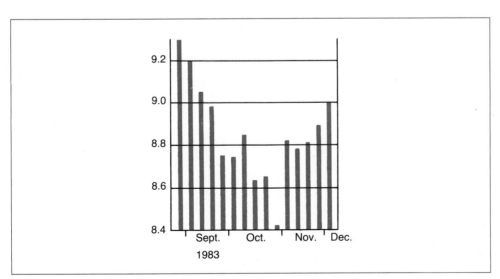

1983 would have a good deal of wasted space between the horizontal axis of the graph, where the interest rate is zero, and the level of the graph representing an 8 percent interest rate. In that area there are simply no data to plot. It is therefore tempting simply to eliminate this wasted space by beginning the graph at an 8 percent interest rate or higher. This was done by *The New York Times* at that time (Figure 2–16), where the lowest points shown in the figure involved an interest rate of 8.4 percent.

What is wrong with the drawing? The answer is that it vastly exaggerates the size of the drop and the rise in the interest rate that are depicted. It makes the drop in the interest rate that occurred in the middle of the period look like a complete crash in the interest rate's level. The more informative graph, which includes the origin as well as the "wasted space" in between is shown in Figure 2–17. Note how this alternative presentation puts matters into perspective. It shows that at the beginning of the period there was a fall in the interest rate, but that it was nowhere near as severe as the graph in *The New York Times* would have suggested to the unwary reader.

Omitting the origin in a graph is dangerous because it always exaggerates the magnitudes of the changes that have taken place.

Sometimes, it is true, the inclusion of the origin would waste so much space that it is undesirable to include it. In that case, a good practice is to put a very clear warning on the graph to remind the reader that this has been done. Figure 2–18 shows one way of doing so.

Unreliability of Steepness and Choice of Units

The last problem we will consider has consequences similar to the one we have just discussed. The problem is that we can never trust the impression we get from the steepness of an economic graph. A graph of stock market prices that

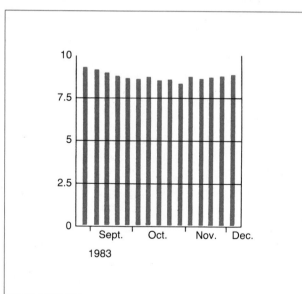

Figure 2–17
INTEREST RATE FIGURES INCLUDING POINT OF ORIGIN
Adding the point of zero interest rate to the previous graph shows that the fall and rise in the interest rate was in fact not so enormous as the earlier graph suggests.

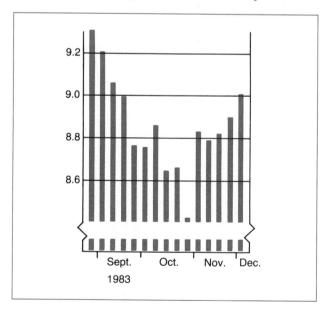

Figure 2–18
A BREAK IN A GRAPH
An alternative way of warning the reader that the zero point has been left out is to put a break in the graph, as illustrated here.

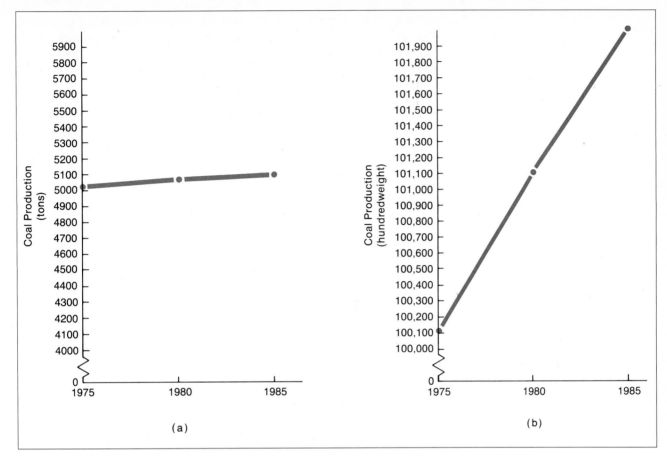

moves uphill sharply (has a large positive slope) appears to suggest that prices are rising rapidly, while another graph in which the rate of climb is much slower seems to imply that prices are going up sluggishly. Yet, depending on how one draws the graph, exactly the same statistics can produce a graph that is rising very quickly or very slowly.

The reason for this possibility is that in economics there are no fixed units of measurement. Coal production can be measured in hundredweight (hundreds of pounds) or in tons. Prices can be measured in cents or in dollars or in millions of dollars. Time can be measured in days or in months or in years. Any of these choices is perfectly legitimate, but it makes all the difference to the speed with which a graph using the resulting figures rises or falls.

An example will bring out the point. Suppose that we have the following (imaginary) figures on daily coal production from a mine, which we measure both in hundredweight and in tons (remembering that 1 ton = 20 hundredweight):

Figure 2–19
SLOPE DEPENDS ON UNITS OF MEASUREMENT
(a) Coal production is measured in tons, and production seems to be rising very slowly.
(b) Production is measured in hundredweight (hundred-pound units) so the same facts now seem to say that production is rising spectacularly.

YEAR	PRODUCTION IN TONS	PRODUCTION IN HUNDRED WEIGHT
1975	5000	100,000
1980	5050	101,000
1985	5090	101,800

Look at Figures 2–19(a) and 2–19(b), one graph showing the figures in tons and the other showing the figures in hundredweight. The line looks quite flat in Figure 2–19(a), but quite steep in Figure 2–19(b).

Unfortunately, we cannot solve the problem by agreeing always to stick to the same measurement units. Pounds may be the right unit for measuring demand for beef, but they will not do in measuring demand for cloth or for coal. A penny may be the right monetary unit for postage stamps, but it is not a very convenient unit for the cost of airplanes or automobiles.

A change in units of measurement stretches or compresses the axis on which the information is represented, which automatically changes the slope of a graph. Therefore, we must never place much faith in the apparent implications of the slope of an ordinary graph in economics.

Later, in Chapter 22 on demand analysis, we will encounter a useful approach economists have adopted to deal with this problem. Instead of calculating changes in "absolute" terms—like tons of coal—they use as their common unit the *percentage* increase. By using percentages rather than absolute figures the problem can be avoided. The reason is simple. If we look at our hypothetical figures on coal production again, we see that no matter whether we measure the increase in output from 1975 to 1980 in tons (from 5000 to 5050) or in hundredweight (from 100,000 to 101,000), the *percentage* increase has been the same. Fifty is 1 percent of 5000, and 1000 is 1 percent of 100,000. Since a change in units affects both the numbers *proportionately*, the result is a washout—it does not do anything to the percentage calculation.

Summary

1. Because graphs are used so often to portray economic models, it is important for students to acquire some understanding of their construction and use. Fortunately, the graphics used in economics are usually not very complex.

2. Most economic models are depicted in two-variable diagrams. We read data from these diagrams just as we read the latitude and longitude on a map: each point represents the values of two variables at the same time.

3. In some instances, three variables must be shown at once. In these cases, economists use contour maps, which, as the name suggests, show "latitude," "longitude," and "altitude" all at the same time.

4. Often, the most important property of a line or curve drawn on a diagram will be its slope, which is defined as the ratio of the "rise" over the "run," or the vertical change divided by the horizontal change. Curves that go uphill as we move to the right have positive slopes, while curves that go downhill have negative slopes.

5. By definition, a straight line has the same slope wherever we choose to measure it. The slope of a curved line changes, but the slope at any point on the curve can be calculated by measuring the slope of a straight line tangent to the curve at that point.

6. A time series graph is a particular type of two-variable diagram that is useful in depicting statistical data. Time is measured along the horizontal axis, and some variable of interest is measured along the vertical axis.

7. While time series graphs are invaluable in helping us condense a great deal of information in a single picture, they can be quite misleading if they are not drawn and interpreted with care. For example, growth trends can be exaggerated by inappropriate choice of units of measurement or by failure to correct for some obvious source of growth (such as rising population). Omitting the origin can make the ups and downs in a time series appear much more extreme than they actually are. Or, by a clever choice of the starting and ending points for the graphs, the same data can be made to tell very different stories. Readers of such graphs—and this includes anyone who ever reads a newspaper—must be on guard for problems like these or they may find themselves misled by "the facts."

Concepts for Review

Variable	Slope of a straight (or curved) line	Ray through the origin, or ray
Two-variable diagram	Negative, positive, zero, and infinite slope	45° line
Horizontal and vertical axes	Tangent to a curve	Contour map
Origin (of a graph)	Y-intercept	Time series graph

Questions for Discussion

1. Look for a graph in your local newspaper, on the financial page or elsewhere. What does the graph try to show? Is someone trying to convince you of something with this graph? Check to see if the graph is distorted in any of the ways mentioned in this chapter.

2. Portray the following hypothetical data on a two-variable diagram:

ENROLLMENT DATA: UNIVERSITY OF NOWHERE

ACADEMIC YEAR	TOTAL ENROLLMENT	ENROLLMENT IN ECONOMICS COURSES
1984–1985	3000	300
1985–1986	3100	325
1986–1987	3200	350
1987–1988	3300	375
1988–1989	3400	400

Measure the slope of the resulting line, and explain what this number means.

3. From Figure 2–5, calculate the slope of the curve at point D.

4. Sam believes that the number of dates he gets per week depends on the number of dabs of aftershave lotion he uses. He concludes from experience that the following figures are typical:

Number of dabs	0	1	2	3	4
Number of dates	1	3	4	5	6

Put these numbers into a graph like Figure 2–1a. Measure and interpret the slopes between adjacent dots.

5. In Figure 2–6, determine the values of X and Y at point K and at point E. What do you conclude?

6. In Figure 2–8, interpret the economic meaning of points A and B. What do the two points have in common? What is the difference in their economic interpretation?

7. Suppose that between 1987 and 1988 expenditures on dog food rose from $35 million to $70 million and that the price of dog food doubled. What do these facts imply about the popularity of dog food?

8. Suppose that between 1980 and 1988 U.S. population went up 10 percent and that the number of people attending professional wrestling matches rose from 3,000,000 to 3,100,000. What do these facts imply about the growth in popularity of professional wrestling?

3

Our necessities are few but
our wants are endless.

INSCRIPTION FOUND IN A
FORTUNE COOKIE

Scarcity and Choice: *The* Economic Problem

This chapter examines a subject that many economists consider to be *the* fundamental issue of economics: the fact that since no resource is available in unlimited supply, people must consequently make decisions consistent with their limited means. A wild-eyed materialist may dream of a world in which everyone owns a yacht and five automobiles, but the earth almost certainly lacks the resources needed to make that dream come true. The scarcity of resources, both natural and man-made, makes it vital that we stretch our limited resources as far as possible.

The chapter introduces a way to analyze the limited choices available to any decision maker. The same sort of analysis, based on the concept of *opportunity cost*, will be shown to apply to the decisions of business firms, of governments, and of society as a whole. Many of the most basic ideas of economics — such as *efficiency, division of labor, exchange*, and the *role of markets* — are introduced here for the first time. These concepts are useful in an analysis of the unpleasant choices forced upon us by the scarcity of resources that constrains all economic decisions. This chapter also introduces a broad question that constitutes the central theme of this text: **What does the market do well and what does it do poorly?**

Application: The "Indispensable Necessity" Syndrome

It is natural but not rational for people to try to avoid facing up to the hard choices which scarcity makes necessary. This happened, for example, when governments at all levels were forced to tighten their belts sharply in the early 1980s. A series of recessions cut into tax revenues. At the same time, the Reagan administration reduced federal grants to state and local governments and looked for ways to trim federal civilian spending. (Actually, government spending rose despite these efforts, but not as much as it would have increased otherwise.)

Budget cuts forced politicians and administrators to make some hard decisions over which services to cut. As they struggled with these decisions, they learned to their dismay that their constituents often were unwilling to accept *any* reductions. Mayors who proposed closing a firehouse or a hospital were confronted by demonstrators decrying the proposed cutback as a "false economy" and describing the firehouse or hospital as "indispensable." Groups marched on Washington to oppose President Reagan's budget cuts. College administrators found that suggestions to eliminate poorly attended courses, cut library hours, or restrict access to the photocopy machine all too frequently were met with the cry that each of these was *absolutely* essential.

Yet, regrettable as it is to have to give up any of these good things, reduced budgets mean that *something* must go. If everyone reacts by declaring *everything* to be indispensable, the decision maker is in the dark and is likely to end up making cuts that are bad for everyone. When the budget must be reduced, it is critical to determine which cuts are likely to prove *least damaging* to the people affected.

It is nonsense to assign top priority to everything. No one can afford everything. An optimal decision is one that chooses the most desirable alternative *among the possibilities permitted by the quantities of scarce resources available*.

Scarcity, Choice, and Opportunity Cost

One of the basic themes of economics is that the **resources** of decision makers, no matter how large they may be, are always limited, and that as a result everyone has some hard decisions to make. The U.S. government has been agonizing over difficult budget decisions for years, though it spends more than a trillion dollars annually! Even Philip II, of Spanish Armada fame, ruler of one of the greatest empires in history, frequently had to cope with rebellion on the part of his troops, whom he was often unable to pay or to supply with even the most basic provisions.

But far more fundamental than the scarcity of funds is the scarcity of physical resources. The supply of fuel, for example, has never been limitless, and a sudden scarcity of fuel would force us to make some hard choices. We might have to keep our homes cooler in winter and warmer in summer, live closer to our jobs, or give up such fuel-using conveniences as dishwashers. While energy is the most widely discussed scarcity these days, the general principle of scarcity applies to all the earth's resources — iron, copper, uranium, and so on.

Even goods that can be produced are in limited supply because their production requires fuel, labor, and other scarce resources. Wheat and rice can be grown. But nations have nonetheless suffered famines because the land, labor, fertilizer, and water needed to grow these crops were unavailable. We can increase our output of cars, but the increased use of labor, steel, and fuel in auto production will mean that something else, perhaps the production of refrigerators, will have to be cut back. This all adds up to the following fundamental principle of economics, one we will encounter again and again in this text.

Virtually all resources are *scarce*, meaning that humanity has less of them than we would like. So choices must be made among a *limited* set of possibilities, in full recognition of the inescapable fact that a decision to have more of one thing means we will have less of something else.

In fact, one popular definition of economics is that it is the study of how best to use limited means in the pursuit of unlimited ends. While this definition, like any short statement, cannot possibly cover the sweep of the entire discipline, it does convey the flavor of the type of problem that is the economist's stock in trade.

Resources are the instruments provided by nature or by people that are used to create the goods and services humans want. Natural resources include minerals, the soil (usable for agriculture, building land, and so on) water, and air. Labor is another resource which is scarce partly because of time limitations (the day has only 24 hours). Factories and machines are resources made by man (or by woman). These three types of resources are often referred to as "land," "labor," and "capital." They are also called the **inputs used in production processes.**

The Principle of Opportunity Cost

Economics examines the options available to households, business firms, governments, and entire societies given the limited resources at their command, and it studies the logic of how **rational decisions** can be made from among the competing alternatives. One overriding principle governs this logic — a principle we have already introduced in Chapter 1 as one of the **12 Ideas for Beyond the Final Exam.** With limited resources, a decision to have more of something is simultaneously a decision to have less of something else. Hence, the relevant *cost* of any decision is its **opportunity cost** — the value of the next best alternative that is given up. Rational decision making, be it in industry, government, or households, must be based on opportunity-cost calculations.

A rational decision is one that best serves the objective of the decision maker, whatever that objective may be. Such objectives may include a firm's desire to maximize its profits, a government's desire to maximize the welfare of its citizens, or another government's desire to maximize its military might. The term "rational" connotes neither approval nor disapproval of the objective itself.

The **opportunity cost** of any decision is the forgone value of the next best alternative that is not chosen.

To illustrate opportunity cost, we continue the example in which production of additional cars requires the production of fewer refrigerators. While the production of a car may cost $6000 per vehicle, or some other money amount, its real cost to society is the refrigerators it must forgo to get an additional car. If the labor, steel, and fuel needed to make a car are sufficient to make eight refrigerators, we say that the opportunity cost of a car is eight refrigerators. The principle of opportunity cost is of such general applicability that we devote most of this chapter to elaborating it.

Opportunity Cost and Money Cost

Since we live in a market economy where (almost) everything "has its price," students often wonder about the connection between the opportunity cost of an item and its market price. What we just said seems to divorce the two concepts. We stressed that the true cost of a car is not its market price but the value of the other things (like refrigerators) that could have been made instead. This *opportunity cost* is the true sacrifice the economy must incur to get a car.

But isn't the opportunity cost of a car related to its money cost? The answer is that the two are often closely tied because of the way a market economy sets the prices of the steel and electricity that go into the production of cars. Steel is valuable because it can be used to make other goods. If the items that steel can make are themselves valuable, the price of steel will be high. But if the goods that steel can make have little value, the price of steel will be low. Thus, if a car has a high opportunity cost, then a well-functioning price system will assign high prices to the resources that are needed to produce cars, and therefore a car will also command a high price. In sum:

If the market is functioning well, goods that have high opportunity costs will tend to have high money costs, and goods whose opportunity costs are low will tend to have low money costs.

Yet it would be a mistake to treat opportunity costs and explicit monetary costs as identical. For one thing, there are times when the market does not function well and hence does not assign prices that accurately reflect opportunity costs. Many such examples will be encountered in this book, especially in Chapters 29 and 34.

Moreover, some valuable items may not bear explicit price tags at all. We have already encountered one such example in Chapter 1, where we contrasted the opportunity cost of going to college with the explicit money cost. We learned that one important item typically omitted from the money-cost calculation is the value of the student's time; that is, the wages he or she could have earned by working instead of attending college. These forgone wages, which are given up by students in order to acquire an education, are part of the opportunity cost of a college education just as surely as are tuition payments.

Other common examples are goods and services that are given away, "free." You incur no explicit monetary cost to acquire such an item. But you may have to pay implicitly by waiting in line. If so, you incur an opportunity cost equal to the value of the next best use of your time.

Production, Scarcity, and Resource Allocation

Consumers do not obtain all the goods and services they would want to acquire if those goods and services were provided free; that is what we mean when we say that outputs are scarce. Scarcity forces consumers to make choices. If Jones buys a motorboat, she may be unable to replace her old coat. The scarcity of goods and services, in turn, is attributed to the scarcity of the land, labor, and capital used to produce **outputs.**

These resources are, after all, the means (instruments) of production, the **inputs** whose services cooperate in the production process, in the farm, and in the factory, to yield both the commodities that people consume, as well as produced means of production (machines, locomotives, and so on).

Scarcity of such input resources, then, means that the economy cannot produce all the bread, hats, cars and computers that consumers would want if they could be made available in limitless amounts. Somehow it must be decided whether or not to assign more fuel to the production of refrigerators, which will mean there is less fuel to use in the production of airplanes or washing machines.

The decision on how to **allocate resources** among the production of different commodities is made in different ways in different types of economies. In a centrally planned economy such as the U.S.S.R., many such decisions are made by government bureaus. In a free market economy such as the United States, Canada, or Great Britain, no one group or individual makes such resource allocation decisions explicitly. Rather, they are made automatically, often unobserved, by what are called "the forces of supply and demand." For example, if consumers want more beef than farmers now supply, that will make it profitable for ranchers to hire more labor to increase their beef herds, thus reallocating labor and other inputs away from other production activities and into increased production of beef.

Outputs are the goods and services that consumers want to acquire. **Inputs** or **means of production** are the natural resources, labor, and produced plant and equipment used to make the outputs.

The **allocation of resources** refers to the decision on how to divide up the economy's scarce input resources among the different outputs produced in the economy and among the different firms or other organizations that produce those outputs.

Scarcity and Choice for a Single Firm

The nature of opportunity cost is perhaps clearest in the case of a single business firm that produces two outputs from a fixed supply of inputs. Given the existing technology and the limited resources at its disposal, the more of one good the firm produces, the less of the other it will be able to produce. And unless management carries out an explicit comparison of the available choices, weighing the desirability of each against the others, it is unlikely that it will make rational production decisions.

Consider the example of a farmer whose available supplies of land, machinery, labor, and fertilizer are capable of producing the various combinations of soybeans and wheat listed in Table 3–1 on page 38. Obviously, the more land and other resources he devotes to production of soybeans, the less wheat he will be able to produce. Table 3–1 indicates, for example, that if he produces only soybeans, he can harvest 40,000 bushels. But, if soybean production

Table 3–1
PRODUCTION POSSIBILITIES OPEN TO A FARMER

BUSHELS OF SOYBEANS	BUSHELS OF WHEAT	LABEL IN FIGURE 3–1
40,000	0	A
30,000	38,000	B
20,000	52,000	C
10,000	60,000	D
0	65,000	E

is reduced to only 30,000 bushels, the farmer can also grow 38,000 bushels of wheat. Thus the opportunity cost of obtaining 38,000 bushels of wheat is 10,000 fewer bushels of soybeans. Or, put the other way around, the opportunity cost of 10,000 more bushels of soybeans is 38,000 bushels of wheat. The other numbers in Table 3–1 have similar interpretations.

Note that Figure 3–1 is a graphical representation of this same information. Point A corresponds to the first line of Table 3–1, point B to the second line, and so on. Curves like AE appear frequently in this book; they are called **production possibilities frontiers.** Any point *on or below* the production possibilities frontier is attainable. Points above the frontier cannot be achieved with the available resources and technology.

The production possibilities frontier always slopes downward to the right. Why? Because resources are limited. The farmer can *increase* his wheat production (move to the right in Figure 3–1) only by devoting more of his land and labor to growing wheat, meaning that he must simultaneously *reduce* his soybean production (move downward) because less of his land and labor remain available for growing soybeans.

Notice that in addition to having a negative slope, our production possibilities frontier AE has another characteristic — it is "bowed outward." Let us consider a bit carefully what this curvature means.

Suppose our farmer is initially producing only soybeans, so that he uses for this purpose even land that is much more suitable for wheat cultivation (point A). Now suppose he decides to switch some of his land from soybean production to wheat production. Which part of his land will he switch? Obviously, if he is sensible, he will use the part best suited to wheat growing. If he shifts to point B, soybean production falls from 40,000 bushels to 30,000 bushels as

A **production possibilities frontier** shows the different combinations of various goods that a producer can turn out, given the available resources and existing technology.

Figure 3–1
PRODUCTION POSSIBILITIES FRONTIER FOR PRODUCTION BY A SINGLE FIRM
With a given set of inputs, the firm can produce only those output combinations given by points in the shaded area. The production possibilities frontier, AE, is not a straight line but one that curves more and more as it nears the axes. That is, when the firm specializes in only one product, those inputs that are especially adapted to the production of the other good lose at least part of their productivity.

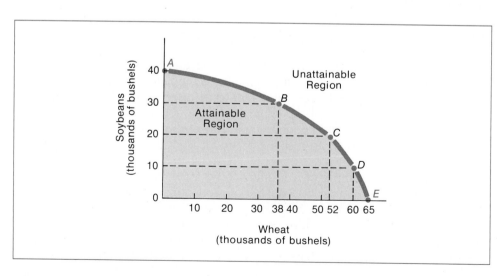

wheat production rises from zero to 38,000 bushels. A sacrifice of only 10,000 bushels of soybeans "buys" 38,000 bushels of wheat.

Imagine now that the farmer wants to produce still more wheat. Figure 3–1 tell us that the sacrifice of an additional 10,000 bushels of soybeans (from 30,000 down to 20,000) will yield only 14,000 more bushels of wheat (see point C). Why? The main reason is that inputs tend to be specialized. As we noted, at point A the farmer was using resources for soybean production that were much more suitable for growing wheat. Consequently, their productivity in soybeans was relatively low, and when they were switched to wheat production, the yield was very high. But this cannot continue forever. As more wheat is produced, the farmer must utilize land and machinery that are better suited to producing soybeans and less well-suited to producing wheat. This is why the first 10,000 bushels of soybeans forgone "buys" the farmer 38,000 bushels of wheat while the second 10,000 bushels of soybeans "buys" him only 14,000 bushels of wheat. Figure 3–1 and Table 3–1 show that these returns continue to decline as wheat production expands: the next 10,000-bushel reduction in soybean production yields only 8000 bushels of additional wheat, and so on.

We can now see that the *slope* of the production possibilities frontier represents graphically the concept of *opportunity cost*. Between points C and B, for example, the opportunity cost of acquiring 10,000 additional bushels of soybeans is 14,000 bushels of forgone wheat; and between points B and A, the opportunity cost of 10,000 bushels of soybeans is 38,000 bushels of forgone wheat. In general, as we move upward to the left along the production possibilities frontier (toward more soybeans and less wheat), the opportunity cost of soybeans in terms of wheat increases. Or, putting the same thing differently, as we move downward to the right, the opportunity cost of acquiring wheat by giving up soybeans increases.

The Principle of Increasing Costs

We have just described a very general phenomenon, which is applicable well beyond farming. The **principle of increasing costs** states that as the production of one good expands, the opportunity cost of producing another unit of this good generally increases.

This principle is not a universal fact; there can be exceptions to it. But it does seem to be a technological regularity that applies to a wide range of economic activities. As our example of the farmer suggests, the principle of increasing costs is based on the fact that resources tend to be specialized, at least in part, so that some of their productivity is lost when they are transferred from doing what they are relatively good at to what they are relatively bad at. In terms of diagrams like Figure 3–1, the principle simply asserts that the production possibilities frontier is bowed outward.

Perhaps the best way to understand this idea is to contrast it with a case in which there are no specialized resources. Figure 3–2 depicts a production possibilities frontier for producing black shoes and brown shoes. Because the labor and capital used to produce black shoes are just as good at producing brown shoes, the frontier is a straight line. If the firm cuts back its production of black shoes by 10,000 pairs, it always gets 10,000 additional pairs of brown shoes. No productivity is lost in the switch because resources are not specialized.

Scarcity and Choice for the Entire Society

Like an individual firm, the entire economy is also constrained by its limited resources and technology. If society wants more aircraft and tanks, it will have to

The **principle of increasing costs** states that as the production of a good expands, the opportunity cost of producing another unit generally increases.

Figure 3–2
PRODUCTION POSSIBILITIES FRONTIER WITH NO SPECIALIZED RESOURCES

Resources that produce black shoes are just as good at producing brown shoes. So there is no loss of productivity when black shoe production is decreased in order to increase brown shoe production. For example, if the firm moves from point *A* to point *B*, black shoe output falls by 10,000 pairs and brown shoe output rises by 10,000 pairs. The same would be true if it moved from point *B* to point *C*, or from point *C* to point *D*. The production possibilities frontier is therefore a straight line.

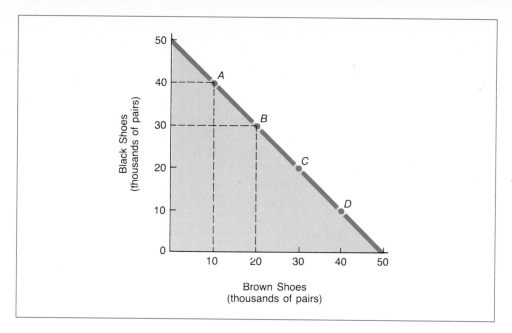

give up some boats and automobiles. If it wants to build more factories and stores, it will have to build fewer homes and sports arenas. In general:

The position and shape of the production possibilities frontier that constrains the choices of the economy are determined by the economy's physical resources, its skills and technology, its willingness to work, and how much it has devoted in the past to the construction of factories, research, and innovation.

Since the debate over increasing our nation's military strength has been so much on the national agenda in recent years, let us illustrate the nature of society's choices by the example of choosing between military might (represented by missiles) and civilian consumption (represented by milk). Just like a single firm, the economy as a whole has a production possibilities frontier for missiles and milk determined by its technology and the available resources of land, labor, capital, and raw materials. This production possibilities frontier may look like curve *BC* in Figure 3–3.

If most workers are employed at dairy farms and supermarkets, the production of milk will be large but the output of missiles will be small. If resources are transferred from farms to factories, the mix of output can be shifted toward increased production of missiles at some sacrifice of milk (the move from *D* to *E*). However, something is likely to be lost in the transfer process — the hay that helped produce the dairy output will not help in missile production. As summarized in the principle of increasing costs, physical resources tend to be specialized, so the production possibilities frontier probably curves downward toward the axes.

We may even reach a point where the only resources left are items that are not very useful outside dairy farms and supermarkets. In that case, even a very large additional sacrifice of milk will enable the economy to produce very few more missiles. That is the meaning of the steep segment, *FC*, on the frontier. At point *C* there is very little more output of missiles than at *F*, even though at *C* milk production has been given up entirely.

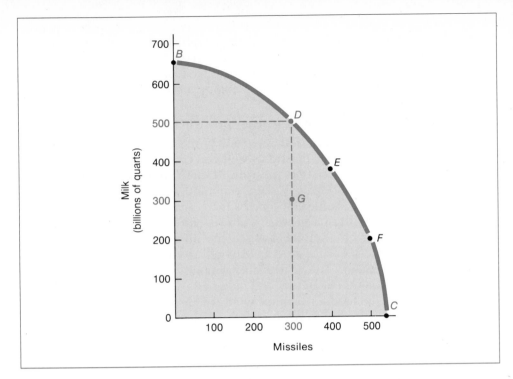

This production possibilities
frontier is curved because
resources are not perfectly
transferable from milk
production to missile
production. The limits on
available rescources place a
ceiling, C, on the output of
one product and a different
ceiling, B, on the output of
the other product.

The downward slope of society's production possibilities frontier implies that hard choices must be made. Our nation's military strength can be increased only by decreasing civilian consumption ("milk"), not by rhetoric nor by wishing it so. The curvature of the production possibilities frontier implies that, as defense spending increases, it becomes progressively more expensive to "buy" additional military strength ("missiles") by sacrificing civilian consumption.

Scarcity and Choice Elsewhere in the Economy

We have stressed that limited resources force hard choices upon business managers and society as a whole. But the same type of choices arise elsewhere—in households, in universities and other nonprofit organizations, and in the government.

The nature of opportunity cost is perhaps most obvious for a household that must decide how to divide its income among the goods and services that compete for the family's trade. If the Higgins family buys an expensive new car, it may be forced to cut back sharply on its other purchases. This does not make it unwise to buy the car. But it does make it unwise to buy the car until the full implications of the purchase for the family's overall budget are considered. If the Higgins family is to use its limited resources most effectively, it must explicitly acknowledge that the opportunity costs of the car are, say, a shorter vacation and making do with the old TV set.

Even a rich and powerful nation like the United States or Japan must cope with the limitations implied by scarce resources. The necessity for choice imposed on the governments of these nations by their limited budgets is similar in character to the problems faced by business firms and households. For the goods and services it buys from others, a government has to prepare a budget similar to that of a very large household. For the items it produces itself—education, police protection, libraries, and so on — it faces a production possibilities frontier much like that of a business firm. Even though the U.S. government will spend over $1100 billion in 1988, some of the most acrimonious debates between the Reagan administration and its critics have been over how to allocate the government's limited resources among competing programs.

Application: Economic Growth in the United States and Japan

Among the economic choices that any society must make, there is one extremely important choice that illustrates well the concept of opportunity cost. This choice is embodied in the question "How fast should the economy grow?"[1] At first, the question may seem ridiculous. Since **economic growth** means, roughly, that the average citizen has more and more goods and services, is it not self-evident that faster growth is always better?

Economic growth occurs when an economy is able to produce more goods and services for each consumer.

Again, the fundamental problem of scarcity intervenes. Economies do not grow by magic. Scarce resources must be devoted to the process of growth. Cement and steel that could be used to make swimming pools and stadiums must be diverted to build more machinery and factories. Wood that could make furniture and skis must be used for hammers and ladders instead. Grain that could be eaten must be used as seed to plant additional acres. By deciding how large a quantity of resources to devote to future needs rather than to current consumption, society in effect *chooses* (within limits) how fast it will grow.

In diagrammatic terms, economic growth means that the economy's production possibilities frontier shifts outward over time — like the move from FF to GG in Figure 3–4(a). Why? Because such a shift means that the economy can produce more of both of the outputs shown in the graph. Thus, in the figure, after growth has occurred it is possible to produce the combination of products represented by points like N. Before growth had occurred point N was beyond the economy's means because it was outside the production possibilities frontier.

How does growth occur? That is, what shifts an economy's production frontier outward? There are many ways. For example, workers may acquire greater skill and learn to produce more output in an hour. Such increases in labor's productivity are discussed in Chapter 7. Perhaps even more important, the economy may construct more capital goods, temporarily giving up some consumption goods to provide the resources to build the factories and machines. Finally, inventions like the steam engine, AC electricity, and industrial robots can and do increase the economy's productive capacity, thereby shifting its production frontier outward.

A consumption good is an item which is available for immediate use by households, and which satisfies wants of members of households without contributing directly to future production by the economy.

A capital good is an item that is used to produce other goods and services in the future, rather than being consumed today. Factories and machines are examples.

Figure 3–4 illustrates the nature of the choice by depicting production possibilities frontiers for **consumption goods**, that are consumed today (like food and electricity) versus **capital goods** that provide for future consumption (like grocery stores and generating plants) for two different societies. Figure 3–4(a) depicts a society like the United States that devotes a relatively small quantity of resources to growth, preferring current consumption instead. It chooses a point like A on this year's production possibilities frontier, FF. At A, consumption is relatively high and production of capital is relatively low, so the production possibilities frontier shifts only to GG next year. Figure 3–4(b) depicts a society much more enamored of growth, like Japan. It selects a point like B on its production possibilities frontier, ff. At B, consumption is much lower and production of capital goods is much higher, so its production possibilities frontier moves all the way to gg by next year. Japan grows faster than the

[1]Economic growth will be studied in detail in Chapter 38.

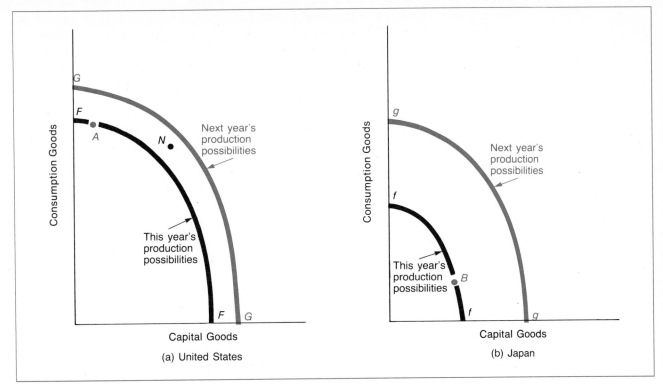

Consumption Goods

This year's production possibilities

Next year's production possibilities

Capital Goods

(a) United States

Consumption Goods

This year's production possibilities

Next year's production possibilities

Capital Goods

(b) Japan

U.S. But the more rapid growth has a price — an *opportunity cost*: The Japanese must give up some of the current consumption that Americans enjoy.

An economy grows by giving up some current consumption and producing capital goods for the future instead. The more capital it produces, the faster will its production possibilities frontier shift outward over time.

The Concept of Efficiency

So far in our discussion of scarcity and choice, we have assumed that either the single firm or the whole economy always operates on its production possibilities frontier rather than *below* it. In other words, we have tacitly assumed that, whatever it decides to do, the firm or economy does so *efficiently*. Economists define *efficiency* as the absence of waste. An efficient economy utilizes all of its available resources and produces the maximum amount of output that its technology permits.[2]

To see why any point on the economy's production possibilities frontier in Figure 3–3 represents an efficient decision, suppose for a moment that society has decided to produce 300 missiles. According to the production possibilities frontier, if 300 missiles are to be produced, then the maximum amount of milk that can be made is 500 billion quarts (point *D* in Figure 3–3). The economy is therefore operating efficiently if it actually produces 500 billion quarts rather than some smaller amount such as 300 billion quarts (as at point *G*). While point *D* is efficient, point *G* is not. This is so because the economy is capable of moving from *G* to *D*, thereby producing 200 billion more quarts of milk without giving up any missiles (or anything else). Clearly, failure to take advantage of the option of choosing point *D* rather than point *G* constitutes a wasted opportunity.

---

[2]A more formal definition of *efficiency* is offered in Chapter 26, page 588.

Figure 3–4
GROWTH IN TWO ECONOMIES
Growth shifts the production possibilities frontiers *FF* and *ff* (black) outward to the frontiers *GG* and *gg* (blue), meaning that each economy can produce more of both goods than it could before. If the shift in both economies occurs in the same period of time, then the Japanese economy [part(b)] is growing faster than the U.S. economy [part (a)] because the outward shift in (b) is much greater than the one in (a).

Note that the concept of efficiency does not tell us which point on the production possibilities frontier is *best*; it only tells us that no point that is *not* on the frontier can be best, because any such point represents wasted resources. For example, should society ever find itself at point G, the necessity of making hard choices would (temporarily) disappear. It would be possible to increase production of *both* missiles *and* milk by moving to a point such as E.

Why, then, would an economy ever find itself at a point below its production possibilities frontier? There are a number of ways in which resources are wasted in real life. The most important of them, unemployment, is an issue that will take up a substantial part of this book (especially in Parts 2 and 3). When many workers are unemployed, the economy finds itself at a point like G, below the frontier, because by putting the unemployed to work in both industries, the economy could produce more missiles *and* more milk. The economy would then move from point G to the right (more missiles) and upward (more milk) toward a point like E on the production possibilities frontier. Only when no resources are wasted by unemployment or misuse is the economy on the frontier.

Analogous problems occur on the farm. For example, if a farmer lets fertilizer fall off the rear end of his truck through sheer carelessness, he will end up at a point *inside* the production possibilities frontier. The farm will not be operating efficiently.

The Three Coordination Tasks of Any Economy

In deciding how to use its scarce resources, society must somehow make three sorts of decisions. First, as we have emphasized, it must figure out **how to utilize its resources efficiently;** that is, it must find a way to get *on* its production possibilities frontier. Second, it must decide **what combination of goods to produce** — how many missiles, how much milk, and so on; that is, it must select one specific point on the production possibilities frontier. Finally, it must decide **how much of each good to distribute to each person,** doing so in a sensible way that does not assign meat to vegetarians and wine to teetotalers.

Certainly, each of these decisions could be made in many ways. For example, a central planner could tell people how to produce, what to produce, and what to consume. [3] But they can also be made without central direction, through a system of prices and markets. Let us consider each task in turn.

Specialization, Division of Labor, and Exchange

Efficiency in production is one of the three basic tasks. Many features of society contribute to efficiency; others interfere with it. While different societies pursue the goal of economic efficiency in different ways, one source of efficiency is so fundamental that we must single it out for special attention: the tremendous gains in productivity that stem from **specialization** and the consequent **division of labor.**

Adam Smith, the founder of modern economics, first marveled at this mainspring of efficiency and productivity on a visit to a pin factory. In a famous passage near the beginning of his monumental book, *The Wealth of Nations* (1776), he described what he saw:

One man draws out the wire, another straightens it, a third cuts it, a fourth points it, a fifth grinds it at the top for receiving the head; to make the head requires two or three

Division of labor means breaking up a task into a number of smaller, more **specialized** tasks so that each worker can become more adept at his or her particular job.

[3] Central planning will be considered in some detail in Chapter 40.

distinct operations; to put it on is a peculiar business, to whiten the pins is another; it is even a trade by itself to put them into the paper . . . .[4]

Smith observed that by dividing the work to be done in this way, each worker became quite skilled in his particular specialty, and the productivity of the group of workers as a whole was enhanced enormously. As Smith related it:

I have seen a small manufactory of this kind where ten men only were employed. . . . Those ten persons . . . could make among them upwards of forty-eight thousand pins in a day. . . . But if they had all wrought separately and independently . . . they certainly could not each of them have made twenty, perhaps not one pin in a day. . . .[5]

In other words, through the miracle of division of labor and specialization, ten workers accomplished what would otherwise have required thousands. This was one of the secrets of the Industrial Revolution, which helped lift humanity out of the abject poverty that had for so long been its lot.

But specialization created a problem. With division of labor, people no longer produced only what they wanted to consume themselves. The workers in the pin factory had no use for the thousands of pins they produced each day; they wanted to trade them for things like food, clothing, and shelter. Specialization thus made it necessary to have some mechanism by which workers producing pins could **exchange** their wares with workers producing such things as cloth and potatoes.

Without a system of exchange, the productivity miracle achieved by the division of labor would have done society little good. With it, standards of living rose enormously. As we observed in Chapter 1:

Mutual Gains from Voluntary Exchange
Unless there is deception or misunderstanding of the facts, a *voluntary* exchange between two parties must make both parties better off. Even though no additional goods are produced by the act of trading, the welfare of society is increased because each individual acquires goods that are more suited to his needs and tastes. This simple but fundamental precept of economics is one of our **12 Ideas for Beyond the Final Exam.**

While goods can be traded for other goods, a system of exchange works better when everyone agrees to use some common item (such as pieces of paper) for buying and selling goods and services. Enter *money*. Then workers in pin factories, for example, can be paid in money rather than in pins, and they can use this money to purchase cloth and potatoes. Textile workers and farmers can do the same.

These two phenomena — specialization and exchange (assisted by money) — working in tandem led to a vast improvement in the well-being of mankind. But what forces induce workers to join together so that the fruits of the division of labor can be enjoyed? And what forces establish a smoothly functioning system of exchange so that each person can acquire what he or she wants to consume? One alternative is to have a central authority telling people what to do. But Adam Smith explained and extolled another way of organizing and coordinating economic activity — the use of markets and prices.

[4]Adam Smith, *The Wealth of Nations* (New York: Random House, Modern Library Edition, 1937), page 4.
[5]*Ibid.*, page 5.

Markets, Prices, and the Three Coordination Tasks

A **market system** is a form of organization of the economy in which decisions on resource allocation are left to the independent decisions of individual producers and consumers acting in their own best interests without central direction.

Smith noted that people are adept at pursuing their own self-interest, and that a **market system** is a fine way to harness this self-interest. As he put it, with pretty clear religious overtones, in doing what is best for themselves, people are "led by an invisible hand" to promote the economic well-being of society as a whole.

Since we live in a market economy, the outlines of the process by which the invisible hand works are familiar to all of us.[6] Firms are encouraged by the profit motive to use inputs efficiently. Valuable resources (like energy) command high prices, and so producers economize on their use. The price (market) system also guides firms' output decisions, and hence those of society. A rise in the price of wheat, for example, will persuade farmers to produce more wheat and fewer soybeans. Finally, a price system determines who gets what goods through a series of voluntary exchanges. Workers with valuable skills and owners of scarce resources will be able to sell what they have at attractive prices. With the incomes they earn, they can then purchase the goods and services they want most, within the limits of their budgets. Those with less to sell will have to live more frugally.

This, in broad terms, is how a market economy solves the three basic problems facing any society: how to produce any given combination of goods efficiently, how to select an appropriate combination of goods, and how to distribute these goods sensibly among the people. As we proceed through the following chapters, you will learn much more about these issues. You will see that they constitute the central theme that permeates not only this text, but the work of economists in general. As you progress through the book, keep in mind the following two questions: **What does the market do well, and what does it do poorly?** There are plenty of answers to both questions. As you will learn in coming chapters:

1. Society has many important goals. Some of them, such as producing goods and services with maximum efficiency (minimum waste), can in certain circumstances be achieved extraordinarily well by letting markets operate more or less freely.

2. Free markets will not, however, achieve all of society's goals. For example, as we will see in Part 3, they often have trouble keeping unemployment and inflation low. And there are even some goals — such as protection of the environment — for which the unfettered operation of markets may be positively harmful. Many observers also believe that markets do not necessarily lead to an equitable distribution of income.

3. But even in cases where the market does not perform at all well, there may be ways of harnessing the power of the market mechanism to remedy its own deficiencies, as you will learn particularly in Parts 4 and 8.

Radicalism, Conservatism, and the Market Mechanism

Since economic debates often have political and ideological overtones, we think it important to close the chapter by stressing that the central theme that we have just outlined is neither a defense of nor an attack upon the capitalist

---

[6]This topic is studied in detail in Chapter 26.

Biographical Note: Adam Smith (1723–1790)

Adam Smith, who was to become the leading advocate of freedom of international trade, was born the son of a customs official in 1723 and ended his career in the well-paid post of collector of customs for Scotland. He received an excellent education at Glasgow College, where, for the first time, some lectures were being given in English rather than Latin. A fellowship to Oxford University followed, and for six years he studied there mostly by himself, since, at that time, teaching at Oxford was virtually nonexistent.

After completing his studies, Smith was appointed professor of logic at Glasgow College and, later, professor of moral philosophy, a field which then included economics as one of its branches. Fortunately, he was a popular lecturer because, in those days, a professor's pay in Glasgow depended on the number of students who chose to attend his lectures. At Glasgow, Smith was responsible for helping young James Watt find a job as an instrument maker. Watt later invented the steam engine, so in this and many other respects, Smith was present virtually at the birth of the Industrial Revolution, whose prophet he was destined to become.

After 13 years at Glasgow, Smith accepted a highly paid post as a tutor to a young Scottish nobleman with whom he spent several years in France, a customary way of educating nobles in the eighteenth century. Primarily because he was bored during these years in France, Smith began working on The Wealth of Nations. Several years after his return to England, in 1776, the book was published and rapidly achieved popularity.

The Wealth of Nations contains many brilliantly written passages. It was one of the first systematic treatises in economics, contributing to both theoretical and factual knowledge about the subject. Among the main points made in the book are the importance for a nation's prosperity of freedom of trade and the division of labor permitted by more widespread markets; the dangers of governmental protection of monopolies and imposition of tariffs; and the superiority of self-interest — the instrument of the "invisible hand" — over altruism as a means of improving the economy's service to the general public.

The British government was grateful for the ideas for new tax legislation Smith proposed, and to show its appreciation appointed him to the lucrative sinecure of collector of customs, which, together with the lifetime pension awarded him by his former pupil, left him very well-off financially, although he eventually gave away most of his money to charitable causes.

The intellectual world was small in the eighteenth century, and among the many people with whom Smith was acquainted were David Hume, Samuel Johnson, James Boswell, Benjamin Franklin, and Jean Jacques Rousseau. Smith got along well with everyone except Samuel Johnson, who was noted for his dislike of Scots. Smith was absent-minded and apparently timid with women, being visibly embarrassed by the public attention of the eminent ladies of Paris during his visits there. He never married, and he lived with his mother most of his life. When he died, the Edinburgh newspapers recalled only that when Smith was four years old he was kidnapped by gypsies. But thanks to his writings, he is remembered for a good deal more than that.

system. Nor is it a "conservative" position. One does not have to be a conservative to recognize that the market mechanism can be a helpful instrument for the pursuit of economic goals. A number of socialist countries, including Yugoslavia and Hungary, have openly and deliberately organized large parts of their economies along market lines, and the People's Republic of China is now rushing in that direction.

The point is not to confuse means and ends in deciding on how much to rely on market forces. Radicals and conservatives surely have different goals, and they may also differ in the means they advocate to pursue these goals. But means should be chosen on the basis of how effective they are in achieving the adopted goals, not on some ideological prejudgments.

For example, radicals may assign a much higher priority to pollution control than conservatives do. Consequently, radicals may favor strict controls even if such controls cut into business profits. Conservatives may prefer things the other way around. Nevertheless, each side may want to use the market mechanism to achieve its goals. Indeed, each side may conclude that, should it lose the political struggle and the other side's position be adopted, less damage will be done to its own goals if market methods are used.

Certainly, there are economic problems with which the market cannot deal. Indeed, we have just noted that the market is the *source* of a number of significant problems. But the evidence leads economists to believe that many economic problems are best handled by market techniques. The analysis in this book is intended to help you identify the strengths and weaknesses of the market mechanism. Forget the slogans you have heard — whether from the left or from the right — and make up your own mind after you have read this book.

Summary

1. Supplies of all resources are limited. Because resources are scarce, a rational decision is one that chooses the best alternative among the options that are possible with the available resources.

2. It is irrational to assign highest priority to everything. No one can afford everything, and so hard choices must be made.

3. With limited resources, if we decide to obtain more of one item, we must give up some of another item. What we give up is called the *opportunity cost* of what we get; this is the true cost of any decision. The concept of opportunity cost is one of the 12 Ideas for Beyond the Final Exam.

4. The allocation of resources refers to division of the economy's scarce inputs (fuel, minerals, machines, labor, and so on) among the economy's different outputs and the enterprises that produce them.

5. When the market is functioning effectively, firms are led to use resources efficiently and to produce the things that consumers want most. In such cases, opportunity costs and money costs (prices) correspond closely. When the market performs poorly, or when important items of cost do not get price tags, opportunity costs and money costs can be quite different.

6. A firm's production possibilities frontier shows the combinations of goods the firm can produce with a given quantity of resources, given the state of technology. The frontier usually is not a straight line, but is bowed outward because resources tend to be specialized.

7. The principle of increasing costs states that as the production of one good expands, the opportunity cost of producing another unit of this good generally increases.

8. The economy as a whole has a production possibilities frontier whose position is determined by its technology and by the available resources of land, labor, capital, and raw materials.

9. If a firm or an economy ends up at a point below its production possibilities frontier, it is using its resources inefficiently or wastefully. This is what happens, for example, when there is unemployment.

10. Economic growth means there is an outward shift in the economy's production possibilities frontier. The faster the growth, the faster this shift will occur. But growth requires a sacrifice of current consumption, and this is its opportunity cost.

11. Efficiency is defined by economists as the absence of waste. It is achieved primarily by gains in productivity brought about through specialization, division of labor, and a system of exchange.

12. If an exchange is voluntary, both parties must benefit even though no new goods are produced. This is another of the 12 Ideas for Beyond the Final Exam.

13. Every economic system must find a way to answer three basic questions: How can goods be produced most efficiently? How much of each good should be produced? How should goods be distributed?

14. The market system works very well in solving some of society's basic problems, but it fails to remedy others and may, indeed, create some of its own. Where and how it succeeds and fails constitute the theme of this book and characterize the work of economists in general.

Concepts for Review

Resources
Scarcity
Choice
Rational decision
Opportunity cost
Outputs
Inputs (means of production)

Production possibilities frontier
Allocation of resources
Principle of increasing costs
Consumption goods
Capital goods
Economic growth

Efficiency
Specialization
Division of labor
Exchange
Market system
Three coordination tasks

Questions for Discussion

1. Discuss the resource limitations that affect:
   a. the poorest person on earth.
   b. the richest person on earth.
   c. a firm in Switzerland.
   d. a government agency in China.
   e. the population of the world.
2. If you were president of your college, what would you change if your budget were cut by 5 percent? By 20 percent? By 50 percent?
3. If you were to drop out of college, what things would change in your life? What, then, is the opportunity cost of your education?
4. A person rents a house for which he pays the landlord $6000 a year and keeps money in a bank account that pays 7 percent interest a year. The house is offered for sale at $80,000. Is this a good deal for the potential buyer? Where does opportunity cost enter the picture?
5. Construct graphically the production possibilities frontier for Lower Slobovia given in the table. Does the principle of increasing cost hold in Lower Slobovia?
6. Consider two alternatives for Lower Slobovia in the year 1988. In case (a) its inhabitants eat 60 million loaves of bread and build only 12,000 ovens. In case (b) the population eats only 15 million loaves but builds 36,000 ovens. Which case will lead to a more generous production possibilities frontier for Slobovia in 1989?

PRODUCTION POSSIBILITIES FOR LOWER SLOBOVIA, 1988

BREAD LOAVES (millions)	OVENS (thousands)
75	0
60	12
45	22
30	30
15	36
0	40

7. Mel's Sports Shop sells two brands of tennis balls. Brand X costs Mel $1.50 per can, and Brand Y costs Mel $2 per can. Draw Mel's production possibilities frontier if he has $60 to spend on tennis balls. Why is it not "bowed out"?

4

The free enterprise system is absolutely too important to be left to the voluntary action of the marketplace.

CONGRESSMAN RICHARD
KELLY OF FLORIDA (1979)

Supply and Demand:
An Initial Look

If the issues of scarcity, choice, and coordination constitute the basic *problem* of economics, then the mechanism of supply and demand is its basic investigative tool. Whether your course concentrates on macroeconomics or microeconomics, you will find that the so-called law of supply and demand is the fundamental tool of economic analysis. Supply and demand analysis is used in this book to study issues seemingly as diverse as inflation and unemployment, the international value of the dollar, government regulation of business, and protection of the environment. So careful study of this chapter will pay rich dividends.

The chapter describes the rudiments of supply and demand analysis in steps. We begin with demand, then add supply, and finally put the two sides together. *Supply and demand curves* — graphs that relate price to quantity supplied and quantity demanded, respectively — are explained and used to show how prices and quantities are determined in a free market. Influences that shift either the demand curve or the supply curve are catalogued briefly. And the analysis is used to explain why airlines often run "sales," and why the home computer industry grew so fast.

One major theme of the chapter is that governments around the globe and throughout recorded history have attempted to tamper with the price mechanism. We will see that these bouts with Adam Smith's invisible hand often have produced undesired side effects that surprised and dismayed the authorities. And we will show that many of these unfortunate effects were no accidents, but were inherent consequences of interfering with the operation of free markets. The invisible hand fights back!

Finally, a word of caution. This chapter makes heavy use of graphs such as those described in Chapter 2. If you encounter difficulties with these graphs, we suggest you review pages 18–24 before proceeding.

Fighting the Invisible Hand

Adam Smith was a great admirer of the price system. He marveled at its intricacies and extolled its accomplishments — both as a producer of goods and a guarantor of individual freedom. Many people since Smith's time have shared his enthusiasm, but many others have not. His contemporaries in the American colonies, for example, were often unhappy with the prices produced by free markets and thought they could do better by legislative decree. (They could not, as the boxed insert on this page shows.) And there have been countless other instances in which the public's sense of justice was outraged by the prices charged on the open market, particularly when the sellers of the expensive items did not enjoy great popularity—landlords, moneylenders, and oil companies are good examples.

Attempts to control interest rates (which may be thought of as the price of borrowing money) go back hundreds of years before the birth of Christ, at least to the code of laws compiled under Hammurabi in Babylonia about 1800 B.C. Our historical legacy also includes a rather long list of price ceilings on foods and other products imposed in the reign of Diocletian, emperor of the declining Roman Empire. More recently, Americans have been offered the "protection" of a variety of price controls. Ceilings have been placed on some prices (such as

Price Controls at Valley Forge

George Washington, the history books tell us, was beset by many enemies during the winter of 1777–1778—including the British, their Hessian mercenaries, and the merciless winter weather. But he had another enemy that the history books ignore, an enemy who meant well but almost destroyed his army at Valley Forge. That enemy was the legislature of the Commonwealth of Pennsylvania, as the following excerpt explains.

In Pennsylvania, where the main force of Washington's army was quartered in 1777, . . . the legislature . . . decided to try a period of price control limited to those commodities needed for use by the army. The theory was that this policy would reduce the expense of supplying the army. . . . The result might have been anticipated by those with some knowledge of the trials and tribulations of other states. The prices of uncontrolled goods, mostly imported, rose to record heights. Most farmers kept back their produce, refusing to sell at what they regarded as an unfair price. Some who had large families to take care of even secretly sold their food to the British who paid in gold.

After the disastrous winter at Valley Forge when Washington's army nearly starved to death (thanks largely to these well-intentioned but misdirected laws), the ill-fated experiment in price controls was finally ended. The Continental Congress on June 4, 1778, adopted the following resolution:

"Whereas . . . it hath been found by experience that limitations upon the prices of commodities are not only ineffectual for the purposes proposed, but likewise productive of very evil consequences to the great detriment of the public service . . . resolved, that it be recommended to the several states to repeal or suspend all laws or resolutions within the said states respectively limiting, regulating or restraining the Price of any Article, Manufacture or Commodity."

SOURCE: Robert L. Schuettinger and Eamonn F. Butler, *Forty Centuries of Wage and Price Controls* (Washington, D.C.: Heritage Foundation, 1979), page 41. Reprinted by permission.

energy) to protect buyers, while floors have been placed under other prices (such as farm products) to protect sellers. Many if not most of these measures were adopted in response to popular opinion, and there is a great outcry whenever it is proposed that any one of them be weakened or eliminated.

Yet, somehow, everything such regulation touches seems to end up in even greater disarray than it was before. Despite rent controls, rents in New York City have considerably more than doubled in the last ten years. Despite laws against ticket "scalping," tickets for popular shows and sports events sell at tremendous premiums—$75 tickets to the 1987 Super Bowl, for example, reportedly were sold for prices as high as $1000. Taxis cost much more in New York City (where they are tightly regulated) than in Washington, D.C. (where they are not). And the list could go on.

Still, legislators continue to turn to controls whenever the economy does not work to their satisfaction, just as they did in 1777. The 1970s and 1980s have seen a return to rent controls in many American cities, a brief experiment with overall price controls by a Republican administration that had vowed never to turn to them, a web of controls over energy prices, and a revival of agricultural price supports.

Interferences with the "Law" of Supply and Demand
Public opinion frequently encourages legislative attempts to "repeal the law of supply and demand" by controlling prices. The consequences usually are quite unfortunate, exacting heavy costs from the general public and often aggravating the problem the legislation was intended to cure. This is another of the **12 Ideas for Beyond the Final Exam,** and it will occupy our attention throughout this chapter.

To understand what goes wrong when markets are tampered with, we must first learn how they operate when they are unfettered. This chapter takes a first step in that direction by studying the machinery of supply and demand. Then, at the end of the chapter, we return to the issue of price controls, illustrating the problems that can arise by case studies of rent controls in New York City and price supports for milk.

Every market has both buyers and sellers. We begin our analysis on the consumers' side of the market.

Demand and Quantity Demanded

Noneconomists are apt to think of consumer demands as fixed amounts. For example, when the production of a new type of machine tool is proposed, management asks "What is its market potential? How many will we be able to sell?" Similarly, government bureaus conduct studies to determine how many engineers will be "required" in succeeding years.

Economists respond that such questions are not well posed—that there is no *single* answer to such a question. Rather, they say, the "market potential" for machine tools or the number of engineers that will be "required" depends on a great number of things, *including the price that will be charged for each*.

The **quantity demanded** is the number of units consumers want to buy.

The **quantity demanded** of any product normally depends on its price. Quantity demanded also has a number of other determinants, including population size, consumer incomes, tastes, and the prices of other products.

Because of the central role of prices in a market economy, we begin our study of demand by focusing on the relationship between quantity demanded and price. Shortly, we will bring the other determinants of quantity demanded back into the picture.

Consider, as an example, the quantity of milk demanded. Almost everyone purchases at least some milk. However, if the price of milk is very high, its "market potential" may be very small. People will find ways to get along with less milk, perhaps by switching to tea or coffee. If the price declines, people will be encouraged to drink more milk. They may give their children larger portions or switch away from juices and sodas. Thus:

There is no *one* demand figure for milk, for machine tools, or for engineers. Rather, there is a different quantity demanded for each possible price.

The Demand Schedule

Table 4–1 displays this information for milk in what we call a **demand schedule**, which indicates how much consumers are willing and able to buy at different possible prices during a specified period of time. The table shows the quantity of milk that will be demanded in a year at each possible price ranging from $1 to 40¢ per quart. We see, for example, that at a relatively low price, like 50¢ per quart, customers wish to purchase 70 billion quarts per year. But if the price were to rise to, say, 90¢ per quart, quantity demanded would fall to 50 billion quarts.

Common sense tells us why this should be so.[1] First, as prices rise, some customers will reduce their consumption of milk. Second, higher prices will induce some customers to drop out of the market entirely—for example, by switching to soda or juice. On both counts, quantity demanded will decline as the price rises.

As the price of an item rises, the quantity demanded normally falls. As the price falls, the quantity demanded normally rises.

The Demand Curve

The information contained in Table 4–1 can be summarized in a graph, which we call a **demand curve**, displayed in Figure 4–1. Each point in the graph corresponds to a line in the table. For example, point B corresponds to the second line in the table, indicating that at a price of 90¢ per quart, 50 billion quarts

[1]This common-sense answer is examined more fully in Chapter 21.

A **demand schedule** is a table showing how the quantity demanded of some product during a specified period of time changes as the price of that product changes, holding all other determinants of quantity demanded constant.

A **demand curve** is a graphical depiction of a demand schedule. It shows how the quantity demanded of some product during a specified period of time will change as the price of that product changes, holding all other determinants of quantity demanded constant.

Table 4–1
DEMAND SCHEDULE FOR MILK

PRICE (dollars per quart)	QUANTITY DEMANDED (billions of quarts per year)	LABEL IN FIGURE 4–1
1.00	45	A
0.90	50	B
0.80	55	C
0.70	60	E
0.60	65	F
0.50	70	G
0.40	75	H

Figure 4-1

DEMAND CURVE
FOR MILK

This curve shows the relationship between price and quantity demanded. To sell 70 billion quarts per year, the price must be only 50¢ (point *G*). If, instead, price is 90¢, only 50 billion quarts will be demanded (point *B*). To sell more milk, the price must be reduced. That is what the negative slope of the demand curve means.

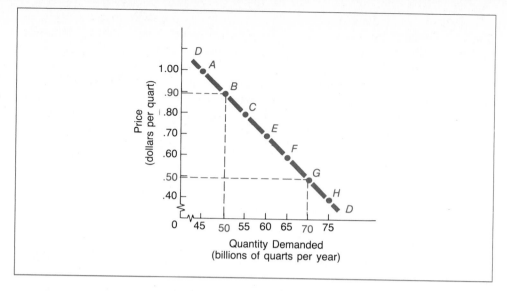

per year will be demanded. Since the quantity demanded declines as the price increases, the demand curve has a negative slope.[2]

Notice the last phrase in the definitions of the demand schedule and the demand curve: "holding all other determinants of quantity demanded constant." These "other things" include consumer incomes and preferences, the prices of soda and orange juice, and perhaps even advertising by the dairy association. We will examine the influences of these factors later in the chapter. First, however, let's look at the sellers' side of the market.

Supply and Quantity Supplied

Like quantity demanded, the quantity of milk that is supplied by dairy farmers is not a fixed number, but also depends on many things. Obviously, if there are more dairy farms, or larger ones, we expect more milk to be supplied. Or if bad weather deprives the cows of their feed, they may give less milk. As before, however, let's turn our attention first to the relationship between **quantity supplied** and one of its major determinants — the price of milk.

> The **quantity supplied** is the number of units sellers want to sell.

Economists generally suppose that a higher price calls forth a greater quantity supplied. Why? Remember our analysis of the principle of increasing cost in Chapter 3 (page 39). According to that principle, as more of any farmer's (or the nation's) resources are devoted to milk production, the opportunity cost of obtaining another quart of milk increases. Farmers will therefore find it profitable to raise milk production only if they can sell the milk at a higher price — high enough to cover the higher costs incurred when milk production expands.

Looked at the other way around, we have just concluded that higher prices normally will be required to persuade farmers to raise milk production. This idea is quite general, and applies to the supply of most goods and services.[3] As long as suppliers want to make profits and the principle of increasing costs holds:

As the price of an item rises, the quantity supplied normally rises. As the price falls, the quantity supplied normally falls.

---

[2]If you need to review the concept of *slope*, refer back to Chapter 2, especially pages 20–23.
[3]This analysis is carried out in much greater detail in Chapters 23 and 24.

The Supply Schedule and the Supply Curve

The relationship between the price of milk and its quantity supplied is recorded in Table 4–2. Tables like this are called **supply schedules**; they show how much sellers are willing to provide (during a specified period) at alternative possible prices. This particular supply schedule shows that a low price like 50¢ per quart will induce suppliers to provide only 40 billion quarts, while a higher price like 80¢ will induce them to provide much more — 70 billion quarts.

As you might have guessed, when information like this is plotted on a graph, it is called a **supply curve**. Figure 4–2 is the supply curve corresponding to the supply schedule in Table 4–2. It slopes upward because quantity supplied is higher when price is higher.

Notice again the same phrase in the definition: "holding all other determinants of quantity supplied constant." We will return to these "other determinants" a bit later in the discussion. But first we are ready to put demand and supply together.

A **supply schedule** is a table showing how the quantity supplied of some product during a specified period of time changes as the price of that product changes, holding all other determinants of quantity supplied constant.

A **supply curve** is a graphical depiction of a supply schedule. It shows how the quantity supplied of some product during a specified period of time will change as the price of that product changes, holding all other determinants of quantity supplied constant.

Table 4–2
SUPPLY SCHEDULE FOR MILK

PRICE (dollars per quart)	QUANTITY SUPPLIED (billions of quarts per year)	LABEL IN FIGURE 4–2
1.00	90	a
0.90	80	b
0.80	70	c
0.70	60	e
0.60	50	f
0.50	40	g
0.40	30	h

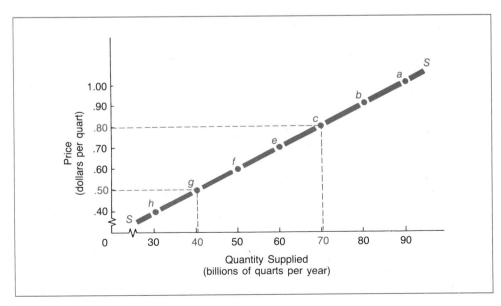

Figure 4–2
SUPPLY CURVE FOR MILK
This curve shows the relationship between the price of milk and the quantity supplied. To stimulate a greater quantity supplied, price must be increased. That is the meaning of the positive slope of the supply curve.

Equilibrium of Supply and Demand

To analyze how price is determined in a free market, we must compare the desires of consumers (demand) with the desires of producers (supply) and see whether the two plans are consistent. Table 4–3 and Figure 4–3 are designed to help us do this.

Table 4–3 brings together the demand schedule from Table 4–1 and the supply schedule from Table 4–2. Similarly, Figure 4–3 puts together the demand curve from Figure 4–1 and the supply curve from Figure 4–2 on a single graph. Such a graphic device is called a **supply–demand diagram**, and we will encounter many of them in this book. Notice that, for reasons already discussed, the demand curve has a negative slope and the supply curve has a positive slope. Most supply–demand diagrams are drawn with slopes like these.

There is only one point in Figure 4–3, point E, at which the supply curve and the demand curve intersect. At the price corresponding to point E, which is 70¢ per quart, the quantity supplied is equal to the quantity demanded. This means that, at a price of 70¢ per quart, consumers are willing to buy just what producers are willing to sell.

Table 4–3
DETERMINATION OF THE EQUILIBRIUM PRICE AND QUANTITY OF MILK

PRICE (dollars per quart)	QUANTITY DEMANDED	QUANTITY SUPPLIED	SURPLUS OR SHORTAGE?	PRICE WILL:
	(billions of quarts per year)			
1.00	45	90	Surplus	Fall
0.90	50	80	Surplus	Fall
0.80	55	70	Surplus	Fall
0.70	60	60	Neither	Remain the same
0.60	65	50	Shortage	Rise
0.50	70	40	Shortage	Rise
0.40	75	30	Shortage	Rise

Figure 4–3
SUPPLY–DEMAND EQUILIBRIUM

In a free market, price and quantity are determined by the intersection of the supply curve and the demand curve. In this example, the equilibrium price is 70¢ and the equilibrium quantity is 60 billion quarts of milk per year. Any other price is inconsistent with equilibrium. For example, at a price of 50¢, quantity demanded is 70 billion (point G), while quantity supplied is only 40 billion (point g), so that price will be driven up by the unsatisfied demand.

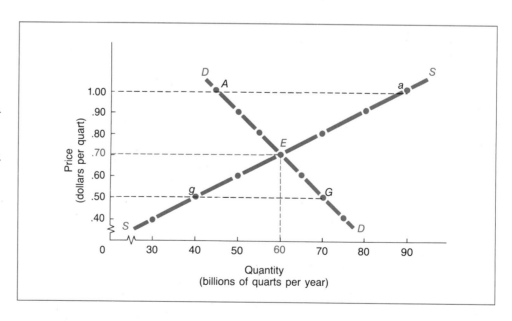

At a lower price, such as 50¢, only 40 billion quarts of milk will be supplied (point g) whereas 70 billion quarts will be demanded (point G). Thus, quantity demanded will exceed quantity supplied. There will be a **shortage** equal to 70 − 40 = 30 billion quarts. Alternatively, at a higher price, such as $1, quantity supplied will be 90 billion quarts (point a) while quantity demanded will be only 45 billion (point A). Quantity supplied will exceed quantity demanded, so there will be a **surplus** equal to 90 − 45 = 45 billion quarts.

Since 70¢ is the price at which quantity supplied and quantity demanded are equal, we say that 70¢ per quart is the **equilibrium price** in this market. Similarly, 60 billion quarts per year is the **equilibrium quantity** of milk.

The term "equilibrium" merits a little explanation, since it arises so frequently in economic analysis. An **equilibrium** is a situation in which there are no inherent forces that produce change; that is, a situation that does not contain the seeds of its own destruction. Think, for example, of a pendulum at rest at its center point. If no outside force (such as a person's hand) comes to push it, the pendulum will remain where it is; it is in *equilibrium*.

But, if someone gives the pendulum a shove, its equilibrium will be disturbed and it will start to move upward. When it reaches the top of its arc, the pendulum will, for an instant, be at rest again. But this is not an equilibrium position. A force known as gravity will pull the pendulum downward, and thereafter its motion from side to side will be governed by gravity and friction. Eventually, we know, the pendulum must return to the point at which it started, which is its only equilibrium position. At any other point inherent forces will cause the pendulum to move.

The concept of equilibrium in economics is similar and can be illustrated by our supply and demand example. Why is no price other than 70¢ an equilibrium price in Table 4–3 or Figure 4–3? What forces will change any other price?

Consider first a low price like 50¢, at which quantity demanded (70 billion) exceeds quantity supplied (40 billion). If the price were this low, there would be many frustrated customers unable to purchase the quantities they desire. They would compete with one another for the available milk. Some would offer more than the prevailing price and, as customers tried to outbid one another, the market price would be forced up. In other words, a price below the equilibrium price cannot persist in a free market because a shortage sets in motion powerful economic forces that push price upward.

Similar forces operate if the market price is *above* the equilibrium price. If, for example, the price should somehow get to be $1, Table 4–3 tells us that quantity supplied (90 billion) would far exceed quantity demanded (45 billion). Producers would be unable to sell their desired quantities of milk at the prevailing price, and some would find it in their interest to undercut their competitors by reducing price. This process of competitive price-cutting would continue as long as the surplus persisted, that is, as long as quantity supplied exceeded quantity demanded. Thus a price above the equilibrium price cannot persist indefinitely.

We are left with only one conclusion. The price 70¢ per quart and the quantity 60 billion quarts is the only price-quantity combination that does not sow the seeds of its own destruction. It is the only *equilibrium*. Any lower price must rise, and any higher price must fall. It is as if natural economic forces place a magnet at point E that attracts the market just like gravity attracts the pendulum.

A **shortage** is an excess of quantity demanded over quantity supplied. When there is a shortage, buyers cannot purchase the quantities they desire.

A **surplus** is an excess of quantity supplied over quantity demanded. When there is a surplus, sellers cannot sell the quantities they desire to supply.

An **equilibrium** is a situation in which there are no inherent forces that produce change. Changes away from an equilibrium position will occur only as a result of "outside events" that disturb the status quo.

The analogy to a pendulum is worth pursuing further. Most pendulums are more frequently in motion than at rest. However, unless they are repeatedly buffeted by outside forces (which, of course, is exactly what happens to pendulums used in clocks), pendulums gradually return to their resting points. The same is true of price and quantity in a free market. Markets are not always in equilibrium, but, if they are not interfered with, we have good reason to believe that they normally are *moving toward equilibrium*.

In principle, in a free market the forces of supply and demand are capable of selecting an equilibrium price and an equilibrium quantity toward which, in practice, we may expect actual price and actual quantity to gravitate.

The last interesting aspect of the analogy concerns the "outside forces" of which we have spoken. A pendulum that is being blown by the wind or pushed by a hand does not remain in equilibrium. Similarly, many outside forces can disturb a market equilibrium. A frost in Florida will disturb equilibrium in the market for oranges. A strike by miners will disturb equilibrium in the market for coal.

Many of these outside influences actually *change the equilibrium price and quantity* by shifting either the supply curve or the demand curve. If you look again at Figure 4–3, you can see clearly that any event that causes *either* the demand curve *or* the supply curve to shift will also cause the equilibrium price and quantity to change. Such events constitute the "other things" that we held constant in our definitions of supply and demand curves. We are now ready to analyze how these outside forces affect the equilibrium of supply and demand, beginning on the demand side.

Shifts of the Demand Curve

Returning to our example of milk, we noted earlier that the quantity of milk demanded is probably influenced by a variety of things other than the price of milk. Changes in population, consumer income, and the prices of alternative beverages such as soda and orange juice presumably cause changes in the quantity of milk demanded, even if the price of milk is unchanged.

Since the demand curve for milk depicts only the relationship between the quantity of milk demanded and the price of milk, holding all other factors constant, a change in any of these other factors produces a *shift of the entire demand curve*. That is:

A change in the price of a good produces a **movement along a fixed demand curve**. By contrast, a change in any other variable that influences quantity demanded produces a **shift of the demand curve**. If consumers want to buy *more* at any given price than they wanted previously, the demand curve shifts to the right (or outward). If they desire *less* at any given price, the demand curve shifts to the left (or inward).

To make this general principle more concrete and to show some of its many applications, let us consider some specific examples.

1. *Consumer incomes.* If average incomes increase, consumers may purchase more of many foods, including milk, even if the price of milk remains the same. That is, *increases in income normally shift demand curves outward to the right*, as depicted in Figure 4–4(a). In this example, the quantity demanded

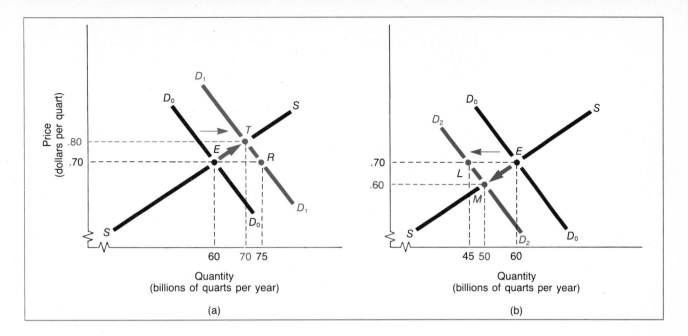

Price
(dollars per quart)

.80

.70

D_1

D_0

S

T

E

R

D_0

D_1

S

60   70 75

Quantity
(billions of quarts per year)

(a)

.70

.60

D_0

D_2

S

E

L

M

D_2

D_0

S

45 50   60

Quantity
(billions of quarts per year)

(b)

at the old equilibrium price of 70¢ increases from 60 billion quarts per year (point E on demand curve $D_0 D_0$) to 75 billion (point R on demand curve $D_1 D_1$). We know that 70¢ is no longer the equilibrium price, since at this price quantity demanded (75 billion) exceeds quantity supplied (60 billion). To restore equilibrium, price will have to rise. The diagram shows the new equilibrium at point T, where the price is 80¢ per quart and the quantity (demanded and supplied) is 70 billion quarts per year. This illustrates a general result.

Any factor that causes the demand curve to shift outward to the right, and does not affect the supply curve, will raise the equilibrium price and the equilibrium quantity.[4]

Everything works in reverse if consumer incomes fall. Figure 4–4(b) depicts a leftward (inward) shift of the demand curve that results from a decline in consumer incomes. For example, the quantity demanded at the previous equilibrium price (70¢) falls from 60 billion quarts (point E) to 45 billion (point L on demand curve $D_2 D_2$). At the initial price, quantity supplied must begin to fall. The new equilibrium will eventually be established at point M, where the price is 60¢ and both quantity demanded and quantity supplied are 50 billion. In general:

Any factor that shifts the demand curve inward to the left, and does not affect the supply curve, will lower both the equilibrium price and the equilibrium quantity.

2. *Population.* Population growth should affect quantity demanded in more or less the same way as increases in average incomes. A larger population will presumably wish to consume more milk, even if the price of milk and

Figure 4–4
THE EFFECTS OF SHIFTS OF THE DEMAND CURVE
A shift of the demand curve will change the equilibrium price and quantity in a free market. In part (a), the demand curve shifts outward from $D_0 D_0$ to $D_1 D_1$. As a result, equilibrium moves from point E to point T; both price and quantity rise. In part (b), the demand curve shifts inward from $D_0 D_0$ to $D_2 D_2$, and equilibrium moves from point E to point M; both price and quantity fall.

[4]This statement, like many others in the text, assumes that the demand curve is downward-sloping and the supply curve is upward-sloping.

average incomes are unchanged, thus shifting the entire demand curve to the right as in Figure 4–4(a). The equilibrium price and quantity both rise. Similarly, a decrease in population should shift the demand curve for milk to the left, as in Figure 4–4(b), causing equilibrium price and quantity to fall.

3. **Consumer preferences.** If the dairy industry mounts a successful advertising campaign extolling the benefits of drinking milk, families may decide to raise their quantities demanded. This would shift the entire demand curve for milk to the right, as in Figure 4–4(a). Alternatively, a medical report on the dangers of high cholesterol may persuade consumers to drink less milk, thereby shifting the demand curve inward, as in Figure 4–4(b).

Again, these are general phenomena. If consumer preferences shift in favor of a particular item, that item's demand curve will shift outward to the right, causing both equilibrium price and quantity to rise [Figure 4–4(a)]. Conversely, if consumer preferences shift against a particular item, that item's demand curve will shift inward to the left, causing equilibrium price and quantity to fall [Figure 4–4(b)].

4. **Prices and availability of related goods.** Because soda, orange juice, and coffee are popular drinks that compete with milk, a change in the price of any of these beverages can be expected to shift the demand curve for milk. If any of these alternative drinks become cheaper, some consumers will switch away from milk. Thus the demand curve for milk will shift to the left, as in Figure 4–4(b). The introduction of an entirely new beverage — like coconut milk — can be expected to have a similar effect.

But other price changes shift the demand curve for milk in the opposite direction. For example, suppose that cookies, a commodity that goes well with milk, become less expensive. This may induce some consumers to drink more milk and thus shift the demand curve for milk to the right, as in Figure 4–4(a).

Common sense normally will tell us in which direction a price change for a related good will shift the demand curve for a good in question. *Increases in the prices of goods that are substitutes for the good in question (as soda is for milk) move the demand curve to the right, thus raising both the equilibrium price and quantity. Increases in the prices of goods that are normally used together with the good in question (such as cookies and milk) shift the demand curve to the left, thus lowering both the equilibrium price and quantity.* (See Discussion Question 11 at the end of the chapter.)

While the preceding list does not exhaust the possible influences on quantity demanded, enough has been said to indicate the principles involved. Let us therefore turn to a concrete example.

Application: Why Airlines Run Sales

Anyone who travels knows that airline companies reduce fares sharply to attract more customers at certain times of the year — particularly in winter (excluding the holiday period), when air traffic is light. Yet there is no reason to think that air transportation gets any cheaper in winter. Our supply and demand diagram makes it easy to understand why airlines run such "sales."

Given the number of planes in airlines' fleets, the supply of seats is relatively fixed, as indicated by the steep supply curve SS in Figure 4–5, and is more or less the same in summer and winter. During seasons when people want to travel less, the demand curve for seats shifts leftward from its normal

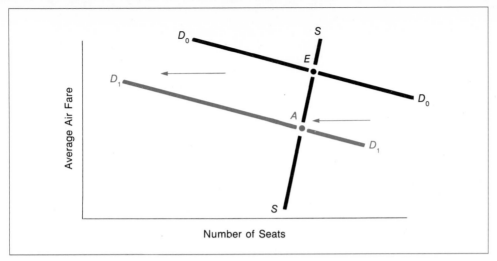

Figure 4–5
SEASONAL CHANGES IN
AIRLINE FARES
During seasons of slack
demand for air travel, the
demand curve shifts leftward
from $D_0 D_0$ to $D_1 D_1$. In
consequence, the market
equilibrium point shifts from E
to A, causing both price and
quantity to decline.

position, $D_0 D_0$, to a position such as $D_1 D_1$. Hence, equilibrium in the air-traffic market shifts from point E to point A. Thus both price and quantity decline at certain times of the year, not because of the generosity of the airlines, but because of the discipline of the market.

Shifts of the Supply Curve

Like quantity demanded, the quantity supplied on a market typically responds to a great number of influences other than price. The weather, the cost of feed, the number and size of dairy farms, and a variety of other factors all influence how much milk will be brought to market. Since the supply curve depicts only the relationship between the price of milk and the quantity of milk demanded, holding all other factors constant, a change in any of these other factors will cause the entire supply curve to shift. That is:

A change in the price of the good causes a **movement along a fixed supply curve.** But price is not the only influence on quantity supplied. And, if any of these other influences changes, the **entire supply curve shifts.**

Let us consider what some of these other factors are, and how they shift the supply curve.

1. *Size of the industry.* We begin with the most obvious factor. If more farmers enter the milk industry, the quantity supplied at any given price probably will increase. For example, if each farm provides 600,000 quarts of milk per year when the price is 70¢ per quart, then 100,000 farmers provide 60 billion quarts, and 130,000 farmers provide 78 billion. Thus, the more farms that are attracted to the industry, the greater will be the quantity of milk supplied at any given price, and hence the farther to the right will be the supply curve.
   Figure 4–6(a) illustrates the effect of an expansion of the industry from 100,000 farms to 130,000 farms — a rightward shift of the supply curve from $S_0 S_0$ to $S_1 S_1$. Notice that at the initial price of 70¢, the quantity supplied after the shift is 78 billion quarts (point I on supply curve $S_1 S_1$), which exceeds the quantity demanded of 60 billion (point E on supply curve $S_0 S_0$).

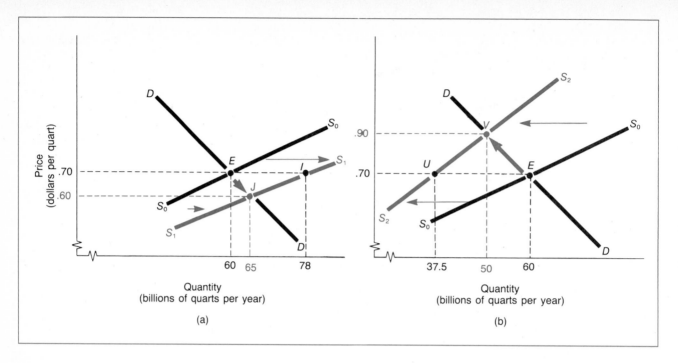

Figure 4–6

EFFECTS OF SHIFTS OF THE SUPPLY CURVE

A shift of the supply curve will change the equilibrium price and quantity in a market. In part (a), the supply curve shifts outward to the right, from $S_0 S_0$ to $S_1 S_1$. As a result, equilibrium moves from point E to point J; price falls as quantity increases. Part (b) illustrates the opposite case—an inward shift of the supply curve from $S_0 S_0$ to $S_2 S_2$. Equilibrium moves from point E to point V, which means that price rises as quantity falls.

We can see in the graph that the price of 70¢ is too high to be the equilibrium price; so the price must fall. The diagram shows the new equilibrium at point J, where the price is 60¢ per quart and the quantity is 65 billion quarts. The general point is that:

Any factor that shifts the supply curve outward to the right, and does not affect the demand curve, will lower the equilibrium price and raise the equilibrium quantity.

This must *always* be true if the industry's demand curve has a negative slope, because the greater quantity supplied can be sold only if price is decreased to induce customers to buy more.[5]

Figure 4–6(b) illustrates the opposite case: a contraction of the industry from 100,000 farms to 62,500 farms. The supply curve shifts inward to the left and equilibrium moves from point E to point V, where price is 90¢ and quantity is 50 billion quarts. In general:

Any factor that shifts the supply curve inward to the left, and does not affect the demand curve, will raise the equilibrium price and reduce the equilibrium quantity.

Even if no farmers enter or leave the industry, results like those depicted in Figure 4–6 can be produced by expansion or contraction of the existing farms. If farms get larger by adding more land, expanding the herds, and so on, the supply curve shifts to the right, as in Figure 4–6(a). If farms get smaller, the supply curve shifts to the left, as in Figure 4–6(b).

[5]Graphically, whenever a positively sloped curve shifts to the right, its intersection point with a negatively sloping curve must always move lower. Just try drawing it yourself.

2. ***Technological progress.*** Another influence that shifts supply curves is technological change. Suppose someone discovers that cows give more milk if Mozart is played during milking. Then, at any given price of milk, farmers will be able to provide a larger quantity of output; that is, the supply curve will shift outward to the right, as in Figure 4–6(a). This, again, illustrates a general influence that applies to most industries: *cost-reducing technological progress shifts the supply curve outward to the right*. Thus, as Figure 4–6(a) shows, the usual consequences of technological progress are lower prices and greater output.

3. ***Prices of inputs.*** Changes in input prices also shift supply curves. Suppose farm workers become unionized and win a raise. Farmers will have to pay higher wages and consequently will no longer be able to provide 60 billion quarts of milk profitably at a price of 70¢ per quart [point E in Figure 4–6(b)]. Perhaps they will provide only 37.5 billion (point U on supply curve S_2S_2). This example illustrates that *increases in the prices of inputs that suppliers must buy will shift the supply curve inward to the left*.

4. ***Prices of related outputs.*** Dairy farms produce more than milk. If cheese prices rise sharply, farmers may decide to use some raw milk to make cheese, thereby reducing the quantity of milk supplied. On a supply–demand diagram, the supply curve would shift inward, as in Figure 4–6(b).

   Similar phenomena occur in other industries, and sometimes the effect goes in the opposite direction. For example, suppose the price of beef goes up, which increases the quantity of meat supplied. That, in turn, will cause a rise in the number of cowhides supplied at any given price of leather. Thus, a rise in the price of beef will lead to a rightward shift in the supply curve of leather. In general: *A change in the price of one good produced by a multiproduct industry may be expected to shift the supply curves of all the other goods produced by that industry.*

Application: A Computer in Every Home?

A dozen years ago, no one owned a home computer. Now there are millions, and enthusiasts look toward the day when computers will be as commonplace as television sets. What happened to bring the computer from the laboratory into the home? Did Americans suddenly develop a craving for computers?

Hardly. What actually happened is that scientists in the early 1970s invented the microchip—a major breakthrough that drastically reduced both the size of computers and, more important, the cost of manufacturing them. Within a few years, microcomputers were in commercial production. And microchip technology continued to improve throughout the 1970s and 1980s, leading to ever smaller, better, and cheaper computers. Today, for a few hundred dollars you can buy a desktop machine whose computing powers rival those of the giant computers of the early 1960s.

In terms of our supply and demand diagrams, the rapid technological progress in computer manufacturing shifted the supply curve dramatically to the right. As Figure 4–7 shows, a large outward shift of the supply curve should bring down the equilibrium price and increase the equilibrium quantity—which is just what happened in the computer industry. The figure calls attention to the fact that consumers naturally buy more computers as the price of computers falls (*a movement along* demand curve DD from E to A), even if the demand curve does not *shift*.

Figure 4–7

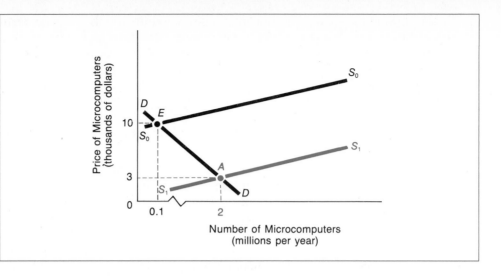

The invention of the
microchip, and subsequent
improvements in microchip
technology, caused the
supply curve of
microcomputers to shift
outward to the right—moving
from $S_0 S_0$ to $S_1 S_1$.
Consequently, equilibrium
shifted from point E to point
A. The price of
microcomputers fell from
$10,000 to $3,000, and the
quantity increased from
100,000 to 2 million per year.
(The numbers in the diagram
are roughly indicative of what
happened in the U.S. market
for microcomputers between
1978 and 1985, before
correcting for the fact that the
1985 computer was vastly
superior to the 1978
computer.)

Restraining the Market Mechanism: Price Ceilings

As we have noted already, lawmakers and rulers have often been dissatisfied
with the outcomes of the operation of the market system. From Rome to Pennsylvania and from biblical times to the space age, they have done battle with
the invisible hand. Sometimes, rather than trying to make adjustments in the
workings of the market, governments have sought to raise or to lower the prices
of specific commodities by decree. In many of these cases, those in authority
felt that the prices set by the market mechanism were, in some sense,
immorally low or immorally high. Penalties were therefore imposed on anyone
offering the commodities in question at prices lower or higher than those determined by the authorities.

But the market has proven itself a formidable foe that strongly resists
attempts to circumvent its workings. In case after case where legal **price ceilings**
are imposed, virtually the same set of consequences ensues:

A **price ceiling** is a legal
maximum on the price
that may be charged for a
commodity.

1. A persistent shortage develops of the items whose prices are controlled.
   Queuing, direct rationing, or any of a variety of other devices, usually inefficient and unpleasant, have to be substituted for the distribution process provided by the price mechanism. *Example:* Price controls on gasoline led to
   long lines at service stations in 1979.

2. An illegal, or "black," market often arises to supply the commodity. There
   are usually some individuals who are willing to take the risks involved in
   meeting unsatisfied demands illegally, if legal means will not do the job.
   Example: Although most states ban the practice, ticket "scalping" occurs at
   most popular sporting events.

3. The prices charged on the black market are almost certainly higher than
   those that would prevail in a free market. After all, black marketeers expect
   compensation for the risk of being caught and punished. *Example:* Goods
   that are illegally smuggled into a country are normally quite expensive.

4. In each case, a substantial portion of the price falls into the hands of the
   black-market supplier instead of going to those who produce the good or
   who perform the service. *Example:* A constant complaint in the series of
   hearings that have marked the history of theater ticket price controls in
   New York City has been that the "ice" (the illegal excess charge) falls into

the hands of ticket scalpers rather than going to those who invested in, produced, or acted in the play.

These points and others are best illustrated by considering a concrete example of price ceilings.

A Case Study: Rent Controls in New York City

New York is the only major city in the United States that has had rent controls continuously since World War II. The objective of rent control is, of course, to protect the consumer from high rents. But most economists believe that rent control does not help the cities or their inhabitants and that, in the long run, it makes almost everyone worse off. Let's use supply–demand analysis to see what actually happens.

Figure 4–8 is a supply–demand diagram for rental units in New York. Curve DD is the demand curve and curve SS is the supply curve. Without controls, equilibrium would be at point E, where rents average $900 per month and 3 million units are occupied. Effective rent controls must set a ceiling price below the equilibrium price of $900, because otherwise the rent level would simply settle at the point determined by market forces. But with a low rent ceiling, such as, say, $500, the quantity of housing demanded will be 3.5 million (point B) while the quantity supplied will be only 2.5 million (point C).

The diagram shows a shortage of 1,000,000 apartments. This theoretical concept of a "shortage" shows up in New York City as an abnormally low vacancy rate—typically about half the national urban average.

As we expect, rent controls have spawned a lively black market in New York. The black market works to raise the effective price of rent-controlled apartments in many ways, including bribes, "key money" paid to move up on the waiting list, and requiring prospective tenants to purchase worthless furniture at inflated prices.

According to the diagram, rent controls reduce the quantity supplied from 3 million to 2.5 million apartments. What do we see in New York? First, some property owners, discouraged by the low rents, have converted apartment buildings into office space or other uses. Second, some apartments have not been maintained adequately. After all, rent controls create a shortage which makes even dilapidated apartments easy to rent. Third, some landlords have actually abandoned their buildings rather than pay rising tax and fuel bills. These abandoned buildings rapidly become eyesores and eventually pose threats to public health and safety.

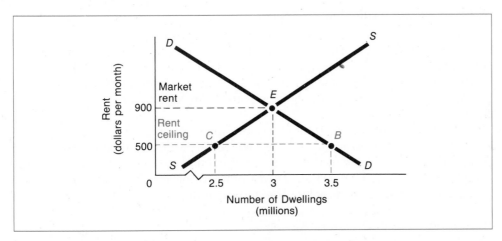

Figure 4–8
SUPPLY–DEMAND DIAGRAM FOR HOUSING
When market forces are permitted to set rents, the quantity of dwellings supplied will equal the quantity demanded. But when a rent ceiling forces rent below the market level, the number of dwellings supplied (point C) will be less than the number demanded (point B). Thus, rent ceilings induce housing shortages.

With all these problems, why do rent controls persist in New York City? And why are some other cities moving in the same direction? Part of the explanation is that many people simply do not understand the problems that rent controls cause. Another part is that landlords are unpopular politically. But a third, and important, part of the explanation is that not everyone is hurt by rent controls. Those who benefit from controls fight hard to preserve them. In New York, for example, many tenants pay rents that are only a fraction of what their apartments would fetch on the open market.

This last point illustrates another very general phenomenon:

Virtually every price ceiling or floor creates a class of people with a vested interest in preserving the regulations because they benefit from them. These people naturally use their political influence to protect their gains, which is one reason why it is so hard to eliminate price ceilings or floors.

Restraining the Market Mechanism: Price Floors

A **price floor** is a legal minimum on the price that may be charged for a commodity.

Interferences with the market mechanism are not always designed to keep prices low. Agricultural price supports and minimum wages are two notable examples in which the law keeps prices *above* free-market levels. **Price floors** are typically accompanied by a standard set of symptoms:

1. A surplus develops as some sellers cannot find buyers. *Example*: The minimum wage law helps create high unemployment among teen-agers.[6]

2. Where goods, rather than services, are involved, the surplus creates a problem of disposal. Something must be done about the excess of quantity supplied over quantity demanded. *Example:* The government has often been forced to purchase, and then store, large amounts of surplus agricultural commodities.

3. To get around the regulations, sellers may offer discounts in disguised—and often unwanted—forms. *Example:* When airline fares were regulated by the government, airlines offered more and better food and stylish uniforms for flight attendants instead of lowering fares. (Some still do; others offer "no frills" service with lower ticket prices.)

Once again, a specific example is useful.

A Case Study: Milk Price Supports

Perhaps you have seen television pictures of government workers giving away cheese to the needy. Perhaps you wondered where all that cheese came from. The answer is that the government's stockpiles of cheese are an indirect result of its efforts to set a floor under the price of milk. Explaining how this works provides a good illustration of the things that can happen when a price floor is imposed.

To help dairy farmers, the U.S. government sets a minimum support price for milk, just as it does for many agricultural products. In most times and places, this support price is well above the free-market level. So a surplus develops, as indicated in Figure 4–9. To maintain the price above the free-market level, the government must buy the surplus milk, which in recent years has

[6]This subject is dealt with more fully in Chapter 36.

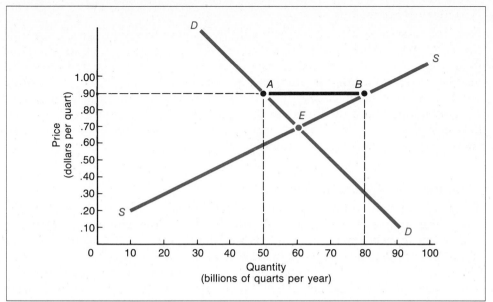

Figure 4–9
PRICE SUPPORTS
FOR MILK
In this diagram, which
repeats the supply and
demand curves from
Figure 4–3, the support price
for milk (90¢ per quart) is
above the equilibrium price
(70¢). Quantity supplied is 80
billion quarts per year (point
B), while quantity demanded
is only 50 billion (point A). To
keep the price at 90¢, the
government must buy 30
billion quarts of milk per year
and store it as cheese.

amounted to 5–10% of all dairy products produced in the United States. But this creates a problem. Milk is so highly perishable that it must be turned into cheese or butter or dried milk before it can be stored. Buying and storing these products costs the U.S. government about $2–$3 billion per year. And every so often, the government accumulates so much cheese in its warehouses that its storage capacity is strained. It may then decide to give the surplus away. That is why the government gives cheese to the poor, instead of something else — such as milk.

A Can of Worms

Our two case studies — rent controls and milk price supports — illustrate some of the major side effects of price floors and ceilings, but barely hint at others. And there are yet more difficulties that we have not even mentioned, for the market mechanism is a tough bird that imposes suitable retribution on those who seek to circumvent it by legislative decree. Here is a partial list of other problems that may arise when prices are controlled.

Favoritism and Corruption
When price ceilings create a shortage, someone must decide who gets the limited quantity that is available. This can lead to political favoritism, to corruption in government, or even to discrimination along racial or religious lines.

Unenforceability
Attempts to control prices are almost certain to fail in industries with numerous suppliers, simply because the regulating agency must monitor the behavior of so many sellers. Some ways will be found to evade or to violate the law, and something akin to the free-market price will generally reemerge. But there is a difference: since the evasion mechanism, whatever its form, will have some operating costs, those costs must be borne by someone. Normally, that someone is the consumer.

Auxiliary Restrictions

Fears that a system of price controls will break down invariably lead to regulations designed to shore up the shaky edifice. Consumers may be told when and from whom they are permitted to buy. The powers of the police and the courts may be used to prevent the entry of new suppliers. Occasionally, an intricate system of market subdivision is imposed, giving each class of firms its protected category of operations in which others are not permitted to compete. Milk marketing orders are one good example. Laws banning conversion of rent-controlled apartments to condominiums are another.

Limitation of Volume of Transactions

To the extent that controls succeed in affecting prices, they can be expected to reduce the volume of transactions. Curiously, this is true whether the regulated price is above or below the free-market's equilibrium price. If it is set above the equilibrium price, quantity demanded will be below the equilibrium quantity. On the other hand, if the imposed price is set below the free-market level, quantity supplied will be cut down. Since sales volume cannot exceed either the quantity supplied or the quantity demanded, a reduction in the volume of transactions is likely to result.

Encouragement of Inefficiency

A price that is above the equilibrium level permits the survival of less-efficient firms whose high operating costs would doom them in an unrestricted market. This invitation to continued inefficiency becomes even more serious if entry of new suppliers is prevented as part of the program of enforcement of price regulations. (This is why deregulation of the airline industry has led to a painful "shake out" of the weaker companies in the 1980s.) Moreover, with the penalties for inefficiency severely restricted, the motivation for continued economy of operation by any firm is reduced.

Misallocation of Resources

Departures from free-market prices are likely to produce misuse of the economy's resources because the connection between production costs and prices is broken. For example, shippers use trucks or barges over routes where the resource cost of rail transportation is lower because artificial restrictions impose floors on railroad rates. In addition, just as more complex locks lead to more sophisticated burglary tools, more complex regulations lead to the use of yet more resources for their avoidance. New jobs are created for executives, lawyers, and economists. It may well be conjectured that at least some of the expensive services of these professionals could have been used more productively elsewhere.

Economists put it this way. Free markets are capable of dealing with the three basic coordination tasks outlined in Chapter 3: deciding *what* to produce, *how* to produce it, and *to whom* the goods should be distributed. Price controls throw a monkey wrench into the market mechanism. Though the market is surely not flawless, and government interferences often have praiseworthy goals, good intentions are not enough. Any government that sets out to repair what it sees as a defect in the market mechanism must take care lest it cause serious damage elsewhere. As a prominent economist once quipped, societies that are too willing to interfere with the operation of free markets soon find that the invisible hand is nowhere to be seen.

The Free Market and the Super Bowl

This excerpt from a newspaper article tells how the free market handled the shortage of tickets to the 1984 Super Bowl. The article uses the concept of opportunity cost from Chapter 3 without using the term. (Can you find where?)

Super Bowl XVIII provides a great illustration of how markets work. There are 72,000 seats in the Tampa stadium and roughly 40 million football fans. This creates a classic confrontation of supply and demand.

On the supply side of the market, quantity is absolutely limited.... Given Tampa's capacity, the supply-of-seats curve for Super Bowl XVIII is vertical.

Demand is another story. Tens of millions of fans would like to be there when the Los Angeles Raiders meet the Washington Redskins... and thus could be included in the market demand for seats....

The NFL does not permit the market to determine the ticket price, however. Instead, it rations tickets.... The market determines neither the initial price nor the initial distribution.

Holders, however, are permitted to resell their tickets, making for a lively market. Many are not willing to pay the full costs of attending the Super Bowl. For Raiders or Redskins home fans, full cost includes round-trip transportation (about $300), lodging ($200), the ticket ($60) and at least two days' time. The cash outlay is at least $600.

The economic cost of attendance is further increased by the implicit price of the ticket itself. The out-of-pocket cost is $60; however, the ticket can be sold for much more. This higher market value represents the ticket's implicit cost.

How high is that cost (price)? In Washington, a major ticket dealer says he bought more than 400 tickets at $350 apiece and resold them for $400 each. The Sunday edition of the *Washington Post* carried 109 ads each offering multiple tickets. The lowest offer was $350 a ticket, the highest $900. So it would appear that the equilibrium price in the aftermarket is about $500 a ticket.*

Are 72,000 fans really willing to pay more than $1,100 each to see the Super Bowl? Probably not. Most fans consider only the cash cost of their tickets, not the true economic cost. They don't realize how much they really are paying for their good fortune. If they acted like economists, the quantity of tickets supplied to the aftermarket would shift markedly to the right and the equilibrium price of a ticket would fall sharply (though not to $60).

SOURCE: Bradley R. Schiller, "Super Bowl Seats: Lucky Draw Costs a Fortune." *THE WALL STREET JOURNAL*, January 19, 1984.

*NOTE: For the 1987 Super Bowl in Los Angeles, ticket prices in the $750–$1000 range were common.

Summary

1. The quantity of a product that is demanded is not a fixed number. Rather, quantity demanded depends on such factors as the price of the product, consumer incomes, and the prices of other products.

2. The relationship between quantity demanded and price, holding all other things constant, can be displayed graphically on a demand curve.

3. For most products, the higher the price, the lower the quantity demanded. So the demand curve usually has a negative slope.

4. The quantity of a product that is supplied also depends on its price and many other influences. A supply curve is a graphical representation of the relationship between quantity supplied and price, holding all other influences constant.

5. For most products, the supply curve has a positive slope, meaning that higher prices call forth greater quantities supplied.
6. A market is said to be in equilibrium when quantity supplied is equal to quantity demanded. The equilibrium price and quantity are shown by the point on a graph where the supply and demand curves intersect. In a free market, price and quantity will tend to gravitate to this point.
7. A change in quantity demanded that is caused by a change in the price of the good is represented by a movement along a fixed demand curve. A change in quantity demanded that is caused by a change in any other determinant of quantity demanded is represented by a shift of the demand curve.
8. This same distinction applies to the supply curve:

Changes in price lead to movements along a fixed supply curve; changes in other determinants of quantity supplied lead to shifts of the whole supply curve.
9. Changes in consumer incomes, tastes, technology, prices of competing products, and many other influences cause shifts in either the demand curve or the supply curve and produce changes in price and quantity that can be determined from supply–demand diagrams.
10. An attempt by government regulations to force prices above or below their equilibrium levels is likely to lead to shortages or surpluses, black markets in which goods are sold at illegal prices, and to a variety of other problems. This is one of the **12 Ideas for Beyond the Final Exam.**

Concepts for Review

Quantity supplied	Supply curve	Equilibrium
Quantity demanded	Supply–demand diagram	Shifts in vs. movements along supply and demand curves
Demand schedule	Shortage	
Demand curve	Surplus	Price ceiling
Supply schedule	Equilibrium price and quantity	Price floor

Questions for Discussion

1. How often do you go to the movies? Would you go less often if a ticket cost twice as much? Distinguish between your demand curve for movie tickets and your "quantity demanded" at the current price.
2. What would you expect to be the shape of a demand curve
   a. for a medicine that means life or death for a patient?
   b. for the gasoline sold by Sam's gas station, which is surrounded by many other gas stations?
3. The following are the assumed supply and demand schedules for footballs:

DEMAND SCHEDULE		SUPPLY SCHEDULE	
PRICE	QUANTITY DEMANDED	PRICE	QUANTITY SUPPLIED
$13	6,000	$13	71,000
11	13,000	11	63,000
9	29,000	9	29,000
7	50,000	7	11,000
5	61,000	5	0

   a. Plot the supply and demand curves and indicate the equilibrium price and quantity.
   b. What effect will an increase in the price of leather (a production input) have on the equilibrium price and quantity of footballs, assuming all other things remain constant? Explain your answer with the help of a diagram.
   c. What effect will a decrease in the price of soccer balls (a substitute commodity) have on the equilibrium price and quantity of footballs, assuming again that all other things are held constant? Use a diagram in your answer.
4. Assume that the supply and demand schedules for economics textbooks at your college are the following:

PRICE	QUANTITY DEMANDED	QUANTITY SUPPLIED
$55	125	1400
45	250	900
35	500	500
25	1000	200
15	2000	0

   a. What is the equilibrium price and quantity of textbooks?
   b. In order to protect the profits of college bookstores, the state government sets a minimum textbook price of $45. How many economics textbooks will be sold now?
   c. Students protest and, as a result, the government abolishes the $45 price floor and imposes instead a $25 maximum price for textbooks. How many economics textbooks will be sold now?

d. While this price ceiling is in effect, computerization of publishing reduces the costs of producing textbooks. What effects will this have on the textbook market?
5. Show how the following demand curves are likely to shift in response to the indicated changes:
   a. The effect on the demand curve for boots when snowfall increases.
   b. The effect on the demand curve for tea when coffee prices rise.
   c. The effect on the demand curve for tea when sugar prices rise.
6. Discuss the likely effects of
   a. rent ceilings on the supply of apartments.
   b. minimum wages on the demand for teen-age workers.
   Use supply–demand diagrams to show what may happen in each case.
7. Drinking water is costly to supply. Draw a supply–demand diagram showing how much water would be bought if water were supplied by a city government at zero charge. What do you conclude from these results about areas of the country in which water is in short supply?
8. On page 68 it is claimed that either price floors or price ceilings reduce the actual quantity exchanged in a market. Use a diagram, or diagrams, to support this conclusion, and explain the common sense behind it.
9. The same rightward shift of the demand curve may produce a very small or a very large increase in quantity, depending on the slope of the supply curve. Explain with diagrams.
10. In 1981, when regulations were holding the price of natural gas below its free-market level, Congressman Jack Kemp of New York said the following in an interview with *The New York Times*: "We need to decontrol natural gas, and get production of natural gas up to a higher level so we can bring down the price."[7] Evaluate the congressman's statement.
11. The two diagrams below show supply and demand curves for two substitute commodities: tapes and compact disks (CDs).
    a. On the left-hand diagram, show what happens when technological progress makes it cheaper to produce CDs.
    b. On the right-hand diagram, show what happens to the market for tapes.
12. (More difficult) Consider the market for milk discussed in this chapter (Tables 4–1 through 4–3 and Figures 4–1 through 4–3). Suppose the government decides to fight kidney stones by levying a tax of 30¢ per quart on sales of milk. Follow these steps to analyze the effects of the tax:
    a. Construct the new supply curve (to replace Table 4–2) that relates quantity supplied to the price consumers pay. (*Hint*: Before the tax, when consumers paid 70¢, farmers supplied 60 billion quarts. With a 30¢ tax, when consumers pay 70¢ farmers will receive only 40¢. Table 4–2 tells us they will provide only 30 billion quarts at this price. This is one point on the new supply curve. The rest of the curve can be constructed in the same way.)
    b. Graph the new supply curve constructed in part (a) on the supply–demand diagram depicted in Figure 4–3. What are the new equilibrium price and quantity?
    c. Does the tax succeed in its goal of reducing the consumption of milk?
    d. How much does the equilibrium price increase? Is the price rise greater than, equal to, or less than the 30¢ tax?
    e. Who actually pays the tax, consumers or producers? (This may be a good question to discuss in class.)

[7]*The New York Times*, December 23, 1981.

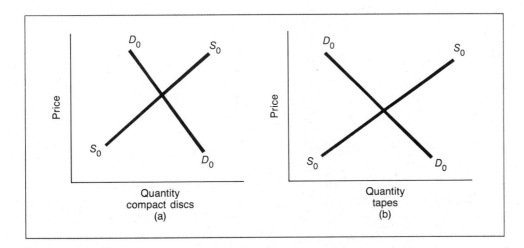

Quantity
compact discs
(a)

Quantity
tapes
(b)

PART 2

The Realm of Macroeconomics

5

Where the telescope ends, the microscope begins. Which of the two has the grander view?

VICTOR HUGO

Macroeconomics and Microeconomics

Economics traditionally has been divided into two fields: microeconomics and macroeconomics. These rather inelegant words are derived from the Greek — "micro" means something small and "macro" means something large. Although they were not specifically described as such, the basic notions and subject matter of **microeconomics** were introduced in Chapters 3 and 4. This chapter does the same for **macroeconomics**.

We begin the chapter by investigating the dividing line between microeconomics and macroeconomics: How do the two parts of the discipline differ and why? Next, we stress that while the *questions* studied by macroeconomists differ from those addressed by microeconomists, the underlying *tools* each group uses are almost the same. Supply and demand provide the basic organizing framework for constructing macroeconomic models, just as they do for microeconomic models. Third, we define some important macroeconomic concepts, like recession, inflation, and gross national product. Fourth, we look briefly at the broad sweep of American economic history to obtain some evaluation of the prevalence and seriousness of the macroeconomic problems of recession and inflation. And, finally, we preview what is to come in subsequent chapters by introducing the notion of government management of the economy.

Drawing a Line Between Macroeconomics and Microeconomics

In microeconomics *we study the behavior of individual decision-making units*. The dairy farmers of Chapter 4 are individual decision-making units; so are the consumers who purchase milk. How do they decide what courses of action are in their own best interests? How are these millions of decisions coordinated by the market mechanism, and with what consequences? Questions like these are the substance of microeconomics and are taken up in Parts 6 through 9.

Although Plato and Aristotle might wince at the abuse of their language, microeconomics applies to the decisions of some astonishingly large units.

Exxon and the American Telephone and Telegraph Company, for instance, have annual sales that exceed the total production of many nations. Yet someone who studies the pricing policies of AT&T is a microeconomist, whereas someone who studies inflation in Trinidad–Tobago is a macro-economist. So the micro versus macro distinction in economics is certainly not based solely on size. What, then, is the basis for this time-honored distinction? Whereas microeconomics focuses on the decisions of individual units (no matter how large), *macroeconomics concentrates on the behavior of entire economies* (no matter how small). Rather than looking at the price and output decisions of a single company, macroeconomists study the overall price level, unemployment rate, and other things that we call *economic aggregates*.

Aggregation and Macroeconomics

What is an "economic aggregate"? Nothing but an *abstraction* that people find convenient in describing some salient feature of economic life. For example, while we observe the prices of butter, telephone calls, and movie tickets every day, we never observe "the price level." Yet many people (not only economists) find it both meaningful and natural to speak of "the cost of living"—so natural, in fact, that the Bureau of Labor Statistics' monthly attempts at measuring it are widely publicized by the news media.

Among the most important of these abstract notions is the concept of *national product,* which represents the total production of a nation's economy. The process by which real objects like hairpins, baseballs, cigarettes, and theater tickets get combined into an abstraction called national product is called **aggregation,** and it is one of the foundations of macroeconomics. We can illustrate it by a simple example.

Aggregation means combining many individual markets into one overall market.

Imagine a nation called Agraria, whose economy is far simpler than the U.S. economy: Business firms in Agraria produce nothing but foodstuffs to sell to consumers. Rather than deal separately with all the markets for pizzas, candy bars, hamburgers, and so on, macroeconomists group them all into a single abstract "market for output." Thus, when macroeconomists in Agraria announce that output in Agraria rose 10 percent this year, are they referring to more potatoes or hot dogs, more soybeans or green peppers? The answer is: They do not care. In the aggregate measures of macroeconomics, output is output, no matter what form it takes.

Amalgamating many markets into one means that distinctions among different products are ignored. Can we really believe that no one cares whether the national output of Agraria consists of $800,000 worth of pickles and $200,000 worth of ravioli rather than $500,000 each of lettuce and tomatoes? Surely this is too much to swallow! Macroeconomists clearly do not believe that no one cares; instead, they rest the case for aggregation on two foundations.

1. While the *composition* of demand and supply in the various markets may be terribly interesting and important for *some* purposes (such as how income is distributed and what kinds of diets the citizens enjoy or endure), it may be of little consequence for the economy-wide issues of inflation and unemployment—the issues that concern macroeconomists.

2. During economic fluctuations, markets tend to move in unison. When demand in the economy rises, there is more demand for potatoes *and* tomatoes, more demand for artichokes *and* pickles, more demand for ravioli *and* hot dogs.

Though there are exceptions to these two principles, both seem serviceable enough as approximations. In fact, if they were not, there would be no discipline called macroeconomics, and this book would be only half as long as it is. (Lest this cause you a twinge of regret, bear in mind that many people feel that unemployment and inflation would be far more difficult to control without macroeconomics — which would be even more regrettable.)

The Line of Demarcation Revisited

These two principles — that markets normally move together and that the composition of demand and supply may be unimportant for some purposes — enable us to draw a different kind of dividing line between the territories of microeconomics and macroeconomics.

In macroeconomics, we typically assume that most details of resource allocation and income distribution are of secondary importance to the study of the overall rates of inflation and unemployment.

In microeconomics, we typically ignore inflation and unemployment and focus instead on how individual markets allocate resources and distribute income.

To use a well-worn metaphor, the macroeconomist analyzes the determination of the size of the economic "pie," paying scant attention to what is inside it or to how it gets divided among the dinner guests. A microeconomist, on the other hand, assumes that the pie is of the right size and shape, and frets over its ingredients and its division. If you have ever baked or eaten a pie, you will realize that either approach alone is a trifle myopic.

In some chapters of this book (especially in Parts 2–4), macroeconomic issues are discussed as if they could be divorced from questions of resource allocation and income distribution. In other chapters (especially those in Parts 6 through 9), microeconomic problems are investigated with scarcely a word about overall inflation and unemployment. Only in certain sections of the book (especially in Parts 5 and 10) are the two modes of analysis brought to bear simultaneously on the same social problems. This is done solely for the sake of pedagogical clarity. In reality, the crucial interconnection between macroeconomics and microeconomics is with us all the time. There is, after all, only one economy.

Supply and Demand in Macroeconomics

Some students reading this book will be taking a course that concentrates on macroeconomics while others will be studying microeconomics. The discussion of supply and demand in Chapter 4 serves as an invaluable introduction to both fields because the basic apparatus of supply and demand is just as important in macroeconomics as it is in microeconomics.

Figure 5–1 shows two diagrams that should look familiar from Chapter 4. In Figure 5–1(a), there is a downward-sloping demand curve, labeled DD, and an upward-sloping supply curve, labeled SS. The axes labeled "Price" and "Quantity" do not specify what commodity they refer to because this is a multipurpose diagram. To start on familiar terrain, first imagine that this is a picture of the market for milk, so the price axis measures the price of milk while the quantity axis measures the quantity of milk demanded and supplied. As we know, if there are no interferences with the operation of a free market, equilibrium will be at point E with a price P_0 and a quantity of output Q_0.

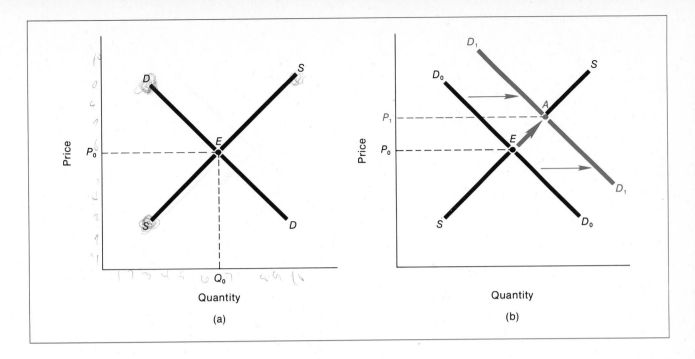

Figure 5–1

TWO INTERPRETATIONS OF A SHIFT IN THE DEMAND CURVE

Part (a) shows an equilibrium at point E, where demand curve DD intersects supply curve SS. Part (b) shows how this equilibrium moves from point E to point A if the demand curve moves outward. If this graph represents the market for milk, as it did in Chapter 4, then it shows an increase in the price of milk. But if the graph represents the aggregate market for "national product," then it shows inflation—a rise in the general price level.

Next, suppose something happens to shift the demand curve outward. For example, we learned in Chapter 4 that an increase in consumer incomes might have this effect. Figure 5–1(b) shows this shift as a rightward movement of the demand curve from $D_0 D_0$ to $D_1 D_1$. Equilibrium has shifted from E to A, so both price and output have risen.

Now let us reinterpret Figure 5–1 as representing an abstract market for "national product." This is one of those abstractions—an economic aggregate—that we described earlier. No one has ever seen, touched, smelled, or eaten a "unit of national product," but these are the kinds of abstractions upon which macroeconomic analysis is built. Consistent with this reinterpretation, think of the price measured on the vertical axis as being another abstraction— the overall price index, or "cost of living."[1] Then curve DD in Figure 5–1(a) is called an **aggregate demand curve**, and curve SS is called an **aggregate supply curve**. We will explain where these curves come from in Chapters 8–11.

With this reinterpretation, Figure 5–1(b) can depict the macroeconomic problem of **inflation.** We see from the figure that the outward shift of the aggregate demand curve, whatever its cause, pushes the price level up from P_0 to P_1. If aggregate demand keeps shifting out month after month, the economy will suffer from inflation, that is, a sustained increase in the general price level.

The other principal problems of macroeconomics, recession and unemployment, also can be illustrated on a supply-demand diagram, this time by shifting the demand curve in the opposite direction. Figure 5–2 repeats the supply and demand curves of Figure 5–1(a) and in addition depicts a leftward shift

The **aggregate demand curve** shows the quantity of national product that is demanded at each possible value of the price level.

The **aggregate supply curve** shows the quantity of national product that is supplied at each possible value of the price level.

Inflation refers to a sustained increase in the general price level.

[1]The appendix to Chapter 6 explains how such price indexes are calculated.

Figure 5–2
AN ECONOMY SLIPPING INTO A RECESSION
In this aggregate supply–demand diagram, there is an initial equilibrium at point E, where demand curve $D_0 D_0$ intersects supply curve SS. When the demand curve shifts inward from $D_0 D_0$ to $D_2 D_2$, equilibrium moves to point B, and output falls from Q_0 to Q_2.

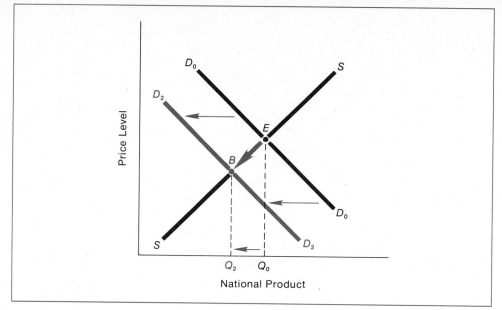

of the aggregate demand curve from $D_0 D_0$ to $D_2 D_2$. Equilibrium now moves from point E to point B so that national product (total output) declines from Q_0 to Q_2. This is what we normally mean by a **recession.**

A **recession** is a period of time during which the total output of the economy declines.

Gross National Product

The economy's total output, we have just seen, is one of the major variables of concern to macroeconomists. While there are several ways to measure it, the most popular choice undoubtedly is the **gross national product**, a term you have probably encountered in the news media. The gross national product, or "GNP" for short, is the most comprehensive measure of the output of all the factories, offices, and shops in the U.S. economy. Specifically, it is the sum of the money values of all final goods and services produced within the year.

Gross national product (GNP) is the sum of the money values of all final goods and services produced by the economy during a specified period of time, usually one year.

Several features of this definition need to be underscored.[2] First, you will notice that:

We add up the *money values* of things.

The GNP consists of a bewildering variety of goods and services: mousetraps and computers, bologna and caviar, ballet performances and rock concerts, tanks and textbooks. How are we to combine all of these into a single number? To an economist, the natural way to do this is first to convert every good and service into *money* terms. If we want to add 10 apples and 20 oranges, we first ask: How much *money* does each cost? If apples cost 20 cents and oranges cost 25 cents, then the apples count for $2 and the oranges for $5, so the sum is $7 worth of "output." The market *price* of each good or service is used as an indicator of its *value* to society simply because *someone* is willing to pay that much money for it.

This decision raises the question of what prices to use in valuing the different outputs. The official data offer two choices. First, we can value each good

[2]Certain exceptions to the definition are dealt with in Appendix B of Chapter 8, especially on page 158. Some instructors may prefer to take up that material here.

and service at the price at which it was actually sold during the year. If we do this, the resulting measure is called **nominal GNP,** or *money GNP,* or *GNP in current dollars*. This seems like a perfectly sensible choice. But as a measure of output, it has one serious drawback: nominal GNP rises when prices rise, even if there is no increase in actual production. For example, if hamburgers cost $1.50 this year but cost only $1.25 last year, then 100 hamburgers will contribute $150 to this year's nominal GNP but only $125 to last year's. But 100 hamburgers are still 100 hamburgers—output has not grown.

Nominal GNP is calculated by valuing all outputs at current prices.

For this reason, government statisticians have devised an alternative measure that corrects for inflation by valuing all goods and services at some fixed set of prices. (Currently, the prices of 1982 are used.) For example, if the hamburgers were valued at $1.25 each in both years, $125 worth of hamburger output would be included in GNP in each year. When we treat every output in this way, we obtain the **real GNP** or *GNP in constant dollars*. The news media often refer to it as "GNP corrected for inflation." Throughout most of this book, and certainly when we are discussing the nation's output, it is the real GNP that we shall be concerned with. The distinction between nominal and real GNP leads us to a working definition of a *recession* as a period in which *real* GNP declines. For example, between 1981 and 1982, nominal GNP rose from $3053 billion to $3166 billion; but real GNP *fell* from $3249 billion to $3166 billion.

The next important aspect of the definition of GNP is that:

Real GNP is calculated by valuing all outputs at the prices that prevailed in some agreed-upon year (currently 1982). Therefore, real GNP is a far better measure of changes in national production.

The GNP for a particular year includes only goods and services produced during that year. Sales of items produced in previous years are explicitly excluded.

For example, suppose you buy a perfectly beautiful 1974 Plymouth next week and are overjoyed by your purchase. The national income statistician will not share your glee because she already counted your car in the GNP in 1974 when it was first produced and sold; the car will never be counted again. The same holds true of houses. An old house (unlike an old car) often will sell for more than its original purchasers paid; yet the resale value of the house does not count in the GNP since it was already counted in the year it was built. For the same reason, exchanges of other existing assets are not included in the GNP.

Third, you will note the use of the phrase **final goods and services** in the definition. The adjective "final" is the key word here. For example, when a supermarket buys milk from a farmer, the transaction is not included in the GNP because the supermarket does not want the milk for itself. It buys milk only for resale to consumers. Only when the milk is sold to consumers is it considered a final product. When the supermarket buys it, economists consider it an **intermediate good.** The GNP does not include sales of intermediate goods or services.[3]

Final goods and services are those that are purchased by their ultimate users.

Finally, although the definition does not state this explicitly:

An **intermediate good** is a good purchased for resale or for use in producing another good.

For the most part, only goods and services that pass through organized markets count in the GNP.

This, of course, excludes many economic activities. For example, illegal activities are not included in the GNP. Thus, gambling services in Chicago are not in the GNP, but gambling services in Atlantic City are. The definition reflects the statisticians' confession that they could not hope to measure the value of

---

[3]Actually, there is another way to add up the GNP by counting a portion of each intermediate transaction. This is explained in Appendix B of Chapter 8, especially pages 161–62.

many of the economy's most important activities, such as housework, do-it-yourself repairs, and leisure time. While these are certainly economic activities that result in currently produced goods or services, they all lack that important measuring rod — a price.

This omission results in certain oddities. For example, suppose that each of two neighboring families hires the other to clean house, generously paying $1000 a week for the services. Each family can easily afford such generosity since it collects an identical salary from its neighbor. Nothing real changes, but GNP goes up by $104,000 a year.

Limitations of the GNP: What GNP Is Not

Having seen in some detail what the GNP *is*, it is worth pausing to expand upon what it *is not*. In particular:

Gross national product is not a measure of the nation's economic well-being.

The GNP is not intended to measure economic well-being, and does not do so for several reasons.

1. ***Only market activity is included in GNP.*** Work done by housewives and do-it-yourselfers certainly contributes to the nation's well-being, but it is not measured in the GNP because it has no price tag.

   One important implication of this exclusion arises when we try to compare the GNPs of developed and less-developed countries. Americans are always incredulous to learn that the per capita GNP of the poorest African countries is less than $250 a year. Surely, no one could survive in America on $5 a week. How can Africans do it? Part of the answer, of course, is that these people are incredibly poor. We shall study their plight in Chapter 38. But another part of the answer is that:

   International GNP comparisons are vastly misleading when the two countries differ greatly in the fraction of economic activity that each conducts in organized markets.

   This fraction is relatively large in the United States and relatively small in the less-developed countries, so when we compare their respective measured GNPs we are not comparing the same economic activities at all. Many things that get counted in the U.S. GNP are not counted in the GNPs of less-developed nations. So it is ludicrous to think that these people, poor as they are, survive on what to Americans would amount to $5 a week.

   A second implication is that GNP statistics take no account of the so-called "underground economy." This includes not just criminal activities, but a great deal of legitimate business activity that is conducted in cash (or by barter) to escape the tax collector. Naturally, we have no good data on the size of the underground economy; but some observers think it may amount to 10 percent or more of U.S. GNP. In some foreign countries, it is surely a much bigger share than this.

2. ***GNP places no value on leisure.*** As a country gets richer, one of the things that happens is that its citizens take more and more leisure time. The steady decrease in the length of the typical workweek in the United States is clear evidence for this. As a result, the gap is steadily widening between official

GNP and some truer measure of national well-being that would include the value of leisure time. For this reason, growth in GNP systematically *understates* the growth in national well-being. But there are also reasons why the GNP *overstates* how well-off we are. We consider these next.

3. **"Bads" as well as "goods" get counted in GNP.** Suppose there is a natural disaster—as when Mt. St. Helens erupted in the state of Washington in 1980. Surely the well-being of the nation was diminished by this catastrophe. Many homes, businesses, and resorts were destroyed; some people were killed; soot covered cities and towns miles from the blast. Yet the disaster probably caused GNP to rise. Consumers spent more to clean up and replace lost possessions. Businesses spent more to rebuild and repair damaged homes and stores. The government spent more for disaster relief and cleanup. Yet no one would think that the nation was better off for its higher GNP.

   Wars represent an extreme example. Mobilization for outright war always causes a country's GNP to rise rapidly. But men called into the army could be producing civilian output. Factories needed to produce armaments could instead be making cars, washing machines, and televisions. A country at war is surely worse off than a country at peace, but this fact will not be reflected in its GNP accounts.

4. **Ecological costs are not netted out of the GNP.** Many of the activities in a modern industrial economy that produce goods and services also have undesirable side effects on the environment. Automobiles provide enjoyment and a means of transportation, but they also despoil the atmosphere. Factories pollute rivers and lakes while manufacturing valuable commodities. Almost everything seems to produce garbage, which creates the problem of what to do with it. None of these ecological costs are deducted from the GNP in an effort to give us a truer measure of the *net* increase in economic welfare that our economy produces. Is this foolishness? Not if we remember the job that national income statisticians are trying to do: They are measuring the economic activity conducted through organized markets, not national welfare.

The Economy on a Roller Coaster

Having defined several of the basic concepts of macroeconomics, let us breathe some life into them by perusing the economic history of the United States. Figures 5–3 and 5–4 provide a capsule summary of this history since the Civil War. Figure 5–3 charts the behavior of the growth rate of real GNP over a period of almost 120 years. The fact that the growth rate has almost always been positive indicates that the main feature has been *economic growth*. In fact, the average annual growth rate over this period has been 3.4 percent. But the figure also shows that recessions—periods of falling real GNP—have been a persistent feature of America's economic performance. The ups and downs that are evident in Figure 5–3 are often referred to as *business cycles*.

The history of the inflation rate displayed in Figure 5–4 also shows more positive numbers than negative ones—more inflation than **deflation.** In total, the price level rose more than eleven-fold since 1869. But we also see some large gyrations in the inflation rate, including sharp bursts of inflation during and right after the two world wars and dramatic deflations in the 1870s, 1880s, 1921–1922, and 1929–1933.

The following exercise may be enlightening. Cover the portions of Figures 5–3 and 5–4 that deal with the period beginning in 1941, the portions to the right of the shaded area in each figure. The picture that emerges for the

Deflation refers to a sustained *decrease* in the general price level.

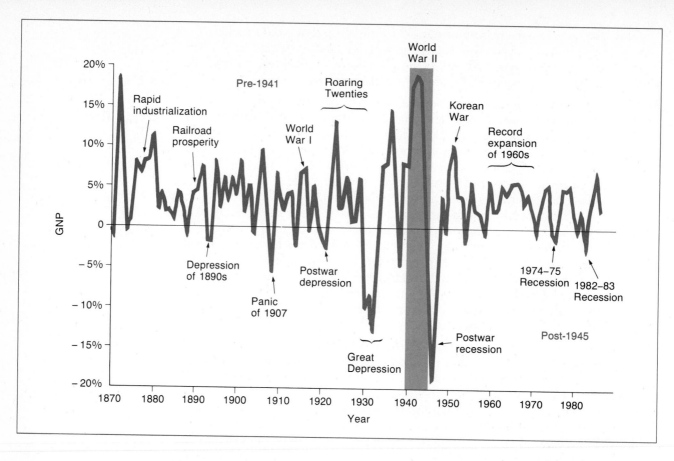

Figure 5–3

THE GROWTH RATE OF
REAL GROSS NATIONAL
PRODUCT OF THE
UNITED STATES,
1870–1987

This time series chart
displays the growth rate of
real gross national product in
the United States from 1870
to 1987. (Here real GNP is
measured in 1982 prices.)
The Great Depression
(1929–1939) stands out
vividly. The years during
World War II are shaded.
Does the growth rate look
smoother to the right of this
shaded area?
SOURCE: Constructed by authors
from Commerce Department data
for 1929–1987. Data for
1869–1928 were kindly provided
by Professor Christina Romer.

1870–1940 period is of an economy on a roller coaster. In Figure 5–3, the ups
and downs of the growth rate of real output are frequent and sometimes quite
pronounced. In Figure 5–4 we see periods of both inflation and deflation with
little or no tendency for one to be more common than the other. Indeed, prices
at the eve of World War II were not much higher than they were at the close of
the Civil War.

Now do the reverse. Cover the data prior to 1946 and look only at the
postwar period. There is, indeed, a difference. Instances of negative real GNP
growth are less common and business cycles are much less severe. While perfection has not been achieved, things do look much better. When we turn to
inflation, however, things look rather worse. Gone are the periods of deflation
and price stability that occurred before World War II. Prices now seem only to
go up.

This quick inspection of the data suggests that something has happened.
The U.S. economy behaved differently in 1946–1987 than it did in 1870–
1940. Many economists attribute this shift in the economy's behavior to lessons
the government has learned about managing the economy—lessons that we
will be learning in Part 4. When you look at the pre-1941 data, you are looking
at an unmanaged economy that went through booms and recessions for
"natural" economic reasons. The government did little about either. When you
examine the post-1945 data, on the other hand, you are looking at an economy
that has been increasingly managed by government policy—sometimes successfully and sometimes unsuccessfully. While the recessions are less severe, a cost
seems to have been exacted: the economy appears to be more inflation-prone
than it was in the more distant past.

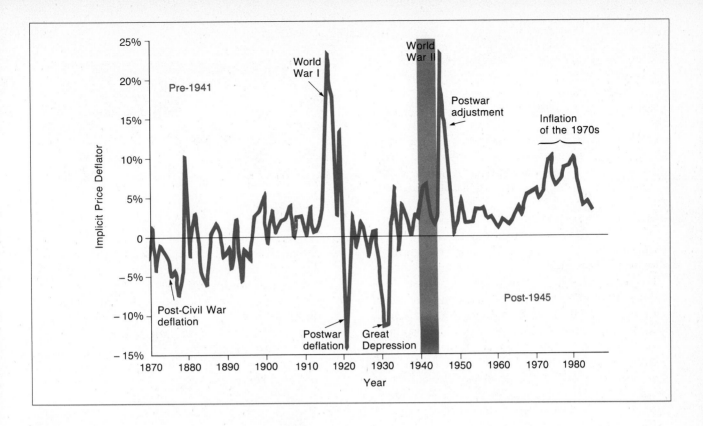

The Great Depression of the 1930s

As you look at these graphs, the Great Depression of the 1930s is bound to catch your eye. The decline in economic activity from 1929 to 1933 (see Figure 5–3) was the most severe in our nation's history, and the rapid deflation (see Figure 5–4) was most unusual. The Depression is but a dim memory now, but those who lived through it will never forget it.

While statistics usually conceal the true drama of economic events, this is not so of the Great Depression—they stand here as bitter testimony to its severity. From its 1929 high to its 1933 low, the production of goods and services dropped 30 percent and the price level fell 23 percent. Business investment almost ceased entirely, and stock market values slumped to less than one-sixth their 1929 level. The unemployment rate rose ominously from about 3 percent in 1929 to 25 percent in 1933—one person in four was jobless. From the data alone, one can virtually conjure up pictures of soup lines, beggars on street corners, closed factories, and homeless families. (See the boxed insert on the next page.)

Unlike many earlier and later recessions that plagued the U.S. economy, the Great Depression was a worldwide event. No country was spared its ravages. This traumatic episode literally changed the history of many nations. In Germany, it facilitated the ascendancy of the Nazi party. In the United States, it enabled Franklin Roosevelt's Democratic party to engineer one of the most dramatic political realignments in history and to push through a host of political and economic reforms.

The worldwide depression also caused a much-needed revolution in the thinking of economists. Up until the 1930s, the prevailing economic theory held that a capitalist economy, while it occasionally misbehaved, had a

Figure 5–4
THE INFLATION RATE IN THE UNITED STATES, 1870–1987
This time series chart portrays the behavior of the U.S. inflation rate from 1870 to 1987. (The specific price index used is called the GNP deflator, and it is defined as the ratio of nominal GNP divided by real GNP.) The difference between the 1870–1940 period and the 1946–1987 period is pronounced.
SOURCE: Constructed by authors from Commerce Department data for 1929–1987. Data for 1869–1928 were kindly provided by Professor Christina Romer.

Life in "Hooverville"

During the worst years of the Great Depression, unemployed workers often congregated in shantytowns on the outskirts of many major cities. Conditions in these slums were deplorable. With a heavy dose of irony, these communities were known as "Hoovervilles," in honor of the president of the United States who preached rugged individualism. A contemporary observer described a Hooverville in New York City as follows:

A Hooverville in New York City.

It was a fairly popular "development" made up of a hundred or so dwellings, each the size of a dog house or chickencoop, often constructed with much ingenuity out of wooden boxes, metal cans, strips of cardboard or old tar paper. Here human beings lived on the margin of civilization by foraging for garbage, junk, and waste lumber. I found some splitting or sawing wood with dull tools to make fires; others were picking through heaps of rubbish they had gathered before their doorways or cooking over open fires or battered oilstoves. Still others spent their days improving their rent-free homes, making them sometimes fairly solid and weatherproof.... Most of them, according to the police, lived by begging or trading in junk; when all else failed they ate at the soup kitchens or public canteens. They were of all sorts, young and old, some of them rough-looking and suspicious of strangers. They lived in fear of being forcibly removed by the authorities, though the neighborhood people in many cases helped them and the police tolerated them for the time being.

SOURCE: Mathew Josephson, *Infidel in the Temple* (New York: Alfred A. Knopf, 1967), pages 82–83.

"natural" tendency to cure recessions or inflations by itself. The roller coaster bounced around but did not normally run off the tracks.

This optimistic view was not confined to academia. It characterized the views of most politicians (certainly including President Herbert Hoover) and business leaders as well. As the great American humorist Will Rogers remarked with characteristic sarcasm:

It's almost been worth this depression to find out how little our big men knew. Mayby [sic] this depression is just "normalcy" and we don't know it. It's made a dumb guy as smart as a smart one.... Depression used to be a state of mind, Now it's a state of coma, now it's permanent. Last year we said, "Things can't go on like this," and they didn't, they got worse.[4]

The stubbornness of the Great Depression shook almost everyone's faith in the ability of the economy to right itself. In Cambridge, England, this questioning attitude led John Maynard Keynes, one of the world's most respected economists, to write *The General Theory of Employment, Interest, and Money* (1936). Probably the most important book in economics of the twentieth century, it carried a rather revolutionary message. Keynes discarded the notion that the economy always gravitated toward high levels of employment, replacing it

[4]From *Sanity Is Where You Find It* by Will Rogers, edited by Donald Day; copyright © 1955 by Rogers Company; reprinted by permission of Houghton Mifflin Company; pages 120–21.

with the assertion that—if a pessimistic outlook led business firms and consumers to curtail their spending plans—the economy might be condemned to stagnation for years and years.

While this doleful prognosis sounded all too realistic at the time, Keynes closed his book on a hopeful note. For he showed how government actions might prod the economy out of its depressed state. The lessons he taught the world then are the lessons we shall be learning in Parts 3 and 4. They show how governments can manage their economies so that recessions will not turn into depressions and depressions will not last as long as the Great Depression. While Keynes was working on *The General Theory*, he wrote his friend George Bernard Shaw that, "I believe myself to be writing a book on economic theory which will largely revolutionize... the way the world thinks about economic problems." In many ways he was right, though parts of the Keynesian message remain controversial to this day.

From World War II to 1973

The Great Depression finally ended when the country mobilized for war in the early 1940s. With total spending at extraordinarily high levels during the war, mostly because of government expenditures, the economy boomed and the unemployment rate fell as low as 1.2 percent.

Wartime spending of this magnitude usually leads to inflation, but much of the potential inflation during World War II was contained by price controls. With prices held below the levels at which quantity supplied equaled quantity demanded, many goods had to be rationed, and shortages of consumer goods were common. All of this ended with a burst of inflation when controls were lifted after the war.

The period from the end of the war until the early 1960s resembled the earlier period of growth with recessions before 1929. The main difference was that the four recessions between 1948 and 1961 were noticeably shorter and less severe than their prewar counterparts. Moderate but persistent inflation also became a fact of life.

When the economy emerged from recession in 1961, it entered what proved to be the longest uninterrupted period of expansion in our nation's history. GNP grew smartly and unemployment declined steadily, while the price level, though continuing to rise, showed no tendency to accelerate. The noninflationary boom was credited widely to the success of what came to be called "The New Economics," a term the media created for the policy of economic management prescribed by Keynes in the 1930s. For a while it looked as if we could avoid both unemployment and inflation. But the optimistic verdicts were premature in both cases.

Inflation was the first problem to crop up, beginning in about 1966. Its major cause, as it had been so many times in the past, was high levels of wartime spending—this time for the Vietnam War. Unemployment came next, when the economic expansion ground to a halt in 1969. Despite a short and mild recession, inflation continued at rates that were considered high at the time—5 to 6 percent a year.

In the face of persistent inflation, and with the economy beginning to pick up steam once again, President Richard Nixon instituted his "New Economic Policy" in a dramatic radio and television address to the nation in August 1971. This sweeping change in policy included America's first experiment with wage and price controls during peacetime. The controls program, which will be discussed in Chapter 17, held the inflation rate in check for a while as economic expansion progressed. But inflation worsened dramatically in 1973, mainly because of an explosion in food prices caused by poor harvests around the world.

The Great Stagflation, 1973–1980

Then things began to get much worse, not only for the United States, but for all the oil-importing nations of the world. A 1973 war between Israel and the Arab nations led to a quadrupling of the price of oil by the Organization of Petroleum Exporting Countries (OPEC). At the same time, continued poor harvests in 1974 in many parts of the globe kept world food prices rising rapidly. Prices of other raw materials also skyrocketed. Naturally, higher costs of fuel and other materials soon were reflected in the prices of manufactured goods.

By unhappy coincidence, these events coincided with the lifting of wage and price controls. Just as had happened after World War II, the elimination of controls led to an acceleration of inflation as prices that had been held artificially below equilibrium levels were allowed to rise. For all these reasons, the inflation rate in the United States soared to above 12 percent during 1974.

Meanwhile, the U.S. economy was slipping into its longest and most severe recession since the 1930s. Real GNP fell by about $4\frac{1}{2}$ percent between late 1973 and early 1975, and the unemployment rate rose from less than 5 percent to nearly 9 percent. Thus, both the twin evils of macroeconomics — inflation and unemployment — were unusually virulent in 1974 and 1975. Indeed, a new term — **stagflation** — was coined to refer to the simultaneous occurrence of economic *stag*nation and rapid in*flation*.

Stagflation is inflation that occurs while the economy is growing slowly ("stagnating") or having a recession.

Thanks partly to government actions, but mostly to natural economic forces, the economic collapse ended in 1975, and a sustained recovery began. On the price front, three forces pushed inflation down rapidly. First, the explosion in food and fuel prices was not repeated. These prices settled down at *levels* far higher than in the early 1970s, but ceased being engines of *inflation*. Second, the adjustment to the end of price controls ended in late 1974, and price behavior returned to normalcy. Third, just as had happened in the past, the severity of the recession put a brake on inflation. The inflation rate tumbled from over 12 percent a year in 1974 to a range of 5 to 7 percent during 1976 and 1977.

But the price of oil began to misbehave again in 1979 when the revolution that deposed the shah of Iran sparked chaos in the world oil market. In a series of price increases, OPEC more than doubled the price of oil during 1979, and government allocation programs led to long lines of motorists at gasoline stations all over the country.

OPEC's actions brought stagflation back again. Inflation accelerated first — from a 9 percent rate in 1978 to over 13 percent in 1979 and then to an astonishing 16 percent during the first half of 1980. Output fell at an extraordinarily rapid rate, but the decline lasted for only about the first six months of 1980. Output began to recover during the second half of 1980.

The Reagan Years

As President Ronald Reagan assumed office in January 1981, the economy was showing signs of life but seemed stuck with a stubborn inflation rate near 10 percent. The new president promised to change things with a package of

The Promise of Reaganomics

President Reagan came to office with a plan to cure stagflation. Here are some excerpts from his first economic message to Congress:

> I believe these proposals will put the Nation on a fundamentally different course — a course leading to less inflation, more growth, and a brighter future for all. . . .
>
> The new policy is based on the premise that . . . government (should) provide a stable and unfettered environment in which private individuals can . . . make appropriate decisions. . . .
>
> As a result of the policies set forth here, our economy's productive capacity is expected to grow significantly faster than could be expected with a continuation of past policies. . . . Concurrently, the general rate of inflation is expected to decline steadily. . . .
>
> The economic assumptions contained in this message may seem optimistic to some observers. Indeed they do represent a dramatic departure from the trends of recent years — but so do the proposed policies.

SOURCE: *America's New Beginning: A Program for Economic Recovery*, White House economic paper, February 18, 1981, pages 1, 24, and 25.

policies he called "supply-side economics."[5] (See the boxed insert above.) And things did indeed change dramatically — though not always in the way President Reagan wanted.

Inflation fell remarkably from over 12 percent in 1980 to only about 4 percent in 1982, the lowest rate in a decade. But the economy did not perk up. Instead, it slumped into its worst recession since the Great Depression. By the time the 1981–1982 recession hit bottom, the unemployment rate was approaching 11 percent, the financial markets were in disarray, and the word "depression" had returned to the vocabulary of some economists.

Recovery from recession began in the winter of 1982–1983 and proceeded vigorously at first. With inflation still tame, proponents of what came to be called "Reaganomics" began to declare victory. But the pace of economic growth slowed markedly after mid-1984 and real GNP growth averaged just 2.8 percent over the ensuing three years. The unemployment rate fell rapidly in 1983, but only slowly thereafter. By mid-1987 it was still 6.1 percent.

The Problem of Macroeconomic Stabilization: A Sneak Preview

This brief look at the historical record shows that our economy has not generally produced a steady pattern of growth without inflation. Rather, it has been buffeted by periodic bouts of unemployment or inflation, and sometimes has

[5]Supply side economics is discussed further in Chapter 12.

been plagued by both. There was also a hint, in the discussion, that government policies may have had something to do with why macroeconomic performance during the years 1946 to 1973 was so vastly superior to what it had been prior to World War II. Let us now expand upon this hint a little bit.

Stabilization policy is the name given to government programs designed to prevent or shorten recessions and to counteract inflation (that is, to *stabilize* prices).

We can provide a preliminary analysis of **stabilization policy,** the name given to government programs designed to prevent or shorten recessions and to counteract inflation, by using the basic tools of aggregate supply and aggregate demand analysis. To facilitate this, we have reproduced as Figures 5–5 and 5–6 two of the diagrams found earlier in this chapter [Figures 5–1(b) and 5–2], but we now give them slightly different interpretations.

Figure 5–5 gives a simplified view of government policy to fight unemployment. We suppose that, in the absence of government intervention, the economy would reach an equilibrium at point E, where demand curve $D_0 D_0$ crosses supply curve SS. Now if the output corresponding to point E is so low that many workers are unemployed, *the government can reduce unemployment if it can increase aggregate demand*. Chapter 12 will consider in detail how the government might try to do this. In the diagram, such an action would shift the demand curve to $D_1 D_1$, causing equilibrium to move to point A. In general:

Recessions and unemployment are often caused by insufficient aggregate demand. When this is so, government policies that successfully augment demand—such as increases in government spending—can be an effective way to increase output and reduce unemployment.

The opposite type of demand management is often called for when inflation is the main macroeconomic problem. Figure 5–6 illustrates this case. Here again, point E, the intersection of demand curve $D_0 D_0$ and supply curve SS, is the equilibrium that would be reached in the absence of government policy. But now we suppose that the price level corresponding to point E is considered "too high," meaning that the *change* in the price level from the previous period to this one would be too rapid if the economy moved to point E. A government program that reduces demand from $D_0 D_0$ to $D_2 D_2$ (for example, a reduction in government spending) can keep prices down and thereby reduce inflation. Thus:

Figure 5–5
STABILIZATION POLICY TO FIGHT UNEMPLOYMENT
This diagram duplicates Figure 5–1(b), but here we assume that Point E — the intersection of demand curve $D_0 D_0$ and supply curve SS — corresponds to high unemployment. With the kind of policy tools that we will study in later chapters, the government can shift the aggregate demand curve outward to $D_1 D_1$. This would raise output and lower unemployment.

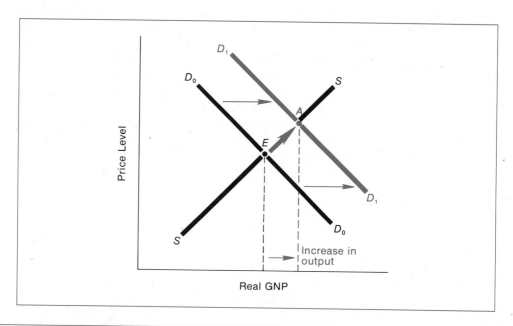

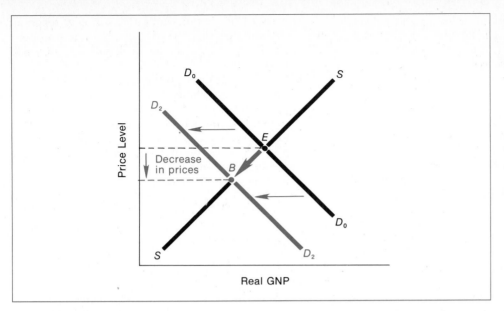

Figure 5-6
STABILIZATION POLICY
TO FIGHT INFLATION
This diagram duplicates
Figure 5–2, but here we
assume that point E — the
equilibrium the economy
would attain without
government
intervention — represents
high inflation (that is, the
price level corresponding to
point E is far above last
year's price level). By using
its policy instruments to shift
the aggregate demand curve
inward to $D_2 D_2$, the
government can keep this
year's price level lower than it
would otherwise have been;
in other words, the
government can reduce
inflation.

Inflation is frequently caused by aggregate demand racing ahead too fast. When this is the case, government policies that reduce aggregate demand can be effective anti-inflationary devices.

This, in brief, summarizes the intent of stabilization policy. When demand behavior is the source of economic instability, the government can limit both recessions and inflations by managing aggregate demand, pushing it ahead when it would otherwise lag, and restraining it when it would otherwise grow too quickly.

Sound simple? It's not. In reality, managing aggregate demand is a lot more complicated — both economically and politically — than shifting around lines on graphs with pencil and paper. We will spend much of Parts 3 and 4 examining the methods of demand management and learning why these methods do not always lead to the results that policymakers hope for.

In addition, the economy is sometimes plagued by both unemployment and inflation *at the same time*. In this case, the tools of demand management, even if wielded with great precision, are simply not up to the task. In Part 4 we will see why demand management is not enough and study some suggestions for dealing with unemployment and inflation at the same time.

Summary

1. Microeconomics studies the decisions of individuals and firms, how these decisions interact, and how they influence the allocation of society's resources and the distribution of income. Macroeconomics looks at the behavior of entire economies and studies the pressing social problems of inflation and unemployment.

2. While their respective subject matters differ greatly, the basic tools of microeconomics and macroeconomics are virtually identical. Both rely on the supply and demand analysis introduced in Chapter 4.

3. Macroeconomic models use abstract concepts like "the price level" and "national product" that are derived by amalgamating many different markets into one. This process is known as aggregation; it should not be taken literally but should be viewed as a useful approximation.

4. The best specific measure of the abstract concept "national product" is the gross national product (GNP), which is obtained by adding up the money values of all final goods and services produced in a given year. These outputs can be evaluated at current market prices (to get nominal GNP) or the prices of some previous year (to get real GNP). Neither intermediate goods nor transactions that take place outside organized markets are included in GNP.

5. The GNP is meant to be a measure of the *production* of the economy, not of the increase in its *well-being*. For example, the GNP places no value on housework and other do-it-yourself activities, nor on leisure time. On the other hand, even commodities that might be considered as "bads" rather than "goods" are counted in the GNP (for example, activities that harm the environment).

6. America's economic history is one of growth punctuated by periodic recessions; that is, periods in which real GNP declined. While the distant past included some periods of falling-prices (deflation), more recent history shows only rising prices (inflation).

7. The Great Depression of the 1930s was the worst in our country's history. It had profound effects both on our nation and on countries throughout the world and led also to a revolution in economic thinking, thanks to the work of John Maynard Keynes.

8. From World War II to the early 1970s, the American economy exhibited much steadier growth than it had in the past. Many observers attribute this to the implementation of the economic policies that Keynes suggested. At the same time, however, the price level seems only to rise, never to fall, in the modern economy. The economy seems to have become more "inflation prone."

9. During the 1970s and early 1980s the U.S. economy suffered through several serious recessions. At the same time, inflation was unusually virulent. This unhappy combination of economic stagnation with rapid inflation was nicknamed "stagflation."

10. One major cause of inflation is that aggregate demand may grow more quickly than aggregate supply. In such a case, a government policy that reduces aggregate demand may be able to check the inflation.

11. Similarly, recessions often occur because aggregate demand grows too slowly. In this case, a government policy that stimulates demand may be an effective way to fight the recession.

Concepts for Review

Microeconomics	Inflation	Final goods and services
Macroeconomics	Deflation	Intermediate goods
National product	Recession	Stagflation
Aggregation	Gross national product (GNP)	Stabilization policy
Aggregate demand and aggregate supply curves	Nominal versus real GNP	

Questions for Discussion

1. Which of the following problems are likely to be studied by a microeconomist and which by a macroeconomist?
   a. The allocation of a university's limited budget.
   b. Why the Great Depression lasted so long.
   c. Why Japan's economy grows faster than the United States' economy, while Britain's grows slower.
   d. Why IBM sells more computers than Apple.

2. You probably use "aggregates" frequently in everyday discussions. Try to think of some examples. (Here is one: Have you ever said, "The student body at this college generally . . ."? What, precisely, did you mean?)

3. Use an aggregate supply and demand diagram to study what would happen to an economy in which the aggregate demand curve never moved while the aggregate supply curve shifted outward year after year.

4. Try asking a friend who has not studied economics in which year he or she thinks prices were higher: 1870 or 1900? 1920 or 1940? (In both cases, prices were higher in the earlier year.) Most people your age think that prices have always risen. Why do you think they have this opinion?

5. When were the two worst recessions of the past 60 years?

6. Which of the following transactions are included in the gross national product, and by how much does each raise GNP?
   a. Smith pays a carpenter $6000 to build a garage.
   b. Smith purchases $1000 worth of lumber and materials and builds himself a garage, which is worth $6000.

c. Smith goes to the woods, cuts down a tree, and uses the wood to build himself a garage that is worth $6000.
d. The Jones family sells its old house to the Reynolds family for $100,000. The Joneses then buy a newly constructed house from a builder for $150,000.
e. Your university purchases a used computer from another university, paying $400,000.
f. Your university purchases a new mainframe computer from IBM, paying $2 million.
g. You lose $200 in an Atlantic City casino.
h. You lose $200 in the stock market.
i. You sell a used economics textbook to your college bookstore for $15.
j. You buy a new economics textbook from your college bookstore for $20.

7. Give some reasons why the gross national product is not a suitable measure of the well-being of the nation. (Have you noticed newspaper accounts in which journalists seem to use GNP for this purpose?)

6

When men are employed, they are best contented.

BENJAMIN FRANKLIN

Inflation is repudiation.

CALVIN COOLIDGE

Macroeconomic Maladies: Unemployment and Inflation

Among the many trials faced by Odysseus, the hero of Homer's *Odyssey*, one of the most difficult was to steer his fragile boat through a narrow strait. On one side lay the rock of the monster Scylla, which threatened to break his craft into pieces, and on the other was the menacing whirlpool of Charybdis. The makers of national economic policy face a similarly difficult task in trying to chart a middle course between the Scylla of unemployment and the Charybdis of inflation. If they steer the economy far from the rocks of unemployment, they run the risk of being swept up in the swift currents of inflation. But if they maintain a safe distance from inflation, they may smash against the rocks of unemployment.

In Parts 3 and 4 we will explain how economic planners attempt to strike a balance between high employment and low inflation, why these goals cannot be attained with machinelike precision, and why improvement on one front generally spells deterioration on the other. A great deal of attention will be paid to the *causes* of inflation and unemployment.

But before getting involved in such weighty issues of theory and policy, we pause in this chapter to take a close look at the twin evils themselves: Why is it that a rise in unemployment is generally considered bad news? Why is inflation so loudly deplored? Can we measure the costs of unemployment and inflation? The answers to some of these questions may at first seem obvious, but we will see that there is more to them than meets the eye.

The chapter is divided into two parts. The first deals with unemployment. After a few words on the human costs of high unemployment, we explain how government statisticians measure unemployment and consider how the elusive concept of "full employment" can be defined. We turn next to our country's system of unemployment insurance, and we conclude by investigating—and quantifying—the economic losses associated with unemployment.

In the second part of the chapter, we turn to inflation. We begin by exploding some persistent myths about inflation, myths that help explain why inflation is so universally deplored. But the costs of inflation are not all mythical. The first real cost we consider is how and why inflation redistributes income and wealth from one group of people to another. Next, we learn how certain laws make inflation impose heavy economic costs that could be avoided if the laws were written differently. This leads us to one of our **12 Ideas for Beyond the Final Exam** mentioned in Chapter 1. We shall see that it is the failure to understand the effect of inflation on interest rates that explains the existence of some of these laws and accounts for other costs of inflation as well. Finally, we define and analyze the difference between creeping and galloping inflation and explode another myth about inflation: the myth that creeping inflation always leads to galloping inflation. An appendix explains how inflation is measured.

The Costs of Unemployment

The human costs of unemployment are probably sufficiently obvious. Years ago, loss of a job meant not only enforced idleness and a catastrophic drop in income, it often led to hunger, cold, ill health, and even death. This is the way one unemployed worker during the Great Depression described his family's plight in a mournful letter to the governor of Pennsylvania:

I have six little children to take care of. I have been out of work for over a year and a half. Am back almost thirteen months and the landlord says if I don't pay up before the 1 of 1932 out I must go, and where am I to go in the cold winter with my children? If you can help me please for God's sake and the children's sakes and like please do what you can and send me some help, will you, I cannot find any work. I am willing to take any kind of work if I could get it now. Thanksgiving dinner was black coffee and bread and was very glad to get it. My wife is in the hospital now. We have no shoes to were [sic]; no clothes hardly. Oh what will I do I sure will thank you.[1]

Nowadays, unemployment does not have such dire consequences for most families, although it still holds these terrors for some. Part of the sting has been taken out of temporary unemployment by our system of unemployment insurance (discussed below), and there are other social welfare programs to support the incomes of the poor (see Chapter 37). Yet most families still suffer a painful loss of income when their breadwinner becomes unemployed.

Even families that are well protected by unemployment compensation suffer when joblessness strikes. Ours is a work-oriented society. A man's "place" has always been in the office or factory or shop, and lately this has become increasingly true for women as well. A worker forced into idleness by a recession endures a psychological cost that is no less real for our inability to measure it. Martin Luther King put it graphically: "In our society, it is murder, psychologically, to deprive a man of a job . . . You are in substance saying to that man that he has no right to exist."[2] High unemployment has been linked to higher incidence of certain types of crimes, psychological disorders, divorces, suicides, and the like.

Nor are the costs only psychological. Accumulated work experience is a valuable asset. When forced into idleness, workers not only cease accumulating experience, but lengthy periods of unemployment may make them "rusty," and thus less productive when they are reemployed. Short periods of unemployment exact different kinds of costs. A record of steady employment is important in

---

[1] From *Brother, Can You Spare a Dime? The Great Depression 1929–1933*, by Milton Meltzer, page 103. Copyright © 1969 by Milton Meltzer. Reprinted by permission of Alfred A. Knopf, Inc.
[2] Quoted in Coretta Scott King (ed.), *The Words of Martin Luther King* (New York: Newmarket Press, 1983), page 45.

applying for a new job. And a worker who has frequently been laid off will lack this record of reliability.

It is important to realize that these costs, whether large or small in total, are distributed most unevenly across the population. At the bottom of the severe recession of 1981–1982, the **unemployment rate** among all workers approached 11 percent, a shockingly high figure. But over 16 percent of blue-collar workers were unemployed, as were 19 percent of nonwhite workers. For teen-agers the situation was worse still, with unemployment above 24 percent, and that of nonwhite teen-agers above 44 percent. Married men had the lowest rate—about 8 percent. Although all these rates were unusually high, the relations among them are typical:

In good times and bad, married men suffer the least unemployment and teen-agers suffer the most; nonwhites are unemployed much more often than whites; blue-collar workers have above-average rates of unemployment; and well-educated people have below-average unemployment rates.

Counting the Unemployed: The Official Statistics

The Bureau of Labor Statistics (BLS) is responsible for measuring unemployment. How do they do it? How accurate are their measurements?

The BLS's basic method for counting the unemployed is quite direct: it asks people. Specifically, a survey of over 50,000 households is conducted each month. The census-taker asks several questions about the employment status of each member of the household. On the basis of these answers, each person is categorized as being *employed, unemployed,* or *not in the labor force.*

The first category is simplest to define. It includes everybody currently working at a job, including part-time workers. Although some part-time workers work less than a full week because they choose to, others do so only because they cannot find a suitable full-time job. Nevertheless, these workers are not considered unemployed, though many would consider them "underemployed."

The second category is a bit trickier. For those not currently working, the BLS first determines whether they are temporarily laid off from a job to which they expect to return. If so, they are counted as unemployed. The remaining workers are asked whether they actively sought work during the previous week. If they did, they are also counted as unemployed. But if they did not, they are classified as *out of the labor force*; that is, since they failed to look for a job they are not considered unemployed.

This seems a reasonable way to draw the distinction—after all, we would not want to count all college students who work during the summer months as unemployed between September and May. Yet, there is a problem: Research has shown that many unemployed workers give up looking for jobs after a time. These so-called **discouraged workers** are victims of poor job prospects, just like the officially unemployed. Ironically, when they give up hope, the official unemployment statistics decline! Some critics have therefore argued that an estimate should be made of the number of discouraged workers and that these people should be added to the roles of the unemployed. In 1986 the BLS estimated that about 1 million workers fell into this category.

Involuntary part-time work, loss of overtime or shortened work hours, and discouraged workers are all examples of "hidden" or "disguised" unemployment. And those who are concerned about these phenomena argue that we should include them in the official unemployment rate because, if we do not, the magnitude of the problem will be *underestimated*.

The **unemployment rate** is the number of unemployed people, expressed as a percentage of the **labor force.**

The **labor force** is the number of people holding or seeking jobs.

A **discouraged worker** is an unemployed person who gives up looking for work and is therefore no longer counted as part of the labor force.

There is, however, an opposing school of thought that argues that the official unemployment rate really *overestimates* the unemployment problem. First, they argue, the unemployment rate of 1988 is not directly comparable to the unemployment rate of, say, 1958 because the composition of the labor force has changed dramatically over these years. Specifically, a larger fraction of all workers are young and female today than was the case 30 years ago. These groups have always had higher rates of unemployment than adult males. Therefore, even if adult men, adult women, and teen-agers each had the *same* unemployment rates in 1988 that they had in 1958, the unemployment rate for the entire population would have been higher in 1988 than in 1958.[3] Second, they argue, to count as unemployed, a person need only *say* that he is looking for work, even if he is not really interested in finding a job. No one knows to what extent the unemployment problem is overstated on account of this, but some think that it may be considerable.

Types of Unemployment

Providing jobs for those willing to work is one principal goal of macroeconomic policy. How are we to define this goal? One clearly *incorrect* answer would be "a zero measured unemployment rate." Ours is a dynamic and highly mobile economy. Households move from one state to another. Individuals quit jobs to look for better positions or to retool for more attractive occupations. These phenomena, and many more, produce some minimal amount of unemployment—people who literally are *between* jobs. Economists call this the level of **frictional unemployment**.

Frictional unemployment is unemployment that is due to the normal workings of the labor market. It includes people who are temporarily between jobs because they are moving or changing occupations, or for similar reasons.

The critical distinguishing feature of frictional unemployment is that it is short-lived. A frictionally unemployed person has every reason to expect to find a new job soon. People tend to think of frictional unemployment as irreducible, but that is not the case. During World War II, for example, unemployment in this country fell below 2 percent—substantially below the frictional level.

Frictional unemployment is irreducible only in the sense that—under normal circumstances—it is socially undesirable to reduce it. Geographical and occupational mobility play important roles in our market economy—enabling people to search for better jobs. Similarly, waste is avoided by allowing inefficient firms, or firms producing items no longer in demand, to be replaced by new firms. Inhibition of either of these phenomena must hamper the workings of the market economy. But, if these adjustment mechanisms are allowed to operate, there will always be some temporarily unemployed workers looking for jobs just as there will always be some firms with unfilled positions looking for workers. This is the genesis of frictional unemployment.

A second type of unemployment is often difficult to distinguish from frictional unemployment, but it has very different implications. **Structural unemployment** arises when jobs are eliminated by changes in the structure of the economy, such as automation or permanent changes in demand. The crucial difference between frictional and structural unemployment is that, unlike a frictionally unemployed worker, a structurally unemployed worker cannot realistically be considered "between jobs." Instead, he may find his skills and experience unwanted in the changing economy in which he lives. He is thus faced with either a prolonged period of unemployment or the necessity of

Structural unemployment refers to workers who have lost their jobs because they have been displaced by automation, because their skills are no longer in demand, or for similar reasons.

[3]If you do not understand why, consider the following analogy. Suppose your college class contains a mixture of "A" students and "C" students. If, between your freshman year and your senior year, more "C" students enter the class as transfers from other colleges, your class's overall grade point average will decline even if every student earns the same grades as a senior that he or she did as a freshman.

making a major change in his occupation. For older workers, learning a new occupation may be nearly impossible.

The remaining type of unemployment, **cyclical unemployment,** will occupy our attention most in this book. Cyclical unemployment arises when the level of economic activity declines. Whenever the unemployment rate rises ominously or falls precipitously, the data are almost certainly reflecting changes in cyclical unemployment.

> **Cyclical unemployment** is the portion of unemployment that is attributable to a decline in the economy's total production. Cyclical unemployment rises during recessions and falls as prosperity is restored.

How Much Employment Is "Full Employment"?

Which of these types of unemployment is considered unavoidable — even under "full employment"? The **Employment Act of 1946,** the landmark piece of legislation in which the U.S. government first committed itself to maintain "conditions under which there will be afforded useful employment opportunities... for those able, willing and seeking to work," was interpreted as a call to hold unemployment close to the frictional level. How much was that? During the prosperous years of the late 1940s and early 1950s, unemployment rates were consistently below 4 percent, dropping as low as 2.9 percent during the Korean War. This led President John F. Kennedy, in 1961, to select a 4 percent unemployment rate as an "interim target." The federal government was, for the first time, committed to a numerical goal.

Starting from a 6.7 percent rate in 1961, unemployment was eroded, more or less steadily, to 3.8 percent in 1966 — surpassing the interim target. Then the additional military spending for the Vietnam War pushed unemployment down still further. The unemployment rate reached 3.5 percent in 1969.

During the 1970s, the 4 percent goal posted by President Kennedy's New Frontier was rejected as being outmoded, although no new numerical target was put in its place. There were several reasons for this rejection of 4 percent.

First, some economists argued that the 4 percent target set during the Kennedy administration had to be adjusted upward for the early and middle 1970s because of the changed composition of the labor force that we have just mentioned. Second, they suggested, the increased generosity of unemployment compensation had reduced any individual's incentive to get himself off the unemployment rolls. Why work if unemployment benefits and other programs provide an income nearly as large as the salary one could earn on the job? This lack of work incentives made 4 percent unemployment much harder to achieve. Finally, these economists claimed, substantial increases in the federal minimum wage during the 1970s made it harder to employ teen-agers and other workers whose productivity was low. If, for example, their productivity was below the legal minimum wage, who would hire them?[4]

The last half of the 1970s saw considerable debate, both in government and in academia, over exactly how much measured unemployment corresponded to full employment. As is so often the case, actual events helped to settle the argument. Throughout 1978 and 1979, the measured unemployment rate hovered near 6 percent and the economy looked to be operating at approximately normal rates. Thus, by the early 1980s, many economists came to believe that **full employment** meant an unemployment rate close to 6 percent. But some felt it might be lower and others thought it was much higher — closer to the 7 percent rates that have prevailed from late 1984 into 1986. The definition of "full employment" remains controversial.

[4]For a full discussion of minimum wage laws, including their effect on unemployment, see Chapter 36.

Unemployment Insurance: The Invaluable Cushion

A surprising feature of the early 1980s was the equanimity with which the electorate tolerated high unemployment rates. One major reason for this was our system of **unemployment insurance.**

One of the most valuable pieces of legislation to emerge from the trauma of the Great Depression was the Social Security Act of 1935. Among other things, it established an unemployment insurance system which is now administered by each of the 50 states under federal guidelines. Thanks to this system, many — but, as we shall see, not all — American workers need never experience the complete loss of income that so many suffered during the 1930s.

While the precise amounts vary substantially, the average weekly benefit check to unemployed workers in 1986 was about $136. This amounted to about 45 percent of average earnings. Though a 55 percent drop in earnings still poses serious problems, the importance of this 45 percent income cushion can scarcely be exaggerated, especially since it may be supplemented by funds from other welfare programs. Families that are covered by unemployment insurance simply do not have to go hungry when they lose their jobs, and they are only rarely dispossessed from their homes.

Who is eligible to receive these benefits? Precise qualifications vary from state to state, but some stipulations apply quite generally. Only experienced workers qualify; so persons just joining the labor force (such as recent graduates of high schools and colleges) or reentering after a prolonged absence (such as women resuming work after years of child rearing) cannot collect benefits. Neither can those who have quit their jobs, except under unusual extenuating circumstances. You must be looking for work to qualify, and benefits end after a stipulated period of time. For all these reasons, only about one-third of the roughly 8.2 million persons who were unemployed during 1986 actually received benefits.

The importance of unemployment insurance to the unemployed is obvious. But there are also significant benefits to citizens who never become unemployed. During recession years many billions of dollars are paid out in unemployment benefits, and since recipients probably spend most of their benefits, unemployment insurance limits the severity of recessions by providing additional purchasing power when and where it is most needed.

The unemployment insurance system is one of several "cushions" that have been built into our economy since 1933 to prevent the possibility of another Great Depression. By giving money to those who become unemployed, the system helps prop up aggregate demand during recessions.

While the U.S. economy is now probably "depression proof," this should not be a cause for too much rejoicing, for the recessions of 1980 and 1981–1982 amply demonstrated that we are far from "recession proof."

The Economic Costs of High Unemployment

The fact that unemployment insurance and other social welfare programs replace a significant fraction of lost income has led some skeptics to claim that unemployment is no longer a serious problem. But the fact is that:

Unemployment insurance is just what the name says — an *insurance* program. And insurance can never prevent a catastrophe from occurring; it can only *spread the costs* of a catastrophe among many people instead of letting them all fall on the shoulders of those few unfortunate souls whom it affects directly.

Fire insurance is an example. If your family is covered by fire insurance and your house burns down, you will probably suffer only a small financial loss because the insurance company will pay most of the expenses. Where does it get the money? It cannot create it out of thin air. Rather, it must have collected the funds from the many other families who purchased insurance but did not suffer any fire damages. Thus, one family's loss of perhaps $80,000 is covered by the insurance payments of 400 families each paying $200 a year. In this way, the costs of the catastrophe are spread among hundreds of families, and in the process, made much more bearable.

But despite the insurance, the family whose house is destroyed by fire suffers anguish and inconvenience. No insurance policy can eliminate this. Furthermore, society loses a valuable resource — a house. It will take much wood, cement, nails, paint, and labor to replace the burnt-out home. *An insurance policy cannot insure society against losses of real resources*.

The case is precisely the same with insurance against unemployment. All workers and employers pay for the insurance policy by a tax that the government levies on wages and salaries. With the funds so collected, the government compensates the victims of unemployment. Thus, instead of letting the costs of unemployment fall entirely on the minority of workers who are out of work, the system of payroll taxes and unemployment benefits *spreads* the costs over the entire population. But it does not eliminate the basic economic cost.

When the economy does not generate enough jobs to employ all those who are willing to work, a valuable resource is lost. Potential goods and services that might have been enjoyed by consumers are lost forever. This is the real economic cost of high unemployment, and no insurance plan can eliminate it.

And these costs are by no means negligible. Table 6–1 summarizes the idleness of workers and machines, and the resulting loss of national output, for some of the years of lowest economic activity in recent decades. The second column lists the civilian unemployment rate, and thus measures unused labor resources. The third lists the percentage of industrial capacity that U.S. manufacturers were actually using, and thus indicates the extent of unused plant and equipment. And the fourth column is an estimate of how much more output (real GNP) could have been produced if these labor and capital resources had been fully employed.

Table 6–1
THE ECONOMIC COSTS OF HIGH UNEMPLOYMENT

YEAR	CIVILIAN UNEMPLOYMENT RATE (percent)	CAPACITY UTILIZATION RATE (percent)	PERCENTAGE OF REAL GNP LOST DUE TO IDLE RESOURCES
1958	6.8	75.0	4.2
1961	6.7	77.3	3.4
1975	8.5	72.3	5.3
1982	9.7	70.3	8.4
1983	9.6	74.0	7.6

SOURCES: Bureau of Labor Statistics; Federal Reserve System; and Robert J. Gordon, *Macroeconomics*, Fourth Edition (Boston: Little, Brown, 1987).

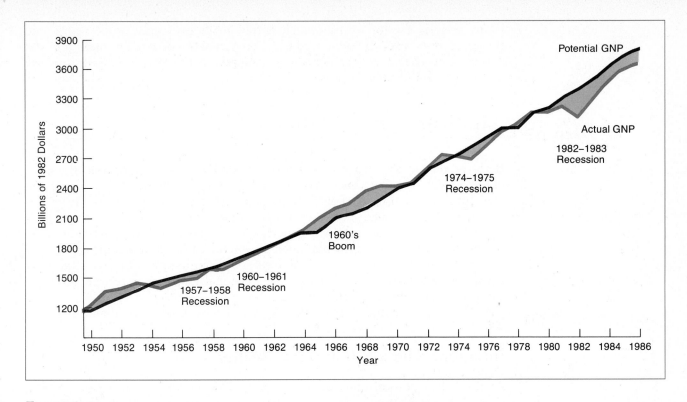

Figure 6–1

ACTUAL AND POTENTIAL GNP IN THE UNITED STATES, 1949–1986

This chart compares the growth of actual GNP (blue line) with that of potential GNP (black line). There have been two lengthy periods during which real GNP remained below its potential (1957–1963, and 1974 to the present), but only one lengthy period during which GNP remained above potential (1965–1970). The large shortfalls of GNP from potential in the 1980s stand out.
SOURCES: U.S. Department of Commerce and Robert J. Gordon, *Macroeconomics*, fourth edition (Boston: Little, Brown, 1987).

While these years are extreme examples, inability to utilize all of the nation's available resources has been a recurrent problem for our economy, especially in the 1980s. The blue line in Figure 6–1 shows the actual real GNP in the United States from 1949 to 1986, while the black line shows the real GNP we *could have* produced if "full employment" had been maintained. This last statement defines a concept called **potential GNP.** As our previous discussion of full employment pointed out, it *is* possible to push employment beyond its normal full employment level. This occurs whenever the unemployment rate dips below the "full employment unemployment rate"—a rate now thought to be 6 percent or so. Consequently, it *is* possible for actual GNP to exceed potential GNP. Figure 6–1 shows several instances where this happened. But it also shows, quite dramatically, that actual GNP has fallen short of potential GNP for most of the past dozen years—sometimes by huge amounts. In fact:

Potential gross national product is the real GNP the economy would produce if its labor and other resources were fully employed.

The cumulative gap between actual and potential GNP over the years 1974–1986 (all evaluated in 1982 prices) is an astounding $1577 billion. At 1988 levels of output, this loss in output as a result of unemployment would be almost five months' worth of production. And there is no way to redeem these losses. The labor wasted in 1985 cannot be utilized in 1989.

Those who argue that unemployment is nothing to worry about today because of unemployment insurance, or because unemployment is concentrated among certain kinds of workers (such as teen-agers), or because many unemployed workers become reemployed within a few weeks, should ponder

Figure 6–1. Is the loss of this much output really no cause for worry? Would these optimists react the same way if the government collected a fraction of the output of every factory in America and dumped it into the sea? Waste is waste no matter who ultimately pays the cost.

The Costs of Inflation

Both the human and economic costs of inflation are less obvious than the costs of unemployment. But this does not necessarily make them any less real, for if one thing is crystal clear about inflation, it is that people do not like it.

Public opinion polls consistently show that inflation ranks high on people's list of major national problems, generally even ahead of unemployment. Surveys also find that inflation, like unemployment, causes a deterioration in consumers' sense of well-being — it makes people unhappy. Finally, studies of voting behavior suggest that during congressional elections voters penalize the party that occupies the White House when inflation is high.

The fact is beyond dispute: People consider inflation to be something bad. Why?

Inflation: The Myth and the Reality

At first, the question may seem ridiculous. During times of inflation, people must keep paying higher prices for the same quantities of goods and services they had before. So more and more income is needed just to maintain the same standard of living. Is it not obvious that this erosion of **purchasing power** — that is, the decline in what money will buy — makes everyone worse off?

The **purchasing power** of a given sum of money is the volume of goods and services it will buy.

This would indeed be the case were it not for one very significant fact. The wages people earn are also prices — prices for labor services. During a period of inflation, wages also rise and, in fact, the average wage typically rises more or less in step with prices. Thus, contrary to popular myth, workers as a group are not usually victimized by inflation.

The **real wage rate** is the wage rate adjusted for inflation. It indicates the volume of goods and services that money wages will buy.

The purchasing power of wages — what is called the **real wage** — is not systematically eroded by inflation. Sometimes wages rise faster than prices, and sometimes prices rise faster than wages. The fact is that in the long run wages tend to outstrip prices as new capital equipment and innovation increase output per worker.

Figure 6–2 illustrates this simple fact. The blue line shows the annual rate of increase of consumer prices in the United States for each year since 1948, while the black line shows the annual rate of wage increase. The difference between the two indicates the rate of growth of *real* wages. Generally, wages rise faster than prices, reflecting the steady advance of technology and of labor productivity; so real wages rise. The years from 1974 to 1981 stand out as an unusual period in which real wages often did not rise. This single fact goes a long way toward explaining why people were so dissatisfied with economic performance when President Reagan took office.

The feature of Figure 6–2 that virtually jumps off the page is the way the two lines dance together. Wages normally rise rapidly when prices rise rapidly, and rise slowly when prices rise slowly. But you should not draw any hasty conclusions from this association. We cannot, for example, learn from this figure whether rising prices cause rising wages or whether rising wages cause rising

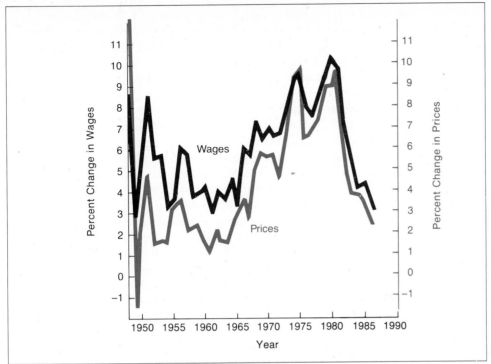

Figure 6–2
RATES OF CHANGE OF
WAGES AND PRICES IN
THE UNITED STATES,
1948–1986
This chart compares the rate
of price inflation (blue line)
with the rate of growth of
nominal wages (black line) in
the postwar period. The
patterns are clearly quite
similar, with wages and
prices normally accelerating
or decelerating together.
Notice that the traditional gap
between wage increases and
price increases did not
prevail in the middle and
late 1970s.
SOURCE: Bureau of Labor
Statistics.

prices. Remember the warnings given in Chapter 1 about trying to infer causation just by looking at data. But analyzing cause and effect is not our purpose right now. We merely want to explode the myth that inflation inevitably erodes real wages.

Why is this myth so widespread? Imagine a world without inflation in which wages are rising 2 percent a year because of the increasing productivity of labor. Now imagine that, all of a sudden, inflation sets in and prices start rising 4 percent a year but that nothing else changes. Figure 6–2 suggests that, with perhaps a small delay, wage increases will accelerate to 2 percent plus 4 percent, or 6 percent a year.

Will workers view this change with equanimity? Probably not. To each worker, the 6 percent wage increase will be seen as something he earned by the sweat of his brow. In his view, he *deserves* every penny of his 6 percent raise. And, in a sense, he is right because "the sweat of his brow" earned him a 2 percent increment in real wages that, when the inflation rate is 4 percent, can only be achieved by increasing his money wages by a total of 6 percent. An economist would divide the wage increase in the following way:

REASON FOR WAGE INCREASE	AMOUNT
Higher productivity	2%
Compensation for higher prices	4%
Total	6%

But the worker will probably keep score differently. Feeling that he earned the entire 6 percent by his own merits, he will view inflation as having "robbed" him of 4 percent of his just deserts. The higher the rate of inflation, the more of his raise the worker will feel has been stolen from him.

"Sure, you're raising my
allowance. But am I actually
gaining any purchasing
power?"

Of course, nothing could be further from the truth. Basically, the economic system is rewarding the worker with *the same 2 percent real wage increment for higher productivity regardless of the rate of inflation*. The "evils of inflation" are often exaggerated because of a failure to understand this mechanism.

A second reason for misunderstanding the effects of inflation is that people are in the habit of thinking in terms of the number of dollars it takes to buy something rather than in terms of the *purchasing power* of these dollars. For example, if inflation doubles both prices and wages, workers will have to labor exactly the same amount of time as before to earn the price of a loaf of bread. But because they now pay $1 a loaf instead of 50 cents, they feel that the price of bread is scandalously high. In fact, nothing really has changed; but people cling to an outmoded idea of what bread *should* cost.

An item's **relative price** is its price in terms of some other item, rather than in terms of dollars.

A third misperception results from failure to distinguish between a *rise in the general price level* and a change in **relative prices,** that is, a rise in the price of one commodity relative to that of another. To see the distinction most clearly, imagine first a *pure inflation* in which *every* price rises by 10 percent during the year, so that relative prices do not change. Table 6–2 gives an example in which movie tickets go up from $4 to $4.40, candy bars from 50 cents to 55 cents, and automobiles from $8000 to $8800. After the inflation, just as before, it will still take 8 candy bars to buy a movie ticket, 2000 movie tickets to buy a car, and so on. A person who manufactures candy bars in order to purchase movie tickets is neither helped nor harmed by the inflation. Neither is a car dealer with a sweet tooth.

But real inflations are not like this. When there is 10 percent general inflation—meaning that the "average price" rises by 10 percent[5]—some prices may jump 20 percent or more while others actually fall. Suppose that, instead of the price increases shown in Table 6–2, prices rise as shown in Table 6–3. Movie prices go up by 25 percent, but candy prices do not change. Surely, candy manufacturers who love movies will be disgruntled because it now costs 10 candy bars instead of 8 to get into the theater. They will blame inflation for raising the price of movie tickets, even though their real problem stems from the *increase in the price of movies relative to candy*. (They would have been hurt as much if movie tickets had remained at $4 while the price of candy fell to 40 cents.)

[5]The way statisticians figure out "average" price increases is discussed in the appendix to this chapter.

Table 6–2

ITEM	LAST YEAR'S PRICE	THIS YEAR'S PRICE	PERCENT INCREASE
Candy bar	$0.50	$0.55	10
Movie ticket	4.00	4.40	10
Automobile	8000	8800	10

Table 6–3

ITEM	LAST YEAR'S PRICE	THIS YEAR'S PRICE	PERCENT INCREASE
Candy bar	$0.50	$0.50	0
Movie ticket	4.00	5.00	25
Automobile	8000	8400	5

Since car prices have risen by only 5 percent, theater owners in need of new cars will be delighted by the fact that an auto now costs only 1680 movie admissions (just as they would have cheered if car prices had fallen to $6720 while movie tickets remained at $4). However, they are unlikely to attribute their good fortune to inflation—as indeed they should not. What has actually happened is that *cars became cheaper relative to movies*.

Because real-world inflation proceeds at *uneven* rates, relative prices are constantly changing. There are gainers and losers, just as some would gain and others lose if relative prices changed without any general inflation. Inflation, however, gets a bad name because losers often blame inflation for their misfortune while gainers rarely credit inflation for their good luck. Alas, nobody loves inflation.

These three kinds of misconceptions may go a long way toward explaining why respondents to public opinion polls consistently list inflation as a major national issue, why higher inflation rates depress consumers, and why voters express their ire at the polls when inflation is high.

Inflation does not systematically erode the purchasing power of wages. Nor does it lead to "unfair" prices. Nor is it usually to blame when some goods become more expensive relative to others.

But not all of the costs of inflation are mythical. Let us now turn to some of the real costs.

Inflation as a Redistributor of Income and Wealth

We have just seen that the *average* person is neither helped nor harmed by inflation. But almost no one is exactly average! Some persons gain from inflation and others lose. It is hard to say anything more systematic than this about the effects of inflation on particular prices and wages.

But inflation does have systematic effects on the distribution of income and wealth. Senior citizens trying to scrape by on pensions or other fixed incomes suffer badly from inflation. Since they earn no wages, it is little solace to them that wages are keeping pace with prices. Their pension incomes are not.[6]

This example actually illustrates a much more general problem. We can think of pensioners as people who "lend" money to an organization (the pension fund) when they are young in order to be "paid back" with interest when they are old. Because of the rise in the price level during the intervening years, the unfortunate pensioners get paid back in less valuable dollars than those they originally loaned. In general:

Those who lend money are usually victimized by rising inflation.

While lenders lose heavily, borrowers do quite well. For example, homeowners who borrowed money from banks in the form of mortgages back in the 1950s, when interest rates were 3 or 4 percent, gained enormously from the surprisingly virulent inflation of the late 1960s and 1970s. They paid back dollars

---

[6]This is not, however, true of recipients of social security. Social security benefits are financed out of tax revenues rather than directly through accumulated savings, and benefit levels are automatically increased to compensate recipients for changes in the price level. For further discussion of the social security system, see Chapter 33.

of much lower value than those that they borrowed. And the same is true of other borrowers.

Borrowers usually gain from rising inflation.

Since the redistribution caused by inflation generally benefits borrowers at the expense of lenders, and since both lenders and borrowers can be found at every income level, we must conclude that:

Inflation does not always steal from the rich to aid the poor, nor does it always do the reverse.

Why, then, is the redistribution caused by inflation so widely condemned? Because its victims are selected capriciously. Nobody legislates this redistribution. Nobody enters into it voluntarily. The gainers do not earn their spoils, and the losers do not deserve their fate. Moreover, there have been particular classes of people whom inflation has systematically robbed of purchasing power year after year — old-age pensioners, people who have saved money and "loaned" it to banks, and workers on long-term contracts or those whose wages and salaries do not adjust easily for some other reason. Even if people "on the average" suffer no damage from inflation, that offers little consolation to those who are hurt by it persistently and systematically. This is the fundamental indictment of inflation.

Inflation redistributes income in an arbitrary way that distorts society's distribution of income. The actual income distribution should reflect the interplay of the operation of free markets and the purposeful efforts of government to alter the distribution. Inflation interferes with and distorts this process.

Real Versus Nominal Interest Rates

But wait. Must inflation always rob lenders to bestow gifts upon borrowers? If both parties see inflation coming, won't lenders demand that borrowers pay a higher interest rate as compensation for the coming inflation? Indeed they will. For this reason, economists draw a sharp conceptual distinction between inflation that is *expected* and inflation that comes as a *surprise*.

What happens when inflation is fully expected by both parties? Suppose Diamond Jim wants to borrow $1000 from Scrooge, and both agree that, in the absence of inflation, which erodes the value of money, a fair rate of interest would be 3 percent on a one-year loan. This means that Diamond Jim would pay back $1030 at the end of the year for the privilege of having $1000 now.

If both expect prices to increase by 6 percent, Scrooge may reason as follows, "If Diamond Jim pays me back $1030 a year from today, that money will buy less than what $1000 buys today. Thus I'll really be *paying him* to borrow from me! I'm no philanthropist. Why don't I charge him 9 percent instead? Then he'll pay back $1090 at the end of the year. With prices 6 percent higher, this will buy roughly what $1030 is worth today. So I'll get the same 3 percent increase in purchasing power that we would have agreed on in the absence of inflation, and won't be any worse off. That's the least I'll accept."

Diamond Jim may follow a similar chain of logic. "With no inflation, I was willing to pay $1030 a year from now for the privilege of having $1000 today, and Scrooge was willing to lend it. He'd be crazy to do the same with a 6 percent inflation. He'll want to charge me more. How much should I pay? If I offer him $1090 a year from now, that will have roughly the same purchasing power as $1030 today, so I won't be any worse off. That's the most I'll pay."

This kind of thinking will lead Scrooge and Diamond Jim to write a contract with a 9 percent interest rate—3 percent as the increase in purchasing power that Diamond Jim pays to Scrooge and 6 percent as compensation for the expected inflation. Then, if the expected 6 percent inflation actually materializes, neither party will have been made better or worse off than was expected at the time the contract was signed.

This example illustrates a very general principle. The 3 percent increase in purchasing power that Diamond Jim agrees to hand over to Scrooge is called the **real rate of interest**. And the 9 percent contractual interest charge that Diamond Jim and Scrooge write into the loan agreement is called the **nominal rate of interest**. The nominal rate of interest is arrived at by adding the **expected rate of inflation** to the real rate of interest. Expected inflation is added to compensate the lender for the loss in purchasing power that he is expected to suffer as a result of inflation. Because of this:

Inflation that is accurately predicted need not redistribute income between borrowers and lenders. If the *expected* rate of inflation that is embodied in the nominal interest rate closely approximates the *actual* rate of inflation, no one gains and no one loses. However, to the extent that expectations prove incorrect, inflation will still redistribute income.[7]

It need hardly be pointed out that errors in predicting the rate of inflation are the norm, not the exception. Published forecasts bear witness to the fact that economists have great difficulty in predicting the rate of inflation. The task is no easier for businesses, consumers, and banks. This is one reason why inflation is so widely condemned as unfair and undesirable. It sets up a guessing game that no one likes.

Inflation and the Tax System

So inflation imposes costs on society because it is hard to predict. But there are other costs of inflation, perhaps even more serious, that arise from high inflation, even when inflation is predicted accurately. These costs stem from the fact that the laws and regulations that govern our financial system were designed for an inflation-free economy; and these laws may malfunction when inflation is high. The tax system is one important example.

Our tax law does not recognize the distinction between nominal and real interest rates. The law simply taxes nominal interest regardless of how much real interest it represents. As a result, strange things happen when there is high inflation. Our example of Scrooge's loan to Diamond Jim will illustrate the problem.

The top line of Table 6–4 shows how taxation affects the loan agreement when there is no inflation and the nominal and real interest rates are both 3 percent. Scrooge earns $30 in nominal interest income (column 3). Since there is no inflation, this also represents $30 in real interest income (column 5). If Scrooge pays one-third of his income in taxes, his tax bill rises by $10 (column 6), leaving him with $20 after tax (column 7). This $20 amounts to 2 percent of the $1000 originally loaned (column 8). Because his $10 tax payment is one-third of his $30 in real interest income, Scrooge's effective tax rate is $33\frac{1}{3}$ percent (column 9), just as Congress intended.

The **real rate of interest** is the percentage increase in purchasing power that the borrower pays to the lender for the privilege of borrowing. It indicates the increased ability to purchase goods and services that the lender earns.

The **nominal rate of interest** is the percentage by which the money the borrower pays back exceeds the money that he borrowed, making no adjustment for any fall in the purchasing power of this money that results from inflation.

[7]EXERCISE: Who gains and who loses if the inflation turns out to be only 4 percent instead of the 6 percent that Scrooge and Diamond Jim expected? What if the inflation rate is 8 percent?

Table 6-4
INFLATION AND THE TAXATION OF INTEREST INCOME

(1) INFLATION RATE (percent)	(2) NOMINAL INTEREST RATE (percent)	(3) INTEREST RATE (dollars)	(4) LOSS OF PURCHASING POWER DUE TO INFLATION (dollars)	(5) REAL INTEREST INCOME (dollars)	(6) TAXES PAID (dollars)	(7) REAL INCOME AFTER TAX (dollars)	(8) (as a percentage $1000 loan)	(9) EFFECTIVE RATE OF TAXATION (percent)
0	3	30	0	30	10	20	2%	33 1/3
6	9	90	60	30	30	0	0	100

Now let's consider the same transaction when the inflation rate is 6 percent and Scrooge and Diamond Jim settle on a 9 percent nominal interest rate. Scrooge collects $90 in interest (column 3). But, with 6 percent inflation, the purchasing power of the $1000 he lends declines by $60 (column 4). Thus his real interest income is again $30 (column 5). However, the tax collector taxes the $90 *nominal* interest income, not the $30 real interest income, so Scrooge must pay $30 (one-third of $90) in taxes (column 6). As we can see in column 7, his after-tax real income on the loan is zero since the tax collector takes all his real income. As column 9 shows, the effective tax rate on Scrooge's real interest income is thus 100 percent, far larger than the $33\frac{1}{3}$ percent rate intended by Congress.

So a tax system that works well at zero inflation misfires at 6 percent inflation because it taxes nominal, rather than real, interest. This little example illustrates a general, and very serious, problem:

Because it fails to recognize the distinction between nominal and real interest rates, our tax system levies high, and presumably unintended, tax rates on interest income when there is high inflation. And similar problems arise in the taxation of dividends, corporate profits, and other items.[8] Many economists feel that these high tax rates discourage saving, lending, and investing, and that high inflation therefore retards economic growth.

The Treasury Department's original tax reform package of 1984 proposed ways to correct most of these problems. But none of these proposals were included in the tax law that Congress passed in 1986. So the problems remain.

Usury Laws, Interest Rate Ceilings, and Other Impediments

A **usury law** sets down a maximum permissible interest rate for a particular type of loan. Loans at rates above the usury ceiling are illegal.

Another example of laws that malfunction under inflation is **usury laws,** which set *maximum* permissible interest rates on particular types of loans. Usury laws date back to biblical days and command rather widespread popular support. The problem is that they place ceilings on *nominal* interest rates, rather than on *real* interest rates and thus can have perverse effects in an inflationary environment.

In our previous example of Scrooge and Diamond Jim, suppose that a usury law sets a maximum rate of 8 percent on consumer loans. When he expects 6

[8]A particularly serious problem arises in the taxation of capital gains. (Capital gains are the difference between the price at which one sells an asset and the price at which one bought it.) In the United States, capital gains are taxed at their nominal values, without any adjustment for changes in their purchasing power resulting from inflation. An example will bring out the point. Between 1970 and 1980 the price level doubled, approximately. Consider some stock that was purchased for $5000 in 1970 and sold for $7500 in 1980. The investor would have lost purchasing power in the transaction because 7500 1980 dollars purchased less than 5000 1970 dollars. Yet, since the tax authorities do not correct for inflation, the investor will be forced to pay tax on the $2500 nominal capital gain as though there had been a profit rather than a loss.

percent inflation, Diamond Jim is willing to pay a 9 percent nominal interest rate and Scrooge is willing to lend at this rate. But the law intervenes. "Thou shalt not charge usurious interest." The deal cannot be completed, and both Diamond Jim and Scrooge go away disappointed.

The problem is that usury ceilings were set in periods of fairly steady prices, when there was no great difference between nominal and real interest rates. If, for example, the usury law had set the legal maximum at an 8 percent *real* rate of interest, it would not have prevented Scrooge from lending to Diamond Jim. As it is, however, a loan carrying a 3 percent real interest rate is perfectly legal at zero inflation but illegal at 6 percent inflation!

Usury laws set in nominal terms created so much havoc during the period of double-digit inflation in 1979–1980 that Congress took drastic action to eliminate them nationwide. Consequently, usury ceilings on interest rates are far less prevalent today than they were a decade ago.

Usury laws and problems with the tax system are just two examples of a general phenomenon:

Many of the laws that govern our financial system become extremely counter-productive in an inflationary environment, causing problems that were never intended by the legislators.

And it is important to note that *these are major costs of inflation that are not purely redistributive*. Society as a whole loses when mutually beneficial transactions are prohibited by law, when saving and investing are discouraged, when loans are not provided to those who need them, and when other useful acts are prevented by obsolete legislation.

Why do such laws stay on the books so long? One reason is a general lack of understanding of the difference between real and nominal interest rates. People seem not to understand that it is normally the *real* rate of interest that matters in an economic transaction because only that rate reveals how much borrowers pay (and lenders receive) *in terms of the goods and services which that money can buy*. They focus on the high nominal interest rates caused by inflation, even if these rates correspond to very low real interest rates. Here are some other examples that may help you appreciate how widespread and important this interest rate illusion is.

Interest Rate Regulations
Interest rate illusion is partly responsible for regulations that impose ceilings around 5 percent on interest paid on many bank accounts. Thus, *by government decree* small savers are condemned to earn *negative* real rates of interest during a period of rapid inflation.

Regulation of Public Utilities
During the early 1960s, when the rate of inflation averaged about $1\frac{1}{4}$ percent a year, interest rates on high-grade corporate bonds hovered just below $4\frac{1}{2}$ percent, yielding a real rate of interest of just over 3 percent. There were few public complaints suggesting that there was anything scandalous about such earning rates.

Yet during 1980 when the rate of inflation rose above 12 percent and corporate interest rates rose to perhaps 11 percent (a *negative* real rate of interest!), there was a public uproar. Regulated utilities, which asked the regulatory agencies to permit them a rate of return closer to 11 percent so that they could afford to borrow the money needed to serve expanding public demand, found that their requests were considered exorbitant by the commissons and by the general public. As a result, they failed to increase their capacities sufficiently.

Record Profit Rates

Amazingly, even business managers were subject to the same form of illusion. Often they were taken aback by the notion that their investors actually lost out (earned a negative *real* rate of return) when the company was earning a 10 percent profit. The managers noted that 10 percent was the company's highest earnings rate in recent history; but with inflation at 12 percent, it turned out that in real terms it was in fact the firm's lowest.

Thus, failure to understand that high *nominal* interest rates can signify low *real* interest rates has been known to impoverish savers during a period of inflation. It has made profits appear high when they were really low. It has sometimes made it impossible for electric companies and other public utilities to raise the capital they need to serve rising consumer demands, and power shortages and failures have been the predictable result.

The Illusion of High Interest Rates

The difference between real and nominal interest (and profit) rates, and the fact that the real rate matters more in terms of economic effects while the nominal rate is politically significant, are matters that are of the utmost importance and yet are understood by very few people, including many persons who make public policy decisions in these areas.

This concept is one of the **12 Ideas for Beyond the Final Exam,** and if you remember it ten years from now, you will truly have gotten a great deal out of studying economics.

Other Costs Of Inflation

Another cost of inflation is that rapidly changing prices make it risky to enter into long-term contracts. In an extremely severe inflation, the "long term" may be only a few days. But even moderate inflations can have remarkable effects on long-term loans. Suppose a corporation wants to borrow $1 million to finance the purchase of some new equipment and needs the loan for 20 years. If the inflation rate averages 4 percent over this period, the $1 million it repays at the end of 20 years will be worth $456,387 in today's purchasing power. If inflation averages 8 percent instead, it will be worth only $214,548. Lending or borrowing for this long a period is obviously a big gamble. With the stakes this high, the outcome may be that neither lenders nor borrowers want to get involved in long-term contracts. But without long-term loans, business investment becomes impossible. The economy stagnates.

Inflation also makes life difficult for the shopper. You probably have a group of stores that you habitually patronize because you know they generally carry the items you want to buy at (roughly) the prices you want to pay. This knowledge saves you a great deal of time and energy. But when prices are changing rapidly, your list quickly becomes obsolete. You return to your favorite clothing store to find that the price of jeans has risen drastically. Should you buy? Should you shop around at other stores? Will they have also raised their prices? Business firms have precisely the same problem with their suppliers. Rising prices force them to shop around more than they are accustomed to, which imposes costs on the firms and, more generally, reduces the efficiency of the whole economy.

Shopping costs may sound frivolous and unimportant, but they are not. Arthur Okun, who chaired the Council of Economic Advisers under President Johnson, suggested an ingenious mental exercise that illustrates the importance of shopping costs. Ask yourself the following question: How much would you have to be paid to promise never again to buy anything from any of the stores you have patronized in the past? When you ponder this for a while, you realize the great value of having normal places to shop. Inflation takes some of this value away.

Creeping Versus Galloping Inflation

The preceding litany of costs of inflation alerts us to one very important fact: *predictable inflation is far less burdensome than is unpredictable inflation*. When will an inflation be most predictable? When it proceeds year after year at more or less the same rate. Thus the *variability of the inflation rate* is a crucial factor. Inflation of 4 percent a year for three consecutive years will exact far lower social costs than inflation that is 2 percent in the first year, zero in the second, and 10 percent in the third. In general:

Steady inflation is much more predictable than variable inflation and therefore has much smaller social and economic costs.

But the *average level of the inflation rate* is also important. Partly because of the interest rate illusions mentioned above and partly because of the more rapid breakdown in normal customer relationships that we have just mentioned, a steady inflation of 6 percent a year is more damaging than a steady inflation of 4 percent a year.

Economists distinguish between **creeping inflations** and **galloping inflations** partly on their average level and partly on their variability. Under creeping inflation, prices rise for a long time at a moderate and fairly steady rate. Postwar Sweden provided a good example. During the 13-year period from 1954 to 1967, prices climbed a total of 64 percent (compared with only 24 percent in the United States), for an average annual inflation rate of 3.9 percent. And the pace of inflation was remarkably steady, rarely dropping below $2\frac{1}{2}$ percent or rising above 5 percent. Closer to home, though for a much shorter time, the U.S. inflation rate hovered near 4 percent during the years 1982–1985.

Galloping inflation refers to an inflation that proceeds at an exceptionally high rate, perhaps for only a relatively brief period. Germany after World War I suffered through one of the more severe inflations in history. Wholesale prices increased over 140 percent in 1921 and a colossal 4100 percent during 1922. At this point, what had been an impressive galloping inflation simply got out of control. Between December 1922 and November 1923, when a hard-nosed reform finally broke the inflationary spiral, wholesale prices in Germany increased by almost 100 million percent! But even this experience was dwarfed by the great Hungarian inflation of 1945–1946, the greatest inflation of them all. For a period of one year, the rate of inflation averaged about 20,000 percent *per month*. And in the final month, the price level skyrocketed 42 quadrillion percent!

While the distinction between creeping and galloping inflation is a quantitative one, we refrained from putting any specific numbers into the definitions. This is because different societies at different points in time hold very different conceptions of what rate constitutes creeping inflation and what rate

Creeping inflation refers to an inflation that proceeds for a long time at a moderate and fairly steady pace.

Galloping inflation refers to an inflation that proceeds at an exceptionally high rate, perhaps for only a relatively brief period. Galloping inflations are generally characterized by accelerating rates of inflation so that the rate of inflation is higher this month than it was last month.

These children in Germany during the hyperinflation of the 1920s are building a pyramid with cash, worth no more than the sand or sticks used by children elsewhere.

constitutes galloping inflation. For example, in the United States today, annual rates of inflation in the 2 to 5 percent range are generally considered to be "creeping," while rates in the 25 to 30 percent range would surely be construed as "galloping." In most Latin American countries, however, inflation consistently in the 25 to 30 percent range is viewed as "creeping." And in the United States of the 1950s, a 6 percent annual inflation might have been branded "galloping."

The Costs of Creeping Versus Galloping Inflation

If you review the costs of inflation that have been discussed in this chapter, you will see why the distinction beween creeping and galloping inflation is so fundamental. Many economists think we can live nicely, indeed can prosper, in an environment of creeping inflation. No one believes we can survive very well under galloping inflation.

Under creeping inflation, the rate at which prices rise is relatively easy to predict and to take into account in setting interest rates (as long as the law allows). Under galloping inflation, where prices are rising at ever-increasing rates, this is extremely difficult, and perhaps impossible, to accomplish. The potential redistributions become monumental, and as a result, lending and borrowing may cease entirely.

Any inflation makes it difficult to write long-term contracts. With creeping inflation, the "long term" may be 20 years, or 10 years, or 5. But with galloping inflation, the "long term" may be measured in weeks or even hours. Restaurant prices may change before you finish your dessert. Railroad fares may go up while you are in the middle of your journey. When it is impossible to enter into contracts of any duration longer than a few hours, economic activity becomes paralyzed. We conclude that:

The horrors of galloping inflation either are absent in creeping inflation or are present in such muted forms that they can scarcely be considered horrors.

Creeping Inflation Does Not Necessarily Lead to Galloping Inflation

We noted earlier that inflation is surrounded by a mythology that bears precious little relation to reality. It seems appropriate to conclude this chapter by disposing of one particularly persistent myth: that creeping inflation invariably leads to galloping inflation.

There is neither statistical evidence nor theoretical support for the myth that creeping inflation inevitably leads to galloping inflation. To be sure, creeping inflations sometimes accelerate. But at other times they slow down.

While creeping inflations have many causes, galloping inflations have occurred only when the government has printed incredible amounts of money, usually to finance wartime expenditures.

In the German inflation of 1923, the government finally found that its printing presses could not produce enough paper money to keep pace with the exploding prices. Not that it did not try. By the end of the inflation, the *daily* output of currency was over 400 quadrillion marks! The Hungarian authorities in 1945–1946 tried even harder. The average growth rate of the money supply was more than 12,000 percent *per month*. Needless to say, these are not the kind of inflation problems that are likely to face the United States in the foreseeable future.

But this should not be interpreted to imply there is nothing wrong with creeping inflation. Much of this chapter has been spent analyzing the very real costs of any inflation, no matter how slow. A case against even moderate inflation can indeed be built, but it does not help this case to shout foolish slogans like "Creeping inflation always leads to galloping inflation." Fortunately, it is simply not true.

Summary

1. Unemployment exacts heavy financial and psychological costs from those who are its victims, costs that are borne quite unevenly by different groups in the population.

2. Unemployment is measured by a government survey. Some critics claim that the survey methods understate the unemployment problem, while others contend that the methods overstate the problem.

3. Frictional unemployment arises when people are between jobs for normal reasons. Thus, most frictional unemployment is desirable.

4. Structural unemployment is due to shifts in the pattern of demand or to technological change that results in certain skills becoming obsolete.

5. Cyclical unemployment is the portion of unemployment that rises in recessions and falls when the economy booms.

6. The Employment Act of 1946 was widely interpreted as committing the government to limiting unemployment to the frictional variety. However, it set no numerical goals.

7. President Kennedy first enunciated the goal of 4 percent unemployment in 1961. But few economists think this is a realistic target for the 1980s. Many think that "full employment" now comes at an unemployment rate near 6 percent.

8. Unemployment insurance replaces nearly one-half the lost income of unemployed persons who are insured. But only about one-third of the unemployed collect benefits, and no insurance program can bring back the lost output that could have been produced had these people been working.

9. In recent decades, the U.S. economy often has produced less output than it could have were it operating at full employment. This shortfall has been particularly large since 1980.

10. People have many misconceptions about inflation. For example, many people believe that inflation systematically erodes real wages, are appalled by rising prices even when wages are rising just as fast, and blame inflation for any unfavorable changes in relative prices. All of these are myths.

11. Other costs of inflation are real, however. For example, inflation often redistributes income from lenders to borrowers.

12. This redistribution can be eliminated by adding the expected rate of inflation to the interest rate. But legal limitations sometimes prevent this, and expectations often prove to be inaccurate.

13. The real rate of interest is the nominal rate of interest minus the expected rate of inflation.

14. Since the real rate of interest indicates the command over real resources that the borrower surrenders to the lender, it is of primary economic importance.

15. Yet public attention often is riveted on nominal rates of interest, and this confusion can lead to costly policy mistakes when high inflation converts high nominal interest rates into very low real interest rates. This is one of the **12 Ideas for Beyond the Final Exam.**

16. Because nominal, not real, interest is taxed, our tax system levies heavy taxes on interest income when inflation is high.

17. Creeping inflation, which proceeds at moderate and fairly predictable rates year after year, carries far lower social costs than galloping inflation, which proceeds at high and variable rates.

18. The notion that creeping inflation inevitably leads to galloping inflation is a myth with no foundation in economic theory and no basis in historical fact.

Concepts for Review

Unemployment rate	Full employment	Real rate of interest
Labor force	Unemployment insurance	Nominal rate of interest
Discouraged workers	Potential GNP	Expected rate of inflation
Frictional unemployment	Purchasing power	Inflation and the tax system
Structural unemployment	Real wage	Usury laws
Cyclical unemployment	Relative prices	Creeping inflation
Employment Act of 1946	Redistribution by inflation	Galloping inflation

Questions for Discussion

1. Why is it not as terrible to become unemployed nowadays as it was during the Great Depression?
2. "Since unemployed workers receive unemployment benefits and other benefits that make up for most of their lost wages, unemployment is no longer a social problem." Comment.
3. Using what you learned about aggregate demand and aggregate supply in Chapter 5, try to explain why the U.S. economy has failed so frequently to produce up to its potential. (You will learn more about this question in later chapters, so don't worry if you find the question difficult now.)
4. Do you think that the Bureau of Labor Statistics overestimates or underestimates the number of people that are unemployed? Why?
5. Why is it so difficult to define "full employment"? What unemployment rate should the government be shooting for today?
6. Show why each of the following complaints is based on a misunderstanding about inflation:
   a. "Inflation must be stopped because it robs workers of their purchasing power."
   b. "Inflation is a terrible social disease. It leads to unconscionably high prices for basic necessities."
   c. "Inflation makes it impossible for working people to afford many of the things they were hoping to buy."
   d. "Inflation must be stopped today, for if we do not stop it, it will surely accelerate to ruinously high rates and lead to disaster."
7. What is the *real interest rate* paid on a loan bearing 16 percent nominal interest per year, if the rate of inflation is
   a. zero
   b. 2 percent
   c. 5 percent
   d. 12 percent
   e. 18 percent
8. Suppose you agree to lend money to your friend on the day you both enter college, at what you both expect to be a zero *real* rate of interest. Payment is to be made at graduation, with interest at a fixed *nominal* rate. If inflation proves to be *lower* during your four years in college than what you both had expected, who will gain and who will lose?
9. You have lived with inflation all your life. Think about the costs that inflation has imposed on you personally. How do these costs relate to the material in this chapter?
10. Add a third line to Table 6–4 showing what would happen if the inflation rate went to 12 percent and the real interest rate remained 3 percent.

Appendix
How Statisticians Measure Inflation

Index Numbers for Inflation

Inflation is generally measured by the change in some index of the general price level. For example, between 1973 and 1986, the Consumer Price Index (CPI), which stood at 100 in 1967, rose from 133.1 to 328.4, an increase of 147 percent. The meaning of the *change* is clear enough. But what is the meaning of the 133.1 figure for 1973 and the 328.4 figure for 1986?

These numbers are **index numbers,** each expresses the cost of a market basket of goods *relative to its cost in some "base" period*. Since the CPI uses 1967 as its base period, the CPI of 328.4 for 1986 means that it cost $328.40 to purchase the same basket of goods and services that cost $100 in 1967.

Now, the particular basket of consumer goods and services under scrutiny really did not cost $100 in 1967. When constructing index numbers, it is conventional to set the index at 100 in the base year. How is this conventional figure used in obtaining index numbers of other years? Very simply. Suppose the budget needed to buy the roughly 250 items included in the CPI was $500 per month in 1967 and $1642 per month in 1986. Then the index is defined by the following rule:

$$\frac{\text{CPI in 1986}}{\text{CPI in 1967}} =$$

$$\frac{\text{Cost of the 250-item market basket in 1986}}{\text{Cost of the 250-item market basket in 1967}}.$$

Since the CPI in 1967 is set at 100:

$$\frac{\text{CPI in 1986}}{100} = \frac{\$1642}{\$500} = 3.284$$

or

$$\text{CPI in } 1986 = 328.4 \, .$$

Exactly the same sort of equation enables us to calculate the CPI in any other year. We have the rule:

CPI in given year =

$$\frac{\text{Cost of market basket in given year}}{\text{Cost of market basket in base year}} \times 100 \, .$$

Of course, not every combination of consumer goods that cost $500 in 1967 rose to $1642 by 1986. For example, a color TV set that cost $500 in 1967 might have sold for $450 in 1986, but a $500 hospital bill in 1967 might have ballooned to $3000. Since no two families buy precisely the same bundle of goods and services, no two families suffer precisely the same increase in their cost of living unless all prices rise at the same rate. Economists refer to this phenomenon as the **index number problem.**

When relative prices are changing, there is no such thing as a "perfect price index" that is correct for every consumer. Any statistical index will understate the increase in the cost of living for some families and overstate it for others. At best, the index can represent the situation of an "average" family.

The Consumer Price Index

The most closely watched price index is surely the **Consumer Price Index,** which is calculated and announced each month by the Bureau of Labor Statistics (BLS). When you read in the newspaper or see on television that the "cost of living rose by 0.4 percent last month," chances are the reporter is referring to the CPI.

The CPI is measured by pricing the items on a list representative of a typical urban household budget. To know what items to include and in what amounts, the BLS conducts an extensive survey of spending habits roughly once every decade (the last one was in 1982–1984). This means that the *same* bundle of goods and services is used as a standard for about 10 years, whether or not spending habits change.[9] Of course, spending habits do

[9]Economists call this a *base-period weight index,* because the relative importance it attaches to each price depends on how much money consumers actually chose to spend on it during the base period.

Table 6–5
RESULTS OF STUDENT EXPENDITURE SURVEY, 1983

ITEM	AVERAGE PRICE	AVERAGE QUANTITY PURCHASED PER MONTH	AVERAGE EXPENDITURE PER MONTH
Hamburger	$ 0.80	70	$ 56
Jeans	24.00	1	24
Movie ticket	5.00	4	20
		Total	$100

Table 6–6
PRICES IN 1988

ITEM	PRICE	PERCENTAGE INCREASE OVER 1973
Hamburger	$ 1.00	25
Jeans	24.00	0
Movie ticket	5.50	10

change; and this introduces a small error into the CPI's measurement of inflation.

A simple example will help us understand how the CPI is constructed. Imagine that college students purchase only three items—hamburgers, jeans, and movie tickets—and that we want to devise a cost-of-living index (call it SPI, for "student price index") for them. First we would conduct a survey of spending habits in the base year (suppose it is 1983). Table 6–5 represents the hypothetical results. You will note that the frugal students of that day spent only $100 per month: $56 on hamburgers, $24 on jeans, and $20 on movies.

Table 6–6 presents hypothetical prices of these same three items in 1988. Each price has risen by a different amount, ranging from zero for jeans up to 25 percent for hamburgers. By how much has the SPI risen? Pricing the 1983 student budget at 1988 prices, we find that what once cost $100 now costs $116, as the following calculation shows:

COST OF 1983 STUDENT BUDGET IN 1988 PRICES

70 hamburgers at $1	$70
1 pair of jeans at $24	24
4 movie tickets at $5.50	22
Total	$116

Thus the SPI, based on 1983 = 100, is

$$SPI = \frac{\text{Cost of budget in 1988}}{\text{Cost of budget in 1983}} \times 100$$

$$= \frac{\$116}{\$100} \times 100 = 116.$$

So the SPI in 1988 stands at 116, meaning that students' cost of living has increased 16 percent over the 5 years.

How to Use a Price Index to "Deflate" Monetary Figures

One of the most common uses of price indexes is in the comparison of monetary figures relating to two different points in time. The problem is that, if there has been inflation, the dollar is not a good measuring rod because it is worth less now than it was in the past.

Here is a simple example. Suppose that the average student spent $100 per month in 1983 and that this monthly spending figure had grown to $110 per month in 1988. If there was an outcry that students had become spendthrifts, how would you answer the charge?

The obvious answer is that a dollar in 1988 does not buy what it did in 1983. Specifically, our SPI shows us that it takes $1.16 in 1988 to purchase what $1 would purchase in 1983. To compare the spending habits of students in the two years, we must divide the 1988 spending figure by 1.16. Specifically, *real* spending per student in 1988 (where "real" is defined by 1983 dollars) is:

Real spending in 1988 =

$$\frac{\text{Nominal spending in 1988}}{\text{Price index of 1988}}.$$

Thus,

$$\text{Real spending in 1988} = \frac{\$110}{1.16} = \$94.83.$$

In sum, this calculation shows that, despite appearances to the contrary, the change in nominal spending from $100 to $110 actually represented a *decrease* in real spending.

This calculation procedure is called **deflating by a price index,** and it serves to translate noncomparable monetary figures into more directly comparable real figures.

Deflating is the process of finding the real value of some monetary magnitude by dividing by some appropriate price index.

A good practical illustration is the real wage, a concept we have discussed in this chapter. Average hourly earnings in the U.S. economy were $2.68 in 1967 and $8.76 in 1986. Since the CPI in 1986 was 328.4 (with 1967 as the base year), the real wage in 1986 (in 1967 dollars) was:

$$\text{Real wage in 1986} = \frac{\text{money wage in 1986}}{\text{price index of 1986}}$$

$$= \frac{\$8.76}{328.4} \times 100 = \$2.67$$

Thus, by this measure, the real wage was essentially the same in 1967 and 1986!

The GNP Deflator

In macroeconomics, one of the most important of the monetary magnitudes that we have to deflate is the nominal gross national product (GNP). The price index used to do this is called the **GNP deflator.** Our general principle for deflating a nominal magnitude tells us precisely how to go from nominal GNP to real GNP:

$$\text{Real GNP} = \frac{\text{Nominal GNP}}{\text{GNP deflator}} \times 100.$$

As with the CPI, the 100 simply serves to establish the base of the index as 100, rather than 1.00.

Economists often consider the GNP deflator to be a better measure of overall inflation in the economy than the Consumer Price Index. The main reason for this is that the two price indexes are based on different market baskets. As already mentioned, the CPI is based on the budget of a typical urban family. By contrast, the GNP deflator is constructed from a market basket that includes *every* item in the GNP—that is, every final good and service produced by the economy. Thus, in addition to prices of consumer goods the GNP deflator includes the prices of airplanes, lathes, and other goods purchased by business. It also includes government services. For this reason, the measures of inflation that these two indexes give are rarely the same. Usually their disagree-ments are minor. But sometimes they can be substantial, as in 1979 when the CPI recorded a 13.3 percent inflation rate while the GNP deflator recorded only 8.9 percent.

Summary

1. Inflation is measured by the percentage increase in an index number of prices, which shows how the cost of some basket of goods has changed over a period of time.
2. Since relative prices are changing all the time, and since different families purchase different items, no price index can represent precisely the change in the cost of living for every family.
3. The Consumer Price Index (CPI) tries to measure the cost of living for an "average" urban household by pricing a "typical" market basket every month.
4. Price indexes like the CPI can be used to *deflate* monetary figures to make them more comparable. This amounts to dividing the monetary magnitude by the appropriate price index.
5. The GNP deflator is a better measure of economy-wide inflation than is the CPI because it includes the price of every good and service in the economy.

Concepts for Review

Index number
Index number problem
Consumer Price Index
Deflating by a price index
GNP deflator

Questions for Discussion

1. Just below you will find the amounts (in billions of dollars) that American consumers spent on various items in 1967 and in 1985. The Consumer Price Index in 1985 (on a base of 1967 = 100) was 322.2. Use this to deflate all the 1985 figures and to compare them with the 1967 figures. Which type of spending has grown most rapidly?

		ITEM	
YEAR	FOOD	GASOLINE AND OIL (billions of dollars)	HOUSING
1967	112.3	17.1	74.1
1985	469.3	91.9	403.3

2. Just below you will find nominal GNP and the GNP deflator for 1966, 1976, and 1986.
   a. Compute real GNP for each year.
   b. Compute the percentage change in nominal and real GNP from 1966 to 1976, and from 1976 to 1986.
   c. Compute the percentage change in the GNP deflator over these two periods.

GNP STATISTICS			
	1966	1976	1986
Nominal GNP (billions of dollars)	772.0	1782.8	4235.0
GNP deflator	35.0	63.1	114.1

3. Fill in the blanks in the following table of GNP statistics.

YEAR	1984	1985	1986
Nominal GNP	3772.2		4235.0
Real GNP	3501.4	3607.5	
GNP deflator		111.2	114.1

4. Use the following data to compute the College Price Index for 1988, using the base 1972 = 100.

ITEM	PRICE IN 1972	QUANTITY PER MONTH IN 1972	PRICE IN 1988
Button-down shirts	$10	1	$22
Loafers	25	1	47
Sneakers	10	3	15
Textbooks	12	12	25
Jeans	12	3	36
Restaurant meals	5	11	12

5. Average hourly earnings in the U.S. economy during several past years were as follows:

1955	1965	1975	1985
$1.71	$2.76	$4.53	$8.57

Use the CPI numbers provided on the inside front cover of this book to calculate the real wage (in 1967 dollars) for each of these years. Which decade had the fastest growth of money wages? Which had the fastest growth of real wages?

6. The example in the appendix showed that the Student Price Index (SPI) rose by 16 percent from 1983 to 1988. You can understand the meaning of this better if you:

a. Use Table 6–5 to compute the fraction of total spending accounted for by each of the three items in 1983. Call these the "expenditure weights."

b. Compute the weighted average of the percentage increases of the three prices shown in Table 6–6, using the expenditure weights you have just computed.

c. You should get 16 percent as your answer. This shows that "inflation," as measured by the SPI, is a weighted average of the percentage price increases of all the items that are included in the index.

7

Productivity, Progress, and Prosperity

Human history has never experienced anything like it. In the industrial countries, the quantity and quality of food, clothing, and comforts have reached levels that were never dreamed possible by earlier generations. The change has been so revolutionary that it is difficult to grasp its magnitude. This chapter helps us envision how great the accomplishment has been. It also suggests the source of the transformation: the fact that a person in the United States today can produce in an hour perhaps 20 times as much as was possible in 1800. Just two figures will suggest the magnitude of the achievement. In 1800 about 90 percent of America's labor force had to work on farms, and all that farm labor barely managed to produce enough food to provide adequate nutrition for the country. Today, in contrast, only about 3 percent of U.S. workers earn their living on farms. Yet those few farm workers provide an outpouring of surpluses which the U.S. government constantly struggles to contain.

Life in the "Good Old Days"

The United States, and the thirteen colonies before it, has always been a privileged land with relatively high levels of nutrition. In the eighteenth century, an average white, native-born male who reached the age of 10 could expect to live to somewhere between age 50 and 55. By contrast, an English *nobleman* at that time could expect to live only to something between age 39 and 46.

In the mid-nineteenth century, low incomes, local weather conditions, crop cycles, an almost complete lack of refrigeration, and limited transport of goods bound a large part of even the U.S. population to a minimal and nutritionally inferior variety of foods. Such uninspiring staples as potatoes, lard, cornmeal, and salt pork were the mainstays of diets, particularly outside the population centers. Most travelers' accounts of meals in nineteenth-century America mentioned the ubiquity of some kind of one-pot stew which constituted the main meal of the day for the family. According to one study, "There were, of course, a few people who knew what it was to . . . eat a meal that consisted of more than one course; but there were very, very few such people, and they were all very rich."[1]

Nevertheless, most Americans were right to feel that they lived in a land of unprecedented abundance, for that one-pot stew was quite sure to be there every day. For many centuries most Europeans had devoted nearly half their food budgets to breadstuffs; and, for most of them, the bread was of inferior quality. Often it took the form of gruel—what we would think of today as a cooked breakfast cereal—which was served in a single bowl with a single spoon, both of which were passed around the table to the entire family.

In bad years, even gruel was unavailable. Famine continued to threaten Europe until the beginning of the nineteenth century, and earlier it had constituted a normal fact of existence. One historian writes,

> ... two consecutive bad harvests spelt disaster.... France, by any standards a privileged country, is reckoned to have experienced 10 general famines during the tenth century; 26 in the eleventh; 2 in the twelfth; 4 in the fourteenth; 7 in the fifteenth; 13 in the sixteenth; 11 in the seventeenth and 16 in the eighteenth.
>
> The same could be said of any country in Europe. In Germany, famine was a persistent visitor to the towns and the flatlands...
>
> ... the countryside sometimes experienced far greater suffering. The peasants... had no solution in case of famine except to turn to the town where they crowded together, begging in the streets and often dying in public squares, as in Venice and Amiens in the sixteenth century.
>
> The towns soon had to protect themselves against these regular invasions.... Beggars from distant provinces appeared in the fields and streets of the town(s) ... starving, clothed in rags and covered with fleas and vermin.[2]

Food shortages were not the only manifestation of unimaginably poor living conditions:

> [I]n Pescara on the Adriatic, a small town with about a thousand inhabitants, an inquiry in 1564 revealed that three-quarters of the families in the town... were virtually homeless, living in makeshift shelters.... In the very rich town of Genoa, the homeless poor sold themselves as galley slaves every winter....
>
> The poor in the towns and countryside of [Europe] lived in a state of almost complete deprivation. Their furniture consisted of next to nothing, at least before the eighteenth century... only a few old clothes, a stool, a table, a bench, the planks of a bed, sacks filled with straw. Official reports for Burgundy between the sixteenth and the eighteenth centuries are full of "references to people [sleeping] on straw... with no bed or furniture" who were only separated "from the pigs by a screen."[3]

Even in the United States, living conditions in the nineteenth century were far from ideal. Most of the homes that travelers saw in rural America were tiny and crudely built, with no glass windows, no lighting except the fireplace,

---

[1]Ruth Schwartz Cowan, *More Work for Mother: The Ironies of Household Technology from the Open Hearth to the Microwave* (New York: Basic Books, 1983), Chapter 4.
[2]Fernand Braudel, *The Structures of Everyday Life: The Limits of the Possible*, vol. 1, *Civilization and Capitalism, 15th–18th Century* (New York: Harper and Row, 1979), pages 73–75 (footnotes omitted, Braudel's emphasis).
[3]*Ibid.*, pages 284–86.

no indoor plumbing, and scanty homemade furniture. Urban housing was not much better. In New York City in the 1860s, it was typical for six people to live in a ten-by-twelve room. In 1890 Jacob Riis wrote of the lower Manhattan tenements,

It is said that nowhere in the world are so many people crowded together on a square mile as here. In [one seven-story tenement building] there were 58 babies and 38 children that were over five years of age. . . . In Essex Street two small rooms in a six-story tenement were made to hold a "family" of father and mother, twelve children, and six boarders. . . .[4]

The worst evils of these overcrowded slums were insufficient light and air—narrow airshafts conveyed foul air and disease and served as inflammatory flues when fire broke out. There were no private water closets or washing facilities in these buildings, and cellars and courtyards were foul.

Like the common man, the rich have also gained much in terms of health and personal comfort in the course of two or three centuries. By the early 1900s, life expectancy at birth for a member of the British nobility had reached 65 years. But in the mid-sixteenth century, that figure was less than 40 years. More remarkable yet is the fact that longevity of the nobility in these centuries was no better than that of the population as a whole, despite the miserable living conditions of the bulk of the nation.

The dramatic improvement in the comforts enjoyed by the rich is illustrated by the development of home heating technology. The role of the draft in fireplace construction was not discovered until early in the eighteenth century. Until then, the huge fireplaces in the homes of the nobles, though beautiful, were extremely ineffective; they roasted nearby persons on one side and froze them on the other. Winter was a serious threat to rich and poor alike. "Cold weather . . . could be a public disaster, freezing rivers, halting mills [with little or no flour having been stored because preservation methods were largely unknown], bringing packs of dangerous wolves out into the countryside, multiplying epidemics."[5] Not even the highest nobility were spared. The Princess Palatine, the German sister-in-law of Louis XIV, reported that in February 1695 "in the Hall of Mirrors at Versailles at the King's table the wine and water froze in the glasses."[6]

Even the housing of relatively well-off nineteenth-century Americans (a very small proportion of the population) was still primitive by modern standards. Baths, for example, were rare even in the cities. No homes had electricity and few had gas. Fewer still had hot running water, and not even 2 percent had indoor toilets and cold running water. Boston, with a population of nearly 200,000 in 1860, had only 31,000 sinks, 4,000 baths, and 10,000 water closets—about half of which were extremely primitive affairs. Albany, with a population in 1860 of 62,000, had only 19 private baths and 160 water closets. Outdoor privies were the norm and baths, for the great majority, a luxury (and were still feared by many to be unhealthy).[7]

[4]Jacob Riis, *How the Other Half Lives* (New York: Hill and Wang, Inc., 1957), page 77. Originally published by Charles Scribner's Sons, New York, 1890.
[5]Braudel, page 299.
[6]*Ibid*. In 19th century rural America, it was not uncommon for ink to freeze in homes of people who were not wealthy.
[7]Edgar W. Martin, *The Standard of Living in 1860* (Chicago: University of Chicago Press, 1942).

Though living conditions were vastly improved from earlier centuries, by today's standards, life in the United States just 100 years ago was hard and primitive.

The Magnitude of Productivity Growth

Today, of course, things are vastly different. In 1980 only 2.2 percent of American housing units lacked complete plumbing—defined as hot and cold piped water, a flush toilet, and a bathtub or shower for the exclusive use of that housing unit. Only 4.5 percent were occupied by more than one person per room. Of the new, privately-owned, one-family houses built in 1981, fully 60 percent had three bedrooms, 46 percent had two bathrooms, and 65 percent had central air conditioning. And, 99.9 percent of all households had an electric vacuum cleaner, an electric toaster, a black and white television (89.8 percent had a color television), a radio, and an electric iron. Similarly, 99.8 percent were equipped with electric refrigerators, 92.8 percent had electric mixers, 77 percent had electric washing machines, 68 percent had electric frypans, 63.6 percent had electric can openers, and 64 percent had electric blankets![8]

This revolution in manner of living was made possible by an unprecedented rate of growth in human efficiency in producing output. Before reporting the facts, it is necessary to describe the two basic concepts, *labor productivity* and *output per capita*, usually employed to measure first, the productive efficiency of the working population, and second, the resulting average level of economic well-being.

Labor Productivity refers to the amount of output turned out by a *given* amount of labor. Obviously, an increase in productivity means that a human being has become a more effective instrument of production. This can be the result of harder work, better training, more or better equipment, innovative technology, or a variety of other causes.

The **standard of living,** on the other hand, is more naturally measured by **GNP per capita,** that is, by total output (GNP) divided by the number of persons among whom it will be distributed. The more output there is for each person, the better off in economic terms the average person must be.

The fantastic magnitude of the increases in both labor productivity and output per capita since, say, 1800 is best appreciated by contrasting it with the dismal average record of many previous centuries. In Europe, after a long decline, living standards had been increasing intermittently since the eleventh century—the century in which William the Conqueror acquired England. Yet, it is estimated that even by the time of the American Civil War neither labor productivity nor GNP per capita had yet reattained the levels that had been achieved in ancient Rome—about 16 centuries earlier! Thus, on the average, productivity and GNP per capita did not grow at all over 1600 years. Even for those wealthy enough to buy them, the number of important new consumer goods innovated in those 16 centuries was remarkably small. Firearms, glass windowpanes, eyeglasses, mechanical clocks, tobacco, and printed books constitute almost the entire list of major new consumer products invented between the fall of the Roman Empire and the beginning of the nineteenth century. Indeed, some significant amenities, notably elaborate bathing facilities and efficient home heating devices, had disappeared since the fall of Rome.

Labor productivity refers to the amount of output a worker turns out in an hour (or a week or a year) of labor. It can be measured as total national output (GNP) in a given year divided by the total number of hours of work performed for pay in the country during that year. That is, labor productivity is defined as GNP per hour of labor.

[8]U.S. Department of Commerce, Bureau of the Census, *Statistical Abstract of the United States, 1982–83* (Washington, D.C.: U.S. Government Printing Office, December 1982), pages 740, 754–55, 758.

In contrast, the period since, say, the 1830s has been characterized by an endless explosion of innovations. The railroad and the steamship revolutionized transportation. Steel-making technology changed drastically. The chemical industry was born and produced scores of new consumer products. The range of personal and household goods that we now take for granted—TV sets, dishwashers, cameras, automobiles, personal computers, and many, many others—appeared in an accelerating stream and became commonplace. This has reached a point where today our one unchanging expectation for the future is that it will be characterized by constant change.

Figure 7–1 shows, for five countries, the impressive growth of labor productivity over the past century. For example, it indicates that in this period Japanese productivity has risen about 2500 percent, French and German productivity levels each went up about 1500 percent, productivity in the United States increased about 1100 percent, and that even British productivity jumped by an astonishing 600 percent.

Figure 7–2 translates this productivity growth into the resulting rise in living standards—in national output per capita [**Gross Domestic Product (GDP)**].[9] In the countries shown, the number of hours worked per year has fallen significantly—by about 40 percent on the average. This is partly the result of a fall in work hours per day; typically from about 12 hours in 1870 down to some $7\frac{1}{2}$ hours per day in 1979. Also, the work week has declined from six days to five days. But most surprising is the almost total absence of any vacations for most of the population in 1870. The two- or four-week vacation is largely a twentieth-century invention—another luxury made possible by the rise in productivity. Largely because of this sharp fall in labor expended, output

[9]It should be noticed that the graphs measure outputs in terms of statistics on GDP (Gross Domestic Product) per capita. GDP, widely used by statisticians outside the United States, is a concept very similar to GNP. The former refers to all outputs produced within the geographic boundaries of a country, whether or not the producers were citizens of that country. GNP, in contrast, excludes all outputs produced by foreigners living or working in the country in question, and it includes outputs produced by citizens (nationals) of the country, even if they were working abroad.

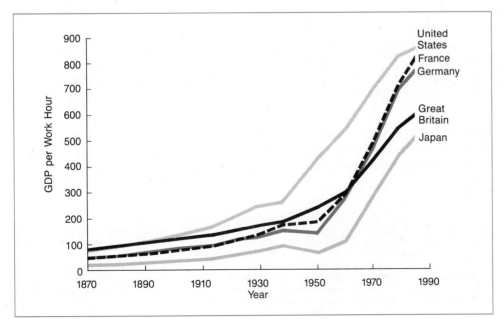

Figure 7–1
LABOR PRODUCTIVITY, 1870–1985
The productivity growth shown here for five industrial countries is typical of today's leading industrial economies. The explosive pattern of increase is unprecedented in previous history.
SOURCE: Angus Maddison, *Phases of Capitalist Development* (New York: Oxford University Press, 1982), page 8 and unpublished Maddison materials.

Figure 7–2
IMPROVEMENT IN LIVING
STANDARDS, SIX
COUNTRIES, 1870
VERSUS 1986
The graph shows how much
higher GDP per capita is
today than it was in 1870 in
each of the six countries
shown. The pattern is typical
for free market industrialized
countries. The numbers are
in dollars adjusted to have
roughly the same purchasing
power in all countries and
both dates listed.
Source: Angus Maddison, *Phases
of Capitalist Development* (New
York: Oxford University Press,
1982), page 8 and unpublished
Maddison materials.

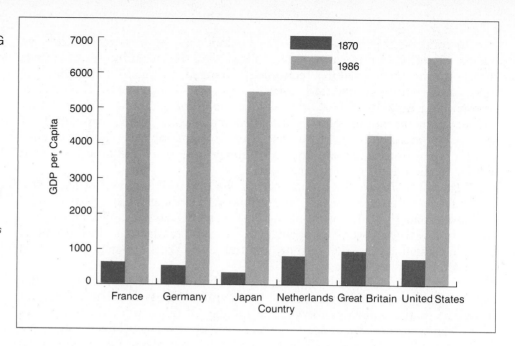

per person did not rise nearly as quickly as productivity. Yet the increases in output per person have also been spectacular. Over the 116-year period reported in the graph, output per person went up 1700 percent in Japan, 800 percent in Germany, 700 percent in the United States and France, and 300 percent in Great Britain.[10]

In other words, to take the U.S. case as an example, the average income of an American in 1870, measured in dollars of constant purchasing power, was only about one-eighth as large as it is today. To imagine what it is like to live with an income so small, one must go to *Egypt, Bolivia, or the Philippines*, whose per capita income today has been calculated to be on a par with that of an average American in 1870! Obviously, the rise in economic well-being of an average American, and of an average resident of the other countries in Figures 7–1 and 7–2, has been substantial. Indeed, it represents a rise to a standard of living a person in an earlier century can hardly have imagined.

Table 7–1 sums up the percentage increases since 1870 in **GDP per labor hour** and in **GDP per capita** for 16 leading industrialized countries. Obviously, the phenomenal growth in productivity and living standards extends to a considerable number of countries.

After some 1600 years of zero average growth in productivity and living standards, growth in both of these areas exploded in the world's industrial countries in the nineteenth and twentieth centuries, reaching levels previously unimaginable.

[10]It is important to notice that all of these numbers have been corrected to eliminate the effects of inflation in the manner already described in Chapter 2, pages 25–26, and in the appendix to Chapter 6. Thus, it is true, of course, that because of the subsequent inflation, a dollar in 1870 could purchase much more bread or many more shoes than it can today, so that a $12 weekly salary in 1870 is not as low, in purchasing power, as it may seem. But the statistics reported here have been corrected to eliminate this source of confusion, using the standard statistical method employed for the purpose. That is, since the statistics indicate that U.S. consumer prices have risen by about 6 times since 1870, a $12 1870 wage is counted as 6 × $12 = $72 in dollars of 1979 purchasing power (for more details on the method for correction for inflation see page 114 in the appendix to Chapter 6).

Table 7–1
Productivity and GDP Per Capita
Total Growth from 1870 to 1979* in 16 Industrialized Countries

	Real GDP per Work Hour	Real GDP Per Capita
Australia	398% growth	221% growth
Great Britain	585	310
Switzerland	830	471
Belgium	887	439
Netherlands	910	429
Canada	1,050	766
United States	1,080	693
Denmark	1,098	684
Italy	1,225	503
Austria	1,270	643
Germany	1,510	824
Norway	1,560	873
France	1,590	694
Finland	1,710	1,016
Sweden	2,060	1,083
Japan	2,480	1,661

Source: Angus Maddison, *Phases of Capitalist Development*. New York: Oxford University Press, 1982: pp. 8, 212.
*In 1970 U.S. dollars.

Significance of the Growth of Productivity

As we pointed out in our list of **12 Ideas for Beyond the Final Exam,** it is hardly an exaggeration to say that, in the long run, almost nothing counts for the determination of a nation's standard of living but its rate of productivity growth—for only rising productivity can raise standards of living in the long run.

Over long periods of time, small differences in rates of productivity growth compound like interest in a bank account, and they can make an enormous difference to a society's prosperity. Nothing contributes more to reduction of poverty, to increases in leisure, and to the country's ability to finance education, public health, environment, and the arts.

Since 1800, productivity in the United States has increased at an average annual rate slightly less than 2 percent. An apparently small change in this figure would have enormous consequences over a long period. Had productivity grown at an average rate of only 1 percent per year instead, an average American today would command about six times as large a quantity of goods and services as his forebears did in 1800. Actually, though it is hard to believe, real per capita income has risen about 20-fold in this period. And if productivity had grown over the entire interval at an annual rate of 3 percent, average living standards would be an incredible 137 times as high as they were in 1800.

Productivity growth can make an enormous difference in a nation's standing in the hierarchy of the world's economies. It has been remarked that the success of the United States in keeping its annual productivity growth about 1 percent ahead of Great Britain for about a century transformed America from a minor, developing country into a superpower and transformed the United Kingdom from the world's preeminent power into a second-rate economy. It is

Japan's 3-percent average annual productivity growth rate since 1870 that transformed it from one of the world's poorest countries into a nation with one of the highest GNP figures in the world.

The Second Major Development: Convergence

Not only have all the industrial countries grown in productivity and income per capita, but these countries have also become more similar to one another both in terms of labor productivity and GNP per capita. In other words, among the industrial countries, those which were furthest behind in 1870 have been catching up with those that were ahead. For example, considering the 16 countries represented in Table 7–1 (these are the only countries for which we have statistics that go back to 1870), the productivity level of the leading country (Australia) was about eight times as high as that of the least productive country (Japan) in 1870. By 1979 that ratio had declined to about two. That is, about three-quarters of the difference between the most productive and the least productive country were eliminated during the 109-year period.

Such a dramatic narrowing of productivity gaps among the industrial countries means that everyone else must be catching up with the leader, and that leader, ever since World War I, has been the United States. This is illustrated in Figure 7–3, which shows what happened to the *relative* living standards of several leading industrialized countries over the period 1950–1986, that is, GDP in each of those countries as a percentage of the U.S. level. It indicates that in 1950, per capita GDP for the average of the countries shown was almost 50 percent of that of the United States. By 1986 the average slightly exceeded 75 percent of the U.S. level. Figure 7–3 also shows that *each* of these countries has been moving closer to the United States (that is, closer to 100 percent of the U.S. level) in this 36-year period because for each country, the right-hand (1986) bar is equal to or taller than the left-hand (1950) bar. (The same is true

Figure 7–3
GDP PER CAPITA IN FIVE COUNTRIES AS PERCENT OF U.S. LEVEL, 1950 VERSUS 1986
The graph shows that four of the countries are approaching U.S. living standards (they have moved much closer to U.S. GDP per capita than they were in 1950). Only Great Britain has failed to come much closer, staying at about 2/3 of the U.S. GDP per capita.
SOURCE: Angus Maddison, *Phases of Capitalist Development* (New York: Oxford University Press, 1982), page 8 and unpublished Maddison materials.

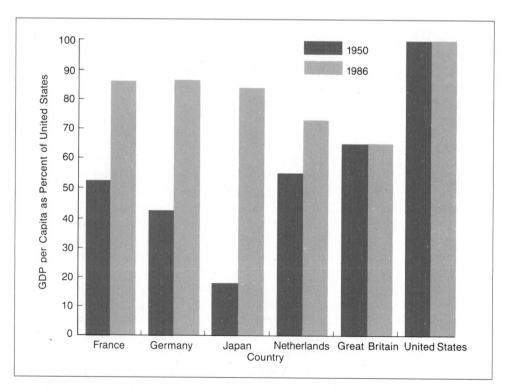

of each and every one of the other ten countries in Table 7–1). To interpret the graph, remember that if the bar representing some country were to reach precisely the top of the graph, it would mean that this country's standard of living is equal to that of the United States.

The data indicate that levels of labor productivity are converging among the leading industrialized countries.[11]

Has the same convergence process applied to countries other than the top industrial nations? Yes it has, at least for many of the medium-wealthy countries and even for the centrally planned economies. We have data on GDP per capita for seven centrally planned economies from 1950 to 1980. They show that GDP per capita of the richest of these countries in 1950 (Czechoslovakia) was more than 7 times as high as that of the poorest (China). By 1980 that distance between the richest (East Germany) and the poorest (still China) had declined to less than 5 to one.

The centrally planned economies have not only been catching up with one another, but they have also (slowly) been reducing the distance between themselves and the rest of the industrialized world. Thus, while GDP per capita in the average of these countries was slightly less than 25 percent of that of the United States in 1950, by 1980 it had reached 44 percent of that of the United States. Again, *every one* of the individual centrally planned economies for which we have data has benefitted from the catch-up.

The centrally planned economies seem to be growing closer to one another and to the United States in terms of income per capita.

Why International Equalization?

Why are all these countries growing more alike in productivity and average standards of living? No one has the entire answer, but a good part of the story is probably the speed-up of the international spread of new technology. Better communications permit innovative techniques to move from one country to another far more quickly than in the past. Better and more widespread education permits countries to learn technical details from one another and to train their labor forces rapidly to make use of them. At the beginning of the eighteenth century when the Newcomen steam engine (the predecessor of Watt's steam engine) was invented in England, it took half a century for the engine to spread to Western European countries and the American colonies. In contrast, the innovations in transistor and semiconductor technology since World War II have, on average, taken about two and one-half years to spread among countries.

All industrial countries benefit from the process of shared information; each learns from the innovations that occur in all the others. The British, the French, and the Germans benefit from American computer technology while the United States and others benefit from Japanese advances in robotics.

But there is one crucial asymmetry. Countries that are behind have a great deal to learn from countries that are ahead, but the leaders have less to learn

---

[11]The reader should be warned that this conclusion has been challenged, at least for the years before World War II, on the grounds that the sample of countries studied happens to include those that have been converging toward the United States because they are the success stories for which statistics are available. Thus, the critics point out, Argentina is omitted from the sample of countries, even though in 1870 many observers would have predicted a brilliant economic future for that country.

from those that have lagged behind. This is generally believed to be a prime explanation of the convergence in living standards. Meanwhile, the growing speed and efficiency of communications speeds up the entire process.

Lagging countries have more to learn from leaders than leaders can learn from laggards. This fact, and the growing speed with which innovations are spread, help explain why the world's economies are growing more equal.

Are All Countries Participating in Equalization?

So far we have seen that a considerable number of countries are growing increasingly similar to one another in terms of productivity and living standards. But we have yet to consider the world's poorest nations—usually referred to as "less developed countries," or LDCs. (See Chapter 38.) Have most of those countries also benefitted from the spread of innovation and closed the gap between themselves and the world's economic leaders? Unfortunately, among the LDCs, where equalization is most desperately needed, the picture is very mixed. Some economies, like Taiwan and South Korea, have achieved spectacular successes. But, as a group, the LDCs have grown less equal among themselves and have fallen further behind the United States. On average, GDP per capita grew about $3\frac{1}{2}$ percent per year in the industrialized countries in the period 1950–1980. But in the LDCs it rose only about $1\frac{1}{2}$ percent a year on average. A number of LDCs have fallen further behind the United States.

While the leading economies in the world are becoming more equal in terms of productivity and living standards, a number of the poorest countries are falling further behind and are holding back the average performance of the LDCs.

Why Some LDCs Are Falling Behind

In Chapter 38 we will discuss in detail the handicaps that have been blamed by specialist observers for the poor performance of many LDCs. Here we will only note briefly why the forces of equalization just described for the more developed countries do not work for a number of the LDCs.

Two influences are pertinent. First, the poor educational levels in the LDCs and the resulting scarcity of qualified engineers and technicians is a serious impediment to imitation and effective use of the complex technological advances of the industrialized countries. So they do not benefit by learning from others to nearly the extent the wealthier countries do. Second, the absence of products to which sophisticated production techniques can readily be applied makes it hard to participate in the growth gains from learning and imitation. A country that depends on products such as bananas, peanuts, and sugar for most of its income has little use for new robot designs or automated manufacturing processes, though it can and often does benefit from agricultural innovations, some of substantial importance. As a result, while the LDCs can and do learn to some degree from the technology of the industrialized economies, they suffer from serious handicaps in this process, handicaps from which the industrial countries are largely immune.

The Recent Productivity Slowdown in the United States

Since the mid-1960s there has been a sharp decline in the rate of growth of productivity in the United States. Some people fear that this threatens to turn America into a third-rate economy unable to compete with other nations. Others take a less alarmist view.

From the end of World War II until about 1965, productivity grew at an average rate of 3.2 percent per year, which is probably faster than it had ever grown before over so long a period. Then, between 1965 and 1972, productivity growth fell to something like 2.2 percent per year. From about 1972 to 1986, it fell to an annual rate of less than 1 percent.

It should be noted carefully that throughout most of this period the *level* of productivity continued to improve. In almost every year, it was higher than the last. But the *rate of improvement* slowed from a gallop to a walk, and finally to a crawl.

Why did U.S. productivity growth slow down? Many statisticians and economists have worked hard to determine why U.S. productivity growth has fallen so much since the mid-1960s. But because so many things have changed at once, no clear and easy answers have emerged. At least seven culprits have been identified.

Low Investment

Probably the most widely accepted cause of the slowdown is the lackluster performance of investment in plant and equipment, which is a prime determinant of labor productivity. The more a society invests, the more plant and equipment an average member of the labor force will have available to work with. More and better equipment will enable her to turn out more output per hour, so productivity will grow. Also, new machines usually incorporate the latest designs, and obsolete equipment tends to be kept longer when investment lags. Thus investment, and the savings that make investment possible, are crucial for productivity growth.

After World War II, business investment in the United States actually rose faster than GNP for a while. However, investment was not large enough to keep pace with the rapidly expanding labor force. Consequently, the amount of capital each worker had to work with fell after the 1960s. Because of differences in measurement procedures, there is some disagreement about the actual magnitude of this decline, but most analysts agree that lagging investment played a substantial role in the general decline in U.S. productivity growth. Most studies attribute from 20 to 40 percent of the slowdown in productivity growth to the shortfall in investment.

Slowdown in Research and Development

Another prime suspect in the slowing of U.S. productivity growth is business expenditure on applied research. Innovation is one of the main sources of productivity growth. New and more efficient productive procedures—from the steam engine to robotics—have multiplied the output a worker is capable of producing. However, innovation requires more than a new idea. It usually needs careful research to get out the "bugs" and to make the new procedures operational. This work is called **research and development (R and D),** and it is usually organized and financed by business firms. Because R and D is a critical step between the original invention and its final adoption by business enterprise, a big drop in R and D expenditures can do substantial damage to productivity growth.

The ratio of R and D outlays to GNP fell about 20 percent between the mid-1960s and the mid-1970s. There has been a decline in the number of scientists and engineers employed by U.S. industry. All in all, the statistical analysts generally attribute some 10 to 20 percent of the U.S. productivity slowdown to lagging R and D outlays.

Research and development (R and D) refers to the activity of business firms in which systematic efforts are undertaken to invent new or improved products or productive techniques and to make them ready to market or for use in production processes.

But what held back such outlays and generally impeded the pace of innovation? No one really knows. One hypothesis is that a decade of stagflation just made innovation and research less attractive to business. Another holds that rising real wages of scientists and engineers discouraged R and D activity by making it more expensive.

Government Regulations

Government regulation is also widely blamed for the slowdown. In the 1960s and 1970s, regulations for protection of the health and safety of workers and for defense of the environment were strengthened. These absorbed some of the investment outlays of business and increased the costs of production. Many business leaders believe that regulation has been a substantial impediment to productivity growth. But, while the statistics do not indicate that this development was completely blameless, they suggest that no more than 10 percent of the slowdown can be attributed to regulation.

Shift to the Service Industries

A **service industry** does not turn out any physical products. Telecommunications, medical care, teaching, police protection, and the work of lawyers are examples of service industries. Some, like telecommunications, use highly sophisticated equipment, and their productivity has grown rapidly. In many other services, such growth has been very slow.

Another possible culprit is the fact that during the period in question the share of the nation's labor force employed in **service industries** may have risen as much as 50 percent. Historically, growth of productivity in many (but by no means all) of the services has been far slower than in manufacturing. This is so in part because the quality of many services depends, or is believed to depend, directly on the amount of time the supplier devotes to the activity. The time devoted by a doctor to an average patient or the amount of faculty time per student are two prominent examples. Also, many services (such as diagnosis and treatment of a sick person) cannot be standardized and put on an assembly line. When workers leave manufacturing, with its relatively rapid productivity growth, and go into service industries where productivity growth is slower, overall productivity growth declines.

How serious is this phenomenon? Unfortunately, statistical estimates vary enormously. We really are not sure. In any event, the shift of the labor force toward the services cannot be considered an example of poor performance by our economy. Unlike lack of innovation, it is not something we must "cure."

Changes in the Makeup of the Labor Force

Discrimination has prevented many women and many members of minority groups from acquiring skills through on-the-job experience. To the extent that they have succeeded, therefore, efforts in recent decades to combat discrimination increased the flow of inexperienced workers into the labor force. The resulting impediment to productivity growth is probably temporary and, in any event, has partially been offset by rising educational attainment of the labor force as a whole.

Rising Energy Prices

The sharply rising price of energy was probably a major contributor to the slowdown in productivity growth. The 1970s was the period of the great petroleum shocks mentioned in Chapter 5. The sudden shortage of oil and the consequent leap in energy prices led to many economic changes. The building insulation business grew. The demand for large, gas-guzzling cars plunged. Much plant and equipment had to be changed to adapt to new patterns of consumer and business demands induced by rising energy prices and to substitute fuel-efficient equipment for items that had been installed when energy was cheap.

Because energy constitutes a small proportion of the nation's total expenditure on inputs, most statistical studies suggest that higher energy prices did not contribute much to the slowdown. A typical estimate is that they account for about 15 percent of the total decline in productivity growth.

Yet there are many, including the authors of this book, who suspect that energy may be responsible for more than that. The equipment which had to be replaced or modified to save on fuel probably used up a far from negligible portion of the country's investment. Moreover, as fuel prices rose, it sometimes became economical throughout the economy to employ more labor instead of using equipment that required expensive energy. So the ratio of labor to output rose, thus cutting directly into labor productivity. In addition, a sharp, sudden crisis and the resulting period of adjustment are never conducive to productivity growth. The fact that productivity growth plunged at just about the same time in most industrial countries suggests that the energy crisis was more important than the statistical studies show. The only explanations that apply to *all* countries are the energy problem and the influence of recession, to which we turn next.

Macroeconomic Conditions

Finally, some portion of the slowdown is probably attributable to the fact that the period since 1974 has not generally been characterized by healthy business conditions. Several recessions and an inflation of unprecedented severity and duration are not conditions that encourage business investment and innovation. There is no clear statistical evidence on the importance of this influence for the long-run behavior of productivity, but it is hard to believe that it was insignificant. Certainly a recession does cut productivity growth and the remaining question is how much of the U.S. economy's miserable productivity growth performance through 1986 was attributable to absence of buoyant prosperity.

The causes of the slowdown in U.S. productivity growth are far from certain. Lagging saving and investment, modest growth in R and D, increased government regulations, the shift to service industries, changes in the labor force, the energy crisis, and repeated recessions and protracted inflation probably all played a part.

More Guarded Interpretations of the Slowdown

Some analysts, however, question whether the U.S. productivity slowdown is as serious as it appears. They argue, first of all, that the U.S. is not alone in suffering a slowdown in productivity growth. The problem has affected virtually every industrial country. Figure 7–4 compares productivity growth rates during 1950–73 with those from 1973–84 for six industrial countries. We find that Great Britain's rate fell 25 percent, that of France declined 33 percent, West Germany's fell 50 percent, Holland's went down 57 percent, and Japan's fell 58 percent. Compared with these, the U.S.'s 60-percent decline does not seem so far out of line.

There is a second reason, based on the longer-run data, why some observers are less alarmed about the slowdown in U.S. productivity growth. Figure 7–5 shows a century of *growth rates* in U.S. labor productivity. The graph as a whole clearly exhibits neither a downward long-term trend nor a marked recent dip below the average growth rate of the preceding century. What we see is that the growth rate of productivity in the United States was virtually constant at

Figure 7–4
FALL IN PRODUCTIVITY GROWTH RATES, 1950–73 VERSUS 1973–84
This graph confirms that productivity growth has declined throughout the industrial world and not just in the United States. The decline is continuing in the 1980s.
SOURCE: Angus Maddison, *Phases of Capitalist Development* (New York: Oxford University Press, 1982), page 8 and unpublished Maddison materials.

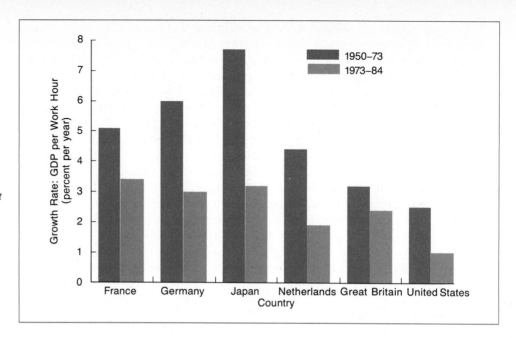

Figure 7–5
ANNUAL GROWTH RATES, U.S. PRODUCTIVITY, (1880–1985)
Aside from the sharp dip during the depression of the 1930s and the sharp rise after World War II, U.S. productivity has grown fairly steadily. However, during the 1980s it has fallen below its historical average of 2 percent improvement per year. No one knows how long the decline is likely to last.
SOURCE: Angus Maddison, *Phases of Capitalist Development* (New York: Oxford University Press, 1982), page 8 and unpublished Maddison materials.

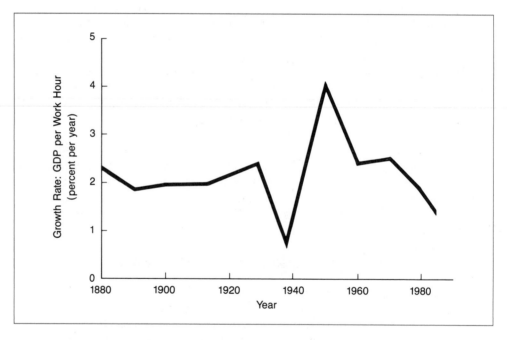

about 2 percent per year between about 1870 and 1930. Then, during the Great Depression of the 1930s, productivity growth plunged. With the advent of World War II and the postwar rebuilding of the devastated countries, U.S. productivity growth leaped upward. After this catch-up period, the growth rate fell back very close to its old historical level of 2 percent. On this view of the matter, then, the deceleration of the 1970s, rather than representing a drop below its historical norms, constitutes a return to that normalcy from a period of extraordinary growth which (in retrospect!) seems to have been predictably temporary. Much more disturbing is the fact that in the past few years productivity growth in the United States has fallen to perhaps half its historical average and has so far shown little sign of improvement. No one has any idea how long this problem, which has beset much of the industrial world, is likely to last.

What about the second disturbing fact about U.S. productivity growth — that it has recently been so much lower than that of other industrial countries? As a matter of fact that, too, is an old story. The growth rate of U.S. productivity has been just middling for the better part of a century. Between 1899 and 1913, the U.S. growth rate was already lower than that of Sweden, France, Germany, Italy, and Japan. Our growth rate was also below theirs (except for France) in 1924–1937. U.S. labor productivity grew rapidly relative to other nations only during both world wars, when many other countries were held back by the demands of their military activities.

There is a plausible explanation for the comparatively slow growth of U.S. productivity. It is the equalization of productivity in the world's industrial countries. If the forces making for equalization did in fact dominate the growth paths of those countries, it is necessarily true that productivity in the lagging countries *had* to grow more quickly than in the countries at the head of the line. Otherwise, they could never have grown more equal. The statistical evidence is consistent with the conjecture that the relative productivity growth rates of the various industrialized countries are largely explained by their distance behind the leader and the growth rates necessary for them to catch up. Viewed in this way, there need be little to be alarmed about in the relatively slow growth rate of U.S. productivity compared to that of other countries.

Viewed in long-term perspective, the recent slowdown in U.S. productivity growth and its lag behind other industrial countries seems somewhat less serious than it appears from an examination of the record of a briefer recent period.

The Costs of Lagging Productivity

Yet, despite what has just been said, there remain good reasons for concern about future productivity prospects. There certainly is no guarantee that productivity growth in the United States will continue at its old historical pace. To do so, the economy will require a continued flow of new and improving technology, new factories, new equipment, and the unslackening effort of engineers, scientists, technicians, management, and labor. None of this is easy or cheap, and none of it is guaranteed.

The costs of failure in this arena are very high. Above all, lagging productivity growth must slow or bring to an end the rising living standards and rising real wages which have so long been a prime accomplishment of the U.S. economy. If there is no rise in output per worker, then it will be impossible to keep increasing the quantity of goods and services provided to each consumer. Indeed, something of the sort has already happened. Since the beginning of the 1970s, the purchasing power of an average American worker's hourly wage has hardly increased at all.

Though we do not know whether long-run U.S. productivity growth has declined, for the past few years it has been well below its historical level. Failure to recoup threatens to hold back the growth in U.S. living standards.

Productivity, Unemployment, and Deindustrialization

Let us now use our long-term data to dispose of some popular myths about productivity growth and its consequences. Popular discussions of productivity growth often warn that rapid increases in labor productivity are not as beneficial as they are cracked up to be. We are told that each productivity increase reduces the demand for labor because it means that fewer work hours are needed to produce a given output. As a result, according to this view, productivity growth must create unemployment. Second, and perhaps somewhat inconsistently, it is argued that if an economy's productivity growth lags behind that of other countries, it will lose jobs to foreign workers, its industry will suffer, and its exports will fall. The resulting decline in industry has been given the catchy label "deindustrialization." However, the data do not support either of these conclusions, at least for the long run.

If the long-run unemployment spectre were a reality, we would expect that the 1100-percent increase in output per labor hour in the United States, its 600-percent increase in Great Britain, and its 1500-percent rise in Germany since 1870 would have had devastating effects on the demand for labor in these countries. After all, with productivity rising twelvefold during the last century, output per capita in the United States could have been kept about constant if employment were cut to one-twelfth its initial share of U.S. population. Even with a 50 percent fall in the number of hours an average person works per year, we might expect unemployment of perhaps five-sixths of the U.S. labor force by now.

Figure 7–6 shows that nothing of the sort has happened. The graph reports unemployment rates for Great Britain, the United States, and Germany in the periods 1874–1914 vs. 1952–1973. It is evident that over this long period there was no upsurge in unemployment, and the trend, if anything, has been somewhat downward. Before 1914, unemployment in the three countries averaged about 4 percent of the labor force, while in the 1952–1973 period it averaged a bit more than 3 percent. Even though there has been a rise in unemployment throughout the industrial world recently, much of it is attributable to short-term influences and reorientation of public policy away from government intervention to reduce unemployment. There is no evidence suggesting any *long-term* rise in unemployment.

How have we maintained unemployment in the face of rising productivity? The answer, of course, is that output per capita has hardly remained constant.

Figure 7–6
UNEMPLOYMENT RATES IN THE UNITED STATES, GREAT BRITAIN, AND GERMANY, 1874–1914 VERSUS 1952–1973
Over the long run, unemployment rates have not increased despite the enormous increase in productivity levels. Unemployment was much higher than is shown here during the 1930s. It has also gone up somewhat during the most recent decade.
SOURCE: R. C. O. Matthews, C. H. Feinstein, and J. C. Odling-Smee, *British Economic Growth 1856–1973* (Stanford: Stanford University Press, 1982), page 94.

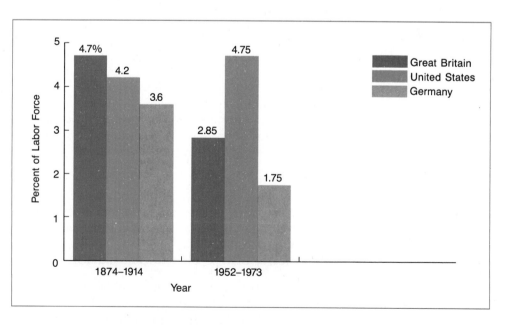

The demand for consumer goods and services, schools, hospitals, and factories has expanded explosively as productivity growth increased the purchasing power in the hands of the American public. That has sufficed to prevent any long-term increase in unemployment.

The same graph also undermines the (nearly) opposite apprehension. It shows that Great Britain, which has been the most noted laggard in productivity growth among industrialized countries, did not suffer from perpetually rising unemployment or unemployment problems more serious than those of other countries. Indeed, comparing the graph's bars for 1874–1914 with those of 1952–73, we see that Great Britain has made out relatively well on that score.

Neither rapid absolute productivity growth nor a slow relative productivity growth rate need subject a country to long-run and persistent increases in unemployment rates.

Before offering an explanation of this behavior of employment, we turn to the widely-held view that a persistent lag in a nation's productivity growth will place it at an increasing competitive disadvantage in international trade, and that it will thereby be excluded increasingly from its export markets, with devastating effects upon its industries.

Here again we use Great Britain, with its exceedingly poor productivity record, to examine these claims. It is true that the British *share* of exports declined from over 40 percent of world trade in 1870 to less than 10 percent a century later. But that is only because other countries' foreign sales rose even more rapidly than Britain's. The fact is that the total exports of Great Britain have risen spectacularly. Table 7–2 shows that between 1870 and 1979 the volume of British exports of goods and services increased about 930 percent; moreover, from 1855 to 1973, British exports of *goods* increased an astonishing 1200 percent.

Nor has Great Britain been forced to deindustrialize internally. In terms of the percent of the labor force employed in the industrial sector of its economy, Britain declined from first place in the sample of 16 countries in 1870 to fourth

Table 7–2
Exports: Total Percentage Growth, 1870–1979, in 15 Industrial Countries

Great Britain	930% growth
Germany	3,700
France	4,100
Switzerland	4,400
Austria	4,700
Sweden	5,100
Italy	6,200
Finland	6,200
Belgium	6,300
Denmark	6,800
Norway	7,700
Netherlands	8,000
United States	9,200
Canada	9,900
Japan	293,000

Source: Angus Maddison, *Phases of Capitalist Development*. New York: Oxford University Press, 1982: pp. 248–53.

place (behind Germany, Austria, and Switzerland) in 1979. But industry's share of employment in Great Britain was still 88 percent of that of Germany, the 1979 leader in terms of industrialization. And Great Britain continued to rank ahead of such countries as Sweden, France, the United States, Belgium, and Japan. If this is deindustrialization, it certainly is not very extreme.

The Real Cost of Lagging Productivity: Lagging Wages

From what has just been said, it may seem that it is not too bad to be a productivity laggard. After all, with no trend toward rising unemployment, with exports increasing, with the share of employment in manufacturing pretty well keeping up with other countries, what is so terrible about Great Britain's fate? Indeed, these observations may make one wonder how Britain was able to score these apparent successes despite its comparatively poor productivity performance.

The secret, which also shows the true price the British had to pay, is to be found in that country's lagging real wages. In the nineteenth century, British workers were the best paid in Europe. According to one estimate, which admittedly is not very reliable, in about 1860 an English worker's wages permitted the purchase of about $2\frac{1}{2}$ times the quantity of goods and services as a German worker's. Yet by 1980, the purchasing power of a German worker's wages was almost twice as great as that of a British worker. In other words, in a little more than a century the relative position of workers in the two countries had almost been reversed.

How are lagging British wages related to its productivity lag? The answer is straightforward. If Britain cannot compete on world markets by virtue of growing efficiency (productivity), it still can sell its products by providing cheap British labor. Of course, Britain does not volunteer to adopt low real wages; rather, market forces make it happen automatically, because inefficiently produced goods cannot be sold on the international marketplace unless those goods are produced by cheaper inputs. Hence, the invisible hand forces British wages to lag behind. Labor simply cannot extract higher wages from an economy that has little to give.

A country with lagging productivity is likely to be condemned to become an exporter of cheap labor. That is the only way it can keep its industry viable, maintain its exports, and preserve domestic jobs. This is the real danger that the United States faces if its productivity performance is unsatisfactory for any substantial period of time.

Concluding Comment

Productivity growth is indeed the stuff of which prosperity is made. The persistent record of U.S. productivity growth is the source of its high standard of living, which is extraordinary both in terms of previous history and in comparison with that of most nations in the world. In the long run, nothing is more important than productivity growth for the economic welfare of the country and for the world. In Chapter 38 we will examine some of the things that can help stimulate this vital ingredient of long-run well-being, which in two centuries transformed the focus of popular and political concerns in many industrial countries from the threat of starvation to the fear of overabundance of products.

Summary

1. Productivity growth over the past century has made a tremendous contribution to standards of living. Real U.S. per capita income is nearly 8 times as large as it was in 1870. Never in previous history have economic conditions improved so much.

2. For the first time in history, famine is no longer a constant threat in the world's industrialized countries. That is because productivity in agriculture has increased greatly. In 1800 about 90 percent of the U.S. labor force was needed to feed the nation poorly. Today, only about 3 percent of the labor force works on farms and yet produces great abundance.

3. Because of compounding, over longer periods a small increase in rate of productivity growth can make an enormous difference in the economic well-being of a nation. This is one of the **12 Ideas for Beyond the Final Exam.**

4. There is evidence suggesting that at least a small set of the world's leading economies are converging toward similar living standards and similar productivity levels.

5. All nations learn about new technological developments from one another. The international spread of inventions means that research in one country also benefits inhabitants in much of the rest of the world.

6. Since the 1960s, there has been a substantial slowdown in productivity growth in most industrial countries.

7. No one is quite sure of the reasons, but slowdown in saving and investment, the fuel crisis of the 1970s, and several recessions all probably played a significant role.

8. Lagging productivity holds back real wages and per capita incomes in a country. However, in the long run it will generally not cause unemployment or inability to export enough to pay for the nation's imports.

9. The growth rate of U.S. productivity has for many decades been slower than that of a number of other industrial countries. However, at least in part, that reflects the fact that the United States is still probably the world's productivity leader; so that while we have much to learn from others, they have even more to learn from us.

10. No one is sure whether or not the current slowdown in U.S. productivity and its lag behind that of other countries is a temporary matter. If it persists it can threaten relative U.S. living standards in the future.

11. The example of Great Britain shows that even if a country's productivity level and level of GDP per capita grow rapidly, it can appear to be depressed if it falls behind relatively, because other countries are growing even more rapidly.

Concepts for Review

Labor productivity
Standard of living
GNP per capita

Gross Domestic Product (GDP)
GDP per labor hour
GDP per capita

Research and development (R and D)
Service industry

Questions for Discussion

1. Try to describe what family budgets were like 120 years ago when U.S. income per person (GDP per capita) was about one-eighth as high as it is today.

2. List some of the inventions that have increased agricultural output in the past century.

3. List some of the inventions that have increased manufacturing output in the last century.

4. List some of the new consumer products of the past century. Which of them became generally available only since World War II?

5. List some foreign inventions widely used in the United States.

6. List some American inventions widely used abroad.

7. If growing productivity has vastly reduced the amount of labor needed to produce a given output, why has it not caused massively growing unemployment?

8. If output per capita in a country doubles every 25 years, how much will it grow in a century?

9. Which do you think are more similar?
   a. Production methods in a U.S. and a German factory today.
   b. Production methods in the same U.S. factory today and the methods used there 25 years ago.

PART 3

Aggregate Supply and Demand Analysis

8

Men are disposed, as a rule and on the average, to increase their consumption as their income increases, but not by as much as the increase in their income.

JOHN MAYNARD KEYNES

Income and Spending: The Powerful Consumer

In Chapter 5 we saw how the strength of aggregate demand influences the performance of the economy. When aggregate demand is growing briskly, the economy is likely to be booming, though it may also be having trouble with inflation. When aggregate demand stagnates, a recession is likely to follow.

This chapter begins our detailed study of the *determination* of aggregate demand. In this and the next few chapters, we will learn why the *aggregate demand curve* of Chapter 5 has a negative slope and how the government can *manage* aggregate demand. Since consumer spending accounts for the lion's share of total demand, it is natural to begin with the consumer. The following chapters will bring investment spending, government spending, and the supply side of the economy into the picture. Still later chapters will add such complications as interest rates, money, and exports and imports.

We start the chapter with some definitions of alternative concepts of economic activity—distinguishing carefully among total *spending* (aggregate demand), total *output*, and total *income*. Next, we turn to the interactions among these three concepts, using a convenient pictorial device that shows how they are all interrelated. Then we note that government attempts to influence consumer spending have sometimes succeeded and sometimes failed, and we pose the question: Why?

The bulk of the chapter is devoted to this question. To answer it, we first describe the important relationship between consumer income and consumer spending, and we use this relationship to show how government policies have worked when they have been successful. Then we discuss some complications that arise from the fact that consumer income, though crucial, is not the only factor governing consumer spending. One of these complications holds the clue to why government policies have sometimes failed to influence consumer spending as expected.

Aggregate Demand, National Product, and National Income

We begin with some definitions. We have already introduced the concept of **gross national product** as the standard measure of the total output of the economy.[1]

For the most part, goods are produced in a market economy only if they can be sold. **Aggregate demand,** another concept encountered in Chapter 5, is the total amount that all consumers, business firms, government agencies, and foreigners wish to spend on all U.S. final goods and services. The downward-sloping aggregate demand curve of Chapter 5 suggested that aggregate demand is a *schedule,* not a fixed number. And several reasons why aggregate quantity demanded depends on the price level will emerge in coming chapters. But the level of aggregate demand also depends on a variety of other factors like consumer incomes, various government policies, and events in foreign countries. We can understand the nature of aggregate demand best if we break it up into its major components.

Consumer expenditure ("consumption" for short) is simply the total demand for all consumer goods and services. This is the focus of the current chapter, and we shall represent it by the letter *C.*

Investment spending, which we represent by the letter *I,* is the amount that firms spend on factories, machinery, and the like plus the amount that families spend on new houses. Notice that this is a very different usage of the word "investment" from that which is found in common parlance. Most people speak of "investing" in the stock market or in a bank account. This kind of "investment" merely swaps one form of financial asset (such as money) for another form (such as a share of stock). When economists speak of "investment," they mean instead the purchase of some *new physical* asset, like a drill press or an oil rig or a home. It is only this kind of investment that leads directly to additional demand for newly produced goods in the economy.

The third major component of aggregate demand is **government purchases** of goods and services; that is, things like paper, typewriters, airplanes, ships, and labor that are bought by all levels of government—federal, state, and local. We use the shorthand symbol *G* to denote this variable.

The final component of aggregate demand is **net exports,** which are simply defined as U.S. exports minus U.S. imports. The reasoning here is simple. Part of the demand for American goods and services originates beyond our borders—as when foreigners buy our wheat, our computers, or our banking services. So this must be added to domestic demand. Similarly, some items included in C and I are not American made—think, for example, of German beer, Japanese cars, and Korean textiles. So these must be subtracted, if we want to measure total spending on U.S. products. Making these two adjustments together amounts to including net exports, which we symbolize by *X − IM* (exports minus imports), as part of aggregate demand.

Given all these abbreviations, we have the following shorthand definition of aggregate demand:

Aggregate demand is the sum $C + I + G + X - IM$.

The last concept we need is a measure of the total *income* of all the individuals in the economy. There are two versions of this: one for before-tax

[1]See Chapter 5, pages 78–80.

Aggregate demand is the total amount that all consumers, business firms, and government agencies are willing to spend on final goods and services.

Consumer expenditure, symbolized by the letter *C,* is the total amount spent by consumers on newly produced goods and services (excluding purchases of new homes, which are considered investment goods).

Investment spending, symbolized by the letter *I,* is the sum of the expenditures of business firms on new plant and equipment, plus the expenditures of households on new homes. Financial "investments" are not included, nor are resales of existing physical assets.

Government purchases, symbolized by the letter *G,* refers to all the goods (such as airplanes and paper clips) and services (such as school teaching and police protection) purchased by all levels of government. It does not include government **transfer payments,** such as social security and unemployment benefits.

Net exports, symbolized by *X − IM,* is the difference between U.S. exports and U.S. imports. It indicates the difference between what we sell to foreigners and what we buy from them.

National income is the sum of the incomes of all the individuals in the economy earned in the forms of wages, interest, rents, and profits. It excludes transfer payments and is calculated before any deductions are taken for income taxes.

Disposable income is the sum of the incomes of all the individuals in the economy after all taxes have been deducted and all transfer payments have been added.

incomes, called **national income,** and one for after-tax incomes, called **disposable income.**[2] The term "disposable income" is meant to be descriptive: it tells us how many dollars consumers actually have available to spend or to save. Because it plays such a prominent role in this chapter, we shall need an abbreviation for it as well; we call it **DI.**

The Circular Flow of Spending, Production, and Income

Enough definitions. How do these three concepts—national product, aggregate demand, and national income—interact in a market economy? We can answer this best with a rather elaborate diagram (Figure 8–1). For obvious reasons, Figure 8–1 is called a **circular flow diagram.** It depicts a large circular tube in which a fluid is circulating in a clockwise direction. There are several breaks in the tube where either some of the fluid leaks out or additional fluid is injected in.

Let us examine this system, beginning on the far left. At point 1 on the circle, we find consumers. Disposable income (*DI*) is flowing into them, and two things are flowing out: consumption (*C*), which stays in the circular flow, and saving (*S*), which "leaks out." This just says that consumers normally spend

[2]More detailed information on these and other concepts is provided in an appendix to this chapter.

Figure 8–1
THE CIRCULAR FLOW OF EXPENDITURE AND INCOME
The upper part of this circular flow diagram depicts the flow of expenditures on goods and services which comes from consumers (point 1), investors (point 2), government (point 3), and foreigners (point 4), and goes to the firms that produce the output (point 5). The lower part of the diagram indicates how the income paid out by firms (point 5) flows to consumers (point 1), after some is siphoned off by the government in the form of taxes and part of this is replaced by transfer payments (point 6).

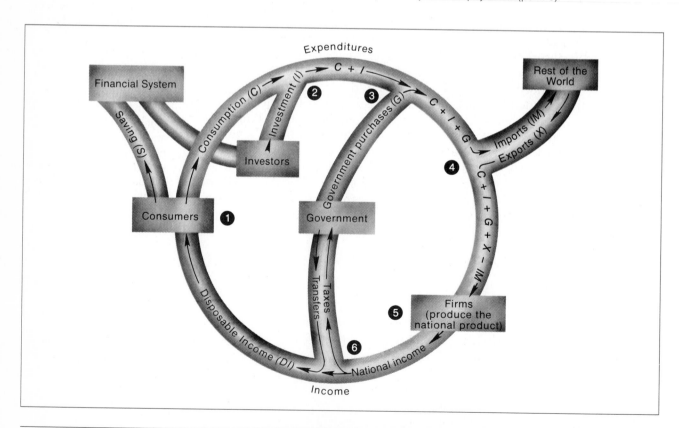

less than they earn and save the balance. The "leakage" to savings, of course, does not disappear, but flows into the financial system. We postpone consideration of what happens there until Chapter 13.

The upper loop of the circular flow represents expenditures, and as we move clockwise to point 2, we encounter the first "injection" into the flow: investment spending (I). The diagram shows this as coming from "investors" — a group that includes both business firms and consumers who buy new homes.[3] As the circular flow moves beyond point 2, it is bigger than it was before. Total spending has increased from C to C + I.

At point 3 there is yet another injection. The government adds its demand for goods and services (G) to those of consumers and investors (C + I). Now aggregate demand is up to C + I + G.

The final leakage and injection comes at point 4. Here we see export spending coming into the circular flow from abroad and import spending leaking out. The net effect of these two forces, net exports, may increase or decrease the circular flow. In either case, by the time we pass point 4 we have accumulated the full amount of aggregate demand, C + I + G + X − IM.

The circular flow diagram shows this aggregate demand for goods and services arriving at the business firms, which are located at point 5 at the southeast portion of the diagram. Responding to this demand, firms produce the national product. As the circular flow emerges from the firms, however, we have renamed it *national income*. Why? The reason is that, except for some complications explained in the appendix:

National income and national product must be equal.

Why is this the case? When a firm produces and sells $100 worth of output, it pays most of the proceeds to its workers, to people who have lent it money, and to the landlord who owns the property on which it is located. All of these payments are *income* to some individuals. But what about the rest? Suppose, for example, that the wages, interest, and rent that the firm pays add up to $90, while its output is $100. What happens to the remaining $10? The answer is that the owners of the firm receive it as *profits*. But these owners are also citizens of the country, so their incomes count in national income, too. Thus, when we add up all the wages, interest, rents, *and profits* in the economy to obtain the national income we must arrive at the value of the national output.

The lower loop of the circular flow diagram traces the flow of income by showing national income leaving the firms and heading for consumers. But there is a detour along the way. At point 6, the government does two things. First, it siphons off a portion of the national income in the form of taxes. Second, it adds back government **transfer payments,** like unemployment compensation and social security benefits, which are sums of money that certain individuals receive as outright *grants* from the government rather than as payments for services rendered to employers.

When taxes are subtracted from GNP, and transfer payments are added, we obtain disposable income.[4]

Transfer payments are sums of money that certain individuals receive as outright *grants* from the government rather than as payments for services rendered to employers.

DI = GNP − Taxes + Transfer Payments.

[3]You are reminded of the specific definition of investment on page 139.
[4]This definition omits a few minor details, which are explained in an appendix to this chapter.

Disposable income flows unimpeded to consumers at point 1, and the cycle repeats.

This diagram raises several complicated questions. Although we pose them here, we will not try to answer them at this early stage. The answers will be made clear in subsequent chapters.

1. Is the output that the firms produce at point 5 (the GNP) equal to aggregate demand? If so, what makes these two quantities equal? If not, what happens?
2. Is the flow of spending and income growing larger or smaller as we move clockwise around the circle, and why?

Chapter 9 provides the answers to questions 1 and 2.

3. Are the government's accounts in balance, so that what flows in at point 6 (taxes minus transfers) is equal to what flows out at point 3 (government purchases)? What happens if they are not?

This important question is first addressed in Chapter 12 and then recurs many times, especially in Chapter 16, which is devoted to discussing budget deficits.

4. Is our international trade balanced, so that exports equal imports? More generally, what factors determine net exports and what are the consequences of trade deficits or surpluses?

These questions, which have been much in the news of late, are postponed until Part 5, which is devoted to international economic issues.

But we cannot discuss any of these issues profitably until we first understand what goes on at point 1, where consumers make decisions, and point 2, where investors make decisions. We turn next, therefore, to the determinants of consumer spending.

Demand Management and the Powerful Consumer

As we suggested in Chapter 5, the government sometimes wants to shift the aggregate demand curve. There are a number of ways in which it can try to do so. One direct approach is to alter its own spending (G), becoming extravagant when private demand is weak and miserly when private demand is strong. But the government can also take a more indirect route by using taxes and other policy tools to influence *private* spending decisions.

A government desiring to change private spending can concentrate its energies on consumer spending (C), on investment spending (I), or on net exports ($X - IM$). At various times in our history, the U.S. government has endeavored to change each of these. Since consumer expenditures constitute nearly two-thirds of gross national product, C presents the most tempting target.

While there are many things it can do to alter consumer spending, the government's principal weapon is the personal income tax. Many of you already have encountered Form 1040, the unwelcome New Year's greeting that every taxpayer receives from the federal government each January. Many more of you probably have been on a payroll and seen a share of your wages deducted and sent to the Internal Revenue Service. It should be no mystery, then, how changes in personal taxes affect consumer spending. Any reduction in personal taxes leaves consumers with more disposable income to spend. Any increase in taxes leaves less.

The linkage from taxes to disposable income to consumer spending seems direct and unmistakable, and, in a certain sense, it is. But a look at the history of some major tax changes aimed at altering C is sobering. The varying degrees of success both of the measures themselves and of the predictions of their effects explain why economic research into the relationship between taxes and consumption continues.

Case 1: The 1964 Tax Reduction

The year 1964 was a good one for economists. For years they had been proclaiming that a cut in personal taxes would be an excellent way to stimulate a stagnating economy. But the plea fell on deaf ears until President John F. Kennedy was persuaded of the basic logic of the argument. Under his successor, Lyndon B. Johnson, Congress reduced personal taxes by about 18 percent. The legislation was designed to spur consumer spending, and it succeeded admirably. Consumers reacted just about as the textbooks of the day predicted, the economic situation improved rapidly and markedly, and economists smiled knowingly.

Case 2: The 1968 Tax Increase

The euphoria of 1964 proved to be short-lived. In 1968–1969 we learned—the hard way—that economists did not have all the answers. Because of the massive defense spending associated with the Vietnam War, the macroeconomic problem of 1966–1968 was precisely the opposite of that in 1964: too much demand rather than too little. It appeared logical, then, to prescribe the opposite medicine; and economists were quick to suggest a rise in personal income taxes to force consumers to spend less.

After a considerable delay, President Johnson recommended a temporary tax increase and Congress enacted a 10 percent rise in personal tax payments (calling it a "surcharge"). However, this attempt to cut aggregate demand by reducing C enjoyed only modest success. While consumer spending probably was below what it would have been in the absence of the surcharge, it was substantially above what the 1964 experience had led economists to predict.

Case 3: The 1975 Tax Reduction

The next major change in tax laws for stabilization purposes also met with partial success at best. In the spring of 1975, as the economy neared the bottom of a recession, President Gerald R. Ford and Congress agreed on a temporary tax cut to spur consumer spending: They returned to each taxpayer part of the taxes paid in 1974 and they reduced income tax rates for the balance of 1975. However, consumers confounded the wishes of the president and Congress by saving a good deal of their rebates rather than spending them.

Case 4: The 1981–1984 Tax Cuts

A series of reductions in personal income tax rates was a major campaign promise of Ronald Reagan, one which was promptly redeemed. Tax rates fell by about 23 percent between 1981 and 1984, and consumer spending increased by more or less the amounts that economists predicted.

What went wrong in 1968 and 1975 but did not go wrong in 1964 and 1981–1984? This chapter will attempt to provide some answers. We begin by exploring the important relationship between consumer income and consumer spending, more or less retracing the chain of logic that led government economists to the right conclusion in 1964. Once this is accomplished, we turn to some of the complications that made things go awry in 1968 and 1975.

Consumer Spending and Income: The Important Relationship

An economist interested in predicting how consumer spending will respond to a change in personal income tax payments must first ask how C is related to disposable income; for an increase in taxes is a decrease in after-tax income, and a reduction in taxes is an increase in after-tax income. This section, therefore, will examine what we know about the response of consumer spending to a change in disposable income.

Figure 8–2 depicts the historical paths of C and DI for the United States since 1929. The association is obviously rather close and certainly suggests that consumption will rise whenever disposable income does, and fall whenever income falls. The difference between the two lines is personal saving. Notice how little saving consumers did during the Great Depression of the 1930s, where the two lines are very close together, and how much they did during World War II, when many consumer goods were either unavailable or rationed so there was little on which to spend money.

Of course, knowing that consumer expenditures, C, will move in the same direction as disposable income, DI, is not enough for policy planners. They need to know how much one will go up when the other rises a given amount.

Figure 8–2
CONSUMER SPENDING AND DISPOSABLE INCOME IN THE UNITED STATES SINCE 1929
This time series chart shows the behavior of consumer spending and disposable income in the United States since 1929. Except for the World War II years, the correspondence between the two variables is remarkably close. The distance between the two lines represents consumer saving which was obviously quite small during the Great Depression of the 1930s and quite large during World War II.
SOURCE: U.S. Department of Commerce.

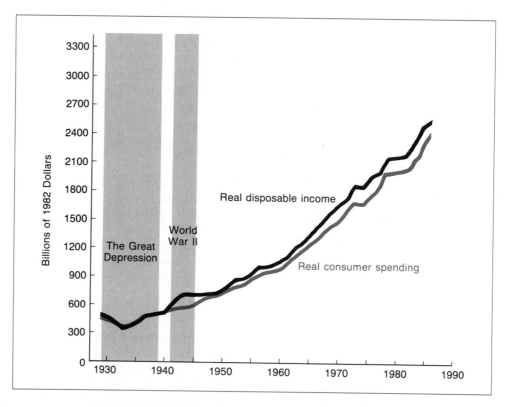

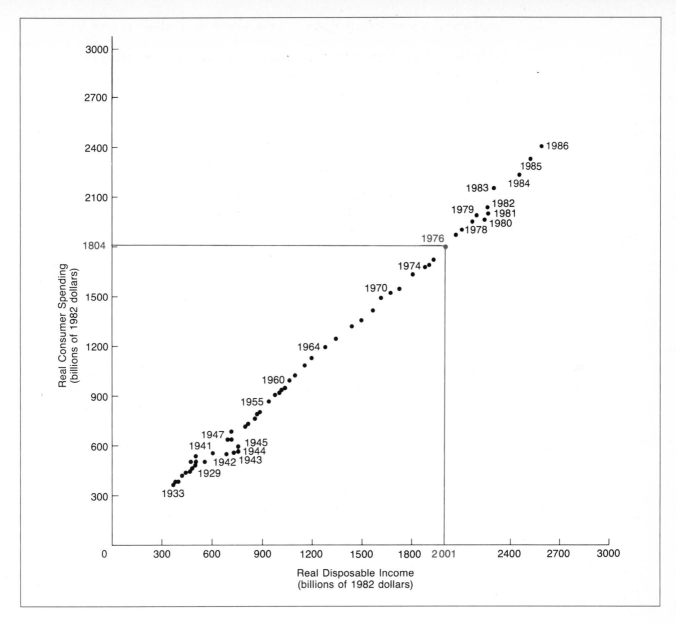

Figure 8–3

SCATTER DIAGRAM OF CONSUMER SPENDING AND DISPOSABLE INCOME IN THE
UNITED STATES, 1929–1986

This diagram shows the same data as depicted in Figure 8–2 but in a different manner. Each point
on the diagram represents the data for both consumer spending and disposable income during a
particular year. For example, the point labeled "1976" indicates that in that year consumer
spending was $1804 billion while disposable income was $2001 billion. Diagrams like this one are
called "scatter diagrams."

Figure 8–3 presents the same data that we saw in Figure 8–2 but in a way
designed to help answer the "how much" question.

Economists call such pictures **scatter diagrams**, and they are very useful in
predicting how one economic variable (in this case, consumer spending) will
change in response to a change in another economic variable (in this case, disposable income). Each dot in the diagram represents the data on C and *DI* corresponding to a particular year. For example, the point labeled "1976" shows

A **scatter diagram** is a
graph showing the
relationship between two
variables (such as
consumption and
disposable income). Each
year is represented by a
point in the diagram.
The coordinates of each
year's point show the
value of the two variables
in that year.

that real consumer expenditures in 1976 were $1804 billion (which we read off the vertical axis), while real disposable incomes amounted to $2001 billion (which we read off the horizontal axis). Similarly, each year from 1929 to 1986 is represented by its own dot in Figure 8–3.

How can such a diagram assist the fiscal policy planner? Imagine that this is 1963 and you must decide whether to recommend to Congress a tax cut of $5 billion, $10 billion, or $15 billion. (It has already been decided that a cut smaller than $5 billion is not worth the legislative effort and that a cut of more than $15 billion is politically infeasible.) You have forecasts of what consumer expenditures are expected to be if taxes are not reduced. This, plus other forecasts of investment and government spending, has led you to conclude that aggregate demand in 1964 will be insufficient if taxes are not reduced.

To assist your imagination, another scatter diagram is given in Figure 8–4. This one removes the points for 1964 through 1986, which appear in Figure 8–3; after all, these were not known in 1963. Years prior to 1947 have also been removed because both the Great Depression and wartime rationing seriously disturbed the normal relationship between DI and C. With no more training in economics than you have right now, what would you do?

One rough-and-ready approach is to get a ruler, set it down on Figure 8–4, and sketch a straight line that comes as close as possible to hitting all the points. Try that now. You will not be able to hit each point exactly, but you will find that you can come remarkably close. The line you have just drawn summarizes, in a very rough way, the consumption-income relationship that is the focus of this chapter. We see at once that it confirms something we might have guessed—that a rise in income is associated with a rise in consumer spending. The slope of the line is certainly positive.

The slope of your line is very important.[5] That line has been drawn into Figure 8–5, and we note that its slope is:

$$\text{Slope} = \frac{\text{Vertical change}}{\text{Horizontal change}} = \frac{\$90 \text{ billion}}{\$100 \text{ billion}} = 0.90 \,.$$

[5]To review the concept of *slope*, turn back to page 20.

Figure 8–4

SCATTER DIAGRAM OF CONSUMER SPENDING AND DISPOSABLE INCOME IN THE UNITED STATES, 1947–1963

This scatter diagram omits some of the data found in Figure 8–3 and indicates the information that policy planners might have used in deciding upon the size of the 1964 income tax cut.

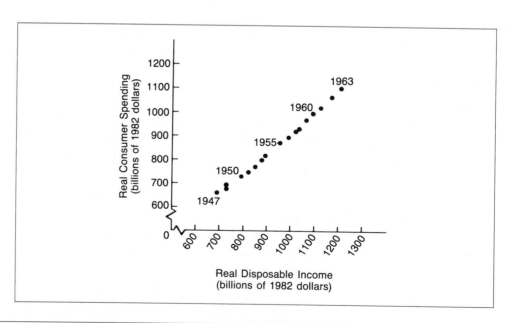

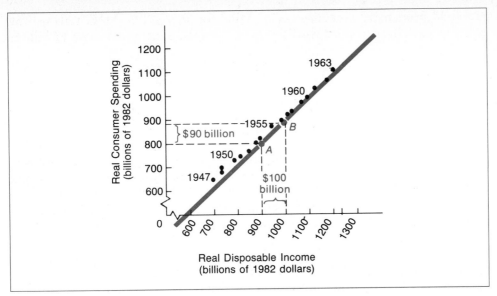

Figure 8–5
SCATTER DIAGRAM OF
CONSUMER SPENDING
AND DISPOSABLE
INCOME IN THE UNITED
STATES, 1947–1963
This diagram is the same as
Figure 8–4 except for the
addition of a straight line that
comes about as close as
possible to fitting all the data
points.

Since the horizontal change involved in the move from A to B represents a rise in disposable income of $100 billion (from $1000 billion to $1100 billion), and the corresponding vertical change represents the associated $90 billion rise in consumer spending (from $900 to $1000 billion), the slope of the line indicates how spending responds to changes in disposable income. In this case, we see that each additional $1 of income leads to 90 cents of additional spending.

In terms of the policy issue of 1964, this line can therefore help provide an answer to the question: How much more consumer spending will be induced by tax cuts of $5 billion, $10 billion, or $15 billion if the effects are similar to those observed in the past? First, we need to keep in mind that each dollar of tax cut increases disposable income by $1. Then we apply Figure 8–5's finding that each additional dollar of disposable income increases consumer spending by 90 cents, and we conclude that proposed tax cuts of $5 billion, $10 billion, or $15 billion would be expected to increase consumer spending by $4.5 billion, $9.0 billion, and $13.5 billion, respectively. Similar questions addressed by economists in 1964 led to a decision to cut taxes by about $9 billion.

Later in this and other chapters, we will encounter several reasons why this procedure, while basically valid, must be used with great caution.

The Consumption Function and the Marginal Propensity to Consume

It has been said that economics is just systematized common sense. Let us, then, try to organize and generalize what has been a completely intuitive discussion thus far. One thing we have learned is that there is a close and apparently reliable relationship between consumer spending, C, and disposable income, DI. Economists call this relationship the **consumption function.**

A second fact we have picked up from these figures is that the slope of the consumption function is fairly constant. We infer this from the fact that the straight line in Figure 8–5 comes close to touching every point. If the slope of the consumption function had changed a lot, it would not be possible to do so well with a single straight line. Because of its importance in such applications as the tax-cut example, economists have given a special name to this slope — the

The **consumption function** is the relationship between total consumer expenditure and total disposable income in the economy, holding all other determinants of consumer spending constant.

The **marginal propensity to consume** (or **MPC** for short) is the ratio of the change in consumption to the change in disposable income that produces the change in consumption. On a graph, it appears as the slope of the consumption function.

marginal propensity to consume, or **MPC** for short. The MPC tells us how many more dollars consumers will spend if disposable income rises by $1 billion.

$$MPC = \frac{\text{Change in consumption}}{\text{Change in disposable income that produces the change in consumption}}$$

The MPC is best illustrated by an example, and for this purpose we turn away from U.S. data for a moment and look at the consumption and income data of a hypothetical country called Macroland (see Table 8–1). The data for Macroland resemble those for the United States, except that in Macroland, C and DI figures happen to be nice round numbers, which facilitates computation.

Columns 1 and 2 of Table 8–1 show annual consumer expenditure and disposable income from 1983 to 1988. These two columns constitute Macroland's consumption function and are plotted in Figure 8–6. Column 3 in the table shows the marginal propensity to consume (MPC), which is the slope of the line in Figure 8–6; it is derived from the first two columns. We can see that between 1985 and 1986, DI rose by $500 billion (from $3000 to $3500) while C rose by $400 billion (from $2500 to $2900). Thus the MPC was:

$$\frac{\text{Change in consumption}}{\text{Change in disposable income}} = \frac{\$400}{\$500} = 0.80.$$

As you can easily verify, the MPC between any other pair of years in Macroland was also 0.80. This explains why the slope of the line in Figure 8–5 was so crucial in estimating the effect of a tax cut. This slope, which we found to be 0.90, is nothing but the MPC for the United States. And it is the MPC that tells us how much *additional* spending will be induced by each dollar *change* in disposable income. For each $1 of tax cut, economists expect consumption to rise by $1 times the marginal propensity to consume.

To estimate the *initial* effect of a tax cut on consumer spending, economists must first estimate the MPC and then multiply the amount of the tax cut by the estimated MPC. But since they never know the true MPC with certainty, this prediction is always subject to some margin of error.[6]

[6]The word "initial" in the first sentence is an important one. Later chapters explain why the effects discussed in this chapter are only the beginning of the story.

Table 8–1
CONSUMPTION AND INCOME IN MACROLAND

YEAR	(1) CONSUMPTION, C (billions of dollars)	(2) DISPOSABLE INCOME, DI (billions of dollars)	(3) MARGINAL PROPENSITY TO CONSUME, MPC
1983	1700	2000	
1984	2100	2500	0.8
1985	2500	3000	0.8
1986	2900	3500	0.8
1987	3300	4000	0.8
1988	3700	4500	0.8

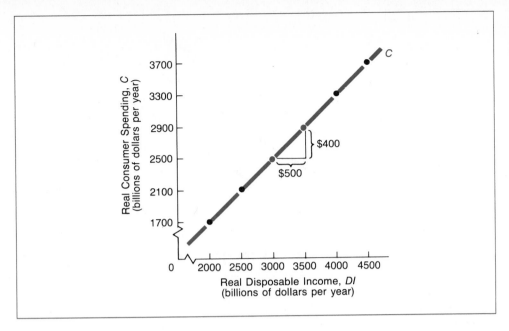

Figure 8–6
THE CONSUMPTION
FUNCTION OF
MACROLAND
This diagram is similar to
Figure 8–5, except that it
applies to a hypothetical (and
blissfully simple!) economy
called Macroland. As can be
seen, a straight-line
consumption function passes
through every point exactly.
The slope of this line is 0.8,
which is the marginal
propensity to consume in
Macroland.

In 1963, for example, economists multiplied the anticipated $9 billion tax cut by the estimated MPC of 0.90 and concluded that consumer spending would rise initially by about $8 billion. Their estimate seems to have been remarkably accurate.

Movements Along Versus Shifts of the Consumption Function

Unfortunately, this sort of calculation does not always yield such precise results. Among the most important reasons for this is that the consumption function does not always stand still; sometimes it shifts.

You will recall from Chapter 4 the important distinction between a *movement along* a demand curve and a *shift* of the curve. A demand curve depicts the relationship between quantity demanded and only *one* of its many determinants — price. Thus, a change in price causes a *movement along the demand curve*, but a change in any other factor that influences quantity demanded causes a *shift of the entire demand curve*.

Because consumer spending is influenced by factors other than disposable income, a similar distinction is vital to understanding real-world consumption functions. Look back at the definition of the consumption function in the margin of page 147. A change in disposable income leads to a **movement along the consumption function** precisely because the consumption function depicts the relationship between C and DI. This is what we have been considering so far. But consumption also has other determinants, and a change in any of these "other determinants" will **shift the entire consumption function** — as indicated in Figure 8–7. These shifts account for many of the errors in forecasting consumption. To summarize:

Any change in disposable income moves us *along* a given consumption function. But a change in any of the other variables that influence consumption *shifts* the entire consumption schedule (see Figure 8–7).

Figure 8–7
SHIFTS OF THE
CONSUMPTION
FUNCTION

An increase in disposable
income causes a movement
along a fixed consumption
function, such as the
movement from point A to
point B on consumption
function C_0. But a change in
any other determinant of
consumer spending will
cause the whole consumption
function to shift upward
(consumption function C_1) or
downward (consumption
function C_2).

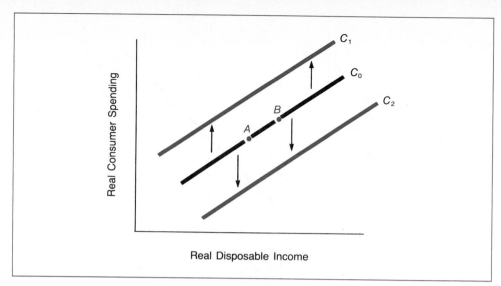

Real Disposable Income

Let us now list some of these "other variables" that can shift the consumption function.

Other Determinants of Consumer Spending

Wealth

One factor affecting consumption is consumers' *wealth*, which is a source of demand in addition to income. Wealth and income are different things. A wealthy person may currently have little *income*. Similarly, a high-income individual who spends all he earns will not accumulate wealth. To appreciate the importance of the distinction, consider two consumers, both earning $35,000 this year. One of them has $100,000 in the bank, while the other has no assets at all. Who do you think will spend more this year? Presumably the one with the big bank account.

The general point is that current income is not the only source of funds that households have; they can also finance spending by withdrawals from their bank accounts or by cashing in other forms of wealth. A stock market boom may therefore raise the consumption function (see the shift from C_0 to C_1 in Figure 8–7), while a collapse of stock prices may lower it (see the shift from C_0 to C_2).

The Price Level

A good deal of consumer wealth is held in forms whose values are fixed in money terms. Money itself is the most obvious example of this, but government bonds, savings accounts, and corporate bonds are all assets with fixed face values in money terms. The purchasing power of any **money fixed asset** obviously declines whenever the price level rises, which means that the asset can buy less. For example, if the price level rises by 10 percent, a $1000 government bond will buy about 10 percent less than it could when prices were lower. Consequently:

A **money fixed asset** is
an asset with a face value
fixed in terms of dollars,
such as money itself,
government bonds, and
corporate bonds.

Higher overall prices, by eroding the purchasing power of consumer wealth, decrease the demand for goods and services.

This is no trivial matter. It has been estimated that consumers in the United States hold money fixed assets worth over $3 *trillion,* so that each 1 percent rise in the price level reduces the purchasing power of consumer wealth by over $30 billion, a tidy sum. The process, of course, operates equally well in reverse. A decline in the price level increases the purchasing power of money fixed assets. So:

Lower overall prices, by enhancing the purchasing power of consumer wealth, increase the demand for goods and services.

For these reasons a change in the price level will shift the entire consumption function. Specifically,

A higher price level leads to lower real wealth and therefore to less spending *at any given level of real income*. Thus, a higher price level leads to a lower consumption function (such as C_2 in Figure 8–7). Conversely, a lower price level leads to a higher consumption function (such as C_1 in Figure 8–7).

Since students are often confused on this point, it is worth repeating that the depressing effect of the price level on consumer spending works through real *wealth,* not through real *income*. The consumption function is a relationship between *real* consumer *income* and *real* consumer *spending*. Thus any decline in *real income,* regardless of its cause, moves the economy *leftward along a fixed consumption function*; it does not shift the consumption function.[7] By contrast, any decline in *real wealth* will *shift the whole consumption function downward,* meaning that there is less spending at any given level of real income.

The Inflation Rate

Prices may be high and rising slowly, or they may be low but rising rapidly. Therefore, the depressing effect of a high *price level* on real consumer spending must be distinguished from any effect on spending of the *rate of inflation* (that is, the rate at which prices are rising).

Any effect of the inflation rate on consumer spending appears to be small; we are not even sure whether inflation stimulates or depresses spending. In the past, economists believed that high rates of inflation caused consumers to spend more to "beat" the inflation. That is, people were thought to purchase goods ahead of their needs in order to avoid the higher prices that loomed on the horizon. But behavior during the period of "double-digit" inflation in 1974 belied this contention: consumer spending was actually unusually *low* during this episode of high inflation, perhaps because of the uncertainty engendered by inflation. However, the opposite happened when inflation returned to double-digit levels in 1979–1980; this time, consumers started spending like mad.

Because there is no strong evidence that the rate of inflation shifts the consumption function systematically in one direction or the other, we shall assume that the position of the consumption function is influenced by the *price level,* but not by the *inflation rate*.

Expectations of Future Incomes

It will hardly be considered earth shattering to suggest that consumers' expectations about future income may affect how they spend today. This final determinant of consumer spending turns out to hold the key to answering the question

---

[7]This is true even if a rise in the price level lies behind the decline in real income. However, wages and prices normally move together, so there is no reason to expect real wages to fall when the price level rises.

we posed earlier. Why did the tax policy that succeeded so well in 1964 and the early 1980s fail to alter consumer spending as much in 1968 and 1975?

Why Tax Policy Failed in 1968 and 1975

To understand how expectations of future incomes affect current consumer expenditures, consider the abbreviated life histories of three consumers given in Table 8–2. The reason for giving our three imaginary individuals such odd names will be apparent shortly.

The consumer named "No Change" earned $100 in each of the four years considered in the table. The consumer named "Temporary Rise" earned $100 in three of the four years, but had a good year in 1975. The consumer named "Permanent Rise" enjoyed a permanent rise in income in 1975 and was clearly the richest.

Now let us use our common sense to figure out how much each of these consumers might have spent in 1975. "Temporary Rise" and "Permanent Rise" had the same income that year. Do you think they spent the same amount? Not if they had some ability to foresee their future income, because "Permanent Rise" was richer in the long run.

Now compare "No Change" and "Temporary Rise." Temporary Rise had 20 percent higher income in 1975 ($120 versus $100) but only 5 percent more over the entire four-year period ($420 versus $400). Do you think her spending was closer to 20 percent above No Change's or closer to 5 percent above it? Most people guess the latter.

The point of this example is that it is reasonable for consumers to decide on their *current* consumption spending by looking at their *long-run* income prospects. This should not be a shocking idea to most college students. How many of you are spending only what you earn this year? Probably not very many. And this is not because you are all foolish spendthrifts. On the contrary, you are rational planners. Knowing that your college education gives you a reasonable expectation of future income prospects much greater than those you now have, you are no doubt spending with that in mind.

Now let us see what all this has to do with the failure of the 1975 income tax rebate. For this purpose, imagine that the three rows in Table 8–2 now represent the entire economy under three different government policies. Recall that 1975 was the year of the rebate. The first row ("No Change") shows the unchanged path of disposable income if no tax cut was enacted. The second ("Temporary Rise") shows an increase in disposable income attributable to a tax cut *for one year only*. The bottom row ("Permanent Rise") shows a policy that increases DI in *every future year* by cutting taxes permanently in 1975. Which

Table 8–2
INCOMES OF THREE CONSUMERS

CONSUMER	INCOMES IN EACH YEAR				TOTAL INCOME
	1974	1975	1976	1977	
No Change	100	100	100	100	400
Temporary Rise	100	120	100	100	420
Permanent Rise	100	120	120	120	460

of the two lower rows do you imagine would have generated more consumer spending in 1975? The bottom row ("Permanent Rise"), of course. What we have concluded, then, is this:

Permanent cuts in income taxes cause greater increases in consumer spending than do temporary cuts of equal magnitude.

The application of this analysis to the case of the 1975 tax cut is immediate. The rebates were clearly one-time increases in income like that experienced by "Temporary Rise" in Table 8–2; no future income was affected. Hence, it is not surprising that statistical studies show that the 1975 tax cut had little effect on consumer spending.

Much the same situation prevailed in 1968, when Congress enacted a temporary 10 percent increase in income taxes to help finance the Vietnam War. Consumers considered the resulting decrease in their disposable income as only a *temporary* loss and did not curtail their spending as much as government officials had hoped. The general lesson is:

A permanent increase in income taxes provides a greater deterrent to consumer spending than does a temporary increase of equal magnitude.

We have, then, what appears to be a general principle, backed up both by historical evidence and common sense. Permanent changes in income taxes have a more significant impact on consumer spending than do temporary changes. Though it may now seem obvious, this is not a lesson you would have learned from the introductory textbooks of 1968. It is one that we learned the hard way, through bitter experience.

The Predictability of Consumer Behavior

We have now learned enough to see why the economist's problem in predicting how consumers will react to an increase or decrease in taxes is not nearly as simple as suggested earlier in this chapter.

The principal problem seems to be anticipating how taxpayers will view any changes in the income tax law. If the government *says* that a tax cut is permanent, will consumers *believe* it and increase their spending accordingly? Perhaps not, if the government has a history of raising taxes after promising to keep them low. Similarly, when (as in 1968) the government explicitly announces that a tax increase is temporary, will consumers always believe this? Or might they greet such an announcement with a hefty dose of skepticism? This is quite possible if there is a long history of "temporary" tax increases that stayed on the books indefinitely.

Thus the effectiveness of any *future* tax policy move may well depend on the government's *past* track record. A government that repeatedly uses a succession of so-called "permanent" tax cuts and tax increases for short-run stabilization purposes may find consumers beginning to ignore the tax changes entirely. The story of the boy who cried wolf is not yet required reading for fiscal policy planners, but it probably should be recommended.

Nor is this the only problem. Economists may fail to take adequate account of large and rapid accumulations of wealth (as happened immediately after World War II, when consumption forecasts were notoriously low) or of sizable losses of wealth (such as the drastic decline in the stock market in 1973–1975, when consumption forecasts were too high). Poor forecasts of future prices may lead consumption forecasts astray. And there are further hazards that we have not even mentioned here. Economic predictions are inexact, and predictions of consumption illustrate this well.

There is much more that can be said about the determinants of consumption, but it is best to leave the rest to more advanced courses. For we are now ready to apply our knowledge of the consumption function to the construction of the first model of the whole economy. While it is true that income determines consumption, the consumption function in turn helps to determine the level of income. If that sounds like circular reasoning, read the next chapter!

Summary

1. Aggregate demand is the total amount of goods and services that consumers, businesses, government units, and foreigners are willing to purchase. It can be expressed as the sum $C + I + G + X - IM$, where C is consumer spending, I is investment spending, G is government purchases, X is exports, and IM is imports.

2. Economists reserve the term "investment" to refer to purchases of newly produced factories, machinery, and houses.

3. National product is the total output of final goods and services of the economy. It is most commonly measured by the gross national product.

4. National income is the sum of the *before-tax* wages, interest, rents, and profits earned by all individuals in the economy. By necessity, it must be equal to national product.

5. Disposable income is the sum of the incomes of all individuals in the economy *after taxes and transfers,* and is the chief determinant of consumer expenditure.

6. All of these concepts, and others, can be depicted in a circular flow diagram that shows expenditures on all four sources flowing into business firms and national income flowing out.

7. The government often has tried to manipulate aggregate demand by influencing private consumption decisions, usually through the personal income tax. Although this policy seemed to work well in 1964 and 1981, it did not work well in 1968 and 1975.

8. The close relationship between consumer spending, C, and disposable income, DI, is called the consumption function. Its slope, which is used to predict the change in consumption that will be caused by a change in income taxes, is called the marginal propensity to consume (MPC).

9. Changes in disposable income move us along a given consumption function. Changes in any of the other variables that affect C shift the entire consumption function. Among the most important of these other variables are total consumer wealth, the price level, and expected future incomes.

10. Because consumers hold so many money fixed assets, they lose out when prices rise, which leads them to reduce their spending.

11. Future income prospects help explain why tax policy did not affect consumption as much as was hoped in 1968 and 1975. This is because the 1968 tax increase and the 1975 tax cut were both temporary, and therefore left future incomes unaffected. By contrast, the 1964 and 1981–1984 tax cuts were permanent, and affected future as well as current incomes. It is no surprise, then, that the 1964 and 1981 actions had stronger effects on spending than did the 1968 or 1975 actions.

Concepts for Review

Aggregate demand
Consumer expenditure (C)
Investment spending (I)
Government purchases (G)
Net exports (X − IM)
C + I + G + X − IM

National income
Disposable income (DI)
Circular flow diagram
Transfer payments
Scatter diagram
Consumption function

Marginal propensity to consume (MPC)
Movements along versus shifts of the consumption function
Money fixed assets
Temporary versus permanent tax changes

Questions for Discussion

1. What are the four components of aggregate demand? Which of these is the largest? Which is the smallest?
2. What is the difference between "investment" as the term is used by most people and "investment" as defined by an economist? Which of the following acts constitute "investment" according to the economist's definition?
   a. General Motors constructs a new assembly line.
   b. You buy 100 shares of General Motors stock.
   c. A small steel company goes bankrupt, and Bethlehem Steel purchases its factory and equipment.
   d. Your family buys a newly constructed home from a developer.
   e. Your family buys an older home from another family. (*Hint:* Are any *new* products demanded by this action?)
3. What would the circular flow diagram (Figure 8–1, page 140) look like in an economy with no government and no foreign trade? Draw one for yourself.
4. The marginal propensity to consume (MPC) for the nation as a whole is roughly 0.90. Explain in words what this means. What is your personal MPC?
5. Look at the scatter diagram in Figure 8–3 (page 145). What does it tell you about what was going on in this country in the years 1942–1945?
6. What is a "consumption function," and why is it a useful device for government economists planning a tax cut?
7. On a piece of graph paper, construct the consumption function for Simpleland from the data given below and determine the MPC.

YEAR	CONSUMER SPENDING	DISPOSABLE INCOME
1984	900	1000
1985	1350	1500
1986	1800	2000
1987	2250	2500
1988	2700	3000

8. In which direction will the consumption function for Simpleland shift if the price level rises? Show this on your graph.
9. Explain why permanent tax cuts are likely to lead to bigger increases in consumer spending than are temporary tax cuts.
10. (More difficult) Between 1984 and 1985, real disposable income (in 1982 dollars) rose from $2470 billion to $2542 billion. Use the data on real consumption expenditures given on the inside front cover of this book to compare the change in C to the change in DI. Explain why dividing the two does not give a good estimate of the marginal propensity to consume.

Appendix A
The Saving Function and the Marginal Propensity to Save

There is an alternative way of looking at the relationships we have discussed in this chapter. Disposable income that is not spent must be saved. Therefore, we can examine the effect of income on *saving* as well as its effect on consumer *spending*.

To see how saving appears on the consumption function diagram, we have repeated the consumption function of Macroland (see Figure 8–6) in Figure 8–8 and added a 45° line. You will recall that a 45° line marks those points where the distances along the horizontal and vertical axes are equal. (If you wish to review, see page 23.) Since the consumption schedule is below the 45° line, the figure shows that consumer spending is less than income, so some is being *saved*.

To find the amount of saving at each level of income, we need only read the vertical distance from the consumption function up to the 45° line. For example, when income is $4000 billion, saving is the distance AB, or $700 billion.

There is also a more direct way to find saving. Table 8–3 repeats the consumption and disposable income data for Macroland from Table 8–1 (page 148). Then, in column 3, we compute the difference between disposable income and consumption, which gives us **aggregate saving.**

Aggregate saving is the difference between disposable income and consumer expenditure. In symbols, $S = DI - C$.

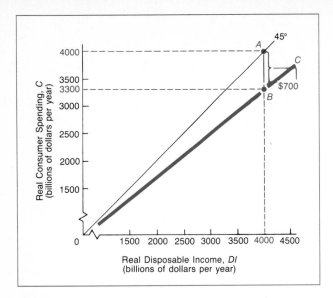

Figure 8–8
THE CONSUMPTION FUNCTION OF MACROLAND
The consumption function of Macroland, which we encountered in Figure 8–6 (page xxx), is repeated here, and a 45° line is added for convenience. Since consumption and saving must always add up to disposable income, the vertical distance between the two lines represents saving. For example, points A and B indicate that when disposable income is $4000 billion, saving is $700 billion.

This subtraction is exactly what we showed graphically in Figure 8–8. Columns 2 and 3 of Table 8–3 constitute what economists call the **saving function.**

The **saving function** is the relationship between total consumer saving and total disposable income in the economy, holding other determinants of saving constant.

The data of Table 8–3 are portrayed in Figure 8–9, which could equally well have been

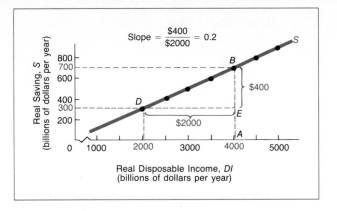

Figure 8–9
THE SAVING FUNCTION OF MACROLAND
The saving function of Macroland, depicted here, can be constructed either from the data in Table 8–3 or from Figure 8–8. This is because when we plot saving against disposable income (as we do here), we are also plotting the difference between consumption and disposable income (the vertical distance between line C and the 45° line in Figure 8–8) against disposable income.

constructed as the difference between the 45° line and the C line in Figure 8–8. (Because saving is so much less than consumption, we have stretched the scale of the vertical axis considerably.) Points A and B correspond to the same points in Figure 8–8. When the consumption function is a straight line, and thus has a constant slope, the same will be true of the saving function. In Figure 8–9, we show this slope as the ratio of distance EB to distance DE or $400/$2000 = 0.2. Economists call this slope the **marginal propensity to save.**

The **marginal propensity to save** (or **MPS**) is the slope of the saving function. It tells us how much more consumers will save if disposable income rises by $1 billion.

Table 8–3
SAVING IN MACROLAND

YEAR	(1) CONSUMPTION, C (billions of dollars)	(2) DISPOSABLE INCOME, DI (billions of dollars)	(3) SAVINGS, S (billions of dollars)	(4) MARGINAL PROPENSITY TO SAVE, MPS
1983	1700	2000	300	
1984	2100	2500	400	0.2
1985	2500	3000	500	0.2
1986	2900	3500	600	0.2
1987	3300	4000	700	0.2
1988	3700	4500	800	0.2

You may have noticed that the MPS is 0.2 while the MPC for Macroland is 0.8. They add up to 1, and not by accident. Since the portion of each additional dollar of disposable income that is not spent must be saved, the MPC and the MPS always add up to 1. It is a simple fact of accounting.

The MPC and the MPS always add up to 1, meaning that an additional dollar of income must be divided between consumption and saving. In symbols:

$$MPC + MPS = 1.$$

This enables us to compute either one of them from the other.

Summary

1. Instead of studying the consumption function, it is possible to study the same data by looking at the saving function, which is defined as the relationship between disposable income and consumer saving.
2. Since consumer saving is merely the difference between disposable income and consumer expenditure, everything we have learned about the consumption function applies to the saving function.
3. The amount of additional saving caused by a $1 increase in disposable income is called the marginal propensity to save, or MPS.
4. Since each additional $1 of disposable income is either spent or saved, the MPC and the MPS must always add up to 1. Thus, knowledge of one implies knowledge of the other.

Concepts for Review

Aggregate saving
Saving function
Marginal propensity to save

Questions for Discussion

1. Look at the circular flow diagram in Figure 8–1 (page 140). Where does the saving function enter the picture?
2. If the MPC in the U.S. economy is about 0.90, how large is the MPS?
3. Take the data from Simpleland in Question 7 on page 140 and use them to construct a saving function for Simpleland on a piece of graph paper.
4. (More difficult) If taxes are cut *temporarily* and consumer spending does not increase much, what must happen to consumer saving? Ask your instructor what happened to consumer saving immediately after the 1975 tax cuts.

Appendix B
National Income Accounting

The type of macroeconomic analysis presented in this book dates from the publication of John Maynard Keynes's *The General Theory of Employment, Interest, and Money* in 1936. But at that time there was really no way to test Keynes's theories because the necessary data did not exist. It took some years for the theoretical notions used by Keynes to find concrete expression in real-world data. The system of measurement devised for this purpose is called **national income accounting.**

The development of this system of accounts ranks as a great achievement in applied economics, perhaps as important in its own right as Keynes's theoretical work. For without it the practical value of Keynesian analysis would be severely limited. Many men and women spent long hours wrestling with the numerous difficult conceptual questions that arose in translating the theory into numbers, but they had one acknowledged leader: Professor Simon Kuznets of Harvard University, who, in 1971, was awarded the Nobel Prize in economics for his contributions to economic measurement techniques. Along the way some more-or-less arbitrary decisions and conventions had to be made. You may not agree with all of them, but the accounting framework that was devised is eminently serviceable, though, inevitably, it has some limitations that must be understood.

Defining GNP: Exceptions to the Rules

We first encountered the concept of **gross national product (GNP)** in Chapter 5.

Gross national product (GNP) is the sum of the money values of all final goods and services produced during a specified period of time, usually one year.

However, the definition of GNP has certain exceptions we have not yet noted.

First, the treatment of government output involves a minor departure from the principle of using market prices. Outputs of private industries are sold on markets, so their prices are observed. But "outputs" of government offices are not sold; indeed, it is sometimes even difficult to define what those outputs are. Lacking prices for outputs, national income accountants fall back on the only prices they have: prices for the inputs from which the outputs are produced. Thus:

Government outputs are valued at the cost of the inputs needed to produce them.

This means, for example, that if a clerk at the Department of Motor Vehicles earns $8 an hour and spends one-half hour torturing you with explanations of why you cannot get a driver's license, that particular government "service" is considered as being worth $4, and will increase GNP by that amount.

Second, some goods that are not actually sold on markets during the year are nonetheless counted in that year's GNP. These are the goods that are produced during the year but not sold; that is, goods that firms stockpile as *inventories*. Goods that are added to inventories count in GNP even though they do not pass through markets.

National income statisticians treat inventories as if they were "bought" by the firms that produced them, even though this "purchase" never takes place.

Finally, the treatment of investment goods runs slightly counter to the rule that only final goods are to be counted. In a broad sense, factories, generators, machine tools, and the like might be considered as intermediate goods. After all, their owners want them only for use in producing other goods, not for any innate value that they possess. But this would present a real problem, for factories and machines normally are never sold to consumers. So when would we count them in GNP? National income statisticians avoid this problem by defining investment goods as final products demanded by the firms that buy them.

Now that we have a more complete definition of what the GNP is, let us turn to the problem of actually measuring it. National income accountants have devised three ways to perform this task, and we consider each in turn.

GNP as the Sum of Final Goods and Services

The first way to measure GNP seems to be the most natural, since it follows so directly from the circular flow diagram in this chapter. It also turns out to be the most useful definition for macroeconomic analysis. We simply add up the final demands of all consumers, business firms, government, and foreigners. Using the symbols C, I, G, and $X - IM$ just as we did in the text, we have:

$$GNP = C + I + G + X - IM.$$

The I that appears in the actual U.S. national accounts is called **gross private domestic investment.** The word "gross" will be explained presently. "Private" indicates that government investment is considered part of G, and "domestic" just means that machinery sold by American firms to foreign companies is included in exports rather than in I. Gross private domestic investment in the United States has three components: business investment in plant and equipment, residential construction (home building),[8] and inventory

---

[8]Thus purchases of new homes are considered part of I rather than part of C.

investment. We repeat again that *only* these three things are **investment** in national income accounting terminology.

As defined in the national income accounts, **investment** includes only newly produced capital goods, such as machinery, factories, and new homes. It does not include exchanges of existing assets.

In common parlance, all sorts of activities that are not part of the GNP are often called "investment." People are said to "invest" in the stock market when they purchase shares. Or wealthy individuals "invest" in works of art. But since transactions like these merely exchange one type of asset (money) for another (stock or art works), they are not included in the GNP.

The symbol G, for government purchases, represents the *volume of current goods and services purchased by all levels of government*. Thus, anything the government pays to its employees is counted in G, as are its purchases of paper, pencils, airplanes, bombs, typewriters, and so forth.

Few citizens realize that *most of what the federal government spends its money on is not for purchases of goods and services*. Instead, it is on **transfer payments** — literally, giving away money — either to individuals or to other levels of government.

The importance of the conceptual distinction lies in the fact that G represents the part of the national product that government uses up for its own purposes — to pay for armies, bureaucrats, paper, and ink — whereas transfer payments merely represent shuffling of purchasing power from one group of citizens to another group. Except for the administrators needed to run the programs, real economic resources are not used up in this process.

In adding up the nation's total output as the sum of $C + I + G + X - IM$, we are summing the shares of GNP that are used up by consumers, investors, government, and foreigners, respectively. Since transfer payments merely give someone the capability to spend on C, it is logical to exclude them from our definition of G, including in C only the portion of these transfer payments that is spent. If we included them in G, the same spending would get counted twice: once in G and then again in C.

The final component of GNP is net exports, which are simply exports of goods and services

minus imports of goods and services. Notice that both goods *and services* count, though the news media devote most attention to the monthly data on trade in goods ("merchandise trade").

Table 8–4 shows GNP for 1986, in both nominal and real terms, computed as the sum of $C + I + G + X - IM$. The most stunning numbers in the table are the large negative figures for net exports. We will have much to say about America's huge trade deficit in Part 5.

GNP as the Sum of All Factor Payments

There is another way to count up the GNP — *by adding up all the incomes in the economy*. Let's see how this method handles some typical transactions. Suppose General Electric builds a generator and sells it to General Motors for $1 million. The first method of calculating GNP simply counts the $1 million as part of *I*. The second method asks: What incomes resulted from the production of this generator? The answer might be something like this:

Wages of G.E. employees	$400,000
Interest to bondholders	$50,000
Rentals of buildings	$50,000
Profits of G.E. stockholders	$100,000

The total is $600,000. The remaining $400,000 is accounted for by inputs that G.E. purchased from

---

Table 8–4
GROSS NATIONAL PRODUCT IN 1986
AS THE SUM OF FINAL DEMANDS

ITEM	AMOUNT (billions of current dollars)	AMOUNT (billions of 1982 dollars)
Personal consumption expenditures (*C*)	2799.8	2450.5
Gross private domestic investment (*I*)	671.0	654.0
Government purchases of goods and services (*G*)	869.7	754.5
Net exports (*X − IM*)	−105.5	−145.8
Exports (*X*)	376.2	377.4
Imports (*IM*)	481.7	523.2
Gross national product (*Y*)	4235.0	3713.3

SOURCE: U.S. Department of Commerce. Totals do not add up precisely due to rounding.

other companies: steel, circuitry, tubing, rubber, and so on.

But if we traced this $400,000 back further, we would find that it is accounted for by the wages, interest, and rentals paid by these other companies, *plus* their profits, *plus* their purchases from other firms. In fact, for *every* firm in the economy, there is an accounting identity that says:

$$\text{Revenues from sales} = \begin{cases} \text{Wages paid} + \\ \text{Interest paid} + \\ \text{Rentals paid} + \\ \text{Profits earned} + \\ \text{Purchases from} \\ \quad \text{other firms.} \end{cases}$$

Why must this always be true? Because profits are the balancing item; they are what is *left over* after the firm has made all its other payments. In fact, this accounting identity is really just the definition of profits: sales revenue less all costs of production.

Now apply this accounting identity to *all the firms in the economy*. Total purchases from other firms are precisely what we call *intermediate goods*. What, then, do we get if we subtract these intermediate transactions from both sides of the equation?

$$\left. \begin{array}{c} \text{Revenues from sales} \\ \text{minus} \\ \text{Purchases from} \\ \text{other firms} \end{array} \right\} = \begin{cases} \text{Wages paid} + \\ \text{Interest paid} + \\ \text{Rentals paid} + \\ \text{Profits earned.} \end{cases}$$

On the right-hand side, we have the sum of all factor incomes: payments to labor, land, and capital. On the left-hand side, we have total sales minus sales of intermediate goods. This means that we have only sales of *final* goods, which is precisely our definition of GNP. Thus, the accounting identity for the entire economy can be rewritten as:

$$\text{GNP} = \text{Wages} + \text{Interest} + \text{Rents} + \text{Profits},$$

and this gives national income accountants another way to measure the GNP.

Table 8–5 shows 1986's GNP measured by the sum of all incomes. Once again, a few details have been omitted in our discussion. The sum of wages, interest, rents, and profits actually adds up

Table 8–5
GROSS NATIONAL PRODUCT IN 1986
AS THE SUM OF INCOMES

ITEM	AMOUNT (billions of dollars)	
Compensation of employees (wages)	2504.9	
plus		
Net interest	326.1	
plus		
Rental income	16.7	
plus		
Profits	574.2	
Corporate profits		284.4
Proprietors' income		289.8
equals		
National income	3422.0	
plus		
Indirect business taxes and miscellaneous items	356.4	
equals		
Net national product	3778.4	
plus		
Depreciation	456.6	
equals		
Gross national product	4235.0	

SOURCE: U.S. Department of Commerce. Totals do not add up precisely due to rounding.

to only $3422 billion (whereas GNP is $4235 billion). We call this sum the **national income** because it is the sum of all factor payments. But the actual selling prices of goods include another category of income that we have ignored so far: sales taxes, excise taxes, and the like. National income statisticians call these *indirect business taxes*, and when we add these to national income we obtain the **net national product (NNP).**

Now we are almost at the GNP. The only difference between GNP and NNP is **depreciation** of the nation's capital stock.

Depreciation is the value of the portion of the nation's capital equipment that is used up within the year. It tells us how much output is needed just to keep the economy's capital stock intact.

The difference between "gross" and "net" simply refers to whether depreciation is included or excluded. We add depreciation to NNP to get GNP. Thus, GNP is a measure of all final output, taking no account of the capital used up in the process (and therefore in need of replacement).

NNP deducts the required replacements to arrive at a *net* production figure.

From a conceptual point of view, most economists feel that NNP is a more meaningful indicator of the economy's output than GNP. After all, the depreciation component of GNP represents the output that is needed just to repair and replace worn out factories and machines; it is not available for anybody to consume.[9] So NNP seems to be a better measure of well-being than GNP. But, alas, GNP is much easier to measure because depreciation is a particularly tricky item. What fraction of his tractor did Farmer Jones "use up" last year? How much did the Empire State Building depreciate during 1987? If you ask yourself these difficult questions, you will understand why most economists feel that GNP is measured more accurately than is NNP. For this reason, most economic models are based on GNP.

In Table 8–5 you can hardly help noticing the preponderant share of employee compensation in total national income — about 73 percent. Labor is by far the most important factor of production. The return on land is truly minute — under 1 percent; and interest accounts for under 10 percent. Profits account for the remaining 17 percent, though the size of corporate profits (less than 9 percent of GNP) is much less than the public thinks. If, by some magic stroke, we could eliminate all corporate profits without upsetting the performance of the economy, the average worker would get a raise of about 11 percent!

GNP as the Sum of Values Added

It may strike you as strange that national income accountants include only *final* goods and services in GNP. Aren't *intermediate* goods part of the nation's product? They are, of course. The problem is that, if all intermediate goods were included in GNP, we would wind up double and triple counting things and therefore get an exaggerated impression of the amount of economic activity that is actually going on.

To explain why, and to show how national income accountants cope with this difficulty, we must introduce a new concept, called **value added.**

The **value added** by a firm is its revenue from selling a product minus the amount paid for goods and services purchased from other firms.

The intuitive sense of the concept is clear: If a firm buys some inputs from other firms, does something to them, and sells the resulting product for a price higher than it paid for the inputs, we say that the firm has "added value" to the product. If we sum up the values added in this way by all the firms in the economy, we must get the total value of all final products. Thus:

GNP can be measured as the sum of the values added by all firms.

To verify that this is so, look back at the last accounting identity on page 160. The left-hand side of this equation, sales revenue minus purchases from other firms, is precisely the firm's value added. Thus:

$$\text{Value added} = \frac{\text{Wages} + \text{Interest} +}{\text{Rents} + \text{Profits.}}$$

Since the second method we gave for measuring GNP is to add up wages, interest, rents, and profits, we see that the value-added approach must also yield the same answer.

The value-added concept is useful in avoiding double counting. Often it is hard to distinguish intermediate goods from final goods. Paint bought by a painter, for example, is an intermediate good. But paint bought by a do-it-yourselfer is a final good. What happens, then, if the professional painter has some paint left over and uses it to refurbish his own garage? The intermediate good becomes a final good. You can see that the line between intermediate goods and final goods is a fuzzy one in practice.

If we measure GNP by the sum of values added, however, it is not necessary to make such subtle distinctions. In this method, *every* purchase of a new good or service counts, but we do not count the entire selling price, only the portion that represents value added.

To illustrate this idea, consider the data in Table 8–6 and how they would affect GNP as the sum of final products. Our example begins when a farmer who grows soybeans sells them to a mill for $3 a bushel. This transaction does *not* count in the GNP, because the miller does not purchase the soybeans for his own use. The miller then

---

[9]If it is used for consumption, the capital stock will decline, and the nation will wind up poorer than before.

Table 8–6
AN ILLUSTRATION OF FINAL
AND INTERMEDIATE GOODS

ITEM	SELLER	BUYER	PRICE
Bushel of soybeans	Farmer	Miller	$ 3
Bag of soy meal	Miller	Factory	4
Gallon of soy sauce	Factory	Restaurant	8
Gallon of soy sauce used as seasoning	Restaurant	Consumers	10
		Total:	$25
Addendum: Contribution to GNP:			**$10**

grinds up the soybeans and sells the resulting bag of soy meal to a factory that produces soy sauce. The miller receives $4, but GNP still has not increased because the ground beans are also an intermediate product. Next, the factory turns the beans into soy sauce, which it sells to your favorite Chinese restaurant for $8. Still no effect on GNP. But then the big moment arrives: The restaurant sells the sauce to you and other customers as a part of your meals, and you eat it. At this point, the $10 worth of soy sauce becomes a final product and is included in the GNP. Notice that if we had also counted the three intermediate transactions (farmer to miller, miller to factory, factory to restaurant), we would have come up with $25 — two and one-half times too much.

Why is it too much? The reason is straight-forward. Neither the miller nor the factory owner nor the restauranteur value the product we have been considering *for its own sake*. Only the customers who eat the final product (the soy sauce) have had an increase in their material well-being. So only this last transaction counts in the GNP. However, as we shall now see, value-added calculations enable us to come up with the right answer ($10) by counting only *part* of each transaction. The basic idea is to count at each step only the contribution to the value of the ultimate final

product that is made at that step, excluding the values of items produced at earlier steps.

Ignoring the minor items (such as fertilizer) that the farmer purchases from others, the entire $3 selling price of the bushel of soybeans is new output produced by the farmer; that is, the whole $3 is value added. The miller then grinds the beans and sells them for $4. He has added $4 − $3 = $1 to the value of the beans. When the factory turns this soy meal into soy sauce and sells it for $8, it has added $8 − $4 = $4 more in value. And finally, when the restaurant sells it to hungry customers for $10, a further $2 of value is added.

Table 8–7 shows this chain of creation of value added by appending another column to Table 8–6. We see that the total value added by all four firms is $10, exactly the same as the restaurant's selling price. This is as it must be, for only the restaurant sells the soybeans as a final product.

Alternative Measures of the Income of the Nation

Economists use the term *national income* in two different ways. The most common usage is as a general term indicating the size of the income of the nation as a whole, without being specific about exactly how this income is to be measured. This is the sense in which the term "national income" is used in this book. The second, and much more precise, use of the term refers to a particular concept in national income accounting which we encountered in Table 8–5 on page 160: the sum of wages, interest, rents, and profits.

Aside from this formal definition of national income, what other accounting concept might be used to measure the total income of the nation? The first and most obvious candidate is the GNP

Table 8–7
AN ILLUSTRATION OF VALUE ADDED

ITEM	SELLER	BUYER	PRICE	VALUE ADDED
Bushel of soybeans	Farmer	Miller	$ 3	$ 3
Bag of soy meal	Miller	Factory	4	1
Gallon of soy sauce	Factory	Restaurant	8	4
Gallon of soy sauce used as seasoning	Restaurant	Consumers	10	2
		Totals:	$25	$10
Addendum: Contribution to GNP				
Final products..			$10	
Sum of values added................................			$10	

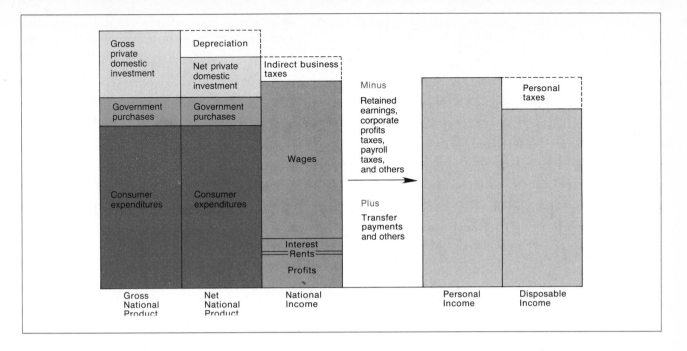

Figure 8–10
ALTERNATIVE MEASURES OF THE INCOME OF THE NATION
This bar chart indicates the relationships among the five alternative measures of the total income of the nation, starting with the largest and most comprehensive measure (GNP) and ranging down to the measure that most closely approximates the spendable income of consumers (disposable income).

itself. GNP, however, is intended to be a measure of *production,* and so has several drawbacks as a measure of *income*. First, it includes some output that represents income to no one — output that simply replaces worn-out machinery and buildings (depreciation). When we deduct this depreciation, we obtain the net national product (NNP), as shown in Figure 8–10. Second, because of sales taxes and related items (indirect business taxes), part of the price paid for each good and service does not represent the income of any individual. When we deduct these indirect business taxes from NNP, we arrive again at the formal definition of national income (refer to Figure 8–10).

There are, however, two other measures of income. **Personal income** is meant to be a better measure of the income that actually accrues to individuals. It is obtained from national income by *subtracting* corporate profits taxes, retained earnings, and payroll taxes (because these items

are never received by individuals), and then *adding in* transfer payments (because these sources of income are not part of the wages, interest, rents, or profits that constitute the national income). As Figure 8–10 suggests, this adding and subtracting normally results in a number that is rather close to national income. Finally, if we subtract personal income taxes from personal income, we obtain **disposable income.**

Among all the concepts of the nation's income depicted in Figure 8–10, only two are used frequently in the construction of models of the economy: gross national product (GNP) and disposable income (*DI*). Since the models presented in this book ignore depreciation and indirect business taxes, GNP is basically identical to national income (see Figure 8–10). Similarly, if we ignore retained earnings, GNP and *DI* differ only by the amounts of taxes and transfers (again, see Figure 8–10).

Summary

1. Gross national product (GNP) is the sum of the money values of all final goods and services produced during a year and sold on organized markets.

There are, however, certain exceptions to this definition.

2. One way to measure the GNP is to add up the final

demands of consumers, investors, government, and foreigners: GNP = C + I + G + X − IM.

3. A second way to measure the GNP is to start with all the factor payments — wages, interest, rents, and profits — that constitute the national income, and then add indirect business taxes and depreciation.

4. A third way to measure the GNP is to sum up the values added by every firm in the economy (and then once again add indirect business taxes and depreciation).

5. Except for possible bookkeeping and statistical errors, all three methods must give the same answer.

Concepts for Review

National income accounting	Transfer payments	Depreciation
Gross National Product (GNP)	Net exports	Value added
Gross private domestic investment	National Income	Personal Income
Government purchases	Net National Product (NNP)	Disposable Income (DI)

Questions for Discussion

1. Which of the following transactions are included in the gross national product, and by how much does each raise GNP?
   a. You buy a new car, paying $8000.
   b. You buy a used car, paying $3000.
   c. IBM builds a $50 million factory to make computers.
   d. An unemployed worker receives a government check for $400 in unemployment compensation.
   e. General Motors builds 2000 Cadillacs at a cost of $14,000 each. Unable to sell them, it holds them as inventories.
   f. Mr. Black and Mr. Blue, each out for a Sunday drive, have a collision in which their cars are destroyed. Black and Blue each hire a lawyer to sue the other, paying the lawyers $1000 each for services rendered. The judge throws the case out of court.
   g. You sell a $400 painting to your roommate.

2. Explain the difference between final goods and intermediate goods. Why is it sometimes difficult to apply this distinction in practice? In this regard, why is the concept of value added useful?

3. Explain the difference between government spending and government purchases of goods and services (G). Which is larger?

4. Explain why national income and gross national product would be exactly equal if there were no depreciation and no indirect business taxes.

5. The following is a complete description of all economic activity in Trivialand for 1987. Draw up versions of Tables 8–4 and 8–5 for Trivialand showing GNP computed in two different ways.
   a. There are thousands of farmers but only two big business firms in Trivialand: Specific Motors (an auto company) and Super Duper (a chain of food markets). There is no government and no depreciation.
   b. Specific Motors produced 1000 small cars, which they sold at $6000 each, and 100 trucks, which

they sold at $8000 each. Consumers bought 800 of the cars, and the remaining 200 cars were exported to the United States. Super Duper bought all the trucks.
   c. Sales at Super Duper markets amounted to $14 million, all of it sold to consumers.
   d. All the farmers in Trivialand are self-employed and sell all their wares to Super Duper.
   e. The costs incurred by all the businesses were as follows:

	SPECIFIC MOTORS	SUPER DUPER	FARMERS
Wages	$3,800,000	$4,500,000	$ 0
Interest	100,000	200,000	700,000
Rent	200,000	1,000,000	2,000,000
Purchases of food	0	7,000,000	0

6. (More difficult) Now complicate Trivialand in the following ways and answer the same questions. In addition, calculate national income, personal income, and disposable income.
   a. The government bought 50 cars, leaving only 150 cars for export. In addition, the government spent $800,000 on wages for soldiers and made $1,200,000 in transfer payments.
   b. Depreciation for the year amounted to $600,000 for Specific Motors and $200,000 for Super Duper. (The farmers had no depreciation.)
   c. The government levied sales taxes amounting to $500,000 on Specific Motors and $200,000 on Super Duper (none on farmers). In addition, the government levied a 10 percent income tax on all wages, interest, and rental income.
   d. In addition to the food and cars mentioned in Question 5, consumers in Trivialand imported 500 computers from the United States at $2,000 each.

9

Demand-Side Equilibrium: Unemployment or Inflation?

Investment... is a flighty bird, which needs to be controlled.

J. R. HICKS

As we learned in Chapter 5, the interaction of aggregate demand and aggregate supply determines whether the economy will stagnate or prosper, whether our resources of labor and capital will be fully employed or unemployed. This is the first of a series of chapters devoted to studying this important process.

A simplified model of aggregate demand is constructed in Chapters 9 and 10, and the supply side is added in Chapter 11. This first model of the economy teaches us much about the causes of unemployment and inflation, but it is too simple to deal with policy issues, because the government and the financial system are largely ignored. Chapters 12–14 remedy these omissions, thereby making it possible to study how government policies affect unemployment and inflation. By the end of Chapter 14 we will have a model that is capable of dealing with a wide variety of policy issues; and we will make extensive use of that model in Chapters 15–17. Then, in Chapters 18–20, we will consider some of the complications that arise from international economic relations.

In Chapter 8 we examined the largest component of aggregate demand, consumer expenditure (C). Here we turn our attention first to the most volatile component, investment (I), and discuss its determinants and the reasons why investment spending is so variable and so difficult to predict.[1] Then, rather than waiting for a full discussion of the other components of aggregate demand, we construct an abbreviated model of the determination of national income based only on the C and I components. We use this model to provide a preliminary description of how the state of aggregate demand influences the level of the gross national product, and to consider a question of great importance to policymakers: Can the economy be expected to achieve full employment of its resources if the government does not intervene?

---

[1] We repeat the warning given in the previous chapter about the meaning of the word *investment*. It *includes* spending by businesses and individuals on *newly produced* factories, machinery, and houses. But it *excludes* sales of used industrial plants, equipment, and homes, and it *also excludes* purely financial transactions, such as the purchase of stocks and bonds.

The Extreme Variability of Investment

The first thing to be said about investment spending is that it is extraordinarily variable.

Unlike consumer spending, which follows movements in disposable income with great (though not perfect) reliability, investment spending swings from high to low levels with annoying rapidity. During recessions, for example, the decline in investment generally constitutes by far the greatest part of the total drop in real GNP, despite the fact that investment is only a small portion of GNP—about 17 percent in the postwar United States. What accounts for these movements of investment demand?

Business Confidence and Expectations About the Future

While many factors influence business people's desires to invest, Keynes himself laid great stress on the *state of business confidence*, which in turn depends on *expectations about the future*.

While tricky to measure, it does seem obvious that businesses will build more factories and purchase more new machines when their expectations are optimistic. Conversely, their investment plans will be very cautious if the economic outlook appears bleak. Keynes pointed out that psychological perceptions like these are subject to abrupt shifts, so that fluctuations in investment can be a major cause of instability in aggregate demand. Hence, Hicks's analogy to a "flighty bird."

Unfortunately, neither economists nor, for that matter, psychologists have any very good ideas about how to *measure*—much less how to *control*—business confidence. Therefore, economists usually focus on several more objective determinants of investment—determinants that are easy to quantify and, perhaps even more important, are more easily influenced by government policy.

The Rate of Interest

The interest rate is the determinant of investment that is most extensively studied by economists, and it will play a pivotal role in later chapters. A good deal of business investment is financed by borrowing, and the interest rate indicates how much firms must pay for that privilege. Some investment projects that look profitable at an interest rate of 7 percent will look disastrous if the firm has to pay 12 percent.

The amount that businesses will want to invest depends on the real interest rate they have to pay on their borrowings. The lower the real rate of interest, the more investment spending there will be.

In Chapter 14 we will study in some detail how the government can influence the rate of interest. Since interest rates affect investment, policymakers have a handle on aggregate demand—a handle they do not hesitate to use. The point is that, unlike business confidence, interest rates are visible and manipulable. Therefore, even if investment responds much more dramatically to changes in confidence than to changes in interest rates, interest rates are nonetheless a more important instrument of government policy.

The State of Demand and Capacity Utilization

There will be a strong incentive to invest when firms find that demand is pressing against their capacity. Under these circumstances, firms are likely to feel that new factories and machinery can be employed profitably. By contrast, if there is a great deal of spare capacity (unused machinery, empty factories, and so on), business managers will not find investment attractive even at low interest rates.

The Growth of Demand

Since it takes a substantial amount of time to order machinery or to build a factory, investment plans are made with an eye on the future. Even when pressures on current capacity are not particularly severe, a firm experiencing rapid growth in sales may start investing now so that it will have adequate capacity when it is needed in the future. In addition, briskly growing sales are likely to make business people more optimistic. Conversely, slow growth of output will discourage investment. We can summarize these last two points by saying that:

High levels of sales in relation to available capacity and rapid economic growth create an atmosphere favorable to investment. On the other hand, low levels of sales and slow growth are likely to discourage investment.

Government stabilization policy thus has another handle on investment spending, for by stimulating aggregate demand it can induce business firms to invest more, though the precise amount may be hard to predict.

Tax Provisions

The government has still another important way to influence investment spending—by altering various provisions of the tax law. Most obviously, there is a tax on corporate profits and the government may reduce the statutory tax rate as a way to spur investment—as it did in 1986. That same tax bill, however, reduced the incentives for many companies to invest by ending the *investment tax credit*, a special subsidy for certain types of investment spending. Finally, the tax law sets maximum **depreciation allowances** which govern how firms may deduct the costs of investment from their taxable income. In 1981, when the Reagan administration wanted to encourage investment spending, it made these allowances more generous as a way to enhance the profitability of investment. To summarize:

Depreciation allowances are tax deductions that businesses may claim when they spend money on investment goods.

The tax law gives the government several ways to influence business spending on investment goods. But influence is far from control. Investment remains a "flighty bird."

A Simplified Circular Flow

Let us now put consumption and investment together and see how they interact, using as our organizing framework the circular flow diagram introduced in the last chapter. For this purpose, we simplify the circular flow somewhat by leaving out the government and the foreign sector.

There are two reasons for doing this. The first is pedagogical: The workings of the model will be clearer if we strip away some complications. But there is an equally important reason. One of the crucial questions surrounding government attempts to stabilize the economy is whether the economy would *automatically* gravitate toward full employment if the government simply left it alone. John Maynard Keynes, contradicting the teachings of generations of economists before him, claimed that it would not. But Keynes' views remain controversial to this day. We can study this issue best by imagining an economy that has no government, so that all the aggregate demand comes from the private sector. This is just what we do in this chapter.

Look now at Figure 9–1, which is the same as Figure 8–1 of the last chapter except that the government and foreign sectors have been omitted. The first thing you may notice is that, with the government out of the picture, there is no longer any leakage out of the national income for taxes (nor are there transfer payments); so there is no important difference between national income and disposable income. Second, there are no government or net export components of total spending; instead, spending is represented by the sum $C + I$.

The Meaning of Equilibrium GNP

We can use Figure 9–1 to begin the construction of a simple model of the determination of national income. A first step is to understand what we mean by "equilibrium income."

As was explained in the last chapter, national *product* and national *income* must, of necessity, be equal. But the same cannot automatically be said of total *spending*. Look again at Figure 9–1 and imagine that, for some reason, the total expenditures $(C + I)$ that are being made at point 3 are greater than the output that is being produced by the business firms at point 4.

Two things may happen in such a situation. Since consumers and firms together are buying (in the forms of C and I) more than firms are producing, business firms are being forced to take goods out of their warehouses to meet customer demands. Thus, inventory stocks must be falling. These inventory reductions are a signal to retailers of a need to increase their orders, and to manufacturers of a need to step up their production. Consequently, production is likely to rise. At some later date, if there is evidence that the high level of

Figure 9–1
A SIMPLIFIED
CIRCULAR FLOW
Here we show a simplified version of the circular flow of income and expenditures that we introduced in Chapter 8. The simplification amounts to shutting off the pipes leading into and out of the government. Thus, this circular flow represents an economy with no government and no foreign trade. Notice that aggregate demand now has only two components (consumer spending and investment spending) and that the entire national income flows to consumers without taxation.

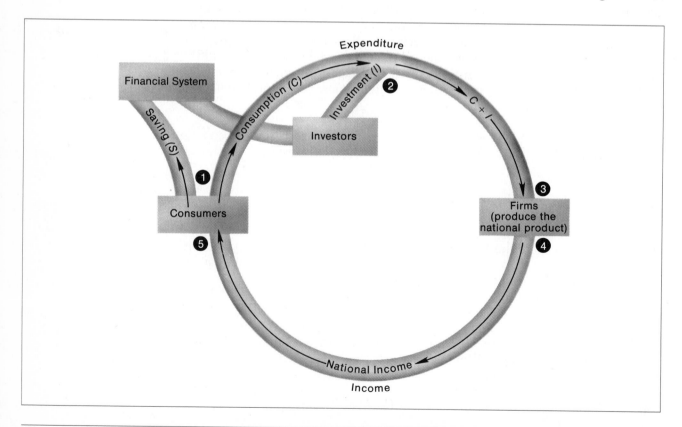

aggregate demand is not just a temporary aberration, either manufacturers or retailers (or both) may also respond to the buoyant sales performances by raising their prices. Economists therefore say that neither output nor the price level is in **equilibrium** when aggregate demand exceeds the current rate of production.

It is clear from the definition of equilibrium that the economy cannot be in equilibrium when aggregate demand exceeds production, for the falling inventories demonstrate to firms that their production and pricing decisions were not quite appropriate.[2] Thus, since we normally use GNP to measure output:

The equilibrium level of GNP cannot be one at which total spending exceeds output because firms will notice that inventory stocks are being depleted. They may first decide to increase production sufficiently to meet the higher demand. Later they may decide to raise prices as well.

Equilibrium refers to a situation in which consumers and firms have no incentive to change their behavior. They are content to continue with things as they are.

Now imagine the other case, in which the flow of spending reaching firms falls short of current production. Some output cannot be sold and winds up as additions to inventories. The inventory pile-up acts as a signal to firms that at least one of their decisions was wrong. Once again, they will probably react first by cutting back on production, causing the GNP to fall. If the imbalance persists, they may also lower prices in order to stimulate sales. But they certainly will not be happy with things as they are. Thus:

The equilibrium level of GNP cannot be one at which total spending is less than output, because firms will not allow inventories to continue to pile up. They may decide to decrease production, or they may decide to cut prices in order to stimulate demand. Normally, firms are reluctant to cut prices until they are certain that the low level of demand is not a temporary phenomenon. So they rely more heavily on reductions in output.

Equilibrium on the Demand Side of the Economy

You may have noticed that we have now determined, through a process of elimination, the level of national income and product that is consistent with peoples' desires to spend. We have reasoned that whenever GNP is below total spending $(C + I)$, the GNP will rise; and that whenever GNP is above $C + I$, the GNP will fall. Equilibrium can only occur, then, when there is just enough spending to absorb the current level of production. Under such circumstances, producers conclude that their price and output decisions are correct, and they have no incentive to change them. We conclude that:

The **equilibrium level of GNP on the demand side** is the one at which total spending equals production. In such a situation, firms find their inventories remaining at desired levels; so there is no incentive to change output or prices.

The simple circular flow diagram, then, has helped us to understand the concept of equilibrium of GNP on the demand side. It has also shown us how the economy is driven toward this equilibrium. It leaves unanswered, however, three important questions:

1. How large is the equilibrium level of GNP?
2. Will the economy suffer from unemployment, inflation, or both?

[2]All the models in this book assume, strictly for simplicity, that firms never want to change their inventories. Deliberate changes in inventories are treated in more advanced courses.

3. Is the equilibrium level of GNP on the demand side also consistent with firms' desires to produce? That is, is it also an equilibrium on the *supply* side?

The first two questions will occupy our attention in this chapter; the third question is reserved to Chapter 11.

Constructing the Expenditure Schedule

Our first objective is to determine precisely the equilibrium level of GNP and to see what factors it depends upon. To make the analysis more concrete, we turn to a numerical example. Specifically, we examine the relationship between aggregate demand and GNP in Macroland, the hypothetical economy that was introduced in the last chapter.

Columns 1 and 2 of Table 9–1 repeat the consumption function of Macroland that we first encountered in Table 8–1. They show how consumer spending, C, depends on national income, which we now begin to symbolize by the letter Y. However, one thing has changed here. The consumption function in Chapter 8 related C to *disposable* income (DI), whereas the consumption function in Table 9–1 relates C to *national* income (Y). This change is legitimate because, in this chapter, we have eliminated the government from the picture. With no taxes and no transfer payments, there is no difference between DI and Y.

Column 3 provides the other component of aggregate demand, I, through the simplifying assumption that investment spending is $700 billion in Macroland, regardless of the level of GNP. By adding together the second and third columns, we calculate C + I, or total expenditure, which is displayed in column 4. Columns 1 and 4, shaded in blue, show how total expenditure depends on income in Macroland. We call this the **expenditure schedule**.

Figure 9–2 shows the construction of the expenditure schedule graphically. The line labeled C is the consumption function of Macroland and simply duplicates Figure 8–6 of the last chapter, except that GNP, not DI, appears on the horizontal axis. It plots on a graph the numbers given in columns 1 and 2 of Table 9–1. The line labeled I displays our assumption that investment is fixed

An **expenditure schedule** shows the relationship between national income (GNP) and total spending.

Table 9–1
TOTAL EXPENDITURE IN MACROLAND (billions of dollars)

(1) INCOME (Y)	(2) CONSUMPTION (C)	(3) INVESTMENT (I)	(4) TOTAL EXPENDITURE (C + I)
2000	1700	700	2400
2500	2100	700	2800
3000	2500	700	3200
3500	2900	700	3600
4000	3300	700	4000
4500	3700	700	4400
5000	4100	700	4800
5500	4500	700	5200
6000	4900	700	5600

This table illustrates the derivation of the expenditure schedule, which is shaded in blue. It is derived from the consumption schedule, columns 1 and 2, and from the investment schedule, columns 1 and 3, by simple addition. This is because total spending is the sum C + I.

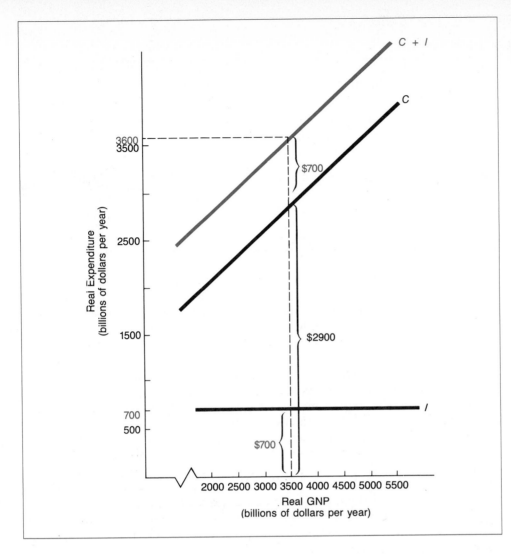

Figure 9–2
CONSTRUCTION
OF THE EXPENDITURE
SCHEDULE
This figure shows in a
diagram what Table 9–1
showed numerically—the
construction of a total
expenditure schedule from its
components. Line C is the
consumption function that we
first encountered in
Figure 8–6 except that GNP,
not disposable income, is
measured along the
horizontal axis. Line I is the
investment schedule
(assumed always to be $700
billion in this example). Line
C + I is the expenditure
schedule and is obtained by
adding investment to the
consumption function. For
example, when GNP is
$3500, C is $2900 and I is
$700, for a total of $3600.

at $700 billion, regardless of the level of GNP. By adding the two lines verti-
cally—that is, by summing consumption and investment at each level of
GNP—we derive the total expenditure schedule that was shown in columns 1
and 4 of Table 9–1. In the diagram, it is the blue line labeled C + I.

In our simple example investment is a fixed number, so the C and C + I
lines are parallel; that is, the distance between them is always the same. This
distance is $700 billion—the volume of investment assumed. If investment
were not always $700 billion, the two lines would either move closer together
(at income levels at which investment was below $700 billion) or grow farther
apart (at income levels at which investment was above $700 billion). For exam-
ple, our list of determinants of investment spending suggested that I might be
larger at higher levels of GNP. Because of this added investment—which is
called **induced investment**—the resulting C + I schedule would have a steeper
slope than the C schedule.

The Mechanics of Income Determination

We are now ready to determine demand-side equilibrium in Macroland. Look
first at Table 9–2, which presents the logic of our circular flow argument in

Induced investment is
the part of investment
spending which rises
when GNP rises and falls
when GNP falls.

Table 9–2
THE DETERMINATION OF EQUILIBRIUM OUTPUT

(1) OUTPUT (Y) (billions of dollars)	(2) TOTAL SPENDING (C + I) (billions of dollars)	(3) BALANCE OF SPENDING AND OUTPUT	(4) INVENTORIES ARE:	(5) PRODUCERS WILL RESPOND BY:
2000	2400	Spending exceeds output	Falling	Producing more
2500	2800	Spending exceeds output	Falling	Producing more
3000	3200	Spending exceeds output	Falling	Producing more
3500	3600	Spending exceeds output	Falling	Producing more
4000	4000	Spending = output	Constant	Not changing production
4500	4400	Output exceeds spending	Rising	Producing less
5000	4800	Output exceeds spending	Rising	Producing less
5500	5200	Output exceeds spending	Rising	Producing less
6000	5600	Output exceeds spending	Rising	Producing less

tabular form. The first two columns of this table reproduce the expenditure schedule that was constructed in Table 9–1. The other columns explain the process by which equilibrium is approached. Let us see why a GNP of $4000 billion must be the equilibrium level.

Consider first any output level below $4000 billion. For example, at output level $Y = \$3500$ billion, total expenditure is $3600 billion (column 2), which is $100 billion more than production. With spending greater than output (column 3), inventories will be falling (column 4). As the table suggests, this will be a signal to producers to raise their output (column 5). Clearly, then, no output level below $Y = \$4000$ billion can be an equilibrium. Output is too low.

A similar line of reasoning can eliminate any output level above $4000 billion. Consider, for example, $Y = \$4500$ billion. The table shows that total spending would be $4400 billion if national income were $4500 billion. So $100 billion of the GNP would go unsold. This would raise producers' inventory stocks and signal them that their rate of production is too high.

Just as we concluded from our circular flow diagram, equilibrium will be achieved only when total spending (C + I) is equal to GNP (Y). In symbols, our condition for equilibrium GNP is:

$$C + I = Y.$$

The table shows that this occurs only at a GNP of $4000 billion. This, then, must be the equilibrium level of GNP.

Figure 9–3 shows this same conclusion graphically, by adding a 45° line to Figure 9–2. Why a 45° line? Recall from Chapter 2 that a 45° line marks all points on a graph at which the value of the variable measured on the horizontal axis is equal to the value of the variable measured on the vertical axis. In this convenient graph of the expenditure schedule, gross national product (Y) is measured on the horizontal axis and total expenditure (C + I) is measured on the vertical axis. So the 45° line shows all the points at which output and spending are equal; that is, where $Y = C + I$. The 45° line therefore displays all the points at which the economy *can possibly* be at equilibrium, for if C + I is not equal to Y, firms will not be content with current output levels.

Now we must compare these potential equilibrium points with the actual combinations of spending and output that the economy can attain, given the behavior of consumers and investors. That behavior, as we have seen, is described by the C + I line in Figure 9–3, which shows how total expenditure

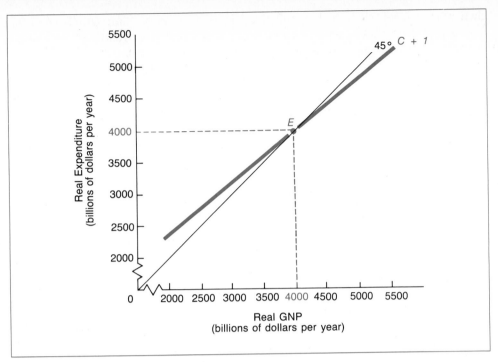

Figure 9–3
INCOME-EXPENDITURE
DIAGRAM
This figure adds a 45°
line—which marks off points
where expenditure and
output are equal—to
Figure 9–2. Since the
condition for equilibrium GNP
is that expenditure and
output must be equal, this
line can be used to
determine the equilibrium
level of GNP. In this example,
equilibrium is at point E,
where GNP is $4000
billion—precisely as we
found in Table 9–2.

varies as income changes. Thus, the economy will *always* be on the C + I line because only points on the C + I line are consistent with the spending plans of consumers and investors. Similarly, *if* the economy is in equilibrium, it *must* be on the 45° line. As Figure 9–3 shows, these two requirements together imply that the only viable equilibrium is at point E, where the C + I line intersects the 45° line. Only this point is consistent both with equilibrium and with the actual desires to consume and invest.

Notice that to the left of the equilibrium point, E, the C + I line lies above the 45° line. This means that total spending exceeds total output, as we have already noted in words and with numbers. Hence inventories will be falling and firms will conclude that they should increase production. The opposite is true to the right of equilibrium point E. Here spending falls short of output, inventories are rising, and firms will cut back production.

Diagrams like this one will recur so frequently in this and the next several chapters that it will be convenient to have a name for them. Let us therefore call them **income-expenditure diagrams** since they show how expenditures vary with income. Sometimes we shall also refer to them simply as **45° line diagrams.**

The Aggregate Demand Curve

Chapter 5 sketched a framework for macroeconomic analysis by introducing aggregate demand and aggregate supply curves which relate aggregate quantities demanded and supplied to the price level. Yet the price level has not even been mentioned so far in our discussion of equilibrium. It is now time to remedy this omission, for only by explicit analysis of the determination of the price level will we be able to deal with important issues relating to inflation.

Fortunately, no further mechanical apparatus is required. The price level can be brought into our income-expenditure analysis by recalling something we learned in the last chapter: At any given level of real income, higher prices lead to lower real consumer spending. The reason, you will recall, is that consumers

An **income-expenditure diagram**, also called a **45° line diagram**, plots total real expenditure (on the vertical axis) against real income (on the horizontal axis). The 45° line marks off points where income and expenditure are equal.

own many assets whose values are fixed in money terms, and which therefore lose purchasing power when prices rise.[3] With real wealth lower, consumers spend less and therefore total spending in the economy falls.

In terms of our 45° line diagram, then, a rise in the price level will lower the consumption function depicted in Figure 9–2 and, hence, will lower the total expenditure schedule as well. Conversely, a fall in the price level will raise both the C and C + I schedules in the diagram. The two parts of Figure 9–4 illustrate both these sorts of shifts.

What, then, do changes in the price level do to the equilibrium level of real GNP on the demand side? Common sense says that, with lower spending, equilibrium GNP should fall. And Figure 9–4 shows that this conclusion is correct. Part (a) shows that a rise in the price level, by shifting the expenditure schedule downward from $C_0 + I$ to $C_1 + I$ leads to a reduction in the equilibrium quantity of real GNP demanded from Y_0 to Y_1. Part (b) shows that a fall in the price level, by shifting the expenditure schedule upward from $C_0 + I$ to $C_2 + I$ leads to a rise in the equilibrium quantity of real GNP demanded from Y_0 to Y_2. In summary:

A rise in the price level leads to a lower equilibrium level of real aggregate quantity demanded. This relationship between the price level and the equilibrium quantity of real GNP demanded is depicted in Figure 9–5 and is precisely what we called the **aggregate demand curve** in earlier chapters. It comes directly from the 45° line diagrams in Figure 9–4. Thus, points E_0, E_1, and E_2 in Figure 9–5 correspond precisely to the points bearing the same labels in Figure 9–4.

Thus we have now learned the first reason why the aggregate demand curve relating the price level to real GNP demanded slopes downward. (More

[3]Two warnings issued in Chapter 8 (pages 150–51) are worth repeating: First, the effect referred to here comes from changes in the *price level*, not from changes in the *inflation rate*. Second, a higher price level does not reduce spending by reducing real income. Quite to the contrary, real income is held constant when we compare consumer expenditures at different price levels.

Figure 9–4

THE EFFECT OF THE PRICE LEVEL ON EQUILIBRIUM AGGREGATE QUANTITY DEMANDED

Because a change in the price level causes the expenditure schedule to shift, it changes the equilibrium quantity of real GNP demanded. Part (a) shows what happens when the price level rises, causing the expenditure schedule to shift downward from $C_0 + I$ to $C_1 + I$. Equilibrium quantity demanded falls from Y_0 to Y_1. Part (b) shows what happens when the price level falls, causing the expenditure schedule to shift upward from $C_0 + I$ to $C_2 + I$. Equilibrium quantity demanded rises from Y_0 to Y_2.

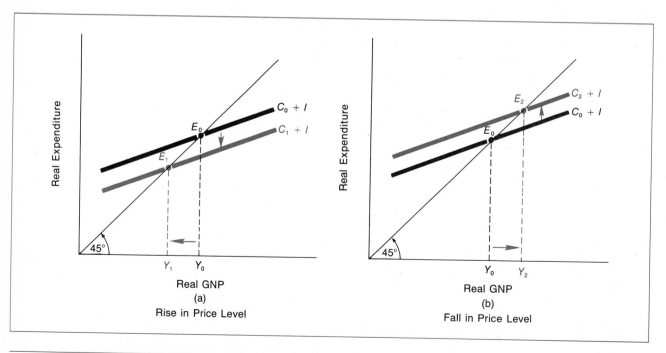

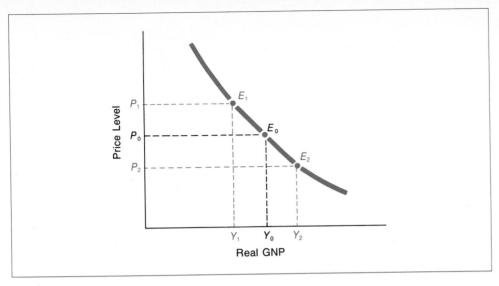

Figure 9–5
THE AGGREGATE
DEMAND CURVE
The graphical analysis in
Figure 9–4 showed that
higher prices lead to lower
aggregate quantity
demanded. This relationship
is called the aggregate
demand curve and is shown
in this figure.

reasons will come later in the book, after we have studied money and interest rates.) We have also been warned that:

An income-expenditure diagram like Figure 9–3 can be drawn up only for a *specific* price level. At different price levels, the $C + I$ schedule will be different and, hence, the equilibrium quantity of GNP demanded will be different.

As we shall now see, this finding is critical to understanding the genesis of unemployment and inflation.

Demand-Side Equilibrium and Full Employment

We now turn to the second major question of this chapter: Will the economy achieve an equilibrium at full employment without inflation, or will there be unemployment, inflation, or both?

In the income-expenditure diagrams used so far, the equilibrium level of GNP demanded has been shown as the intersection of the expenditure schedule and the 45° line, regardless of whatever level of GNP might correspond to full employment. However, as we will see now, when equilibrium GNP falls above full employment, the economy probably will be plagued by inflation. And when equilibrium falls below full employment, there will be unemployment and recession.

This remarkable fact was one of the principal messages of Keynes's *General Theory of Employment, Interest, and Money*. Writing during the Great Depression, it was natural for him to stress the case in which equilibrium falls short of full employment so that there are unemployed resources. Figure 9–6 illustrates this possibility. A vertical line has been erected at the full-employment level of GNP (called "potential GNP"), which is assumed to be $5000 billion in the example. We see that the $C + I$ curve cuts the 45° line at point E, which corresponds to a GNP ($Y = \$4000$ billion) below potential GNP. In this case, the $C + I$ curve is too low to lead to full employment. Such a situation might arise because either consumers or investors are unwilling to spend at normal rates, or because the price level is "too high," thereby depressing the $C + I$ curve. Unemployment must occur because not enough output will be demanded to keep the entire labor force busy.

Figure 9-6

A RECESSIONARY GAP
Sometimes equilibrium GNP may fall below potential GNP, so that some workers are unemployed. This diagram illustrates such a case. The horizontal distance *EB* between equilibrium GNP and potential GNP is called the recessionary gap.

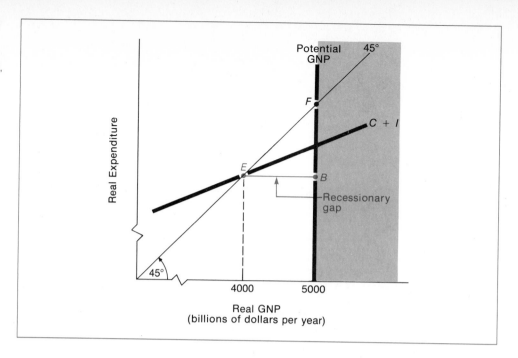

The **recessionary gap** is the amount by which the equilibrium level of real GNP falls short of potential GNP.

The distance between the equilibrium level of output demanded and the full-employment level of output (that is, potential GNP) is called the **recessionary gap** — and is shown by the horizontal distance from *E* to *B*.

It is clear from Figure 9-6 that full employment can be reached only by raising the total spending schedule to eliminate the recessionary gap. Specifically, the *C + I* schedule must move upward until it cuts the 45° line at point *F*. Can this happen without government intervention? We know that a sufficiently large drop in the price level could do the job. But is that a realistic prospect? We shall return to this question after we have brought the supply side into the picture. But first let us consider the other case, in which equilibrium GNP exceeds full employment.

Figure 9-7 illustrates this possibility. The expenditure schedule intersects the 45° line at point *E*, where GNP is $6000 billion. But this exceeds the full employment level, Y = $5000 billion. A case like this can arise when consumer or investment spending is unusually buoyant or when a "low" price level pushes the *C + I* curve upward.

The **inflationary gap** is the amount by which equilibrium real GNP exceeds the full-employment level of GNP.

To reach an equilibrium at full employment, the price level would have to rise enough to drive the *C + I* schedule *down* until it passed through point *F*. The horizontal distance *BE* — which indicates the amount by which the quantity of GNP demanded exceeds potential GNP — is called the **inflationary gap.** If there is an inflationary gap, a higher price level or some other means of reducing total expenditure is necessary to reach an equilibrium at full employment.

In sum, only if the price level and the spending plans of consumers and investors are "just right" will the *C + I* curve intersect the 45° line precisely at full employment, so that neither a recessionary gap nor an inflationary gap occurs. Are there reasons to expect this outcome? Does the economy have a self-correcting mechanism that automatically eliminates recessionary or inflationary gaps and propels it toward full employment? And how is it that inflation and unemployment sometimes occur together? These are questions we are not ready to address because we have not brought *aggregate supply* into the picture.

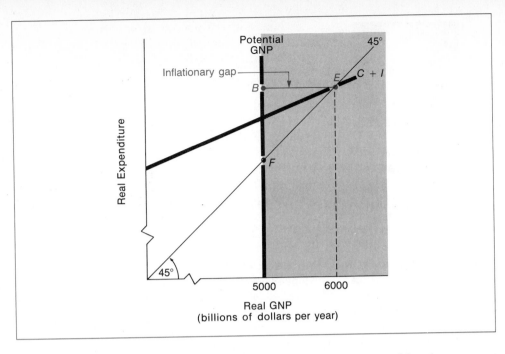

Figure 9–7

AN INFLATIONARY GAP
Sometimes equilibrium GNP may lie above potential GNP, meaning that there are more jobs than required for full employment. This diagram illustrates such a case. The horizontal distance *BE* between potential GNP and equilibrium GNP is called the inflationary gap. It is gradually eliminated by rising prices, which pull the *C + I* schedule down until it passes through point *F*.

And, as we learned in Chapter 5, the price level is determined by the interaction of *both* aggregate demand *and* aggregate supply. However, it is not too early to get an idea about why things can go wrong, why the economy can find itself far away from full employment.

The Coordination of Saving and Investment

To understand what goes wrong with the economy in a recession, it is useful to pose the following question: How can the full-employment level of GNP fail to be an equilibrium?

To find an answer, look back at the simplified circular flow diagram (Figure 9–1 on page 168). Suppose that firms produce the full-employment level of GNP, and this becomes the national income that emerges at point 4 in the diagram. This full-employment level of income then flows to consumers at point 5, who save some of it and spend the rest. The saving, you will note, "leaks out" of the circular flow at point 1. So, once we pass this point, consumption is less than full-employment GNP. But then, at point 2, an additional source of spending enters: investment. Recalling that the condition for equilibrium is that the sum *C + I* equals the GNP, we have the following conclusion:

The economy will reach an equilibrium at full employment only if the amount that consumers wish to save out of full-employment incomes is precisely equal to the amount that investors want to invest. If these two magnitudes happen to be unequal, then full employment will not be an equilibrium for the economy.

Specifically, we can see from the circular flow diagram that if saving exceeds investment at full employment, then the total demand arriving at the firms (point 3) will fall short of total output because the added investment spending is not enough to replace the leakage to saving. With demand inadequate to support production at full employment, we know that the GNP must fall below potential. There will be a recessionary gap. Conversely, if investment

Biographical Note: John Maynard Keynes (1883–1946)

John Maynard Keynes was something of a child prodigy. After an outstanding scholastic career at Eton and Cambridge, Keynes took the civil service examination. His second-place score was not good enough to land him the position he wanted (in the Treasury), so in 1907 he found himself in the India Office. Some years later, reflecting on the fact that his lowest score on the exam was in the economics section, he suggested with characteristic immodesty that, "The examiners presumably knew less than I did." He was probably right.

During World War I, Keynes was called to the Treasury to assist in planning various financial aspects of the war. There his "unique combinations of the guts of a burglar and the intellect of a first-class economist" quickly established him as a dominant figure. At the war's end, he represented the British Treasury at the peace conference in Versailles. The conference was a turning point in Keynes's life, though it was one of his few failures. He sought unsuccessfully to persuade the Allies to take a less punitive attitude toward the vanquished Germans, and then left the conference in protest in June 1919 to work on his *Economic Consequences of the Peace*, which created a furor when it was published. In it Keynes argued that the Germans could never meet the harsh economic terms of the treaty and that its viciousness posed the threat of continued instability and perhaps another war in Europe.

No longer welcome in government, Keynes returned to Cambridge and to his circle of literary and artistic friends in London's Bloomsbury district—a group that included Virginia Woolf, Lytton Strachey, and E. M. Forster. In 1925 he married the beautiful ballerina Lydia Lopokova, who gave up her stage career for him (though she later acted in a theater that Keynes himself established).

Between the wars, Keynes devoted himself to making money, to economic theory, and to political economy. He managed to make both himself and King's College rich by speculating in international currencies and commodities—allegedly by studying the newspapers while still in bed each morning! As a scholar, he wrote the *Tract on Monetary Reform* (1923), a stunning denunciation of the gold standard, which was published two years before Churchill once again tied the pound to gold. In 1936, he published his masterpiece, *The General Theory of Employment, Interest, and Money*, on which modern macroeconomics is based.

A heart attack in 1937 reduced Keynes's activities somewhat, but he returned to the Treasury during World War II and conducted several delicate financial negotiations with the Americans. Then as the capstone to a truly remarkable career, he represented the United Kingdom—and by all accounts dominated the proceedings—at the conference in Bretton Woods, New Hampshire, in 1944 that established an international financial system that served the Western world for 27 years. (See Chapter 19.)

He died of a heart attack at his home on Easter Sunday of 1946 as Lord Keynes, Baron of Tilton, a man who had achieved almost everything that he sought, and who had only one regret: He wished he had drunk more champagne.

---

exceeds saving when the economy is at full employment, then total demand ($C + I$) will exceed potential GNP and production will rise above the full-employment level. There will be an inflationary gap.

Now this discussion does nothing but restate what we already know in different words.[4] But these words hold the key to understanding why the economy can find itself stuck below full employment (or above it, for that matter), for *the people who do the investing are not the same people who do the saving*. In a modern capitalist economy, investing is done by one group of individuals (corporate

---

[4]In symbols, our previous equilibrium condition was $C + I = Y$. If we note that Y is also the sum of consumption plus saving, $Y = C + S$, it follows that $C + I = C + S$, or $I = S$, is a restatement of the equilibrium condition. The saving = investment approach is described in an appendix to this chapter.

executives and home buyers) while saving is done by another group.[5] It is easy to imagine that their plans may not be well coordinated. If they are not, we have just seen how either unemployment or inflation can arise.

Notice that these problems would never arise if the acts of saving and investing were not separated. Imagine a primitive economy of farmers, each of whom invests only in his own farm. There is no borrowing or lending, and no financial system. In this world, any farmer wanting to buy a new plow or tractor (that is, wanting to invest) would have to refrain from consuming part of his income (that is, would have to *save*). Therefore, the amount that all farmers together planned to save out of full-employment income would of necessity be equal to the amount of planned investment. Total spending and production would always have to be equal at full employment.

Almost the same holds true in a centrally planned economy like that of Soviet Russia. There, the state decides how much will be invested and has a great deal of leverage over how much saving people do. If the planners do their calculations correctly, they can force saving to be equal to investment at full employment. Consequently, business fluctuations are not a major problem in the Soviet Union. (They have plenty of others!)

Keynes observed that modern market economies differ from either primitive societies or centrally planned societies in this fundamental way, and that this flaw in the market mechanism is what leaves them vulnerable to recessions. However, one should not conclude that in order to avoid unemployment and recession the U.S. economy should revert to either a primitive form of capitalism or to rigid central planning. These "remedies" are far worse than the disease. Fortunately, there are policies the government can follow in an advanced capitalist economy to ease the pain of unemployment and recession — policies that we shall be studying in the following chapters.

[5]In a modern economy, it is not only households that save. Businesses save also, in the form of retained earnings. Nonetheless, households are the ultimate source of the saving needed to finance investment.

Summary

1. Investment is the most volatile component of aggregate demand, largely because it is tied so closely to the state of business confidence and to expectations about the future performance of the economy.

2. Government policy cannot influence business confidence in any reliable way, so policies designed to alter investment spending are aimed at more objective, though possibly less important, determinants of investment. Among these are interest rates, the overall state of aggregate demand, and tax incentives.

3. The equilibrium level of national income on the demand side is the level at which total spending just equals production (GNP). In this chapter we ignore government and foreign demand, so total spending is the sum of consumption plus investment. Thus, in symbols, the condition for equilibrium is $Y = C + I$.

4. Income levels below equilibrium are bound to rise because, when spending exceeds output, firms will see their inventory stocks being depleted and will react by stepping up production.

5. Income levels above equilibrium are bound to fall because, when total spending is insufficient to absorb total output, inventories will pile up and firms will react by curtailing production.

6. The determination of the equilibrium level of GNP on the demand side can be portrayed on a convenient "income-expenditure diagram" as the point at which the expenditure schedule — defined as the sum of the consumption and investment schedules — crosses the 45° line. The 45° line is significant because it marks off points at which spending and output are equal (that is, at which $C + I = Y$), and this is the basic condition for equilibrium.

7. An income-expenditure diagram can only be drawn up for a specific price level, however. Thus the equilibrium GNP so determined depends on the price level.

8. Because higher prices reduce the purchasing power of consumers' wealth and hence reduce their spending, equilibrium real GNP demanded is lower when prices are higher. This downward-sloping relationship is known as the aggregate demand curve.

9. Equilibrium GNP can be above or below potential GNP, which is defined as the GNP that would be produced if the labor force were fully employed.
10. If equilibrium GNP exceeds potential GNP, the difference is called an inflationary gap. If equilibrium GNP falls short of potential GNP, the resulting difference is called a recessionary gap.
11. Such gaps can occur because the saving that consumers want to do at full-employment income levels may differ from the investing that investors want to do. This problem is not likely to arise in a planned economy or in a primitive economy.

Concepts for Review

Depreciation allowances
Equilibrium level of GNP
Expenditure schedule
Induced investment
$C + I = Y$

Income-expenditure
  (or 45° line) diagram
Aggregate demand curve
Full-employment level of GNP
  (or potential GNP)

Recessionary gap
Inflationary gap
Coordination of saving and investment

Questions for Discussion

1. Why would someone interested in stabilization policy want to study a model of an economy in which there is no government?
2. When President Reagan took office, there was a feeling that the rate of business investment in the United States was too low. Does this chapter give you any ideas about what is meant by the phrase "too low"? What factors do you think accounted for the low level of investment spending? (You may want to discuss this last issue with your instructor.)
3. Why is not any arbitrary level of GNP an equilibrium for the economy? (Do not give a mechanical answer to this question, but explain the economic mechanism involved.)
4. From the following data, construct an expenditure schedule on a piece of graph paper. Then use the income-expenditure (45° line) diagram to determine the equilibrium level of GNP.

INCOME	CONSUMPTION	INVESTMENT
1100	990	120
1150	1035	120
1200	1080	120
1250	1125	120
1300	1170	120

5. From the following data, construct an expenditure schedule on a piece of graph paper. Then use the income-expenditure (45° line) diagram to determine the equilibrium level of GNP. Compare your answer with your answer to Question 4.

INCOME	CONSUMPTION	INVESTMENT
1100	1020	90
1150	1050	105
1200	1080	120
1250	1110	135
1300	1140	150

6. Suppose investment spending were always $250, government spending were always $150, and consumer spending depended on the price level in the following way:

PRICE LEVEL	CONSUMER SPENDING
80	740
90	720
100	700
110	680
120	660

On a piece of graph paper, use these data to construct an aggregate demand curve. Why do you think this example supposes that consumption declines as the price level rises?
7. Does the economy this year seem to have an inflationary gap or a recessionary gap? (If you do not know the answer from reading the newspaper, ask your instructor.)
8. Why are there no recessions in the Soviet Union?
9. (More difficult)* Consider an economy in which the consumption function takes the following simple algebraic form:

$$C = 100 + 0.8Y$$

and in which investment (I) is always 700. Find the equilibrium level of GNP from the requirement that $C + I = Y$. Compare your answer to Table 9–2 and Figure 9–3.

*The answer to this question is provided in Appendix B.

Appendix A
The Saving and Investment Approach

As we mentioned in the chapter, there is another way of looking at the determination of the equilibrium level of GNP on the demand side. Instead of studying the condition that total expenditure ($C + I$) is equal to production (Y), we can study the condition that saving (S) is equal to investment (I). This is what we will do in this appendix.

It must be emphasized at the outset that this is not a *new* approach. It is merely another way of looking at precisely the same phenomenon. The reason is that income (Y) must be either spent on consumer goods (C) or saved (S). Since $Y = C + S$ *always*, and since $Y = C + I$ when Y is at its equilibrium value, we can describe equilibrium by the condition that $C + S = C + I$, or simply:

$$S = I .$$

Graphical Analysis

This way of looking at equilibrium has a different graphical representation: It does not use the 45° line diagram, but it contains precisely the same information. Recall that in an appendix to Chapter 8 we constructed the saving schedule, which we repeat here as Figure 9–8. Since the equilibrium condition now under scrutiny is $S = I$, we can complete the story by using the investment schedule shown in Figure 9–2 (page 171).

To find the point at which saving and investment are equal, we need only put both curves on the same diagram, which we have done in Figure 9–9. Point E shows the equilibrium level of GNP, which is at an income level of $4000 billion. As must be the case, this is the same answer we obtained with the 45° line diagram.

You will notice that at income levels below $4000 billion, investment exceeds saving, just as $C + I$ exceeded output in the 45° line diagram. Similarly, at income levels above $4000 billion, S exceeds I. (In the 45° line diagram, Y exceeded $C + I$ in this range.) This must be the case since the two graphs are alternative depictions of the same phenomena. The economic analyses behind them are precisely the same.

Induced Investment

In the chapter we mentioned the possibility of *induced investment*, that is, of an investment schedule that rises as GNP rises, but we did not examine this possibility in our graphs. (However, this case did arise in Discussion Question 5.) The reason is that what matters in the 45° line diagram is the slope of the *combined* $C + I$ schedule, not

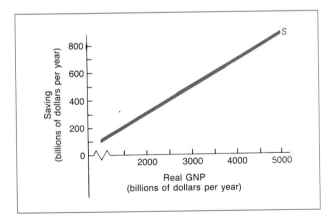

Figure 9–8
THE SAVING SCHEDULE
This diagram shows the relationship between saving and income in Macroland and duplicates Figure 8–9 (page 156).

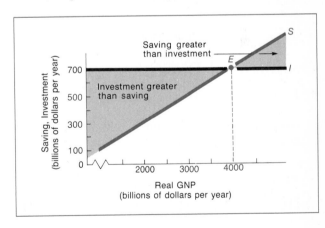

Figure 9–9
DETERMINATION OF EQUILIBRIUM GNP BY SAVING = INVESTMENT
This diagram depicts the equilibrium of the economy at point E, where the saving and investment schedules intersect. The equilibrium is at a real GNP of $4000 billion, which, as must be the case, is the same conclusion that we reached with the aid of the 45° line diagram (Figure 9–3 on page 173).

the *individual* slopes of the C and I schedules. So an upward-sloping investment schedule makes little difference to the analysis.

When using the saving and investment approach, however, the slope of the investment schedule becomes more apparent, if not more important. So Figure 9–10 illustrates the case of induced investment. In this diagram, the investment schedule is upward sloping. Equilibrium, however, is still at point E — where the S and I schedules cross. Thus, allowance for induced investment does not change our analysis in any significant way.[6]

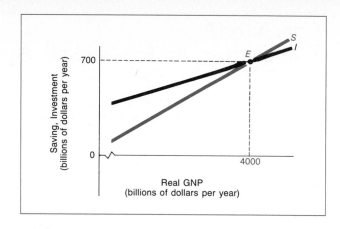

Figure 9–10
INCOME DETERMINATION WITH INDUCED INVESTMENT
When investment rises with GNP ("induced investment"), the investment schedule acquires a positive slope. Apart from this, the determination of equilibrium output is precisely as it was before. Point E, where the S and I schedules cross, is the equilibrium.

[6]Some students may wonder what happens if the slope of the investment schedule exceeds that of the saving schedule. This is a difficult question that is best reserved for more advanced courses. Suffice it to say here that the simple model of income determination constructed in this chapter will not work in such a case.

Summary

1. The condition for equilibrium GNP — which we gave in the chapter as the equation of total spending with output ($C + I = Y$) — can be restated as the requirement that saving and investment be equal ($S = I$). This does not change anything, but simply says the same thing in different words.
2. These different words lead to a different graphical presentation, in which we look for equilibrium at the point where the saving schedule crosses the investment schedule.
3. Induced investment — that is, investment that rises as the GNP rises — leads to an upward-sloping investment schedule, but requires no other change in the analysis.

Concepts for Review

$S = I$ Investment schedule
Saving schedule   Induced investment

Questions for Discussion

1. From the data in Discussion Question 4 at the end of the chapter, construct the saving schedule and the investment schedule on a piece of graph paper. (In doing so, remember that any income that is not consumed must have been saved.) Use these constructions to find the equilibrium level of GNP.
2. Do the same thing with the data in Discussion Question 5.

Appendix B
The Simple Algebra of Income Determination

The model of demand-side equilibrium that the chapter presented graphically and in tabular form can also be handled with some simple algebra.

Written as an equation, the consumption function in our example is:

$$C = 100 + 0.8Y.$$

This is simply the equation of a straight line with intercept 100 and slope 0.8. Investment in the example was assumed to be 700, regardless of the level of income. So the sum $C + I$ is:

$$C + I = 100 + 0.8Y + 700 = 800 + 0.8Y,$$

which describes the C + I curve in Figure 9–3. Since the equilibrium quantity of GNP demanded is defined by:

$$Y = C + I,$$

we can solve for the equilibrium value of Y by substituting 800 + 0.8Y for C + I, to get:

$$Y = C + I = 800 + 0.8Y.$$

To solve this equation for Y, first subtract 0.8Y from both sides to get:

$$0.2Y = 800.$$

Then divide both sides by 0.2 to obtain the answer:

$$Y = 4000.$$

This, of course, is precisely the solution we found by graphical and tabular methods in the chapter.

The method of solution is easily generalized to deal with any set of numbers in our equations. Suppose the consumption function is:

$$C = a + bY.$$

(In the example, $a = 100$ and $b = 0.8$.) Then the equilibrium condition that $Y = C + I$ implies:

$$Y = a + bY + I.$$

Subtracting bY from both sides leads to:

$$(1 - b)Y = a + I,$$

and dividing through by $1 - b$ gives:

$$Y = \frac{a + I}{1 - b}.$$

This formula, which is certainly not to be memorized, is valid for any numerical values of a, b, and I (so long as b is between zero and one.)

Questions for Discussion

1. Find the equilibrium level of GNP demanded in an economy in which investment is always $300 and the consumption function is described by the following algebraic equation:

$$C = 150 + 0.8Y.$$

2. Do the same for an economy in which investment is fixed at $250 and the consumption function is:

$$C = 250 + 0.5Y.$$

3. In each of the above cases, how much saving is there in equilibrium? (*Hint:* Income not consumed must be saved.) Is saving equal to investment?

4. Imagine an economy in which consumer expenditure is represented by the following equation:

$$C = 50 + .75Y.$$

Imagine also that investors want to spend 500 at every level of income: $I = 500$.

a. What is the equilibrium level of income?
b. If the full employment level of income is 2000, is there a recessionary or inflationary gap? If so, how much?
c. What will happen to the equilibrium level of income if investors become pessimistic about the country's future and reduce their investment to 400?
d. Is there a recessionary or inflationary gap now? How much?

5. Ivyland has the following consumption function:

$$C = 100 + .75Y.$$

Firms in Ivyland always invest $200.
a. Find the equilibrium level of GNP.
b. How much is saved? Is saving equal to investment?
c. Suppose consumers are given an inducement to save, so that the consumption function falls to $C = 50 + .75Y$, but at the same time firms boost investment spending to $240. Answer (a) and (b) under these new circumstances.

10

A definite ratio, to be called the *Multiplier*, can be established between income and investment.

JOHN MAYNARD KEYNES

Changes on the Demand Side: Multiplier Analysis

In the last chapter we derived the economy's *aggregate demand curve*, which shows how the equilibrium quantity of real GNP demanded depends on the price level — holding all other factors constant. But often these "other factors" do not remain constant and, as a consequence, the entire aggregate demand curve shifts. This chapter is the first of several that are devoted to enumerating these "other factors" and explaining how and why they make the aggregate demand curve shift.

The central concept of this short chapter is the *multiplier* — the idea that an increase in spending will bring about an *even larger* increase in equilibrium GNP. We approach this idea from three different perspectives, each of which provides different and significant insights into the multiplier process. First, the multiplier is illustrated graphically using the income-expenditure diagram from Chapter 9. Next, we reach the same conclusion through the use of a numerical example, and finally, we offer an algebraic statement. Each of these is an expression of the remarkable multiplier result.

Near the end of the chapter, we use multiplier analysis to explain why a drive to increase national saving might not succeed.

The Magic of the Multiplier

Because it is subject to such abrupt swings, investment spending is often the cause of business fluctuations in the United States and elsewhere. Let us, therefore, ask what would happen to equilibrium income in our fictitious country, Macroland, if firms there suddenly decided to spend more on investment goods. As we shall see, such a decision would have a *multiplied* effect on GNP in Macroland. The same would be true in the U.S. economy.

The **multiplier** is the ratio of the change in equilibrium GNP (Y) divided by the original change in spending that causes the change in GNP.

For simplicity, we begin by assuming that the price level is fixed — an assumption we maintain *only* for this short chapter. Refer first to Table 10–1, which looks very much like Table 9–1 (page 170). The only difference is that we assume here that, for some reason, firms in Macroland now want to invest $200 billion more than they previously did — for a total of $900 billion. The **multiplier** principle says that Macroland's GNP will rise by more than the $200

Table 10–1
TOTAL EXPENDITURE AFTER THE RISE IN INVESTMENT SPENDING
(billions of dollars)

(1) INCOME (Y)	(2) CONSUMPTION (C)	(3) INVESTMENT (I)	(4) TOTAL EXPENDITURE (C + I)
2000	1700	900	2600
2500	2100	900	3000
3000	2500	900	3400
3500	2900	900	3800
4000	3300	900	4200
4500	3700	900	4600
5000	4100	900	5000
5500	4500	900	5400
6000	4900	900	5800

This table shows the construction of a total expenditure schedule for Macroland after investment has risen to $900 billion. As indicated by the shaded numbers, only income level Y = $5000 billion is an equilibrium on the demand side of the economy because only at this level is total spending (C + I) equal to production (Y).

billion increase in investment. Specifically, the multiplier is defined as the ratio of the change in equilibrium GNP (Y) divided by the original change in spending that causes the change in GNP. In shorthand, when we deal with the multiplier for investment (I), the formula is:

$$\text{Multiplier} = \frac{\text{Change in } Y}{\text{Change in } I}.$$

Let us verify that the multiplier is indeed greater than 1. Table 10–1 shows how to derive a new expenditure schedule by adding up C and I at each level of Y, just as we did in Chapter 9. If you compare the last column of Table 10–1 to that of Table 9–1, you will see that the new expenditure schedule lies uniformly above the old one by $200 billion. Figure 10–1 illustrates this diagrammatically. The schedule marked $C + I_0$ is derived from the last column of Table 9–1, while the higher schedule marked $C + I_1$ is derived from the last column of Table 10–1. The two $C + I$ lines are parallel and $200 billion apart.

So far no act of magic has occurred — things look just as you might expect. But one more step will bring the multiplier rabbit out of the hat. Let us see what the upward shift of the $C + I$ line does to equilibrium income. In Figure 10–1, equilibrium moves outward from point E_0 to point E_1, that is, from $4000 billion to $5000 billion. The difference is an increase in national income of $1000 billion. All this from a $200 billion stimulus to investment? That is the magic of the multiplier.

Because the change in I is $200 billion and the change in equilibrium Y is $1000 billion, by applying our definition, the multiplier is:

$$\text{Multiplier} = \frac{\text{Change in } Y}{\text{Change in } I} = \frac{\$1000}{\$200} = 5.$$

This tells us that, in our example, every additional dollar of investment demand will add $5 to the equilibrium GNP!

This does indeed seem mysterious. Can something be created from nothing? Let us, therefore, check to be sure that the graph has not deceived us. The first and last columns of Table 10–1 show in numbers what Figure 10–1 shows

Figure 10–1

ILLUSTRATION OF
THE MULTIPLIER

This figure depicts the
multiplier effect of a rise in
investment spending of $200
billion. The expenditure
schedule shifts upward from
$C + I_0$ to $C + I_1$, thus moving
equilibrium from point E_0 to
point E_1. The rise in income
is $1000 billion, so the
multiplier is $1000/$200 = 5.

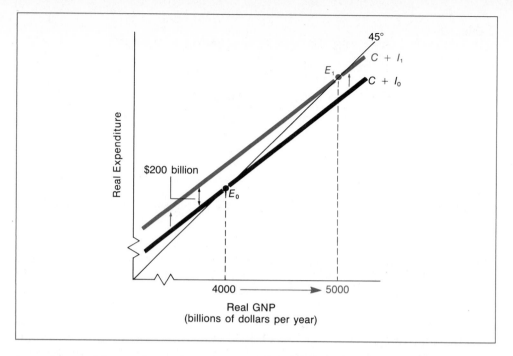

in a picture. Notice that, at any income level below $5000, spending $(C + I)$
exceeds output (Y). As we know, this cannot be an equilibrium situation
because inventories would be disappearing. On the other hand, at any income
level above $5000 inventories would be piling up, since $C + I$ is less than Y.

Only at $Y = $5000 billion are spending and production in balance, as
Table 10–1 shows. This is $1000 billion higher than the $4000 billion equilibrium GNP obtained in the discussion of Table 9–1, where investment was
only $700 billion. Thus a $200 billion rise in investment leads to a $1000 bil-
lion rise in equilibrium GNP. The multiplier really is 5.

Demystifying the Multiplier: How It Works

The multiplier result seems peculiar at first, but it loses its mystery once we
remember the circular flow of income and expenditure and the simple fact that
one person's spending is another person's income. To illustrate the logic of the
multiplier, and see why it is exactly 5 in our model economy, let us look more
closely at what actually happens if businesses decide to spend an additional $1
million on investment goods. If GNP is to rise by $5 million, and $Y = C + I$,
then consumer spending must rise by $4 million. Let's see how.

Suppose that Generous Motors—a major corporation in Macroland—
decides to spend $1 million to retool a factory to manufacture pollution-free,
electronically powered automobiles. Its $1 million expenditure goes to construc-
tion workers and owners of construction companies as wages and profits. That
is, it becomes their *income*.

But the owners and workers of the construction firms will not simply keep
their $1 million in the bank. They will spend some of it. If they are "typical"
consumers, their spending will be $1 million times the marginal propensity to
consume (MPC). In our example, the MPC is 0.8. So let us assume that they
spend $800,000 and save the rest. *This $800,000 expenditure is a net addition to
the nation's demand for goods and services exactly as GM's original $1 million expen-
diture was.* So, at this stage, the $1 million investment has already pushed GNP
up some $1.8 million.

But the process by no means stops here. Shopkeepers receive the $800,000 spent by construction workers, and these shopkeepers in turn also spend 80 percent of their new income. This accounts for $640,000 (80 percent of $800,000) in additional consumer spending in the "third round." Next follows a fourth round in which the recipients of the $640,000, in their turn, spend 80 percent of this amount, or $512,000, and so on. At each stage in the spending chain, people spend 80 percent of the additional income they receive, and the process continues. Consumption grows in each round.

Where does it all end? Does it all end? The answer is that it does, indeed, eventually end—with GNP a total of $5 million higher than it was before Generous Motors spent the original $1 million. The multiplier, as stated, is 5.

Table 10–2 displays the basis for this conclusion. In the table, "round 1" represents GM's initial investment, which creates $1 million in income for construction workers; "round 2" represents the construction workers' spending which creates $800,000 in income for shopkeepers. The rest of the table proceeds accordingly. Each entry in column 2 is 80 percent of the previous entry, and column 3 tabulates the running sum of column 2.

We see that after 10 rounds of spending, the initial $1 million investment has mushroomed to nearly $4.5 million, and the sum is still growing. After 20 rounds, the total increase in GNP is over $4.9 million—near its eventual value of $5 million. While it takes quite a few rounds of spending before the multiplier chain is near 5, we see from the table that it approaches 4 rather quickly. If each income recipient in the chain waits, say, two months before spending his new income, the multiplier will reach 4 in only about 14 months.

Table 10–2
THE MULTIPLIER SPENDING CHAIN

(1) ROUND NUMBER	(2) SPENDING IN THIS ROUND	(3) CUMULATIVE TOTAL
1	$1,000,000	$1,000,000
2	800,000	1,800,000
3	640,000	2,440,000
4	512,000	2,952,000
5	409,600	3,361,600
6	327,680	3,689,280
7	262,144	3,951,424
8	209,715	4,161,139
9	167,772	4,328,911
10	134,218	4,463,129
⋮	⋮	⋮
20	14,412	4,942,354
⋮	⋮	⋮
50	18	4,999,929
⋮	⋮	⋮
"Infinity"	0	5,000,000

This table shows how the multiplier unfolds through time. Round 1 is GM's initial spending, which leads to $1 million in additional income to construction workers. Round 2 shows the construction workers spending 80 percent of this amount, since the marginal propensity to consume is 0.8. The other rounds proceed accordingly, with spending in each successive round equal to 80 percent of that in the previous round. Technically, the full multiplier of 5 is reached only after an "infinite" number of rounds. But, as can be seen, we are close to the full amount after 20 rounds.

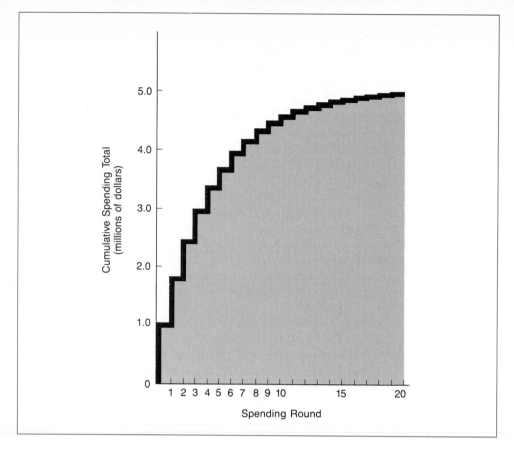

Figure 10–2
HOW THE
MULTIPLIER BUILDS
This diagram portrays the numbers from Table 10–2 and shows how the multiplier builds through time. Notice how the effect grows quickly at first and how the full effect is almost reached after 20 rounds.

Figure 10–2 provides a graphical presentation of the numbers in the last column of Table 10–2. Notice how the multiplier builds up rapidly at first and then tapers off to approach its ultimate value (5 in this example) gradually.

Algebraic Statement of the Multiplier

Figure 10–2 and Table 10–2 probably make a persuasive case for the fact that the multiplier eventually reaches 5. But for the remaining skeptics we offer a simple algebraic proof.[1] Most of you learned about an "infinite geometric progression" in high school. This is simply an infinite series of numbers, each one of which is a fixed fraction of the previous one. This fraction is called the "common ratio." A geometric progression beginning with 1 and having a common ratio equal to 0.8 would look like this:

$$1 + 0.8 + (0.8)^2 + (0.8)^3 + \dots.$$

More generally, a geometric progression beginning with 1 and having a common ratio R would be:

$$1 + R + R^2 + R^3 \dots$$

[1]Students who blanch at the sight of algebra should not be put off. Anyone who can balance a checkbook (even many who cannot!) will be able to follow the argument.

A simple formula enables us to sum such a progression as long as R is less than 1.[2] The formula is:[3]

$$\begin{matrix} \text{Sum of infinite} \\ \text{geometric progression} \end{matrix} = \frac{1}{1 - R}.$$

Now we can recognize that the multiplier chain in Table 10–2 is just an infinite geometric progression with 0.8 as its common ratio. That is, each $1 spent by GM leads to a $(0.8) \times \$1$ expenditure by construction workers, which in turn leads to a $(0.8) \times (0.8 \times \$1) = (0.8)^2 \times \$1$ expenditure by the shopkeepers, and so on. Thus, for each initial dollar of investment spending, the progression is:

$$1 + 0.8 + (08)^2 + (0.8)^3 + (0.8)^4 + \dots.$$

Applying the formula for the sum of such a series, we find that:

$$\text{Multiplier} = \frac{1}{1 - 0.8} = \frac{1}{0.2} = 5.$$

Notice how this result can be generalized. If we did not have a specific numerical value for the marginal propensity to consume, but simply called it "MPC," the geometric progression in Table 10–2 would have been:

$$1 + \text{MPC} + (\text{MPC})^2 + (\text{MPC})^3 + \dots,$$

which has the MPC as its common ratio. Applying the same formula for summing a geometric progression to this more general case gives us the following general result:

OVERSIMPLIFIED FORMULA FOR THE MULTIPLIER

$$\text{Multiplier} = \frac{1}{1 - \text{MPC}}.$$

We call this formula "oversimplified" because it ignores many factors that are important in the real world. One of them is *inflation,* a complication to which we will turn in the next chapter. A second is *income taxation,* a point we will elaborate in Chapter 12. A third factor arises from the *financial system* and, after we discuss money and banking in Chapters 13 and 14, we will explain it in

---

[2] If R exceeds 1, nobody can possibly sum it — not even with the aid of a modern computer!
[3] The proof is simple. Let the symbol S stand for the (unknown) sum of the series:

$$S = 1 + R + R^2 + R^3 + \dots.$$

Then, multiplying by R,

$$RS = R + R^2 + R^2 + R^3 + \dots.$$

By subtracting RS from S, we obtain:

$$S - RS = 1$$

or

$$S = \frac{1}{1 - R}.$$

Chapter 15. A final factor relates to *international trade*, and will wait until Chapter 20. As it turns out, each of these factors *reduces* the size of the multiplier.

We can begin to appreciate just how unrealistic the "oversimplified" formula is by considering some real numbers for the U.S. economy. The marginal propensity to consume (MPC) has been estimated many times and is about 0.9. From our oversimplified formula, then, it would seem that the multiplier should be:

$$\text{Multiplier} = \frac{1}{1 - 0.9} = \frac{1}{0.1} = 10 \, .$$

In fact, the actual multiplier for the U.S. economy is believed to be less than 2. This is quite a discrepancy! But it does not mean that anything we have said about the multiplier so far is incorrect. Our story is simply incomplete. As we progress through the following chapters, you will learn why the multiplier is below 2 even though the MPC is close to 0.9. For now we simply point out that:

While the multiplier is larger than 1 in the real world, it cannot be calculated with any degree of accuracy from the oversimplified formula. The actual multiplier is *lower* than the formula suggests.

The Multiplier Effect of Consumer Spending

Business firms that invest are not the only ones that can work the magic of the multiplier; so can consumers. Let us see how the multiplier works when the process is initiated by an upsurge in consumer spending.

First, we need to distinguish between two types of change in consumer spending. When C rises because income rises — that is, when consumers move outward *along a fixed consumption function* — we call the increase in C an **induced increase in consumption.** However, if instead C rises because the entire consumption function *shifts* up, we call this an **autonomous increase in consumption.** The name indicates that consumption changes independently of income, and Chapter 8's discussion pointed out that a number of events, such as a change in the price level or in the value of the stock market, can initiate such a shift.

An **induced increase in consumption** is an increase in consumer spending that stems from an increase in consumer incomes. It is represented on a graph as a movement along a fixed consumption function.

An **autonomous increase in consumption** is an increase in consumer spending without any increase in incomes. It is represented on a graph as a shift of the entire consumption function.

Let us suppose that, for some reason, consumer spending rises autonomously by $200 billion. In this case, our table of aggregate demand would have to be revised to look like Table 10–3. Comparing this to Table 10–1 on page 185, we note that each entry in column 2 is $200 billion *higher* than the corresponding entry in Table 10–1 (because consumption is higher), and each entry in column 3 is $200 billion *lower* (because investment is lower).

The equilibrium level of income is clearly Y = $5000 billion once again. Indeed the entire expenditure schedule is the same as it was in Table 10–1. The initial rise of $200 billion in spending leads to an ultimate rise of $1000 billion in GNP, just as occurred in the case of higher investment spending. In fact, Figure 10–1 applies to this case without any changes. The multiplier for autonomous changes in consumer spending, then, is also 5 ($1000/$200).

Table 10–3

TOTAL EXPENDITURE AFTER CONSUMERS DECIDE TO SPEND $200 BILLION MORE
(billions of dollars)

(1) INCOME (Y)	(2) CONSUMPTION (C)	(3) INVESTMENT (I)	(4) TOTAL EXPENDITURE (C + I)
2000	1900	700	2600
2500	2300	700	3000
3000	2700	700	3400
3500	3100	700	3800
4000	3500	700	4200
4500	3900	700	4600
5000	4300	700	5000
5500	4700	700	5400
6000	5100	700	5800

This table shows the construction of the total expenditure schedule for Macroland following an autonomous increase of $200 billion in consumption rather than in investment. Notice that columns 2 and 3 differ from the corresponding columns in Table 10–1, but column 4 is the same in both tables. Thus the expenditure schedule in the 45° line diagram is the same as in the earlier example.

The reason is straightforward. It does not matter who injects an additional dollar of spending into the economy, whether it is business investors or consumers. Wherever it comes from, 80 percent of it will be respent if the MPC is 0.8, and the recipients of this second round will in turn spend 80 percent of their additional income, and so on and on. And that is what constitutes the multiplier process.

The Multiplier in Reverse

A good way to check your understanding of the multiplier process is to run it in reverse: What happens if, for example, consumers autonomously decide to spend less? For example, suppose a wave of thriftiness comes over the people of Macroland so that, no matter what their total income, they now want to spend $200 billion *less* than they did previously.

A decision to spend $200 billion less out of any given level of income is, by definition, a *downward* shift of the total expenditure schedule by $200 billion. This is shown in Figure 10–3, where the $C + I$ schedule falls from $C_0 + I$ to $C_1 + I$. The horizontal distance between these two parallel lines is the $200 billion drop in spending.

There are two ways of calculating the multiplier. First, our oversimplified multiplier formula tells us that the multiplier is

$$\frac{1}{1 - \text{MPC}} = \frac{1}{1 - 0.8} = \frac{1}{0.2} = 5.$$

So a $200 billion drop in spending will lead to a multiplier effect of $1000 billion. Alternatively, we can read this conclusion from Figure 10–3. Here the economy's equilibrium point moves down the 45° line from point E_0 to E_1; income drops from $4000 billion to $3000 billion—a decline of $1000 billion.

Figure 10-3

THE MULTIPLIER IN REVERSE

This diagram shows the multiplier effect of an autonomous decline in consumer spending of $200 billion. The decline appears as a downward shift of $200 billion in the expenditure schedule, which falls from $C_0 + I$ to $C_1 + I$. Equilibrium, which is always at the intersection of the expenditure schedule and the 45° line, moves from point E_0 to point E_1, and income falls from $4000 billion to $3000 billion.

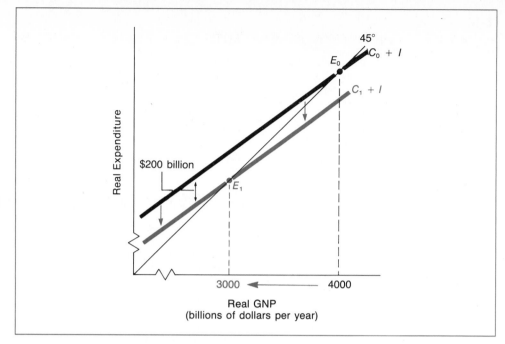

Now compare the analysis of a decline in spending that is summarized in Figure 10–3 with our previous analysis of an increase in spending, as shown in Figure 10–1 on page 186. You will see that everything is simply turned in the opposite direction. The multiplier works in both directions.

The Paradox of Thrift

This last example of multiplier analysis teaches us an important lesson: It shows that an increase in the desire to save will lead to a cumulative fall in GNP. And, *because saving depends on income,* the resulting decline in national income will pull saving down.

Let us be a bit more specific about this. Before the upsurge in saving, consumers were spending $3300 billion out of a total national income of $4000 billion, as we can see in Table 9–1 on page 170. Hence $700 billion was being saved. In Figure 10–3, income falls to $3000 billion. Since investment is still $700 billion, and $C + I$ must add up to Y, we know that consumption at point E must be $2300. So total saving is still $700 (= $3000 − $2300) billion. The effort to save more has been totally frustrated by the decline in GNP.[4]

The **paradox of thrift** is the fact that an effort by a nation to save more may simply reduce national income and fail to raise total saving.

This remarkable result is called the **paradox of thrift,** because it shows that, while saving may pave the road to riches for an individual, if the nation as a whole decides to save more, the result may be a recession and poverty for all. The paradox of thrift is important because it is contrary to most people's thinking, and it means that greater saving may be a mixed blessing if it is not accompanied by equally greater investment.

---

[4]It is even possible to devise examples in which total saving goes *down* when people attempt to save more. Just suppose there is *induced investment;* that is, suppose that investment spending rises with GNP. Then, when GNP falls, so does *I.* Since $S = I$ in equilibrium, savings must decline.

The Multiplier and the Aggregate Demand Curve

At this point we must recall something that was mentioned at the start of the chapter: Income-expenditure diagrams such as Figure 10–1 or 10–3 can be drawn up only for a given price level. A different price level leads to a different total expenditure curve. This means that our oversimplified multiplier formula measures *the increase in real GNP demanded that would occur if the price level were fixed*. That is, it measures the *horizontal shift* of the economy's aggregate demand curve.

Figure 10–4 illustrates this conclusion by supposing that the price level that underlies Figure 10–1 is $P = 100$. The top panel simply repeats Figure 10–1 and shows how an increase in investment spending from $700 to $900 billion leads to an increase in GNP from $4000 to $5000 billion.

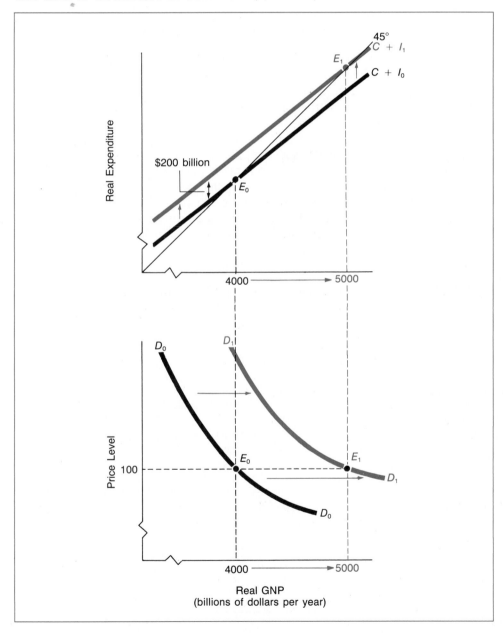

Figure 10–4
TWO VIEWS OF THE MULTIPLIER
The top panel repeats Figure 10–1. The bottom panel shows two aggregate demand curves. Curve D_0D_0, which applies when investment is $700 billion, shows that equilibrium GNP on the demand side comes at $Y = $4000 billion when $P = 100$ (point E_0). Curve D_1D_1, which applies when investment is $900 billion, shows that equilibrium GNP on the demand side comes at $Y = $5000 billion when $P = 100$ (point E_1). The horizontal distance between points E_0 and E_1 in the bottom panel indicates the oversimplified multiplier effect.

The bottom panel shows two downward-sloping aggregate demand curves. The first, labeled D_0D_0, depicts the situation when investment is $700 billion. Point E_0 on this curve indicates that, at the given price level ($P = 100$), the equilibrium quantity of GNP demanded is $4000 billion. It corresponds exactly to point E_0 in the top panel. The second aggregate demand curve, D_1D_1, depicts the situation after investment has risen to $900 billion. Point E_1 on this curve indicates that the equilibrium quantity of GNP demanded when $P = 100$ has risen to $5000 billion, which corresponds exactly to point E_1 in the top panel.

As Figure 10–4 shows, the horizontal distance between the two aggregate demand curves is exactly equal to the increase in real GNP shown in the income-expenditure diagram—in this case, $1000 billion. Thus:

An autonomous increase in spending leads to a horizontal shift of the aggregate demand curve by an amount given by the oversimplified multiplier formula.

Thus everything we have said about the multiplier applies to shifts of the economy's aggregate demand curve. If businesses decide to increase their investment spending, or if the consumption function shifts up, the aggregate demand curve moves horizontally to the right—as indicated in Figure 10–4. If either investment decreases or the consumption function shifts down, the aggregate demand curve moves horizontally to the left. In subsequent chapters we will learn, not surprisingly, that the same applies to changes in either of the other two components of total spending: government purchases and net exports.

Thus the economy's aggregate demand curve cannot be expected to stand still. Autonomous changes in spending by consumers, investors, government units, or foreigners all cause the aggregate demand curve to move around. But to understand the consequences of shifts of aggregate demand, we must bring the aggregate supply curve into the picture. That is the task of the next chapter.

Summary

1. Any autonomous increase in expenditure has a multiplier effect on GNP; that is, it increases GNP by more than the original increase in spending.
2. The reason for this multiplier effect is that one person's additional expenditure constitutes a new source of income for another person, and this additional income leads to still more spending, and so on.
3. The multiplier also works in reverse: an autonomous decrease in any component of aggregate demand leads to a multiplied decrease in national income.

4. A simple formula for the multiplier says that its numerical value is $1/(1 - \text{MPC})$. This formula, which is too simple to give accurate results, measures the horizontal shift of the aggregate demand curve.
5. If the nation as a whole decides to save more, that is, to consume less, the resulting decline in national income may serve to make everyone poorer. This possibility that thriftiness, while a virtue for the individual, may be disastrous for an entire nation, is called the paradox of thrift.

Concepts for Review

The multiplier
Induced increase in consumption

Autonomous increase in consumption

Paradox of thrift

Questions for Discussion

1. Try to remember where you last spent a dollar. Explain how this dollar will lead to a multiplier chain of increased income and spending. (Who received the dollar? What will he or she do with it?)
2. Use both numerical and graphical methods to find the multiplier effect of the following shift in the consumption function in an economy in which investment is always $110.

INCOME	CONSUMPTION BEFORE SHIFT	CONSUMPTION AFTER SHIFT
$510	$430	$470
540	450	490
570	470	510
600	490	530
630	510	550
660	530	570
690	550	590
720	570	610

(*Hint:* What is the marginal propensity to consume?)

3. Turn back to Discussion Question 4 in Chapter 9 (page 180). Suppose investment spending rises to $130, and the price level is fixed. By how much will the equilibrium GNP increase? Derive the answer both numerically and graphically.
4. Explain the paradox of thrift. Why do you think it is called a paradox?
5. (More difficult) Suppose the consumption function is as given in Discussion Question 9 of Chapter 9 (page 180)

$$C = 100 + 0.8Y$$

and investment (I) rises to 900. Use the equilibrium condition $Y = C + I$ to find the equilibrium level of GNP. (In working out the answer, assume the price level is fixed.) Compare your answer to Table 10–1 and Figure 10–1. Now compare your answer to the answer to Discussion Question 9 of Chapter 9. What do you learn about the multiplier?

Appendix
The Simple Algebra of the Multiplier

In Appendix B to Chapter 9, we worked out a general expression for the equilibrium level of GNP when the price level is fixed, investment is some fixed number, I, and the consumption function is:

$$C = a + bY.$$

The answer obtained there (which can be found on page 183) was:

$$Y = \frac{a + I}{1 - b}.$$

From this formula, it is easy to derive the oversimplified multiplier formula algebraically and to show that it applies equally well to a change in investment or to a change in autonomous consumer spending. To do this, suppose that *either* I

or a increases by 1 unit. In either case, the sum $C + I$ would rise from:

$$C + I = a + bY + I,$$

to:

$$C + I = a + bY + I + 1.$$

Using the equilibrium condition that Y must be equal to $C + I$, we can solve for Y just as we did in Appendix B of Chapter 9:

$$Y = C + I$$

so that:

$$Y = a + bY + I + 1$$

and therefore:

$$(1 - b)Y = a + I + 1,$$

or:

$$Y = \frac{a + I + 1}{1 - b}.$$

By comparing this with our previous expression for Y, we see that a 1 unit change in *either a or I* changes equilibrium GNP by:

$$\text{change in } Y = \frac{a + I + 1}{1 - b} - \frac{a + I}{1 - b}$$

$$\text{change in } Y = \frac{a + I + 1 - (a + I)}{1 - b}$$

or:

$$\text{change in } Y = \frac{1}{1 - b}.$$

Recalling that b is the marginal propensity to consume, we see that this is precisely the over-simplified multiplier formula.

11

Supply-Side Equilibrium: Unemployment *and* Inflation?

We might as well reasonably dispute whether it is the upper or the under blade of a pair of scissors that cuts a piece of paper, as whether value is governed by [demand] or [supply].

ALFRED MARSHALL

In Chapter 9 we learned that the level of prices, in conjunction with the economy's consumption and investment schedules, governs whether the economy will experience a recessionary or an inflationary gap. If the $C + I$ schedule is "too low," a *recessionary gap* will arise, while a $C + I$ schedule that is "too high" leads to an *inflationary gap*. Which sort of gap actually occurs is of some importance because, as we shall confirm in this chapter, a recessionary gap normally spells unemployment while an inflationary gap means inflation.

The tools provided in Chapter 9, however, are not sufficient to determine which sort of gap will arise because, as we know, the position of the $C + I$ schedule depends on the price level. And the price level is determined by *both aggregate demand and aggregate supply*. Thus, the task of the present chapter is to bring the supply side of the economy into the picture.

We begin by explaining how the *aggregate supply* curve is derived from business costs. Next we consider the interaction of aggregate supply and aggregate demand, and the joint determination of output and the price level. With this apparatus in hand, we return to the phenomena of recessionary and inflationary gaps and study how the economy adjusts to each type. Doing this puts us in a position to deal with the crucial question raised in earlier chapters: Does the economy have an efficient self-correcting mechanism? As we shall see, the economy is better at curing inflationary gaps than recessionary gaps. Finally, we use aggregate supply–aggregate demand analysis to explain the vexing problem of *stagflation* — the simultaneous occurrence of high unemployment *and* high inflation — that has plagued the economy so often since the mid-1970s. The chapter ends by explaining how inflation affects the multiplier.

The Supply Side Matters

The Reagan administration took office in January 1981 espousing a new doctrine called "supply-side economics" — an allegedly new theory designed to supplant the Keynesian theory we have studied in the last two chapters. Supply-side economics was controversial from the start, and it remains so to this day. Supporters credit it with spurring economic growth and conquering inflation. Detractors blame it for many of our current problems, especially the huge federal budget and foreign trade deficits.

Actually, however, supply-side economics was not a new theory at all. Rather, it was a collection of activist policies aimed at the supply side of the economy—plus a claim that these policies were just what the U.S. economy needed after the inflationary 1970s. The policies naturally provoked considerable debate; and we will review that debate in the next chapter. But one supply-side proposition never was controversial: that what happens on the supply side of the economy matters a great deal for inflation, unemployment, and economic growth. It is therefore time for us to consider the origins of the aggregate supply curve and the factors that can make it shift.

The Aggregate Supply Curve

In earlier chapters we noted that aggregate demand is a schedule, not a fixed number. The quantity of real GNP that will be demanded depends on the price level, as summarized in the economy's *aggregate demand* curve.

Analogously, the concept of *aggregate supply* does not refer to a fixed number but, rather, to a schedule (to a supply curve). The volume of goods and services that will be provided by profit-seeking enterprises depends on the prices they obtain for their outputs, on wages and other production costs, on the state of technology, and on other things. The relationship between the price level and the quantity of real GNP supplied, *holding all other determinants of quantity supplied constant*, is called the economy's **aggregate supply curve.**

A typical aggregate supply curve is drawn in Figure 11–1. It slopes upward, meaning that as prices rise more output is produced, *other things held constant*. It is not difficult to understand why this is so. Producers in the U.S. economy are motivated mainly by profit. Since the profit made by producing a unit of output is simply the difference between the price at which it is sold and the unit cost of production,

$$\text{profit per unit} = \text{price} - \text{cost per unit},$$

The **aggregate supply curve** shows, for each possible price level, the quantity of goods and services that all the nation's businesses are willing to produce, holding all other determinants of aggregate quantity supplied constant.

Figure 11–1
AN AGGREGATE SUPPLY CURVE
This graph shows a typical aggregate supply curve. It has a positive slope (that is, it rises as we move to the right), meaning that the quantity of output supplied rises as the price level rises.

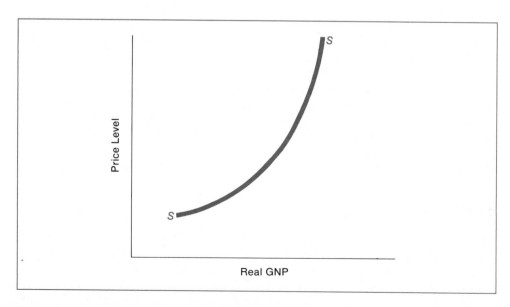

it is clear that the response of production to a rising price level (henceforth, P) depends on the response of costs.[1]

One critical fact affecting this response is that labor and other inputs used by firms normally are available at *relatively fixed prices* for some period of time — though certainly not forever. There are many reasons for this. Some workers and firms enter into long-term labor contracts that set money wages up to three years in advance. Even where there are no explicit contracts, employees typically have their wages increased only about once per year. During the interim period, money wages are fixed. Much the same is true of other factors of production. Many firms get deliveries of raw materials under long-term contracts according to which suppliers have agreed to provide the materials at pre-arranged prices. None of these contracts lasts forever, of course, but many of them last long enough to matter.

Why is it significant that firms often purchase inputs like labor and raw materials at prices that stay fixed for considerable periods? Because firms decide how much to produce by comparing selling prices with costs of production; and production costs obviously depend on input prices. If the selling prices of the firm's products rise while wages and other factor costs are relatively fixed, production becomes more profitable, and so firms are persuaded to increase output.

A simple example will illustrate the idea. Suppose a firm uses one hour of labor time to manufacture a gadget that sells for $9. If workers earn $8 per hour, and the firm has no other production costs, its profit per unit is:

$$\text{profit per unit} = \text{price} - \text{cost per unit}$$
$$= \$9 \quad - \$8$$
$$= \$1.$$

Now what happens if the price of a gadget rises to $10, but wage rates remain constant? The firm's profit per unit becomes:

$$\text{profit per unit} = \text{price} - \text{cost per unit}$$
$$= \$10 \quad - \$8$$
$$= \$2.$$

With production more profitable, it is likely that the firm will supply more gadgets.

The same process operates in reverse. Suppose selling prices fall while input costs are relatively fixed. Since this squeezes their profit margins, firms may react by cutting back on production. For example, if the price of a gadget fell from $9 to $8.50, profit per unit would fall from $1 to 50 cents, and firms would probably produce less.

The behavior we have just described is summarized by the upward slope of the aggregate supply curve: Production rises when the price level (P) rises, and falls when P falls. In other words:

The aggregate supply curve slopes upward because firms normally can purchase labor and other inputs at fixed costs for some period of time. Thus, higher selling prices make production more attractive.

---

[1] For a full discussion of business output decisions and how they respond to costs, see Chapter 24.

The phrase "for some period of time" alerts us to the possibility that the aggregate supply curve may not stand still for long. If wages or prices of other inputs change, as they surely will during inflationary times, then the aggregate supply curve will shift.

Shifts of the Aggregate Supply Curve

We have concluded so far that, for any given levels of wages and other input prices, there will be an upward-sloping aggregate supply curve relating the price level to aggregate quantity supplied. But what factors determine the *position* of this curve? What things can make it shift?

The Money Wage Rate

Our previous discussion suggests that the most obvious determinant of the position of the aggregate supply curve is the money wage rate. Wages are the major element of cost for most firms, typically accounting for something like 70 percent of all expenses. Higher wages spell higher costs, thereby lowering profits at any given prices.

Let us return to our example and consider what would happen to a gadget producer if the money wage rose to $8.75 per hour while the price of a gadget remained $9. Profit per unit would decline from:

$$\$9 - \$8 \quad = \$1$$

to:

$$\$9 - \$8.75 = \$0.25 .$$

With profits squeezed, the firm would probably cut back on production.

This is the typical reaction of firms in our economy to a rise in wages. Therefore, a wage increase leads to a decrease in aggregate quantity supplied at current prices. Graphically, the aggregate supply curve shifts to the left (or inward), as shown in Figure 11–2. In this diagram, when wages are low, firms

Figure 11–2
A SHIFT OF THE AGGREGATE SUPPLY CURVE
This diagram shows what happens to the economy's aggregate supply curve when money wages rise. Higher wages shift the supply curve inward from $S_0 S_0$ to $S_1 S_1$, leading, for example, to an output level of $3500 billion (point B), rather than $4000 (point A), when the price level is 100. The aggregate supply curve will shift inward in the same manner if the price of any other input (such as energy) increases.

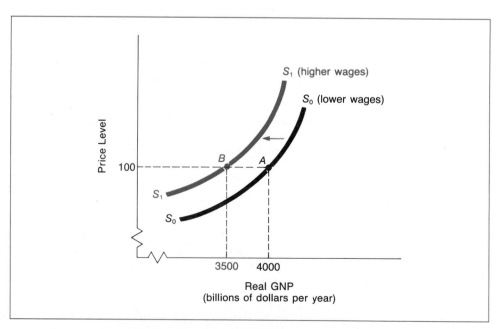

are willing to supply $4000 billion in goods and services at a price level of 100 (point A). After wages increase, however, these same firms are willing to supply only $3500 billion at this price level (point B). By similar reasoning, the aggregate supply curve will shift to the right (or outward) if wages fall. Thus:

A rise in the money wage rate causes the aggregate supply curve to shift *inward*, meaning that the quantity supplied at any price level declines. A fall in the money wage rate causes the aggregate supply curve to shift outward, meaning that the quantity supplied at any price level increases.

Prices of Other Inputs

In this regard, there is nothing special about wages. An increase in the price of *any* input that firms buy will shift the aggregate supply curve in the same way. That is:

The aggregate supply curve is shifted inward by an increase in the price of any input to the production process, and it is shifted outward by a decrease.

While there are many inputs other than labor, the one that has attracted the most attention in recent years is energy. We shall have much to say about energy in this book, including further discussion in this chapter and in Chapter 34. But for present purposes the important thing to realize is that increases in the price of energy, such as those that took place in the 1970s and early 1980s, push the aggregate supply curve inward more or less as shown in Figure 11–2. By the same token, a rise in the price of *any* input we import from abroad would have the effect shown in the figure.

Technology and Productivity

Another factor that determines the position of the aggregate supply curve is the state of technology. Suppose, for example, that a technological breakthrough increases the **productivity** of labor. If wages do not change, such an improvement in productivity will *decrease* business costs and thus improve profitability and encourage more production.

Productivity is the amount of output produced by a unit of input.

Once again, our gadget company will help us understand how this works. Suppose the price of a gadget stays at $9 and the hourly wage rate stays at $8, but gadget workers become much more productive. Specifically, suppose the labor input required to manufacture a gadget falls from one hour (which costs $8) to three-quarters of an hour (which costs $6). Then profit per unit rises from $9 − $8 = $1 to $9 − $6 = $3. The lure of higher profits should induce gadget manufacturers to increase production. In brief, we have concluded that:

Improvements in productivity shift the aggregate supply curve outward.

Figure 11–2 can be viewed as applying to a *decline* in productivity. As we noted earlier in Chapter 7, slow growth of productivity has been a problem for the United States of late, and it remains a source of great concern. Many people feel that the productivity slowdown contributed to the stagflation of the 1970s.

Available Supplies of Labor and Capital

The last determinant of the position of the aggregate supply curve is obvious, but we list it anyway both for the sake of completeness and for its importance in the debate over supply-side economics. The bigger the economy — as measured by its available supplies of labor and capital—the more it is capable of producing. So:

As the labor force grows, and as the capital stock is increased by investment, the aggregate supply curve shifts outward (to the right), meaning that more output can be produced at any given price level.

These, then, are the major "other things" that we hold constant when drawing up an aggregate supply curve: wage rates, prices of other inputs (like energy), technology, labor force, and capital stock. While a change in the price level moves the economy *along a given supply curve,* a change in any of these other determinants of aggregate quantity supplied *shifts the entire supply schedule.*

The Shape of the Aggregate Supply Curve

One other feature of the aggregate supply curve depicted in Figure 11–1 merits comment. We have drawn our supply curve with a characteristic curvature: It is relatively flat at low levels of output and gets steeper at high levels of output (as we move to the right). There is a reason for this.

When economic activity is weak, product demand slack, and capacity utilization low, firms are likely to respond to an upsurge in demand by bringing their unused capital and labor resources back into production. They will find, therefore, that unit costs of production do not rise much as output expands. As a result, they will find it neither necessary nor advisable to raise prices much. Rapidly rising output with relatively unchanged prices means an aggregate supply curve that is relatively flat.

By contrast, if the economy is booming, demand is buoyant, and production is straining capacity, firms will be able to increase output only by hiring more workers, acquiring more capital, or putting workers on overtime. Whatever they do, unit costs of production rise. Price increases will thus be encouraged by cost developments and, incidentally, will not be resisted forcefully on the demand side. In this case, the aggregate supply curve is steep. Thus:

The slope of the aggregate supply curve, which tells us the price increase that is associated with a unit increase in quantity supplied, generally rises as the degree of resource utilization rises.

Equilibrium of Aggregate Demand and Supply

In Chapter 9 we learned that the level of prices is a crucial determinant of whether equilibrium GNP is below full employment (a "recessionary gap"), precisely at full employment, or above full employment (an "inflationary gap"). We are now in a position to analyze which type of gap, if any, will actually occur in any particular case by combining the analysis of aggregate supply just completed with the analysis of aggregate demand from the last two chapters to determine *simultaneously* the equilibrium level of real GNP (Y) and the equilibrium price level (P).

Figure 11–3 displays the mechanics. The aggregate demand curve DD and the aggregate supply curve SS intersect at point E, where real GNP is $4000 billion and the price level is 100. As can be seen in the graph, at any higher price level, such as 120, aggregate quantity supplied would exceed aggregate quantity demanded. There would be a glut on the market as firms found themselves unable to sell all their output. As inventories piled up, firms would compete

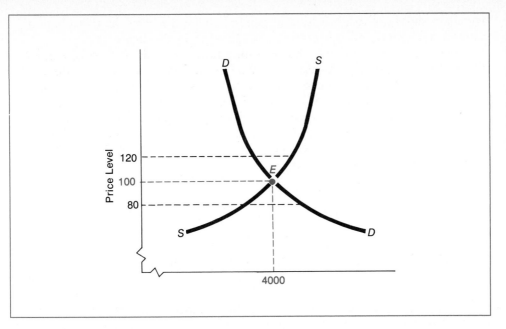

Figure 11–3
EQUILIBRIUM OF REAL
GNP AND THE PRICE
LEVEL
This diagram shows how the
equilibrium levels of real GNP
and the price level are
simultaneously determined by
the intersection of the
aggregate demand curve
(*DD*) and the aggregate
supply curve (*SS*). In this
example, equilibrium occurs
at point *E*, with a real GNP of
$4000 billion and a price
level of 100.

more vigorously for the available customers, thereby forcing prices down. The
price level would fall, as would production.

At any price level lower than 100, such as 80, quantity demanded would
exceed quantity supplied. There would be a shortage of goods on the market.
With inventories disappearing and customers knocking on their doors, firms
would be encouraged to raise prices. The price level would rise, and so would
output.

Only when the price level is 100 are the quantities of real GNP demanded
and supplied equal. Hence, only the combination $P = 100$, $Y = 4000 is an
equilibrium.

Table 11–1 illustrates the same conclusion in another way, using a tabular
analysis similar to that of Chapter 9 (refer back to Table 9–2, page 172).
Columns 1 and 2 constitute an aggregate demand schedule corresponding to the
aggregate demand curve *DD* in Figure 11–3. Columns 1 and 3 constitute an

Table 11–1
THE DETERMINATION OF THE EQUILIBRIUM PRICE LEVEL

(1) PRICE LEVEL	(2) AGGREGATE QUANTITY DEMANDED (billions of dollars)	(3) AGGREGATE QUANTITY SUPPLIED (billions of dollars)	(4) BALANCE OF SUPPLY AND DEMAND	(5) PRICES WILL:
75	4400	3600	Quantity demanded exceeds quantity supplied	Rise
80	4300	3700	Quantity demanded exceeds quantity supplied	Rise
100	4000	4000	Quantity demanded equals quantity supplied	Remain the same
120	3800	4200	Quantity supplied exceeds quantity demanded	Fall
150	3600	4400	Quantity supplied exceeds quantity demanded	Fall

aggregate supply schedule with the general shape discussed in this chapter. It corresponds exactly to aggregate supply curve SS in the figure.

It is clear from the table that equilibrium occurs only at $P = 100$ and $Y = \$4000$. At any other price level, aggregate quantities supplied and demanded would be unequal, with consequent upward or downward pressure on prices. For example, at a price level of 80, customers demand \$4300 billion worth of goods and services, but firms wish to provide only \$3700 billion. The price level is too low and will be forced upward. Conversely, at a price level of, say, 120, quantity supplied (\$4200 billion) exceeds quantity demanded (\$3800 billion), implying that the price level must fall.

Recessionary and Inflationary Gaps Revisited

Let us now reconsider a question we posed, but could not answer, in Chapter 9: Will equilibrium occur at, below, or beyond full employment?

We could not give a complete answer to this question in Chapter 9 because we had no way to determine the equilibrium price level, and therefore no way to tell which type of gap, if any, would arise. The aggregate supply and demand analysis summarized in Figure 11–3 gives us the information we need to determine the price level. But we find that our answer is nonetheless the same as it was in Chapter 9: Anything can happen.

The reason is that nothing in Figure 11–3 tells us where full employment is; it could be above the \$4000 billion equilibrium level or below it. Depending on the locations of the aggregate demand and aggregate supply curves, then, we can reach equilibrium above full employment (an inflationary gap), at full employment, or below full employment (a recessionary gap).

All three possibilities are illustrated in Figure 11–4. The three upper panels are familiar from Chapter 9. As we move from left to right, the $C + I$ schedule rises from $C + I_0$ to $C + I_1$ to $C + I_2$, leading respectively to a recessionary gap, an equilibrium at full employment, and an inflationary gap. In fact, the upper left-hand diagram is a repeat of Figure 9–6 (page 176), and the upper right-hand diagram repeats Figure 9–7 (page 177). We stressed in Chapter 9 that any one of the three cases is possible, depending on the price level and on the consumption and investment schedules.

In the three lower panels, the equilibrium price level is determined at point E by the intersection of the aggregate supply curve (SS) and the aggregate demand curve (DD). But the same three possibilities emerge nonetheless.

In the lower left-hand panel, aggregate demand is too small to provide jobs for the entire labor force, so there is a recessionary gap equal to distance EB, or \$1000 billion. This corresponds precisely to the situation depicted on the income-expenditure diagram immediately above it.

In the lower right-hand panel, aggregate demand is so high that the economy reaches an equilibrium well beyond full employment. There is an inflationary gap equal to BE, or \$1000 billion, just as in the diagram immediately above it.

In the lower middle panel, the aggregate demand curve $D_1 D_1$ is at just the right level to produce an equilibrium at full employment. There is neither an inflationary nor a recessionary gap, as in the diagram just above it.

It may seem, therefore, that we have done nothing but restate our previous conclusions. But, in fact, we have done much more. Because now that we have studied the determination of the equilibrium price level, we are able to examine how the economy adjusts to either a recessionary gap or an inflationary gap.

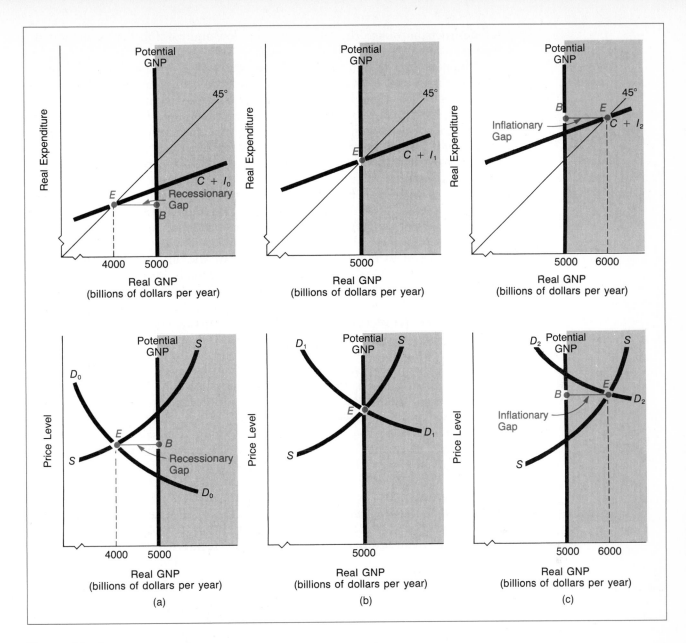

Figure 11–4
RECESSIONARY AND INFLATIONARY GAPS REVISITED

This diagram shows three possible types of equilibrium on two different diagrams. In the top row, income-expenditure diagrams from Chapter 9 are used to depict a recessionary gap, an equilibrium at full employment, and an inflationary gap. In the bottom row, these same three situations are shown on aggregate supply and demand diagrams. In each case, the aggregate supply curve is the same (SS), equilibrium occurs at point E, and full employment GNP is $5000 billion. In part (a), the aggregate demand curve $D_0 D_0$ is relatively low, so that equilibrium falls below full employment. There is a recessionary gap measured by the distance EB, or $1000 billion. In part (b), the aggregate demand curve $D_1 D_1$ is higher, and equilibrium occurs precisely at full employment. There is no gap of either kind. In part (c), the aggregate demand curve $D_2 D_2$ is so high that equilibrium occurs beyond full employment. There is an inflationary gap measured by the distance BE, or $1000 billion.

Adjusting to an Inflationary Gap: Inflation

We have already suggested that an inflationary gap sets the stage for inflation. As we shall see now, the economy, if left to its own devices, produces an inflation that eventually eliminates an inflationary gap. In other words, the gap self-destructs, although the process may be slow and painful. Let us see how this works.

Suppose equilibrium GNP is above potential, as in the lower right-hand panel of Figure 11–4. Jobs are plentiful and labor is in great demand. Although some workers are unemployed, this minimal unemployment is less than the frictional levels — that is, less than the number we usually expect to be jobless because they are moving, changing occupations, and so on. Many firms, on the other hand, are having trouble finding workers. They may even be having trouble hanging on to their current employees, as other firms try to lure them away with higher wages.

Such a situation is bound to lead to rising money wages, and rising wages add to business costs, thus shifting the aggregate supply curve inward. (Remember, the aggregate supply curve is drawn for a *given* money wage.) But as the aggregate supply curve shifts inward — eventually moving from $S_0 S_0$ to $S_1 S_1$ in Figure 11–5, for example — the size of the inflationary gap steadily declines. Thus, inflation erodes the inflationary gap, eventually leading the economy to an equilibrium at full employment (point F in Figure 11–5).

There is a straightforward way of looking at the economics that underlies the self-correcting process. The trouble arises because consumers and investors are demanding more output than the economy is capable of producing at normal operating rates. To paraphrase an old cliché, there is too much demand chasing too little supply. Naturally, prices will be rising in such an environment. And rising prices will eat away at the purchasing power of consumers' wealth, forcing them to cut back on consumption, as explained in Chapter 8. Eventually, consumers' appetites for goods will be scaled down to the economy's capacity to provide those goods; and at this point, the self-correcting process stops. That, in essence, is the unhappy process by which the economy cures itself of the problem of excessive aggregate demand.

One caveat should be entered. The conclusion that an inflationary gap sows the seeds of its own destruction holds *only in the absence of further forces propelling the aggregate demand curve outward*. But in Chapter 10 we have already encountered several forces that might shift the aggregate demand curve outward. As you can see by manipulating the aggregate demand-aggregate supply

Figure 11–5
THE ELIMINATION OF AN INFLATIONARY GAP
When the aggregate supply curve is $S_0 S_0$ and the aggregate demand curve is *DD*, the economy will initially reach equilibrium (point E) with an inflationary gap. The resulting inflation of wages will push the supply curve inward until it has shifted to the position indicated by curve $S_1 S_1$. Here, with equilibrium at point F, the economy is at normal full employment. But, during the adjustment period from E to F, there will have been inflation.

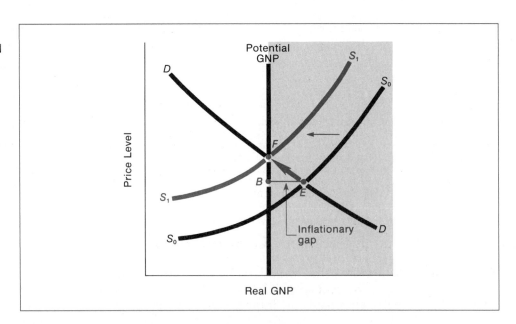

diagram, if aggregate demand is shifting out at the same time that aggregate supply is shifting in, there will certainly be inflation, but the inflationary gap may not shrink. (Try this as an exercise, to make sure you understand how to use the apparatus.) So not all inflations come to a natural end.

Demand Inflation and Stagflation

Simple as it is, this adjustment model teaches us a number of important lessons about inflation in the real world. First of all, Figure 11–5 reminds us that the real culprit in this particular inflation is the excessive level of aggregate demand. The aggregate demand curve is initially so high that it intersects the aggregate supply curve at an output level higher than full employment. The resulting intense demand for workers pushes wages higher; and higher wages spell higher prices. While excessive demand is not the only possible cause of inflation in the real world, it certainly is the cause in our example.

However, business managers and journalists are likely to blame inflation on rising wages. In a superficial sense, of course, they are right, because higher wages do indeed lead firms to raise their prices. But in a deeper sense they are wrong. Both rising wages and rising prices are only symptoms of an underlying malady: too much aggregate demand. Blaming labor for inflation in such a case is a bit like blaming high doctor bills for making you ill.

Second, we see that output falls while prices rise as the economy adjusts from point E to point F in Figure 11–5. This process thus provides our first (but not our last!) explanation of the phenomenon of **stagflation.** We see that:

Stagflation is inflation that occurs while the economy is growing slowly or having a recession.

A period of stagflation is part of the normal aftermath of a period of excessive aggregate demand.

It is easy enough to understand why stagflation occurs in this case. When aggregate demand is excessive, the economy will temporarily produce beyond its normal capacity. Labor markets tighten and wages rise. Machinery and raw materials may also become scarce and so start rising in price. Faced by higher costs, the natural reaction of business firms is to produce less and to charge a higher price. That is stagflation.

It may be useful to review what we have learned about inflationary gaps thus far.

If aggregate demand is exceptionally high, the economy may reach an equilibrium above full employment (an inflationary gap). When this occurs, the tight situation in the labor market soon forces wages to rise. Since wages are business costs, prices rise and there is inflation. With cuts in consumer purchasing power, the inflationary gap begins to close. As the inflationary gap is closing, output falls while prices continue to rise, so the economy experiences stagflation until the inflationary gap is eliminated. At this point, a long-run equilibrium is established with a higher price level and with GNP equal to potential GNP.

An Example from U.S. History: 1966 to 1970

The stagflation that follows a period of excessive aggregate demand is, you will note, a rather benign form of the dreaded disease. After all, while output is falling, it nonetheless remains above potential GNP; and unemployment is low. The U.S. economy has not experienced anything like this for many years. In fact, you have to go back to the late 1960s to find a "textbook" example of an inflationary gap that extinguished itself in this way.

During 1966–1968, the U.S. economy was booming, unemployment was below 4 percent, and jobs were plentiful. There was an inflationary gap, like that shown in the lower right-hand panel of Figure 11–4. Our analysis suggests that wages should have been accelerating, and indeed they were. The gray bars in Figure 11–6 illustrate this acceleration. The blue bars show that, with one minor exception, the rate of inflation followed the rate of increase of wages — rising from about 2 percent a year to over 5 percent. This is, again, in line with what our model predicts.

The upsurge in inflation naturally ate away at the inflationary gap, as shown in Figure 11–5, and the gap was gone by the end of 1970. Yet inflation continued unabated through a mild recession in 1969–1970. The U.S. economy was in the stagflation phase. Despite outcries of "excessive" wage demands that "caused" inflation, it is clear that the ultimate cause of the acceleration in both wages and prices was the excessive aggregate demand of the Vietnam War episode. The economy behaved just as our simple model suggests.

Adjusting to a Recessionary Gap: Deflation or Unemployment?

Let us now consider what can happen when the economy finds itself in equilibrium *below* full employment — that is, when there is a *recessionary* gap. This might be caused, for example, by inadequate consumer spending or by anemic investment spending.

Figure 11–7 illustrates such a case and gives an impression of the economic situation we faced at the bottom of the 1981–1982 recession. According to one estimate, real GNP was about $265 billion below potential GNP. And the unemployment rate stood at 10.7 percent.

You might expect that we could just run our previous analysis in reverse: High unemployment leads to falling wages; falling wages reduce business costs and shift the aggregate supply curve outward, so firms cut prices (see Figure 11–7); falling wages and prices eliminate the recessionary gap by propping up

Figure 11–6
GROWTH RATES OF WAGES AND PRICES IN THE UNITED STATES, 1965–1970
These data illustrate what happened when an inflationary gap arose in the United States during 1966–1968. Notice the acceleration of both wages and prices. By 1970, the gap was eliminated, and wage increases leveled off. There was a minor recession in 1969–1970, but inflation continued.
SOURCE: *Economic Report of the President*, 1987.

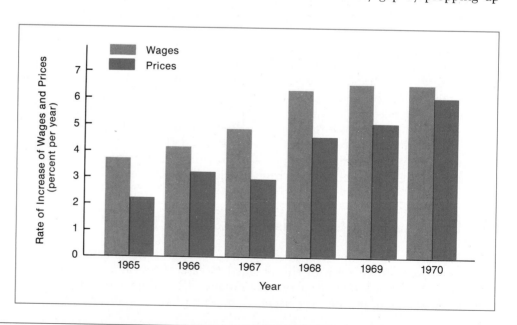

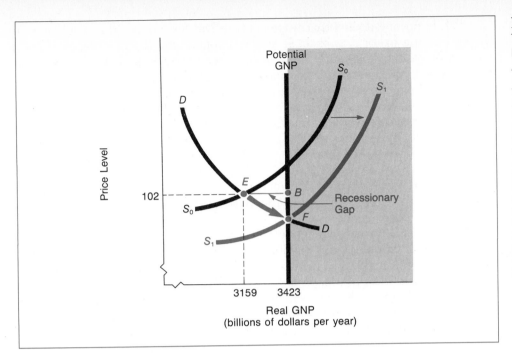

Figure 11–7
THE ELIMINATION OF A
RECESSIONARY GAP?
At point *E* there is a
recessionary gap because
the aggregate demand curve
DD crosses the aggregate
supply curve $S_0 S_0$ below the
level of potential GNP. If
wages fall, the aggregate
supply curve gradually shifts
outward until it reaches the
position indicated by supply
curve $S_1 S_1$. Here the
economy has attained a
full-employment equilibrium
at point *F*. But if wages
refuse to fall, the economy
gets stuck with a
recessionary gap and a long
period of unemployment.

consumer spending; and full employment is restored. The economy moves
smoothly from point *E* to point *F* in Figure 11–7. Very simple. And very misleading in our modern economy!

Why is it misleading? Our brief review of the historical record in
Chapter 5 showed that, while the economy may have operated like this long
ago, it certainly does not work this way now. The history of the United States
shows many examples of falling wages and prices before World War II but none
since then. Not even the severe recession of 1981–1982, during which unemployment climbed above 10 percent, was able to force average prices and wages
down—though it certainly slowed their rate of increase.

Exactly why wages and prices are rigid in the downward direction in our
modern economy has been a subject of intense and continuing controversy
among economists for years.

Some economists emphasize institutional features like minimum wage laws,
union contracts, and a variety of government regulations that place legal floors
under particular wages and prices. Because most of these institutions are of relatively recent vintage, this theory successfully explains why wages and prices are
more rigid now than they were before World War II. However, most of the
U.S. economy is not subject to legal restraints on wage and price cutting. So it
seems doubtful that legal restrictions can provide a complete explanation.

Other observers subscribe to the theory that workers have a profound psychological resistance to accepting a wage reduction. This theory certainly has
the ring of truth. Think how you would react if your boss announced that she
was cutting your hourly wage rate. You might quit, or you might devote less
care and attention to your job. Genuine wage reductions are rare enough to be
newsworthy. For example, Chrysler workers accepted hefty pay cuts in the early
1980s, but only when it appeared that the company was in grave danger of
going bankrupt. In 1983, the Greyhound bus company grabbed the headlines by
insisting that its drivers accept a large wage reduction; the drivers refused, and a
nasty strike followed. In more recent years, money wages have been cut by several airline companies as the industry suffered through a painful shakeout.

While no one doubts that wage cuts are bad for morale, the psychological theory has one major drawback. It fails to explain why the psychological resistance to wage cuts apparently started only after World War II. Until a satisfactory answer to this question is provided, many economists will remain skeptical.

A third explanation is based on a fact we emphasized in Chapter 5 — that business cycles were less severe in the postwar period than they were in the prewar period. Because workers and firms came to believe that recessions would not turn into depressions, the argument goes, they may have decided to wait out the bad times rather than accept wage or price reductions that they would later regret.

There are other theories as well, none of which commands anything like universal assent. But, regardless of the cause, we might as well accept the fact that, in our modern economy, prices and wages will rise when demand is strong but generally will not fall when demand is weak.

The implications of this rigidity are quite serious, for a recessionary gap cannot cure itself without some deflation. And if wages and prices will not fall, *the economy gets stuck at a point like E in Figure 11–7, that is, at an equilibrium below full employment*. Keynes was the first economist to point out that wage rigidity could lead to a long-lasting equilibrium below full employment and to distinguish it from the full-employment equilibrium that we have just been considering.

When aggregate demand is low, the economy may get stuck in an *unemployment equilibrium*. There is a recessionary gap, but wages and prices refuse to fall; so the gap persists. The economy endures a prolonged period of production below potential GNP.

Does the Economy Have a Self-Correcting Mechanism?

Now a situation like this would, presumably, not last forever. As the recession lengthened, and perhaps deepened, more and more workers would be unable to obtain jobs at the prevailing high wages. Eventually their resistance to wage cuts, whatever the cause, would be worn down by their need to be employed.

Firms, too, would become increasingly willing to cut prices as the period of weak demand lasted longer and longer and managers became convinced that the slump was not merely a temporary aberration. Prices and wages did, in fact, fall during the Great Depression of the 1930s. And they might fall again if a sufficiently drastic depression were allowed to occur. They certainly slowed markedly in the weak markets of the early 1980s.

Nowadays, political leaders of both parties believe it is folly to wait for falling wages and prices to eliminate a recessionary gap. But while they agree that *some* government action is both necessary and appropriate under recessionary conditions, there is still vocal — and highly partisan! — debate over how much and what kind of intervention is warranted.

One reason for this disagreement is that the **self-correcting mechanism** does operate — if only weakly — to cure recessionary gaps. Recent history provides a vivid illustration.

Disinflation and Recovery in the 1980s: A Case Study

The recession of 1981–1982 opened up the largest recessionary gap since the Great Depression. By the end of 1982, when the slump hit bottom, real GNP was estimated to be some $265 billion (in 1982 dollars) below potential. (See

Figure 11–7.) Our theory suggests that such a large gap should push inflation-down strongly, and it did. While wages and prices did not actually decline, their rates of increase tumbled from 9–10 percent in 1981 to about 4 percent by 1983. (See Figure 11–8.)

But what about the self-correcting mechanism? Did falling inflation eat away at the recessionary gap? Yes, but slowly and painfully. Recovery from recession began in the winter of 1982–1983 and proceeded rapidly at first: the civilian unemployment rate tumbled from its peak of 10.7 percent to only 7.2 percent within about two years. But then it stalled out, and unemployment hovered near 7 percent of the labor force for some time. Some observers at the time claimed that 7 percent was now the "full employment" unemployment rate. If so, the self-correcting mechanism worked just as our simple model says—although millions of unemployed workers and thousands of bankrupted businesses suffered along the way. However, most economists believe that full employment today corresponds to an unemployment rate closer to 5.5 or 6 percent. In that case, the self-correcting mechanism still had some way to go. And, indeed, unemployment started falling again in late 1986 and early 1987.

Our overall conclusion about the economy's ability to right itself, then, seems to run something like this:

The economy does indeed have a self-correcting mechanism that tends to eliminate either unemployment or inflation. However, this mechanism is much more efficient at curing inflationary gaps through inflation than at curing recessionary gaps through deflation. In addition, its beneficial effects on inflation are sometimes swamped by strong inflationary forces (such as rapid increases in aggregate demand). Thus the self-correcting mechanism cannot always be relied upon.

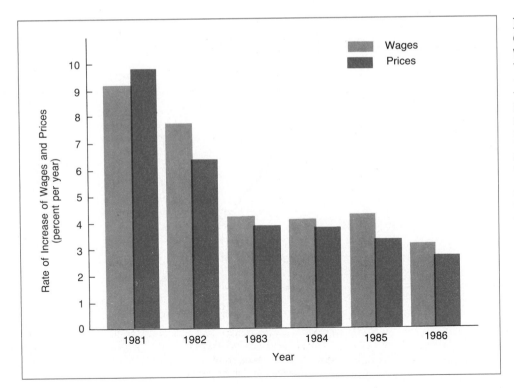

Figure 11–8
GROWTH RATES OF WAGES AND PRICES IN THE UNITED STATES, 1981–1986
These data illustrate what happened when the U.S. economy developed a large recessionary gap in 1981–1982. Notice that wage and price inflation slowed down dramatically in 1981–1983, but then stabilized.
SOURCE: *Economic Report of the President, 1987.*

Stagflation from Supply Shifts

We have so far encountered one type of stagflation in this chapter — the stagflation that often follows in the aftermath of an inflationary boom. However, that is not what happened in the more serious stagflationary episodes of 1973–1975 and 1979–1981. What was going on during those years that caused so much more unemployment and inflation than was expected? What were the causes of this new, more virulent type of stagflation? Several things, but the principal villain was the rising price of energy.

In 1973 the Organization of Petroleum Exporting Countries (OPEC) reached a collusive agreement to limit production that succeeded in quadrupling the price of crude oil in only a few months. American consumers soon found the prices of gasoline and home heating fuels increasing sharply. American businesses found that one of the important inputs to the production process — energy — rose drastically in price, thus increasing the cost of doing business. In 1979, the world oil market went into a panic again following the ouster of the Shah of Iran. Oil prices escalated as buyers scrambled to secure supplies and build inventories. Seizing the opportunity, OPEC this time doubled the price of oil.

Higher energy prices, we observed earlier, make the economy's aggregate supply curve shift inward in the manner shown in Figure 11–2 (page 200). If the aggregate supply curve shifts inward, as it surely did in 1973–1974 and again in 1979–1980, production will be reduced. And in order to reduce demand to the available supply, prices will have to rise. The result is the worst of both worlds: falling production and rising prices.

This conclusion is shown in Figure 11–9, which superimposes an aggregate demand curve, *DD*, on the two aggregate supply curves of Figure 11–2. The economy's equilibrium shifts upward to the left, from point *E* to point *A*. Thus, output falls while prices rise. In brief:

Stagflation is the typical result of adverse supply shifts.

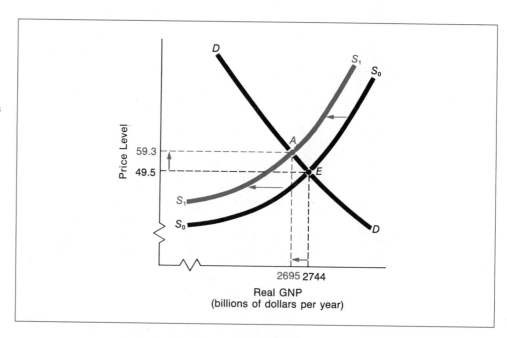

Figure 11–9
STAGFLATION FROM A SHIFT IN AGGREGATE SUPPLY
This diagram illustrates how stagflation arises if the aggregate supply curve shifts inward to the left (from $S_0 S_0$ to $S_1 S_1$). If the aggregate demand curve does not change, equilibrium moves from point *E* to point *A*. Output falls as prices rise, which is what we mean by stagflation. The diagram indicates roughly what happened in the U.S. during 1973–1975, when higher energy prices caused stagflation.

The numbers used in Figure 11–9 are roughly indicative of what happened in the United States between 1973 (represented by supply curve S_0S_0 and point E) and 1975 (represented by supply curve S_1S_1 and point A). Real GNP, in 1982 prices, fell by about $50 billion, while the price level rose almost 20 percent.

The story of the early 1980s is more complicated because so many other things were going on at the same time — especially the sharp changes in national economic policy ushered in by President Reagan. But, in broad outline, the 1979–1982 economy followed the script that had been written in 1973–1975 (see Figure 11–9). The inflation rate rose to an astonishing 13.3 percent in 1979 and to a sizzling 16 percent in the first half of 1980. Americans were almost panic-stricken over these unprecedented inflation rates, which exceeded even the worst months of 1974. Recession followed inflation. The economy began to weaken slightly in 1979, slipped into a small recession in early 1980, and experienced a huge recession in 1981–1982.

The general lesson to be learned from the experience of the 1970s and early 1980s is as important as it is clear:

The typical results of an adverse supply shock are a fall in output and an acceleration in inflation. This is one reason why the world economy was plagued by stagflation in the mid-1970s and early 1980s. And it can happen again if another series of supply-reducing events takes place.

Of course, supply shifts can work in the other direction as well. The world oil market softened in 1982–1983, OPEC weakened, and oil prices declined. At the same time, bountiful harvests around the world depressed agricultural prices. The aggregate supply curve was shifting outward, which helped the U.S. and other countries to reduce inflation rapidly. Then in early 1986 OPEC collapsed and oil prices plummeted. For a few months, the Consumer Price Index actually fell; and the inflation rate for 1986 as a whole was only 1.1 percent.

Favorable supply shocks tend to push output up and reduce inflation.

Inflation and the Multiplier

When we introduced the concept of the multiplier in Chapter 10, we said that there were several reasons why its actual value is smaller than suggested by the oversimplified multiplier formula. We are now in a position to understand one of these reasons: Inflation reduces the size of the multiplier.

The basic idea is simple. In Chapter 10, we described a multiplier process in which one person's spending became another person's income, which led to further spending by the second person, and so on. But this story is confined to the demand side of the economy. Let us therefore consider what is likely to happen on the supply side as the multiplier process unfolds. Will the additional demand be taken care of by firms without raising prices?

If the aggregate supply curve is upward sloping, the answer is no; more goods will only be provided at higher prices. Thus, as the multiplier chain progresses, pulling income and employment up, prices will also be rising. And this, as we know from Chapter 8, will dampen consumer spending because rising prices reduce the purchasing power of consumers' wealth. So the multiplier chain will not proceed as far as it would have in the absence of inflation.

How much inflation results from the rise in demand? How much of the multiplier chain is cut off by inflation? The answers depend on the slope of the economy's aggregate supply curve.

For a concrete example of the analysis, let us return to the $200 billion increase in investment spending used in Chapter 10. As we learned there (see especially page 185), $200 billion in additional investment spending eventually leads—through the multiplier process—to *a horizontal shift of $1000 billion in the aggregate demand curve*. But to know the actual quantity that will ultimately be produced, and the actual price level, we must bring the aggregate supply curve into the picture.

Figure 11–10 does this. Here we show the $1000 billion horizontal shift of the aggregate demand curve, from $D_0 D_0$ to $D_1 D_1$, that is derived from the over-simplified multiplier formula (which ignores rising prices). The aggregate supply curve, SS, then tells us how this expansion of demand is apportioned between higher output and higher prices. We see that as the economy's equilibrium moves from point E_0 to point E_1, real GNP does not rise by $1000 billion. Instead, prices rise, which, as we know, tends to cancel out part of the rise in quantity demanded. So output increases only from $4000 billion to $4800 billion—an increase of $800 billion. Thus, in our example, inflation reduces the multiplier from $1000/$200 = 5 to $800/$200 = 4. In general:

As long as the aggregate supply curve is upward sloping, any increase in aggregate demand will push up the price level. This will, in turn, drain off some of the higher real demand by eroding the purchasing power of consumer wealth. Thus, inflation reduces the value of the multiplier below that suggested by the oversimplified formula.

Notice also that the price level in this example has been pushed up (from 100 to 120, or 20 percent) by the rise in investment demand. This, too, is a general result:

As long as the aggregate supply curve is upward sloping, any outward shift of the aggregate demand curve will cause some rise in prices in the economy.

Figure 11–10

INFLATION AND THE MULTIPLIER

This figure illustrates the complete analysis of the multiplier, including the effect of inflation. The simple multiplier of Chapter 10, which ignored changes in the price level, appears here as a *horizontal* shift of $1000 billion in the aggregate demand curve, meaning that the multiplier would be $1000/$200 = 5 if prices did not rise. However, when aggregate demand shifts from $D_0 D_0$ to $D_1 D_1$, prices rise. In the diagram, the price level increases from 100 to 120 or by 20 percent. Consequently, equilibrium real income increases from $4000 billion to only $4800—for a rise of $800 billion, or a multiplier of $800/$200 = 4.

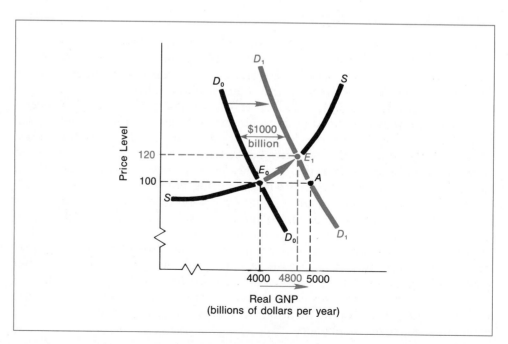

The economic behavior behind these results certainly cannot be considered surprising. Firms faced with large increases in quantity demanded at their original prices respond to these changed circumstances in two natural ways: They raise production (so GNP rises), and they raise prices (so the price level rises). But this rise in the price level reduces the purchasing power of the bank accounts and bonds held by consumers, and they too react in the natural way: They cut down on their spending. Such a reaction amounts to a movement *along* aggregate demand curve $D_1 D_1$ in Figure 11–10 from point A to point E_1.

Higher prices thus play their usual dual role in a market economy: They encourage suppliers to produce more and, at the same time, encourage demanders to consume less. In this way, equilibrium is reestablished at higher levels of output and higher prices through the process of inflation.

Figure 11–10 also shows us exactly where the oversimplified multiplier formula goes wrong. By ignoring the effects of the higher price level, the oversimplified formula supposes the economy moves horizontally from point E_0 to point A. As the diagram clearly shows, output does not actually rise this much. Output *would* rise this much only if the aggregate supply curve were horizontal. (Verify this for yourself by penciling in an imaginary horizontal aggregate supply curve through points E_0 and A in Figure 11–10.) That is, the oversimplified multiplier formula tacitly assumes that the aggregate supply curve is horizontal. Normally, this is an unrealistic assumption, and that is one reason why the oversimplified formula exaggerates the size of the multiplier.

As a summary, it may be useful to put together what we have learned about multiplier analysis in Chapters 10 and 11.

STEPS IN CALCULATING THE MULTIPLIER

1. Shift the expenditure schedule in the 45° line diagram vertically by the amount of the autonomous shift in spending (as, for example, in Figure 10–1 on page 186).

2. Use the 45° line diagram, or the oversimplified multiplier formula, to calculate the multiplier effect on GNP that *would* occur *if* the price level did not change (again, see Figure 10–1).

3. Now move from the 45° line diagram to an aggregate supply and demand diagram like Figure 11–10 to see how the price level will react. Enter the multiplier effect calculated in step 2 as a horizontal shift of the aggregate demand curve in the supply-demand diagram.

4. The supply-demand diagram will now show the actual effect on real output as well as the resulting inflation or deflation.[2]

A Role for Stabilization Policy

Chapter 9 emphasized the volatility of investment spending, and Chapter 10 noted that changes in investment have multiplier effects on aggregate demand. This chapter took the next step by showing how shifts in the aggregate demand curve cause fluctuations in both real GNP growth and inflation—fluctuations which are widely decried as undesirable. It also suggested that the economy's self-correcting mechanism works rather slowly, thereby leaving room for government stabilization policy to improve the workings of the free market. Can the government really do this? If so, how? These are the questions for Part 4.

[2] The change in the price level reacts back on the 45° diagram. See Discussion Question 11 at the end of the chapter.

Summary

1. The economy's aggregate supply curve relates the quantity of goods and services that will be supplied to the price level. It normally slopes upward to the right because the costs of labor and other inputs are relatively fixed in the short run, meaning that higher selling prices make input costs relatively "cheaper" and therefore encourage greater production.

2. The position of the aggregate supply curve can be shifted by changes in money wage rates, prices of other inputs, technology, or quantities of labor and capital available for employment.

3. The aggregate supply curve normally gets steeper as output increases. This means that, as output and capacity utilization rise, any given increase in aggregate demand leads to more inflation and less growth of real output.

4. The equilibrium price level and the equilibrium level of real GNP are jointly determined by the intersection of the economy's aggregate supply and aggregate demand schedules. This intersection may come at full employment, below full employment (a recessionary gap), or above full employment (an inflationary gap).

5. If there is an inflationary gap, the economy has a mechanism that erodes the gap through a process of inflation. Specifically, unusually strong job prospects push wages up, which shifts the aggregate supply curve to the left and reduces the inflationary gap.

6. One consequence of this self-correcting mechanism is that, if a surge in aggregate demand opens up an inflationary gap, part of the economy's natural adjustment to this event will be a period of stagflation; that is, a period in which prices are rising while output is falling.

7. The economy also has a self-correcting mechanism that erodes a recessionary gap. However, this mechanism works much more slowly and less reliably than the inflationary-gap mechanism because it relies on falling wages to shift the aggregate supply curve outward, and wages do not fall easily.

8. An inward shift of the aggregate supply curve will cause output to fall while prices rise; that is, it will cause stagflation. Among the events that have caused such a shift are the abrupt increases in the price of foreign oil.

9. Adverse supply shifts like this apparently plagued our economy in 1973–1974 and again in 1979–1980, leading to stagflation both times.

10. Among the reasons why the oversimplified multiplier formula is wrong is the fact that it ignores any inflation that may be caused by an increase in aggregate demand. Such inflation decreases the multiplier by reducing consumer spending, because consumers as a group suffer a loss of purchasing power when prices rise.

Concepts for Review

Aggregate supply curve
Productivity
Equilibrium of real GNP and the price level

Inflationary gap
Self-correcting mechanism
Stagflation

Recessionary gap
Inflation and the multiplier

Questions for Discussion

1. In an economy with the following aggregate demand and aggregate supply schedules, find the equilibrium levels of real output and the price level. Graph your solution. If full employment comes at $1600 billion, is there an inflationary or a recessionary gap?

AGGREGATE QUANTITY DEMANDED (in billions)	PRICE LEVEL	AGGREGATE QUANTITY SUPPLIED (in billions)
2000	75	1400
1950	80	1450
1800	90	1600
1700	110	1700
1600	140	1800

2. Suppose a worker receives a wage of $10 per hour. Compute the real wage (money wage deflated by the price index) corresponding to each of the following possible price levels: 85, 95, 100, 110, 120. What do you notice about the relationship between the real wage and the price level? Relate this to the slope of the aggregate supply curve.

3. In 1986, capacity utilization averaged 80 percent. In 1982, it averaged 72 percent. In which year do you think the economy found itself on a steeper portion of its aggregate supply curve? Explain why.

4. Explain why a decrease in the price of foreign oil shifts the aggregate supply curve outward to the right. What are the consequences of such a shift?

5. Comment on the following statement: "Inflationary and recessionary gaps are nothing to worry about because the economy has a built-in

mechanism that cures either type of gap automatically."

6. Give *two* different explanations of how the economy can suffer from stagflation.

7. Why do you think wages tend to be rigid in the downward direction?

8. Add the following aggregate supply and demand schedules to the data in Question 3 of Chapter 10 (page 195) to see how inflation affects the multiplier.

(1)	(2)	(3)	(4)
	AGGREGATE DEMAND (when investment	AGGREGATE DEMAND (when investment	AGGREGATE
PRICE LEVEL	is $120)	is $130)	SUPPLY
90	$1210	$1310	$1110
95	1205	1305	1155
100	1200	1300	1200
105	1195	1295	1245
110	1190	1290	1290
115	1185	1285	1335

Draw these schedules on a piece of graph paper. Then:

a. Notice that the difference between columns 2 and 3 (the aggregate demand schedule at two different levels of investment) is always $100. Discuss how this relates to your answer in the previous chapter.

b. Find the equilibrium GNP and the equilibrium price level both before and after the increase in investment. What is the value of the multiplier?

9. Explain in words why rising prices reduce the multiplier effect of an autonomous increase in aggregate demand.

10. Use an aggregate supply and demand diagram to show that multiplier effects are smaller when the aggregate supply curve is steeper. Which case gives rise to more inflation — the steep aggregate supply curve or the flat one? What happens to the multiplier if the aggregate supply curve is vertical?

11. (More difficult) Assume that investment spending rises. Draw a set of graphs illustrating the Steps in Calculating the Multiplier listed on page 215. Your aggregate supply and demand diagram from steps 3 and 4 will show a change in the price level. How would this change in the price level react back on the 45° line diagram you used in step 1? In view of this, use the 45° line diagram to show that inflation reduces the multiplier.

PART 4

Fiscal and Monetary Policy

12

Next, let us turn to the
problems of our fiscal policy.
Here the myths are legion
and the truth hard to find.

JOHN F. KENNEDY

Fiscal Policy and
Supply-Side Economics

In Part 3, we constructed and analyzed a model of an economy with no government. We concluded that such an economy has only weak tendencies to move toward high employment with low inflation. Furthermore, we hinted that well-designed government policies might improve the economy's performance. It is now time to pick up that hint—and to get acquainted with some of the difficulties the government must overcome if it is to conduct a successful stabilization policy.

Traditionally, the government has used its taxing and spending powers to influence the demand side of the economy. So this chapter begins there, in the domain of conventional *fiscal policy*. Specifically, we expand the basic model to allow, first, for government purchases of goods and services as a component of aggregate demand, and second, for taxes that make disposable income less than national income. As we shall see, neither of these complications requires any fundamental change in the way we analyze the determination of GNP and the price level, although taxes do reduce the multiplier.

When President Reagan assumed office in 1981, he rejected the customary emphasis on aggregate demand management and argued that the government could and should use tax policy to influence aggregate *supply*. So the last parts of the chapter examine "supply-side economics"—the controversial analysis that was used to explain the president's program and to predict its effects.

Tax Reform and Fiscal Policy

In January 1987 a sweeping revision of the U.S. income tax code went into effect. The tax reform act that President Reagan signed into law in October 1986 was the culmination of an epic two-year legislative struggle during which legislators and the administration locked horns over numerous provisions. But, as the tax reform debate progressed, one ground rule was observed by all the participants: The bill was to be "revenue neutral," meaning that total tax collections were to neither rise nor fall.

Why was revenue neutrality so important? Because the president and members of Congress wanted to separate heated debates over the *structure* of taxation—which is what tax reform was all about—from equally heated debates over the government's **fiscal policy,** that is, the overall balance of spending and taxation. Many senators and representatives felt that taxes should be raised to reduce the budget deficit. The president agreed that the deficit was too large, but insisted that raising taxes was not the way to reduce it. Had the total volume of taxation been at issue, the White House and Congress probably never would have reached agreement on a tax bill.

The government's **fiscal policy** is its plan for spending and taxation. It is designed to steer aggregate demand in some desired direction.

But why all this fuss about fiscal policy? How do our political leaders decide how much spending or taxation is the right amount? Perhaps more to the point, how can you as a voter decide whether your elected representatives have made sound decisions? These are the questions for this chapter.

Government Purchases and Equilibrium Income

Before attempting to answer such difficult questions, we must integrate the government into our model of the determination of national income and the price level. We do this in stages, starting first with **government purchases of goods and services (G),** and then adding taxes. Thus, in bringing the government back into the circular flow of income and expenditure (see Figure 12–1), we ignore for the moment the flows of tax revenues and transfer payments at point 5. How would the equilibrium level of GNP be determined in an economy in which the state bought goods but did not levy taxes or make transfers?

The circular flow diagram shows us the answer, just as it did in an economy with no government (Chapter 9). If the size of the circular flow of income and expenditure is to be maintained, then the total amount of new goods and services that firms produce at point 4 (Y) must be equal to the sum of the demands of consumers at point 1 (C), investors at point 2 (I), and government

Figure 12–1
THE CIRCULAR FLOW OF EXPENDITURE AND INCOME WITH NO FOREIGN TRADE

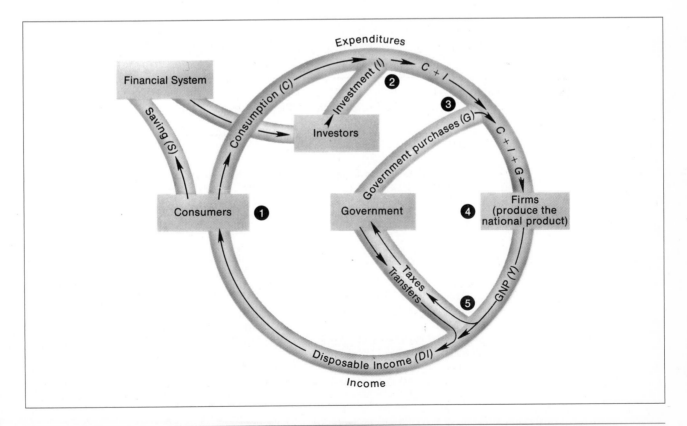

at point 3 (G). We thus obtain the following restatement of the condition for equilibrium on the demand side of the economy:[1]

For any given price level, equilibrium GNP on the demand side of the economy occurs when the sum of consumption demand, investment demand, and government demand for goods and services just equals output. In symbols:

$$Y = C + I + G.$$

The reasoning behind this equilibrium condition is precisely the same as it was in Chapter 9. At income levels below equilibrium, the sum $C + I + G$ would exceed Y; and so inventories would be disappearing, signaling firms that they should raise their production. Conversely, at income levels above equilibrium, $C + I + G$ would be less than Y, so that unwanted inventories would be accumulating and firms would have incentives to cut back production.

Table 12–1, which may usefully be compared to Table 9–1 in Chapter 9 (page 170), illustrates this process. The first three columns give the same consumption and investment schedules that we worked with there. The fourth column reflects the assumption that government purchases are $800 billion irrespective of the level of GNP. Summing these three components gives us our new total expenditure schedule in columns 1 and 5.

What, then, is the equilibrium level of GNP? As the table indicates, only a GNP of $8000 billion can be an equilibrium, for only at this level is total spending in balance with production.

Figure 12–2 shows the same conclusion graphically. The line labeled C is the same consumption function we used in previous chapters. The line labeled $C + I$ adds the fixed $700 billion in investment to this; again, this amount is taken from previous chapters. Finally, the line labeled $C + I + G$ adds an additional $800 billion in government spending to the $C + I$ line, which gives us our new total expenditure schedule.

[1]We are still leaving exports and imports out of the picture. They are the subject of Part 5.

Table 12–1
DERIVATION OF A TOTAL EXPENDITURE SCHEDULE WITH GOVERNMENT PURCHASES

(1)	(2)	(3)	(4)	(5)
NATIONAL INCOME (Y) (billions)	CONSUMPTION (C) (billions)	INVESTMENT (I) (billions)	GOVERNMENT PURCHASES (G) (billions)	TOTAL EXPENDITURE (C + I + G) (billions)
$4000	$3300	$700	$800	$4800
4500	3700	700	800	5200
5000	4100	700	800	5600
5500	4500	700	800	6000
6000	4900	700	800	6400
6500	5300	700	800	6800
7000	5700	700	800	7200
7500	6100	700	800	7600
8000	6500	700	800	8000
8500	6900	700	800	8400

This table adds government purchases of $800 billion to our model economy. Notice that the equilibrium level of GNP grows to $8000 billion, for this is the level at which output is equal to total spending (the sum of $C + I + G$).

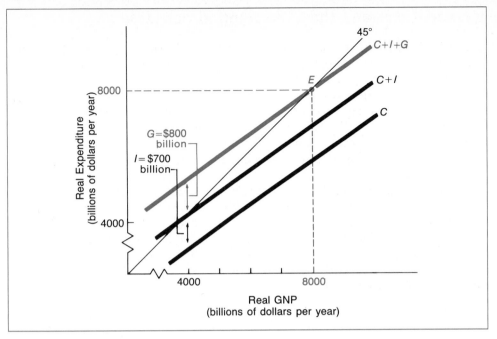

Figure 12–2
INCOME
DETERMINATION WITH
GOVERNMENT
SPENDING
This diagram adds
government purchases of
goods and services (G) to
the income expenditure
diagrams that we have been
using. The C + I + G curve
is the total expenditure
schedule for an economy
with no foreign trade, and the
point where it crosses the 45°
line (point E) marks the
equilibrium level of GNP. The
C + I + G line is parallel to
the C + I line because of the
assumption that whatever the
level of GNP, government
spending remains at $800
billion.

Just as in previous chapters, the equilibrium of the economy is at point *E*, where the total expenditure schedule crosses the 45° line. This is because the 45° line includes all the points at which C + I + G add up to Y. The diagram shows that equilibrium is at a GNP of $8000 billion, which consists of $6500 billion in consumption, $700 billion in investment, and $800 billion in government purchases. This agrees precisely with Table 12–1, as it must. If all this seems familiar from previous chapters, it should; for the analysis is precisely the same.[2]

In Chapter 10 we stated that when government spending was introduced, the multiplier for G would be the same as the multiplier for autonomous changes in C and I. We can now demonstrate this conclusion.

If you turn back to page 173, you will see that the equilibrium reached there was at a level of output Y = $4000 billion. Now, in an economy that is identical with the one in Chapter 9 except for the $800 billion in government spending, we see that the equilibrium is at Y = $8000 billion. Thus an $800 billion increment in G (from zero to $800 billion) has pushed up GNP by $4000 billion. In this example, then, the multiplier for government spending is $4000/$800 = 5, which, you will recall, was also the value of the multiplier for autonomous increases in investment or consumption.

The two multipliers are identical because the logic behind them is identical. In Chapter 10 we studied an example of a multiplier spending chain set in motion when Generous Motors spent $1 million to build a factory. This process could equally well have been kicked off by the federal government buying $1 million worth of new cars from GM. Thereafter, each recipient of additional income would spend 80 percent of it (the assumed marginal propensity to consume), until $5 million in new income had eventually been created.

And the qualification that we placed on the oversimplified multiplier formula in Chapter 11 also applies here. Government spending normally leads to some inflation, which pulls down consumer spending and thus reduces the value of the multiplier below our illustrative figure of 5.

[2]An algebraic version of this and other topics discussed here can be found in the appendix to this chapter.

Income Taxes and the Consumption Schedule

You can see, then, that it takes little effort to bring government purchases into our model of income determination. Let us turn our attention next to taxes and, in particular, to the personal income tax.

For present purposes, the most important aspect of taxes is that they create a discrepancy between gross national product (GNP) and disposable income (*DI*), as can be seen in the circular flow diagram (Figure 12–1). Tax revenues flow out of the circular flow and into the hands of the government. (The effects of transfer payments, which enter the circular flow at point 5, will be considered presently.)

We learned in Chapter 8 that there is a close and reliable relationship between consumer spending and *disposable* income. Therefore, if we want to construct a relationship between consumer spending and GNP, we first have to allow for the fact that taxes are deducted from GNP before *DI* is arrived at. The importance of this piece of accounting is that when taxes are increased, disposable income falls—and hence so does consumption—*even if GNP is unchanged*. As a result:

An increase in personal income taxes shifts the consumption schedule in our 45° line diagram downward. Similarly, a reduction in taxes shifts the consumption schedule upward.

The specific manner in which the consumption schedule shifts depends on the nature of the tax change. One way to reduce taxes is to increase the per person exemption, as was done in the 1986 tax reform act. The increase in disposable income from this provision is the *same* regardless of the level of GNP; hence the increase in consumer spending is the same. In a word, the C schedule shifts upward in a parallel manner, as shown in Figure 12–3(a).

But often tax policy is designed to make the change in disposable income depend on the level of income, normally being larger at high income levels than at low ones. This is true, for example, when Congress reduces the bracket

Figure 12–3
HOW TAX POLICY SHIFTS THE CONSUMPTION SCHEDULE
Because consumption depends on disposable income, not GNP, any change in taxes will shift the consumption schedule relating consumption to GNP. Part (a) shows how the curve shifts for changes in taxes of fixed amounts. Part (b) shows how the C curve shifts if the tax cut (or tax increase) is larger at high incomes than at low incomes.

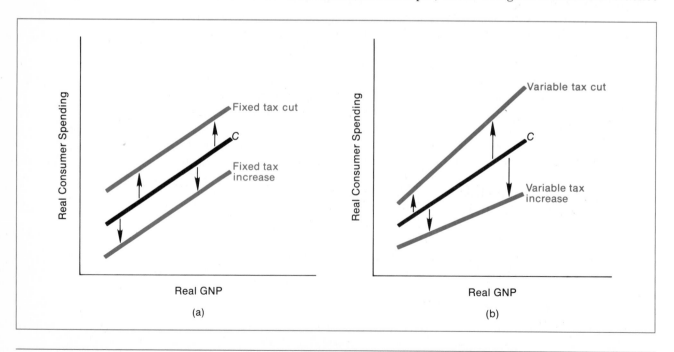

rates in the personal income tax code, which it also did in the 1986 tax act.[3] Since this sort of tax policy raises disposable income more when GNP is higher, the downward shift in the C schedule is sharper at high income levels than at low ones. Figure 12–3(b) illustrates how this type of tax policy shifts the consumption schedule.

Tax Policy and Equilibrium Income

We are now in a position to put taxes into our model of income determination. To do so, we must first adjust the consumption schedule we have been using to allow for an income tax.

Table 12–2 does this on the assumption that taxes are 25 percent of GNP. Column 1 shows alternative values of GNP ranging from $2.5 trillion to $5.5 trillion, and column 2 indicates that taxes are always one-quarter of this amount. Column 3 subtracts column 2 from column 1 to arrive at disposable income (DI). Column 4 then shows the amount of consumer spending corresponding to each level of DI. Note that columns 3 and 4 just repeat the consumption function that we studied in Chapter 8. But the consumption schedule that we need for our 45° line diagram relates C to Y, not to DI — that is, it relates spending to *total* consumer income, not to income net of taxes — and that schedule is therefore found in columns 1 and 4.

To derive the new expenditure schedule for an economy with taxes, we need only replace the old consumption schedule with this new one — that is, we must replace column 2 of Table 12–1 with column 4 of Table 12–2. This is done numerically in Table 12–3, and the results are shown diagrammatically in Figure 12–4. In particular, the expenditure schedule contained in columns 1 and 5 of Table 12–3 is shown as the C + I + G line in Figure 12–4. Naturally, the inclusion of taxes has lowered the expenditure schedule.

Since the 45° line is given in the diagram, we can immediately locate the equilibrium level of GNP at point E. Here, gross national product is

[3]You may be wondering how a tax law could raise the personal exemption, lower bracket rates, and yet remain revenue neutral. The answer is that the 1986 tax act closed many loopholes and raised taxes on corporations.

Table 12–2
DERIVATION OF A CONSUMPTION SCHEDULE WITH INCOME TAXATION

(1)	(2)	(3)	(4)
		DISPOSABLE INCOME	
GROSS NATIONAL PRODUCT (billions)	TAXES (billions)	(GNP minus taxes) (billions)	CONSUMPTION (billions)
$2500	$ 625	$1875	$1600
3000	750	2250	1900
3500	875	2625	2200
4000	1000	3000	2500
4500	1125	3375	2800
5000	1250	3750	3100
5500	1375	4125	3400

Because taxes (column 2) must be subtracted from gross national product (column 1) to get disposable income (column 3), this table shows how an income tax lowers the consumption schedule (column 4) in a concrete example. (Compare column 4 with the consumption schedule in Table 12–1 to see that the C schedule has indeed fallen.)

Table 12–3
TOTAL EXPENDITURE SCHEDULE WITH TAXES AND GOVERNMENT PURCHASES

(1) NATIONAL INCOME (Y) (billions)	(2) CONSUMPTION (C) (billions)	(3) INVESTMENT (I) (billions)	(4) GOVERNMENT PURCHASES (G) (billions)	(5) TOTAL EXPENDITURE (C + I + G) (billions)
$2500	$1600	$700	$800	$3100
3000	1900	700	800	3400
3500	2200	700	800	3700
4000	2500	700	800	4000
4500	2800	700	800	4300
5000	3100	700	800	4600
5500	3400	700	800	4900

This table replaces the previous consumption schedule with a new one that adjusts for the income tax (as shown in Table 12–2) and shows that the equilibrium level of income is $4000 billion.

Figure 12–4
INCOME DETERMINATION WITH GOVERNMENT SPENDING AND TAXATION

This diagram adds a 25 percent income tax to the model economy portrayed in Figure 12–2. Because of this, the C schedule is shifted down (and hence the C + I and C + I + G schedules are also shifted down). Equilibrium is at point E, where the C + I + G schedule crosses the 45° line. Thus equilibrium GNP is $4000 billion, the same as it was in the economy with no government. This however, is certainly not a general result; government actions can either raise or lower GNP.

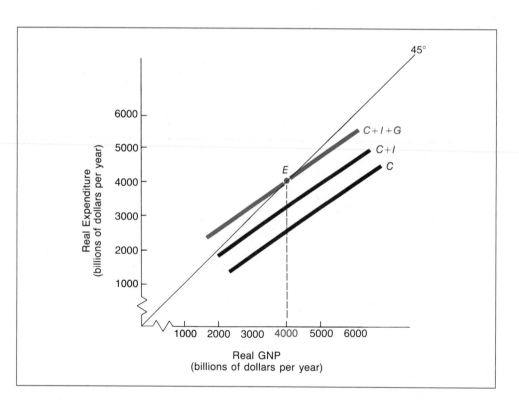

$4000 billion, consumption is $2500 billion, investment is $700 billion, and government purchases are $800 billion. As we know, full employment may occur above or below Y = $4000 billion. If below, there is an inflationary gap. Prices probably will start to rise, pulling the expenditure schedule down and reducing equilibrium GNP. If above, there is a recessionary gap, and history suggests that prices will fall only slowly. In the interim, there will be a period of high unemployment.

In short, once we adjust the expenditure schedule to include the effects of taxes, the determination of national income proceeds exactly as before. The effects of government spending and taxation, therefore, are fairly straightforward and can be summarized as follows:

Government purchases of goods and services *add* to total spending directly through the G component of C + I + G. Taxes indirectly reduce total spending by lowering disposable income and thus reduce the C component of C + I + G. On balance, then, the government's actions may raise or lower the equilibrium level of GNP, depending on how much spending and taxing it does.

Notice one interesting feature of our example. With government purchases of $800 billion and taxes equal to 25 percent of GNP, the economy's equilibrium is at Y = $4000 billion (see Figure 12–4 or Table 12–3), the same as it was with G = 0 and no taxes. But tax receipts are $1000 billion when GNP is $4000 billion. This means that $1000 billion in taxes must have decreased GNP by the same amount as $800 billion in spending increased it. Apparently:

The multiplier for changes in taxes is smaller than the multiplier for changes in government purchases.

Let us see why.

Multipliers for Tax Policy

Because they work indirectly via consumption, multipliers for tax changes must be worked out in two steps.

Step 1. Before turning to the 45° line diagram, we must figure out what any proposed change in the tax law is likely to do to the consumption schedule.

Step 2. We can then enter this effect as a shift of the C + I + G schedule in the 45° line diagram and work out the multiplier.

A reduction in income taxes provides a convenient example of this two-step analysis, because we have already done step 1 in an earlier chapter. Specifically, in Chapter 8 we studied how consumer spending would respond to a cut in income taxes. We concluded that if the tax reduction were viewed as permanent, consumers would increase their spending by an amount equal to the tax cut times the marginal propensity to consume. (If you need review, turn back to pages 144–48.)

This is the shift that must be entered in the 45° line diagram to complete step 2, and Figure 12–5 displays such a shift. The tax cut raises the expenditure schedule from $C_0 + I + G$ to $C_1 + I + G$ by raising its C component. The diagram then shows the multiplier effect on GNP, which rises from Y_0 to Y_1.

In our numerical example, income tax receipts rise from zero to $1000 billion. So step 1 instructs us to multiply the $1000 billion in added income taxes by the marginal propensity to consume (MPC), which is 0.8, to get $800 billion as the estimated vertical shift of the consumption schedule at Y = $4000 billion. Notice that this is precisely equal to the $800 billion increase in government purchases. So, in this example, the *downward* shift of the C schedule exactly offsets the *upward* shift of the G schedule when Y = $4000, leading to no net change in the C + I + G schedule. That is why the equilibrium level of GNP did not change when we introduced the government.

Figure 12–5
THE MULTIPLIER FOR A
REDUCTION IN INCOME
TAXES
In this example, the $C + I + G$ schedule is shifted upward from $C_0 + I + G$ to $C_1 + I + G$, by a tax cut. Equilibrium GNP therefore increases from Y_0 to Y_1.

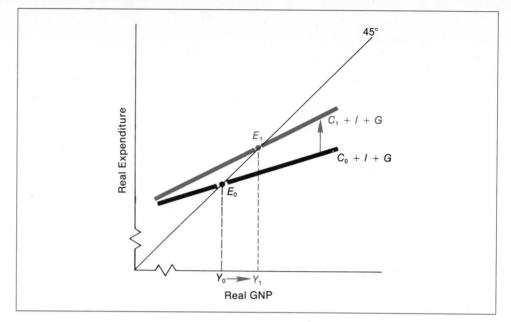

Thus we see the reason why the multiplier for income taxes is lower than the multiplier for government purchases: while G is a direct component of $C + I + G$, taxes are not. Taxes work indirectly, first by changing disposable income and then by changing C. That is why we had to multiply the $1000 billion change in taxes by 0.8 to get the $800 billion shift of the C schedule. Economically, some of the change in disposable income affects *saving* rather than *spending*; so a one-dollar tax cut does not pack as much punch as a dollar of G. The fact that the multipliers for G and taxes differ in this way has an interesting implication:

If government purchases and taxes rise by equal amounts, the equilibrium level of GNP on the demand side will rise. If G and taxes fall by equal amounts, the equilibrium level of GNP on the demand side will fall.

Thus fiscal policies that keep the deficit the same do not keep aggregate demand the same—a lesson that politicians frequently forget.

Government Transfer Payments

Finally, we should mention the last major tool of fiscal policy: **government transfer payments.** How are transfers treated in our models of income determinations—like purchases of goods and services (G) or like taxes?

The answer follows readily from the circular flow diagram on page 221 or the accounting identity back on page 140. The important thing to understand about transfer payments is that they intervene between gross national product (Y) and disposable income (DI) in precisely the *opposite* way from income taxes. Specifically, starting with the wages, interest, rents, and profits that constitute the national income, we *subtract* income taxes to calculate disposable income. We do so because these taxes represent the portion of incomes that are *earned* but never *received* by consumers. But then we must *add* transfer payments because they represent sources of income that are *received* though they were not *earned* in the process of production. Thus, *transfer payments are basically negative taxes;* giving a consumer $1 in the form of a transfer payment is equivalent to reducing her taxes by $1.

So, in terms of the 45° line diagram, increases in transfer payments can be treated simply as decreases in taxes. And we see that Figure 12–5, which we devised to illustrate a tax cut, can also be used to illustrate a rise in unemployment benefits, or in social security benefits, or in any other such transfer payment. Similarly, the analysis of a decrease in transfer payments would proceed exactly like the analysis of an increase in taxes.

The Multiplier Revisited

We have now acquired most of the tools we need to understand how fiscal policy decisions are made. But, before senators or congressmen vote on the budget, they should have an idea of the magnitude of the multiplier. Our figure of 5 is too high, and we can now understand how the income tax works to lower its value. But before getting involved in the mechanics, let us understand the basic reason.

As we learned in Chapter 10, the multiplier works through a chain of spending and respending, as one person's expenditure becomes another's income. But, through taxation, some of the additional income leaks out of the circular flow at each stage. Specifically, if the income tax rate is 25 percent, when Generous Motors spends $1 million on salaries, workers actually receive only $750,000 in *after-tax* (or disposable) income. If workers spend 80 percent of this amount (based on an MPC of 0.8), spending in the next round will be only $600,000. Notice that this is only 60 *percent* of the original expenditure, not 80 *percent* as in our earlier example. Thus the multiplier chain for each original dollar of spending shrinks from:

$$1 + 0.8 + (0.8)^2 + (0.8)^3 + \ldots = \frac{1}{1 - 0.8} = \frac{1}{0.2} = 5$$

to:

$$1 + 0.6 + (0.6)^2 + (0.6)^3 + \ldots = \frac{1}{1 - 0.6} = \frac{1}{0.4} = 2\tfrac{1}{2}.$$

This is clearly a very large reduction in the multiplier. We thus have a second reason why our oversimplified multiplier formula of Chapter 10 gives an exaggerated impression of the size of the multiplier:

REASONS WHY THE OVERSIMPLIFIED MULTIPLIER FORMULA IS WRONG

1. It ignores price-level changes, which serve to reduce the size of the multiplier.
2. It ignores income taxes, which serve to reduce the size of the multiplier.

Of the two reasons, the second is much the more important in practice. In later chapters, we shall encounter still more reasons.

This conclusion about the multiplier is shown graphically in Figure 12–6, where we have drawn our $C + I + G$ schedules with a slope of 0.6 to reflect an MPC of 0.8 and a tax rate of 25 percent rather than the 0.8 slope that we used previously. The figure depicts the effect of an increase in government purchases

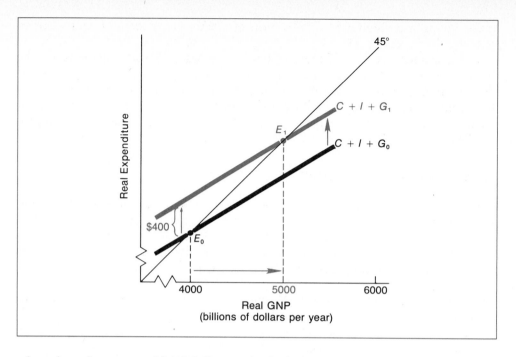

Figure 12-6

THE MULTIPLIER IN THE PRESENCE OF AN INCOME TAX

This diagram illustrates that an economy with an income tax (in this case a 25 percent income tax) has a lower multiplier than an economy without one. Specifically, the $C + I + G$ curve is shifted upward by a $400 billion increase in G, and the diagram shows that equilibrium GNP rises by $1000 billion — from $4000 billion to $5000 billion. The multiplier is therefore $1000/$400 = $2\frac{1}{2}$, whereas without an income tax it was 5.

of goods and services of $400 billion, which shifts the $C + I + G$ schedule from $C + I + G_0$ to $C + I + G_1$. Equilibrium moves from point E_0 to point E_1 — a growth in GNP from $Y = $4000 billion to $Y = $5000 billion. Thus, if we ignore for the moment any increases in the price level (which would reduce the multiplier shown in Figure 12-6), a $400 billion increment in government spending leads to a $1000 billion increment in GNP. So when taxes are included in our model, the multiplier is only $1000/$400 = $2\frac{1}{2}$, just as we concluded before.

Planning Expansive Fiscal Policy

Now, at last, you are ready to pretend that you are a member of Congress deciding how to respond to the president's proposed budget. Suppose that the economy would have a GNP of $4000 billion if last year's budget were simply repeated. Suppose further that your goal is to achieve a fully employed labor force and that staff economists tell you that your goal can be achieved with a GNP of approximately $5000 billion. Finally, just to keep the calculations manageable, suppose the price level is fixed. (We will drop this unrealistic assumption in just a few pages.) What budget should you vote for?

This question is far from hypothetical. When President Ronald Reagan took office in January 1981, the unemployment rate was 7.4 percent, and the gap between actual and potential GNP (in current prices) was estimated to be about $40 billion. He immediately scrapped President Carter's proposed budget and urged Congress to enact an entirely different fiscal policy, one which led to the largest peacetime budget deficits in American history. The ensuing debate over the budget has continued to this day.

Returning to our hypothetical example, what options are available if we want to raise GNP by $1000 billion? This chapter has taught us that Congress can raise government purchases, reduce taxes, or increase transfer payments by enough to close the recessionary gap between actual and potential GNP.

Figure 12-7 illustrates the problem, and its cure through higher government spending, on our 45° line diagram. Figure 12-7(a) shows the equilibrium

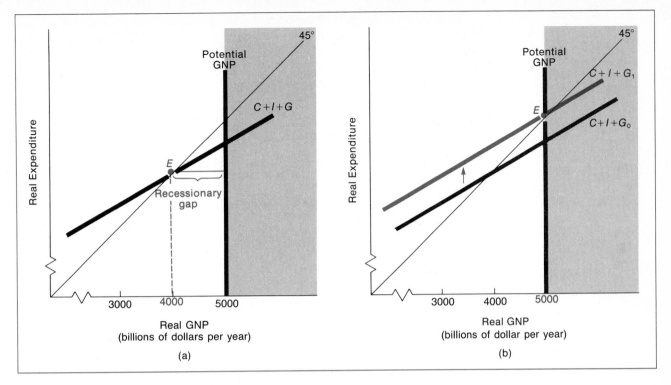

of the economy if no changes are made in the budget. Except for the full-employment line at $Y = \$5000$ and the corresponding recessionary gap, it looks just like Figure 12–4. With an expenditure multiplier of $2\frac{1}{2}$, you can figure out that an additional \$400 billion of government spending will be needed to push the GNP up \$1000 billion and eliminate this gap ($\$1000 \div 2\frac{1}{2} = \$400$).

So you might vote to raise G from $G_0 = \$800$ billion to $G_1 = \$1200$ billion, hoping to move the $C + I + G$ curve in Figure 12–7(a) out to the position indicated in Figure 12–7(b), thereby achieving full employment. Of course, you might prefer to achieve this fiscal stimulus by lowering income taxes rather than by increasing expenditures, as President Reagan did in 1981. Or you might prefer to rely on more generous transfer payments. The point is that there are a variety of budgets capable of pushing the economy up to full employment by increasing GNP by \$1000 billion. Figure 12–7 applies equally well to any of them.

Planning Restrictive Fiscal Policy

The preceding example assumed that the basic problem of fiscal policy is to overcome a deficiency of aggregate demand, as was the case at the start of the Reagan administration. Often this is so. But at other times the problem is that demand is excessive relative to the economy's capacity to produce. In this case, fiscal policy should assume a restrictive stance in order to reduce inflation.

It does not take much imagination to run our previous analysis in reverse. If, under a continuation of current budget policies, there would be an inflationary gap, contractionary fiscal policy tools can eliminate it. Either by cutting spending programs out of the budget, or by raising taxes, or by some combination of these policies, the government can pull the $C + I + G$ schedule down to a noninflationary position and achieve an equilibrium at full employment.

Figure 12–7
FISCAL POLICY TO ELIMINATE A RECESSIONARY GAP
This diagram shows, with more precision than can actually be achieved in practice, how fiscal policy can eliminate a recessionary gap. Part (a) shows the gap: Equilibrium GNP (\$4000 billion) falls short of potential GNP (\$5000 billion). Part (b) shows how fiscal policy—by moving the $C + I + G$ curve up just enough—can wipe out this gap and restore full employment. With a multiplier of $2\frac{1}{2}$, a rise in G of \$400 billion or a cut in taxes large enough to shift C up by \$400 billion would do the trick.

Notice the difference between this way of eliminating an inflationary gap and the natural self-correcting mechanism of the economy that we discussed in Chapter 11. There we observed that, if the economy were left to its own devices, a cumulative but self-limiting process of inflation eventually would eliminate the inflationary gap and return the economy to full employment. Here we see that it is not necessary to put the economy through the inflationary wringer. Instead, a restrictive fiscal policy can limit aggregate demand to the level that the economy can produce at full employment.

The Choice Between Spending Policy and Tax Policy

In principle, fiscal policy can nudge the economy in the desired direction equally well by changing government spending or by changing taxes. For example, if the government wants to expand the economy, it can raise G or lower taxes. Either policy shifts the total expenditure schedule upward, as depicted in Figure 12–7, thereby raising the equilibrium GNP on the demand side.

In terms of our aggregate demand and supply diagram, either policy shifts the aggregate demand curve outward, from $D_0 D_0$ to $D_1 D_1$ in Figure 12–8. As a result, the economy's equilibrium moves from point E to point A. Both real GNP and the price level rise. As this diagram points out, any combination of higher spending and lower taxes that produces the same aggregate demand curve leads to the same increases in real GNP and prices.

How, then, do we decide whether it is better to raise spending or to cut taxes? The answer depends mainly on how large a public sector we want, and this is a contentious issue.

One point of view, expressed most eloquently in the writings of John Kenneth Galbraith, is that there is something amiss when a country as wealthy as the United States has such an impoverished public sector. In Galbraith's view, America's most pressing needs are not for more designer jeans, sports cars, and VCRs, but rather for better schools, more efficient public transportation systems, and cleaner and safer city streets. Those who agree with him believe that we should *increase* G when the economy needs stimulus, and pay for these improved public services by *increasing taxes* when the economy needs to be reined in.

Figure 12–8
EXPANSIONARY FISCAL POLICY
Any of a variety of expansionary fiscal policies will push the aggregate demand curve outward to the right as depicted by the shift from $D_0 D_0$ to $D_1 D_1$ in this aggregate supply and demand diagram. The economy's equilibrium moves upward to the right along aggregate supply curve SS, from point E to point A. Comparing A with E, we note that output is higher but prices are also higher. The expansionary policy has caused some inflation.

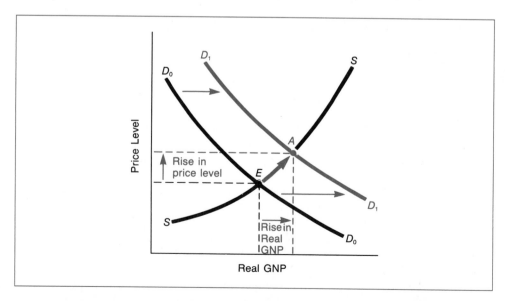

An opposing opinion, advocated most forcefully by President Ronald Reagan, gained the ascendancy in the 1980s. In this view, the government sector is already too large; we are foolish to rely on government to do things that private individuals and businesses could do better on their own; and the growth of government interferes too much in our everyday lives, and in so doing circumscribes our freedom. Those who hold this view argue for *tax cuts* when macroeconomic considerations call for expansionary fiscal policy, and for *reductions in public spending* when restrictive policy is required. That is precisely what President Reagan tried to do.

Too often the use of fiscal policy for economic stabilization is erroneously associated with a large and growing public sector—that is, with "big government." This need not be the case. Individuals favoring a smaller public sector can advocate an active fiscal policy just as well as those who favor a larger public sector. Advocates of big government budgets should seek to expand demand (when appropriate) through higher government spending and contract demand (when appropriate) through tax increases. By contrast, advocates of small public budgets should seek to expand demand by cutting taxes and reduce demand by cutting expenditures.

Some Harsh Realities

The mechanics outlined so far in this chapter make the fiscal policy planner's job look rather simple. The elementary diagrams suggest, rather misleadingly, that the authorities can drive GNP to any level they please simply by manipulating spending and tax programs. It seems as though they should be able to hit the full-employment bull's eye every time.

But, in fact, a better analogy is to shooting through dense fog at an erratically moving target with an inaccurate gun. The target is moving because, in the real world, the investment schedule (and, to a lesser extent, the consumption schedule) is constantly shifting on account of changes in expectations, new technological breakthroughs, changes in consumers' tastes, and the like. This means that the policies decided upon today, which are to take effect at some future date, may no longer be appropriate by the time that future date rolls around. Policy must be based, to some extent, on *forecasting*, and no one has yet discovered a foolproof method of economic forecasting.[4] Since our forecasting ability is so modest, and because fiscal policy decisions sometimes take a long time to be carried out, the government may occasionally find itself fighting the last inflation just when the new recession gets under way.

A second misleading feature of our diagrams is that multipliers are not known with as much precision as our examples suggest. Thus while the "best guess" may be that a $20 billion cut in government purchases will reduce GNP by $40 billion, the actual outcome may be as little as $24 billion or as much as $56 billion. It is therefore impossible to "fine tune" every wobble out of the economy's growth path through fiscal policy; economic science is simply not that precise. The point is even more cogent with respect to tax policy, for here we get involved in trying to guess whether consumers will view tax changes as permanent or temporary.

A third complication is that our target—full-employment GNP—may be only dimly visible, as if through a fog. Especially when the economy's last experience with full employment is far in the past, economists may have difficulty

[4]Some problems and techniques of economic forecasting are considered in Chapter 15.

estimating the GNP level that represents full employment. In fact, as mentioned in Chapter 6, there is much controversy right now over how much unemployment constitutes "full employment."

Finally, in trying to decide whether to push the unemployment rate lower, legislators would like to know what the inflationary costs are likely to be. As Figure 12–8 reminds us, any expansionary fiscal policy that closes a recessionary gap by increasing aggregate demand also pushes prices higher, that is, causes more inflation. This undesired side effect may make the government hesitant to use fiscal policy to end a recession.

Is there a way out of this dilemma? Can we stimulate the economy by fiscal policy without worsening inflation? During the late 1970s and 1980s, a small but influential minority of economists, journalists, and politicians argued that we could. They called their approach "supply-side economics."

The Idea Behind Supply-Side Tax Cuts

The central idea of supply-side economics is that certain types of tax cuts can be expected to increase aggregate supply. What kinds of measures are these? The basic principle is simple to state but not so simple to carry out in practice.

If taxes can be cut in a way that increases people's incentives to work, *and if people actually respond to these incentives,* then the tax system can be used to increase the total amount of labor that is available for employment. Similarly, if the tax system is changed in ways that encourage households to save more and businesses to invest more, *and if people respond to these changes in the way policymakers hope,* then the total amount of capital that is available for use will begin to rise. Both sorts of tax policies, then, if successful, will increase aggregate supply.

Figure 12–9 illustrates this conclusion on an aggregate supply and demand diagram. If policy measures can shift the economy's aggregate supply to position $S_1 S_1$, then prices will be lower and output higher than if the aggregate supply curve were $S_0 S_0$. Policymakers will have succeeded in reducing inflation and raising real output (lowering unemployment) at the same time. The trade-off between inflation and unemployment will have been defeated. This is the goal of supply-side economics.

Figure 12–9
THE IDEA BEHIND SUPPLY-SIDE TAX CUTS
The basic idea of supply-side cuts is that if they achieve their desired objective they will cause the economy's aggregate supply curve to shift outward to the right. For example the aggregate supply curve might be $S_1 S_1$ under a program of supply-side tax cuts, whereas it would only be $S_0 S_0$ without such tax cuts. In this case, if aggregate demand is the same in either case, the tax cuts would lead to the equilibrium point B instead of the equilibrium point A. Comparing B with A, we see that the program leads to lower prices and higher output.

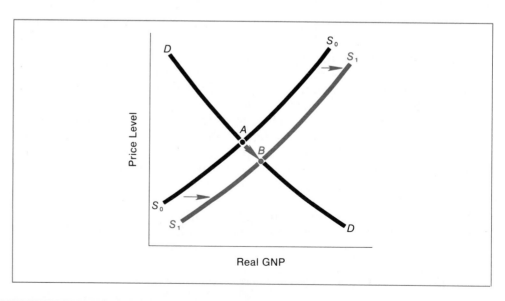

What sorts of policies do supply siders advocate? There is a long list, but most supply-side tax cuts are aimed at stimulating capital formation. For example:

1. **Accelerated Depreciation.** As mentioned in Chapter 9, a company investing in a machine or factory is not permitted to take the entire cost of that asset as a tax write-off in the year it is purchased. Instead, it must spread the cost over the lifetime of the asset in a series of **depreciation allowances** — annual tax deductions that in total add up to the value of the asset. Naturally, firms prefer to take their depreciation allowances sooner rather than later, because higher depreciation allowances in the early years of an investment mean lower immediate tax burdens.

   Many supply siders argue that an effective way to provide greater incentives for investment is to speed up ("accelerate") depreciation allowances. There are many ways to do this, and the details are best left to courses on accounting. However, one straightforward way is simple enough to explain right here. If Congress reduces the "lifetime" of a machine for tax purposes from, say, seven years to five years, then firms will get the tax savings from depreciation faster. That is precisely what President Reagan and Congress did in 1981.

2. **Reducing the Corporation Income Tax.** Another type of tax cut that supply siders often favor is reducing the statutory rates of taxation on corporate income. By letting companies retain more of their pre-tax income, it is argued, government will provide both greater investment incentives (by raising the profitability of investments) and more investable funds (by letting companies keep more of their earnings). This step was taken as part of the 1986 tax reform.[5]

3. **Reducing Taxes on Capital Gains.** Many investments, particularly financial investments such as stocks and bonds, often lead to **capital gains and losses.** For example, if Mr. Cabot purchases 100 shares of IBM stock in 1960 for $10,000 and sells them in 1988 for $100,000, the law says he has reaped a $90,000 *capital gain*, and must pay tax accordingly. Supply siders argue that lower taxes on capital gains provide greater incentives for individuals and firms to invest more, and, partly for these reasons, Congress reduced taxes on capital gains in 1979 and again in 1981. However, capital gains taxes were raised as part of the 1986 tax reform.

   > A **capital gain** is an increase in the market value of a piece of property, such as a common stock or a parcel of land, that occurs during the period between when it is bought and when it is sold. A **capital loss** is a decrease in that property's value.

   Not all supply-side tax cuts are aimed at spurring investment. If there is to be more investment, someone must be providing the saving to finance it. Thus, supply siders typically favor:

4. **Reducing Taxes on Income from Savings.** One extreme form of this proposal would simply exempt from taxation all income from interest and dividends. Since income must be either consumed or saved, this would, in effect, change our present personal income tax into a tax on consumer spending. While this has not been adopted, the income tax changes introduced in 1981 did contain several significant steps in this direction — including, most notably, permitting almost all wage-earners to shelter limited amounts of saving from taxation in Individual Retirement Accounts (IRAs). Supply siders promoted and applauded these changes. Nonetheless, the use of IRAs was restricted by the 1986 tax bill.

---

[5]However, in return, Congress eliminated the investment tax credit, an investment subsidy mentioned in Chapter 9.

Supply siders recognize that capital is not the only factor of production. Aggregate supply can be expanded by increasing the supply of labor services as well. For this reason, they generally advocate:

5. **Lowering Personal Income Tax Rates.** Such cuts, they argue, will encourage people to work harder and for longer hours, and will induce them to spend more time at productive activities and less time worrying about how to avoid taxes. In fact, sharp cuts in personal taxes have been the cornerstone of President Reagan's economic strategy. At the urging of the president, Congress passed a massive three-stage reduction in personal income taxes under which tax rates were reduced by 5 percent in 1981, an additional 10 percent in 1982, and a final 10 percent in 1983. Five years later, bracket rates were slashed again in the Tax Reform Act of 1986. Now, except in unusual circumstances, no American is in a tax bracket above 33 percent, and most taxpayers are in the 15 percent bracket. Such low tax rates, supply siders argue, should bolster incentives to work, to save, and to invest.

Finally, aggregate supply depends on the state of technology. So supply siders are interested in using the tax system to encourage technological progress by such measures as:

6. **Tax Credits for Research and Development.** Under a law enacted in 1981, companies that spend money on research and development (R & D) are entitled to reductions in their tax bills. The hope is obvious: Tax incentives should increase spending on R & D, and more R & D should lead to improvements in technology.

Let us suppose, for the moment, that a successful supply-side tax cut is enacted to help close a recessionary gap. Since *both* aggregate demand *and* aggregate supply increase simultaneously, the economy may be able to avoid the painful inflationary consequences of an expansionary fiscal policy that were shown in Figure 12–8.

Figure 12–10 illustrates this conclusion. The two aggregate demand curves and the initial aggregate supply curve $S_0 S_0$ are carried over directly from Figure 12–8. But we have introduced an additional supply curve, $S_1 S_1$, to

Figure 12–10

A SUCCESSFUL SUPPLY-SIDE TAX REDUCTION

A tax cut specifically aimed at the supply side, if successful, will shift *both* aggregate demand *and* aggregate supply to the right. In this diagram, equilibrium is initially at point E, where demand curve $D_0 D_0$ intersects supply curve $S_0 S_0$. After the supply-side tax cut, the aggregate demand curve is $D_1 D_1$ and the aggregate supply curve is $S_1 S_1$, so equilibrium is at point C. As compared with the results of a tax cut that works only on the demand side (point A), the supply-side tax cut raises output more and prices less

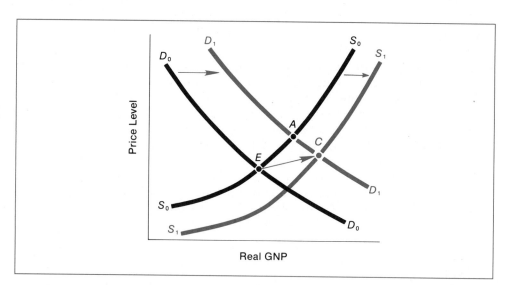

reflect the successful supply-side tax cut depicted in Figure 12–9. The equilibrium of the economy moves from E to C, whereas with a conventional demand-side tax cut it would have moved from E to A. As compared with point A, output is higher and prices are lower at point C.

A good deal, you say! Indeed it is. The supply-side argument is extremely attractive. It certainly appealed to candidate Ronald Reagan in 1980 and, as a consequence, it has had a profound influence on our nation's economic policy. But will it work in practice? Can we actually do what is depicted in Figure 12–10? Let us consider some difficulties.

Some Flies in the Ointment

Supply-side economics was, and remains, controversial. Supporters have touted it as a painless remedy for all our economic ills. Detractors have derided it as wishful thinking and branded it "voodoo economics."

Although supply-side economics has its critics, the critics rarely question the goals of the program or the basic idea that the tax system can be used to improve incentives. They argue, instead, that supply siders exaggerate the beneficial effects of supply-side tax cuts and ignore some undesirable side effects. Here is a list of the main objections to supply-side tax cuts that have fueled the great national debate since the late 1970s, a debate that is by no means over.

1. *Small Magnitude of Supply-Side Effects.* The first objection is that supply siders are simply too optimistic: We really do not know how to do what Figure 12–9 shows. It is easy to design tax cuts that, for example, make working more *attractive* financially, that is, which raise take-home pay. All you have to do is cut tax rates. Doing this, however, does not guarantee that people will actually work more. Instead, they may find themselves able to afford the goods and services they want with fewer hours of labor, and react by working *less*. Similarly, if tax cuts raise the return on savings, people may find their savings goals easier to achieve, and react by saving less.

   Most of the statistical evidence suggests that it is unrealistic to expect tax reductions to lead to substantial increases in either labor supply or household savings. Consequently, most economists expected President Reagan's tax cuts to lead to only modest increases in labor supply and saving—far less than avid supply siders predicted. As Charles Schultze, chief economic adviser to President Carter, quipped: "There's nothing wrong with supply-side economics that division by ten couldn't cure."

2. *Demand-Side Effects.* The second objection is that supply siders underestimate the effects of tax cuts on aggregate demand. If you cut personal taxes, individuals *may possibly* work more, but they *will certainly* spend more. If you reduce business taxes and thereby encourage expansion of industrial capacity, business firms will demand more investment goods.

   Two responses to this criticism have been made. Some of the more extreme proponents of supply-side economics have sought to deny the obvious, that is, to deny that supply-side tax cuts will stimulate aggregate demand. For example, according to supply-side advocate George Gilder: "The supply-sider denies that a tax cut can have any immediate effect on total disposable income or real aggregate demand."

   This wishful thinking was, fortunately, not President Reagan's response—at least in principle. His plan was to link the tax cuts to reductions in government spending that would cancel out the demand-side effects. Let us review the reasoning briefly. We learned in earlier chapters that tax cuts raise aggregate demand while reductions in government spending reduce it. Thus, whatever demand stimulus is caused by the tax cuts, there is some expenditure reduction big enough to cancel its demand-side effects. By combining these two programs into a fiscal package, it may be possible to obtain the situation depicted in Figure 12–9: a rise in aggregate supply with no accompanying rise in aggregate demand.

The problem with this strategy is that if *large* tax cuts are made, then *large* spending cuts must accompany them. Many observers in the early 1980s worried that the expenditure cuts proposed by President Reagan, while substantial, were much smaller than the tax cuts. In fact, we learned later that the president's own budget director, David Stockman, was among the skeptics. (See the boxed insert on page 240.) We also learned that the skeptics were right: The Reagan program actually cut taxes far more than it cut spending.

If we put these two objections together, we are led to Figure 12–11. Here we depict a small outward shift in the aggregate supply curve (which reflects the first objection) and a large outward shift of the aggregate demand curve (which reflects the second). The result is that the economy's equilibrium moves from point A (the intersection of $S_0 S_0$ and $D_0 D_0$) to point E (the intersection of $S_1 S_1$ and $D_1 D_1$). Prices rise as output expands. The outcome differs only a little from the straight "demand-side" fiscal stimulus depicted in Figure 12–8 (page 232).

3. ***Problems in Timing.*** The most promising types of supply-side tax cuts seek to encourage greater business investment by, for example, making depreciation allowances more generous. But investment does not create new industrial capacity overnight. It takes time to plan new investment projects, arrange the financing, get delivery on machinery, build factories, and then actually put these things into operation. The crucial point is that the *expenditures* on investment goods come before the *expansion of capacity*. Thus, even a supply-side optimist, if he is realistic, should recognize that supply-side tax cuts have their primary effects on aggregate demand in the short run. Effects on aggregate supply come later.

Figure 12–11
A MORE PESSIMISTIC VIEW OF SUPPLY-SIDE TAX CUTS
If the effect of supply-side tax initatives on the aggregate supply curve is actually much smaller than suggested by Figure 12–9, the anti-inflationary impact will be correspondingly smaller. As you can see in this diagram, it is possible that a large shift in the aggregate demand curve could overwhelm the favorable effects of the tax cuts on the price level.

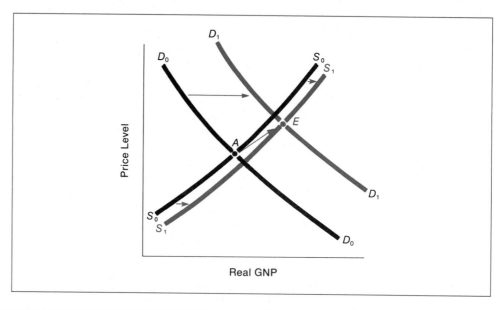

4. **Limited Effect on Inflation.** Supply-side policies were offered as a cure for inflation. Unfortunately, even a very successful supply-side program can be expected to make only a small dent in the inflation rate. The reason is a matter of simple arithmetic.

Inflation depends on the *difference* between the rates at which the *aggregate demand* and *aggregate supply* curves are shifting outward over time. Aggregate supply is, as a matter of definition, the product of the amount of labor available times the amount of output produced by each hour of labors—the **productivity** of labor. There is little that can be done to affect the long-run growth rate of labor supply, which depends fundamentally on population growth. Thus, if supply-side policies are to increase the growth rate of aggregate supply, they must focus on productivity.

But we learned in Chapter 7 that the historical growth rate of productivity in the United States is only about 2 percent per year. A 50 percent improvement in productivity growth would constitute a remarkable achievement. No serious economist thinks we really know how to achieve such a feat. But even a supply-side miracle of this magnitude would add only 1 percentage point to the growth rate of aggregate supply and therefore would lower the inflation rate by only about 1 percentage point—a very small effect.

5. **Effect on the Distribution of Income.** The preceding objections all pertain to the likely effects of supply-side policies on aggregate supply and demand. But there is a very different problem that bears mention: Most supply-side initiatives would increase income inequality. Why? Because, while raising the incomes of the wealthiest members of our society may not be their primary aim, most supply-side cuts cannot help but concentrate benefits on the rich simply because it is the rich who earn most of the capital gains, interest, and dividends, and who own most of the corporations.

Indeed, this tilt toward the rich is almost an inescapable corollary of supply-side logic. The basic aim of supply-side economics is to increase the incentive for working and investing, that is, to increase the gap between the rewards of those who succeed in the economic game (by working hard, investing well, and so on) and those who fail. It can hardly be surprising, therefore, that supply-side policies tend to increase economic inequality.

6. **Losses of Tax Revenue.** You can hardly help noticing that most of the policies suggested by supply siders involve reductions in one tax or another. Thus, unless some other tax is raised or spending is cut, supply-side tax cuts are bound to raise the government budget deficit. Critics of President Reagan's program, for example, argued that such large tax cuts would leave monstrous budget deficits for years to come.

Once again, extreme supply siders answered this objection by denying the obvious. Lower tax rates, they argued, need not lead to lower tax revenues if the tax base grows quickly enough. For example, suppose the GNP starts at $4000 billion when the tax rate is 25 percent; so the government collects $1000 billion in tax revenues. Then, if the tax rate is cut to 20 percent, but GNP grows to $5000 billion as a result, tax receipts will remain at $1000 billion. Reasoning like this led extreme supply siders like Professor Arthur Laffer to predict that the Reagan tax cuts would actually lead to more tax revenue and smaller budget deficits![6]

---

[6]The famous Laffer Curve is a graph showing how tax revenues first rise, but then fall, as the tax rate rises from zero, to 10 percent, then 20 percent, and so on up to 100 percent. Therefore, if tax rates are high enough, the reasoning goes, we can actually raise more revenue by cutting rates.

Reaganomics and the Budget: An Insider's View

President Reagan's original economic package was advertised as an equal reduction in taxes and spending. The incoming administration actually promised to balance the budget by fiscal year 1984*—a promise greeted with disbelief by those outside the administration. Later we learned that the most knowledgeable insider, Budget Director David Stockman, was the biggest skeptic of all. He told his story in his controversial book, *The Triumph of Politics: Why the Reagan Revolution Failed* (New York: Harper & Row, 1986), from which the following quotations are taken.

Even before he took over the Office of Management and Budget (OMB) in January 1981, Stockman realized that supply-side tax cuts would open a huge budget gap that could be closed only by gigantic budget cuts. Though worried that "I was the only one who had done even a minimal degree of . . . homework on the fundamental fiscal math," he welcomed the opportunity. "We would have the . . . politicians pinned to the wall. They would have to dismantle . . . bloated, wasteful, and unjust spending enterprises—or risk national ruin." Only in retrospect did he realize that, "Designing a comprehensive plan to bring about a sweeping change in national economic governance in forty days is a preposterous, wantonly reckless notion."

Energized by an ideological commitment to smaller government, Stockman prepared thick books of proposed budget cuts "chock-a-block with details and apparent precision (to) give the impression that the economic program was being launched with . . . admirable preparation. In fact, . . . critical loose ends were left unresolved everywhere." Then, in early February, bad news came: The OMB's computer models said the tax cuts would leave a 1984 deficit of $130 billion even with an optimistic forecast and all the proposed cuts. After that, Stockman "became a veri-

table incubator of shortcuts, schemes, and devices to overcome the truth."

Time was short, however, for the president was to present his program to Congress on February 18th. "As we went into the final ten days, the President of the United States was not even given the slightest warning that his economic policy revolution was bursting at the seams . . . the final week of White House deliberations on the economic plan gave new meaning to the concept of chaos." The document issued on February 18th claimed that the tax cuts would reduce revenues in fiscal year 1982 by $54 billion, most of which would be paid for by $41 billion in budget cuts. It projected budget balance by 1984 even though Stockman's internal calculations were showing a deficit of $130 billion or more. "The original budget plan I had devised . . . had been fatally flawed . . . the massive tax cut . . . never stood a chance of being paid for by a commensurate shrinkage of the welfare state."

Negotiations with Congress widened the budget gap as spending cuts were trimmed and tax cuts fattened. Stockman's budgeteers tried to square the circle with accounting gimmicks, but by November 1981 "it had become overwhelmingly clear that the . . . original political and economic assumptions were wrong by a country mile. . . . Now even the most outlandishly optimistic forecast . . . gave us triple-digit deficits . . . as far as the eye could see." We still have them.

*The fiscal year of the U.S. government runs from October 1st to September 30th. Thus fiscal year 1984 began on October 1, 1983.

To the vast majority of economists, this claim was implausible on its face. In the preceding example, if the GNP starts at $4000 billion, a cut in the tax rate from 25 percent to 20 percent lowers tax revenues initially by $200 billion (from $1000 billion to $800 billion). For this to cause a $1000 billion increase in the GNP (from $4000 billion to $5000 billion), the tax multiplier would have to be $1000/$200 = 5. This is about three times as large as the actual multiplier is believed to be. Turning from hypothetical examples to reality, federal tax revenues did not rise, but rather fell sharply after the 1982–1983 tax cuts—just as the critics had predicted. And the large budget deficits that ensued have been a major economic issue ever since.[7]

Toward Assessment of Supply-Side Economics

On balance, most economists have reached the following conclusions about supply-side tax initiatives:

1. The likely effectiveness of supply-side tax cuts depends very much on what kinds of taxes are cut. Tax reductions aimed at stimulating business investment are likely to pack more punch than tax reductions aimed at getting people to work longer hours or to save more.

2. Such tax cuts probably will increase aggregate supply, but the increase in aggregate supply will come much more slowly than the increase in aggregate demand. Thus supply-side policies should not be thought of as a substitute for short-run stabilization policy, but rather as a way to promote (slightly) faster economic growth in the long run.

3. Demand-side effects of supply-side tax cuts are likely to be much larger than supply-side effects, especially in the short run.

4. Supply-side policies can be expected to make, at most, only a small dent in the inflation rate.

5. Supply-side tax cuts are likely to benefit the rich more than the poor.

6. Supply-side tax cuts are almost certain to lead to bigger, not smaller, budget deficits.

But this list does not close the books on the issue. It does not even tell us whether supply-side tax cuts are a good idea or a bad one. Some people will look over this list and decide that they favor supply-side tax cuts; indeed, many economists and most of the Congress supported President Reagan's program in 1981. Others, perusing the same facts, will reach the opposite conclusion. We cannot say that either group is "wrong" because, like almost every economic policy, supply-side economics has its pros and cons.

Why, then, did so many economists and politicians react so negatively to supply-side economics in the early 1980s? The main reason seems to be that the claims made by the most ardent supply siders were clearly excessive. Naturally, these claims were proven wrong. But showing that wild claims are wild does not dispose of the kernel of truth in supply-side economics: Reductions in marginal tax rates do improve economic incentives. Any specific supply-side tax cut must be judged on its individual merits.

How did things work out after the Reagan tax cuts of 1981? Although supply siders had predicted an exuberant boom, the U.S. economy in 1981–1982 suffered through its worst recession since the Great Depression. But, when recovery finally came, the economy grew rapidly in 1983 and into 1984—

[7]Chapter 16 is devoted to the causes and consequences of budget deficits.

Are Marginal Tax Rates of Marginal Importance?

When Congress passed President Reagan's program of supply-side tax cuts in 1981, not everyone was convinced that they would have the dramatic effects that the president predicted. Here's how two humorists greeted the president's policy.

The Reagan administration has launched a radical economic experiment based on top officials' Promethean understanding of the psyches of American workers. The new economic team has divined that only one question burns in the mind of the modern American worker: What is my marginal tax rate?

Let us look in on a typical American family as they make crucial economic decisions. The digital alarm woke John Galt Workingstiff at 7:14 A.M., confronting him with the first of many rational choices of the day. Could he increase his family's economic well-being more by resting, thus boosting his productivity later in the day, or by rising early to check the economic indicators?

Kemp, 10, and Roth, 8, were at their Radio Shack microcomputer consoles. "We're going short in rutabagas today, Dad," said the eldest, his shoe-button eyes alight with glee. Workingstiff was stern. "You know the rules," he said. "If you can't net enough income today to offset my property tax, you have to recoup it by going to school."

Workingstiff glanced at the digital clock. 8:36. His shift at the Wonder Widget factory was set to start at 9. But what did it matter if he was a little late? Venal union officials would protect his featherbedding habits. And his union dues were fully deductible.

Anyway, why shouldn't he stay home and miss a half day's work? The worst that could happen was that he would lose his job. Unemployment benefits, after all, were tax free.

Suddenly, burbles of excitement echoed from Kemp and Roth. "Daddy!" they cried. "In a dramatic late-night session, Congress passed a major tax-cut bill! It's retroactive! President Reagan is to sign it this morning!"

But Workingstiff was apathetic. "I don't care about a general tax bill," he grumbled. "What does it do to my marginal tax rate?"

"That's cut 10 percent in the first year!" said Kemp.

"And there's more to come. And it's predictable!" chimed in Roth.

The effect was galvanic. Workingstiff reached for his coat, calculator and lunch pail. As he swung behind the wheel, he felt bullish on America. "Don't wait dinner for me," he shouted, "I think I'll work the second shift."

He backed down the drive and into Elm Street. Around him spread the productive pageant of his beloved Anytown, U.S.A., bustling with economic vigor and unleashed productive energy. Before him, in the direction of the Wonder Widget factory, loomed high vistas of achievement: zooming productivity, tranquil labor management relations, victory over the Japanese and Germans. As his father had before him in 1941, he turned toward those mountains, and his face was bright with hope.

SOURCE: Excerpted with permission from Garrett Epps and Walter Shapiro, "You're the Marginal Tax Rate of My Eye," *The Washington Post*, March 1, 1981.

confounding many pessimistic forecasters. Since then, however, the expansion has been sluggish. There has been little if any evidence to date that supply-side incentives have increased saving, investment, or labor supply to any noticeable degree. But inflation did fall rapidly in the early 1980s and has remained low. Finally, income inequality did grow larger and, as already mentioned, the budget deficit grew ominously.

In a nutshell, then, the specific supply-side tax cuts enacted in 1981 appear to have had some beneficial effects and some harmful ones—as was to be expected. Was the program a good idea, on balance? America is still making that judgment.

Summary

1. The government's fiscal policy is its plan for managing aggregate demand through its spending and taxing programs. It is made jointly by the president and Congress.
2. Government purchases of goods and services (G) are a direct component of total spending. Therefore, they have the same multiplier as do autonomous changes in consumption or investment.
3. When income taxes are introduced, there is a difference between GNP and disposable income. Since consumer spending (C) depends on disposable income, any change in taxes will shift the consumption schedule on a 45° line diagram.
4. Shifts in the consumption function caused by tax policy are subject to the same multiplier as autonomous shifts in the consumption schedule. However, the income tax reduces the size of this common multiplier just as it reduces the size of the multiplier for G or for I.
5. Government transfer payments are treated like negative taxes, not like government purchases of goods and services, because they influence total spending only indirectly through their effect on consumption.
6. The net effect of the government on aggregate demand—and hence on equilibrium output and prices—depends on whether the expansionary effects of its spending are greater or smaller than the contractionary effects of its taxes.
7. The multiplier for changes in taxes is smaller than the multiplier for changes in government purchases.
8. If the multipliers were known precisely, it would be possible to plan any of a variety of fiscal policies to eliminate either a recessionary or an inflationary gap. Recessionary gaps can be cured by raising G, cutting taxes, or increasing transfers. Inflationary gaps can be cured by cutting G, raising taxes, or reducing transfers.
9. Active stabilization policy can be carried out either by means that tend to expand the size of government (by raising either G or taxes when appropriate) or by means that hold back the size of government (by reducing either G or taxes when appropriate).
10. Expansionary fiscal policy can cure recessions, but it normally exacts a cost in terms of higher inflation. This dilemma has led to a great deal of interest in "supply-side" tax cuts designed to stimulate aggregate supply.
11. Supply-side tax cuts aim to push the economy's aggregate supply curve outward to the right. If successful, they can expand the economy and reduce inflation at the same times—a highly desirable outcome.
12. But critics point out five problems of supply-side tax cuts: They also stimulate aggregate demand; the beneficial effects on aggregate supply may be small; the demand-side effects occur before the supply-side effects; they make the income distribution more unequal; and large tax cuts lead to large budget deficits.
13. Supply-side policies can be expected to make only a small contribution to the long-term battle against inflation.

Concepts for Review

Fiscal policy
Goverment purchases of goods
    and services (G)

Government transfer payments
Effect of income taxes on the multiplier
Supply-side tax cuts

Depreciation allowances
Capital gains and losses
Productivity

Questions for Discussion

1. Where in its annual budget cycle is the federal government right now? (Bring yourself up to date by reading the financial page of your local newspaper.)

2. Consider an economy in which tax collections are always $200 and in which the three components of aggregate demand are as follows:

GNP	TAXES	DI	C	I	G
$480	$200	$280	$210	$100	$200
540	200	340	255	100	200
600	200	400	300	100	200
660	200	460	345	100	200
720	200	520	390	100	200

Find the equilibrium of this economy graphically. What is the marginal propensity to consume? What is the multiplier? What would happen to equilibrium GNP if government purchases were raised by $15 and the price level were unchanged?

3. Now consider a related economy in which investment is also $100, government purchases are also $200, and the price level is also fixed. But taxes now vary with income, and as a result the consumption schedule looks like the following:

GNP	TAXES	DI	C
$480	$160	$320	$240
540	180	360	270
600	200	400	300
660	220	440	330
720	240	480	360

Find the equilibrium graphically. What is the marginal propensity to consume? What is the tax rate? Use your diagram to show the effect of an increase of $30 in government purchases. What is the multiplier? Compare this answer to your answer to Question 2 above. What do you conclude?

4. Explain why G has the same multiplier as autonomous shifts in C or I, while taxes have a different multiplier.

5. Return to the hypothetical economy in Question 2 and suppose that *both* taxes and government purchases are increased by $60. Find the new equilibrium under the assumption that consumer spending continues to be exactly three-quarters of disposable income (as it is in Question 2).

6. If the government today decides that aggregate demand is excessive and is causing inflation, what options are open to it? What if it decides that aggregate demand is too weak instead?

7. Discuss the difference between a government purchase of a good or service and a government transfer payment.

8. Suppose that you are in charge of the fiscal policy of the economy in Question 2. There is an inflationary gap with income at $600, and you want to reduce income to $540. What specific actions can you take to achieve this goal?

9. Now put yourself in charge of the economy in Question 3, and suppose that full employment comes at a GNP of $720. How can you push income up to that level?

10. Which of the proposed supply-side tax cuts appeals to you most? Draw up a list of arguments for and against enacting such a cut right now.

11. (More difficult) Consider an economy with a horizontal aggregate supply curve. Investment is fixed at $700, government purchases are $800, the consumption function is:

$$C = 100 + 0.8 \, DI \, ,$$

and taxes are one-quarter of GNP—making disposable income (*DI*) equal to three quarters of GNP. Find the equilibrium level of GNP. How would this equilibrium change if taxes were abolished? Compare your answer with the examples in this chapter.

Appendix
Algebraic Treatment of Fiscal Policy and Aggregate Demand

In this appendix we explain the simple algebra behind the fiscal policy multipliers discussed in the chapter. In so doing, we deal only with a simplified case in which prices do not change. While it is possible to work out the corresponding algebra for the more realistic aggregate demand–aggregate supply analysis with variable prices, the analysis is rather complicated and is best left to more advanced courses.

We start with the example used in the chapter (especially on pages 222–23 and 225–28). The government spends $800 billion on goods and services (G = 800) and levies an income tax equal to 25 percent of GNP. So if the symbol T denotes tax receipts:

$$T = .25\,Y.$$

Since the consumption function we have been working with is

$$C = 100 + 0.8\,DI,$$

where DI is disposable income, and since disposable income and GNP are related by the accounting identity

$$DI = Y - T,$$

it follows that the C schedule used in the 45° line diagram is described by the algebraic equation:

$$
\begin{aligned}
C &= 100 + 0.8(Y - T) \\
&= 100 + 0.8(Y - .25Y) \\
&= 100 + 0.8(.75Y) \\
&= 100 + 0.6\,Y.
\end{aligned}
$$

We can now apply the equilibrium condition for an economy with a government, which is:

$$Y = C + I + G.$$

Since investment in this example is $I = 700$, substituting for C, I, and G into this equation gives:

$$
\begin{aligned}
Y &= 100 + 0.6\,Y + 700 + 800 \\
0.4Y &= 1600 \\
Y &= 4000.
\end{aligned}
$$

This is all there is to finding equilibrium GNP in an economy with a government.

To find the multiplier for government spending, increase G by 1 and resolve the problem:

$$
\begin{aligned}
Y &= C + I + G \\
Y &= 100 + 0.6Y + 700 + 801 \\
0.4Y &= 1601 \\
Y &= 4002.5
\end{aligned}
$$

So the multiplier is $4002.5 - 4000 = 2.5$, as stated in the text.

To find the multiplier for an increase in fixed taxes, change the tax schedule to:

$$T = .25Y + 1.$$

Disposable income is then

$$DI = Y - T = Y - (.25Y + 1) = .75Y - 1,$$

so the consumption function is

$$
\begin{aligned}
C &= 100 + 0.8DI \\
&= 100 + 0.8(.75Y - 1) \\
&= 99.2 + 0.6Y.
\end{aligned}
$$

Solving for equilibrium GNP as usual gives:

$$
\begin{aligned}
Y &= C + I + G \\
Y &= 99.2 + 0.6Y + 700 + 800 \\
0.4Y &= 1599.2 \\
Y &= 3998.
\end{aligned}
$$

So a $1 increase in fixed taxes lowers Y by $2. The tax multiplier is -2.

Now let us proceed to a more general solution, using symbols rather than specific numbers. The equations of the model are as follows:

$$(1) \quad Y = C + I + G$$

is the equilibrium condition, as usual;

$$(2) \quad C = a + bDI$$

is the same consumption function we have used in the appendixes of Chapters 9 and 10;

$$(3) \quad DI = Y - T$$

is the accounting identity relating disposable income to GNP;

$$(4) \quad T = T_0 + tY$$

is the tax function, where T_0 represents fixed taxes (which were zero in our numerical example) and t represents the tax rate (which was 0.25 in the example). Finally, I and G are just fixed numbers.

We begin the solution by substituting (3) and (4) into (2) to derive the consumption schedule relating C to Y:

$$C = a + b\,DI$$

$$C = a + b(Y - T)$$

$$C = a + b(Y - T_0 - tY)$$

$$(5) \quad C = a - b\,T_0 + b(1 - t)Y.$$

You will notice that a change in fixed taxes (T_0) shifts the *intercept* of the C schedule while a change in the tax rate (t) changes its *slope*, as explained in the text (pages 224–25).

Next substitute (5) into (1) to find equilibrium GNP:

$$Y = C + I + G$$

$$Y = a - b\,T_0 + b(1 - t)Y + I + G$$

$$[1 - b(1 - t)]Y = a - b\,T_0 + I + G$$

or

$$(6) \quad Y = \frac{a - bT_0 + I + G}{1 - b(1 - t)}.$$

Equation (6) shows us that G has the same multiplier as I or a, and that this multiplier is:

$$\text{Multiplier} = \frac{1}{1 - b(1 - t)}.$$

To see that this is in fact the multiplier, raise G or I or a by 1 unit. In each case, equation (6) would be changed to read:

$$Y = \frac{a - b\,T_0 + I + G + 1}{1 - b(1 - t)}.$$

Subtracting equation (6) from this expression gives the change in Y stemming from a one-unit change in G or I or a:

$$\text{Change in Y} = \frac{1}{1 - b(1 - t)}.$$

We noted in Chapter 10 (page 190) that if there were no income tax ($t = 0$), a realistic value for b (the marginal propensity to consume) would yield a multiplier of 10, which is much bigger than the true multiplier. Now that we have added taxes to the model, our multiplier formula produces much more realistic numbers. Reasonable values for the parameters for the U.S. economy are $b = \frac{9}{10}$ and $t = \frac{1}{3}$. The multiplier formula then gives:

$$\text{Multiplier} = \frac{1}{1 - \frac{9}{10}\left(1 - \frac{1}{3}\right)} = \frac{1}{1 - \frac{9}{10} \times \frac{2}{3}}$$

$$= \frac{1}{1 - \frac{6}{10}} = \frac{1}{\frac{4}{10}} = 2.5,$$

which is not far from its actual estimated value, nearly 2.

Finally, we can see from equation (6) that the multiplier for a change in fixed taxes (T_0) is:

$$\text{Tax multiplier} = \frac{-b}{1 - b(1 - t)}.$$

For the example considered in the text and earlier in this appendix, $b = 0.8$ and $t = 0.25$, so the formula gives:

$$\frac{-.8}{1 - .8(1 - .25)} = \frac{-.8}{1 - .8(.75)}$$

$$= \frac{-.8}{1 - .6} = \frac{-.8}{.4} = -2.$$

According to these figures, each $1 *increase* in T_0 *reduces* Y by $2.

Questions for Discussion

1. In an economy described by the following set of equations:

$$C = 10 + .9DI$$

$$I = 200$$

$$G = 360$$

$$T = 100 + (1/3)Y,$$

find the equilibrium level of GNP. Then find the multipliers for government purchases and for fixed taxes. If it is desired to lower GNP by 100, what are some policies that would do the trick?

2. This is a variant of the previous problem that approaches things the way a fiscal policy planner might. In an economy whose consumption function and tax function are as given in Question 1, and

with investment fixed at 200, find the value of G that would make GNP equal to 1400.

3. You are given the following information about an economy.

$$C = 20 + .8(Y - T)$$

$$I = 100$$

$$G = 520$$

$$T = .25Y$$

a. Find equilibrium GNP and the budget deficit.
b. Suppose the government, unhappy with the budget deficit, decides to cut government spending by precisely the amount of the deficit in (a). What actually happens to the budget deficit and why?

4. (More difficult) In the economy considered in Question 3, suppose the government, seeing that it has not wiped out the deficit, keeps cutting G until it succeeds in balancing the budget. What levels of GNP will then prevail?

13

Money and the Banking System

[Money] is a machine for doing quickly and commodiously what would be done, though less quickly and commodiously, without it.

JOHN STUART MILL

The circular flow diagrams that were used in earlier chapters to explain equilibrium GNP (see, for example, Figure 12–1 on page 221) had a "financial system" in their upper left-hand corners. Savings flowed into this system and investment flowed out. Something obviously goes on inside the financial system to channel the saving into investment, and it is time we learned just what this something is.

There is another, equally important, reason for studying the financial system. *Fiscal policy* is not the only lever the government has on the economy's aggregate demand curve: It also exercises significant control over aggregate demand by manipulating *monetary policy*. If we are to understand monetary policy (the subject of Chapters 14 and 15), we must first acquire some understanding of the financial system.

The present chapter has three major objectives. It first seeks to explain the nature of money: what it is, what purposes it serves, and how it is measured. Once this is done, we turn our attention to the banking system, explaining its historical origins, the nature of banking as a business, and why this industry is so heavily regulated. Finally, we learn how banks create money—a subject that is of great importance because it is simply impossible to understand monetary policy without knowing how money is created.

At the end of the chapter, we will see why government authorities must exercise control over the supply of money in a modern economy, and this leads naturally into the discussion in Chapter 14 of *central banking*, that is, the techniques used to implement monetary policy. Then, we will integrate what we will by then have learned about money and monetary policy into our model of income determination.

Policy Issue: Deregulating the Banks

The United States is in the process of deregulating its banking system. Almost all legal limitations on interest rates have been abolished, and the government is allowing banks to engage in an ever-widening spectrum of financial activities. As a result, banks are rapidly becoming supermarkets of finance where, in addition to normal banking services like keeping an account and taking out loans, you can buy or sell stocks and bonds, purchase life insurance, have your electric bill paid, and many other things.

Bank deregulation has sparked controversy. Most observers applaud deregulation and believe it will make our economy more efficient. But some fear that deregulation will change our financial system in unpredictable ways, perhaps making it more fragile and harder to control. To make an informed judgment on deregulation, we must first ask a basic question: Why were banks so heavily regulated in the first place?

Banking is certainly not heavily monopolized. While there are financial giants such as Citibank (New York) and Bank of America (California), the industry is populated by literally thousands of small banks located in cities and towns throughout the country. There are more than 14,000 commercial banks and over 5000 savings institutions nationwide. So why did government regulations formerly tell banks, to some degree, how much they could accept in deposits, how much interest they could pay on these deposits, what types of investments they could make, and so on?

A first reason is that the major "output" of the banking industry — the nation's supply of money — is an important determinant of aggregate demand, as we will see in Chapter 14. Bank managers presumably do what is best for their stockholders. That, at any rate, is their job. But as we shall see, what is best for bank stockholders may not be best for the whole economy. For this reason, the government does not allow bankers to determine the level of the nation's money supply by profit considerations alone.

A second reason for the extensive regulation of banks is concern for the safety of depositors. In a free-enterprise system, new businesses are born and die every day; and no one save those people immediately involved takes much notice of these goings-on. When a firm goes bankrupt, stockholders lose money and employees may lose their jobs. (The latter may not even happen if new management takes over the assets of the bankrupt firm.) But, except for the case of very large firms, that is about it.

But banking is different. If banks were treated like other firms, depositors would lose money whenever one went bankrupt. That is bad enough by itself, but the real danger comes in the case of a **run on a bank.** When depositors get jittery about the security of their money, they may all rush in at once to cash in their accounts. For reasons we will learn in this chapter, most banks could not survive a "run" like this and would be forced into insolvency. Worse yet, this disease is highly contagious. If Mrs. Smith hears that her neighbor has just lost her life savings because the Main Street National Bank went broke, she is quite likely to rush to her own bank to make a hefty withdrawal. In fact, that is precisely what happened in 1985 when savings banks in Ohio and Maryland got into trouble.

A **run on a bank** occurs when many depositors withdraw cash from their accounts all at once.

Without modern forms of bank regulation, therefore, one bank failure might lead to another; and indeed, bank failures were common throughout most of American history (see Figure 13–1 on page 250). But despite the upsurge in bank failures in recent years, the failure of a major bank nowadays is still rare enough to be newsworthy. The reason is that government has taken steps to ensure that such an infectious disease, if it occurs, will not spread. It has done this in several ways that will be mentioned in this chapter.

Barter Versus Monetary Exchange

Money is so much a part of our day-to-day existence that we are likely to take it for granted, failing to appreciate all that it accomplishes. But it is important to

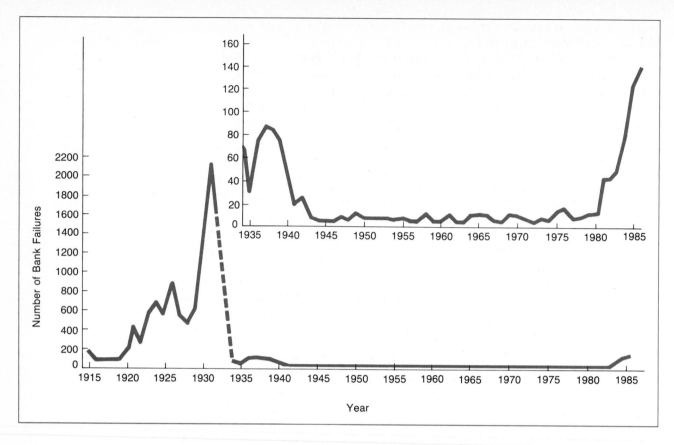

Figure 13–1
BANK FAILURES IN THE UNITED STATES, 1915–1986
This chart shows the number of commercial banks that failed each year from 1915 through 1986. Notice the sharp drop in the number of failures from 1932 to 1934 and the steep rise in recent years. Failures clearly are much less common in the postwar period than they were in earlier years.
SOURCE: Federal Deposit Insurance Corporation.

Barter is a system of exchange in which people directly trade one good for another, without using money as an intermediate step.

realize that money is very much a social contrivance. Like the wheel, it had to be invented. The most obvious way to trade commodities is not by using money, but by **barter**—a system in which people exchange one good directly for another. And the best way to appreciate what monetary exchange accomplishes is to imagine a world without it.

Under a system of direct barter, if Farmer Jones grows corn and has a craving for peanuts, he has to find a peanut farmer, say, Farmer Smith, with a taste for corn. If he finds such a person (this was called the *double coincidence of wants* by the classical economists), they make the trade. If this sounds easy, try to imagine how busy Farmer Jones would be if he had to repeat the sequence for every commodity he consumed in a week. For the most part, the desired double coincidences of wants are more likely to turn out to be double wants of coincidence, where Jones gets no peanuts and Smith gets no corn. Worse yet, with so much time spent looking for trading partners, Jones would have far less time to grow corn. Thus:

Money greases the wheels of exchange, and thus makes the whole economy more productive.

Under a monetary system, Farmer Jones gives up his corn for money. He does so not because he wants the money per se, but because of what that money can buy. Money makes his shopping tasks much easier, for it allows him simply to locate a peanut farmer who wants money. And what peanut farmer does not? For these reasons, monetary exchange replaced barter at a very early stage of human civilization, and only extreme circumstances, like massive wars and runaway inflations, have been able to bring barter (temporarily) back.

The Conceptual Definition of Money

Monetary exchange is the alternative to barter. In a system of monetary exchange, people trade **money** for goods when they purchase something and trade goods for money when they sell something; but they do not trade goods directly for other goods. This defines money's principal role as the **medium of exchange.** But once it has become accepted as the medium of exchange, whatever object is serving as money is bound to take on other functions as well. For one, it will inevitably become the **unit of account,** that is, the standard unit for quoting prices. Thus, if inhabitants of an idyllic tropical island used coconuts as money, they would be foolish to quote prices in terms of sea shells.

Money may also come to be used as a **store of value.** If Farmer Jones temporarily produces and sells corn of more value than he wants to consume, he may find it convenient to store the difference in the form of money until he wants to use it. This is because he knows that money can be "sold" easily for goods and services at a later date, whereas land, gold, and other stores of value might not be. Of course, if money pays no interest and inflation is substantial, he may decide to forgo the convenience of money and store his wealth in some other form rather than see its purchasing power rapidly eroded. So this role of money is far from inevitable.

Since money may not always serve as a store of value, and since there are many stores of value other than money, it is best not to include the store-of-value function as part of our conceptual definition of money. Instead, we simply label as "money" whatever serves as the medium of exchange.

What Serves as Money?

Anthropologists and historians will testify that a bewildering variety of things have served as money in different times and places. Cattle, stones, candy bars, cigarettes, woodpecker scalps, porpoise teeth, and giraffe tails are a few of the more colorful examples.

In primitive or less organized societies, the commodities that served as money generally had value in themselves. If not used as money, cattle could be slaughtered for food, cigarettes could be smoked, and so on. But such **commodity money** generally runs into several severe difficulties. To be useful as a medium of exchange the commodity must be divisible. This makes cattle a poor choice. It must also be of uniform, or at least readily identifiable, quality so that inferior substitutes are easy to recognize. This may be why woodpecker scalps never achieved great popularity. The medium of exchange must also be storable and durable, which presents a serious problem for candy-bar money. Finally, because commodity money needs to be carried and stored, it is helpful if the item is compact, that is, has high value per unit of volume and weight. (See the boxed insert on page 253).

All of these traits make it sensible that gold and silver have circulated as money since the first coins were struck about 2500 years ago. As they have high value in nonmonetary uses, a lot of purchasing power can be carried without too much weight. Pieces of gold are also storable, divisible (with a little trouble), and of identifiable quality (with a little more trouble).

The same characteristics suggest that paper would make an ideal money. Since we can print any number on it that we please, we can make paper money as divisible as we like and also make it possible to carry a large value in a lightweight and compact form. Paper is easy to store and, with a little cleverness, we can make counterfeiting hard (though never impossible). The Chinese

Money is the standard object used in exchanging goods and services. In short, money is the **medium of exchange.**

The **unit of account** is the standard unit for quoting prices.

A **store of value** is an item used to store wealth from one point in time to another.

A **commodity money** is an object in use as a medium of exchange, but which also has a substantial value in alternative (nonmonetary) uses.

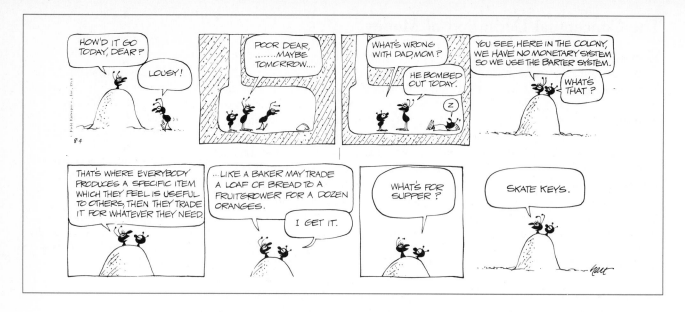

originated paper money in the eleventh century and Marco Polo brought word of this invention to Europe.

Paper cannot, however, serve as a commodity money because its value per square inch in alternative uses is so small. A paper currency that is repudiated by its issuer can, perhaps, be used as wallpaper or to wrap fish, but these uses will surely represent only a small fraction of the paper's value as money.[1] Contrary to the popular expression, such a currency literally *is* worth the paper it is printed on, which is to say that it is not worth much. Thus paper money is always **fiat money.**

Fiat money is money that is decreed as such by the government. It is of little value as a commodity, but it maintains its value as a medium of exchange because people have faith that the issuer will stand behind the pieces of printed paper and limit their production.

Money in the contemporary United States is almost entirely fiat money. Look at a dollar bill. Next to George Washington's picture it states: "This note is legal tender for all debts public and private." Nowhere on the certificate is there a promise, stated or implied, that the U.S. government will exchange it for anything else. A dollar bill is convertible into 4 quarters, 10 dimes, 20 nickels, or any other similar combination, but not into gold, chocolate, or any other commodity.

Why do people hold these pieces of paper? Only because they know that others are willing to accept them for things of intrinsic value—food, rent, shoes, and so on. If this confidence ever evaporated, these dollar bills would cease serving as a medium of exchange and, given that they make ugly wallpaper, would become virtually worthless.

But don't panic. This is not likely to occur. Our current monetary system has evolved over hundreds of years during which *commodity* money was first replaced by *full-bodied paper money* — paper certificates that were backed by gold or silver of equal value held in the issuer's vaults. Then the full-bodied paper money was replaced by certificates that were only partially backed by gold and silver. Finally, we arrived at our present system, in which paper money has no "backing" whatsoever. Like a hesitant swimmer who first dips her toes, then her legs, then her whole body into a cold swimming pool, we have "tested the water" at each step of the way—and found it to our liking. It is unlikely that we will ever take a step back in the other direction.

[1]The first paper money issued by the federal government, the Continental dollar, was essentially repudiated. (Actually, the new government of the United States redeemed the Continentals for 1 cent on the dollar in the 1790s.) This gave rise to the derisive expression, "It's not worth a Continental."

Dealing by Wheeling on Yap

Primitive forms of money still exist in some remote places, as this extract from a newspaper article shows.

Stone wheel money from Yap.

YAP, Micronesia — On this tiny South Pacific Island . . . the currency is as solid as a rock. In fact, it is rock. Limestone to be precise.

For nearly 2,000 years the Yapese have used large stone wheels to pay for major purchases, such as land, canoes and permission to marry. Yap is a U.S. trust territory, and the dollar is used in grocery stores and gas stations. But reliance on stone money . . . continues.

Buying property with stones is "much easier than buying it with U.S. dollars," says John Chodad, who recently purchased a building lot with a 30-inch stone wheel. "We don't know the value of the U.S. dollar."

Stone wheels don't make good pocket money, so for small transactions, Yapese use other forms of currency, such as beer. . . .

Besides stone wheels and beer, the Yapese sometimes spend *gaw*, consisting of necklaces of stone beads strung together around a whale's tooth. They also can buy things with *yar*, a currency made from large sea shells. But these are small change.

The people of Yap have been using stone money ever since a Yapese warrior named Anagumang first brought the huge stones over from limestone caverns on neighboring Palau, some 1,500 to 2,000 years ago. Inspired by the moon, he fashioned the stone into large circles. The rest is history. . . .

By custom, the stones are worthless when broken. You never hear people on Yap musing about wanting a piece of the rock . . .

SOURCE: Adapted from Art Pine, "Hard Assets, or Why a Loan in Yap is Hard to Roll Over," *The Wall Street Journal*, March 29, 1984, page 1.

How the Quantity of Money Is Measured

Since the amount of money in circulation is of profound importance for the determination of national product and the price level, it is important for the government to know how much money there is, that is, to devise some *measure* of the money supply.

Our conceptual definition of money describes it as the medium of exchange. But this raises questions about just what items should be included and what items excluded when we count up the money supply. Some items are easy. All of our coins, the small change of our economic system, clearly should count as money. So should paper money, which accounts for a far greater volume of transactions. But we cannot stop here if we want to include the main vehicle for making payments in our society, for the lion's share of our nation's payments are made neither in metal nor in paper money, but by check.

Checking deposits are actually no more than bookkeeping entries in bank ledgers. Many people think of checks simply as a convenient way to give coins or dollar bills to someone else. But that is not so. In fact, the volume of money held in the form of checking deposits far exceeds the volume of currency. For example, when you pay the grocer $50 by check, dollar bills rarely change hands. Instead, that check normally travels back to your bank, where $50 is deducted from the bookkeeping entry that records your account and added to the bookkeeping entry for your grocer's account. (If you and the grocer hold accounts at different banks, more books get involved; but still no coins or bills are likely to be moved.)

Since so many transactions are made by check, it seems imperative that checking deposits be included in any specific definition of the money supply. Unfortunately, this is not an easy task nowadays because of the bewildering variety of checkable accounts that are available to depositors. Traditional checking accounts in commercial banks are the most familiar; they offer unlimited check writing privileges, often free of charge, but pay no interest.

In the past decade, however, many other financial institutions have gotten into the act. For example, both banks and savings institutions offer *NOW* (negotiable order of withdrawal) accounts that pay a low, fixed rate of interest (about $5\frac{1}{2}$ percent) in return for certain service charges. These institutions also offer so-called *Super NOW* accounts, which pay market-determined interest rates that are higher than the rates paid by NOW accounts.

One popular definition of the money supply stops here and includes coins, paper money, travelers' checks, and *only* these three types of checking accounts. In the official U.S. statistics, this narrowly defined concept of money is called **M1.** The left-hand side of Figure 13–2 shows the composition of M1 as of August 1987.

But there are other types of accounts that allow withdrawals by check and which therefore are candidates for inclusion in the money supply. Most prominently, *money market deposit accounts* allow only a few checks per month but pay market-determined interest rates. Consumers have found these accounts extremely attractive vehicles for short-term investment, and balances in them now exceed all the checkable deposits included in M1.

[2]This includes travelers' checks and both NOW (negotiable order of withdrawal) and Super NOW accounts.

The narrowly defined money supply, usually abbreviated **M1,** is the sum of all coins and paper money in circulation, plus certain checkable deposit balances at banks and savings institutions.[2]

Figure 13–2
DEFINITIONS OF THE MONEY SUPPLY
(September 1987)
SOURCE: Federal Reserve.

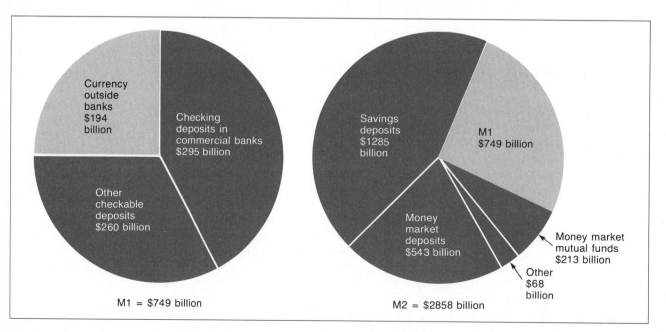

In addition, many mutual fund organizations and brokerage houses offer *money market mutual funds.* These funds sell shares and use the proceeds to purchase a variety of short-term securities. But the important point, for our purposes, is that owners of shares in money market mutual funds can withdraw their funds simply by writing a check. So depositors can use their holdings of fund shares just like checking accounts—and they do.

Finally, although you cannot write a check on a *savings account,* many economists feel that modern banking procedures have blurred the distinction between checking balances and savings balances. For example, many banks offer convenient electronic transfers of funds from one account to another, either by telephone or by pushing a button on an automated teller. Consequently, savings balances can serve the same purposes as checking balances. For this reason, savings accounts are included—along with money market deposit accounts, money market mutual fund shares, and a few other small items—in the broader definition of the money supply known as **M2.**

The composition of M2 as of August 1987 is shown on the right-hand side of Figure 13–2. You can see that savings accounts predominate, dwarfing everything that is included in M1. Figure 13–2 illustrates two points that are worth remembering. First, our money supply comes not only from banks, but also from savings institutions, brokerage houses, and mutual fund organizations. Second, however, banks still play a predominant role.

Some economists do not want to stop counting at M2; they prefer still broader definitions of money (M3, and so on) which include more types of bank deposits and other closely related assets. The problem with this approach is that there is no obvious place to stop, no clear line of demarcation between those assets that *are* money and those that are merely *close substitutes* for money—so called **near moneys.**

If we define an asset's **liquidity** as the ease with which it can be converted into cash, there is a range of assets of varying degrees of liquidity. Everything in M1 is completely "liquid"; the money market fund shares and passbook savings accounts included in M2 are a bit less so; and so on, until we encounter such things as short-term government bonds, which, while still quite liquid, would not normally be included in the money supply. Any number of different "Ms" can be defined—and have been—by drawing the line in different places.

And there are still more complexities. For example, credit cards clearly serve as a medium of exchange. So should they be included in the money supply? Yes, you say. But how would we do this? How much money does your credit card represent? If you think about questions like this for a while, you will realize that there are no easy answers—which is one reason why research on the definition of money continues.

But we do not want to get bogged down in complex definitional issues in a first course in economics. So we will simply adhere to the convention that *"money" consists only of coins, paper money, and checkable deposits.*

Now that we have defined money and seen how it can be measured, we turn our attention to the principal creators of money—the banks.

The broadly defined money supply, usually abbreviated **M2,** is the sum of all coins and paper money in circulation, plus all types of checking account balances, plus most forms of savings account balances, plus shares in money market mutual funds, and a few other minor items.

Near moneys are liquid assets that are close substitutes for money.

An asset's **liquidity** refers to the ease with which it can be converted into cash.

How Banking Began

When Adam and Eve left the Garden of Eden, they did not encounter a branch of Citibank. Banking had to be invented, and some time passed before it came to be practiced as it is today. With a little imagination, we can see how the first banks must have begun.

When money was made of gold it was most inconvenient for consumers and merchants to carry it around and weigh and assay it for purity every time a transaction was made. So it is not surprising that the practice developed of leaving one's gold in the care of a goldsmith, who had safe storage facilities, and carrying in its place a receipt from the goldsmith stating that John Doe did indeed own five ounces of gold of a certain purity. When people began trading goods and services for the goldsmiths' receipts, rather than for the gold itself, the receipts became an early form of paper money.

At this stage, paper money was fully backed by gold. But gradually the goldsmiths began to notice that the amount of gold they were actually required to pay out in a day was but a small fraction of the total gold they had stored in their warehouses. Then one day some enterprising goldsmith hit upon a momentous idea that must have made him fabulously wealthy.

His thinking probably ran something like this. "I have 2000 ounces of gold stored away in my vault, for which I collect storage fees from my customers. If I get much more, I'll need an expensive new vault. But in the last year, I was never called upon to pay out more than 100 ounces on a single day. What harm could it do if I lent out, say, half the gold I now have? I'll still have more than enough to pay off any depositors that come in for a withdrawal, so no one will ever know the difference. And I could earn 30 additional ounces of gold each year in interest on the loans I make (at 3 percent interest on 1000 ounces). With this profit, I could lower my service charges to depositors and so attract still more deposits. I think I'll do it."

With this resolution, the modern system of **fractional reserve banking** was born. This system has three important features — features that are crucially important to this chapter.

Fractional reserve banking is a system under which bankers keep as reserves only a fraction of the funds they hold on deposit.

1. *Bank profitability.* By getting deposits at zero interest and lending some of them out at positive interest rates, goldsmiths made a profit. The history of banking as a profit-making industry was begun and has continued to this date. *Banks, like other enterprises, are in business to earn profits.*

2. *Bank discretion over the money supply.* When goldsmiths decided that they could get along by keeping only a fraction of their total deposits on reserve in their vaults and lending out the balance, they acquired the ability to *create money*. As long as they kept 100 percent reserves, each gold certificate represented exactly one ounce of gold. So whether people decided to carry their gold or leave it with their goldsmith did not affect the money supply, which was set by the volume of gold.

   With the advent of fractional reserve banking, however, new paper certificates were added whenever goldsmiths lent out some of the gold they held on deposit. The loans, in effect, created new money. In this way, the total amount of money came to depend on the amount of gold that each goldsmith felt compelled to maintain as reserves in his vault. For any given volume of gold on deposit, the lower the reserves the goldsmiths kept, the more loans they could make, and therefore the more money there would be. While we no longer use gold to back our money, this principle remains true today. *Bankers' business decisions influence the supply of money.*

3. *Exposure to runs.* A goldsmith who kept 100 percent reserves never had to worry about a run on his vault. Even if all his depositors showed up at the door at once, he always had enough gold to return their deposits. But as soon as the first goldsmith decided to get by with only fractional reserves, the possibility of a run on the vault became a real concern. If that first

goldsmith who lent out half his gold had found 51 percent of his customers at his door one unlucky day, he would have had a lot of explaining to do. Similar problems have worried bankers for centuries. *The danger of a run on the bank has induced bankers to keep prudent reserves and to lend out money carefully.*

Principles of Bank Management: Profits Versus Safety

Bankers have a reputation, probably deserved, for conservatism in politics, dress, and business affairs. From what has been said so far, the economic rationale for this conservatism should be clear. Checking deposits are pure fiat money. Years ago, these deposits were "backed" by nothing more than the bank's promise to convert them into currency on demand. If people lost trust in a bank, the bank was doomed.

Thus, it has always been imperative for bankers to acquire a reputation for prudence. This they did (and continue to do) in two principal ways. First, they had to maintain a sufficiently generous level of reserves to minimize their vulnerability to runs. Second, they had to be somewhat cautious in making loans and investments, since any large losses on their loans would undermine the confidence of depositors.

It is important to realize that banking under a system of fractional reserves is an inherently risky business that is rendered relatively safe only by cautious and prudent management. America's continuing history of bank failures bears sober testimony to the fact that many bankers have been neither cautious nor prudent. Why? Because this is not a recipe for high profits. Bank profits are maximized by keeping reserves as low as possible, by making at least some risky investments, and by giving loans to borrowers of questionable credit standing (because these borrowers will pay the highest interest rates). The art of bank management is to strike the appropriate balance between the lure of profits and the need for safety. When a banker errs by being too stodgy, his bank will earn inadequate profits. When he errs by taking unwarranted risks, his bank may not survive at all. Many banks have perished in this latter way in recent years.

Bank Regulation

The public authorities, however, apparently have decided that the balance struck by profit-minded bankers often would not be at the place where society would like it struck. So government has thrown up a web of regulations designed to insure the safety of depositors and to control the supply of money.

The principal innovation guaranteeing the safety of bank deposits is **deposit insurance.** Today most bank deposits are insured against loss by the **Federal Deposit Insurance Corporation (FDIC)** or by the **Federal Savings and Loan Insurance Corporation (FSLIC)** — two agencies of the United States government. If your bank belongs to the FDIC or the FSLIC (and most do), your checking account is insured for up to $100,000 regardless of what happens to the bank. Thus, while bank failures may spell disaster for the bank's stockholders, they do not give many depositors cause for concern. Deposit insurance eliminates the motive for customers to rush to their bank just because they hear some bad news about the bank's finances. Many observers give this innovation much of the credit for the pronounced decline in bank failures since 1933, the year in which the FDIC was established. (Refer back to Figure 13–1 on page 250.) But the recent rash of bank failures has put a strain on the deposit insurance system.

Deposit insurance is a system that guarantees that depositors will not lose money even if their bank goes bankrupt.

In addition to insuring depositors against loss, the government takes steps to see that banks do not get into financial trouble. For one thing, various regulatory authorities conduct periodic *bank examinations and audits* in order to keep tabs on the financial condition and business practices of the banks under their purview. For another, laws and regulations *limit the kinds and quantities of assets in which banks may invest.* For example, most banks are prohibited from purchasing common stock. Both these forms of regulation are clearly aimed at maintaining bank safety.

A final type of regulation also has some bearing on safety but is motivated primarily by the government's desire to control the money supply. We have seen that the amount of money any bank will issue depends on the amount of reserves it elects to keep. For this reason, most banks are subject by law to minimum **required reserves.** While banks may (and sometimes do) keep reserves in excess of these legal minimums, they may not keep less. It is this regulation that places an upper limit on the money supply. The rest of this chapter is concerned with the details of this mechanism.

How Bankers Keep Books

Before we can fully understand the mechanics of modern banking and the process by which money is "created," we must acquire at least a nodding acquaintance with the way in which bankers keep their books. The first thing to know is how to distinguish assets from liabilities.

An **asset** of a bank is something of value that the bank *owns*. This "thing" may be a physical object, such as the bank building, a computer, or a vault, or it may be just a piece of paper, such as an IOU of a customer to whom the bank has made a loan. A **liability** of a bank is something of value that the bank *owes*. Most bank liabilities take the form of bookkeeping entries. For example, if you have a checking account in the Main Street Bank, your bank balance is a liability of the bank. (It is, of course, an asset to you.)

There is an easy test to see whether some piece of paper or bookkeeping entry is a bank's asset or liability. Ask yourself whether, if this paper were converted into cash, the bank would receive the cash (if so, it is an asset) or pay it out (if so, it is a liability). This test makes it clear that loans to customers are bank assets (when loans are repaid, the bank collects), while customers' deposits are bank liabilities (when deposits are cashed in, the bank must pay). Of course, things are just the opposite to the bank's customers: the loans are liabilities and the deposits are assets.

When accountants draw up a complete list of all the bank's assets and liabilities, the resulting document is called the bank's **balance sheet.** Typically, the value of all the bank's assets exceeds the value of all its liabilities. (On the rare occasions when this is not the case, the bank is in serious trouble.) In what sense, then, do balance sheets "balance"?

They balance because accountants have invented the concept of **net worth** to balance the books. Specifically, they have defined the net worth of a bank to be the difference between the value of all its assets and the value of all its liabilities. Thus, by definition, when accountants add net worth to liabilities, the sum they get must be the same as the value of the bank's assets. In short:

$$\text{Assets} = \text{Liabilities} + \text{Net Worth}.$$

Table 13–1 illustrates this with the balance sheet of a fictitious bank, Bank-a-mythica, whose finances are extremely simple. On December 31, 1987,

Required reserves are the minimum amount of reserves (in cash or the equivalent) required by law. Normally, required reserves are proportional to the volume of deposits.

An **asset** of an individual or business firm is an item of value that the individual or firm owns.

A **liability** of an individual or business firm is an item of value that the individual or firm owes. Many liabilities are known as "debts."

A **balance sheet** is an accounting statement listing the values of all the assets on the left-hand side and the values of all the liabilities and **net worth** on the right-hand side.

Net worth is the value of all assets minus the value of all liabilities.

Table 13–1
BALANCE SHEET OF BANK-A-MYTHICA, DECEMBER 31, 1987

ASSETS		LIABILITIES AND NET WORTH	
Assets		**Liabilities**	
Reserves	$1,000,000	Checking deposits	$5,000,000
Loans outstanding	4,500,000		
Total	$5,500,000		
Addendum: Bank Reserves		**Net Worth**	
Actual reserves	$1,000,000	Stockholders' equity	500,000
Required reserves	1,000,000		
Excess reserves	0		
		Total	$5,500,000

it had only two kinds of assets (listed on the left-hand side of the balance sheet) — $1 million in cash, which it held as reserves, and $4,500,000 in outstanding loans to its customers, that is, in customers' IOUs. And it had only one type of liability (listed on the right-hand side) — $5 million in checking deposits. The difference between total assets ($5.5 million) and total liabilities ($5 million) was the bank's net worth ($500,000), shown on the right-hand side of the balance sheet.

The Limits to Money Creation by a Single Bank

Let us now turn to the process of deposit creation. Many bankers will deny that they have any ability to "create" money. (The phrase itself has a suspiciously hocus-pocus sound to it.) But they are not quite right. For although any individual bank's ability to create money is severely limited in a system with many banks, the banking system as a whole can achieve much more than the sum of its parts. Through the modern alchemy of **deposit creation,** it can turn one dollar into many dollars. But to understand this important process, we had better proceed in steps, beginning with the case of a single bank, our hypothetical Bank-a-mythica.

According to the balance sheet in Table 13–1, Bank-a-mythica is holding cash reserves that are equal to 20 percent of its deposits ($1 million in cash is equal to 20 percent of the $5 million in deposits). Let us assume that this is the minimum reserve ratio prescribed by law and that the bank strives to keep its reserves down to the legal minimum; that is, it strives to keeps its **excess reserves** down to zero.

Now let us suppose that on January 2, 1988, an eccentric widower comes into Bank-a-mythica and deposits $100,000 in cash in his checking account. The bank now has acquired $100,000 more in cash reserves, and $100,000 more in checking deposits. But since deposits are up by $100,000, *required* reserves are up only by 20 percent of this amount, or $20,000, leaving $80,000 in *excess* reserves. Table 13–2 illustrates the effects of this transaction on Bank-a-mythica's balance sheet. It is tables such as this, which show *changes* in balance sheets rather than the balance sheets themselves, that will help us follow the money-creation process.[3]

Excess reserves are any reserves held in excess of the legal minimum.

[3]Notice that in all such tables, which are frequently called "T accounts," the two sides of the ledger must balance. This is because changes in assets and changes in liabilities must be equal if the balance sheet is to balance both before and after the transaction.

Table 13-2

CHANGES IN BANK-A-MYTHICA'S BALANCE SHEET, JANUARY 2, 1988

ASSETS		LIABILITIES	
Reserves	+ $100,000	Checking deposits	+ $100,000
Addendum: Changes in Reserves			
Actual reserves	+ $100,000		
Required reserves	+ 20,000		
Excess reserves	+ $ 80,000		

Bank-a-mythica receives a $100,000 cash deposit. It now holds excess reserves of $80,000, since required reserves rise by only $20,000 (20 percent of $100,000).

If Bank-a-mythica does not want to hold excess reserves, it will be unhappy with the situation illustrated in Table 13–2, for it is holding $80,000 in excess reserves on which it earns no interest. So as soon as possible it will lend out the extra $80,000 — let us say to Hard-Pressed Construction Company. This loan leads to the balance sheet changes shown in Table 13–3: Bank-a-mythica's loans rise by $80,000 while its holdings of cash reserves fall by $80,000.

By combining Tables 13–2 and 13–3, we arrive at Table 13–4, which summarizes all the bank's transactions for the week. Reserves are up $20,000, loans are up $80,000, and now that the bank has had a chance to adjust to the inflow of deposits, it no longer holds excess reserves.

Looking at Table 13–4 and keeping in mind our specific definition of money, it appears at first that the chairman of Bank-a-mythica is right when he claims not to have engaged in the nefarious practice of "money creation." All that happened was that, in exchange for the $100,000 in cash it received, the bank issued the widower a checking balance of $100,000. This does not change M1; it merely converts one form of money into another.

But wait. What happened to the $100,000 in cash that the eccentric man brought to the bank? The table shows that $20,000 was retained by Bank-a-mythica in its vault. Since this currency is no longer in circulation, it no longer counts in the official money supply. (Notice that Figure 13–2 included only "currency outside banks.") But the other $80,000, which the bank lent out, is still in circulation. It is held by Hard-Pressed Construction, which probably will redeposit it in some other bank. But even before this happens, the original

Table 13-3

CHANGES IN BANK-A-MYTHICA'S BALANCE SHEET, JANUARY 3–6, 1988

ASSETS		LIABILITIES
Loans outstanding	+ $80,000	No change
Reserves	− 80,000	
Addendum: Changes In Reserves		
Actual reserves	− $80,000	
Required reserves	No change	
Excess reserves	− $80,000	

Bank-a-mythica gets rid of its excess reserves by making a loan of $80,000 to Hard-Pressed Construction Company.

Table 13-4
CHANGES IN BANK-A-MYTHICA'S BALANCE SHEET, JANUARY 2–6, 1988

ASSETS		LIABILITIES	
Reserves	+ $20,000	Checking deposits	+ $100,000
Loans outstanding	+ 80,000		
Addendum: Changes in Reserves			
Actual reserves	+ $20,000		
Required reserves	+ $20,000		
Excess reserves	No change		

When it receives $100,000 in cash deposits, Bank-a-mythica keeps only the required $20,000 in reserves and lends out the remaining $80,000 to Hard-Pressed Construction Company. Its excess reserves return to zero.

$100,000 in cash has supported a rise in the money supply: there is now $100,000 in checking deposits and $80,000 in cash in circulation, making a total of $180,000. The money-creation process has begun.

Multiple Money Creation by a Series of Banks

Let us now trace the $80,000 in cash and see how the process of money creation gathers momentum. Suppose that Hard-Pressed Construction Company, which banks across town at the First National Bank, deposits the $80,000 into its bank account. First National's reserves increase by $80,000. But because deposits are up by $80,000, *required* reserves rise by only 20 percent of this amount or $16,000. If the management of First National Bank behaves like that of Bank-a-mythica, the $64,000 of excess reserves will be lent out.

Table 13–5 shows the effects of these events on First National Bank's balance sheet. (The preliminary steps corresponding to Tables 13–2 and 13–3 are not shown separately.) At this stage in the chain, the original $100,000 in cash has led to $180,000 in deposits—$100,000 at Bank-a-mythica and $80,000 at First National Banks—and $64,000 in cash, which is still in circulation (in the hands of the recipient of First National's loans—Al's Auto Shop). Thus, from the original $100,000, a total of $244,000 has been added to the money supply ($180,000 in checking deposits plus $64,000 in cash).

But, to coin a phrase, the bucks do not stop here. Al's Auto Shop will presumably deposit the proceeds from its loan into its own account at Second

Table 13-5
CHANGES IN FIRST NATIONAL BANK'S BALANCE SHEET

ASSETS		LIABILITIES	
Reserves	+ $16,000	Checking deposits	+ $80,000
Loans outstanding	+ 64,000		
Addendum: Changes In Reserves			
Actual reserves	+ $16,000		
Required reserves	+ 16,000		
Excess reserves	No change		

Hard-Pressed deposits its $80,000 in First National Bank, which sets aside the required $16,000 in reserves (20 percent of $80,000) and lends $64,000 to Al's Auto Shop.

Table 13–6
CHANGES IN SECOND NATIONAL BANK'S BALANCE SHEET

ASSETS		LIABILITIES	
Reserves	+ $12,800	Checking deposits	+ $64,000
Loans outstanding	+ 51,200		
Addendum: Changes In Reserves			
Actual reserves	+ $12,800		
Required reserves	+ 12,800		
Excess reserves	No change		

When Al deposits his $64,000 in Second National Bank, that bank retains $12,800 as required reserves (20 percent of $64,000) and lends out the remaining $51,200.

National Bank, leading eventually to the balance sheet adjustments shown in Table 13–6 when Second National makes an additional loan rather than hold on to excess reserves. You can see how the money-creation process continues.

Table 13–7 is a convenient tabular summary of the balance-sheet changes of the first five banks in the chain (from Bank-a-mythica through the Fourth National Bank) on the assumptions that each bank holds exactly the 20 percent required reserves (no excess reserves), and that each loan recipient redeposits the proceeds in the next bank. But the chain does not end there. For the Main Street Movie Theatre, which received the $32,768 loan from the Fourth National Bank, then deposits these funds into the Fifth National Bank. Fifth National has to keep only 20 percent of this deposit, or $6,553.60, on reserve and will lend out the balance. And so the chain continues.

Where does it all end? The last two lines of Table 13–7 show what eventually happens to all other banks and to the entire banking system. The initial deposit of $100,000 in cash ultimately leads to a total of $500,000 in new deposits (column 1) and a total of $400,000 in new loans (column 4). The money supply (column 5) rises by $400,000 because the initial transaction at Bank-a-mythica merely exchanges one form of money (currency in circulation) for another (checking deposits) and hence has no net effect on the money supply. But all the other transactions in the chain increase the money supply by the amount of new deposits.

Table 13–7
THE PROCESS OF MULTIPLE MONEY CREATION

BANK	(1) DEPOSIT RECEIVED	(2) REQUIRED RESERVES	(3) EXCESS RESERVES	=	(4) NEW LOANS	(5) ADDITION TO MONEY SUPPLY
Bank-a-mythica	+ $100,000	+ $20,000	+ $80,000		+ $80,000	0
First National Bank	+ 80,000	+ 16,000	+ 64,000		+ 64,000	+ $80,000
Second National Bank	+ 64,000	+ 12,800	+ 51,200		+ 51,200	+ 64,000
Third National Bank	+ 51,200	+ 10,240	+ 40,960		+ 40,960	+ 51,200
Fourth National Bank	+ 40,960	+ 8,192	+ 32,768		+ 32,768	+ 40,960
. . .						
All other banks	+ 163,840	+ 32,768	—		+ 131,072	+ 163,840
TOTALS	+ $500,000	+ $100,000	0		+ $400,000	+ $400,000

So there really is some hocus-pocus. Somehow, an initial deposit of $100,000 leads to $500,000 in new bank deposits—a multiple expansion of $5 for every original dollar—and a net increase of $400,000 in the money supply. We had better understand why this is so. But first let us verify that the calculations in Table 13–7 are correct.

If you look carefully at the table, you will see that each column of numbers forms a *geometric progression;* specifically, each entry is equal to exactly 80 percent of the entry that preceded it. Recall that in our discussion of the multiplier in Chapter 10 we learned how to sum an infinite geometric progression, which is just what each of these chains eventually will be. In particular, if the common ratio is R, the sum of an infinite geometric progression is

$$1 + R + R^2 + R^3 + \ldots = \frac{1}{1 - R}.$$

By applying this formula to the chain of checking deposits in column 1 of Table 13–7, we get:

$$\$100,000 + \$80,000 + \$64,000 + \$51,200 + \ldots$$
$$= \$100,000 \times (1 + 0.8 + 0.64 + 0.512 + \ldots)$$
$$= \$100,000 \times (1 + 0.8 + 0.8^2 + 0.8^3 + \ldots)$$
$$= \$100,000 \times \frac{1}{1 - 0.8} = \frac{\$100,000}{0.2} = \$500,000.$$

Proceeding similarly, we can verify that both columns 4 and 5 sum to $400,000 and that column 2 sums to $100,000. (Check these as exercises.)

So the numbers in Table 13–7 seem to be correct. Let us, therefore, think through the logic behind them. The chain of deposit creation can end only when there are no more excess reserves to be loaned out; that is, when the entire $100,000 in cash is tied up in *required* reserves. That explains the last entry in column 2. But, with a reserve ratio of 20 percent, excess reserves disappear only when checking deposits expand by $500,000—which is the last entry in column 1. Finally, since balance sheets must balance, the sum of all newly-created assets (reserves plus loans) must equal the sum of all newly-created liabilities ($500,000 in deposits). That leaves $400,000 for new loans—which is the last entry in column 4.

More generally, if the reserve ratio is some number R (rather than the $\frac{1}{5}$ in our example) each dollar of deposits requires only a fraction R of a dollar in reserves. Hence, deposits must expand by $1/R$ for each dollar of new reserves that are injected into the system. This suggests the general formula for multiple money creation when the required reserve ratio is some number R:

OVERSIMPLIFIED MONEY MULTIPLIER FORMULA

If the required reserve ratio is some fraction, R, an injection of $1 of excess reserves into the banking system can lead to the creation of $1/R$ in new money. That is, the so-called "money multiplier" is given by:

Change in deposits $= (1/R) \times$ Change in excess reserves.

Notice that this formula correctly describes what happens in our example. The initial deposit of $100,000 in cash at Bank-a-mythica creates $80,000 in *excess* reserves (the top entry in column 3 of Table 13–7). Applying a multiplier of $1/R = 1/0.2 = 5$ to this $80,000, we conclude that the money supply will rise by $400,000—which is just what happens.

The Process in Reverse: Multiple Contractions of the Money Supply

Let us now briefly consider how this deposit-creation mechanism operates in reverse—as a system of deposit *destruction*. In particular, suppose that our eccentric widower came back to Bank-a-mythica to withdraw $100,000 from his checking account and return it to his mattress, where it rightfully belongs. Bank-a-mythica's *required* reserves would fall by $20,000 as a result of this transaction (20 percent of $100,000), but its *actual* reserves would fall by $100,000. The bank would be $80,000 short, as indicated in Table 13–8(a).

How does it react to this discrepancy? As some of its outstanding loans are routinely paid off, the bank will cease granting new ones until it has accumulated the necessary $80,000 in required reserves. The data for Bank-a-mythica's contraction are shown in Table 13–8(b), assuming that borrowers pay off their loans in cash.[4]

But where did the borrowers get this money? Probably by making withdrawals from other banks. In this case, let us assume it all came from First National Bank, which loses an $80,000 deposit and $80,000 in reserves. It finds itself short some $64,000 in reserves [see Table 13–9(a)] and therefore must reduce its loan commitments by $64,000 [see Table 13–9(b)]. This, of course, causes some other bank to suffer a loss of reserves and deposits of $64,000, and the whole process repeats just as it did in the case of deposit expansion.

After the entire banking system had become involved, the picture would be just as shown in Table 13–7, except that all the *plus* signs would be *minus* signs. Deposits would shrink by $500,000, loans will fall by $400,000, bank reserves would be reduced by $100,000, and the money supply would fall by

[4]In reality, they would probably pay with checks drawn on other banks. Bank-a-mythica would then cash these checks to acquire the reserves.

Table 13–8
CHANGES IN THE BALANCE SHEET OF BANK-A-MYTHICA

(a)			(b)	
ASSETS	LIABILITIES		ASSETS	LIABILITIES
Reserves − $100,000	Checking deposits − $100,000		Reserves + $80,000 Loans outstanding − 80,000	
Addendum: Changes In Reserves			**Addendum: Changes In Reserves**	
Actual reserves − $100,000			Actual reserves + $80,000	
Required reserves − 20,000			Required reserves No change	
Excess reserves − $ 80,000			Excess reserves + $80,000	

When Bank-a-mythica loses a $100,000 deposit, it must reduce its loans by $80,000 to replenish its reserves.

Table 13–9
CHANGES IN THE BALANCE SHEET OF FIRST NATIONAL BANK

(a)			(b)	
ASSETS	LIABILITIES		ASSETS	LIABILITIES
Reserves − $80,000	Checking deposits − $80,000		Reserves + $64,000	
			Loans outstanding − 64,000	
Addendum: Changes In Reserves			**Addendum: Changes In Reserves**	
Actual reserves − $80,000			Actual reserves + $64,000	
Required reserves − 16,000			Required reserves No change	
Excess reserves − $ 64,000			Excess reserves + $64,000	

First National Bank's loss of an $80,000 deposit forces it to cut back its loans by $64,000.

$400,000. As suggested by our money multiplier formula with $R = 0.2$, the decline in the money supply is $1/0.2 = 5$ times as large as the decline in excess reserves.

During the height of the radical student movement of the late 1960s, a circular appeared in Cambridge, Massachusetts, urging citizens to withdraw all funds from their checking accounts on a prescribed date, hold them in cash for one week, and then redeposit them. This act, the circular argued, would surely wreak havoc upon the capitalist system. Obviously, some of these radicals were well-schooled in modern money mechanics, for the argument was basically correct. The tremendous multiple contraction of the banking system and consequent multiple expansion that a successful campaign of this sort could have caused might have seriously disrupted the local financial system. But history records that the appeal met with little success. Checking-account withdrawals are not the stuff of which revolutions are made.

Why the Money Creation Formula is Oversimplified

So far, our discussion of the process of money creation has made it all seem rather mechanical. If all proceeds according to formula, each $1 in new excess reserves will lead to a $1/R$ increase in the money supply. But in reality things are not this simple. Just as we did in the case of the expenditure multiplier, we must stress that the oversimplified formula for money creation is accurate only under very particular circumstances. These circumstances require that:

1. Every recipient of a bank loan must redeposit the proceeds of that loan into another bank rather than hold it in cash.

2. Every bank must hold reserves no larger than the legal minimum.

Let us see what happens to the chain of deposit creation when either of these assumptions is violated.

Suppose first that the business firms and individuals who receive bank loans decide not to redeposit all of the proceeds into their bank accounts. For example, Hard-Pressed Construction Company and all the other borrowers might decide to hold half of their loan proceeds in cash and deposit only the remaining half. Then First National Bank would receive only a $40,000 deposit and could, therefore, make only a $32,000 loan. Second National Bank would then receive only $16,000 (half of $32,000), and so on. The whole chain of money creation would be reduced drastically. Thus:

If individuals and business firms decide to hold more cash, the multiple expansion of the money supply will be curtailed because fewer dollars of cash will be available to be used as reserves to support new checking deposits. Consequently, the money supply will be smaller.

The basic idea here is simple. Each $1 of cash held by a bank can support several dollars (specifically, $1/R$) of money. But $1 of cash held by an individual is exactly one dollar of money; it supports no bank deposits. Hence, any time cash leaves the banking system, the money supply will decline. And any time cash enters the banking system, the money supply will rise.

Next, suppose that Bank-a-mythica's management becomes more conservative, or that the outlook for loan repayments worsens because of a recession. The bank might then decide to keep more reserves than the legal requirement (say, 30 percent) and lend out less than the $80,000 assumed in Table 13–4 (say, $70,000). If this happens, then First National Bank will receive a smaller injection of cash reserves than that shown in Table 13–5. And if First National's management is as jittery as Bank-a-mythica's, it too will hold more in reserves and lend out less. Thus:

If banks wish to keep excess reserves, the multiple expansion of the money supply will be restricted. A given amount of cash will support a smaller supply of money than would be the case if banks held no excess reserves.

The Need for Monetary Control

If we pursue this point a bit further, we will see why government regulation of the money supply is so important for economic stability. We have just suggested that banks will wish to keep excess reserves when they do not foresee profitable and secure opportunities to make loans. This is likely to happen during the downswing and around the bottom of a business contraction. If it occurs, the propensity of banks to hold excess reserves will turn the money creation process into one of money destruction. Thus:

During a recession, profit-oriented banks would be prone to reduce the money supply by increasing their excess reserves — if the monetary authorities did not intervene. As we will learn in subsequent chapters, the money supply is an important influence on aggregate demand, so such a contraction of the money supply would exacerbate the severity of the recession.

On the other hand, banks will want to squeeze the maximum possible money supply out of any given amount of cash reserves by keeping their reserves at the bare minimum when the demand for bank loans is buoyant, profits are high, and many investments suddenly start to look profitable. This reduced incentive to hold excess reserves in prosperous times means that:

During an economic boom, the behavior of profit-oriented banks is likely to make the money supply expand, adding undesirable momentum to the booming economy and paving the way for a burst of inflation. The authorities must intervene to prevent this.

Regulation of the money supply, then, is necessary because bankers, in the pursuit of profit, might otherwise provide the economy with a wildly gyrating money supply that dances to the tune of the business cycle. Precisely how the authorities can keep the money supply under control is the subject of the next chapter.

Summary

1. It is more efficient to exchange goods and services by using money as a medium of exchange than by bartering them directly.
2. In addition to being the medium of exchange, whatever serves as money is likely to become the standard unit of account and a popular store of value.
3. Throughout history, all sorts of things have served as money. Commodity money gave way to fullbodied paper money (certificates backed 100 percent by some commodity, like gold), which in turn gave way to partially backed paper money. Nowadays our paper money has no commodity backing whatsoever; that is, it is pure fiat money.
4. The most widely used definition of the U.S. money supply is M1, which includes coins, paper money, and several types of checking deposits. However, many economists prefer the M2 definition, which adds to M1 most savings deposits and several other types of checkable accounts, some of which are not held in banks.
5. Under our modern system of fractional reserve banking, banks keep cash reserves equal to only a fraction of their total deposit liabilities. This is the key to their profitability, since their remaining funds can be loaned out at interest. But it also leaves them potentially vulnerable to runs.
6. Because of this vulnerability, bank managers are generally conservative in their investment strategy, and they also keep a prudent level of reserves. Even so, the government keeps a watchful eye over banking practices.
7. Before 1933, bank failures were common; but they are rare today. Many observers attribute this development to deposit insurance. Nonetheless, recent years have witnessed an upsurge of bank failures.
8. Because it holds only fractional reserves, even a single bank can create money. But its ability to do so is severely limited because the funds it lends out probably will be deposited in another bank.
9. As a whole, the banking system can create several dollars of money for each dollar of excess reserves it receives. Under certain assumptions, the ratio of new money to new excess reserves will be $1/R$, where R is the required reserve ratio.
10. The same process works in reverse, as a system of money destruction, when cash is withdrawn from the banking system.
11. Because banks and individuals may want to hold more cash when the economy is shaky, the money supply would probably contract under such circumstances if the monetary authorities did not intervene. Similarly, the money supply would probably expand rapidly in boom times if it were unregulated.

Concepts for Review

Run on a bank
Barter
Unit of account
Money
Medium of exchange
Store of value
Commodity money
Fiat money

M1 versus M2
Near moneys
Liquidity
Fractional reserve banking
Deposit insurance
Federal Deposit Insurance Corporation (FDIC)
Federal Savings and Loan Insurance Corporation (FSLIC)

Required reserves
Asset
Liability
Balance sheet
Net worth
Deposit creation
Excess reserves

Questions for Discussion

1. If ours were a barter economy, how would you pay your tuition bill? What if your college did not want the goods or services you offered in payment?
2. How is "money" defined, both conceptually and in practice? Does the U.S. money supply consist of commodity money, full-bodied paper money, or fiat money?
3. What is fractional reserve banking, and why is it the key to bank profits? (Hint: What opportunities to make profits would banks have if reserve

requirements were 100 percent?) Why does fractional reserve banking give bankers discretion over how large the money supply will be? Why does it make banks potentially vulnerable to runs?

4. Do you hold a checking account in a bank? If so, what will happen to your account if the bank goes bankrupt?

5. Suppose that no banks keep excess reserves and no individuals or firms hold on to cash. If someone suddenly discovers $4 million in buried treasure, explain what will happen to the money supply if the required reserve ratio is one-sixth (16.67 percent).

6. How would your answer to Question 5 differ if the reserve ratio were 25 percent? If the reserve ratio were 100 percent?

7. Each year during Christmas shopping season, consumers and stores wish to increase their holdings of cash. Explain how this could lead to a multiple contraction of the money supply. (As a matter of fact, the authorities prevent this contraction from occurring by methods explained in the next chapter.)

8. Excess reserves make a bank less vulnerable to runs. Why, then, don't bankers like to hold excess reserves? What circumstances might persuade them that it would be advisable to hold excess reserves?

9. Use tables such as Tables 13-2 and 13-3 to illustrate what happens to bank balance sheets when each of the following transactions occurs:
   a. You withdraw $100 from your checking account to purchase textbooks at the university book store.
   b. Paul steals $150 in cash from Peter and deposits it into his checking account.
   c. Mary Q. Contrary withdraws $600 in cash from her account at Hometown Bank, carries it to the city, and deposits it into her account at Big City Bank.

10. For each of the transactions listed in Question 9, what will be the ultimate effect on the money supply if the required reserve ratio is 10 percent? (Assume that the oversimplified money multiplier formula applies.)

14

Monetary Policy and the National Economy

Victorians heard with grave attention that the Bank Rate had been raised. They did not know what it meant. But they knew that it was an act of extreme wisdom.

J. K. GALBRAITH

This chapter adds our analysis of money and the banking system from Chapter 13 to the model of income determination and the price level that we have been developing since Chapter 8. By the end of the chapter, we will have in hand a complete model of the macroeconomy. We will then use this model to see how *monetary policy* affects aggregate demand and hence influences unemployment and inflation.

We begin by learning about the operations of America's *central bank*, the *Federal Reserve System*. The "Fed," as it is often called, is a very special kind of bank. Its customers are banks rather than individuals, and it performs some of the same services for them as your bank performs for you. Though it turns out to be an effective profit maker, its actions are not guided by the profit motive. Instead, the Fed tries to manage the money supply in what it perceives to be the national interest. Just how the Fed does its job, and why its performance has fallen short of perfection, are the first subjects of this chapter.

Next we integrate money into the Keynesian $C + I + G$ model. The mechanisms through which monetary policy affects aggregate demand are spelled out and analyzed in detail, and we learn an additional reason why the aggregate demand curve slopes downward. This sets the stage for the rest of Part 4, where we use the model to investigate a variety of important policy issues.

The Federal Reserve System: Origins and Structure

When the **Federal Reserve System** was established in 1914, the United States joined the company of most of the other advanced industrial nations. Up until then, the United States, distrustful of centralization of economic power, was almost the only important nation without a **central bank.** Britain's central bank, the Bank of England, for example, dates from 1694.

A **central bank** is a bank for banks. America's central bank is the **Federal Reserve System.**

The impetus for the establishment of a central bank in the United States came not from the power of economic logic but from some painful experiences with economic reality. Four severe banking panics between 1873 and 1907 convinced legislators and bankers alike that a central bank that would regulate credit conditions was not a luxury but a necessity. After the 1907 crisis, the National Monetary Commission was established to find out just what was wrong with America's banking system. Its report in early 1912 led directly to the establishment of the Federal Reserve System.

Although the basic idea of central banking came from Europe, some changes were made when it was imported, making the Federal Reserve System a uniquely American institution. Owing to the vastness of our country, the extraordinarily large number of commercial banks, and our tradition of dual state–federal regulations, it was decided that the United States should have not one central bank but 12. The boundaries of the 12 Federal Reserve districts and the location of each of the 12 district banks are shown in Figure 14–1.

Technically, each of the Federal Reserve banks is a corporation; its stockholders are the banks that belong to it. But your bank, if it is a member of the System, does not enjoy the privileges normally accorded to stockholders: It receives only a token share of the Federal Reserve's immense profits (the bulk is donated to the U.S. Treasury), and it has no say in the decisions of the corporation. The private banks are more like customers of the Fed than like owners.

Who, then, controls the Fed? Most of the power resides in the seven-member Board of Governors of the Federal Reserve System, headquartered in Washington, and especially in its chairman, who is now Alan Greenspan, an economist. Members of the board are appointed by the president of the United States, with the advice and consent of the Senate, for 14-year terms. The president also designates one of the members to serve a four-year term as chairman of the board, and thus to be the most powerful central banker in the world; for the United States differs from many other countries in that the Federal Reserve Board, once appointed by the president, is *independent* of the rest of the government. So long as it stays within the statutory authority delineated by Congress, it alone has responsibility for determining the nation's monetary policy. The power of appointment, however, gives the president considerable long-run influence over Federal Reserve policy.

Figure 14–1
THE TWELVE FEDERAL RESERVE DISTRICTS
This map shows the boundaries of the 12 Federal Reserve districts and the locations of the 12 Federal Reserve banks. In which Federal Reserve district do you live?

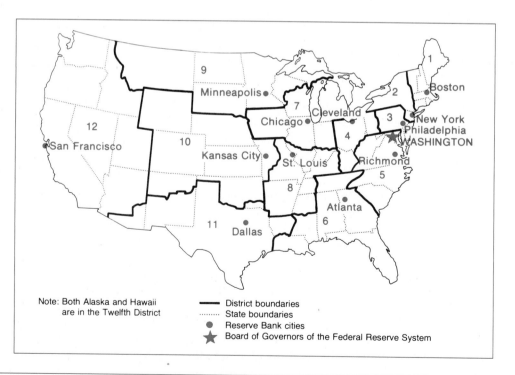

Note: Both Alaska and Hawaii are in the Twelfth District

— District boundaries
...... State boundaries
● Reserve Bank cities
★ Board of Governors of the Federal Reserve System

Closely allied with the Board of Governors is the powerful **Federal Open Market Committee (FOMC),** which meets periodically in Washington. For reasons to be explained shortly, the decisions of the FOMC largely determine the size of the U.S. money supply. This 12-member committee consists of the seven governors of the Federal Reserve System and the presidents of five of the district banks.

The Independence of the Fed

The institutional independence of the Federal Reserve System is looked upon as a source of pride by some and as an antidemocratic embarrassment by others. The proponents of Federal Reserve independence argue that it enables monetary policy decisions to be made on objective, technical criteria and keeps monetary control out of the "political thicket." Without this independence, it is argued, there would be a tendency for politicians to force the Fed to expand the money supply too rapidly, thereby contributing to chronic inflation and undermining faith in America's financial system.

Opponents of this view counter that there is something profoundly undemocratic about having a group of unelected bankers and economists make decisions that affect the well-being of 240 million Americans. Monetary policy, they argue, ought to be formulated by the elected representatives of the people, just like fiscal policy. Those who argue for executive or congressional control over the Fed can point to historical instances in which monetary and fiscal policy have been at loggerheads—with the Fed undoing or even overwhelming the effects of fiscal policy decisions.

There is plenty of middle ground between the two extremes. One less drastic proposal would simply shift the term of the chairman of the Federal Reserve Board to make it coincide with that of the president. As things stand today, a newly elected president must retain the chairman that his predecessor appointed whether or not he agrees with his policies.

Another suggested reform would require the Fed to announce its ultimate targets for unemployment and inflation and explain how it expects its monetary policy actions to promote these goals. An extreme version of this proposal would require that the Fed adhere to the goals of the administration or of Congress. But a softer version simply would require that the Fed announce its own goals and subject them to public scrutiny. A small step in this direction was taken in 1975 when the Fed, in response to congressional wishes, began announcing "ranges of tolerance" for growth rates of the money supply (by several definitions!). That is, the chairman of the Federal Reserve Board now periodically tells Congress *in advance* what the maximum and minimum permissible growth rates for the money stock are in the coming months.

How people view these and other reform proposals that revolve around the issue of the Fed's independence depends on how they perceive the office. Are governors of the Federal Reserve System akin to judges and therefore, at least in principle, best thought of as nonpartisan and independent technocrats? The 14-year term of office certainly suggests an analogy to the judiciary, but the board's role is most assuredly one that involves policy making, not just "impartial" interpretation of the law. Or are the governors more like members of the Cabinet, that is, policy-making officials who should properly serve only at the pleasure of the president? Since neither analogy fits precisely, the issue is a vexing one.

Controlling the Money Supply: Open-Market Operations

Open-market operations refer to the Fed's purchase or sale of government securities through transactions in the open market.

Partly for historical reasons, the Fed normally relies on what are called **open-market operations** to manipulate the money supply. Open-market operations have the effect of giving the banks more reserves or taking reserves away from them, thereby triggering a multiple expansion or contraction of the money supply as in Chapter 13.

How does this work? Suppose the Federal Open Market Committee decides that the money supply is too low. It can issue instructions that the money supply be expanded through operations in the open market. Specifically, this means that the Federal Reserve System *purchases* U.S. government securities (generally short-term securities called "Treasury bills") from any individual or bank that wishes to sell, thus putting more reserves in the hands of the banks.[1]

An example will illustrate the mechanics of open-market operations. Suppose the order is to purchase $100 million worth of securities and that commercial banks are the sellers. *The Fed makes payment by giving the banks $100 million in new reserves.* So, if they held only the required amount of reserves initially, the banks now have $100 million in excess reserves, as shown in Table 14–1.

Where does the Fed get the money that it gives to the banks in return for the securities? It could pay in cash, but normally does not. Instead, it manufactures the funds out of thin air or, more literally, by punching the keyboard of a computer terminal. Specifically, the Fed pays the banks for the securities by adding the appropriate sums to the accounts that the banks maintain at the Fed. Balances held in these accounts constitute bank reserves, just like cash in bank vaults.

While this process of creating bookkeeping entries at the Federal Reserve is commonly referred to as "printing money," the Fed does not literally run the

[1] In fact, the Fed almost always deals with one of a small group of dealers who "make a market" in government securities. However, this detail has no effect on the basic principles. The dealers are simply intermediaries, intervening between the ultimate buyer (the Fed) and the ultimate seller.

Table 14–1
EFFECTS OF AN OPEN-MARKET PURCHASE OF SECURITIES ON THE BALANCE SHEETS OF BANKS AND THE FED

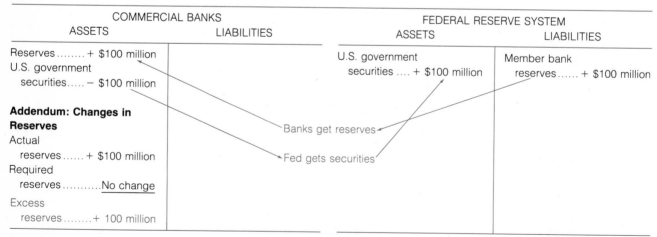

COMMERCIAL BANKS		FEDERAL RESERVE SYSTEM	
ASSETS	LIABILITIES	ASSETS	LIABILITIES
Reserves........ + $100 million		U.S. government securities .... + $100 million	Member bank reserves...... + $100 million
U.S. government securities..... − $100 million			
Addendum: Changes in Reserves			
Actual reserves...... + $100 million			
Required reserves...........No change			
Excess reserves........+ 100 million			

Banks get reserves
Fed gets securities

When the Fed buys $100 million worth of securities from the banks, it adds this amount to the bookkeeping entries that represent the banks' accounts at the Fed (called "member bank reserves"). Since deposits have not increased at all, required reserves are unchanged by this transaction. But actual reserves are increased by $100 million, so there are $100 million in excess reserves. This will trigger a multiple expansion of the banking system.

printing presses. Instead, it simply exchanges its IOUs for an existing asset (a government security). But unlike your IOUs, the Fed's IOUs constitute legal bank reserves, and thus are the equivalent of cash in their ability to support a multiple expansion of the money supply. The banks, not the Fed, actually increase the money supply; but the Fed's actions give the banks the wherewithal to do it.

Once the excess reserves are created, multiple expansion of the banking system proceeds in the usual way. It is not hard for the Fed to estimate the ultimate increase in the money supply that will result from its actions. As we saw in the last chapter, each dollar of excess reserves can support $1/R$ dollars of checking deposits if R is the required reserve ratio. In our example, $R = 0.20$; so $100 million in new reserves can support $100/0.2 = $500 million in new money.

But *estimating* the ultimate monetary expansion is a far cry from *knowing it* with certainty. As we know from Chapter 13, the simple money multiplier formula is predicated on the assumptions that people will want to hold no more cash, and that banks will want to hold no more excess reserves, as the monetary expansion proceeds. In practice, these assumptions are unlikely to be literally true. So, if the Fed is to predict the eventual effect of its action on the money supply correctly, it must estimate both the amount that firms and individuals will want to add to their currency holdings and the amount that banks will want to add to their excess reserves. Neither of these can be estimated with great precision. In summary:

When the Federal Reserve System wants to increase the money supply, it purchases U.S. government securities in the open market. It pays for these securities by creating new bank reserves, and these additional reserves lead to a multiple expansion of the money supply.

However, because of fluctuations in people's desires to hold cash and banks' desires to hold excess reserves, the Fed cannot predict the consequences of these actions with perfect accuracy. Thus, over short periods, control over the money supply must of necessity be imperfect.

The procedures followed when the FOMC wants to *contract* the money supply are just the opposite of those we have just explained. In brief, it orders a *sale* of government securities in the open market. This takes reserves *away* from banks, since banks pay for the securities by drawing down their deposits at the Fed. A multiple *contraction* of the banking system ensues. The principles are exactly the same as when the process operates in reverse—and so are the uncertainties.

Open-Market Operations, Bond Prices, and Interest Rates

By offering more government bonds for sale on the open market, the Federal Reserve will normally depress the price of bonds. This is illustrated by Figure 14–2, which shows a rightward shift of the (vertical) supply curve of bonds—from $S_0 S_0$ to $S_1 S_1$—with an unchanged demand curve, DD. The price of bonds falls from P_0 to P_1 as equilibrium in the bond market shifts from point A to point B.

Falling bond prices translate into rising interest rates. You cannot have one without the other. Why is that? Most bonds pay a fixed number of dollars of interest per year. For concreteness, consider a bond that pays $90 each year. If the bond sells for $1000, bondholders earn a 9 percent return on their

Figure 14–2

OPEN-MARKET SALES
AND BOND PRICES

If the Fed offers bonds for
sale in the open market, the
supply curve of bonds shifts
rightward from S_0S_0 to S_1S_1.
In consequence, equilibrium
in the bond market shifts
from point A to point B. The
price of bonds declines from
P_0 to P_1. By the same
reasoning, an open-market
purchase drives bond prices
up.

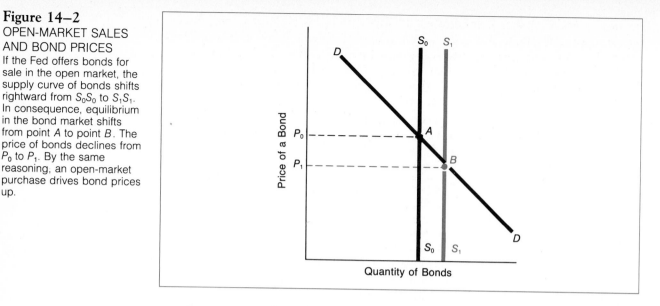

investment since $90 is 9 percent of $1000. We say that *the interest rate on the
bond is 9 percent*. Now suppose the price of the bond falls to $900. The annual
interest payment is still $90, so bondholders now earn 10 percent on their
money ($90 is 10 percent of $900). *The effective interest rate on the bond has risen
to 10 percent*. This relationship between bond prices and interest rates is completely general:

When bond prices fall, interest rates rise. When bond prices rise, interest rates
fall.

In fact, the relationship amounts to nothing more than two ways of saying the
same thing. Higher interest rates *mean* lower bond prices; lower interest rates
mean higher bond prices.

     We thus see that the Fed, through its open-market operations, exercises
direct influence over interest rates. Specifically:

An open-market purchase of bonds by the Fed not only raises the money supply
but also drives up bond prices and pushes interest rates down. Conversely, an
open-market sale of bonds, which reduces the money supply, lowers bond prices
and raises interest rates.

Controlling the Money Supply: Reserve Requirements

The Fed also has another way to control the money supply: by varying the minimum required reserve ratio. To see how this works, consider the balance sheet
of a hypothetical bank shown in Table 14–2. If the minimum required reserve
ratio is 20 percent, and the bank wishes to hold only the legal minimum in
reserves, Middle American Bank is in equilibrium on October 25, 1988. Its $1
million in checking deposits mean that its required reserves amount to
$200,000, which just matches its actual reserves. Excess reserves are zero.

     Now suppose that the Federal Reserve Board decides that the money sup-
ply needs to be increased. One action it can take is to lower the required
reserve ratio. As an exaggerated example, suppose it reduces reserve requirements to 15 percent of deposits.

Table 14–2
BALANCE SHEET OF MIDDLE AMERICAN BANK, October 25, 1988

ASSETS		LIABILITIES AND NET WORTH	
Reserves	$ 200,000	Checking deposits	$1,000,000
Loans outstanding	1,000,000	Net worth	200,000
Total assets	$1,200,000	Total liabilities plus net worth	$1,200,000

If the required reserve ratio is 20 percent, Middle American Bank holds exactly its required reserved on October 25, 1988—no more and no less. However, if the reserve ratio falls to 15 percent, its required reserves will fall to only $150,000 (15 percent of $1 million), and it will have $50,000 in excess reserves.

Middle American Bank's balance sheet is unaffected by this action, but the bank's managers are sure to react to it. For now required reserves are only $150,000 (15 percent of $1 million), so the bank is holding $50,000 in excess reserves—funds that are earning no interest for the bank. The effect is the same as if a new depositor had brought in cash: The bank now has more money to lend. Once it lends out this $50,000, its balance sheet will be as shown in Table 14–3; it now holds $50,000 less in reserves and $50,000 more in loans.

Although no new deposits are created by this transaction, we know from the previous chapter that the wheels of a multiple expansion of the banking system have been set in motion. For the recipient of the loan will deposit the proceeds in his own bank, giving that bank excess reserves and, therefore, the ability to grant more loans, and so on.

Once again, while the Fed's control over banks' excess reserves may be quite precise, its control over the money supply is a good deal looser. It can and will rely on its past experience to *estimate* the ultimate effect of any change in reserve requirements on the money supply. In normal times, these estimates are quite accurate (that, presumably, is the definition of "normal times"). But at other times banks may surprise the Fed by holding larger or smaller excess reserves than anticipated, or businesses and consumers may surprise it by holding more or less currency. In such cases, the Fed will not get the money supply it was shooting for and will have to readjust its policies.

It does not take much imagination to see what the Fed must do to reserve requirements when it wants to engineer a *contraction* of the money supply. If banks are not holding excess reserves, an increase in the required reserve ratio will force them to contract their loans and deposits until their reserve deficiencies are corrected. Of course, if banks do have sufficient excess reserves, they can flout the Fed's wishes. But the Fed normally will be trying to rein in the money supply when the economy is booming, and these are precisely the times when banks will not want to hold more idle reserves than they have to.

Table 14–3
BALANCE SHEET OF MIDDLE AMERICAN BANK, October 26, 1988

ASSETS		LIABILITIES AND NET WORTH	
Reserves	$ 150,000	Checking deposits	$1,000,000
Loans outstanding	1,050,000	Net worth	200,000
Total assets	$1,200,000	Total liabilities plus net worth	$1,200,000

If Middle American Bank does not wish to hold excess reserves, its balance sheet will look like this after it loans out the extra $50,000 in excess reserves. At this point, it once again has no excess reserves.

In fact, the Fed has not relied much on the reserve ratio as a weapon of monetary control. Current legislation provides for a basic reserve ratio of 12 percent against checking deposits, which is not expected to change frequently.

Controlling the Money Supply: Lending to Banks

When the Federal Reserve System was first established, its founders did not intend it to pursue an active monetary policy to stabilize the economy. Indeed, the basic ideas of stabilization policy were foreign at the time, dating only from Keynes's *General Theory of Employment, Interest, and Money* in 1936. Instead, the Fed's founders viewed it as a means of preventing the supplies of money and credit from drying up during economic contractions, as had happened so often in the pre-1914 period.

One of the principal ways in which the Fed was to provide such insurance against financial panics was to act as a "lender of last resort." That is, when risky business prospects made commercial banks hesitant to extend new loans, or when banks were in trouble, the Fed would step in by lending money to the banks, thus inducing the banks to lend more money to their customers.

Loans from the Federal Reserve banks to individual commercial banks have existed from the first days of the System. When the Fed extends borrowing privileges to a bank in need of reserves, that bank receives a credit in its deposit account at the Fed (see Table 14–4). This addition to bank reserves may lead to an expansion of the money supply; or it may eliminate a reserve deficiency and thereby prevent a multiple contraction of the banking system. In either case, the Fed makes monetary conditions more expansive by making borrowing easier.

The **discount rate** is the interest rate the Fed charges on loans it makes to banks.

Federal Reserve officials can influence the volume of member bank borrowing by setting the *rate of interest charged on these loans*. For historical reasons, this is called the **discount rate** in the United States. In most foreign countries, it is known as the "bank rate." If the Fed wants to give banks more reserves, it can reduce the interest rate that it charges, thereby tempting banks to borrow more. Alternatively, it can soak up reserves by raising its rate and persuading the banks to reduce their borrowings.

Table 14–4
BALANCE SHEET CHANGES FOR BORROWING FROM THE FED

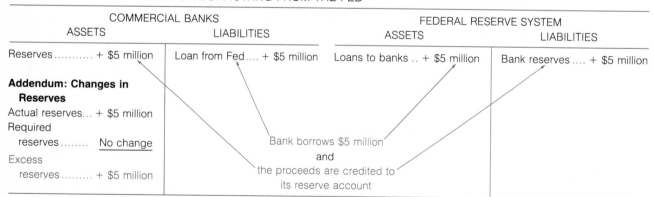

COMMERCIAL BANKS		FEDERAL RESERVE SYSTEM	
ASSETS	LIABILITIES	ASSETS	LIABILITIES
Reserves .... + $5 million	Loan from Fed.... + $5 million	Loans to banks .. + $5 million	Bank reserves .... + $5 million
Addendum: Changes in Reserves			
Actual reserves... + $5 million			
Required reserves .... No change			
Excess reserves .... + $5 million			

Bank borrows $5 million and the proceeds are credited to its reserve account

When the Fed lends $5 million to a bank, it simply adds this amount to the bookkeeping entry that represents that bank's account at the Fed. Once again, actual reserves increase while required reserves do not change (because commercial bank deposits do not change). Hence this loan would be expected to initiate a multiple expansion of the banking system.

While this type of *active* manipulation of the discount rate is practiced widely in foreign countries, where the bank rate is often the centerpiece of monetary policy, it is much less common in the United States, where the Fed usually relies on open market operations in conducting its monetary policy. More often the Fed adjusts the discount rate *passively* to keep it in line with market interest rates. Nonetheless, changes in the discount rate have important psychological effects on financial markets, where they are widely interpreted as signals of the Fed's attitude toward interest rates.

As in the case of changes in reserve requirements and open market operations, the Fed cannot know for sure how banks will react to changes in the discount rate. Sometimes they may respond vigorously to a cut in the rate, borrowing a great deal from the Fed and lending a correspondingly large amount to their customers. At other times they may essentially ignore the Fed's actions. The link between the lending rate and the money supply is a loose one.

Often, though, the Fed tries to tighten this link by using a more direct way of controlling the volume of bank borrowing—**moral suasion.** This phrase refers to some not-so-subtle methods that the Fed has for letting banks know when it thinks they are borrowing too much. Since banks are anxious to maintain the good will of the Fed, they often respond to warnings that they they have overused their borrowing privileges—especially when such warnings are accompanied by a veiled threat that these privileges might be suspended if the offending bank does not mend its ways. As the Fed often reminds the banks, borrowing is "a privilege, not a right."

Moral suasion refers to informal requests and warnings designed to persuade banks to limit their borrowings from the Fed.

Proposals for Tightening Monetary Control

The fact that each of the Federal Reserve's principal instruments of monetary control is somewhat imperfect has led to a number of suggestions designed to improve the System's ability to regulate the supply of money.

Because banks' discretion over the amount of reserves they hold (subject only to the legal minimums) makes the link between changes in Federal Reserve policy and changes in the money supply rather slippery, some economists would like to see a return to a system of 100 percent reserve requirements. Under such a rule, no bank could add to or subtract from its excess reserves because there would never be any excess reserves. Each dollar of bank reserves would support exactly one dollar of deposits, no more and no less; so there would be no such thing as a multiple expansion or contraction of the banking system. The Fed can now control bank reserves with great precision; and under a system of 100 percent reserve requirements, its control over the money supply would be equally precise.

While such a change in banking regulations undoubtedly would make the Fed's job easier, it would also change the face of banking in dramatic and possibly unpredictable ways. It will be recalled from Chapter 13 that banking as we know it today evolved from that first goldsmith's momentous discovery that he could get along with only fractional reserves. This discovery has been the mainspring of bank profits ever since. Abolition of fractional reserve banking should therefore be viewed as a major overhaul of the financial system. This does not necessarily mean that it is a bad idea, only that it should be approached with some caution.

Some observers have suggested that lending to banks, far from aiding the Fed's monetary control, actually undermines it, and therefore the Fed should stop lending except in emergency cases. Their reasoning is as follows: When the Fed tries to force a contraction of the banking system, some banks may resist this desire by borrowing the reserves they need. Similarly, some banks may relinquish reserves to pay back loans just when the Fed wants the money supply to expand.

No doubt this occasionally happens. But there are also times when Federal Reserve lending is a valuable supplement to open market policy. Since it is by no means clear that monetary control would be tighter if lending were abolished, the Fed is understandably reluctant to give up one of its major traditional weapons.

The Money Supply Mechanism

This completes our discussion of the Fed's methods of controlling the money supply and the limitations of these methods. One point, however, merits further emphasis. We have noted several times that the Fed's control of the money supply is imperfect because banks can and do vary their holdings of excess reserves. Since reserves earn no interest, banks will hold substantial *excess* reserves only when they feel that funds cannot be put to profitable uses. This may happen if shaky business conditions make loans to customers look unusually risky or if interest rates are very low. Conversely, banks will work hard to hold reserves to the legal minimum when loans to customers look safe and when interest rates are high. Thus:

As interest rates rise, banks normally find it more profitable to expand their volume of loans and deposits, thus increasing the supply of money. However, the Fed can shift the relationship between the money supply and interest rates by employing any of its principal weapons of monetary control: open market operations, changes in reserve requirements, or changes in lending policy to banks.

These ideas are depicted graphically in Figure 14–3. Figure 14–3(a) shows a typical money supply schedule labeled MS, illustrating the fact that bank behavior makes the money stock rise as interest rates rise.[2] Notice that the sensitivity of the money supply to interest rates is rather weak in the diagram—a

[2]There are many interest rates in the economy. However, they all tend to move up and down together. Hence, for present purposes, we can speak of "the" rate of interest.

Figure 14–3
THE SUPPLY SCHEDULE FOR MONEY
Part (a) shows a typical supply schedule for money. It is rising as we move toward the right, meaning that banks will supply more money when interest rates are higher. Part (b) illustrates what happens to the money supply schedule when the Fed purchases securities in the open market, or lowers required reserves, or provides banks with more loans. The supply schedule shifts outward. Part (c) depicts the effect of using these same policy instruments in the opposite (contractionary) direction. The supply schedule shifts inward.

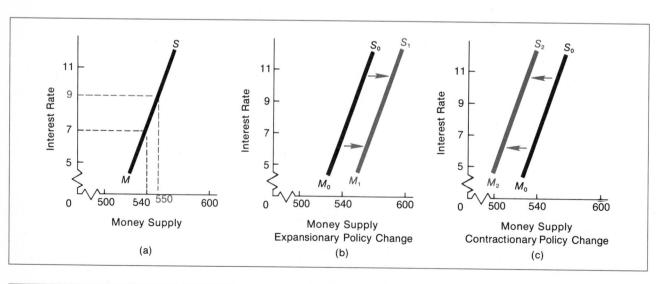

large rise in the rate of interest (from 7 percent to 9 percent) induces only a small increase in the supply of money (from \$540 billion to \$550 billion). The drawing is deliberately constructed that way because that is what the statistical evidence shows.

The curve in Figure 14–3(a) shows the money supply schedule corresponding to some specific monetary policy. Figure 14–3(b) portrays how the money supply schedule responds to an *expansionary change in monetary policy,* such as an open market purchase of government bonds, a reduction in reserve requirements, or a drop in the Fed's lending rate. The money supply schedule shifts outward from $M_0 S_0$ to $M_1 S_1$, as indicated by the arrows. After banks have adjusted to the change, there is more money at any given interest rate.

Figure 14–3(c) shows what happens in the reverse case — *contractionary monetary policy,* such as an open market sale of securities, an increase in reserve requirements, or a rise in the lending rate. The money supply shifts inward from $M_0 S_0$ to $M_2 S_2$.

As we have stressed, the diagrams make things look rather more precise than they actually are. Since the Fed's control over the money supply schedule is imperfect in the short run, the actual MS schedule is obscured by a bit of fog. In what follows, we portray all the graphs as clean straight lines only for pedagogical simplicity. The Fed wishes things were so simple in the real world!

The Demand for Money

Just as we must know something about both the supply of and the demand for wheat before we can predict how much will be sold and at what price, it is necessary to know something about the **demand for money** if we are to understand the amount of money actually in existence and the prevailing interest rate.

The definition of money given in Chapter 13 suggests the most important reason why people hold money balances: the medium of exchange is needed to carry out purchases and sales of goods and services. More dollars are needed to conduct the nation's business if more purchases and sales are made or if each transaction takes place at a higher price. Since the real gross national product (GNP) is normally considered to be the best measure of the total volume of goods and services traded in the economy, it seems safe to assume that the demand for money will rise as real GNP rises. And, indeed, an impressive amount of statistical evidence supports this supposition. In addition, both common sense and mountains of evidence point to the conclusion that a higher price level leads to a higher demand for money simply because more dollars are needed to conduct the same transactions.

But real output and the price level are not the only factors affecting the demand for money; interest rates matter, too. At first, that may seem surprising because most forms of money pay either no interest or an interest rate which is fixed by law. Why, then, are interest rates relevant? They are relevant because money is only one of a variety of forms in which individuals can hold their wealth. Holders of money *give up* the opportunity to hold one of these other assets, such as government bonds, in order to gain the convenience of money. In so doing, they *give up* the interest that they could have earned on one of these alternative assets.

This is another example of the concept of **opportunity cost.**[3] On the surface, it seems virtually costless to hold money. But, *compared with the next best alternative,* this action is not costless at all. For example, if the best alternative

---

[3]If you need to review this concept, see Chapter 3.

to holding $100 in cash is to put those funds into a government bond that pays 8 percent interest, then the opportunity cost of holding that money is $8 per year (8 percent of $100).

How, then, should the rate of interest influence the quantity of money that people demand? It is natural to assume that when interest rates are high people will make strenuous efforts to economize on their holdings of money balances, efforts that would not be worthwhile at lower interest rates. In a word, rational behavior of consumers and business firms should make the demand to hold money *decline* as the interest rate *rises*. And, once again, careful analysis of the data shows this to be true. To summarize:

People and business firms hold money primarily to finance their transactions. Therefore, the quantity of money demanded increases as real output rises or as prices rise. However, the quantity of money demanded decreases as the rate of interest rises because the rate of interest is the opportunity cost of holding money balances.

It is possible to portray the demand for money by a graphical device, as shown in the three panels of Figure 14–4. In panel (a) we show a downward-sloping demand schedule for money (the curve labeled MD)—the quantity of money demanded decreases as the rate of interest rises. But since the quantity of money demanded also depends on real output and the price level, we must hold both real output and the price level constant in drawing up such a curve. Changes in either of these variables will shift the MD curve in the manner indicated in the other two panels because at higher levels of real GNP and higher prices, demand for money is greater; and at lower levels of real GNP and lower prices, demand for money is smaller.

Figure 14–4
THE DEMAND SCHEDULE FOR MONEY
The downward-sloping line MD in part (a) is a typical demand curve for money. It slopes down because money is a less-attractive asset when interest rates on alternative assets are higher. However, such a curve can be drawn up only for particular levels of output and prices. A rise in either real output or the price level will shift the money-demand curve outward, as shown in part (b). Conversely, a fall in either real output or the price level will shift the curve inward, as in part (c).

Equilibrium in the Money Market

As is usual in supply and demand analysis, it is useful to put both sides of the market together on a single graph. Figure 14–5 combines the money supply schedule of Figure 14–3(a) (labeled MS) with the money demand schedule of Figure 14–4(a) (labeled MD). Point E is the equilibrium of the money market. The diagram thus shows that *given* real output and the price level (which locates the MD curve) and *given* the Federal Reserve's monetary policy (which locates the MS curve), the money market is in equilibrium at an interest rate of

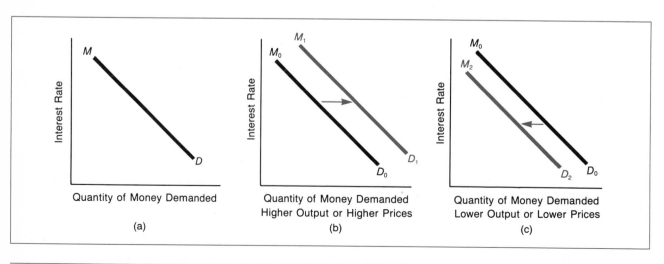

	(a)	(b)	(c)
Interest Rate	Quantity of Money Demanded	Quantity of Money Demanded — Higher Output or Higher Prices	Quantity of Money Demanded — Lower Output or Lower Prices

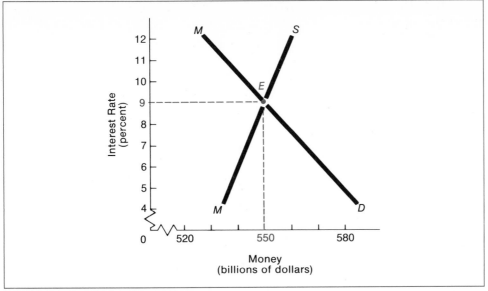

Figure 14–5
EQUILIBRIUM IN THE
MONEY MARKET
Equilibrium in the market for
money is determined by the
intersection of demand curve
MD and supply curve MS. At
point E, the interest rate is 9
percent, and the money
supply is $550 billion. At no
other interest rate would the
demand for and the supply of
money be in balance.

9 percent and a money stock of $550 billion. At any interest rate above 9 percent, the quantity of money supplied would exceed the quantity demanded and the interest rate — which is the price for renting money — would therefore decline. At any interest rate below 9 percent, more money would be demanded than supplied, and so the interest rate would rise. This is familiar ground.

Since the Fed can shift the MS curve, it can alter this equilibrium through its **monetary policy.** Expansionary monetary policy actions include purchasing government securities in the open market, reducing reserve requirements, and encouraging banks to borrow. Any of these actions will provide additional excess reserves to the banking system, thus encouraging banks to increase their loans and deposits. As money becomes more plentiful, interest rates drop.

Our supply-demand analysis of the money market shows this in Figure 14–6(a). By shifting the money supply schedule outward from $M_0 S_0$ to $M_1 S_1$, the Fed moves the market equilibrium from point E to point A — thus forcing the interest rate down.

Contractionary monetary policy actions, such as selling securities in the open market, raising reserve requirements, and discouraging borrowing, have the opposite effect. They push interest rates up, as Figure 14–6(b) shows. Thus:

Monetary policies that expand the money supply normally lower interest rates. Monetary policies that reduce the money supply normally raise interest rates.

Monetary policy refers to actions that the Federal Reserve System takes in order to change the equilibrium of the money market; that is, to alter the money supply, move interest rates, or both.

Money and Income: The Important Difference

We are now ready to see precisely how the Federal Reserve's monetary policy decisions affect unemployment, inflation, and the overall state of the economy. But first a review of some important vocabulary. As pointed out in Chapter 1, the words "money" and "income" are used almost interchangeably in common parlance. This is a pitfall we must learn to avoid.

Money is a snapshot concept. It is the answer to questions like: "How much money do you have right now?" or "How much money did you have at 3:32 P.M. on Friday, November 5th?" To answer questions like these, you would add up the cash you are (or were) carrying and whatever checking balances you

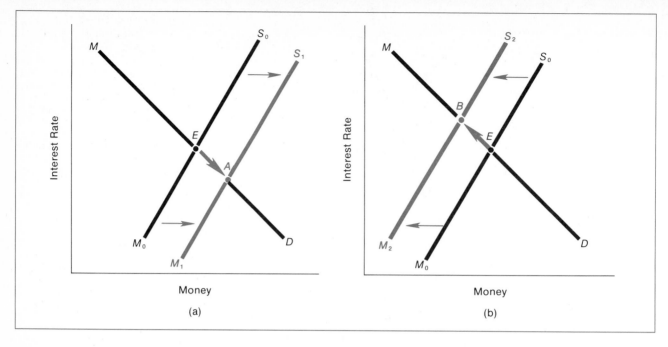

Figure 14–6

THE EFFECTS OF MONETARY POLICY ON THE MONEY MARKET
The two parts of this figure show the effects of monetary policy on the money supply (M) and the rate of interest (r). In part (a), expansionary monetary policies shift the supply schedule from M_0S_0 to M_1S_1 and push the equilibrium from point E to point A; M rises while r falls. In part (b), contractionary policies pull the supply schedule in from M_0S_0 to M_2S_2 causing equilibrium to move up from point E to point B; M falls as r rises.

have (or had), and answer something like: "I have $126.33," or "On Friday, November 5th, at 3:32 P.M., I had $31.43."

Income, by contrast, is more like a motion picture; it comes to you only over a period of time. If you are asked "What is your income?" you must respond by saying "$150 *per week*," or "$600 *per month*," or "$7200 *per year*," or something like that. Notice that there is a unit of time attached to each of these responses. If you just say "My income is $452," without indicating whether it is per week or per month or per year, no one will understand what you mean.

That the two concepts are very different is easy to see. A typical American family has an *income* of about $30,000 per year, but its holdings of *money* at any point in time (using the M1 definition) are under $2000. Similarly, at the national level, nominal GNP in 1987 was around xxx billion, while the money stock (M1) in the middle of the year was only about $4500 billion.

While money and income are very different, they are certainly related. The rest of this chapter is precisely about that relationship. Specifically, we will look at how the stock of *money* in existence at any moment of time influences the rate at which people will be earning *income*, that is, how money affects the GNP.

Interest Rates and Total Expenditure

To begin, we go back to the analysis of Chapters 8–12, where we learned that aggregate demand is the sum of consumption spending (C), investment spending (I), and government purchases of goods and services (G).[4] We know that *fiscal policy* controls G directly and exerts influence over both C and I through the tax laws. We now want to find out how *monetary policy* affects C + I + G.

Most economists agree that, of the three components of aggregate demand, investment (I) is the most sensitive to monetary policy. *Business investment* in new factories and machinery is sensitive to interest rates for reasons that have

[4]We continue to ignore exports and imports until Part 5.

been explained in earlier chapters.[5] Since the rate of interest that must be paid on borrowings is one element of the cost of making an investment, business executives will find investment prospects less attractive as interest rates rise. Therefore, they will spend less. For similar reasons, *investment in housing* by individuals may also be deterred by high interest rates. Since the interest cost of a home mortgage is the major component of the total cost of owning a home, fewer families will want to buy a new home when interest rates are high than when interest rates are low. We conclude that:

Higher interest rates lead to lower investment spending. But investment (I) is a component of total spending ($C + I + G$). Therefore, when interest rates rise, total spending falls. In terms of the 45° line diagram of previous chapters, a higher interest rate leads to a lower $C + I + G$ schedule. Conversely, a lower interest rate leads to a higher $C + I + G$ schedule. (See Figure 14–7.)

Monetary Policy and Aggregate Demand in the Keynesian Model

The effect of interest rates on spending provides the mechanism by which monetary policy affects aggregate demand in the Keynesian model. We know from our analysis of the money market that monetary policy can have a profound effect on the rate of interest. Let us, therefore, outline the effects of monetary policy, starting first on the demand side of the economy.

Suppose the Federal Reserve, seeing the economy stuck with unemployment and a recessionary gap, raises the money supply. It would normally do this by purchasing government securities in the open market, but the specific weapon that the Fed uses is not terribly important for present purposes. What matters is that the money supply (M) expands.

With the demand schedule for money (temporarily) fixed, such an increase in the supply of money has the effect that an increase in supply always has in a

[5]See, for example, Chapter 9, page 166.

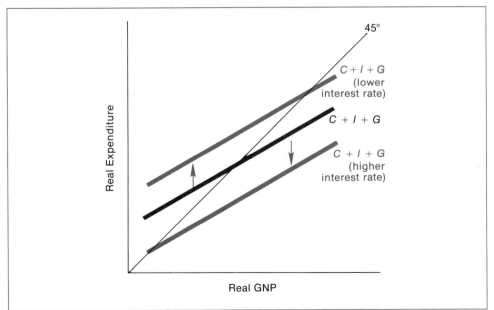

Figure 14–7
THE EFFECT OF INTEREST RATES ON AGGREGATE DEMAND
Because interest rates are an important determinant of investment spending, *I*, the *C + I + G* schedule shifts whenever the rate of interest changes. Specifically, as shown here, lower interest rates shift the curve upward and higher interest rates shift it downward.

Figure 14–8

THE EFFECT OF
EXPANSIONARY
MONETARY POLICY ON
THE MONEY SUPPLY
AND RATE OF INTEREST
An expansionary monetary
policy pushes the money
supply schedule outward
from $M_0 S_0$ to $M_1 S_1$, causing
equilibrium in the money
market to shift from point E_0
to point E_1. The money
supply rises from $550 billion
to $590 billion, while the
interest rate falls from 9
percent to 7 percent.

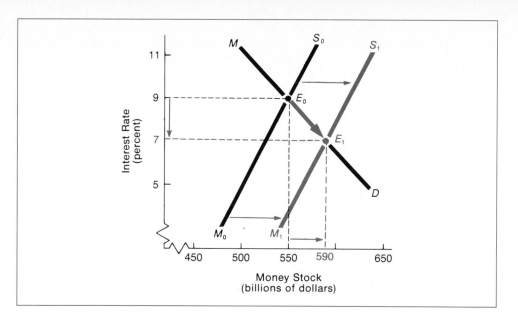

free market—it lowers the price. (See Figure 14–8.) In this case, the price of renting money is the rate of interest, r; so r falls.

Next, for reasons we have just outlined, investment spending (I) rises in response to the lower interest rates. But, as we learned in Chapter 10, such an autonomous rise in investment kicks off a multiplier chain of increases in output and employment. Thus, finally, we have completed the links from the money supply to the level of aggregate demand. In brief, monetary policy works as follows:

A higher money supply leads to lower interest rates, and these lower interest rates encourage investment, which has multiplier effects on aggregate demand.

The process operates equally well in reverse. By contracting the money supply, the Fed can force interest rates up, causing investment spending to fall and pulling down aggregate demand via the multiplier mechanism.

This, in outline form, is how monetary policy operates in the Keynesian model. Since the chain of causation is fairly long, the following schematic diagram may help clarify it.

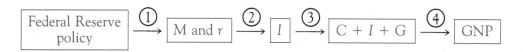

In this causal chain, link 1 indicates that the actions of the Federal Reserve affect money and interest rates. Link 2 stands for the effect of interest rates on investment. Link 3 simply notes that investment is one component of total spending. And link 4 is the multiplier, relating an autonomous change in investment to the ultimate change in aggregate demand.

Let us next review what we know about each of these links and fill in some illustrative numbers. In the process, we will see what economists must study if they are to estimate the effects of monetary policy.

Link 1 is the subject of this chapter and of Figure 14–8. Given the initial level of real GNP and prices, the demand schedule for money is shown by curve

MD. The Fed's expansionary action shifts the supply schedule out from M_0S_0 to M_1S_1, resulting in an increase in the money stock from \$550 billion to \$590 billion in this example, and a decline in the interest rate from 9 percent to 7 percent. Thus the first thing an economist must know is how sensitive interest rates are to changes in the supply of money.

Link 2 translates the drop in the interest rate into an increase in investment spending (I), which we take to be \$100 billion in this example. To estimate this effect in practice, economists must study the sensitivity of investment to interest rates.

Link 3 instructs us to enter this \$100 billion rise in I as an autonomous shift in the $C + I + G$ schedule of a 45° line diagram. Figure 14–9 carries out this step. The expenditure schedule rises from $C + I_0 + G$ to $C + I_1 + G$.

Finally, link 4 applies multiplier analysis to this vertical shift in the expenditure schedule in order to predict the eventual increase in real GNP demanded. In our examples, we have been using a multiplier of 2.5, so multiplying \$100 billion by 2.5 gives the final effect on aggregate demand—a rise of \$250 billion. This is shown in Figure 14–9 as a shift in equilibrium from E_0 (where GNP is \$4000 billion) to E_1 (where GNP is \$4250 billion). Of course, the size of the multiplier itself must also be estimated. To summarize:

The effect of monetary policy on aggregate demand depends on the sensitivity of interest rates to the money supply, on the responsiveness of investment spending to the rate of interest, and on the size of the multiplier.

Money and the Price Level in The Keynesian Model

One need only recall the inflation of the 1970s to realize that we have forgotten something. What happens to the price level? To answer this, we must simply remember once again that prices and output are determined jointly by aggregate demand *and* aggregate supply. The analysis of monetary policy that we have completed so far has shown us how an increase in the money supply shifts the aggregate demand curve, that is, increases the *aggregate quantity demanded at any*

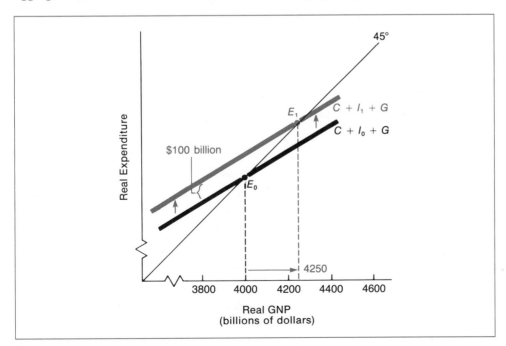

Figure 14–9
THE EFFECT OF EXPANSIONARY MONETARY POLICY ON AGGREGATE DEMAND
Expansionary monetary policies, which lower the rate of interest, will cause the $C + I + G$ schedule to shift upward from $C + I_0 + G$ to $C + I_1 + G$, as shown here. In this example, since the multiplier is 2.5, a \$100 billion rise in investment leads, via the multiplier process, to a \$250 billion rise in GNP.

given price level. But to learn what happens to the price level and to real output, we must consider *aggregate supply* as well.

Specifically, in considering shifts in aggregate demand caused by *fiscal* policy in Chapter 12, we noted that an upsurge in total spending normally induces firms to increase output somewhat *and* to raise prices somewhat. This is just what an aggregate supply curve shows. Whether prices or real output exhibit the greater response depends mainly on the degree of capacity utilization. An economy operating near full employment has but a limited ability to increase production; it therefore responds to greater demand mainly by raising prices. On the other hand, an economy with a substantial amount of unemployed labor and unused capital can produce a great deal more output without raising prices.

Now this analysis of output and price responses applies equally well to monetary policy or, for that matter, to anything else that raises aggregate demand. We conclude, then, that:

Expansionary monetary policy causes some inflation under normal circumstances. But how much inflation it causes depends on the state of the economy. If the money supply is expanded when unemployment is high and there is much unused industrial capacity, then the result may be little or no inflation. If, however, increases in the money supply occur when the economy is fully employed, then the main result is likely to be inflation.

The effect of a rise in the money supply on the price level is depicted graphically on an aggregate supply and demand diagram in Figure 14–10. The curved shape of aggregate supply curve SS reflects the assumptions that output rises with little inflation when the economy is depressed, while prices rise with little gain in output when the economy is near full employment.

In the example we have been using, the Fed's actions raise the money supply by \$40 billion, and this increases aggregate demand (through the multiplier) by \$250 billion. We enter this in Figure 14–10 as a horizontal shift of \$250 billion in the aggregate demand curve, from D_0D_0 to D_1D_1. The diagram shows that this expansionary monetary policy raises the economy's equilibrium from

Figure 14–10

THE INFLATIONARY EFFECTS OF EXPANSIONARY MONETARY POLICY
Raising the money supply normally causes inflation. When expansionary monetary policy causes the aggregate demand curve to shift outward from D_0D_0 to D_1D_1, the economy's equilibrium shifts from point E to point B. Real output expands (in this case by \$200 billion), but prices also rise (in this case by 3 percent).

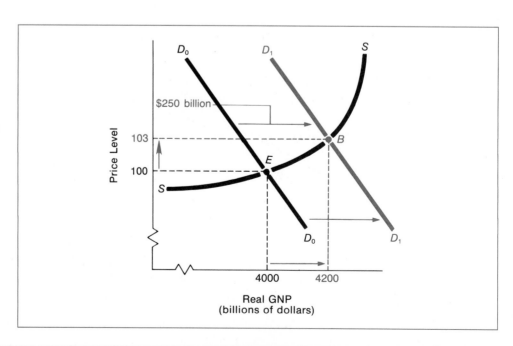

point E to point B — the price level therefore rises from 100 to 103, or 3 percent. The diagram also shows that real GNP rises by only $200 billion, which is less than the $250 billion stimulus to aggregate demand. The reason, as we know from earlier chapters, is that rising prices stifle demand.

By taking account of the effect of an increase in the money supply on the price level, we have completed our story about the role of monetary policy in the Keynesian model. We can thus expand our schematic diagram of monetary policy as follows:

$$\boxed{\begin{array}{c}\text{Federal Reserve}\\\text{policy}\end{array}} \xrightarrow{\;①\;} \boxed{M \text{ and } r} \xrightarrow{\;②\;} \boxed{I} \xrightarrow{\;③\;} \boxed{C + I + G} \xrightarrow{\;④\;} \boxed{Y \text{ and } P}$$

The last link now recognizes that *both* output *and* prices normally are affected by changes in the money supply.

Application: Why the Aggregate Demand Curve Slopes Downward

This analysis of the effect of money on the price level puts us in a better position to understand why higher prices reduce aggregate quantity demanded; that is, why the aggregate demand curve slopes downward. In earlier chapters, we explained this phenomenon by observing that rising prices reduce the purchasing power of certain assets held by consumers, especially money and government bonds, and that this in turn retards consumption spending. There is nothing wrong with this analysis. But higher prices have a much more important effect on aggregate demand through a channel that we are now in a position to understand.

Money is demanded primarily to conduct transactions and, as we have noted in this chapter, a rise in the *average money cost* of each transaction — as a result of a rise in the price level — will increase the quantity of money demanded. This means that when expansionary policy of any kind pushes the price level up, more money will be demanded at any given interest rate.

But, if the supply of money is *not* increased, an increase in the quantity of money demanded at any given interest rate must force the cost of borrowing money — the rate of interest — to rise. As we know, increases in interest rates reduce investment and, hence, reduce aggregate demand. This, then, is the main reason why the economy's aggregate demand curve has a negative slope, meaning that aggregate quantity demanded is lower when prices are higher. In sum:

At higher price levels, the quantity of money demanded is greater. Given a fixed supply schedule, therefore, a higher price level must lead to a higher interest rate. Since high interest rates discourage investment, aggregate quantity demanded is lower when the price level is higher. That is, the aggregate demand curve slopes downward to the right.

From Models to Policy Debates

You will no doubt be relieved to hear that we have now developed just about all the technical apparatus we need to analyze stabilization policy. To be sure, you will encounter many graphs in the next few chapters. But most of them are repeats of diagrams with which you are already familiar. Our attention now turns from *building* models to *using* models to understand important policy issues. The next three chapters take up a trio of important and controversial policy debates that surface regularly in the newspapers: the Keynesian–monetarist debate over stabilization policy (Chapter 15), the Reagan-era debate over the government budget deficit (Chapter 16), and the controversy over the tradeoff between inflation and unemployment (Chapter 17).

Summary

1. A central bank is a bank for banks.

2. The Federal Reserve System is America's central bank. There are 12 Federal Reserve banks, but most of the power is held by the Board of Governors in Washington and by the Federal Open Market Committee.

3. The Federal Reserve is independent of the rest of the government. There is controversy over whether this independence is a good idea, and a number of reforms have been suggested in recent years that would make the Fed more accountable to the president or to Congress.

4. The Fed has three major weapons for control of the money supply: open-market operations, reserve requirements, and its lending policy to the banks.

5. By lowering or raising reserve requirements, the Fed makes it possible for each dollar of reserves to support more or fewer dollars of deposits. Thus, lowering or raising the reserve ratio is one way to increase or decrease the money supply.

6. But the Fed does not do this very often. More typically, it raises the money supply by purchasing government securities in the open market. The Fed's payments to the banks for such purchases provide banks with new reserves and, hence, lead to a larger money supply. Conversely, open market sales of securities take reserves from the banks and lead to a smaller money supply.

7. When the Fed buys bonds, bond prices rise and interest rates fall. When the Fed sells bonds, bond prices fall and interest rates rise.

8. The Fed can also increase the money supply by allowing banks to borrow more reserves, perhaps by reducing the interest rate it charges on such loans. Alternatively, by discouraging borrowing, it can make the money supply contract.

9. None of these weapons, however, gives the Fed perfect control over the money supply in the short run, because it cannot predict perfectly how far the process of deposit creation or destruction will go.

10. The money supply schedule shows that more money is supplied at higher interest rates because, as interest rates rise, banks find it more profitable to expand their loans and deposits. This schedule can be shifted by Federal Reserve policy.

11. The money demand schedule shows that less money is demanded at higher interest rates because interest is the opportunity cost of holding money. This schedule shifts when output or the price level changes.

12. The equilibrium money stock (M) and the equilibrium rate of interest (r) are determined by the intersection of the money supply and money demand schedules.

13. Federal Reserve policy can shift this equilibrium. Expansionary policies cause M to rise and r to fall. Contractionary policies reduce M and increase r.

14. Investment spending (I), including business investment and investment in new homes, is sensitive to interest rates (r). Specifically, I is lower when r is higher.

15. This fact explains how monetary policy works in the Keynesian model. Raising the money supply (M) leads to lower r; the lower interest rates stimulate more investment spending; and this investment stimulus, via the multiplier, then raises aggregate demand.

16. However, prices are likely to rise as output rises. The amount of inflation caused by increasing the money supply depends on the levels of unemployment and of capacity utilization. There will be much inflation when the economy is near full employment, but little inflation when there is a great deal of slack.

17. The main reason why the aggregate demand curve slopes downward is that higher prices increase the demand to hold money in order to finance transactions. Given the money supply, this pushes interest rates up; and this, in turn, discourages investment.

Concepts for Review

Central bank
Federal Reserve System
Federal Open Market Committee (FOMC)
Independence of the Fed
Reserve requirements
Open-market operations

Bond prices and interest rates
Contraction and expansion of the money supply
Federal Reserve lending to banks
Moral suasion
Supply of money

Demand for money
Opportunity cost
Equilibrium in the money market
Monetary policy
Why the aggregate demand curve slopes downward

Questions for Discussion

1. Why does a modern industrial economy need a central bank?

2. Do you think it is a good idea to have an independent central bank? Explain your reasons.

3. Suppose there is $60 billion of cash in existence, and that half of it is held in bank vaults as *required* reserves (that is, banks hold no *excess* reserves). How large will the money supply be if the required reserve ratio is $16\frac{2}{3}$ percent? 20 percent? 25 percent?

4. Show the balance sheet changes that would take place if the Federal Reserve Bank of San Francisco purchased an office building from the Bank of America for a price of $100 million. Compare this to the effect of an open-market purchase of securities shown in Table 14–1. What do you conclude?

5. Suppose that the Fed purchases $8 million worth of government bonds from David Rockefeller, who banks at the Chase Manhattan Bank of New York. Show the effects on the balance sheets of the Fed, the Chase Manhattan Bank, and David Rockefeller. (*Hint:* What will Rockefeller do with the $8 million check he receives from the Fed?) Does it make any difference if the Fed buys bonds from a bank or from an individual?

6. Why would the Fed's control over the money supply be tighter under a system of 100 percent reserves?

7. Explain why the quantity of money supplied normally is higher and the quantity of money demanded normally is lower at higher interest rates.

8. What steps can the Fed take if it wants to drive the interest rate down? Illustrate on a diagram.

9. Explain why both business investments and purchases of new homes are expected to decline when interest rates rise.

10. Explain what a $40 billion increase in the money supply will do to real GNP under the following assumptions:
    a. Each $20 billion increase in the money supply reduces the rate of interest by 1 percentage point.
    b. Each 1 percentage point decline in interest rates stimulates $30 billion of new investment spending.
    c. The expenditure multiplier is 2.5.
    d. There is so much unemployment that prices do not rise noticeably when demand increases.

11. Explain how your answer to Question 10 would differ if each of the assumptions were changed. Specifically, what sorts of changes in the assumptions would make monetary policy very weak?

12. Use graphs like Figures 14–5 and 14–7 to explain why the aggregate demand curve has a negative slope.

13. (More difficult) Consider an economy in which government purchases and taxes are both zero, the consumption function is:

$$C = 100 + 0.8\,Y,$$

and investment spending (I) depends on the rate of interest (r) in the following way:

$$I = 500 - 800\,r.$$

Find the equilibrium GNP if the Fed makes the rate of interest (a) 5 percent ($r = 0.05$), (b) 10 percent, (c) zero.

15

The Keynesian–Monetarist Debate

Up to now our discussion of stabilization policy has been almost entirely objective and technical. In seeking to understand how the national economy works and how government policies affect it, we have mostly ignored the intense economic and political controversies that surround the actual conduct of stabilization policy. Chapters 15 through 17 are about precisely these issues. The present chapter derives its name from the fact that the protagonists in several of these debates are groups of economists that the news media have dubbed *Keynesians* and *monetarists*.

We begin the chapter by explaining the monetarist view of how money affects the economy. Although the monetarist and Keynesian theories seem to be two contradictory views of how monetary and fiscal policy work, we will see that the conflict is more apparent than real. In fact, the disagreement is akin to hearing a Briton say, "Yes," and a Frenchman say, "Oui." The uninitiated hear two different languages, but knowledgeable listeners understand that they mean the same thing.

However, while one major objective of this chapter is to show that the differences between the two theories are greatly exaggerated, there *are* significant differences between the two schools of thought—not outright contradictions but differences in emphasis. These differences occupy the rest of the chapter. We shall see that monetarists and Keynesians disagree over the nature of aggregate supply, over the relative importance of monetary and fiscal policy, over whether the Federal Reserve should try to control the money stock or interest rates, and, indeed, over whether the government should try to conduct any stabilization policy at all. Since economists' abilities to forecast the future is critical to the success or failure of stabilization efforts, considerable time is spent in this chapter on the techniques and accuracy of economic forecasting.

Velocity and the Quantity Theory of Money

We saw in the last chapter how money influences real output and the price level in the Keynesian model. But there is another way to look at these matters, using a model that is much older than the Keynesian model and yet is at the heart of modern critiques of Keynesian economics. This model is known as the

quantity theory of money, and it is easy to understand once we have introduced one new concept — *velocity*.

We learned in Chapter 13 that because barter is so cumbersome, virtually all economic transactions in advanced economies are conducted by the use of money. This means that if there are, say, $4500 billion worth of transactions in the economy during a particular year, and there is an average money stock of $900 billion during that year, then each dollar of money must get used an average of five times during the year (since 5 × $900 billion = $4500 billion).

The number 5 in this example is called the **velocity of circulation,** or just **velocity** for short, because it indicates the speed at which money circulates. For example, a particular dollar bill might be used to buy a haircut in January; the barber might use it to buy a sweater in March; the storekeeper might then use it to pay for gasoline in May; the gas station owner could pay it out to the painter who paints his house in October; and the painter might spend it on a Christmas present in December. This would mean that the dollar was used five times during the year. If it were used only four times during the year, its velocity would be only 4, and so on. Similarly, a $20 bill circulating with a velocity of 8 would be the monetary instrument used to finance $160 worth of transactions in that year.

Velocity indicates the number of times per year that an "average dollar" is spent on goods and services. It is the ratio of nominal GNP to the number of dollars in the money stock. That is:

$$\text{Velocity} = \frac{\text{Nominal GNP}}{\text{Money stock}}$$

No one has data on all the transactions in the economy. To make velocity an operational concept, we must settle on a precise definition of transactions that we can actually measure. The most popular choice is gross national product in current dollars (nominal GNP), even though it ignores many transactions which use money — such as sales of existing assets. If we accept nominal GNP as a measure of the money value of transactions, we are lead to a concrete definition of velocity as the ratio of nominal GNP to the number of dollars in the money stock. Since nominal GNP is the product of real GNP times the price level, we can write this definition in symbols as:

$$\text{Velocity} = \frac{\text{Value of transactions}}{\text{Money Stock}} = \frac{\text{Nominal GNP}}{M} = \frac{P \times Y}{M}.$$

By multiplying both sides of the equation by M, we arrive at an identity called the **equation of exchange** that relates the money supply and nominal GNP:

$$\text{Money supply} \times \text{Velocity} = \text{Nominal GNP}.$$

Alternatively, stated in symbols, we have:

$$M \times V = P \times Y.$$

The **equation of exchange** states that the money value of GNP transactions must be equal to the product of the average stock of money times velocity. That is:

$$M \times V = P \times Y.$$

Here we have quite an obvious link between the stock of money, M, and the nominal value of the nation's output. But it is only a matter of arithmetic, not of economics. For example, it does not imply that the Fed can raise nominal GNP by increasing M. Why not? Because V might simultaneously fall by enough to prevent M × V from rising. That is, if there were more dollar bills in circulation than before, but each bill changed hands more slowly, total spending would not necessarily rise. Thus:

The *quantity theory of money* transforms the equation of exchange from an accounting identity into an economic model by assuming that changes in velocity are so minor that velocity can be taken to be virtually constant.

You can see that if V never changed, the equation of exchange would be a marvelously simple model of the determination of nominal GNP—far simpler than the Keynesian model. To see this, we need only to turn the equation of exchange around to read,

$$P \times Y = V \times M.$$

This equation says, for example, that if the Federal Reserve wants to increase nominal GNP by 12.7 percent, it need only raise the money supply by 12.7 percent. In such a simple world, economists could use the equation of exchange to *predict* nominal GNP simply by predicting the quantity of money. And policymakers could *control* nominal GNP simply by controlling the money supply.

In the real world things are not so simple because velocity is not a fixed number. But this does not necessarily destroy the usefulness of the quantity theory. We explained in Chapter 1 why all economic models make assumptions that are at least mildly unrealistic—without such assumptions they would not be models at all, just tedious descriptions of reality. The question is really whether the assumption of constant velocity is a useful abstraction from annoying detail or a gross distortion of facts.

Figure 15–1 sheds some light on this question by showing the behavior of velocity since 1929. You will undoubtedly notice a downward trend in the graph from 1929 until 1946, an upward trend until 1981, and a downward movement in recent years. Clearly, *velocity is not constant over long periods of time*. Closer examination of monthly or quarterly data reveals some rather substantial fluctuations of velocity about its trend. Such fluctuations have led most economists to the conclusion that *velocity is not constant in the short run either*. Nor have predictions of nominal GNP based on the product of V times M fared very well. It seems, then, that the strict quantity theory of money is not an adequate model of aggregate demand.

Figure 15–1
VELOCITY OF
CIRCULATION,
1929–1986
During a period of American history of nearly 60 years, velocity fell from 3.5 in 1930 to about 2 in 1946, and then rose to almost 7 in 1981 before falling again. Clearly, velocity is not constant over long periods of time.
NOTE: This graph uses the M1 definition of money.

SOURCE: Constructed by the authors; data from Bureau of Economic Analysis and Federal Reserve Board.

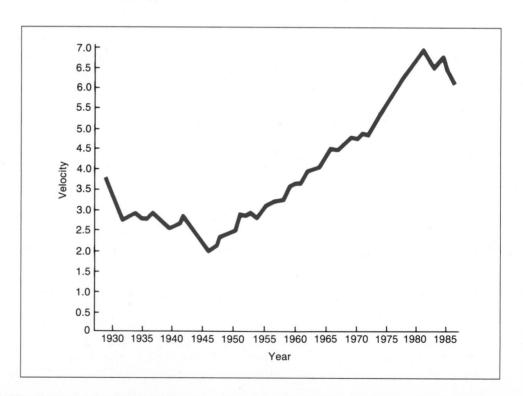

The Determinants of Velocity

Since it is abundantly clear that velocity is a variable, not a constant, we can use the equation of exchange as a model of GNP determination only by examining the determinants of velocity. What factors decide whether V will be 4 or 5 or 6; that is, whether a dollar will be used to buy goods and services four or five or six times a year?

Perhaps the principal factor is the *frequency with which paychecks are received*. This can best be explained through a numerical example. Consider a worker who earns $24,000 a year, paid to her in 12 monthly paychecks of $2000 each. Suppose that she spends the whole $2000 over the course of each month and maintains a minimum balance in the checking account of $500. Each payday her bank balance will shoot up to $2500 and then be gradually whittled down as she makes withdrawals to purchase goods and services. Finally, on the day before her next paycheck arrives, her checking balance will be just $500. Over the course of a typical month, then, her average checking account balance will be $1500 (halfway between $2500 and $500).

Now suppose her employer switches to a twice-a-month payroll. Her paychecks come twice as often, but are reduced to $1000 each. There is no reason for her rate of spending to change, but her *cash balances* will change. For now her checking balance will rise only to $1500 on payday (the $500 minimum balance plus the $1000 paycheck), and it will still be drawn down gradually to $500. Her average cash balance will therefore decline to $1000 (halfway between $1500 and $500). Why is this so? Because, with the next paycheck coming sooner than before, it is not necessary to keep as much cash in the bank in order to carry out a given quantity of transactions.

But what does this have to do with velocity? Notice that when she was on a monthly payroll, this worker's personal velocity was:

$$V = \frac{\text{Annual income}}{\text{Average cash balance}} = \frac{\$24,000}{\$1500} = 16.$$

When she switched to a semimonthly payroll, velocity rose to:

$$V = \frac{\text{Annual income}}{\text{Average cash balance}} = \frac{\$24,000}{\$1000} = 24.$$

The general lesson to be learned is that:

More frequent wage payments mean that people can conduct their transactions with lower average cash balances. Since they will want to hold less cash, money will circulate faster. In other words, velocity will rise.

A second factor influencing velocity is the *efficiency of the payments mechanism,* including how quickly checks clear banks, the use of credit cards, and other methods of transferring funds. It is easy to see how this works.

The example in the previous paragraph assumed that our worker holds her entire paycheck in the form of money until she uses it to make a purchase. But, given that many forms of money pay little or no interest, this method may not be the most rational behavior. If it is possible to convert interest-bearing assets into money on short notice and at low cost, a rational individual might use her paycheck to purchase such assets and then use credit cards for most purchases, making periodic transfers to her checking account as necessary. For the same amount of total transactions, then, she would require lower money balances. This means that money would circulate faster: Velocity would rise.

The incentive to limit cash holdings depends on the ease and speed with which it is possible to exchange money for other assets. This is what we mean by the "efficiency of the payments mechanism." As computerization has speeded up the bookkeeping procedures of banks, as financial innovations have made it possible to transfer funds rapidly between checking accounts and other assets, and as credit cards have come to be used instead of cash, the need to hold money balances has declined. By definition, then, velocity has risen.

Fortunately such basic changes in the payments mechanism usually take place only gradually, and thus often are easy to predict. But this is not always so. For example, a host of financial innovations in the 1970s and 1980s — some of which were mentioned in Chapter 13's discussion of the definitions of money — have given analysts fits in predicting velocity.

A third determinant of velocity is the *rate of interest*. The basic motive for economizing on money holdings is that most money (at least M1) pays little or no interest, while many alternative stores of value pay higher rates. The higher these alternative rates of interest, the greater the incentive to economize on holding money. Therefore, as interest rates rise, people want to hold less money. So the existing stock of money circulates faster, and velocity rises.

It is this factor that most directly undercuts the usefulness of the quantity theory of money as a guide for monetary policy. For in the last chapter we learned that expansionary monetary policy, which increases M, normally also decreases the interest rate. But if interest rates fall, other things being equal, velocity (V) will also fall. Thus, *when the Fed raises the money supply (M), the product* M × V *may go up by a smaller percentage than does M itself.*

One component of the interest rate is worth singling out for special attention: *the expected rate of inflation*. We explained in Chapter 6 why an "inflation premium" equal to the expected inflation rate often gets built into market interest rates.[1] Thus, in many instances, high inflation is the principal cause of high nominal interest rates. High rates of inflation, which erode the purchasing power of money, therefore lead both individuals and businesses to hold as little money as they can get by on — actions that increase velocity. To summarize this discussion of the determinants of velocity:

Velocity is not a strict constant but depends on such things as the frequency of payments, the efficiency of the financial system, the rate of interest, and the rate of inflation. Only by studying these determinants of velocity can we hope to predict the level of nominal GNP from knowledge of the money supply.

Monetarism: The Quantity Theory Modernized

The foregoing does not mean, however, that the equation of exchange cannot be a useful framework within which to organize macroeconomic analysis. Under the right circumstances, it can be. And during the past 30 years or so a group of economists called *monetarists* has convincingly demonstrated that this is so.

Monetarists recognize that velocity is not a constant. But they stress that it is fairly *predictable* — certainly in the long run and probably also in the short

[1]If you need review, turn back to pages 104–105.

run. This leads them to the conclusion that the best way to study economic activity is to start with the *equation of exchange:* $M \times V = P \times Y$. From here, careful study of the determinants of M (which we provided in the previous two chapters) and of V (which we just completed) can be used to *predict* the behavior of nominal GNP. Similarly, given an understanding of movements in V, control over the money supply gives the Fed *control* over nominal GNP.

These are the central tenets of **monetarism**. When something happens in the economy, monetarists ask two questions:

1. What does this event do to the stock of money?
2. What does this event do to velocity?

From the answers, they assert that they can predict the path of nominal GNP.

By comparing the monetarist approach with the Keynesian approach that we described in the previous chapter, we can put both doctrines into perspective and understand the limitations of each. As we mentioned earlier, they differ more in style than in substance. Keynesians divide economic knowledge into three neat compartments — marked "C," "I," and "G" — and unite them all with the equilibrium condition that $C + I + G = Y$. In Keynesian analysis, money affects the economy by first affecting interest rates.

Monetarists, on the other hand, organize their knowledge into two alternative boxes — labeled "M" and "V" — and then use a simple identity that says $M \times V = P \times Y$ to bring this knowledge to bear in predicting aggregate demand. In the monetarist model, the role of money in the national economy is not necessarily limited to working through interest rates.

The bit of arithmetic that multiplies M and V to get $P \times Y$ is neither more nor less profound than the one that adds up C and I and G to get Y. And certainly both identities are correct. The only substantive difference is that the monetarist equation leads to a prediction of *nominal* GNP, that is, the demand for goods and services measured in money terms, while the Keynesian equation leads to a prediction of *real* GNP, that is, the demand for goods and services measured in dollars of constant purchasing power.

Why, then, do we not simply mesh the two theories — using the monetarist approach to study nominal GNP and the Keynesian approach to study real GNP? It seems that by doing so we could use the separate analyses of real and nominal GNP to obtain a prediction of the future behavior of the price level, which, of course, is the source of any difference in behavior between real and nominal GNP.

The reason that this appealing procedure will not work helps point out the major limitation of each theory. *Taken by itself, either theory is incomplete*. Each gives us a picture of the *demand* side of the economy without saying anything about the *supply* side. To try to predict both the price level and real output solely from these demand-oriented models would be like trying to predict the price of peanuts by studying only the behavior of consumers and ignoring that of farmers. It just will not work. In terms of our earlier aggregate supply and demand analysis:

Both the monetarist and Keynesian analyses are ways of studying the *aggregate demand curve*. In neither case is it possible to learn anything about both output and the price level without also studying the *aggregate supply curve*.

Economists thus are forced to choose between two alternative ways of predicting aggregate demand. Those who choose the monetarist route will use

Monetarism is a mode of analysis that uses the equation of exchange to organize and analyze macroeconomic data.

velocity and the money supply to study the demand for *nominal* GNP, and then turn to the supply side to estimate how any predicted change in nominal income gets apportioned between changes in production and changes in prices. The schematic diagram on page 284, with its emphasis on interest rates, plays little role in the monetarist analysis of the transmission mechanism for monetary policy.

On the other hand, an economist working with the Keynesian $C + I + G$ approach will start by using the schematic diagram on page 284 to predict how monetary policy affects the demand for *real* GNP. Then he will turn to the aggregate supply curve to estimate the inflationary consequences of this real demand.

Which approach works better? There is no generally correct answer for all economies in all periods of time. Therefore, it is not surprising that some economists prefer one approach while others favor the alternative. However, velocity has behaved in an erratic, and to some extent inexplicable, manner in the U.S. during the 1980s—which has led many economists to abandon monetarism.

Reconciling the Keynesian and Monetarist Views

We have already come a long way toward reconciling the Keynesian and monetarist views of how the economy operates. Keynesian analysis lends itself naturally to the study of fiscal policy, since G is a part of $C + I + G$. But we learned in the previous chapter that Keynesian economics also provides a powerful and important role for monetary policy: An increase in the money supply reduces interest rates, which, in turn, stimulates the demand for investment.

Monetarist analysis provides an obvious and direct route by which monetary policy influences both output and prices. But can the monetarist approach also handle fiscal policy? It can, because fiscal policy has an important effect on the rate of interest. And it is not hard to understand how this effect operates.

Let's see what happens to real output and the price level following, say, a rise in government purchases of goods and services. We learned in Chapter 12 that both real GNP (Y) and the price level (P) rise. But Chapter 14's analysis of the demand for money taught us that rising Y and P push the demand curve for money outward to the right. With no change in the supply curve for money, the rate of interest must rise. So expansionary fiscal policy raises interest rates.

If the government uses its spending and taxing weapons in the opposite direction, the same process works in reverse. Falling output and (possibly) falling prices shift the demand curve for money inward to the left. With a fixed supply curve for money, equilibrium in the money market leads to a lower interest rate. Thus:

Monetary policy is not the only type of policy that affects interest rates. Fiscal policy also affects interest rates. Specifically, increases in government spending or tax cuts normally push interest rates up, whereas restrictive fiscal policies normally pull interest rates down.

The fact that fiscal policy affects interest rates gives it a role in the monetarist model despite the fact that the equation of exchange, $M \times V = P \times Y$, does not include either government spending or taxation among its variables. Any fiscal policy that a Keynesian would call expansionary—higher spending, lower taxes, and so on—pushes up the rate of interest. And rising interest rates push up velocity because people want to hold less money when the interest they can earn on alternative assets increases. So it is through the V term in M × V that fiscal policy does its work in the monetarist framework. The equation of exchange, M × V = P × Y, then implies that nominal GNP must rise when, say, government spending increases—even if M is fixed. The given supply of money can finance more transactions when velocity is higher.

Conversely, restrictive fiscal policies like tax increases and expenditure cuts reduce the quantity of money demanded and lower interest rates. The consequent drop in velocity reduces income through the equation of exchange, because the money supply circulates more slowly.

The translation, then, seems to be complete. The Keynesian story about how fiscal policy works can be phrased in the monetarist dialect. And the monetarist tale about monetary policy can be told with a Keynesian accent. Furthermore, both modes of analysis help only to explain the mysteries of aggregate *demand* and must be supplemented by an analysis of aggregate *supply* to be complete. We must conclude, then, that:

The differences between Keynesians and monetarists have been grossly exaggerated by the news media. Indeed, when it comes to matters of basic economic theory, there are hardly any differences at all.

But this does not mean that Keynesians and monetarists must agree on everything any more than the fact that English prose can be translated into French implies that the English and the French always see eye to eye. There are important differences of emphasis and policy that we will take up in the remainder of this chapter.

Application: The Multiplier Formula Once Again

But first the fact that expansionary fiscal policy pushes up interest rates has another important consequence that we should mention. Recall that higher interest rates deter private investment spending. This means that when the government raises the G component of C + I + G, one of the side effects of its action will be to reduce the I component (by raising interest rates). Consequently, the sum C + I + G will not rise as much as simple multiplier analysis might suggest. The fact that a surge in government demand (G) discourages some private demand (I) provides another reason why the oversimplified multiplier formula, 1/(1 − MPC), exaggerates the size of the multiplier:

Because any rise in G (or, for that matter, any autonomous rise in C or I) pushes interest rates higher, and hence deters some investment spending, the increase in the sum C + I + G is smaller than what the oversimplified multiplier formula predicts.

Combining this observation with our previous analysis of the multiplier, we now have the following list of:

REASONS WHY THE OVERSIMPLIFIED MULTIPLIER FORMULA IS WRONG

1. It ignores price-level changes, which reduce the size of the multiplier.
2. It ignores the income tax, which reduces the size of the multiplier.
3. It ignores the rising interest rates that accompany any autonomous increase in spending, which also reduce the size of the multiplier.

Keynesians Versus Monetarists: Fiscal Versus Monetary Policy

Although the Keynesian and monetarist approaches can be thought of as two languages, it is well known that language can influence attitudes in many subtle ways. And it must be admitted that Keynesians and monetarists have not lacked things to argue about.

For years they conducted a spirited, and well publicized, debate over whether the government should rely mainly on fiscal policy or monetary policy to manage aggregate demand. While one would guess from reading the newspapers that this is the most important issue in the Keynesian–monetarist debate today, it is in fact the *least* important. It is unimportant because, as we have seen, each approach allows a role for each type of policy.

Nonetheless, the Keynesian language biases things subtly toward thinking that fiscal policy is central simply because fiscal actions influence aggregate demand so directly. G is, after all, a part of $C + I + G$. Monetarists, on the other hand, see a more indirect channel that works through interest rates and velocity, and they wonder if something might not go wrong along the way.

The roles are reversed in the analysis of monetary policy. To monetarists, the effect of the money supply on aggregate demand is simple — it follows directly from velocity through the equation of exchange: $M \times V = P \times Y$. While monetary policy also affects aggregate demand in the Keynesian model, the mechanisms are rather complex, and there is obviously room for a slip-up. Monetary expansion might not affect the interest rate much, or a fall in the interest rate might not induce much additional investment. Thus, some Keynesians have had their doubts when monetarists attributed great powers to monetary policy.

During the 1960s and early 1970s the choice between fiscal and monetary policy dominated the debate between the more partisan Keynesians and monetarists. Extreme monetarists claimed that fiscal policy was futile, while extreme Keynesians argued that monetary policy was useless. But during the 1970s, accumulating evidence made each extreme view seem less and less tenable. More and more monetarists had to admit that fiscal policy did affect output and prices, and more and more Keynesians had to concede the same to monetary policy. By 1976, two economists surveying the debate could write that "the shift has been so great that we wonder whether anything more than machismo and habit propels the controversy today." Nonetheless, echoes of this battle are occasionally heard today.

While Keynesians and monetarists agree that both fiscal and monetary policy have significant effects on aggregate demand, Keynesians tend to look more toward fiscal policy while monetarists tend to rely more on monetary policy.

This, however, is not a major difference.

Keynesians Versus Monetarists: Lags in Fiscal and Monetary Policy

More important than the issue of which type of policy is more *powerful* is the question of which type of medicine — fiscal or monetary — cures the patient more *quickly*. In our discussions of fiscal and monetary policy so far, we have ignored such subtle questions of timing and proceeded as if the authorities instantly noticed the need for stabilization policy, decided upon a course of action, and administered the appropriate medicine. In reality, each of these steps takes time.

First, delays in data collection and processing mean that the latest macroeconomic data pertain to the economy as it was a few months ago. Second, one of the prices of democracy is that the government often takes a distressingly long time to decide what should be done, to muster the necessary political support, and to put its decisions into effect. Finally, our $5 trillion economy is a bit like a sleeping elephant—it reacts rather sluggishly to moderate fiscal and monetary prods. As it turns out, these **lags in stabilization policy**, as they are called, play a pivotal role in the choice between fiscal and monetary policy. It is not hard to see why.

The main policy tool for manipulating consumer spending (C) is the personal income tax, and Chapter 8 documented why the fiscal policy planner can feel fairly secure that each $1 of tax reduction will lead to about 90 to 95 cents of additional spending *eventually*. But not all of this will happen at once.

First, consumers must learn about the tax change. Then more time may elapse before many consumers are convinced that the change is permanent. Finally, there is the simple force of habit: Households need time to adjust their spending habits when circumstances change. For all these reasons, consumers may increase their spending by only 30 to 50 cents for each $1 of additional income within the first few months after a tax cut. Only gradually, over a period of perhaps several years, will they raise their spending until they are finally consuming 90 to 95 cents of each additional dollar of income.

Lags are much longer for investment (I), which, while it also can be influenced by fiscal policy (tax incentives), provides the main vehicle by which monetary policy affects aggregate demand. Planning for capacity expansion in a large corporation is a long, drawn-out process. Ideas must be submitted and approved. Plans must be drawn up, funding acquired, orders for machinery or contracts for new construction placed. And most of this occurs *before* any appreciable amount of money is spent. Economists have found that much of the response of investment to changes in interest rates or tax provisions is delayed for several years.

The fact that C responds more quickly than I has important implications for the choice among alternative stabilization policies. The reason is that the most common varieties of fiscal policy affect aggregate demand either directly (G is a component of C + I + G) or work through consumption with a relatively short lag, while monetary policy has its major effects on investment. Therefore:

Conventional types of fiscal policy actions, such as changes in G or in personal taxes, probably affect aggregate demand much more promptly than do monetary policy actions.

Notice that the statement says nothing about which instrument is more *powerful*. It simply asserts that the fiscal weapon, whether it is stronger or weaker, acts more *quickly*. This important fact has been used to build a case that fiscal policy should bear the major burden of economic stabilization. But before you jump to such a conclusion, you should realize that the sorts of lags we have been discussing are not the only ones affecting the timing of stabilization policy.

Apart from these lags in expenditure, which are beyond the control of policymakers, there are further lags that are due to the behavior of the policymakers themselves! We are referring here to the delays that occur while the policymakers are studying the state of the economy, contemplating what steps they should take, and putting their decisions into effect. And here most observers believe that monetary policy has an important edge; that is:

Policy lags are normally much shorter for monetary policy than for fiscal policy.

The reasons are apparent. The Federal Open Market Committee (FOMC) meets frequently, so monetary policy decisions are made almost every month. And once the Fed decides on a course of action, it normally can be executed almost instantly by buying or selling bonds on the open market.

Contrast this with fiscal policy. Federal budgeting procedures operate on an annual budget cycle. Except in rare circumstances, *major* fiscal policy initiatives that affect spending can occur only at the time of the annual budget. Tax laws can be changed at any time, but the wheels of Congress grind slowly and it may take many months before Congress acts on a presidential request to change taxes. In sum, one has to be very optimistic to suppose that important fiscal policy actions can be taken on short notice.

Where does the combined effect of expenditure lags and policy lags leave us? With nothing conclusive, we are afraid. As the late Arthur Okun put it, the debate over whether the nation should rely only on monetary policy or only on fiscal policy is a bit like arguing whether a safe car is one with good headlights or one with good brakes. It is unwise to drive at night unless you have both.

Keynesians Versus Monetarists: Control of the Money Supply Versus Control of Interest Rates

But the Keynesian–monetarist battles did not end there. As the debate over fiscal versus monetary policy fizzled, the two schools of thought regrouped along new, and more productive, battle lines.

One major controversy that is very much alive today is over how the Federal Reserve should conduct monetary policy. Keynesians argue that the Fed should use open-market operations and its other tools to control the rate of interest (r) while monetarists insist that the Fed should concentrate on controlling the money supply (M). To appreciate the nature of the debate, we must first understand why the Fed cannot do both. That is, why can it not control both M and r at the same time?

Figure 15–2 will help us see the answer. It shows an initial equilibrium in the money market at point E, where money demand curve $M_0 D_0$ crosses money supply curve MS. Here the interest rate is $r = 9$ percent and the money stock is $M = \$550$ billion. Let us assume that these are the Fed's targets for M and r; it wants to keep the money supply and interest rates just where they are.

If the demand curve for money holds still, this is possible. But suppose the demand for money is not so obliging. Suppose, instead, that the demand curve shifts outward to the position indicated by $M_1 D_1$ in Figure 15–2. As we learned in the last chapter (see, especially, Figure 14–4 on page 280) this might happen because output increases or because prices rise. Or it might happen simply because people decide to hold more money. Whatever the reason, the Fed can no longer achieve both of its previous targets.

If the Fed takes no action, the outward shift in the demand curve will push up both the quantity of money (M) and the rate of interest (r). Figure 15–2 shows this graphically. If the demand curve for money shifts outward from $M_0 D_0$ to $M_1 D_1$ and there is no change in monetary policy (so that supply

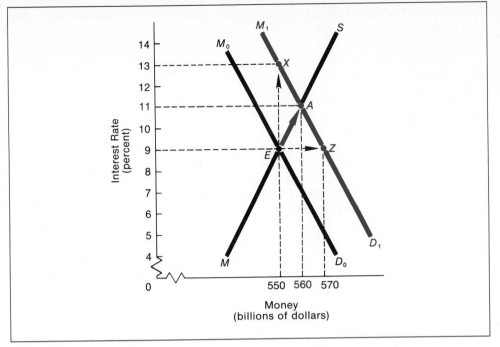

Figure 15–2
THE FEDERAL RESERVE'S POLICY DILEMMA
This diagram illustrates the dilemma facing the Fed when the demand schedule for money shifts. In this case, we suppose that it increases from $M_0 D_0$ to $M_1 D_1$. If the equilibrium at point E satisfied its goals both for the money supply ($550 billion) and for the rate of interest (9 percent), either one or both of these goals will have to be abandoned after the demand schedule shifts. Points X, A, and Z illustrate three of the many choices. At X, the Fed is keeping the money supply at $550 billion through contractionary policies, but at a cost of skyrocketing interest rates. At Z, the Fed is holding interest rates at 9 percent, but the required expansionary monetary policies raise the money supply to $570 billion. At A, the Fed is not adjusting its policy and is accepting an increase in both the money supply and the rate of interest.

schedule MS does not move), equilibrium moves from point E to point A. The money stock rises to $560 billion and the interest rate rises to 11 percent.

However, the supply of money is one of the major determinants of aggregate demand. Consequently, if the economy is already operating near full employment, the Fed might be unwilling to let M rise. In that case, it can use any of its contractionary weapons to prevent M from rising. But, if it does this, it will push r up even higher because, with no increase in the money supply, an even higher interest rate is necessary to keep quantity supplied and quantity demanded equal.

This is also shown in Figure 15–2. After the demand curve for money shifts, point E is unattainable. The Fed must choose from among the points on $M_1 D_1$, and point X is the point on this curve that keeps the money supply at $550 billion. If the supply curve is pushed inward so that it passes through point X, M will remain at $550 billion. However, the interest rate will skyrocket to 13 percent.

Alternatively, if the economy is operating at low levels of resource utilization, the Fed might decide that a rise in M is permissible, but that a rise in r is to be avoided. Why? Because, as we know, investment spending normally declines when interest rates rise. In this case, the Fed would be forced to engage in expansionary monetary policy to prevent the outward shift of the demand curve for money from pushing up r. The reason is that only by providing additional money can the Fed equate supply to the higher demand without a rise in interest rates. In terms of Figure 15–2, the interest rate can be held at 9 percent by shifting the supply curve outward to pass through point Z. But to do this, the Fed will have to push the money supply up to $570 billion. To summarize this discussion:

When the demand curve for money shifts outward, the Fed must tolerate a rise in interest rates, a rise in the money stock, or both. It simply does not have the weapons to control *both* the supply of money *and* the interest rate. If it tries to keep M steady, then r will rise sharply. Conversely, if it tries to stabilize r, then M will shoot up.

This explains why the Fed often finds it impossible to control both the money supply and the rate of interest. A shift in the demand schedule for money supply may make previously selected targets for M and r unattainable.

What Should the Fed Do?

Keynesians and monetarists have argued for years over what the Fed should do about this dilemma. Should it adhere rigidly to its target growth path for the money supply, regardless of the consequences for interest rates? Should it hold interest rates steady even if that causes wild gyrations in the money stock? Or is some middle ground more appropriate? Let us explore the issues before considering what has actually been done.

The main problem with rigid targets for the *supply* of money is that the *demand* for money does not cooperate by growing smoothly and predictably from month to month; instead it dances about quite a bit in the short run. This confronts the monetarist recommendation to control the money supply with two problems:

1. It is almost impossible to achieve. Since the volume of money in existence depends on *both* the demand *and* supply schedules, it would require exceptional dexterity on the part of the Fed to keep M on target in the face of significant fluctuations in demand for money.

2. For reasons that were just explained, rigid adherence to money-stock targets might lead to wide fluctuations in interest rates, which could create an unsettled atmosphere for business decisions.

By the same token, even more powerful objections can be raised against exclusive concentration on interest rate movements. Since increases in nominal GNP shift the demand schedule for money outward (as Figure 15–2 shows), a central bank determined to keep interest rates from rising would have to expand the money supply in response. Conversely, when GNP sagged, it would have to contract the money supply to keep rates from falling. Thus, interest rate *pegging* would make the money supply expand in boom times and contract in recessions—with potentially grave consequences for the stability of the economy. Ironically, this is precisely the sort of monetary behavior the Federal Reserve System was designed to prevent. Hence, if the Fed is to control interest rates, it had better formulate flexible targets, not fixed ones.

What Has the Fed Done?

In the early part of the postwar period, the predominant view held that the interest rate target was much the more important of the two. The rationale for this view was that gyrating interest rates would cause abrupt and unsettling changes in investment spending, and this in turn would make the whole economy fluctuate. In this view, stabilization of interest rates was the best way to stabilize GNP. If fluctuations in the money supply were required to keep interest rates on a steady course, that would be nothing to worry about. Consequently, the Fed looked mostly at interest rates.

In the 1960s, this prevailing view came under increasing attack by Professor Milton Friedman and other monetarists. They argued that the Fed's obsession with stabilization of interest rates actually *destabilized* the economy because it led to undue fluctuations in the money supply. The monetarist prescription was simple. The Fed should stop worrying about fluctuations in interest rates and make the money supply grow at a constant rate from month to month and year to year.

Monetarism made important inroads at the Fed during the inflationary 1970s. Early in the decade, the central bank began to keep much closer tabs on the money stock than it previously had. More important, a major change in the conduct of monetary policy was announced by then-Chairman Paul Volcker in October 1979. Henceforth, he asserted, the Fed would stick more closely to its target for money stock growth regardless of the implications for interest rates. Interest rates would go wherever the law of supply and demand took them.

According to our analysis, this change in policy should have led to wider fluctuations in interest rates. And it did. Unfortunately, the Fed ran into some bad luck. The ensuing three years were marked by unusually severe gyrations in the demand for money, so the ups and downs of interest rates were far more extreme than anyone had expected. Figure 15–3 gives an indication of just how volatile interest rates were between late 1979 and late 1982. Naturally, this erratic performance led to some heavy criticism of the Fed.

Then, in October 1982, Chairman Volcker announced that the Fed was temporarily abandoning its attempts to stick to a target growth path for the money supply. Although he did not say so, his announcement presumably meant that the Fed would once again pay more attention to interest rate targets. As you can see in Figure 15–3, interest rates have been much more stable—though certainly not constant—since the change in policy. Most observers think this is no coincidence.

Since late 1982, the Fed has distanced itself more and more from the monetarist position on control of the money supply. In early 1987, it actually stopped posting growth targets for M1. The central bank has essentially adopted the Keynesian position—though without saying so. In truth, it had little choice. The demand curve for money behaved so erratically and so

Figure 15–3
THE BEHAVIOR OF INTEREST RATES, 1979–1987
This chart traces interest rate movements from 1979 through 1987. Notice the extreme volatility of rates during the period from late 1979 to mid-1982—the period in which the Fed was concentrating more on stabilizing the money supply. Since mid-1982, interest rates have been much less volatile.

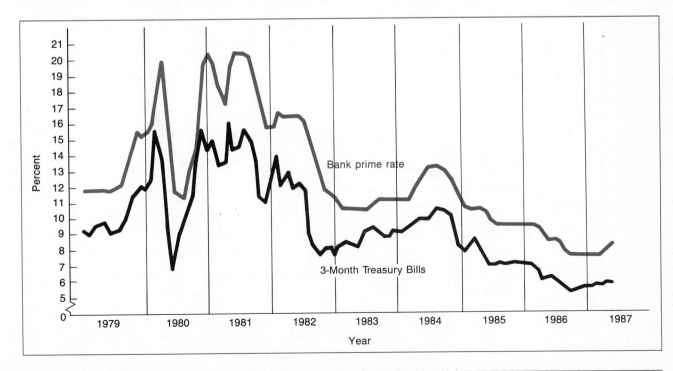

unpredictably between, say, 1981 and 1987 that stabilizing the money stock was probably impossible and certainly undesirable. Whether this situation will continue for the rest of the decade is anyone's guess.

Keynesians Versus Monetarists: The Aggregate Supply Curve

Another lively battleground in the Keynesian–monetarist debate today is over the shape of the economy's aggregate supply curve. As we have noted, either the Keynesian or the monetarist model must be supplemented by an aggregate supply curve if it is to tell us anything about output and prices. Most Keynesians tend to think of the aggregate supply curve as fairly flat in the short run, as in Figure 15–4(a), so that large increases in output can be achieved with little inflation. Monetarists, by contrast, envision the supply curve as steep, as in Figure 15–4(b), so that prices are very responsive to changes in output. The differences for public policy are substantial.

In the Keynesian view, expansionary fiscal or monetary policy that raises the aggregate demand curve can buy large gains in real GNP at little cost in terms of inflation. This is shown in Figure 15–5(a). Here, stimulation of demand raises the aggregate demand curve from $D_0 D_0$ to $D_1 D_1$ and moves the economy's equilibrium from point E to point A. There is a substantial rise in output ($400 billion) with only a pinch of inflation (1 percent).

Conversely, when the supply curve is flat, a restrictive stabilization policy is not a very effective way to cure inflation; instead, it serves mainly to reduce real output, as Figure 15–5(b) shows. Here, a leftward shift of the aggregate demand curve moves equilibrium from point E to point B, lowering real GNP by $400 billion but cutting the price level by merely 1 percent.

The monetarists see things differently. To them, the aggregate supply curve is so steep that expansionary fiscal or monetary policies are likely to cause a good deal of inflation without adding much to real GNP. [See

Figure 15–4
ALTERNATIVE VIEWS OF THE AGGREGATE SUPPLY CURVE
Keynesians tend to think of the economy's aggregate supply schedule as very flat, as in part (a), whereas monetarists tend to think of it as quite steep, as in part (b).

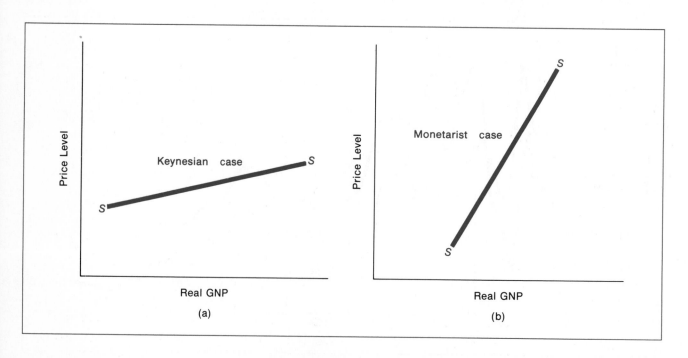

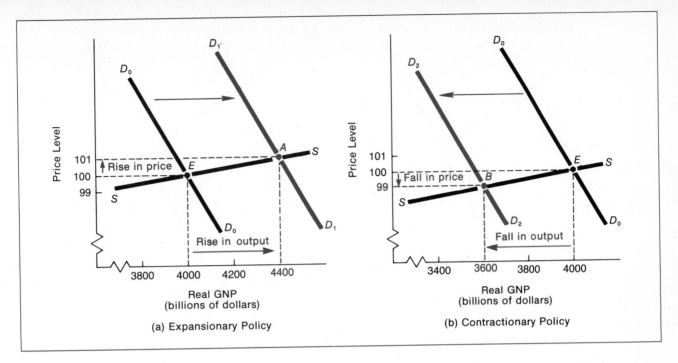

(a) Expansionary Policy

(b) Contractionary Policy

Figure 15–6(a), where expansionary policies shift equilibrium from E to A.] Similarly, contractionary policies are effective ways of bringing down the price level without much sacrifice of output, as shown by the shift from E to B in Figure 15–6(b).

The resolution of this debate is of fundamental importance for the proper conduct of stabilization policy. If the Keynesian view is right, stabilization policy is much more effective at combating recession than inflation. If the monetarist view is correct, the reverse is true.

But why does the argument persist? Why cannot economists determine whether the aggregate supply curve is flat or steep, and stop arguing? The answer is that supply conditions in the real world are far more complicated than our simple diagrams suggest. Some industries may have flat supply curves while others have steep ones. For reasons explained in Chapter 11, supply curves shift over time. And, unlike many laboratory scientists, economists cannot perform the controlled experiments that would reveal the shape of the aggregate supply curve directly. Instead, they must use statistical inference to make educated guesses.

Although empirical research on aggregate supply is proceeding, our understanding of aggregate supply remains much less settled than our understanding of aggregate demand. Nevertheless, many economists believe that the dim outline of a consensus view has emerged. This view stresses that the steepness of the aggregate supply schedule depends on the degree of slack in the economy.

If industry has a great deal of spare capacity, then increases in demand will not call forth large price increases. Similarly, when many workers are unemployed, employment can rise without causing much acceleration in the rate at which wages are growing. In a word, the aggregate supply curve is quite flat. On the other hand, when businesses are producing near capacity and unemployment is near the frictional level, greater demand for goods will induce firms to raise prices; and greater demand for labor will push wages up faster. In brief, the aggregate supply schedule will be steep.

Figure 15–5
STABILIZATION POLICY WITH A FLAT AGGREGATE SUPPLY CURVE: THE KEYNESIAN CASE
These two diagrams show that stabilization policy is much more effective as an antirecession policy than as an anti-inflation policy when the aggregate supply curve is flat. In part (a), monetary or fiscal policies push the aggregate demand curve outward from $D_0 D_0$ to $D_1 D_1$, causing equilibrium to shift from point E to point A. It can be seen that output rises substantially (from $4000 billion to $4400 billion), while prices rise only slightly (from 100 to 101, or 1 percent). So the policy is quite successful. In part (b), contractionary policies are used to combat inflation by pushing the aggregate demand curve inward from $D_0 D_0$ to $D_2 D_2$. Prices do fall slightly (from 100 to 99) as equilibrium shifts from point E to point B, but real output falls much more dramatically (from $4000 billion to $3600 billion); so the policy has had little success. Keynesians tend to believe in this case.

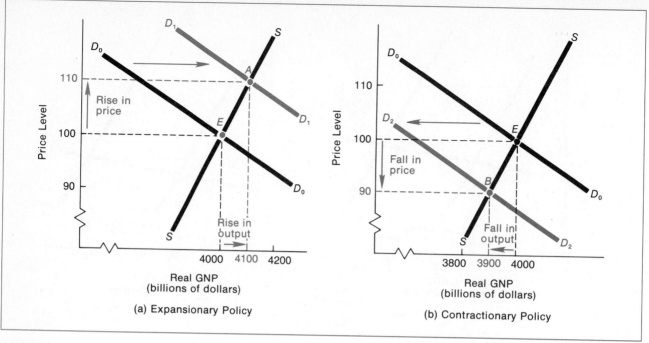

(a) Expansionary Policy

(b) Contractionary Policy

Figure 15–6

STABILIZATION POLICY WITH A STEEP AGGREGATE SUPPLY CURVE: THE MONETARIST CASE

These two diagrams show that stabilization policy is much more effective at fighting inflation than at fighting recession when the aggregate supply curve is steep. In part (a), expansionary policies that push aggregate demand outward from $D_0 D_0$ to $D_1 D_1$ raise output by only $100 billion but push up prices by 10 percent as equilibrium moves from point E to point A. So demand management is not a good way to end a recession. In part (b), contractionary policies that pull aggregate demand inward to $D_2 D_2$ are successful in that they lower prices markedly (from 100 to 90, or about 10 percent) but reduce output only slightly (from $4000 billion to $3900 billion). Monetarists tend to believe in this case.

Figure 15–7 shows a version of the aggregate supply curve that embodies these ideas. It has the same general shape as most of the supply curves that we have used in this book. At low levels of GNP, like Y_1, it is nearly horizontal; then its slope starts to rise gradually until at very high levels of GNP, like Y_2, it becomes almost vertical. The implication is that any change in aggregate demand will have most of its effect on *output* when economic activity is slack (the Keynesian case) but on *prices* when the economy is operating near full employment (the monetarist case). In summary:

1. Keynesians believe that the aggregate supply curve is rather *flat* in many circumstances, especially when the economy is operating at low levels of resource utilization. They therefore stress the effects of demand management on output and belittle the effects on prices.

2. Monetarists believe that the aggregate supply curve is rather *steep* in many circumstances, especially when the economy has little slack. They therefore emphasize the effects of demand management on prices and belittle the effects on real output.

3. A middle-of-the-road view would hold that the Keynesian case is stronger when there is a great deal of unemployment, while the monetarist case is stronger when the economy is near full employment. Not all economists accept this middle-of-the-road view, but many do.

Keynesians Versus Monetarists: Should the Government Intervene?

We have yet to consider what may be the most fundamental and controversial issue of all: Is it likely that the government can conduct a successful stabilization policy? Or are its well-intentioned efforts likely to be harmful, so that it would be better to adhere to fixed rules?

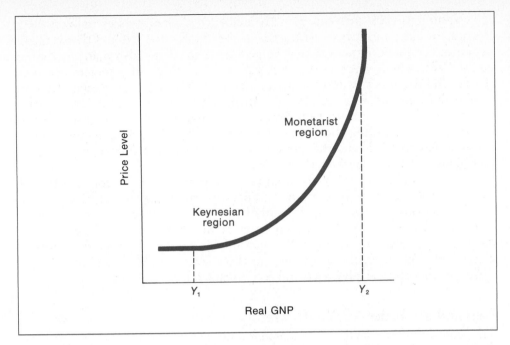

Figure 15–7
AN AGGREGATE SUPPLY
CURVE WITH BOTH
STEEP AND FLAT
REGIONS
As this diagram suggests,
either the Keynesians or the
monetarists may be right
under the appropriate
circumstances. The
Keynesian view of a flat
supply curve is likely to be
most accurate when there is
much unemployment and
unused capacity. The
monetarist view of a steep
supply curve is likely to be
more accurate when there is
full employment and high
capacity utilization.

This controversy has raged for several decades now, with no end in sight. That Keynesians favor discretionary stabilization policy while monetarists favor noninterventionist rules is not surprising, given their political differences. As it happens, monetarists tend to be politically conservative while many Keynesians are liberal. So it is natural that Keynesians should be more intervention-minded and monetarists more inclined to keep the government's hands off the economy. But much more than political ideology propels the debate. We want to understand the economic issues.

Monetarists point to the lags and uncertainties that surround the operation of both fiscal and monetary policies—lags and uncertainties that we have stressed repeatedly in this and earlier chapters. Will the Fed's actions have the desired effects on the money supply? What will these actions do to interest rates? How will they affect spending, and how long will it take before the effects appear? Can fiscal policy actions be taken promptly? Will consumers view tax changes as temporary or permanent? How large is the expenditure multiplier? The list could go on and on.

Monetarists look at this formidable catalogue of difficulties, add a dash of skepticism about our ability to forecast the future state of the economy (see page 314), and conclude that stabilization policy is likely to do more harm than good. They advise both the fiscal and monetary authorities to pursue a passive policy rather than an active one—adhering to fixed rules that, while they will not iron out all the bumps in the economy's growth path, will at least keep it roughly on track in the long run.

Keynesians, though they admit that perfection is unattainable, are much *more optimistic* about the possibility of achieving a successful stabilization policy. And they are much *less optimistic* than the monetarists about how smoothly the economy would function in the absence of demand management. They therefore advocate discretionary increases in government spending (or decreases in taxes) and more rapid growth of the money supply when the economy has a recessionary gap. By this policy mix, they believe, government can keep the economy closer to its full-employment growth path.

Naturally, each side can point to evidence that buttresses its own view. Keynesians like to look back with pride at the tax cut of 1964 and the sustained period of economic growth that it helped usher in. They also point to the tax cut of 1975, which was enacted at just about the trough of a severe recession, the Federal Reserve's switch to easy money in 1982, and the accidentally Keynesian tax cuts of 1983 and 1984 — all of which were helpful. Monetarists remind us of the government's refusal to curb what was obviously a situation of runaway demand during the 1966–1968 Vietnam buildup, its overexpansion of the economy in 1972, and the monetary overkill that helped bring on the sharp recessions of 1974–1975 and 1981–1982.

The historical record of fiscal and monetary policy is far from glorious. It shows that while there were many instances in which appropriate stabilization policy *could have been* helpful, the authorities instead either took inappropriate steps or did nothing at all. The question of whether the government should adopt passive rules or attempt an activist stabilization policy therefore merits a closer look. As we shall see, the lags in the effects of policy that we discussed earlier in this chapter play a pivotal role in the debate.

Lags and the Rules-Versus-Discretion Debate

The reason that lags lead to a fundamental difficulty for stabilization policy — a difficulty so formidable that it has led many economists to conclude that attempts to stabilize economic activity are likely to do more harm than good — can be explained best by reference to Figure 15–8. Here we chart the behavior of both actual and potential GNP over the course of a business cycle in a hypothetical economy in which no stabilization policy is attempted. At point A, the economy begins to slip into a recession and does not recover to full employment until point D. Then, between points D and E, it overshoots and is in an inflationary boom.

The case for stabilization policy runs like this. The recession is recognized to be a serious problem at point B, and appropriate actions are taken. These actions have their major effects around point C and therefore curb both the depth and the length of the recession.

Figure 15–8

A TYPICAL BUSINESS CYCLE

This is a stylized representation of the relationship between actual and potential GNP during a typical business cycle. The imaginary economy slips into a recession at point A, bottoms out around point B, and is in a recovery period until point D. After point D, it enters an inflationary boom that lasts until point E.

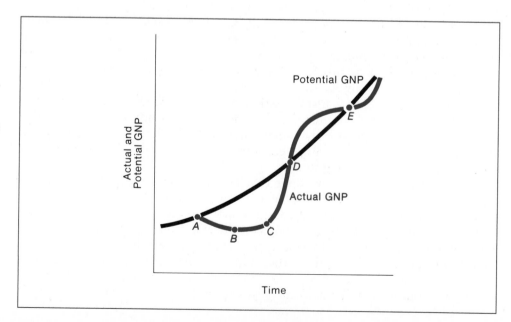

But suppose the lags are really much longer than this. Suppose, for example, that delays in taking action postpone policy initiatives until point C and that stimulative policies do not have their major effects until after point D. Then policy will be of little help during the recession and will actually do harm by overstimulating the economy during the ensuing boom. Thus:

In the presence of long lags, attempts at stabilizing the economy can actually succeed in destabilizing it.

Because of this, some economists, like Milton Friedman, have argued that we are better off letting the economy alone and relying on its natural self-corrective forces to cure recessions and inflations. Instead of embarking on periodic programs of monetary and fiscal stimulus or restraint, they advise policymakers to stick to fixed rules; that is, to rigid formulas that ignore current economic events.

Automatic Stabilizers

The rule most emphasized by monetarists is that the Fed keep the money supply growing at a constant rate. For fiscal policy, monetarists generally recommend that the government resist temptations to manage aggregate demand actively and rely instead on **automatic stabilizers**—features of the economy that reduce its sensitivity to shocks. Examples of automatic stabilizers are not hard to find in the federal budget. The personal income tax is the most obvious example.

An **automatic stabilizer** is any arrangement that automatically serves to support aggregate demand when it would otherwise sag and to hold down aggregate demand when it would otherwise surge ahead. In this way, an automatic stabilizer reduces the sensitivity of the economy to shifts in demand.

The ability of the income tax to act as a shock absorber derives from the fact that it makes disposable income, and thus consumer spending, less sensitive to fluctuations in GNP. When GNP rises, disposable income (*DI*) rises also, but by less than the rise in GNP because part of the income is siphoned off by the U.S. Treasury. This helps limit the upward fluctuation in consumption spending. And when GNP falls, *DI* falls less sharply because part of the loss is absorbed by the Treasury rather than by consumers. So consumption does not drop as much as it otherwise might. Thus, as we noted in Chapter 12, income taxes lower the value of the multiplier. In truth, the unloved personal income tax is one of several modern institutions that help ensure us against a repeat performance of the Great Depression.

There are many other automatic stabilizers in our economy. For example, in Chapter 6 we studied the U.S. system of unemployment insurance. This serves as an automatic stabilizer in a similar way. When GNP begins to fall and people lose their jobs, unemployment benefits prevent the disposable incomes of the jobless from falling as much as their earnings. As a result, unemployed workers can maintain their spending, and consumption need not fluctuate as dramatically as employment.

And the list could continue. The basic principle is the same: Each of these automatic stabilizers, in one way or another, serves as a shock absorber, thereby lowering the multiplier. And each does so without the need for any decision-maker to take action. In a word, they work *automatically*.

Stabilization Policy: Discretionary Measures or Fixed Rules?

Believers in fixed rules assert that we should forget about discretionary policy and rely solely on automatic stabilizers and the economy's natural, self-correcting mechanisms. Are they right? As usual, the answer depends on many factors.

How Fast Does the Economy's Self-Correcting Mechanism Work?

We stressed in Chapter 11 that the economy does have a self-correcting mechanism. If the economy can cure recessions and inflations quickly by itself, then the case for intervention is weak. For if such problems typically last only a short time, then lags in discretionary stabilization policy mean that the medicine will often have its major effects only after the disease is over. (In terms of Figure 15–8, this would be a case where point D comes very close to point A.)

While the more extreme advocates of rules argue that this is what indeed happens, most economists agree that the economy's self-correcting mechanism is slow and not terribly reliable, even when supplemented by the automatic stabilizers. On this count, then, a point is scored for the Keynesians and for discretionary policy.

How Long Are the Lags in Stabilization Policy?

As we explained, long lags before stabilization measures are adopted or take effect make it unlikely that policy can do much good, while short lags point in the other direction. Thus, advocates of fixed rules emphasize the length of lags while proponents of discretion discount them.

Who is really right depends on the circumstances. In the most optimistic scenario, fiscal policy actions are taken promptly, and the economy feels much of the stimulus from expansionary policy in less than a year after slipping into a recession. While far from an instant cure, such timely actions certainly would be felt soon enough to do some good. But, as we have seen, more pessimistic scenarios raise the possibility that policy may actually be destabilizing. History offers examples of both types of scenarios. No general conclusion can be drawn.

How Accurate Are Economic Forecasts?

One way to cut down the policy-making lag enormously is to have good economic forecasts. If we could see a recession coming a full year ahead of time (which we certainly *cannot* do), even a rather sluggish policy response would still be timely. (In terms of Figure 15–8, this would be a case where the recession is predicted well before point A.)

It therefore behooves us to take a look at the techniques that economists in universities, government agencies, and private businesses have developed over the years to assist them in predicting what the economy will do. There are a variety of techniques, none of them foolproof.

Techniques of Economic Forecasting

The Use of Econometric Models

An **econometric model** is a set of mathematical equations that embody the economist's model of the economy.

Among the most widely publicized forecasts are those generated by the use of **econometric models** of the economy. Put simply, an econometric model is merely a mathematical version of the models of macroeconomic activity that we have described in Parts 2–4. The difference is that the basic notions are cast in the form of mathematical equations rather than in diagrams. For example, our consumption function could have been expressed by the formula:

$$C = a + bDI,$$

where C is consumer spending and DI is disposable income, instead of by a graph.[2]

---

[2]This is nothing but the formula for a straight line with a slope of b and an intercept of a.

The builder of an econometric model takes equations like these and uses actual data to estimate the sizes of a and b. For example, statistical analysis may lead a forecaster to the conclusion that the correct magnitude of a in the previous formula is approximately 100 and that the most reasonable value of b is 0.8. Then the consumption function formula is:

$$C = 100 + 0.8\, DI\,.$$

This says that consumer spending is $100 (billion) plus 80 percent of disposable income. The economist can complete his model by adding a definition of disposable income as GNP minus tax receipts:

$$DI = Y - T,$$

and appending the fact that GNP is the sum of C, I, and G:

$$Y = C + I + G\,.$$

In this simple model, then, we have a total of three equations. If we hypothesize that government purchases, tax receipts, and investments are all unaffected by the relationships in the model, these three equations are just enough to determine the values of the three remaining variables: C, DI, and Y. These last three variables are called the model's *endogenous variables*, meaning that their values are determined *inside* the model. The remaining variables — G, T, and I — are called the model's *exogenous variables* because they must be provided from *outside* the model. With this nomenclature, it is easy to describe how the user of an econometric model forecasts the state of the economy:

An econometric forecaster uses a model to transform forecasts of the exogenous variables into corresponding forecasts of the endogenous variables.

Models actually used to forecast the behavior of the U.S. economy have hundreds of variables and equations. Because of their complexity, the only practical way to solve them for forecasts of all the endogenous variables is to use a high-speed computer. But making the forecasts accurate is another thing entirely because of the "garbage in, garbage out" problem: If you feed junk into a computer, that's exactly what comes out at the end. In the forecasting context, this "junk" can be either a bad set of predictions of the exogenous variables or an inaccurate set of equations. This is why model builders are constantly seeking to improve their equations. But they have yet to achieve anything like perfection. And, even if they did, their forecasts would still not be infallible because there is a certain amount of unavoidable randomness in macroeconomic behavior. After all, we are dealing with literally millions of individuals and business firms, and events essentially outside our control can sometimes exert a profound influence on our economy. (Example: Political turmoil in Iran in 1979 helped bring on the stagflation of 1979–1980.) So forecasts of the exogenous variables are bound to be wide of the mark at times.

Leading Indicators

A second forecasting method, pioneered at the National Bureau of Economic Research, exploits observed historical timing relationships through the use of certain **leading indicators** that have in the past given advance warning of economic events.

A **leading indicator** is a variable that, experience has shown, normally turns down before recessions start and turns up before expansions begin.

For example, the stock market is a leading indicator because stock market downturns normally begin several months before downturns in industrial production. Why does this happen? Does the decline in the stock market cause economic downturns by reducing consumer spending? Or are both the stock market and industrial production just reacting to some other influence, with the stock market's reaction coming sooner? Certainly these are fascinating questions. But the answers may not be crucial to a forecaster *if* the stock market continues to be as good a leading indicator for industrial production in the future as it has been in the past. In that event, we will be able to make use of the observed relationship between stock prices and industrial production for forecasting even if we do not entirely understand its origins.

As it turns out, however, excessive reliance on any single leading indicator produces an unimpressive forecasting record. An obvious solution is to look at many indicators. But once we start to do this, we will often receive conflicting signals. If one indicator is rising rapidly while another is falling, what are we to do?

One way to resolve this conflict is to form an average of several leading indicators. For example, every month the news media report the latest reading on the Commerce Department's composite index, which is a weighted average of 11 of their leading indicators. (See the boxed insert on page 313.) Figure 15–9 compares the behavior of this index with movements in real GNP. As you can see, the agreement is usually quite good. The leading indicators occasionally call for a recession that never comes (as in 1966), and occasionally they give clear early warning signals of a downturn (as in 1973 and 1979). But often movements of the leading indicators are followed so closely by movements in real gross national product that the advance warning they provide comes too late to be of much use to policymakers.

Figure 15–9
REAL GNP AND THE
LEADING INDICATORS,
1950–1986
This diagram compares the path of the leading indicators (in blue) with that of real GNP (in black). The scales have been adjusted to make the two series comparable. It can be seen that the leading indicators sometimes give advance warning of a turning point in economic activity (for example, in 1979) but often give false signals of turning points that never occur (for example, 1966).
SOURCE: *Business Conditions Digest* and *Survey of Current Business*.

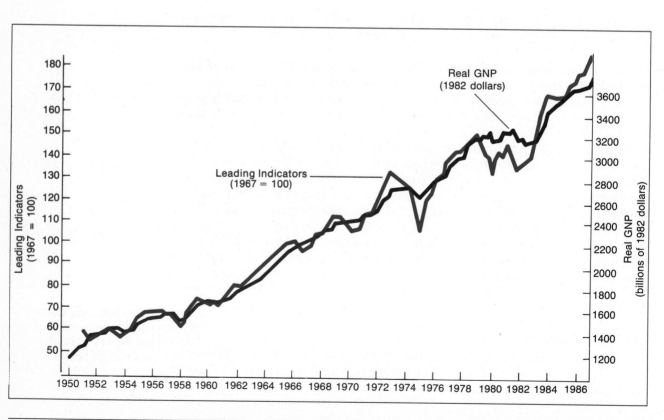

Survey Data

A third method of forecasting utilizes periodic surveys of the intentions of business and consumers. The Bureau of Economic Analysis of the Commerce Department and the Securities and Exchange Commission regularly ask firms how much money they plan to invest in factories and machinery over the next 3 to 12 months. These data are published in the financial press and are widely used by economists in industry, government, and academia. The Survey Research Center of the University of Michigan regularly conducts a survey of how consumers feel about both their personal finances and the general state of the economy. Some economists have found that this information on consumer sentiment helps improve forecasts of consumer spending.

Judgmental Forecasts

This term is used to describe the forecasts of those desperate (and probably prudent!) forecasters who refuse to rely on any one method, but look instead at every scrap of evidence they can get their hands on. They study the outputs of the econometric models; they watch the leading indicators; and they scrutinize the findings of surveys. At times, it seems, they even gaze at the stars. In any case, judgmental forecasters distill all this information in their heads and somehow arrive at a forecast of GNP and other key variables. How do they go about it? An outside observer can never really tell, since the very nature of judgmental forecasting precludes the existence of a formula that can be written down or described.

The Index of Leading Indicators

The Commerce Department's widely publicized index of leading indicators is a weighted average of 11 economic variables that have been shown to be useful in predicting business fluctuations. While the components of the index sometimes change, at the time of this writing they are:

1. Stock market prices.
2. The money supply (M2), expressed in 1982 dollars.
3. The change in business inventories.
4. The percentage change in sensitive commodity prices.
5. The average work week of production workers in manufacturing.
6. Initial claims for unemployment insurance. (This component enters negatively since rising unemployment is a sign of bad times.)
7. Building permits for private housing.
8. New orders for consumer goods and materials, in 1982 dollars.
9. Contracts and orders for investment goods, in 1982 dollars.
10. Change in business and consumer borrowing.
11. Vendor performance (an indicator of how easy or difficult it is for firms to get deliveries of inputs).

The Accuracy of Economic Forecasts

Which method wins the prize for the most accurate forecasts? First, no technique is clearly superior all the time. If it were, no one would do it any other way. Second, because econometric forecasters use surveys, lead–lag patterns, and judgment in forming their predictions of exogenous variables, and since judgmental forecasters watch the models closely, a clean comparison is impossible. In recent years, however, it seems that the most accurate forecasts have been derived by judgmental adjustment of forecasts from econometric models.

How accurate are economic forecasts? That depends both on the variable being forecast (consumption, for example, is easier than investment) and on the time period (for example, 1982–1983 were tough years for forecasters; 1984–1986 were much easier).

To give a rough idea of magnitudes, forecasts of the inflation rate for the year ahead typically err by plus or minus 1 to $1\frac{1}{2}$ percentage points. But in a rough year for forecasters, errors of 3 percentage points or so are common. Forecasts of real GNP for the coming year made during the 1970s and 1980s have also typically erred by between 1 and $1\frac{1}{2}$ percent. The biggest errors by far came in recession years like 1974–1975 and 1981–1982. Apart from these periods, errors of under 1 percent have been typical.[3]

Is this record good enough? That depends on what the forecasts are used for. It is certainly not good enough to support so-called fine tuning, that is, attempts to keep the economy always within a hair's breadth of full employment. But it probably is good enough if our interest in using discretionary stabilization policy is to close persistent and sizable gaps between actual and potential GNP.

Other Dimensions of the Rules-Versus-Discretion Debate

While lags and forecasting play major roles in the debate between advocates of rules and advocates of discretionary policy, these are not the only battlegrounds.

The Size of Government

One bogus argument that is nonetheless often heard is that an activist fiscal policy must inevitably lead to a growing public sector. Since proponents of fixed rules tend also to be opponents of big government, they view this as undesirable. Of course, others think that a large public sector is just what society needs. This argument, however, is completely beside the point because, as we pointed out in Chapter 12 (page 233): *One's opinion about the proper size of government should have nothing to do with one's view on stabilization policy*. For example, the Reagan administration promoted an extremely *activist* policy to spur the economy by *shrinking* the size of the public sector through reductions in taxes.

Uncertainties Caused by Government Policy

Advocates of rules are on stronger ground when they argue that frequent changes in tax laws, government spending programs, or monetary conditions make it difficult for firms and consumers to formulate and carry out rational plans. They argue that by adhering to fixed rules, which are known to businesses and consumers, the authorities can provide a more stable environment for the private sector.

[3]Victor Zarnowitz, "The Record and Improvability of Economic Forecasting," National Bureau of Economic Research, Working Paper No. 2099, December 1986.

While no one disputes that a more stable environment is better for private planning, supporters of discretionary policy point out the difference between stability in the government budget (or in Federal Reserve operations) and stability in the economy. The goal of stabilization policy is to help *prevent* gyrations in the pace of economic activity by *causing* timely gyrations in the government budget (or in monetary policy). Which atmosphere is better for business, they ask, one in which fiscal and monetary rules keep things peaceful on Capitol Hill and at the Federal Reserve System while recessions and inflations rack the economy, or one in which policy instruments are changed abruptly on occasion but the economy grows more steadily? They think that the answer is self-evident.

A Political Business Cycle?

A final argument used by advocates of rules is political rather than economic in nature. Fiscal policy, they note, is decided upon by elected politicians: the president and members of Congress. When elections are on the horizon (and for members of the House of Representatives they *always* are), these men and women are likely to be at least as concerned with keeping their offices as with doing what is right for the economy. This leaves fiscal policy subject to all sorts of "political manipulations," meaning that inappropriate actions may be taken to attain short-run political goals. In a system of purely automatic stabilization, its proponents argue, a rule of law would replace the rule of men, and this peril would be eliminated.

There is certainly a *possibility* that politicians could deliberately *cause* economic instability to help their own reelection. And some observers of these "political business cycles" have claimed that several American presidents have taken full advantage of the opportunity. Furthermore, even if there is no insidious intent, politicians may take the wrong actions for perfectly honorable reasons. Decisions in the political arena are never clear-cut, and it certainly is easy to find examples of grievous errors in the history of U.S. fiscal policy.

So, taken as a whole, the political argument against discretionary policy seems to have a great deal of merit. But what are we to do about it? It is foolhardy to believe that fiscal and monetary decisions could or should be made by a group of objective and nonpartisan technicians. Steering the economy is not like steering a rocket to the moon. Because policy actions that help on the employment front normally do harm on the inflation front, and vice versa, the "correct" policy action is almost always an inherently political matter. In a democracy, if we take such decisions out of the hands of elected officials, in whose hands shall we put them?

This harsh fact may seem worrisome in view of the possibilities for political chicanery, but it should not bother us any more (or any less!) than similar maneuvering in other areas of policy making. After all, the same thing applies to international relations, issues of national defense, formulation and enforcement of the law, and so on. Politicians make all these decisions for us, subject only to sporadic accountability at election times. Is there really any reason why economic decisions should be different?

Conclusion: What Should Be Done?

Where do all these considerations leave us? On balance, is it better to conduct discretionary policy as best we can, knowing full well that we will never do it perfectly? Or is it wiser to rely on fixed rules and the automatic stabilizers?

In weighing the pros and cons that we have discussed in this chapter, one's basic view of the economy is central. Some economists believe that the economy, if left unmanaged, would generate a series of ups and downs that are hard to predict, but that it would correct each of them by itself in a relatively short period of time. They conclude that, because of long lags and poor forecasts, our ability to anticipate whether the economy will be heading up or down by the time policy actions have their effects is quite limited. And so they are led to advocate fixed rules.

Other economists liken the economy to a giant glacier with a great deal of inertia. This means that if we observe an inflationary or recessionary gap today, it is likely still to be there a year or two from now because the self-correcting mechanism works so slowly. In such a world, accurate forecasting is not imperative, even if policy lags are long. If we base policy on a forecast of a $100 billion gap between actual and potential GNP a year from now, and the gap turns out to be only $50 billion, then we still will have done the right thing despite the horrible forecast. Holders of this view of the economy, then, are likely to advocate the use of discretionary policy.

While there is no consensus on this issue either among economists or among politicians, a prudent view might be that:

The case for active discretionary policy is strong when the economy has a serious deficiency or excess of aggregate demand. However, advocates of fixed rules are right that it is unwise to try to iron out every little wiggle in the growth path of GNP.

But the decision cannot be made solely on economic grounds. Political judgments enter as well. In the end:

The question of whether the government should take an active hand in managing the economy, which is one of the main bones of contention between Keynesians and monetarists today, is as much a matter of ideology as of economics. Liberals have always looked to government activism to solve social problems, while conservatives have consistently pointed out that many efforts of government fail despite the best intentions.

Table 15–1

MAJOR ISSUES IN THE KEYNESIAN–MONETARIST DEBATE

ISSUE	MONETARIST POSITION	KEYNESIAN POSITION	POSSIBLE COMPROMISE POSITION
View of velocity	stable	unstable	stable in some time periods; unstable in others
Best way to conduct monetary policy	control the money supply	control interest rates	watch both variables without rigidly controlling either
View of aggregate supply curve	steep	flat	flat in slack economy, steep near full employment
Should government try to stabilize the economy?	no	yes	only when gap between actual and potential GNP is large

Since no one can decide whether liberal or conservative political attitudes are the "correct" ones on purely objective criteria, the rules-versus-discretion debate is likely to go on for quite some time.

For your convenience, Table 15–1 summarizes the major issues in the Keynesian–monetarist debate and indicates a possible compromise position for each.

Summary

1. Monetarist and Keynesian analyses are two different ways of studying the determination of aggregate demand. Neither is a complete theory of the behavior of the economy until aggregate supply is brought into the picture.

2. Velocity (V) is the ratio of nominal GNP to the stock of money (M). It indicates how quickly money circulates, that is, how many times money changes hands in a year.

3. Among the determinants of velocity is the rate of interest (r). At higher interest rates, people find it less attractive to hold money because most money pays no interest. Thus, when r rises, money circulates faster, and V rises.

4. Monetarism is a type of analysis that focuses attention on velocity and the money supply (M). Though monetarists realize that V is not constant, they believe that it is predictable enough to make it a useful tool for policy analysis and forecasting.

5. Because it raises output and prices, and hence increases the demand for money, expansionary fiscal policy pushes interest rates higher. This is how a monetarist explains the effect of fiscal policy. Because higher r leads to higher velocity, it leads to a higher product $M \times V$ even if M is unchanged.

6. While Keynesian and monetarist theory both lead us to expect that fiscal *and* monetary policy can each affect aggregate demand, Keynesians tend to believe more in the effectiveness of fiscal policy while monetarists tend to believe more in the effectiveness of monetary policy.

7. Because fiscal policy actions affect aggregate demand either directly through G or indirectly through C, the expenditure lags between fiscal actions and their effects on aggregate demand are probably fairly short. By contrast, monetary policy operates mainly on investment, I, which responds slowly to changes in interest rates.

8. However, the policy-making lag normally is much longer for fiscal policy than for monetary policy. Hence, when the two lags are combined, it is not clear which type of policy acts more quickly.

9. Because it cannot control the demand curve for money, the Federal Reserve cannot control *both* M and r. If the demand for money changes, the Fed must decide whether it wants to hold M steady, hold r steady, or adopt some compromise position.

10. Monetarists emphasize the importance of stabilizing the growth path of the money supply while Keynesians put more emphasis on keeping interest rates on target.

11. In practice, the Fed has changed its views on this issue several times. For decades, it attached primary importance to interest rates. Between 1979 and 1982, it stressed its commitment to stable growth of the money supply. But since 1982 it has deemphasized money growth.

12. Keynesians believe that the aggregate supply curve is flat in the short run. This means that increases in aggregate demand will add much to the nation's real output and add little to the price level. Stabilization policy thus has much to recommend it as an antirecession device, but it has little power to combat inflation.

13. Monetarists believe that the aggregate supply curve is steep. This means that increases in aggregate demand increase real output rather little and succeed mostly in pushing up prices. Consequently, while stabilization policy can do much to fight inflation, it is not a very effective way to cure unemployment.

14. The Keynesian view probably is most applicable to an economy with much unemployment, while the monetarist view applies best to an economy producing near capacity levels.

15. When there are long lags in the operation of fiscal and monetary policy, it becomes possible that attempts to stabilize economic activity may actually succeed in destabilizing it.

16. The U.S. economy has a number of automatic stabilizers which make it less vulnerable to shocks than it would otherwise be. Among these are the personal income tax and unemployment benefits.

17. Economic forecasts are made by econometric models, by exploiting leading indicators, and by judgment. Each method seems to play a role in arriving at good forecasts; but no method is foolproof, and economic forecasts are not as accurate as many people would like them to be.

18. Many monetarists believe that our imperfect knowledge of the channels through which stabilization policy works, and the long lags involved, make it unlikely that discretionary stabilization

policy can succeed.

19. Keynesians recognize these difficulties but do not believe they are as serious as monetarists think. On the other hand, Keynesians place much less faith in the economy's ability to cure recessions and inflations on its own. They therefore think that discretionary policy is not only advisable, but essential.

20. Stabilizing the economy by fiscal policy does *not* imply a tendency toward "big government."

Concepts for Review

Quantity theory of money
Velocity
Equation of exchange
Effect of interest rate on velocity
Monetarism

Effect of fiscal policy on interest rates
Lags in stabilization policy
Shape of the aggregate supply curve
Controlling M versus controlling r
Automatic stabilizers

Econometric models
Leading indicators
Judgmental forecasts
Rules versus discretionary policy

Questions for Discussion

1. How much money (including cash and checking account balances) do you typically have at any particular moment? Divide this into your total income over the past 12 months to obtain your own personal velocity. Are you typical of the nation as a whole?

2. In the next column you will find data on nominal gross national product and the money supply (M1 definition) for selected years. Compute velocity in each year. Can you see any trend?

YEAR	NOMINAL GNP (billions of dollars)	MONEY SUPPLY (M1) (billions of dollars) (end of year)
1966	772	174
1976	1783	310
1986	4235	731

3. Use the concept of opportunity cost to explain why velocity is higher at higher interest rates.

4. How does monetarism differ from the quantity theory of money? How does it differ from Keynesian analysis?

5. Distinguish between the expenditure lag and the policy lag in stabilization policy. Does monetary or fiscal policy have the shorter expenditure lag? What about the policy lag?

6. Explain why their contrasting views on the shape of the aggregate supply curve lead Keynesians to argue much more strongly for stabilization policies to fight unemployment while monetarists argue much more strongly for stabilization policies to fight inflation.

7. Use a supply and demand diagram similar to Figure 15–2 (page 301) to show the choices open to the Fed following an unexpected decline in the demand for money. If the Fed is following a monetarist policy rule, what will happen to the rate of interest?

8. Explain why lags make it possible for policy actions intended to stabilize the economy actually to destabilize it instead.

9. Name some automatic stabilizers and explain how and what they "stabilize."

10. Which of the following events would strengthen the argument for the use of discretionary policy, and which would strengthen the argument for rules?
   a. Structural changes make the economy's self-correcting mechanism faster and more reliable than before.
   b. New statistical methods are found that improve the accuracy of economic forecasts.
   c. A Republican president is elected when there is an overwhelmingly Democratic Congress. The Congress and the president differ sharply on what should be done about the national economy.

11. (More difficult) Use the following hypothetical econometric model of the U.S. economy to obtain a forecast of the GNP in 1991:

$$C = 100 + 0.8DI$$
$$DI = Y - T$$
$$Y = C + I + G.$$

T, I, and G are the exogenous variables, and their forecasted values for 1991 are $T = 1000$, $I = 700$, $G = 800$.

12. (More difficult) Answer the same question for an economy described by:

$$C = 18 + 0.9DI$$
$$DI = Y - T$$
$$T = 10 + \tfrac{1}{3}Y$$
$$Y = C + I + G$$

with forecasts $I = 200$, $G = 880$.

16

Budget Deficits and the National Debt: Fact and Fiction

Blessed are the young, for they shall inherit the national debt.

HERBERT HOOVER

There is a belief that runs deep in the American character that there is something inherently wrong with government budget deficits. Opinion polls consistently show that the public wants smaller deficits. Yet under President Reagan, surely the most conservative president in decades, the federal government has run the largest deficits in history.

How could such a thing have happened under a president who says he believes in balanced budgets? What kinds of problems do large deficits pose for the economy, both now and in the future? Should we strive to balance the budget? And if so, by what means? These are the questions to be addressed in this chapter.

We begin by explaining why the principles of stabilization policy that we have learned in Part 4 do not lead to the conclusion that the budget should always be balanced. (Neither, however, do they lead to the conclusion that it should always have a massive deficit!) Next we try to get the facts straight. We discuss the size of the national debt, and how it grew so large. Then we turn to the federal budget deficit and why some economists claim that it is badly mismeasured.

With the facts established, we examine the alleged ill effects of deficits. We shall see that many popular arguments against deficits are based on faulty reasoning. But not all are. In particular, we devote special attention to two potentially severe costs of deficit spending: It can be inflationary, and it can "crowd out" private investment spending.

The Partisan Political Debate over the Budget Deficit

Never has the budget deficit been more in the news than during the presidency of Ronald Reagan. Whatever else you think of President Reagan's controversial economic policies, it is clear that they have brought with them the biggest budget deficits in our history—a fact that has not been lost on his political foes. The endless debate between the president's supporters and opponents over the causes and consequences of large deficits, and how best to reduce them, has probably been the major public policy issue of the 1980s.

Critics of the president blame the large deficits directly on the tax cuts of 1981–1984, complain that the president has done little to stem the tide of red ink, argue that the deficit is a ticking time bomb that will ultimately cause grievous harm to the economy, and advocate higher taxes and lower defense spending to close the budget gap.

The president and his supporters have replied that the problem was inherited from the past, blamed Congress for refusing to trim civilian spending, and, at times, argued that a big deficit is the lesser evil if the alternatives are raising taxes or reducing military spending. They have frequently suggested that economic growth will eventually bring in enough tax revenue to balance the budget—provided that civilian spending is reduced enough.

The result of this partisan political struggle has been stalemate and continuing high deficits. The president has blocked tax increases and has bitterly, though unsuccessfully, opposed cutbacks in planned defense spending. Congress has slashed the president's requests for military spending, but turned down most of the large civilian budget cuts he has proposed. While the two sides argued over budget priorities, the deficit ballooned from $128 billion in fiscal year 1982 to $221 billion in fiscal 1986.

In this chapter, we will try to put politics aside and concentrate on the economic issues. You should keep in mind, however, that political, not economic, considerations have kept the deficit as large as it is for so long.

Should the Budget Be Balanced?

In December 1985, Congress passed a law—which it has since ignored—mandating a balanced budget by 1991. (See the boxed insert on page 340.) Is a zero deficit an appropriate target for fiscal policy?

The basic principles that we discussed in Chapter 12 certainly do not lead to the conclusion that the budget should always be balanced. Instead, they point to the desirability of budget *deficits* when private demand (C + I) is too weak and budget *surpluses* when private demand is too strong. The budget should be balanced, according to these principles, only when C + I + G under a balanced-budget policy approximately equals full-employment levels of output. This may sometimes occur, but it will not necessarily be the norm.

In brief, according to this approach, the focus of fiscal policy should be on *balancing aggregate supply and aggregate demand,* not on balancing the budget. The reason why a balanced budget may not achieve a balanced economy is clear from our earlier discussion of stabilization policy.

Consider the fiscal policy that would be followed if we lived under an effective balanced-budget law. If private spending sagged for some reason, the multiplier would pull GNP down. Since personal and corporate tax receipts fall sharply when GNP declines, the budget would start to swing into the red. That would require either lower spending or higher taxes—exactly the opposite of the appropriate policy response. Thus:

Attempts to balance the budget—as done, say, by President Hoover during the Great Depression—will prolong and deepen recessions.

Budget balancing can also lead to inappropriate fiscal policy when an economic boom begins. If rising tax receipts induce a budget-balancing government to spend more or cut taxes, fiscal policy will "boom the boom"—with disastrous inflationary consequences. Fortunately, believers in budget balancing usually are not alarmed by surpluses.

Actually, the issue is even more complicated than we have indicated so far. As we learned in Chapter 14, fiscal policy is not the only way the government affects aggregate demand. The government also influences aggregate demand through its monetary policy. For this reason:

The appropriate fiscal policy depends, among other things, on the stance of monetary policy. While a balanced budget may be appropriate under one monetary policy, a deficit or a surplus may be appropriate under another monetary policy.

An example will illustrate the point. Suppose Congress and the president believe that the aggregate supply and demand curves will intersect approximately at full employment if the budget is balanced. That would seem to call for a balanced-budget fiscal policy.

But suppose now that monetary policy turns contractionary, pulling the aggregate demand curve inward to the left as shown in Figure 16–1 and creating a recessionary gap. If the fiscal authorities wish to restore real GNP to its original level, they must shift the aggregate demand curve back out to its original position, $D_0 D_0$. To do this, they must either raise spending or cut taxes, thereby opening up a budget deficit. Thus the change in monetary policy changes the appropriate fiscal policy from a balanced budget to a deficit.

By the same token, a given target for aggregate demand implies that any change in fiscal policy will alter the appropriate monetary policy. For example, suppose Figure 16–1 indicates the effects of reducing the budget deficit by cutting government spending. If the authorities do not want real GNP to fall, monetary policy must become sufficiently more expansionary to restore the aggregate demand curve to $D_0 D_0$. As we shall see at the end of the chapter, it is precisely this outcome — a smaller budget deficit balanced by easier money — that many economists have sought in the 1980s.

So a balanced budget should not be expected to be the norm. Then how do we know whether any particular deficit is too large or too small? That is a good question, but a complicated one. Before attempting an answer, we should get some facts straight.

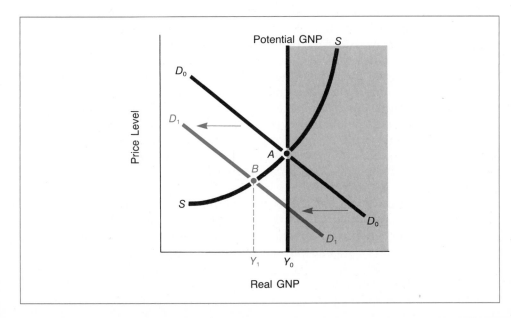

Figure 16–1
THE INTERACTION OF MONETARY AND FISCAL POLICY
Both monetary and fiscal policy affect the aggregate demand curve. If monetary policy turns contractionary, the aggregate demand curve shifts inward from $D_0 D_0$ to $D_1 D_1$ thereby lowering real GNP from Y_0 to Y_1. If Y_0 represented full employment with a balanced budget, then Y_1 represents a recessionary gap. Expansionary fiscal policy can push the aggregate demand curve back to $D_0 D_0$ but only by opening up a deficit in the government budget.

Deficits and Debt: Some Terminology

First some critical terminology. The title of this chapter contains two terms that seem similar but mean different things: *budget deficits* and the *national debt*. We must learn to distinguish between the two.

The **budget deficit** is the amount by which the government's expenditures exceed its receipts during some specified period of time, usually one year. For example, during fiscal year 1987, the government raised about $860 billion in taxes but spent almost $1020 billion, leaving a deficit of almost $160 billion.[1]

The **national debt,** also called the public debt, is the total value of the government's indebtedness at a moment in time. Thus, for example, the national debt at the end of fiscal year 1987 was over $2.3 trillion.

The two concepts—debt and deficits—are closely related because the government accumulates *debt* by running *deficits* or reduces its debt by running surpluses. The relationship between the debt and the deficit can be explained by a simple analogy. As you run water into a bathtub ("run a deficit"), the accumulated volume of water in the tub ("the debt") rises. Alternatively, if you let water out of the tub ("run a surplus"), the level of the water ("the debt") falls. Analogously, budget deficits raise the national debt while budget surpluses lower it.

Having made this distinction, let us look first at the size and nature of the accumulated public debt, and then at the annual budget deficit.

> The **budget deficit** is the amount by which the government's expenditures exceed its receipts during a specified period of time, usually one year.
>
> The **national debt** is the federal government's total indebtedness at a moment in time. It is the result of previous deficits.

Some Facts About the National Debt

How large a public debt do we have? How did we get it? Who owns it? Is it really growing rapidly?

To begin with the simplest question, the public debt is enormous. At the end of 1987 it amounted to over $2400 billion, almost $10,000 for every man, woman, and child in America. But nearly 30 percent of this outstanding debt was owned by agencies of the U.S. government—in other words, one branch of the government owed it to another. If we deduct this portion, the net national debt was only about $1750 billion, or around $7200 per person.

Furthermore, when we compare the debt with the gross national product—the volume of goods and services our economy produces in a year—it does not seem so large after all. With a GNP of over $4500 billion in late 1987, the net debt was just over one-third of the nation's yearly income. By contrast, many families who own homes owe *several years'* worth of income to the bank that granted them a mortgage. Many U.S. corporations also owe their bondholders much more than one-third of a year's sales.

But before these analogies make you feel too comfortable, we should point out that simple analogies between public and private debt are almost always misleading. A family with a large mortgage debt also owns a home with a value that presumably exceeds the mortgage. A solvent business firm has assets (factories, machinery, inventories, and so forth) that far exceed its outstanding bonds in value.

Is the same thing true of the U.S. government? Nobody knows for sure. How much is the White House worth? Or the national parks? And what about military bases, both here and abroad? Simply because these government assets are *not* sold on markets, no one can tell whether the federal government's assets

---

[1]*Reminder:* The fiscal year of the U.S. government ends on September 30. Thus, fiscal year 1987 ran from October 1, 1986, to September 30, 1987.

exceed its debt or not. One heroic attempt to measure the value of the government's assets concluded that they far exceeded the national debt in 1980, but fell slightly below the national debt by 1984.[2]

Figure 16–2 charts the irregular increase in the national debt from 1915 to 1987. You will notice that most of the debt was acquired either during wars, especially World War II, or during the last 15 years, which included two severe recessions. When economic activity falls, tax receipts of the federal government fall because of the heavy reliance on income taxes. As we shall see later, the

[2]Robert Eisner, *How Real Is the Federal Deficit?* (New York: Free Press, 1986), page 29.

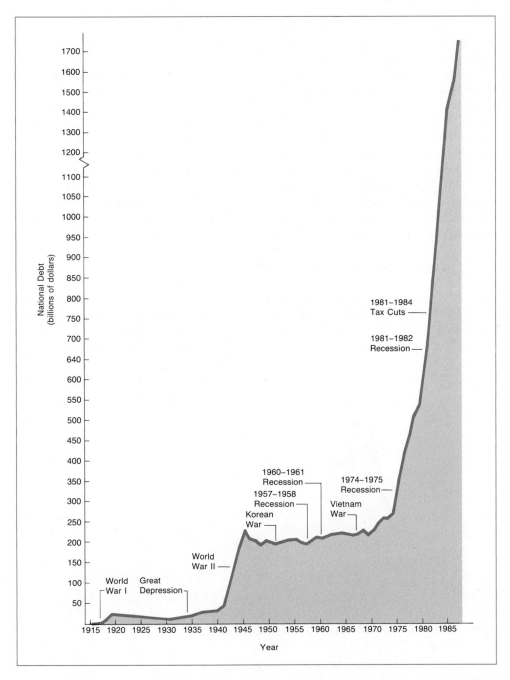

Figure 16–2
THE U.S. NATIONAL DEBT, 1915–1987
This graph charts the behavior of the public debt in the United States, after subtracting out the portion of the debt that is held by government agencies. It is clear that, until very recently, just about all the increases could be accounted for by wars and recessions. Few people realize that the public debt was about the same in 1972 as it was in 1945. But since 1972, it has grown rapidly.
SOURCE: Constructed by the authors from data in *Historical Statistics of the United States* and *Economic Report of the President*.

cause of the debt is quite germane to the question of whether or not the debt is a burden. So it is important to remember that:

Until about 1983, almost all of the U.S. national debt stemmed from financing wars and from losses of tax revenues that accompany recessions.

The growth of the debt looks enormous in Figure 16–2. But we must remember that everything grows in a growing economy. Private debt and business debt have grown rapidly since 1915; it would be surprising indeed if the public debt had not grown also. The fact is that federal debt grew less rapidly than private debt during most of the period since World War II—until about 1980.

In addition, the debt is measured in dollars and, in an inflationary environment, the amount of purchasing power that each dollar represents declines each year. A good way to put the numbers into perspective is to express each year's national debt as a fraction of that year's nominal GNP. This is done in Figure 16–3. Here, in contrast to Figure 16–2, we see an unmistakable downward trend from the dizzying heights of World War II until the recession of 1974–1975. In 1945, the national debt was the equivalent of 13 months' national income. By 1974 this figure had been whittled down to two months. If we use this as a crude indicator of the nation's ability to "pay off" its debt, then the burden of the debt was certainly far smaller in 1974 than it was in 1945.

This last graph also calls attention to a fact which is less comforting. During the 1980s, the national debt has been growing faster than GNP. By 1987, the debt was up to five months' GNP and growing. This is one reason why many economists are alarmed by continued large budget deficits.

Interpreting the Budget Deficit

We have observed that the federal government's annual budget deficits have been extremely large under President Reagan. As Figure 16–4 shows, the budget deficit for fiscal year 1981, which was affected in only minor ways by President Reagan's policies, was $79 billion. By fiscal year 1983, it had grown to a

Figure 16–3
RATIO OF PUBLIC DEBT TO GROSS NATIONAL PRODUCT
This graph takes the data from Figure 16–2 and divides each year's debt by the gross national product of that year. We can see that the debt grew relative to GNP during the two world wars, during the Great Depression, during the 1974–1975 recession, and since 1981. Other than that, the debt generally has fallen relative to GNP.

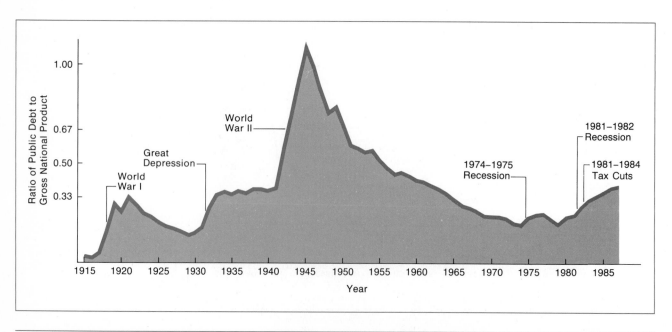

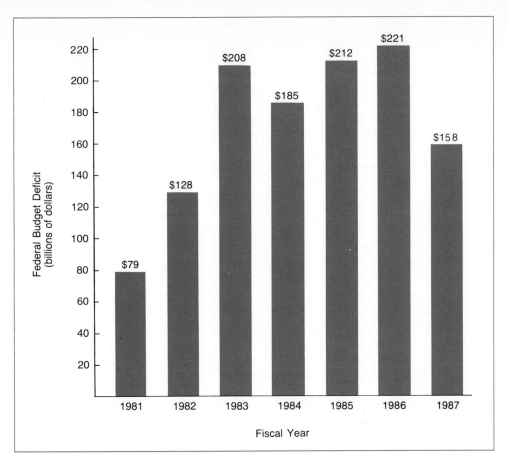

Figure 16–4
OFFICIAL BUDGET
DEFICITS SINCE 1981
(FISCAL YEARS)
The budget deficit almost
tripled between fiscal year
1981 and fiscal year 1983
and did not change much
between then and fiscal
1986. In fiscal year 1987, it
declined somewhat.

record $208 billion. But that record was broken in 1985 and again in 1986. The budget for fiscal year 1987, which ended just before this book went to press, still showed a deficit of $158 billion.

These are enormous, even mind-boggling, numbers. But what do they mean? In interpreting them, we begin with what many economists view as a serious measurement problem — the way interest payments are treated in the government's budget.

Inflation Accounting for Interest Payments*

At first blush, government accountants seem to treat interest payments in the sensible way: Every dollar of interest that the government pays on the national debt is counted as a dollar of spending — just like military purchases, social security payments, and the salaries of members of Congress. This seems the natural thing to do. But it ignores the fundamental distinction between real and nominal interest rates that we emphasized in Chapter 6. To review the analysis:

The **real interest rate** tells us the amount of purchasing power the borrower turns over to the lender for the privilege of borrowing. To this we must add an **inflation premium**, equal to the expected rate of inflation, to get the **nominal interest rate**. The inflation premium compensates the lender for the expected erosion of the purchasing power of her money and is best thought of as repayment of principal.[3]

*This section contains difficult material which may be skipped in shorter courses.
[3]If you need review, see pages 104–105.

The last sentence has important implications for the government budget — implications that few people understand.

From an economic point of view, the portion of the government's interest payments that merely compensates lenders for inflation should be counted as *repayment of principal,* not as *interest expense,* because it simply returns to lenders the purchasing power of their original loans. Only the *real* interest that the government pays should be treated an expenditure item in the budget. Breaking up interest payments in this way is called **inflation accounting**. Since even sophisticated people have trouble understanding inflation accounting, it is worth taking the time to illustrate the idea with an analogy and a simple example.

Imagine that you lend a roommate, who is enrolled in a chemistry course, a bar of radium that you happen to own. Your roommate uses the radioactive bar in experiments for a year, and then returns it to you. Has your loan been repaid in full? Certainly not. Because of the natural process of radioactive decay, the bar you get back is smaller than the bar you originally loaned. To pay you back in full, your roommate must give you enough additional radium to replace the portion that eroded during the year.

The analogy to interest rates on loans is straightforward: Inflation erodes the purchasing power of money just as radioactive decay erodes radium. So, in figuring out how many dollars constitutes repayment of principal, we must take inflation into account. Let's illustrate this by a concrete example, comparing a loan made at zero inflation (no decay) with a loan made at 10 percent inflation (rapid decay).

First, suppose the government borrows $1000 for a year when the inflation rate is zero, paying 2 percent interest. At the end of the year it must pay back $1000 in principal and $20 in interest, for a total of $1020. Of this, only $20 — the interest payment — is an expenditure item in the budget. The repayment of principal does not appear in the budget since it is not spending. The loan transaction is summarized simply in column 1 of Table 16–1.

Now let us see how inflation (radioactive decay of money) complicates the accountant's job. Suppose the same transaction takes place when the rate of inflation is 10 percent. If the real rate of interest is still 2 percent, the nominal rate of interest must be about 12 percent.

Inflation accounting means adjusting standard accounting procedures for the fact that inflation lowers the purchasing power of money.

Table 16–1
ACCOUNTING FOR A $1000 LOAN AT A 2 PERCENT REAL INTEREST RATE

ITEM	(1) AT ZERO INFLATION	(2) AT 10% INFLATION CONVENTIONAL ACCOUNTING	(3) AT 10% INFLATION INFLATION ACCOUNTING
Interest (included in budget)	$ 20	$ 122	$ 22
plus			
Principal (excluded from budget)	1,000	1,000	1,100
equals			
Total payment	$1,020	$1,122	$1,122
Addendum:			
Purchasing power of principal repayment	$1,000	$ 909	$1,000

More precisely, to compensate the lender for 10 percent inflation, and nothing more, the government must return $1.10 for each dollar originally borrowed. A real interest rate of 2 percent means that the government must return 2 percent more than this, or $1.02 \times \$1.10 = \$1.122$ per dollar borrowed. Thus, each dollar of lending earns 12.2 cents in interest, making the nominal interest rate 12.2 percent.

If the nominal interest rate is 12.2 percent, a government that borrows $1000 at the start of the year will have to repay $1,122 at year's end. Conventional accounting procedures will treat $1000 of this as repayment of principal (and hence not as an expenditure) and $122 as interest (which *is* an expenditure). This conventional accounting treatment is indicated in column 2 of Table 16–1.

But these numbers are misleading since $1000 at the end of the year is not adequate repayment of principal because inflation has eroded the real value of money. The correct inflation accounting treatment recognizes that it takes $1100 at the end of the year to buy what $1000 bought at the beginning of the year. So $1100 is treated as repayment of principal, leaving only $22 ($1122 − $1100) to be treated as interest. The correct inflation accounting treatment of the loan is shown in column 3 of Table 16–1.

To recapitulate, the proper economic treatment of a loan in an inflationary environment must recognize that more dollars (in our example, $1100) must be returned to the lender in order to give back the purchasing power of the original loan ($1000). Only the excess of the nominal interest payment ($122) over the compensation for inflation ($100) should be counted as interest.

This example holds the following lesson for interpreting budget deficit figures:

Inflation distorts the government budget under conventional accounting procedures by exaggerating interest expenses.

The example also suggests how this error can be corrected:

To correct the deficit for inflation, we must subtract the inflation premium from the interest paid on the national debt, thereby counting only *real* interest payments.

This treatment, by the way, corresponds exactly to the way inflation accounting is done by major corporations.

As Table 16–2 shows, making the inflation adjustment to interest payments would have reduced reported deficits by an average of about $45 billion in recent years, enough to turn apparently large deficits in 1980 and 1981 into small deficits. The table also shows that the years starting in fiscal 1982 stand out as exceptions to previous norms: The federal government began running large deficits *even after correction for inflation accounting.*

The High-Employment Budget

The second major issue in making sense of the budget deficit is not a problem of measurement, but rather one of interpretation.

As we learned in Chapter 12, the government's taxing and spending decisions profoundly affect the level of economic activity. For example, higher spending or lower taxes leads — via the multiplier process — to higher aggregate

Table 16–2
INFLATION ACCOUNTING AND THE DEFICIT

FISCAL YEAR	OFFICIAL DEFICIT (billions of dollars)	INFLATION ADJUSTMENT FOR INTEREST PAID (billions of dollars)	INFLATION ADJUSTED DEFICIT (−) OR SURPLUS (+) (billions of dollars)
1979	−40	+44	+4
1980	−74	+52	−22
1981	−79	+51	−28
1982	−128	+38	−90
1983	−208	+35	−173
1984	−185	+40	−145
1985	−212	+39	−173
1986	−221	+41	−180
1987	−158	+50	−108

SOURCE: Robert Eisner, *How Real Is the Federal Deficit?*, and authors' estimates.

demand and therefore to a higher GNP. This makes it natural to think that big deficits signify expansionary fiscal policy.

But that view may be incorrect because the state of the economy also affects the budget. In particular, *recessions tend to enlarge the budget deficit*. The reason is simple. Remember that the deficit is the difference between government expenditures and tax receipts, that is:

$$\text{Deficit} = G + \text{Transfers} - \text{Taxes}.$$

The government's most important sources of tax revenue — income taxes, corporate taxes, and payroll taxes — all shrink when GNP falls because firms and people pay less tax when they earn less. Similarly, some government spending, notably transfer payments like unemployment benefits, rises when GNP falls because more people are out of work. Since spending goes up and tax receipts go down as GNP falls:

The deficit rises in a recession and falls in a boom, even when there is no change in fiscal policy.

Because the deficit changes even when policy does not, the deficit is a poor measure of the government's fiscal policy. For this reason, many economists feel that we should pay less attention to the actual deficit or surplus and more attention to the deficit or surplus in what is called the **high-employment budget**. This is a hypothetical construct that replaces both the spending and taxes in the *actual* budget by estimates of how much the government *would be* spending and receiving, given current tax rates and expenditure rules, if the economy were operating near full employment.

Since it is based on the spending and taxing the government would be doing near full employment rather than on actual expenditures and receipts, the high-employment budget is not sensitive to the state of the economy. It will change only when policy changes. For this reason, most economists believe it is a better measure of the thrust of fiscal policy than the actual deficit. This new concept helps us understand the genesis of the large budget deficits of the 1980s: They were partly attributable to the consistently high unemployment rates that marked this period. Table 16–3 shows just how important the distinction between the actual deficit and the high-employment deficit has been in

The **high-employment budget** is the hypothetical budget we *would have* if the economy were operating near full employment.

Table 16–3
UNEMPLOYMENT AND THE DEFICIT

FISCAL YEAR	OFFICIAL DEFICIT (billions of dollars)	ADJUSTMENT TO HIGH EMPLOYMENT (billions of dollars)	HIGH-EMPLOYMENT DEFICIT (billions of dollars)
1980	−74	+23	−51
1981	−79	+31	−48
1982	−128	+77	−51
1983	−208	+102	−106
1984	−185	+55	−130
1985	−212	+41	−171
1986	−221	+36	−185
1987	−158	+36	−122

SOURCE: Congressional Budget Office.

recent years, particularly in the deep recession years 1982 and 1983. But since fiscal year 1983, even the high-employment budget has shown triple-digit deficits.

Other Measurement Issues

There are other complicated issues in measuring and interpreting the federal budget deficit. We conclude this section by mentioning just two of them.

1. *State and local budget surpluses.* Part of the reason for the federal deficit is that the federal government gives a good deal of money (over $100 billion in recent years) to state and local governments in the form of *grants-in-aid* each year. These funds have helped state and local governments run substantial surpluses — averaging between $30 and $50 billion annually in recent years. Thus, the *combined* deficits of governments at *all* levels has been considerably smaller than the *federal* deficit.

2. *Capital expenditures.* Some federal spending goes to purchase capital of various sorts — government buildings, military equipment, and so on. There is nothing unusual about borrowing to purchase assets. Private businesses and individuals do it all the time. For this reason, many people have suggested that the federal government compile a separate capital budget — which is precisely what most state and local governments do. The Office of Management and Budget is evaluating the merits of this idea.

Conclusion: What's New About the Recent Deficits?

Table 16–4 puts our two major adjustments — for inflation accounting and for unemployment — together and compares recent deficits (column 1) with corresponding figures on the high-employment, inflation-corrected deficit (column 4). The difference between the two columns is startling. The apparently substantial budget deficits of 1980–1982 were actually roughly balanced on the high-employment, inflation-corrected basis. Only since fiscal year 1983 has the high-employment, inflation-corrected budget been in deficit; and this concept of the deficit grew steadily from 1983 to 1986.

This, then, is the true swing in the federal budget position under President Reagan. Whereas the high-employment, inflation-corrected budget has historically shown an approximate balance, since fiscal 1983 it has shown a large deficit.

Table 16–4
ACTUAL AND ADJUSTED BUDGET DEFICITS

FISCAL YEAR	(1) OFFICIAL DEFICIT (billions of dollars)	(2) ADJUSTMENT FOR INFLATION (billions of dollars)	(3) ADJUSTMENT TO HIGH EMPLOYMENT (billions of dollars)	(4) ADJUSTED DEFICIT (−) OR SURPLUS (+) (billions of dollars)
1980	−74	+52	+23	+1
1981	−79	+51	+31	+3
1982	−128	+38	+77	−13
1983	−208	+35	+102	−71
1984	−185	+40	+55	−90
1985	−212	+39	+41	−132
1986	−221	+41	+36	−144
1987	−158	+50	+36	−72

SOURCE: Congressional Budget Office, Robert Eisner, and authors' calculations.

But what does all this mean? It certainly does *not* mean that in 1987, for example, only $72 billion in additional tax revenue (column 4) would have balanced the budget. What the numbers *do* mean is this. Of the $158 billion deficit in 1987 (column 1), about $50 billion was an artifact of poor accounting procedures and about $36 billion was attributable to the fact that the unemployment rate was still above full employment. This does not make the deficit disappear, but it does put it into some perspective.

Bogus Arguments About the Burden of the Debt

Having gained some perspective on the facts, let us now turn to some of the arguments advanced by those who claim that by running budget deficits we are placing an intolerable burden on future generations.

Argument 1: Our children and grandchildren will be burdened by heavy interest payments. To meet these payments there will have to be higher taxes.

Answer: It is certainly true that a higher debt will necessitate higher interest payments and, other things being equal, this will lead to higher taxes paid by our children and grandchildren. But think who will receive the higher interest payments as income: our children and grandchildren! Thus one group of future Americans will, essentially, be making interest payments to another group of future Americans. While some people will gain and others will lose, the future generation as a whole will come out even. We conclude that:

As long as the national debt is owned by domestic citizens, which the bulk of the U.S. debt is, future interest payments will merely shuffle money from one group of Americans to another. These transfers may or may not be desirable, but they hardly constitute a burden to the nation as a whole.

However, this argument *is* valid for the roughly 16 percent of our debt that is held by foreigners. Paying the interest on this portion of the debt will be a burden on future generations of Americans.

Argument 2: It will ruin the nation when we repay the enormous debt.

Answer: A first answer to this merely rephrases the answer to the previous argument: Only the part owned by foreigners involves any burden; the rest is paid by one group of Americans to another. But there is a much more fundamental point. *Unlike a private family, the nation need never pay off its debt.* Instead, each time the principal is due, the U.S. Treasury can simply "roll it over" by floating more debt. Indeed, this is precisely what the Treasury does.

Is this a bit of chicanery? How can the U.S. government get away with making loans that it never intends to pay back? The answer is found by recognizing the fallacy of comparing the U.S. government to a family or individual. People cannot be extended credit in perpetuity because they will not live that long. Sensible lenders will not extend long-term credit to very old people because their heirs cannot be forced to pay up. But the U.S. government will never "die"; at least, we hope not! So this problem does not arise. In this respect, the government is in much the same position as a large corporation. The American Telephone and Telegraph Company never worries about paying off its debt. It too rolls it over by floating new debt all the time.

Argument 3: Like any family or any business firm, a nation has a limited capacity to borrow. If it exceeds this limit, it is in danger of being unable to pay its creditors. It may go bankrupt with calamitous consequences for everyone.

Answer: This is another example of a false analogy. What is claimed about private debtors is certainly true. But the U.S. government need never fear defaulting on its debt. Why? First, because it has enormous power to raise revenues by taxation. If you had such power, you would never have to fear bankruptcy either.

But there is a still more fundamental point—one that distinguishes the U.S. debt from that of many foreign nations. *The American national debt is an obligation to pay U.S. dollars:* Each debt certificate obligates the Treasury to pay the holder so many U.S. dollars on a prescribed date. But the U.S. government is the source of these dollars; it prints them! *No nation need ever fear defaulting on debts that call for repayment in its own currency.* At the very worst, it can always print whatever money it needs to pay off its creditors.

It does not follow, however, that acquiring debt through budget deficits is therefore always a good idea. Sometimes it is clearly a bad idea. Printing money to pay the debt will expand aggregate demand and cause inflation, and this often will be undesirable. The point is not that budget deficits are either good or bad—we already know that they can be either under the appropriate circumstances. Rather, the point is that worrying about a possible default on the national debt is unnecessary and even foolish.

Having cleared the air of these fallacious arguments, we are now in a position to explore some real problems that may arise when the government spends more than it takes in through taxation.

Budget Deficits and Inflation

One indictment of deficit spending that certainly *does* have validity under most circumstances is the charge that it is inflationary. Why? Because when government policy pushes up aggregate demand, firms may find themselves unwilling or unable to produce the higher quantities that are being demanded at the going prices. Prices will therefore have to rise.

Figure 16–5
THE INFLATIONARY EFFECTS OF DEFICIT SPENDING

In this diagram, expansionary fiscal policy pushes the aggregate demand curve out from D_0D_0 to D_1D_1, causing equilibrium to move from E_0 (where there is unemployment) to E_1 (where there is full employment). But because aggregate supply curve SS slopes upward, the price level is pushed up from 100 to 106; that is, there is a 6 percent inflation.

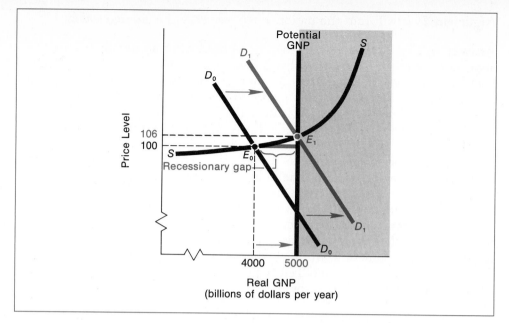

Figure 16–5 is an aggregate supply and demand diagram that shows this analysis graphically. Initially, equilibrium is at point E_0 — where demand curve D_0D_0 and supply curve SS intersect. Output is \$4000 billion, and the price index is at 100. The diagram indicates that the economy is operating below full employment; there is a recessionary gap. If the government does nothing to reduce the resulting unemployment, we know from Chapter 11 that this recessionary gap will linger for a long time. The economy will suffer through a prolonged period of unemployment.

Rather than permit such a long recession, we know that the government can raise its spending or cut its taxes enough to shift the aggregate demand schedule upward from D_0D_0 to D_1D_1. Such a policy can wipe out the recessionary gap and the associated unemployment — but not without an inflationary cost. The diagram shows that the new equilibrium price level is at 106, or 6 percent higher than before the government acted.

Thus the cries that budget deficits are "inflationary" have the ring of truth. How much truth, of course, depends on the slope of the aggregate supply curve. Deficit spending will not cause much inflation if the economy has lots of slack and the aggregate supply curve consequently is flat. But deficit spending will be highly inflationary in a fully-employed economy with a steep aggregate supply curve.

The Monetization Issue

Some people worry about the inflationary consequences of deficits for a rather different reason. They fear that the Federal Reserve may have to "monetize" part of the deficit, by which they mean that the Fed may feel compelled to purchase some of the newly issued government debt. Let us explain, first, why the Fed might make such purchases, and second, why these purchases are called **monetizing the deficit**.

The central bank is said to **monetize the deficit** when it purchases the bonds that the government issues.

Deficit spending, we have just noted, normally drives up both real GNP and the price level. As we have emphasized before, such an economic expansion shifts the demand curve for money outward to the right — as depicted in Figure 16–6. The figure shows that, if the Federal Reserve takes no actions to shift the money supply curve, interest rates will rise.

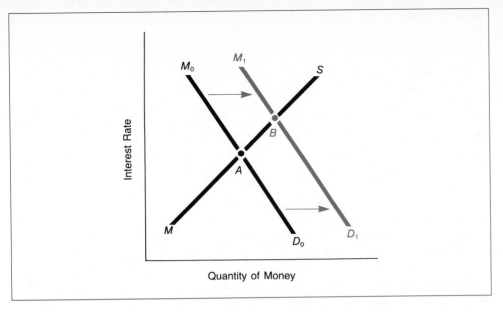

Figure 16–6
FISCAL EXPANSION AND
INTEREST RATES
If expansionary fiscal policy
pushes real GNP and the
price level higher, the
demand curve for money will
shift outward from $M_0 D_0$ to
$M_1 D_1$. Equilibrium in the
money market shifts from
point A to point B, so interest
rates rise.

Suppose now that the Fed does not want interest rates to rise. What can it do? To prevent the incipient rise in r, it must engage in *expansionary monetary policies* that shift the supply curve for money outward to the right — as indicated in Figure 16–7. And, as noted in Chapter 14, expansionary monetary policies normally take the form of open-market purchases of government bonds. For this reason, deficit spending sometimes induces the Federal Reserve to increase its purchases of government bonds, that is, to buy up some of the newly issued debt.

But why is this called *monetizing* the deficit? The reason is simple. As we learned in Chapter 14, open-market purchases of bonds by the Fed give banks more reserves, which leads, eventually, to an increase in the money supply. This is also shown in Figure 16–7: The outward shift of the money supply schedule from $M_0 S_0$ to $M_1 S_1$ leads to an increase in the money supply. By this

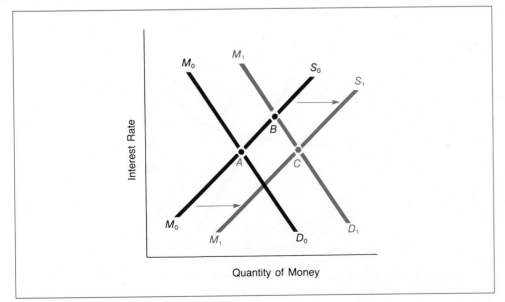

Figure 16–7
MONETIZATION AND
INTEREST RATES
If the Federal Reserve does
not want a fiscal expansion to
raise interest rates, it must
increase the money supply.
In this diagram, the fiscal
expansion shifts the demand
curve for money from $M_0 D_0$
to $M_1 D_1$, precisely as it did in
Figure 16–6. To keep the
rate of interest constant the
Fed will have to shift the
money supply curve outward
from $M_0 S_0$ to $M_1 S_1$. Points A
and C correspond to the
same rate of interest.

indirect route, then, larger budget deficits may lead to an expansion of the money supply. To summarize:

If the Federal Reserve takes no countervailing actions, an expansionary fiscal policy that raises the budget deficit will raise real GNP and prices, thereby shifting the demand curve for money outward and driving up interest rates. If the Fed does not want interest rates to rise, it can engage in expansionary open-market operations, that is, purchase more government debt. If the Fed does this, the money supply will increase. In this case, we say that part of the deficit is *monetized*.

Monetized deficits are more inflationary than nonmonetized deficits for the simple reason that expansionary monetary and fiscal policy *together* is more inflationary than expansionary fiscal policy *alone*. Figure 16–8 illustrates this conclusion. The aggregate supply curve and aggregate demand curves $D_0 D_0$ and $D_1 D_1$ are carried over without change from Figure 16–5. The shift from $D_0 D_0$ to $D_1 D_1$ represents the effect of expansionary fiscal policy (raising the budget deficit). If, in addition, the Fed monetizes part of the deficit, the aggregate demand curve will shift out still further — perhaps to the position indicated by $D_2 D_2$. Thus the price level will rise even more (compare points B and C).

Is this a real worry? Does the Fed actually monetize any substantial portion of the deficit? Sometimes it does, but normally it does not. For example, during the decade ending in 1986, the total federal debt held outside the government increased by about $1275 billion, but the Federal Reserve's holdings of government bonds increased by only about $85 billion. By this crude measure, less than 7 percent of the typical deficit was monetized.

Nonetheless, many economists and business leaders have been concerned about monetization in the 1980s. The reason is simple arithmetic. When budget deficits are extremely large, even a small percentage of monetization can lead to substantial increases in bank reserves and the money supply.

Figure 16–8
MONETIZED DEFICIT SPENDING
Expansionary fiscal policies that raise the budget deficit push the aggregate demand curve outward from $D_0 D_0$ to $D_1 D_1$. If the Fed monetizes some of the deficit, then expansionary monetary policy pushes the aggregate demand curve out even further — to $D_2 D_2$. Monetized deficits (point C) are therefore more inflationary than deficits that are not monetized (point B).

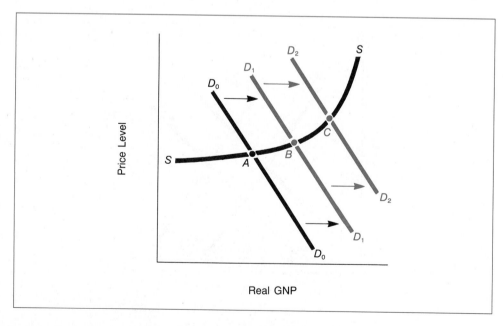

Deficits, Interest Rates, and Crowding Out

So far we have been looking for possible burdens of the national debt on the *demand* side of the economy. But the more serious burden probably comes on the *supply* side because large budget deficits discourage investment and therefore retard the growth of our nation's capital stock. The mechanism is easy to understand.

We have just seen that budget deficits tend to raise interest rates unless the Fed engages in substantial monetization. But the rate of interest (r) is a major determinant of investment spending (I). In particular, higher r leads to lower I. And if we spend less on I today, we will have a smaller capital stock tomorrow. This, according to most economists, is the true sense in which a large national debt may put a burden on future generations:

Because of the large national debt, we may bequeath less physical capital to future generations. If they inherit less plant and equipment, these generations will be burdened by a lower productive capacity—a lower potential GNP.

There is another way of looking at this problem—a way that explains why it is often called the **crowding-out effect.** Consider what happens in financial markets when the government engages in deficit spending. When it spends more than it takes in through tax revenues, the government must borrow the balance from private citizens. It does this by issuing bonds, and these bonds compete with corporate bonds and other financial instruments for the available supply of funds. When some private savers are persuaded to buy government bonds, there must be a decline in the funds remaining to invest in private bonds. Thus some private borrowers will get "crowded out" of the financial markets as the government claims an increasing share of the economy's total saving.

Some critics of deficits who have taken this lesson to its illogical extreme argue that each $1 of deficit spending by government crowds out exactly $1 of private spending, so that expansionary fiscal policy has no net effect on total demand. In their view, when G rises, I falls by the same amount, so that C + I + G is unchanged.

Under normal circumstances, this would not be expected to occur. Why? First, moderate budget deficits will push up interest rates only moderately. Second, the sensitivity of private spending to interest rates is not that great. Even at the higher interest rates that government deficits cause, most corporations will continue to borrow to finance their investments.

Furthermore, there is a counterforce that might be called the **crowding-in effect.** Deficit spending in time of economic slack presumably quickens the pace of economic activity; that, at least, is its purpose. As the economy expands, businesses find it both necessary and profitable to add to their capacity in order to meet the greater demands of consumers. Because of this *induced investment,* as we called it in earlier chapters, any increase in G tends to *increase* investment rather than *decrease* it as predicted by the crowding-out hypothesis.

The strength of the crowding-in effect depends on how much additional real GNP is stimulated by government spending (that is, on the size of the multiplier) and on how sensitive investment spending is to the improved profit opportunities that accompany rapid growth. It is even conceivable that the crowding-in effect can dominate the crowding-out effect, so that I rises on balance when G rises.

Crowding out occurs when deficit spending by the government forces private investment spending to contract.

Crowding in occurs when government spending, by raising real GNP, induces increases in private investment spending.

But how can this be true in view of the crowding-out argument? Certainly, if government is borrowing more *and the total volume of private saving is fixed*, then private industry must be borrowing less. While this little bit of arithmetic is correct, the fallacy in the strict crowding-out argument comes in supposing that the economy's flow of saving is really fixed. If government deficits succeed in their goal of raising production, there will be more income and therefore more saving. In that way *both* government *and* industry can borrow more.

Which effect dominates, crowding out or crowding in? The crowding-out hypothesis stems from the increases in interest rates that deficit spending causes; this is certainly bad for investment. But the crowding-in hypothesis stems from the increases in production and profitability, which are good for investment. Under different sets of circumstances, one or the other force may prove to be stronger.

For example, a report issued by the Congressional Budget Office near the bottom of the deep recession of 1974–1975 argued that "on balance . . . it appears likely that more investments would be 'crowded in' by a stimulative fiscal policy than would be 'crowded out,' given the present state of the economy."[4] The report explained that, with so much slack in the economy, a surge in G would likely lead to a considerable increase in real output because the higher demand would not cause much inflation and, consequently, the multiplier would be large. In terms of our graphical apparatus, the aggregate supply curve would be rather flat when the economy is in the range indicated by Region I in Figure 16–9.

But the same report hastened to add, "The opposite conclusion might well be drawn if resources were more fully employed." This is because the economy would then be operating in the steep portion of Region III of the aggregate supply curve shown in Figure 16–9 so that demand stimulation would lead to only limited gains in real output.[5] If real GNP growth is minor, then so must be the

[4]Congressional Budget Office, *Inflation and Unemployment: A Report on the Economy* (Washington, D.C.: U.S. Government Printing Office, June 30, 1975), page 58.
[5]EXERCISE: Show that any given horizontal shift in the aggregate demand curve has a smaller effect on real GNP in Region III than it does in Region I.

Figure 16–9
A TYPICAL AGGREGATE SUPPLY CURVE
The aggregate supply curve depicted here has three regions. In Region I, output can increase with almost no change in prices because there is a great deal of unused labor and spare industrial capacity. Thus the supply curve is virtually horizontal. In Region III, resources are more or less fully employed, so even rather small increases in output necessitate substantial price increases; the supply curve is very steep. Region II is intermediate between these two extremes.

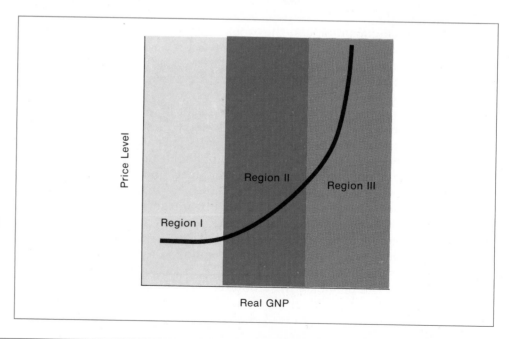

amount of induced investment. The crowding-in effect therefore would be weak. Instead, government spending would push up the price level, raise the demand for cash balances, and crowd out private borrowers.

Let us summarize what we have learned about the crowding-out controversy.

SUMMARY

1. The basic argument of the crowding-out hypothesis is sound: *Unless there is enough additional saving*, more government borrowing will force out some private borrowers who are discouraged by the high interest rates. This will reduce investment spending and cancel out some of the expansionary effects of higher government spending.
2. This force is rarely strong enough to cancel out the *entire* expansionary thrust of government spending, however. Some net stimulus to the economy remains.
3. If the deficit spending induces substantial growth in GNP, then there will be more saving. There might even be so much more that private industry could borrow *more* than before, despite the increase in government borrowing.
4. The crowding-out effect is likely to dominate when the economy is operating near full employment. The crowding-in effect is likely to dominate when there is a great deal of slack.

The True Burden of the National Debt

This analysis of crowding out versus crowding in, puts us in a position to understand why budget deficits might or might not impose a burden on future generations:

"Would you mind explaining again how high interest rates and the national deficit affect my allowance?"

When government budget deficits take place in a high-employment economy, the crowding-out effect will probably dominate. So deficits will exact a burden by leaving a smaller capital stock to future generations. However, deficits in a slack economy may well lead to *more* investment rather than *less*. In this case, where the crowding-in effect dominates, the new debt is a blessing rather than a burden.

Which case applies to the U.S. national debt? To answer this, let us go back to the historical facts and recall how we accumulated such a large debt. The first cause was the financing of wars, especially World War II. This debt was contracted in a fully-employed economy, and thus undoubtedly constituted a burden in the formal sense. It left future generations with less capital because some of our nation's resources were diverted from private investment into government production. The bombs, ships, and planes that it financed were used up in the war, not bequeathed as capital to future generations.

Yet what were the alternatives? We could have financed the entire war by taxation and thus placed the burden on consumption rather than on investment. But that would truly have been ruinous, and maybe even impossible, given the colossal wartime expenditures. Or we could have printed money. But that would have unleashed an inflation that nobody wanted. Or we could have just done much less government spending and perhaps not have won the war. So, in retrospect, the generations alive today and in the future may not feel unduly burdened by the decisions of the people in power in the 1940s. One need only imagine the sort of burden that would have been inherited had the United States not won the war.

The second major contributor to the national debt has been a series of recessions. But these are precisely the circumstances under which increasing the debt might prove to be a blessing rather than a burden. So, if we look for the classic type of deficit to which the valid burden-of-the-debt argument applies— deficits acquired in a fully-employed peacetime economy—we do not find many in the U.S. record until recently.

It is in this context that current budget deficits are a sharp departure from the past. Since 1986, the U.S. economy has been approaching the full employment zone. And it has been doing so in peacetime with deficits in the neighborhood of $200 billion per year. This is something that has never happened before, and it poses a real threat of severe crowding out and a serious potential burden on future generations.

The Burden of the National Debt

Let us now summarize our evaluation of the burden of the national debt and thereby clarify one of the **12 Ideas for Beyond the Final Exam** introduced in Chapter 1.

First, the arguments that a large national debt may lead the nation into bankruptcy, or unduly burden future generations who have to make onerous payments of interest and principal, are mostly bogus.

Second, the national debt *will* be a burden if it is contracted in a fully-employed peacetime economy, because in that case it will reduce the nation's capital stock.

Third, there are circumstances in which budget deficits are appropriate for stabilization reasons.

Fourth, until recently, the actual public debt of the U.S. government was mostly contracted as a result of wars and recessions—precisely the circumstances under which the valid burden-of-the-debt argument does not apply. However, the large deficits of recent years are worrisome from this point of view.

The Economic Effects of Budget Deficits: Causation Versus Correlation

Anyone who has followed the debate over budget deficits in the press is bound to have been confused by the contradictory claims and counter-claims. Do deficits lead to high interest rates? Some say yes, others say no. Are deficits inflationary? Some say yes, others say no. Are large deficits a roadblock to economic expansion? Some say yes, others say no. And somehow each participant in the debate finds data to support his or her view.

Who is right? Let us use what we have learned about the economic effects of budget deficits to make some sense of this confusion. We can do so by contrasting two imaginary case studies which, however, bear a certain resemblance to events in the United States in the early 1980s.

Case 1: A Tax Cut

Suppose the government opens up a budget deficit by reducing taxes. What should happen? According to the theory we have developed, aggregate demand should increase, and that should increase both real GNP (Y) and the price level

(P) — as in Figure 16–5 (page 332). The rise in Y and P should shift the demand curve for money outward, thereby raising the rate of interest (r) — as in Figure 16–6 (page 333) — and subsequently lowering investment. Thus, in response to the large deficit, the economy should experience rapid GNP growth, high inflation, and high interest rates. The general conclusion is:

If the government undertakes expansionary fiscal policies, like cutting taxes or raising spending, the deficit should rise and:

1. Real GNP should grow faster;
2. Interest rates should rise (which harms investment);
3. Inflation should rise.

This conclusion is recorded for future reference in the first column of Table 16–5.

Case 2: A Recession

Now suppose that the budget deficit increases for an entirely different reason. For example, suppose consumer spending declines sharply. What will happen? The decline in aggregate demand will lower both real GNP and prices. With both Y and P falling, the quantity of money demanded will decline. And the decrease in the demand for money will pull down interest rates, which will stimulate investment. Finally, as we have noted in this chapter, when GNP falls so do tax receipts; so the deficit will widen.[6] Thus, in this case, we expect larger deficits to be accompanied by weaker GNP growth, slower inflation, and lower interest rates. The general conclusion is:

If the economy experiences a recession for reasons having nothing to do with fiscal policy, the deficit should rise and:

1. Real GNP should fall;
2. Interest rates should fall;
3. Inflation should fall.

This conclusion is recorded in the second column of Table 16–5.

Table 16–5 shows how different the two cases are. The deficit rises in both cases. But in the first case Y, P, and r all rise, while in the second case they all fall.[7] In the real world, of course, deficits are sometimes caused by fiscal policy actions (as in Case 1) and sometimes caused by other factors (as in Case 2).

[6]EXERCISE: Test your understanding by working out the diagrams for this example.
[7]EXERCISE: To test your understanding, construct a version of Table 16–5 that applies to *falling* deficits caused by (a) a tax increase or (b) an autonomous increase in consumer spending. Be sure you can explain each entry in the table.

Table 16–5
DEFICITS AND THE ECONOMY: A SUMMARY

EXPECTED EFFECT ON:	CASE 1 FISCAL POLICY ACTIONS RAISE THE DEFICIT	CASE 2 A RECESSION RAISES THE DEFICIT
Real GNP growth	Up	Down
Interest rate	Up	Down
Inflation rate	Up	Down

Balancing The Budget
By Outlawing Deficits

The U.S. Congress has seriously considered enacting a balanced-budget amendment to the Constitution several times in the past decade. And a majority of the state legislatures has petitioned Congress to call a constitutional convention for precisely that purpose. If a few more states join the call, the first constitutional convention since 1787 may be convened. So some sort of constitutional prohibition of budget deficits, presumably with escape clauses, may one day become law.

Congress took a step in that direction in December 1985 when it passed the Balanced Budget Act, commonly known as the Gramm-Rudman-Hollings Act for its three senatorial sponsors. The act sets a strict numerical schedule for reducing the budget deficit from the $212 billion recorded in fiscal year 1985 to zero by fiscal year 1991. Despite the important effect of economic activity on the budget deficit that was discussed in this chapter (see especially pages 327–29), Congress made the deficit limit for each year a fixed number to apply whether the economy is booming or limping along. It did, however, provide for exceptional circumstances (such as a forecast of recession) under which the limits could be suspended.

The law set out a list of deadlines for Congress to follow in handling each year's budget. But its most stunning and important provision was a mechanical formula for cutting government spending by computer in the event that Congress failed to make the necessary deficit reductions by the specified date.

Early returns on the operation of the law have not been favorable. Congress set a $172 billion deficit limit for fiscal year 1986. But, since Gramm-Rudman was enacted after fiscal 1986 had started, the limit was not binding. In fact, the 1986 deficit turned out to be $221 billion—even higher than the 1985 deficit. An inauspicious beginning.

Then things got worse. In August 1986, as the House and Senate were nearing agreement over how to abide by Gramm-Rudman's fiscal 1987 deficit limit of $144 billion, the Supreme Court declared the automatic budget-cutting mechanism unconstitutional. The law had lost its teeth. Nonetheless, House Democrats and Senate Republicans miraculously agreed on a budget that claimed to produce a $144 billion deficit, and many observers gave Gramm-Rudman credit for disciplining Congress.

But the congratulations proved premature. First the president rejected Congress's budget proposal as too stingy on defense spending. Then the Congressional Budget Office reported that the budget failed to abide by the Gramm-Rudman deficit limit anyway. Discouraged, Congress simply ignored all the Gramm-Rudman deadlines. Then, after the fiscal year had begun, a jerry-built budget—replete with an embarrassing number of accounting gimmicks and other budgetary tricks—was rushed through both houses and signed into law by the president. In the end, the fiscal 1987 deficit came in at $158 billion despite surprisingly high revenues. Throughout the deliberations over the fiscal 1988 budget, both the administration and Congress more or less ignored the Gramm-Rudman deficit limit of $108 billion.

And that is why different people, looking at the same facts, can reach different conclusions about deficits.

The point is that "looking at the facts" is not enough. Simple correlations between the budget deficit and some other economic variable are not terribly informative. You must be able to distinguish between *cause* and *effect*. In

Case 1, changes in fiscal policy were the driving force; in a sense, a higher deficit *caused* Y, P, and r to rise. But in Case 2, there was no change in fiscal policy; a higher deficit was an *effect* of a recession.

Recent U.S. history has had elements of both cases. In the first years of the Reagan administration, we experienced a terrible recession that had very little to do with the president's fiscal policies (analogous to Case 2). Starting in 1983, however, the Reagan tax cuts began to have major effects on the deficit (as in Case 1). No wonder the charges and countercharges were so confused, and the evidence so confusing. (See Discussion Question 10 at the end of the chapter.)

Conclusion: The Partisan Debate over the Budget Deficit

Given what we have learned about the theory and facts of budget deficits, we are now in a position to address the issues debated by President Reagan and his critics.

1. *How did we get such a large deficit?* As we have seen in this chapter, triple-digit deficits began in 1982. At first, the most important cause was not Mr. Reagan's policies, but rather the steep recession. While the budget showed titanic deficits in 1982 and 1983, the high-employment deficits were roughly half as large (see Table 16–3 on page 329).

    But by 1984, with the economy improving and the tax cuts fully effective, the high-employment deficit was tremendous. Deliberate fiscal policy actions account for most of the 1984 deficit as well as subsequent deficits. Whether the blame should rest with the president or the Congress is a matter of politics, not economics.

2. *Is the deficit a problem?* Once again, the answer to the question was different in 1981–1983 from what it has been since. In 1981–1982, the economy went through a deep recession. And in 1983, the first year of the recovery, unemployment was still far above full employment. Under these circumstances, crowding out would not be expected to be a serious problem and actions to close the deficit would have threatened the recovery. According to the basic principles of fiscal policy, a large deficit was probably appropriate.

    But things are different now. Crowding out becomes a more serious issue as the economy nears full employment. So budget deficits should fall. But the actual deficit did not fall from 1983 to 1986 and the high-employment deficit rose dramatically. Since 1983 we have had large high-employment deficits in peacetime for the first time in our history; and worries about the burden of the national debt, once mostly myths, are becoming all too realistic.

3. *What should be done about the deficit?* It is a matter of simple arithmetic that you close a budget deficit by raising taxes and/or by reducing spending. Either of these routes is a contractionary fiscal policy and will retard the growth of real GNP and make it harder to return to full employment.

Is there any way around this problem? There is, if fiscal and monetary policies can be coordinated better. If fiscal policy must turn contractionary to reduce the deficit, monetary policy can turn expansionary to counteract the effects on aggregate demand. In this way, we can hope to shrink the deficit without shrinking the economy in the process. Such a change in the policy "mix" would also bring down interest rates, since both tighter budgets and easier money tend to push interest rates down.

For these reasons, many economists—both liberal and conservative—have long advocated a shift in the policy mix toward tighter budgets and easier monetary policy. Some progress has been made in this direction. But, at this writing, most economists still feel that the federal deficit is too high.

Summary

1. Rigid adherence to budget balancing would make the economy less stable by reducing aggregate demand (via tax increases and reductions in government spending) when private spending is low, and raising aggregate demand when private spending is high.

2. Since both monetary and fiscal policy influence aggregate demand, the appropriate budget deficit or surplus depends on monetary policy. Similarly, the appropriate monetary policy depends on budget policy.

3. The national debt has grown dramatically since the mid-1970s. But until recently it was generally growing less rapidly than GNP.

4. Inflation makes the deficit look bigger than it really is because all nominal interest payments are counted as expenditures. Under inflation accounting, only real interest payments would count as expenditures, and the deficit would be seen to be much smaller.

5. Part of the reason for the large budget deficits of the 1980s is the fact that the economy has operated well below full employment. The high-employment deficit, which uses estimates of what the government's receipts and outlays would be at full employment, has been much smaller than the official deficit.

6. If we correct the official deficit for inflation and adjust it to high levels of employment, we find that deficits in the high-employment inflation-corrected budget began only in 1983. Before that there were balanced budgets or surpluses.

7. Arguments that the public debt will burden future generations, who will have to make huge payments of interest and principal, are based on false analogies. In fact, most of these payments are simply transfers from some Americans to other Americans. Besides, the Treasury can, and normally does, "roll over" its debt rather than pay it off.

8. The bogus argument that a large national debt can bankrupt a country like the United States ignores the fact that our national debt consists of obligations to pay U.S. dollars—a currency the government can raise by taxation or create by printing money.

9. Under normal circumstances, budget deficits are somewhat inflationary. They are even more inflationary if they are "monetized," that is, if the Federal Reserve buys some of the newly issued government debt in the open market.

10. Unless the deficit is substantially monetized, deficit spending forces interest rates higher and discourages private investment spending. This is called the crowding-out effect. If there is a great deal of crowding out, then deficits really do impose a burden on future generations by leaving them a smaller capital stock to work with.

11. But there is also a crowding-in effect from higher government spending (G). If expansionary fiscal policy succeeds in raising real output (Y), more investment will be induced by the higher Y.

12. Which effect is stronger, crowding out or crowding in, depends mainly on the state of the economy. When unemployment is high, crowding in probably dominates, so higher G does not cause lower investment. But when the economy is near full employment, the proponents of the crowding-out hypothesis are probably right: High government spending just displaces private investment.

13. Whether or not deficits are a burden therefore depends on how and why the government ran these deficits in the first place. If deficits are contracted to fight recessions, it is possible that more investment is crowded in by the increases in income that these deficits make possible than is crowded out by the increases in interest rates. Deficits contracted to carry on wars certainly impair the future capital stock, though they may not be considered a burden for noneconomic reasons. Since these two cases account for most of America's national debt, our debt cannot reasonably be considered a serious burden. This is one of the **12 Ideas for Beyond the Final Exam.**

14. If deficits arise from deliberate fiscal policy actions, then larger deficits should lead to more rapid growth of real output, higher prices, and higher interest rates.

15. But if deficits arise from a recession, we should find larger deficits accompanied by declining GNP, lower inflation, and lower interest rates.

Concepts for Review

Budget deficit
National debt
Real versus nominal interest rates
Inflation accounting

High-employment budget
Monetization of deficits
Crowding out

Crowding in
Burden of the national debt
Mix of monetary and fiscal policy

Questions for Discussion

1. Explain the difference between the budget deficit and the national debt. If we reduce the deficit, will the debt stop growing?
2. Explain how the U.S. government has managed to accumulate a debt of more than $2400 billion. To whom does it owe this debt? Can this debt be considered a burden on future generations?
3. Comment on the following: "Deficit spending paves the road to ruination. If we keep it up, the whole nation will go bankrupt. Even if things do not go this far, what right have we to burden our children and grandchildren with these debts while we live high on the hog?"
4. Calculate the budget deficit and the inflation-corrected deficit for an economy with the following data:

   Government expenditures other than interest = 90
   Tax receipts = 75
   Interest payments = 64
   Interest rate = 8 percent
   Inflation rate = 5 percent
   National debt at start of year = 800

   (*Note:* 8 percent interest on an $800 debt is $64.)
5. Explain why the high-employment budget might show a surplus while the actual budget is in deficit.
6. If the Federal Reserve begins to increase the money supply more slowly than before, what will happen to the government budget deficit? (*Hint:*

What will happen to tax receipts and interest expenses?) If the government wants to offset the effects of the Fed's actions on aggregate demand, what might it do? How will this affect the deficit?

7. Given the current state of the economy, do you think the Fed should monetize more of the deficit? (*Note:* There is no one correct answer to this question. It is a good question to discuss in class.)
8. Explain the difference between crowding out and crowding in. Given the current state of the economy, which effect would you expect to be dominant right now?
9. Suppose the Balanced Budget Act had been in effect in 1982, during the worst of the recession. What might have happened to the economy?
10. Evaluate each of the following statements. (*Note:* The facts in each case are correct; concentrate on the conclusion that is reached.)
    a. "In 1982, the deficit was larger than in 1981. But interest rates were lower. Therefore, larger deficits do not cause higher interest rates."
    b. "In 1978 we had a small deficit and strong GNP growth. In 1982, we had a huge deficit and a recession. Therefore, deficit spending does not stimulate the economy."
    c. "If we compare 1980–1981 with 1985–1986, we find much larger deficits but much lower inflation in the last two years than in the first two. Therefore, it is clear that deficit spending is not inflationary."

17

The Trade-Off Between Inflation and Unemployment

The worldwide trend toward higher inflation was arrested during the first half of the 1980s. The rate of inflation in the United States declined from about 10 percent to under 4 percent. In Great Britain inflation fell from 20 percent to 4 percent; in Italy from 21 percent to 11 percent; in West Germany from $4\frac{1}{2}$ percent to about zero. As this was happening, the Western economies all suffered severe recessions. In the United States, for example, the unemployment rate topped 10 percent for the first time since the Great Depression.

Most economists believe that this conjunction of events was no coincidence. Rather, they insist, the period of high unemployment was the price we paid to reduce the rate of inflation. Although some optimists claim that it is possible to reduce inflation without suffering from unemployment, the world clearly paid a heavy price for the disinflation of the 1980s. Was this price inevitable, or could we have avoided it? That is the question for this chapter.

You may recall from Chapter 1 that the existence of an agonizing trade-off between inflation and unemployment is one of the **12 Ideas For Beyond the Final Exam.** The importance of this trade-off can hardly be overestimated. It is probably the one area of macroeconomics where confusion is most widespread. And because this confusion can have disastrous consequences for the conduct of stabilization policy, the trade-off merits the comprehensive examination that we give it in this chapter. Without a thorough understanding of the dimensions of this trade-off, it is impossible for a citizen to make an informed judgment about macroeconomic policy.

Demand-Side Inflation Versus Supply-Side Inflation: A Review

Let us begin our investigation of the trade-off by reviewing some of what we have learned about inflation in earlier chapters.

One major cause of inflation, though certainly not the only one, is *excessive growth of aggregate demand*. What happens if, for some reason, either consumers or investors or the government decides to increase spending? We know, first of all, that such an autonomous increase in spending will have a multiplier effect on aggregate demand; that is, each additional $1 of C or I or G will lead to more than $1 of additional demand. Second, we know that firms normally find it profitable to supply the additional output only at higher prices. Hence, such a stimulus to aggregate demand will normally pull up *both* real output *and* prices.

Figure 17–1, which is familiar from earlier chapters, reviews this conclusion. Initially, the economy is at point A, where aggregate demand curve D_0D_0 intersects aggregate supply curve SS. Then something happens to increase demand, and the aggregate demand curve shifts horizontally to D_1D_1. The new equilibrium is at point B, where both prices and output are higher than they were at A.

The slope of the aggregate supply curve measures the amount of inflation that accompanies any specified rise in output and therefore embodies the trade-off between unemployment and inflation. We concluded in the last chapter that this trade-off will be favorable when the economy is operating at low levels of capacity utilization and high levels of unemployment. Under such circumstances, firms can expand their operations substantially without running into higher costs. On the other hand, if the demand stimulus occurs in a fully employed economy, firms will find it difficult to raise output and so will respond mostly by raising prices. Thus, the tradeoff is unfavorable when unemployment is low.

But we have learned in this book (especially in Chapter 11) that inflation need not always emanate from the demand side. Restrictions in the growth of aggregate supply—caused, for example, by an increase in the price of foreign oil—can shift the economy's aggregate supply curve inward. This is illustrated in Figure 17–2, where the aggregate supply curve shifts from S_0S_0 to S_1S_1, and the economy's equilibrium consequently moves from point A to point B. Prices rise as output falls. We have *stagflation*.

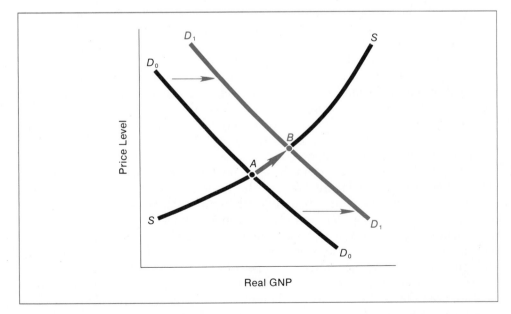

Figure 17–1
INFLATION FROM THE DEMAND SIDE
An increase in aggregate demand, whether it comes from consumers, investors, or the government, shifts the aggregate demand curve outward from D_0D_0 to D_1D_1. The economy's equilibrium moves from point A to point B. Since point B corresponds to a higher price level than does point A, there is inflation (that is, a rising price level) as the economy moves from A to B.

Figure 17–2

INFLATION FROM THE SUPPLY SIDE

A decrease in aggregate supply—which can be caused by such factors as an autonomous increase in wages, or by an increase in the price of foreign oil—can cause inflation. When the aggregate supply curve shifts to the left, from S_0S_0 to S_1S_1, the equilibrium point moves from A to B. Comparing B with A, we see that the price level is higher, which means there must have been *inflation* (rising prices) in the interim. Notice also that adverse supply shifts make real ouput decline while prices are rising; that is, they produce *stagflation*.

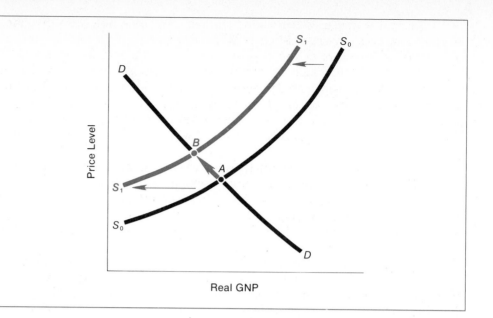

Thus, while inflation can be initiated from either the *demand* side or the *supply* side of the economy, there is a crucial difference. Demand-side inflation is normally accompanied by rising real GNP (see Figure 17–1), while supply-side inflation may well be accompanied by falling GNP (see Figure 17–2). This is an important distinction, as we shall see in this chapter.

Applying the Model to a Growing Economy

You may have noticed that our simple model of aggregate supply and aggregate demand determines an equilibrium *price level* and an equilibrium *level of real GNP*. But, in the real economy, we do not see an unchanged price level and an unchanged level of real GNP for long periods of time. Instead, the price level and the level of real GNP change every year.

This is illustrated in Figure 17–3, which is a scatter diagram of the U.S. price level and the level of GNP for every year from 1963 to 1986. The points are labeled to show the clear upward march of the economy through time—toward higher prices and higher levels of output.

It is certainly no mystery why this occurs. The normal state of affairs is for *both* the aggregate demand curve *and* the aggregate supply curve to shift to the right each year. Aggregate supply grows because there are more workers, more machinery, and more factories each year, and because technology is improving. Aggregate demand grows because a growing population means more demand for both consumer and investment goods, because the government increases its spending, and because the Federal Reserve increases the money supply. We can think of each point in Figure 17–3 as the intersection of an aggregate supply curve and an aggregate demand curve for that particular year. To help you visualize this, the curves for 1978 are sketched in the diagram.

Figure 17–4 illustrates how our theoretical model of aggregate supply and aggregate demand applies to a growing economy. The numbers are chosen so that curves D_0D_0 and S_0S_0 roughly represent the end of 1985, and the curves D_1D_1 and S_1S_1 roughly represent the end of 1986, except that nice round numbers are used. Thus the equilibrium late in 1985 was at point A, with real GNP

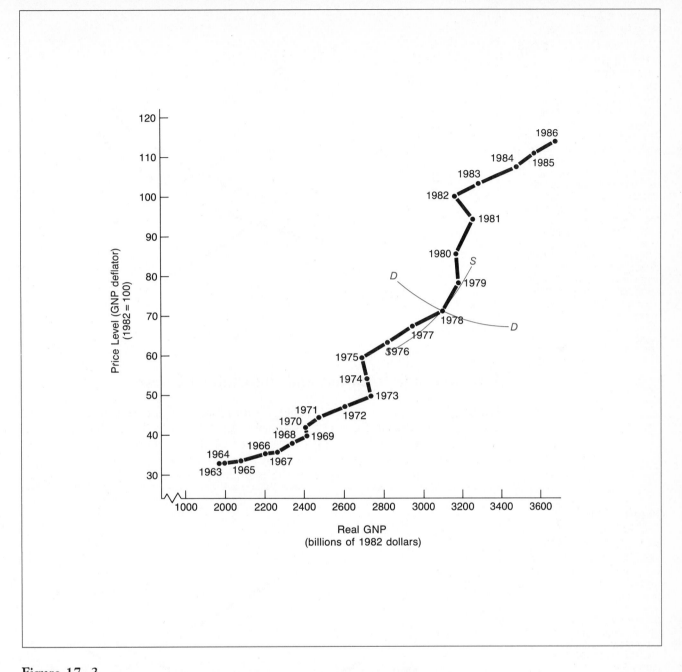

Figure 17–3
THE PRICE LEVEL AND REAL OUTPUT IN THE UNITED STATES, 1963–1986
This scatter diagram shows, for each year from 1963 to 1986, the price level (GNP deflator) and real GNP for the United States.
Clearly the normal state of affairs is for both variables to rise from one year to the next.
SOURCE: U.S. Department of Commerce, Bureau of Economic Analysis

of $3600 billion (in 1982 dollars) and a price level of 113, while the equilibrium a year later was at point B, with real GNP at $3700 billion and the price level at 115, or 1.8 percent higher. The blue arrow in the diagram shows how equilibrium moved during 1986. It points upward and to the right, meaning that both prices and output increased.

Figure 17–4

AGGREGATE SUPPLY AND DEMAND ANALYSIS OF A GROWING ECONOMY

This diagram illustrates how the aggregate supply and demand analysis of earlier chapters can be applied to a real-world economy, in which both the supply curve and the demand curve normally shift outward from one year to the next. In this example, demand curve D_0D_0 and supply curve S_0S_0 represent the U.S. economy in late 1985. Equilibrium was at point A, with a price level of 113 and real GNP of $3600 billion. Demand curve D_1D_1 and supply curve S_1S_1 represent the end of 1986. During the year, the price index rose by 2 points (almost 2 percent) and output increased by $100 billion (almost 3 percent).

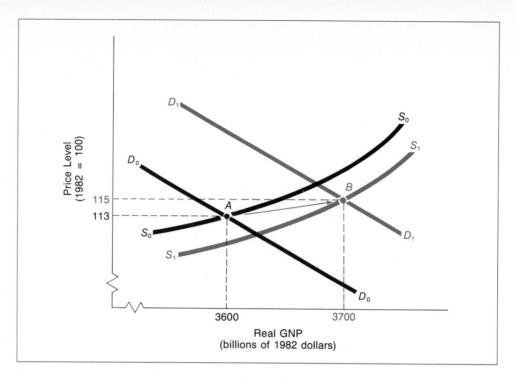

Demand-Side Inflation and the Phillips Curve

Let us now use our theoretical model to rerun history. Suppose that during 1986 the aggregate demand curve grew *faster* than it actually did. What difference would this have made for the performance of the national economy? Figure 17–5 provides the answers. Here the demand curve D_0D_0 and both supply curves are exactly as they were in the previous diagram, but the demand curve

Figure 17–5

THE EFFECTS OF FASTER GROWTH OF AGGREGATE DEMAND

In this hypothetical example, we imagine that because either private citizens spent more or the government pursued more expansionary policies, aggregate demand grew faster between late 1985 and late 1986 than it did in Figure 17–4. The consequence is that, in this diagram, the price level rises 6 points (almost 6 percent) during 1986 compared with the 2 points (under 2 percent) in Figure 17–4. Growth of real output is also greater: $200 billion here versus only $100 billion in the previous figure.

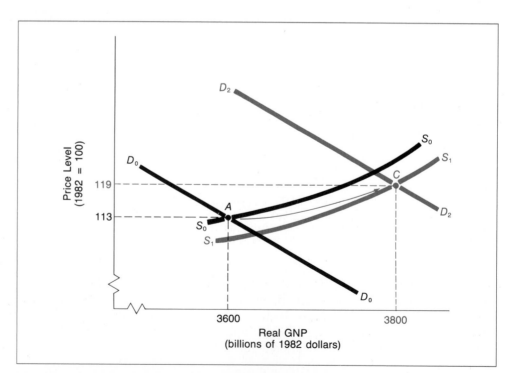

D_2D_2 is farther to the right than the demand curve D_1D_1 in Figure 17–4. Equilibrium is at point A late in 1985 and point C late in 1986. Comparing point C in Figure 17–5 with point B in Figure 17–4, we see that output would have increased more during 1986 ($200 billion versus $100 billion) and prices would also have increased more (to 119 instead of 115); that is, there would have been more *inflation*. This is generally what happens when the growth rate of aggregate demand speeds up.

For any given rate of growth of the aggregate supply curve, a faster rate of growth of the aggregate demand curve will lead to more inflation and faster growth of real output.

Figure 17–6 illustrates the opposite case. Here we imagine that the aggregate demand curve shifted out *less* than in Figure 17–4. That is, demand curve D_3D_3 in Figure 17–6 is to the left of demand curve D_1D_1 in Figure 17–4. The consequence, we see, is that the shift of the economy's equilibrium during 1986 (from point A to point E) would have entailed *less inflation* and *slower growth of real output* than actually took place. This again is generally the case.

For any given rate of growth of the aggregate supply curve, a slower rate of growth of the aggregate demand curve will lead to less inflation and slower growth of real output.

If we put these two findings together, we have a clear prediction from our theory:

If fluctuations in the economy's real growth rate from year to year are caused primarily by variations in the rate at which aggregate demand increases, then the data should show the most rapid inflation occurring when output expands most rapidly and the slowest inflation occurring when output expands most slowly.

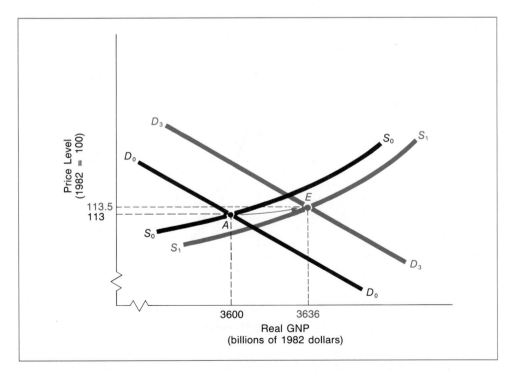

Figure 17–6
THE EFFECTS OF SLOWER GROWTH OF AGGREGATE DEMAND
Here, the aggregate demand curve is assumed to shift outward less than it did in Figure 17–4. Consequently, the movement from equilibrium point A to equilibrium point E during 1986 entails a smaller rise in the price level and a smaller increase in real output than actually occurred.

Does the theory fit the facts? We will put it to the test in a moment, but first let us translate it into a prediction about the relationship between inflation and unemployment. Faster growth of real output naturally means faster growth in the number of jobs and, hence, *lower unemployment*. Conversely, slower growth of real output means slower growth in the number of jobs and, hence, *higher unemployment*. So we conclude that, if business fluctuations emanate from the demand side, unemployment should be low when inflation is high and inflation should be low when unemployment is high.

Figure 17–7 illustrates this idea. The actual unemployment rate in the United States in late 1986 was about 6.5 percent, and the inflation rate during the year was about 1.8 percent. This is point *b* in Figure 17–7, which corresponds to equilibrium point *B* in Figure 17–4. The faster growth rate of demand depicted by point *C* in Figure 17–5 would have led to higher inflation and lower unemployment. For the sake of a concrete example, we suppose that unemployment would have been 5.5 percent and inflation would have been 5.3 percent; this is point *c* in Figure 17–7. Point *E* in Figure 17–6 summarized the results of slower growth of aggregate demand: Unemployment would have been higher and inflation lower. In Figure 17–7, this is represented by point *e*, with an unemployment rate of 7.5 percent and an inflation rate of about 1 percent. This figure shows graphically the principal empirical implication of our theoretical model:

If fluctuations in economic activity are primarily caused by variations in the rate at which the aggregate demand curve shifts outward from year to year, then the data should show an inverse relationship between unemployment and inflation, as in Figure 17–7.

Now we are ready to look at real data. Do we actually observe such an inverse relationship between inflation and unemployment? About 30 years ago,

Figure 17–7
ORIGINS OF THE PHILLIPS CURVE
The three previous diagrams indicated three different rates of growth of real GNP between late 1985 and late 1986 and three different inflation rates. Since each different real growth rate corresponds to a different rate of unemployment, we can put the information contained in the three preceding diagrams together in a scatter diagram to show the relationship between inflation and unemployment. Points *b, c,* and *e* in this figure correspond to points *B, C,* and *E* in Figures 17–4, 17–5, and 17–6, respectively. The inflation numbers are read directly from the previous three graphs. The unemployment numbers are fabricated to represent the fact that faster growth (Figure 17–5) is associated with lower unemployment (point *c*), while slower growth (Figure 17–6) is associated with higher unemployment (point *e*). Scatter diagrams like this one are called "Phillips curves," after their inventor, A. W. Phillips.

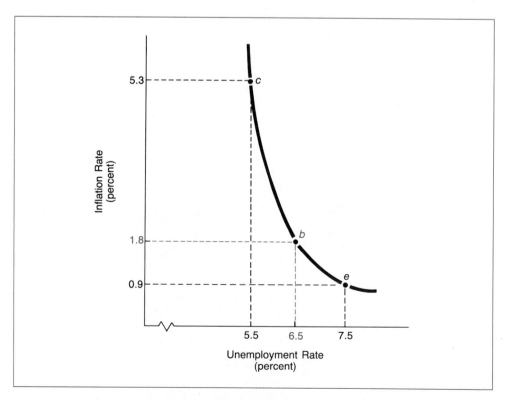

economist A. W. Phillips plotted data on unemployment and the rate of change of *wages* (not prices) for several extended periods of British history on a series of scatter diagrams, one of which is reproduced as Figure 17–8. He then sketched in a curve that seemed to "fit" the data. This type of curve, which is now called a **Phillips curve,** shows that wage inflation normally is high when unemployment is low and is low when unemployment is high. So far, so good.

Phillips curves have also been constructed for *price* inflation, and one of these for the postwar United States is shown in Figure 17–9. The curve appears to fit the data well, though not perfectly. As viewed through the eyes of our theory, these facts suggest that economic fluctuations in England between 1861 and 1913 and in the United States between 1954 and 1969 probably were accounted for primarily by changes in the growth of aggregate demand. The simple model of demand-side inflation really does seem to describe what happened.

During the 1960s and early 1970s, economists often thought of the Phillips curve as a "menu" of the choices available to policymakers. In this view, policymakers could opt for low unemployment and high inflation—as in 1969. Or

A **Phillips curve** is a graph depicting the rate of unemployment on the horizontal axis and either the rate of inflation or the rate of change of money wages on the vertical axis. Phillips curves are normally downward sloping, indicating that higher inflation rates are associated with lower unemployment rates.

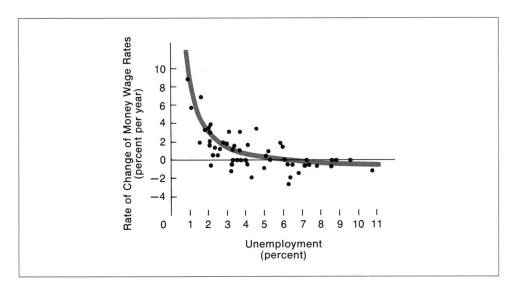

Figure 17–8
THE ORIGINAL
PHILLIPS CURVE
This scatter diagram, reproduced from the original article by A. W. Phillips, shows the rate of change of money wages and the rate of unemployment in the United Kingdom between 1861 and 1913. Each year is represented by a point in the diagram.
SOURCE: A. W. Phillips, "The Relation Between Unemployment and the Rate of Change of Money Wages in the United Kingdom, 1861–1957." *Economica,* New Series, vol. 25, November 1958.

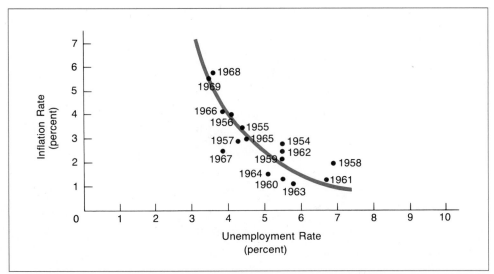

Figure 17–9
A PHILLIPS CURVE FOR THE UNITED STATES
This Phillips curve relates *price* inflation (rather than wage inflation) to the unemployment rate in the United States for the years 1954–1969. Though it misses badly in a few instances (for example, 1958), it generally "fits" the data well.

they might prefer higher unemployment coupled with lower inflation—as, for example, in 1961. The Phillips curve, it was thought, described the *quantitative* trade-off between inflation and unemployment. And, for a number of years, it worked rather well.

Then something happened. The economy in the 1970s behaved far worse than expected in terms of the Phillips curve shown in Figure 17–9. In particular, given the unemployment rates in each of those years, inflation was astonishingly high by historical standards. This is shown in Figure 17–10, which simply adds to Figure 17–9 the points for 1970–1986. Clearly something had gone wrong with the old view of the Phillips curve as a menu for policy choices. But what?

Supply-Side Inflation and the Collapse of the Phillips Curve

There are two major answers to this question, and the truth no doubt contains elements of each. We begin with the simpler explanation which claims that much of the inflation of the 1970s did not emanate from the demand side. Instead, the 1970s were full of adverse "supply shocks"—events like the crop failures of 1972–1973 and the oil price increases of 1973–1974 and 1979–1980—that pushed the economy's aggregate supply curve inward to the left. What kind of Phillips curve will be generated when economic fluctuations come from the supply side?

Figure 17–10
A PHILLIPS CURVE FOR THE UNITED STATES?

This scatter diagram adds the points for 1970–1986 to the scatter diagram shown in Figure 17–9. It is clear that inflation in each of those years was higher than the Phillips curve would have led us to predict.

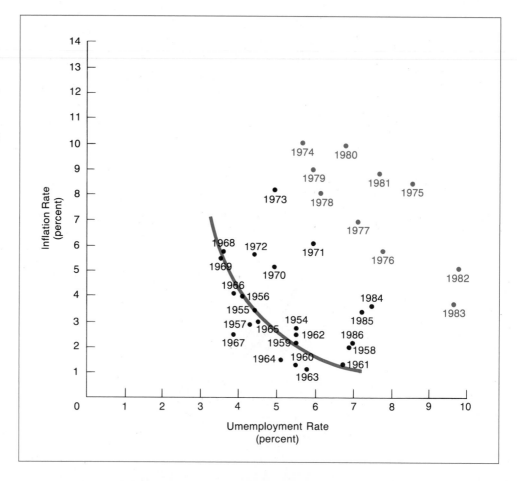

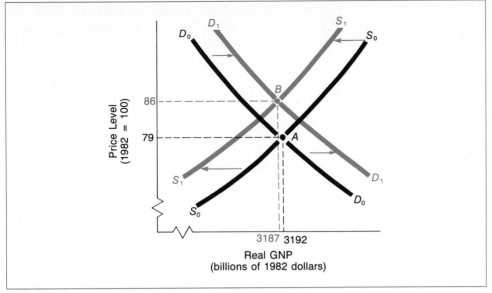

Figure 17–11
STAGFLATION FROM A
SUPPLY SHOCK
Instead of shifting outward as
it normally does, the
aggregate supply curve
shifted inward — from S_0S_0 to
S_1S_1 — between 1979 and
1980. Coupled with fairly
slow growth of the aggregate
demand curve — from D_0D_0 in
1979 to D_1D_1 in
1980 — equilibrium moved
from point A to point B.
There was a slight decline of
real output, and prices rose
rapidly.

To find out, let us take the events of 1979 and 1980 as an example. In Figure 17–11, aggregate demand curve D_0D_0 and aggregate supply curve S_0S_0 represent the economic situation in 1979. Equilibrium was at point A, with a price level of 79 and real output of $3192 billion. By 1980, the aggregate demand curve had shifted out to the position indicated by D_1D_1, and, under normal conditions, the aggregate supply curve would have shifted out as well. But 1979 was anything but normal. The Iranian revolution led to a shutdown of Iran's oilfields for months. The resulting worldwide scramble for oil led OPEC to double the price of its product during the year.

Thus, instead of shifting *outward* as it normally does from one year to the next, the aggregate supply curve shifted *inward* during 1979, to S_1S_1. The equilibrium for 1980 (point B in the figure) therefore wound up almost vertically above the equilibrium point for 1979. Real output declined slightly and prices — led by energy costs — rose rapidly.

Now, in a growing population with more people looking for jobs each year, a stagnant economy that is not generating new jobs suffers a rise in the unemployment rate. This is precisely what happened in the United States; the unemployment rate averaged 5.8 percent in 1979 and 7.1 percent in 1980. Thus, inflation and unemployment increased at the same time: The Phillips curve basically shifted upward. A general conclusion is that:

If fluctuations in economic activity emanate from the supply side, higher rates of inflation will be associated with higher rates of unemployment, and lower rates of inflation will be associated with lower rates of unemployment.

The instances of major supply shocks during the 1970s stand out clearly in Figure 17–10. (Remember these are *real* data; they are not made up by some textbook writer.) Food prices boomed between 1972 and 1974 and again in 1978. Energy prices soared in 1973–1974 and again in 1979–1980. It is clear that the inflation and unemployment data generated by the U.S. economy between 1972 and 1974, and again between 1978 and 1980, are consistent with our theoretical model of supply-side inflation. Indeed, if you look at Figure 17–10 carefully, you can almost see the outlines of three separate Phillips curves: a low one for 1954–1969 (shown in the diagram), a high one for 1974–1983, and an intermediate one for 1970–1973 and 1984–1986. Many economists believe that the supply shocks of the 1970s account for these shifts of the Phillips curve.

What the Phillips Curve Is Not

But there is another view of what went wrong in the 1970s. This one holds that policymakers misinterpreted the Phillips curve and tried to pick unsustainable combinations of inflation and unemployment. Specifically, the Phillips curve is a *statistical relationship* between inflation and unemployment that we expect to emerge *if changes in the growth of aggregate demand are the predominant factor accounting for economic fluctuations*. But the curve was widely misinterpreted as depicting a number of *alternative equilibrium points* that the economy could achieve and from which policymakers could choose.

We can understand the flaw in this reasoning by quickly reviewing an earlier lesson. We know from Chapter 11 that the economy has a **self-correcting mechanism** that will cure both inflations and recessions *eventually* even if the government does nothing. Why is this relevant here? Because it tells us that many combinations of output and prices cannot be maintained indefinitely. Some will "self-destruct." Specifically, if the economy finds itself far away from the normal full-employment level of unemployment, forces will be set in motion that tend to erode the inflationary or recessionary gap.

For example, consider the case of a recessionary gap where aggregate supply curve S_0S_0 intersects aggregate demand curve DD at point A in Figure 17–12. With equilibrium output well below potential GNP, there is unused industrial capacity and unsold output. So firms will not raise prices much. At the same time, the availability of unemployed workers eager for jobs limits the rate at which labor can push up wage rates. But wages are the main component of business costs, so when wages decline (relative to what they would have been without a recession) so do costs. And lower costs stimulate greater production. This idea is depicted in Figure 17–12 as an outward shift of the aggregate supply curve—from S_0S_0 to S_1S_1.

Figure 17–12
THE ELIMINATION OF A RECESSIONARY GAP
When the aggregate supply curve is S_0S_0 and the aggregate demand curve is *DD*, the economy will reach an equilibrium with a recessionary gap (point *A*). The resulting deflation of wages will cause the aggregate supply curve to shift outward (downward) from S_0S_0 to S_1S_1 and eventually to S_2S_2. Here, with equilibrium at point *C*, the recessionary gap is gone and the economy is back at normal full employment.

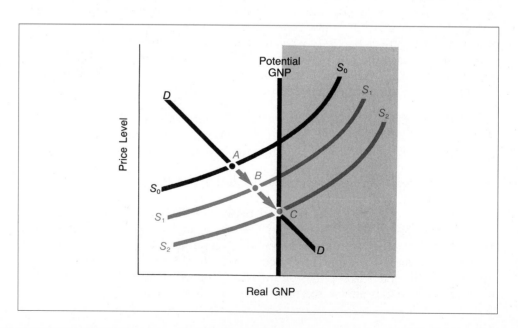

As can be seen in the figure, the outward shift of the aggregate supply curve brought on by the recession causes equilibrium output to rise as the economy moves from point A to point B. Thus the size of the recessionary gap begins to shrink. This process continues until the aggregate supply curve reaches the position indicated by S_2S_2 in Figure 17–12. Here wages have fallen enough to eliminate the recessionary gap, and the economy has reached a full-employment equilibrium at point C.[1]

We can relate this to our discussion of the origins of the Phillips curve with the help of Figure 17–13, which is a hypothetical Phillips curve.

Point a in Figure 17–13 corresponds to point A in Figure 17–12: it shows the initial recessionary gap with unemployment (at 8 percent) above full employment, which we assume to occur at 6 percent. But we have just seen that point A in Figure 17–12 — and therefore also point a in Figure 17–13 — is not sustainable. The economy tends to rid itself of the recessionary gap through the disinflation process we have just described. The adjustment path from A to C that we analyzed in Figure 17–12 would appear on our Phillips curve diagram as a movement toward less inflation and less unemployment — something like the blue arrow from point a to point c in Figure 17–13.

Similarly, points representing inflationary gaps — such as point d in Figure 17–13 — are not sustainable. They are also gradually eliminated by the self-correcting mechanism that we studied in Chapter 11. Wages are forced up by the abnormally low unemployment, and this in turn pushes prices higher. Higher prices deter investment spending by forcing up interest rates and deter consumer spending by lowering the purchasing power of consumer wealth. The inflationary process continues until the amount people want to spend is brought into balance with the amount firms want to supply at normal full employment.

[1]This simple analysis assumes that the aggregate demand curve does not move during the adjustment period. If it is shifting to the right, the recessionary gap will disappear even faster, but inflation will not slow down as much.

EXERCISE: Construct the diagram for this case by adding a shift in the aggregate demand curve to Figure 17–12.

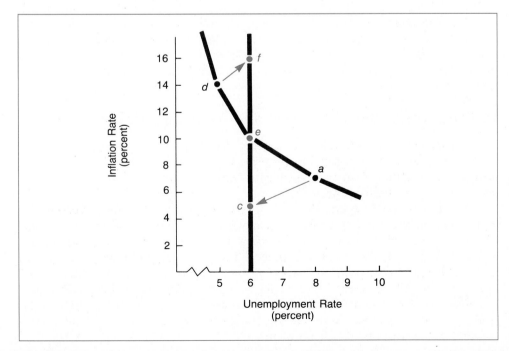

Figure 17–13
THE VERTICAL LONG-RUN PHILLIPS CURVE
In the long run, points like a, where unemployment is above the normal "full-employment" unemployment rate, are unsustainable. The economy's natural self-correcting mechanism (which was described in Figure 17–12) will erode the recessionary gap by reducing both inflation and unemployment. In the diagram, this will force the economy toward a point like c. The long-run choices, therefore, are among points like c and f, which constitute what is called the vertical (long-run) Phillips curve, not among points like d and a on the downward-sloping (short-run) Phillips curve.

During such an adjustment period, unemployment and inflation are both rising—as indicated by the blue path from point d to point f in Figure 17–13.

Putting these two conclusions together, we see that:

On a Phillips curve diagram, neither points corresponding to an inflationary gap (like d in Figure 17–13) nor points corresponding to a recessionary gap (like a in Figure 17–13) can be maintained indefinitely. Inflationary gaps lead to rising unemployment and rising inflation. Recessionary gaps lead to falling inflation and falling unemployment. All the points that are sustainable in the long run (such as c, e, and f in Figure 17–13) correspond to the same rate of unemployment, which is therefore called the **natural rate of unemployment.** The natural rate corresponds to what we have so far been calling the "full employment" unemployment rate.

The economy's self-correcting mechanism always tends to push the unemployment rate back toward a specific rate of unemployment that we call the **natural rate of unemployment.**

Thus the Phillips curve connecting points d, e, and a is not a menu of policy choices. While we can move from a point like e to a point like d by stimulating aggregate demand sufficiently, there is no way that we can stay at point d. Unemployment cannot be kept this low indefinitely. Instead, policymakers must choose from among points like c, e, and f, all of which are vertically above one another at the natural rate of unemployment. For rather obvious reasons, the line connecting these points has been dubbed the **vertical (long-run) Phillips curve.** It is this vertical Phillips curve (connecting points like e and f), that represents the true long-run menu of policy choices. We thus conclude that:

The **vertical (long run) Phillips curve** shows the menu of inflation/unemployment choices available to society in the long run. It is a vertical straight line at the natural rate of unemployment.

In the short-run, it is possible to "ride up the Phillips curve" toward lower levels of unemployment by stimulating aggregate demand. Conversely, by restricting the growth of demand, it is possible to "ride down the Phillips curve" toward lower rates of inflation (see, for example, point a in Figure 17–13). There is, thus, a *trade-off between unemployment and inflation*. Stimulating demand will improve the unemployment picture but worsen inflation; restricting demand will lower inflation but aggravate the unemployment problem.

However, there is no such trade-off in the long run. The economy's self-correcting mechanism ensures that unemployment eventually will return to the "natural rate," no matter what happens to aggregate demand. In the long run, faster growth of demand leads only to higher inflation, not to lower unemployment; and slower growth of demand leads only to lower inflation, not to higher unemployment.

Fighting Inflation with Fiscal and Monetary Policy

Now let us apply this analysis to a concrete policy problem, one that has troubled every president from Lyndon Johnson to Ronald Reagan. How should the government's ability to manage aggregate demand through fiscal and monetary policy be used to fight inflation?

We have already spent many chapters discussing how the government's monetary and fiscal policy tools—tax rates, government spending, open market operations, and so on—can be used to increase or decrease aggregate demand. We have also discussed some of the practical problems that arise in using each of these weapons and some of the issues involved in choosing among them. Rather than repeat all this, let us just suppose that the government somehow controls aggregate demand and wishes to use this ability to fight inflation. What has our discussion of the trade-off between inflation and unemployment taught us about this problem?

To create an example that comes close to that inherited by President Reagan in early 1981, let us imagine that a new president takes office when the inflation rate is 10 percent and the unemployment rate is 6 percent—point *e* in Figure 17–13.[2] Suppose the new president adopts a policy of restricting the growth of aggregate demand by contractionary fiscal and monetary policies, thereby opening up a recessionary gap. In a word—though no politician would ever use such blunt language—he decides to fight inflation by causing a recession.

At first, the economy "rides down" the short-run Phillips curve from point *e* to point *a* in Figure 17–13. The recession pushes unemployment up from 6 percent to 8 percent, but it reduces inflation from 10 percent to 7 percent. This scenario roughly describes what happened in the United States between early 1981 and late 1982, except that the recession was much more severe than in the example. Unemployment in the United States hit 10.7 percent.

But the anti-inflation dividends of recession do not end there. The economy's self-correcting mechanism begins to work and gradually erodes the recessionary gap. Inflation continues to decline as the economy recovers and unemployment falls. In the example, inflation falls from 7 percent to 5 percent as the economy recovers along the path from *a* to *c* in Figure 17–13. In the actual U.S. case, inflation continued to decline as recovery progressed, but the economy had still not returned to full employment when this book went to press in 1987.

When all the dust has settled, the economy in our hypothetical example has moved from point *e* to point *c* in Figure 17–13. Comparing these two points shows that, in the end, there is less inflation and no more unemployment. In what sense, then, do policymakers have to face up to a *trade-off* between inflation and unemployment? The answer is that:

The cost of reducing inflation by restrictive fiscal and monetary policies is a *temporary* rise in unemployment.

Figures 17–14 and 17–15 are intended to give the flavor of what the real menu of choices looks like to a policymaker who is considering embarking on such a program. Figure 17–14 contrasts the behavior of the inflation rate over time under a "status quo policy," which keeps the unemployment rate unchanged at 6 percent, with the behavior under a restrictive anti-inflationary policy, which deliberately slows the growth rate of aggregate demand and makes unemployment rise.

Inflation will continue at 10 percent per year if the government does not restrain the growth of demand and unemployment remains at 6 percent. This is the "status quo policy" path shown in black in Figure 17–14. It corresponds to the case where the economy stays indefinitely at point *e* in Figure 17–13.

On the other hand, if a restrictive policy is followed and the growth of aggregate demand is restrained, inflation will begin to fall, slowly at first but then with increasing speed. In the example, we suppose that the inflation rate falls little in the first year, more in the second year, and is essentially down to 5 percent after three years. This is the blue "restrictive policy" path in Figure 17–14. It corresponds to the path from *e* to *a* to *c* in Figure 17–13.

---

[2] The actual inflation rate was about 10 percent; but the unemployment rate was above 7 percent, so President Reagan had both inflation and unemployment to worry about. Our example will be easier to analyze, however, if we depart from reality by pretending that unemployment was not a problem initially.

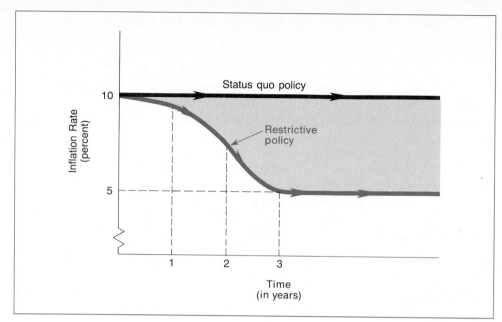
The shaded area in the figure summarizes the difference between these two paths and therefore depicts the payoff to anti-inflation policy. But there are also costs.

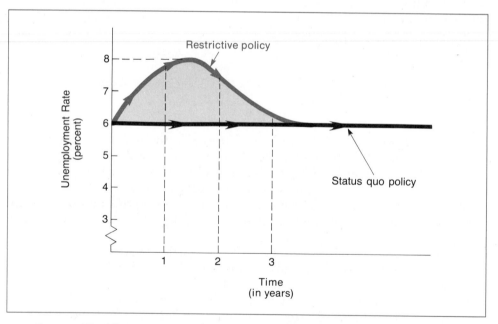
Figure 17–15 gives a rough impression of how the unemployment rate might behave under the two alternative policies. The "status quo policy" keeps the unemployment rate at 6 percent, which is the natural rate. The restrictive policy results in a recession: Unemployment rises from 6 percent to 8 percent, and then gradually falls back to the natural rate of 6 percent. The shaded area in Figure 17–15 shows what it costs to get the inflation rate down: For over three years unemployment is above the natural rate.

Notice the differences in timing between Figure 17–14 and Figure 17–15. In the early stages of the disinflation program (say, the first year), progress against inflation is meager even though the losses on the unemployment front are substantial. This reflects an underlying reality that we have mentioned before: Inflation gives way only grudgingly to economic slack. This, of course, makes anti-inflation policy politically distasteful. The costs of higher unemployment, though temporary, come right away; the benefits of lower inflation, though more durable, may not arrive until after the next election.

What Should Be Done?

Should the government pay the recessionary cost of fighting inflation? When the benefits depicted in Figure 17–14 are balanced against the costs shown in Figure 17–15, have we made a good bargain? While each of you will have to answer this question for yourself, our analysis highlights three critical issues on which your answer should rest.

The Costs of Inflation and Unemployment

We spent an entire chapter early in the book (Chapter 6) examining the social costs of inflation and unemployment. Most of the costs of the extra unemployment depicted in Figure 17–15, we concluded, are easy to translate into dollars and cents. Basically, we need only estimate the real GNP that is lost each year. However, the costs of inflation are harder to put a price tag on, and hence the benefits from reducing inflation are harder to measure. Thus there is considerable controversy over the costs and benefits of using recession to fight inflation.

Some economists and public figures believe that inflation is extremely costly, and so they look with favor on the trade-off that is embodied in Figures 17–14 and 17–15. Others have a lower estimate of the costs of inflation and find recession a terribly high price to pay. In particular, some observers believe that we paid an excessively high price to reduce inflation in the 1980s, while others applaud the policy and maintain that the price was worth paying.

The Position of the Economy

We have stated several times in this book that the shape of the economy's aggregate supply curve, and hence the shape of the short-run Phillips curve, depends on the degree of resource utilization. If resources are virtually fully employed, the aggregate supply curve (and thus the Phillips curve) will be steep, which means that the inflation gains will be substantial and the unemployment costs will be minimal. On the other hand, if there is a great deal of unemployed labor and unutilized industrial capacity, the aggregate supply curve (and hence the short-run Phillips curve) may be nearly horizontal. In that case, a great deal of unemployment will be needed to achieve even a slight reduction in inflation. The Phillips curves we have drawn in this chapter have this characteristic shape.

Because the Phillips curve is shaped this way, the trade-off for inflation-fighters looks more favorable when the economy is in a boom and less favorable when there is already a good deal of unemployment. This, of course, complicated the task faced by President Reagan, who took office at a time when inflation was high but unemployment was already above the natural rate.

The Efficiency of the Economy's Self-Correcting Mechanism

We have stressed that once government policy causes a recession, it is the economy's natural self-correcting mechanism that cures the recessionary gap.

The obvious question here is: How long do we have to wait? If the self-correcting mechanism — which works through reductions in the rate of wage inflation — is slow and halting, the costs of fighting inflation will be enormous. On the other hand, if wage inflation responds promptly, the recession necessary to bring down inflation may not be severe.

This is another issue that is surrounded by controversy. Most economists believe that the weight of the evidence points to extremely sluggish wage behavior. The rate of wage inflation appears to respond only slowly to economic slack. In terms of our Figure 17–13 (page 355), this means that the economy will traverse the path from a to c at an agonizingly slow pace, so that a long period of weak economic activity will be necessary if there is to be any appreciable effect on inflation.

But a significant minority opinion finds this assessment far too pessimistic. Economists in this group argue that the costs of reducing inflation are not nearly so severe and that the key to a successful anti-inflation policy is its effects on people's *expectations*. To understand this argument, we must first examine why expectations are relevant to the Phillips-curve trade-off.

Inflationary Expectations and the Phillips Curve

The explanation starts with more review. Recall from Chapter 11 that the main reason why the economy's aggregate supply curve slopes upward — that is, why output increases as the price level rises — is that businesses typically purchase labor and other inputs under long-term contracts that stipulate the cost of the input in *money* terms (for example, the money wage rate). If such contracts are in force when prices go up, then *real* wages fall as prices rise. From businesses' point of view, labor becomes cheaper in real terms, and firms are induced to expand employment and output. Buying cheaply and selling dearly is, after all, the route to higher profits. Long-term contracts that fix the money wage, then, explain why higher prices lead to more output; that is, why the aggregate supply curve slopes upward.

Table 17–1 illustrates how this works in a concrete example. We suppose that workers and firms agree today that the money wage to be paid a year from now will be $10 per hour. The table then shows the real wage that corresponds to each alternative rate of inflation. Clearly, the higher the inflation rate, the higher the price level at the end of the year and the lower the real wage.

Lower real wages provide an incentive for the firm to increase output, as we have just noted. But lower real wages also impose losses of purchasing power

Table 17–1
MONEY AND REAL WAGES UNDER INFLATION

INFLATION RATE (percent)	PRICE LEVEL ONE YEAR FROM NOW	MONEY WAGE ONE YEAR FROM NOW (dollars per hour)	REAL WAGE ONE YEAR FROM NOW (dollars per hour)
0	100	10.00	10.00
2	102	10.00	9.80
4	104	10.00	9.62
6	106	10.00	9.43

NOTE: Each real wage figure is obtained by dividing the $10 nominal wage by the corresponding price level a year later and multiplying by 100. Thus, for example, when the inflation rate is 4 percent, the real wage at the end of the year is ($10/104) × 100 = $9.62.

on workers. Thus, there is a sense in which workers are being "cheated" by inflation if they sign a contract specifying a fixed money wage in an inflationary environment.

Many economists doubt that workers would sign such a contract if they can see inflation coming. Would it not be more reasonable, these economists ask, to insist on being compensated for inflation in advance? After all, firms should be willing to offer higher money wages when they expect inflation because they realize that higher money wages need not imply higher *real* wages.

Table 17–2 illustrates how the money wage specified in a contract can be adjusted for expected inflation. For example, if 4 percent inflation is expected, the contract could stipulate that the wage rate be increased to $10.40 (which is 4 percent more than $10) at the end of the year. That would keep the real wage at $10, the same as it would be under zero inflation. The remaining money wage figures in Table 17–2 are derived similarly.

If workers and firms actually adjust money wages in the way suggested in Table 17–2, then the expected real wage will not decline as the expected price level rises. In the example, the expected future real wage is always $10 per hour. Prices and wages will go up together if expectations prove correct, leaving the real wage unchanged. Workers will not lose from inflation, and firms will not gain. But, of course, that means that there will be no reason for firms to produce more as prices rise. In a word, the aggregate supply curve would become *vertical*. In general:

If workers can see inflation coming, and if they receive compensation for it in advance so that inflation does not erode *real* wages, then the economy's aggregate supply curve will not slope upward. It will be a vertical line at the level of output corresponding to potential GNP.

Such a curve is shown in part (a) of Figure 17–16. Since we derived the Phillips curve from the aggregate supply curve earlier in the chapter, it follows that even the *short-run* Phillips curve will become vertical under these circumstances [see part (b) of Figure 17–16].[3]

If this analysis is correct, it has profound implications for the costs and benefits of inflation fighting. This can be seen by referring back to Figure 17–13 on page 355, where we depicted the strategy of fighting inflation by causing a recession. We concluded there that in order to move from point *e* (representing 10 percent inflation) to point *c* (representing 5 percent inflation), the economy would have to take a long and unpleasant detour through point *a*; that is,

[3]See Discussion Question 10 at the end of the chapter.

Table 17–2
MONEY AND REAL WAGES UNDER EXPECTED INFLATION

EXPECTED INFLATION RATE (percent)	EXPECTED PRICE LEVEL ONE YEAR FROM NOW	MONEY WAGE ONE YEAR FROM NOW (dollars per hour)	EXPECTED REAL WAGE ONE YEAR FROM NOW (dollars per hour)
0	100	10.00	10.00
4	104	10.40	10.00
8	108	10.80	10.00
12	112	11.20	10.00

Figure 17–16

A VERTICAL AGGREGATE SUPPLY CURVE AND THE CORRESPONDING VERTICAL PHILLIPS CURVE

If workers foresee inflation, and if they also receive full compensation for it in advance, then inflation will no longer erode real wages. In that case, firms will have no incentive to raise production as prices rise, and the aggregate supply curve will be vertical as in part (a). Since we derived the short-run Phillips curve from the aggregate supply curve, the short-run Phillips curve will also become vertical [part (b)].

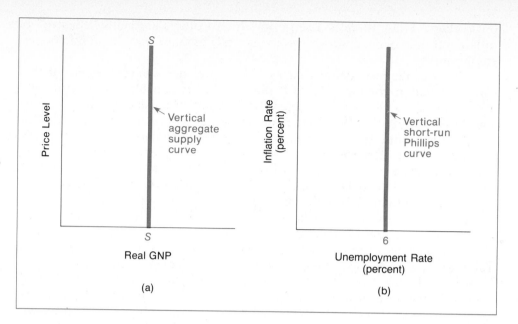

(a)

(b)

it would have to endure a recession. If, however, even the *short-run* Phillips curve were *vertical* rather than downward sloping, this detour would not be necessary. It would be possible for inflation to fall without unemployment rising. The economy could jump directly from point *e* to point *c*.

Is this analysis correct? Can we really slay the inflationary dragon so painlessly? As a piece of pure logic, the argument is impeccable. Yet things do not seem to work out this way. In practice, inflation fighting looks to be very costly. We must therefore ask ourselves whether the premises on which the analysis rests are realistic. There are several reasons why many economists think the expectations argument should not be applied uncritically to the modern economy.

Point 1. The argument is predicated on the notion that inflation can be accurately foreseen. But many contracts for labor and other raw materials cover such long periods of time that the expectations that were held when the contracts were written may be very different from current reality. If a restrictive policy reduces inflation below the rate firms and workers expected when they made their wage agreements, real wages wind up *higher* than intended, and hence firms want to reduce employment and produce less.

Point 2. Many people believe that inflationary expectations are sluggish, that they do not adapt quickly to changes in the economic environment. If, for example, the government embarks on an anti-inflation policy, workers will continue to expect high inflation for quite a while. Thus they will continue to insist on high rates of increase in money wages. Then, if inflation actually slows down, real wages will wind up rising faster than anyone expected. Firms will therefore find labor "too expensive" relative to current selling prices, and unemployment will result. With lags in the reaction of expectations, then, the short-run Phillips curve retains its downward slope, and inflation fighting is costly.

The Theory of Rational Expectations

These two points, and others we have not mentioned, have persuaded most economists that the expectations argument, while valid in part, should not be taken to extremes. Most economists nowadays accept the notion that the Phillips curve is downward sloping in the short run, and hence that a short-run trade-off does exist.

But a vocal minority of economists disagrees. This group, believers in the doctrine of **rational expectations,** insists that the only type of inflation that leads to *increases* in output is *unexpected* inflation, because only unexpected inflation reduces real wages. (To see this, compare Tables 17–1 and 17–2.) Similarly, they argue, the only type of reduction in inflation that leads to recession is an *unexpected* reduction.

To explain this point of view, we must first explain what *rational expectations* are. Once we do this, we will be in a position to understand why rational expectations have such radical implications for the Phillips curve.

What Are *Rational* Expectations?

In many economic contexts, people must formulate expectations about what the future will bring. For example, those who invest in the stock market need to forecast the future prices of the stocks they buy and sell. And we have just discussed why workers and businesses may want to forecast future prices before they agree on a money wage. *Rational expectations* is a controversial hypothesis about how such forecasts are made.

As used by economists, a forecast (an "expectation") of a future variable is considered rational if the forecaster makes *optimal* use of all information that is both *available* and *relevant*. Let us elaborate on the italicized words in this definition, using as an example a hypothetical stock market investor who has rational expectations.

First, believers in the doctrine of rational expectations recognize that *information is limited*. An investor who is interested in buying General Motors stock would like to know how much profit the company will make in the coming years. Armed with such information, she could predict the future price of GM stock more accurately. But that information is simply not available. Her forecast of the future price of GM stock is not "irrational" just because she does not know GM's future profits. On the other hand, if GM stock normally goes down on Fridays and up on Mondays, she should be aware of this fact.

Second, *not all information is important*. Some publicly available facts may be irrelevant to predicting the variables of interest. If so, a rational forecaster can afford to be ignorant of them. For example, anyone who cares to can find out how many babies were born last year in Peoria, Illinois. But this fact may not tell you much about the future performance of General Motors. So our investor need not have this information to be rational. However, if there is a clear Friday/Monday pattern in GM stock prices, she had better know what day of the week it is!

Finally, we have the word *optimal*. As used by economists, this means using proper statistical inference to process all the relevant information that is available before making a forecast. In a word, to have rational expectations, your forecasts do not have to be correct, but they cannot have systematic errors that could be avoided by applying better statistical methods. This requirement, while exacting, is not quite as outlandish as it may seem. A good billiards player makes expert use of the laws of physics, even though he may have no

> **Rational expectations** are forecasts which, while not necessarily correct, are the best that can be made given the available data. Rational expectations, therefore, cannot err systematically. If expectations are rational, forecasting errors are pure random numbers.

understanding of the theory. Similarly, an experienced stock market investor may make good use of information even without formal training in statistics.

Rational Expectations and the Trade-Off

Let us now see how the doctrine of rational expectations has been applied to deny that there exists any trade-off between inflation and unemployment—even in the short run.

Though they recognize that inflation cannot always be predicted accurately, rational expectationists claim that workers will not make *systematic* errors in forecasting inflation. Note that Point 2 above suggests that inflationary expectations are typically *too low* when inflation is rising and *too high* when inflation is falling. Rational expectationists deny that this is possible. Workers, they argue, will always make the best possible forecast of inflation, using all the latest data and the best available economic models. Such forecasts will not err systematically in one direction or the other regardless of whether inflation is rising or falling. Consequently:

If expectations are rational, the difference between the *actual* rate of inflation and the *expected* rate of inflation (the forecasting error) will be a pure random number.

Now recall the basic expectationist argument summarized in the previous section: Employment is affected by inflation only to the extent that inflation *differs* from what was expected. But, under rational expectations, no *predictable* change in inflation can make the *expected* rate of inflation deviate from the *actual* rate of inflation. Hence, according to the rational expectationists, unemployment will always remain at the natural rate—except for random, and therefore totally unpredictable, gyrations due to forecasting errors.

The implications of rational expectations for the conduct of economic policy are revolutionary. For one thing:

If expectations are rational, the inflation rate can be reduced without the need for a period of high unemployment because the short-run Phillips curve is vertical.

According to the rational expectations view, the government's ability to manipulate aggregate demand gives it no ability to control real output and unemployment because the aggregate supply curve is vertical—even in the short run. [To see why, experiment by moving an aggregate demand curve when the aggregate supply curve is vertical, as in Figure 17–16(a).] Any *predictable* change in aggregate demand will lead to a change in the expected rate of inflation, and hence will leave real wages unaffected.

The government therefore can influence output only by making *unexpected* changes in aggregate demand. But this is not easy to do when expectations are rational because people understand what policymakers are up to. According to the rational expectationists, if the monetary and fiscal authorities typically react to high inflation by reducing aggregate demand, people will soon come to anticipate this reaction. And, as just mentioned, anticipated reductions in aggregate demand do not affect unemployment because they do not cause *unexpected* changes in inflation.

An Evaluation

Since rational expectationists believe that inflation can be reduced without losses of output, they tend to be hawks in the war against inflation. Though the doctrine has attracted many adherents, rational expectationists remain in the minority. There are several reasons for this.

For one, Point 1 above remains valid even if expectations are rational. When long-term contracts are made, people get locked into provisions which, while rational when they were made, may seem irrational from today's point of view. For example, consider a labor contract drawn up late in 1980 that specified money wages to be paid in 1981–1984. Given what people knew then, it may have been rational to expect the 1984 price level to be 30 percent higher than the 1981 price level. So the money wage may have been set to rise 33 percent over the three years. But, in fact, the price level rose only 15 percent. If the money wages specified in the contract were actually paid, the real wage wound up 15 percent higher than intended. But no one behaved irrationally.

Second, many observers of the labor market continue to believe that inflationary expectations are sluggish; that is, they are not *rational* expectations. Workers or managers may not be as well-informed as the rational expectations hypothesis assumes. Or they may not have a good understanding of how the economy works. Or they may not behave like the expert statisticians that the rational expectations hypothesis envisions.

Finally, the facts have not been kind to the rational expectations point of view. The theory suggests that unemployment should hover around the natural rate most of the time, with random gyrations in one direction or the other. Yet this does not seem to be the case. The theory also denies that predictable monetary and fiscal policy actions will have effects on real output. Yet most observers think they can identify episodes in the past where such actions had significant effects on real GNP and unemployment. And many direct tests of the rationality of expectations have cast doubt on the hypothesis. For example, survey data on peoples' expectations rarely meet the exacting requirements of rationality.

At this writing, there is a great deal of controversy over how best to apply the idea of rational expectations to macroeconomic issues. The issues are far from resolved. But the evidence to date leads most economists to reject the extreme rational expectationist position for short-run analysis. In the long run, however, the rational expectations view should be more or less correct since people will not hold systematically wrong expectations indefinitely. As Abraham Lincoln said, you cannot fool all of the people all of the time.

Fighting Recessions with Fiscal and Monetary Policy

At this point it may be useful to pause and take stock of what we have learned. A good way to test your understanding is to run the analysis in reverse. We have been considering the use of monetary and fiscal policies to combat *inflation*. Let us now suppose instead that the crucial macroeconomic problem is *unemployment*.

We again turn to the Phillips curve diagram, Figure 17–13 on page 355, for a concrete example. Suppose that the economy somehow finds itself at a point like *a*, in a recession. And suppose that the president and Congress want to get the economy back to full employment. What should they do?

We know from our previous analysis what will happen if the current rate of growth of aggregate demand is simply maintained. Since point *a* on the short-run Phillips curve represents a recessionary gap, the economy's self-correcting mechanism begins to work. High unemployment slows the rate of increase of money wages, which tends to push the aggregate supply curve outward — compared with where it would have been if full employment were maintained.

The slowdown in wages both puts a brake on inflation and stimulates employment. The economy slowly travels down the path indicated by the blue arrow in Figure 17–13, from point *a* to point *c*. But, as we have noted before, the road from *a* to *c* may be slow and bumpy.

Is there a better way out of our economic problems? Perhaps. As we know, expansionary measures such as tax cuts, increases in government spending, or open market purchases of government securities can speed up the rate at which the aggregate demand curve moves to the right. (Compare Figures 17–4 and 17–5 on page 348.) Such a policy would enable the economy to "ride up" the short-run Phillips curve toward point *e*.

Figure 17–17
THE PAYOFF TO ANTIRECESSION POLICY
By stimulating aggregate demand through monetary and fiscal policy, the government can reduce unemployment more rapidly. If it relies exclusively on the economy's ability to right itself, unemployment will follow the black "status quo policy" path. If, instead, the government takes an active hand in fighting the recession, unemployment will follow the blue "expansionary policy" path. The shaded area measures the reduction in unemployment that the expansionary policy achieves.

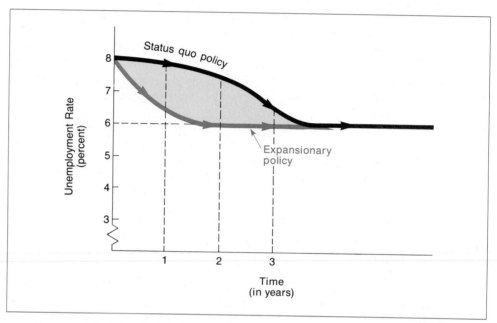

Figures 17–17 and 17–18 will help us compare this active antirecession policy with the more passive "status quo policy." Under the status quo policy of

Figure 17–18
THE COST OF ANTIRECESSION POLICY
The unemployment gains depicted in the previous figure are not obtained without cost. By stimulating the economy, the government policies cause a rise in the inflation rate—as shown by the blue "expansionary policy" path. If, instead, the government had simply waited for the economy's natural self-correcting mechanism to work, inflation would have fallen—see the black "status quo policy" path. The difference between these two paths (the shaded area) represents the inflationary cost of fighting the recession.

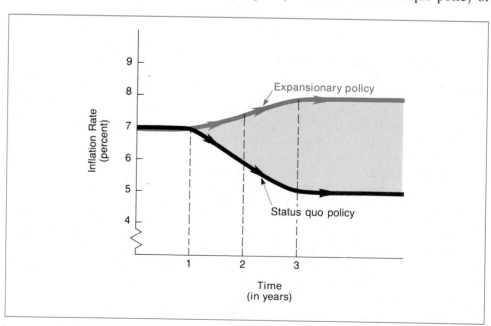

relying on the economy's self-correcting mechanism, the unemployment rate gradually falls from the 8 percent that corresponds to point a on the Phillips curve to the 6 percent that corresponds to point c. But progress is agonizingly slow. The "status quo policy" path shown in black in Figure 17–17 indicates that it takes more than three uncomfortable years to return to full employment.

By contrast, if expansionary monetary and fiscal policy actions are taken, the return to full employment is much quicker. According to the blue "expansionary policy" path in Figure 17–17, we get there in about one and one-half years. The shaded area in the figure measures the payoff to antirecession policy; it shows how much unemployment we save during the three-year period.

But, as we have by now come to expect, these gains are made at some cost. The black "status quo policy" path in Figure 17–18 shows the likely behavior of the inflation rate under the policy of waiting for the economy's self-corrective forces to work. Inflation falls gradually from the 7 percent rate that corresponds to point a on the Phillips curve to the 5 percent rate that corresponds to point c. But if expansionary policy is pursued, inflation will not creep downward; instead it will creep upward, as indicated by the blue "expansionary policy" path in Figure 17–18. The shaded area in this figure shows the cost of fighting recession with monetary and fiscal policy: We wind up with more inflation.

In considering whether or not to fight a recession, policymakers face a tradeoff between unemployment and inflation. If they take expansionary actions to reduce unemployment, they may end up with a higher inflation rate.

Are the inflationary costs depicted in Figure 17–18 worth the benefits of lower unemployment shown in Figure 17–17? This is not a question that can be answered with any assurance. The answer hinges on the same three issues we isolated in discussing anti-inflation policy:

1. **The social costs of inflation and unemployment.** Those who regard inflation as extremely costly will not want to pay the price of shortening the recession. Those who are more concerned with unemployment will find recession fighting a good idea.

2. **The position of the economy.** As we have noted, the Phillips curve is likely to be flatter at higher rates of unemployment. As you can see by studying Figure 17–13, if the Phillips curve is rather flat, the extra inflation caused by fighting a recession will be minimal. On the other hand, if the short-run Phillips curve is steep, the inflationary price tag will be high. Thus the case for fighting deep recessions is stronger than the case for fighting shallow ones.

3. **The efficiency of the economy's self-correcting mechanism,** which works as unemployment slows the rate of growth of wages. Naturally, if the economy's self-corrective forces work rapidly, there is little reason for the government to try to speed things up. On the other hand, if the mechanism is slow and unreliable or, worse yet, if it breaks down entirely, the case for government intervention is much stronger.

Why Economists (and Politicians) Disagree

These three factors help explain why economists sometimes differ so radically from one another in their recommendations as to the proper conduct of national economic policy. And they also help account for disagreements among politicians.

The question is: When a recession occurs, should the government take actions to bring it to a rapid end? You will say *yes* if you believe that (1) unemployment is more costly than inflation, (2) the short-run Phillips curve is rather flat, and (3) the economy's self-correcting mechanism is slow and unreliable. These views on the economy tend to be associated with economists of the Keynesian school, and with the (generally liberal) politicians who listen to them.

But you will say *no* if you believe that (1) inflation is more costly than unemployment, (2) the short-run Phillips curve is steep, and (3) the self-correcting mechanism works smoothly and quickly. These views are held by most monetarists and rational expectationists, so it is not surprising that the (generally conservative) politicians who follow their advice typically oppose strong measures to fight recessions.

The tables turn, however, when the question is whether or not to use policy to fight inflation. The Keynesian view of the world—that unemployment is costly, that the short-run Phillips curve is flat, and that the self-correcting mechanism is unreliable—leads to the conclusion that the costs of fighting inflation are high while the benefits are low. The monetarist and rational expectationist positions on these three issues are just the reverse, and so are the policy conclusions.

The Dilemma of Demand Management

So we have seen that the makers of monetary and fiscal policy face an agonizing trade-off. If they stimulate aggregate demand to reduce unemployment, they will aggravate inflation. If they restrict aggregate demand to fight inflation, they will cause higher unemployment.

But wait. Early in the chapter we learned that when inflation comes from the supply side, inflation and unemployment are *positively* associated: We suffer from more of both or enjoy less of each. Does this mean that monetary and fiscal policymakers can escape the trade-off between inflation and unemployment? Certainly not.

Adverse shifts in the aggregate supply curve can cause both inflation and unemployment to rise together, and thus can destroy the Phillips curve relationship. Nevertheless, anything that monetary and fiscal policy can do will make unemployment and inflation move in opposite directions because monetary and fiscal policy give the government control only over the *aggregate demand* curve, not over the *aggregate supply* curve.

Thus, no matter what the source of inflation, and no matter what happens to the Phillips curve, the makers of monetary and fiscal policy must still face up to the disagreeable trade-off between inflation and unemployment. This is a principle that many policymakers have failed to recognize, and one of the **12 Ideas** that we hope you will remember well **Beyond the Final Exam.**

Naturally, the unpleasant nature of this trade-off has led to a vigorous search for a way out of the dilemma. Both economists and public officials have sought a policy that might offer improvements on both fronts simultaneously, or that might ease the pain of either unemployment or inflation. The rest of this chapter considers some of these ideas.

Attempts to Improve the Trade-Off Directly

One class of policies aims to reduce the natural rate of unemployment. For example, vocational training and retraining programs, if successful, help unemployed workers with obsolete skills acquire abilities that are currently in demand. In doing so, they help alleviate upward pressures on wage rates in jobs where qualified workers are in short supply. For example, if an unemployed steelworker is taught to assemble computers, then progress is made against both inflation and unemployment, since one former steelworker leaves the ranks of the unemployed while one new worker helps alleviate the shortage of skilled labor in the computer industry. A similar role is played by the United States Employment Service and similar agencies at the state and local levels—which try to improve the match of workers to jobs by funneling information from prospective employers to prospective employees.

Although the idea sounds appealing and has attracted many adherents, successes achieved through training and placement programs have, in practice, been limited. Too often, people are trained for jobs that do not exist by the time they finish their training—if indeed they ever existed. Even when successful, these programs are expensive, which restricts the number of workers that can be accommodated.

Over the last decade, many government regulations over prices and provision of service have been reduced or made more flexible in such industries as airlines, trucking, railroads, telecommunications, and energy. Presidents Ford, Carter, and Reagan have all vigorously promoted deregulation, and each has cited the anti-inflationary impact as one of his reasons.[4] In addition, the Reagan administration halted the rise of the minimum wage and generally sought to reduce the amount of red tape imposed on businesses.

Prices have generally fallen in the deregulated industries. But most economists, while applauding deregulation on microeconomic grounds, doubt that it has had a large impact on the economy-wide inflation rate. The Reagan administration also sparked acrimonious debate by extending the deregulation drive into the areas of environmental protection and occupational health and safety.

Incomes Policy

Yet another way to improve the trade-off, one that has been tried intermittently in the United States, is incomes policy. As practiced in this country, incomes policy has run the gamut from verbal admonitions all the way to President Nixon's outright prohibition of wage and price increases in 1971. And in some foreign countries that rely upon incomes policy far more heavily than we do, a still more bewildering variety of alternative measures has emerged. Indeed, there may be only one common thread linking these disparate policies: No hard evidence exists that any of them has succeeded *permanently* in improving the trade-off between unemployment and inflation. Note that the emphasis here is on the word "permanently," for many attempts at incomes policy—including some in this country—have had temporary success.

Incomes policy is a generic term used to describe a wide variety of measures aimed at curbing inflation *without* reducing aggregate demand.

Jawboning

The mildest form of incomes policy is commonly referred to as **jawboning.** The term is meant to conjure up in your mind an image of the president of the

Jawboning refers to informal pressures on firms and unions to slow down the rates at which prices and wages are rising.

[4]For a full discussion of regulation and deregulation, see Chapter 31.

United States calling some corporate executive on the carpet for announcing a price increase deemed to be contrary to the national interest. Since corporate executives are likely to feel surrounded, perhaps even threatened, under these circumstances, jawboning has occasionally induced businesses to rescind previously-announced price increases.

Perhaps the most spectacular success was President Kennedy's confrontation with the steel industry in 1962. But President Johnson jawboned more than anyone else, and it was President Nixon who first established an official agency to monitor price increases and "blow the whistle" on those that were unwarranted. Since then, jawboning has become a partisan affair. President Ford rejected "open mouth policy," President Carter reinstated it, and President Reagan rejected it once again.

The main argument in favor of jawboning is that it is a relatively painless way to try to improve the trade-off between inflation and unemployment. Large corporations, it is argued, have the market power to raise prices even when price rises are not justified by cost increases. But, since these corporate giants are also public-relations conscious, proponents of jawboning argue, why not use the prestige of the federal government to dissuade them from exercising their market power?

Opponents of jawboning respond that market power can only explain *high* prices, not *rising* prices. Why, they ask, would a firm with market power wait until this month to raise prices when it could have done so last month? They answer that large corporations raise prices only when changes in demand or cost considerations make it profitable to do so, not because they have a residue of unused market power.

On balance, a fair assessment of jawboning would probably conclude that it does little good and little harm.

Wage–Price Guideposts

Wage–price guideposts are numerical standards for permissible wage and price increases.

The next step up from jawboning is the establishment of an official standard for "permissible" rates of increase in wages and prices. These so-called **wage–price guideposts** were initiated by the Kennedy administration in early 1962 but used most notably by the Johnson administration. Lacking an enforcement mechanism, they collapsed amid the inflationary pressures of 1967. Late in 1978, guideposts were resurrected by President Carter, who was by then convinced that jawboning was not enough. But inflation accelerated in 1979 and 1980 anyway, and President Reagan abandoned the guideposts immediately upon assuming office.

The logic behind guideposts is both simple and compelling. In an ideally functioning economy, if worker productivity rises by 2 percent a year, then wages can rise by 2 percent a year with no increase in costs or prices. Alternatively, wages can increase at a 4 percent annual rate while prices rise at 2 percent a year, and so on. In general, price inflation proceeds at a rate roughly 2 percentage points below wage inflation. A set of wage–price guideposts is obtained by picking a target rate of inflation, say 3 percent a year, and adding 2 percent to get a consistent target for wage increases—5 percent in this example. The government then announces that (a) wage increases that exceed this standard will be deemed "inflationary," (b) firms enjoying productivity increases faster than the national average are expected to raise their prices more slowly than 3 percent a year while, (c) firms obtaining sub-par productivity improvements are allowed to have higher-than-average price increases so that, (d) the overall price level can increase at a rate of 3 percent a year.

Such guideposts are logically sound. The problem comes in deciding what to do if some union or corporation violates them. Experience shows that voluntarism goes only so far when economic self-interest is threatened. If the government responds by jawboning—as frequently happened in the 1960s—we are back to the first type of incomes policy. Alternatively, we can give the guideposts the force of law, which brings us to the next variety of incomes policy.

Wage–Price Controls

Once the government is given the legal authority to *force* labor and industry to adhere to a set of guideposts, we have moved to a system of mandatory **wage–price controls.** While the United States used such a policy with great success during World War II and again during the Korean War, the Nixon administration's efforts to apply wage–price controls in peacetime is generally considered to have failed. This experience has soured many people on the idea of ever using them again.

Wage–price controls are legal restrictions on the ability of industry and labor to raise wages and prices.

Before considering some pros and cons of controls, let us be clear about what economists mean when they say that the 1971–1974 price controls "failed." They surely do *not* mean that inflation was not reduced by controls; most studies of the period have found that in fact it *was* reduced. Instead, they mean that the *lower* inflation rates that prevailed while controls were in effect were counterbalanced by *higher* inflation rates during the year or so after controls were lifted. Thus, instead of improving the tradeoff, the controls managed to increase the *variability* of inflation—making it lower in 1972–1973 and higher in 1974 than it would otherwise have been. In Chapter 6 we pointed out that the *variability* of inflation often exacts more serious social costs than the *average level*. In this sense, then, the controls program was counterproductive.

A major justification for controls, to which spokesmen for the Nixon administration appealed, is that inflation gathers a substantial momentum once workers, consumers, and business managers begin to expect that it will continue. **Inflationary expectations** encourage workers to demand higher wage increases. Firms, in turn, are willing to grant the workers' demands because they believe they will be able to pass the cost increases on to consumers in a general inflationary evironment. Thus, to a great extent, *inflation occurs because people expect it to occur*. Phrased in terms of our Phillips curve analysis, *inflationary expectations shift the Phillips curve upward*, so that any given rate of unemployment corresponds to a higher rate of inflation.

This analysis provides the best intellectual case for controls. A tough and thorough program of wage and price controls, it is argued, can break the vicious cycle of inflationary expectations. By announcing controls, the government serves notice on workers that they do not need anticipatory wage increases to preserve their purchasing power. And firms are warned that they may not be able to pass on higher costs to consumers. By breaking inflationary expectations, supporters argue, a controls program can shift the Phillips curve down and reduce the rate of inflation.

Under the right conditions, this argument may be correct. Several economists, for example, believe that controls helped both Argentina and Israel reduce galloping inflations in the 1980s. However, what if astute workers and business executives realize that no controls program can remain in force forever—at least not in a free-market economy like ours? They may then view the temporary dip in the inflation rate caused by controls as an aberration soon to be corrected, and therefore not as a major event that warrants changing their long-term expectations.

Why cannot wage–price controls be a permanent feature of the U.S. economy? We learned the answer to this back in Chapter 4. When price ceilings are effective, they force the price below the equilibrium price, so that quantity demanded exceeds quantity supplied. This is shown in Figure 17–19, where the equilibrium price of hamburgers is assumed to be $1. If controls do not allow the price of hamburgers to rise above 75 cents, quantity demanded will exceed quantity supplied by one million hamburgers.

With price no longer serving as the rationing device, some other method of rationing is necessary. One possibility is long lines of eager eaters waiting their turn for burgers. Scenes like this are typical in the Soviet Union, and they were witnessed in this country at gas stations during 1979, when gasoline was in short supply. Another is government ration coupons, giving the owner the right to buy a hamburger—a device used successfully for many goods during World War II. Neither of these measures is likely to be popular with the electorate in peacetime. And both are likely to spawn a black market, which erodes respect for law and order at the same time that it abrogates the effects of controls. As critics are fond of pointing out, controls give perfectly law-abiding citizens an incentive to break the law in an effort to circumvent the controls.

And the problems spawned by price controls go deeper than this. Among the principal factors determining the equilibrium price of hamburgers are the prices of raw agricultural commodities like beef. But prices of raw agricultural commodities cannot be controlled by the government because they depend on the weather and other acts of nature. If price controls hold the price of hamburgers at 75 cents while the price of beef skyrockets, it may become unprofitable to sell hamburgers. If so, firms will start leaving the hamburger industry.

With hamburgers unavailable, consumers will shift to other goods, thereby putting upward pressure on the prices of goods such as fish and soybeans. Thus, price controls on hamburgers will cause the hamburger industry to contract and necessitate additional price controls on fish and soybeans. And so it goes. Each extension of price controls to a new commodity requires additional controls to support it, in a never-ending chain. Thus, for price controls to be effective, they must be nearly universal—which is, of course, next to impossible except in times of acute national crisis.

Figure 17–19
THE EFFECTS OF PRICE CONTROLS
This diagram portrays the market for hamburgers under an effective price control system. Since the equilibrium price is $1 per hamburger, a regulation that holds the price at 75 cents makes the quantity of hamburgers demanded (2,500,000 per year) exceed the quantity supplied (1,500,000 per year). There is a shortage of one million hamburgers per year, and some sort of rationing scheme probably is necessary.

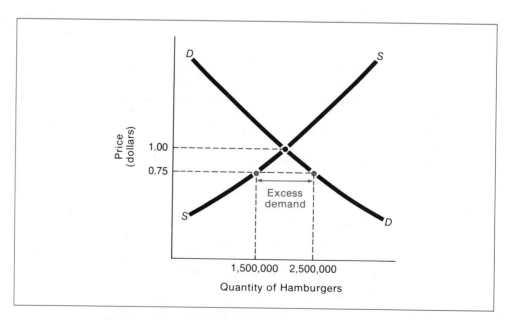

Wage–Price Freezes

An extreme case of mandatory controls is a **wage–price freeze**—a statute making it illegal to increase wages or prices above their levels on some specified date. President Nixon ushered in his controls program with a three-month freeze beginning in mid-August 1971. Such an action cannot last long, for it ossifies the market mechanism. It is meant to be a shock treatment—a dramatic action intended to break inflationary expectations. A wage–price freeze is generally a prelude to some milder form of incomes policy.

A **wage–price freeze** is an outright ban on wage or price increases.

Tax-Based Incomes Policy

A different approach to incomes policy—called **tax-based incomes policy** or TIP—seeks to use the tax system to fight inflation. The idea behind TIP is simple, though its practical implementation might be complex. TIP would give employers and employees a financial stake in fighting inflation by lowering taxes for firms or workers who abide by national guideposts for wage–price behavior, or by raising taxes for those who violate them.

Tax-based incomes policy uses the tax system to provide incentives favoring noninflationary behavior.

While there are many TIP plans, one particular example will bring out the flavor of them all. Suppose the government wants to limit wage increases to 5 percent a year. It could pass legislation granting a 2 percent payroll tax rebate to employees in firms in which average wages increase by no more than 5 percent. Then, for example, workers who settled for a $4\frac{1}{2}$ percent raise would actually wind up with *more* after-tax income than those who settled for a 6 percent raise. They would get $4\frac{1}{2}$ percent more from their employers, plus 2 percent more from the government in the form of lower taxes, for a total gain of $6\frac{1}{2}$ percent. This incentive, it is hoped, would lead labor and management to settle for slower growth in wages; and these slower wage increases, in turn, would lead to slower price increases.

Other TIP plans focus on corporation taxes rather than on payroll taxes, or utilize the "stick" rather than the "carrot" by penalizing violators of the wage–price guideposts rather than rewarding those who obey. But the basic goal is always the same: to make noninflationary behavior profitable for either firms or workers, or both.

Is TIP workable? Since it has never been tried, we have no idea how serious the many practical problems of implementation would be. For example, how would the government deal with a firm that simply promoted many workers into higher-paying job classifications rather than raising its wage scale?

The Share Economy

Recently, a new and imaginative approach to improving the trade-off has attracted the attention of politicians both here and abroad. Professor Martin Weitzman of M.I.T. has suggested that the introduction of **profit sharing,** a system in which workers are paid a base wage plus a share of company profits, would make the economy more resistant to unemployment.[5] His reasoning is as follows. If part of workers' pay comes from profit sharing rather than in straight wages, then labor costs automatically fall whenever business turns sour. With labor therefore "cheaper," firms will have less reason to lay workers off. In consequence, what Weitzman calls *a share economy* should normally have lower unemployment than an otherwise identical economy without profit sharing.

Profit sharing is a system of compensating labor in which workers receive both a fixed base wage and a share of the company's profits.

[5]Martin Weitzman, *The Share Economy* (Harvard University Press: 1984).

And because it would produce more goods, it should also normally have lower prices.

Weitzman's theoretical arguments are ingenious. And he bolsters his case by pointing to the low unemployment and low inflation of Japan—which has had extensive profit sharing for years. But organized labor has been cool to the idea of letting their earnings fluctuate with company profits. Furthermore, since we have no experience with widespread profit sharing, we can only guess at the practical problems that would arise in a share economy. Nonetheless, the potential benefits are large enough to justify the intensive scrutiny that profit sharing is now receiving.

Indexing

Indexing refers to provisions in a law or a contract whereby monetary payments are automatically adjusted whenever a specified price index changes. Wage rates, pensions, interest payments on bonds, income taxes, and many other things can be indexed in this way, and have been. Sometimes such contractual provisions are called *escalator clauses*.

Indexing—which refers to provisions in a law or contract whereby monetary payments are automatically adjusted whenever a specific price index changes—presents a very different approach to the inflation–unemployment dilemma. Whereas the other proposals discussed in this chapter are all designed *to lower the inflation rate*, the primary purpose of indexing is *to reduce the social costs of inflation*.

The mechanics of indexing are best explained by an example, and the most familiar example in the United States is an *escalator clause* in a wage agreement. An escalator clause provides for an automatic increase in money wages—without the need for new contract negotiations—any time the price level rises by more than a specified amount. Suppose that with the Consumer Price Index (CPI) sitting at 340, a union and a firm agree on a three-year contract setting wages at $8 per hour this year, $9 next year, and $10 in the third year. They might then add an escalator clause stating that wages will be increased above these stipulated amounts by 5 cents per hour for each point by which the CPI exceeds 370 in any future year of the contract. Then, if the CPI reaches 380 in the third year of the contract, workers will receive an additional 50 cents per hour (5 cents for each of the 10 points by which 380 exceeds 370), for a total wage of $10.50 per hour. In this way, workers are partly protected from inflation. Nowadays, less than half of all workers employed by large unionized firms in the United States are covered by some sort of escalator clause. And very few nonunion workers or employees of small firms enjoy such protection.

Interest payments on bonds or savings accounts can also be indexed, although this is not currently done in the United States.[6] The most extensive indexing to be found in the United States today is in government transfer payments. Social security benefits, for instance, are fully indexed so that retirees are not victimized by inflation. A variety of government income maintenance and social insurance programs also pay benefits that are tied directly to prices.

Indexing and the Social Costs of Inflation

Some economists believe that the United States should follow the example of several foreign countries and adopt a much more widespread system of indexing. Why? Because, they argue, it would take most of the sting out of inflation. To see how indexing would accomplish this, let us review some of the social costs of inflation that we enumerated in Chapter 6.

One important cost is the capricious redistribution of income caused by unexpected inflation. We saw that borrowers and lenders normally incorporate

---

[6]Some other countries, with much higher inflation than ours, do extensive indexing of interest rates. Brazil and Israel are notable examples.

an *inflation premium* equal to the *expected rate of inflation* into the nominal interest rate. Then, if inflation turns out to be higher than expected, the borrower has to pay to the lender only the agreed-upon nominal interest rate, including the premium for *expected* inflation; he does not have to compensate the lender for the (higher) *actual* inflation. Thus the borrower enjoys a windfall gain and the lender loses out. The opposite happens if inflation turns out to be lower than was expected. But if interest rates on loans were indexed, none of this would occur. Borrowers and lenders would agree on a fixed *real* rate of interest, and then the borrower would compensate the lender for whatever *actual inflation* occurred. No one would have to guess what the inflation rate would be.[7]

A second social cost we mentioned in Chapter 6 stems from the fact that our tax system levies taxes on nominal interest and nominal capital gains. As we learned, this flaw in the tax system leads to extremely high effective tax rates in an inflationary environment. But indexing could fix this problem easily. We need only rewrite the tax code so that only *real* interest payments and *real* capital gains are taxed.

A final problem noted in Chapter 6 is that uncertainty over future price levels makes it difficult to enter into long-term contracts—rental agreements, construction agreements, and so on. One way out of this problem is to write indexed contracts, which specify all future payments in real terms.

In the face of all these benefits, and others we have not mentioned here, why do many economists oppose indexing? Probably the major reason is the fear that indexing will lead to an acceleration of inflation. With the costs of inflation reduced so markedly, they argue, what will persuade governments to pay the price of fighting inflation? What will stop them from inflating more and more? They fear that the answer to these questions is, Nothing. Voters who stand to lose nothing from inflation are unlikely to pressure their legislators into stopping it. Opponents of indexing worry that a mild inflationary disease could turn into a ravaging epidemic in a highly indexed economy.

[7]For example, an indexed loan with a 2 percent real interest rate would require a 5 percent nominal interest payment if inflation were 3 percent, a 7 percent nominal interest payment if inflation were 5 percent, and so on.

Summary

1. Inflation can be caused either by rapid growth of aggregate demand or by sluggish growth of aggregate supply.

2. When fluctuations in economic activity emanate from the demand side, prices will rise rapidly when real output grows rapidly. Since rapid growth means more jobs, unemployment and inflation will be inversely related.

3. This inverse relationship between unemployment and inflation is called the Phillips curve. It explains U.S. data for the 1950s and 1960s rather well but fails miserably to account for the 1970s.

4. One reason for this failure is that the Phillips curve was misinterpreted as a menu of *long-run* policy choices for the economy. This view is incorrect because the economy's self-correcting mechanism guarantees that neither an inflationary gap nor a recessionary gap can last indefinitely.

5. Because of the self-correcting mechanism, the economy's true long-run choices lie along a *vertical* Phillips curve, which shows that the so-called *natural rate of unemployment* is the only unemployment rate that can persist indefinitely.

6. In the short-run, the economy can move up or down its short-run Phillips curve. *Temporary* reductions in unemployment can be achieved at the cost of higher inflation. Similarly, *temporary* increases in unemployment can be used to fight inflation.

7. Whether it is advisable to use unemployment to fight inflation depends on three principal factors: the relative social costs of inflation versus unemployment, the efficiency of the economy's self-correcting mechanism, and the current position of the economy.

8. If workers expect inflation to occur, and if they

demand (and receive) compensation for inflation, output will be independent of the price level. Both the aggregate supply curve and the short-run Phillips curve are vertical in this case.

9. However, errors in predicting inflation will still change real wages and hence will still change the quantity of output that firms wish to supply. Thus, *unpredicted* movements in the price level will lead to a normal, upward-sloping aggregate supply curve.

10. According to the doctrine of rational expectations, errors in predicting inflation are purely random. This means that, except for some random (and uncontrollable) gyrations, the aggregate supply curve is vertical even in the short run.

11. Many economists reject the rational expectations view of the world. Some deny that expectations are "rational" and believe instead that people tend, for example, to underpredict inflation when it is rising. Others point out that contracts signed years ago cannot possibly embody expectations that are "rational" in terms of what we know today.

12. When fluctuations in economic activity are caused by shifts of the aggregate supply curve, output will grow slowly (causing unemployment to rise) when inflation speeds up. Hence, the rates of unemployment and inflation will be positively related.

13. Many observers feel that the adverse supply shifts during the 1970s help explain why the Phillips curve collapsed.

14. Even if inflation is initiated by supply-side problems, so that inflation and unemployment occur together, the monetary and fiscal authorities still face this trade-off: Anything they do to improve unemployment is likely to worsen inflation, and anything they do to reduce inflation is likely to aggravate unemployment. The reason is that monetary and fiscal policy mainly influence the aggregate demand curve, not the aggregate supply curve. This is one of our **12 Ideas for Beyond the Final Exam.**

15. Policies that improve the functioning of the labor market — including retraining programs and employment services — can lower the natural rate of unemployment. To date, however, the U.S. government has had only modest success with these measures.

16. Some small amount of progress against inflation may also be made by eliminating government regulations that keep prices high. Indeed, some of this has already been done.

17. Many varieties of incomes policies have been used in this and other countries in an effort to improve the trade-off between inflation and unemployment. While some have led to notable temporary improvements, their lasting effects have been minimal.

18. The weakest varieties of incomes policies simply set up standards for permissible wage and price increases (wage–price guideposts) and apply verbal admonitions against violators (jawboning). Stronger variants may actually set legal limits on wage and price increases or even ban them outright (a wage–price freeze). But such policies seriously interfere with the workings of our market economy.

19. One argument in favor of short-term wage–price controls is that they can reduce inflationary expectations and thereby rob inflation of some of its momentum.

20. A new and different approach to incomes policy would use tax incentives to encourage more moderate wage and price increases. This so-called tax-based income policy has yet to be tried.

21. Some economists argue that we could improve both unemployment and inflation by including an important profit-sharing component in labor earnings.

22. Indexing is another way to approach the trade-off problem. Instead of trying to improve the trade-off, it concentrates on reducing the social costs of inflation — perhaps eliminating them, altogether. Opponents of indexing worry, however, that the economy's resistance to inflation may be lowered by indexing.

Concepts for Review

Demand-side inflation	Phillips curve	Jawboning
Vertical (long-run) Phillips curve	Stagflation caused by supply shocks	Tax-based incomes policy (TIP)
Rational expectations	Self-correcting mechanism	Wage–price guideposts
Supply-side inflation	Natural rate of unemployment	Profit sharing
Trade-off between unemployment and inflation in the short run and in the long run	Inflationary expectations	Indexing (escalator clauses)
	Incomes policy	Wage–price controls
	Wage–price freezes	Real versus nominal interest rates

Questions for Discussion

1. Some observers during the 1970s claimed that policymakers no longer face a trade-off between inflation and unemployment. Why did they think this? Were they correct?

2. "There is no sense in trying to shorten recessions through fiscal and monetary policy because the effects of these policies on the unemployment rate are sure to be temporary." Comment on both the truth of this statement and its relevance for policy formulation.

3. Why is the economy's self-correcting mechanism more efficient at eliminating inflationary gaps than it is at eliminating recessionary gaps?

4. Why is it said that decisions on fiscal and monetary policy are, at least in part, political decisions that cannot be made on "objective" economic criteria?

5. Does the economy have a recessionary gap or an inflationary gap today? What should be done about this? What facts would you want to know in preparing an answer to this question?

6. What is a "Phillips curve"? Why did it seem to work so much better in the 1954–1969 period than it did in the 1970s?

7. Explain the dilemma that policymakers face when there is an episode of supply inflation. What do you think should have been done in 1979? What would you recommend if there were a severe bout of supply inflation today?

8. Explain why expectations about inflation affect the wages that result from labor–management bargaining.

9. What is meant by "rational" expectations? Why does the doctrine of rational expectations have such stunning implications for economic policy? Would believers in rational expectations want to shorten a recession by expanding aggregate demand? Would they want to fight inflation by reducing aggregate demand?

10. Show that, if the economy's aggregate supply curve is vertical, fluctuations in the growth of aggregate demand produce only fluctuations in inflation with no effect on output. Relate this to your answer to the previous question.

11. Do you think it is proper for the president of the United States to "jawbone" some corporations into reducing their price increases?

12. Explain some of the differences between wage–price guideposts and wage–price controls.

13. Suppose that a program of wage–price controls is under consideration by the government. What are the possible benefits to the nation from such a program? What are the possible costs? How would you balance the benefits against the costs?

14. Explain the basic idea behind "TIP" (tax-based incomes policy). Try to devise a TIP plan of your own. Can you foresee some practical difficulties with your plan?

15. Ordinary savings accounts now pay approximately $5\frac{1}{2}$ percent *nominal* interest. Would you prefer to trade yours in for an indexed bank account that paid a zero *real* rate of interest? What if the real interest rate offered were 1 percent? What if it were −1 percent? What do your answers to these questions reveal about your personal attitudes toward inflation?

PART 5

The United States in the World Economy

18

No nation was ever ruined by trade.

BENJAMIN FRANKLIN

International Trade and Comparative Advantage

While the United States can satisfy its own requirements for such goods as coal and sugar, it is almost *entirely* dependent on the rest of the world for other products, such as rubber and coffee. For these and many other vital inputs the United States must depend on trade with other countries. Though imports and exports are not nearly as important for the United States as they are for smaller nations such as Great Britain, Israel, and the Netherlands, they nonetheless make substantial contributions to both employment and standards of living here. Furthermore, as we shall see in Chapter 20, our international trade has profound effects on the health of our national economy.

In this chapter, we examine the purposes of foreign trade and the ways in which governments seek to influence or limit it. First, we examine why countries engage in trade. Second, we learn why the populations of both exporting and importing countries generally benefit from trade even though they are, in effect, merely "swapping goods." Third, we study the crucial *law of comparative advantage*, which determines what commodities a country finds advantageous to export and what commodities it finds advantageous to import. Fourth, we see how the prices of internationally traded goods are determined by supply and demand. And, finally, we examine the pros and cons of quotas, tariffs, and other devices designed to protect a country's industries from foreign competition.

Issue: The Competition of "Cheap Foreign Labor"

When analyzing international trade, common sense can be extremely valuable; indeed, there is no substitute for it. Yet sometimes conclusions based on common sense without factual confirmation and careful analysis can be misleading.

One important example is the argument that buying products made by cheap foreign labor is unfair and destructive to domestic interests. Some U.S. business people and union leaders argue that imports take bread out of the mouths of American workers and depress standards of living in this country. According to this view, cheap foreign goods cause job losses and put pressure on

U.S. businesses to lower wages. Moreover, imports allegedly encourage the continued exploitation of foreign workers by sweatshop proprietors abroad by making clear to them that low prices and, consequently, low wages are the only basis on which they can compete.

Yet, the facts are not consistent with this scenario. For one thing, wages in industrial countries that export to the United States rose spectacularly during the 1970s and 1980s. Table 18–1 shows that wages in seven leading industrial countries rose from an average of only 46 percent of American wages in 1970 to 82 percent by 1986. In fact, by 1986 labor costs in West Germany exceeded our own, and Sweden and the Netherlands were not far behind. Since 1986, this trend has continued, for the dollar is worth less now than it was then.[1] The fact is that American imports of Volkswagens from Germany, Volvos from Sweden, and Mazdas from Japan grew despite the fact that wages rose in those countries relative to those in the United States.

Although foreign labor became more expensive relative to U.S. labor during the 1960s and 1970s, America's position in the international marketplace deteriorated. In the 1950s, when European and Japanese wages were far below those in the United States, we had no trouble marketing our products abroad. In fact, the main problem then was to bring our imports up to the level at which they roughly balanced our bountiful exports. Then, as wages in Europe and Japan began to rise closer to those in the United States, America encountered serious trouble in its ability to sell goods abroad.

Clearly, then, cheap foreign labor need not serve as a crucial obstacle to U.S. sales abroad—as a "common sense" view of the matter suggests. In this chapter we will see what is wrong with that view.

Why Trade?

The main reason that countries trade with one another rather than try to run completely independent economies is that the earth's resources are not equally distributed across its surface. The United States has an abundant supply of coal, an energy source that is scarce in most of the rest of the world. Saudi Arabia has little land that is suitable for farming, but it sits atop a huge pool of oil. Because of the seemingly whimsical distribution of vital resources, every nation must trade with others to acquire what it lacks. In general, the more varied the

[1]Changes in international currency values are considered in the next chapter.

Table 18–1
LABOR COSTS IN INDUSTRIALIZED COUNTRIES

	1970	1986
	(percentage of U.S. labor costs)	
France	41	80
Great Britain	35	57
Italy	42	78
Japan	24	73
Netherlands	51	92
Sweden	70	93
West Germany	56	103

Data are compensation estimates per hour and relate to production workers in the manufacturing sector.
SOURCE: U.S. Bureau of Labor Statistics.

endowment of a particular country, the less it will have to depend on others to make up for its deficiencies.

Even if countries had all the resources they need, other differences in natural endowments — such as climate, terrain, and so on — would lead them to engage in trade. Americans *could,* with great difficulty, grow their own banana trees and coffee shrubs in hothouses; but these items are much more efficiently grown in such places as Honduras and Brazil, where the climate is appropriate. On the other hand, wheat grows in the United States with little difficulty, while mountainous Switzerland is not a good place to grow either bananas or wheat.

The skills of a country's labor force also play a role. If Argentina has a large group of efficient farmers and few workers with industrial experience while the opposite is true in Great Britain, it makes sense for Argentina to specialize in agriculture and let Great Britain concentrate on manufacturing.

This last point suggests one other important reason why countries trade — the advantages of **specialization.** If a small country were to try to produce every product, it would end up with many industries in which output was too small to utilize mass-production techniques, specialized training facilities, and other arrangements that give a cost advantage to large-scale operations. This is an acute problem for some countries, whose operation of their own international airlines or their own steel mills, for example, seems explainable only in political rather than economic terms. Inevitably, small nations that insist on operating in industries that are economical only when their scale of operation is large find that these enterprises can survive only with the aid of large government subsidies. To summarize:

International trade is essential for the prosperity of the trading nations because:

1. every country lacks some vital resources that it can get only by trading with others;

2. each country's climate, labor force, and other endowments make it a relatively efficient producer of some goods and an inefficient producer of other goods; and

3. specialization permits larger outputs and can therefore offer economies of large-scale production.

Mutual Gains from Trade

Centuries ago, it was believed that one nation could gain from an exchange only at the expense of another. Early writers on international trade pointed out that, since nothing is produced by the act of trading, the total collection of goods in the hands of the two parties at the end of an exchange is no greater than before the exchange took place. Therefore, they incorrectly argued, if one country gains from a swap, the other country must necessarily lose.

One of the consequences of this mistaken view was a policy prescription calling for each country to do its best to act to the disadvantage of its trading partners — in Adam Smith's terms, to "beggar its neighbors." The idea that one nation's gain must be another's loss means that a country can promote its own welfare only by harming others.

Yet, as Adam Smith and others after him emphasized, in any *voluntary exchange,* unless there is misunderstanding or misrepresentation of the facts,

Specialization means that a country devotes its energies and resources to only a small proportion of the world's productive activities.

both parties *must* gain (or at least expect to gain) something from the transaction. Otherwise why would both parties agree to the exchange?

But how can mere exchange, in which no production takes place, leave *both* parties better off? The answer is that while trade does not increase the physical quantities of the goods available, it does allow each party to acquire items better suited to their needs and tastes. Suppose Scott has four sandwiches and nothing to drink, while William has four bottles of Coke and nothing to eat. A trade of two of Scott's sandwiches for two of William's Cokes does not increase the total supply of either food or beverages, but it clearly produces a net increase in the welfare of both boys.

Mutual Gains from Voluntary Exchange
Both parties must expect to gain from any *voluntary exchange*. Trade brings about mutual gains by redistributing products in such a way that both participants end up holding a combination of goods that is better adapted to their preferences than the goods they held before. This principle, which is one of our **12 Ideas for Beyond the Final Exam,** applies to nations just as it does to individuals.

International Versus Intranational Trade

The 50 states of the United States may be the most eloquent testimony to the gains from specialization and free trade. Florida specializes in growing oranges, Iowa in growing corn, Pennsylvania makes steel, and Michigan builds cars. All these states trade freely with one another and enjoy great material prosperity. Try to imagine how much lower living standards would be if your own state had to make all of these goods, plus the thousands of other things you consume each year.

The logic of international trade is essentially no different from that underlying trade among different states; the basic reasons for trade are equally applicable *within* a country or *among* countries. If we can learn about trade from strictly domestic exchanges, why study international trade as a special subject? There are at least three reasons.

Political Factors in International Trade
First, domestic trade takes place under a single national government, while foreign trade must involve at least two governments. At least in theory, the government of a nation is concerned with the welfare of all its citizens. But governments are usually much less deeply concerned with the welfare of citizens of other countries. For example, the Constitution of the United States prohibits overt tariffs and other impediments to domestic trade, barriers which seek to increase the gains from trade of some citizens at the expense of others. But the Constitution does not prohibit the United States from imposing tariffs on imports from abroad. A major issue in the economic analysis of international trade, and therefore of this chapter, is the use and misuse of impediments to free international trade.

The Many Currencies Involved in International Trade
Second, all trade within the borders of the United States is carried out in U.S. dollars. But trade across national borders must involve at least two currencies. Rates of exchange between different currencies can and do change. Thirty-five

years ago the pound was worth more than $4; now it is worth about $1.60. This variability in exchange rates brings with it a host of complications and policy problems that are discussed in the next chapter.

Impediments to Mobility of Labor and Capital

Third, it is usually much easier for labor and capital to move about within a country than to move from one country to another. If there are jobs in California but none in Michigan, workers can move freely to follow the job opportunities. Of course, there are personal costs—not only the dollar cost of moving, but also the psychological cost of giving up friends and familiar surroundings. But such relocations are not inhibited by immigration quotas, by laws restricting the employment of foreigners, or by the need to learn a new language, as are moves from one country to another.

There are also greater impediments to the transfer of capital from one country to another than to its movement within a country. The shipment of plant and equipment between countries can be expensive, and the international shipment of funds to be invested in foreign firms is likely to encounter many restrictions. For example, many countries have rules limiting the share of foreign ownership in a company. Foreign investment is also subject to special risks, such as the danger of outright expropriation if, say, after a political revolution the new government decides to take over all foreign properties without compensation. But even if nothing so extreme occurs, capital invested abroad faces risks from possible variations in exchange rates. An investment yielding a million pounds a year will be worth $2 million to American investors if the pound is worth $2 but only $1 million if the pound should fall to $1.

While labor, capital, and other factors of production do move from country to country when offered an opportunity to increase their earnings abroad, they are less likely to do so than to move from one region of a country to another to gain similar increases.

Comparative Advantage: The Fundamental Principle of Specialization

Some of the reasons why trade is beneficial to both parties are obvious. We now turn to an important source of mutual benefit which is far from obvious.

Coffee can be produced in Colombia using less labor and smaller quantities of other inputs than would be needed to grow it in the United States. And we know that the United States can produce large passenger aircraft at a lower resource cost than can Colombia. We say then that Colombia has an **absolute advantage** over the United States in coffee production, and the United States has an absolute advantage over Colombia in aircraft production.

A numerical example will illustrate the idea. According to Table 18–2, one year of labor time in the United States can produce either 50 pounds of

One country is said to have an **absolute advantage** over another in the production of a particular good if it can produce that good using smaller quantities of resources than can the other country.

Table 18–2
ALTERNATIVE OUTPUTS FROM ONE YEAR OF LABOR INPUT

	IN THE UNITED STATES	IN COLUMBIA
Coffee (pounds)	50	300
Airplanes	1/20	1/100

coffee or 1/20 of an airplane. By contrast, one year of labor time in Colombia can produce 300 pounds of coffee or 1/100 of an airplane. Thus, six years of labor input would be required to produce 300 pounds of coffee in the United States, whereas Colombia could do the job with only one year's worth of labor. On the other hand, it would take Colombia 100 years of labor to produce an airplane, a job the United States could do with only 20 years.

Obviously, if the United States wants coffee and Colombia wants airplanes, each can save resources by specializing in what it does best and trading with one another—each exporting the good in which it has an *absolute advantage*.

Suppose, however, that one country is more efficient than another in producing *every* item. Can they still gain by trading? The surprising answer is *definitely yes,* and a simple parable will help explain why.

The work of a highly paid business consultant frequently requires computer analysis. Suppose the consultant began her career as a computer operator, doing her own keypunching and programming, and is extremely good at it. She may sometimes grow impatient with the slow, sloppy work of some of the low-paid keypunchers who work for her and be tempted to do all the work herself. Good judgment, however, tells her that though she is better *both* at giving business advice *and* at keypunching than are her employees, it is foolish to devote any of her valuable time to the low-skilled keypunching job. That is because the opportunity cost of an hour devoted to keypunching is an hour less devoted to business consulting, which is a far more lucrative proposition.

This is an example of the principle of **comparative advantage** at work. The consultant specializes in business advice despite her absolute advantage in keypunching because she has a still greater absolute advantage as a business consultant. She suffers some direct loss by not doing her own keypunching. But that loss is more than compensated for by the earnings she makes selling her services to clients.

This example brings out the fundamental principle that underlies the economic analysis of patterns of specialization and exchange among different nations and is one of our **12 Ideas for Beyond the Final Exam.** The principle, called the *law of comparative advantage,* was discovered by David Ricardo, one of the giants in the history of economic analysis.

> One country is said to have a **comparative advantage** over another in the production of a particular good relative to other goods it can produce if it produces that good least inefficiently as compared with the other country.

The Law of Comparative Advantage

Even if one country is at an absolute disadvantage relative to another country in the production of *every* good, it is said to have a *comparative advantage* in making the good in whose production it is *least inefficient* in comparison with the other country.

Ricardo's basic finding was that two countries can still gain by trading even if one country is more efficient than another in the production of *every* commodity (that is, has an absolute advantage in every commodity).

In determining the most efficient patterns of production, what matters is *comparative* advantage, not *absolute* advantage. Thus one country will often gain by importing a certain good even if that good can be produced at home more efficiently than it can be produced abroad. Such imports will be profitable if the country is even more efficient at producing the goods that it exports in exchange.

The Arithmetic of Comparative Advantage

Let's see precisely how this works using numbers based on Ricardo's original example. Suppose labor is the only input used to produce wine and cloth in two countries, England and Portugal. Suppose further that Portugal has an absolute advantage in both goods, as indicated in Table 18–3. In this example, a week's worth of labor can produce either 12 yards of cloth or 6 barrels of wine in Portugal, but only 10 yards of cloth or 1 barrel of wine in England. So Portugal is the more efficient producer of both goods. Nonetheless, as our consultant-keypuncher example suggests, it pays for Portugal to specialize and trade with England.

We verify that this is so in two steps. First, we note that Portugal has a comparative advantage in wine while England has a comparative advantage in cloth. Then we show that both countries can gain if Portugal specializes in producing wine, England specializes in producing cloth, and the two countries trade with one another.

According to the numbers in Table 18–3, Portugal is 20 percent more efficient than England in producing cloth: It can produce 12 yards with a week's labor, whereas England can produce only 10. However, Portugal is six times as efficient as England in producing wine: It can produce 6 barrels per week rather than 1. Thus Portugal's competitive edge is far greater in wine than in cloth. That is precisely what we mean by saying that Portugal has a *comparative advantage* in wine. Looked at from the British perspective, these same numbers indicate that England is only slightly less efficient than Portugal in cloth production but drastically less efficient in wine production. So England's comparative advantage is in cloth. According to Ricardo's law of comparative advantage, then, the two countries can benefit if Portuguese wine is traded for English cloth. Let us check that this is true.

Suppose Portugal transfers a million weeks of labor out of the textile industry and into winemaking. According to the figures in Table 18–3, its cloth output falls by 12 million yards while its wine output rises by 6 million barrels. (See Table 18–4.) Suppose, at the same time, England transfers two million weeks of labor out of winemaking (thereby losing 2 million barrels of wine) and into clothmaking (thereby gaining 20 million yards of cloth). Table 18–4 shows us that these transfers of resources in the two countries increase the world's production of both outputs! Together, the two countries now have 4 million

Table 18–3
ALTERNATIVE OUTPUTS FROM ONE WEEK OF LABOR INPUT

	IN ENGLAND	IN PORTUGAL
Cloth (yards)	10	12
Wine (barrels)	1	6

Table 18–4
EXAMPLE OF THE GAINS FROM TRADE

	ENGLAND	PORTUGAL	TOTAL
Cloth (millions of yards)	+20	−12	+8
Wine (millions of barrels)	−2	+6	+4

additional barrels of wine and 8 million additional yards of cloth—surely a nice outcome.

But there seems to be some sleight of hand here. All that has taken place is an exchange. Yet, somehow Portugal and England gain both cloth and wine. How can such gains in physical output be possible? The explanation is that the trade process we have just described involves more than just a swap of a fixed

Biographical Note: David Ricardo (1772–1823)

David Ricardo was born four years before publication of Adam Smith's *Wealth of Nations*. Descended from a family of well-to-do stockbrokers of the Jewish faith who migrated to London from Amsterdam and were, in turn, descended from Portuguese Jews, he had about twenty brothers and sisters. At a school in Amsterdam, Ricardo's formal education ended at the age of 13, and so he was largely self-educated. He began his career by working in his father's brokerage firm. At age 21, Ricardo married a Quaker woman and decided to become a Unitarian, a sect then considered "little better than atheist." By Jewish custom, Ricardo's father broke with him, though apparently they remained friendly.

Ricardo then decided to go into the brokerage business on his own and was enormously successful. During the Napoleonic Wars he regularly scored business coups over leading British and foreign financiers, including the Rothschilds. After gaining a huge profit on government securities that he had bought just before the Battle of Waterloo, Ricardo decided to retire from business when he was just over 40 years old.

He purchased a country estate, Gatcomb (now owned by the royal family), where a brilliant group of intellectuals met regularly. Particularly remarkable for the period was the number of women included in the circle, among them Maria Edgeworth, the novelist (who wrote extravagant praise of Ricardo's mind), and Jane Marcet, an author of textbooks, one of which was probably the first text in economics. Ricardo's close friends included the economists T. R. Malthus and James Mill, father of John Stuart Mill, the noted philosopher-economist. Malthus remained a close friend of Ricardo even though they disagreed on many subjects and continued their arguments in personal correspondence and in their published works.

James Mill persuaded Ricardo to go into Parliament. As was then customary, Ricardo purchased his seat by buying a piece of land that entitled its owner to a seat in Parliament. There he proved to be a noteworthy advocate of many causes that were against his personal interests.

James Mill also helped persuade Ricardo to write his masterpiece, *The Principles of Political Economy and Taxation*, which may have been the first book of pure economic theory. It was noteworthy that Ricardo, the most practical of practical men, had little patience with empirical economics and preferred instead to rest his analysis explicitly and exclusively on theory. His book made considerable contributions to the analysis of pricing, wage determination, and the effects of various types of taxes, among many other subjects. It also gave us the law of comparative advantage. In addition, the book described what has come to be called the Ricardian rent theory—even though Ricardo did not discover the analysis and explicitly denied having done so.

Ricardo died in 1823 at the age of 51. He seems to have been a wholly admirable person—honest, charming, witty, conscientious, brilliant—altogether too good to be true.

bundle of commodities. It is also a *change in the production arrangements*, with some of England's wine production taken over by the more efficient Portuguese wine producers, and with some of Portugal's cloth production taken over by English weavers who are *less* inefficient at producing cloth than English vintners are at producing wine.

When every country does what it can do best, all countries can benefit because more of every commodity can be produced without increasing the amounts of labor used.

If this result still seems a bit mysterious, the concept of opportunity cost will help remove the remaining mystery. If the two countries do not trade, Table 18–3 shows that England can acquire a barrel of wine on its own only by giving up 10 yards of cloth. Thus the opportunity cost of a barrel of wine in England is 10 yards of cloth. But in Portugal the opportunity cost of a barrel of wine is only 2 yards of cloth (see, again, Table 18–3). Thus, in terms of real resources foregone, it is cheaper — for *either* country — to acquire wine in Portugal. By a similar line of reasoning, the opportunity cost of cloth is higher in Portugal than in England, so it makes sense for both countries to acquire their cloth in England.[2]

The Graphics of Comparative Advantage

The gains from trade can also be displayed graphically, and doing so helps us to understand how these gains arise.

The lines *UK* and *PG* in Figure 18–1 are the production possibilities frontiers of the two countries, drawn on the assumption that each country has 6 million weeks of labor available.[3] For example, with 6 million weeks of labor, Table 18–3 tells us that England can produce 6 million barrels of wine and no cloth (point *K*), 60 million yards of cloth and no wine (point *U*), or any combination between (the line *UK*). Similar reasoning shows that *PG* is Portugal's production possibilities frontier.

[2]As an exercise, provide this line of reasoning.
[3]To review the concept of the production possibilities frontier, see Chapter 3.

Figure 18–1
ABSOLUTE AND COMPARATIVE ADVANTAGE SHOWN BY TWO COUNTRIES' PRODUCTION POSSIBILITIES FRONTIERS
Portugal's absolute advantage is shown by its ability to produce more of every commodity using the same quantity of labor as does England. Therefore, Portugal's production possibilities frontier, *PG*, is higher than England's, *UK*. But Portugal has a comparative advantage in wine production in which it is six times as productive as England. (It can produce 36 million barrels, point *P*, compared with England's 6 million, point *K*.) On the other hand, Portugal is only 20 percent more productive in cloth production (point *G*) than England (point *U*). Thus, England is less inefficient in producing cloth, where it consequently has a comparative advantage.

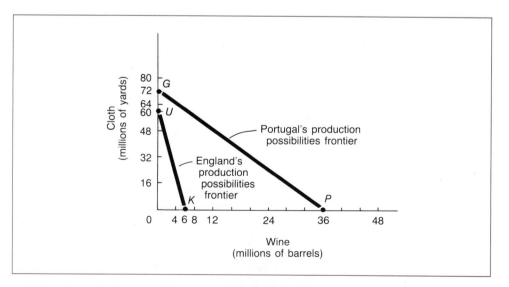

Note that Portugal's production possibilities frontier lies *above* England's throughout the diagram. That is because Portugal is the more efficient producer of *both* commodities. With the same amount of labor, it can obtain more wine and more cloth than England. Thus, the higher position of Portugal's frontier is the graph's way of showing Portugal's *absolute* advantage in both wine and cloth.

Portugal's comparative advantage in wine production and England's comparative advantage in cloth production are shown in a different way — by the relative *slopes* of the two production possibilities frontiers. Portugal's frontier is not only higher than England's, it is also flatter. What does this mean economically? One way of looking at the difference is to remember that while Portugal can produce six times as much wine as England (compare points P and K), it can produce only 20 percent more cloth than England (points G and U). England is, relatively speaking, much better at cloth production than at wine production. That is what is meant when we say it has a *comparative* advantage in the former.

We may express this difference more directly in terms of the slopes of the two lines. The slope of Portugal's production possibilities frontier is $OG/OP = 72/36 = 2$. This means that if Portugal reduces its wine production by one barrel, it will obtain two yards of cloth. Thus, the *opportunity cost* of a barrel of wine in Portugal is two yards of cloth, as we observed earlier.

In the case of England, the slope of the production possibilities frontier is $OU/OK = 60/6 = 10$. That is, if England reduces wine production by one barrel, it gets 10 additional yards of cloth. So in England the *opportunity cost* of a barrel of wine is 10 yards of cloth.

A country's absolute advantage in production over another country is shown by its having a higher production possibilities frontier. The difference in the comparative advantages of the two countries is shown by the difference in the slopes of their frontiers.

Because opportunity costs differ in the two countries, gains from trade are possible. How these gains are divided between the two countries depends on the prices for wine and cloth that emerge from world trade, which is the subject of the next section. But we already know enough to see that world trade must leave a barrel of wine costing less than 10 yards of cloth and more than 2 yards. Why? Because, if a barrel of wine cost more than 10 yards of cloth (its opportunity cost in England), England would be better off producing its own wine rather than trading with Portugal. Similarly, if a barrel of wine fetched less than two yards of cloth (its opportunity cost in Portugal), Portugal would prefer to produce its own cloth rather than trade with England.

We conclude, therefore, that if both countries are to trade, the rate of exchange between cloth and wine must be somewhere between 10 to 1 and 2 to 1. To illustrate the gains from trade in a concrete example, suppose the world price ratio settles at 4 to 1; that is, one barrel of wine costs 4 yards of cloth. How much, precisely, do England and Portugal gain from world trade?

Figure 18–2 is designed to help us see the answer. Production possibilities frontiers UK in part (a) and PG in part (b) are the same as in Figure 18–1. But England can do better than UK. Specifically, with a world price ratio of 4 to 1, England can buy a barrel of wine by giving up only 4 yards of cloth, rather than 10 (which is the opportunity cost of wine in England). Hence, if England produces only cloth [point U in Figure 18–2(a)] and buys its wine from Portugal, Britain's *consumption possibilities* will be as indicated by the blue line that begins

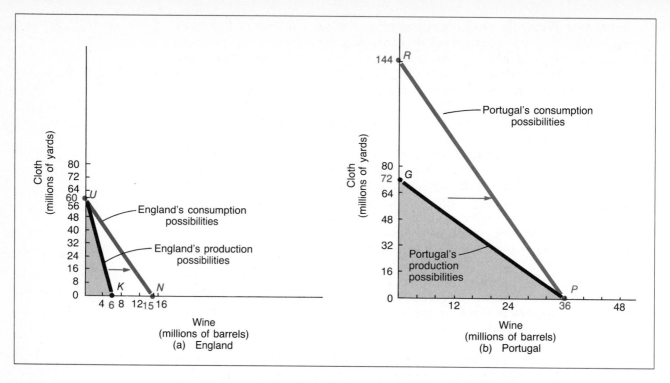

Figure 18–2

THE GAINS FROM TRADE
In this diagram, we suppose that trade opens up between England and Portugal and that the world price of wine is four times the world price of cloth. Now England's consumption possibilities are all the points on line *UN* (which starts at *U* and has a slope of 4), rather than just the points on its own production possibilities frontier, *UK*. Similarly, Portugal can choose any point on line *PR* (which begins at *P* and has a slope of 4), rather than just points on *PG*. Thus both nations gain from trade.

at point *U* and has a slope of 4—indicating that each additional barrel of wine costs England 4 yards of cloth. Since trade allows England to choose a point on *UN* rather than on *UK*, trade opens up consumption possibilities that were simply not available before.

The story is similar for Portugal. If the Portuguese produce only wine [point *P* in Figure 18–2(b)], they can acquire 4 yards of cloth from England for each barrel of wine they give up as they move along the blue line *PR* (whose slope is 4). This is better than they can do on their own, since a sacrifice of one barrel of wine yields only 2 yards of cloth in Portugal. Hence world trade enlarges Portugal's consumption possibilities from *PG* to *PR*.

Figure 18–2 shows graphically that gains from trade arise to the extent that world prices (4 to 1 in our example) differ from domestic opportunity costs (10 to 1 and 2 to 1 in our example). So it is a matter of some importance to understand how prices in international trade are established. Supply and demand is a natural place to start.

Supply–Demand Equilibrium and Pricing in Foreign Trade

When applied to international trade, the supply–demand model runs into several new complications. First, it involves at least two demand curves: that of the exporting country and that of the importing country. Second, it may also involve two supply curves, since the importing country may produce some part of its own consumption. Third, equilibrium does not take place at the intersection point of *either* pair of supply–demand curves. Why? Because if there is any trade, the exporting country's quantity supplied must be *greater* than its quantity demanded, while the quantity supplied by the importing country must be *less* than its quantity demanded.

These complications are illustrated in Figure 18–3, where we show the supply and demand curves of a country that exports wine, in part (a), and those

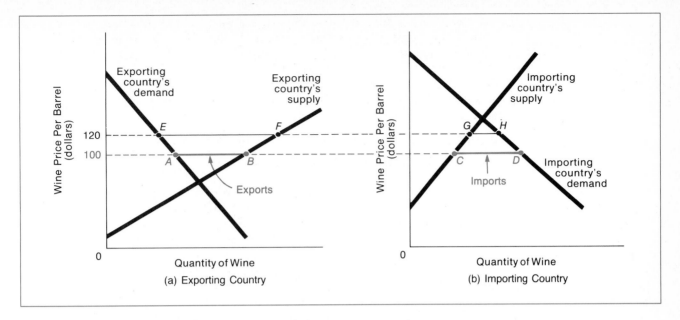

Exporting country's demand

Exporting country's supply

120

100

E

F

A

B

Exports

Wine Price Per Barrel (dollars)

0

Quantity of Wine

(a) Exporting Country

Importing country's supply

G H

C D

Imports

Importing country's demand

Wine Price Per Barrel (dollars)

0

Quantity of Wine

(b) Importing Country

of one that imports wine, in part (b). For simplicity, we assume that these countries do not deal in wine with anyone else.

Where will the two-country wine market reach equilibrium? The equilibrium price in a free market must satisfy two requirements:

1. The price of wine must be the same in both countries.

2. The quantity of wine exported must equal the quantity of wine imported.

In Figure 18–3, this happens at a price of $100 per barrel. At that price, the distance AB between what the exporting country produces (point B) and what it consumes (point A) equals the distance CD between the quantity demanded of the importing country (point D) and its quantity supplied (point C). At a price of $100 per barrel, the amount the exporting country has available to sell abroad is exactly equal to the amount the importer wants to buy, and so matters are in balance.

At any price above $100, producers in both countries will want to sell more and consumers in both countries will want to buy less. For example, if the price rises to $120 per barrel, the exporter's quantity supplied will rise from B to F, and the exporter's quantity demanded will fall from A to E, as shown in Figure 18–3(a). As a result, there will be a rise in the amount available for export, from AB to EF. For exactly the same reason, the price increase will cause higher production and lower sales in the importing country, leading to a shrinkage in the amount the importing country wants to import—from CD to GH in part (b). This means that the new price, $120 per barrel, cannot be sustained if the international market is free and competitive. With export supply EF far greater than import demand GH, there must be downward pressure on price and a move back toward the $100 equilibrium price. Similar reasoning shows that prices below $100 also cannot be sustained.

We can now see the straightforward role of supply–demand equilibrium in international trade:

In international trade, the equilibrium price must be at a level at which the amount the exporting country wants to export is exactly equal to the amount

Figure 18–3
SUPPLY–DEMAND
EQUILIBRIUM IN THE
INTERNATIONAL WINE
TRADE
Equilibrium requires that exports, AB (which is the exporting nation's quantity supplied, B, minus the exporter's quantity demanded, A), exactly balance imports, CD, by the importing country. At $100 per barrel of wine, there is equilibrium. But at a higher price, say $120, there is disequilibrium because export supply, EF, exceeds import demand, GH.

the importing country wants to import. Equilibrium will thus occur at a price at which the horizontal distance AB in Figure 18–3(a) (the excess of the exporter's quantity supplied over its quantity demanded) is equal to the horizontal distance CD in Figure 18–3(b) (the excess of the importer's quantity demanded over its quantity supplied). At this price, the *world's* quantity demanded is equal to the *world's* quantity supplied.

Comparative Advantage and Competition of "Cheap Foreign Labor"

The principle of comparative advantage takes us a good part of the way toward an explanation of the fallacy in the "cheap foreign labor" argument described earlier in the chapter. Given the assumed productive efficiency of Portuguese labor and the inefficiency of British labor, we would expect wages to be much higher in Portugal than in England.

In these circumstances, one can expect Portuguese workers to be apprehensive about an agreement to permit trade between the countries — "How can we hope to meet the unfair competition of those underpaid British workers?" And British laborers are also likely to be concerned — "How can we hope to meet the competition of those Portuguese, who are so efficient in producing everything?"

The principle of comparative advantage shows us that both fears are unjustified. As we have just seen, when trade is opened up between Portugal and England *workers in both countries will be able to earn higher real wages than before* because of the increased productivity that comes about through specialization.

Figure 18–2 (page 390) shows this fact directly. We have seen from our illustration that, with trade, England can end up with more wine and more cloth than it had before. So the living standards of its workers can rise even though they have been left vulnerable to the competition of the superefficient Portuguese. Portugal also can end up with more wine and with more cloth; so the living standards of its workers can rise even though they have been exposed to the competition of cheap British labor. These higher standards of living are, of course, a reflection of the higher real wages earned by workers in both countries.

The lesson to be learned here is elementary: Nothing helps raise standards of living more than does a greater abundance of goods.

Tariffs, Quotas, and Other Interferences with Trade

Despite the mutual gains obtained, international trade has historically been subjected to unrelenting pressure for government interference. In fact, until the rise of a free-trade movement in England at the end of the eighteenth and the beginning of the nineteenth centuries (with such economists as Adam Smith and David Ricardo as its vanguard), it was taken for granted that one of the essential tasks of government was to impose regulations that impede trade — presumably in the national interest.

There were many who argued then (and some who still argue today) that a nation's wealth consists of the amount of gold or other monies at its command. Consequently, the proper aim of government policy was to do everything it could to promote exports as a way to increase the amount foreigners would owe to it. Similarly the government was to discourage imports in order to decrease the amount the country owed to foreigners.

Obviously, there are limits to which this policy can be carried out. A country *must* import vital foodstuffs or critical raw materials that it cannot supply for itself; for if it does not, it must suffer a severe fall in living standards as well as a deterioration in its military strength. Morever, it is mathematically impossible for *every* country to sell more than it buys—one country's exports *must* be some other country's imports. If everyone competes in this game and cuts imports to the bone, then obviously exports must go the same way. The result will be that everyone is deprived of the mutual gains that trade can provide.

In more recent times, notably in the United States during the first three decades of the twentieth century, there was a return to an active policy designed to reduce competition from foreign imports. Since then, the United States has gradually assumed a leading role in attempts to promote freedom of trade, and barriers have gradually been reduced. However, recently a combination of high unemployment rates and a deterioration in America's competitive position in world trade has led to political pressures to move back in the other direction. The 1980s have seen new restrictions on U.S. trade in automobiles, lumber, semiconductors, and a variety of other products. Were it not for the free-trade proclivities of the Reagan administration, even more trade restrictions probably would have been enacted.

Three main devices have been used by modern governments seeking to control trade: tariffs, quotas, and export subsidies.

A **tariff** is simply a tax on imports. An importer of wine, for example, may be charged $10 for each barrel of wine he brings into the country. The United States is generally a low-tariff country. Although there are a few notable exceptions, most of our tariff rates are below 10 percent, and many items have no tariff at all. However, many other countries rely on heavy tariffs to protect their industries. Tariff rates of 100 percent or more are not unheard of.

A **quota** is a legal limit on the amount of a good that may be imported. For example, the government might allow no more than 5 million barrels of wine to be imported in a year. In some cases, governments ban the importation of certain goods outright—a quota of zero. (See the accompanying boxed insert for an example.) The United States imposes quotas on a smattering of goods, including steel, Japanese automobiles, textiles, sugar, and meat. But most imports are free of quotas.

An **export subsidy** is a payment by the government to an exporter. By reducing the exporter's costs, such subsidies permit exporters to lower their selling prices and compete more effectively in world trade. While export subsidies are minor in the United States, they are used extensively by some foreign governments to assist their industries—a practice that provokes bitter complaints from American manufacturers about "unfair competition."

How Tariffs and Quotas Work

Both tariffs and quotas restrict supplies coming from abroad and drive up prices. The tariff works by raising prices and hence cutting the demand for imports, while the sequence associated with a quota goes the other way—restriction in supply forces prices up.

Let us use our international trade diagrams to see what a quota does. The supply and demand curves in Figure 18–4 are like those of Figure 18–3. Just as in Figure 18–3, equilibrium in a free international market occurs at a price of $100 per barrel (in both countries). At this price, the exporting country produces 10 million barrels [point *B* in part (a)] and consumes 5 million (point *A*),

A **tariff** is a tax on imports.

A **quota** specifies the maximum amount of a good that is permitted into the country from abroad per unit of time.

An **export subsidy** is a payment by the government to exporters to permit them to reduce the selling price of their goods so they can compete more effectively in foreign markets.

Yes, Greeks Have No Bananas

ATHENS—Are there no bananas in Olympia? Yes.

Are there no bananas in Thebes? Yes. In Corinth? Yes. In Sparta, Marathon, Delphi? Yes, yes, yes.

Are there no bananas on Crete?

That depends on your definition of banana. Little green pods do grow on that Greek island, on scorched, drooping plants that look as though they want to be banana trees. They are called bananas, but they don't taste much like bananas—or, at least, that's what people say. A foreigner can't easily get a taste of a ripe Cretan banana. They are all sold secretly, on the black market. To buy a banana anywhere in Greece, you need a connection. All over the world, people take bananas for granted. A bunch of bananas off the boat from Panama isn't exactly what dreams are made of, right? Well, in this country, dreams *are* made of bananas. Alien bananas are contraband in Greece. For Greeks, a sweet, yellow, pulpy Panamanian banana is the forbidden fruit.

"Greece no banana," says the taxi driver at the Athens airport, ecstatically accepting an exotic beauty as a tip. A traveler has just slipped through customs with a bunch in a brown paper bag, defying a five-pound limit. The driver tenderly places his in the glove compartment. "I show it to my grandson," he says.

It has been 12 years now since the last banana boat sailed away from Piraeus. There are children in Greece today who don't even know what a banana is. Greece was a dictatorship in 1971, and dictatorships sometimes do strange things. The one in Greece outlawed the traffic in foreign bananas.

The head of internal security, Col. Stelios Pattakos, gave the order. He was born on Crete, a

bone-dry island, and was friendly toward some farmers there who had it in their heads to try growing a fruit native to equatorial jungles. The colonel got rid of the competition. Still, the Cretan crop was so puny it couldn't satisfy a 50th of the Greek passion for bananas. The price went up. The government imposed controls. And then the banana peddlers went underground.

When the dictatorship collapsed in 1974, Col. Pattakos was sentenced to life imprisonment for nonbanana-related offenses. Democracy returned—but bananas didn't. Bureaucrats do strange things, too.

A banana avalanche, they determined, would hurt the Greek apple business. Everybody would suddenly stop eating apples and start eating bananas. It didn't do any good to argue that comparing apples and bananas was like comparing apples and oranges. So Col. Pattakos got life, and the Greek people got life without bananas.

SOURCE: *The Wall Street Journal*, July 28, 1983, page 1.

---

so that exports are 5 million barrels—the distance AB. Similarly, the importing country consumes 8 million barrels [point D in part (b)] and produces only 3 million (point C), so that its imports are also 5 million barrels—the distance CD.

Now suppose the government of the importing nation imposes an import quota of (no more than) 3 million barrels. The free-trade equilibrium is no longer possible. Instead, the market must equilibrate at a point where both exports and imports are 3 million barrels. As Figure 18–4 indicates, this requires different prices in the two countries.

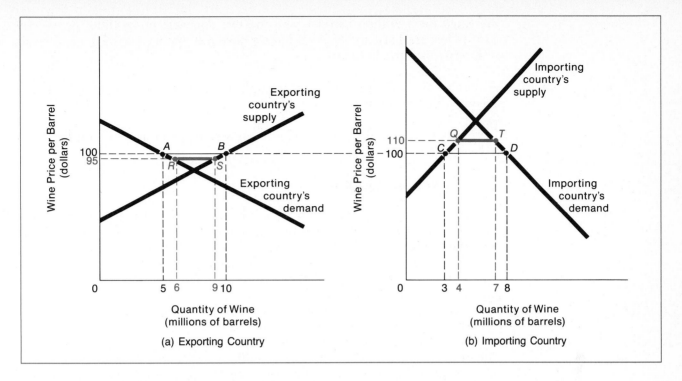

(a) Exporting Country

(b) Importing Country

Imports in part (b) will be 3 million — the distance QT — only when the price of wine in the importing nation is $110 per barrel, because only at this price will quantity demanded exceed domestic quantity supplied by 3 million barrels. Similarly, exports in part (a) will be 3 million barrels — the distance RS — only when the price in the exporting country is $95 per barrel. At this price, quantity supplied exceeds domestic quantity demanded by 3 million barrels in the exporting country. Thus the quota *raises* the price in the importing country to $110 and *lowers* the price in the exporting country to $95. In general:

An import quota on a product normally will reduce the volume of that product traded, raise the price in the importing country, and reduce the price in the exporting country.

The same restriction of trade can be accomplished through a tariff. In the example we have just completed, a quota of 3 million barrels resulted in a price that was $15 higher in the importing country than in the exporting country ($110 − $95). Suppose that, instead of a quota, the importing nation posts a $15 per barrel tariff. International trade equilibrium then must satisfy the following two requirements:

1. The price that consumers in the importing country pay for wine must exceed the price that suppliers in the exporting country receive by $15 (the amount of the tariff).

2. The quantity of wine exported must equal the quantity of wine imported.

By consulting the graphs in Figure 18–4, you can see exactly where these two requirements are satisfied. If the exporter produces at S and consumes at R, while the importer produces at Q and consumes at T, then exports and imports

Figure 18–4

QUOTAS AND TARIFFS IN INTERNATIONAL TRADE

Under free trade, the equilibrium price of wine is $100 per barrel. The exporting country, in part (a), sends *AB*, or 5 million barrels, to the importing country (distance *CD*). If a quota of 3 million barrels is imposed by the importing country, these two distances must shrink to 3 million barrels. The solution is shown by distance *RS* for exports and distance *QT* for imports. Exports and imports are equal, as must be the case, but the quota forces prices to be unequal in the two countries. Wine sells for $110 per barrel in the importing country but only $95 per barrel in the exporting country. A tariff achieves the same result differently. It *requires* that the prices in the two countries be $15 apart. And this, as the graph shows, dictates that exports (= imports) will be equal at 3 million barrels.

are equal (at 3 million barrels), and the two domestic prices differ by exactly $15. (They are $110 and $95.) What we have just discovered is a general result of international trade theory:

Any restriction of imports that is accomplished by a quota normally can also be accomplished by a tariff.

In this case, the tariff corresponding to an import quota of 3 million barrels is $15 per barrel.

Tariffs versus Quotas

But while tariffs and quotas can accomplish the same reduction in international trade and lead to the same domestic prices in the two countries, there *are* some important differences between the two types of restrictions.

First, under a quota, profits from the price increases in the importing country usually go into the pockets of the foreign and domestic sellers of the product. Because supplies are limited by quotas, customers in the importing country must pay more for the product. So the suppliers, be they foreign or domestic, receive more for every unit they sell. For example, the U.S. quota on imports of Japanese automobiles that began in 1981 raised the "profits" of both American and Japanese automakers by billions of dollars per year.

On the other hand, when trade is restricted by a tariff, some of the profits go instead as tax revenues to the *government* of the importing country. In effect, the government increases its tax revenues partly at the expense of its citizens and partly at the expense of foreign exporters, who must accept a reduced price because of the resulting decrease in quantity demanded in the importing country. (Domestic producers again benefit, because they are exempt from the tariff.) In this respect, a tariff is certainly a better proposition than a quota from the viewpoint of the country that enacts it.

Another important distinction between the two measures is the difference in their implications for productive efficiency and prices in the long run. A tariff handicaps all foreign suppliers equally. It still awards sales to the firms and nations who are most efficient and can therefore supply the goods most cheaply.

A quota, on the other hand, necessarily awards its import licenses more or less capriciously—perhaps on a first-come, first-served basis or in proportion to past sales or even on political criteria. There is not the slightest reason to expect the most efficient and least costly suppliers to get the import permits. In the long run, the population of the importing country is likely to end up with significantly higher prices, poorer products, or both.

The U.S. quota on Japanese cars illustrates all of these effects. Japanese automakers responded to the limit on the number of cars by shipping bigger models equipped with more "optional" equipment. The "stripped down" Japanese car became a thing of the past. And the newer, smaller Japanese automakers—like Subaru and Mitsubishi—found it difficult to compete in the U.S. market because their quotas were so much smaller than those of Toyota, Datsun, and Honda.

If a country must inhibit imports, there are two important reasons for it to give preference to tariffs over quotas: (1) some of the resulting financial gains from tariffs go to the government of the importing country rather than to foreign and domestic producers; and (2) unlike quotas, tariffs offer no special benefits to inefficient exporters.

Why Inhibit Trade?

To state that tariffs are a better way to inhibit international trade than quotas leaves open a far more basic question: Why limit trade in the first place? There are two primary reasons for adopting measures that restrict trade: First, they may help the importing country get more advantageous prices for its goods, and second, they protect particular industries from foreign competition.

Shifting Prices in Your Favor

How can a tariff make prices more advantageous for the importing country if it raises consumer prices there? The answer is that it forces foreign exporters to sell more cheaply. Because their market is restricted by the tariff, they will be left with unsold goods unless they cut their prices. Suppose, as in Figure 18–4(b), that a $15 tariff on wine raises the price of wine in the importing country from $100 to $110 per barrel. This rise in price drives down imports from an amount represented by the length of the black line CD to the smaller amount represented by the blue line QT. And to the exporting country, this means an equal reduction in exports [see the change from AB to RS in Figure 18–4(a)].

As a result, the price at which the exporting country can sell its wine is driven down (from $100 to $95 in the example) while producers in the importing country—being exempt from the tariff—can charge $110 per barrel. In effect, such a tariff amounts to government intervention to rig prices in favor of domestic producers and to exploit foreign sellers by forcing them to sell more cheaply than they otherwise would.

However, this technique works only as long as foreigners accept tariff exploitation passively. And, as the accompanying boxed insert suggests, they rarely do. Instead, they retaliate, usually by imposing tariffs or quotas of their own on their imports from the country that first began the tariff game. This can easily lead to a trade war in which no one gains in terms of more favorable prices and everyone loses in terms of the resulting reductions in overall trade. Something like this happened to the world economy in the 1930s and helped prolong the worldwide depression. At present, it is threatening to happen again.

Tariffs or quotas can benefit particular domestic industries in a country that is able to impose them without fear of retaliation. But when every country uses them, everyone is likely to lose in the long run.

Protecting Particular Industries

The second, and probably more frequent, reason why countries restrict trade is to protect particular industries from foreign competition. If foreigners can produce steel or watches or shoes more cheaply, domestic businesses and unions in these industries are quick to demand protection; and their government is often reluctant to deny it to them. It is here that the cheap foreign labor argument is most likely to be invoked.

The fact is, however, that the firms that are unable to compete in the market are the ones whose relative inefficiency does not permit them to beat foreign exporters at their own game. In Ricardo's example of comparative advantage, one can well imagine the complaints from Portuguese clothmakers as the opening of trade led to increased importation of English cloth. At the same time, English grape growers would probably have expressed equal concern over the flood of imported wine from Portugal. Protective tariffs and quotas

An Eye for an Eye...and a Book for a Shingle?

Trade wars have a way of gathering momentum and moving in unpredictable directions, as the following excerpt shows.

As the authorities in the United States prepare to announce a decision on whether to impose a duty on imports of softwood lumber from Canada, the Canadian Government is threatening retaliation.

The lumber dispute is by far the biggest trade battle between Canada and the United States, the world's largest trading partners. A tariff of the magnitude requested by the American lumber industry would add more than $1 billion to the $3.5 billion price of softwood lumber imported from Canada each year.

"I think you can expect a strong response, but I'm not going to tell you what it is," Pat Carney, Canada's Minister for International Trade, said in an interview today.

She called the American lumber producers' request for a duty "total harassment."

After Washington imposed a tariff on Canadian cedar shingles last May, Ottawa imposed duties on a number of imports from the United States ranging from books to Christmas trees. But trade experts say it is unclear what retaliatory steps the Canadians could take now.

SOURCE: *The New York Times,* October 9, 1986.

are designed to undercut harsh competition coming from abroad. But it is precisely this competition that gives consumers the benefits of international specialization.

Usually, when an industry feels itself threatened by foreign competition, it is argued that some form of protection against imports is needed to prevent loss of jobs. We know from Part 4 that there are better ways to stimulate employment. But a program that limits foreign competition will do a better job of preserving employment in the particular protected industry. It will work, but often at a considerable cost to consumers in the form of higher prices and to the economy in the form of inefficient use of resources. Table 18–5 gives some

Table 18–5
ESTIMATED COSTS OF PROTECTIONISM

INDUSTRY	COST PER JOB SAVED
Automobiles	$105,000
Book manufacturing	100,000
Dairy products	220,000
Steel	750,000
Sugar	60,000
Textiles	42,000

SOURCE: Gary C. Hufbauer, Diane T. Berliner, and Kimberly Ann Elliott, *Trade Protection in the United States: 31 Case Studies* (Washington: Institute for International Economic Studies), 1986, Table 1.2.

recent estimates of the costs to American consumers of using tariffs and quotas to save jobs in selected industries. In every case, the costs far exceed the wages of the workers in the protected industries—ranging as high as a colossal $750,000 per job for the current quotas on steel products.

Nevertheless, union complaints over proposals to reduce a tariff or a quota are justified unless something is done to ease the cost to the individual workers of switching to those lines of production that trade has now made profitable.

The argument for free trade between countries cannot be considered compelling if there is no adequate program to assist the minority of citizens in each country who will be harmed whenever patterns of production change drastically, as would happen, for example, if tariff and quota barriers were suddenly brought down.

Owners of wineries in Britain and of textile mills in Portugal may see heavy investments suddenly rendered unprofitable. So would workers whose investments in acquiring special skills and training are no longer marketable. Nor are the costs to displaced workers only monetary. They may have to move to new locations as well as to new industries, uprooting their families, losing old friends and neighbors, and so on. That the *majority* of citizens undoubtedly will gain from free trade will be no consolation to those who are its victims.

To help alleviate this problem, the United States (and other countries) has set up programs to assist workers who lose jobs because of changing patterns of world trade. In the United States such **trade adjustment assistance** is provided to firms or workers who suffer idle facilities, unprofitability, and unemployment because of sharp increases in imports.

Firms may be eligible for technical assistance designed to improve their efficiency, financial assistance in the form of government loans or government guarantees of private loans, and permission to delay tax payments. Workers are eligible for retraining programs, lengthened periods of eligibility for unemployment compensation, and allowances to help pay for the cost of moving to other jobs. Each form of assistance is designed to ease the burden on the victims of free trade so that the rest of us can enjoy its considerable benefits.

Trade adjustment assistance in the U.S. began in 1962, and benefits to displaced workers had grown to be extremely generous by the 1970s. However, the Reagan administration—objecting that the program put too much emphasis on *assistance* and not enough on *adjustment*—cut benefits drastically in 1981. Now, very few workers qualify.

> **Trade adjustment assistance** provides special unemployment benefits, loans, retraining programs, and other aid to workers and firms that are harmed by foreign competition.

Other Arguments for Protection

National Defense and Other Noneconomic Considerations

There are times when a tariff or some other measure to interfere with trade may be justified on noneconomic grounds. If a country considers itself vulnerable to military attack, it may be perfectly rational to keep alive industries whose outputs can be obtained more cheaply abroad but whose supplies might be cut off in an emergency. For example, airplane production by small countries makes sense only on these grounds.

The danger is that every industry, even those with the most peripheral relationship to defense, is likely to invoke this argument on its behalf. For instance, the U.S. watchmaking industry claimed protection for itself for many years on the grounds that its skilled craftsmen would be invaluable in wartime. Perhaps so, but a technicians' training program probably could have done the job more cheaply and even more effectively by teaching exactly the skills needed for military purposes.

Similarly, the U.S. has occasionally banned either exports to or imports from nations like Cuba, the Soviet Union, Libya, and Afghanistan on political grounds. Such actions often have important economic effects, creating either bonanzas or disasters for particular American industries. But they are justified by politics, not by economics. Noneconomic reasons also explain quotas on importation of whaling products and on the furs of other endangered species.

The Infant-Industry Argument

Another common argument for protectionism is the so-called infant-industry argument. Promising new industries, it is alleged, often need breathing room to flourish and grow. If we expose these infants to the rigors of international competition too soon, the argument goes, they may never develop to the point where they can survive on their own in the international marketplace.

The argument, while valid in certain instances, is less defensible than it at first appears. It makes sense only if the industry's prospective future gains are sufficient to repay the social losses incurred while it is being protected. But if the industry is likely to be so profitable in the future, why doesn't private capital rush in to take advantage of the prospective net profits? The annals of business are full of cases in which a new product or a new firm lost money at first but profited handsomely later. Only where funds are not available to a particular industry for some reason, despite its glowing profit prospects, does the infant-industry argument for protection stand up to scrutiny. And even then it may make more sense to provide a government loan than to provide trade protection.

It is hard to think of examples where the infant-industry argument applies. But even if such a case were found, one would have to be careful that the industry not remain in diapers forever. There are too many cases in which new industries were awarded protection when they were being established and, somehow, the time to withdraw that protection never arrived. One must beware of infant industries that never grow up.

Strategic Trade Policy

A new argument for (one hopes temporary) protectionism has become popular in recent years. Advocates of this argument agree that free trade for all is the best system. But they point out that we live in an imperfect world in which many nations refuse to play by the rules of the free-trade game. And they fear that a nation that pursues free trade in a protectionist world is likely to lose out. It therefore makes sense, they argue, to threaten to protect your markets unless other nations agree to open theirs. (See the article by columnist William Safire on page 401.)

This is a hard argument for economists to deal with. While it accepts the superiority of free trade, it argues that threatening protectionism is the best way to establish free trade. Such a strategy might work, but it clearly involves great risks. If threats that America will turn protectionist induce other countries to scrap existing protectionist policies, then the gamble will have succeeded. But, if the gamble fails, the world ends up with even more protection than it started with.

The analogy to arms negotiations with the Soviet Union is pretty obvious—and a little frightening. We threaten to install new missiles unless the Russians agree to dismantle some of theirs. If they do, the world is a safer place

Can Protectionism Save Free Trade?

In this 1983 column, William Safire shook off his longstanding attachment to free trade and argued eloquently for retaliation against protectionist nations.

WASHINGTON—Free trade is economic motherhood. Protectionism is economic evil incarnate... Never should government interfere in the efficiency of international competition.

Since childhood, these have been the tenets of my faith. If it meant that certain businesses in this country went belly-up, so be it... If it meant that Americans would be thrown out of work by overseas companies paying coolie wages, that was tough...

The thing to keep in mind, I was taught, was the Big Picture and the Long Run. America, the great exporter, had far more to gain than to lose from free trade; attempts to protect inefficient industries here would ultimately cost more American jobs.

While playing with my David Ricardo doll and learning nursery rhymes about comparative advantage, I was listening to another laissez-fairy tale: Government's role in the world of business should be limited to keeping business honest and competitive. In God we antitrusted. Let businesses operate in the free marketplace.

Now American businesses are no longer competing with foreign companies. They are competing with foreign governments who help their local businesses. That means the world arena no longer offers a free marketplace; instead, most other governments are pushing a policy that can be called *helpfulism*.

Helpfulism works like this: A government like Japan decides to get behind its baseball-bat industry. It pumps in capital, knocks off marginal operators, finds subtle ways to discourage imports of Louisville Sluggers, and selects target areas for export blitzes. Pretty soon, the favored Japanese companies are driving foreign competitors batty.

How do we compete with helpfulism? One way is to complain that it is unfair; that draws a horselaugh. Another way is to demand a "Reagan Round" of trade negotiations under GATT, the Gentlemen's Agreement To Talk, which is equally laughable. Yet another way is to join the helpfuls by subsidizing our exports and permitting our companies to try monopolistic tricks abroad not permitted at home. But all that makes us feel guilty, with good reason.

The other way to deal with helpfulism is through—here comes the dreadful word—*protection*. Or, if you prefer a euphemism, *retaliation*. Or if that is still too severe, *reciprocity*. Whatever its name, it is a way of saying to the cutthroat cartelists we sweetly call our trading partners: "You have bent the rules out of shape. Change your practices to conform to the agreed-upon rules, or we will export a taste of your own medicine."

A little balance, then, from the free trade theorists. The demand for what the Pentagon used to call "protective reaction" is not demagoguery, not shortsighted, not self-defeating.

On the contrary, the overseas pirates of protectionism and exemplars of helpfulism need to be taught the basic lesson in trade, which is: tit for tat.

SOURCE: William Safire, "Smoot-Hawley Lives," *The New York Times*, March 17, 1983. Copyright © 1983 by The New York Times Company. Reprinted by permission.

and everyone is better off. But, if they do not, the arms race accelerates and everyone is worse off. Is our threat to build new missiles therefore a wise or a foolish policy? There is no agreement on this question, and so we should not expect agreement on the advisability of using protectionist measures in a strategic way.

What Import Prices Benefit a Country?

Dumping means selling goods in a foreign market at lower prices than those charged in the home market.

One of the most curious features of the protectionist position is the fear of low prices charged by foreign sellers. Countries that subsidize exports are accused of **dumping**—of getting rid of their goods at unconscionably low prices. For example, Japan has frequently been accused of dumping various goods on the U.S. market—most recently, semiconductors.

Unfair Foreign Competition

Satire and ridicule are often more persuasive than logic and statistics. Exasperated by the spread of protectionism to so many industries under the prevailing Mercantilist philosophy, French economist Frédéric Bastiat decided to take the protectionist argument to its illogical conclusion. The fictitious petition of the French candlemakers to the Chamber of Deputies, written in 1845 and excerpted below, has become a classic in the battle for free trade.

We are subject to the intolerable competition of a foreign rival, who enjoys, it would seem, such superior facilities for the production of light, that he is enabled to *inundate* our *national market* at so exceedingly reduced a price, that, the moment he makes his appearance, he draws off all custom for us; and thus an important branch of French industry, with all its innumerable ramifications, is suddenly reduced to a state of complete stagnation. This rival is no other than the sun.

Our petition is, that it would please your honorable body to pass a law whereby shall be directed the shutting up of all windows, dormers, skylights, shutters, curtains, in a word, all openings, holes, chinks, and fissures through which the light of the sun is used to penetrate our dwellings, to the prejudice of the profitable manufactures which we flatter ourselves we have been enabled to bestow upon the country...

We foresee your objections, gentlemen; but there is not one that you can oppose to us...which is not equally opposed to your own practice and the principle which guides your policy...

Labor and nature concur in different proportions, according to country and climate, in every article of production...If a Lisbon orange can be sold at half the price of a Parisian one, it is because a natural and gratuitous heat does for the one what the other only obtains from an artificial and consequently expensive one...

Does it not argue the greatest inconsistency to check as you do the importation of coal, iron, cheese, and goods of foreign manufacture, merely because and even in proportion as their price approaches *zero*, while at the same time you freely admit, and without limitation, the light of the sun, whose price is during the whole day at *zero*?

SOURCE: F. Bastiat, *Economic Sophisms* (New York: G. P. Putnam's Sons, 1922).

A moment's thought should indicate why this fear must be considered curious. As a nation of consumers, we should be indignant when foreigners charge us *high* prices, not *low* ones. That is the common-sense rule that guides every consumer, and the consumers of imported commodities should be no exception. Only from the topsy-turvy viewpoint of an industry seeking protection from competition are high prices seen as being in the public interest.

Ultimately, it must be in the best interest of a country to get its imports as cheaply as possible. It would be ideal for the United States if the rest of the world were willing to provide its exports to us free or virtually so. We could then live in luxury at the expense of the rest of the world.

But, of course, what benefits the United States as a whole does not necessarily benefit every single American. If quotas on, say, steel imports were dropped, American consumers and industries that purchase steel would gain from lower prices. But owners of steel companies and steelworkers would suffer serious losses in the form of lower profits, lower wages, and lost jobs—losses they will fight hard to prevent. For this reason, politics often leads to the adoption of protectionist measures that would likely be rejected on strictly economic criteria.

The notion that low import prices are bad for a country is a fitting companion to the idea—so often heard—that it is good for a country to export much more than it imports. True, this means that foreigners will end up owing us a good deal of money. But it also means that we will have given them large quantities of our products and have gotten relatively little in foreign products in return. That surely is not an ideal way for a country to reap gains from international trade.

Our gains from trade do not consist of accumulations of gold or of heavy debts owed us by foreigners. Rather, our gains are composed of goods and services that others provide minus goods and services we must provide in return.

Conclusion: A Last Look at the "Cheap Foreign Labor" Argument

The preceding discussion should indicate the fundamental fallacy in the argument that American workers have to fear cheap foreign labor. If workers in other countries are willing to supply their products to us with little compensation, this must ultimately *raise* the standard of living of the average American worker. As long as the government's monetary and fiscal policies succeed in maintaining high levels of employment at home, how can we possibly lose by getting the products of the world at bargain prices?

There are, however, some important qualifications. First, our employment policy may not be effective. If workers who are displaced by foreign competition cannot find jobs in other industries, then American workers will indeed suffer from international trade. But that is a shortcoming of the government's employment program, not of its international trade policies.

Second, we have noted that an abrupt stiffening of foreign competition resulting from a major innovation in another country, or from a discovery of a new and better source of raw materials, or from a sharp increase in export subsidies by a foreign country, *can* hurt U.S. workers by not giving them an adequate chance to adapt gradually to the new conditions. The more rapid the change, the more painful it will be. If it occurs fairly gradually, workers can retrain and move on to the industries that now require their services. If the change is even more gradual, no one may have to move. People who retire or leave the threatened industry for other reasons simply need not be replaced. But competition that inflicts its damage overnight is certain to impose real costs upon the affected workers, costs that are no less painful for being temporary.

But these are, after all, qualifications to an overwhelming argument. They call for intelligent monetary and fiscal policies and for transitional assistance to unemployed workers, not for abandonment of free trade.

In the long run, labor will be "cheap" only where it is not very productive. Wages will tend to be highest in countries in which high labor productivity keeps costs down and permits exporters to compete effectively despite high wages. It is thus misleading to say that the United States held its own in the international marketplace until recently *despite* the high wages of its workers. Rather it is much more illuminating to point out that the high wages of American workers were a result of high worker productivity, which gave the United States a heavy competitive edge.

We note that in this matter it is *absolute* advantage, not *comparative* advantage, that counts. The country that is most efficient in every output can pay its workers more in every industry.

Summary

1. Countries trade because differences in their natural resources and other inputs create discrepancies in the efficiency with which they can produce different goods, and because specialization may offer them greater economies of large-scale production.

2. Voluntary trade will generally be advantageous to both parties in an exchange. This is one of our **12 Ideas for Beyond the Final Exam.**

3. International trade is more complicated than trade within a nation because of political factors, different national currencies, and impediments to the movement of labor and capital across national borders.

4. Both countries will gain from trade with one another if each exports goods in which it has a comparative advantage. That is, even a country that is generally inefficient will benefit by exporting the goods in whose production it is *least inefficient*. This is another of the **12 Ideas for Beyond the Final Exam.**

5. When countries specialize and trade, each can enjoy consumption possibilities that exceed its production possibilities.

6. The prices of goods traded between countries are determined by supply and demand, but one must consider explicitly the demand curve and the supply curve of *each* country involved. Thus, in international trade, the equilibrium price must be where the excess of the exporter's quantity supplied over its domestic quantity demanded is equal to the excess of the importer's quantity demanded over its quantity supplied.

7. The "cheap foreign labor" argument ignores the principle of comparative advantage, which shows that real wages can rise in both the importing and exporting countries as a result of specialization.

8. Tariffs and quotas are designed to protect a country's industries from foreign competition. Such protection may sometimes be advantageous to that country, but not if foreign countries adopt tariffs and quotas of their own as a means of retaliation.

9. While the same restriction of trade can be accomplished by either a tariff or a quota, tariffs offer at least two advantages to the country that imposes them: (1) some of the gains go to the government rather than to foreign producers; and (2) there is greater incentive for efficient production.

10. When a nation shifts from protection to free trade, some industries and their workers will lose out. Equity then demands that these people and firms be compensated in some way. The U.S. government offers various forms of trade adjustment assistance to do this, but these programs are small at present.

11. Several arguments for protectionism can, under the right circumstances, have validity. These include the national defense argument, the infant-industry argument, and the use of trade restrictions for strategic purposes. But each of these arguments is frequently abused.

12. Dumping may hurt domestic producers, but it always benefits domestic consumers.

Concepts for Review

Imports
Exports
Specialization
Mutual gains from trade
Absolute advantage

Comparative advantage
"Cheap foreign labor" argument
Tariff
Quota

Export subsidy
Trade adjustment assistance
Infant-industry argument
Dumping

Questions for Discussion

1. You have a dozen eggs worth 80 cents and your neighbor has a pound of bacon worth about the same. You decide to swap six eggs for a half pound of bacon. In financial terms, neither of you gains anything. Explain why you are nevertheless both likely to be better off.

2. In the eighteenth century, some writers argued that one person in a trade could be made better off only by gaining at the expense of the other. Explain the fallacy in the argument.

3. Country A has lots of hydroelectric power, a cold climate, and a highly skilled labor force. What sorts of products do you think it is likely to produce? What are the characteristics of the countries with which you would expect it to trade?

4. Upon removal of a tariff on watches, a U.S. watch-making firm goes bankrupt. Discuss the pros and cons of the tariff removal in the short and long runs.

5. Country A's government believes that it is best always to export more (in money terms) than the value of its imports. As a consequence, it exports more to country B every year than it imports from country B. After 100 years of this arrangement, both countries are destroyed in an earthquake. What were the advantages and disadvantages of the surplus to country A? To country B?

6. The table below describes the number of red socks and white socks that can be produced with an hour of labor in two different cities:

	IN BOSTON	IN CHICAGO
Red socks (pairs)	3	2
White socks (pairs)	3	1

   a. If there is no trade, what is the price of white socks relative to red socks in Boston?
   b. If there is no trade, what is the price of white socks relative to red socks in Chicago?

   c. Suppose each city has 1000 hours of labor available per year. Draw the production possibilities frontier for each city.
   d. Which city has an absolute advantage in the production of which good(s)? Which city has a comparative advantage in the production of which good(s)?
   e. If the cities start trading with each other, which city will specialize and export which good?
   f. What can be said about the price at which trade will take place?

7. Suppose that the United States and Mexico are the only two countries in the world. In the United States, a worker can produce 6 bushels of wheat or 1 barrel of oil in a day. In Mexico, a worker can produce 2 bushels of wheat or 4 barrels of oil per day.
   a. What will be the price ratio between the two commodities (that is, the price of oil in terms of wheat) in each country if there is no trade?
   b. If free trade is allowed and there are no transportation costs, what commodity would the U.S. import? What about Mexico?
   c. In what range will the price ratio have to fall under free trade? Why?
   d. Picking one possible post-trade price ratio, show clearly how it is possible for both countries to benefit from free trade.

8. The table below presents the demand and supply curves for watches in Switzerland and the United States.
   a. Draw the demand and supply curves for the United States on one diagram and those for Switzerland on another one.
   b. If there is no trade between the United States and Switzerland, what are the equilibrium price and quantity in the watch market in the United States? In Switzerland?
   c. Now suppose trade is opened up between the two countries. What will be the equilibrium price in the world market for watches? What has happened to the price of watches in the United States? In Switzerland?

d. Which country will export watches? How many?
e. When trade opens, what happens to the quantity of watches produced, and therefore employment, in the watch industry in the United States? In Switzerland? Who benefits and who loses *initially* from free trade?

PRICE PER WATCH (dollars)	QUANTITY DEMANDED IN U.S. (thousands)	QUANTITY SUPPLIED IN U.S. (thousands)	QUANTITY DEMANDED IN SWITZERLAND (thousands)	QUANTITY SUPPLIED IN SWITZERLAND (thousands)
10	110	0	80	30
20	90	20	50	50
30	70	40	35	65
40	60	60	20	80
50	50	80	5	95
60	40	95	0	105
70	30	105	0	110
80	20	110	0	115

19

The International Monetary System: Order or Disorder?

Cecily, you will read your
Political Economy in my
absence. The chapter on the
Fall of the Rupee you may
omit. It is somewhat too
sensational.

MISS PRISM IN
*THE IMPORTANCE
OF BEING EARNEST*

In the last chapter, we discussed the reasons for international trade and the benefits that accrue to all nations when countries specialize in producing those goods in which they have a comparative advantage. But the movement of goods across national borders generally requires the movement of *money* in the opposite direction. For example, when the United States buys coffee from Brazil, we must send money to the Brazilians. When Japan purchases petroleum from Saudi Arabia, it must send money to the Saudis, and so on. This chapter takes a look at the system that has been set up to handle these international movements of money — the **international monetary system**.

We begin by investigating a system in which rates of exchange among national currencies are determined in free markets by the laws of supply and demand. Here the key concept to be studied is the *exchange rate*. We shall see that the main macroeconomic variables studied in Parts 2–4 — output, the price level, and the rate of interest — each play a role in the determination of a country's exchange rate. This discussion sets the stage for Chapter 20, where we will learn how movements of the exchange rate, in turn, affect the national economy.

Next, we turn to the opposite polar form — an international monetary system in which exchange rates are fixed by government authority, rather than by the market. We do not now live in such a world. Yet studying it will help us understand the current international monetary system, which is a curious hybrid of fixed and floating exchange rates. Furthermore, by comparing how the two types of currency systems work, we can gain an understanding of the continuing controversy over whether the major trading nations should seek greater stability in exchange rates.

What Are Exchange Rates?

We noted in the previous chapter that international trade is more complicated than domestic trade. There are no national borders to be crossed when, say, California lettuce is shipped to Massachusetts. The consumer in Boston pays with *dollars*, just the currency that the farmer in Salinas wants. But if that same farmer ships his lettuce to Japan, consumers there will have only Japanese *yen* with which to pay, rather than the dollars the farmer in California wants. Thus if international trade is to take place, there must be a way to transform one currency (yen) into another (dollars). The rates at which such transformations are made are called **exchange rates**.

There is an exchange rate between every pair of currencies. For example, $1 is currently the equivalent of about 6 French francs. The exchange rate between the franc and the dollar, then, may be expressed as "6 francs to the dollar" (meaning that it costs 6 francs to buy a dollar) or about "17 cents to the franc" (meaning that it costs 17 cents to buy a franc).

Although exchange rates change all the time, Table 19–1 gives an indication of exchange rates prevailing in July 1980, February 1985, and September 1987, showing how many dollars or cents it cost at each of those times to buy each unit of foreign currency. You will note some dramatic changes in the international value of the dollar over time. In a nutshell, the dollar soared in the period from mid-1980 to early 1985 and has fallen against most major currencies since then. This chapter seeks to explain such currency realignments.

Under our present system, currency rates change frequently. When other currencies get more expensive in terms of dollars, we say that they have **appreciated** relative to the dollar. Alternatively, we can look at this same event as the dollar buying less foreign currency, meaning that the dollar has **depreciated** relative to another currency.

What is a depreciation to one country must be an appreciation to the other.

For example, if the dollar cost of a German mark rises from $33\frac{1}{3}$ cents to 50 cents, the cost of a U.S. dollar in terms of marks simultaneously falls from 3 marks to 2 marks. The Germans have had a currency *appreciation* while we have had a currency *depreciation*.

Notice also that, when many currencies are changing in value, the dollar may be appreciating with respect to one currency but depreciating with respect to another.

Table 19–1 shows that, between February 1985 and September 1987, the dollar *depreciated* sharply relative to the Japanese yen and most European

The **exchange rate** states the price, in terms of one currency, at which another currency can be bought.

A nation's currency is said to **appreciate** when exchange rates change so that a unit of its own currency can buy more units of foreign currency. The currency is said to **depreciate** when exchange rates change so that a unit of its currency can buy fewer units of foreign currency.

Table 19–1
EXCHANGE RATES WITH THE U.S. DOLLAR
(dollars per unit of foreign currency)

COUNTRY	CURRENCY UNIT	SYMBOL	JULY 1980	COST IN DOLLARS FEBRUARY 1985	SEPTEMBER 1987
Australia	dollar	$	$1.16	$0.74	$0.73
Canada	dollar	$	0.87	0.74	0.76
France	franc	FF	0.25	0.10	0.16
Germany	mark	DM	0.57	0.30	0.55
Italy	lira	L	0.0012	0.00049	0.00076
Japan	yen	¥	0.0045	0.0038	0.0069
Mexico	peso	$	0.044	0.0050	0.00065
Sweden	krona	Kr	0.24	0.11	0.16
Switzerland	franc	S. Fr.	0.62	0.36	0.66
United Kingdom	pound	£	2.37	1.10	1.64

SOURCE: International Financial Statistics and *The Wall Street Journal*.

currencies. For example, the British pound rose from $1.10 to $1.64. Yet during that same period the dollar *appreciated* dramatically relative to the Mexican peso; it bought about 200 pesos in 1985 but over 1500 in 1987.

While this is the terminology used to describe movements of exchange rates in free markets, another set of terms is used to describe decreases and increases in currency values when those values are set by government decree. When an officially set exchange rate is altered so that a unit of a nation's currency can buy *fewer* units of foreign currency, we say there has been a **devaluation** of that currency. When the exchange rate is altered so that the currency can buy *more* units of foreign currency, we say there has been a **revaluation**.

Exchange Rate Determination in a Free Market

Why is it that a German mark costs 56 cents and not 46 cents or 66 cents? In a world of **floating exchange rates**, with no government interferences, the answer would be fairly straightforward. Exchange rates would be determined by the forces of supply and demand, just like the prices of apples, or typewriters, or haircuts.

In a leap of abstraction, imagine that the United States and West Germany were the only countries on earth, so there was only one exchange rate to be determined. Figure 19–1 depicts the determination of this exchange rate at the point (denoted *E* in the figure) where demand curve *DD* crosses supply curve *SS*. At this price (56 cents per mark), the number of marks demanded is equal to the number of marks supplied.

In a free market, exchange rates are determined by the law of supply and demand. If the rate were below the equilibrium level, the quantity of marks demanded would exceed the quantity of marks supplied, and the price of a mark would be bid up. If the rate were above the equilibrium level, quantity supplied would exceed quantity demanded, and the price of a mark would fall. Only at the equilibrium exchange rate is there no tendency for the rate to change.

As usual, supply and demand determine price. What we must ask in this case is: Where do the supply and demand come from? Why does anyone demand a German mark? The answer comes in three parts:

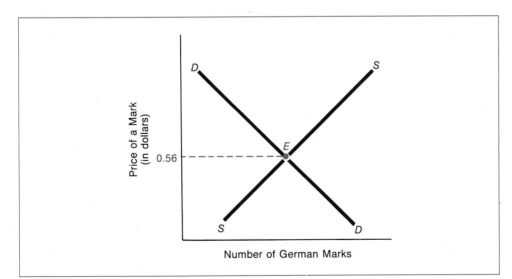

1. *International trade in goods and services.* This was the subject of the last chapter. If, for example, Jane Doe, an American, wants to buy a German automobile, she will first have to buy marks with which to pay the dealer in Munich.[1] So Jane's demand for a German *car* leads to a demand for German *marks*. In general, *demand for a country's export goods and services leads to a demand for its currency.*[2]

2. *International trade in financial instruments like stocks and bonds.* For example, if American investors want to purchase German stocks, they will first have to acquire the marks that the sellers will insist upon. In this way, demand for German financial assets leads to demand for German marks. Thus, *demand for a country's financial assets leads to a demand for its currency.*

3. *Purchases of physical assets like factories and machinery overseas.* If IBM wants to buy out a small German computer manufacturer, the owners will no doubt want to receive marks. So IBM will first have to acquire German currency. In general, *direct foreign investment leads to a demand for a country's currency.*

Now, where does the supply come from? To answer this, we need only turn all of these transactions around. Germans wanting to buy U.S. goods and services, or to invest in U.S. financial markets, or to make direct investments in America will have to offer their marks for sale in the foreign-exchange market (which is similar to the stock market) to acquire the needed dollars. To summarize:

The *demand* for a country's currency is derived from the demands of foreigners for its export goods and services and for its assets, including financial assets, factories, and machinery. The *supply* of a country's foreign currency arises from its imports, and from foreign investment by its own citizens.

To appreciate the usefulness of even this simple supply and demand analysis, let us consider how the exchange rate between the dollar and the mark would change if there were an economic boom in the United States. One important effect of such a boom would be to stimulate American demand for German products, such as automobiles, cameras, and wines. In terms of the supply-demand diagram shown in Figure 19–2, the increased desires of Americans for German products would shift the demand curve for German marks out from $D_1 D_1$ (the black line in the figure) to $D_2 D_2$ (the blue line). Equilibrium would shift from point E to point A, and the exchange rate would rise from 56 cents per mark to 60 cents per mark. In a word, the increased demand for marks by U.S. citizens causes the mark to *appreciate* relative to the dollar.

EXERCISE

Test your understanding of the supply and demand analysis of exchange rates by showing why each of the following events would lead to a depreciation of the mark (appreciation of the dollar) in a free market:

1. A recession in the United States cuts American purchases of German goods.

2. German investors are attracted by prospects for profit in the American stock market.

[1] Actually she will not do this because banks generally handle foreign exchange transactions for consumers. An American bank probably will buy the marks for her. But the effect is exactly the same as if Jane had done it herself.
[2] See Discussion Question 2 at the end of the chapter (page 429).

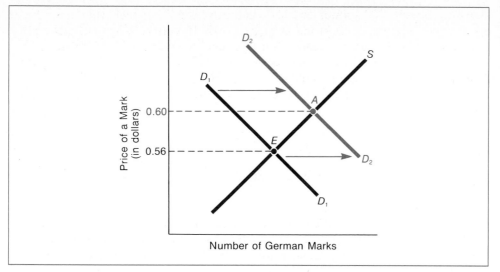

Figure 19–2
THE EFFECT OF AN ECONOMIC BOOM ON THE EXCHANGE RATE
If the U.S. economy suddenly booms, Americans will spend more on imports from Germany. Thus the demand curve for German marks will rise from $D_1 D_1$ to $D_2 D_2$ as Americans seek to acquire the marks they need. The diagram shows that this will cause the mark to appreciate, from 56 cents to 60 cents, as equilibrium shifts from point E to point A. Looked at from the U.S. perspective, the dollar will depreciate.

3. Interest rates on government bonds rise in the United States but are stable in Germany (*Hint:* Which country's citizens will be attracted by high interest rates in the other country?)

To say that supply and demand determine exchange rates in a free market is at once to say everything and to say nothing. If we are to acquire some understanding of the reasons why some currencies appreciate while others depreciate, we must look into the factors that move the supply and demand curves. Economists believe that the principal determinants of exchange rate movements are rather different in the long, medium, and short runs. So we turn in the next three sections to the analysis of exchange rate movements over these three "runs," beginning with the long run.

The Purchasing-Power Parity Theory: The Long Run

As long as there is free trade across national borders, exchange rates should eventually adjust so that the same product costs the same number of dollars (or the same amount of any other currency) in every country, except for differences attributable to transportation costs and the like. This simple statement forms the basis of the major theory of exchange rate determination in the long run.

The **purchasing-power parity theory of exchange rate determination** holds that the exchange rate between any two national currencies adjusts to reflect differences in the price levels in the two countries.

An example will bring out the basic truth in this theory and also suggest some of its limitations. Suppose that Swedish and American steel are identical and that these two nations are the only producers of steel for the world market. Suppose further that steel is the only tradable good that either country produces.

Question: If American steel costs $160 per ton and Swedish steel costs 1000 kronor per ton, what must be the exchange rate between the dollar and the krona?

Answer: Since 1000 kronor or $160 each buys a ton of steel, they must be of equal value. Hence, each krona must be worth 16 cents. Why? A higher price of a krona, like 20 cents, would mean that steel would cost $200 per ton (1000 kronor at 20 cents each) in Sweden but only $160 per ton in the United States. Then all foreign customers would shop for their steel in the United States. Similarly, any exchange rate below 16 cents per krona would send all the steel business to Sweden.

EXERCISE
Show why an exchange rate of 12 cents per krona is too low.

The purchasing-power parity theory is used to make long-run predictions about the effects of inflation on exchange rates. To continue our example, suppose that over a five-year period, prices in the United States rise by 25 percent while prices in Sweden rise by 100 percent. The purchasing-power parity theory predicts that the krona will depreciate relative to the dollar. It also predicts the amount of the depreciation. After the inflation, American steel costs $200 per ton (one-fourth more than $160), while Swedish steel costs 2000 kronor per ton (100 percent more than 1000 kronor). For these two prices to be equivalent, 2000 kronor must be worth $200, or one krona must be worth 10 cents. The krona, therefore, must have fallen from 16 cents to 10 cents.

According to the purchasing-power parity theory, differences in domestic inflation rates are a major cause of adjustments in exchange rates. If one country has a faster rate of inflation than another, then its exchange rate should be depreciating.

For many years, the theory seemed to work tolerably well. While precise numerical predictions based on purchasing power parity calculations were not very accurate (see the accompanying box), nations with higher inflation did at least experience depreciating currencies. But in the 1980s, even this broke down. For example, while the U.S. inflation rate was higher than both West Germany's and Japan's between 1980 and 1985, the dollar nonetheless rose relative to both the mark and the yen. Clearly, the theory is missing something. There are a number of complications which the purchasing-power theory ignores.

First, changes in any of the interferences with free trade, such as tariffs and quotas, can upset simple calculations based on purchasing-power parity. For example, if Swedish prices rise faster than American prices but, at the same time, foreign countries erect tariff barriers to keep American (but not Swedish) steel out, then the krona might not have to depreciate.

Second, some goods and services cannot be traded across national frontiers. Land and buildings are only the most obvious examples; most services can be traded only to a limited extent (as when tourists from one country have their hair cut in another). Inflation rates for goods and services that are *not tradable* have little bearing on exchange rates.

Third, few of the goods that different nations produce and trade are as uniform as the Swedish and American steel in our example. A Volvo and a Buick, for example, are not identical products. So the price of a Volvo *in U.S. dollars*

Purchasing-Power Parity and the Big Mac

In 1983, *The New York Times* used a well-known international commodity to assess the purchasing-power parity theory. As this article shows, the theory did not work very well.

The French have been most vociferous in complaining that the dollar's value has been too high. But if the cost of lunch at McDonald's is any guide, it is the franc, more than the dollar, that should be devalued.

Theoretically, at least, if all exchange rates were where they should be, prices of the same goods should be identical in every country. Using McDonald's as an example, exchange rates, indeed, are out of line and the dollar is overvalued against all the major currencies, except the franc.

Last Wednesday in New York, it cost $3.39 to buy a Big Mac, a small order of fries and a small Coke. This was substantially higher than the cost of a comparable McDonald's lunch in five major foreign cities.

In Paris, however, the dollar-equivalent price was $3.82, based on the franc's June 28 value of 13.08 cents. The biggest bargain was in Amsterdam, where the price of a McDonald's lunch was only $2.40. In Switzerland, the cost of a comparable meal was $3.23; in Tokyo, $2.62; in Germany, $2.57; and in London, $2.40.

If the seven currencies were to be made equal on the "MacIndex," using the New York price as a yardstick, the Swiss franc would have to be revalued upward by 4.7 percent against the dollar; the Japanese yen 22.7 percent; the German mark 24 percent; the British pound 25.7 percent and the Dutch guilder 29.2 percent. The French franc would have to be devalued 11.3 percent.

SOURCE: *The New York Times*, July 3, 1983.

AUTHORS' NOTE: Actually, the theory did not do all that badly. Over the next several months, the French franc depreciated 10.9 percent relative to the dollar.

---

can rise faster than the price of a Buick without driving Volvos out of the market entirely. On balance:

Most economists believe that other factors are much more important than relative price levels for exchange rate determination in the short run. But in the long run, purchasing-power parity plays an important role.

Economic Activity and Exchange Rates: The Medium Run

Since consumer spending increases when income expands and decreases when income contracts, the same is likely to happen to spending on imported goods. For this reason:

A country's imports will rise quickly when its economy is booming and slowly when its economy is stagnating.

We have already illustrated this point with Figure 19–2. There we saw that a boom in the United States would shift the demand curve for marks outward and therefore lead to an appreciation of the mark (depreciation of the dollar) as American imports from Germany surge. However, if Germany were booming at the same time, German citizens would be buying more American exports, which would shift the supply curve of marks outward. On balance, the value of the dollar might or might not fall. What matters is whether exports are growing faster than imports. The general lesson is that:

Holding other things equal, a country that grows faster than the rest of the world normally finds its currency depreciating because its imports grow faster than its exports, so that its demand curve for foreign currency shifts outward more rapidly than its supply curve.

A recent policy controversy involving the United States, West Germany, and Japan is a case in point. As the dollar fell in 1986 and 1987, the U.S. government tried to persuade the Germans and Japanese to give their economies a boost as a way of spurring U.S. exports and propping up the dollar.

Interest Rates and Exchange Rates: The Short Run

While economic activity is important for exchange rate determination in the medium run, "other things" often are not equal in the short run. Specifically, one factor that often seems to call the tune in determining exchange rate movements in the short run is *interest rate differentials*. There is an enormous fund of so-called hot money — owned by banks, multinational corporations, and wealthy individuals of all nations, and amounting to perhaps a trillion dollars — that travels around the globe in search of the highest interest rates.

Thus suppose that British government bonds are paying an 8 percent rate of interest when yields on equally safe American government securities rise to 10 percent. British investors will be attracted by the high interest rates in the United States and will offer pounds for sale in order to buy dollars, planning to use those dollars to buy American securities. At the same time, American investors will find investing in the United States more attractive than ever, so fewer pounds will be demanded by Americans.

When the demand schedule falls and the supply curve rises, the effect on price is predictable: The pound will depreciate, as Figure 19–3 shows. In the figure, the supply curve of pounds shifts outward from $S_1 S_1$ to $S_2 S_2$ when British

Figure 19–3
THE EFFECT OF A RISE IN U.S. INTEREST RATES
When the U.S. raises its interest rates, more English investors will want to buy American bonds, and so the supply curve of pounds will shift outward from $S_1 S_1$ to $S_2 S_2$. At the same time, fewer Americans will seek to buy British bonds, so the demand curve for pounds will shift inward from $D_1 D_1$ to $D_2 D_2$. The combined effect of these two shifts is to move the market equilibrium from point E_1 to point E_2. The British pound depreciates, and the dollar appreciates.

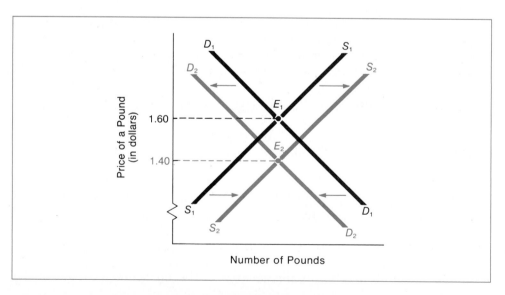

investors seek to sell pounds in order to purchase U.S. securities. At the same time, American investors wish to buy fewer pounds because they no longer wish to invest in British securities. Thus the demand curve shifts inward from $D_1 D_1$ to $D_2 D_2$. The result, in our example, is a depreciation of the pound from \$1.60 to \$1.40. In general:

Holding other things equal, countries with high interest rates are able to attract more capital than are countries with low interest rates. Thus a rise in interest rates often will lead to an appreciation of the currency, and a drop in interest rates will lead to a depreciation.

This factor, most experts in international finance believe, is the major determinant of exchange rates in the short run. It certainly played a predominant role in the stunning movements of the U.S. dollar during the 1980s. Beginning in 1980, American interest rates rose well above comparable interest rates abroad. In consequence, foreign capital was attracted here, American capital stayed at home, and the dollar soared. Then, in the mid-1980s, the gap between U.S. and foreign interest rates narrowed and the dollar fell.

Market Determination of Exchange Rates: Summary

We can summarize this discussion of exchange rate determination in free markets as follows:

1. Currency values generally will be *appreciating* in countries whose inflation rates are lower than the rest of the world because buyers in foreign countries will demand their goods, and thus drive up the currency.

2. Exchange rates would also be expected to rise in countries whose levels of economic activity are lower than average, because these countries will be importing rather little.

3. We expect to find appreciating currencies in countries whose interest rates are high because these countries will attract capital from all over the world.

Reversing each of these, we expect that currencies will be *depreciating* in countries with relatively high inflation rates, or high levels of economic activity, or low interest rates.

Fixed Exchange Rates and the Definition of the Balance of Payments

Some exchange rates today are truly floating, determined by the forces of supply and demand without government interference. But many are not. For this reason, we turn our attention next to the opposite of floating exchange rates, a system of **fixed exchange rates**, or rates that are set by government. Naturally, under such a system the exchange rate, being fixed, is not closely watched. Instead, international financial specialists focus on a country's **balance of payments** — a term we must now define.

> Fixed exchange rates are rates set by government decisions and maintained by government actions.

To understand what the balance of payments is, look at Figure 19–4, which depicts a situation that might represent, say, Great Britain before its major devaluation in 1967 — an *overvalued* currency. While the supply and demand curves for British pounds indicate an equilibrium exchange rate of \$2.40 to the pound (point E), the British government is keeping the rate at

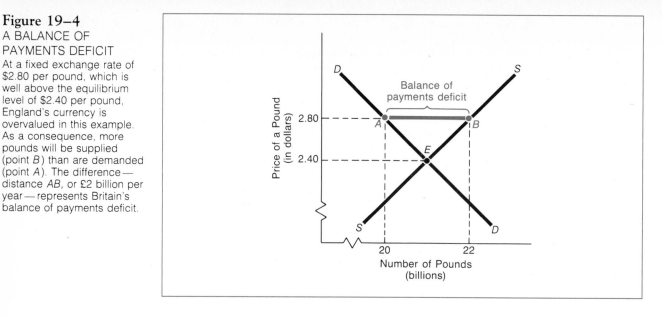

Figure 19–4

A BALANCE OF PAYMENTS DEFICIT

At a fixed exchange rate of $2.80 per pound, which is well above the equilibrium level of $2.40 per pound, England's currency is overvalued in this example. As a consequence, more pounds will be supplied (point *B*) than are demanded (point *A*). The difference— distance *AB*, or £2 billion per year—represents Britain's balance of payments deficit.

The **balance of payments deficit** is the amount by which the quantity supplied of a country's currency (per year) exceeds the quantity demanded. Balance of payments deficits arise whenever the exchange rate is pegged at an artificially high level.

The **balance of payments surplus** is the amount by which the quantity demanded of a country's currency (per year) exceeds the quantity supplied. Balance of payments surpluses arise whenever the exchange rate is pegged at an artificially low level.

$2.80. Notice that at $2.80 more people are supplying pounds than are demanding them. In the example, suppliers are selling £22 billion per year, but demanders are purchasing only £20 billion.

This gap between the £22 billion that some people sell and the £20 billion that other people buy is what we mean by Britain's **balance of payments deficit**—£2 billion per year in this case. It is shown by the horizontal distance between points *A* and *B* in Figure 19–4.

How can market forces be flouted in this way? Since sales and purchases on any market must be equal, as a simple piece of arithmetic, the excess of quantity supplied over quantity demanded of British currency (£2 billion per year in this example) must be bought by the Bank of England, Britain's central bank. In buying these pounds, it must give up some of the gold and foreign currencies that it keeps as *reserves*. Thus the Bank of England would be losing £2 billion in reserves per year as the cost of keeping the pound at $2.80.

Naturally, this cannot go on forever; the reserves eventually will run out. And this is the fatal flaw in the system of fixed exchange rates. Once speculators become convinced that the exchange rate can be held only a short while longer, they will sell pounds in massive amounts rather than hold on to a currency whose value they soon expect to fall sharply. The supply curve of pounds will shift outward drastically, as shown in Figure 19–5, causing a sharp rise in the balance of payments deficit (from £2 billion to £4 billion in the example). This is called a "run" on the currency. Lacking sufficient reserves, the central bank will have to permit the exchange rate to fall to its equilibrium level, and this might amount to an even larger devaluation than would have been required before the speculative run on the pound began.

For an example of the reverse case, a severely *undervalued* currency, let us consider Germany in 1973. Figure 19–6 depicts demand and supply curves for marks that intersect at an equilibrium price of 40 cents per mark (point *E* in the diagram). Yet, in the example, we suppose that the German authorities are holding the rate at 35 cents. At this rate, the quantity of marks demanded (50 billion) greatly exceeds the quantity supplied (40 billion). The difference is Germany's **balance of payments surplus**, and is shown by the horizontal distance *AB*.

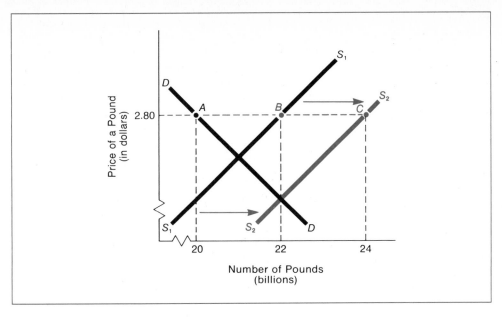

Figure 19–5
A SPECULATIVE RUN ON
THE POUND
When speculators become
convinced that a devaluation
of the pound is in the offing,
they will rush to sell pounds.
Their actions shift the supply
curve outward from $S_1 S_1$ to
$S_2 S_2$ and, in the process,
widen England's balance of
payments deficit from AB to
AC.

Germany can keep the rate at 35 cents only by providing the marks that foreigners want to buy: 10 billion marks per year in this example. In return, it receives U.S. dollars, British pounds, French francs, gold, and so on. All of this serves to increase Germany's reserves of foreign currencies. But notice the important difference between this case and Britain's overvalued pound.

The accumulation of reserves rarely will *force* a central bank to revalue in the way that depletion of reserves can force a devaluation.

This was another weakness of the system of fixed exchange rates that prevailed between 1944 and 1971. In principle, imbalances in exchange rates could be cured either by a devaluation by the country with a balance of payments deficit or by an upward revaluation by the country with a balance of

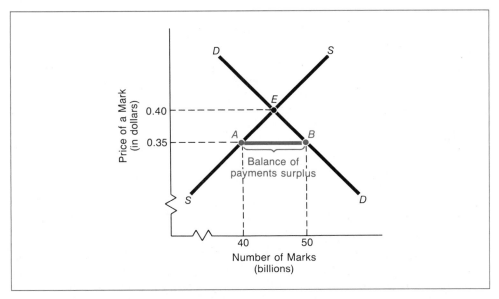

Figure 19–6
A BALANCE OF
PAYMENTS SURPLUS
In this example, Germany's
currency is undervalued at
35 cents per mark since the
equilibrium exchange rate is
40 cents per mark.
Consequently, more marks
are being demanded (point
B) than are being supplied
(point A). The gap between
quantity demanded and
quantity supplied — distance
AB, or 10 billion marks per
year — measures Germany's
balance of payments surplus.

payments surplus. In practice, though, it was almost always the deficit countries that were forced to act.

Why did the surplus countries refuse to revalue? One reason was a stubborn refusal to recognize some basic economic realities. They viewed the disequilibrium as the problem of the deficit countries and believed that the deficit countries, therefore, should take the corrective steps. This, of course, is nonsense. Some currencies are overvalued *because* some other currencies are undervalued. In fact, the two statements mean exactly the same thing.

The other reason why exporters in Germany, Japan, and other surplus countries resisted upward revaluations is that such actions would make their products more expensive to foreigners and thus cut into their sales. And these exporters had the political clout to make their views stick. Meanwhile, since the values of the mark and the yen on world markets were artificially held down, German and Japanese consumers were put in the unenviable position of having to pay more for imported goods than they need have paid. Rather than buy these excessively expensive foreign goods, they watched domestically produced goods go overseas in return for pieces of paper (dollars, francs, pounds, and so on).

Defining the Balance of Payments in Practice

From the preceding discussion it may seem that measuring a nation's balance of payments position is a simple task: We simply count up the private demand for and supply of its currency and subtract quantity supplied from quantity demanded. Conceptually, this is all there is to it. But in practice, the difficulties are great because we never have statistics on the number of dollars demanded and supplied. There is no way to observe these directly.

If we look at actual market transactions, we will see that the number of U.S. dollars actually *purchased* and the number of U.S. dollars actually *sold* are identical. Unless someone has made a bookkeeping error, this must always be so. How, then, can we recognize a balance of payments surplus or deficit? Easy, you say. Just look at the transactions of the central bank, whose purchases or sales must make up the difference between private demand and private supply. If the Federal Reserve is buying dollars, its purchases measure our balance of payments deficit. If it is selling, its sales represent our balance of payments surplus.

Thus the suggestion is to measure the balance of payments by *excluding official transactions among governments*. This is roughly how the balance of payments surplus or deficit is defined today, though, for a variety of complicated reasons, the U.S. government decided long ago to stop publishing any official statistic called "the balance of payments deficit." Instead, all foreign transactions are listed, and readers are invited to define the balance of payments in any way they wish. Let us now see just what data are published in these official accounts.

The U.S. Balance of Payments Accounts

Using 1986 as an example, Table 19–2 shows the official U.S. balance of payments accounts. There is nothing that purports to measure America's overall balance of payments surplus or deficit. The top section of the table summarizes America's trade in currently produced goods and services—the so-called *current account*. The positive or negative sign attached to each entry indicates whether the transaction represented a *gain* (+) or a *loss* (−) of foreign currency.

Table 19–2
U.S. BALANCE OF PAYMENTS ACCOUNTS, 1986 (billions of dollars)

Current Account

(1) Balance of trade		−$144.3
(2) Merchandise exports	+224.4	
(3) Merchandise imports	−368.7	
(4) Net military transactions		−3.7
(5) Travel and transportation (net)		−9.9
(6) Net income from investments and other services		+32.2
(7) Balance on goods and services (Lines 1 plus 5 plus 6)		−125.7
(8) Unilateral transfers		−15.7
(9) Private	−1.7	
(10) U.S. government (nonmilitary)	−14.0	
(11) Balance on current account (Lines 7 plus 8)		−141.4

Capital Account

(12) Net private capital flows		+84.3
(13) Change in U.S. assets abroad	−94.4	
(14) Change in foreign assets in the U.S.	+178.7	
(15) Net governmental capital flows		+33.1
(16) Change in U.S. government assets	−1.6	
(17) Change in foreign official assets in the U.S.	+34.7	
(18) Balance on capital account (Lines 12 plus 15)		+117.4

Addendum

(19) Sum of lines (11) and (18)	−24.0
(20) Statistical discrepancy	−24.0

SOURCE: *Survey of Current Business*, June 1987. Organization of table changed by authors.

Looking first at the top of the table, we see that in merchandise transactions, Americans imported about $144 billion more than they exported, leading to a whopping deficit in what is called the *balance of trade* (see lines 1–3). Because it is available on a monthly basis, this is the number reported most frequently by the news media. The incredibly large trade deficit shown in line 1, probably the largest ever run by any nation, caused great consternation and political controversy. For example, it was a major factor behind the drive for more trade protection that we discussed in Chapter 18.

The entry in line 4 indicates the net effect of a large number of dollars spent by U.S. military installations abroad (transactions that cost us foreign currency) and a large amount of foreign currency earned by selling armaments. On balance, these cost the United States about $3.7 billion in foreign currency. Line 5 shows that in 1986 American tourists and shippers spent about $10 billion more on foreign services than foreign tourists and shippers spent here. Line 6 displays our major source of foreign currency earnings in the services category: We earned about $32 billion more on our investments overseas (and on some other miscellaneous services) than foreign investors earned here.

Line 7 gives the net result of all trading in goods and services — *the balance on goods and services*. The entry in line 7 means that the United States spent over $125 billion more than it received during 1986. Lines 8–10 indicate the so-called unilateral transfers, including both private gifts to foreigners and official foreign aid. Together these cost us over $15 billion in foreign currency. When these unilateral transfers are subtracted from the deficit on goods and services, we find (in line 11) a huge deficit of $141.4 billion in America's *current account*. Many economists take the balance on current account to be the most basic measure of a nation's international transactions.

But this hardly represents our "balance of payments," as it leaves out all purchases and sales of assets. This group of transactions is shown in the *capital account* (lines 12–18). Line 12 shows that, on balance, foreign individuals and businesses bought about $84 billion more in assets here than private American investors bought from foreigners. The net entry is *plus* $84.3 billion because $94.4 billion dollars flowed *out of* the United States to buy foreign assets (line 13), while $178.7 billion in foreign money flowed *into* the United States to buy American assets (line 14).

This large surplus in private capital flows, coupled with a much larger deficit in the current account, left the United States with a gigantic balance of payments deficit in 1986. How are such deficits financed? Normally, by government capital flows in the opposite direction (such as when foreign governments buy U.S. government bonds). Line 15 tells us that such was the case in 1986. Foreign governments bought $34.7 billion worth of U.S. assets (line 17), while our government bought only $1.6 billion in foreign assets (line 16), leaving a large surplus in governmental capital flows of $33.1 billion (line 15).

You may notice that the accounts do not balance. When we add up the current account (line 11) plus the overall (private plus government) capital account (line 18), we get a $24.0 billion deficit (line 19). But, of course, this is impossible. Since it is a simple matter of arithmetic that the two accounts together must balance (dollars purchased = dollars sold), the difference is considered a *statistical discrepancy* (line 20). While part of this huge discrepancy simply comes from errors in data collection and computation, the lion's share reflects the U.S. government's inability to monitor all the flows of money, goods, and services across its borders. When we fail to record the cargo of a truck hauling U.S. goods to Canada, we overstate our current account deficit. When we fail to record foreign capital movements into the United States, we understate our capital account surplus. Such errors and omissions have left a big statistical discrepancy in the U.S. balance of payments accounts for years.

A Bit of History: The Gold Standard

It is hard to find examples of strictly fixed exchange rates in the historical record. About the only time exchange rates were truly fixed was under the old **gold standard**, at least when it was practiced in its ideal form.[3] Under the gold standard, fixed exchange rates were maintained by an automatic equilibrating mechanism that went something like this: All currencies were defined in terms of gold; indeed, some were actually made of gold. When a nation had a deficit in its balance of payments, this meant, essentially, that more gold was flowing *out* than was flowing *in*. Since the domestic money supply was based on gold, losing gold to foreigners meant that the quantity of money *automatically* fell. This raised interest rates and attracted foreign capital. At the same time, the restrictive "monetary policy" pulled down national output and prices, thus discouraging imports and encouraging exports. The balance of payments problem quickly rectified itself. This meant, however, that:

Under the gold standard, no nation had control of its domestic monetary policy, and therefore no country could control its domestic economy very well.

[3]As a matter of fact, while the gold standard lasted (on and off) for hundreds of years, it was rarely practiced in its ideal form. Except for a brief period of fixed exchange rates in the late nineteenth and early twentieth centuries, there were periodic adjustments of exchange rates even under the gold standard.

At least in principle, the effects on surplus countries were perfectly symmetrical under the gold standard. A balance of payments surplus led, via gold inflows, to an increase in the domestic money supply, whether the surplus country liked the idea or not. This raised prices and output, thereby increasing imports and decreasing exports. And it also lowered interest rates, thereby encouraging outflows of capital. Because of these automatic adjustments, nations rarely reached the point at which devaluations or revaluations were necessary. Exchange rates were fixed as long as countries abided by the rules of the gold standard game.

In addition to the loss of control over domestic monetary conditions, the gold standard posed one other serious difficulty.

A fundamental problem with the gold standard was that the world's commerce was at the mercy of gold discoveries.

Discoveries of gold meant higher prices in the long run and higher real economic activity in the short run, through the standard monetary-policy mechanisms that we studied in Part 4. And when the supply of gold did not keep pace with growth of the world economy, prices had to fall in the long run and employment had to fall in the short run.

The Bretton Woods System and the International Monetary Fund

The gold standard, which had faltered many times before, finally collapsed for good amid the financial chaos of the Great Depression of the 1930s and the Second World War. Without it, the world struggled through an almost complete breakdown in international trade.

Then, as World War II drew to a close, with much of Europe in ruins and with the United States holding the lion's share of the free world's reserves, officials of the industrial nations met at Bretton Woods, New Hampshire, in 1944 to try to establish a stable monetary environment that would facilitate world trade. Since the dollar was the only "strong" currency at that time, it was natural for them to turn to the dollar as the basis of the new international economic order.

That is just what they did. The Bretton Woods agreements reestablished a system of fixed exchange rates based not on the old gold standard but on the free convertibility of the U.S. dollar into gold. The United States agreed to buy or sell gold to maintain the $35 per ounce price that had been established by President Franklin Roosevelt in 1933. The other signatory nations, which had almost no gold in any case, agreed to buy and sell dollars to maintain their exchange rates at agreed-upon levels. Thus all currencies were indirectly on a modified "gold standard." A holder of French francs, for example, could exchange these for dollars at (roughly) 5 francs per dollar and then exchange these into gold at $35 per ounce. In this way, the value of the franc was fixed at 175 francs per ounce of gold (5 francs per dollar times 35 dollars per ounce). The new system was dubbed the **gold-exchange system**, and it was often referred to as the **Bretton Woods system**.

The **International Monetary Fund (IMF)** was set up to police and manage this new system. Using funds that had been contributed by member countries, the IMF was empowered to make loans to countries that were running low on reserves. A change in exchange rates was to be permitted only in the case of a "fundamental disequilibrium" in a nation's balance of payments—for it was believed that only relatively fixed exchange rates could provide the stable climate needed to restore world trade.

Of course, the Bretton Woods conferees did not define clearly what a "fundamental disequilibrium" was, nor could they have. As the system evolved, it came to mean a chronic *deficit* in the balance of payments of sizable proportions. Such nations would then *devalue* their currencies relative to the dollar. So the system was not really one of fixed exchange rates but rather one where rates were "fixed until further notice."

Several flaws in the Bretton Woods system have already been mentioned in our discussion of the pure system of fixed exchange rates. First, since devaluations were permitted only after a long run of balance of payments deficits, these devaluations (a) could be clearly foreseen and (b) normally had to be large. Speculators then saw opportunities for profit and would "attack" weak currencies with a wave of selling.

This problem led many economists to question whether the system of fixed exchange rates was really providing the stable climate for world trade that had been intended. Was a system where rates were constant for long periods and then altered by large amounts really more conducive to international trade than one where overvalued currencies would gradually depreciate, as they would under a system of floating rates?

The second problem arose from the custom that deficit nations were expected to devalue when forced to, while surplus nations (mainly Germany and Japan) could resist upward revaluations. Since the U.S. dollar defined the monetary value of gold (at $35 per ounce), America was the one nation in the world that had no way to devalue its currency relative to gold, no matter how "fundamental" the disequilibrium became. The only way exchange rates between the dollar and foreign currencies could change was if the surplus nations revalued their currencies upward relative to the dollar. They did not do this frequently enough, so the United States, with its chronically overvalued currency, ran persistent balance of payments deficits in the 1960s.

Adjustment Mechanisms Under the Bretton Woods System

Under the Bretton Woods system, devaluation was viewed as a last resort, to be used only after other methods of adjusting to payments imbalances had failed. What were these other methods?

We have already encountered most of them in our discussion of exchange rate determination in free markets (see pages 409–15). Any factor that increases the demand for, say, British pounds or that reduces the supply will push the value of the pound upward if it is free to adjust. If, however, the exchange rate is pegged, it is the balance of payments deficit rather than the exchange rate that will adjust when supply of or demand for a nation's money changes. Specifically, the British balance of payments deficit will shrink if either the demand for pounds increases or the supply decreases.

The two panels of Figure 19–7 illustrate this adjustment. In each case, Great Britain has a payments deficit, since the official exchange rate ($2.80) exceeds the equilibrium rate ($2.40). The deficit starts at *AB* in each diagram. Then either the demand curve moves outward as in part (a), or the supply curve moves inward as in part (b). With the exchange rate held at $2.80, the balance of payments deficit shrinks—to *CB* in part (a) or to *AC* in part (b).

Referring back to our earlier discussions of the factors that underlie the demand and supply curves, then, we see that one way a deficit nation can

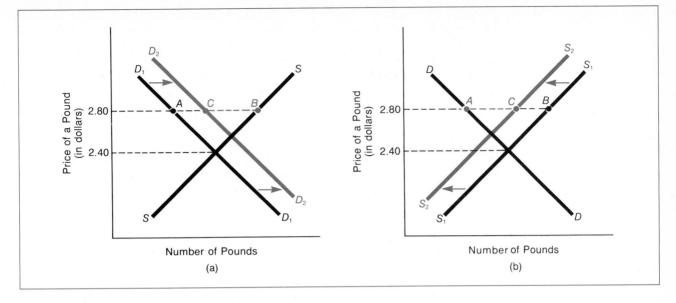

Number of Pounds
(a)

Number of Pounds
(b)

improve its balance of payments is to *reduce its aggregate demand,* thus discouraging imports and cutting down its demand for foreign currency. Another is to *slow its rate of inflation,* thus encouraging exports and discouraging imports. Finally, it can *raise its interest rates* in order to attract more foreign capital.

In a word, deficit nations were expected to follow restrictive monetary and fiscal policies *voluntarily* just as they would *automatically* have done under the old gold standard. However, just as under the gold standard, this medicine was often unpalatable, so deficit nations frequently resorted to a bewildering variety of **exchange controls** — laws and regulations that made it very difficult for its nationals to sell their own currency to get foreign exchange. Many countries still have such controls.

Surplus nations could, of course, have taken the opposite measures: pursuing expansive monetary and fiscal policies to increase economic growth and lower interest rates. Such actions, by increasing the supply of the country's currency and reducing the demand for it, would have reduced the balance of payments surplus. But often the countries did not relish the inflation that accompanies expansionary policies; and so, once again, they left the burden of adjustment to the deficit nations. The general point about fixed exchange rates is that:

Under a system of fixed exchange rates, the government of a country loses some control over its domestic economy. There may be times when balance of payments considerations force it to contract its economy in order to cut down its demand for foreign currency, even though domestic needs are calling for expansion. Conversely, there may be times when the domestic economy needs to be reined in, but balance of payments considerations suggest expansion.

The Bretton Woods system worked fairly well for a number of years, but it finally broke down over its inability to devalue the U.S. dollar. In August 1971, the rapid depletion of America's reserves and the accumulation of foreign debts resulting from America's chronic balance of payments deficits forced President Richard M. Nixon to end fixed exchange rates. He unilaterally abolished the gold exchange system by announcing that the United States would no longer peg the value of the dollar by buying and selling gold. After some futile

Figure 19–7
ADJUSTING TO BALANCE OF PAYMENTS DEFICITS
The two parts of this diagram illustrate alternative ways to cut England's balance of payments deficit while maintaining the exchange rate at $2.80 per pound. Part (a) might represent a reduction in British inflation, which would increase world demand for her export products. Or it could represent a rise in British interest rates, which would attract foreign capital. Part (b) might represent a reduction in British incomes, which would diminish English appetites for foreign goods. In either case, whether demand rises or supply falls, the balance of payments deficit is reduced: from *AB* to *CB* in part (a) and from *AB* to *AC* in part (b).

Exchange controls are laws restricting the exchange of one nation's currency for another's.

attempts by the major trading nations to reestablish fixed rates in 1971 and 1972, the Bretton Woods system ended in 1973.

Most observers today agree that the gold-exchange system could not have survived the incredible events of the 1970s in any case. The worldwide inflationary boom of 1972, the poor food harvests in 1972–1974, the huge increases in the price of oil in 1973–1974 and again in 1979–1980, and the great worldwide recessions of 1974–1976 and the 1980s created a world in which the major countries were experiencing dramatically different inflation rates.

For example, between 1975 and 1985, inflation averaged 4 percent per year in Germany, 7 percent in the United States, 11 percent in Great Britain, and 15 percent in Italy. As the purchasing-power theory reminds us, large differences in inflation rates call for *major* changes in currency values. The Bretton Woods system was ill-suited to handle such major changes.

Why Try to Fix Exchange Rates?

In view of these and other severe problems with the Bretton Woods system, why did the international financial community work so hard to maintain fixed rates for so many years? The answer is that floating exchange rates, determined in free markets by supply and demand, also pose problems.

Chief among these is the possibility that freely floating rates might prove to be highly variable rates, which add an unwanted element of risk to foreign trade. For example, if the exchange rate is 16 cents to the French franc, then a 2000-franc Parisian dress will cost $320. But should the franc appreciate to 20 cents, this same dress would cost $400. An American department store thinking of buying this dress may need to place its order far in advance and will want to know the cost *in dollars*. It may be worried about the possibility that the value of the franc will rise, so that the dress will cost more than $320. And such worries might inhibit trade.

"Then it's agreed. Until the dollar firms up, we let the clamshell float."
Drawing by Ed Fisher © 1971, The New Yorker Magazine, Inc.

There are two answers to this concern. First, we could hope that freely floating rates would prove not to be very volatile. Prices of many domestic consumer goods, for example, are determined by supply and demand in free markets and yet do not fluctuate unduly.

Second, speculators might relieve business firms of exchange rate risks—for a fee, of course. Consider the deparment store example. If French francs cost 16 cents today, the department store manager can assure herself of paying exactly $320 for the dress several months from now by arranging for a speculator to deliver francs to her at 16 cents on the day she needs them. If the franc appreciates in the interim, it is the speculator, not the department store, that will take the financial beating. (And, of course, if the franc depreciates, the speculator will pocket the profits.) Thus speculators play an important role in a system of floating exchange rates.

The widespread fears that speculative activity in free markets will lead to wild gyrations in prices, while occasionally valid, are more often unfounded. The reason is simple. International currency speculators, if they are to make profits, must buy a currency when its value is low (thus helping to support the currency by pushing up its demand curve) and sell it when its value is high (thus holding down the price by adding to the supply curve).

This means that, if they are successful, speculators will be coming into the market as *buyers* just when demand is weak (or when supply is strong), and coming in as *sellers* just when demand is strong (or supply is scant). In doing so, they will help limit price fluctuations. Looked at the other way around, speculators can destabilize prices only if they are systematically willing to lose money.[4]

Notice the stark contrast to the system of fixed exchange rates in which speculation often led to wild "runs" on currencies that were on the verge of devaluation. Speculative activity, which may well be destabilizing under fixed rates, is likely to be stabilizing under floating rates.

We do not mean to imply here that there are no difficulties at all under floating exchange rates. At the very least, speculators will demand a fee for their services—a fee that adds to the costs of trading across national borders. In addition, it may be impossible to eliminate all exchange-rate risks through speculation. Currently, for example, contracts on foreign currencies offered in speculative markets cover at most a few months. Thus no business can protect itself from exchange-rate changes over periods measured in years.

The experience under floating rates since 1973 has delivered clear verdicts on these two issues. First, exchange rates have in fact proven to be extremely volatile—much more volatile than advocates of floating rates anticipated. This volatility has led, in recent years, to more and more talk about moving back toward fixed exchange rates. Second, however, international trade has flourished despite all this volatility.

The Current Mixed System

Our current international financial system—where some currencies are still pegged in the old Bretton Woods manner, others are floating freely, and many more are floating subject to government interferences—has evolved gradually since President Nixon severed the dollar's link to gold. Though it continues to change and adapt, at least three features are evident.

The first is the decline in the notion that exchange rates should be fixed for relatively long periods of time. The demand by many countries in the early 1970s that the world quickly return to fixed exchange rates had largely subsided by the mid-1970s. Even where rates are still pegged to the dollar, devaluations and revaluations are now much more frequent—and smaller—than they were in the 1944–1971 period. Most free-world currency rates change slightly on a day-to-day basis, and market forces generally determine the basic trends, up or down. Even advocates of greater fixity in exchange rates generally propose that governments keep rates within certain *ranges*, rather than literally fix them as under Bretton Woods.

Second, however, some central banks do not hesitate to intervene to moderate exchange movements whenever they feel that such actions are appropriate. Typically, these interventions are aimed at ironing out transitory fluctuations. But there are times in which central banks oppose basic trends in exchange rates. Deficit nations buy their own currencies to prevent them from depreciating. Surplus nations sell their own currencies to prevent them from appreciating. While we certainly no longer have many fixed exchange rates, many of the major currencies are floating less than freely. The terms **"dirty float"** or **"managed float"** have been coined to describe this mongrel system.

The third unmistakable feature of the present international monetary system is the virtual elimination of any role for gold. The trend away from gold actually began before President Nixon's dramatic announcement in 1971, and

[4]See Discussion Question 11 at the end of the chapter.

by now it is only a minor exaggeration to say that gold plays no role in the world's financial system. Nowadays there is a *free market* in gold, which enables those who wish to invest in gold—dentists, jewelers, industrial users, speculators, and ordinary citizens who think of gold as a good store of value—to buy or sell as they wish. The price of gold, determined each day by the law of supply and demand, has proved to be quite volatile. Fortunes have been made and lost by investors in gold.

Figure 19–8
THE UPS AND DOWNS OF THE DOLLAR, 1970–1987
This graph charts the behavior of the international value of the dollar relative to a basket of ten major foreign currencies since 1970. (The index is based on March 1973 = 100.) The net change in the value of the dollar since 1972 has not been large, but the ups and downs have been pronounced. The stunning climb of the dollar from its 1980 low to its 1985 high stands out on the graph, as do the sharp declines in 1971–1973, 1977–1978, and 1985–1986.
SOURCE: Federal Reserve System.

Recent Developments in International Financial Markets

The Dancing Dollar

We mentioned earlier that floating exchange rates have not been stable exchange rates. No currency illustrates this better than the U.S. dollar. (See Figure 19–8.)

After several years of considerable stability, the international value of the dollar plummeted from late 1977 until late 1978. Compared to a weighted average of currencies of other nations, the dollar depreciated by 17 percent— enough to grab headlines in the United States. Where would it all end, Americans wondered? Then a rescue mission arrested the fall, and the dollar stabilized for almost two years.

Starting in mid-1980, however, the dollar began rising like a rocket. For example, in 1980 a U.S. dollar bought less than 2 German marks, about 4 French francs, and about 830 Italian lira. By the time it peaked in February 1985, the dollar could buy more than 3 German marks, about 10 French francs, and over 2000 Italian lira. The mighty dollar was a blessing to Americans who

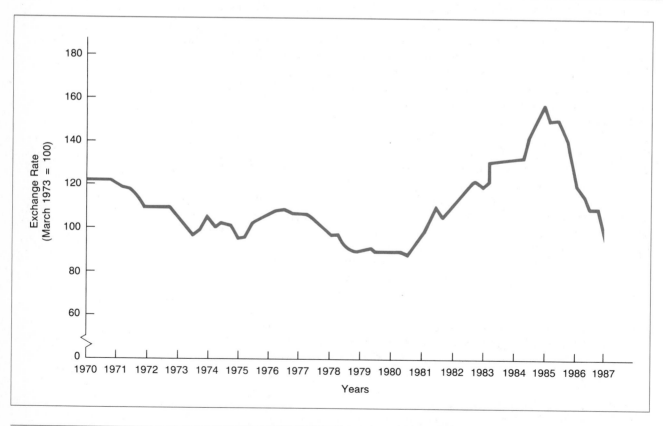

traveled abroad or who bought foreign goods because foreign prices, when translated to dollars by the exchange rate, looked cheap to Americans.[5]

But the arithmetic worked the other way for U.S. firms seeking to sell their goods abroad; foreign buyers found everything American very expensive.[6] It was no surprise, therefore, that as the dollar climbed our exports fell, our imports rose, and our current account registered all-time record deficits. An expensive currency, Americans came to learn, is a mixed blessing.

Since early 1985, the value of the dollar has generally been falling against most major currencies and is now back down to 1981 levels. The cheaper dollar is curbing American appetites for imports and alleviating some of the problems of our export industries. However, rising prices for imported goods and foreign vacations have been a source of consternation to many American consumers. An uncertainty over the future of the dollar may have contributed to the stock market crash of October 1987.

The European Monetary System

As noted earlier, floating exchange rates are no magical cure-all. One particular problem beset the members of the European Economic Community (EEC). These Common Market countries seek a unified market like the United States and have a long-range goal of establishing a single currency for all member countries. Floating rates would make this goal impossible. So in 1973 some of the member countries entered into an agreement whereby exchange rates among their currencies would remain relatively *fixed* while Common Market currencies as a group would rise or fall *relative to the rest of the world*.

Within a short time, however, both Britain and Italy found themselves unable to maintain parity with the strong currencies of Germany and the Netherlands. Britain was the first to let the pound float, but soon Italy and France also had to devalue relative to the mark. In 1979 the arrangement was strengthened and formalized into the **European Monetary System (EMS),** which currently has eight member nations. The EMS makes periodic adjustments to exchange rates which get out of line with the others, and it is widely regarded as the first step, albeit a small one, toward a unified European currency. In practice, the German mark is the dominant currency in the EMS, playing a role within Europe analogous to that played by the dollar under the Bretton Woods system.

The LDC Debt Problem[7]

The enormous debts of many less developed countries (LDCs), and the difficulties they are having in meeting their burdensome interest payments, have frequently grabbed the headlines during the 1980s. Many experts feel that the still-unresolved LDC debt problem poses the most serious threat to the stability of the international monetary system.

The seeds of the problem were sown in the 1970s. When real interest rates were low, many of these countries, particularly in Latin America, borrowed heavily to finance their development. In some cases, the money was put to good use. But, in others, unwise policies frittered away the funds. Then, in the 1980s, well-managed and poorly managed countries alike were hit by three common shocks. First, the worldwide recession of the 1980s made it harder for them to earn foreign currency by exporting goods to the industrial countries;

[5]EXAMPLE: How much does a 200-franc hotel room in Paris cost in dollars when the franc is worth 20 cents? 16 cents? 10 cents?
[6]EXAMPLE: How much does a $55 American camera cost a German consumer when the mark is worth 55 cents? 44 cents? 33.33 cents?
[7]For more on this problem, see Chapter 38, especially pages 862–63.

their markets simply contracted. Second, real interest rates rose dramatically, making the burden of paying interest on the debt much harder to bear. Third, the value of the dollar rose, making their international debts—which were denominated in dollars—more onerous.

Beginning with Mexico's problems in 1982, the 1980s have been marked by a series of near-crises in the international financial system as countries like Argentina, Brazil, Peru, the Phillipines, and others have postponed or scaled back payments and renegotiated their debt obligations. Citizens of many of these countries have suffered severe declines in their standards of living as the LDCs scramble to meet their interest and principal payments. Some banks have absorbed sizable losses. But, so far, a series of special arrangements negotiated by governments and banks has managed to keep the system afloat and avoid a panic.

However, no one is declaring the problem solved. Many business people, politicians, and economists doubt that the LDCs will ever be able to repay their debts in full and advocate some sort of partial forgiveness of interest or principal, perhaps on a selective basis. To date, American banks have opposed such plans. But there is continued concern that widespread defaults on loans by LDCs could threaten the solvency of some major U.S. banks.

Summary

1. Exchange rates state the value of one currency in terms of another and thus influence the patterns of world trade in important ways.

2. If governments do not interfere, exchange rates will be determined in free markets by the usual laws of supply and demand. Such a system is called floating exchange rates.

3. Demand for a nation's currency is derived from foreigners' desires to purchase that country's goods and services or to invest in its assets. Any change that increases the demand for a nation's currency will cause its exchange rate to appreciate under floating rates.

4. Supply of a nation's currency is derived from the desire of that country's citizens to purchase foreign goods and services or to invest in foreign assets. Any change that increases the supply of a nation's currency will cause its exchange rate to depreciate under floating rates.

5. In the long run, purchasing-power parity plays a major role in exchange rate movements. The purchasing-power parity theory states that relative price levels in any two countries determine the exchange rate between their currencies. Therefore, countries with relatively low inflation rates normally will have appreciating currencies.

6. Over shorter periods, the pace of economic activity and the level of interest rates exert a greater influence on the exchange rate. In particular, interest rate movements are typically the dominant factor in the short run.

7. Exchange rates can be fixed at nonequilibrium levels by governments that are willing and able to mop up any excess of quantity supplied over quantity demanded, or provide any excess of quantity demanded over quantity supplied. In the first case, the country is suffering from a balance of payments deficit because of its overvalued currency. In the second, an undervalued currency has given it a balance of payments surplus.

8. In the early part of this century, the world was on a particular system of fixed exchange rates called the gold standard, in which the value of every nation's currency was fixed in terms of gold. But this created problems because nations could not control their own money supplies and because the world could not control its total supply of gold.

9. After World War II, the gold standard was replaced by the gold-exchange (or Bretton Woods) system where rates were again fixed, or rather, fixed until further notice. In this system, the U.S. dollar was the basis of international currency values.

10. The gold-exchange system served the world well and helped restore world trade, but it got into trouble when the dollar became chronically overvalued since the system provided no way to remedy this situation.

11. After 1971, the world gradually moved toward a system of relatively free exchange rates, though there are plenty of exceptions. We now have a thoroughly mixed system of "dirty" or "managed" floating which continues to evolve and adapt.

12. Floating rates are not without their problems. For

example, importers and exporters justifiably worry about fluctuations in exchange rates. Though these problems seem manageable, some people think that a return to fixed exchange rates is desirable.

13. Under floating exchange rates, investors who speculate on international currency values provide a valuable service by assuming the risks of those who do not wish to speculate. Normally, speculators stabilize rather than destabilize exchange rates, because that is how they make profits.

14. The U.S. dollar rose dramatically in value from 1980 to 1985, making our imports cheaper and our exports more expensive. Since 1985, however, the dollar has been tumbling.

Concepts for Review

International monetary system	Floating exchange rates	Gold standard
Exchange rate	Purchasing-power parity theory	Gold-exchange system
Appreciation	Fixed exchange rates	(Bretton Woods system)
Depreciation	Balance of payments deficit	International Monetary Fund (IMF)
Devaluation	and surplus	Exchange controls
Revaluation	Current account	"Dirty" or "managed" floating
Supply of and demand for	Capital account	The European Monetary System (EMS)
foreign exchange	Balance of trade	The LDC debt problem

Questions for Discussion

1. What items do you own or routinely consume that are produced abroad? What countries do these come from? How have your purchases affected the exchange rates between the dollar and these currencies?

2. If the dollar depreciates relative to the Japanese yen, will the Sony stereo you have longed for become more or less expensive? What effect do you imagine this will have on American demands for Sonys? Does the American demand curve for yen, therefore, slope upward or downward? Explain.

3. During the 1980s, inflation in West Germany has generally been below that in the United States. What, then, does the purchasing-power parity theory predict should have happened to the exchange rate between the mark and the dollar? (Look at Table 19–1 to see what actually has happened.)

4. Use supply and demand diagrams to analyze the effect on the exchange rate between the dollar and the British pound if:
   a. Britain's flow of North Sea oil increases.
   b. British dockworkers refuse to unload ships that arrive with cargo from America but continue to load ships that sail from Britain.
   c. The Federal Reserve raises interest rates in America.
   d. The U.S. government, to help settle the problems of the Middle East, gives huge amounts of foreign aid to Israel and her Arab neighbors.
   e. Both Britain and the United States slip into recession, but the British recession is far more severe.

   f. Polls suggest that Britain's conservative government will be replaced by radicals, who vow to nationalize all foreign-owned assets.

5. How are the problems of a country faced with a balance of payments deficit similar to those posed by a government regulation that holds the price of peanuts above the equilibrium level? (*Hint:* Think of each in terms of a supply-demand diagram.)

6. Look at the U.S. balance of payments accounts table in the text (Table 19–2 on page 419). Figure out where each of the following actions you could have taken in 1986 would have been recorded in these accounts:
   a. You spent the summer traveling in Europe.
   b. Your uncle in Canada sent you $25 as a birthday present.
   c. You bought a new Volvo.
   d. You sold your stock on the Japanese stock market.
   e. You drove over the Canadian border carrying American records in your trunk and sold them to a friend in Canada. (*Hint:* Would your sale have been recorded anywhere?)

7. For each of the transactions listed in Question 6, indicate how it would affect:
   a. the U.S. balance of payments, if exchange rates were fixed;
   b. the international value of the dollar, if exchange rates were floating.

8. Under the old gold standard, what do you think happened to world prices when there was a huge gold strike in California in 1849? What do you think happened when the world went without any

important new gold strikes for 20 years or so?

9. Explain why the members of the Bretton Woods conference in 1944 wanted to establish a system of fixed exchange rates. What was the flaw that led to the ultimate breakdown of the system in 1971?

10. Suppose you want to reserve a hotel room in Paris for the coming summer but are worried that the value of the franc may rise between now and then, making the rooms too expensive for your budget. Explain how a speculator could relieve you of this worry. (Don't actually try it. Speculators deal only in very large sums!)

11. On page 425, it is pointed out that successful speculators buy a currency when demand is weak and sell it when demand is strong. Use supply and demand diagrams for two different periods (one with weak demand, the other with strong demand) to show why this will limit price fluctuations.

12. Use the following statistics to produce a balance of payments table for the United States, identifying separately the current and capital accounts. (Assume no statistical discrepancy.)

U.S. income on foreign investment	20
U.S. government grants to foreigners	40
Merchandise exports	400
U.S. tourist expenditures abroad	30
U.S. private direct investment abroad	200
Merchandise imports	600

a. Does the balance of payments show a surplus or a deficit?

b. What would happen to the exchange rate under flexible exchange rates?

20

Macroeconomics in a World Economy

No man is an island, entire of itself.

JOHN DONNE

America is no longer an isolated economy immune to foreign influences, if indeed it ever was one. More than ever before, the nations of the world are locked together in an uneasy economic union. Fluctuations in foreign GNP growth, foreign inflation, and foreign interest rates profoundly affect the U.S. economy. Economic events that originate within our borders reverberate around the globe. Before we complete our study of macroeconomics, we must become acquainted with these international linkages, for otherwise it is truly impossible to understand many of the most important economic developments of the 1980s.

One simple fact will drive home the point. Between 1981 and 1986, the sum of $C + I + G$ in the United States, measured in constant 1982 dollars, advanced by about $660 billion, or 3.8 percent per year. Yet during this same five-year period, real GNP grew only about $465 billion, or 2.7 percent per year. (See Figure 20–1.) The large gap between these two numbers suggests that a model that equates Y to $C + I + G$ must be missing something important. It is, and this chapter is designed to remedy the omissions.

The analysis is explained in a step by step manner. We begin by studying how international trade in goods and services affects macroeconomic activity in different countries, paying no attention to changes in exchange rates or to international movements of capital. Then we bring in exchange rate adjustments, which change the price of one country's goods in terms of the currency of another. In Chapter 19, we learned how changes in major macroeconomic variables like GNP, prices, and interest rates affect exchange rates. In this chapter, we complete the circle by looking at international linkages in the opposite direction—studying how changes in the exchange rate affect the domestic economy. Finally, we bring international capital flows into the picture and learn how monetary and fiscal policy work in an international economy.

Policy Issue: The U.S. Trade Deficit

Everybody knows that the United States has been importing much more than it has been exporting in recent years. In 1986, for example, our real imports of Japanese automobiles, Korean textiles, French wine, and other products

Figure 20–1

GROWTH IN DOMESTIC DEMAND AND GNP, 1981–1986

Between 1981 and 1986, real GNP in the United States expanded by about $465 billion, or almost $200 billion less than the growth of the sum of C + I + G. The difference between Y and C + I + G is net exports, X − IM, which fell by almost $200 billion over this period. SOURCE: U.S. Bureau of Economic Analysis.

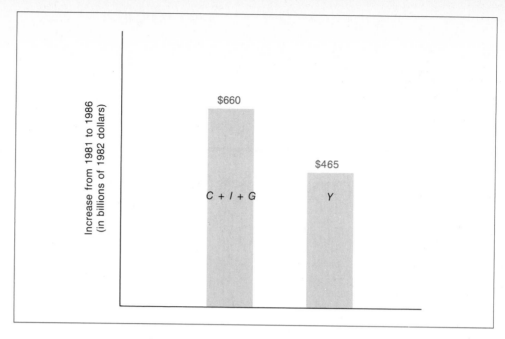

amounted to $523 billion while our real exports of wheat, computers, banking services, and the like were just $377 billion. In absolute magnitude, this trade deficit was the largest ever run by any nation in the history of the world. Naturally, it attracted a great deal of attention not only from economists, but also from politicians, the business community, and the news media. Indeed, America's gaping trade deficit rivals the federal budget deficit as the major economic news story of the 1980s. And both have been blamed by some for the October 1987 stock market crash.

Yet few people realize that American foreign trade was roughly in balance as recently as 1982–1983. And fewer still understand how we came to acquire such a mammoth trade deficit in so short a time. This lack of knowledge, however, has not inhibited these same people from prescribing—and in some cases seeking to legislate—"cures" for our trade problems. By the end of this chapter, you will have acquired an understanding of the origins of America's trade deficit and will be able to make up your own mind about how it can best be cured.

International Trade and National Incomes

If you turn back to the circular flow diagram of Chapter 8 (see page 140), you will see that there is an additional source of spending aside from the usual C + I + G. That final component of aggregate demand is *net exports*, which we symbolize by $X - IM$, where X is **exports** and IM is **imports**. The condition for equilibrium on the demand side of the economy remains what it was: Total spending must equal total production. But in an **open economy,** the total output available for purchase consists of domestic production plus imports (which are foreign goods that we purchase):

An **open economy** is one that trades with other nations in goods and services, and perhaps also in financial assets.

$$\text{Total available output} = Y + IM.$$

And total expenditure consists of domestic demand plus exports (foreign demand for our products):

$$\text{Total expenditure} = C + I + G + X.$$

So, in the presence of international trade, output and expenditure are in balance when:

$$Y + IM = C + I + G + X,$$

or, rearranging slightly:

$$Y = C + I + G + X - IM.$$

In a strictly arithmetic sense, this revised equilibrium condition for an open economy explains how Y could have expanded by $200 billion less than $C + I + G$ in the United States between 1981 and 1986: Real net exports, $X - IM$, fell by about $200 billion. But this is a rather shallow explanation. To gain a deeper understanding, we must study the determinants of exports and imports.

While both exports and imports depend on many factors, the predominant one is national income. Some of the additional consumption and investment goods that American consumers and firms buy as their spending rises are foreign goods. So:

Our imports rise as our GNP rises and fall as our GNP falls.

Similarly, our *exports* are the *imports* of other countries, so it is natural to assume that our exports depend on *their* GNPs, not on our own. Thus:

Our exports are relatively insensitive to our own GNP, but are quite sensitive to the GNPs of other countries.

These two observations enable us to bring international trade into our model of income determination and the multiplier. Table 20–1 displays the mechanics in a concrete example adapted from Chapter 12. The first two columns are an abbreviated version of Table 12–3 on page 226; they show the sum of $C + I + G$ — now labelled "Domestic Expenditure" at alternative levels of GNP.

Columns 3 and 4 record specific numerical versions of the assumed behavior of exports and imports. Exports are fixed at $400 billion regardless of (our)

Table 20–1
INCOME DETERMINATION WITH INTERNATIONAL TRADE

(1) GROSS NATIONAL PRODUCT (Y) (billions)	(2) DOMESTIC EXPENDITURE ($C + I + G$) (billions)	(3) EXPORTS (X) (billions)	(4) IMPORTS (IM) (billions)	(5) NET EXPORTS ($X - IM$) (billions)	(6) TOTAL EXPENDITURE ($C + I + G + X - IM$) (billions)
$2500	$3100	$400	$250	$150	$3250
3000	3400	400	300	100	3500
3500	3700	400	350	50	3750
4000	4000	400	400	0	4000
4500	4300	400	450	−50	4250
5000	4600	400	500	−100	4500
5500	4900	400	550	−150	4750

GNP, and imports are assumed to rise by $50 billion for every $500 billion rise in GNP. Column 5 simply subtracts imports from exports to get net exports, X − IM, and column 6 adds net exports to domestic expenditure to get total expenditure, C + I + G + X − IM.

The equilibrium, you can see, occurs at Y = $4000 billion. At any lower level of GNP, Y is less than C + I + G + X − IM, so output will rise. At any higher level of GNP, Y is greater than C + I + G + X − IM, so output will fall.

Figures 20–2 and 20–3 derive the same conclusion graphically. The upper panel of Figure 20–2 shows that exports are fixed at $400 billion regardless of GNP while imports increase as GNP rises, just as in Table 20–1. The difference between exports and imports, or net exports, is positive until GNP reaches $4000 billion and negative once GNP surpasses that amount. The bottom panel of Figure 20–2 shows the subtraction explicitly and makes it clear that:

Net exports decline as GNP rises.

Figure 20–3 carries this analysis over to the 45° line diagram. We begin with a familiar C + I + G line, in black; this simply duplicates the C + I + G line from Figure 12–4 (page 226). Equilibrium in an open economy occurs where Y = C + I + G + X − IM, so we must now add net exports to domestic expenditure. Figure 20–3 does this by first repeating the X − IM line from Figure 20–2 at the bottom of the graph and then adding the two black lines vertically to produce the blue line labelled C + I + G + X − IM. The C + I

Figure 20–2

THE DEPENDENCE OF NET EXPORTS ON GNP

This graph displays the data on exports, imports, and net exports found in Table 20–1. Exports, X, are independent of GNP while imports, IM, rise as GNP rises (top panel). As a result, net exports, X − IM, decline as GNP rises (bottom panel).

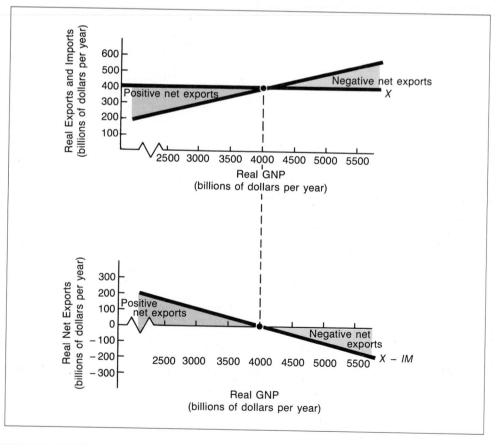

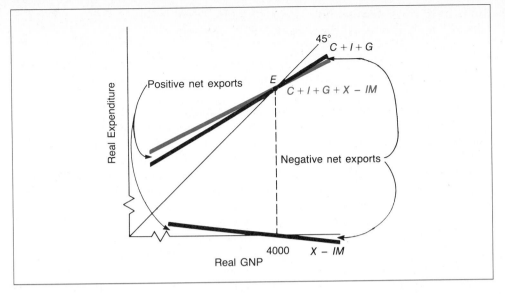

Figure 20–3
EQUILIBRIUM GNP WITH
FOREIGN TRADE
In the presence of foreign
trade, equilibrium GNP
occurs where the $C + I + G + X - IM$ line crosses the
45° line, for here $Y = C + I + G + X - IM$. In the graph,
equilibrium is at point E,
where GNP is $4000 billion.
This matches the equilibrium
we found in Chapter 12
(Figure 12–4 on page xxx)
without international trade
because our example
assumes that net exports are
zero when $Y = \$4000$. In the
diagram, net exports are
shown by the vertical
distance—positive or
negative—between the
$C + I + G + X - IM$ line
and the $C + I + G$ line. The
$C + I + G + X - IM$ line is
flatter than the $C + I + G$ line
because net exports decline
as GNP rises.

A **closed economy** is one
that does not trade with
other nations in either
goods or assets.

$+ G + X - IM$ line crosses the 45° line at point E, which is the equilibrium level of GNP with international trade.

If you turn back to page 226 in Chapter 12, you will see that $Y = \$4000$ is also the equilibrium we found in a **closed economy** with no international trade. (Figure 20–3 shows this quite clearly, since the $C + I + G$ and $C + I + G + X - IM$ lines both cross the 45° line at $Y = \$4000$.) Does international trade therefore not affect domestic income?

Hardly. Notice in the table or in the figure that we have constructed our example so that exports exactly balance imports ($X - IM = 0$) when GNP is $4000 billion. This is just an artifact of our example. It is because of this artifact that net exports have no effect on equilibrium GNP.

When net exports are zero, foreign trade has no net effect on domestic GNP.

The Multiplier in the Presence of Foreign Trade

But this is not the normal state of affairs. Let us consider what happens if exports rise to $650 billion while imports remain as in Table 20–1. Table 20–2

Table 20–2
EQUILIBRIUM GNP AFTER A RISE IN EXPORTS

GROSS NATIONAL PRODUCT (Y) (billions)	DOMESTIC EXPENDITURE (C + I + G) (billions)	EXPORTS (X) (billions)	IMPORTS (IM) (billions)	NET EXPORTS (X − IM) (billions)	TOTAL EXPENDITURE (C + I + G + X − IM) (billions)
$2500	$3100	$650	$250	$400	$3500
3000	3400	650	300	350	3750
3500	3700	650	350	300	4000
4000	4000	650	400	250	4250
4500	4300	650	450	200	4500
5000	4600	650	500	150	4750
5500	4900	650	550	100	5000

shows us that equilibrium now occurs at a GNP of $Y = \$4500$ billion. So international trade has raised domestic GNP. In general:

When net exports are positive, international trade raises equilibrium GNP. When net exports are negative, international trade lowers equilibrium GNP.

The reason is hardly mysterious. When foreigners buy U.S. products, they put income into the hands of Americans, just as domestic investment does. As this income is spent and respent, a multiplier process is set in motion, raising GNP. Specifically, in this example an increase of $250 billion in exports (from $400 billion to $650 billion) leads to an increase of $500 billion in GNP (from $4000 billion to $4500 billion). So the multiplier is 2 (= $500/$250).[1] This same conclusion is shown graphically in Figure 20–4, where the line $C + I + G + X_0 - IM$ represents the original expenditure schedule and the line $C + I + G + X_1 - IM$ represents the expenditure schedule after the rise in exports. Equilibrium shifts from point E to point A, and GNP rises by $500 billion.

Notice that the multiplier in this example is 2, whereas in the absence of international trade (in Chapter 12) it was $2\frac{1}{2}$. There is nothing special that makes the multiplier for exports different from any other multiplier. The same multiplier of 2 would apply to an autonomous change in *any* component of total expenditure.[2] What we have discovered is that:

International trade lowers the value of the multiplier.

Figure 20–3 shows us graphically why this is true. Because net exports decline as GNP rises, the total expenditure line is *flatter* in the presence of international trade ($C + I + G + X - IM$) than in its absence ($C + I + G$). As we know from earlier chapters, the *size* of the multiplier depends on the *slope* of the expenditure schedule — steeper expenditure schedules lead to larger

[1] EXERCISE: Construct a version of Table 20–1 to show what would happen if imports rose by $250 billion at every level of GNP while exports remained at $400 billion. You should be able to show that the new equilibrium would be $Y = \$3500$ billion.

[2] EXERCISE: Construct a version of Table 20–1 that shows the effects of a rise in domestic expenditure by $250 billion at every level of GNP. Show that the new equilibrium occurs at $Y = \$4500$.

Figure 20–4
THE MULTIPLIER WITH FOREIGN TRADE
This diagram shows a $250 billion increase in exports as a vertical shift of the total expenditure schedule from $C + I + G + X_0 - IM$, to $C + I + G + X_1 - IM$. As a result, equilibrium shifts from point E to point A, and GNP rises from $4000 billion to $4500 billion. The multiplier is therefore 2 (= $500/$250).

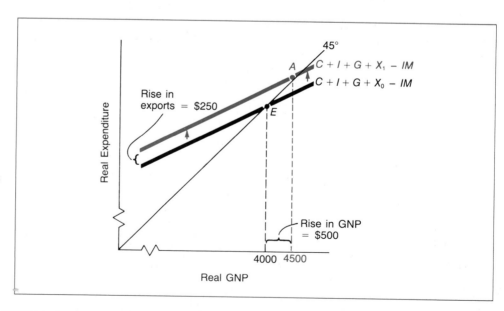

mulipliers. Since international trade flattens the expenditure schedule, it lowers the multiplier.[3]

Thus international trade gives us yet another reason why the oversimplified multiplier formula first given in Chapter 10 (page 189) overstates the true value of the multiplier. We now have accumulated four such reasons:

REASONS WHY THE OVERSIMPLIFIED MULTIPLIER FORMULA IS WRONG

1. It ignores price-level changes, which reduce the size of the multiplier.
2. It ignores the income tax, which reduces the size of the multiplier.
3. It ignores the rising interest rates that accompany any autonomous increase in spending, which reduce the size of the multiplier.
4. It ignores international trade, which also reduces the size of the multiplier.

Although we have much more to learn about how the U.S. economy is linked to the economies of other countries, this simple analysis of the multiplier in the presence of foreign trade already teaches us an important lesson: *Booms and recessions tend to be transmitted across national borders*.

Why is that? Figure 20–4 shows how a rise in our exports will, via the multiplier, raise GNP in the United States. But we have said nothing so far about what might cause our exports to rise. One possibility is that a boom abroad raises aggregate demand and GNP in foreign countries. With rising incomes, foreigners will buy more American goods—which means that United States exports will rise. By this mechanism, rapid economic growth abroad contributes to rapid economic growth here.

Of course, the same mechanism also operates in the downward direction. Suppose some of the foreign countries that trade with us slip into recession. As their GNPs decline, so do their imports. But this means that the U.S. will experience a decline in exports which, through the multiplier, will pull down GNP in the U.S. Hence a recession abroad can contribute to recessionary conditions in the United States.

Naturally, what foreign countries do to us, we also do to them. Thus rapid economic growth in the U.S. tends to produce boom conditions in the countries from which we buy, and recessions here tend quickly to spill beyond our borders. In summary:

The GNPs of the major economies are linked by trade. A boom in one country tends to raise its imports and hence push up exports and GNP in other countries. Similarly, a recession in one country tends to pull GNP down in other countries.

[3]For those who like formulas, we can amend the multiplier formula given in the appendix to Chapter 12 (page 246) to allow for international trade. That formula was:

$$\text{Multiplier} = \frac{1}{1 - b(1 - t)}$$

where b is the marginal propensity to consume and t is the tax rate. If we define the marginal propensity to import as the rise in imports per dollar of GNP (the marginal propensity to import is 0.1 in our example) and symbolize it by the letter m, the formula for the multiplier with foreign trade is:

$$\text{Multiplier} = \frac{1}{1 - b(1 - t) + m}.$$

This formula clearly shows that a higher value of m leads to a lower multiplier.

Relative Prices, Exports, and Imports

While GNP levels at home and abroad are important influences on a country's net exports, they are not the only relevant factor. International prices matter, too. To make things concrete, let us focus on trade between the United States and Japan and assume — just for this short section — that the yen/dollar exchange rate is *fixed*.

Suppose now that the prices of American export goods rise while Japanese prices are constant. This makes U.S. products more expensive *relative to Japanese goods* than was true previously. If American consumers react to the new relative price structure by buying more Japanese goods, our *imports rise*. If Japanese consumers react to the same relative price changes by buying fewer American products, our *exports fall*. Both reactions reduce America's net exports. And since $X - IM$ is a component of $C + I + G + X - IM$, the result is less aggregate demand and GNP in the United States.

Figure 20–5 shows this conclusion graphically. In the figure, the black lines labelled $X_0 - IM_0$ and $C + I + G + X_0 - IM_0$ are carried over without change from Figure 20–3. A rise in American prices, we have just concluded, shifts the $X - IM$ schedule (and hence the $C + I + G + X - IM$ schedule) downward as shown in the diagram. Equilibrium therefore shifts from E_0 to E_1, leading to lower GNP in the United States.

Naturally, the effects of a decline in American prices are precisely the opposite of those depicted in Figure 20–5. Net exports are stimulated, the $C + I + G + X - IM$ line shifts up, and GNP rises. Thus:

For given foreign prices, a rise in the prices of a country's exports will lead to a reduction in that country's net exports, and hence to a decline in its real GNP. Analogously, a fall in the prices of a country's exports will raise that country's net exports and GNP.

Notice that this analysis leads us to conclude that a *higher* domestic price level leads, other things equal, to a *lower* equilibrium GNP on the demand side.

Figure 20–5
RELATIVE INTERNATIONAL PRICES AND EQUILIBRIUM GNP
If American prices rise or foreign prices fall, U.S. exports decline and U.S. imports rise. Hence, America's net export schedule declines from the black $X_0 - IM_0$ line to the blue $X_1 - IM_1$ line. In the upper part of the diagram, the total expenditure curve shifts downward correspondingly. As a result, equilibrium GNP falls.

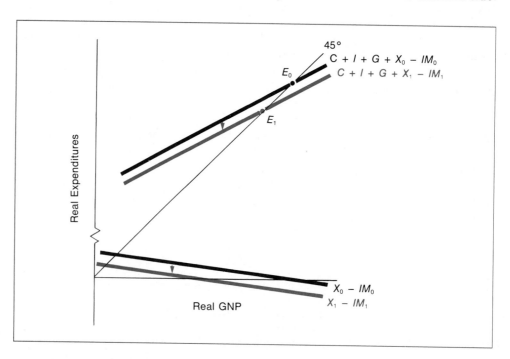

(See Figure 20–5.) That is simply a long-winded way of saying that the economy's *aggregate demand curve slopes downward,* something we have previously concluded on other grounds. Hence:

International trade provides yet another reason for a downward-sloping aggregate demand curve. As the price level rises, domestic goods become more expensive relative to foreign goods, which reduces net exports and lowers equilibrium real GNP on the demand side of the economy.

Since trade patterns are governed by the prices of U.S. goods *relative to* Japanese goods, precisely the same logic applies to changes in Japanese prices. Suppose Japanese prices fall. Americans will import more and export less. So X − IM will decline, dragging down GNP in the United States. Figure 20–5 applies to this case without change. By similar reasoning, rising Japanese prices increase U.S. net exports and stimulate our economy. Thus:

Price increases abroad raise a country's net exports and hence its GNP. Price decreases abroad have the opposite effects.

The Effects of Changes in Exchange Rates

From here it is a simple matter to figure out how changes in *exchange rates* affect a country's net exports, for currency appreciations or depreciations are like changes in international relative prices.

Recall that the basic role of an exchange rate is to convert one country's prices into the currency of another. Table 20–3 uses two examples of U.S.–Japanese trade to remind us of this role. Suppose the dollar depreciates from 150 yen to only 120 yen. Then, from the viewpoint of American consumers, a television set that costs ¥60,000 in Japan goes up in price from $400 to $500. To Americans, it is just as if TV prices in Japan had risen by 25 percent. Naturally, Americans react by purchasing fewer Japanese products. So American imports go down.

Now consider the implications for Japanese consumers interested in buying American microcomputers that cost $2000. When the dollar falls from 150 yen to 120 yen, they see the price of this computer falling from ¥300,000 to ¥240,000. To them, it is just as if American producers had offered a 20 percent markdown. Under such circumstances, we expect U.S. sales to the Japanese to rise. So U.S. exports should increase. Putting these two findings together, we conclude that:

A currency depreciation should raise net exports and therefore increase aggregate demand. Conversely, a currency appreciation should reduce net exports and therefore decrease aggregate demand. (Figure 20–5 can be thought of as applying to an *appreciation* of the currency.)

Table 20–3
EXCHANGE RATES AND HOME-CURRENCY PRICES

	60,000 YEN JAPANESE TV SET		$2000 U.S. HOME COMPUTER	
EXCHANGE RATE	PRICE IN JAPAN	PRICE IN U.S.	PRICE IN U.S.	PRICE IN JAPAN
$1 = 150 yen	¥60,000	$400	$2,000	¥300,000
$1 = 120 yen	¥60,000	$500	$2,000	¥240,000

For later reference, this conclusion is depicted on an aggregate supply and demand diagram in Figure 20–6. If the currency depreciates, net exports rise and the aggregate demand curve shifts outward from D_0D_0 to D_1D_1. Both prices and output rise as the economy's equilibrium moves from E_0 to E_1. If the currency appreciates, everything operates in reverse: net exports fall, the aggregate demand curve shifts inward to D_2D_2, and both prices and output decline.

Now we are in a position to understand one of the main reasons why the U.S. trade deficit grew so large in the 1980s. Recall from Chapter 19 that the international value of the dollar soared from mid-1980 until early 1985. (You may wish to refer back to Figure 19–8 on page 426.) According to the analysis we have just completed, such a stunning appreciation of the dollar should have encouraged U.S. imports, damaged U.S. exports, and been a drag on aggregate demand. That is precisely what happened. In real 1982 dollars, American imports soared by 52 percent between 1981 and 1986 while American exports declined by 4 percent. The result is that a $49 billion net export surplus turned into a $146 billion deficit. In consequence, strong growth in $C + I + G$ translated into only mediocre growth in GNP.

Lags in International Trade and the J Curve

The exchange value of the dollar peaked in early 1985 and began to decline. Yet our trade deficit continued to climb in 1985 and through most of 1986. Something seems wrong here. Since the dollar was falling, our analysis predicts that America's net export position should have improved. Instead, it continued to deteriorate.

Actually, there is nothing wrong with our analysis. It is simply incomplete, for we have failed to note that international trade patterns take time to respond to changes in exchange rates. These lags in international trade give rise to a phenomenon known as the **J curve**. (See Figure 20–7.) The J curve indicates that, following a devaluation or depreciation, a country's trade deficit actually deteriorates for a while (from A to B in Figure 20–7) before improving (beyond point B). Thus a considerable period of time may elapse before any

The **J curve** shows the typical pattern of response of net exports to a change in currency values. Following a depreciation or a devaluation, net exports usually decline at first and then rise.

Figure 20–6
THE EFFECTS OF EXCHANGE RATE CHANGES ON AGGREGATE DEMAND
A depreciation of the exchange rate raises net exports and hence shifts the aggregate demand curve outward to the right, from D_0D_0 to D_1D_1 in the diagram. An appreciation of the currency shifts the aggregate demand curve inward to the left, to D_2D_2. Thus depreciations are expansionary and appreciations are contractionary.

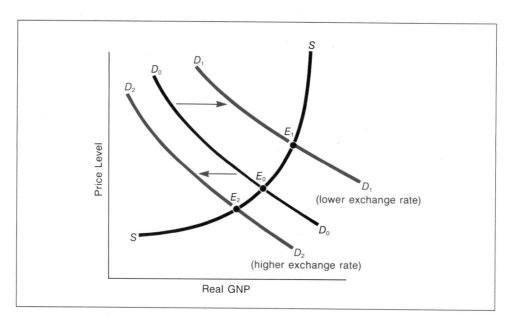

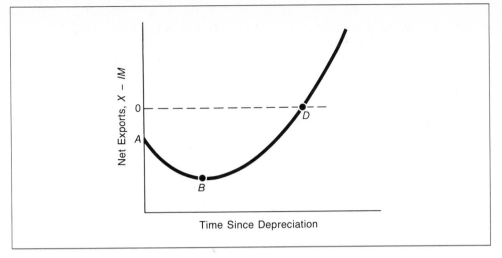

Figure 20-7
THE J CURVE
The response of a country's net exports to a decline in the value of its currency tends to follow a J-shaped pattern. In the period immediately following the depreciation or devaluation, everyone imports and exports about the same volume of goods as they did before. But imports cost more in terms of home currency, so net exports decline. This is the descending portion of the J curve, from point *A* to point *B*. After a while, however, imports decline and exports rise, so net exports improve. This is the rising portion of the curve, beyond point *B*.

improvement in net exports is apparent. In the U.S. case, net exports first began to turn around late in 1986.

To explain the origins of the J curve, let us continue the example of an appreciating yen (depreciating dollar). On the day after the yen rises in value, the dollar prices of, say, Sony television sets in American stores and warehouses will be the same as they were on the previous day. Similarly, the yen prices of IBM PCs in Japan will be the same. Hence there is no reason for Americans to buy fewer Japanese TVs nor for Japanese to buy more American computers. Gradually, however, the profit motive will force Sony to raise its U.S. dollar prices and induce IBM to cut its Japanese yen prices. Only then do international trade patterns start to adjust. But that, too, takes time. American wholesalers and retailers with long-term contracts with Japanese TV manufacturers will only gradually redirect their orders to American suppliers. Similarly, Japanese merchants accustomed to dealing with local computer manufacturers will only gradually begin to place orders with American firms.

These gradual adjustments of international trade patterns lead to a J curve in the following manner. In the short run, Americans will be buying almost as many Japanese TV sets after the dollar depreciates as they did before. But we will be paying more—in U.S. dollars—for each set. Hence our imports from Japan, *when measured in U.S. dollars*, actually rise while our exports are unchanged. So our trade deficit deteriorates at first. Only after the passage of some time will the volume of U.S. imports decline enough to improve America's trade position with Japan.[4]

Some illustrative numbers will clarify the arithmetic behind the J curve. Suppose that, when the dollar was worth 150 yen, the United States was importing 1 million TV sets at $400 each and exporting 150,000 computers at $2000 each. Then the dollar value of our imports was $400 million and the dollar value of our exports was $300 million, leading to a trade deficit with Japan of $100 million.

Now the dollar depreciates to 120 yen and the dollar price of Japanese TVs rises to $500 (see Table 20–3). At first, purchases are unchanged; so our import bill for the 1 million Japanese TVs increases to $500 million. With exports

---

[4]Actually, improvement occurs only if consumers in the two countries are sufficiently responsive to price changes. The precise condition is best left to more advanced courses in international economics.

remaining at $300 million, our trade deficit balloons to $200 million. We are on the downward portion of the J, between A and B in Figure 20–7.

After some time, however, Americans curtail their purchase of Japanese TVs and the Japanese buy more American computers. For the sake of concreteness, suppose that we now import 800,000 TVs and export 200,000 computers. At a price of $500 each, our TV imports cost $400 million. At a price of $2000 each, our computer exports earn us $400 million. Thus our trade with Japan is now balanced. In terms of Figure 20–7, we have reached point D.

Applying the J-curve analysis to the recent U.S. experience is no easy matter because the dollar did not decline all at once, but rather in stages beginning in early 1985. Each depreciation set in motion its own little J curve, forming a complex pattern. However, there is no doubt that the J-curve phenomenon goes a long way toward explaining why U.S. net exports responded so sluggishly to the falling dollar.

Aggregate Supply in an Open Economy

So we have concluded that, after a lag described by the J curve, a currency depreciation increases aggregate demand while a currency appreciation decreases it. To complete our model of macroeconomics in an open economy, we must now turn to the implications of international trade for *aggregate supply*.

Part of the story is familiar. As we know from previous chapters, the U.S., like all economies, purchases some of its productive inputs from abroad. Oil is only the most prominent example. We also rely on foreign suppliers for various metals (like titanium), many raw agricultural products (like coffee beans), and thousands of other items that are used by American industry. If these imported inputs rise in price, American firms will charge higher prices at any given level of output. Graphically, this means that *the aggregate supply curve will shift upward*.

There are also direct inflationary effects of rising foreign prices. First, prices of imported goods are included in American price indexes like the Consumer Price Index (CPI). So when prices of Japanese cars, French wine, and Swiss watches increase, the CPI goes up even if no American price rises. Second, higher import prices provide less foreign competition for American producers of cars, wine, and watches, who may react by raising their own prices. All of this can be summarized by saying:

When foreign prices rise, the U.S. aggregate supply curve is likely to shift inward, pushing up U.S. prices. When foreign prices fall, the U.S. aggregate supply curve shifts outward, pushing U.S. prices down.

Similarly, rising or falling prices in the U.S. contribute to inflation or deflation in other countries.

This analysis makes it easy to think through the consequences of a change in the *exchange rate*. Suppose the dollar depreciates. Then foreign goods cost more in terms of dollars, just as if foreign prices had risen. The consequence, we now know, is that the aggregate supply curve shifts *inward*. Similarly, an appreciation of the dollar makes foreign goods less expensive to Americans and shifts the aggregate supply curve *outward*. Thus (refer to Figure 20–8):

A currency depreciation shifts the aggregate supply curve inward and drives up the domestic price level. A currency appreciation has the opposite effects.

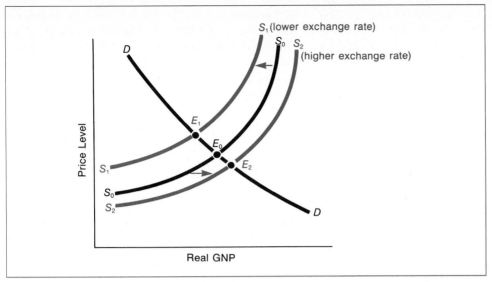

Figure 20–8
THE EFFECTS OF
EXCHANGE RATE
CHANGES ON
AGGREGATE SUPPLY
A depreciation of the
currency pushes the
aggregate supply curve
inward, from S_0S_0 to S_1S_1 in
the diagram, and is therefore
inflationary. A currency
appreciation has a
deflationary effect because it
pushes the aggregate supply
curve outward, from S_0S_0 to
S_2S_2.

The Macroeconomic Effects of Exchange Rates

We can now put aggregate demand and aggregate supply together and study the macroeconomic effects of changes in exchange rates.

First suppose that the international value of the dollar falls. Referring back to Figures 20–6 and 20–8, we see that this will shift the aggregate demand curve *outward* and the aggregate supply curve *inward*. The result, as Figure 20–9 shows, is that the U.S. price level certainly rises. Whether real GNP rises or falls depends on whether the supply or demand shift is the dominant influence. The evidence strongly suggests that aggregate *demand* shifts are usually more important, so we expect GNP to rise.

A currency depreciation is inflationary and probably also expansionary.

What is the intuitive explanation for this result? When the dollar falls, foreign goods become more expensive to Americans. That is directly inflationary.

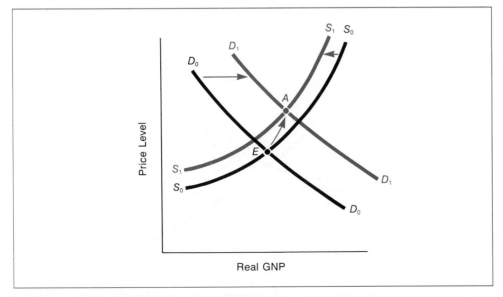

Figure 20–9
THE EFFECTS OF A
CURRENCY
DEPRECIATION
If the currency depreciates,
aggregate demand increases
because net exports are
stimulated and aggregate
supply decreases because
foreign goods become more
expensive. Prices rise as
equilibrium moves from point
E to point *A*. If the demand
shift is the more important
influence, output increases,
too.

At the same time, aggregate demand in the U.S. is stimulated by rising net exports. As long as the expansion of demand outweighs the adverse shift of the aggregate supply curve brought on by the depreciation, real GNP should rise.

Now let's reverse things. Suppose the dollar *appreciates*. In this case, net exports *fall* so the aggregate demand curve shifts *inward*. At the same time, foreign goods become cheaper, so the aggregate supply curve shifts *outward*. (See Figure 20–10.) Once again, we can be sure of the movement of the price level: It falls. Output will also fall if the demand shift is more important than the supply shift, as is likely. Hence:

A currency appreciation is certainly disinflationary and is probably contractionary.

In the rest of the chapter, we shall assume that the effect of the exchange rate on aggregate *demand* dominates its effect on aggregate *supply*, because that is what the evidence suggests.

Interest Rates and International Capital Flows

There is one important piece left in our international economic puzzle. We have analyzed international trade in goods and services rather fully, but have ignored international movements of capital.

For some nations, this omission is of little concern because they are rarely involved in international capital flows. But things are quite different for the United States, whose dollar is the world's major international currency. The vast majority of international capital flows involve either the buying or the selling of assets whose values are stated in dollars. Fortunately, given what we have just learned about the effects of exchange rates, it is not difficult to add international capital flows to our analysis.

Recall from Chapter 19 that interest-rate differentials and capital flows are typically the most important determinants of exchange rate movements in the short run. Specifically, suppose interest rates in the United States rise while foreign interest rates remain unchanged. We learned in Chapter 19 that this will attract capital to the United States and cause the dollar to appreciate. This

Figure 20–10
THE EFFECTS OF A CURRENCY APPRECIATION

If the currency appreciates, aggregate demand declines because net exports fall and aggregate supply increases because foreign goods become cheaper. Prices fall as equilibrium moves from point *E* to point *B*. If the demand shift is the more important influence, output also falls.

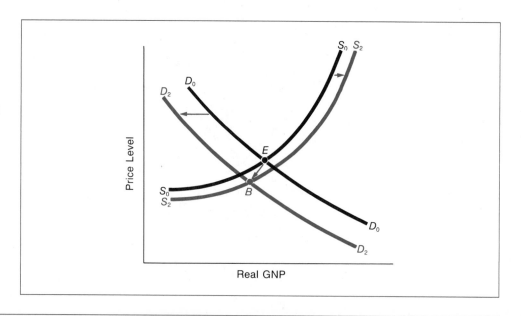

Real GNP

chapter has taught us that an appreciating dollar, in turn, will reduce net exports, prices, and output in the U.S. — as indicated in Figure 20–10. Thus:

A rise in interest rates tends to contract the economy by appreciating the currency and reducing net exports.

Notice that this conclusion has a familiar ring. In Chapter 14, while studying how monetary policy works, we observed that higher interest rates deter investment spending and hence reduce the I component of $C + I + G + X - IM$. Now, in studying an open economy with international capital flows, we see that higher interest rates also reduce the $X - IM$ component. Thus *international capital flows strengthen the negative effects of interest rates on aggregate demand*.

If interest rates in the United States fall, or if those abroad rise, everything we have just said is turned in the opposite direction. There is no need to repeat the analysis. The conclusion is:[5]

A fall in interest rates tends to expand the economy by depreciating the exchange rate and raising net exports.

Fiscal Policy in an Open Economy

Now we are ready to use our model to study how fiscal and monetary policy work when the exchange rate is floating and capital is internationally mobile. In addition to teaching us how international economic relations modify the effects of stabilization policies, this discussion will serve as a review of what we have learned up to this point in the chapter, for no new theoretical apparatus is necessary. We begin with fiscal policy.

Suppose the government cuts taxes or raises spending. Aggregate demand increases, which pushes up both real GNP and the price level in the usual manner. This is shown as the shift from D_0D_0 to D_1D_1 in Figure 20–11. In a closed economy, that is the end of the story. But in an open economy with international capital flows, the fact that a fiscal expansion pushes up interest rates assumes great importance.

[5]EXERCISE: Provide the reasoning behind this conclusion.

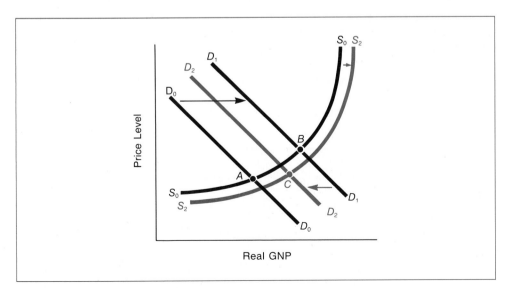

Figure 20–11

A FISCAL EXPANSION IN AN OPEN ECONOMY

A fiscal expansion pushes the aggregate demand outward, from D_0D_0 to D_1D_1 in the diagram. But it also raises interest rates which attracts international capital and appreciates the currency. The currency appreciation, in turn, reduces aggregate demand and raises aggregate supply — as shown by the blue curves S_2S_2 and D_2D_2. The result is that equilibrium occurs at point C rather than at point B. Output and prices both rise less than they would in a closed economy.

What happens in international financial markets as a result of higher U.S. interest rates? American securities become more attractive to foreign investors who then go to the foreign exchange market to buy dollars for use in purchasing American securities. That drives up the value of the dollar. The rising dollar, in turn, makes American goods more expensive abroad and foreign goods cheaper here. So exports fall and imports rise. The $X - IM$ component of aggregate demand therefore falls.

The fiscal expansion thus winds up increasing both America's *capital* account *surplus* and *current* account *deficit*. In fact, the two must rise by equal amounts because, under floating exchange rates, it is always true that:[6]

$$\text{current account surplus} + \text{capital account surplus} = 0.$$

Since a fiscal expansion leads to a trade deficit, many economists believe that the U.S. trade deficit of the 1980s was a side-effect of the Reagan tax cuts. We will come back to that issue shortly.

But first note that the induced rise in the dollar will shift the aggregate supply curve *outward* and the aggregate demand curve *inward*, as we saw in Figure 20–10 (page 444). Figure 20–11 adds these two shifts (in blue) to the effect of the original fiscal expansion (in black). The final equilibrium in an open economy is point C, whereas in a closed economy it would be point B. By comparing points B and C we can see how international linkages change the picture of fiscal policy that we painted in Part 4.

There are two main differences. First, a rising exchange rate offsets part of the inflationary effect of a fiscal expansion by making imports cheaper. Second, a rising exchange rate reduces the expansionary effect on real GNP by reducing $X - IM$. Here we have a new kind of "crowding out," different from the one we studied in Chapter 16. In the earlier chapter, we learned that an increase in G, by raising interest rates, will crowd out some private investment spending. Here a rise in G crowds out *net exports*. But the effect is the same: The fiscal multiplier is reduced. Thus, we conclude that:

International capital flows reduce the power of fiscal policy.

Table 20–4 shows that this new international variety of crowding out has been much more important than the traditional type of crowding out in the 1980s. Between 1981 and 1986, the share of investment in GNP actually *increased* (from 16.8 percent to 17.6 percent) despite the rise in the share of government purchases (from 19.4 percent to 20.3 percent). Only the share of net exports, $X - IM$, fell—from 1.5 percent to −3.9 percent.

[6]If you need review, turn back to Chapter 19, pages 415–20.

Table 20–4
PERCENTAGE SHARES OF REAL GNP IN THE UNITED STATES: 1981 AND 1986

YEAR	C	I	G	X − IM
1981	62.3%	16.8%	19.4%	1.5%
1986	66.0%	17.6%	20.3%	−3.9%
Change	+3.7	+0.8	+0.9	−5.4

Monetary Policy in an Open Economy

Now let us consider how monetary policy works in an open economy with floating exchange rates and international capital mobility.

As we know from earlier chapters, expansionary monetary policy raises aggregate demand, which pushes up both Y and P. This is shown in Figure 20–12 by the shift from D_0D_0 to D_1D_1, and it looks exactly the same as a fiscal expansion. However, we know that a monetary expansion pushes interest rates *down*, whereas a fiscal expansion pushes them *up*. Hence the ramifications in international capital markets are reversed. Funds start to flow *out of* the United States in search of better rates of return abroad. The exchange rate *falls*. The depreciating dollar discourages imports and encourages exports; so $X - IM$ *rises*.

America therefore winds up with capital flowing out (a deficit on capital account) and an increase in its trade surplus—or a reduction in its trade deficit. This time, as you will notice from Figure 20–12:

International capital flows increase the power of monetary policy.

International Aspects of Reaganomics

This completes our theoretical analysis of the macroeconomics of open economies. Now let us put the theory through its paces by applying it to the changes in U.S. macroeconomic policy since 1981. In the process, we will see that Reaganomics had important international implications that we did not mention in Part 4.

In broadest outline, the Reagan administration engineered a dramatic change in the policy mix toward tighter money and much easier fiscal policy. The Federal Reserve's tight monetary policy was already in progress when President Reagan was elected; the new administration simply encouraged the Fed to

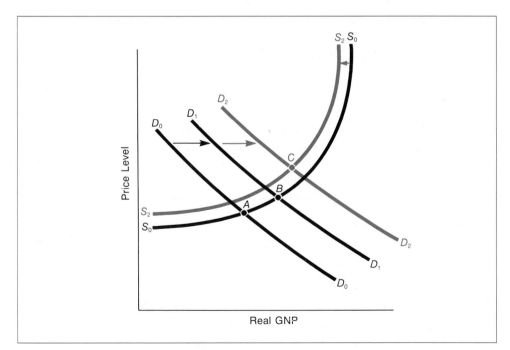

Figure 20–12
A MONETARY EXPANSION IN AN OPEN ECONOMY
A monetary expansion pushes the aggregate demand outward, from D_0D_0 to D_1D_1, just like a fiscal expansion. But it lowers, rather than raises, interest rates which leads to international capital outflows and a currency depreciation. The depreciation increases net exports and therefore raises aggregate demand—which shifts outward from D_1D_1 to D_2D_2. But it also raises foreign prices and reduces aggregate supply—as indicated by the shift from S_0S_0 to S_2S_2. The result is that output and prices both rise more in an open economy (point C) than they would in a closed economy (point B).

persevere. The expansionary fiscal policy was mainly the result of the tax cuts of 1981–1984, which led to very large and persistent federal budget deficits.

Table 20–5 indicates what the theory predicts should have happened under such circumstances. Look first at column 1. We have just concluded that a fiscal expansion should raise real interest rates, make the dollar appreciate, raise real GNP (though perhaps weakly because the rising dollar should reduce net exports), and be less inflationary than normal because of the rising dollar. This information is recorded by entering + signs for increases and − signs for decreases.

Our analysis of a monetary *expansion* can be turned on its head to predict the likely effects of a monetary *contraction*. Column 2 notes that the theory says that the tight money component of Reaganomics should have raised real interest rates, made the dollar appreciate, reduced real GNP (probably strongly because the rising dollar should reduce net exports), and been more disinflationary than usual because of the rising dollar.

Column 3 puts the two pieces together. We conclude that the Reaganomics policy mix of fiscal expansion and monetary contraction should have raised interest rates strongly, pushed the value of the dollar up dramatically, devastated our foreign trade, and had uncertain effects on output and inflation—the balance depends on whether fiscal expansion overwhelmed monetary contraction or vice-versa.

How well do these predictions square with the facts? Let us take them one at a time. We know from Chapter 19 that the international value of the dollar soared—rising about 80 percent from its low in mid-1980 to its high in early 1985. We have also observed in this chapter that American foreign trade was clobbered. Real net exports fell from about +$49 billion in 1981 to about −$146 billion in 1986—a swing of $195 billion in just five years. These two facts accord extremely well with the theory.

What about interest rates? Figure 20–13 shows an estimate of the real interest rate on long-term U.S. government bonds from 1978 to 1987. (The historic norm for this rate is between 2 and 3 percent.) The real rate of interest rose dramatically between the time of the 1980 election campaign and the time the Reagan economic program was enacted into law (by September 1981). It then fell during the 1982 recession, but rose again to very high levels in mid-1984. Again, this is just as our theory predicts.

What about real GNP? As we know, the U.S. economy suffered through a terrible recession in 1981–1982. However, it then rebounded and grew strongly for about a year and a half. Thus output growth sagged at first and then spurted. To appraise the effects of Reaganomics on real output, we must look over a longer period. If we take the full five-year period from 1981 to 1986, the average annual growth rate of real GNP was 2.7 percent. Since this almost precisely

Table 20–5
EXPECTED EFFECTS OF POLICY

VARIABLE	(1) FISCAL EXPANSION	(2) MONETARY CONTRACTION	(3) REAGANOMICS
Real interest rate	+	+	+
Exchange rate	+	+	+
Real GNP	+ (small)	− (large)	?
Net exports	−	−	−
Inflation	+ (small)	− (large)	?

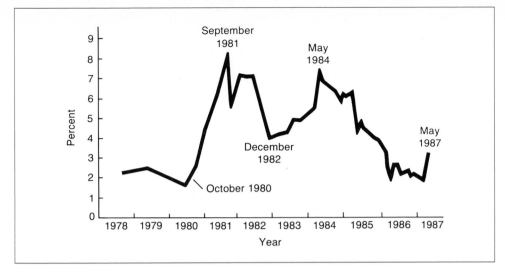

Figure 20–13
REAL INTEREST RATES
IN THE UNITED STATES,
1978–1987
This figure charts the
behavior of the real interest
rate on ten-year U.S.
government bonds on the
basis of a survey of
inflationary expectations. It
rises steeply in 1980–1981.
SOURCE: Richard B. Hoey,
Drexel Burnham Lambert.

matches the average growth rate achieved during the preceding 15 years, the conclusion seems to be that the monetary contraction cancelled out the demand-increasing effects of the fiscal expansion, leaving no net effect on the growth rate of aggregate demand.

If this is so, that would leave only the supply shifts caused by the appreciating dollar. Figures 20–11 and 20–12 show that fiscal expansions and monetary contractions both *increase* aggregate supply by appreciating the currency. (Remember, Figure 20–12 applies to a monetary *expansion*.) The rising dollar certainly helped slow inflation in the early 1980s. In addition, the fact that the deep recession came early in President Reagan's term of office meant that the economy had a recessionary gap throughout the 1981–1986 period. Finally, as we saw in earlier chapters, energy prices were falling rapidly. Each of these factors played a role in the rapid disinflation.

The Link Between the Budget Deficit and the Trade Deficit

There is another useful way to look at the connection between fiscal policy and the trade deficit. But to understand it we need to do some simple arithmetic.

We begin by recalling two definitions: that GNP equals disposable income (*DI*) plus taxes (*T*):

$$Y = DI + T,$$

and that disposable income can either be consumed or saved:

$$DI = C + S.$$

These two definitions jointly imply that:

$$Y = C + S + T,$$

which simply says that national income can be spent, saved, or taxed away.

Now remember the equilibrium condition for GNP in an open economy:

$$Y = C + I + G + X - IM.$$

Equating these two expressions for Y gives:

$$C + I + G + X - IM = C + S + T.$$

Subtracting C from both sides and grouping terms in a natural way leads to this conclusion:

$$G - T = (S - I) - (X - IM).$$

In words, the government budget deficit must be equal to the surplus of savings over investment plus the trade deficit.

This fundamental equation suggests that there is a potentially tight connection between the budget deficit and the trade deficit. Let us examine how this link worked out in the case of Reaganomics.

Since the Reagan tax cuts led to a large budget deficit, the United States could have avoided a large trade deficit only by saving much more or investing much less. The latter is not a very appetizing option and, in any case, generous business tax cuts in 1981 shielded investment spending from the ravages of high real interest rates. (As we saw in Table 20–4, investment *rose* as a share of GNP.) That leaves saving. Supply-siders did indeed promise that the tax cuts would raise savings by extraordinary amounts. Had these promises been redeemed, the budget deficit need not have caused a trade deficit. But they were not. With S not rising and I not falling, our equation leaves only one possibility: A rise in $G - T$ must be reflected in a fall in $X - IM$. The government budget deficit thus led to a massive trade deficit.

This story seems overly mechanical. It may also appear to differ from the one we told earlier; after all, the last paragraph never mentioned interest rates or exchange rates. One last piece of arithmetic, however, will both show that the two stories are equivalent and bring out the intuition behind our fundamental equation.

As we noted in Chapter 19 and earlier in this chapter, the current account and capital account surpluses must sum to zero under floating rates. Thus:

$$(X - IM) + \text{Capital inflows} = 0.$$

Using this to replace $X - IM$ in the previous equation gives:

$$G - T = (S - I) + \text{Capital inflows}.$$

This last equation is simply common sense: If American savers will not save enough to meet the borrowing requirements of both the U.S. government and American investors, then the balance must be borrowed from foreigners.

And it is no mystery how this happens. To attract foreign capital, we must offer interest rates higher than those available abroad. As capital flows into the United States, the exchange rate is driven up. And the high exchange rate leads to a trade deficit. Thus the adjustments of interest rates and exchange rates that we discussed earlier are precisely the way the economy matches the budget deficit with a trade deficit.

On Curing the Trade Deficit

We now have a thorough understanding of how the United States acquired its massive twin deficits and became the world's most indebted nation. Next comes the hard question that we raised at the beginning of the chapter: What can be done about it; how can we cure our foreign trade problem and end our addiction to foreign borrowing?

The answer, of course, is highly controversial. Both economists and politicians disagree over the appropriate course of action. The best we can do here is outline some alternatives.

1. **Reduce the Government Budget Deficit:** The equation:

$$G - T = (S - I) - (X - IM)$$

points to a reduction in the budget deficit as one good way to reduce the trade deficit. Lower G or higher T would lead to lower real interest rates in the United States, a depreciating dollar and, after a lag summarized by the J curve, a shrinking trade deficit.

In fact, American policymakers have been trying to follow this route for some years now, the dollar has come down considerably, and our trade deficit has begun to shrink. However, partisan political bickering over how best to reduce the budget deficit has made progress on this front agonizingly slow and painful.

2. **Expansionary Monetary Policy:** When the government curtails its spending or raises taxes to reduce its budget deficit, aggregate demand falls. If we do not want deficit reduction to contract the U.S. economy, we must compensate for it by monetary stimulus. Like contractionary fiscal policy, expansionary monetary policy also lowers interest rates and depreciates the dollar.

Once again, American policymakers have been pursuing this policy for years. Interest rates here have generally been falling since mid-1984 and the money supply has been growing rapidly. In 1987, however, the Fed became concerned about the possible inflationary consequences of rapid money growth (and of the falling dollar) and grew more cautious.

Notice that these two remedies, in combination, amount to undoing the Reaganomics policy mix of tight money and loose budgets. Between 1980 and 1984, the United States experienced a monetary contraction followed by a fiscal expansion. What we need now to cure the trade deficit, according to many economists, is precisely the reverse: a monetary expansion coupled with a fiscal contraction.

3. **Rapid Economic Growth Abroad:** If foreign economies grew faster, residents of these countries would buy more American goods. That would raise American exports and GNP and reduce our trade deficit. Since about 1985, the U.S. has been urging our major trading partners — especially West Germany and Japan — to stimulate their economies, though with little success.

4. **Raise Domestic Savings or Reduce Domestic Investment:** Our fundamental equation calls attention to two other routes to a smaller trade deficit: higher savings or lower investment.

U.S. personal saving rates are now near all-time lows. If Americans would save more, we could finance more of our government budget deficit at home and therefore would need to borrow less abroad. This, too, would lead to a cheaper dollar and a smaller trade deficit. The only trouble is that no one has yet found a reliable way to induce Americans to save more. We seem to be a nation of consumers.

If the other cures for our trade deficit fail to work in time, the trade deficit may cure itself in a particularly unpleasant way: by dramatically

Saving Patterns and Trade Deficits: The Arithmetic Of U.S.–Japanese Economic Relations

The huge U.S. trade deficit with Japan is a significant source of friction between the two countries and has led to frequent calls for protectionist measures in this country. Our fundamental equation,

$$G - T = (S - I) - (X - IM),$$

teaches us that part of the problem traces to different saving habits in the two countries.

The Japanese people are among the biggest savers in the world. So $S - I$ is a large positive number in Japan. Like the U.S. government, the Japanese government has a budget deficit. However, Japan's $G - T$ is far smaller than its $S - I$. It therefore follows that, in order to balance the international books, Japan must generate a trade surplus.

The contrast between the United States and Japan in this regard is marked. While the American people and government together are big net *borrowers*, the Japanese people and government together are big net *savers*. In an integrated world financial system, it is therefore natural that the Japanese should be lending to us. In short, Japan should have capital *outflows* and we should have capital *inflows* — which is just what has been happening in recent years. Remembering that:

$$\text{current account} + \text{capital account} = 0,$$
$$\text{surplus} \qquad\qquad \text{surplus}$$

the implication is that Japan should have a current account *surplus,* and we should have a current account *deficit*.

Once again this is only natural. In fact, the United States has had a trade deficit with Japan for a long time — even when our overall trade position and Japan's were nearly balanced. Being an island nation almost devoid of natural resources, Japan must run huge trade deficits in primary products. Much of this trade is with developing countries. To offset this trade deficit in primary products, Japan needs a surplus in trade in manufactured goods. And who is likely to be the leading customer for these goods? The biggest consumers on earth, of course — the Americans.

So it is natural for the United States to run a bilateral deficit in trading goods with Japan. However, that does not imply that an annual deficit of $60 billion or more is appropriate, nor that the Japanese are blameless.

For one thing, Japan has long been among the most protectionist of all the advanced industrial nations. Much of this protectionism has been subtle, coming not through high tariffs but through bureaucratic regulations that make importing difficult. But Japan also has its share of high tariffs and quotas. So one possible solution to the U.S.–Japan trade problem is to persuade Japan to open its markets more. But no one really thinks that, even in a completely free market, we could sell in Japan nearly as much as they sell here.

Macroeconomic policy might be a more effective tool. Look once again at the fundamental equation:

$$G - T = (S - I) - (X - M).$$

If Japan stimulated its economy by more expansionary fiscal policy, $G - T$ would rise and $X - M$ would fall. If, at the same time, the U.S. reduced its budget deficit, $G - T$ would fall here and $X - M$ would rise. In all likelihood, our bilateral trade deficit with Japan would narrow.

reducing U.S. domestic investment. Let us see how this might work. As our trade deficits and foreign borrowing persist, foreigners wind up holding more and more U.S. dollar assets. At some point, their willingness to acquire yet more dollar assets will begin to wear thin and they will start charging us much higher interest rates. Of course, higher interest rates lead to lower investment in the United States. Some economists fear a worst-case scenario in which foreigners cease lending to the United States, interest rates here shoot up, and we experience a severe recession. A recession, of course, would reduce our trade deficit substantially by curbing our appetite for imports. But it is a painful cure.

5. **Protectionism:** We have saved the worst approach for last. One seemingly obvious way to cure our trade deficit is to limit imports by imposing stiff tariffs, strict quotas, and other protectionist devices. We discussed protectionism, and the reasons why almost all economists oppose it, in Chapter 18. Despite the economic arguments against it, protectionism has an undeniable political allure. It seems, superficially, to "save American jobs." And it conveniently shifts the blame for our trade problems onto foreigners.

In addition to robbing s and other countries of the benefits of comparative advantage studied in Chapter 18, there are reasons why protectionism might not even succeed in reducing our trade deficit. One is that other nations may retaliate. We erect trade barriers to reduce our imports, thereby reducing IM. But if foreign countries erect corresponding barriers to our exports, X declines. On balance, our *net* exports, $X - IM$, may or may not improve. But world trade will surely suffer. This is a game that may have no winners, only losers.

Even if other nations do not retaliate, tariffs and quotas may not improve our trade deficit much. Why? If they succeed in reducing American spending on imports, tariffs and quotas thereby reduce the supply of dollars on the world market and push the value of the dollar up. A rising dollar, of course, hurts U.S. exports and encourages more imports. The fundamental equation,

$$G - T = (S - I) - (X - M),$$

reminds us that protectionism can raise $X - IM$ only if it reduces the budget deficit, raises saving, or reduces investment.[7]

Conclusion: We Are Not Alone

We do indeed live in a world economy. The major trading nations of the world are linked by exports and imports, by capital flows, and by exchange rates. What happens to national income, prices, and interest rates in one country affects other nations.

Thus policymakers in Europe, Asia, and South America take a keen interest in developments in the U.S. economy. If the U.S. economy expands, these other countries have better markets for their exports. If we pursue policies that make the dollar depreciate, they find their currencies appreciating. If interest rates rise in the United States, they see capital flowing out of their countries into ours. As the "big guy on the block," America bears a special responsibility for the health of the world economy.

[7]Here tariffs, which raise revenue for the government, have a clear advantage over quotas, which do not.

Coordinating Economic Policies: The Group of Seven

Six somberly suited men and one, the Italian, who invariably arrives in open sports coats, convene every three months or so in the opulent gilded chambers of the Louvre Palace, in the clubby rooms of No. 11 Downing Street or beneath the swooping brass chandeliers of the American Treasury's third-floor conference room. All ministers of finance, they . . . come armed with briefing books, kept at their fingertips, and with the weight of their economies on their backs . . .

Collectively, they are known as the Group of Seven, for the industrial democracies—the United States, Japan, West Germany, France, Britain, Canada and Italy—that join in the annual economic summit conferences. Formed only a year ago, the group has an impressive mandate: to devise a way the countries can work together to manage the world economy. That is easier said than done.

In a simpler era . . . when the world's economies were less interdependent . . . a similar group of men wrote the treaty of Bretton Woods, which tied the finances of the Western world to gold and kept them in some kind of balance. That era is now past; most financial experts agree that the same volatile forces that pushed that system to its limits by the early 1970's, leading President Richard M. Nixon to abandon the gold standard, make it impossible to return to such simple mechanisms as rigidly fixed relationships among currencies.

But finding a workable replacement . . . pushes economic theory to its limits . . . [and] assumes a hefty dose of political clout among its participants, if they are to put into effect at home the promises they make to each other. "One of the most difficult jobs in the world," said Treasury Secre-

tary James A. Baker 3d, "is coordinating economic policy. Of necessity, a country's domestic agenda has to come first unless you're going to cede sovereignty, and we're not going to do that."

. . . What the Western finance ministers have established so far is a "framework," they call it, for holding their economies on course . . . Already, the countries have put into effect one feature of the broader concept of policy coordination. They have been setting ranges for currency exchange rates, a partial step back to the system of fixed exchange rates that prevailed from 1944 until the early 1970's . . .

The idea is that when a currency departs from the range, the countries will act in some way . . . For all the ministers' progress, the most important component of an attempt to coordinate economic policies—a willingness to alter countries' fiscal policies of taxation and spending—has yet to be demonstrated. So far, they have been willing only to alter monetary policies—mainly interest rates—in response to unwanted changes in exchange rates.

SOURCE: Excerpted from Peter Kilborn, "Can the Big Seven Learn to Waltz?" *The New York Times* (business section), May 31, 1987.

But we are not the *only* guys on the block. What happens in Germany, Japan, and elsewhere affects the U.S. economy, too. The depression in Latin America and the near-depression in Europe during the 1980s damaged our export markets and contributed to our trade deficit. As mentioned in the previous section, the U.S. government has been urging the Japanese and the Germans to pursue more expansionary policies to help the world economy get back on its feet.

That the major economies of the world are linked suggests the need for greater policy coordination among nations. But since the national interests of particular countries often differ, countries are understandably reluctant to surrender any of their sovereignty. Hence international policy coordination remains an elusive goal. (See the boxed insert on page 454.) Economically speaking, we all live in one world. Politically, however, we live in a world of separate nation-states.

Summary

1. The nations of the world are linked together economically because national income, prices, and interest rates in one country affect those in another.
2. Equilibrium in an open economy requires that $Y = C + I + G + X - IM$. Thus international trade raises GNP if net exports $(X - IM)$ are positive and reduces GNP if net exports are negative.
3. Because imports rise as GNP rises while exports are insensitive to (domestic) GNP, net exports decline as GNP rises.
4. International trade reduces the value of the multiplier.
5. Rapid (or sluggish) economic growth in one country contributes to rapid (or sluggish) growth in other countries.
6. Net exports depend on a country's prices relative to prices in other countries. This provides another reason why the aggregate demand curve slopes downward.
7. If the currency depreciates, net exports rise and aggregate demand increases, thereby raising both real GNP and the price level. A depreciating currency also reduces aggregate supply by making imported goods more expensive.
8. If the currency appreciates, net exports fall and aggregate demand, real GNP, and the price level all decrease. But an appreciating currency also increases aggregate supply by making imports cheaper.
9. Because there are lags in international trade, net exports follow a J-shaped pattern after a currency depreciation; that is, the trade deficit gets worse before it gets better.
10. International capital flows respond strongly to interest rate differentials among countries. Hence higher domestic interest rates lead to currency appreciations and lower interest rates lead to depreciations.
11. For this reason, international capital flows make monetary policy more powerful and fiscal policy less powerful.
12. Since Reaganomics combined tight money with highly expansionary fiscal policy, it raised interest rates, pushed the dollar up, and caused a large trade deficit in the United States.
13. Budget deficits and trade deficits are linked by the fundamental equation $G - T = (S - I) - (X - IM)$. This also implies that $G - T = S - I +$ capital inflows.
14. It follows from this equation that the U.S. trade deficit must be cured by some combination of lower budget deficits, higher savings, and lower investment.
15. A change in the policy mix toward easier monetary policy and smaller budget deficits is one way to reduce the U.S. trade deficit without contracting the U.S. economy.
16. Protectionist policies might not cure the U.S. trade deficit because (a) they will cause the dollar to appreciate and (b) they may provoke foreign retaliation.
17. International coordination of economic policies is important. But it is also elusive in a world of sovereign nations.

Concepts for Review

Questions for Discussion

1. Suppose exports and imports of a country are given by:

GNP	EXPORTS	IMPORTS
$500	$300	$ 50
750	300	100
1000	300	150
1250	300	200
1500	300	250
1750	300	300

Calculate net exports at each level of GNP.

2. If domestic expenditure in the economy described in Question 1 is as shown below, construct a 45°-line diagram and locate the equilibrium level of GNP.

GNP	DOMESTIC EXPENDITURES
$ 500	$ 450
750	650
1000	850
1250	1050
1500	1250
1750	1500

3. Now raise exports to $400 and find the equilibrium again. How large is the multiplier?
4. For years, the U.S. government has been trying to get West Germany to expand its economy faster. Explain how more rapid growth in Germany would affect the U.S. economy.
5. If inflation is higher in the United States than in Taiwan, and the exchange rate between the two countries is fixed, what is likely to happen to the balance of trade between the two countries?
6. Explain why a currency depreciation leads to an improvement in a country's trade balance. If there is a "J curve," what happens in the short run? Why?
7. Explain why American fiscal policy is less powerful and American monetary policy is more powerful than indicated in the closed-economy model of Part 4.
8. Use an aggregate supply-and-demand diagram to analyze the effects of a currency appreciation.
9. Explain why $G - T = (S - I) - (X - IM)$.
10. Given what you now know, evaluate Reaganomics.
11. What, in your view, is the best way for America to reduce its trade deficit?
12. (More difficult) Suppose consumption and investment are described by:

$$C = 120 + .8DI \qquad (DI = \text{disposable income})$$

$$I = 1100 + .1Y - 100r \qquad (Y = GNP)$$

Here r, the interest rate, is measured in percentage points (for example, a 9 percent interest rate is $r = 9$). Exports and imports are as follows:

$$X = 250$$

$$IM = 110 + .2Y$$

Government purchases are $G = 500$ and taxes depend on income as follows:

$$T = -50 + .25Y.$$

The price level is fixed and the demand for money is:

$$M^D = 50 + .2Y - 20r.$$

a. The central bank (called the "Fed") uses its monetary policy to peg the interest rate at $r = 9$. Find equilibrium GNP, the budget deficit or surplus, and the trade deficit or surplus.
b. Suppose the currency depreciates and, as a result, exports and imports change to:

$$X = 400$$

$$IM = -40 + .2Y.$$

Now find equilibrium GNP, the budget deficit or surplus, and the trade deficit or surplus.

Essentials of Microeconomics: Consumers and Firms

21

Everything is worth what its purchaser will pay for it.

PUBLILIUS SYRUS
(1ST CENTURY B.C.)

Consumer Choice and the Individual's Demand Curve

It is clear from our initial look at supply and demand in Chapter 4 that if we are to understand how markets function and how they react to changes in the economic environment, we will have to delve more deeply into the nature of both demand and supply. What influences determine the shapes and positions of the demand and supply curves? How do the curves shift in response to various events? The purpose of Part 6 is to answer questions like these and thereby to provide the analytical tools we will need to pursue the central theme of this book: the virtues and shortcomings of the market mechanism.

We begin on the demand side of the market. In this chapter we emphasize that the market demand curves of Chapter 4 depend on choices made by individual consumers, and we explore the logic underlying these choices. Thus, in contrast with Chapter 4, where we dealt with curves describing the combined demand of all consumers in the market, here we will consider the demand curve of an individual consumer. Since such a demand curve tells us how much of a good a consumer wants to purchase at each possible price, its origins must in some sense rest in consumer psychology. But since economists claim no qualifications for making deep pronouncements about consumer psychology, our exploration will not go very far below the surface. It will, however, describe some powerful tools used in the analysis of consumer choice and cast some light on a number of important issues, including the negative slope of the individual consumer's demand curve.

In Chapter 22 we take up some further aspects of demand curves that are essential for understanding the workings of the market mechanism and expand our analysis from demand curves for single consumers to demand curves for a total market. Then, in Chapters 23 and 24, we turn our attention to the supply side of the market.

A Puzzle: Should Water Be Worth More than Diamonds?

When Adam Smith was lecturing at the University of Glasgow in the 1760s, he introduced the study of demand by posing a puzzle. Common sense, he said, suggests that the price of a commodity must somehow depend on what that good is worth to consumers—on the amount of *utility* that commodity offers. Yet, Smith pointed out, there are cases in which a good's utility apparently has little influence on its price.

Two examples he gave were diamonds and water. He noted that water, which is essential to life and therefore undoubtedly of enormous value to most consumers, generally sells at a very low price, while diamonds, on the other hand, cost thousands of dollars even though their uses are quite limited. A century later, this puzzle, called the **diamond–water paradox,** helped stimulate the invention of what is perhaps the most powerful set of tools in the economist's toolkit—*marginal analysis*. Fortunately, we need only wait a few pages, not a century, to learn how marginal analysis—a general method for making optimal decisions—helps to resolve the paradox.

Total and Marginal Utility

In the American economy, millions of consumers make millions of decisions every day. You decide to buy a movie ticket instead of a paperback novel. Your roommate decides to buy two pounds of cheese rather than one or three. How are these decisions made?

Economists have constructed a simple theory of consumer choice based on the hypothesis that each consumer spends his or her income in the way that yields the greatest amount of satisfaction, or *utility*. This seems a reasonable starting point, since it says little more than that people do what they prefer. But, to make the theory operational, we need a way to measure utility.

A century ago, economists thought that utility could be measured directly in some kind of psychological units (sometimes called "utils"), after somehow reading the consumer's mind. But gradually it came to be realized that this was an unnecessary and, perhaps, impossible task. How many utils did you get from the last movie you saw? You probably cannot answer that question because you have no idea what a util is.

But you may be able to answer a different question like, How many hamburgers would you give up to get that movie ticket? If you answer "three," we still do not know how many utils you get from a film. But we do know that you get more than you get from a hamburger. Hamburgers, rather than utils, become the unit of measurement, and we can say that the utility of a movie (to you) is three hamburgers.

Early in the twentieth century, economists concluded that this more indirect way of measuring utility was all they needed to build a theory of consumer choice. We can measure the utility of a movie ticket by asking how much of some other commodity (like hamburgers) you are willing to give up for it. Any commodity will do for this purpose. But the simplest choice, and the one we will use in this book, is money.[1]

Thus we are led to define the **total utility** of some bundle of goods to some consumer as *the largest sum of money she will voluntarily give up in exchange for it*. For example, suppose Jennifer is considering purchasing six pounds of bananas. She has determined that she will not buy them if they cost more than $2.22, but she will buy them if they cost $2.22 or less. Then the *total utility* of six pounds of bananas to her is $2.22—the maximum amount she is willing to spend to have them.

The **total utility** of a quantity of goods to a consumer (measured in money terms) is the maximum amount of money he or she is willing to give in exchange for it.

[1]NOTE TO INSTRUCTORS: You will recognize that while not using the terms, we are distinguishing between neoclassical *cardinal utility* and *ordinal utility*. Moreover, throughout the book, marginal utility in money terms or money marginal utility is simply a synonym for the marginal rate of substitution between money and the commodity in question.

Total utility measures the benefit Jennifer derives from her purchases. It is total utility that really matters. But to understand which decisions most effectively promote *total* utility we must consider the related concept of **marginal utility.** This term refers to the *additional utility that an individual derives by consuming one more unit of any good*.

The **marginal utility** of a commodity to a consumer (measured in money terms) is the maximum amount of money he or she is willing to pay *for one more unit* of it.

Table 21–1 helps clarify the distinction between marginal and total utility and shows how the two are related. The first two columns show how much *total* utility (measured in money terms) Jennifer derives from various quantities of bananas, ranging from zero to eight. For example, a single pound is worth (no more than) 60 cents to her, two pounds are worth $1.16, and so on. The *marginal* utility is the *difference* between any two successive total utility figures. For example, if the consumer already has three pounds (worth $1.60 to her), an *additional* pound brings her total utility up to $1.96. Her marginal utility is thus the difference between the two, or 36 cents.

Remember: Whenever we use the terms *total utility* and *marginal utility*, we are defining them in terms of the consumer's willingness to part with money for the commodity — not in some unobservable (and imaginary) psychological units.

The "Law" of Diminishing Marginal Utility

The **"law" of diminishing marginal utility** asserts that additional units of a commodity are worth less and less to a consumer in money terms. As the individual's consumption increases, the marginal utility of each additional unit declines.

With these definitions we can now propose a simple hypothesis about consumer tastes: The more of a good a consumer has, the less will be the *marginal* utility of an additional unit.

In general, this is a plausible proposition. The idea is based on the assertion that every person has a hierarchy of uses to which he or she will put a particular commodity. All of these uses are valuable, but some are more valuable than others. Let's consider bananas again. Jennifer may use them to feed her family, to feed a pet monkey, to make a banana cream pie (which is a bit rich for her tastes), or to give to a brother-in-law for whom she has no deep affection. If she has only one pound, it will be used solely for the family to eat. The second, third, and fourth pounds may be used to feed the monkey; and the fifth may go into the banana cream pie. But the only use she has for the sixth pound, alas, is to give it to her brother-in-law.

The point is obvious. Each pound of bananas contributes something to the satisfaction of Jennifer's needs for the product. But each additional pound

---

Table 21–1
TOTAL AND MARGINAL UTILITY OF BANANAS (MEASURED IN MONEY TERMS)

(1) NUMBER OF POUNDS	(2) TOTAL UTILITY (in dollars)	(3) MARGINAL UTILITY* (in dollars)	(4) POINT IN FIGURE 21–1
0	0		
1	.60	.60	A
2	1.16	.56	B
3	1.60	.44	C
4	1.96	.36	D
5	2.14	.18	E
6	2.22	.08	F
7	2.26	.04	G
8	2.26	0	H

*Each entry in this column is the difference between successive entries in column (2).

contributes less (relative to money) than its predecessor because the use to which it can be put has a lower priority. This, in essence, is the logic behind the **"law" of diminishing marginal utility.**

The third column of Table 21–1 illustrates this concept. The marginal utility (abbreviated MU) of the first pound of bananas is 60 cents; that is, Jennifer is willing to pay *up to* 60 cents for the first pound. The second pound is worth no more than 56 cents, the third pound only 44 cents, and so on until, after the fifth pound, Jennifer is willing to pay only 8 cents for an additional pound (the MU of the sixth pound is 8 cents).

The numbers in the first and third columns in the table are shown in Figure 21–1 by points A, B, C, and so on. We note that the graph of marginal utility is negatively sloped; this again illustrates how marginal utility diminishes as the quantity of product rises.

The assumption upon which this "law" is based is plausible for most consumers and for most commodities. But, like most laws, there are exceptions. For some people, the more they have of a particular good, the more they want. Consider the needs of alcoholics and stamp collectors, for example. The stamp collector who has a few stamps may consider the acquisition of one more to be mildly amusing. The person who has a large and valuable collection may be prepared to go to the ends of the earth for another stamp. Similarly, the alcoholic who finds a dry martini quite pleasant when he first starts drinking may find one more to be absolutely irresistible once he has already consumed four or five. Economists, however, generally treat such cases of *increasing marginal utility* as anomalies. For most goods and most people, marginal utility probably declines as consumption increases.

The Optimal Purchase Rule

Now let us put the concept of marginal utility to work in analyzing consumer choice. Every consumer has a limited amount of money to spend. Which items will she buy, and in what quantities? The theory of consumer choice is based on the hypothesis that she will spend her money in the way that *maximizes her total utility*. This hypothesis leads to the following **optimal purchase rule:**

It always pays the consumer to buy more of any commodity whose marginal utility (measured in money) exceeds its price, and less of any commodity whose marginal utility is less than its price. When possible, the consumer should buy

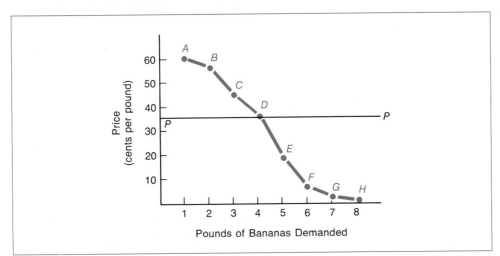

Figure 21–1
A TYPICAL MARGINAL UTILITY OR DEMAND CURVE
This demand curve is derived from the consumer's table of marginal utilities by following the optimal purchase rule. The points in the graph correspond to the numbers in Table 21–2.

the quantity of each good at which price (P) and marginal utility (MU) are exactly equal, that is, at which

$$P = MU,$$

because only these quantities will maximize the *total utility* she gains from her purchases given the fact that the money she has available must be divided among all the goods she buys.[2]

Notice that while our concern is with *total* utility, the rule is framed in terms of *marginal* utility. Marginal utility is not important for its own sake, but rather as an instrument used to calculate the level of purchases that maximizes total utility.

To see why this rule works, refer back to the table and graph of marginal utilities of bananas (Table 21–1 and Figure 21–1). Suppose the supermarket is selling bananas for 36 cents a pound (line *PP* in the graph) and Jennifer considers buying only two pounds. We see that this is not a wise decision, because the marginal utility of the third pound of bananas (44 cents, point C,) is greater than its 36-cent price. If Jennifer were to increase her purchase to three pounds, the additional pound would cost 36 cents but yield 44 cents in marginal utility; thus the additional purchase would bring her a clear net gain of 8 cents. Obviously, at the 36-cent price she is better off with three pounds of bananas than with two.

Similarly, at this price, five pounds (point *E*) is *not* an optimal purchase because the 18-cent marginal utility of the fifth pound is less than its 36-cent price. Jennifer would be better off with only four pounds, since that would save her 36 cents with only an 18-cent loss in utility—a net gain of $36 - 18 = 18$ cents from the decision to buy one pound less. In sum, our rule for optimal purchases tells us that Jennifer should *not* end up buying a quantity at which MU is higher than price (points like *A, B,* and *C*) because a larger purchase would make her better off. Similarly, she should not end up at points *E, F, G,* and *H*, at which MU is below price because from any such point she would be better off buying less. Rather, Jennifer should buy four pounds (point *D*), where $P = MU$.

It should be noted that price is an objective, observable figure determined by the market, while marginal utility is subjective and reflects the tastes of the consumer. Since the consumer lacks the power to influence the price, she must adjust her purchases to make the marginal utility of each good equal to the price given by the market.

From Marginal Utility to the Demand Curve

We can use the optimal purchase rule to show that the "law" of diminishing marginal utility implies that demand curves typically slope downward to the right, that is, they have negative slopes.[3] For example, it is possible to use the

[2]We can equate a dollar price with marginal utility only because we measure marginal utility in money terms (or, as the matter is more usually put by economists, because we deal with the marginal rate of substitution of money for the commodity in question). If marginal utility were measured in some psychological units not directly translatable into money terms, a comparison of *P* and MU would have no meaning. However, MU could also be measured in terms of any commodity other than money. (Example: How much root beer is Jennifer willing to trade for an additional banana?)
[3]If you need review, turn back to pages 20–23 in Chapter 2.

Table 21–2
LIST OF OPTIMAL QUANTITY TO PURCHASE AT ALTERNATIVE PRICES

PRICE* (in dollars)	QUANTITY TO PURCHASE
.04	7
.08	6
.18	5
.36	4
.44	3
.56	2
.60	1

*Note that for simplicity of explanation the prices shown have been chosen to equal the marginal utilities in Table 21–1. In-between prices would make the optimal choices involve fractions of a pound (say 2.6 pounds).

list of marginal utilities in Table 21–1 to determine how many bananas Jennifer would buy at any particular price. Table 21–2 gives several alternative prices, and the optimal purchase quantity corresponding to each. (To make sure you understand the logic behind the optimal purchase rule, verify that the entries in the right-hand column of Table 21–2 are in fact correct.) This *demand schedule,* which relates quantity demanded to price, may be translated into Jennifer's *demand curve* shown in Figure 21–1. This demand curve is simply the blue marginal utility curve. You can see that it has the characteristic negative slope commonly associated with demand curves.

Let us examine the logic underlying the negatively sloped demand curve a bit more carefully. If Jennifer is purchasing the optimal number of bananas, and then the price falls, she will find that her marginal utility of bananas is now above the suddenly reduced price. For example, Table 21–1 tells us that at a price of 44 cents per pound it is optimal to buy three pounds, because the marginal utility (MU) of the fourth pound is 36 cents. But, if price is reduced to anything less than 36 cents, it then pays to purchase the fourth pound because its MU exceeds its price. This additional pound of bananas will lower the marginal utility of the next (fifth) pound of bananas (to 18 cents in the example), and so if the price is above 18 cents it will not pay the consumer to buy that fifth pound, just as prescribed in the optimal purchase rule.

Note the critical role of the "law" of diminishing marginal utility. If *P* falls, a consumer who wishes to maximize total utility will see to it that MU falls. According to the "law" of diminishing marginal utility, the only way to do this is to increase the quantity purchased.

While this explanation is a bit abstract and mechanical, it can easily be rephrased in practical terms. We have seen that the various uses to which an individual puts a commodity have different priorities. For Jennifer, giving bananas to her family has a higher priority than using them to make a pie, which in turn is of higher priority than giving them to her brother-in-law. If the price of bananas is high, Jennifer will buy only enough for the high-priority uses—those that offer a high marginal utility. When price declines, however, it pays to purchase more of the good—enough for some low-priority uses. This is the essence of the analysis. It tells us that the same assumption about consumer psychology underlies both the "law" of diminishing marginal utility and the negative slope of the demand curve. They are really two different ways of describing the assumed attitudes of consumers.

The Diamond–Water Paradox: The Puzzle Resolved

We can use marginal utility analysis to solve the mystery of Adam Smith's diamond–water paradox — his observation that diamonds are generally considered very expensive, while water is usually considered cheap, even though water seems to offer far more utility. The resolution of the diamond–water paradox is based on the distinction between marginal and total utility.

The *total* utility of water — its life-giving benefit — is indeed much higher than that of diamonds, just as Smith observed. But price, as we have seen, is not related directly to total utility. Rather, the optimal purchase rule tells us that price will tend to be equal to *marginal* utility. And there is every reason to expect the marginal utility of water to be very low while the marginal utility of diamonds is very high.

Water is extremely plentiful in many parts of the world, and so its price is generally quite low. Consumers thus use correspondingly large quantities of water. By the principle of diminishing marginal utility, therefore, the marginal utility of water to a typical household will be pushed down to a low level.

On the other hand, diamonds are scarce. As a result, the quantity of diamonds consumed is not large enough to drive the MU of diamonds down very far, and so buyers are willing to pay high prices for them. The scarcer the commodity, the higher its *marginal* utility and its market price will be, regardless of the size of its *total* utility.

Thus, like many paradoxes, the diamond–water puzzle has a straightforward explanation. In this case, all one has to remember is that:

Scarcity raises price and *marginal* utility but not necessarily *total* utility.

Prices, Income, and Quantity Demanded

Our study of marginal analysis has enabled us to examine the relation between the price of a commodity and the quantity that will be purchased. But the amount of money a consumer is willing to pay for an additional unit of a good does not depend only on the consumer's tastes, but also on how much that person can afford to spend. Consequently, the quantity of the good demanded by a consumer also depends on the consumer's income. Let us first consider briefly how a change in income affects quantity purchased. Then we will use this information to learn more about the effect of a price change.

The Two Effect of a Change in Income

The consumer's purchase of basketball tickets depends on both his income and the price of tickets. Let us consider what happens to the number of tickets a consumer will buy when his real income rises. It may seem almost certain that he will buy more tickets than before, but that is not necessarily so. A rise in real income can either increase or decrease the quantity of tickets purchased.

Why might it do the latter? There are some goods and services which people buy only because they cannot afford any better. They eat bologna three days a week and filet mignon twice a year, but they would rather have it the other way around. They use margarine instead of butter, or purchase most of their clothing secondhand. If their real income rises, they may then buy more filet mignon and less bologna, more butter and less margarine, more new shirts and fewer secondhand shirts. Thus, a rise in real income will reduce the quantities of bologna, margarine, and secondhand shirts demanded. Economists have given the rather descriptive name **inferior goods** to the class of commodities for which quantity demanded falls when income rises.

The upshot of this discussion is that we cannot draw definite conclusions about the effects of a rise in consumer incomes on quantity demanded. For most commodities, if incomes rise and prices do not change, there will be an increase in quantity demanded. (Such items are often called *normal goods*.) But for the inferior goods there will be a decrease in quantity demanded.

The Two Effects of a Change in Price*

When the price of some good, say heating oil, falls, it has two consequences. First, it makes fuel oil cheaper relative to electricity, gas, or coal. We say, then, that the *relative price* of fuel oil has fallen. Second, this price decrease leaves homeowners with more money to spend on movie admissions, soft drinks, or clothing. In other words, the decrease in the price of fuel oil *increases the consumer's real income* — his power to purchase other goods.

While a fall in the price of a commodity always produces these two effects simultaneously, our analysis will be easier if we separate the effects from one another and study them one at a time.

1. **The income effect.** As we have just noted, a fall in the price of a commodity leads to a rise in the consumer's *real* income — the amount that his wages will purchase. The consequent effect on quantity demanded is called the **income effect** of the price fall. The income effect caused by a fall in a commodity's price is much the same as if the consumer's wages had risen: he will buy more of any commodity that is not an inferior good. The process producing the income effect has three stages: (1) the price of the good falls; causing (2) an increase in the consumer's real income; which leads to (3) a change in quantity demanded. Of course, if the price of a good rises, it will produce the same effect in reverse. The consumer's real income will decline, leading to the opposite change in quantity demanded.

2. **The substitution effect.** A change in the price of a commodity produces another effect on quantity demanded that is rather different from the income effect. This is the **substitution effect,** which is the effect on quantity demanded attributable to the fact that the new price is now higher or lower than before *relative to the prices of other goods*. The substitution effect of a price change is the portion of the change in quantity demanded that can be attributed *exclusively* to the resulting change in relative prices rather than to the associated change in real income.

   There is nothing mysterious or surprising about the effect of a change in relative prices when the consumer's real income remains unchanged. Whenever it is possible for the consumer to switch between two commodities, he can be expected to buy more of the good whose relative price has fallen and less of the good whose relative price has risen. For example, a few years ago AT&T instituted sharp reductions in the prices of evening long distance telephone calls relative to daytime calls. The big decrease in the relative price of evening calls brought about a large increase in calling during the evening hours and a decrease in daytime calling, just as the telephone company had hoped. Similarly, a fall in the relative price of fuel oil will induce more of the people who are building new homes to install oil heat instead of electric heat.

An **inferior good** is a commodity whose quantity demanded falls when the purchaser's real income rises, all other things remaining equal.

The **income effect** is a *portion* of the change in quantity of a good demanded when its price changes. A rise in price cuts the consumer's purchasing power (real income), which leads to a change in the quantity demanded of that commodity. That change is the income effect.

The **substitution effect** is the change in quantity demanded of a good resulting from a change in its relative price, exclusive of whatever change in quantity demanded may be attributable to the associated change in real income.

*This section contains rather more difficult material, which, in shorter courses, may be omitted without loss of continuity.

When the price of any commodity X rises relative to the price of some other commodity Y, a consumer whose real income has remained unchanged can be expected to buy less X and more Y than before. Thus, *if we consider the substitution effect alone,* a decline in price always increases quantity demanded and a rise in price always reduces quantity demanded.

These two concepts, the income effect and the substitution effect, which many beginning economics students think were invented to torture them, are really quite useful. Let us consider an example of how economists use them. Suppose the price of hamburgers declines while the price of cheese remains unchanged. The *substitution effect* clearly induces the consumer to buy more hamburgers in place of grilled cheese sandwiches, because hamburgers are now comparatively cheaper. What of the *income effect?* Unless hamburger is an inferior good, it leads to the same decision. The fall in price makes consumers richer, which induces them to increase their purchases of all but inferior goods. This example alerts us to two general points:

If a good is not inferior, it must have a downward-sloping demand curve, since income and substitution effects reinforce each other. However, an inferior good may violate this pattern of demand behavior because the income effect of a decline in price leads consumers to buy less.

Do *all* inferior goods, then, have upward-sloping demand curves? Certainly not, for we have the substitution effect to reckon with; and the substitution effect always favors a downward-sloping demand curve. Thus we have a kind of tug-of-war in the case of an inferior good. If the *income effect* predominates, the demand curve will slope upward; if the *substitution effect* prevails, the demand curve will slope downward.

Economists have concluded that the substitution effect generally wins out; so while there are many examples of inferior goods, there are few examples of upward-sloping demand curves. When might the income effect prevail over the substitution effect? Certainly not when the good in question (say, margarine) is a very small fraction of the consumer's budget, for then a fall in price makes the consumer only slightly "richer," and therefore creates a very small income effect. But the demand curve could slope upward if an inferior good constitutes a substantial portion of the consumer's budget.

We conclude this discussion of income and substitution effects with a warning against an error that is frequently made. Many students mistakenly close their books thinking that price changes cause substitution effects while income changes cause income effects. This is incorrect. As the foregoing example of hamburgers made clear:

Any change in price sets in motion both a substitution effect and an income effect, both of which affect quantity demanded.

This completes our discussion of the logic behind consumer choice. In the next chapter we will use this analysis as a base upon which to build a theory of demand, thereby taking our first major step toward understanding how the market system operates.

The Theory of Consumer Choice and White Rats

A few years ago a team of economists and psychologists studied whether the theory of consumer choice that we have just outlined—including the different income and substitution effects of a price change—applies to animal species other than *homo sapiens*. According to their research, it does.[*]

In one experiment, standard laboratory rats were placed in experimental chambers equipped with two levers; pressing one lever rewarded them with a prescribed amount of commodity A (say, water) while pressing the other rewarded them with a prescribed amount of commodity B (say, food). The rats were given a limited "budget" because they could only press the levers a fixed number of times per day. Once they had exhausted their "income" by pressing the levers, say, 250 times, the lights above the levers would go out, signaling the rats that their presses would no longer result in rewards. Apparently, the little creatures learned the meaning of the lights quite quickly.

In this controlled environment, *income effects* could be observed by varying the permitted number of lever presses per day. The results showed clearly that when more lever presses were allowed, rats chose to consume more of both goods. Apparently, none of the goods such as food, water, root

[*]John H. Kagel, Raymond C. Battalio, Howard Rachlin, and Leonard Green, "Demand Curves for Animal Consumers," *Quarterly Journal of Economics*, vol. XCVI, February 1981, pages 1–16.

beer, and Tom Collins mix are inferior goods from the point of view of rats.

Measuring *substitution effects* was a bit trickier since, as we have stressed, a price change sets in motion *both* an income effect *and* a substitution effect. In the experiment, the "price" of each commodity was controlled by the amount of food or liquid produced by each lever press. Substitution effects were measured, for example, by raising the "price" of food (that is, reducing the amount of food yielded by each press), while at the same time allowing the rat enough additional lever presses to compensate him for his loss of purchasing power. As the analysis of this chapter has suggested, the rats responded to this change in their environment by "buying" less food.

Putting the two effects together, then, a higher price of food led to less consumption of food via the income effect and also to less consumption of food via the substitution effect. The demand curves of these rats were indeed negatively sloped.

Summary

1. Economists distinguish between total and marginal utility. Total utility, or the benefit a consumer derives from a purchase, is measured by the maximum amount of money he or she would give up in order to have the good in question. Rational consumers seek to maximize total utility.

2. Marginal utility is the maximum amount of money a consumer is willing to pay for an additional unit of a particular commodity. Marginal utility is useful in calculating what set of purchases maximizes total utility.

3. The "law" of diminishing marginal utility is a psy-

chological hypothesis stating that as a consumer acquires more and more of a commodity, the marginal utility of additional units of the commodity will decrease.

4. To maximize the total utility obtained by spending money on some commodity X, given the fact that other goods can be purchased only with the money that remains after buying X, the consumer must purchase a quantity of X such that the price is equal to the commodity's marginal utility (in money terms).

5. If the consumer acts to maximize utility, and if his

marginal utility of some good declines when larger quantities are purchased, then his demand curve for the good will have a negative slope. A reduction in price will induce the purchase of more units, leading to a lower marginal utility.

6. Abundant goods tend to have a low price and low marginal utility regardless of whether their total utility is high or low. That is why water can have a low price despite its high total utility.

7. An inferior good, such as secondhand clothing, is a commodity consumers buy less of when they get richer, all other things held equal.

8. A rise in the price of a commodity has two effects on quantity demanded: (a) a substitution effect, which makes the good less attractive because it has become more expensive than it was previously, and (b) an income effect, which decreases the consumer's total utility because higher prices cut his purchasing power.

9. Any increase in the price of a good always has a *negative* substitution effect; that is, considering only the substitution effect, a rise in price must reduce the quantity demanded.

10. The income effect of a rise in price may, however, push quantity demanded up or down. For normal goods, the income effect of a higher price (which makes consumers poorer) reduces quantity demanded; for inferior goods, the income effect of higher prices actually increases quantity demanded.

Concepts for Review

Diamond–water paradox	The "law" of diminishing marginal utility	Inferior goods
Marginal analysis	Optimal purchase rule ($P = MU$)	Income effect
Total utility	Scarcity and marginal utility	Substitution effect
Marginal utility		

Questions for Discussion

1. Describe some of the different things you do with water. Which would you give up if the price of water rose a little? If it rose by a fairly large amount? If it rose by a very large amount?

2. Which is greater: your *total* utility from 12 gallons of water per day or from 18 gallons per day? Why?

3. Which is greater: your *marginal* utility at 12 gallons per day or your marginal utility at 18 gallons per day? Why?

4. Suppose you wanted to measure the marginal utility of a commodity to a consumer by determining the consumer's psychological attitude or strength of feeling for the commodity directly, rather than seeing how much money the consumer is willing to give up for the commodity. How might you go about such a psychological measurement? (*Note:* No one has a good answer to this question.)

5. Some people who do not understand the optimal purchase rule argue that if a consumer buys so much of a good that its price equals its marginal utility, he could not possibly be behaving optimally. Rather, they say, he would be better off quitting when ahead; that is, buying a quantity such that marginal utility is much greater than price. What is wrong with this argument? (*Hint:* What opportunity does the consumer then miss? Is it maximization of marginal or total utility that serves the consumer's interests?)

6. What inferior goods do you purchase? Why do you buy them? Do you think you will continue to buy them when your income is higher?

7. Which of the following items are likely to be normal goods to a typical consumer? Which are likely to be inferior goods?
   a. Vintage champagne
   b. Paper napkins
   c. Secondhand clothing
   d. Overseas trips

8. Suppose that gasoline and safety pins each rise in price by 20 percent. Which will have the larger income effect on the purchases of a typical consumer? Why?

9. Around 1850, Sir Robert Giffen observed that Irish peasants actually consumed more potatoes as the price of potatoes increased. Use the concepts of income and substitution effects to explain this phenomenon.

Appendix
Indifference Curve Analysis

The analysis of consumer demand presented in this chapter, while correct as far as it goes, has one shortcoming: By treating the consumer's decision about the purchase of each commodity as an isolated event, it conceals the necessity of choice imposed on the consumer by his limited budget. It does not indicate explicitly the hard choice behind every purchase decision—the sacrifice of some goods to obtain others. The idea, of course, is implicit because the purchase of a commodity involves a trade-off between that good and money. If you spend more money on rent, you have less to spend on entertainment. If you buy more clothing, you have less money for food. But to represent the consumer's choice problem explicitly, economists have invented two geometric devices, the *budget line* and the *indifference curve*, which this appendix describes.

Geometry of the Available Choices: The Budget Line

Suppose, for simplicity, that there were only two commodities produced in the world, cheese and records. The decision problem of any household then would be to determine the allocation of its income between these two goods. Clearly, the more it spends on one, the less it can have of the other. But just what is the trade-off? A numerical example will answer this question and also introduce the graphical device that economists use to portray the trade-off.

Suppose that cheese costs $2 per pound, records sell at $3 each, and our consumer has $12 at his disposal. He obviously has a variety of

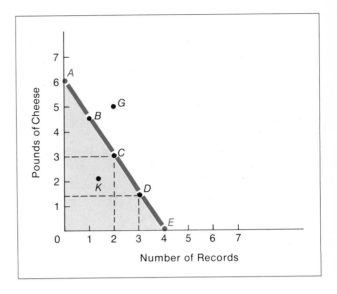

Figure 21–2
A BUDGET LINE
This budget line shows the different combinations of cheese and records the consumer can buy with $12 if cheese costs $2 per pound and records cost $3 each. At point A the consumer buys six pounds of cheese and has nothing left over for records. At point E he spends the entire budget on records. At intermediate points (such as C) on the budget line, the consumer buys some of both goods (two records and three pounds of cheese).

choices—as displayed in Table 21–3. For example, if he buys no records, he can go home with six pounds of cheese, and so on. Each of the combinations of cheese and records that the consumer can afford can be shown in a diagram in which the axes measure the quantities of each commodity that are purchased. In Figure 21–2, pounds of

Table 21–3
ALTERNATIVE PURCHASE COMBINATIONS FOR A $12 BUDGET

NUMBER OF RECORDS (at $3 each)	EXPENDITURE ON RECORDS (in dollars)	REMAINING FUNDS (in dollars)	NUMBER OF POUNDS OF CHEESE (at $2 each)	LABEL IN FIGURE 21–2
0	0	12	6	A
1	3	9	$4\frac{1}{2}$	B
2	6	6	3	C
3	9	3	$1\frac{1}{2}$	D
4	12	0	0	E

cheese are measured along the vertical axis, number of records is measured along the horizontal axis, and each of the combinations enumerated in Table 21–3 is represented by a labeled point. For example, point A corresponds to spending everything on cheese, point E corresponds to spending everything on records, and point C corresponds to buying two records and three pounds of cheese.

If we connect points A through E by a straight line, the blue line in the diagram, we can trace all the possible ways to divide the $12 between the two goods. For example, point D tells us that if the consumer buys three records, there will be only enough money left to purchase one and one-half pounds of cheese. This is readily seen to be correct from Table 21–3. Line AE is therefore called the **budget line.**

The **budget line** for a household represents graphically all the possible combinations of two commodities that it can purchase, given the prices of the commodities and some fixed amount of money at its disposal.

Properties of the Budget Line

Let us now use r to represent the number of records purchased by our consumer and c to indicate the amount of cheese he acquires. Thus, at $2 per pound, he spends on cheese a total of 2 × (number of pounds of cheese bought) = 2c dollars. Similarly, he spends 3r dollars on records, making a total of 2c + 3r = $12, if the entire $12 is spent on the two commodities. This is the equation of the budget line. It is also the equation of the straight line drawn in the diagram.[4]

We note also that the budget line represents the *maximal* amounts of the commodities that the consumer can afford. Thus, for any given purchase of records, it tells us the greatest amount of cheese his money can buy. If our consumer wants to be thrifty, he can choose to end up at a point below the budget line, such as K. Clearly, then, the choices he has available include not only those points on the budget line AE, but also any point

in the shaded triangle formed by the budget line AE and the two axes. By contrast, points above the budget line, such as G, are not available to the consumer given his limited budget. A bundle consisting of five pounds of cheese and two records would cost $16, which is more than he has to spend.

The position of the budget line is determined by two types of data: the prices of the commodities purchased and the income at the buyer's disposal. We can complete our discussion of the graphics of the budget line by examining briefly how a change in either of these magnitudes affects its location.

Obviously, any increase in the income of the household increases the range of options available to it. Specifically, *increases in income produce parallel shifts in the budget line*, as shown in Figure 21–3. The reason is simply that a, say, 50 percent increase in available income, if entirely spent on the two goods in question, would permit the family to purchase exactly 50 percent more of *either* commodity. Point A in Figure 21–2 would shift upward by 50 percent of its distance from the origin, while point E would move to the right by

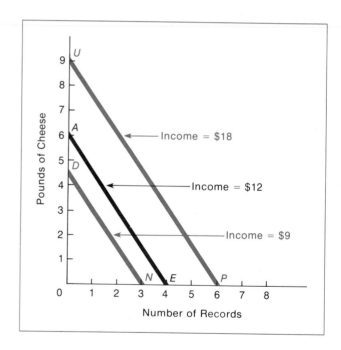

Figure 21–3
THE EFFECT OF INCOME CHANGES ON THE BUDGET LINE
A change in the amount of money in the consumer's budget causes a parallel shift in the budget line. A rise in the budget from $12 to $18 raises the budget line from *AE* to *UP*. A fall from $12 to $9 lowers the budget line from *AE* to *DN*.

[4]The reader may have noticed one problem that arises in this formulation. If every point on the budget line AE is a possible way for the consumer to spend his money, there must be some manner in which he can buy fractional records. Perhaps the purchase of one and one-half records can be interpreted to include a down payment of $1.50 on a record on his next shopping trip! Throughout this book it is convenient to assume that commodities are available in fractional quantities when drawing diagrams. This makes the graphs clearer and does not really affect the analysis.

50 percent.[5] Figure 21–3 shows three such budget lines corresponding to incomes of $9, $12, and $18, respectively.

Finally, we can ask what happens to the budget line when there is a change in the price of some commodity. In Figure 21–4, we see that when the price of the records *decreases*, the budget line moves outward, but the move is no longer parallel because the point on the cheese axis remains fixed. Once again, the reason is fairly straightforward. A 50 percent reduction in the price of records permits the family's $12 to buy twice as many records as before: point E is moved rightward to point H, at which eight records are shown to be obtainable. However, since the price of cheese has not changed, point A, the amount

[5] An algebraic proof is simple. Let M (which is initially $12) be the amount of money available to our household. The equation of the budget line can be solved for c, obtaining

$$c = -(3/2)r + M/2.$$

This is the equation of a straight line with a slope of $-3/2$ and a vertical intercept of $M/2$. A change in M, the quantity of money available, will not change the *slope* of the budget line; it will lead only to parallel shifts in that line.

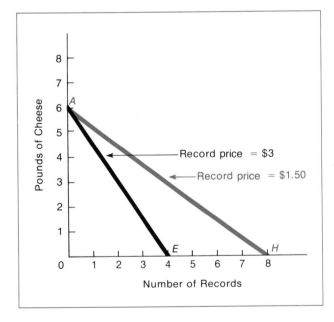

Figure 21–4
THE EFFECT OF PRICE CHANGES ON THE BUDGET LINE
A fall in the price of records causes the end of the budget line on the records axis to swing away from the origin. A fall in record price from $3 to $1.50 swings the price line from *AE* to blue line *AH*. This happens because at the higher price, $12 buys only four records, but at the lower price, it can buy eight records.

of cheese that can be bought for $12, is unaffected. Thus we have the general result that *a reduction in the price of one of the two commodities swings the budget line outward along the axis representing the quantity of that item while leaving the location of the other end of the line unchanged*.

What the Consumer Prefers: The Indifference Curve

The budget line tells us what choices are *available* to the consumer. We next must examine the consumer's *preferences* in order to determine which of these possibilities he will want to choose.

After much investigation, economists have determined what they believe to be the minimum amount of information they need about a purchaser in order to analyze his choices. This information consists of the consumer's *ranking* of the alternative bundles of commodities that are available. Suppose, for instance, the consumer is offered a choice between two bundles of goods, bundle W, which contains three records and one pound of cheese, and bundle T, which contains two records and three pounds of cheese. The economist wants to know for this purpose only whether the consumer prefers W to T, T to W, or whether he is *indifferent* about which one he gets. Note that the analysis requires no information about *degree* of preference—whether the consumer is wildly more enthusiastic about one of the bundles or just prefers it slightly.

Graphically, the preference information is provided by a group of curves called **indifference curves** (Figure 21–5).

An **indifference curve** is a line connecting all combinations of the commodities in question that are equally desirable to the consumer.

But before we examine these curves, let us see how such a curve is interpreted. A single point on an indifference curve tells us nothing about preferences. For example, point R on curve I_a simply represents the bundle of goods composed of four records and one-half pound of cheese. It does *not* suggest that the consumer is indifferent between one-half pound of cheese and four records. For the curve to tell us anything, we must consider at least two of its points, for example, points S and W. Since they represent two different combinations that are on the same indifference curve, they are equally desirable to our consumer.

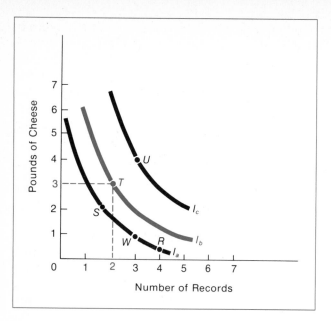

Figure 21-5
THREE INDIFFERENCE CURVES FOR CHEESE
AND RECORDS
Any point in the diagram represents a combination of cheese
and records (for example, *T* represents two records and three
pounds of cheese). Any two points on the same indifference
curve (for example, *S* and *W*) represent two combinations of
the goods that the consumer likes equally well. If two points
such as *T* and *W*, lie on different indifference curves, the one
on the higher indifference curve is preferred by the consumer.

Properties of the Indifference Curves

We do not know yet which bundle our consumer
prefers; we know only that a choice between certain bundles will lead to indifference. So before
we can use an indifference curve to analyze the
consumer's choice, we must examine a few of its
properties. Most important for us is the fact that:

As long as the consumer desires *more* of each of
the goods in question, *every* point on a higher
indifference curve (that is, a curve farther from
the origin in the graph) will be preferred to *any*
point on a lower indifference curve.

In other words, among indifference curves,
higher is better. The reason is obvious. Given two
indifference curves, say I_b and I_c in Figure 21-5,
the higher curve will contain points lying above
and to the right of some points on the lower
curve. Thus, point *U* on curve I_c lies above and to
the right of point *T* on curve I_b. This means that
at *U* the consumer gets more records *and* more

cheese than at *T*. Assuming that he desires both
commodities, our consumer must prefer *U* to *T*.
Since every point on curve I_c is, by definition,
equal in preference to point *U*, and the same relation holds for point *T* and all other points along
curve I_b, *every* point on curve I_c will be preferred
to *any* point on curve I_b.

This at once implies a second property of
indifference curves: they never intersect. This is
so because if an indifference curve, say I_b, is anywhere above another, say I_a, then I_b must be
above I_a everywhere, since every point on I_b is
preferred to every point on I_a.

Another property that characterizes the indifference curve is its *negative slope*. Again, this
holds only if the consumer wants more of both
commodities. Consider two points, such as *S* and
R, on the same indifference curve. If the consumer is indifferent between them, one cannot
contain more of *both* commodities than the other.
Since point *S* contains more cheese than *R*, *R*
must offer more records than *S*, or the consumer
would not be indifferent about which he gets.
This means that if, say, we move toward the one
with the larger number of records, the quantity of
cheese must decrease. The curve will always slope
downhill toward the right, a negative slope.

A final property of indifference curves is the
nature of their curvature—the way they round
toward the axes. As drawn, they are "bowed in"—
they flatten out (their slopes decrease in absolute
value) as they extend from left to right. To understand why this is so we must first examine the
economic interpretation of the slope of an indifference curve.

The Slopes of an Indifference Curve and of a Budget Line

In Figure 21-6 the average slope of the indifference curve between points *M* and *N* is represented
by *RM/RN*. *RM* is the quantity of cheese the consumer gives up in moving from *M* to *N*. Similarly,
RN is the increased number of records acquired in
this move. Since the consumer is indifferent
between bundles *M* and *N*, the gain of *RN* records
must just suffice to compensate him for the loss of
RM pounds of cheese. Thus the ratio *RM/RN* represents the terms on which the consumer is just
willing—*according to his own preference*—to trade
one good for the other. If *RM/RN* equals two, the
consumer is willing to give up (no more than) two
pounds of cheese for one additional record.

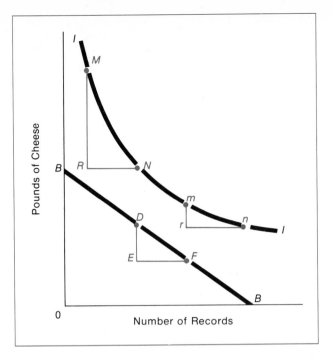

Figure 21–6
SLOPES OF A BUDGET LINE AND AN
INDIFFERENCE CURVE
The slope of the budget line shows how many pounds of
cheese, *ED,* can be exchanged for *EF* records. The slope of
the indifference curve shows how many pounds of cheese,
RM, the consumer is just willing to exchange for *RN* records.
When the consumer has more records and less cheese (point
m as compared with *M*), the slope of the indifference curve
decreases, meaning that the consumer is only willing to give
up *rm* pounds of cheese for *rn* records.

The **slope of an indifference curve,** referred to as
the **marginal rate of substitution** between the
commodities involved, represents the maximum
amount of one commodity the consumer is willing
to give up in exchange for one more unit of
another commodity.

    The slope of budget line *BB* in Figure 21–6 is
also a rate of exchange between cheese and
records. But it no longer reflects the consumer's
subjective willingness to trade. Rather, the slope
represents the rate of exchange *the market* offers to
the consumer when he gives up money in
exchange for cheese and records. Recall that the
budget line represents all commodity combinations a consumer can get by spending a fixed
amount of money. The budget line is thus a curve
of constant expenditure. At current prices, if the
consumer reduces his purchase of cheese by
amount *DE* in Figure 21–6, he will save just
enough money to buy an additional amount, *EF*,

of records, since at points *D* and *F* he is spending
the same total number of dollars.

    The **slope of a budget line** is the amount of one
commodity the market requires an individual to
give up in order to obtain one additional unit of
another commodity without any change in the
amount of money spent.

    The slopes of the two types of curves, then, are
perfectly analogous in their meaning. The slope of
the indifference curve tells us the terms on which
the *consumer* is willing to trade one commodity for
another, while the slope of the budget line reports
the *market* terms on which the consumer can trade
one good for another.
    It is useful to carry our interpretation of the
slope of the budget line one step further. Common
sense tells us that the market's rate of exchange
between cheese and records would be related to
their prices, p_c and p_r, and it is easy to show that
this is so. Specifically, the slope of the budget line
is equal to the ratio of the prices of the two commodities. The reason is straightforward. If the
consumer gives up one record, he has p_r more dollars to spend on cheese. But the lower the price of
cheese the greater the quantity of cheese this
money will enable him to buy — that is, his
cheese purchasing power will be inversely related
to its price. Since the price of cheese is p_c per
pound, the additional p_r dollars permit him to buy
p_r/p_c more pounds of cheese. Thus the slope of the
budget line is p_r/p_c.
    Before returning to our main subject, the
study of consumer choice, we pause briefly and use
our interpretation of the slope of the indifference
curve to discuss the third of the properties of the
indifference curve — its characteristic curvature —
which we left unexplained earlier. With indifference curves being the shape shown, the slope
decreases as we move from left to right. We can
see in Figure 21–6 that at point *m*, toward the
right of the diagram, the consumer is willing to
give up far less cheese for one more record (quantity *rm*) than he is willing to trade at point M,
toward the left. This is because at M he initially
has a large quantity of cheese and few records,
while at *m* his initial stock of cheese is low and he
has many records. In general terms, the curvature
premise on which indifference curves are usually
drawn asserts that consumers are relatively eager
to trade away a commodity of which they have a
large amount but are more reluctant to trade goods

of which they hold small quantities. This psychological premise is what is implied in the curvature of the indifference curve.

The Consumer's Choice

We can now use our indifference curve apparatus to analyze how the consumer chooses among the combinations he can afford to buy; that is, the combinations of records and cheese shown by the budget line. Figure 21–7 brings together in the same diagram the budget line from Figure 21–2 and the indifference curves from Figure 21–5.

Since, according to the first of the properties of indifference curves, the consumer prefers higher to lower curves, he will go to the point on the budget line that lies on the highest indifference curve attainable. This will be point T on indifference curve I_b. He can afford no other point that he likes as well. For example, neither point K below the budget line nor point Z on the budget line gets him on as high an indifference curve, and any point on an indifference curve above I_b, such as point U, is out of the question because it lies beyond his financial means. We end up with a simple rule of consumer choice:

Consumers will select the most desired combination of goods obtainable for their money. The choice will be that point on the budget line at which the budget line is tangent to an indifference curve.

We can see why no point except the point of tangency, T (two records and three pounds of cheese), will give the consumer the largest utility that his money can buy. Suppose the consumer were instead to consider buying four records and no cheese. This would put him at point Z on the budget line and on indifference curve I. But then, by buying fewer records and more cheese (a move to the left on the budget line), he could get to an indifference curve that was higher and hence more desirable without spending any more money. It clearly does not pay to end up at Z. Only at the point of tangency, T, is there no room for improvement.

At a point of tangency where the consumer's benefits from purchasing cheese and records are maximized, the slope of the budget line equals the slope of the indifference curve. This is true by the definition of a point of tangency. We have just seen that the slope of the indifference curve is the marginal rate of substitution between cheese and records, and that the slope of the budget line is the ratio of the prices of records and cheese. We can therefore restate the requirement for the optimal division of the consumer's money between the two commodities in slightly more technical language:

Consumers will get the most benefit from their money by choosing a combination of commodities whose marginal rate of substitution is equal to the ratio of their prices.

It is worth reviewing the logic behind this conclusion. Why is it not advisable for the consumer to stop at a point like Z, where the marginal rate of substitution (slope of the indifference curve) is less than the price ratio (slope of the budget line)? Because by moving upward and to the left along his budget line, he can take advantage of market opportunities to obtain a commodity bundle that he likes better. And this will always be the case if the rate at which the consumer is *personally* willing to exchange cheese for records (his marginal rate of substitution) differs from the rate of exchange offered *on the market* (the slope of the budget line).

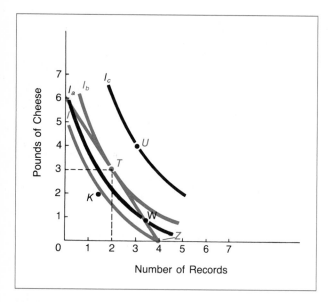

Figure 21–7
OPTIMAL CONSUMER CHOICE
Point T is the combination of records and cheese that gives the consumer the greatest benefit for his money. I_b is the highest indifference curve that can be reached from the budget line. T is the point of tangency between the budget line and I_b.

Consequences of Income Changes: Inferior Goods

Next, consider what happens to the consumer's purchases when there is a rise in income. We know that a rise in income produces a parallel outward shift in the budget line, such as the shift from BB to CC in Figure 21–8. This moves the consumer's equilibrium from tangency point T to tangency point E on a higher indifference curve.

A rise in income may or may not increase the demand for a commodity. In the case shown in Figure 21–8, the rise in income does lead the consumer to buy more cheese *and* more records. But his indifference curves need not always be positioned in a way that yields this sort of result. In Figure 21–9 we see that as the consumer's budget line rises from BB to CC, the tangency point moves leftward from H to G, so that when his income rises he actually buys *fewer* records. In this case we infer that records are an **inferior good.**

Consequences of Price Changes: Deriving the Demand Curve

Finally, we come to the main question underlying demand curves: How does our consumer's choice

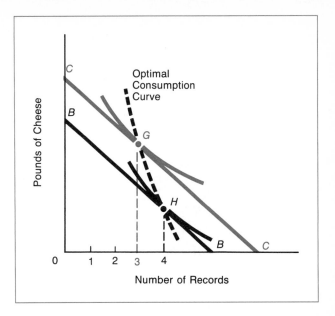

Figure 21–9
EFFECTS OF A RISE IN INCOME WHEN RECORDS ARE AN INFERIOR GOOD
The upward shift in the budget line from BB to CC causes the quantity of records demanded to fall from four (point H) to three (point G).

change if the price of one good changes? We learned earlier that a reduction in the price of a record causes the budget line to swing outward along the horizontal axis while leaving its vertical intercept unchanged. In Figure 21–10, we depict the effect of a decline in the price of records on the quantity of records demanded. As the price of records falls, the budget line swings from BC to BD. The tangency points, T and E, also move in a corresponding direction, causing the quantity demanded to rise from two to three. The price of records has fallen, and the quantity demanded has risen: the demand curve for records is negatively sloped.

The demand curve for records can be constructed directly from Figure 21–10. Point T tells us that two records will be bought when the price of a record is $3. Point E tells us that when the price of a record falls to $1.50, quantity demanded rises to three records.[6] These two pieces of information are shown in Figure 21–11 as points t and e on the demand curve for records. By examining the effects of other possible prices for records

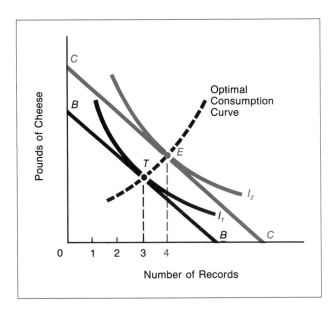

Figure 21–8
EFFECTS OF A RISE IN INCOME WHEN NEITHER GOOD IS INFERIOR
The rise in income causes a parallel shift in the budget line from BB to CC. The quantity of records demanded rises from three to four, and the quantity demanded of cheese also increases.

[6]How do we know that the price of records corresponding to budget line BD is $1.50? Since the $12 total budget will purchase at most eight records (point D), the price per record must be $12 ÷ 8 = $1.50.

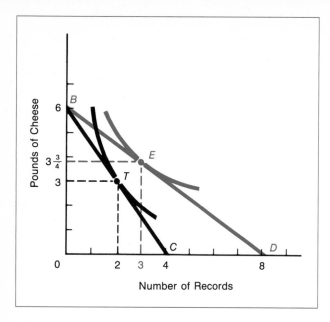

Figure 21–10
CONSEQUENCES OF PRICE CHANGES
A fall in record price swings the budget line outward from line *BC* to *BD*. The consumer's equilibrium point (the point of tangency between the budget line and an indifference curve) moves from *T* to *E*. The desired purchase of records increases from two to three, and the desired purchase of cheese increases from three pounds to three and three-fourths pounds.

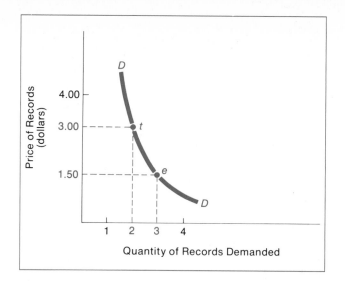

Figure 21–11
DERIVING THE DEMAND CURVE FOR RECORDS
The demand curve is derived from the indifference curve diagram by varying the price of the commodity in question. Specifically, when the price is $3 per record, we know from Figure 21–10 that the optimal purchase is two records (point *T*). This information is recorded here as point *t*. Similarly, the optimal purchase is three records when the price of records is $1.50 (point *E* in Figure 21–10). This is shown here as point *e*.

(other budget lines emanating from point *B* in Figure 21–10), we can find all the other points on the demand curve in exactly the same way.

The indifference curve diagram also brings out an important point that the demand curve does not show. A change in the *price of records* also has consequences for the *quantity of cheese demanded* because it affects the amount of money left over for cheese purchases. In the example illustrated in Figure 21–10, the decrease in the price of records increases the demand for cheese from three to three and three-fourths pounds.

Summary

1. Indifference-curve analysis permits us to study the interrelationships of the demands for two (or more) commodities.

2. The basic tools of indifference-curve analysis are the consumer's budget line and indifference curves.

3. A budget line shows all combinations of two commodities that the consumer can afford, given the prices of the commodities and the amount of money the consumer has available to spend.

4. The budget line is a straight line whose slope equals the ratio of the prices of the commodities. A change in price changes the slope of the budget line. A change in the consumer's income causes a parallel shift in the budget line.

5. Two points on an indifference curve represent two combinations of commodities such that the consumer does not prefer one of the combinations over the other.

6. Indifference curves normally have negative slopes and are "bowed in" toward the origin. The slope of an indifference curve indicates how much of one commodity the consumer is willing to give up in order to get an additional unit of the other commodity.

7. The consumer will choose the point on his budget line that gets him to the highest attainable indifference curve. Normally this will occur at the point of tangency between the two curves. This choice indicates the combination of commodities that gives him the greatest benefits for the amount of money he has available to spend.

8. The consumer's demand curve can be derived from his indifference curve.

Concepts for Review

Budget line
Indifference curves

Marginal rate of substitution
Slope of an indifference curve

Slope of a budget line

Questions for Discussion

1. John Q. Public spends all his income on gasoline and hot dogs. Draw his budget line when:
   a. his income is $80 and the cost of one gallon of gasoline and one hot dog is $1.60 each.
   b. his income is $120 and the two prices are as in part (a).
   c. his income is $80 and hot dogs cost $1.60 each and gasoline costs $1.20 per gallon.
2. Draw some hypothetical indifference curves for John Q. Public on a diagram identical to the one you constructed for part (a) of Question 1.
   a. Approximately how much gasoline and how many hot dogs will Public buy?
   b. How will these choices change if his income increases to $120, as in part (b) of Question 1? Is either good an inferior good?
   c. How will these choices change if gasoline prices fall to $1.20 per gallon, as in part (c) of Question 1?
3. Explain what information the *slope* of an indifference curve conveys about a consumer's preferences. Use this to explain the typical U-shaped curvature of indifference curves.

22

Things are worth as much as
they are valued.

MOLIÈRE

Market Demand
and Elasticity

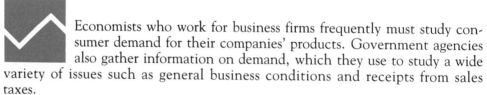

Economists who work for business firms frequently must study consumer demand for their companies' products. Government agencies
also gather information on demand, which they use to study a wide
variety of issues such as general business conditions and receipts from sales
taxes.

The quantity demanded in any market depends on many things: the
incomes of consumers, the price of the good, the prices of other goods, the volume and effectiveness of advertising, and so on. Demand analysis deals with all
these influences, but it has traditionally focused on the price of the good in
question. The reason is that the market price of a commodity plays a crucial
role in influencing both quantity supplied and quantity demanded, and, in
equilibrium, price is set at the level that makes these two quantities equal. This
role of price was studied in Chapter 4, and we will return to it time and again
throughout the book.

We begin this chapter by showing how the market demand curve for a
product is derived from the demand curves of the individual consumers. Next
we turn to the "law" of demand, which tells us that quantity demanded
decreases as price increases. Third, the important concept of elasticity is introduced and studied in detail as a way to measure the responsiveness of quantity
demanded to price. And, finally, in an appendix, we explain the importance of
the time period to which a demand curve applies and how this can create problems in obtaining demand information from statistical data.

From Individual Demand Curves to
Market Demand Curves

A **market demand curve**
shows how the total
quantity demanded of
some product during a
specified period of time
changes as the price of
that product changes,
holding other things
constant.

In the last chapter, we studied how *individual demand curves* are derived from
the logic of consumer choice. But to understand how the market system works
we must derive the relationship between price and quantity demanded *in the
market as a whole* — the **market demand curve.**

If each individual pays no attention to other people's purchase decisions
when making his own, it is straightforward to derive the market demand curve

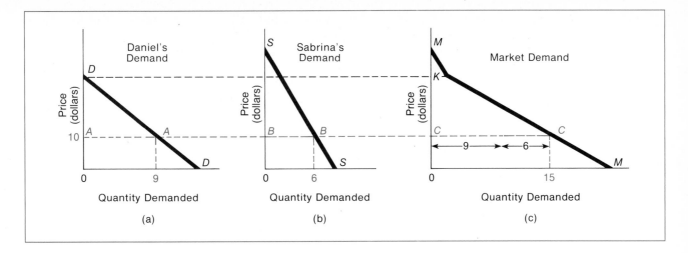

Figure 22-1
THE RELATIONSHIP BETWEEN TOTAL MARKET DEMAND AND THE DEMAND
OF INDIVIDUAL CONSUMERS WITHIN THAT MARKET
If Daniel and Sabrina are the customers for a product, and at a price of $10 Daniel demands 9 units [line *AA* in part (a)] and
Sabrina demands 6 units [line *BB* in part (b)], then total quantity demanded by the market at that price is 9 + 6 = 15 [line *CC* in
part (c)]. In other words, we obtain the market demand curve by adding horizontally all points on each consumer's demand curve
at each given price. Thus, at a $10 price we have length *CC* on the market demand curve, which is equal to *AA* + *BB* on the
individual demand curves. (The sharp angle at point *K* on the market curve occurs because it corresponds to the price at which
Dan, whose demand pattern is different from Sabrina's, first enters the market. At any higher price, only Sabrina is willing to buy
anything.)

from the customers' individual demand curves. We simply *add* the negatively
sloping individual demand curves *horizontally* as shown in Figure 22-1. There
we see the individual demand curves *DD* and *SS* for two people, Daniel and
Sabrina, and the total (market) demand curve *MM*.

Specifically, this market demand curve is constructed as follows. *Step 1:*
Pick any relevant price, say $10. *Step 2:* At that price, determine Daniel's
quantity demanded (9 units) from Daniel's demand curve in part (a) and
Sabrina's quantity demanded (6 units) from Sabrina's demand curve in part (b).
Note that these quantities are indicated by line segment *AA* for Daniel and line
segment *BB* for Sabrina. *Step 3:* Add Sabrina's and Daniel's quantities
demanded at the $10 price (segment *AA* + segment *BB* = 9 + 6 = 15) to yield
the total quantity demanded by the market at that price [line segment *CC*,
with total quantity demanded equal to 15 units, in part (c)]. Now repeat the
process for all alternative prices to obtain other points on the market demand
curve until the shape of the entire curve *MM* is indicated. That is all there is to
the adding-up process. (Question: What happens to the market demand curve
if, say, population grows, and another consumer enters the market?)

The "Law" of Demand

A formal definition of the demand curve for an entire market was given in
Chapter 4 and again on the opposite page. We shall pay much attention in this
chapter to the "other things" referred to in this definition. But for now, let us
focus on price, and note that the total quantity demanded by the market normally moves in the opposite direction from price. Economists call this relationship the **"law" of demand.**

Notice that we have put the word *law* in quotation marks. By now you will
have observed that economic laws are not always obeyed, and we shall see in a

The **"law" of demand**
states that a lower price
generally increases the
amount of a commodity
that people in a market
are willing to buy. So, for
most goods, demand
curves have a negative
slope.

moment that the "law" of demand is not without its exceptions. But first let us see why the "law" usually holds.

In Chapter 21 we learned that individual demand curves are usually downward sloping because of the "law" of diminishing marginal utility. If individual demand curves slope downward, then we see from the preceding discussion of the adding-up process that the market demand curve must also slope downward. This is just common sense: If every consumer in the market buys fewer bananas when the price of bananas rises, then the total quantity demanded in the market must surely fall.

But market demand curves may slope downward even when individual demand curves do not, because not all consumers are alike. For example, if a bookstore reduces the price of a popular novel, it may draw many new customers, but few customers will be induced to buy two copies. Similarly, people differ in their fondness for bananas. True devotees may maintain their purchases of bananas even at exorbitant prices, while others will not eat a banana even if it is offered free of charge. As the price of bananas rises, the less-enthusiastic banana eaters drop out of the market entirely, leaving the expensive fruit to the more devoted consumers. Thus the quantity demanded declines as price rises simply because higher prices induce more people to kick the banana habit. Indeed, for many commodities, it is the appearance of new customers in the *market* when prices are lower, rather than the negative slope of *individual* demand curves, that accounts for the law of demand.

This is also illustrated in Figure 22–1 where we see that at a price higher than D only Sabrina will buy the product. However, at a price below D Daniel is also induced to make some purchases. Hence, below point K the market demand curve lies further to the right than it would have if Daniel had not been induced to enter the market. Put the other way, a rise in price from a level below D to a level above D will cut quantity demanded for two reasons: First because Sabrina's demand curve has a negative slope and, second, because it drives Daniel out of the market.

We conclude, therefore, that the law of demand stands on fairly solid ground. If individual demand curves are downward sloping, then the market demand curve surely will be, too. And the market demand curve may slope downward even when individual demand curves do not.

Nevertheless, exceptions to the law of demand have been noted. One common exception occurs when quality is judged on the basis of price — the more expensive the better. For example, some people buy vegetables labeled "organic" even though they are more expensive than other vegetables. Even if the two kinds of vegetables are identical to a biologist, some consumers may assume that the "organic" vegetables are superior simply because they are more expensive. If organic vegetables then become cheaper, consumers might assume that they are no longer superior and actually reduce their purchases.

Another possible cause of an upward-sloping demand curve is snob appeal. If part of the reason for purchasing a Rolls Royce is to advertise one's wealth, a decrease in the car's price may actually reduce sales, even if the quality of the car is unchanged. Other types of exceptions have also been noted by economists; but, for most commodities, it seems quite reasonable to assume that demand curves have a negative slope, an assumption that is supported by the data.

Application: Who Pays an Excise Tax?

The law of demand has many applications. Suppose, for example, that 18 million records are sold per year, and the government considers placing a $4 tax on each record sold (called an **excise tax**), hoping to collect $72 million in revenue per year ($4 per record times 18 million records). The law of demand tells us that the government will collect less than $72 million. Why? Because the excise tax will push up the price, and that will reduce quantity demanded below 18 million.

An **excise tax** is a tax which is levied as a fixed amount of money per unit of product sold, or as a fixed percentage of the purchase price.

Knowing that revenues will rise by less than $72 million is useful, but it is not enough. If quantity demanded is highly responsive to price, a rise in price will cause consumers to cut back sharply on record purchases and the government will get less money from its tax than if consumers are less sensitive to price. So, to determine its tax receipts, the government needs to estimate *how much* the price will rise and *how much* quantity demanded will fall. For this purpose, the government needs a *quantitative measure* of the responsiveness of quantity demanded to price. Such a measure is the main subject of this chapter. But to see how tax revenues can be estimated, we must detour briefly. In the process, we will also learn who really pays the excise tax.*

Table 22–1 presents hypothetical supply and demand schedules for records in a format that is familiar from Chapter 4. You can see that the equilibrium price is $6 per record and the equilibrium quantity is 18 million records per year [point A in Figure 22–2(a)]. Now, what happens if the government imposes a $4 per record excise tax? To find the answer, we must first determine what a $4 excise tax does to the supply curve.

The Effect of the Tax on the Supply Curve

We do this by answering a series of hypothetical questions about how sellers would react to the tax at different levels of market price.

First, if records sell for $12, including the tax, how many will be supplied? The key point here is that suppliers will receive only $8 per record—$12 minus the $4 tax. Therefore, the tax-free supply schedule in Table 22–1 tells us (third line) that quantity supplied will be 24 million records per year. Thus, at a price to customers of $12, quantity supplied is 24 million. This information is recorded in the top row of Table 22–2.

The rest of the supply schedule in Table 22–2 is constructed similarly. For example, a $10 price nets the seller $6 which, according to Table 22–1, leads to a quantity supplied of 18 million. And so on.

*The remainder of this section is an illustrative application of the concept of responsiveness of demand to price and it can be skipped on a first reading.

Table 22–1
DEMAND AND SUPPLY SCHEDULES FOR RECORDS

PRICE (dollars)	QUANTITY SUPPLIED	QUANTITY DEMANDED
	(millions of records per year)	
10	30	0
9	27	1
8	24	3
7	21	9
6	18	18
5	15	27
4	12	36
3	9	45

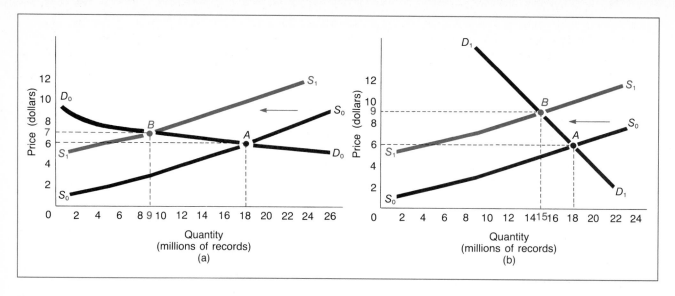

Figure 22–2

WHO PAYS AN EXCISE TAX?

A $4 excise tax shifts the supply curve vertically upward by $4—from $S_0 S_0$ to $S_1 S_1$. The market equilibrium therefore shifts from point A to point B. In part (a), the demand curve $D_0 D_0$ is rather flat, so the price rises only $1 (from $6 to $7) while the quantity falls dramatically (from 18 million to 9 million). Producers pay most of the tax. In part (b), the demand curve $D_1 D_1$ is much steeper, so the price rises by $3 and quantity falls by much less (only 3 million records). Consumers pay most of the tax.

A pattern is apparent in Table 22–2. At any given price, suppliers will provide the same quantity after the tax as they previously provided at a price $4 lower. Thus, we conclude that:

An excise tax shifts the supply curve upward by the amount of the tax.

This conclusion is just common sense. After all, suppliers care about the price they receive, not about the price buyers pay. Graphically, our conclusion is depicted in part (a) of Figure 22–2, which shows the demand curve $D_0 D_0$ and the two supply curves—$S_0 S_0$ before tax and $S_1 S_1$ after the tax. The two supply curves are parallel and $4 apart.

The Role of the Shape of the Demand Curve

Now we can answer the questions of interest: How much will the market price rise as a result of the tax? How much will the quantity fall? And how much revenue will the government collect?

The answers depend on the responsiveness of quantity demanded to price changes, that is, on the shape of the demand curve. We start with a case in which demand is relatively responsive [part (a) of Figure 22–2], that is, a small

Table 22–2

EFFECT OF $4 EXCISE TAX ON THE RECORD MARKET

PRICE INCLUDING TAX (dollars)	PRICE RECEIVED BY SUPPLIERS (dollars)	QUANTITY SUPPLIED	QUANTITY DEMANDED
		(millions of records per year)	
12	8	24	0
11	7	21	0
10	6	18	0
9	5	15	1
8	4	12	3
7	3	9	9
6	2	6	18
5	1	3	27

(vertical) change in price leads to a large (horizontal) change in quantity, making the demand curve rather flat.

Figure 22–2(a) shows that in this case the $4 excise tax raises the equilibrium price from $6 (point A) to $7 (point B). Because this lowers the quantity sold from 18 million to 9 million per year, the government will collect only $36 million ($4 times 9 million), rather than $72 million.

In this example, the price rises by only one-fourth as much as the tax (from $6 to $7), so consumers wind up paying only one-fourth of the tax. The other $3 of tax is paid by businesses, which now collect only $3 per record ($7 less $4 tax) instead of $6. But consumers do not always pay such a small fraction of an excise tax. The way the tax burden is shared depends on how responsive quantity demanded is to price. In this example, quantity demanded responds very strongly.[1]

Part (b) of Figure 22–2 shows that things work out quite differently if quantity demanded is much less responsive to price. Demand curve D_1D_1 is much steeper than demand curve D_0D_0, meaning that a given change in price elicits a much smaller quantity response.[2] As a result, the equilibrium price rises by much more ($3 instead of $1), and the quantity demanded falls by much less (only 3 million instead of 9 million).

With the unresponsive demand curve D_1D_1, consumers pay three-quarters of the tax and firms pay only one-quarter. And, since the decline in quantity is much smaller in part (b) than in part (a), the government collects more revenue — $60 million per year ($4 times 15 million) in part (b) rather than the $36 million in part (a). Thus we conclude that the less responsive consumer demand is to a change in price, the larger the share of any excise tax that is paid by consumers, and the more total tax revenue the government collects, other things being equal. Clearly we need a good way to measure the responsiveness of quantity demanded to price changes — a subject to which we turn next.

Elasticity: The Measure of Responsiveness

It is not only governments that need a way to measure the responsiveness of quantity demanded to price. So do other users of demand information, such as business firms, which need it for decisions on pricing of products, on whether to add new models of their products, and so on. Economists measure this responsiveness by means of a concept they call **elasticity.** A demand curve indicating that consumers respond sharply to a change in price is said to be "elastic" (or "highly elastic"). A demand curve involving a relatively small or insignificant response by consumers to a given price change is called "inelastic."

The precise measure used for this purpose is called the **price elasticity of demand,** or sometimes simply the **elasticity of demand,** and it is defined as the ratio of the *percentage* change in quantity demanded to the associated *percentage* change in price. Specifically:

$$\text{Elasticity of demand} = \frac{\text{\% change in quantity demanded}}{\text{\% change in price}}.$$

The **(price) elasticity of demand** is the ratio of the *percentage* change in quantity demanded to the *percentage* change in price that brings about the change in quantity demanded.

[1]The distribution of the tax burden also depends on the responsiveness of quantity *supplied* to price. But we are concentrating on demand here.

[2]The reader should verify that a fall in price from $7 to $6 raises quantity demanded by 9 million records in part (a) of Figure 22–2 but only by about 1 million records in part (b).

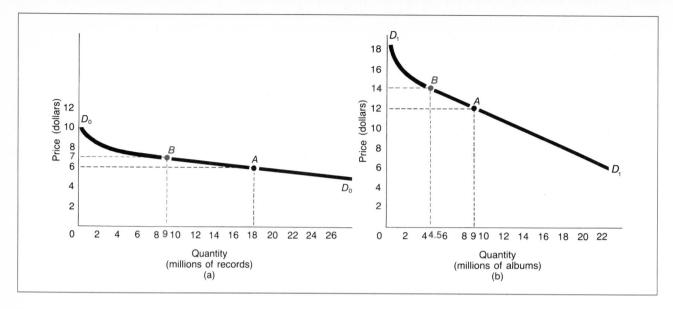

Figure 22–3
THE SENSITIVITY OF SLOPE TO UNITS OF MEASUREMENT
The slope of a curve changes whenever we change units of measurement. Part (a) repeats Figure 22–2(a); the demand curve looks very flat. In Part (b) we measure quantity in two record albums, so all the quantities are cut in half and all the prices are doubled. As a result, the demand curve looks rather steep. But the two demand curves present exactly the same information.

Thus, demand is called **elastic** if, say, a 10 percent rise in price leads to a reduction in quantity demanded that is greater than 10 percent. The demand is called **inelastic** if such a rise in price reduces quantity demanded by any amount less than 10 percent.

Let us now consider how these definitions can be used to analyze a demand curve. At first, it may seem that the *slope* of the demand curve conveys the information we need: curve D_0D_0 is much steeper than curve D_1D_1 in Figure 22–3, so that any given change in price corresponds to a much larger change in quantity demanded in the case of Figure 22–3(a) than in Figure 22–3(b), so it is tempting to call (a) "more elastic." But slope will not do the job because the slope of any curve depends on the units of measurement, as we saw in Chapter 2; and in economics there are no standardized units of measurement. Cloth output may be measured in yards or meters; milk in quarts or liters; and coal in tons or kilograms.[3]

It is because of this problem that economists use the elasticity measure, which is based on *percentage* changes in price and quantity rather than on *absolute* changes. The elasticity formula solves the units problem because percentages are unaffected by units of measurement. If the defense budget doubles, it

---

[3]An example will illustrate the problem. Figure 22–3(a) repeats the demand curve D_0D_0 from Figure 22–2(a). It looks flat. Specifically, its slope between points A and B is:

$$\text{Slope} = \frac{\text{change in price}}{\text{change in quantity demanded}} = \frac{\$1.00}{9} = 0.11 .$$

But suppose we measure quantity in millions of two-record albums, instead of in millions of records. This is done in Figure 22–3(b), and here the demand curve looks very steep. Between points A and B, price changes by $2 per album (that is, $1 per record) and quantity demanded changes by 4.5 million albums (9 million records); so the slope is now:

$$\text{Slope} = \frac{\text{change in price}}{\text{change in quantity demanded}} = \frac{\$2.00}{4.5} = 0.44 .$$

This is quite a change in slope. But nothing has really changed. Points A and B represent exactly the same quantities and prices in both figures. Only the units of measurement have changed.

goes up by 100 percent, whether measured in millions or billions of dollars. If a person's height doubles between the ages of 5 and 15, it goes up 100 percent, whether measured in inches or centimeters.[4]

In the formula that is actually used to measure price elasticity of demand, then, both the change in quantity demanded and the change in price are expressed as *percentages*.* In addition to using percentages, the elasticity formula usually used in practice has a second important attribute: The change in quantity is not calculated either as a percentage of the "initial" quantity or as a percentage of the "subsequent" quantity, but *as a percentage of the average of the two quantities*. Similarly, the change in price is expressed as a percentage of the average of the two prices in question. To see why the issue arises, consider, as an example, the demand information presented in Table 22–1 (page 481). At a price of $6, quantity demanded is 18 million records; at a price of $7, quantity demanded is 9 million. Suppose a record company is deciding whether to price its product at $7 or $6. The difference in sales volume is 18 million − 9 million = 9 million. This 9 million difference in sales is 50 percent of 18 million, but 100 percent of 9 million. Which is the correct figure to use as the percentage change in quantity?

This problem is always with us because any given change in quantity must involve some larger quantity Q_L (18 million in our example) and some smaller quantity Q_S (9 million) so that a given change in quantity must be a relatively small percentage of Q_L and a relatively large percentage of Q_S. Obviously, neither of these can claim to be *the* right percentage change in quantity. It turns out to be convenient to use what appears to be a compromise — the *average* of the two quantities. In terms of our example, we use the average of 18 million and 9 million, that is, 13.5 million, in our calculation of the percentage change in quantity. Thus:

$$\text{Percent change in quantity} = 9 \text{ million as a percent of } 13.5 \text{ million}$$
$$= 66\tfrac{2}{3} \text{ percent.}$$

Similarly, in calculating the percentage change in price, we take the $1 change in price as a percentage of the average of $7 and $6, giving us $1/$6.50, or 15.4 percent, approximately.

Summary   The elasticity formula has two basic attributes:

1. It deals only in percentages.
2. It calculates percentage change in terms of the average value of the quantities or prices at issue.

---

[4]Application of the elasticity formula given above to our example illustrates that it really does solve the units problem. In moving from point A to point B in either version of Figure 22–3, quantity demanded declines by 50 percent — from 18 million to 9 million in part (a), or from 9 million to 4.5 million in part (b). Similarly, the percentage rise in price from $6 to $7 in part (a) or from $12 to $14 in part (b) is 16.67 percent whether we use dollars, dimes, or pennies. Mathematically, the reason is straightforward. If H_a and H_b represent height at age 5 and age 15, respectively, the formula for the percentage rise in height is $(H_b - H_a)/H_a$. If we switch from inches to centimeters, in this formula both the numerator and the denominator are multiplied by 2.5, since an inch is about 2.5 centimeters. These 2.5s then cancel out, leaving the percentage figure unaffected by the switch from inches to centimeters.

*The remainder of this section involves fairly technical computational issues, so that on a first reading you may prefer to go directly to the new section that begins on page 486.

In addition, the formula usually drops all minus signs.[5]

We can now state the formula for price elasticity of demand. Keeping in mind all three features of the formula, we have:

Price elasticity of demand

$$= \frac{\text{change in quantity as \% of average of the two quantities in question}}{\text{change in price as \% of average of the two prices in question}},$$

so that in our example,

$$\text{Elasticity} = \frac{9 \text{ million as \% of } (18 \text{ million} + 9 \text{ million})/2}{\$1 \text{ as \% of } (\$7 + 6)/2}$$

$$= \frac{66.67\%}{15.38\%} = 4.33.$$

Example: When P is 12, Q is 17; and when P is 8, Q is 23. Then the change in P is $12 - 8 = 4$, and average P is $(12 + 8)/2 = 10$, so the change in P is 4 as a percentage of 10, or 40%. Similarly, the change in Q is $23 - 17 = 6$, and average Q is $(23 + 17)/2 = 20$, so the change in Q is 6 as a percentage of 20, or 30%. Hence:

$$\text{Elasticity} = 30/40 = 0.75.$$

This calculation is summarized in Table 22–3.

Elasticity and the Shape of Demand Curves

Figure 22–4 indicates how elasticity of demand is related to the shape of the demand curve. We begin with two extreme but important cases. Part (a) depicts a demand curve that is simply a vertical line. This curve is called *perfectly inelastic* throughout because its elasticity is zero. That is, since quantity

---

[5]This is, then, a third attribute of the elasticity formula as usually used—the removal of all minus signs. Recall that, by the law of demand, when price increases, quantity demanded will normally decrease, and vice versa. That is, when the percentage change in price is positive, the percentage change in quantity demanded will be negative, and vice versa. So our elasticity formula would normally produce a *negative* number. In calculating elasticity it is customary to disregard the minus sign to make the elasticity a *positive* number. That way, a *larger* elasticity number means that demand is *more* responsive to price.

Table 22–3
CALCULATION OF PRICE ELASTICITY OF DEMAND

	PRICE	QUANTITY
Situation 1	$P_1 = 12$	$Q_1 = 17$
Situation 2	$P_2 = 8$	$Q_2 = 23$
Change	$P_1 - P_2 = 12 - 8 = 4$	$Q_2 - Q_1 = 23 - 17 = 6$
Average	$(P_1 + P_2)/2 = 20/2 = 10$	$(Q_2 + Q_1)/2 = 40/2 = 20$
% change	4 as % of 10 = 40%	6 as % of 20 = 30%
Elasticity = % change in quantity/% change in price = 30/40 = 0.75		

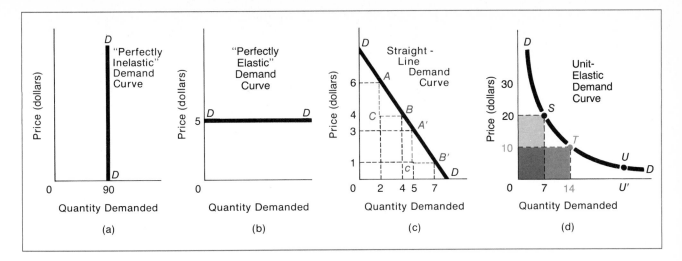

demanded remains at 90 units no matter what the price, the percentage change in quantity is always zero, and hence the elasticity is zero. That is, in this case, consumer purchases do not respond at all to any change in price. Such a demand curve is quite unusual. It may perhaps be expected when the price range being considered already involves very low prices from the point of view of the consumer. (Will anyone use more salt if its price is lowered?) It may also occur when the item (such as medicine) is considered absolutely essential by the consumer, although even here the demand curve will remain vertical only so long as price does not exceed what the consumer can afford.

Part (b) of Figure 22–4 shows the opposite extreme: a horizontal demand curve. It is said to be *perfectly elastic* (or "infinitely elastic"). If there is the slightest rise in price, quantity demanded will drop to zero; that is, the percentage change in quantity demanded will be infinitely large. This may be expected to occur where a rival product that is just as good in the consumer's view is available at the going price ($5 in our diagram). In cases where no one will pay more than the going price, the seller will lose all his customers if he raises his price even one penny. Thus, this is the opposite extreme case of consumer responsiveness to price changes: the case where elasticity is infinite.

Part (c) depicts a case between these two extremes: a *straight-line* demand curve, which is neither vertical nor horizontal. Though the *slope* of a straight-line demand curve is constant throughout its length, its *elasticity* is not. For example, the elasticity of demand between points A and B in Figure 22–4(c) is:

$$\frac{\text{Change in } Q \text{ as \% of average } Q}{\text{Change in } P \text{ as \% of average } P} = \frac{2 \text{ as \% of } (2 + 4)/2}{2 \text{ as \% of } (4 + 6)/2}$$

$$= \frac{2/3}{2/5} = \frac{66 \ 2/3\%}{40\%} = 1.67 \text{ (approx.)}.$$

But the elasticity of demand between points A' and B' is:

$$\frac{2 \text{ as \% of } (5 + 7)/2}{2 \text{ as \% of } (3 + 1)/2} = \frac{2/6}{2/2} = \frac{33 \ 1/3\%}{100\%} = 0.33 \text{ (approx.)}.$$

Along a straight-line demand curve, the price elasticity of demand grows steadily smaller as we move from left to right. That is so because the quantity

Figure 22–4
DEMAND CURVES WITH DIFFERENT ELASTICITIES
The vertical demand curve in part (a) is *perfectly inelastic* (elasticity = 0)—quantity demanded remains the same regardless of price. The horizontal demand curve in part (b) is *perfectly elastic*—at any price above $5, quantity demanded falls to zero. Part (c) shows a *straight-line demand curve*. Its *slope* is constant, but its *elasticity* is not. Part (d) depicts a *unit-elastic* demand curve whose constant elasticity is 1.0 throughout. A change in price pushes quantity demanded in the opposite direction but does not affect total expenditure. When price equals $20, total expenditure is price times quantity, or $20 × 7 = $140; and when price equals $10, expenditure equals $10 × 14 = $140.

keeps getting larger, so that a given numerical change in quantity becomes an ever smaller percentage change, while the price keeps going lower so that a given numerical change in price becomes an ever larger percentage change.[6]

If the elasticity of a straight-line demand curve varies from one part of the curve to another, what is the appearance of a demand curve with the same elasticity throughout its length? For reasons given in the next section, it looks like the curve in Figure 22–4(d), which is a curve with elasticity equal to one throughout (a *unit-elastic* demand curve). That is, a unit-elastic demand curve bends in the middle toward the origin of the graph, and at either end moves closer and closer to the axes but never touches or crosses the axes.

As we have seen, it is conventional to speak of a curve whose elasticity is greater than one (percentage change in quantity greater than percentage change in price) as an *elastic* demand curve, and of one whose elasticity is less than one as an *inelastic* curve. When elasticity is exactly one, we say the curve is *unit elastic*. This terminology is convenient for discussing the last important property of the elasticity measure.

Elasticity and Total Expenditure

The elasticity of demand conveys useful information about the effect of a price change on the buyer's *total expenditure*. In particular, it can be shown that:

If demand is elastic, a fall in price will increase total expenditure. If demand is unit elastic, a change in price will leave total expenditure unaffected. If demand is inelastic, a fall in price will reduce total expenditure. The opposite will be true when price rises.

These relationships hold because total expenditure equals price times quantity demanded, $P \times Q$, and a fall in price has two opposing effects on $P \times Q$. It decreases P and, if the demand curve is negatively sloped, it increases Q.

That is, a price decrease has two effects on expenditures: (1) *The price effect*, which decreases expenditure by cutting the amount of money a consumer spends on each unit of the good, and (2) *the quantity effect*, which increases the consumer's total expenditure on the good by raising the number of units of the good that he buys. The net consequence for expenditure depends on the elasticity. If price goes down 10 percent and quantity demanded declines 10 percent (a case of *unit elasticity*), the two effects will cancel out: $P \times Q$ will remain constant. On the other hand, if price goes down 10 percent and quantity demanded rises 15 percent (a case of *elastic* demand), $P \times Q$ will increase. Finally, if a 10-percent price fall leads to a 5-percent rise in quantity demanded (an *inelastic* case), $P \times Q$ will fall.

[6]In detail, the reason why the price elasticity of demand grows steadily smaller is that the elasticity formula deals in *percentage* changes in quantity and in price, which behave in a curious way on a straight-line demand curve. At a point near the top of the curve [such as point A in part (c)], price is relatively high ($6), while at a point nearer the bottom of the curve (such as A′), price is lower ($3). Thus a $2 reduction in price from the $6 price at point A will represent a smaller *percentage* price decrease ($2 = 33 1/3% of $6) than the same $2 reduction from the $3 price at point A′ ($2 = 66 2/3% of $3). In other words, as we move down a demand curve to successively lower initial prices, a given reduction in price (a $2 price decrease) becomes a larger and larger *percentage* price reduction. The opposite is true of percentage changes in quantity.

(To simplify the discussion in these paragraphs, we have ignored the complication that the elasticity calculation is based on the *average* of the "initial" and "subsequent" prices and on the average of the two corresponding quantities.)

The connection between elasticity and total expenditure is easily seen in a graph. First we note that:

The total expenditure represented by any point on a demand curve (any price–quantity combination), such as point S in Figure 22–5, is equal to the area of the rectangle under that point (the area of rectangle ORST in the figure). This is so because the area of a rectangle equals height times width = OR times OT = price times quantity, and, by definition, price times quantity equals total expenditure.

To illustrate the connection between elasticity and consumer expenditure, Figure 22–5 shows an elastic portion of a demand curve, DD. At a price of $6 per unit, the quantity sold is four units, so total expenditure is 4 × $6 = $24. This is represented by the vertical rectangle whose upper right corner is point S, because the formula for the area of a rectangle is area = height × width, which in this case is equal to 4 × $6 = $24. When price falls to $5 per unit, 12 units are bought. Consequently, the new expenditure ($60 = $5 × 12), now measured by the blue rectangle, will be larger than the old. In contrast, Figure 22–4(d), the unit elastic demand curve, shows a case in which expenditure remains constant even though selling price changes. Total spending is $140 whether the price is $20 and 7 units are sold (point S) or the price is $10 and 14 units are sold (point T).

This discussion also indicates why a unit-elastic demand curve must have the shape depicted in Figure 22–4(d), hugging the axes closer and closer but never touching or crossing them. We have seen that when demand is unit-elastic, total expenditure must be the same at every point on the curve. It must be the same ($140) at point S and point T and point U. Suppose that at point U (or some other point), the demand curve were to touch the horizontal axis. We will see now that this is impossible if expenditure at this point is to remain $140. It is impossible because if U' lies on the axis, the price at that point must be zero. Therefore, at that point we must have total expenditure = P × Q = 0 × Q = zero. We conclude that if the demand curve is unit-elastic throughout, it can never cross the horizontal axis (where P = 0) or the vertical axis (where Q = 0). Since the slope of the demand curve is negative, the curve simply must get closer and closer to the axes as one moves away from its middle

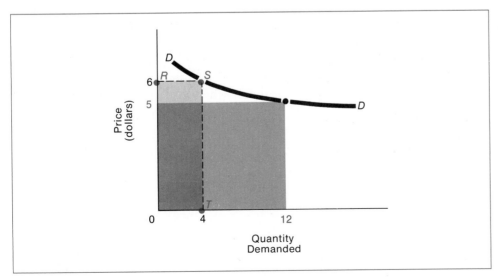

Figure 22–5
AN ELASTIC DEMAND CURVE
When price falls, quantity demanded rises by a greater percentage, increasing the total expenditure. Thus when the price falls from $6 to $5, quantity demanded rises from 4 to 12, and total expenditure rises from $6 × 4 = $24 to $5 × 12 = $60.

points. That is why a unit-elastic demand curve must always have the shape illustrated in Figure 22–4(d).

What Determines Elasticity of Demand?

What kinds of goods have elastic demand curves, meaning that quantity demanded responds strongly to price? And what kinds of goods have inelastic demand curves? Several considerations are relevant.

Nature of the Goods

Necessities, such as basic foodstuffs, have very inelastic demand curves, meaning they are not very responsive to changes in prices. For example, the quantity of potatoes demanded does not decline much when the price of potatoes rises. One study estimates that the price elasticity of demand for potatoes is as low as 0.3, meaning that when their price rises 10 percent, the quantity of potatoes purchased falls only 3 percent. In contrast, many *luxury goods*, such as restaurant meals, have rather elastic demand curves. One estimate is that the price elasticity of demand for restaurant meals is 1.6, so that a ten percent rise in their price will cut purchases of such meals by 16 percent.

Availability of Close Substitutes

If consumers can easily get a good substitute, Y, for a product, X, they will switch readily to Y if the price of X rises sharply. Thus the closer the substitutes for X that are available, the more elastic its demand will be. This factor is a critical determinant of elasticity. The demand for gasoline is inelastic because it is not easy to run a car without it. But the demand for *any particular brand* of gasoline is quite elastic, because another company's product will work just as well. This example suggests a general principle: The demand for narrowly defined commodities (like iceberg lettuce) is more elastic than the demand for more broadly defined commodities (like vegetables).

Fraction of Income Absorbed

The fraction of income absorbed by a particular item is also important. Who will buy less salt if the price of salt rises? But many families will buy fewer cars if auto prices go up.

Passage of Time

This factor is relevant because the demand for many products is more elastic in the long run than in the short run. For example, when the price of home heating oil rose in the 1970s, some homeowners switched from oil heat to gas heat. But, at first, very few homeowners switched; so the demand for oil was quite inelastic. As time passed and more homeowners had the opportunity to purchase and install new equipment, the demand curve gradually became more elastic.

We will see in the appendix to this chapter that the price elasticity of demand is not easy to calculate statistically. But first we give some other examples of important elasticity measures.

Elasticity is a General Concept

While we have spent much time studying the *price* elasticity of demand, elasticity is a very general measure of the responsiveness of one economic variable to another.

It is clear from what we have said that a firm will be very interested in the price elasticity of its demand curve. But this is not where its interest in demand ends, for, as we have noted, quantity demanded depends on other things besides price. Business firms will be interested in consumer responsiveness to changes in these variables as well. For example, we know that quantity demanded depends, in addition to price, upon the consumer's income. The firm's management will therefore want to know how much a change in consumer income affects the demand for its product. Fortunately, the elasticity measure can be helpful here too.

An increase in consumer incomes clearly raises the quantity demanded of most goods. To measure the response we use the *income elasticity of demand,* defined as the ratio of the percentage change in quantity demanded to the percentage change in income.

Prices of Related Goods: Substitutes and Complements

There are many products whose quantities demanded depend on the quantities and prices of other products. Certain goods make one another more desirable. For example, cream and sugar can increase the desirability of coffee, and vice versa. The same is true of mustard or ketchup and hamburgers. In some extreme cases, neither of two products ordinarily has any use without the other — an automobile and tires, a pair of shoes and shoelaces, and so on. Such goods, each of which makes the other more valuable, are called **complements.**

> Two goods are called **complements** if an increase in the price of one reduces the quantity demanded of the other, all other things remaining constant.

The demand curves of complements are interrelated, meaning that a rise in the price of coffee is likely to affect the quantity of sugar demanded. Why? When coffee prices rise, less coffee will be drunk and therefore less sugar will be demanded. The opposite will be true of a fall in coffee prices. A similar relationship holds for other complementary goods.

At the other extreme, there are goods that make one another *less* valuable. These are called **substitutes.** Ownership of a motorcycle, for example, may decrease the desire for a bicycle. If your pantry is stocked with cans of tuna fish, you are less likely to rush out and buy cans of salmon. As you might expect, demand curves for substitutes are also interrelated, but in the opposite direction. When the price of motorcycles falls people may demand fewer bicycles, so the quantity demanded falls. When the price of salmon goes up, people eat more tuna.

> Two goods are called **substitutes** if an increase in the price of one raises the quantity demanded of the other, all other things remaining constant.

There is another elasticity measure which can be used in determining whether two products are substitutes or complements: their **cross elasticity of demand.** This measure is defined much like the ordinary price elasticity of demand, only instead of measuring the responsiveness of the quantity demanded of, say, coffee to a change in the price of coffee, cross elasticity of demand measures the responsiveness of the quantity demanded of coffee to a change in the price of, say, sugar. For example, if a 20-percent rise in the price of sugar reduces the quantity of coffee demanded by 5 percent (a change of *minus* 5 percent in quantity demanded), then the cross elasticity of demand will be

> The **cross elasticity of demand** for product X to a change in the price of another product, Y, is the ratio of the percentage change in quantity demanded of product X to the percentage change in the price of product Y that brings about the change in quantity demanded.

$$\frac{\% \text{ change in quantity of coffee demanded}}{\% \text{ change in sugar price}} = \frac{-5\%}{20\%} = -.25 .$$

Obviously, the producers of breakfast cereal X care a great deal about the cross elasticity of the demand for product X with respect to the price of rival cereal Y.

Using the cross elasticity of demand measure, we come to the following rule about complements and substitutes:

If two goods are substitutes, a rise in the price of one of them raises the quantity demanded of the other; so their cross elasticities of demand will normally be positive. If two goods are complements, a rise in the price of one of them tends to decrease the quantity demanded of the other item, so their cross elasticities will normally be negative.[7]

This result is really a matter of common sense. If the price of a good goes up and there is a substitute available, people will tend to switch to the substitute. If the price of Coke goes up and the price of Pepsi does not, at least some people will switch to Pepsi. Thus, a *rise* in the price of Coke causes a *rise* in the quantity of Pepsi demanded. Both percentage changes are positive numbers and so their ratio, the cross elasticity of demand, is also positive.

On the other hand, if two goods are complements, a rise in the price of one will discourage its own use and will also discourage use of the complementary good. Automobiles and car radios are obviously complements. A large increase in the price of cars will depress the sale of cars, and this in turn will reduce the sale of car radios. Thus, a positive percentage change in the price of cars leads to a negative percentage change in the quantity of car radios demanded. The ratio of these numbers, the cross elasticity of demand for cars and radios, is therefore negative.

Advertising, Prices of Complements and Substitutes, and Demand Curve Shifts

Demand is obviously a complex phenomenon. We have studied in detail the dependence of quantity demanded on price, and we have just seen that quantity demanded depends on other variables such as incomes and the prices of complementary and substitute products. Because of these "other variables," demand curves often do not retain the same shape and position as time passes. Instead, they shift about. And, as we learned in Chapter 4, shifts in demand curves have predictable consequences for both quantity and price. But in public or business discussions, we often hear vague references to a "change in demand." By itself, this expression does not really mean anything. Remember from our discussion in Chapter 4 that it is vital to distinguish between a response to a price change (*which is a movement along the demand curve*) and a change in the relationship between price and quantity demanded (*which is a shift in the demand curve*).

When price falls, quantity demanded generally responds by rising. This is a movement *along* the demand curve. On the other hand, an effective advertising campaign may mean that more goods will be bought at *any given price*. This would be a rightward *shift* in the demand curve. In fact, such a shift can be caused by a change in the value of any of the variables affecting quantity demanded other than price. While the distinction between a shift in a demand curve and a movement along it may at first seem trivial, it is a significant difference in practice and can cause confusion if it is ignored. So let us pause for a moment to consider how changes in some of these other variables shift the demand curve.

---

[7]Because cross elasticities can be positive or negative, it is *not* customary to drop minus signs as we do when calculating ordinary price elasticity of demand.

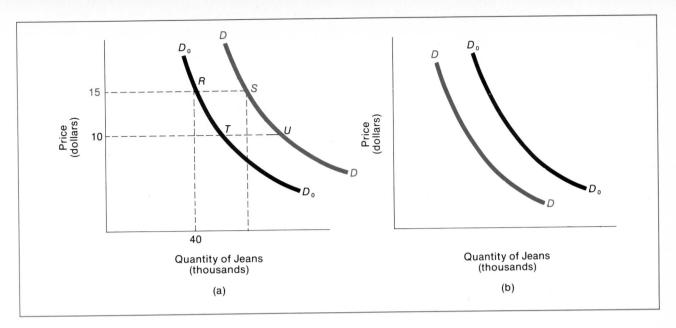

Quantity of Jeans
(thousands)

(a)

Quantity of Jeans
(thousands)

(b)

As an example, consider the effect of a change in consumer income on the demand curve for jeans. In Figure 22–6(a), the black curve $D_0 D_0$ is the original demand curve for jeans. Now suppose that parents start sending more money to their needy sons and daughters in college. If the price of jeans were to stay the same, we would expect students to use some of their increased income to buy more jeans. For example, if the price were to remain at $15, quantity demanded might rise from 40,000 (point R) to 60,000 (point S). Similarly, if price had instead been $10, and had remained at that level, there might be a corresponding change from T to U. In other words, the rise in income would be expected to *shift* the entire demand curve to the right from $D_0 D_0$ to $D_1 D_1$. In exactly the same way, a fall in consumer income can be expected to lead to a leftward shift in the demand curve for jeans, as shown in Figure 22–6(b).

Other variables that affect quantity demanded can be analyzed in the same way. For example, a rise in TV advertising for jeans might lead to a rightward (outward) shift in the demand curve for jeans, as in Figure 22–6(a). The same thing might occur if there were an increase in the price of a substitute product, such as skirts or corduroy trousers, because that would put jeans at a competitive advantage. That is, if two goods are substitutes, a rise in the price of one of them will tend to cause the demand curve for the other one to shift outward (to the right). Conversely, if a product that is complementary to jeans (perhaps a certain type of belt) becomes more expensive, we would expect the demand curve for jeans to shift to the left, as in Figure 22–6(b). In summary:

A demand curve is expected to shift to the right (outward) if consumer incomes rise, if tastes change in favor of the product, if substitute goods become more expensive, or if complementary goods become cheaper. A demand curve is expected to shift to the left (inward) if any of these factors goes in the opposite direction.

The Time Dimension of the Demand Curve and Decision Making

There is one more feature of a demand curve that does not show up on a graph but that is very important nevertheless. A demand curve indicates, at each

Figure 22–6
SHIFTS IN A DEMAND CURVE
A rise in consumer income or an increase in advertising or a rise in the price of a competing product can all produce a rightward (outward) shift of the demand curve for a product as depicted by the shift from the black curve $D_0 D_0$ to the blue curve $D_1 D_1$ in part (a). This means that at any fixed price (say, $15), the quantity of the product demanded will rise. (In the figure, it rises from 40,000 to 60,000 units.) Similarly, a fall in any of the variables, such as consumer income, will produce a leftward (inward) shift in the demand curve, as in part (b) of the figure.

Cross Elasticity in Practice: The Supreme Court's Decision in the DuPont Antitrust Case

In 1956 the Supreme Court decided a historic antitrust case. The Department of Justice had sued DuPont, charging that it "monopolized trade in cellophane." DuPont sold about 75 percent of the cellophane used in the United States, so it was clear that it produced most of the product. But the Supreme Court also considered whether substitute products provided enough competition to prevent DuPont from acting like a monopolist. It used cross elasticity of demand as an important piece of evidence on the matter and concluded that DuPont was not guilty—that it did not "monopolize." Here is an excerpt from the Court's decision:

Sec.2-B DuPont & Co. (Cellophane) 247

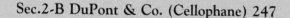

An element for consideration as to cross elasticity of demand between products is the responsiveness of the sales of one product to price changes of the other. If a slight decrease in the price of cellophane causes a considerable number of customers of other flexible wrappings to switch to cellophane, it would be an indication that a high cross elasticity of demand exists between them; that the products compete in the same market. The court below held that the "[g]reat sensitivity of customers in the flexible packaging markets to price or quality changes" prevented DuPont from possessing monopoly control over price. The record sustains these findings.

SOURCE: *U.S. Reports*, vol. 351 (Washington, D.C., 1956), page 400.

---

possible price, the quantity of the good that is demanded *during a particular period of time*. That is, all the alternative prices considered in a demand curve must refer to *the same* time period. We do not compare a price of $10 for January with a price of $8 for September. This feature imparts a peculiar character to the demand curve and makes statistical estimates more difficult because the data we actually observe show different prices and quantities only for different dates. Why, then, do economists adopt this apparently peculiar approach? The answer is that the time dimension of the demand curve is dictated inescapably by the logic of decision making.

When a business undertakes to find the best price for one of its products for, say, the next six months, it must consider the range of alternative prices available to it for that six-month period and the consequences of each possible choice. For example, if management is reasonably certain that the best price lies somewhere between $3.50 and $5.00, it should perhaps consider each of the four possibilities, $3.50, $4.00, $4.50, and $5.00, and estimate how much it can expect to sell at each of these potential prices during the six-month period in question. The result of these estimates may appear in a format similar to that shown in the table below.

Potential price	$3.50	$4.00	$4.50	$5.00
Expected quantity demanded	75,000	73,000	70,000	60,000

This table, which supplies management what it needs to know to make a pricing decision, also contains precisely the information an economist uses to draw a demand curve.

The demand curve describes a set of hypothetical responses to a set of potential prices, only one of which can actually be charged. All of the points on the demand curve refer to alternative possibilities for the *same* period of time — the period for which the decision is to be made.

Thus the demand curve as just described is no abstract notion that is useful primarily in academic discussion. Rather it offers precisely the information that businesses need for rational decision making. However, as already noted, the fact that all points on the demand curve are hypothetical possibilities, all for the same period of time, causes problems for statistical evaluation of demand curves. These problems are discussed in the appendix to this chapter.

Summary

1. A market demand curve for a product can be obtained by summing horizontally the demand curves of each individual in the market; that is, by adding up at each price the quantities demanded by each consumer.
2. The "law" of demand says that demand curves normally have a negative slope, meaning that a rise in price reduces quantity demanded.
3. To measure the responsiveness of quantity demanded to price we use the elasticity of demand, which is defined as the percentage change in quantity demanded divided by the percentage change in price.
4. If demand is elastic (elasticity greater than one), a rise in price will reduce total expenditure. If demand is unit elastic (elasticity equal to one), a rise in price will not change total expenditure. If demand is inelastic (elasticity less than one), a rise in price will increase total expenditure.
5. Demand is not a fixed number. Rather, it is a relationship showing how quantity demanded is affected by price and other pertinent influences. If one or more of these other variables change, the demand curve will shift.
6. Goods that make each other more desirable (hot dogs and mustard, wristwatches and watch straps) are called *complements*. Goods such that if we have more of one we usually want less of another (steaks and hamburgers, Coke and Pepsi) are called *substitutes*.
7. Cross elasticity of demand is defined as the percentage change in the quantity demanded of one good divided by the percentage change in the price of the other good. Two substitute products normally have a positive cross elasticity of demand. Two complementary products normally have a negative cross elasticity of demand.
8. A rise in the price of one of two substitute commodities can be expected to shift the other's demand curve to the right. A rise in the price of one of two complementary goods is apt to shift the other's demand curve to the left.
9. All points on a demand curve refer to the *same* time period — the time during which the price will be in effect.

Concepts for Review

Market demand curve	(Price) elasticity of demand	Substitutes
Excise tax	Elastic, inelastic, and unit-elastic demand curves	Cross elasticity of demand
"Law" of demand	Complements	Shift in a demand curve

Questions for Discussion

1. What variables besides price and advertising are likely to affect the quantity of a product that is demanded?

2. Describe the probable shifts in the demand curves for
   a. railroad trips when there is an improvement in the trains' on-time performance.
   b. automobiles when railroad fares rise.
   c. automobiles when gasoline prices rise.
   d. electricity when average temperature in the U.S. rises during a particular year. (Note: The demand curve for electricity in Maine and the demand curve for electricity in Florida should respond in different ways. Why?)

3. Which of the following goods may conceivably have positively sloping demand curves? Why?
   a. Diamonds.
   b. Copper.
   c. Milk.
   d. Ball-point pens.

4. Explain why elasticity of demand is measured in *percentages*.

5. Explain why the elasticity of demand formula normally eliminates minus signs.

6. Give examples of commodities whose demand you expect to be elastic and some you expect to be inelastic.

7. Explain why the elasticity of a straight-line demand curve varies from one part of the curve to another.

8. A rise in the price of a certain commodity from $10 to $20 reduces quantity demanded from 30,000 to 20,000 units. Calculate the price elasticity of demand.

9. Calculate the price elasticity of demand when price falls from $6 to $5 in Table 22–1.

10. If the price elasticity of demand for gasoline is 0.15, and the current price is $1.00 a gallon, what rise in the price of gasoline will reduce its consumption by 10 percent?

11. A rise in the price of a product whose demand is elastic will reduce the total revenue of the firm. Explain.

12. How many things can you think of that will cause a demand curve to shift?

13. Which of the following product pairs would you expect to be substitutes and which would you expect to be complements?
    a. Shoes and shoelaces.
    b. Gasoline and big cars.
    c. Bread and crackers.
    d. Butter and margarine.

14. For each of the previous product pairs, what would you guess about their cross elasticity of demand?
    a. Do you expect it to be positive or negative?
    b. Do you expect it to be a large or small number? Why?

15. Explain why the following statement is true. "A firm with a demand curve which is inelastic at its current output level can always increase its profits by raising its price and selling less." (*Hint:* Refer back to the discussion of elasticity and total expenditure on pages 488–90.)

Appendix
Statistical Analysis of Demand Relationships

The peculiar time dimension of the demand curve, in conjunction with the fact that many variables other than price can influence quantity demanded, makes it suprisingly hard to discover the shape of the demand curve from statistical data. It can be done, but the task is full of booby traps and can usually be carried out successfully only by using advanced statistical methods. Let us see why these two characteristics of demand curves cause problems.

The most obvious way to go about estimating a demand curve statistically is to collect a set of figures on prices and quantities sold in different periods, like those given in Table 22–4. These points can then be plotted on a diagram with price and quantity on the axes, as shown in Figure 22–7. One can then proceed to draw in a line (the dotted line *TT*) that connects these points reasonably well and that appears to be the demand curve. Unfortunately, line *TT*, which summarizes the historical data, may bear no relationship to the demand curve we are after.

You may notice at once that the prices and quantities represented by the historical points in Figure 22–7 refer to different periods of time and that they all have been *actual*, not *hypothetical*, prices and quantities at some time. The distinction is not insignificant. Over the period covered by the historical data, the true demand curve, which is what we really want, may well have

Table 22–4
HISTORICAL DATA ON PRICE AND QUANTITY

	JANUARY	FEBRUARY	MARCH	APRIL	MAY
Price	$7.20	$8.00	$7.70	$8.00	$8.20
Quantity sold	95,000	91,500	95,000	90,000	91,000

shifted because some of the other variables affecting quantity demanded changed.

What actually happened may be as shown in Figure 22–8. Here we see that in January the demand curve was given by JJ, but by February the curve had shifted to FF, by March to MM, and so on. That is, there was a separate and distinct demand curve for each of the relevant months, and none of them need have any resemblance to the plot of historical data, TT.

In fact, the slope of the historical plot curve, TT, can be very different from the slopes of the true underlying demand curves, as is the case in Figure 22–8. This means that the decision maker can be seriously misled if he selects his price on the basis of the historical data. He may, for example, think that demand is quite insensitive to changes in price (as line TT in the diagram seems to indicate), and so he may reject the possibility of a price reduction when in fact the true demand

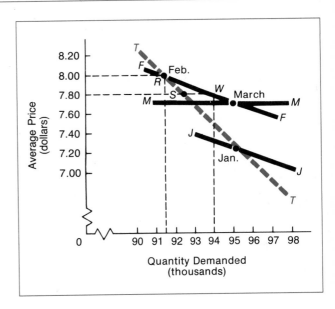

Figure 22–8
PLOT OF HISTORICAL DATA AND TRUE DEMAND CURVES FOR JANUARY, FEBRUARY, AND MARCH
An analytical demand curve shows how quantity demanded in a particular month is affected by the different prices considered during that month. In the case shown, the true demand curves are much flatter (more elastic) than is the line plotting historical data. This means that a cut in price will induce a far greater increase in quantity demanded than the historical data suggest.

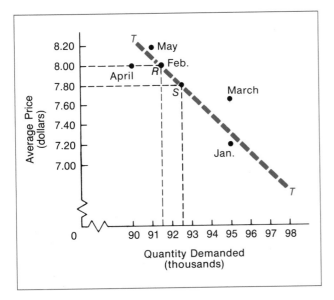

Figure 22–7
PLOT OF HISTORICAL DATA ON PRICE AND QUANTITY
The dots labeled Jan., Feb., and so on represent actual prices and quantities sold in the months indicated. The blue line TT is drawn to approximate the dots as closely as possible.

curves show that a price reduction will increase quantity demanded substantially. For example, if in February he were to charge a price of $7.80 rather than $8, the historical plot would suggest to him a rise in quantity demanded of only 1000 units. (Compare point R, with sales of 91,500 units, and point S, with sales of 92,500 units, in Figure 22–7.) However, as can be seen in Figure 22–8, the true demand curve for February (line FF in Figure 22–8) promises him an increment in sales of 2500 units (from point R, with sales of 91,500, to point W, with sales of 94,000) if he reduces February's price from $8 to $7.80. A manager who based his decision on the historical plot, rather than on the true demand curve, might be led into serious error.

In light of this discussion, it is astonishing how often in practice one encounters demand studies that use apparently sophisticated techniques to arrive at no more than a graph of historical data. One must not allow oneself to be misled by the apparent complexity of the procedures employed to fit a curve to historical data. If these merely plot historical quantities against historical prices, the true underlying demand curve is unlikely to be found.

An Illustration: Did the Advertising Program Work?

A few years ago one of the nation's largest producers of packaged foods conducted a statistical study to determine the effectiveness of its advertising expenditures, which amounted to nearly $100 million a year. A company statistician collected year-by-year figures on company sales and advertising outlays and discovered, to his delight, that they showed a remarkably close relationship to one another: quantity demanded rose as advertising rose. The trouble was that the relationship seemed just too perfect. In economics, data about demand and any one of the elements that influence it almost never make such a neat pattern. Human tastes and other pertinent influences are just too variable to permit such regularity.

Suspicious company executives asked one of the authors of this book to examine the analysis. A little thought showed that the suspiciously close statistical relationship between sales and advertising expenditure resulted from a disregard for the principles just presented. The investigator had in fact constructed a graph of *historical* data on sales and advertising expenditure, analogous to TT in Figures 22–7 and 22–8 and therefore not necessarily similar to the truly relevant relationship.

The stability of the relationship actually arose from the fact that, in the past, the company had based its advertising outlays on its sales, automatically allocating a fixed percentage of its sales revenues to advertising. The *historical* advertising–demand relationship therefore described only the company's budgeting practices, not the effectiveness of its advertising program. If management had used this curve in planning its advertising campaigns, it might have made some regrettable decisions. *Moral:* Avoid the use of historical curves like TT in making economic decisions.

23

Input Decisions and Production Costs

You realize this cost figure is only an estimate. Of course, the actual cost will be higher.

ARCHITECT TO HIS CLIENT IN AN OLD *NEW YORKER* CARTOON

Having discussed the consumers' side of the market, we now turn to that of the producers. Just as the consumer must decide what combination of products to buy and how much of each to purchase, the producer must decide how much to produce (the size of the firm's *output*) and what combination of *inputs* (labor, raw materials, machinery, and so on) to buy. And just as there is a key concept — the consumer's utility or preferences — which is crucial for the analysis of the buyer's behavior, there is a fundamental phenomenon — production cost — which underlies the analysis of the seller's decisions.

The costs of producing any given output depends on the quantities of inputs needed to produce that output. If output can be increased with only very small increases in input usage, then cost *per unit* will fall when output rises. On the other hand, if, say, a 10 percent increase in output requires a 20 percent increase in input use, then cost per unit will increase.

Because the firm's decision on how much output to produce depends on its costs, we must first analyze how costs are determined in order to understand the choice of output level. This chapter will therefore consider the logic of a firm's input decisions and how those input decisions determine costs. The next chapter will analyze output choices.

For pedagogical purposes this chapter is divided into two parts. In the first part we begin with the simple case in which the firm only varies the quantity of a single input. This will vastly simplify the analysis and enable us to see how the production relation between inputs and outputs gives the producer the cost information he needs to determine output and price.

The second part of the chapter goes over the same territory but deals with the more realistic case in which several input quantities can be changed. Many new insights emerge from the multi-input analysis.[1] Throughout the chapter we also assume that the price of each input is fixed by the market and is beyond the control of the firm that buys it.

---

[1]*NOTE*: Some instructors may prefer to postpone this part until later in the course.

Figure 23–1
HISTORICAL COSTS FOR
LONG-DISTANCE
TELEPHONE
TRANSMISSION
By 1986, the dollar cost per
circuit mile had fallen to
about 9 percent of what it
was in 1942. Because prices
had more than tripled in that
period the decline in *real*
cost was even more
sensational. In constant
dollars, in 1986 the
investment cost per circuit
mile was about 2 percent of
its 1942 level. Yet this
diagram of historical costs is
not legitimate evidence
one way or the other about
economies of scale in
telecommunications.
SOURCE: AT&T. Recent data
estimated.

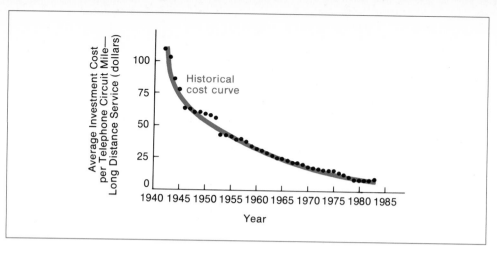

Illustrative Issue: Do Large Firms Produce at Lower Cost?

Economies of large-scale production are thought to be a pervasive feature of modern industrial society. Automation, assembly lines, and sophisticated machinery are widely believed to reduce production costs dramatically. But if this equipment has enormous capacity and requires a very large investment, small companies will not be able to benefit much from these products of modern technology. In this case, only large-scale production can offer the associated savings in costs. Where such *economies of scale,* as economists call them, exist, production costs per unit will decline as output expands.

But this favorable relationship between low costs and large size does not characterize every industry. When a court is called upon to decide whether a giant firm should be broken up into smaller units, officials need to know whether the industry has significant economies of scale. Those who want to break up large firms argue that industrial giants concentrate economic power, which is something these individuals wish to avoid. Those who oppose such breakups point out that if significant economies of scale are present, large firms will be much more efficient producers than will a number of small firms. It is crucial, therefore, to be able to decide whether economies of scale are present. What kind of evidence will speak to this issue?

Sometimes data like those shown in Figure 23–1 are offered to the courts when they consider such cases. These figures, provided by AT&T, indicate that since 1942, as the volume of messages rose, the capital cost of long-distance communication by telephone dropped enormously. Yet economists maintain that while this graph may be valid evidence of efficiency, innovation, and perhaps other virtues of the telecommunications industry, it does *not* constitute legitimate evidence, one way or another, about the presence of economies of scale. Specifically, though this information shows that costs fell as the telephone company's volume of business grew, it does *not* show that a large firm is more efficient than a small one. At the end of this chapter we will see precisely what is wrong with such evidence and what sort of evidence really is required.

The One Variable-Input Case

We begin our discussion with the unrealistic single variable-input case. That is, while any business firm uses many different inputs, we will assume for simplicity that it can only change the quantity of one of them. In other words, we are trying to replicate in our theoretical analysis what a physicist or a biologist does in the laboratory when conducting a *controlled* experiment, in which only one variable is permitted to change at a time in order to study the influence of that variable alone.

Total, Average, and Marginal Physical Products

Consider, as an example of a firm, Farmer Phil Pfister, who grows corn by himself on a 40-acre plot of land. Ultimately, he can vary all his input quantities: He can hire many or few farmhands, buy more land, or sell some of the land he owns. But suppose for the moment that his only choice is how much fertilizer to apply to his land.

Farmer Pfister has studied the relationship between his **input** of fertilizer and his **output** of corn, and he has concluded that, at least up to a point, more fertilizer leads to more output. The relevant data are displayed in Table 23–1. We can see that 1000 bushels of corn will grow on the 40 acres even with no fertilizer at all but that use of some fertilizer yields additional output; for instance, with four tons of fertilizer, output is 2200 bushels. Eventually, however, a saturation point is reached beyond which additional fertilizer actually reduces the corn crop (any amount beyond eight tons). These data are portrayed graphically in Figure 23–2 in what we call a **total physical product (TPP) curve.** This curve shows how much corn Farmer Pfister can produce on 40 acres of land when different quantities of fertilizer are used.

Two other physical product concepts are added in Table 23–2. **Average physical product (APP)** is the measure of output per unit of input; it is simply the total physical product divided by the total quantity of variable input used. In our example, it is total corn output divided by number of tons of fertilizer used. APP is shown in the last column of Table 23–2, in which the TPP schedule is reproduced for convenience. For example, since 4 tons of fertilizer yield 2200 bushels of corn, the APP of 4 tons of fertilizer is 2200/4 = 550 bushels per ton of fertilizer. (For a real example, see the box on page 503.)

If Farmer Pfister is to decide how much fertilizer to use, he must know how much *additional* corn output he can expect from each *additional* ton of fertilizer.

An **input** is any item which the firm uses in its production process. Labor, fuel, raw materials, machinery and factories are all examples of inputs.

The firm's **output** is the good or service it produces. Sometimes the word "output" is used to mean the *quantity* of the good or service that the firm produces.

The firm's **total physical product (TPP) curve** shows what happens to the quantity of the firm's output, as one changes the quantity of one of the firm's inputs while holding the quantities of all other inputs unchanged.

The **average physical product (APP)** is the total physical product (TPP) divided by the total quantity of input used. Thus, APP = TPP/Q where Q = the quantity of input.

Table 23–1
FARMER PFISTER'S TOTAL PHYSICAL PRODUCT SCHEDULE

CORRESPONDING LABEL IN FIGURE 23–2	FERTILIZER INPUT (tons)	CORN OUTPUT (bushels)
A	0	1000
B	1	1250
C	2	1550
D	3	1900
E	4	2200
F	5	2450
G	6	2600
H	7	2650
I	8	2650
J	9	2600

*Data of the sort provided in this table do not represent the farmer's subjective opinion. They are *objective* information of the sort a soil scientist could supply from experimental evidence.

Figure 23–2

TOTAL PHYSICAL PRODUCT WITH DIFFERENT QUANTITIES OF FERTILIZER

This graph shows how Farmer Pfister's corn crop varies as he uses more and more fertilizer on his fixed plot of land. (Other inputs, such as labor, are also held constant in this graph.)

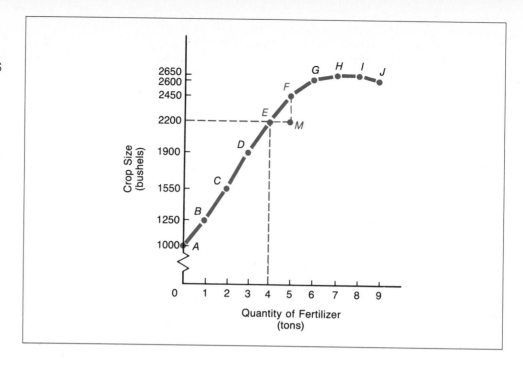

Table 23–2

FARMER PFISTER'S TOTAL, AVERAGE, AND MARGINAL PHYSICAL PRODUCT SCHEDULES

FERTILIZER INPUT (tons)	TOTAL PHYSICAL PRODUCT (corn output in bushels)	MARGINAL PHYSICAL PRODUCT (bushels per ton)	AVERAGE PHYSICAL PRODUCT (bushels per ton)
0	1000	—	—
1	1250	250	1250
2	1550	300	775
3	1900	350	633.3
4	2200	300	550
5	2450	250	490
6	2600	150	433.3
7	2650	50	378.6
8	2650	0	331.3
9	2600	−50	288.9

The **marginal physical product (MPP)** of an input is the increase in total output that results from a one-unit increase in the input, holding the amounts of all other inputs constant.

This concept is known as **marginal physical product (MPP).** The marginal physical product of, for example, the fourth ton of fertilizer, is the total output of corn when four tons of fertilizer are used *minus* the total output when three tons are used.

The marginal physical product schedule of fertilizer on Farmer Pfister's land is given in the third column of Table 23–2. For example, since 3 tons of fertilizer yield 1900 bushels of corn and 4 tons yield 2200 bushels, the MPP of the fourth ton is 2200 − 1900 = 300 bushels. The other MPP entries in Table 23–2 are calculated from the total product data in the same way. Figure 23–3 displays these numbers graphically in a **marginal physical product curve.**

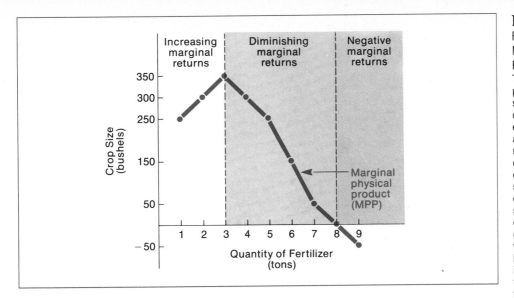

Figure 23–3
FARMER PFISTER'S MARGINAL PHYSICAL PRODUCT (MPP) CURVE
This graph of marginal physical product (MPP) shows how much *additional* corn Farmer Pfister gets from each application of an additional ton of fertilizer. The relation between the MPP curve and the total product curve in Figure 23–2 is simple and direct: the MPP curve at each level of input shows the *slope* of the corresponding total product curve. To see why, suppose we want to know what happens when Farmer Pfister increases fertilizer usage from four tons to five tons; that is, we want to determine the MPP of the fifth ton. In Figure 23–2 this takes us from point *E* to point *F* on the total product curve so that output increases from 2200 bushels to 2450 bushels. The difference, 250 bushels, is the marginal physical product of the fifth ton of fertilizer. It is measured by the slope of the total product curve between points *E* and *F* because it corresponds to the rise in the curve (distance *MF*) resulting from a move to the right by one unit (distance *EM*)—which is precisely the definition of slope.

The "Law" of Diminishing Marginal Returns

The marginal physical product curve in Figure 23–3 shows a pattern that will prove significant for our analysis. Until three tons of fertilizer are used, the marginal physical product of fertilizer is *increasing*; between three tons and eight tons it is *decreasing*, but still *positive*; and beyond eight tons the MPP of fertilizer actually becomes *negative*. The graph has been divided into three zones to illustrate these three cases. The left zone is called the region of **increasing marginal returns,** the middle zone is the region of **diminishing marginal returns,** and the right zone is the region of **negative marginal returns.** In this graph, the marginal returns to fertilizer increase at first and then diminish. This is a typical pattern.

In the increasing returns zone, each additional ton of fertilizer adds more to TPP than the previous ton added. This corresponds to points A through D in Figure 23–2 where the curve is rising with increasing rapidity. In the diminishing returns area, each additional ton of fertilizer adds less to TPP than the previous ton added. This corresponds to points E through H, where the TPP curve

The U.S. Productivity Problem and Average Physical Product

In recent years there has been increasing concern in the United States that the productivity of Japanese workers is outstripping the productivity of American workers. (See Chapter 7 for further discussion of these issues.) For example, statistics for two auto plants suggest that a Japanese auto worker, on the average, turns out nine engines per day, while his U.S. counterpart turns out only two. Thus, the productivity of labor in the auto industry is widely measured as the number of units of output produced per hour of labor.

But you will now recognize that the number of engines produced divided by the number of labor hours expended is exactly the same as the average physical product of an hour of labor in auto engine production. In other words, when you read in the newspapers about trends in the productivity of U.S. labor, or comparisons between that productivity and productivity in other countries, you will know that the report refers to the average physical product, which we discuss in this chapter.

in Figure 23–2 is still rising but at a diminishing rate. Finally, in the zone of negative marginal returns (inputs greater than 8) additional fertilizer actually reduces production by damaging the plants.

The **"law" of diminishing marginal returns,** which has played a key role in economics for two centuries,[2] asserts that when we increase the amount of any one input, *holding the amounts of all others constant,* the marginal returns to the expanding input ultimately begin to diminish. The so-called law is no more than an empirical regularity based on some observation of the facts; it is not a theorem deduced analytically.

The reason why returns to a single input are usually diminishing is straight-forward. As we increase the quantity of one input while holding all others constant, the input whose quantity we are increasing gradually becomes more and more abundant compared with the others. As the farmer uses more and more fertilizer with his fixed plot of land, the soil gradually becomes so well fertilized that adding yet more fertilizer does little good. Eventually the plants are absorbing so much fertilizer that any further increase in fertilizer will actually harm them. At this point the marginal physical product of fertilizer becomes *negative*.

Production, Input Quantities, and Cost

In order to decide how much to produce and what combination of inputs to use, the farmer must consider how these decisions affect his costs. We now will see how these costs are determined by the production relations that have just been studied and the prices of the inputs. We use our two basic assumptions— that the price of fertilizer is beyond the control of the firm and that the quantities of all inputs other than fertilizer are fixed—to deduce the firm's costs from the physical product schedules in Table 23–1 and Figure 23–2. We need simply record, for each quantity of output, the amount of fertilizer required to produce it, multiply that quantity of fertilizer by its price, and add this to the costs of the other inputs whose quantities we are holding constant. It is critical to recognize that these additional costs must include the opportunity costs of any inputs the farmer contributes himself—such as his labor or his capital, which he could instead have used elsewhere to earn wages or interest.

Suppose that fertilizer costs $350 per ton and that the cost of the inputs whose quantities we are holding constant (capital, labor, and land) is $2200. Then, from Table 23–1, we have the table of total costs shown in Table 23–3. For example, to produce 1900 bushels of corn, we know from the fourth row of Table 23–1 that it requires 3 tons of fertilizer at $350 per ton, which when added to the $2200 cost of other inputs gives us the total cost, $3250. The point of this exercise is that:

The total product curve tells us the input quantities needed to produce any given output. And from those input quantities and the price of the inputs, we can determine the *total cost* (TC) of producing any level of output. This is the amount the firm spends on the inputs needed to produce the output, plus any opportunity costs that arise in that production activity. Thus, the relation of total cost to output is determined by the technological production relations between inputs and outputs, and by input prices.

[2] The "law" is generally credited to Anne Robert Jacques Turgot (1727–1781), one of the great Comptrollers-General of France before the Revolution, whose liberal policies, it is said, represented the old regime's last chance to save itself. But, with characteristic foresight, the king fired him.

Table 23–3

A PORTION OF FARMER PFISTER'S TOTAL COST SCHEDULE
(Obtained from the production data in Table 23–1, assuming fertilizer is the only variable input)

OUTPUT OF CORN (bushels)	TOTAL COST (cost of fertilizer plus other inputs)
1000	$2200
1250	$2200 + $350 = $2550
1550	$2200 + 2 × $350 = $2900
1900	$2200 + 3 × $350 = $3250
2200	$2200 + 4 × $350 = $3600
2450	$2200 + 5 × $350 = $3950
2600	$2200 + 6 × $350 = $4300
2650	$2200 + 7 × $350 = $4650

The Three Cost Curves

The behavior of the firm's costs as output changes is obviously critical for output decisions. There are three interrelated cost curves that contain the pertinent information: the **total cost curve,** the **average cost curve,** and the **marginal cost curve,** where marginal cost is a concept analogous to marginal physical product. As we shall see shortly, average and marginal costs are obtained directly from total costs (which we have just determined).

Total cost (TC) was just explained. But it is worth stressing that TC is not quite the same as the total expenditure of the firm. Expenditure and cost are not equal because, to an economist, "cost" must include the *opportunity costs* of inputs provided by owners of the firm—even though the owners do not explicitly "charge" for those inputs. Thus, if in producing his corn, Farmer Pfister purchases $2600 in inputs, and in addition he himself provides labor time, capital, and land whose opportunity cost is $1700 (that is, it could have earned $1700 elsewhere), then the total cost of his output equals $2600 in input expenditures plus $1700 in opportunity cost, or $4300.

Average cost (AC), also called unit cost, is simply total cost divided by output; that is:

$$\text{Average cost} = \frac{\text{Total cost}}{\text{Quantity of output}},$$

or in symbols:

$$AC = \frac{TC}{Q}.$$

To determine the *marginal cost* (MC), we must know what would happen to TC if output were to increase by one unit. For example, the marginal cost of a fifth unit of output is the amount that production of this unit increases total cost. That is, it is equal to the excess of the total cost of the fifth unit over the total cost of the fourth unit. Table 23–4 presents the calculation systematically. For variety, we deal this time with the number of houses built per month by a construction firm that turns out standardized homes. We assume that the firm's total costs have already been determined from the relation between its inputs

A firm's **total cost (TC) curve** shows, for each possible quantity of output, the total amount which the firm must spend for its inputs to produce that amount of output plus any opportunity cost incurred in the process.

A firm's **average cost (AC) curve** shows, for each output, the cost per unit, that is, total cost divided by output.

A firm's **marginal cost (MC) curve** shows, for each output, the increase in the firm's total cost required if it increases its output by an additional unit.

Table 23-4

HYPOTHETICAL TOTAL, AVERAGE, AND MARGINAL COSTS OF A HOME CONSTRUCTION FIRM

TOTAL HOUSES BUILT PER PERIOD (Q)	MARGINAL COST (TC) (thousands of dollars)	COST (MC) (thousands of dollars)	AVERAGE COST (AC) (thousands of dollars)
0	0		—
1	210	210	210
2	270	60	135
3	306	36	102
4	360	54	90
5	425	65	85
6	516	91	86
7	700	184	100

and its outputs, just as we did in the case of Farmer Pfister. For example, the entries in blue show that the total cost of four houses is $360,000, and of five houses is $425,000.

From the TC data we can next obtain the AC figure for each output. For example, we see that the AC of four houses is $360,000/4 = $90,000. We can also obtain the MC figures from the TC numbers. For example, by subtracting the TC of five houses from the TC of four houses, we see that the MC of producing the fifth house is $425,000 − $360,000 = $65,000. In general:

Once we know a firm's total costs for its various outputs, we can calculate its average costs and its marginal costs from the same information.[3]

Figure 23-4 plots the numbers in this table and thus shows the total, average, and marginal cost curves for the construction firm. The shapes of the curves depicted here are considered typical. The TC curve is generally assumed to rise fairly steadily as the firm's output increases. After all, one cannot expect to produce three houses at a lower total cost than two houses. The AC curve and the MC curve are both shown to be shaped roughly like the letter U—first going downhill, then gradually turning uphill again.

To explain these characteristic shapes, we must first distinguish between two important types of costs.

Fixed Costs and Variable Costs

Total, average, and marginal costs are often divided into two components: **fixed costs** and **variable costs.** A *fixed cost* is the cost of the inputs which the firm needs to produce any output at all, and where the total cost of such inputs does not change when the firm changes its outputs by an amount that does not exceed the inputs' production capacity. Any other cost of the firm's operation is called *variable* because the total amount of that cost will increase when the firm's output rises.

The difference between fixed costs and variable costs can be illustrated by comparing the cost of a railroad's fuel with that of its track construction. To operate between St. Louis and Kansas City, a railroad must lay a set of tracks. It

A **fixed cost** is the cost of the indivisible inputs which the firm needs to produce any output at all. The total cost of such indivisible inputs does not change when the output changes. Any other cost of the firm's operation is called **variable cost.**

[3]The process also works the other way. If we know AC we can work backwards to find TC from the formula TC = AC × Q. Similarly, if we know all of the firm's marginal costs, we can work backwards and find its total costs.

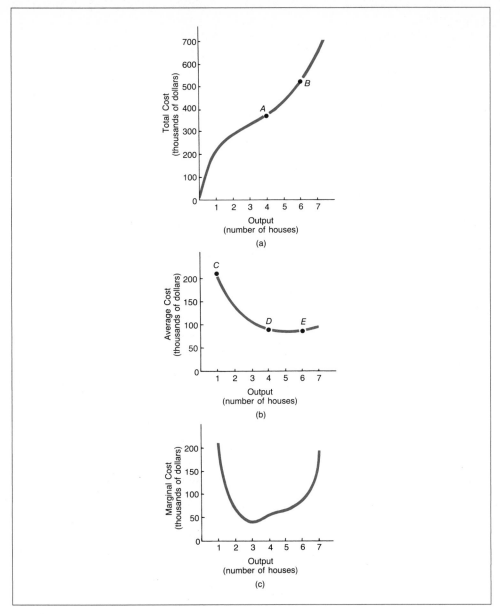

Figure 23–4
TOTAL, AVERAGE, AND
MARGINAL COSTS
These cost curves of a
hypothetical home
construction firm are based
on figures presented in
Table 23–4. The curves show
how the firm's total, average,
and marginal costs behave
when the firm changes its
decision on how many
houses to produce.

cannot lay half a set of tracks or a quarter set of tracks. We therefore call such an input "indivisible."

We see that at any output *greater than zero* the firm has no choice — it must incur its fixed costs. The construction cost of the railroad's tracks will be the same whether one train per month or five trains per day travel the route.[4] Thus, up to a point, track construction cost is not affected by output size, that is, by volume of traffic. On the other hand, the more trains that pass over those tracks, the higher the railroad's total fuel bill will be. We therefore say that fuel costs are variable.

Though variable costs are only part of overall costs (fixed plus variable costs), the variable costs of a firm exhibit patterns of behavior like those already

[4]Note, however, that an increase in traffic will increase annual maintenance and replacement cost, so that replacement and maintenance are variable costs. Note also that opportunity costs can be fixed, variable, or a combination of the two.

Table 23–5
HYPOTHETICAL FIXED COSTS OF A HOME CONSTRUCTION FIRM

HOUSES BUILT PER PERIOD	TOTAL FIXED COST (TFC) (thousands of dollars)	AVERAGE FIXED COST (AFC) (thousands of dollars)
0	—	—
1	120	120
2	120	60
3	120	40
4	120	30
5	120	24
6	120	20

shown in Table 23–4 and Figure 23–4. However, curves of *total fixed costs* (TFC) and *average fixed costs* (AFC) have very special patterns which are illustrated in Table 23–5 and Figure 23–5. We see that TFC remains the same, whether the firm produces a lot or a little, so long as it produces anything at all.[5] As a result, any TFC curve, like the one in Figure 23–5(a), is horizontal — it has the same height at every output.

Average fixed cost, however, gets smaller and smaller as output increases because, with TFC constant, AFC = TFC/Q gets smaller and smaller as output (the denominator) increases. Put another way, any increase in output permits the fixed cost to be spread among more units, leaving less and less of it to be carried by any one unit. For example, when only one house is built, the entire $120,000 of the firm's fixed cost must be borne by that one house. But if the firm constructs two homes, each of them need only cover half the total — $60,000.

However, AFC can never reach zero since even if the firm were to produce, say, a million houses; each would have to bear, on the average, one millionth of the TFC, which is still a positive number, even if it is a very small one. It follows that the AFC curve goes lower and lower as output increases, moving closer and closer to the horizontal axis, but never crossing it. This is the pattern shown in Figure 23–5(b).

[5]Here we assume that the fixed costs are also what economists call "sunk" meaning that the firm has already spent the money in question or signed a contract to do so. Consequently, if the firm decides to go out of business (produce zero output), it must still spend the money.

Figure 23–5
FIXED COSTS: TOTAL AND AVERAGE
The total fixed cost curve [part (a)] is horizontal because, by definition, TFC does not change when output changes. AFC in part (b) decreases steadily as the TFC is spread among more and more units of output, but because AFC never reaches zero, the AFC curve never crosses the horizontal axis.

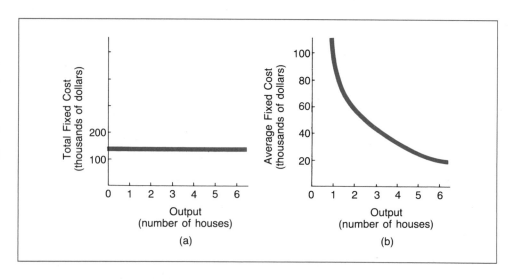

Since we have simply divided costs into two parts, fixed costs (FC) and variable costs (VC), we also have the rules:[6]

$$TC = TFC + TVC \qquad AC = AFC + AVC$$

The total fixed cost curve is always horizontal because, by definition, total fixed cost does not change when output changes. The average fixed cost curve declines when output increases, moving closer and closer to the horizontal axis, but never crossing it.

Shapes of the Average Cost and Total Cost Curves

The preceding discussion of fixed and variable costs enables us to complete our investigation of the shapes of the total, average, and marginal cost curves.

We have drawn the AC curve to be U-shaped in Figure 23–4(b): the leftward portion of the curve is downward sloping, and the rightward portion is upward sloping. Why should we expect AC to decline when output increases in the leftward portion of the AC curve? Fixed costs are a major element in the answer. As we have seen in Figure 23–5(b), the average *fixed* cost curve always falls as output increases, and it falls very sharply at the leftward end of the AFC curve. But AC = AFC + AVC, so that the AC curve of virtually any product contains a fixed cost portion, AFC, which falls when output increases. That is the main reason we can expect the AC curve for any product to have a downward sloping portion such as *CD* in Figure 23–4(b) — a portion which is said to be characterized by decreasing average cost.

All of this is related to the concept of economies of scale which is discussed later in the chapter. We must postpone discussion of that concept because so far in our analysis we have allowed only one input quantity to vary, while the economies of scale concept refers to the consequence of changing all input quantities simultaneously.

Similarly, in the range of the curve to the right of point *E* in the same figure, AC is rising. This, then, is the zone of increasing average cost — a given percentage rise in output requires a greater percentage rise in TC, so that AC = TC/Q must rise.

But why does the portion of the AC curve with decreasing average cost come to an end? There are two reasons: (1) the law of diminishing returns, and (2) the administrative (bureaucratic) problems of large organizations.

The first of these phenomena is crucial for our present discussion in which we are expanding one input (quantity of fertilizer) while holding all other input quantities constant. In that case we can be sure that the law of diminishing returns will work to increase marginal (and average) costs, for reasons we have already considered. Moreover, in reality, where firms can and do vary more than one input quantity, the law of diminishing returns also works to raise MC and AC because a firm may not be able to expand all of its inputs in proportion as its output increases. For example, it may not be able to expand the time the top management of the company devotes to its operation because there are limits to the number of hours the president can put in. Even if all other inputs double, the president may not be able to double the amount of time she puts in. With some inputs not expanding while others are, diminishing returns to the

[6]The reader may wonder if there is such a thing as marginal fixed cost. The answer is "yes," but it doesn't matter because marginal fixed cost must generally equal zero. Why? Because, by definition, an increase in output never adds anything to total fixed cost. For example, for both 2 and 3 units of output TFC must be the same, so that $MFC_3 = TFC_3 - TFC_2 = 0$.

expanding inputs can be expected because the proportions between the various inputs will grow less and less efficient and that will tend to raise average costs.

The second, and probably more important, source of increasing average cost in practice is sheer size. Large firms tend to be relatively bureaucratic, impersonal, and costly to manage. As the personal touch of top management is lost and the firm becomes very large, costs will ultimately rise disproportionately, and average cost will ultimately be driven upward.

The point at which average cost begins to rise varies from industry to industry. It occurs at a much larger volume of output in automobile production than in farming—which is why no farms are as big as even the smallest of automobile producers. A large part of the reason is that the fixed costs of automobile production are far greater than those in farming, so the resulting spreading of the fixed cost over an increasing number of units of output keeps AC falling in auto production for a far larger range of output than it does in farming. Thus, although firms in both industries may have U-shaped AC curves, the bottom of the U occurs at a far larger output in auto production than in farming.

The typical AC curve of a firm is U-shaped. Its downward sloping segment is attributable to the fact that the firm's fixed costs are spread over larger and larger outputs. The upward sloping segment is largely attributable to the disproportionate rise in administrative cost that occurs as the firm grows larger. The output at which decreasing average cost ends, or at which increasing average cost begins, varies from industry to industry. The greater the relative size of fixed costs, the higher will tend to be the output at which the switchover occurs.

This, then, indicates the basis for economists' conclusion that AC curves tend to be U-shaped.[7] Since the shape of the TC curve does not play a major role in introductory discussions in microeconomics, only a few words will be said on this subject.

Going back to Figure 23–4(a), we see that between points 0 and A the TC curve is rising, but at a declining rate (its slope keeps falling). Roughly speaking, this means that in this region TC goes up less rapidly than Q. Further to the right, however, TC rises at an increasing rate, so that TC goes up more rapidly than Q. Looked at in another way, what has just been said amounts to the assertion that portion 0A of the TC curve corresponds to the falling portion of the AC curve. On the other hand, region AB of the TC curve is the portion of the TC curve corresponding to the rising portion of the AC curve. Thus, the shape of the 0A region of the TC curve corresponds to that of the region CD of the AC curve—both reflect the spreading of fixed costs over an increasing output. And, similarly, disproportionate increases in administrative costs can account for segment AB of the TC curve, just as it helps explain the rising portion of the AC curve.

Long-Run Versus Short-Run Costs

The cost to the firm of a change in its output depends very much on the period of time under consideration. The reason is that, at any point in time, many input choices are *precommitted* by past decisions. If, for example, the firm

---

[7]Empirical evidence confirms this view, though it suggests that the bottom of the U is often long and flat. That is to say, there is often a considerable range of outputs between the regions of decreasing and increasing average cost. In this intermediate region the AC curve is approximately horizontal, meaning that there AC does not change when output increases.

purchased machinery a year ago, it is committed to that decision for the remainder of the machine's economic life, unless the company is willing to take the loss involved in getting rid of it sooner. The cost is then said to be **sunk**.

An input to which the firm is committed for a short period of time, however, is not a fixed commitment when a longer planning horizon is considered. For example, a two-year-old machine with a nine-year economic life is a fixed commitment, part of whose cost is still sunk for the next seven years, but it is not a fixed commitment in plans that extend beyond the seven years. Economists summarize this notion by speaking of two different "runs" for decision making — the **short run** and the **long run.**

These terms will recur time and again in this book. They interest us now because of their relationship to the shape of the cost curve. In the short run, there is relatively little opportunity for the firm to adapt its production processes to the size of its current output because the size of its plant has largely been predetermined by its past decisions. Over the long run, however, all inputs, including the size of the plant, become adjustable.

Consider the example of Farmer Pfister. Once the crop is planted, he has little discretion over how much of the various inputs to use. Over a somewhat longer planning horizon, he can decide how much labor to employ and how much seed to use. Over a still longer period, he can acquire new equipment and increase or decrease the size of his farm. Much the same is true of big industrial firms. In the short run, management has little control over the production technique. But with some advance planning, different types of machines using different amounts of labor and energy can be acquired, factories can be redesigned, and other choices can be made. Indeed, over the longest run, no inputs remain committed; all of them can be varied in both quantity and design.

It should be noted that the short and long runs do not refer to the same period of time for all firms; rather, they vary in length depending on the nature of the firm's sunk commitments. If, for example, the firm can change its work force every week, its machines every two years, and its factory every 20 years, then 20 years will be the long run, and any period less than 20 years will constitute the short run.

The **sunk cost** is a cost to which a firm is precommitted for some limited period, either because the firm has signed a contract to make the payments or because the firm has already paid for some durable item (such as a machine or a factory) and cannot get its money back except by using that item to produce output for some period of time.

The **long run** is a period of time long enough for all the firm's sunk commitments to come to an end.

The **short run** is a shorter period of time than the long run, so that some, but not all, of the firm's commitments will have ended.

The Average Cost Curve in the Short and Long Runs

As we just observed, which inputs can be varied and which are precommitted depends on the time horizon under consideration. It follows that:

The average (and marginal and total) cost curve depends on the firm's planning horizon. The average (and total) cost curve pertinent to the long run differs from that for the short run because more inputs become variable.

We can, in fact, be much more specific about the relationships between short-run and long-run average cost (AC) curves. Consider, as an example, the publisher of a small newspaper. In the short run, the firm can choose only the number of typesetters, printers, paper, and ink it uses; but in the long run, it can also choose between two different sizes of printing presses. If the firm purchases the smaller press, the AC curve looks like curve *SL* in Figure 23–6. That means that if the paper is pleasantly surprised and its circulation grows to 50,000 copies per day, its cost will be 12 cents per copy (point *V*). It may then wish it had purchased the bigger press (whose AC curve is shown as *BG*), which would have enabled the firm to cut unit cost to 9 cents (point *W*).

Figure 23–6

SHORT- AND LONG-RUN AVERAGE COST CURVES FOR A NEWSPAPER

The publisher has a choice of two printing plants, a small one with AC curve *SL*, and a big one with AC curve *BG*. These are the short-run curves that apply as long as the newspaper is stuck with its chosen plant. But in the long run, when it has its choice of plant size, it can pick any point on the blue lower boundary of these curves. This lower boundary, *STG*, is the long-run average cost curve.

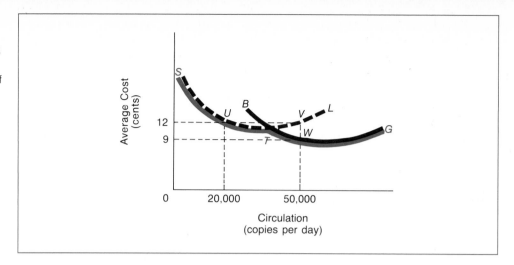

However, in the short run nothing can be done about this decision; the AC curve remains *SL*. Similarly, had it bought the larger press, its short-run AC curve would have been *BG* and it would have been committed to this cost curve even if business were to decline sharply.

In the long run, however, the machine must be replaced, and management has its choice once again. If it expects a circulation of 50,000 copies, it will purchase the larger press and its cost will be 9 cents per copy. Similarly, if it expects sales of only 20,000 copies, it will arrange for the smaller press and for average costs of 12 cents (point *U*). In sum, in the long run, the firm will select the plant size (that is, the short-run AC curve) that is most economical for the output level it expects to produce. The long-run average cost curve then consists of all the *lower* segments of the short-run AC curves. In Figure 23–6, this composite curve is the blue curve *STG*.

The Choice of Input Combination*

We come next to the more realistic case in which the firm decides on the quantities of several inputs—labor, land, and capital, as well as fertilizer.

So far, since only one input, fertilizer, was assumed to be controlled by the farmer, the quantity of the input that must be used by the firm has appeared to follow directly from the magnitude of output. With the quantities of all other inputs fixed by assumption, the only way the farmer could increase his output was to buy whatever additional amount of fertilizer that rise in output required, no more and no less. But that is not how things work in reality. Even given their output quantities, firms have some choices they can make about inputs. Next we will analyze how those choices can be made.

Substitutability: The Choice of Input Combinations

Casual observation of industrial processes deludes many people into thinking that management really has very little discretion in choosing its inputs. Technological considerations alone, it would appear, dictate such choices. A particular type of furniture-cutting machine may require two operators working for an

---

*Instructors may want to teach this part of the chapter (up to page 518) now, or they may prefer to wait until they come to Chapters 35 and 36 on the determination of wages, interest rates, profit, and rent.

hour on a certain amount of wood to make five desks, no more and no less. But this is an overly narrow view of the matter; whoever first declared that there are many ways to skin a cat saw things more clearly.

The furniture manufacturer may have several alternative production processes for making desks. For example, there may be simpler and cheaper machines that can change the same pile of wood into five desks using more than two hours of labor. Or still more workers could eventually do the job with simple hand tools, using no machinery at all. The firm will seek the *least costly* method of production. In advanced industrial societies, where labor is expensive and machinery is cheap, it may pay to use the most automated process; in more primitive societies, where machinery is scarce and labor abundant, making desks by hand may be the most economical solution.

In other words, one input can generally be *substituted* for another. A firm can produce the same number of desks with less labor, *if* it is prepared to sink more money into machinery. But whether it *pays* to make such a substitution depends on the relative costs of labor and machinery. Several general conclusions follow from this discussion.

1. Normally, there are different options available to a firm wanting to produce a particular volume of output. Input proportions are rarely fixed immutably by technological considerations.
2. Given a target level of production, if a firm cuts down on the use of one input (say, labor), it will normally have to increase its use of another input (say, machinery). This is what we mean when we speak of *substituting* one input for another.
3. Which combination of inputs represents the *least costly* way to produce the desired level of output depends on the relative prices of the various inputs.

A method of analysis that a business firm can use to select the least costly production process is described next. But you should know at the outset that the analysis is applicable well beyond the confines of business enterprises. Nonprofit organizations, like your own college, are interested in finding the least costly ways to accomplish a variety of tasks (for example, maintaining the grounds and buildings); government agencies are concerned with meeting their objectives at minimum costs. Even in the household, there are many "cats" that can be "skinned" in different ways. Thus our present analysis of **cost minimization** is widely applicable.

We begin by dealing with one input at a time. Then we will deal with several at once.

Diminishing Returns and the Optimal Quantity of an Input

The first two columns of Table 23–6 repeat Farmer Pfister's marginal physical product schedule from Table 23–2. (The third column will be explained presently.) Suppose fertilizer costs $350 per ton, the farmer's product is worth $2 per bushel, and he is using three tons of fertilizer. Is this optimal for him? The answer is no, because the marginal physical product of the fourth ton is 300 bushels (fourth entry in the marginal physical product column of Table 23–6). This means that although a fourth ton of fertilizer would cost $350, it would yield an additional 300 bushels, which at the price of $2 would add $600 to his revenue. Thus he comes out $600 − $350 = $250 ahead if he adds a fourth ton.

Table 23–6

MARGINAL PHYSICAL PRODUCTS AND MARGINAL REVENUE PRODUCTS OF FARMER PFISTER'S FERTILIZER

FERTILIZER (tons)	MARGINAL PHYSICAL PRODUCT (bushels)	MARGINAL REVENUE PRODUCT (dollars)
1	250	500
2	300	600
3	350	700
4	300	600
5	250	500
6	150	300
7	50	100
8	0	0
9	−50	−100

It is convenient to have a specific name for the additional revenue that accrues to a firm when it increases the quantity of some input by one unit; we call it **marginal revenue product.** So if Farmer Pfister's crop sells at a fixed price (say, $2 per bushel), the marginal revenue product (MRP) of the input equals its marginal physical product (MPP) multiplied by the price of the product:

$$\text{MRP} = \text{MPP} \times \text{Price of output}.$$

The **marginal revenue product (MRP)** of an input is the additional revenue the producer is able to earn as a result of increased sales when he uses an additional unit of the input. MRP = MPP × price of product.

For example, we have just seen that the marginal revenue product of the fourth ton of fertilizer to Farmer Pfister is $600, which we obtained by multiplying the MPP of 300 bushels by the price of $2 per bushel. The other entries in Table 23–6 are obtained in precisely the same way. The concept of MRP enables us to formulate a simple **rule for the optimal use of any input.** Specifically:

When the marginal revenue product of an input exceeds its price, it pays the producer to expand his use of that input. Similarly, when the marginal revenue product of the input is less than its price, it pays the producer to use less of that input.

Let us test this rule in the case of Farmer Pfister. We have observed that three tons of fertilizer cannot be enough because the MRP of the fourth ton ($600) exceeds its price ($350). What about the fifth ton? Table 23–6 tells us that the MRP of the fifth ton ($500) also exceeds its price; thus, stopping at four tons cannot be optimal. The same cannot be said of the sixth ton, however. A sixth ton is not a good idea, since its MRP is only $300, which is less than its $350 cost.

Notice the crucial role of diminishing returns in this analysis. Because the "law" of diminishing marginal returns holds true for Pfister's farm, the marginal *physical* product of fertilizer eventually begins to decline. Therefore, the marginal *revenue* product also begins to decline. At the point where MRP falls below the price of fertilizer, it is appropriate for Pfister to stop increasing his purchases. In sum, it always pays the producer to expand his input use until diminishing returns set in and reduce the MRP to the price of the input.

A common expression suggests that it does not pay to continue doing something "beyond the point of diminishing returns." As we see from this analysis, quite to the contrary, it normally pays to do so! Only when the marginal revenue product of an input has been reduced (by diminishing returns) to the level of the input's price has the proper amount of the input been employed. Thus, the optimal quantity of an input is that at which the MRP is equal to its price (P). In symbols:

$$\text{MRP} = P \text{ of input}.$$

Choice of Input Proportions: The Production Function

So far we have dealt with the choice of each input quantity as if it could be decided separately from the others by setting the MRP of each input equal to its price. This is somewhat misleading, for the choices of how much fertilizer, labor, and land to employ depend on one another. For example, the amount of fertilizer it pays Farmer Pfister to use clearly depends on the number of acres he farms, because the marginal physical product of fertilizer depends on the amount of land that is used, and vice versa. Decisions about how much of each different input to employ are therefore interdependent.

To help select the combination of inputs that can produce the desired output most cheaply, economists have invented a concept they call the **production function.** The production function summarizes the technical and engineering information about the relationship between inputs and output in a given firm, taking *all* the firm's inputs into account. It indicates, for example, just how much output Farmer Pfister can produce if he has a given amount of land, labor, fertilizer, and so on.

When there are only two inputs—which are enough to indicate the basic principles involved—a production function can be represented graphically (which we do in the appendix to this chapter) or by a simple table. Table 23–7 indicates Farmer Pfister's production function for the use of labor and fertilizer to produce corn on his farm. To make the table easier to read, most of the numbers that normally would be entered (but that are irrelevant for our purposes) have been omitted and replaced by dashes.

The table is read like a mileage chart. Thus, if we want to see how much can be produced with two tons of fertilizer and three months of labor, we locate the 2 in the column of numbers on the left, which indicates the quantity of fertilizer, and the 3 in the row of numbers across the top, which represents the

The **production function** indicates the *maximum* amount of product that can be obtained from any specified *combination* of inputs, given the current state of knowledge. That is, it shows the *largest* quantity of goods that any particular collection of inputs is capable of producing.

Table 23–7
A PRODUCTION FUNCTION

QUANTITY OF FERTILIZER (tons)	QUANTITY OF LABOR (months)					
	0	1	2	3	4	5
0	0	1000	—	—	—	2600
1	0	1250	1900	2400	2600	—
2	0	1550	2250	2600	2800	—
3	0	1900	2450	2750	—	—
4	0	2200	2600	—	—	—
5	0	2450	3000	—	—	—
6	0	2600	—	—	4900	—
7	0	2650	—	—	—	—
8	0	2650	3700	4600	5400	6000
9	0	2600	—	—	—	—

months of labor. Then, in the spot horizontally to the right of the 2 and vertically below the 3 we find the number 2600, meaning that this input combination can produce 2600 bushels of output per month. Similarly, you should be able to verify that with eight tons of fertilizer and three months of labor, 4600 bushels per month can be produced.

The zero entries in the first column of Table 23–7 tell us that Farmer Pfister can produce nothing with no labor. The second column, which corresponds to alternative amounts of fertilizer used in combination with *one* month of labor, is familiar to us already — it is just the total physical product schedule that we have been using for Farmer Pfister working alone with various amounts of fertilizer. The other columns represent alternative production arrangements in which Pfister hires one or more farmhands to help him.

How much labor and fertilizer should Farmer Pfister use if he wants to grow 2600 bushels of corn? The production function table shows us that there are a variety of alternatives available to him. He can, for example, work alone and use six tons of fertilizer. Or he can hire a second worker and use only four tons. Or, at the other extreme, he can grow 2600 bushels without fertilizer by using five workers. The blue numbers in Table 23–7 indicate the different ways in which Farmer Pfister can meet his 2600-bushel production target.

Which will he choose? Naturally, the one that costs him the least. Table 23–8 shows Farmer Pfister's cost calculations. It is assumed here that fertilizer costs $350 per ton, that farm labor costs $500 per month, and that Pfister's sunk costs on such items as land and machinery amount to $1700 per month. Thus, for example, the first line tells us that Pfister can produce 2600 bushels using only his own labor (which costs $500), six tons of fertilizer (which cost $2100), and land and machinery that cost $1700 per month, for a total cost of $500 + $2100 + $1700 = $4300. The other lines in Table 23–8 can be read the same way. We see that the cheapest way to produce 2600 bushels of corn is by using three workers and two tons of fertilizer, for a total cost of $3900, which is less than any other alternative.

Notice that two types of information are relevant to Farmer Pfister's decision. The *technological information* embodied in the production function tells Pfister all the possible ways that 2600 bushels can be produced; that is, it tells him about the possibilities for factor substitution. Then *financial information* — the prices of the two inputs — is needed to tell him which alternative is least costly. If either set of data changes, Farmer Pfister's decision on input combinations is likely to change as well. For example, if fertilizer gets much more expensive, he might switch to an alternative that uses more labor and less fertilizer.

Table 23–8
PRODUCTION COSTS UNDER ALTERNATIVE INPUT COMBINATIONS CAPABLE OF PRODUCING 2600 BUSHELS

QUANTITY OF LABOR (months)	COST OF LABOR (at $500 per month)	QUANTITY OF FERTILIZER (tons)	COST OF FERTILIZER (at $350 per ton)	SUNK COSTS (for land, machinery, etc.)	TOTAL COST
1	$ 500	6	$2100	$1700	$4300
2	1000	4	1400	1700	4100
3	1500	2	700	1700	3900
4	2000	1	350	1700	4050
5	2500	0	0	1700	4200

Does the "marginal revenue product equals price" rule continue to hold when there are two or more inputs? Let us see by testing whether the rule is satisfied when Pfister uses three months of labor and two tons of fertilizer. (Table 23–8 has just shown us that this input combination is the least costly way to produce 2600 bushels.) We know from Table 23–7 that when three months of labor are used, the marginal *physical* product (MPP) of the second ton of fertilizer is 200 bushels (2600 bushels minus 2400 bushels). Since the price of a bushel of corn is $2, the marginal *revenue* product (MRP) of the second ton of fertilizer is $400, which exceeds its price ($350). Therefore, Farmer Pfister should purchase the second ton. But should he purchase the third? Its MPP is 150 bushels (2750 minus 2600), so its MRP is $2 × 150 = $300. This is less than what the third ton would cost, so Pfister should stop at two tons.

What about months of labor? Reading across the row corresponding to two tons of fertilizer, we see that the MPP of the third month of labor is 350 bushels (2600 − 2250) while the MPP of the fourth month of labor is only 200 bushels. At a $2 price for corn, the corresponding MRPs are $700 for the third month of labor and only $400 for the fourth month. Since labor costs $500 per month, it is optimal to stop at three months.

Because we have not considered fractional amounts in our production function table, we have not been able to satisfy the MRP = *P* rule exactly. But we can see that Farmer Pfister has indeed followed the basic logic of the rule and has come as close as possible to setting:

$$\text{MRP of fertilizer} = P \text{ of fertilizer}$$

$$\text{MRP of labor} = P \text{ of labor}.$$

If we remember that the MRP of each input is its marginal *physical* product times the price of corn, we can see that these rules are just a formalization of common sense. They say, for example, that if one input costs twice as much as another, then optimal input use requires that the first input be twice as productive (on the margin) as the second.[8]

This common-sense reasoning leads to an important conclusion. Suppose the price of fertilizer rises while the price of labor remains the same. The rule

$$P \text{ of fertilizer} = \text{MRP of fertilizer} = \text{MPP of fertilizer} \times \text{price of corn}$$

[8]A little algebra is helpful in restating this rule. Letting P_F, P_L and P_C represent the prices of fertilizer, labor, and corn, respectively, and letting MRP_F and MPP_F represent the marginal revenue product and the marginal physical product of fertilizer, respectively, with similar notation for labor, our two rules for optimal input use become:

$$P_F = \text{MRP}_F = P_C \times \text{MPP}_F \text{ and } P_L = \text{MRP}_L = P_C \times \text{MPP}_L.$$

Then if we divide the first optimality rule by the second, we obtain:

$$\frac{P_F}{P_L} = \frac{\text{MRP}_F}{\text{MRP}_L} = \frac{\text{MPP}_F \times P_C}{\text{MPP}_L \times P_C}.$$

Since P_C can be divided out of both numerator and denominator, the general rule for optimal input combinations is:

$$\frac{P_F}{P_L} = \frac{\text{MPP}_F}{\text{MPP}_L}.$$

In words, variable inputs should always be combined in such a way that their prices are proportional to their marginal physical products.

tells us that optimal use of fertilizer now requires that the MPP of fertilizer must be higher than before. (The price of corn has not changed.) By the "law" of diminishing returns, the MPP of fertilizer is *higher* only when *less* fertilizer is used. Thus a rise in the price of fertilizer leads the farmer to use *less* fertilizer and, if he still wants to produce 2600 bushels of output, to use *more* labor. In general:

As any one input becomes more costly relative to other competing units, the firm is likely to substitute one input for another; that is, to reduce its use of the input that has become more expensive and to increase its use of competing inputs.[9]

This general principle of input substitution applies in industry just as it does on Farmer Pfister's farm. For some applications of the analysis, see the box on page 520.

The Firm's Cost Curves

Earlier we calculated the firm's cost curves in the special case where the quantity of only one input — fertilizer — was selected by the firm. Now we can see how the cost curves can be determined in the more realistic case of multiple inputs.

In deciding on the quantity of output that serves its objectives best, the firm must consider alternative production levels and compare their costs. In the present example, an output of 2600 bushels is not likely to be the only possible production level that Farmer Pfister is considering. He might wonder, for example, about the least costly way to produce 2100 bushels or 3100 bushels.

By the same procedures outlined in Table 23–8 (page 516), Farmer Pfister can compute the minimum cost of producing *any* quantity of output, using the logic of the requirement that in such a cost-minimizing decision the relative marginal revenue products of any two inputs must equal their relative prices.

Let us suppose that Farmer Pfister has calculated the minimum total costs for alternative production levels displayed in Table 23–9. Here we have the numbers Pfister needs to plot five different points on his *total cost curve* (columns 1 and 2 of the table), which is the curve shown in Figure 23–7. Point A shows the $2880 total cost of 1600 bushels of output, point B shows the

[9]*EXERCISE*: Suppose that fertilizer rises in price to $600 per ton. Construct a new version of Table 23–8 (page 516) and use it to show that it will be optimal to reduce fertilizer use from two tons to zero and to increase the use of labor from three months to five months.

Table 23–9
DATA FOR FARMER PFISTER'S TOTAL COST CURVE

(1) OUTPUT LEVEL (bushels)	(2) TOTAL COST (TC) (dollars)
1600	2880
2100	3360
2600	3900
3100	4805
3600	5940

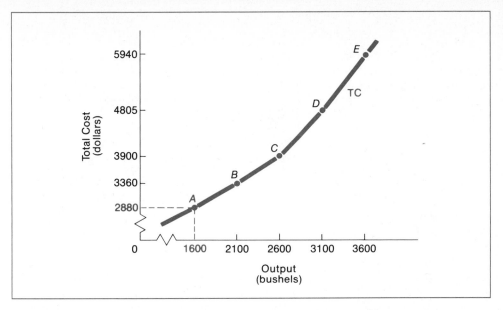

Figure 23–7
TOTAL COST CURVE,
FROM THE COST AND
OUTPUT DATA IN
TABLE 23–9
Point A shows that to
produce 1600 bushels per
month, a total of $2880 in
cost must be incurred, just as
Table 23–9 indicates.

$3360 total cost of 2100 bushels, and so on. As before, by dividing the total cost for each output by the quantity of the output, we obtain the corresponding *average cost*; that is, the cost per unit of output. For example, when output is 2600 bushels, total cost is $3900; so average cost is $3900/2600, or $1.50. Similarly, we can deduce the marginal cost curve from the total cost figures, just as we did before.[10]

Economies of Scale

We are now beginning to put together the apparatus we need to address the question posed at the start of this chapter: How can we tell if a firm has substantial **economies of scale?** We are now in a position to give a definition of this concept.

   The scale of operation of a business enterprise is defined by the quantities of the various inputs it uses. To see what happens when the firm doubles its scale of operations, we inquire about the effect on output of doubling every one of the firm's input quantities. As an example of economies of scale, turn back to the production function for Farmer Pfister in Table 23–7 on page 515 and assume that labor and fertilizer are the only two inputs.[11] Notice that with two months of labor and four tons of fertilizer, output is 2600 bushels. What happens if we double both inputs — to four months of labor and eight tons of fertilizer? The table shows us that output rises to 5400 — that is, it more than doubles. So Farmer Pfister's production function, at least in this range, is said to display **increasing returns to scale** (economies of scale).

   We can relate this definition of economies of scale to the shape of the *long-run* average cost curve instead of the production function. Notice that the definition requires that a doubling of *every* input bring about more than a doubling of output. If all input quantities are doubled, then total cost must double.

Production is said to involve **economies of scale,** also referred to as **increasing returns to scale,** if, when all input quantities are doubled, the quantity of output is more than doubled.

[10]*EXERCISE*: Provide the average and marginal cost columns for Table 23–9 and draw the AC and MC curves.

[11]This is necessary because the table deals with only two inputs and the definition requires that *all* inputs be doubled simultaneously. So, to be true to the definition, because labor, fertilizer, *land, and machinery* were all used by the farmer, their quantities would all have to be doubled.

Input Substitution on the Range

When the second fuel crisis hit the United States at the end of the 1970s, the newspapers carried a story about ranchers in the Southwest reportedly hiring additional cowhands to drive cattle on foot instead of carrying them on trucks. In other words, the rising price of oil had led ranchers to substitute the work of cowboys for the gasoline formerly used in driving cattle-carrying trucks. This is no scenario from a Wild West movie but an illustration of the way in which life follows the analytical principles described in the text, substituting inputs whose relative price has not risen for inputs whose relative price has risen.

There are many other illustrations of this phenomenon. It helps to explain the disappearance, in half a century, of personal servants who were once commonplace in the homes of middle-class families (in the 1920s "every" such home had at least a full-time maid) and the substitution of washing machines, clothes dryers, and dishwashers

as real wages rose in the United States. It also helps to account for the disappearance of wooden houses in England as forests disappeared and wood became increasingly expensive compared with other building materials. You can undoubtedly come up with other examples without difficulty.

But if output *more* than doubles as a result, then cost per unit (average cost) must decline. In other words:

Production functions with economies of scale lead to long-run average cost curves that decline as output expands.

An example will clarify the arithmetic behind this rule. We saw earlier (Table 23–8) that it costs $4100 to produce 2600 bushels with two months of labor and four tons of fertilizer. The average cost is thus $4100/2600, or approximately $1.58 per bushel. If, as the production function states, doubling all inputs (and thus doubling costs to $8200) leads to production of 5400 bushels, then cost per unit will become $8200/5400, or approximately $1.52. Economies of scale in the production function thus lead to *decreasing* average cost as output expands; in this case, average cost decreases by 6 cents—from $1.58 to $1.52.

A decreasing average cost curve is depicted in Figure 23–8(a). But this is only one of three possible shapes the long-run average cost curve can take. A second possibility is shown in part (b) of the figure. In this case, if all input quantities change proportionately, we have an example of **constant returns to scale,** where both total cost (TC) and quantity of output (Q) double, so average cost (AC = TC/Q) remains constant. Finally, it is possible that output less than doubles when all inputs double. This would be a case of **decreasing returns to scale,** which leads to a rising long-run average cost curve like the one depicted in part (c) of Figure 23–8. Thus there is an association between the slope of the AC curve and the nature of the firm's return to scale. The correspondence is precise if the firm does find it efficient to carry out any changes in its output by means of proportionate changes in all of its inputs.

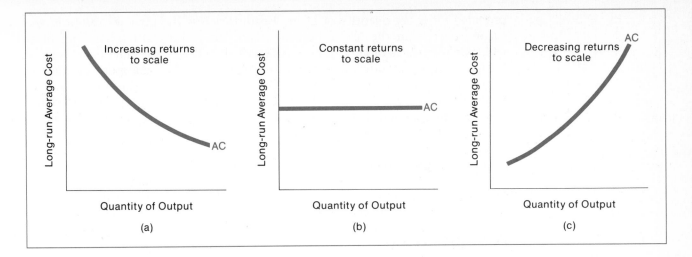

Figure 23–8

THREE POSSIBLE
SHAPES FOR THE
LONG-RUN AVERAGE
COST CURVE
In part (a), long-run average
costs are decreasing as
output expands because the
firm has significant
economies of scale
(increasing returns to scale).
In part (b), constant returns
to scale lead to a long-run
AC curve that is flat; costs
per unit are the same for any
level of output. In part (c),
which pertains to a firm with
decreasing returns to scale,
long-run average costs rise
as output expands.

It should be pointed out that the same production function can display increasing returns to scale in some ranges, constant returns to scale in others, and decreasing returns to scale in yet others. Farmer Pfister's production function in Table 23–7 provides an illustration of this. We have already seen that it displays increasing returns to scale when inputs are doubled from two months of labor and four tons of fertilizer to four months of labor and eight tons of fertilizer. But, looking back at Table 23–7 (page 515), we can see that there are constant returns to scale when inputs double from two months of labor and three tons of fertilizer (2450 bushels of output) to four months of labor and six tons of fertilizer (4900 bushels). We can also find a region of decreasing returns to scale. Notice that with two months of labor and one ton of fertilizer the yield is 1900 bushels, while with double those inputs—four months of labor and two tons of fertilizer—the yield is only 2800 bushels.

Diminishing Returns and Returns to Scale

Earlier in this chapter we discussed the "law" of diminishing marginal returns. Is there any relationship between economies of scale and the phenomenon of diminishing returns? It may seem at first that the two are contradictory. After all, if a producer gets diminishing returns from his inputs as he uses more of each of them, doesn't it follow that by using more of *every* input, he cannot obtain economies of scale? The answer is that there is no contradiction, for the two principles deal with fundamentally different issues.

1. ***Returns to a single input.*** Here we must ask the question: How much can output expand if we increase the quantity of just *one* input, *holding all other input quantities unchanged?*
2. ***Returns to scale.*** Here the question is: How much can output expand if *all* inputs are increased *simultaneously* by the same percentage?

The "law" of diminishing returns provides an answer to the first question while economies of scale pertains to the second.

Table 23–7 shows us that Farmer Pfister's production function satisfies the "law" of diminishing returns to a single input. To see this, we must hold the quantity of one input constant while letting the other vary. The row corresponding to eight tons of fertilizer will serve as an example, since an entry is provided for every quantity of labor. Reading across the row, we see from the second entry that the use of one month of labor and eight tons of fertilizer yields 2650 bushels of corn. The next entry shows that the same eight tons of fertilizer plus one additional month of labor produces a marginal product of 1050 bushels (that is, the total of 3700 bushels produced by the two months of labor minus the 2650 bushels obtained from the first month's labor). In the third column we find that another month of labor (still holding fertilizer use at eight tons) brings in a smaller marginal product of 900 (4600 total bushels minus 3700 bushels from the first two months). The "law" of diminishing returns is clearly satisfied.

Returns to scale, on the other hand, describe the production response to a proportionate increase in *all* inputs. We have already seen that this production function displays increasing returns to scale in some ranges, constant returns to scale in others, and decreasing returns to scale in yet others. Thus the "law" of diminishing returns (to a single input) is compatible with *any* sort of returns to scale. In summary:

Returns to scale and returns to a single input (holding all other input quantities constant) refer to two distinct aspects of a firm's technology. A production function that displays diminishing returns to *a single input* may show diminishing, constant, or increasing returns when *all input quantities are increased proportionately*.

Historical Costs Versus Analytical Cost Curves

Toward the end of Chapter 22, we made much of the fact that all points on a demand curve pertain to the *same* period of time, and that a plot of historical data on prices and quantities is normally *not* the demand curve that the decision maker needs. A similar point relating to cost curves will resolve the problem posed at the beginning of the chapter as to whether declining historical costs are evidence of economies of scale.

All points on any of the cost curves used in economic analysis refer to the same period of time.

One point on the cost curve of an auto manufacturer tells us, for example, how much it would cost it to produce 2.5 million cars during 1988. Another point on the curve tells us what happens to the firm's costs if, *instead,* it produces, say, 3 million cars in 1988. Such a curve is called an **analytical cost curve** or, when there is no possibility of confusion, simply a cost curve. This curve must be distinguished from a diagram of **historical costs,** which shows how costs have changed from year to year.

The different points on an analytical cost curve represent *alternative possibilities,* all for the same time period. In 1988, the car manufacturer will produce either 2.5 or 3 million cars (or some other amount), but certainly not both. Thus, at most, only one point on this cost curve will ever be observed. The company may, indeed, produce 2.5 million in 1988 and 3 million in 1989; but the latter is not relevant to the 1988 cost curve. By the time 1989 comes around, the cost curve may well have shifted, so the 1988 cost figure will not apply to the 1989 cost curve. We can, of course, draw a different sort of graph that indicates, year by year, how costs and outputs have varied. Such a graph, which gathers together the statistics for a number of different periods, is not, however, a *cost curve* as that term is used by economists. An example of such a diagram of historical costs was given in Figure 23–1.

But why do economists rarely use historical cost diagrams and instead deal primarily with analytical cost curves, which are much more difficult to explain and to obtain statistically? The answer is that analysis of real policy problems—such as the desirability of having a single supplier of telephone services—leaves no choice in the matter. Rational decisions require analytical cost curves. Let us see why.

Resolving the Economies of Scale Puzzle

Since the 1940s there has been great technical progress in the telephone industry. From ordinary open wire, the industry has gone to microwave systems, telecommunications satellites and coaxial cables of enormous capacity, and new techniques using laser beams are on the way. Innovations in switching techniques and in the use of computers to send messages along uncrowded routes are equally impressive. All of this means that the *entire* analytical cost curve of telecommunications must have shifted downward quite dramatically from year to year. Innovation must have reduced not only the cost of large-scale operation *but also the cost of smaller-scale operations*.

Now if we are to determine whether in 1988 a single supplier can provide telephone service more cheaply than can a number of smaller firms, we must compare the costs of *both* large- and small-scale production *in 1988*. It does no good to compare the cost of a large supplier in 1988 with its own costs as a smaller firm back in 1942, because that cannot possibly give us the information we need. The cost situation in 1942 is irrelevant for today's decision between large and small suppliers because no small firm today would use the obsolete techniques of 1942. Until we compare the costs of the large and small supplier *today* we cannot make a rational choice between single-firm and multifirm production. It is the analytical cost curve, all of whose points refer to the same period, that, by definition, supplies this information.

Figures 23–9 and 23–10 show two extreme hypothetical cases, one in which economies of scale are present and one in which they are not. Yet both of them are based on the same historical cost data (in black) with their very sharply declining costs. (This curve is reproduced from Figure 23–1.) They also show (in blue) two possible average cost curves, one for 1942 and one for 1988. In Figure 23–9 the analytical AC curve (in blue) has shifted downward very

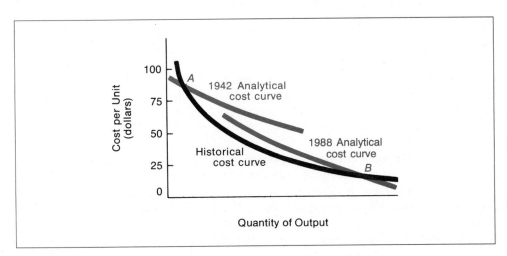

Quantity of Output

Figure 23–9
DECLINING HISTORICAL COST CURVE WITH THE ANALYTICAL AVERAGE COST CURVE ALSO DECLINING IN EACH YEAR
The two analytical cost curves shown indicate how the corresponding points (*A* and *B*) on the historical cost diagram are generated by that year's analytical curve. Because the analytical cost curves are declining, we know that there are economies of scale in the production activity whose costs are shown.

Figure 23–10
DECLINING HISTORICAL
COST CURVE WITH
U-SHAPED ANALYTICAL
COST CURVES IN
EACH YEAR
Here the shape of the
average cost curve does not
show economies of scale.

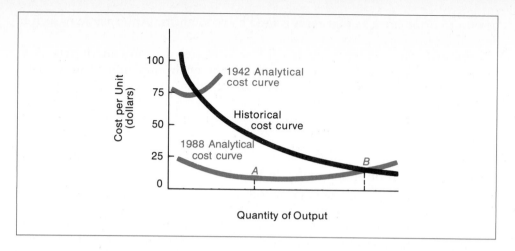

sharply from 1942 to 1988, as technological change reduced all costs. More-over, both of the AC curves slope downward to the right, meaning that, in either year, the larger the firm the lower its average costs. Thus, the situation shown in Figure 23–9 really does represent a case in which there are economies of large-scale production so that one firm can produce at lower cost than many.

But now look at Figure 23–10, which shows exactly the same historical costs as Figure 23–9. Here, both analytical AC curves are U-shaped. In particular, we note that the 1988 AC curve has its minimum point at an output level, A, that is less than one-half the current output, B, of the large supplier. This means that in the situation shown in Figure 23–10, despite the sharp downward trend of historical costs, a smaller company can produce more cheaply than a large one can. In this case, one cannot justify domination of the market by a single large firm on the grounds that its costs are lower. In sum, the behavior of historical costs tells us nothing about the cost advantages or disadvantages of a single large firm. More generally:

Because a diagram of historical costs does not compare the costs of large and small firms at the same point in time, it cannot be used to determine whether there are economies of large-scale production. Only the analytical cost curve can supply this information.

Cost Minimization in Theory and Practice

Lest you be tempted to run out and open a business, confident that you now understand how to minimize costs, we should point out that decision making in business is a good deal harder than we have indicated here. Rare is the business executive who knows for sure what his production function looks like, or the exact shapes of his marginal revenue product schedules, or the precise nature of his cost curves. No one can provide a cookbook for instant success in business. What we have presented here is a set of principles that constitutes a guide to good decision making.

Business management has been described as the art of making critical decisions on the basis of inadequate information, and in our complex and ever-changing world there is often no alternative to an educated guess. Actual business decisions will at best approximate the cost-minimizing ideal outlined in this chapter. Certainly, there will be mistakes. But when management does its job well and the market system functions smoothly, the approximation may prove amazingly good. While no system is perfect, inducing firms to produce at the lowest possible cost is undoubtedly one of the jobs the market system does best.

Summary

1. A firm's total cost curve shows the lowest possible cost for producing any given level of output. It is derived from the input combination used to produce any given output and the prices of the inputs.

2. A firm's average cost (AC) curve shows the lowest possible cost per unit at which it is possible to produce any given level of output. It is derived from the total cost (TC) curve by simple arithmetic: AC = TC/Q.

3. A firm's marginal cost (MC) curve shows for each output level the increase in total cost resulting from a one-unit increase in output.

4. The long run is a period sufficiently long for the firm's plant to require replacement and for all its current contractual commitments to expire. The short run is any period briefer than that.

5. Fixed costs are costs whose total amounts do not vary when output increases. All other costs are called *variable*.

6. At all outputs the total fixed cost (TFC) curve is horizontal and the average fixed cost (AFC) curve declines toward the horizontal axis but never crosses it.

7. TC = TFC + TVC;
   AC = AFC + AVC.

8. It is normally possible to produce the same quantity of output in a variety of ways by substituting more of one input for less of another. Firms normally seek the least costly way to produce any given output.

9. The marginal physical product of an input is the increase in total output resulting from a one-unit increase in the use of that input, holding the quantities of all other inputs constant.

10. The "law" of diminishing marginal returns states that if we increase the amount of one input (holding all other input quantities constant), the marginal physical product of the expanding input will eventually begin to decline.

11. The marginal revenue product of an input is the additional revenue the firm earns from the increased sales resulting from the use of one more unit of the input.

12. A firm that wants to minimize costs will use each input up to the point where its marginal revenue product (MRP) is equal to its price (P).

13. The production function shows the relationship between inputs and output. It indicates the maximum quantity of output obtainable from any given combination of inputs.

14. If a doubling of all the firm's inputs *just* permits it to double its output, the firm is said to have constant returns to scale. If with doubled inputs it can *more than* double its output, it has increasing returns to scale (or, economies of scale). If a doubling of inputs produces *less than* double the output, the firm has decreasing returns to scale.

15. With increasing returns to scale, the firm's long-run average costs are decreasing; constant returns to scale are associated with constant long-run average costs; and decreasing returns to scale are associated with increasing long-run average costs.

16. We cannot tell if there are economies of scale (increasing returns to scale) simply by inspecting a diagram of historical cost data. Only the underlying analytical cost curve can supply this information.

Concepts for Review

Total physical product
Average physical product (APP)
Marginal physical product (MPP)
"Law" of diminishing marginal returns
Total cost curve
Average cost curve
Marginal cost curve
Fixed cost
Variable cost

Increasing (decreasing) average cost
Sunk cost
Short and long runs
Substitutability of inputs
Cost minimization
Marginal revenue product (MRP)
Rule for optimal input use
   (MRP = P of input)
Production function

Economies of scale (increasing returns to scale)
Constant returns to scale
Decreasing returns to scale
Historical versus analytical cost relationships

Questions for Discussion

1. A firm's total fixed cost is $44,000. Construct a table of total and average fixed costs for this firm for output levels varying from 0 to 6 units. Draw the corresponding TFC and AFC curves.

2. With the following data, calculate the firm's AVC and MVC and draw the graphs for TVC, AVC, and MVC.

QUANTITY	TOTAL VARIABLE COSTS (thousands of dollars)
1	$ 20
2	40
3	60
4	88
5	120
6	180

3. From the figures in Questions 1 and 2, calculate TC and AC for each of the output levels from 1 to 6, and draw the two graphs.

4. If a firm's commitments in 1988 include machinery that will need replacement in five years, a factory building rented for 10 years, and a two-year union contract specifying how many workers it must employ, when, from its point of view in 1988, does the firm's long run begin?

5. If the marginal revenue product of a kilowatt hour of electric power is 8 cents and the cost of a kilowatt hour is 12 cents, what can a firm do to increase its profits?

6. A firm hires two workers and rents 15 acres of land for a season. It produces 100,000 bushels of crop. If it had doubled its land and labor, production would have been 300,000 bushels. Does it have constant, diminishing, or increasing returns to scale?

7. Suppose wages are $20,000 per season and land rent per acre is $4000. Calculate the average cost of 100,000 bushels and the average cost of 300,000 bushels, using the figures in Question 6 above. (Note that average costs diminish when output increases.) What connection do these figures have with the firm's returns to scale?

8. Farmer Pfister has bought a great deal of fertilizer. Suppose he now buys more *land,* but not more fertilizer, and spreads the fertilizer evenly over all his land. What may happen to the marginal physical product of fertilizer? What, therefore, is the role of input proportions in the determination of marginal physical product?

9. Labor costs $10 per hour. Nine workers produce $180 of product per hour. Ten workers produce $196 of product; 11 workers produce $208; and 12 workers produce $215. Draw up a table of the marginal revenue products of 10, 11, and 12 workers. What is the optimal amount of labor to hire?

10. (More difficult) A firm finds there is a sudden increase in the demand for its product. In the short run, it must operate longer hours and pay higher overtime wage rates. In the long run, however, it will pay the firm to install more machines and not operate them for longer hours. Which do you think will be lower, the short-run or the long-run average cost of the increased output? How is your answer affected by the fact that the long-run average cost includes the new machines the firm buys, while the short-run average cost includes no machine purchases?

Appendix
Production Indifference Curves

To describe a production function — that is, the relationship between input combinations and size of total output — we can use a graphic device called the **production indifference curve** instead of the sort of numerical information described in Table 23–7 in the chapter.

A **production indifference curve** (sometimes called an *isoquant*) is a curve in a graph showing quantities of *inputs* on its axes. Each indifference curve indicates *all* combinations of input quantities capable of producing *a given* quantity of output; thus, there must be a separate indifference curve for each quantity of output.

If you have read the appendix on indifference curves in Chapter 21 (on consumer demand), you will recognize a close analogy in logic (and in geometric shape) between consumers' and producers' indifference curves. Figure 23–11 represents

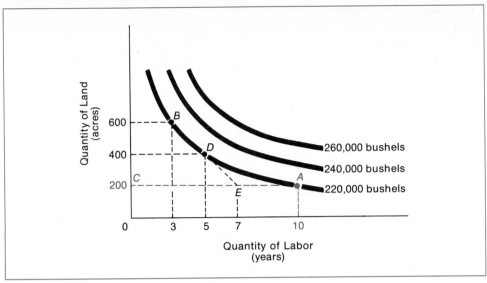

Figure 23–11
A PRODUCTION
INDIFFERENCE MAP
The figure shows three
indifference curves, one for
the production of 220,000
bushels of wheat, one for
240,000 bushels, and one for
260,000 bushels. For
example, the lowest curve
shows all combinations of
land and labor capable of
producing 220,000 bushels
of wheat. Point A on that
curve shows that 10 years of
labor and 200 acres of land
are enough to do the job.

different quantities of labor and capital capable of producing given amounts of wheat. The indifference curve labeled 220,000 bushels indicates that an output of 220,000 bushels of wheat can be obtained with the aid of *any one* of the combinations of inputs represented by points on that curve. For example, it can be produced by 10 years of labor and 200 acres of land (point A) or, instead, it can be produced by the labor-capital combination shown by point B on the same curve. Because it lies considerably below and to the right of point B, point A represents a productive process that uses more labor and less land than shown at point B.

Points A and B can be considered *technologically* indifferent because each represents a bundle of inputs capable of yielding the same quantity of finished goods. However, "indifference" in this sense does not mean that the producer will be unable to make up his mind between input combinations A and B. Input prices will permit him to arrive at that decision, because the two input choices are not *economically* indifferent.

The production indifference curves in a diagram such as Figure 23–11 constitute a complete description of the production function. For each combination of inputs, they show how much output can be produced. Since it is drawn in two dimensions, the diagram can deal with only two inputs at a time. In more realistic situations, there may be more than two inputs, and an algebraic analysis must be used. But all the principles we need to analyze such a situation can be derived from the two-variable case.

Characteristics of the Production Indifference Curves

Before discussing input pricing and quantity decisions, we first examine what is known about the shapes of production indifference curves. The main characteristics are straightforward and entirely analogous to the properties of consumer indifference curves discussed in the appendix to Chapter 21.

Characteristic 1: Higher curves correspond to larger outputs. Points on a higher indifference curve represent larger quantities of *both* inputs than the corresponding points on a lower curve. Thus, the higher the curve, the larger the output it represents.

Characteristic 2: The indifference curve will generally have a negative slope. It goes downhill as we move toward the right. This means that if we reduce the quantity of one input used, and we do not want to cut production, we must use more of another input. For example, if we want to use less labor to produce 220,000 bushels of wheat, we will have to farm more land to make up for the reduced labor input.

Characteristic 3: The curves are typically assumed to curve inward toward the origin near their "middle." This is a reflection of the "law" of diminishing returns to a single input. For example, in Figure 23–11, points B, D, and A represent three different input combinations capable of producing the same quantity of output. At point B a large amount of land and relatively little labor is used, while the opposite is true at point A. Point D is intermediate between the two. Indeed, point D is chosen so that its use of land is exactly halfway between the amounts of land used at A and at B.

Now consider the choice among these input combinations. As the farmer considers first the input combination at B, then the one at D, and finally the one at A, he is considering the use of less and less land, making up for it by the use of more and more labor so that he can continue to produce the same output. But the trade-off does not proceed at a constant rate because of diminishing returns in the substitution of labor for land.

When the farmer considers moving from point B to point D, he gives up 200 acres of land and instead hires two additional years of labor. Similarly, the move from D to A involves giving up another 200 acres of land. But this time, hiring an additional two years of labor does not make up for the reduced use of land. Diminishing returns to labor as he hires more and more workers to replace more and more land means that now a much larger quantity of additional labor, five years rather than two, is needed to make up for the reduction in the use of land. If there had been no such diminishing returns, the indifference curve would have been a straight line, DE. The curvature of the indifference curve through points D and A reflects diminishing returns to substitution of inputs.

The Choice of Input Combinations

A production indifference curve only describes what input combinations *can* produce a given output; it indicates the technological possibilities. A business cannot decide which of the available options suits its purposes best without the corresponding cost information: that is, the relative prices of the inputs.

Just as we did for the consumer in the appendix to Chapter 21, we can construct a **budget line** — a representation of equally costly input combinations — for the firm. For example, if farmhands are paid $9000 a year and land rents for $1000 per acre a year, then a farmer who spends $360,000 can hire 40 farmhands but rent no land (point K in Figure 23–12), or he can rent 360 acres but have no money left for farmhands (point J). But it is undoubtedly more sensible for him to pick some intermediate point on his budget line,

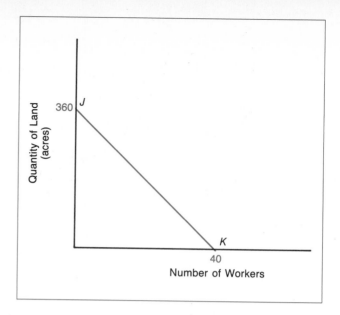

Figure 23–12
A BUDGET LINE
The firm's budget line, *JK*, shows all the combinations of inputs it can purchase with a fixed amount of money — in this case $360,000.

JK, at which he divides the $360,000 between the two inputs.

There is an important difference, however, in how this budget line is used. The consumer had a fixed budget and sought the highest indifference curve attainable with these limited funds. The firm's problem in minimizing costs is just the reverse. Its budget is not fixed. Instead, it wants to produce a given quantity of output (say, 240,000 bushels) with the *smallest possible budget*.

A way to find the minimum budget capable of producing 240,000 bushels of wheat is illustrated in Figure 23–13, which combines the indifference curve for 240,000 bushels from Figure 23–11 with a variety of budget lines similar to JK in Figure 23–12. The firm's problem is to find the lowest budget line that will allow it to reach the 240,000-bushel indifference curve. Clearly, an expenditure of $270,000 is too little; there is no point on budget line AB that permits production of 240,000 bushels. Similarly, an expenditure of $450,000 is too much, because the firm can produce its target level of output more cheaply. The solution is at point T, meaning that 15 workers and 225 acres of land are used to produce the 240,000 bushels of wheat. In general:

The least costly way to produce any given level of output is indicated by the point of tangency

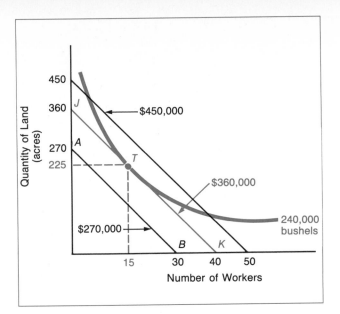

Figure 23–13
COST MINIMIZATION
The least costly way to produce 240,000 bushels of wheat is shown by point *T*, where the production indifference curve is tangent to budget line *JK*. Here the farmer is employing 15 workers and using 225 acres of land. It is not possible to produce 240,000 bushels on a smaller budget, and any larger budget would be wasteful.

between a budget line and the production indifference curve corresponding to that level of output.

Cost Minimization, Expansion Path, and Cost Curves

Figure 23–13 shows how to determine the input combination that minimizes the cost of producing 240,000 bushels of output. We can repeat this procedure exactly for any other output quantity, such as 200,000 bushels or 300,000 bushels. In each case, we draw the corresponding production indifference curve and find the lowest budget line that permits it to be produced. For example, in Figure 23–14, budget line *BB* is tangent to the indifference curve for 200,000 units of output and budget line *B'B'* is tangent to the indifference curve for 300,000 units of output. In this way, we obtain three tangency points: *S*, which gives us the input combination that produces a 200,000-bushel output at lowest cost; *T*, which gives the same information for a 240,000-bushel output; and *S'*, which indicates the cost-minimizing input combination for the production of 300,000 bushels.

This process can be repeated for as many other levels of output as we like. For each such output we draw the corresponding production indifference curve and find its point of tangency with a budget line. That tangency point will show the input combination that produces the output in question at lowest cost.

Curve *EE* in Figure 23–14 connects all these cost-minimizing points, that is, it is the locus of *S*, *T*, and *S'* and all the other points of tangency between a production indifference curve and a budget line. Curve *EE* is called the firm's **expansion path,** which is defined as the locus of the firm's cost-minimizing input combinations for all relevant output levels.

In Figure 23–13 we were able to determine for tangency point *T* the quantity of output (from the production indifference curve through that point) and the total cost (from the tangent budget line). Similarly, we can determine the output and total cost for every other point on the expansion path, *EE*, in Figure 23–14. For example, at point *S* we see that output is 200,000 and total cost is $270,000. This is precisely the sort of information we need to find the firm's total cost curve; that is, it is just the sort of information contained in Table 23–4, from which we first calculated the total cost curve and then the average and marginal cost curves in Figure 23–4. Thus we see that:

The points of tangency between a firm's production indifference curves and its budget lines yield its expansion path. The expansion path shows the firm's cost-minimizing input combination for each pertinent output level. This information also yields the output and total cost for each point on the expansion path, which is just what we need to draw the firm's cost curves.

Effects of Changes in Input Prices

Suppose that the cost of renting land increases and the wage rate of labor decreases. This means that the budget lines will differ from those depicted in Figure 23–13. Specifically, with land now more expensive, any given sum of money will rent fewer acres, so the intercept of each budget line on the vertical (land) axis will shift *downward*. Conversely, with labor cheaper, any given sum of money will buy more labor, so the intercept of the budget line on the horizontal (labor) axis will shift to the *right*. A series of budget lines

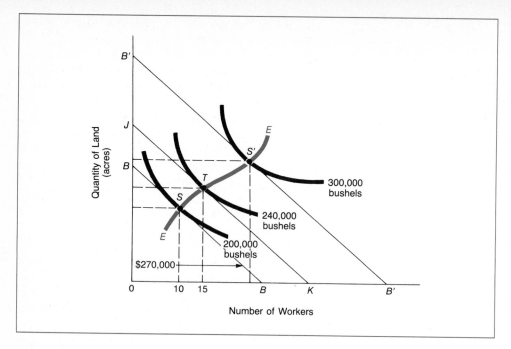

Figure 23–14
THE FIRM'S EXPANSION
PATH
Each point of tangency such
as S, between a production
indifference curve and a
budget line shows the
combination of inputs which
can produce the output
corresponding to that
indifference curve at lowest
cost. The locus of all such
tangency points is EE, the
firm's expansion path.

corresponding to a $1500 per acre rental rate for land and a $6000 annual wage for labor is depicted in Figure 23–15. We see that these budget lines are less steep than those shown in Figure 23–13, and that the least costly way to produce 240,000 bushels of wheat is now given by point E.

To assist you in seeing how things change, Figure 23–16 combines, in a single graph, budget line JK and tangency point T from Figure 23–13 and budget line WV and tangency point E from Figure 23–15. Notice that point E lies below and to the right of T, meaning that as wages decrease

and rents increase, the firm will hire more labor and rent less land. As common sense suggests, when the price of one input rises in comparison with that of others, it will pay the firm to hire less of this input and more of other inputs to make up for its reduced use of the more expensive input.

In addition to this substitution of one input for another, a change in the price of an input may induce the firm to alter the level of output that it decides to produce. But this is the subject of the next chapter.

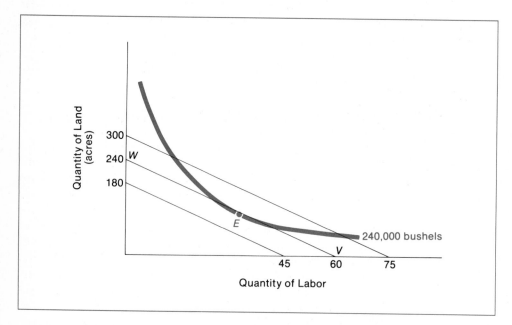

Figure 23–15
OPTIMAL INPUT CHOICE
AT A DIFFERENT SET OF
INPUT PRICES
If input prices change, the
combination of inputs that
minimizes costs will normally
change, too. In this diagram,
land rents for $1500 per acre
(more than in Figure 23–13)
while labor costs $6000 per
year (less than in
Figure 23–13). As a result,
the least costly way to
produce 240,000 bushels of
wheat shifts from point T in
Figure 23–13 to point E here.

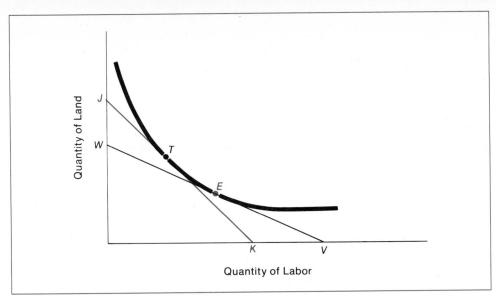

Figure 23–16
HOW CHANGES IN INPUT PRICES AFFECT INPUT PROPORTIONS
When land becomes more expensive and labor becomes cheaper, the budget lines (such as *JK*) become less steep than they were previously (see *WV*). As a result, the least costly way to produce 240,000 bushels shifts from point *T* to point *E*. The firm uses more labor and less land.

Summary

1. A production function can be fully described by a family of production indifference curves, each of which shows all the input combinations capable of producing a specified amount of output.
2. As long as each input has a positive marginal physical product, production indifference curves will have a negative slope and the higher curves will represent larger amounts of output than the lower curves. Because of diminishing returns, these curves characteristically bend toward the origin near their middle.
3. The optimal input combination for any given level of output is indicated by the point of tangency between a budget line and the appropriate production indifference curve.
4. The firm's expansion path shows, for each of the firm's possible output levels, the combination of input quantities that minimizes the cost of producing that output.
5. From the production indifference curves and the budget lines tangent to them along the expansion path, one can find the total cost for each output level. From these figures one can determine the firm's total cost, average cost, and marginal cost curves.
6. When input prices change, firms will normally use more of the input that becomes relatively less expensive and less of the input that becomes relatively more expensive.

Concepts for Review

Production indifference curve
Budget line
Expansion path

Point of tangency between the budget line and the corresponding production indifference curve

Questions for Discussion

1. Typical Manufacturing Corporation (TMC) produces gadgets with the aid of two inputs: labor and glue. If labor costs $5 per hour and glue costs $5 per gallon, draw TMC's budget line for a total expenditure of $100,000. In this same diagram, sketch a production indifference curve indicating that TMC can produce no more than 1000 gadgets with this expenditure.

2. With respect to Question 1, suppose that wages rise to $10 per hour and glue prices rise to $6 per gallon. How are TMC's optimal input proportions likely to change? (Use a diagram to explain your answer.)

3. What happens to the expansion path of the firm in Question 2?

24

Output–Price Decisions: The Importance of Marginal Analysis

Annual income twenty pounds, annual expenditure nineteen six, result happiness. Annual income twenty pounds, annual expenditure twenty pounds ought and six, result misery.

CHARLES DICKENS

When IBM introduced its new line of personal computers in 1987, the company had to decide on the prices at which each would be offered and the number of each to produce. These were clearly among the most crucial decisions the firm ever made. They had a vital influence on IBM's labor requirements, on the reception given the product by consumers, and indeed, on the future success of the company.

This chapter describes the tools that firms like IBM can use to make decisions on outputs and prices—tools that are equally useful to government agencies and nonprofit organizations in making analogous decisions. We begin the chapter by examining the relationship between the firm's price decisions and the quantity of product it sells. We then discuss the assumption of profit maximization before turning to the techniques firms can use to achieve the largest possible profit. We will explore, in words, with numerical examples, and with graphs, several methods of finding the level of output that maximizes profits. Each of these methods teaches us something else about the nature of the firm's decision-making process and provides some general lessons about the use of marginal analysis.

The analysis will also yield two conclusions which may be somewhat surprising and show that unaided common sense can sometimes be misleading in business decisions. Specifically, it will be shown that a change in fixed costs does not change the price and output that maximize a firm's profits, and that it may be possible for a firm to make a profit by selling at a price below cost.

Two Illustrative Cases*

Price and output decisions can perplex even the most experienced business people, as the following real-life illustrations show. At the end of the chapter we will see how the tools described here helped solve the problems.

*The figures in these examples are doctored to help preserve the confidentiality of the information and to simplify the calculations. The cases, however, are real.

CASE 1: PRICING A SIX-PACK

The managers of one of America's largest manufacturers of soft drinks became concerned when a rival company introduced a cheaper substitute for one of their leading products. As a result, some of the firm's managers advocated a reduction in the price of a six-pack from $1.50 to $1.35. This stimulated a heated debate. It was agreed that the price should be cut if it was not likely to reduce the company's profits. Although some of the managers maintained that the cut made sense because of the demand it would stimulate, others held that the price cut would hurt the company by cutting profit per unit of output. The company had reliable information about costs, but knew rather little about their consumers' responsiveness to price changes. At this point a group of consultants was called in to offer their suggestions. We will see how economic analysis enabled them to solve the problem even though the vital demand elasticity figures were unavailable.

CASE 2: SAVING THE COMPANY BY SELLING BELOW COSTS

A supplier of a canned meat product was selling 10 million units per year at a wholesale price of $11 per unit. It found that rising wages and raw material prices had increased its costs to $13 per unit, which was clearly a losing proposition. Yet the availability of competing canned meats convinced the firm's managers that they could not get away with a price increase. At this point a purchasing agent for a foreign government approached the firm and offered to buy an additional 10 million units, but at a price of only $7 per unit. At first, management considered the offer ludicrous, since the $7 price came nowhere near covering the unit cost of $13. But after some analysis, management was able to show that the firm could actually clear up its financial problem by agreeing to the proposed sale even though it was "below cost." At the end of the chapter we will explain just how this was possible.

Price and Quantity: One Decision, Not Two

This chapter is about how firms like those in the preceding cases select a *price* and a *quantity* of output that best serve their financial interests. While it would seem that firms must choose two numbers, in fact they can pick only one. Once they have selected the *price*, the *quantity* they will sell is up to consumers. Alternatively, firms may decide *how much* they want to sell, but then they must leave it to the market to determine the *price* at which this quantity can be sold.

Management gets its two numbers by making only one decision because the firm's demand curve tells it, for any quantity it may decide to market, the highest possible price its product can fetch. For purposes of illustration, consider a hypothetical firm, Computron, Inc., which produces giant computers. Computron's demand curve, *DD* in Figure 24–1, shows that if the company decides to charge the relatively high price of $15 million per computer (point *a* on the curve), then it can sell only one unit per year. On the other hand, if it wants to sell as many as six computers per year, it can do so only by offering its product at the low price of $8 million (point *f*). In summary:

Each point on the demand curve represents a price–quantity pair. The firm can pick any such pair. But it can never pick the price corresponding to one point on the demand curve and the quantity corresponding to another point, since such an output would never be sold at the selected price.

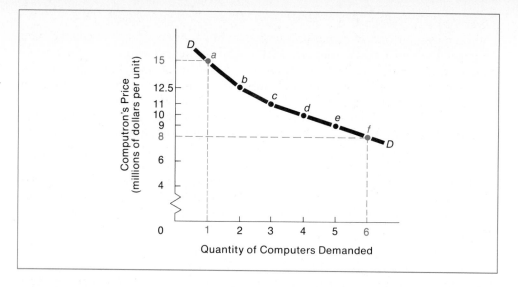

Figure 24–1
COMPUTRON'S
DEMAND CURVE
This graph shows the
quantity of product
demanded at each price. For
example, the curve shows
that at a price of $8 million
(point *f*), six units will be
demanded.

Throughout this chapter, then, we will not discuss price and output decisions separately, for they are merely two different aspects of the same decision. To analyze this decision, we will make a strong assumption about the behavior of business firms, which, while not literally correct, seems to be a useful simplification of a much more complex reality — the assumption that firms strive for the largest possible total profit.

Do Firms Really Maximize Profits?

Naturally, many people have questioned whether firms really try to maximize profits, to the exclusion of all other goals. Business people are like other human beings: their motives are varied and complex. Given the choice, many executives might prefer to control the largest firm rather than the most profitable one. Some may be influenced by envy, others by a desire to "do good." Different managers within the same firm may not always agree with one another. Thus, any attempt to summarize the objectives of management in terms of a single number (profit) is bound to be an oversimplification.

In addition, the exacting requirements for maximizing profits are tough to satisfy. In practice, the required calculations are rarely carried out fully. In deciding on how much to invest, on what price to set for a product, or on how much to allocate to the advertising budget, the range of available alternatives is enormous. And information about each alternative is often expensive and difficult to acquire. As a result, when a firm's management decides on an $18 million construction budget it rarely compares the consequences of that decision in any detail with the consequences of all the possible alternatives — such as budgets of $17 million or $19 million. But unless all the available possibilities are compared, there is no way management can be sure it has chosen the one that brings in the highest possible profit.

Often management studies with care only the likely effects of the proposed decision itself: What sort of plant will it obtain for the money? How costly will it be to operate the plant? How much revenue is it likely to obtain from the sale of the plant's output? Management's concern is *whether the decision will produce results that satisfy the firm's standards of acceptability* — whether its risks will not be unacceptably great, whether its profits will not be unacceptably low, and so on. Such analysis does not necessarily lead to the maximum possible profit, because, though the decision may be good, some of the alternatives that have *not* been investigated may be better.

Decision making that seeks only acceptable solutions has been called **satisficing** to contrast with optimizing. Some analysts, such as Carnegie-Mellon University's Nobel Prize winner Herbert Simon, have concluded that decision making in industry and government is often of the satisficing variety.

But even if this is true, it does not necessarily make profit maximization a bad assumption. Recall our discussion of abstraction and model-building in Chapter 1. A map of Los Angeles that omits thousands of roads is no doubt "wrong" if interpreted as a literal description of the city. Nonetheless, by capturing the most important elements of reality, it may help us understand the city better than a map that is cluttered with too much detail. Similarly, we can learn much about the behavior of business firms by assuming that they try to maximize profits, even though we know that *all* of them do not act this way *all* of the time.

We will therefore assume throughout this and the next few chapters that the firm has only one objective. It wants to make its *total* profit as large as possible. Our analytic strategy will be to determine what output level (or price) achieves this goal.

Total Profit: Keep Your Eye on the Goal

Total profit, then, is assumed here to be *the* goal of the profit-maximizing firm. It is, by definition, the difference between what the company earns in the form of sales revenue and what it pays out in the form of costs:

$$\text{Total profit} = \text{Total revenue} - \text{Total costs}.$$

Total profit defined in this way is called **economic profit,** to distinguish it from the accountant's definition of profit. The two concepts of profit differ because total cost, in the economist's definition, includes the opportunity cost of any capital, labor, or other inputs supplied by the owner of the firm. Thus, if a small business earns just enough to pay the owner the normal fee for her labor and the use of her capital (say, $35,000 a year), and not a penny more, an economist will say she is earning zero *economic* profit (she is just covering all her costs). In contrast, most accountants will say her profit is $35,000.

To analyze how total profit depends on output, we must study the behavior of the two components of total profit: total revenue (TR) and total cost (TC). We know from preceding chapters that both **total revenue** and **total cost** depend on the output–price combination the firm selects.

Total revenue can be calculated directly from the demand curve, since by definition it is the product of price times the quantity that will be bought at that price:

$$\text{TR} = P \times Q.$$

Table 24–1 shows how the total revenue schedule is derived from the demand schedule for our illustrative firm, Computron. The first two columns simply express the demand curve of Figure 24–1 in tabular form. The third column gives, for each quantity, the product of price times quantity. For example, if

Table 24-1

DEMAND SCHEDULE AND TOTAL MARGINAL REVENUE SCHEDULES FOR COMPUTRON, INC.

(data corresponding to Figure 24–1)

NUMBER OF COMPUTERS (per year)	PRICE = AVERAGE REVENUE (millions of dollars per computer)	TOTAL REVENUE (millions of dollars per year)	MARGINAL REVENUE (millions of dollars per computer)
0	—	0	—
1	15	15	15
2	12.5	25	10
3	11	33	8
4	10	40	7
5	9	45	5
6	8	48	3

Computron markets three computers per year at a price of $11 million per computer, its annual sales revenue will be 3 × $11 million = $33 million.

Figure 24–2 displays Computron's total revenue schedule in graphical form as the black TR curve. This graph shows precisely the same information as the demand curve in Figure 24–1, but in a somewhat different form. For example, point *d* on the demand curve in Figure 24–1, which shows a price–quantity combination of P = $10 million and Q = 4 computers, appears as point *D* in Figure 24–2 as a total revenue of $40 million ($10 million price per unit times 4 units) corresponding to a quantity of four computers. Similarly, each point on the TR curve in Figure 24–2 corresponds to the similarly labeled point in Figure 24–1.

The relationship between the demand curve and the TR curve can be rephrased in a slightly different way. Since the price of the product is the revenue *per unit* that the firm receives, we can view the demand curve as the curve of **average revenue.** Average revenue (AR) and total revenue (TR) are related

Average revenue (AR) is total revenue (TR) divided by quantity.

Figure 24–2

COMPUTRON'S TOTAL REVENUE CURVE

The total revenue curve for Computron, Inc., is derived directly from the demand curve, since total revenue is the product of price times quantity. Points A, B, C, D, E and F in this diagram correspond to points a, b, c, d, e and f, respectively, in Figure 24–1.

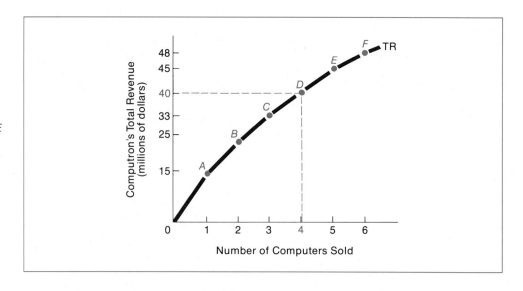

to one another in the same way as average cost and total cost.[1] Specifically, since

$$AR = \frac{TR}{Q} = \frac{P \times Q}{Q} = P \, ,$$

average revenue and price are two names for the same thing.

Finally, the last column of Table 24–1 shows the **marginal revenue** for each level of output, that is, the *addition* to total revenue resulting from the addition of one unit to total output. Its definition and calculation are precisely analogous to those of marginal cost, which were described at length in Chapter 23 (pages 505–509). Thus, in Table 24–1 we see that when output rises from two to three units, total revenue goes up from $25 million to $33 million, so that marginal revenue is $33 million − $25 million = $8 million.

The revenue side is, of course, only one-half of the profit picture. We must turn to the cost side for the other half. The last chapter explained how the total cost (TC), average cost (AC), and marginal cost (MC) schedules are determined by the firm's production techniques and the prices of the inputs it buys. Rather than repeat this analysis, we simply list the total, average, and marginal cost schedules for Computron in Table 24–2. Figure 24–3 depicts the total cost curve as the blue TC curve.

Notice that total costs at zero output are not zero, because Computron incurs sunk costs of $2 million per year even if its produces nothing.[2] For example, Computron will have to pay the upkeep of its factory, even if it happens to be (temporarily) unused.

To study how total profit depends on output, we bring together in Table 24–3 the total revenue and total cost schedules. The last column in Table 24–3, total profit, is just the difference between total revenue and total cost for each level of output. Remembering that Computron's assumed objective is to maximize its profits, it is a simple matter to determine the level of production it will choose if a table such as 24-3 is available. By producing and selling three computers per year, Computron achieves the highest level of profits it is capable of achieving—some $12 million per year. Any higher or lower rate of production would lead to lower profits. For example, profits would drop to $8 million if output were expanded to four units.

> Marginal revenue, often abbreviated MR, is the *addition* to total revenue resulting from the addition of one unit to total output. Geometrically, marginal revenue is the *slope* of the total revenue curve. Its formula is $MR_1 = TR_1 - TR_0$, and so on.

[1]See the appendix to this chapter for a general discussion of the relationship between totals and averages.
[2]The concept of sunk cost will be discussed further in Chapter 25, page 563.

Table 24–2
TOTAL, AVERAGE, AND MARGINAL COSTS FOR COMPUTRON, INC.

NUMBER OF UNITS (per year)	TOTAL COST (millions of dollars)	MARGINAL COST (millions of dollars per unit)	AVERAGE COST (millions of dollars per unit)
0	2		—
1	9	7	9
2	14	5	7
3	21	7	7
4	32	11	8
5	45	13	9
6	60	15	10

Figure 24-3

COMPUTRON'S TOTAL COST CURVE

The graph shows, for each possible level of output, Computron's total costs. Because Computron has some fixed costs, the level of total cost at zero output is $2 million, not zero.

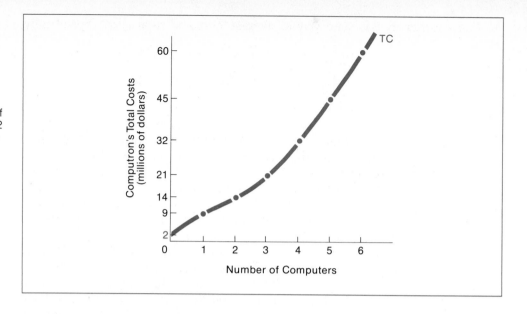

Table 24-3

TOTAL REVENUES, COSTS, AND PROFIT FOR COMPUTRON, INC.

NUMBER OF UNITS (per year)	TOTAL REVENUE	TOTAL COST (millions of dollars per year)	TOTAL PROFIT
0	0	2	−2
1	15	9	6
2	25	14	11
3	33	21	12
4	40	32	8
5	45	45	0
6	48	60	−12

Profit Maximization: A Graphical Interpretation

Precisely the same analysis can be presented graphically. In the upper portion of Figure 24–4 we bring together into a single diagram the total revenue curve from Figure 24–2 and the total cost curve from Figure 24–3. Total profit, which is the difference between total revenue and total cost, appears in the diagram as the *vertical* distance between the TR and TC curves. For example, when output is four units, total revenue is $40 million (point *A*), total cost is $32 million (point *B*), and total profit is the distance between points *A* and *B*, or $8 million.

In this graphical view of the problem, Computron wants to maximize total profit, which is the vertical distance between the TR and TC curves. The curve of total profit is drawn in the lower portion of Figure 24–4. We see that it reaches its maximum value, $12 million, at an output level of approximately three units per year. This is the same conclusion we reached with the aid of Table 24–3.

The total profit curve in Figure 24–4 is shaped like a hill. Though such a shape is not inevitable, we expect a hill shape to be typical for the following reason. If a firm produces nothing, it certainly earns no profit, and it will probably incur a loss if it has an idle factory on its hands and must spend money to

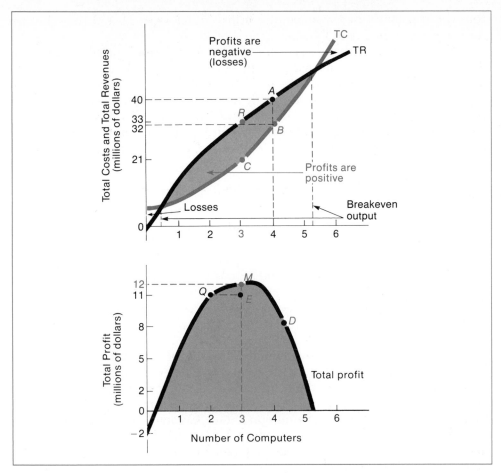

Figure 24–4
PROFIT MAXIMIZATION:
A GRAPHICAL
INTERPRETATION
Computron's profits are
maximized when the vertical
distance between its total
revenue curve, TR, and its
total cost curve, TC, is at its
maximum. In the diagram,
this occurs at an output of
three units per year; total
profits are CR, or $12 million.
The total profit curve is also
shown in the figure. Naturally,
it reaches its maximum value
($12 million) at three units
(point *M*).

guard it and keep it from deteriorating. At the other extreme, a firm can produce so much output that it swamps the market, forcing price down so low that it again loses money. Only at intermediate levels of output — something between zero and the amount that floods the market — will the company earn a positive profit. Consequently, the total profit curve will rise from zero (or negative) levels at a very small output, to positive levels in between; and, finally, it will fall to negative levels when output gets too large. Thus, the total profit curve will normally be a hill like the one in Figure 24–4.

Marginal Analysis and Maximization of *Total* Profit

We see that there may be many levels of output that yield a positive profit. But the firm is not aiming for just any level of profit. It wants the largest profit that is obtainable. The profit graph shows that the hill reaches its summit ($12 million) when output is approximately 3 units. If the firm produces only 2 units, it earns only $11 million in profit. If it produces 4, its profit falls to $8 million. The firm's goal is to get to the top of the hill, where profit is maximized.

If management really knew the exact shape of its profit hill, that is, if it had a table such as 24–3, choosing the optimal level of output would be a simple task indeed. It would only have to locate the point such as M in Figure 24–4, the top of its profit hill. However, management rarely if ever has its information in such a simple form, so a different technique for finding the optimum is required. That technique is **marginal analysis** — the same set of tools that the consumer used to maximize utility in Chapter 21 and that the firm used to minimize costs in Chapter 23.

To see how marginal analysis helps solve Computron's problem, we introduce an expository concept: **marginal profit.** Referring back to Table 24–3, for example, we see that an increase in Computron's annual output from two to three computers would raise total profit from $11 million to $12 million. That is, it would generate $1 million in *additional* profits, which we call the *marginal profit* resulting from the addition of the third unit. Similarly, marginal profit from the fourth unit would be:

$$\text{Total profit} \atop \text{from 4 units} \; - \; {\text{Total profit} \atop \text{from 3 units}} = \$8 \text{ million} - \$12 \text{ million} = -\$4 \text{ million}.$$

The marginal rule for finding the optimal level of output is easy to understand:

If the marginal profit from increasing output by one unit is positive, then output should be increased. If the marginal profit from increasing output by one unit is negative, then output should be decreased. Thus, an output level can maximize *total* profit only if at that output *marginal* profit equals zero.

In the Computron example, the marginal profit from the third unit is +$1 million. This means that going from the second to the third unit *adds* $1 million to profit, so it pays to produce the third unit. But marginal profit from the fourth unit is −$4 million, so the firm should not produce the fourth because that would reduce total profit by $4 million. Since Computron is dealing in whole numbers (for example, it cannot produce 3.12 computers) it cannot achieve a marginal profit of exactly zero. But by producing three units per year it comes quite close.

The profit hill in Figure 24–4 gives us a graphical interpretation of the "marginal profit equals zero" condition. Marginal profit is defined as the additional profit that accrues to the firm when output rises by one unit. So, when output is increased, say, from two units to three units (the distance *QE* in Figure 24–4), total profit rises by $1 million (the distance *EM*) and marginal profit is therefore *EM/QE*. This is precisely the definition of the *slope* of the total profit curve between points *Q* and *M*. In general:

Marginal profit is the slope of the total profit curve.

With this geometric interpretation in hand, we can easily understand the logic of the marginal profit rule. At a point such as *Q*, where the total profit curve is rising, marginal profit (= slope) is positive. Profits cannot be maximal at such a point, because we can increase profits by moving farther to the right. A firm that decided to stick to point *Q* would be wasting the opportunity to increase profits by increasing output. Similarly, the firm cannot be maximizing profits at a point like *D*, where the slope of the curve is negative, because there marginal profit (=slope) is negative. If it finds itself at a point like *D*, the firm can raise its profit by decreasing its output.

Only at a point such as *M*, where the total profit curve is neither rising nor falling, can the firm possibly be at the top of the profit hill rather than on one of the sides of the hill. And point M is precisely where the slope of the curve — and hence the marginal profit — is zero. *An output decision cannot be optimal unless the corresponding marginal profit is zero*.

Marginal profit is the *addition* to total profit resulting from one more unit of output.

The firm is not interested in marginal profit for its own sake, but rather for what it implies about *total* profit. Marginal profit is like the needle on the pressure gauge of a boiler: The needle itself is of no concern to anyone, but if one fails to watch it the consequences may be quite dramatic.

One common misunderstanding that arises in discussions of the marginal criterion of optimality is the idea that it seems foolish to go to a point where marginal profit is zero. "Isn't it better to earn a positive marginal profit?" This notion springs from a confusion between the quantity one is seeking to maximize (*total* profit) and the gauge that indicates whether such a maximum has in fact been attained (*marginal* profit). Of course it is better to have a positive *total* profit than zero total profit. But a zero value on the *marginal* profit gauge merely indicates that all is apparently well, that *total* profit may be at its maximum.

Marginal Revenue and Marginal Cost: Guides to an Optimum

There is a more conventional version of the marginal analysis of profit maximization which proceeds directly in terms of the cost and revenue components of profit. For this purpose refer back to Figure 24–4, where the profit hill was constructed from the total revenue (TR) and total cost (TC) curves. Observe that there is another way of finding the profit-maximizing solution. We want to maximize the vertical distance between the TR and TC curves. This distance, we see, is not maximal at an output level such as two units, because there the two curves are growing farther apart. If we move farther to the right, the vertical distance between them (which is total profit) will increase. Conversely, we have not maximized the vertical distance between TR and TC at an output level such as four units, because there the two curves are coming closer together. We can add to profits by moving farther to the left (reducing output).

The conclusion from the graph, then, is that total profit (the vertical distance between TR and TC) is maximized only when the two curves are neither growing farther apart nor coming closer together; that is, when their *slopes* are equal. While this conclusion is rather mechanical, we can breathe some life into it by interpreting the slopes of the two curves as **marginal revenue** and **marginal cost.** These concepts, which have been defined and illustrated in previous chapters (see pages 505–506 and 536–37), permit us to restate the geometric conclusion we have just reached in an economically significant way:

Profit can be maximized only at an output level at which marginal revenue is (approximately) equal to marginal cost. In symbols:

$$MR = MC.$$

The logic of the MC = MR rule for profit maximization is straightforward.[3] When MR is *not* equal to MC, profits cannot possibly be maximized because the firm can increase its profits either by raising its output or by reducing it. For example if MR = \$16 and MC = \$12, an additional unit of output *adds* \$16 million to revenues but only \$12 million to cost. Hence the firm can increase its net profit by \$4 million by producing and selling one more unit. Similarly, if MC exceeds MR, say MR = \$7 and MC = \$10, then the firm

---

[3]You may have surmised by now that just as total profit = total revenue − total cost, it must be true that marginal profit = marginal revenue − marginal cost. This is in fact correct. It also shows that when marginal profit = 0, we must have MR = MC.

Table 24–4

MARGINAL REVENUE AND MARGINAL COST FOR COMPUTRON, INC.

NUMBER OF UNITS (per year)	MARGINAL REVENUE	MARGINAL COST
	(millions of dollars per year)	
0	—	—
1	15	7
2	10	5
3	8	7
4	7	11
5	5	13
6	3	15

loses $3 million on its marginal unit, so it can add $3 million to its profit by reducing output by one unit. Only when MR = MC is it impossible for the firm to add to its profit by changing its output level.

Table 24–4 reproduces marginal revenue and marginal cost data for Computron, Inc., from Tables 24–1 and 24–2. The table shows, as must be true, that the MR = MC rule leads us to the same conclusion as Figure 24–4 and Table 24–3. Computron should produce and sell three computers per year.

The marginal revenue of the third computer is $8 million ($33 million from selling three computers less $25 million from selling two) while the marginal cost is only $7 million ($21 million minus $14 million). So the firm should produce the third unit. But the fourth computer brings in only $7 million in marginal revenue while its marginal cost is $11 million — clearly a losing proposition.

Because the graphs of marginal analysis will prove so useful in the following chapters, Figure 24–5(a) shows the MR = MC condition for profit maximization graphically. The black curve labeled MR in the figure is the marginal revenue schedule from Table 24–4. The blue curve labeled MC is the marginal cost schedule. They intersect at point E, which is therefore the point where marginal revenue and marginal cost are equal. The optimal output for Computron is three units.[4] Figures 24–5(b) and 24–5(c), respectively, are reproductions of the TR and TC curves from the upper part of Figure 24–4 and the total profit curve from the lower portion of that figure. Note how MC and MR intersect at the same output at which the distance of TR above TC is greatest, which is the output at which the profit hill reaches its summit.

Application: Fixed Cost and the Profit-Maximizing Price

Our analytic apparatus can now be used to offer a surprising insight. Suppose there is a rise in the firm's fixed cost; say, the rented cost of an indispensible air filtering machine doubles. What will happen to the profit-maximizing price and output? Should price go up to cover the increased cost? Should the firm push for a larger output (even if that requires a fall in price)? The answer is: neither.

When a firm's fixed cost increases, its profit-maximizing price and output remain completely unchanged, so long as it pays the firm to stay in business.

[4]One important qualification must be entered. Sometimes marginal revenue and marginal cost curves do not have the nice shapes depicted in Figure 24–5(a), and they may intersect more than once. In such cases, while it remains true that MC = MR at the output level that maximizes profits, there may be other output levels at which MC is also equal to MR but at which profits are not maximized.

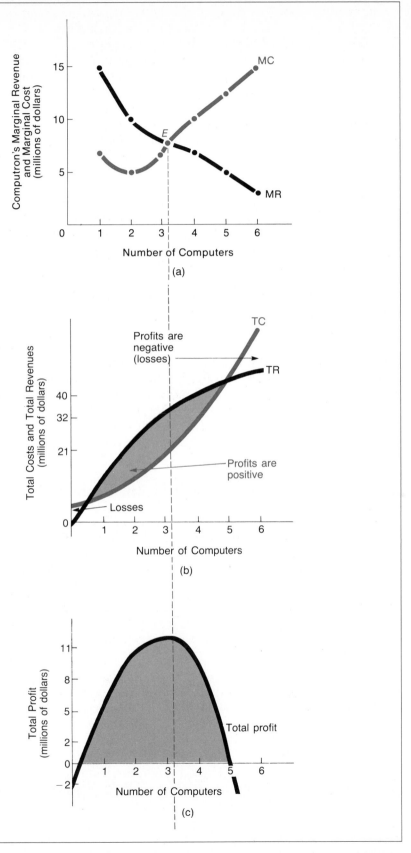

Figure 24–5
PROFIT MAXIMIZATION:
ANOTHER GRAPHICAL
INTERPRETATION
Profits are maximized where
marginal revenue (MR) is
(approximately) equal to
marginal cost (MC), for only
at such a point will *marginal
profit* be zero. Part (a) shows
the MR = MC condition for
profit maximization
graphically as point *E*, where
output is close to three
computers. Since Computron
does not produce fractions of
computers, the best it can do
is to produce three of them.
The diagram also reproduces
from Figure 24–4 the TR and
TC curves [part (b)] and the
total profit curve [part (c)],
showing how all three agree
that the profit-maximizing
output is a bit larger than
three units.

In other words, there is nothing the firm's management can do to offset the effect of the rise in fixed cost. It must just lie back and take it.

Why is this so? Remember that, by definition, a fixed cost is a cost that does not change when output changes. Computron's air filtering cost increase is the same whether business is slow or booming, whether production is 2 or 6 computers. This is illustrated in Table 24–5, which also reproduces Computron's total profits from Table 24–3. The third column of the table shows that total fixed cost has risen by $2 million per year, no matter what the firm's output. As a result, for each possible output of the firm, total profit is $2 million less than what it would have been otherwise. For example, when output is 4 units, we see that total profit must fall from $8 million (second column) to $6 million (last column).

Now, because profit is reduced by the same amount at each and every output level, the output level which was most profitable to the firm before the fixed cost increase must still be the output that yields the highest profit. In Table 24–5 we see that $10 million is the largest entry in the last column showing profits after the rise in fixed cost. The highest profit is attained, as it was before, when output equals three units. Given the firm's demand curve (Figure 24–1) this, of course, means that the profit-maximizing price will remain $11 million—the price at which it sells 3 units (point c on the demand curve).

All of this is also shown in Figure 24–6, which shows the firm's total profit hill before and after the rise in fixed cost (reproducing Computron's initial profit hill from Figure 24–4). We see that the cost increase simply moves the profit hill straight downward by $2 million, so that the highest point on the hill is just lowered from point M to point N. But the top of the hill is shifted neither toward the left nor toward the right. It remains at the 3-unit output level. Just as we saw before, the profit-maximizing output level remains unchanged when fixed costs rise.

Marginal Analysis in Real Decision Problems

We can now put the marginal analysis of profit determination to work to unravel the puzzles with which we began this chapter. These are both examples drawn from reality, and reality never works as neatly as a textbook illustration. In particular, neither example involves a mechanical application of the MC =

Table 24–5
TOTAL PROFIT BEFORE AND AFTER A RISE IN FIXED COST

NUMBER OF UNITS (per year)	TOTAL PROFIT BEFORE FIXED COST INCREASE (millions of dollars per year)	INCREASE IN FIXED COST (millions of dollars per year)	TOTAL PROFIT AFTER COST INCREASE (millions of dollars per year)
0	−2	2	−4
1	6	2	4
2	11	2	9
3	12	2	10
4	8	2	6
5	0	2	−2
6	−12	2	−14

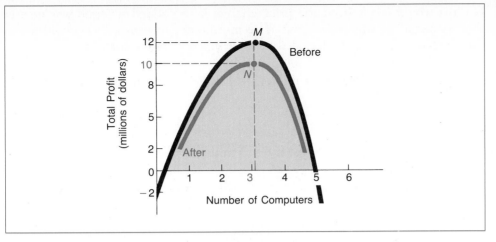

Figure 24–6
FIXED COST DOES
NOT AFFECT
PROFIT-MAXIMIZING
OUTPUT

The graph reproduces
Computron's initial profit hill
from Figure 24–4 (the black
curve labeled "before"). A $2
million increase in fixed cost
shifts the profit hill downward,
to the blue curve marked
"after." But the original point
of maximum profit (point M)
and the new one (point N)
are at the same output level.
This is so because the cost
increase pushes the profit hill
straight downward.

MR rule. However, as these cases show, the reasoning underlying the rule *does* help to deal with real problems.

CASE 1: THE SODA-PRICING PROBLEM

Our first problem dealt with a firm's choice between keeping the price of a brand of soda at $1.50 per six-pack or reducing it to $1.35 when a competitor entered the market. The trouble was that to know what to do, the firm needed to know its demand curve (and hence its marginal revenue curve). However, the firm did not have enough data to determine the shape of its demand curve. How, then, could a rational decision be made?

As we indicated, the debate among the firm's managers finally reached agreement on one point: The price should be cut if, as a result, profits were not likely to decline; that is, if *marginal profit* were not negative. Fortunately, the data needed to determine whether marginal profit was positive were obtainable. Initial annual sales were 10 million units, and the firm's engineers maintained emphatically that marginal costs were very close to constant at $1.20 per six-pack over the output range in question. Instead of trying to determine the *actual* increase in sales that would result from the price cut, the team of consultants decided to try to determine the *minimum necessary* increase in quantity demanded required to avoid a decrease in profits.

It was clear that the firm needed additional revenue at least as great as the additional cost of supplying the added volume, if profits were not to decline. The consultants knew that sales at the initial price of $1.50 per six-pack were $15 million ($1.50 per unit times 10 million units). Letting Q represent the (unknown) quantity of six-packs that would be sold at the proposed new price of $1.35, the economists compared the added revenue with the added cost of providing the Q new units. Since MC was constant at $1.20 per unit, the added cost amounted to:

$$\text{Added cost} = \$1.20 \times (Q - 10 \text{ million}).$$

This was to be compared with the added revenue:

$$\text{Added revenue} = \text{New revenue} - \text{Old revenue}$$
$$= \$1.35Q - \$15 \text{ million}.$$

No loss would result from the price change if the added revenue was greater than or equal to the added cost. The minimum Q necessary to avoid a loss therefore was that at which added revenue equaled added cost, or

$$1.35Q - 15 \text{ million} = 1.2Q - 12 \text{ million},$$

or

$$0.15Q = 3 \text{ million}.$$

This would be true if, and only if, Q, the quantity sold at the lower price, would be

$$Q = 20 \text{ million units}.$$

In other words, this calculation showed that the firm could break even from the 15-cent price reduction only if the quantity of its product demanded rose at least 100 percent (from 10 to 20 million units). Since past experience indicated that such a rise in quantity demanded was hardly possible, the price reduction proposal was quickly abandoned. Thus the logic of the MC = MR rule, plus a little ingenuity, enabled the consultants to deal with a problem that at first seemed baffling—even though they had no estimate of marginal revenue.

CASE 2: THE UNPROFITABLE CANNED MEAT PRODUCER

Our second case study concerned a firm that was losing money (because the price of its canned meat product was less than its average cost) and that was then offered the questionable opportunity to sell more of its product to a foreign buyer at a price that was lower still. The relevant information is summarized in Table 24–6.

Obviously, this firm was in a bad way financially. Its average cost was $13, and yet the price it was charging for its product was only $11 per unit; so it was losing money on this product. Indeed, we see that it lost $20 million on the 10 million units of output it sold. Management might well have reasoned this way: It would be desirable to expand our volume, but we can't afford to do so. Instead, we must raise our price above our $13 average cost, even if it cuts down our sales.

While the managers were pondering their dilemma, a foreign purchasing group offered to buy an additional 10 million units of the company's canned meat product if the company would supply the units at a discount price of $7. On an average cost calculation this arrangement seem disastrous. After all, AC

Table 24–6

INITIAL COSTS AND REVENUES OF THE CANNED MEAT PRODUCER

UNITS SOLD (millions)	TOTAL COST (millions of dollars)	AVERAGE COST	MARGINAL COST	PRICE (dollars)	TOTAL REVENUE	TOTAL COST	PROFIT OR LOSS
			(dollars)			(millions of dollars)	
10	130	13	3	11	110	130	−20

Table 24–7
COST AND REVENUES OF THE SUPPLIER OF CANNED MEAT AFTER SALES "BELOW COST"

UNITS SOLD (millions)	TOTAL COST (millions of dollars)	AVERAGE COST	MARGINAL COST	TOTAL REVENUE	TOTAL COST	PROFIT OR LOSS
		(dollars)		(millions of dollars)		
20	160	8	3	180	160	+20

was $13 and the company was already losing money at a price of $11. How could it possibly afford to sell at an even lower price?

But was the proposition so ludicrous? With its marginal costs approximately constant at $3, by accepting the offer the company could change its situation from that shown in Table 24–6 to that shown in Table 24–7. We see that the total numbers of units sold will have doubled, from 10 to 20 million. Total costs will have risen from $130 million to $160 million. That is, they will have gone up $30 million (the MC of $3 on each of the 10 million additional units). The arithmetic shows that, as a consequence, AC *must* have fallen from $13 = $130/10 to $8 = $160/20.

The last three columns report the resulting "miracle." The apparently ridiculous proposition that 10 million additional units of canned meat be sold at a price below either the old or the new average cost in fact succeeded in eliminating the deficit and actually put the company into the black, to the tune of $20 million in net profits. Just how was this "miracle" accomplished? The answer becomes clear when we apply the rules we have learned in this chapter. In Table 24–6, it can be seen that AC was indeed $13; but the corresponding MC figure was only $3. Therefore, every *additional* unit sold to the foreign buyer at a price of $7 brought in a marginal profit of $7 − $3 = $4. On such terms the more one sells the better off one is.

This case illustrates a point that is encountered frequently. The canned meat supplier was offered an opportunity to deal with a new class of customers at a price that appeared not to cover costs but really did. The same sort of issue frequently faces a firm considering the introduction of a new product or the opening of a new branch office. In many such cases the new operation may not cover *average* costs as measured by standard accounting methods. Yet to follow the apparent implications of those cost figures would amount to throwing away a valuable opportunity to add to the net earnings of the firm and, perhaps, to contribute to the welfare of the economy. Only *marginal* analysis can reveal whether the contemplated action is really worthwhile.

Conclusion: The Fundamental Role of Marginal Analysis

We have seen in Chapter 21 how marginal analysis helps us to understand the consumer's purchase decisions. In Chapter 23 it helped us understand the firm's input choices. And in this chapter it enabled us to examine output decisions. The logic of marginal analysis applies not only to economic decisions by consumers and firms, but also to those of governments, universities, hospitals, and other organizations. In short, the analysis applies to any individual or group that must make economic choices for the use of scarce resources. Thus, one of the most important conclusions that can be drawn from the last four chapters, a conclusion brought out vividly by the two examples we have just discussed, is that:

The Importance of Marginal Analysis
In any decision about whether to expand an activity, it is always the *marginal* cost and *marginal* revenue that are the relevant factors. A calculation based on *average* figures is likely to lead the decision maker to miss all sorts of opportunities, some of them critical.

More generally, if one wants to make *optimal* decisions, *marginal analysis* should be used in the planning calculations. This is true whether the decision applies to a business firm seeking to maximize profit or minimize cost, to a consumer trying to maximize utility, or to a less developed country striving to maximize per capita output. It applies as much to decisions on input proportions and advertising as to decisions about output levels and prices. Indeed, this is such a general principle of economics that it is one of the **12 Ideas for Beyond the Final Exam.**

A real-life example far removed from profit maximization will illustrate the way in which marginal criteria are useful in decision making. For some years before women were admitted to Princeton University (and to several other colleges), the cost of the proposed change was frequently cited as a major obstacle. It had been decided in advance that any women coming to the university would constitute a net addition to the student body because, for a variety of reasons involving relations with alumni and other groups, a reduction in the number of male students was not feasible. Presumably on the basis of a calculation of average cost, some critics spoke of figures as high as $80 million.

To economists it was clear, however, that the relevant figure was the *marginal cost,* the addition to total cost that would result from the introduction of the additional students. The women students would, of course, bring to Princeton additional tuition fees (marginal revenues). If these fees were just sufficient to cover the amount they would add to costs, the admission of the women would leave the university's financial picture unaffected.

A careful calculation showed that the admission of women would add far less to the university's financial problems than the *average cost* figures indicated. One reason was that women's course preferences are characteristically different from men's and hence women frequently elect courses that are undersubscribed in exclusively male institutions. Therefore, the admission of one thousand women to a formerly all-male institution may require fewer additional classes than if one thousand more men had been admitted.[5] More important, it was found that a number of classroom buildings were underutilized. The cost of operating these buildings was nearly fixed — their total utilization cost would be changed only slightly by the influx of women. The corresponding marginal cost was therefore almost zero and certainly well below the average cost (cost per student).

For all these reasons, it turned out that the relevant marginal cost figure was much smaller than the figures that had been bandied about earlier. Indeed, this cost was something like a third of the earlier estimates. There is little doubt that this careful marginal calculation played a critical role in the admission of

[5]See Gardner Patterson, "The Education of Women at Princeton," *Princeton Alumni Weekly*, vol. 69, September 24, 1968.

women to Princeton and to some other institutions that made use of the calculations in the Princeton analysis. Subsequent data, incidentally, confirmed that the marginal calculations were amply justified.

A Look Back and a Look Forward

We have now completed four chapters describing how consumers and business managers can make optimal decisions. Can you go to Wall Street or Main Street and find executives calculating marginal cost and marginal revenue in order to decide how much to produce? Hardly. Not any more than you can find consumers in stores computing their marginal utilities in order to decide what to buy. Like consumers, successful business people often rely heavily on intuition and "hunches" that cannot be described by any set of rules.

However, we have not sought a literal *description* of consumer and business behavior, but rather a *model* to help us analyze and predict this behavior. Just as astronomers construct models of the behavior of objects that do not think at all, economists construct models of consumers and business people who do think, but whose thought processes may be rather different from those of economists. In the chapters that follow we will use these models to serve the purposes for which they were designed: to analyze the functioning of a market economy, and to see what things it does well and what things it does poorly.

Summary

1. A firm can choose the quantity of its product it wants to sell or the price it wants to charge. But it cannot choose both because price affects the quantity demanded.
2. In economic theory, it is usually assumed that firms seek to maximize profits. This should not be taken literally, but rather interpreted as a useful simplification of reality.
3. Marginal revenue is the additional revenue earned by increasing sales by one unit. Marginal cost is the additional cost incurred by increasing production by one unit.
4. Maximum profit requires the firm to choose the level of output at which marginal revenue is equal to marginal cost.
5. Geometrically, the profit-maximizing output level occurs at the highest point of the total profit curve. There the slope of the total profit curve is zero, meaning that marginal profit is zero.
6. A change in fixed cost will not change the profit-maximizing level of output.
7. It may pay a firm to expand its output if it is selling at a price greater than marginal cost, even if that price happens to be below average cost.
8. Optimal decisions must be made on the basis of marginal cost and marginal revenue figures, not average cost and average revenue figures. This is one of the **12 Ideas for Beyond the Final Exam.**

Concepts for Review

Profit maximization	Total revenue and cost	Fixed cost
Satisficing	Average revenue and cost	Marginal analysis
Total profit	Marginal revenue and cost	Marginal profit
Economic profit		

Questions for Discussion

1. "It may be rational for a firm not to try to maximize profits." Discuss the circumstances under which this statement may be true.

2. Suppose the firm's demand curve indicates that at a price of $8 per unit, customers will demand two million units of its product. Suppose management decides to pick *both* price and output, produces three million units of its product, and prices it at $10. What will happen?

3. Suppose a firm's management would be pleased to increase its share of the market, but if it expands its production the price of its product will fall and so its profits will decline somewhat. What choices are available to this firm? What would you do if you were president of this company?

4. Why does it make sense for a firm to seek to maximize *total* profit, rather than to maximize *marginal* profit?

5. A firm's marginal revenue is $23 and its marginal cost is $12. What amount of profit does the firm fail to pick up by refusing to increase output by one unit?

6. Calculate average revenue (AR) and average cost (AC) in Table 24–3. How much profit does the firm earn at the output at which AC = AR? Why?

7. A firm's total cost is $200 if it produces one unit, $350 if it produces two units, and $450 if it pro-

duces three units of output. Draw up a table of total, average, and marginal costs for this firm.

8. Draw an average and marginal cost curve for the firm in Question 7. Describe the relationship between the two curves.

9. A firm with no fixed costs has the demand and total cost schedules given in the table below. If it wants to maximize profits, how much output should it produce?

QUANTITY	PRICE (dollars)	TOTAL COST (dollars)
1	6	1
2	5	2.5
3	4	6
4	3	7
5	2	11

10. Review the concept of fixed cost in Chapter 23. Suppose Computron's total costs are increased by $10 million per year. Show in Table 24–2 how this affects Computron's total and average costs.

11. Why does it make sense for a change in a firm's fixed cost not to change the output level that maximizes its profit?

Appendix
The Relationships Among Total, Average, and Marginal Data

You may have surmised that there is a close connection between the average revenue and average cost curves and the corresponding marginal revenue and marginal cost curves. After all, we deduced our total revenue figures from the average revenue and then calculated our marginal revenue figures from the total revenues; and a similar chain of deduction applied to costs. In fact:

Marginal, average, and total figures are inextricably bound together. From any one of the three, the other two can be calculated. Total, average, and marginal figures bear relationships to one another that hold for *any* variable — such as revenue, cost, or profit — that is affected by the number of units in question.

To illustrate and emphasize the wide applicability of marginal analysis, we switch our exam-

ple from profits, revenues, and costs to a noneconomic variable, human body weights. We do so because calculation of weights is more familiar to most people than calculation of profits, revenues, or costs, and we can use this example to illustrate several fundamental relationships between average and marginal figures. The necessary data are in Table 24–8.[6] We begin with an empty room (total weight of occupants is equal to zero). A person weighing 100 pounds enters; marginal and average weight are both 100 pounds. If the person is followed by a person weighing 140 pounds (marginal weight equals 140 pounds), the average weight rises to 120 pounds (240/2), and so on.

---

[6]Note that in this illustration, "persons in room" is analogous to units of output, "total weight" to total revenue or cost, and so on.

Table 24–8

WEIGHTS OF PERSONS IN A ROOM

NUMBER OF PERSONS IN ROOM	TOTAL WEIGHT	AVERAGE WEIGHT (pounds)	MARGINAL WEIGHT
0	0	—	—
1	100	100	100
2	240	120	140
3	375	125	135
4	500	125	125
5	600	120	100
6	660	110	60

The way to calculate average weight from total weight is quite clear. When, for example, there are four persons in the room with a total weight of 500 pounds, the average weight must be 500/4 = 125 pounds, as shown in the corresponding entry of the third column. In general, the rule for converting totals to averages, and vice versa, is:

Rule 1a. Average weight equals total weight divided by number of persons.

Rule 1b. Total weight equals average weight times number of persons.

And this rule naturally applies equally well to cost, revenue, profit, or any other variable of interest.

Calculation of *marginal* weight from *total* weight follows the *subtraction* process we have already encountered in the calculation of marginal utility, marginal cost, and marginal revenue. Specifically:

Rule 2a. The marginal weight of, say, the third person equals the total weight of three people minus the total weight of two people.

For example, when the fourth person enters the room, *total* weight rises from 375 to 500 pounds, and hence the corresponding marginal weight is 500 − 375 = 125 pounds, as is shown in the last column of Table 24–8. We can also go in the opposite direction—from marginal to total—by the reverse, *addition*, process.

Rule 2b. The total weight of, say, three people equals the marginal weight of the first person plus the marginal weight of the second person plus the marginal weight of the third person.

Rule 2b can be checked by referring to Table 24–8. There it can be seen that the total weight of three persons, 375 pounds, is indeed equal to 100 + 140 + 135 pounds, the sum of the preceding marginal weights. A similar relation holds for any other total weight figure in the table, as the reader should verify.[7]

In addition to these familiar arithmetic relationships, there are two other useful relationships. The first of these may be stated as:

Rule 3. In the absence of fixed weight (costs), the marginal, average, and total figures for the first person must all be equal.

This rule holds because when there is only one person in the room, whose weight is X pounds, the average weight will obviously be X, the total weight must be X, and the marginal weight must also be X (since the total must have risen from 0 to X pounds). Put another way, when the marginal person is alone, he or she is obviously also the average person, and also represents the totality of all relevant persons.

Now for the final and very important relationship:

Rule 4. If marginal weight is lower than average weight, then average weight must fall when the number of persons increases. If marginal weight exceeds average weight, average weight must rise when the number of persons increases; and if marginal and average weight are equal, the average weight must remain constant when the number of persons increases.

These three possibilities are all illustrated in Table 24–8. Notice, for example, that when the third person enters the room, the average weight rises from 120 to 125 pounds. That is because this person's (marginal) weight is 135 pounds, which is above the average, as Rule 4 requires. Similarly, when the sixth person—who is a 60-pound child—enters the room, the average falls from 120 to 110 pounds because marginal weight, 60 pounds, is below average weight.

The reason Rule 4 works is easily explained with the aid of our example. When the third person enters, we see that the average rises. At once

---

[7]There is an exception in the case of costs. Summing up marginal cost figures as in Rule 2b leads to total *variable* cost. If there are *fixed* costs, these must be added in to arrive at total (variable plus fixed) costs.

we know that this person must be above average weight, for otherwise his arrival would not have pulled up the average. Similarly, the average will be pulled down by the arrival of a person whose weight is below the average (marginal weight is less than average weight). And the arrival of a person of average weight (marginal equals average weight) will leave the old average figure unchanged. That is all there is to the matter.

It is essential to avoid a common misunderstanding of this rule: it does *not* state, for example, that if the average figure is rising, the marginal figure must be rising. When the average rises, the marginal figure may rise, fall, or remain unchanged. The arrival of two persons both well above average will push the average up in two successive steps even if the second new arrival is lighter than the first. We see such a case in Table 24–8, where the arithmetic shows that while average weight rises successively from 100 to 120 to 125, the marginal weight falls from 140 to 135 to 125.

Graphic Representation of Marginal and Average Curves

We have shown how, from a curve of total profit (or total cost or total anything else), one can determine the corresponding marginal figure. We noted several times in the chapter that the marginal value at any particular point is equal to the *slope* of the corresponding total curve at that point. But for some purposes it is convenient to use a graph that records marginal and average values directly rather than deriving them from the curve of totals.

We can obtain such a graph by plotting the data in a table of average and marginal figures, such as Table 24–8. The result looks like the graph shown in Figure 24–7. Here we have indicated the number of persons in the room on the horizontal axis and the corresponding average and marginal figures on the vertical axis. The solid dots represent average weights; the small circles represent marginal weights. Thus, for example, point A shows that when two persons are in the room, their average weight is 120 pounds, as was reported on the third line of Table 24–8. Similarly, point B on the graph represents information provided in the next column of the table; that is, that the marginal weight of the third person who

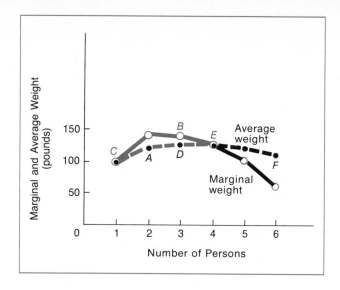

Figure 24–7
THE RELATIONSHIP BETWEEN MARGINAL AND AVERAGE CURVES
If the marginal curve is above the average curve, the average curve will be pulled upward. Thus, wherever the marginal is above the average, the average must be going upward (blue segment of curves). The opposite is true where the marginal curve is below the average curve.

enters the room is 135 pounds. For visual convenience these points have been connected into a marginal curve and an average curve, represented respectively by the solid and the broken curves in the diagram. This is the representation of marginal and average values that economists most frequently use.

Figure 24–7 illustrates two of our rules. Rule 3 says that, for the first unit, the marginal and average values will be the same. And that is precisely why the two curves start out together at point C. When there is only one person in the room, marginal and average weight *must* be the same. The graph also obeys Rule 4: between points C and E, where the average curve is *rising*, the marginal curve lies *above* the average. (Notice, however, that over part of this range the marginal curve *falls* even though the average curve is rising—Rule 4 says nothing about the rise or fall of the marginal curve.) We see also that over range EF, where the average curve is falling, the marginal curve is below the average curve, again in accord with Rule 4. Finally, at point E, where the average curve is neither rising nor falling, the marginal curve meets the average curve: average and marginal weights are equal at that point.

Questions for Discussion

1. Suppose the following is your record of exam grades in Principles of Economics:

EXAM DATE	GRADE	COMMENT
September 30	65	A slow start.
October 28	75	A big improvement.
November 26	90	Happy Thanksgiving!
December 13	85	Slipped a little.
January 24	95	A fast finish!

Use these data to make up a table of total, average, and marginal grades for the five exams.

2. From the data in your table, illustrate each of the rules mentioned in this appendix. Be sure to point out an instance where marginal grade falls but average grade rises.

PART 7

The Market System:
Virtues and Vices

25

The Firm and the Industry Under Perfect Competition

In Chapter 23 we analyzed how a firm's input decisions determine its cost curves, and in Chapter 24 we saw that cost and demand curves together lead to a decision about how much to produce. It may seem, therefore, that we have completed the analysis of the supply side of the market. This is not so, however, because firms do not operate in a vacuum. A single firm is but one component of a market, and what one firm does may affect the others. Thus our discussion of supply is not complete until we have analyzed how *all* the firms in an industry interact in the marketplace.

Industries differ dramatically in how populated they are and in the size of a typical firm. Some industries, like fishing, contain a great many very small firms; others, like autos, are composed of a few industrial giants. This chapter deals with a very particular type of market structure — called *perfect competition* — in which firms are numerous and small. The chapter begins by comparing alternative market forms and defining perfect competition precisely. We then use the tools acquired in Chapter 24 to analyze the behavior of the perfectly competitive firm and derive its supply curve. Next, we consider the supply curve of *all* the firms in an industry — the *industry supply curve* — and we investigate how developments in the industry affect the individual firms.

A Puzzle: Can Good Weather Be Bad for Farmers?

If you do your own gardening, you no doubt hope for the best possible weather — a nice mixture of sunshine and rain to help the plants grow. Drought and frost are your mortal enemies. For farmers, however, ideal weather sometimes spells disaster. After a bumper crop, farmers often trek to Washington to picket the White House and complain about the low prices that result. Legislators are urged to "protect" farmers from these low prices, which is to say, to protect them from the consequences of good weather. On the other hand, adverse weather often leaves farmers *as a whole* rather well off. Even though it ruins some particular farmers, picket lines typically do not appear after droughts, floods, and premature frosts. What accounts for this strange behavior? The tools we are about to describe — the analysis of competitive supply — will permit us to answer this question at the end of the chapter.

Varieties of Market Structure: A Sneak Preview

It will be helpful to open our discussion by explaining clearly what is meant by the word **market**. Economists do not reserve the term to denote only an organized exchange operating in a well-defined physical location. In its more general and abstract usage "a market" refers to a set of sellers and buyers whose activities affect the price at which a *particular commodity* is sold. For example, two separate sales of General Motors stock in different parts of the country may be considered as taking place on the same market, while the sale of bread and carrots in neighboring stalls of a market square may, in our sense, occur on totally different markets.

So far, we have talked only about firms in general without worrying about the sort of market in which they operate. But in this chapter and the next few we will see that market form makes a great deal of difference for the way in which firms can and do behave. Under some market forms, for example, the firm has no control over price. In others the firm has the power to adjust price in a way that adds to its profits and which, in the opinion of some, constitutes exploitation of consumers. Economists distinguish among different kinds of markets according to (1) how many firms they include, (2) whether the products of the different firms are identical or somewhat different, and (3) how easy it is for new firms to enter the market. Table 25–1 summarizes the main features of the four market structures we will study in this and subsequent chapters. It is provided here as a kind of road map of where we are going. *Perfect competition* is obviously at one extreme (many small firms selling an identical product), while *pure monopoly* (a single firm) is at the other. In between are hybrid forms — called *monopolistic competition* (many small firms each selling products slightly different from the others') and *oligopoly* (a few large rival firms) — that share some of the characteristics of perfect competition and some of the characteristics of monopoly.

Perfect competition is far from the typical market form in the U.S. economy. Indeed, it is quite rare. Many farming and fishing industries approximate perfect competition, as do many financial markets (such as the New York Stock

A **market** refers to the set of all sale and purchase transactions that affect the price of some commodity.

Table 25–1
VARIETIES OF MARKET STRUCTURE

| TYPE OF MARKET STRUCTURE | DEFINITION | | BARRIERS TO ENTRY | WHERE TO FIND IT | |
	NUMBER OF SELLERS	NATURE OF THE PRODUCT		IN THE U.S. ECONOMY	IN THIS TEXTBOOK
Perfect competition	Many	All firms produce identical products (example: wheat)	None	Some agricultural markets and parts of retailing come close	Chapter 25
Monopolistic competition	Many	Different firms produce somewhat different products (example: restaurant meals)	Minor	Most of the retailing sector, textiles, and restaurants	Chapter 28
Oligopoly	Few	Firms may produce identical or differentiated products (example: brands of toothpaste)	May be considerable	Much of the manufacturing sector, especially autos, steel and cigarettes	Chapter 28
Pure monopoly	One	Unique product	May be considerable	Public utilities	Chapter 27

Exchange). Pure monopoly—literally *one* firm—is also infrequently encountered. Most of the products you buy are no doubt supplied by oligopolies or monopolistic competitors—terms we will be defining precisely in Chapter 28.

Perfect Competition Defined

You can appreciate just how special perfect competition is once we provide a comprehensive definition. A market is said to operate under **perfect competition** when the following four conditions are satisfied:

1. *Numerous participants.* Each seller and purchaser constitutes so small a portion of the market that their decisions have no effect on the price. This requirement rules out trade associations or other collusive arrangements strong enough to affect price.

2. *Homogeneity of product.* The product offered by any seller is identical to that supplied by any other seller. (Example: wheat of a given grade is a homogeneous product; different brands of toothpaste are not.) Because the product is homogeneous, consumers do not care from which firm they buy.

3. *Freedom of entry and exit.* New firms desiring to enter the market face no special impediments that the existing firms can avoid. Similarly, if production and sale of the good proves unprofitable, there are no barriers preventing firms from leaving the market.

4. *Perfect information.* Each firm and each customer is well informed about the available products and their prices. They know whether one supplier is selling at a price lower than another is.

These are obviously exacting requirements that are met infrequently in practice. One example might be a market for common stock: there are literally millions of buyers and sellers of AT&T stock; all of the shares are exactly alike; anyone who wishes can enter the market easily; and most of the relevant information is readily available in the daily newspaper. But other examples are hard to find. Our interest in perfect competition is surely not for its descriptive realism.

Why, then, do we spend time studying perfect competition? The answer takes us back to the central theme of this book. It is under perfect competition that the market mechanism performs best. So, if we want to learn what markets do well, we can put the market's best foot forward by beginning with perfect competition.

As Adam Smith suggested some two centuries ago, perfectly competitive firms use society's scarce resources with maximum efficiency. And as Friedrich Engels suggested in the opening quotation of this chapter, perfectly competitive firms serve consumers' tastes effectively. So by studying perfect competition, we can learn just how much an *ideally functioning* market system might accomplish. This is the topic of the present chapter and the next one. Then, in Chapters 27 and 28, we will consider other market forms and see how they deviate from the perfectly competitive ideal. Still later chapters (especially Chapter 29 and Parts 8 and 9) will examine many important tasks that the market does not perform at all well, even under perfect competition. These chapters combined should provide a balanced assessment of the virtues and vices of the market mechanism.

The Competitive Firm and Its Demand Curve

To discover what happens in a market in which perfect competition prevails, we must deal separately with the behavior of the *individual firms* and the behavior of the *industry* that is constituted by those firms. One basic difference between the firm and the industry under competition relates to *pricing*. We say that:

Under perfect competition, the firm is a *price taker*. It has no choice but to accept the price that has been determined in the market.

The fact that a firm in a perfectly competitive market has no control over the price it charges follows from the definition of perfect competition. The presence of a vast number of competitors, each offering identical products, forces each firm to meet but not exceed the price charged by the others. Like a stockholder with 100 shares of General Electric, the firm simply finds out the prevailing price on the market and either accepts that price or refuses to sell. But while the individual firm has no influence over price under perfect competition, the industry does. This influence is not conscious or planned — it happens spontaneously through the impersonal forces of supply and demand, as we observed in Chapter 4.

With two important exceptions, the analysis of the behavior of the firm under perfect competition is exactly the same as that pertaining to any other firm, so the tools described in Chapters 23 and 24 can be applied directly. The two exceptions are the special shape of the competitive firm's demand curve and the effects on the firm's profits of freedom of entry and exit. We will consider them in turn, beginning with the demand curve.

In Chapter 24, we always assumed that the firm's demand curve sloped downward; if a firm wished to sell more (without increasing its advertising or changing its product specifications), it had to reduce the price of its product. The competitive firm is an exception to this general principle.

A perfectly competitive firm has a **horizontal demand curve**. This means it can double or triple its sales without any reduction in the price of its product.

How is this possible? The answer is that the competitive firm is so insignificant relative to the market as a whole that it has absolutely no influence over price. The farmer who sells his corn through an exchange in Chicago must accept the current quotation his broker reports to him. Because there are thousands of farmers, the Chicago price per bushel will not budge because Farmer Jones decides he doesn't like the price and holds back a truckload for storage. Thus, the demand curve for Farmer Jones's corn is as shown in Figure 25–1; the price he is paid in Chicago will be $8 per bushel whether he sells one truckload (point A) or two (point B) or three (point C). That is so because price is determined by the *industry's* supply and demand curves shown in the right-hand portion of the graph.

Short-Run Equilibrium of the Competitive Firm

We have pointed out that economists consider the short run to be a period so brief that some commitments cannot be changed. For example, the firm may have signed a five-year rental lease, so that the firm's long run must be a period

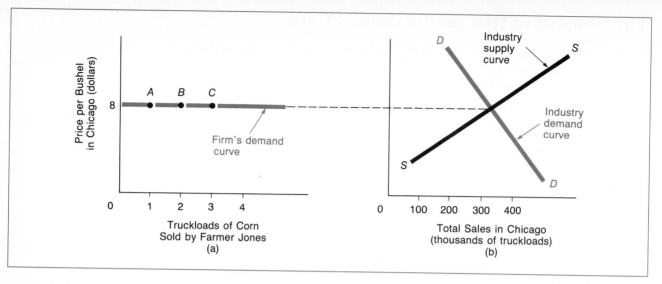

Figure 25–1
Figure 25–1
DEMAND CURVE FOR A
FIRM UNDER PERFECT
COMPETITION
Under perfect competition
the size of the output of a
firm is so small a portion of
the total industry output that it
cannot affect the market
price of the product. Even if
the firm's output increases
many times, market price
remains $8, where it is set by
industry supply and demand.

greater than five years. Another critical element that cannot change in the short run is the number of firms in the industry. Even if an industry is making profits so high that new entrants are attracted into the business, that will usually take time. In the short run, then, we can ignore the possibility of entry or exit and study the decisions of the firms already in the industry. We already have sufficient background to do this. To begin, recall from Chapter 24 that profit maximization requires the firm to pick an output level that makes its *marginal cost equal to its marginal revenue*: MC = MR. The only feature that distinguishes the profit-maximizing equilibrium of the competitive firm from that of any other type of firm is its horizontal demand curve.

Because the demand curve is horizontal, the competitive firm's marginal revenue curve is a horizontal straight line that coincides with its demand curve; hence, MR = price (P). It is easy to see why this is so. If the price does not depend on how much the firm sells (which is what a horizontal demand curve means), then each *additional* unit sold brings in an amount of revenue (the *marginal* revenue) exactly equal to the market price. So marginal revenue always equals price under perfect competition; the demand curve and the MR curve coincide because the firm is a price taker.

Once we know the shape and position of a firm's marginal revenue curve, we can use this information and the marginal cost curve to determine its optimal output and profit, as shown in Figure 25–2. As usual, the profit-maximizing output is that at which MC = MR (point B). This competitive firm produces 50,000 bushels per year—the output level at which MC and MR are both equal to the market price, $8. Thus:

Because it is a price taker, the *equilibrium* of a profit-maximizing firm in a perfectly competitive market must occur at an output level at which marginal cost is equal to price, or in symbols:

$$MC = P.$$

The same information is shown in Table 25–2, which gives the firm's total revenue, total cost, and profit for different output quantities. We see from the last column that total profit is maximized at an output of about 50,000 bushels,

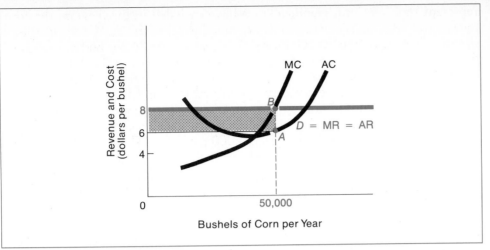

Figure 25–2
SHORT-RUN
EQUILIBRIUM OF THE
COMPETITIVE FIRM
The profit-maximizing firm will
select the output (50,000
bushels per year) at which
marginal cost equals
marginal revenue (point B).
The demand curve, D, is
horizontal because the firm's
output is too small to affect
market price, thus it is also
the marginal revenue curve.
In the short run, demand may
be either high or low in
relation to cost. Therefore
each unit it sells may return a
profit (AB) or a loss.

Table 25–2
REVENUES, COSTS, AND PROFITS OF A COMPETITIVE FIRM

QUANTITY (thousands of bushels)	TOTAL REVENUE	MARGINAL REVENUE	TOTAL COST	· MARGINAL COST	TOTAL PROFIT
			(thousands of dollars)		
0	0				
10	80	80	85		−5
20	160	80	150	65	10
30	240	80	180	30	60
40	320	80	230	50	90
50	400	80	300	70	100
60	480	80	450	150	30
70	560	80	700	250	−140

where total profit is $100,000. Table 25–2 also gives marginal costs and
marginal revenues. We see that an increase in output from 40,000 to 50,000
bushels incurs a marginal cost ($70,000) which is approximately equal to the
corresponding marginal revenue ($80,000),[1] confirming that 50,000 bushels is
the profit-maximizing output.

Short-Run Profit: Graphic Representation

Our analysis so far tells us how the firm can pick the output that maximizes its
profit. But even if it succeeds in doing so, the firm may conceivably find itself
in trouble. If the demand for its product is weak or its costs are high, even the
firm's most profitable option may lead to a loss. To determine whether the firm
is making a profit or incurring a loss we must compare total revenue (TR =
P × Q) with total cost (TC = AC × Q). Since Q is common to both of these,
that is equivalent to comparing P with AC.

The firm's profit can therefore be shown in Figure 25–2. By definition,
profit per unit of output is revenue per unit minus cost per unit. To enable us to

---

[1]To calculate marginal costs and marginal revenues accurately we should increase output one bushel at a time,
instead of proceeding in leaps of 10,000 bushels. But that would require too much space! In any event, that
is why MR and MC are not exactly equal.

represent profit per unit graphically we have included in the diagram the firm's *average cost* (AC) curve, which was explained in Chapter 23. We see in the figure that average cost at 50,000 bushels per year is only $6 per bushel (point A). Since the price, or *average revenue* (AR), is $8 per bushel (point B), the firm is making a profit of AR − AC = $2 per bushel. This profit margin appears in the graph as the vertical distance between points A and B.

Notice that in addition to showing the *profit per unit*, the graph can be used to show the firm's *total profit*. Total profit is the profit per unit ($2 in this example) times the number of units (50,000 per year). Therefore, total profit is represented as the *area* of the shaded rectangle whose height is the profit per unit ($2) and whose width is the number of units (50,000).[2] That is, total profit at any output is the area of the rectangle whose base equals the level of output and whose height equals AR − AC. Thus, in this case, profits are $100,000 per year.

The MC = P condition gives us the output that maximizes the perfectly competitive firm's profit. It does not, however, tell us whether the firm is making a profit or incurring a loss. To determine this, we must compare price with average cost.

The Case of Short-Term Losses

The market is obviously treating the farmer in the graph rather nicely. But what if the market were not so generous in its rewards? What if, for example, the market price were only $4 per bushel instead of $8? Figure 25–3 shows the equilibrium of the firm under these circumstances. The firm still maximizes profits by producing the level of output at which marginal cost is equal to price—point B in the diagram. But this time "maximizing" profits really means keeping the loss as small as possible.

At the optimal level of output (30,000 bushels per year), average cost is $6 per bushel (point A), which exceeds the $4 per bushel price (point B). The firm is therefore running a loss of $2 per bushel times 30,000 bushels, or $60,000 per year. This loss, which is represented by the area of the shaded

[2]Recall that the formula for the area of a rectangle is area = height × width.

Figure 25–3
SHORT-RUN
EQUILIBRIUM OF THE
COMPETITIVE FIRM WITH
A LOWER PRICE
In this diagram, the cost curves are the same as in Figure 25–2 but the demand curve (D) has shifted down to a market price of $4 per bushel. The firm still does the best it can by setting MC = P (point B). But since its average cost at 30,000 bushels per year is $6 per bushel, it runs a loss (shown by the shaded rectangle).

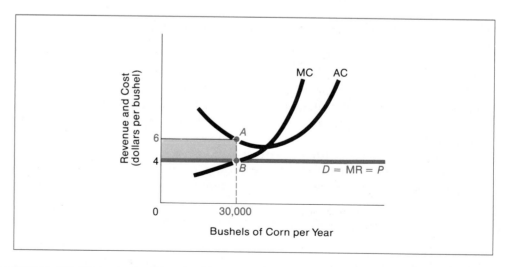

rectangle in Figure 25–3, is the best the firm can do. If it selected any other output level, its loss would be even greater.

Shut-Down and Break-Even Analysis

There is, however a limit to the loss the firm can be forced to accept. If losses get too big, the firm can simply go out of business. To understand the logic of the decision between shutting down and remaining in operation, we must return to the distinction between costs that are sunk and those that are variable in the short run. It will be recalled from the discussion of Chapter 23 that costs are sunk if the firm cannot escape them in the short run, either because of a contract (say, with the landlord or the union) or because it has already bought the item whose cost is sunk (say, a machine).

If the firm stops producing, its revenue will fall to zero. Its short-run variable costs will also fall to zero. But its sunk costs — such as rent — will remain to plague it. If the firm is losing money, sometimes it will be better off continuing to operate until its obligations to pay sunk costs expire; but sometimes it will do better by shutting down and producing nothing. Two rules govern the decision:

Rule 1. The firm will make a profit if total revenue (TR) exceeds total cost (TC). In that case, it should not plan to shut down either in the short run or in the long run.

Rule 2. The firm should continue to operate in the short run if TR exceeds total short-run variable cost (TVC). It should nevertheless plan to close in the long run if TR < TC.

The first rule is obvious. If the firm's revenues cover its total costs, then it does not lose money.

The second rule is a bit more subtle. Suppose TR is less than TC. If our unfortunate firm continues in operation, how much will it lose? Clearly it will lose the difference between total cost and total revenue; that is:

$$\text{Loss if the firm stays in business} = TC - TR.$$

However, if the firm stops producing, both its revenues and short-run variable costs become zero, leaving only the *sunk* costs to be paid:

$$\text{Loss if the firm shuts down} = \text{sunk costs}.$$

Rule 2 is illustrated by the two cases in Table 25–3.[3] Case I deals with a firm which loses money but is better off staying in business in the short run. If it closes down, it will lose its $60,000 sunk cost. But if it continues in operation, it will lose only $40,000 because TR ($100,000) exceeds total variable cost (TVC) ($80,000) by $20,000, so that its operation contributes $20,000 toward meeting its sunk costs. In case II, on the other hand, it pays the firm to shut down because continued operation only adds to its losses. If the firm operates, it

---

[3]More generally, we see that the firm will then find it advisable to shut down if it is better to lose its sunk costs than to lose TC − TR. In other words, it will shut down if TC − TR > sunk costs or TC − sunk costs > TR. Remembering that TC = TVC + sunk costs in the short run, we can express this condition as if TVC > TR, which is Rule 2.

Table 25–3
THE SHUT-DOWN DECISION

	CASE I	CASE II
	(thousands of dollars)	
Total revenue (TR)	$100	$100
Total variable cost (TVC)	80	130
Sunk cost	60	60
Total cost (TC)	140	190
Loss if firm shuts down (= sunk cost)	60	60
Loss if firm does not shut down	40	90

will lose $90,000 (last entry in Table 25–3) whereas if it shuts down it will lose only the $60,000 in sunk costs which it must pay in any case, whether it operates or not.

The shut-down decision can also be analyzed graphically. In Figure 25–4 the firm will run a loss whether the price is P_1, P_2, or P_3, because none of these prices is high enough to reach the minimum level of average cost (AC). The *lowest* price that keeps the firm from shutting down can be shown in the graph by introducing one more short-run cost curve: the **average variable cost** (AVC) curve. Why is this curve relevant? Because, as we have just seen, it pays the firm to remain in operation if its total revenue (TR) exceeds its total short-run variable cost (TVC). If we divide both TR and TVC by quantity (Q), we get $TR/Q = P$ and $TVC/Q = AVC$, so this condition may be stated equivalently as the requirement that price exceed AVC. The conclusion is:

The firm will produce nothing unless price lies above the minimum point on the AVC curve.

Figure 25–4 illustrates this principle by showing an MC curve, an AVC curve, and several alternative demand curves corresponding to different possible prices. Price P_1 is below the minimum average variable cost. With this price, the firm cannot even cover its variable costs and is better off shutting down (producing zero output). Price P_3 is higher. While the firm still runs a loss if it sets MC = P at point A (because AC exceeds P_3), it is at least covering its short-run variable costs, and so it pays to keep operating in the short run. Price

Figure 25–4
SHUT-DOWN ANALYSIS
At a price as low as P_1, the firm cannot even cover its short-run average variable costs, and it is better off shutting down entirely. At a price as high as P_3, the firm selects point A but operates at a loss (because P_3 is below AC). However, it is more than covering its average variable costs (since P_3 exceeds AVC), so it pays to keep producing. Price P_2 is the borderline case. With this price, the firm selects point B and is indifferent between shutting down and staying open.

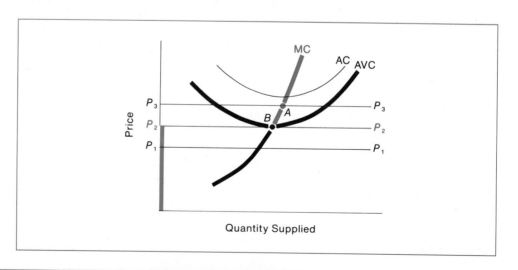

P_2 is the borderline case. If the price is P_2, the firm is indifferent between shutting down and staying in business and producing at a level where MC = P (point B). P_2 is thus the *lowest* price at which the firm will produce anything. As we see from the graph, P_2 corresponds to the minimum point on the AVC curve.

The Short-Run Supply Curve of the Competitive Firm

Without realizing it, we have now derived the **supply curve of the competitive firm** in the short run. Why? Recall that a supply curve summarizes the answers to such questions as, If the price is so and so, how much will the firm produce? We have now discovered that there are two possibilities, as indicated by the thick blue line in Figure 25–4.

1. In the short run, if the price exceeds the minimum AVC, it pays a competitive firm to produce the level of output that equates MC and P. Thus, for any price above point B, we can read the corresponding quantity supplied from the firm's MC curve.

2. If the price falls below the minimum AVC, then it pays the firm to produce nothing. Quantity supplied falls to zero.

Putting these two observations together, we conclude that:

The short-run supply curve of the perfectly competitive firm is its marginal cost curve above the point where it intersects the average (short-run) variable cost curve; that is, above the minimum level of AVC. If price falls below this level, the firm's quantity supplied drops to zero.

The Short-Run Supply Curve of the Competitive Industry

Having completed the analysis of the competitive *firm's* supply decision, we turn our attention next to the competitive *industry*. Again we need to distinguish between the short run and the long run, but the distinction is different here. The short run for the *industry* is defined as a period of time too brief for new firms to enter the industry or for old firms to leave, so the number of firms is fixed. By contrast, the long run for the industry is a period of time long enough for any firm that so desires to enter (or leave). In addition, in the long run each firm in the industry can adjust its output to its own long-run costs.[4] We begin our analysis of industry equilibrium in the short run.

With the number of firms fixed, it is a simple matter to derive the **supply curve of the competitive industry** from those of the individual firms. At any given price, we simply *add up* the quantities supplied by each of the firms to arrive at the industry-wide quantity supplied. For example, if each of 1000 identical firms in the corn industry supplies 45,000 bushels when the price is $6 per bushel, then the quantity supplied by the industry at a $6 price will be 45,000 bushels per firm × 1000 firms = 45 million bushels.

This process of deriving the *market* supply curve from the *individual* supply curves of firms is perfectly analogous to the way we derived the *market* demand curve from the *individual* demand curves of consumers in Chapter 22. Graphically, what we are doing is *summing the individual supply curves horizontally*, as

---

[4]The relationship between short-run and long-run cost curves for the firm was discussed in Chapter 23, pages 511–12.

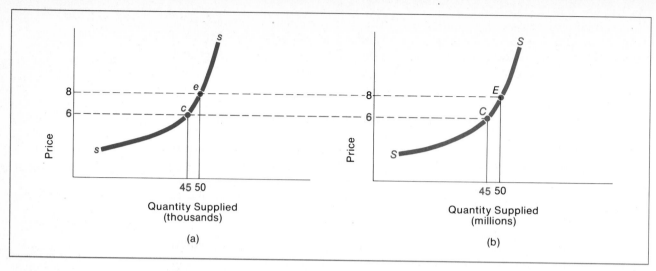

Figure 25–5
DERIVATION OF THE INDUSTRY SUPPLY CURVE FROM THE SUPPLY CURVES OF THE INDIVIDUAL FIRMS
In this hypothetical industry of 1000 identical firms, each individual firm has the supply curve ss in part (a). For example, quantity supplied is 45,000 bushels when the price is $6 per unit (point c). By *adding up* the quantities supplied by each firm at each possible price, we arrive at the industry supply curve SS in part (b). For example, at a unit price of $6, total quantity supplied by the industry is 45 million units (point C).

illustrated in Figure 25–5. At a price of $6, each of the 1,000 firms in the industry supplies 45,000 bushels [point c in part (a)], so the industry supplies 45 million bushels [point C in part (b)]. At a price of $8, each firm supplies 50,000 bushels [point e in part (a)], and so the industry supplies 50 million bushels [point E in part (b)]. Similar calculations can be carried out for any other price. This adding-up process indicates, incidentally, that the supply curve of the industry will shift to the right whenever a new firm enters the industry.

The supply curve of the competitive industry in the short run is derived by *summing* the short-run supply curves of all the firms in the industry *horizontally*.

Notice that if the short-run supply curves of individual firms are upward sloping, then the short-run supply curve of the competitive industry will be upward sloping, too. We have seen that the firm's supply curve is its marginal cost curve (above the level of minimum average variable cost), so it follows that rising marginal costs lead to an upward sloping short-run *industry* supply curve.

Industry Equilibrium in the Short Run

Now that we have derived the industry supply curve, we need only add a market demand curve to determine the price and quantity that will emerge. This is done for our illustrative corn industry in Figure 25–6, where the industry supply curve [carried over from Figure 25–5(b)] is SS and the demand curve is DD. Note that for the competitive industry, unlike the competitive firm, the demand curve is normally downward sloping. Why? Each firm by itself is so small that if it alone were to double its output the effect would hardly be noticeable. But if *every* firm in the industry were to expand its output, that would make a substantial difference. Customers can be induced to buy the additional quantities arriving at the market only if the price of the good falls.

Point E is the equilibrium point for the competitive industry, because only at the combination of price, $8, and quantity, 50 million bushels, are neither purchasers nor sellers motivated to upset matters. At a price of $8, sellers are willing to offer exactly the amount consumers want to purchase.

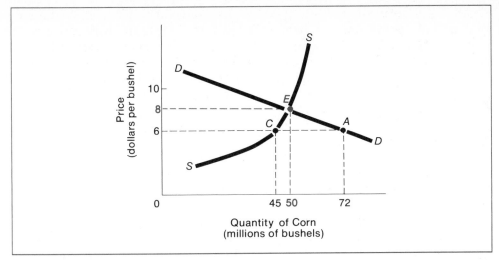

Figure 25–6
SUPPLY–DEMAND
EQUILIBRIUM OF A
COMPETITIVE INDUSTRY
The only equilibrium
combination of price and
quantity is a price of $8 and
a quantity of 50 million
bushels, at which the supply
curve SS and the demand
curve DD intersect (point E).
At a lower price such as $6,
quantity demanded (72
million bushels as shown by
point A on the demand
curve) will be higher than the
45 million bushel quantity
supplied (point C). Thus the
price will be driven back up
toward the $8 equilibrium.
The opposite will happen at a
price such as $10, which is
above equilibrium.

Should we expect price actually to reach, or at least to approximate, this equilibrium level? The answer is yes. To see why, we must consider what happens when price is not at its equilibrium level. Suppose it takes a lower value, such as $6. The low price will stimulate customers to buy more; and it will also lead firms to produce less than at a price of $8. Our diagram confirms that at a price of $6, quantity supplied (45 million bushels) is lower than quantity demanded (72 million bushels). Thus, unsatisfied buyers will probably offer to pay higher prices, which will force price *upward* in the direction of its equilibrium value, $8.

Similarly, if we begin with a price higher than the equilibrium price, we may readily verify that quantity supplied will exceed quantity demanded. Under these circumstances, frustrated sellers are likely to reduce their prices, so price will be forced downward. In the circumstances depicted in Figure 25–6, then, there is in effect a magnet at the equilibrium price of $8 that will pull the actual price in its direction if for some reason the actual price starts out at some other level.

In practice, there are few cases in which competitive markets, over a long period of time, seem not to have moved toward equilibrium prices. Matters eventually appear to work out as depicted in Figure 25–6. Of course, numerous transitory influences can jolt any real-world market away from its equilibrium point—a strike that cuts production, a sudden change in consumer tastes, and so on. And there also have been periods, sometimes of distressingly long duration, when the "bottom has dropped out" of some nearly competitive markets, such as stock exchanges. During such market "crashes," it certainly did not seem that prices were moving toward equilibrium.

Yet, as we have just seen, there are powerful forces that do push prices back toward equilibrium—toward the level at which the supply and demand curves intersect. These forces are of fundamental importance for economic analysis, for if there were no such forces, prices in the real world would bear little resemblance to equilibrium prices, and there would be little reason to study supply–demand analysis. Fortunately, the required equilibrating forces do exist.

Industry and Firm Equilibrium in the Long Run

The equilibrium of a competitive industry in the long run may differ from the short-run equilibrium that we have just studied for two reasons. First, the number of firms in the industry (1000 in our example) is not fixed in the long run. Second, as we saw in Chapter 23 (pages 511–12), the firm can vary its plant size and make other changes in the long run that were prevented by temporary commitments in the short run. Hence the firm's (and the industry's) long-run cost curves are not the same as its short-run cost curves.

What will lure new firms into the industry or repel old ones? Profits. Remember that when a firm selects its optimal level of output by setting MC = P it may wind up with either a profit or a loss. Such profits or losses must be *temporary* for a competitive firm, because the freedom of new firms to enter the industry or of old firms to leave it will, in the long run, eliminate them.

Suppose very high profits accrue to firms in the industry. Then new companies will find it attractive to enter the business, and expanded production will force the market price to fall from its initial level. Why? Recall that the industry supply curve is the horizontal sum of the supply curves of individual firms. Under perfect competition, new firms can enter the industry *on the same terms as existing firms*. This means that new entrants will have the *same* individual supply curves as old firms. If the market price did not fall, entry of new firms would lead to an increased number of firms with no change in output *per firm*. Consequently, the total quantity supplied on the market would be higher, and would exceed quantity demanded. But, of course, this means that in a free market entry of new firms *must* push the price down.

Figure 25–7 shows how the entry process works. In this diagram, the demand curve DD and the original (short-run) supply curve $S_0 S_0$ are carried over from Figure 25–6. The entry of new firms seeking high profits *shifts the industry's short-run supply curve outward to the right*, to $S_1 S_1$. The new market equilibrium is at point A (rather than at point E), where price is $6 per bushel and 72 million bushels are produced and consumed. Entry of new firms reduces price and raises total output. (Had the price not fallen, quantity supplied after entry would have been 80 million bushels—point F.) Why must the price fall? Because the demand curve for the industry is downward sloping—an increase in output will be purchased by consumers only if the price is reduced.

To see where the entry process stops, we must consider how the entry of new firms affects the behavior of old firms. At first, this may seem to contradict the notion of perfect competition; perfectly competitive firms are not supposed

Figure 25–7

A SHIFT IN THE INDUSTRY SUPPLY CURVE CAUSED BY THE ENTRY OF NEW FIRMS

This diagram shows what happens to the industry equlibrium when new firms enter the industry. Quantity supplied at any given price increases; that is, the supply curve shifts to the right, from $S_0 S_0$ to $S_1 S_1$ in the figure. As a result the market price falls (from $8 to $6) and the quantity increases (from 50 million bushels to 72 million bushels).

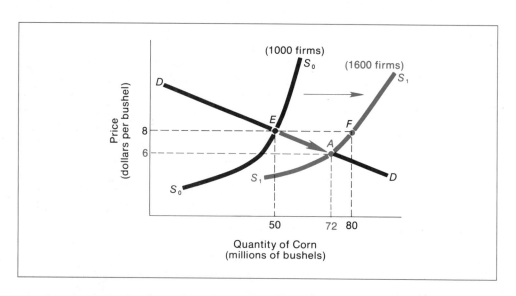

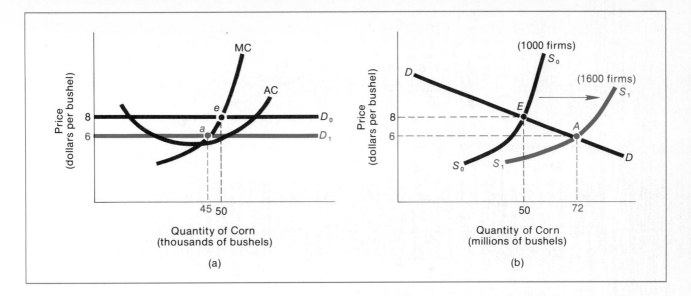

Quantity of Corn
(thousands of bushels)

(a)

Quantity of Corn
(millions of bushels)

(b)

to care what their competitors are doing. Indeed, these corn farmers do not care. But they *do* care very much about the market price of corn, and, as we have just seen, the entry of new firms into the corn-farming industry lowers the price of corn.

In Figure 25–8 we have juxtaposed the diagram of the equilibrium of the competitive firm (Figure 25–2 on page 561) and the diagram of the equilibrium of the competitive industry (Figure 25–7). Before entry, the market price was $8 [point E in Figure 25–8(b)] and each of the 1000 firms was producing 50,000 bushels—the point where marginal cost and price were equal [point e in Figure 25–8(a)]. The demand curve facing each firm was the horizontal line D_0 in Figure 25–8(a). There were profits because average costs (AC) at 50,000 bushels per firm were less than price.

Now suppose 600 new firms are attracted by these high profits and enter the industry. Each has the cost structure indicated by the AC and MC curves in Figure 25–8(a). As we have noted, the industry supply curve in Figure 25–8(b) shifts to the right, and price falls to $6 per bushel. Firms in the industry cannot fail to notice this lower price. As we see in Figure 25–8(a), each firm reduces its output to 45,000 bushels in reaction to the lower price (point a). But now there are 1600 firms, so total industry output is 45,000 × 1600 = 72 million bushels [point A in Figure 25–8(b)].

At point *a* in Figure 25–8(a), there are still profits to be made because the $6 price exceeds average cost. Thus the entry process is not yet complete. When will it end? Only when all profits have been competed away. Only when entry shifts the industry supply curve so far to the right [$S_2 S_2$ in Figure 25–9(b)] that the demand curve facing individual firms falls to the level of minimum average cost [point *m* in Figure 25–9(a)] will all profits be eradicated and entry cease.

The two panels of Figure 25–9 show the competitive firm and the competitive industry in long-run equilibrium.[5] Notice that at the equilibrium point [*m* in part (a)], each firm picks its own output level so as to maximize its profit.

Figure 25–8
THE COMPETITIVE FIRM AND THE COMPETITIVE INDUSTRY
Here we show the interaction between developments at the industry level [in part (b)] and developments at the firm level [in part (a)]. An outward shift in the industry supply curve from $S_0 S_0$ to $S_1 S_1$ in part (b) lowers the market price from $8 to $6. In part (a), we see that a profit-maximizing competitive firm reacts to this decline in price by curtailing output. When the demand curve of the firm is D_0 ($8), it produces 50,000 bushels (point e). When the firm's demand curve falls to D_1 ($6), its output declines to 45,000 bushels (point a). However, there are now 1600 firms rather than 1000 so total industry output has expanded from 50 million bushes to 72 million bushels [part (b)]. Entry has reduced profits. But since *P* still exceeds AC at an output of 45,000 bushels per firm in part (a), some profits remain.

[5]If the original short-run equilibrium had involved losses instead of profits, firms would have exited from the industry, shifting the industry supply curve inward, until all losses were eradicated and we would end up in a position exactly like Figure 25–9. EXERCISE: To test your understanding, draw the version of Figure 25–8 that corresponds to this case.

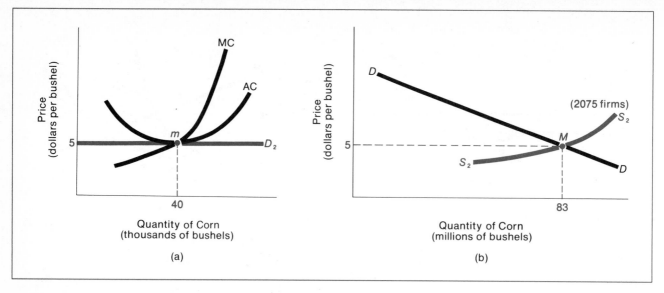

(a)

(b)

Figure 25–9

LONG-RUN EQUILIBRIUM OF THE COMPETITIVE FIRM AND INDUSTRY

By the time 2075 firms have entered the industry, the industry supply curve is S_2S_2 and the market price is $5 per bushel. At this price, the horizontal demand curve facing each firm is D_2 in part (a), so the profit-maximizing level of output is 40,000 bushels (point m). Here, since average cost and price are equal, there is *no* economic profit.

This means that for each firm $P = MC$. But free entry forces AC to be equal to P in the long run [point M in part (b) of the graph], for if P were not equal to AC, firms would either earn profits or suffer losses. Thus:

When a perfectly competitive industry is in long-run equilibrium, firms maximize profits so that $P = MC$, and entry forces the price down until it is tangent to the long-run average cost curve ($P = AC$). As a result, in competitive equilibrium it is always true that:

$$P = MC = AC.$$

The Long-Run Industry Supply Curve

We have now basically seen what lies behind the supply–demand analysis that was first introduced in Chapter 4 and its determination of the long-run equilibrium price and quantity sold. Only one thing remains to be explained. Figures 25–5 through 25–8 depicted short-run industry supply curves and short-run equilibrium. However, since Figure 25–9 describes long-run competitive equilibrium, its industry supply curve must also, obviously, pertain to the long run.

How is the long-run industry supply curve related to the short-run supply curve? The answer is implicit in what has just been discussed. The long-run industry supply curve evolves from the short-run supply curve via two simultaneous processes. First, there is the entry of new firms or the exit of old ones, which shifts the short-run industry supply curve toward its long-run position. Second, and concurrently, as each firm in the industry is freed from its sunk commitments, the cost curves that become pertinent for its decisions are its long-run cost curves rather than its short-run cost curves. For example, consider a company that was stuck in the short run with a plant designed to serve 20,000 customers even though it was fortunate enough to have 25,000 customers. When the old plant wears out and it is time to replace it, management will obviously build a new plant that can serve the larger number of customers more conveniently and efficiently. The reduced cost that results from the larger plant is the cost that is pertinent to both the firm and to the industry in the long run. In sum:

The industry attains its long-run supply curve both through the exit and entry of firms to the industry and through the behavior of firms already in the industry taking advantage of the opportunities for enhanced efficiency. These opportunities are made possible by the expiration of those firm's sunk commitments.

Finally, we can characterize the long-run supply curve of the competitive industry ($S_2 S_2$ in Figure 25–9) and its relation to cost. That supply curve must be identical to the industry's long-run average cost curve. Why? Because in the long run, as we have seen, economic profit must be zero. There can be no output level such that the price the industry would charge to supply that output quantity exceeds the long-run average cost (LRAC) of supplying that quantity. This must be so because any such excess of price over LRAC would constitute a profit that would attract new firms. Similarly, price cannot remain below LRAC because that would induce firms to exit from the industry. Therefore, at each point on the long-run supply curve for the industry the price for that output level must equal its long-run average cost. It is this long-run industry supply curve that is relevant to the determination of long-run equilibrium price and quantity in the standard supply–demand diagram.

The long-run supply curve of the competitive industry is also the industry's long-run average cost curve. The industry is driven to that supply curve by the entry or exit of firms and by the adjustment of firms already in the industry.

Zero Economic Profit: The Opportunity Cost of Capital

In our discussions of the long run, something may be troubling to you. Why would there be any firms in the industry *at all* if in the long run there were no profits to be made? What sense does it make to call a position of zero profit a "long-run equilibrium"? The answer is that the zero profit concept used in economics does not mean the same thing that it does in ordinary usage.

As has been noted repeatedly, when economists measure average cost, they include the cost of *all* the firm's inputs, *including the opportunity cost of the capital or any other inputs, such as labor, provided by the firm's owners*. Since the firm may not make explicit payments to some of those who provide it with capital, this element of cost may not be picked up by the firm's accountants. So what economists call *zero economic profit* may correspond to some positive amount of profit as measured by conventional accounting techniques. For example, if investors can earn 15 percent by lending their funds elsewhere, then the firm must earn a 15-percent rate of return to cover its opportunity cost of capital.

Because economists consider this 15-percent opportunity cost to be the *cost of the firm's capital*, they include it in the AC curve. If the firm cannot earn at least 15 percent on its capital, funds will not be made available to it, because investors can earn greater returns elsewhere. So, in the economist's language, in order to break even — earn zero **economic profit** — a firm must earn enough not only to cover the cost of labor, fuel, and raw materials, but also the cost of its funds, including the opportunity cost of any funds supplied by the owners of the firm.

Economic profit equals net earnings, in the accountant's sense, minus the opportunity costs of capital and of any other inputs supplied by the firm's owners.

To illustrate the difference between economic profits and accounting profits, suppose U.S. government bonds pay 15 percent, and the owner of a small shop earns 10 percent on her business investment. The shopkeeper might say she is making a 10-percent profit, but an economist would say she is *losing* 5 percent on every dollar she has invested in her business. The reason is that by keeping her money tied up in the firm, she gives up the chance to buy government bonds and receive a 15-percent return. With this explanation of the meaning of economic profit we can now understand the logic behind the zero-profit condition for the long-run industry equilibrium.

Zero profit in the economic sense simply means that firms are earning the normal economy-wide rate of profit in the accounting sense. This result is guaranteed, in the long run, under perfect competition by freedom of entry and exit.

Freedom of entry guarantees that those who invest in a competitive industry will receive a rate of return on their capital *no greater than* the return that capital could earn elsewhere in the economy. If economic profits were being earned in some industry, capital would be attracted into it. The new capital would shift the industry supply curve to the right, which would drive down prices and profits. This process would continue until the return on capital in this industry was reduced to the return that capital could earn elsewhere — its opportunity cost.

Similarly, freedom of exit of capital guarantees that in the long run, once capital has had a chance to move, no industry will provide a rate of return *lower than* the opportunity cost of capital. For if returns in one industry were particularly low, resources would flow out of it. Plant and equipment would not be replaced as it wore out. As a result, the industry supply curve would shift to the left, and prices and profits would rise toward their opportunity cost level.

Perfect Competition and Economic Efficiency

Economists have long admired perfect competition as a thing of beauty, like one of King Tut's funerary masks (and just as rare!). Adam Smith's invisible hand produces results that are considered *efficient* in a variety of senses that we will examine carefully in the next chapter. But one aspect of the great efficiency of perfect competition follows immediately from the analysis we have just completed.

We have seen earlier, when we discussed Figure 25–9(a), that when the firm is in long-run equilibrium we must have P = MC = AC. This implies that long-run competitive equilibrium of the firm will occur at the lowest point on the firm's long-run AC curve, which is also where that curve is tangent to the firm's horizontal demand curve.

In long-run competitive equilibrium, every firm produces at the minimum point on its average cost curve. Thus the outputs of competitive industries are produced at the lowest possible cost to society.

Why is it always most efficient if each firm in a competitive industry produces at the point where AC is as small as possible? An example will bring out the point. Suppose the industry is producing 12 million bushels of corn. This amount can clearly be produced by 120 farms each producing 100,000 bushels, or by 100 farms each producing 120,000 bushels, or by 200 farms each producing 60,000 bushels. This is so since $120 \times 100{,}000 = 100 \times 120{,}000 = 60 \times$

Table 25–4

AVERAGE COST FOR THE FIRM AND TOTAL COST FOR THE INDUSTRY

FIRM'S OUTPUT (bushels)	FIRM'S AVERAGE COST (dollars)	NUMBER OF FIRMS	INDUSTRY OUTPUT (bushels)	TOTAL INDUSTRY COST (dollars)
60,000	0.90	200	12,000,000	$10,800,000
100,000	0.70	120	12,000,000	8,400,000
120,000	0.80	100	12,000,000	9,600,000

200,000 = 12 million. (Of course the job can also be done instead by other numbers of farms, but for simplicity let us consider only these three possibilities.) Suppose the AC figures for the firm are as shown in Table 25–4. Suppose, moreover, that an output of 100,000 bushels corresponds to the lowest point on the AC curve, with an AC of 70 cents per bushel. Which is the cheapest way for the industry to produce its 12 million bushel output? That is, what is the cost-minimizing number of firms for the job? Looking at the last column of Table 25–4, we see that the industry's total cost of producing the 12-million-bushel output is reduced to as low an amount as possible if it is done by 120 firms each producing the cost-minimizing output of 100,000 bushels.

Why is this so? The answer is not difficult to see. For a given industry output, it is obvious that *total* industry cost will be as small as possible if and only if AC for *each* firm is as small as possible, that is, if the number of firms doing the job is such that each is producing the output at which AC is as low as possible.

That this kind of cost efficiency characterizes perfect competition in the long run can be seen in Figures 25–8 and 25–9. Before full long-run equilibrium is reached (Figure 25–8), firms may not be producing in the least costly way. For example, the 50 million bushels being produced by 1000 firms at points *e* and *E* in Figures 25–8(a) and (b) could be produced more cheaply by more firms, each producing a smaller volume, because the point of minimum average cost lies to the left of point *e* in Figure 25–8(a). This problem is rectified, however, in the long run by entry of new firms seeking profit. We see in Figure 25–9 that after the entry process is complete, every firm is producing at its most efficient (lowest AC) level — 40,000 bushels. As Adam Smith might have put it, even though each farmer cares only about his own profits, the corn-farming industry as a whole is guided *by an invisible hand* to produce the amount of corn that society wants at the lowest possible cost.

Why Good Weather Can Be Bad for Farmers

The interactions between the competitive firm and the competitive industry that we have just studied permit us to resolve the puzzle with which we began the chapter: Why is it that farm incomes often decline when the harvest is good and increase when the harvest is bad?

First, we should clarify the point. The statement is not that *every* farmer benefits from a drought or a flood. Obviously, these calamities can ruin the particular farmers who are Mother Nature's victims. The claim is that farmers who are not severely affected by bad weather, *including those with average damage*, come out ahead, and the reason is not hard to understand.

Once crops are planted, the supply curve of the farming industry is very nearly vertical. The harvest will be almost the same whether the price is high or low. A bumper crop means that the supply curve is far to the right, like $S_1 S_1$

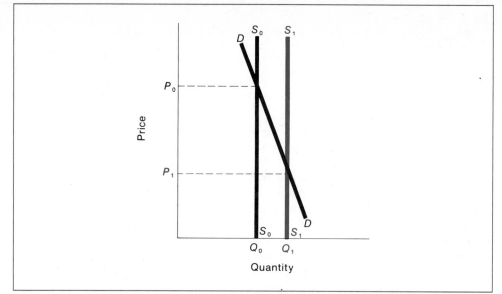

Figure 25–10

THE PROBLEM WITH FARM INCOMES

The demand curve for most farm products is quite inelastic. Thus if good weather conditions lead to a bumper crop (the supply curve shifts outward from $S_0 S_0$ to $S_1 S_1$), the market price typically falls so much that farm income (the product of price times quantity sold) actually declines. Conversely, farm income often rises when the weather is bad and farm prices are high.

in Figure 25–10, instead of in its "normal" position (which is indicated by $S_0 S_0$ in the figure). Consequently, a bumper crop leads to low prices — equilibrium will be at price P_1 instead of price P_0. As the graph indicates, the drop in price is often quite severe because the demand curves for most farm products are rather *inelastic*. Each farmer's quantity produced may be increased by the good weather. But because the market price falls *by an even greater percentage*, the farmers' total income declines.[6] As noted at the outset of this chapter, this often sends farmers scurrying off to Washington crying "Foul!"

On the other hand, suppose bad weather damages the crop but all farmers lose about 25 percent of their crops. Because of the inelastic market demand curve, the market price shoots up. (To see this, just use Figure 25–10 in reverse: suppose $S_1 S_1$ is the supply curve under normal weather conditions and $S_0 S_0$ is the supply curve when the weather is bad.) Each farmer's harvest falls slightly, but the price he gets for each unit rises smartly, and he comes out ahead of the game. Nothing is quite so good for all farmers as a drought that cuts everyone's crop.

[6]This is a consequence of the inelasticity of the demand curve. Recall that in Chapter 22 (page 488) we showed that a reduction in price *lowers* total revenue if the demand curve is inelastic. This is the result we are using here.

Summary

1. Markets are classified into several types depending on the number of firms in the industry, the degree of similarity of their products, and the possibility of impediments to entry.

2. The four main market structures discussed by economists are monopoly (single-firm production), oligopoly (production by a few firms), monopolistic competition (production by many firms with somewhat different products), and perfect competition (production by many firms with identical products and free entry and exit).

3. Few industries satisfy the conditions of perfect competition exactly, although some come close. Perfect competition is studied because it is easy to analyze and because it is useful as a yardstick to measure the performance of other market forms.

4. The demand curve of the perfectly competitive firm is horizontal because its output is so small a share of the industry's production that it cannot affect price. With a horizontal demand curve,

price, average revenue, and marginal revenue are all equal.

5. The short-run equilibrium of the perfectly competitive firm is at the level of output that maximizes profits; that is, where MC equals MR equals price. This equilibrium may involve either a profit or a loss.

6. The short-run supply curve of the perfectly competitive firm is the portion of its marginal cost curve that lies above its average variable cost curve.

7. The industry's short-run supply curve under perfect competition is the horizontal sum of the supply curves of all its firms.

8. In the long run, freedom of entry forces the perfectly competitive firm to earn zero economic profit; that is, no more than the firm's capital could earn elsewhere (the opportunity cost of the capital).

9. Industry equilibrium under perfect competition is at the point of intersection of the industry supply and demand curves.

10. In long-run equilibrium under perfect competition, the firm's output is chosen so that average cost, marginal cost, and price are all equal. Output is at the point of minimum average cost, and the firm's demand curve is tangent to its average cost curve at its minimum point.

11. The competitive industry's long-run supply curve coincides with its long-run average cost curve.

Concepts for Review

Market	Price taker	Supply curve of the firm
Perfect competition	Horizontal demand curve	Supply curve of the industry
Pure monopoly	Short-run equilibrium	Long-run equilibrium
Monopolistic competition	Sunk cost	Opportunity cost
Oligopoly	Variable cost	Economic profit

Questions for Discussion

1. Explain why a perfectly competitive firm does not expand its sales without limit if its horizontal demand curve means that it can sell as much as it wants to at the current market price.

2. Explain why a demand curve is also a curve of average revenue. Recalling that when an average revenue curve is neither rising nor falling, marginal revenue must equal average revenue, explain why it is always true that $P = MR = AR$ for the perfectly competitive firm.

3. Explain why in the short-run equilibrium of the perfectly competitive firm $P = MC$, while in long-run equilibrium $P = MC = AC$.

4. Which of the four attributes of perfect competition (many small firms, freedom of entry, standardized product, perfect information) are primarily responsible for the fact that the demand curve of a perfectly competitive firm is horizontal?

5. Which of the four attributes of perfect competition is primarily responsible for the firm's zero economic profits in long-run equilibrium?

6. It is indicated in the text (page 564) that the MC curve cuts the AVC curve at the *minimum* point of the latter. Explain why this must be so. (*Hint:* Since marginal costs are, by definition, entirely composed of variable costs, the MC curve can be considered the curve of *marginal variable costs*. Apply the general relationships between marginals and averages explained in Chapter 24.)

7. Explain why it is not sensible to close a business firm if it earns zero economic profits.

8. If the firm's lowest average cost is $7, and the corresponding average variable cost is $4, what does it pay a perfectly competitive firm to do if
   a. the market price is $9?
   b. the price is $5?
   c. the price is $2?

9. If the market price in a competitive industry is above its equilibrium level, what would you expect to happen?

10. (More difficult) A decade ago when oil prices were very high, it was proposed to mix alcohol distilled from corn with gasoline to make "gasohol." This obviously would have caused an upward shift in the demand for corn. Use Figure 25–9 to analyze the effects on corn-growing profit and output
    a. in the short run.
    b. in the long run.

26

The Price System and the Case for Laissez Faire

If there existed the universal mind that . . . would register simultaneously all the processes of nature and of society, that could forecast the results of their inter-reactions, such a mind . . . could . . . draw up a faultless and an exhaustive economic plan. . . . In truth, the bureaucracy often conceives that just such a mind is at its disposal; that is why it so easily frees itself from the control of the market.

LEON TROTSKY
(A LEADER OF THE
RUSSIAN REVOLUTION)

Early in the book, we posed a question that provides an organizing framework for our study of microeconomics: What does the market do well, and what does it do poorly? Given what we have learned about demand in Chapters 21 and 22 and about supply in Chapters 23–25, we are now in a position to offer a fairly comprehensive answer to the first part of this question: What does the market do well?

We begin by returning to two important themes raised in Chapters 3 and 4: First, that because all resources are scarce, it is critical to utilize them *efficiently;* second, that an economy must have some way to *coordinate* the actions of many individual consumers and producers. Specifically, we emphasize that society must somehow choose *how much* of each good to produce, *what input quantities* to use in the production process, and *how to distribute* the resulting outputs among consumers.

As the opening quotation suggests, these tasks are exceedingly difficult for central planners to accomplish effectively. But they are rather simple for a market system, which is why observers with philosophies as diverse as those of Adam Smith and Leon Trotsky have been admirers of the market. But the chapter should not be misinterpreted as a piece of salesmanship, for that is not its purpose.

The version of the price system we shall study here is an idealized one in which every good is produced under the exacting conditions of perfect competition. While, as we have seen, a number of industries are reasonable approximations to perfect competition, other industries in our economy are as different from this idealized world as the physical world is from a frictionless vacuum tube. But just as the physicist uses the vacuum tube to illustrate the laws of gravity with a clarity that is otherwise unattainable, the economist uses the theoretical concept of a perfectly competitive economy to illustrate the virtues of the market. There will be plenty of time in later chapters to study the vices.

Efficient Resource Allocation: The Concept

The fundamental fact of scarcity limits the volume of goods and services that any economic system can produce. In Chapter 3 we illustrated the concept of

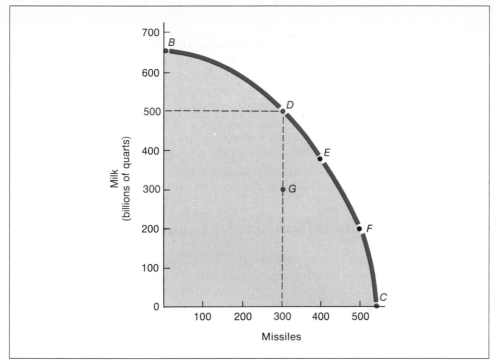

Figure 26–1
THE PRODUCTION
POSSIBILITIES FRONTIER
AND EFFICIENCY
Every point on the production
possibilities frontier, BC,
represents an efficient
allocation of resources
because it is impossible to
get more of one item without
giving up some of the other.
Any point below the frontier,
like G, is inefficient, since it
wastes the opportunity to
obtain more of both goods.

scarcity with a graphical device called a *production possibilities frontier*, which we repeat here for convenience as Figure 26–1. The frontier, curve *BC*, depicts all combinations of missiles and milk that this society can produce given the limited resources at its disposal. For example, if it decides to produce 300 missiles, it will have enough resources left over to produce *no more than* 500 billion quarts of milk (point *D*). Of course, it is always possible to produce fewer than 500 billion quarts of milk—at a point, such as G, below the production possibilities frontier. But if society does this, it is wasting some of its productive potential; that is, it is not operating *efficiently*.

In Chapter 3 we defined efficiency rather loosely as the absence of waste. Since the main subject of this chapter is how a competitive market economy allocates resources efficiently, we now need a more precise definition. It is easiest to define an **efficient allocation of resources** by saying what it is *not*. Suppose it were possible to rearrange things so that some people would have more of the things they want and no one would have to give up anything. Then failure to change the allocation of resources to take advantage of this opportunity would surely be wasteful—that is, *inefficient*. When there are no such possibilities for reallocating resources to make some people better off without making anyone else worse off, we say that the allocation of resources is *efficient*.

Figure 26–1 illustrates the idea. Points below the frontier, like G, are inefficient because, if we start at G, we can make *both* milk lovers *and* missile lovers better off by moving to a point *on* the frontier, like *E*. Thus *no point below the frontier* can represent an efficient allocation of resources. By contrast, *every point on the frontier* is efficient because, no matter where on the frontier we start, it is impossible to get more of one good without giving up some of the other.

This example brings out two important features of the concept of efficiency. First, it is strictly a technical concept; there are no value judgments stated or implied, and tastes are not questioned. An economy is judged efficient if it is good at producing *whatever* people want. Thus the economy in the

An **efficient allocation of resources** is one that takes advantage of every opportunity to make some individuals better off in their own estimation while not worsening the lot of anyone else.

example can be as efficient when it produces only missiles at point C as when it produces only milk at point B.

Second, there are normally many efficient allocations of resources; in the example, *every* point on frontier BC can be efficient. As a rule, the concept of efficiency does not permit us to tell which allocation is "best" for society. In fact, the most amazing thing about the concept of efficiency is that it gets us anywhere at all. At first blush, the criterion seems vacuous. It seems to assert, in effect, that anything agreed to unanimously is desirable. If some people are made better off *in their own estimation,* and none are harmed, then society is certainly better off by anyone's definition. Yet, as we shall see in this chapter, the concept of efficiency can be used to formulate surprisingly detailed rules to steer us away from situations in which resources are being wasted.

Pricing to Promote Efficiency: An Example

Let us first give an intuitive picture of the meaning of efficiency and its connection with pricing, using a real-life example — the prices (tolls) that are charged to use the bridges in the San Francisco Bay area. We will see that although proper pricing of these scarce resources (the bridges) can enhance efficiency, people nonetheless have often resisted the efficient solution.

Figure 26–2 shows a map of the San Francisco Bay area, featuring the five bridges that serve the bulk of the traffic in and around the bay. A traveler going from north of Berkeley (point A) to Palo Alto (point B) has a choice of at least three routes:

1. Over the Richmond–San Rafael Bridge, across the Golden Gate Bridge, through San Francisco, and on southward.
2. Cross the bay on the San Francisco–Oakland Bay Bridge, and continue on southward as before.
3. Come down the eastern side of the bay, cross on the San Mateo–Hayward Bridge or the Dumbarton Bridge, and then head on to Palo Alto.

Let's consider which of these three choices utilizes society's resources most efficiently. The most crowded of the five bridges is the Golden Gate, followed closely by the San Francisco–Oakland Bay Bridge. The first carries nearly 16,000 cars per lane per day, and the second nearly 10,000. During rush hours, delays are frequent and traffic barely crawls across these bridges. In other words, space is scarce, and every car that uses these bridges makes it that much harder for others to get across. On the other hand, the San Mateo and Dumbarton bridges carry approximately 3000 and 4000 cars per lane per day, respectively. From the efficiency point of view, it is best if any driver who has a choice of routes takes the one using the least crowded bridges. This will help reduce the amount of time wasted by the population as a whole in getting where they are going. Specifically, in our illustration, Route 1, using the Golden Gate Bridge, is not a socially desirable way for our driver to get to Palo Alto. Route 2, with its use of the San Francisco–Oakland Bay Bridge, is almost as bad because of the added delays it contributes to everyone else. Route 3 is the best choice from the viewpoint of the public interest.

It is here that prices can be used to promote efficiency in the utilization of bridges. Specifically, if we charge higher prices (very likely substantially higher

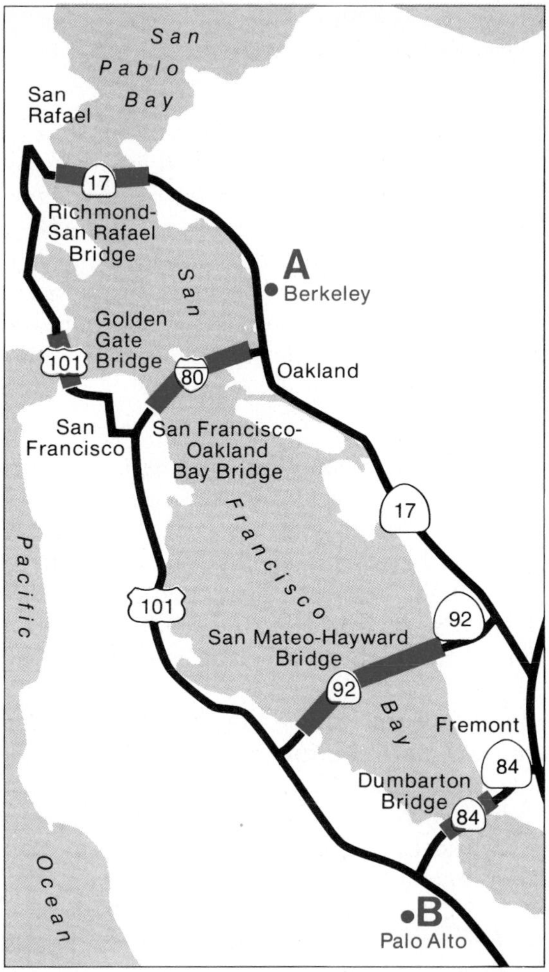

Figure 26–2
TOLL BRIDGES OF THE
SAN FRANCISCO BAY
AREA

prices) for the use of the most crowded bridges, on which space is a scarce resource, balanced by lower prices on the uncrowded bridges, we can induce more drivers to use the uncrowded bridges. This is just the same reasoning that leads economists to advocate low prices for abundant minerals and high prices for scarce ones.

Can Price Increases Ever Serve the Public Interest?

This last discussion raises a point that people untrained in economics always find difficult to accept: *low prices may not always be in the public interest*. The reason is clear enough. If a price, such as the price of crossing a crowded bridge or the price of oil, is set "too low," then consumers will receive the "wrong" signals. They will be encouraged to crowd the bridge even more or to consume more oil, thereby squandering society's precious resources.

A historic illustration is perhaps the most striking way to bring out the point. In 1834, some ten years before the great potato famine caused unspeakable misery and death by starvation and brought so many people from Ireland to the United States, a professor of economics named Mountifort Longfield lectured at the University cf Dublin about the price system. He offered the following remarkable illustration of his point:

Suppose the crop of potatoes in Ireland was to fall short in some year one-sixth of the usual consumption. If [there were no] increase of price, the whole . . . supply of the year would be exhausted in ten months, and for the remaining two months a scene of misery and famine beyond description would ensue. . . . But when prices [increase] the sufferers [often believe] that it is not caused by scarcity. . . . They suppose that there are provisions enough, but that the distress is caused by the insatiable rapacity of the possessors . . . [and] they have generally succeeded in obtaining laws against [the price increases] . . . which alone can prevent the provisions from being entirely consumed long before a new supply can be obtained. [1]

Longfield's reasoning can usefully be rephrased. If the crop fails, potatoes become scarcer. If society is to use its very scarce resources efficiently, it must cut back on the consumption of potatoes—which is just what rising prices would do *automatically* if the market mechanism were left to its own devices. However, if the price is held artificially low, then consumers will be using society's resources inefficiently. In this case, the inefficiency shows up in the form of famine and suffering when the year's crop is consumed months before the next crop arrives.

It is not easy to accept the notion that higher prices can serve the public interest better than lower ones. Politicians who voice this view are put in the position of the proverbial father who, before spanking his child, announces, "This is going to hurt me much more than it hurts you!" Since advocacy of higher prices courts political disaster, the political system often rejects the market solution when resources suddenly become more scarce.

The pricing of oil in the United States in the 1970s provided an excellent example. For years after the oil cartel (OPEC) drastically raised prices, legislation in the United States held domestic oil prices below free-market levels. The consequence, as economists were quick to point out, was that American consumers faced a market price for oil that was below the true marginal cost of oil to society. Consumers were therefore encouraged to use too much oil, and our dependence on imported oil increased. Suggestions to end the price controls, first by President Ford and later by President Carter, were rebuffed by lawmakers who feared the political consequences. Only in 1979 did President Carter begin the decontrol process, a process that was completed by President Reagan in 1981—more than seven years after OPEC's actions had caused a scarcity of oil.

Prevention of a rise in prices where a rise is appropriate can have serious consequences indeed. We have seen from Longfield's example that it can contribute to famine. We know that it caused nationwide chaos in gasoline distribution after the sudden fall in Iranian oil exports in 1979. It has contributed to the surrender of cities under military siege when effective price ceilings discouraged the efforts of those who were taking the risk of smuggling food supplies through enemy lines. And it has discouraged the construction of housing in cities, when rent controls made building a losing proposition.

---

[1] Mountifort Longfield, *Lectures on Political Economy* (Dublin, 1834), pages 53–56.

Of course there are cases in which it is appropriate to resist price increases—where unrestrained monopoly would otherwise succeed in gouging the public; where taxes are imposed on products capriciously and inappropriately; and where rising prices fall so heavily on the poor that rationing becomes the more acceptable option. But it is important to recognize that artificial restrictions on prices can produce serious and even tragic consequences—consequences that should be taken into account before a decision is made to tamper with the market mechanism.

Scarcity and the Need to Coordinate Economic Decisions

Efficiency becomes a particularly critical issue for the general welfare when we concern ourselves with the workings of the economy as a whole rather than a narrower topic such as choice among several bridge routes or the output decision of a single firm. An economy may be thought of as a complex machine with literally millions of component parts. If this machine is to function efficiently, some way must be found to make the parts work in harmony.

A consumer in Peoria may decide to purchase two dozen eggs, and on the same day similar decisions are made by thousands of shoppers throughout the country. None of these purchasers knows or cares about the decisions of the others. Yet, scarcity requires that these demands must somehow be coordinated with the production process so that the total quantity of eggs demanded does not exceed the total quantity supplied. The supermarkets, wholesalers, shippers, and chicken farmers must somehow arrive at consistent decisions, for otherwise the economic process will deteriorate into chaos. And there are many other such decisions that must be coordinated. One cannot run machines that are completed except for a few parts that have not been delivered. Refrigerators and cars cannot be used unless there is an adequate supply of fuel.

In an economy that is planned and centrally directed, it is easy to imagine how such coordination takes place—though the implementation turns out to be far more difficult than the idea. Central planners set production targets for firms and may even tell firms how to meet these targets. In extreme cases, consumers may even be told, rather than asked, what they want to consume.

In a market system, prices are used to coordinate economic activity instead. High prices discourage consumption of the resources that are most scarce, while low prices encourage consumption of the resources that are comparatively abundant. For example, if supplies of oil begin to run out while enormous reserves of coal remain, the price of oil can be expected to rise in comparison with the price of coal. As the price of oil rises, only those for whom oil offers the greatest benefits will continue to buy it. Firms or individuals that can get along almost equally well with coal or gas will switch to these more economical fuels. Some business firms will transform their equipment, and new homes will be built with heating systems that use gas. Only those who find alternative fuels a poor or unacceptable substitute for oil will continue to use oil despite its higher price. In this way, prices are the instrument used by Adam Smith's invisible hand to organize the economy's production.

The invisible hand has an astonishing capacity to handle a coordination problem of truly enormous proportions — one that will remain beyond the capabilities of electronic computers at least for the foreseeable future. It is true that like any mechanism this one has its imperfections, some of them rather serious. But without understanding the nature of the overall task performed by the market system, it is all too easy to lose sight of the tremendously demanding task that it constantly accomplishes — unnoticed, undirected, and at least in some respects, amazingly well. Let us, then, examine in more detail just what this coordination problem is like.

Three Coordination Tasks in the Economy

We noted in Chapter 3 that any economic system, whether planned or unplanned, must find answers to three basic questions of resource allocation:

1. *Output Selection:* How much of each commodity should be produced?
2. *Production Planning:* What quantities of each of the available inputs should be used to produce each good?
3. *Distribution:* How should the resulting products be divided among the consumers?

These coordination tasks may at first appear to be tailor-made for a regime of governmental central planning like that in the U.S.S.R. Yet most economists believe that it is in these tasks that central planning performs most poorly and, paradoxically, that the free market, with its utter lack of conscious planning and central direction, performs best. To understand how the unguided market manages the miracle of creating order of what might otherwise have been chaos, let us look at how each of these questions is answered by a system of free and unfettered markets — the method of economic organization that the eighteenth-century French economists named **laissez faire.** Under laissez faire, the government would prevent crime, enforce contracts, and build roads and other types of public works; but it would not set prices and would interfere as little as possible with the operation of free markets. How does such an unmanaged economy solve the three coordination problems?

Laissez faire refers to a program of minimal interference with the workings of the market system. The term means that people should be left alone in carrying out their economic affairs.

Output Selection

In a free-market system, the price mechanism decides what to produce via what we have called the "law" of supply and demand. Where there is a *shortage* — that is, where quantity demanded exceeds quantity supplied — the market mechanism pushes the price up, thereby encouraging more production and less consumption of the commodity in short supply. Where there is a *surplus* — that is, where quantity supplied exceeds quantity demanded — the same mechanism works in reverse: the price falls, which discourages production and stimulates consumption.

We can make these abstract ideas more concrete by looking at a particular example. Suppose millions of people wake up one morning with a craving for omelettes. For the moment, the quantity of eggs demanded exceeds the quantity supplied. But within a few days the market mechanism swings into action to meet this sudden change in demand. The price of eggs rises, which stimulates the production of eggs. In the first instance, farmers simply bring more eggs to market by taking them out of storage. Over a somewhat longer period of time, chickens that otherwise would have been sold for meat are kept in the chicken coops laying eggs. Finally, if the high price of eggs persists, farmers begin to increase their flocks, build more cages, and so on. Thus, a shift in consumer demand leads to a shift in society's resources; more eggs are wanted, and so the market mechanism sees to it that more of society's resources are devoted to the production of eggs.

Similar reactions follow if a technological breakthrough reduces the input quantities needed to produce some item. Electronic calculators are a marvelous example. Only 15 years ago, calculators were so expensive that they could be found only in business firms and scientific laboratories. Then advances in science and engineering reduced their cost dramatically, and the market went to work. With costs sharply reduced, prices fell dramatically and the quantity demanded skyrocketed. Electronics firms flocked into the industry to meet this demand, which is to say that more of society's resources were devoted to producing the calculators that were suddenly in such great demand. These examples lead us to conclude that:

Under laissez faire, the allocation of society's resources among different products depends on two basic influences: consumer preferences and the relative difficulty of producing the goods, that is, their production costs. Prices vary so as to bring the quantity of each commodity produced into line with the quantity demanded.

Notice that no bureaucrat or central planner arranges the allocation of resources. Instead, allocation is guided by an unseen force — the lure of profits, which is the invisible hand that guides chicken farmers to increase their flocks when eggs are in greater demand and guides electronics firms to build new factories when the cost of electronic products falls.

Production Planning

Once the composition of output has been decided, the next coordination task is to determine just how those goods are going to be produced. The production-planning problem includes, among other things, the assignment of inputs to enterprises — that is, which farm or factory will get how much of which materials. These decisions can be crucial. If a factory runs short of an essential input, the entire production process may grind to a halt.

As a matter of fact, inputs and outputs cannot be selected separately. The inputs assigned to the growing of coffee rather than to bananas determine the quantities of coffee and bananas that can be obtained. However, it is simpler to think of these decisions as if they occurred one at a time.

Once again, under laissez faire it is the price system that apportions fuels and other raw materials among the different industries in accord with those industries' requirements. The firm that needs a piece of equipment most urgently will be the last to drop out of the market for that product when prices rise. If more grain is demanded by millers than is currently available, the price will rise and bring quantity demanded back into line with quantity supplied, always giving priority to those users who are willing to pay the most for grain. Thus:

In a free market, inputs are assigned to the firms that can make the most productive (most profitable) use of them. Firms that cannot make a sufficiently productive use of some input will be priced out of the market for that item.

This task, which sounds so simple, is actually almost unimaginably complex. It is also one on which many centrally planned systems have foundered. We will return to it shortly, as an illustration of how difficult it is to replace the market by a central planning bureau. But first let us consider the third of our three coordination problems.

Distribution of Products Among Consumers

The third task of any economy is to decide which consumer gets each of the goods that has been produced. The objective is to distribute the available supplies so as to match the differing preferences of consumers as well as possible. Coffee lovers must not be flooded with tea while tea drinkers are showered with coffee.

The price mechanism solves this problem by assigning the highest prices to the goods in greatest demand and then letting individual consumers pursue their own self-interests. Consider our example of the rising price of eggs. As the price of eggs rises, those whose craving for omelettes is not terribly strong will begin to buy fewer eggs. In effect, the price acts as a rationing device, which apportions the available eggs among the consumers who are willing to pay the most for them.

But the price mechanism has one important advantage over other rationing devices: It is able to pay attention to consumer preferences. If eggs are rationed by the most obvious and usual means (say, two to a person), everyone ends up with the same quantity—whether he thinks eggs the more unpleasant component of his breakfast or the ingredients of his evening's soufflé, for which he pangs all day long. The price system, on the other hand, permits each consumer to set his own priorities. If you just barely tolerate eggs, a rise in their price quickly induces you to get your protein from some other source. But the egg lover is not induced to switch so readily. Thus:

The price system carries out the distribution process by rationing goods on the basis of preferences *and relative incomes*.

Notice the last three words. This rationing process *does* favor the rich, and this is a problem that market economies must confront. However, we may still want to think twice before declaring ourselves opposed to the price system. If equality is our goal, might not a more reasonable solution be to use the tax system to equalize incomes, and *then* let the market mechanism distribute goods in accord with preferences?

We have just seen, in broad outline, how a laissez faire economy addresses the three basic issues of resource allocation: what to produce, how to produce it, and how to distribute the resulting products. Since it performs these tasks quietly, without central direction, and with no apparent concern for the public interest, many radical critics have predicted that such an unplanned system must degenerate into chaos. Yet that does not seem to be the way things work out. Unplanned the market may be, but its results are far from chaotic. In fact,

— Наверное, в проекте произошла неувязка...

Рисунок В. ТИЛЬМАНА

quite ironically, it is the centrally planned economies that often find themselves in economic chaos. Perhaps the best way to appreciate the accomplishments of the market is to consider how a centrally planned system copes with the three coordination problems we have just outlined. For this purpose, we will concentrate on just one of them: production planning.

Input–Output Analysis: The Near Impossibility of Perfect Central Planning

Of the three coordination tasks of any economy, the assignment of inputs to specific industries and firms has claimed the most attention of central planners. The reason is this: Because the production processes of the various industries are *interdependent,* the whole economy can grind to a halt if the production planning problem is not solved satisfactorily.

Let's take a simple example. Gasoline is used both by consumers to run cars and by the trucking industry. Unless the planners allocate enough gasoline to trucking, products will not get to market; and unless they allocate enough trucks to haul the gasoline to gas stations, consumers will not be able to get to the market to buy the products. Thus, trucking activity depends on gasoline production but gasoline production depends on trucking activity. We seem to be caught in a circle. Though it turns out not to be a vicious circle, both problems must be dealt with together, not separately.

Because the output required from any one industry depends on the output desired from every other industry, planners can be sure that the production of the various outputs is sufficient to meet both consumer and industrial demands only by taking explicit account of the interdependencies among industries. If they change the output target for one industry, every other industry's output target also must be adjusted.

For example, if planners decide to provide consumers with more electricity, then more steel must be produced for more electric generators. But an increase in steel output requires more coal to be mined. More mining in turn means that still more electricity is needed to light the mines, to run the elevators, and perhaps even to run some of the trains that carry the coal, and so on and on. Any single change in production sets off a chain of adjustments throughout the economy that require still further adjustments.

To decide how much of each output an economy must produce, the planner must use statistics to form a set of equations, one equation for each product, and then solve those equations *simultaneously*. (The simultaneous solution process prevents the circularity of the analysis — electricity output depends on steel production, but steel output depends on electricity production — from becoming a vicious circle.) The technique used to solve these complicated equations — **input–output analysis** — was invented by economist Wassily Leontief, and it won him the Nobel Prize in 1973.

The equations of input–output analysis, which are illustrated in the boxed insert on page 587, take account of the interdependence among industries by describing precisely how each industry's target output depends on every other industry's target. Only by solving these equations *simultaneously* for the required outputs of electricity, steel, coal, and so on, can one be sure of a consistent solution that produces the required amounts of each product — including the amount of each product needed to produce every other product.

The example of input–output analysis that appears in the box is not provided so that you can learn how to apply the technique yourself. Its real purpose is to illustrate the *very complicated* nature of the problem that faces a central planner. For the problem faced by a real planner, while analogous to the one in the box, is enormously more complex. In any real economy, the number of commodities is far greater than the three outputs in the example. In the United States, some large manufacturing companies individually deal in hundreds of thousands of items, and the armed forces keep several *million* different items in inventory. In planning, it is ultimately necessary to make calculations for each single item. It is not enough to plan the right number of bolts *in total*; we must make sure that the required number *of each size* is produced. (Try to put five million large bolts into five million small nuts.) So, to be sure our plans will really work, we need a separate equation for every size of bolt and one for every size and type of nut. But then, to replicate the analysis described in the boxed insert, we will have to solve simultaneously several *million* equations! Unfortunately, there is as yet no electronic computer capable of doing this.

Worse still is the data problem. Each of our three equations requires *three* pieces of statistical information, making 3×3, or 9, numbers in total. This is because the equation for electricity must indicate on the basis of statistical information how much electricity is needed in steel production, how much in coal production, and how much is demanded by consumers. Therefore, in a five-industry analysis, 5×5, or 25, pieces of data are needed, a 100-industry analysis requires 100^2, or 10,000 numbers, and a million-item input–output study might need one *trillion* pieces of information. The data-gathering problems are therefore no easy task, to put it mildly. There are still other complications, but we have seen enough to conclude that:

A full, rigorous central-planning solution to the production problem is a tremendous task, requiring an overwhelming quantity of information and some incredibly difficult calculations. Yet this very difficult job is carried out automatically and unobtrusively by the price mechanism in a free-market economy.

Input–Output Equations: An Example

Imagine an economy with only three outputs: electricity, steel, and coal; and let E, S, and C represent the dollar value of their respective outputs. Suppose that for every dollar's worth of steel, $0.20 worth of electricity is used up, so that the total electricity demand of steel manufacturers is $0.2S$. Similarly, assume the coal manufacturers use up $0.30 of electricity in producing $1 worth of coal, or a total of $0.3C$ units of electricity. Since E dollars of electricity are produced in total, the amount left over for consumers, after subtraction of industrial demands for fuel, will be

$$
\begin{array}{ccc}
E & 0.2S & 0.3C \\
\text{(available} - & \text{(use in steel} - & \text{(use in coal} \\
\text{electricity)} & \text{production)} & \text{production).}
\end{array}
$$

Suppose further that the central planners have decided to supply $15 million worth of electricity to consumers. We end up with the electricity output equation

$$E - 0.2S - 0.3C = 15 .$$

The planner will also need such an equation for each of the two other industries, specifying for each of them the net amounts intended to be left for consumers after the industrial uses of these products. The full set of equations might then be:

$$
\begin{aligned}
E - 0.2S \ - 0.3C \ &= 15 \\
S - 0.1E \ - 0.06C &= 7 \\
C - 0.15E - 0.4S \ &= 10 .
\end{aligned}
$$

These are typical equations in an input–output analysis. Only, in practice, a typical analysis has dozens and sometimes hundreds of equations with similar numbers of unknowns. This, then, is the logic of input–output analysis.

Perfect Competition and Efficiency: What to Produce

We have now indicated how the market mechanism solves the three basic coordination problems of any economy — what to produce, how to produce, and how to distribute the goods to consumers. And we have suggested that these same tasks pose almost insurmountable difficulties for central planners. One critical question remains. Is the allocation of resources that the market mechanism selects *efficient,* according to the precise definition of efficiency presented at the start of this chapter? The answer is that, under the idealized circumstances of perfect competition, it is. Since a detailed proof of this assertion for all three coordination tasks would be long and time-consuming, we will present the proof only for the first of the three tasks — output selection. The corresponding analyses for the production planning and distribution problems are quite similar and are reserved for the appendix.

Our question is this: Given the output combination selected by the market mechanism, is it possible to improve matters by producing more of one good and less of another? Might it be "better," for example, if society produced more beef and less lamb? We shall answer this question in the negative, thus showing that, at least in theory, perfect competition does guarantee efficiency in production.

We will do this in two steps. First, we will derive a criterion for efficient output selection, that is, a test which tells us whether or not production is being carried out efficiently. Second, we will examine why that test is *automatically* passed by the prices that emerge from the market mechanism under perfect competition.

Step 1: Rule for Efficient Output Selection

We begin by stating the rule for efficient output selection:

Efficiency in the choice of output quantities requires that, for each of the economy's outputs, the marginal cost (MC) of the last unit produced be equal to the marginal utility (MU) of the last unit consumed.[2] In symbols:

$$MC = MU.$$

Let us use an example to see why this rule *must* be satisfied for the allocation of resources to be efficient. Suppose the marginal utility of an additional pound of beef to consumers is $8, while its marginal cost is only $5. Then the value of the resources that would have to be used up to produce one more pound of beef (its MC) would be $3 less than the money value of that additional pound to consumers (its MU). By expanding the output of beef by one pound, society could get more (the MU) out of the economic production process than it was putting in (the MC). It follows that the output at which MU > MC cannot be optimal, since society would be made better off by an increase in that output level.

The opposite is true if the MC of beef exceeds the MU of beef. In that case, the last pound of beef must have used up more value (MC) than it produced (MU). It would therefore be better to have less beef and more of something else.

We have therefore shown that, if there is *any* product for which MU is not equal to MC, the economy must be wasting an opportunity to produce a net improvement in consumers' welfare. This is exactly what we mean by using resources *inefficiently*. Just as was true at point G in Figure 26–1, if MC ≠ MU for any commodity, it is possible to rearrange things so as to make some people better off while harming no one. It follows that efficiency in the choice of outputs is achieved only when MC = MU for *every* good.[3]

Step 2: The Critical Role of the Price System

The next step in the argument is to show that under perfect competition the price system *automatically* leads buyers and sellers to behave in a way that makes MU and MC equal. To see this, recall from the last chapter that under perfect competition it is most profitable for each beef-producing firm to produce the quantity of beef at which the marginal cost of the beef is equal to the price of beef:

$$MC = P.$$

This must be so because, if the marginal cost of beef were less than the price, the farmer could add to his profits by increasing the size of his herd (or the amount of grain that he feeds his animals); and the reverse would be true if the

---

[2]It will be recalled from Chapter 21 that we measure marginal utility in money terms, that is, the amount of money that a consumer is willing to give up for an additional unit of the commodity. Economists usually call this the marginal rate of substitution between the commodity and money.

[3]Warning: We will find in Chapter 29 that one reason markets sometimes perform imperfectly is the fact that the marginal cost to the individual decision maker (this is called "private marginal cost") is not the same as the marginal cost to society ("social marginal cost"). This occurs when the individual whose actions cause the cost is able to escape paying it herself and instead lets someone else bear the burden. Example: Firm X's production causes pollution emissions which increase the laundry bills of households in the neighborhood. In such a case the efficiency rule requires MU = marginal social cost and that rule will obviously be violated if the behavior of the market makes MU = marginal private cost, so that inefficiency will result.

marginal cost of beef were greater than its price. Thus, under perfect competition, the lure of profits leads each producer of beef (and of every other product) to supply the quantity that makes MC = P.

We also learned, in Chapter 21, that it is in the interest of each consumer to purchase the quantity of beef at which the marginal utility of beef in terms of money is equal to the price of beef:

$$MU = P.$$

If he did not do this, as we saw, either an increase or a decrease in his purchase of beef would leave him better off.

Putting these last two equations together, we see that the invisible hand enforces the following string of equalities:

$$MC = P = MU.$$

But if both the MC of beef and the MU of beef are equal to the same price, P, then they must surely be equal to each other. That is, it must be true that the quantity of beef produced and consumed in a perfectly competitive market satisfies the equation:

$$MC = MU,$$

which is precisely our rule for efficient output selection. Since the same must be true of every other product supplied by a competitive industry:

Under perfect competition, the uncoordinated decisions of producers and consumers can be expected *automatically* to produce a quantity of each good that satisfies the MC = MU rule for efficiency in deciding what to produce. That is, under the idealized conditions of perfect competition, the market mechanism, *without any government intervention*, is capable of allocating society's scarce resources efficiently.

The Invisible Hand at Work

This is truly a remarkable result. How can the price mechanism automatically satisfy all the exacting requirements for efficiency — requirements that no central planner can hope to handle because of the masses of statistics and the enormous calculations they require? The conclusion seems analogous to the rabbit suddenly pulled from the magician's hat. But, as always, rabbits come out of hats only if they were hidden there in the first place. What really is the machinery by which our act of magic works?

The secret is that the price system lets consumers and producers pursue their own best interests — something they are probably very good at doing. Prices are the dollar costs of commodities to consumers. So, in pursuing their own best interests, consumers will buy the commodities that give them the most satisfaction *per dollar*. As we learned in Chapter 21, this means that each consumer will continue to buy beef until the marginal utility of beef is equal to the market price. And since every consumer pays the same price in a perfectly competitive market, the market mechanism ensures that *every consumer's MU will be equal to this common price*.

Turning next to the producers, we know from Chapter 25 that competition equates prices with marginal costs. And, once again, since every producer faces the same market price, the forces of competition will bring the MC *of every producer into equality with this common price*. Since MC measures the resource cost (in every firm) of producing one more unit of the good and MU measures the money value (to every consumer) of consuming one more unit, then when MC = MU *the cost of the good to society is exactly equal to the value that consumers place on it*. Therefore:

When all prices are set equal to marginal costs, the price system is giving the correct cost signals to consumers. It has set prices at levels that induce consumers to use the resources of the society with the same care they devote to watching their own money.

This is the magic of the invisible hand. Unlike central planners, consumers need not know how difficult it is to manufacture a certain product, nor how scarce are the inputs required by the production process. Everything the consumer needs to know to make his or her decision is embodied in the market price, which, under perfect competition, accurately reflects marginal costs.

Other Roles of Prices: Income Distribution and Fairness

So far we have stressed the role of prices most emphasized by economists: prices guide the allocation of resources. But a different role of prices often commands the spotlight in public discussions: prices influence the distribution of income between buyers and sellers. For example, high rents often make tenants poorer and landlords richer.

This rather obvious role of prices draws the most attention from the public, politicians, and regulators, and is one we should not lose sight of.[4] Markets only serve demands that are backed up by consumers' desire *and ability* to pay. Though the market system may do well in serving a poor family, giving that family more food and clothing than a less efficient economy would provide, it offers far more to the family of a millionaire. Many observers object that such an arrangement represents a great injustice, however efficient it may be.

Often, recommendations made by economists for improving the economy's efficiency are opposed on the grounds that they are unfair. For example, economists frequently advocate higher prices for transportation facilities at the time of day when they are most crowded. They propose a pricing arrangement called *peak, off-peak pricing* under which prices for public transportation are higher during rush hours than during other hours.

The rationale for this proposal should be clear from our discussion of efficiency. A seat on a train is a much scarcer resource during rush hours than during other times of the day when the trains run fairly empty. Thus, according to the principles of efficiency outlined in this chapter, seats should be more expensive during rush hours to discourage consumers from using the trains during peak periods. The same notion applies to other services. Charges for nighttime long-distance telephone calls are lower than those in the daytime and, in some places, electricity is sold more cheaply at night, when demand does not strain the supplier's generating capacity.

Yet the proposal that higher fares should be charged for public transportation during peak hours—say, from 8:00 A.M. to 9:30 A.M., and from 4:30 P.M. to 6 P.M.—often runs into stiff opposition on the grounds that most of the burden will fall on lower-income working people who have no choice about the timing of their trips. For example, a survey in Great Britain of members of

---

[4]Income distribution is the subject of Part 9.

Table 26–1
REPLIES TO A QUESTIONNAIRE

QUESTION: In order to make the most efficient use of a city's resources, how should subway and bus fares vary during the day?	Economists (percent)	Conservative Party M.P.'s (percent)	Labor Party M.P.'s (percent)
a. They should be relatively low during rush hour to transport as many people as possible at lower costs.	1	—	40
b. They should be the same at all times to avoid making travelers alter their schedules because of price differences.	4	60	39
c. They should be relatively high during rush hour to minimize the amount of equipment needed to transport the daily travelers.	88	35	19
d. Impossible to answer on the data and alternatives given.	7	5	2

SOURCE: Adapted from Samuel Brittan, *Is There an Economic Consensus?*, page 93. Copyright Samuel Brittan, 1973. Reproduced by permission of Curtis Brown Ltd.

Parliament and of economists found that while high peak-period fares were favored by 88 percent of the economists, only 35 percent of the Conservative Party M.P.'s and just 19 percent of the Labor Party M.P.'s approved of this arrangement (see Table 26–1). We may surmise that the M.P.'s reflected the views of the public more accurately than did the economists. In this case, people simply find the efficient solution unfair, and so refuse to adopt it.

Our earlier example of bridges in the San Francisco area also raises issues of fairness. As will be recalled, we concluded from our analysis that efficient use of bridges requires higher tolls on the more crowded bridges such as the San Francisco–Oakland Bay and Golden Gate Bridges. Since this principle seems so clear and rational, the reader may be interested to see at what levels the actual bridge tolls were set when this book was first written. Travel on the crowded Golden Gate Bridge required a $1.25 toll for a round trip. But the San Francisco–Oakland Bay, Dumbarton, and San Mateo–Hayward bridges each carried a 75-cent toll even though the Bay Bridge was far more crowded than the others. Even stranger, the Richmond–San Rafael Bridge, which was about as sparsely used as any, charged a $1 toll.

From the point of view of efficiency, this pattern of tolls obviously seems quite irrational. Some of the least crowded bridges were assigned the highest tolls! Yet some widely held notions of "fairness" explain why the authorities placed rather low tolls on some highly congested bridges.

Many people feel that it is fair for those who travel on a bridge to pay for its costs. In this view, it would be unjust for those who use the crowded San Francisco–Oakland Bay Bridge to pay for the less-crowded Richmond–San Rafael Bridge. Naturally, a bridge that is traveled heavily more quickly takes in the revenue necessary to recoup the cost of building, maintaining, and running it. That is why fairness is believed to dictate low tolls on crowded bridges. On the other hand, the relatively few users of a less-crowded bridge must pay higher tolls in order to make a fair contribution toward its costs.

Of course, such a pattern of tolls slows traffic and lures even more drivers to the already overcrowded bridges, thereby contributing to inefficiency. But one cannot legitimately conclude that advocates of such prices are "stupid." Whether this pattern of tolls is or is not desirable must be decided, ultimately, on the basis of the public's sense of what constitutes fairness and justice in pricing and the amount it is willing to pay in terms of delays, inconvenience, and other inefficiencies in order to avoid apparent injustices.[5]

Economics alone cannot decide the appropriate trade-off between fairness and efficiency. It cannot even pretend to judge which pricing arrangements are fair and which are unfair. But it can and should indicate whether a particular pricing decision, proposed because it is considered fair, will impose heavy inefficiency costs upon the community. Economic analysis also can and should indicate how to evaluate these costs, so that the issues can be decided on the basis of an understanding of the facts.

Toward Assessment of the Price Mechanism

Our analysis of the case for laissez faire is not meant to imply that the free-enterprise system is an ideal of perfection, without flaw or room for improvement. In fact, it has a number of serious shortcomings that we will explore in subsequent chapters. But recognition of these imperfections should not conceal the enormous accomplishments of the price mechanism.

We have shown that, given the proper circumstances, it is capable of meeting the most exacting requirements of allocative efficiency, requirements that go well beyond the capacity of any central planning bureau. The market mechanism has provided an abundance of goods unprecedented in human history. Even centrally planned economies use the price mechanism to carry out considerable portions of the task of allocation, most notably the distribution of goods among consumers. No one has invented an instrument for directing the economy that can replace the price mechanism, which no one ever designed or planned for, but that simply grew by itself, a child of the processes of history.

---

[5]Since this material was first published, the tolls have been changed, and it is interesting to note that their magnitudes now correspond more closely to the relative crowding of the bridges. This suggests that in public pricing policy, efficiency considerations do carry *some* weight.

Summary

1. An allocation of resources is considered *inefficient* if it wastes opportunities to change the use of the economy's resources in any way that makes consumers better off. Resource allocation is called *efficient* if there are no such wasted opportunities.

2. Under perfect competition, the free-market mechanism adjusts prices so that the resulting resource allocation is efficient. It induces firms to buy and use inputs in ways that yield the most valuable outputs per unit of input; it distributes products among consumers in ways that match individual preferences; and it produces commodities whose value to consumers exceeds the cost of producing them.

3. Resource allocation involves three basic coordination tasks: (a) How much of each good to produce, (b) What quantities of the available inputs to use in producing the different goods, and (c) How to distribute the goods among different consumers.

4. Efficient decisions about what goods to produce require that the marginal cost (MC) of producing each good be equated to its marginal utility (MU) to consumers. If the MC of any good differs from its MU, then society can improve resource allocation by changing the level of production.

5. Because the market system induces firms to set MC equal to price, and induces consumers to set MU equal to price, it automatically guarantees that the MC = MU condition is satisfied.

6. Sometimes improvements in efficiency require some prices to increase in order to stimulate supply or to prevent waste in consumption. This is why price increases can sometimes be beneficial to consumers.

7. In addition to allocating resources, prices also influence the distribution of income between buyers and sellers.

8. The workings of the price mechanism can be criticized on the grounds that it is unfair because of the preferential treatment it accords wealthy consumers.

Concepts for Review

Efficient allocation of resources
Coordination tasks: output selection, production planning, distribution of goods

Laissez faire
Input–output analysis

MC = P requirement of perfect competition
MC = MU efficiency requirement

Questions for Discussion

1. What are the possible social advantages of price rises in each of the two following cases?
   a. Charging higher prices for electrical power on very hot days when many people use air conditioners.
   b. Raising water prices in drought-stricken areas.
2. Discuss the fairness of the two preceding proposals.
3. Discuss the nature of the inefficiency in each of the following cases:
   a. An arrangement whereby relatively little coffee and much tea is made available to people who prefer coffee and that accomplishes the reverse for tea lovers.
   b. An arrangement in which skilled mechanics are assigned to ditchdigging and unskilled laborers to repairing cars.
   c. An arrangement that produces a large quantity of trucks and few cars, assuming both cost about the same to produce and to run but that most people in the community prefer cars to trucks.
4. In reality, which of the following circumstances might give rise to each of the preceding problem situations?
   a. Regulation of output quantities by a government.
   b. Rationing of commodities.
   c. Assignment of soldiers to different jobs in an army.
5. In a free market, how will the price mechanism deal with each of the inefficiencies described in Question 3?
6. Suppose a given set of resources can be used to make either one handbag or two wallets, and the MC of a handbag is $23 while the MC of a wallet is $9. If the MU of a wallet is $9 and the MU of a handbag is $30, what can be done to improve resource allocation? What can you say about the gain to consumers?

Appendix
The Invisible Hand in the Distribution of Goods and in Production Planning

On pages 587–89 of this chapter we offered a glimpse of the way economists analyze the workings of the invisible hand by showing how the market handles the problem of efficiency in one of the three tasks of resource allocation: the selection of outputs. We explained the MC = MU rule that must be followed for a set of outputs to be efficient, and showed how a free market can induce people to act in a way that satisfies that rule. In this appendix we complete the story, examining how the price mechanism handles the other two tasks of resource allocation: the distribution of goods among consumers and the planning of production.

Efficient Distribution of Commodities: Who Gets What?

While decisions about distribution among consumers depend critically on value judgments, a surprising amount can be said purely on grounds of efficiency. For example, consumers' desires are not being served efficiently if large quantities of milk are given to someone whose preference is for apple cider, while gallons of cider are assigned to a milk lover. Deciding how much of which commodity goes to whom is a matter that requires delicate calculation. It causes great difficulties during wartime when planners must ration goods. The planners generally end up utilizing a crude egalitarianism: the same amount of butter to everyone, the same amount of coffee to everyone, and so on. This may be justified, to paraphrase the statement of a high official in another country, by an "unwillingness to pander to acquired tastes," but it is easy to see that such fixed rations are unlikely to produce an efficient result.

The analysis of the efficient distribution of the economy's different products among its many consumers turns out to be quite similar to our previous analysis of efficient output selection. Suppose there are two individuals, Mr. Steaker and Ms. Chop, and that Steaker wants lots of beef and little lamb, while the opposite is true of Chop. Suppose each is getting one pound of lamb and one pound of beef per week. It is then possible to make *both* people better off without increasing their total consumption of two pounds of beef and two pounds of lamb if Mr. Steaker trades some of his lamb to Ms. Chop in return for some beef. The initial distribution of goods was not efficient because it wasted opportunities for trades that yield *mutual* gains.

It is easy enough to think of allocations of commodities among consumers that are *inefficient* — simply assign to each person only what he does not like. But how does one recognize an allocation that *is* efficient? After all, there are many of us whose preferences have much in common. If two individuals both like beef and lamb, how should the available amounts of the two commodities be divided between them? We will now show that, as in the analysis of efficient output selection, there is a simple rule that must be satisfied by *any* efficient distribution of products among consumers. Consider any two commodities in the economy, such as beef and lamb, and any two consumers, like Steaker and Chop, each of whom likes to eat some of each type of meat. Then:

The basic rules for the efficient distribution of beef and lamb between Steaker and Chop are that

Steaker's MU of beef = Chop's MU of beef

and

Steaker's MU of lamb = Chop's MU of lamb.

Analogous equations must be satisfied for every other pair of individuals, and for every other pair of products.

Why are these equalities required for efficiency? Recall that a distribution of commodities among consumers can be efficient only if it has taken advantage of every potential gain from trade. That is, if two people can trade in a way that makes them *both* better off, then the distribution cannot be efficient. We can show that if *either* of the previous equations is not satisfied, then such trades are possible.

Suppose, for example, that the following are the relevant marginal utilities:

Steaker's MU of beef = $4

Chop's MU of beef = $2

Steaker's MU of lamb = $1

Chop's MU of lamb = $1

In such a case a mutually beneficial exchange of beef and lamb can be arranged. For example, if Steaker gives Chop three pounds of lamb in return for one pound of beef, they will both be better off. Steaker loses three pounds of lamb, which are worth $3 to him, and gets a pound of beef, which is worth $4 to him. So he winds up $1 ahead. Similarly, Chop gives up one pound of beef, which is worth $2 to her, and gets in return three pounds of lamb, worth $3 to her. So she also gains $1.

Such a mutually beneficial exchange is possible here because the two consumers have different marginal utilities for beef. Each can benefit by giving up what he or she considers less valuable in exchange for something valued more highly. The initial position in which the two equations were not both satisfied was therefore not efficient because *without any increase in the total amounts of beef and lamb available to them, both could be made better off*. The lesson of this example is quite general:

Any time that two persons have unequal MU's for any commodity, the welfare of both parties can be increased by an exchange of commodities. Efficiency requires that any two individuals have the same MU's for any pair of goods.

The great virtue of the price system is that it induces people to carry out *voluntarily* all opportunities for mutually beneficial swaps. Without the price system, Steaker and Chop might not make the trade because they do not know each other. But the price system enables them to trade with each other by trading with the market. Remember from our discussion of consumer choice in Chapter 21 that it pays any consumer to buy any commodity up to the point where the good's money marginal utility is just equal to its price. In other words, in equilibrium:

$$\begin{aligned} \text{Mr. Steaker's MU of beef} &= \text{Price of beef} \\ &= \text{Ms. Chop's MU} \\ &\quad \text{of beef.} \end{aligned}$$

This is so because, if, say, Mr. Steaker's MU of beef were greater than the price of beef, he could improve his lot by exchanging more of his money for beef. And the reverse could be true if Steaker's MU of beef fell short of the price of beef. For the same reason, since the price of lamb is the same to both individuals, each will choose voluntarily to buy quantities of lamb at which:

$$\begin{aligned} \text{Mr. Steaker's MU of lamb} &= \text{Price of lamb} \\ &= \text{Ms. Chop's MU} \\ &\quad \text{of lamb.} \end{aligned}$$

Thus, we see that as long as both consumers face the same prices for lamb and beef, their independent decisions *must* satisfy our criterion for efficient distribution of beef and lamb between them:

Steaker's MU of beef = Chop's MU of beef

Steaker's MU of lamb = Chop's MU of lamb .

Given any prices for two commodities, each consumer, acting only in accord with his or her preferences and with no necessary consideration of the effects on the other person, will automatically make the purchases that efficiently serve the mutual interests of both purchasers.

This time, where have we sneaked the rabbit into our price system argument? The answer is that the market acts as a middleman between any pair of consumers. Given the prices offered by the market, each consumer will use his or her dollars in a way that exhausts all opportunities for gains from trade *with the market*. Mr. Steaker and Ms. Chop each take advantage of every such opportunity to gain by trading with the market,

and in the process they automatically take advantage of every opportunity for advantageous trades between themselves.

Efficient Production Planning: Allocation of Inputs

Finally, we note briefly that a similar analysis shows how the price system leads to an efficient allocation of inputs among the different production processes—the third of our allocative issues. For precisely the same reasons as in the case of the distribution of products among consumers:

Efficient use of two inputs (say, labor and fertilizer) in the production of two goods (say, wheat and corn) requires that

$$\begin{aligned} &\text{Marginal revenue product} & &\text{MRP of fertilizer} \\ &\text{(MRP) of fertilizer} = &&\text{in corn} \\ &\text{in wheat production} & &\text{production} \end{aligned}$$

$$\frac{\text{MRP of labor}}{\text{in wheat production}} = \frac{\text{MRP of labor in}}{\text{corn production}}.$$

By the same logic as before, it can be shown that if these equations do not hold, it is possible to produce more corn and more wheat using no more labor and fertilizer than before but merely by redistributing the quantities of the two inputs between the two crops. [6] Similarly, since we learned in Chapter 23 that maximum profits require each farmer to hire each input until the input's marginal revenue product equals its price, and since the price of a ton of fertilizer is the same for both wheat farmers and corn growers, it follows that we must have:

$$\begin{aligned} &\text{MRP of fertilizer in wheat production} \\ = &\text{Price of fertilizer} \\ = &\text{MRP of fertilizer in corn production} . \end{aligned}$$

The same relationship must be true for labor inputs:

$$\begin{aligned} &\text{MRP of labor in wheat production} \\ = &\text{Price of labor} \\ = &\text{MRP of labor in corn production} . \end{aligned}$$

[6]See Discussion Question 2 at the end of this appendix.

Thus, we conclude that by making the independent choices that maximize their own profits, and without necessarily considering the effects on anyone else, each farmer (firm) will *automatically* act in a way that satisfies the efficiency condition for the allocation of inputs among different products.

Summary

1. The condition for efficient distribution of commodities among consumers is that every consumer have the same marginal utility (MU) for every product. If this condition is not met, then two consumers can arrange a swap that makes both of them better off.
2. In a free market, all consumers pay the same prices. So, if they pursue their own self-interest by setting $MU = P$, they automatically satisfy the condition for efficient distribution of commodities.
3. The condition for efficient allocation of inputs to the various production processes is that the marginal revenue product (MRP) of any input be the same in every industry.
4. Since all producers pay the same prices for inputs under perfect competition, if each firm pursues its own self-interest by setting its MRP of any input equal to that input's market price, the condition for efficient production planning will be satisfied automatically.

Questions for Discussion

1. Show that commodities are not being distributed efficiently if Mr. Olson's marginal utilities of a pound of tomatoes and a pound of potatoes are, respectively, 60 cents and 30 cents while Mr. Johnson's are, respectively, 50 cents and 40 cents.
2. Suppose the marginal revenue product of a gallon of petroleum in the trucking industry is $2.15 while the marginal revenue product of petroleum in the auto-racing industry is $1.70. Show that petroleum inputs are being allocated inefficiently. How would a market system tend to prevent this situation from occurring?

27

Monopoly

The price of monopoly is
upon every occasion the
highest which can be got.

ADAM SMITH*

In Chapters 25 and 26 we described an idealized market system in
which all industries are perfectly competitive, and we extolled the
beauty of that system. In this chapter, we turn to one of the blemishes — the possibility that some industries may be monopolized, and the consequences of such monopolization.

We begin by defining *monopoly* and investigating some of the reasons for
its existence. Then, using the tools of Chapter 24, we consider the monopolist's
choice of an optimal price–output combination. As we shall see, while it is possible to analyze how much a monopolist will choose to produce, a monopolist
has no "supply curve" in the usual sense. This and other features of monopolized markets require basic modification of our supply–demand analysis of the
market mechanism. That modification leads us to the central message of this
chapter — monopolized markets do not match the ideal performance of perfectly competitive ones. In the presence of monopoly the market mechanism no
longer allocates society's resources efficiently. This opens up the possibility that
government actions to constrain monopoly might actually improve the workings of the market — a possibility we will study in detail in Chapters 31 and 32.

Application: Monopoly and Pollution Charges

We begin, as usual, with a real-life problem. Chapter 1 noted that most
economists want to control pollution by charging the polluter heavily, making
him pay more money the more pollution he emits. Making it sufficiently expensive for firms to pollute, it is said, will force them to cut their emissions.[1]

A common objection to this proposal is that it simply will not work when
the polluter is a monopolist: "The monopolist can just raise the price of his
product, pass the pollution charge on to his customers, and go on polluting as
before, with total impunity." After all, if a firm is a monopoly, what is to stop it
from raising its price when it is hit by a pollution charge?

Yet observation of the behavior of firms threatened with pollution charges
suggests that there is something wrong with this objection. If the polluter could
escape the penalty completely, we would expect him to acquiesce or to put up

---

*But Adam Smith's statement is incorrect! See Discussion Question 7 at the end of the chapter.
[1]Details on this method of pollution control are provided in Chapter 34.

only token opposition. Yet wherever it has been proposed to levy a charge on the emission of pollutants, the outcries have been enormous, even among firms with no important rivals. Lobbyists are dispatched at once to do their best to stop the legislation. In fact, rather than agree to being charged for their emissions, firms usually indicate a preference for direct controls that *force* them to adopt specific processes that are less polluting than the ones they are now using—that is, the firms seem to prefer to have government tell them what they must do!

In this chapter we will see how to analyze the issue, and why monopolies cannot make their customers pay the pollution charge—or at least not all of it. We will see how the monopolist's downward-sloping demand curve keeps him from passing on all of a pollution tax or any other increase in his costs (any upward shift in his cost curves).

Monopoly Defined

A **pure monopoly** is an industry in which there is only one supplier of a product for which there are no close substitutes, and in which it is very hard or impossible for another firm to coexist.

Pure monopoly was defined in Table 25–1 on page 557; the definition is quite stringent. First, there must be only one firm in the industry—the monopolist must be "the only supplier in town." Second, there must be no close substitute for the monopolist's product. Thus, even the sole provider of natural gas in a city would not be considered a pure monopoly, since other firms offer close substitutes like heating oil and coal. Third, there must be some reason why survival of a potential competitor is extremely unlikely, for otherwise monopoly could not persist.

These rigid requirements make pure monopoly a rarity in the real world. The local telephone company and the post office are good examples of one-firm industries that face little or no effective competition. But most firms face competition from substitute products. Even if only one railroad serves a particular town, it must compete with bus lines, trucking companies, and airlines. Similarly, the producer of a particular brand of beer may be the only supplier of that specific product but is not a monopolist by our definition. Since many other beers are close substitutes for its product, the company will lose much of its business if it tries to raise its price much above the prices of other brands.

And there is one further reason why the unrestrained pure monopoly of economic theory is rarely encountered in practice. We will learn in this chapter that pure monopoly can have a number of undesirable features. As a consequence, in markets where pure monopoly might otherwise prevail, the government has intervened to prevent monopolization or to limit the discretion of the monopolist to set its price.

If we do not study pure monopoly for its descriptive realism, why do we study it? Because, like perfect competition, pure monopoly is a market form that is easier to analyze than the more common market structures that we will consider in the next chapter. Thus, pure monopoly is a stepping stone toward models of greater reality. Also, the "evils of monopoly" stand out most clearly when we consider monopoly in its purest form, and this greater clarity will help us understand why governments have rarely allowed unfettered monopoly to exist.

Causes of Monopoly: Barriers to Entry and Cost Advantages

The key element in preserving a monopoly is keeping potential rivals out of the market. One possibility is that some specific impediment prevents the establishment of a new firm in the industry. Economists call such impediments **barriers to entry.** Some examples are:

1. *Legal restrictions.* The U.S. Postal Service has a monopoly position because Congress has given it one. Private companies that might want to compete with the postal service are prohibited from doing so by law. Local monopolies of various kinds are sometimes established either because government grants some special privilege to a single firm (for example, the right to operate a food concession in a municipal stadium) or prevents other firms from entering the industry (for instance, by licensing only a single local radio station).

2. *Patents.* A special, but important, class of legal impediments to entry are **patents.** To encourage inventiveness, the government gives exclusive production rights for a period of time to the inventor of certain products. As long as the patent is in effect, the firm has a protected position and is a monopoly. For example, Xerox had for many years (but no longer has) a monopoly in plain paper copying.

3. *Control of a scarce resource or input.* If a certain commodity can be produced only by using a rare input, a company that gains control of the source of that input can establish a monopoly position for itself. For example, some years ago a group of firms tried to get together to control the world's supply of uranium, but the attempt failed.

Obviously, such barriers can keep rivals out and ensure that an industry is monopolized, but monopoly can also occur in the absence of barriers to entry if a single firm has important cost advantages over its potential rivals. Two examples of this are:

4. *Technical superiority.* A firm whose technological expertise vastly exceeds that of potential competitors can, for a period of time, maintain a monopoly position. For example, IBM for many years had little competition in the computer business mainly because of its technological virtuosity. Eventually, however, competitors began to catch up.

5. *Economies of scale.* If mere size gives a large firm a cost advantage over a smaller rival, it is likely to be impossible for anyone to compete with the largest firm in the industry.

Natural Monopoly

This last type of cost advantage is important enough to merit special attention. In some industries, economies of large-scale production or economies from simultaneous production of a large number of items (for example, car motors and bodies, truck parts, and so on) are so extreme that the industry's output can be produced at far lower cost by a single firm than by a number of smaller firms. In such cases, we say there is a **natural monopoly,** because once a firm gets large enough relative to the size of the market for its product, its natural cost advantage will enable it to drive the competition out of business.

A natural monopoly need not be a large firm if the market is small enough. *What matters is the size of a single firm relative to the total market demand for the product.* Thus a small bank in a rural town or a gasoline station at a lightly traveled intersection may both be natural monopolies even though they are very small firms.

A **natural monopoly** is an industry in which advantages of large-scale production make it possible for a single firm to produce the entire output of the market at lower average cost than a number of firms each producing a smaller quantity.

Figure 27–1

NATURAL MONOPOLY
When the average cost curve of a firm is declining, as depicted here, natural monopoly may result. A firm producing two million widgets will have average costs of $2.50, which are well below those of a smaller competitor producing one million widgets (average cost = $3). It can cut its price to a level (lower than $3) that its competitior cannot match and thereby drive the competitor out of business.

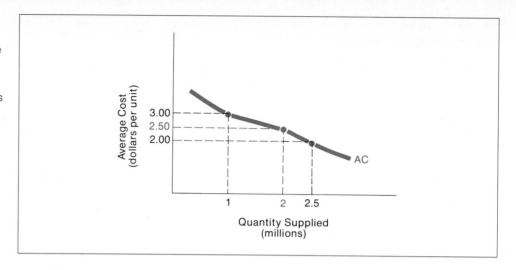

Figure 27–1 shows the sort of average cost (AC) curve that leads to natural monopoly. Suppose that any firm producing widgets would have this AC curve and that, initially, there are two firms in the industry. Suppose also that the large firm is producing two million widgets at an average cost of $2.50, and the small firm is producing one million widgets at an average cost of $3. Clearly the large firm can drive the small firm out of business by offering its output for sale at a price below $3 (so the small firm can match the price only by running a loss) but above $2.50 (so it can still make a profit). The managers of the large firm will no doubt be smart enough to realize this possibility, and hence a monopoly will arise "naturally" even in the absence of barriers to entry. Once the monopoly is established (producing, say, 2.5 million widgets) the economies of scale act as a very effective deterrent to entry because no new entrant can hope to match the low average cost ($2) of the existing monopoly firm.

Many public utilities are permitted to operate as monopoly suppliers for exactly this reason. It is believed that the technology of producing or distributing their output enables them to achieve substantial cost reductions when they produce large quantities. It is therefore often considered desirable to permit these firms to obtain the lower costs they achieve by having the entire market to themselves, and to subject them to regulatory supervision rather than break them up into a number of competing firms. The issue of regulating natural monopolies will be examined in detail in Chapter 31. To summarize this discussion:

There are two basic reasons why a monopoly may exist: barriers to entry, such as legal restrictions and patents, and cost advantages of large-scale operation, such as those that lead to natural monopoly.

The rest of this chapter will analyze how such a monopoly may be expected to behave if its freedom of action is not limited by the government.

The Monopolist's Supply Decision

A monopolist does not have a "supply curve," as we usually define the term. He does not say to himself: "The price of my product is $6. How much should I produce?" For, unlike the case of a perfect competitor, a monopolist is not at the mercy of the market; he does not have to take the market price as given and react to it. Instead, the monopolist has the power to set the price, or rather to select the price–quantity combination on his demand curve that he prefers. That is, the monopolist is not a *price taker* who must simply adapt himself to whatever price the forces of supply and demand decree for him. Rather, the monopolist is a *price maker* who can, if he wishes, raise his price. For any price that the monopolist might choose, the demand curve for his product tells him how much consumers will buy. Thus the standard supply–demand analysis described in Chapter 4 does not apply to the determination of price or output when the industry is a monopoly.

Unlike the perfectly competitive firm, the monopolist's demand curve is normally downward sloping, not horizontal. Unlike the case of perfect competition, a price rise will not cause him to lose all his customers. But it will cause him to lose *some* business. The higher his price, the less he can expect to sell.

It is because of the downward-sloping demand curve that the sky is not the limit in pricing by a monopolist. Some price increases are not profitable. In deciding what price best serves his interests, the monopolist must consider whether his profits can be increased by raising or lowering his price.

In our analysis, we shall assume that the monopolist wants to maximize his profits. We note two things about that. First, even a monopolist is not guaranteed a positive profit. If the demand for its product is low or the firm is inefficient, it may lose money and may eventually be forced to go out of business. Second, if the monopolist does earn a positive profit he may be able to keep on doing so even in the long run if entry of new competitors on profitable terms is difficult or impossible. This is so because absence of entry can permit the monopolist to keep his price well above his average cost.

The methods of Chapter 24 can be used to determine which price the profit-maximizing monopolist will prefer. To maximize his profits, he must compare his marginal revenue (the addition to total revenue resulting from a one-unit rise in output) with his marginal cost (the addition to total cost resulting from that additional unit). For this purpose, a marginal cost (MC) curve and a marginal revenue (MR) curve for a typical monopolist are drawn in Figure 27–2, which also contains the monopolist's demand curve (*DD*).

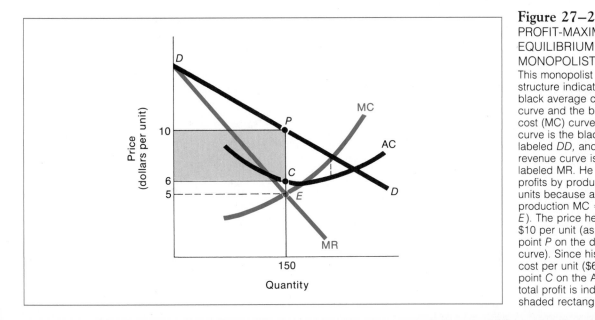

Figure 27–2
PROFIT-MAXIMIZING EQUILIBRIUM FOR A MONOPOLIST
This monopolist has the cost structure indicated by the black average cost (AC) curve and the blue marginal cost (MC) curve. His demand curve is the black line labeled *DD,* and his marginal revenue curve is the blue line labeled MR. He maximizes profits by producing 150 units because at this level of production MC = MR (point *E*). The price he charges is $10 per unit (as given by point *P* on the demand curve). Since his average cost per unit ($6) is given by point *C* on the AC curve, his total profit is indicated by the shaded rectangle.

The Monopolist's Price and Marginal Revenue

Notice that the marginal revenue curve is always *below* the demand curve, meaning that MR is always less than price (P). This is an important fact and is easy to explain. A monopolist normally must charge the same price to all his customers. So, if he wants to raise his sales by one unit, he must lower his price somewhat to *all* his customers. When he cuts his price to attract new sales, all his previous customers also benefit from the price reduction. Thus the *additional* revenue that he takes in when he increases sales by one unit (his *marginal revenue*) is the price he collects from his new customer *minus the revenue he loses by cutting the price paid by all his old customers*. This means that MR is necessarily *less than* price; graphically, it implies that the MR curve is *below* the demand curve, as in Figure 27–2.

Figure 27–3 illustrates the relationship between price and marginal revenue in a specific example. Suppose a monopolist is initially selling 15 units at a price of $2.10 per unit (point A), and he wishes to increase sales by one unit. The demand curve tells him that in order to sell the 16th unit, he must reduce his price to $2 (point B). How much revenue will he gain from this increase in sales; that is, how large is his marginal revenue?

As we know, *total revenue* at point A is the area of the rectangle whose upper right-hand corner is point A, or $2.10 \times 15 = 31.50$. Similarly, total revenue at point B is the area of the rectangle whose upper right-hand corner is point B, or $2 \times 16 = 32$. The *marginal revenue* of the 16th unit is, by definition, total revenue when 16 units are sold minus total revenue when 15 units are sold, or $32 - 31.50 = 0.50$.

In Figure 27–3, marginal revenue appears as the area of the tall blue rectangle ($2) *minus* the area of the flat gray rectangle ($1.50). We can see that MR is less than price by observing that the price is shown in the diagram by the area of the blue rectangle.[2] Clearly, the price (area of the blue rectangle) must exceed the marginal revenue (area of the blue rectangle *minus* area of the gray rectangle), as was claimed.[3]

[2]Because the width of this rectangle is one unit, its area is height × width = ($2 per unit) × (1 unit) = $2.
[3]There is another way to arrive at this conclusion. Recall that the demand curve is the curve of *average revenue*. Since the average revenue is declining as we move to the right, it follows from one of the rules relating marginals and averages (see the appendix to Chapter 24) that the marginal revenue curve must always be below the average.

Figure 27–3
THE RELATIONSHIP BETWEEN MARGINAL REVENUE AND PRICE
Line *DD* is the demand curve of a monopolist. In order to raise his sales from 15 to 16 units he must cut his price from $2.10 (point *A*) to $2 (point *B*). If he does this, his revenues go up by the $2 price he charges the buyer of the 16th unit (the area of the tall blue rectangle), but go down by the 10-cent price reduction he offers to his previous customers (the area of the flat gray rectangle). His marginal revenue therefore, is the difference between these two areas. Since the price is the area of the blue rectangle it follows that marginal revenue is less than price for a monopolist.

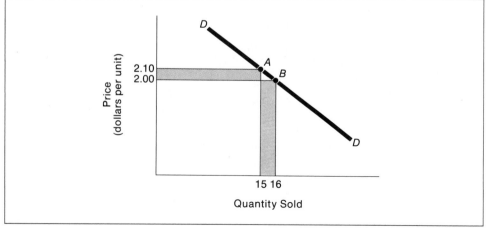

Determining the Profit-Maximizing Output

We return now to the supply decision of the monopolist depicted in Figure 27–2. Like any other firm, the monopoly maximizes its profits by setting marginal revenue (MR) equal to marginal cost (MC). It selects point E in the diagram, where output is 150 units. But point E does not tell us the monopoly price because, as we have just seen, price exceeds MR for a monopolist. To learn what price the monopolist charges, we must use the demand curve to find the price at which consumers are willing to purchase 150 units. The answer, we see, is given by point P. The monopoly price is $10 per unit, which naturally exceeds both MR and MC (which are equal at $5).

The monopolist depicted in Figure 27–2 is earning a tidy profit. This profit is shown in the graph by the shaded rectangle whose height is the difference between price (point P) and average cost (point C) and whose width is the quantity produced (150 units). In the example, profits are $4 per unit, or $600.

To study the decisions of a profit-maximizing monopolist, we must:

1. find the output at which MR = MC, to select the profit-maximizing output level;

2. find the height of the demand curve at that level of output, to find the corresponding price;

3. compare the height of the demand curve with that of the AC curve at that output to see whether the net result is a profit or a loss.

A monopolist's profit-maximization calculation can also be shown numerically. In Table 27–1, the first two columns show the price and quantity figures that constitute the monopolist's demand curve. Column 3 shows total revenue (TR) for each output, which is the product of price and quantity. Thus, for three units of output we have TR = $92 × 3 = $276. Column 4 shows marginal revenue (MR). For example, when output rises from 3 to 4 units, TR increases from $276 to $320, so MR is $320 − $276 = $44. Column 5 gives the monopolist's total costs for each level of output. Column 6 derives marginal cost (MC) from total cost (TC) in the usual way. Finally, by subtracting TC from TR for each level of output, we derive total profit in column 7.

This table brings out a number of important points. We note first (columns 2 and 3) that a cut in price sometimes raises total revenue. For

Table 27–1
A PROFIT-MAXIMIZING MONOPOLIST'S PRICE–OUTPUT DECISION

Demand Curve		Revenue		Cost		Total Profit
(1)	(2)	(3)	(4)	(5)	(6)	(7)
Q	P	TR = P × Q	MR	TC	MC	TR − TC
0	—	$ 0		$ 10		$−10
1	$140	140	$140	70	$60	70
2	107	214	74	120	50	94
3	92	276	62	166	46	110
4	80	320	44	210	44	110
5	66	330	10	253	43	77
6	50	300	−30	298	45	2

example, when output rises from 1 to 2, *P* falls from $140 to $107 and TR rises from $140 to $214. But sometimes a fall in *P* reduces TR; when (between 5 and 6 units of output) *P* falls from $66 to $50, TR falls from $330 to $300. Next we observe, by comparing columns 2 and 4, that after the first unit, price always exceeds marginal revenue. Finally, from columns 4 and 6 we see that MC = MR = $44 when *Q* is between 3 and 4 units, indicating that this is the level of output that maximizes the monopolist's total profit. That is confirmed in the last column of the table, which shows that at those outputs profit reaches its highest level, $110, for any of the output quantities considered in the table.

Comparison of Monopoly and Perfect Competition

This completes our analysis of the monopolist's price–output decision. At this point it is natural to wonder whether there is anything distinctive about monopoly and whether its consequences are desirable or undesirable. For the purpose of finding out, we need a standard of comparison. Perfect competition provides this standard because, as we learned in Chapters 25 and 26, it is a benchmark of ideal performance against which other market structures can be judged. By comparing the results of monopoly with those of perfect competition, we will see why economists since Adam Smith have condemned monopoly as inefficient.

A Monopolist's Profit Persists

The first difference between competition and monopoly is a direct consequence of the absence of barriers to entry in the former. Profits such as those shown in Figure 27–2 would be competed away by free entry in a competitive market. In the long run, a competitive firm must earn zero economic profit; that is, it can earn only enough to cover its costs, including the opportunity cost of the owner's capital and labor. But higher profits can persist under monopoly — if the monopoly is protected by barriers to entry. The fates can be kind to a monopolist and allow him to grow wealthy at the expense of the consumer. Because people find such accumulations of wealth objectionable, monopoly is widely condemned, and when monopolies are regulated by government, limitations are usually placed on the profits monopolists can earn.

Monopoly Restricts Output to Raise Short-Run Price

Excess monopoly profits may be a problem, but the second difference between competition and monopoly is even more worrisome in the opinion of economists:

As compared with the perfectly competitive ideal, the monopolist restricts his output and charges a higher price.

To see that this is so, let us conduct the following thought experiment. Imagine that a court order breaks up the monopoly firm depicted in Figure 27–2 (reproduced here as Figure 27–4) into a large number of competitive firms. Suppose further that the industry demand curve is unchanged by this event and that the MC curve in Figure 27–4 is also the (horizontal) sum of the MC curves of all the newly created competitive firms. Under these assumptions, we can easily compare the output–price combinations that would emerge in the short run under monopoly and perfect competition.

Since the short-run supply curve of the competitive industry is the sum of the MC curves of all the individual firms (above minimum average variable

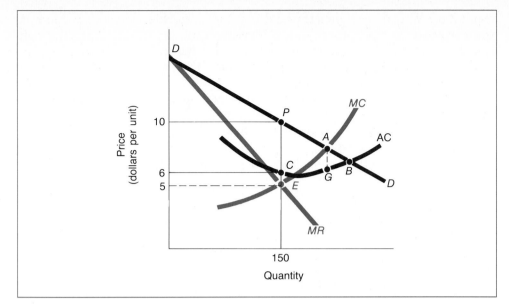

Figure 27–4
COMPARISON OF A
MONOPOLY AND A
COMPETITIVE INDUSTRY
The monopoly output is point
E at which MC = MR. The
short-run competitive output
is point A, at which MC = P,
and so is greater than the
monopoly output. The
long-run competitive output is
even greater (point B)
because it must be
sufficiently large to yield zero
profit (P = AC).

costs), the MC curve in Figure 27–4 would constitute the supply curve of the competitive industry. Equilibrium under perfect competition would occur at point A, where quantity demanded (which we read from the demand curve) and quantity supplied (which we read from the MC = supply curve) are equal.

By comparing point A with the monopolist's equilibrium (point E), we can see that the monopolist produces fewer units of output than would a competitive industry with the same demand and cost conditions. Since the demand curve slopes downward, producing less output means charging a higher price. The monopolist's price, indicated by point P, exceeds the price that would result from perfect competition at point A. This is the essence of the truth behind the popular view that monopolists "gouge the public."

Monopoly Restricts Output to Raise Long-Run Price

In fact, the reduction in output and increase in price may be even greater than we have indicated. Our analysis so far is correct, but only for the short run. In the short run, monopoly output is determined by MC = MR (point E) while competitive output is determined by MC = P (point A). But in the long run, as we learned in Chapter 25, the lure of profits will attract more firms into a perfectly competitive industry. In Figure 27–4, we can see that there *are* profits to be made. When the industry produces at point A, the market price (point A) clearly exceeds the average cost of production (point G). Each competitive firm will then be earning profits in excess of the opportunity cost of capital.

But, as we know, such a situation cannot persist if there is free entry. New firms will enter the industry, thereby pushing the supply (= MC) curve outward to the right. (The AC curve will also shift rightward as total industry capacity expands.) Long-run competitive equilibrium will eventually be established at a point similar to B, where price and average cost are equal (and hence economic profits are zero). Comparing point B with point A, we see that competitive output is *even higher* and competitive price is *even lower* than we indicated at first.

Monopoly Leads to Inefficient Resource Allocation

We conclude, then, that a monopoly will charge a higher price and produce a smaller output than will a competitive industry with the same demand and cost conditions. Why do economists find this situation so objectionable? Because, as you will recall from Chapter 26, a competitive industry devotes "just the right amount" of society's scarce resources to the production of its particular commodity. Therefore, if a monopolist produces less than a competitive industry, it must be producing too little.

Remember from Chapter 26 that efficiency in resource allocation requires that the marginal utility (MU) of each commodity be equal to its marginal cost, and that perfect competition guarantees that:

$$MU = P \text{ and } MC = P, \text{ so } MU = MC.$$

Under monopoly, consumers continue to maximize their own welfare by setting MU equal to P. But the monopoly producer, we have just learned, sets MC equal to MR. Since MR is *below* the market price, P, we conclude that in a monopolized industry:

$$MU = P \text{ and } MC = MR < P, \text{ so } MU > MC.$$

Because MU exceeds MC, too few of society's resources are being used to produce the monopolized commodity. Adam Smith's invisible hand is sending out the wrong signals. Consumers are willing to pay an amount for an additional unit of the good (its MU) that exceeds what it costs to produce that unit (its MC). But the monopolist refuses to increase his production, for if he raises output by one unit, the revenue he will collect (the MR) will be less than the price the consumer will pay for the additional unit (P). So the monopolist does not increase his production and resources are allocated inefficiently. To summarize this discussion of the consequences of monopoly:

Because it is protected from entry, a monopoly firm earns profits in excess of the opportunity cost of capital. At the same time, monopoly breeds inefficiency in resource allocation by producing too little output and charging too high a price. For these reasons, some of the virtues of laissez faire evaporate if an industry becomes monopolized.

Can Anything Good Be Said About Monopoly?

Except for the case of natural monopoly — where a single firm offers important cost advantages — it is not easy to find arguments in favor of monopoly. But the comparison between monopoly and perfect competition in the real world is not quite as clean as it is in our example.

Monopoly May Shift Demand

For one thing, we have assumed that the market demand curve is the same whether the industry is competitive or monopolized. But is this necessarily so? The demand curve will be the same if the monopolist does nothing about his demand, but that hardly seems likely.

Under perfect competition, purchasers consider the products of all suppliers in an industry to be identical, and so no single supplier has any reason to advertise. A farmer who sells wheat through one of the major markets has absolutely no motivation to spend money on advertising because he can sell all the wheat he wants to at the going price.

When the monopolist takes over, however, it may very well pay him to advertise. If he believes that the touch of Madison Avenue can make consumers' hearts beat faster as they rush to the market to purchase the wheat whose virtues have been extolled on television, the monopolist will allocate a substantial sum of money to accomplish this feat. This should shift his demand curve outward; after all, that is the purpose of these expenditures. The monopolist's demand curve and that of the competitive industry will then no longer be the same. The higher demand curve for the monopolist's product will perhaps induce him to expand his volume of production and to reduce the difference between the competitive and the monopolistic output levels indicated in Figure 27–4. It will also, however, induce him to charge even higher prices.

Monopoly May Shift the Cost Curves

Similarly, the advent of a monopoly may produce shifts in the average and marginal cost curves. One reason for higher costs is the advertising we have just been discussing. Another is that the sheer size of the monopolist's organization may lead to bureaucratic inefficiencies, coordination problems, and the like. On the other hand, the monopolist may be able to eliminate certain types of duplication that are unavoidable for a number of small independent firms: one purchasing agent may do the job where many buyers were needed before; and a few large machines may replace many small items of equipment in the hands of the competitive firms. In addition, the large scale of his input purchases may permit the monopolist to avail himself of quantity discounts not available to small competitive firms.

If the unification achieved by monopoly does succeed in producing a downward shift in the marginal cost curve, monopoly output will thereby tend to move up closer to the competitive level, and the monopoly price will tend to move down closer to the competitive price.

Monopoly May Aid Innovation

In addition to this, some economists, most notably Joseph Schumpeter, have argued that it is potentially misleading to compare the cost curves of a monopoly and a competitive industry *at a single point in time*. Because it is protected from rivals, and therefore sure to capture the benefits from any cost savings it can devise, a monopoly has a particularly strong motivation to invest in research, they argue. If this research bears fruit, then the monopolist's costs will be lower than those of a competitive industry in the long run, even if they are higher in the short run. Monopoly, according to this view, may be the handmaiden of innovation. While the argument is an old one, it remains controversial. The statistical evidence is decidedly mixed.

Natural Monopoly — Where Single-Firm Production is Cheapest

Finally, we must remember that the monopoly depicted in Figure 27–2 is not a natural monopoly. But some of the monopolies you find in the real world are. Where the monopoly is natural, costs of production would, by definition, be higher and possibly much higher if the single large firm were broken up into many smaller firms. (Refer back to Figure 27–1 on page 600.) In such cases, it may be in society's best interest to allow the monopoly to exist so that consumers can benefit from the economies of large-scale production. But then it may be appropriate to place legal limitations on the monopolist's ability to set a price; that is, to *regulate* the monopoly. Regulation of business is an issue that will occupy our attention in Chapter 31.

Monopoly and the Shifting of Pollution Charges

We conclude our discussion of monopoly by returning to the application that began this chapter—the effectiveness of pollution charges as a means to reduce emissions. Recall that the question is whether a monopoly can raise its price enough to cover any pollution fees, thus shifting these charges entirely to its customers and evading them altogether.

The answer is that any firm or industry can usually shift *part* of the pollution charge to its customers. Economists argue that this shifting is a proper part of a pollution-control program since it induces consumers to redirect their purchases from goods that are highly polluting to goods that are not. For example, a significant increase in taxes on leaded gasoline with, perhaps, a simultaneous decrease in the tax on unleaded gasoline will send more motorists to the unleaded-gas pumps, and that will reduce dangerous lead emissions into the atmosphere.

But more important for our discussion here is the other side of the matter. While some part of a pollution charge is usually paid by the consumer, *the seller will usually be stuck with some part of the charge, even if he is a monopolist*. Why? Because of the negative slope of his demand curve. If he raises his price, he will lose customers, and that will eat into his profits. He will then always be better off if he absorbs *some* of the charge himself rather than try to pass all of it on to his customers.

This is illustrated in Figure 27–5. In part (a) we show the monopolist's demand, marginal revenue, and marginal cost curves. As in Figure 27–2, equilibrium output is 150 units—the point at which marginal revenue (MR) equals marginal cost (MC). And price is again $10—the point on the demand curve corresponding to 150 units of output (point A).

Now, let a charge of $5 per unit be put on the firm's polluting output, shifting the marginal cost curve up uniformly to the curve labeled "MC plus fee" in Figure 27–5 (b). Then the profit-maximizing output falls to 100 units (point F), for here MR = MC + pollution fee. The new output, 100 units, is

Figure 27–5
MONOPOLY PRICE AND OUTPUT WITH AND WITHOUT A POLLUTION CHARGE

Part (a) shows the monopoly equilibrium without a pollution charge, with price equal to $10 and quantity equal to 150. In part (b) a $5 fee is levied on each unit of polluting output. This raises the marginal cost curve by the amount of the fee, from the black to the blue line. As a result, the output at which MC = MR falls from 150 to 100. Price rises from $10 to $12. Note that this $2 price rise is less than the $5 pollution fee, so the monopolist will be stuck with the remaining $3 of the charge.

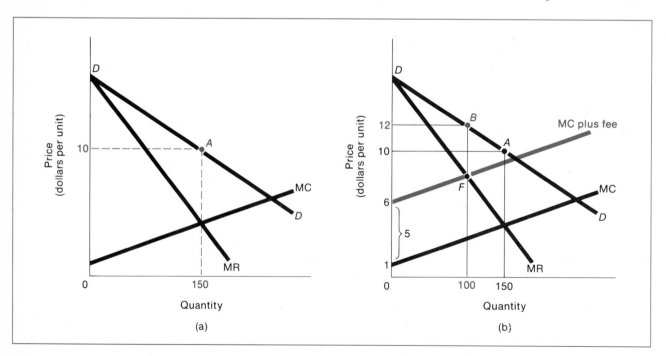

lower than the precharge output, 150 units. Thus, the charge leads the monopolist to restrict his polluting output. The price of his product rises to $12 (point B), the point on the demand curve corresponding to 100 units of output. But the rise in price from $10 to $12 is less than half the $5 pollution charge per unit. Thus:

The pollution charge *does* hurt the polluter even if he is a profit-maximizing monopolist, and it *does* force him to cut his polluting outputs.

No wonder the polluters' lobbyists fight so vehemently! Polluters realize that they often will be far better off with direct controls that impose a financial penalty *only* if they are caught in a violation, prosecuted, and convicted—and even then the fines are often negligible, as we will see in Chapter 34.

We may note, finally, that *any* rise in a monopolist's costs will hurt him and reduce his profits. The reason is exactly the same as in the case of a pollution charge. Even though he is a monopolist, he cannot simply raise his price and make up for any cost increase. For consumers can and will respond by buying less of the monopolist's commodity—after all, that is what the negative slope of the demand curve means:

If a monopoly already charges the price that maximizes its profits, a rise in cost will always hurt because any attempt to offset it by a price rise must reduce profit. The monopolist cannot pass the entire burden of the cost increase to consumers.

Summary

1. A pure monopoly is a one-firm industry producing a product for which there are no close substitutes.
2. Monopoly can persist only if there are important cost advantages to single-firm operation or barriers to free entry. These barriers may be legal impediments (patents, licensing) or some unique advantage the monopolist acquires for himself (control of a scarce resource).
3. One important case of cost advantages is natural monopoly: instances where only one firm can survive because of important economies of large-scale production.
4. A monopoly has no supply curve. It maximizes its profit by producing an output at which its marginal revenue equals its marginal cost. Its price is given by the point on its demand curve corresponding to that output.
5. In a monopolistic industry, if demand and cost curves are the same as those of a competitive industry, and if the demand curve has a negative slope and the supply curve a positive slope, output will be lower and monopoly price will be higher than those of the competitive industry.
6. Advertising may enable the monopolist to shift his demand curve above that of a comparable competitive industry's, and through economies such as large scale input purchases, he may be able to shift his cost curves below those of a competitive industry.
7. If a pollution charge is imposed on the product of a profit-maximizing monopoly, that monopoly will raise its price, but normally not by the full amount of the charge. That is, the monopolist will end up paying part of the pollution fee.
8. Any rise in his costs generally hurts a monopolist. Because of his negatively sloping demand curve, he cannot simply pass them on to consumers.

Concepts for Review

Pure monopoly	Natural monopoly	Inefficiency of monopoly
Barriers to entry	Monopoly profits	Shifting of pollution charges
Patents		

Questions for Discussion

1. Which of the following industries are pure monopolies?
   a. The only supplier of water in an isolated desert town.
   b. The only supplier of Rolex watches in town.
   c. The only supplier of fuel oil in town.
   Explain your answers.
2. Suppose a monopoly industry produces less output than a similar competitive industry. Discuss why this may be considered "socially undesirable."
3. If a competitive firm earns zero economic profits, explain why anyone would invest money in it. (*Hint:* What is the role of the opportunity cost of capital in economic profit?)
4. The following are the demand and *total* cost schedules for Company Town Water Company, a local monopoly.

OUTPUT (gallons)	PRICE (dollars per gallon)	TOTAL COST (dollars)
50,000	.11	3,000
100,000	.10	6,500
150,000	.09	11,000
200,000	.08	16,000
250,000	.07	23,000
300,000	.05	32,000

How much output will Company Town produce, and what price will it charge? Will it earn a profit? How much? (*Hint:* You will first have to compute its MR and MC schedules.)

5. Show from the preceding table that for the water company, marginal revenue (per 50,000 gallon unit) is always less than price.
6. Suppose a tax of $12 is levied on each item sold by a monopolist, and as a result he decides to raise his price by exactly $12. Why may this decision be against his own best interest?
7. Use Figure 27–2 to show that Adam Smith was wrong when he claimed that a monopoly would always charge "the highest price which can be got."

28

Between Competition and Monopoly

I was grateful to be able to
answer promptly and I did.
I said I didn't know.

MARK TWAIN

Most productive activity in the United States, as in any advanced industrial society, can be found between the two theoretical poles considered so far: perfect competition and pure monopoly. Thus, if we want to understand the workings of the market mechanism in a real, modern economy, we must look between competition and monopoly, at the hybrid market structures first mentioned in Chapter 25: *monopolistic competition* and *oligopoly*.

This chapter begins with a precise definition of monopolistic competition, a market structure characterized by many small firms selling somewhat different products. Here each firm's output is so small relative to the total output of closely related and, hence, rival products that it does not expect its rivals to respond to or even to notice any changes in its own behavior. Monopolistic competition or something close to it is widespread in the retail sector of our economy; shoe stores, restaurants, and gasoline stations are some good examples. We will use the theory of the firm described in Chapter 24 to analyze the price–output decision of a monopolistically competitive firm, and then consider industry-wide adjustments, as we did in Chapter 25.

Then we turn to oligopoly, a market structure in which a few large firms dominate the market. Industries like steel, automobiles, and tobacco are good examples of oligopoly in our economy. The critical feature distinguishing an oligopolist from either a monopolist or a perfect competitor is that the oligopolist cares very much about what other firms in his industry do. And the resulting interdependence of decisions, we will see, makes oligopoly very hard to analyze. Consequently, economic theory contains not one but many models of oligopoly (some of which will be reviewed in this chapter), and it is often hard to know which model to apply in any particular situation.

At several points in this chapter we will raise the following critical question: How good is the market mechanism at allocating resources when a commodity is produced under monopolistic competition or under oligopoly? A definitive answer is not usually possible, but we shall see that the case for laissez faire is seriously compromised by the existence of either monopolistic competition or oligopoly.

Some Puzzling Observations

It is easy to see that we need to study the hybrid market structures considered in this chapter, for many things we observe in the real world defy understanding within the framework of either perfect competition or pure monopoly. Here are some examples:

1. *Advertising.* While some advertising is primarily informative (for example, help-wanted ads), much of the advertising that bombards us on TV and in magazines is part of a competitive struggle for our business. Many big companies use advertising as the principal weapon in their battle for customers, and advertising budgets can constitute a very large share of their expenditures. Yet oligopolistic industries containing a few giant firms are often accused of being "uncompetitive" while farming is considered as close to perfect competition as any industry in our economy, even though most individual farmers spend nothing at all on advertising.[1] Why do the allegedly "uncompetitive" oligopolists make such heavy use of advertising while very competitive farmers do not?

2. *"Excessive" Number of Firms.* You have all seen intersections with three or four gasoline stations in close proximity. Often, two or three of them may have no cars waiting to be served and the attendants are unoccupied. There seem to be more gas stations than the available amount of traffic warrants, with a corresponding waste of labor time, equipment, and other resources. Why do they all stay in business?

3. *Sticky Prices.* Many prices in the economy change from minute to minute. Every day the latest prices of such items as soybeans, cocoa, and copper are published. But if you want to buy one of these at 11:45 A.M. some day, you cannot use yesterday's price because it has probably changed since then. Yet prices of other products, such as cars and refrigerators, generally change at most several times a year, even when inflation is proceeding at a double-digit pace. The firms that sell cars and refrigerators know that market conditions change all the time. Why don't they adjust their prices more often?

This chapter will offer explanations of each of these three phenomena.

Monopolistic Competition

For years, most economic theorists dealt with only two workable models of the behavior of firms: the monopoly model and the perfectly competitive model. This gap was partially filled, and the realism of economic theory was thereby greatly increased, by the work of Edward Chamberlin of Harvard University and Joan Robinson of Cambridge University during the 1930s. The market structure they first analyzed is called **monopolistic competition.**

A market is said to operate under conditions of *monopolistic competition* if it satisfies four conditions, three of which are the same as under perfect competition: (1) *Numerous participants* — that is, many buyers and sellers, all of whom are small; (2) *heterogeneity of products* — as far as the buyer is concerned, each seller's product is at least somewhat different from every other's; (3) *freedom of exit and entry;* and (4) *perfect information*.

---

[1] But farmers' *associations*, like Sunkist and various dairy groups, do spend money on advertising.

Monopolistic competition is a market form that we encounter frequently in our economy. It is particularly characteristic of retailing, where the small shopkeeper still plays a significant role, and of many of the economy's services, such as medical and legal, which are provided under similar conditions. Gas stations and restaurants are other good examples.

Notice that monopolistic competition differs from perfect competition in only one respect (item 2 in the definition). While all products are identical under perfect competition, under monopolistic competition products differ from seller to seller—in quality, in packaging, or in supplementary services offered (for example, length of the guarantee, car window washing by a gas station, and so on). The factors that serve to differentiate products need not be "real" in any objective or directly measurable sense. For example, differences in packaging or in associated services can and do distinguish products that are otherwise identical. On the other hand, two products may perform quite differently in quality tests, but if consumers know nothing about this difference, it is irrelevant.

Since products under monopolistic competition are not identical, there is no reason to expect the price of any firm's product to remain unchanged when the quantity supplied varies. Each seller, in effect, deals in a market slightly separated from the others and caters to a set of customers who vary in their "loyalty" to his product. If he raises his price somewhat, he may expect to drive some but not all of his customers into the arms of his competitors. If he lowers his price, he may expect to attract some trade from his rivals. But since his product is not a perfect substitute for theirs, if he undercuts them slightly he will not attract away *all* their business as he would in the perfectly competitive case.

Thus, if Harry's Hot Dog House reduces its price slightly, it will attract those customers of Sam's Sausage Shop who were nearly indifferent between the two. A bigger price cut by Harry will bring in some customers who have a slightly greater preference for Sam's product. But even a big cut in Harry's price will not bring him the hard-core sausage lovers who hate hot dogs. So the monopolistic competitor's demand curve is negatively sloped, like that of a monopolist, rather than horizontal, like that of a perfect competitor.

Since his product is distinguished from all others, a monopolistic competitor appears to have something akin to a small monopoly. Can we therefore expect him to earn more than zero economic profit? Like a perfect competitor, perhaps he will in the short run. But in the long run, high economic profits will attract new entrants into a monopolistically competitive market—not entrants with products *identical* to an existing firm's, but with products sufficiently similar to hurt.

If one ice-cream parlor's location enables it to do a thriving business, it can confidently expect another, selling a *different* brand, to open nearby. When one seller adopts a new, attractive package, he can be sure that his rivals will soon follow suit, with a slightly different design and color of their own. In this way freedom of entry ensures that the monopolistically competitive firm earns no higher return on its capital in the long run than it could earn elsewhere. Just as under perfect competition, price will be driven to the level of average cost, including the opportunity cost of capital. In this sense, though its product is somewhat different from that of everyone else, the firm under monopolistic competition has no more monopoly power than one operating under perfect competition.

Let us now examine the process which assures that economic profits will be driven to zero in the long run, even under monopolistic competition.

Price and Output Determination Under Monopolistic Competition

The *short-run* equilibrium of the firm under monopolistic competition differs little from the case of monopoly. Since the firm faces a downward-sloping demand curve (labeled *D* in Figure 28–1), its marginal revenue (MR) curve will lie below its demand curve. Profits are maximized at the output level at which marginal revenue and marginal cost (MC) are equal. In Figure 28–1, the profit-maximizing output for a hypothetical gasoline station is 12,000 gallons per week, and it sells this output at a price of $1.00 per gallon (point *P* on the demand curve).

This diagram, you will note, looks much like Figure 27–2 (page 601) for a monopoly. The only difference is that the demand curve of a monopolistic competitor is likely to be much flatter than the pure monopolist's because there are many close substitutes for the monopolistic competitor's product. If our gas station raises its price to $1.30 per gallon, most of its customers will go across the street. If it lowers its price to $.70, it will have long lines at its pumps.

The gas station depicted in Figure 28–1 is making economic profits. Since average cost at 12,000 gallons per week is only $.90 per gallon (point *C*), the station is making a profit on gasoline sales of 10 cents per gallon, or $1200 per week in total (the shaded rectangle). Under monopoly, such profits can persist. But under monopolistic competition they cannot, because new firms will be attracted into the market. While the new stations will not offer the identical product, they will offer products that are close enough to take away some business from our firm (for example, they may sell Mobil or Shell gasoline instead of Exxon).

When more firms share the market, the demand curve facing any individual must fall. But how far? The answer is basically the same as it was under

Figure 28–1
SHORT-RUN
EQUILIBRIUM OF THE
FIRM UNDER
MONOPOLISTIC
COMPETITION
Like any firm, a monopolistic competitor maximizes profits by equating marginal cost (MC) and marginal revenue (MR). In this example, the profit-maximizing output level is 12,000 gallons per week and the profit-maximizing price is $1.00 per gallon. The firm is making a profit of 10 cents per gallon, which is depicted by the vertical distance from *C* to *P*.

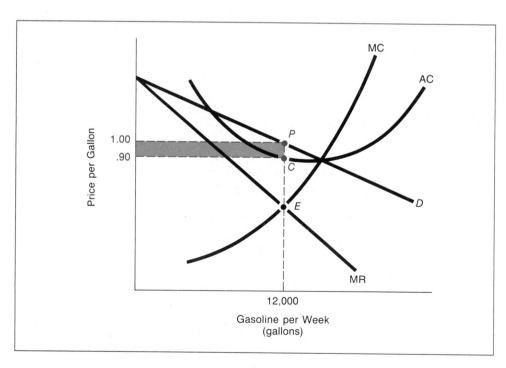

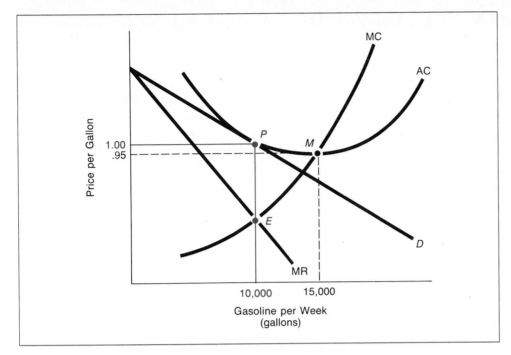

Figure 28–2
LONG-RUN EQUILIBRIUM
OF THE FIRM UNDER
MONOPOLISTIC
COMPETITION
In this diagram the cost
curves are identical to those
of Figure 28–1, but the
demand curve (and hence
also the MR curve) has been
depressed by the entry of
new competitors. When the
firm maximizes profits by
equating marginal revenue
and marginal cost (point E),
its average cost is equal to
its price ($.95), so economic
profits are zero. For this
reason, the diagram depicts
a *long-run* equilibrium
position.

perfect competition: Market entry will cease only when the most that the firm can earn is zero economic profit.

Figure 28–2 depicts the same monopolistically competitive firm as in Figure 28–1 *after* the adjustment to the long run is complete. The demand curve has been pushed down so far that when the firm equates MC and MR in order to maximize profits (point E), it simultaneously equates price (P) and average cost (AC) so that profits are zero (point P). As compared with the short-run equilibrium depicted in Figure 28–1, price in long-run equilibrium is *lower* ($.95 per gallon versus $1.00), there are *more firms* in the industry, and each firm is producing a *smaller* output (10,000 gallons versus 12,000) at a *higher* average cost per gallon ($.95 versus $.90).[2] In general:

Long-run equilibrium under monopolistic competition requires that the firm's demand curve be tangent to its average cost curve.

Why? Because if the two curves intersected, there would be output levels at which price exceeded average cost, which means that economic profits could be earned and there would be an influx of new substitute products. Similarly, if the average cost curve failed to touch the demand curve altogether, the firm would be unable to obtain returns equal to those that its capital can get elsewhere, and firms would leave the industry.

This analysis of entry is quite similar to the perfectly competitive case. Moreover, the notion that firms under monopolistic competition earn exactly zero economic profits seems to correspond fairly well to what we see in the real world. Filling station operators, whose market has the characteristics of monopolistic competition, do not earn notably higher profits than do small farmers, who operate under conditions closer to perfect competition.

[2]*EXERCISE:* Show that if the demand curve fell still further, the firm would incur a loss. What would then happen in the long run?

The Excess Capacity Theorem and Resource Allocation

But there is one important difference between perfect and monopolistic competition. Look at Figure 28–2 again. The tangency point between the average cost and demand curves, point P, occurs along the *negatively sloping portion* of the average cost curve, since only there does the AC curve have the same (negative) slope as the demand curve. If the AC curve is U-shaped, the tangency point must therefore lie above and to the left of the *minimum point* on the average cost curve, point M. By contrast, under perfect competition the firm's demand curve is horizontal, so tangency must take place at the minimum point on the average cost curve, as is easily confirmed by referring back to Figure 25–9(a) on page 570. This observation leads to the following important conclusion:

Under monopolistic competition, the firm in the long run will tend to produce an output lower than that which minimizes its unit costs, and hence unit costs of the monopolistic competitor will be higher than is necessary. Since the level of output corresponding to minimum average cost is naturally considered to be the firm's optimal capacity, this result has been called the **excess capacity theorem of monopolistic competition.**

It follows that if every firm under monopolistic competition were to expand its output, cost per unit of output would be reduced. But we must be careful about jumping to policy conclusions from that observation. It does *not* follow that *every* monopolistically competitive firm *should* produce more. After all, such an overall increase in industry output means that a smaller portion of the economy's resources will be available for other uses; and from the information at hand we have no way of knowing whether that leaves us ahead or behind in terms of social benefits.

Yet the situation represented in Figure 28–2 can still be interpreted to represent a substantial *inefficiency*. While it is not clear that society would gain if *every* firm were to achieve lower costs by expanding its production, society *can* save resources if firms combine into a smaller number of larger companies that produce the same total output. For example, suppose that in the situation shown in Figure 28–2 there are 15 monopolistically competitive firms each selling 10,000 gallons of gas per week. The total cost of this output, according to the figures given in the diagram, would be

$$\text{(Number of firms)} \times \text{(Output per firm)} \times \text{(Cost per unit)}$$
$$= 15 \times 10,000 \times \$.90 = \$135,000.$$

If, instead, the number of stations were cut to 10, and each sold 15,000 gallons, total production would be unchanged. But total costs would fall to $10 \times 15,000 \times \$.80 = \$120,000$, a net saving of \$15,000 *for the same total output.*

This result is not dependent on the particular numbers used in our illustration. It follows directly from the observation that lowering the cost per unit must always reduce the total cost of producing any *given* industry output. The economy must gain in the sense of getting the same total output as before but at a lower cost. After all, which do you prefer—a dozen bottles of soda for 50 cents each or a dozen bottles of soda at 35 cents each?

The excess capacity theorem explains one of the puzzles mentioned at the start of this chapter. The intersection with four filling stations, where two could serve the available customers with little increase in delays and at lower costs, is a practical example of excess capacity.

The excess capacity theorem seems to imply that there are too many sellers in monopolistically competitive markets and that society would benefit from a reduction in their numbers. However, such a conclusion would be a bit hasty. Even if a smaller number of larger firms could reduce costs, society may not benefit from the change because it would leave consumers a smaller range of choice. Since all products are at least slightly different under monopolistic competition, a reduction in the number of firms means that the number of different products falls as well. We achieve greater efficiency at the cost of greater standardization. In some cases consumers may agree that this trade-off represents a net gain, particularly where the variety of products available was initially so great that it only served to confuse them. But for other products, most consumers would probably agree that the diversity of choice is worth the extra cost involved. After all, we would probably save money on clothing if every student were forced to wear the same uniform. But since the uniform is likely to be too hot for student A, too cool for student B, and aesthetically displeasing to everyone, would the cost saving really be a net benefit?

Oligopoly

In terms of the dollar value of all manufactured goods produced in our economy, there seems little doubt that first place must be assigned to our final market form — oligopoly. An *oligopoly* is a market dominated by a few sellers at least several of which are large enough relative to the total market to be able to influence the market price.

An **oligopoly** is a market dominated by a few sellers at least several of which are large enough relative to the total market to be able to influence the market price.

In highly developed economies, it is not monopoly, but oligopoly, that is virtually synonymous with "big business." Any oligopolistic industry includes a group of giant firms, each of which keeps a watchful eye on the actions of the others.[3] It is under oligopoly that rivalry among firms takes its most direct and active form. Here one encounters such actions and reactions as the frequent introduction of new products, free samples, and aggressive — if not downright nasty — advertising campaigns. One firm's price decision is likely to elicit a cry of pain from its rivals, and firms are engaged in a continuing battle in which strategies are planned day by day and each major decision can be expected to induce a direct response.

The manager of a large oligopolistic firm who has occasion to study economics is somewhat taken aback by the notion of perfect competition, because it is devoid of all harsh competitive activity as he knows it. Remember that under perfect competition the managers of firms make no price decisions — they simply accept the price dictated by market forces and adjust their output accordingly. As we observed at the beginning of the chapter, a competitive firm does not advertise; it adopts no sales gimmicks; it does not even know who most of its competitors are. But since oligopolists are not as dependent on market forces, they do not enjoy such luxuries. They worry about prices, spend fortunes on advertising, and try to understand their rivals' behavior patterns.

The reasons for such divergent behavior should be clear. First, a perfectly competitive firm can sell all it wants at the current market price. So why should it waste money on advertising? By contrast, Ford and Chrysler cannot sell all

---

[3]Notice that nothing is said in the definition about the degree of product differentiation. Some oligopolies sell products that are essentially identical (such as steel plate from different steelmakers) while others sell products that are quite different in the eyes of consumers (for example, Chevrolets, Fords, and Plymouths).

the cars they want at the current price. Since their demand curves are negatively sloped, if they want to sell more they must either reduce prices or advertise more (to shift their demand curves outward).

Second, since the public believes that the products supplied by firms in a perfectly competitive industry are identical, if seller A advertises his product, the advertisement is just as likely to bring customers to seller B. Under oligopoly, however, products are usually not identical. Ford advertises to try to convince consumers that its automobiles are better than GM's or Toyota's. And if the advertising campaign succeeds, GM and Toyota will be hurt and probably will respond by more advertising of their own. Thus, it is the firm in an oligopoly with differentiated products that is forced to compete via advertising, while the perfectly competitive firm gains little or nothing by doing so.

Why Oligopolistic Behavior Is So Hard to Analyze

The relative freedom of choice in pricing of at least the largest firms in an oligopolistic industry, and the necessity for them to take direct account of their rivals' responses, are potentially troublesome. Producers that are able to influence the market price may find it expedient to adjust their outputs so as to secure more favorable prices. Just as in the case of monopoly, such actions are likely to be at the expense of the consumer and detrimental to the economy's efficient use of resources.

It is not easy to reach definite conclusions about resource allocation under oligopoly, however. The reason is that oligopoly is much more difficult to analyze than the other forms of economic organization. The difficulty arises from the interdependent nature of oligopolistic decisions. For example, Ford's management knows that its actions will probably lead to reactions by General Motors, which in turn may require a readjustment in Ford's plans, thereby producing a modification in GM's response, and so on. Where such a sequence of moves and countermoves may lead is difficult enough to ascertain. But the fact that Ford executives know all this in advance, and may try to take it into account in making their initial decision, makes even that first step difficult, if not impossible, to analyze and predict.

The truth is that almost anything can happen under oligopoly, and sometimes does. The early railroad kings went so far as to employ gangs of hoodlums who engaged in pitched battles to try to prevent the operation of a rival line. At the other extreme, overt or more subtle forms of collusion have been employed to avoid rivalry altogether—to transform an oligopolistic industry, at least temporarily, into a monopolistic one. Arrangements designed to make it possible for the firms to live and let live have also been utilized: price leadership (see below) is one example; an agreement allocating geographic areas among the different firms is another.

Because of this rich variety of behavior patterns it is not surprising that economists have been unable to agree on a single, widely accepted model of oligopoly behavior. Nor should they. Since oligopolies in the real world are so diverse, oligopoly models in the theoretical world should also come in various shapes and sizes. The theory of oligopoly contains some really remarkable pieces of economic analysis, some of which we will review in the following sections.

A Shopping List

An introductory course cannot hope to explain all the different models of oligopoly; nor would that serve any purpose but to confuse you. Since economists differ in their opinions about which approaches to oligopoly theory are the most interesting and promising, we offer in this section a quick catalogue of some models of oligopolistic behavior. Then, in the remainder of the chapter, we will describe in greater detail a few other models.

Ignore Interdependence

One simple approach to the problem of oligopolistic interdependence is to assume that the oligopolists themselves ignore it; that they behave as if their actions will not elicit reactions from their rivals. It *is* possible that an oligopolist, finding the "if he thinks that I think that he thinks..." chain of reasoning just too complex, will decide to ignore his rivals' behavior. He may then just maximize profits on the assumption that his decisions will not affect those of his rivals. In this case, the analysis of oligopoly is identical to the analysis of monopoly in the previous chapter.

Strategic Interaction

While it is possible that *some* oligopolies ignore interdependence *some* of the time, it is very unlikely that such models offer a general explanation for the behavior of *most* oligopoly behavior *most* of the time. The reason is quite simple. Because they operate in the same market, the price and output decisions of the makers of Brand X and Brand Y soap suds *really are* interdependent. Suppose, for example, that the management of Brand X, Inc., decides to cut its price to $1.05 on the assumption that Brand Y, Inc., will continue to charge $1.12 per box, to manufacture five million boxes per year, and to spend $1 million per year on advertising. It may find itself surprised when Brand Y, Inc., cuts its price to $1 per box, raises production to eight million boxes per year, and sponsors the Super Bowl. If so, Brand X's profits will suffer, and the company will wish it had not cut its price. Most important for our purposes, it will learn not to ignore interdependence in the future. For many oligopolies, then, competition may resemble military operations involving tactics, strategies, moves and countermoves. Thus it seems imperative to consider models that deal explicitly with oligopolistic interdependence. We will study several such models, probably the most notable of them being those provided by the theory of games.

Cartels

The opposite end of the spectrum from ignoring interdependence is for all the firms in an oligopoly to recognize their interdependence and agree to a peace treaty under which they collude overtly with one another, thereby transforming the industry into a giant monopoly—a **cartel.**

A notable example of the formation of a cartel is the Organization of Petroleum Exporting Countries (OPEC), which first began to make decisions in unison in 1973. OPEC, for a while, was one of the most spectacularly successful cartels in history. By restricting output, the member nations managed to quadruple the price of oil in 1973–1974. Then, unlike most cartels, which come apart in internal bickering or for other reasons, OPEC held together through two worldwide recessions and a variety of unsettling political events, and struck again with huge price increases in 1979–1980. Only in the mid-1980s did it run into trouble.

But the story of OPEC is not the norm. Cartels are not easy to organize and are even more difficult to preserve. Firms find it hard to agree on such things as the amount by which each will reduce its output in order to help push up the price. For a cartel to survive, each member must agree to produce no

A **cartel** is a group of sellers of a product who have joined together to control its production, sale, and price in the hope of obtaining the advantages of monopoly.

more than the level of output that has been assigned to it by the group. Yet once price is driven up and profitability is increased, it becomes tempting for each seller to offer secret discounts in order to lure some of the profitable business away from other members of the cartel. (Indeed, some of this happened to OPEC in the early 1980s.) When this happens, or is even suspected by cartel members, it is often the beginning of the end of the collusive arrangement. Each member begins suspecting the others and is tempted to cut price first, before the others beat him to the punch.

Cartels, therefore, usually adopt elaborate policing arrangements, in effect spying on each member firm to make sure it does not sell more than it is supposed to or shave the price below that chosen by the cartel. This means that cartels are unlikely to succeed or to last very long if the firms sell many varied products whose prices are difficult to compare and whose outputs are difficult to keep track of. In addition, if prices are frequently negotiated on a customer-by-customer basis, and special discounts are common, a cartel may be almost impossible to arrange.

Many economists consider cartels to be one of the least desirable forms of market organization. If a cartel is successful, it may end up charging the monopoly price and obtaining monopoly profits. But because the firms do not actually combine their operations but continue to produce separately, the cartel offers the public no offsetting benefits in the form of economies of large-scale production. For these and other reasons, open collusion among firms is illegal in the United States, as we will see in Chapter 32, and outright cartel arrangements are rarely found. (However, in many other countries cartels are common.) There is only one major exception in the United States: regulated industries such as telecommunications and oil pipeline transportation, which the government sometimes forces to behave as a cartel would, never charging prices lower than those the regulatory agency sets. This exception will be discussed in Chapter 31.

Price Leadership

Though overt collusion is quite rare, some observers think that *tacit collusion* is quite common among oligopolists in our economy. Oligopolists who do not want to rock what amounts to a very profitable boat may seek to develop some indirect way of communicating with one another and signaling their intentions. Each tacitly colluding firm hopes that if it behaves in a way that does not make things too difficult for its competitors, then its rivals will return the favor.

One common example of tacit collusion is **price leadership,** an arrangement in which one firm in the industry is, in effect, assigned the task of making pricing decisions for the entire group. It is expected that other firms will adopt the prices set by the price leader, even though there is no explicit agreement, only tacit consent. Typically, the price leader will be the dominant firm in the industry. But in some price-leadership arrangements the role of leader may rotate from one firm to another. For example, it has been suggested that the steel industry for many years conformed to the price leadership model, with U.S. Steel and Bethlehem Steel assuming the role of leader at different times.

Price leadership *does* overcome the problem of oligopolistic interdependence, though it is not the only possible way of doing so. If Brand X, Inc., is the price leader for the soap suds industry, it can predict how Brand Y, Inc., will react to any price increases it announces. (Brand Y will match the increases.) Similarly, Brand Z executives will be able to predict Brand Y's behavior as long as the price-leadership arrangement holds up.

Under **price leadership,** one firm sets the price for the industry and the others follow.

But one problem besetting price leadership is that, while the oligopolists as a group may benefit by avoiding a damaging **price war,** one of them may benefit more than the others. The firm that is the price leader is clearly in a better position to maximize its own profits than are any of the rival firms, which must simply fall in line. It is thus the responsibility of the price leader to take into account its rivals' welfare when making its price decision—or else it may find itself dethroned! For this reason, a price-leadership arrangement, if effective, can lead to the same sort of price and production decisions as would a cartel. Alternatively, leadership can break down entirely.

Sales Maximization*

Early in our analysis of the theory of the firm, we discussed the hypothesis that firms try to maximize profits and noted that other objectives are possible (see pages 534–35). Among these alternative goals, the one that has achieved the most attention is **sales maximization.**

Modern industrial firms are managed and owned by entirely different groups of people. The managers are paid executives who work for the company on a full-time basis and may grow to identify their own welfare with that of the company. The owners may be a large and diffuse group of stockholders, most of whom own only a tiny fraction of the outstanding stock, take little interest in the operations of the company, and do not feel that the company is "theirs" in any real sense. In such a situation, it is not entirely implausible that the company's decisions will be influenced more heavily by management's goals than by the goal of the owners (which is, presumably, to maximize profit).

It has been suggested, for example, that management's salary and prestige may be tied more directly to the company's *size*, as measured by its sales volume, rather than to its *profits*. Therefore, the firm's managers may select a price–output combination that maximizes sales rather than profits. But does sales maximization lead to different decisions than does profit maximization? We shall see now that the answer is yes.

Figure 28–3 is a diagram that should be familiar by now. It shows the marginal cost (MC) and average cost (AC) curves for a firm—in this case Brand X, Inc.—along with its demand and marginal revenue (MR) curves. We have used such diagrams before and know that if the company wants to maximize profits, it will select point A, where MC = MR. This means that it will produce 2.5 million boxes of soap suds per year and sell them at a price of $1 each (point E). Since average cost at this level of output is only 80 cents per box, profit per unit is 20 cents. Total profits are therefore $.20 × 2,500,000 = $500,000 per year. This is the highest attainable profit level for Brand X, Inc.

Now what if Brand X wants to maximize sales revenue instead? In this case, it will want to keep producing until MR is depressed to *zero*; that is, it will select point B. Why? By definition, MR is the *additional* revenue obtained by raising output by one unit. If the firm wishes to maximize revenue, then any time it finds that MR is positive it will want to increase output further, and any time it finds that MR is negative it will want to decrease output. Only when MR = 0 can the maximum sales revenue have possibly been achieved.[4]

Thus if Brand X, Inc., is a sales maximizer, it will produce 3.75 million boxes of soap suds per year (point B), and charge 75 cents per box (point F).

In a **price war** each competing firm is determined to sell at a price that is lower than the prices of its rivals, usually regardless of whether that price covers the pertinent cost. Typically, in such a price war firm A cuts its price below Firm B's; then B retaliates by undercutting A, and so on and on until one or more of the firms surrender and let themselves be undersold.

---

*The three sections that follow may be read in any combination, and in any order, without loss of continuity.
[4]The logic here is exactly the same as the logic that led to the conclusion that a firm maximized *profits* by setting *marginal profit* equal to zero. If you need review, consult Chapter 24, especially pages 539–41.

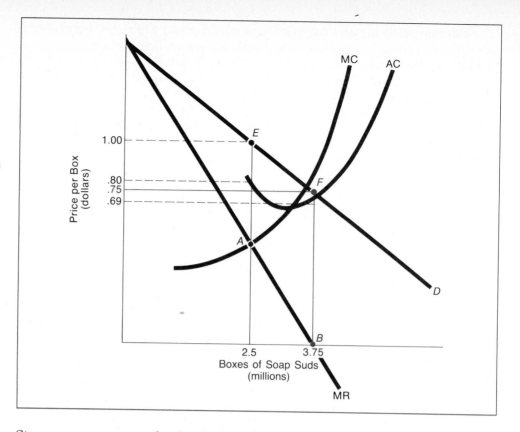

Figure 28–3

SALES-MAXIMIZATION
EQUILIBRIUM

A firm that wishes to maximize sales revenue will expand output until marginal revenue (MR) is zero—point B in the diagram, where output is 3.75 million boxes per year. This is a greater output level than it would choose if it were interested in maximizing profits. In that case, it would select point A, where MC = MR, and produce only 2.5 million boxes. Since the demand curve is downward sloping, the price corresponding to point B (75 cents) must be less than the price corresponding to point A ($1).

Since average costs at this level of production are only 69 cents per box, profit per unit is 6 cents and, with 3.75 million units sold, total profit is $225,000. Naturally, this level of profit is less than what the firm can achieve if it reduces output to the profit-maximizing level. But this is not the firm's goal. Its sales revenue at point B is 75 cents per unit times 3.75 million units, or $2,812,500, whereas at point A it was only $2,500,000 (2.5 million units at $1 each). What we conclude, then, is that:

If a firm is maximizing sales revenue, it will produce more output and charge a lower price than it would if it were maximizing profits.

We see clearly in Figure 28–3 that this result holds for Brand X, Inc. But does it always hold? The answer is yes. Look again at Figure 28–3, but ignore the numbers on the axes. At point A, where MR = MC, marginal revenue must be positive because it is equal to marginal cost (which, we may assume, is *always* positive). At point B, MR is equal to zero. Since the marginal revenue curve is negatively sloped, the point where it reaches zero (point B) must necessarily correspond to a higher level of output than the point where it cuts the marginal cost curve (point A). Thus, sales-maximizing firms always produce more than profit-maximizing firms and, to sell this greater volume of output, they must charge a lower price.

The Game-Theory Approach

Game theory, contributed in 1944 by mathematician John von Neumann (1903–1957) and economist Oskar Morgenstern (1902–1977), adopts a more imaginative approach than any other analysis of oligopoly. It attacks the issue of interdependence directly by assuming that each firm's managers proceed on the assumption *that their rivals are extremely ingenious decision makers*. In this model, each oligopolist is seen as a competing player in a game of strategy. Since managers believe their opponents will always adopt the most profitable countermove to any move they make, they seek the optimal defensive strategy.

Two fundamental concepts of game theory are the *strategy* and the *payoff matrix*. A strategy represents an operational plan for one of the participants. In its simplest form it may refer to just one of a participant's possible decisions. For example, "I will add to my product line a car with a TV set that the driver can watch," or "I will cut the price of my car to $5500." Since much of the game-theory analysis of oligopoly has focused on an oligopoly of two firms—a *duopoly*—we illustrate the payoff matrix for a two-person game in Table 28–1.

This matrix is a table of numbers reporting the payoffs that our firm will receive for each possible pair of its own and its rival's strategies. It is read like a mileage chart. For example, if our firm selects strategy B (cut price to $5500) and its rival chooses W (offer diesel engine), we see that our company will end up with 70 percent of the market (third column, second row). The special case of pure rivalry, in which every gain for our firm means an *exactly* equal loss for its competitor, and vice versa, is referred to as a *zero-sum game*. In the zero-sum case, the payoff matrix has the convenient property of telling us all we need to know about our competitor's payoff matrix as well as our own. Given the market share of one firm, we can immediately deduce the other firm's market share by subtraction. For example, if the matrix tells us that our firm's market share will be 70 percent, we know that the rival's market share must be 30 percent.

We can now begin to discuss optimal strategy choices for the two firms. Since our firm is in direct conflict with the other firm, we know that our rival will try to keep our market share as low as possible, and vice versa. Thus, in evaluating its strategies, the management of our firm may reason as follows: "If I select strategy A, the worst that can happen to me is that my adversary will select counterstrategy W, which would cut my market share to its minimum level, 30 percent (the blue number in the first row of the payoff matrix). Similarly, if I utilize strategy B, the outcome I must be prepared for is 28 percent, which is the (blue) minimum payoff to that strategy. Finally, if I use strategy C, my rival can damage me most by using strategy V, which gives me 50 percent."

What, if anything, can the management of our firm do to maximize its chances for success? Game theory suggests that it should select the strategy whose *minimum* payoff is higher than the minimum payoff for any other

Table 28–1
A PAYOFF MATRIX

	Rival's Strategy		
	U: Set Price at $6000	V: Set Price at $5000	W: Offer Diesel Engine
A: Install TV set	80	35	30
B: Cut price to $5500	45	28	70
C: Offer three-year loan	60	50	90

The entries represent the share of market our firm will receive under any combination of strategies offered by itself and its competitor.

At the Frontier: Game Theory and Entry Deterrence

Game theory continues to yield valuable insights, as researchers working on the analysis of oligopoly use it in their work. An example is the game theory model of strategic decisions by firms already inside an industry ("old firms") whose primary purpose is to prevent the entry of new rivals ("new firms"). One way in which this can be done is for the old firm to build a bigger factory than it would want to construct otherwise, in the belief that the output of the excessive factory capacity will force prices down and in the process make entry unprofitable. By doing so, the old firm may recognize that it, too, gives up some profit, compared to what it would earn if no new firm even threatened to enter. However, the old firm hopes nevertheless that it will be better off than if entry did occur.

Some hypothetical numbers and a graph typical of those used in game theory will make the story clear. There are two options for the old firm: to build a small factory or a big one. There are also two options for the potential new firm: to open for business (that is, to enter) or not to enter. The accompanying table shows the four resulting combinations of decisions that are possible and the accompanying profits or losses the two firms may expect in each case.

The table shows (line 1) that the best arrangement of all for the old firm is one in which it builds a small factory and the new firm decides not to enter. For in that case the old firm will earn $6 million while the new firm (since it never starts up) will earn zero. However, (line 2) if the old firm does decide to build a small factory, it can be pretty sure the new firm *will* open up for business because then that new firm will earn $2 million (rather than zero), and in the process it will reduce the old firm's profits to $2 million.

On the other hand, if the old firm selects its other option and builds a big factory, the increased output will depress prices and profits. The old firm will now earn only $4 million if the new firm stays out while *each* firm will *lose* $2 million (line 4) if the new firm enters. Obviously, if the old firm builds a big factory, the new firm will be better off staying out of the business rather than subjecting itself to a $2 million loss.

What size factory, then, will it pay the old firm to build? When we consider the matter it becomes clear that it will be profitable for the old firm to build the large factory with its excessive capacity. For then it can expect the new firm to stay out so that the big factory will enable the old firm to earn $4 million. In contrast, if a small factory is built the new firm will open for business and reduce the old firm's profit to $2 million.

Thus, if we take the new firm's strategic choices into account, it is obvious that it would pay the old firm to build the oversized factory and take the $4 million in profits it would earn by deterring the other firm from entering.

The accompanying figure illustrates the possible choices.

Possible Decisions		Profits (millions of dollars)	
for old firm	for new firm	old firm	new firm
1) small factory	don't enter	6	0
2) small factory	enter	2	2
3) big factory	don't enter	4	0
4) big factory	enter	-2	-2

This graph shows the possible choices of an old firm and the possible responses of a potential entrant. If the old firm builds a big factory the entrant will avoid $2 million in losses by staying out of the business, leaving the old firm with $4 million in profit (asterisk lines). On the other hand, with a small factory the new firm will enter the business (dashed lines) so the old firm would be worse off, with only $2 million in profit.

Possible Choices of Old Firm	Possible Reactions of New Firm	Profits	
		Old Firm	New Firm
Big Factory	Enter	-2	-2
	Don't enter	4	0
Small Factory	Enter	2	2
	Don't enter	6	0

strategy. This is called the **maximin criterion** — one seeks the *max*imum of the *min*imum payoffs to the various strategies, the highest of the blue entries. In this case, the maximin payoff is 50 percent and leads to the choice of strategy C by our firm (and V by its adversary).

The **maximin criterion** means selecting the strategy that yields the maximum payoff, on the assumption that your opponent does as much damage to you as he can.

There is, of course, a great deal more to game theory than we have been able to suggest in a few paragraphs. We have only sought to suggest a little of its flavor. Game theory provides, for example, an illuminating analysis of coalitions, indicating, for cases involving more than two firms, which firms would do well to align themselves together against which others. The theory of games has also been used to analyze a variety of complicated problems outside the realm of oligopoly theory. It has been employed in management training programs and by a number of government agencies. It is used in political science and in formulating military strategy. It has been presented here to offer the reader a glimpse of the type of work that is taking place on the frontiers of economic analysis and to suggest how economists think about complex analytical problems.

The Kinked Demand Curve Model[5]

As our final example of oligopoly analysis, we describe a model designed to account for the alleged stickiness in oligopolistic pricing, meaning that prices in oligopolistic markets change far less frequently than do prices in competitive markets. It will be recalled that this is one of the puzzling phenomena with which we began this chapter. The prices of corn, soybeans, cocoa, and silver, all of which are sold in markets with large numbers of buyers and sellers, change minute by minute. But prices of such items as cars, TV sets, and dishwashers, all of which are supplied by oligopolists, may change only every few months. These prices seem to resist frequent change even in periods of inflation.

One reason may be that, when an oligopolist cuts his price, he is never sure how his rivals will react. One extreme possibility is that Firm Y will ignore the price cut of Firm X, that is, Y's price will not change. Alternatively, Y may reduce its price, precisely matching that of Firm X. Accordingly, the model makes use of two different demand curves: one curve represents the quantities a given oligopolistic firm can sell at different prices *if competitors match its price moves*, and the other demand curve represents what happens when competitors stubbornly *stick to their initial price levels*.

Point A in Figure 28–4 represents the initial price and output of our firm: 1000 units at $10 each. Through that point pass two demand curves: *DD*, which represents our company's demand if competitors keep their prices fixed, and *dd*, the curve indicating what happens when competitors match our firm's price changes.

The *DD* curve is the more elastic (flatter) of the two, and a moment's thought indicates why this should be so. If our firm cuts its price from its initial level of $10 to, say, $8, and if competitors do not match this cut, we would expect our firm to get a large number of new customers — perhaps its quantity demanded will jump to 1400. However, if its competitors respond by also reducing their prices, its quantity demanded will rise by less — perhaps only to 1100. Conversely, when it raises its price, our firm may expect a larger loss of sales if

[5]Variants of this model were constructed by Hall and Hitch in England and by Sweezy in the United States. See R. L. Hall and C. J. Hitch, "Price Theory and Business Behavior," *Oxford Economic Papers*, No. 2, May 1939, and P. M. Sweezy, "Demand Under Conditions of Oligopoly," *Journal of Political Economy*, vol. 47, August 1939.

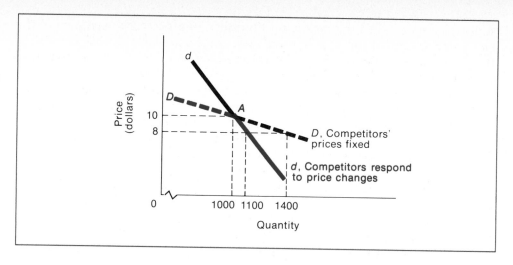

Figure 28–4
THE KINKED
DEMAND CURVE
It has been suggested that oligopolists are deterred from changing prices frequently because they fear the reactions of their rivals. If they raise prices they will lose many customers to competitors because the competitors will not match the price increase. (Elastic demand curve *DD* therefore applies to price increases.) But if they cut prices, competitors will be forced to match the price cut so that price cut will not bring many new customers. (The inelastic demand curve *dd* applies to price cuts.) Thus, the demand curve facing the firm is the kinked, blue curve *DAd*.

its rivals fail to match its increase, which the reader may readily verify by observing the relative steepness (inelasticity) of the curve *dd* in Figure 28–4.

How does this relate to sticky oligopolistic prices? Here our firm's fears and expectations must be brought into the matter. The hypothesis of those who designed this model was that a typical oligopolistic firm has good reason to fear the worst. If it lowers its prices and its rivals do not, its sales will seriously cut into its competitor's volume, and so the rivals will *have* to match the price cut in order to protect themselves. The inelastic demand curve, *dd*, will therefore apply if our firm decides on a price reduction (points below and to the right of point *A*).

On the other hand, if our company chooses to *increase* its price, management will fear that its rivals will continue to sit at their old price levels, calmly collecting the customers that have been driven to them. Thus, the relevant demand curve for price increases will be *DD*.

In sum, our firm will figure that it will face a segment of the elastic demand curve *DD* if it raises its price and a segment of the inelastic demand curve *dd* if it decreases its price. Its true demand curve will then be given by the heavy blue line. For obvious reasons, this is called a **kinked demand curve.**

In these circumstances, it will pay management to vary its price only under extreme provocation, that is, only if there is an enormous change in costs. For the kinked demand curve represents a "heads you lose, tails you lose" proposition in terms of any potential price change. If it raises its price, the firm will lose many customers (demand is elastic); if it lowers its price, the increase in volume will be comparatively small (demand is inelastic).

Figure 28–5 illustrates this conclusion graphically. The two demand curves, *dd* and *DD*, are carried over precisely from the previous diagram. The dashed curve, labeled MR, is the marginal revenue curve associated with *DD*, while the solid curve, labeled mr, is the marginal revenue curve associated with *dd*. Since the marginal revenue curve relevant to the firm's decision making is MR for any output level *below* 1000 units but mr for any output level *above* 1000 units, the composite marginal revenue curve facing the firm is shown by the thin blue line.

The marginal cost curve drawn in the diagram cuts this composite marginal revenue curve at point *E*, which indicates the profit-maximizing combination of output and price for this oligopolist. Specifically, the quantity supplied at point *E* is 1000 units, and the price is $10, which we read from curve *DAd*.

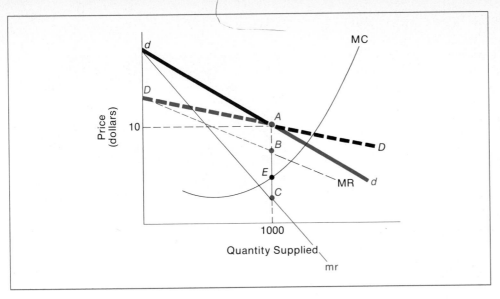

Figure 28–5
THE KINKED DEMAND
CURVE AND STICKY
PRICES
The kinked demand curve
DAd that we derived in the
previous diagram leads to a
marginal revenue curve that
follows MR down to point B
then drops directly down to
point C, and finally follows mr
thereafter. Consequently,
marginal cost curves a little
higher or a little lower than
the MC curve shown in the
diagram will lead to the same
price–output decision.
Oligopoly prices are "sticky,"
then, in the sense that they
do not respond to minor
changes in costs. Only cost
changes large enough to
push the MC curve out of the
range BC will lead to a
change in price.

The unique aspect of this diagram is that the kinked demand curve leads to a marginal revenue curve that takes a sharp plunge between points B and C. Consequently, moderate upward or downward shifts of the MC curve will still leave it intersecting the marginal revenue curve somewhere between B and C, and thus will *not* lead the firm to change its price–output decision. (Try this for yourself in Figure 28–5.) This is the sense in which the kinked demand curve makes prices "sticky."

If this is in fact the way oligopolists feel about their competitors' behavior, it is easy to see why they may be reluctant to make frequent price changes. We can also understand why a system of price leadership might arise. The price leader can, in times of inflation for instance, raise prices when he thinks it appropriate, confident that he will not be left out on a limb (a kink?) by others' unwillingness to follow.

Monopolistic Competition, Oligopoly, and Public Welfare

How good or bad, from the viewpoint of the general welfare, is the performance of firms that are monopolistically competitive or oligopolistic?

We have seen that their performance *can* leave much to be desired. For example, the excess capacity theorem showed us that monopolistic competition can lead to inefficiently high production costs. Similarly, because market forces may not be sufficiently powerful to restrain their behavior, oligopolists' prices and outputs may differ substantially from those that are socially optimal. Moreover, there are those who believe that misleading advertising by corporate giants often distorts the judgments of consumers, leading them to buy things they do not need and would otherwise not want. It is said that such corporate giants wield political power, economic power, and power over the minds of consumers—and that all of these undermine the beneficent workings of Smith's invisible hand.[6]

But because oligopoly behavior is so varied, we cannot generalize with confidence. Because one oligopolist decides on price, output, and advertising in a manner very different from another, the implications for social welfare vary from case to case.

[6]See, for example, the discussion of Galbraith in Chapter 41.

The New Theory of Contestable Markets

Perfect competition has long been used as a standard for the structure and behavior of an industry, though it is widely recognized to be unattainable in reality, except in a few activities such as agriculture. Recently, some economists have tried to supplement this concept with the aid of a generalized criterion, called a *perfectly contestable market*. Some markets which contain a few relatively large firms are highly contestable, though they are certainly not perfectly competitive. Because perfect competition requires a large number of firms, all of them negligible in size relative to the size of the industry, no industry with economies of large-scale production can be perfectly competitive.

A market is defined as perfectly contestable if firms can enter it and, if they choose, exit without losing the money they invested. Note that the crucial issue is not the amount of capital that is required to enter the industry, but whether or not an entrant can get his investment out if he wishes—whether that expenditure is a *sunk* cost. For example, if entry involves investing in highly mobile capital—such as airplanes, barges, or trucks—the entrant may be able to exit quickly and cheaply. If an airline enters the St. Louis–Denver route and finds business disappointing, it can easily transfer its airplanes to, say, the Chicago–Los Angeles route.

A profitable market which is contestable is therefore attractive to *potential* entrants. Because of the absence of barriers to entry or exit, firms undertake little risk by going into such a market. If their entry turns out to have been a mistake, they can move to another market without loss.

Contestable Markets' Performance

The constant threat of entry elicits good performance by oligopolists, or even by monopolists, in a contestable market. In particular, highly contestable markets have at least two desirable characteristics.

First, profits exceeding the opportunity cost of capital are eliminated in the long run by freedom of entry, just as they are in a perfectly competitive market. If the current opportunity cost of capital is 12 percent while the firms in a contestable market are earning a return of 18 percent,

new firms will enter the market, expand the industry's outputs, and drive down the prices of its products to the point where all excess profit has been removed. To avoid this outcome, established firms must expand output to a level that precludes excess profit.

Second, inefficient enterprises cannot survive in a perfectly contestable industry because cost inefficiencies invite replacement of the incumbents by entrants who can provide the same outputs at lower cost and lower prices. Only firms operating at the lowest possible cost, using the most efficient techniques, can survive.

In sum, firms in a perfectly contestable market will be forced to operate as efficiently as possible, and to charge as low prices as long-run financial survival permits. Though first published only a few years ago, these ideas are already widely used by courts and government agencies concerned with the performance of business firms. For they provide workable guidelines for improved or acceptable behavior in industries in which economies of scale mean that only a small number of firms can or should operate.

How many industries in reality approximate perfect contestability? No one knows yet, because only a few industries have so far been studied with this issue in mind. But even for a market which is far from contestable the analysis can be useful. This is so because if the government decides the industry needs regulation to prevent it from behaving like a monopoly, contestable markets provide a model of good behavior for regulation to try to achieve. All this is discussed in Chapter 31.

Yet, recent analysis has provided one case in which both the behavior and the quality of performance of an oligopolistic or monopolistically competitive firm can be predicted and judged. This is the case in which entry into or exit from the market is costless and unimpeded. In such a case, called a **perfectly contestable market** (see the accompanying boxed insert), the constant threat of entry forces even the largest firm to behave well—to produce efficiently and never to overcharge. For if that firm is inefficient, or sets its prices too high, it will be threatened with replacement by an entrant.

A market is **perfectly contestable** if entry and exit are costless and unimpeded.

Of course, many industries are not perfectly contestable or even nearly so. But in those industries which are highly contestable—that is, in which entry and exit costs are negligible—market forces can do a good job of forcing business to behave in the manner that most effectively promotes the public interest. And where an industry is not very contestable, but there are ways to reduce entry and exit costs, the new theory of contestable markets suggests that this may sometimes be a more promising approach than any attempt by government to interfere with the behavior of the oligopolistic firms in order to improve their performance.

Summary

1. Under monopolistic competition, there are numerous small buyers and sellers; each firm's product is at least somewhat different from every other firm's product—that is, each firm has a partial "monopoly" of some product characteristics, and thus a downward-sloping demand curve; there is freedom of entry and exit; and there is perfect information.

2. In long-run equilibrium under monopolistic competition, free entry eliminates economic profits by forcing the firm's demand curve into a position of tangency with its average cost curve. Therefore, output will be below the point at which average cost is lowest. This is why monopolistic competitors are said to have "excess capacity."

3. An oligopolistic industry is composed of a few large firms selling similar products in the same market.

4. Under oligopoly, each firm carefully watches the major decisions of its rivals and will often plan counterstrategies. As a result, rivalry is often vigorous and direct, and the outcome is difficult to predict.

5. One model of oligopoly behavior assumes that the oligopolists ignore interdependence and simply maximize profits or sales. Another assumes that they join together to form a cartel and thus act like a monopoly. A third possibility is price leadership, where one firm sets prices and the others follow suit. A fourth is that each firm might assume that its rivals will adopt the optimal countermove to any move it makes.

6. A firm that maximizes sales will continue producing up to the point where marginal revenue is driven down to zero. Consequently, a sales maximizer will produce more than a profit maximizer and will charge a lower price.

7. Game theory provides new tools for analyzing business strategies under conditions of oligopoly.

8. If a firm thinks that its rivals will match any price cut but fail to match any price increase, its demand curve becomes "kinked" and its price will be sticky—that is, it will be adjusted less frequently than would be the case under either perfect competition or pure monopoly.

9. Monopolistic competition and oligopoly can be harmful to the general welfare. But if the market is perfectly contestable, that is, if entry and exit are easy and costless, the threat of entry will lead to optimal performance.

Concepts for Review

Monopolistic competition
Excess capacity theorem
Oligopoly
Oligopolistic interdependence

Cartel
Price leadership
Sales maximization
Game theory

Maximin criterion
Kinked demand curve
Sticky price
Perfectly contestable markets

Questions for Discussion

1. How many real industries can you name that are oligopolies? How many that operate under monopolistic competition? Perfect competition? Which of these is hardest to find in reality? Why do you think this is so?

2. Consider some of the products that are widely advertised on TV. By what kind of firm is each produced—a perfectly competitive firm, an oligopolistic firm, or what? How many major products can you think of that are *not* advertised on TV?

3. In what ways may the small retail sellers of the following products differentiate their goods from those of their rivals to make themselves monopolistic competitors: hamburgers, radios, cosmetics?

4. Pricing of securities on the stock market is said to be done under conditions in many respects similar to perfect competition. The auto industry is an oligopoly. How often do you think the price of a share of Ford Motor Company's common stock changes? How about the price of a Ford Pinto? How would you explain the difference?

5. Suppose Chrylser hires a popular singer to advertise its compact automobiles. The campaign is very successful and the company increases its share of the compact-car market substantially. What is Ford likely to do?

6. Using game theory, set up a payoff matrix similar to one Chrysler's management might employ in analyzing the problem presented in Question 5.

7. Discussion Question 4 at the end of Chapter 27 presented cost and demand data for a monopolist, and asked you to find the profit-maximizing solution. Use these same data to find the sales-maximizing solution. Are the answers different? Explain.

8. Can you think of any aspects of the behavior of some particular oligopolistic firm that in your view is not in the public interest?

9. Do all oligopoly firms behave in the ways described in your answer to Question 8?

10. A new entrant, Bargain Airways, cuts air fares between Eastwich and Westwich by 20 percent. Biggie Airlines, which has been operating on this route, responds by cutting fares by 35 percent. What does Biggie hope to achieve?

11. If air transportation is perfectly contestable, why will Biggie fail to achieve the ultimate goal of its price cut?

12. Which of the following industries are most likely to be contestable?
    a. Aluminum production.
    b. Barge transportation.
    c. Automobile manufacturing.
    d. Air transportation.
    Explain your answers.

29

The Market Mechanism: Shortcomings and Remedies

When she was good
She was very, very good,
But when she was bad she
was horrid.

HENRY WADSWORTH
LONGFELLOW

What does the market do well, and what does it do poorly? These questions constitute the central theme of our study of microeconomics and we are by now well on our way toward getting some answers. We began in Chapters 25 and 26 by explaining and extolling the workings of Adam Smith's invisible hand—the mechanism by which a perfectly competitive economy allocates resources efficiently without any guidance from government. While the theoretical model studied there was an idealized one, observation of the real world confirms the accomplishments of the market mechanism. Free-market economies have achieved levels of output, productive efficiency, variety in available consumer goods, and general prosperity that are unprecedented in history.

Yet the market mechanism also displays some glaring weaknesses. One of these—the fact that large and powerful business firms can interfere with the invisible hand and lead both to concentrations of wealth and to misallocation of resources—was the subject of Chapters 27 and 28. Now we take a more comprehensive view of the failures of the market and some of the things that can be done to remedy these failures.

That the market cannot do everything we would like it to do is quite apparent. Amid the outpouring of goods and services, we find areas of depressing poverty, cities choked with traffic and pollution, and educational institutions and artistic organizations in serious financial trouble. Our economy, although capable of yielding an overwhelming abundance of material wealth, seems far less capable of eradicating social ills and controlling environmental damage. In this chapter, we will examine the reasons for the market's failings in these areas and indicate specifically why the price system *by itself* may be incapable of dealing with them.

What Does the Market Do Poorly?

While it is probably impossible to come up with an exhaustive list of the imperfections of the market mechanism, we can identify seven major areas in which the market has been accused of failing:

1. Market economies suffer from severe business fluctuations.

2. The market distributes income quite unequally.

3. Where markets are monopolized, they allocate resources inefficiently.

4. The market cannot deal properly with the incidental side effects of many economic activities.

5. The market cannot provide public goods, such as national defense.

6. The market mechanism makes public and personal services increasingly expensive, thereby handicapping their supply, particularly when financed by government.

7. The market does a poor job of allocating resources between the present and the future.

The first three of these issues — business fluctuations, income inequality, and monopoly — have already been discussed or will be discussed in detail later.

The remaining four items on our list constitute the subject matter of this chapter. Each of these, like monopoly, is an instance in which the efficiency of the market mechanism is compromised. Therefore, to help us analyze these problems, we offer next a brief review of the concept of efficient resource allocation, which was discussed in detail in Chapter 26.

Efficient Resource Allocation: A Review

The basic problem of resource allocation is deciding how much of each commodity the economy should produce. At first glance, it may seem that the solution is simple: the more the better; so we should produce as much of each good as we can. But careful thinking tells us that this is not necessarily the right decision.

Outputs are not created out of thin air. They are produced from the available supplies of labor, fuel, raw materials, and machinery. And if we use these resources to produce, say, more handkerchiefs, we must take them away from some other products, such as linens. So, to decide whether increasing the production of handkerchiefs is a good idea, we must compare the utility of that increase with the loss of utility caused by having to produce less hospital linen. The increased output will be a good thing only if society considers the additional handkerchiefs more valuable than the forgone hospital linen.

Opportunity Cost and Resource Allocation
Here it is worth remembering the concept of *opportunity cost*, one of our **12 Ideas for Beyond the Final Exam.** The opportunity cost of an increase in the output of some product is the value of the other goods and services that must be forgone when inputs (resources) are taken away from their production in order to increase the output of the product in question. In our example, the opportunity cost of the increased handkerchief output is the decrease in output of hospital linen that results when resources are reallocated from the latter to the former. The general principle is that an increase in some output represents a *misallocation* of resources if the utility of that increased output is less than its opportunity cost.

To illustrate this idea, we repeat a graph encountered several times in earlier chapters — a *production possibilities frontier* — but we put it to a somewhat different use. Curve ABC in Figure 29–1 is a production possibilities frontier

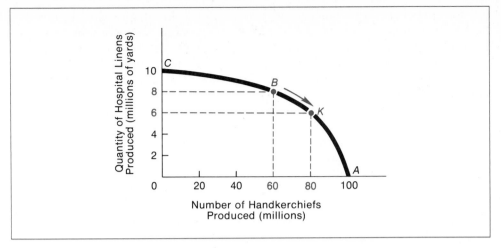

Figure 29–1
THE ECONOMY'S
PRODUCTION
POSSIBILITIES FRONTIER
FOR THE PRODUCTION
OF TWO GOODS
This graph shows
combinations of outputs of
the two goods that the
economy can produce with
the resources available to it.
If *B* is the most desired
output combination among
those that are possible, it will
correspond to a market
equilibrium in which each
good's price is equal to its
marginal cost. If the price of
linen is above its marginal
cost, or the price of a
handkerchief is below its
marginal cost, then linen
output will be inefficiently
small and handkerchief
output inefficiently large
(point *K*).

showing the alternative combinations of handkerchiefs and hospital linens the
economy can produce by reallocating its resources between the production of
the two goods. For example, point A amounts to allocation of all the resources
to handkerchief production, so that 100 million of these items and no hospital
linens are produced. Point C represents the reverse situation, with all resources
allocated to hospital linens and none to handkerchiefs. Point B represents an
intermediate allocation, resulting in the production of eight million yards of
linen and 60 million handkerchiefs.

Suppose now that point B represents the *optimal* resource allocation — that
is, the only combination of outputs that best satisfies the wants of society
among all the possibilites that are *attainable* (given the technology and resources
as represented by the production frontier). Two questions are pertinent to our
discussion of the price system:

1. What prices will get the economy to select point B; that is, what prices will
   yield an *efficient* allocation of resources?
2. How can the wrong set of prices lead to a misallocation of resources?

The first question was discussed extensively in Chapter 26. There we saw
that:

An efficient allocation of resources requires that each product's price be equal
to its marginal cost; that is:

$$P = MC.$$

The reasoning, in brief, is as follows. In a free market, the price of any
good reflects the money value to consumers of an additional unit; that is, its
marginal utility (MU). Similarly, if the market mechanism is working well, the
marginal cost (MC) measures the value (the opportunity cost) of the resources
needed to produce an additional unit of the good. Hence, if prices are set equal
to marginal costs, then consumers, by using *their own money* in the most effective way to maximize *their own* satisfaction, will automatically be using *society's
resources* in the most effective way. That is, as long as it sets prices equal to
marginal costs, the market mechanism automatically satisfies the MC = MU

rule for efficient resource allocation that we studied in Chapter 26.[1] In terms of Figure 29–1, this means that if $P = $ MC for both goods, the economy will automatically gravitate to point B, which we assumed to be the optimal point.

This chapter is devoted mainly to the second question: How can the "wrong" prices cause a misallocation of resources? The answer to this question is not too difficult, and we can use the case of monopoly as an illustration.

The "law" of demand tells us that a rise in the price of a commodity normally will reduce the quantity demanded. Suppose, now, that the linen industry is a monopoly, so the price of linens exceeds their marginal cost.[2] This will decrease the quantity of linens demanded below the eight million yards that we have assumed to be socially optimal (point B in Figure 29–1). So the economy will move from point B to a point like K, where too few linens and too many handkerchiefs are being produced for maximal consumer satisfaction. By setting the "wrong" prices, then, the market fails to achieve the most efficient use of the economy's resources.

If the price of a commodity is above its marginal cost, the economy will tend to produce less of that item than maximize consumer benefits. The opposite will occur if an item's price is below its marginal cost.

In the remainder of this chapter, we will encounter several other instances in which the market mechanism may set the "wrong" prices.

Externalities

We come now to the fourth item on our list of market failures—one of the least obvious yet one of the most consequential of the imperfections of the price system. Many economic activities provide incidental benefits to others for whom they are not specifically intended. For example, a homeowner who plants a beautiful garden in front of her house incidentally and unintentionally provides pleasure to her neighbors and to those who pass by—people from whom she receives no payment. We say then that her activity generates a **beneficial externality.**

Similarly, there are activities that indiscriminately impose costs on others. For example, the operator of a motorcyle repair shop, from which all sorts of noise besieges the neighborhood and for which he pays no compensation to others, is said to produce a **detrimental externality.** Pollution constitutes the classic illustration of a detrimental externality.

To see why the presence of externalities causes the price system to misallocate resources, we need only recall that the system achieves efficiency by rewarding producers who serve consumers well—that is, at as low a cost as possible. This argument breaks down, however, as soon as some of the costs and benefits of economic activities are left out of the profit calculation.

When a firm pollutes a river, it uses up some of society's resources just as surely as when it burns coal. However, if it pays for coal but not for the use of water, it is natural for management to be economical in its use of coal and wasteful in its use of water. Similarly, a firm that provides benefits to others for which it receives no payment is unlikely to be generous in allocating resources to the activity, no matter how socially desirable it may be.

An activity is said to generate a **beneficial or detrimental externality** if that activity causes incidental benefits or damages to others, and no corresponding compensation is provided to or paid by those who generate the externality.

[1] If you need review, consult pages 588–90.
[2] To review why price under monopoly may be expected to exceed marginal cost, you may want to reread pages 605–606.

In an important sense, the source of the difficulty is to be found in the definition of "property rights." Coal mines are *private property;* their owners will not let anyone take coal without paying for it. Thus, coal is costly and so is not used wastefully. But waterways are not private property. Since they belong to everyone in general, they belong to no one in particular. They therefore can be used free of charge as dumping grounds for wastes by anyone who chooses to do so. Because no one pays for the use of the oxygen in a public waterway, that oxygen will be used wastefully. That is the source of detrimental externalities.

Externalities and Inefficiency

Using these concepts, we can see precisely why an externality has undesirable effects on the allocation of resources. In discussing externalities, it is crucial to distinguish between *social* and *private* marginal cost. We define **marginal social cost** (MSC) as the sum of two components: (1) **marginal private cost** (MPC), which is the share of marginal cost caused by an activity that is paid for by the persons who carry out the activity; and (2) *incidental cost,* which is the share borne by others.

If increased output by a firm increases the smoke it emits, then, in addition to its direct private costs as recorded in the company accounts, expansion of its production imposes incidental costs on others in the form of increased laundry bills, medical expenditures, outlays for air conditioning and electricity, as well as the unpleasantness of living in a cloud of noxious fumes. These are all part of the activity's marginal *social* cost.

Where the firm's activities generate detrimental externalities, its marginal social cost will be greater than its marginal private cost. In symbols, MSC > MPC. Since, in equilibrium, the market will yield an output at which consumers' marginal utility (MU) is equal to the firm's marginal private cost (MU = MPC), it follows that the marginal utility is *smaller* than marginal social cost. Society would then necessarily benefit if output of that product were *reduced*. It would lose the marginal utility but save the marginal social cost. And, since MSC > MU means that the production of the marginal unit of the good entails a cost to society larger than the benefit contributed by that unit of the good, society would come out ahead. We conclude that:

Where the firm's activity causes detrimental externalities, free markets will leave us in a situation where marginal benefits are less than marginal social costs. Smaller outputs than those that maximize profits will be socially desirable.

We have already indicated why this is so. Private enterprise has no motivation to take into account costs that it causes to others but for which it does not have to pay. So goods that cause such externalities will be produced in undesirably large amounts by private firms. For precisely analogous reasons:

Where the firm's activity generates beneficial externalities, free markets will produce too little output. Society would be better off with larger output levels.

These principles can be illustrated with the aid of Figure 29–2. This diagram repeats the two basic curves needed for the analysis of the equilibrium of the competitive firm: a demand-marginal revenue curve and a marginal cost curve (see Chapter 24). These represent the *private* costs and revenues accruing to a particular firm (in this case, a paper mill). The mill's maximum profit is

The **marginal social cost** of an activity is the sum of **marginal private cost** plus the incidental cost (positive or negative) which is borne by others.

Figure 29–2

EQUILIBRIUM OF A FIRM WHOSE OUTPUT PRODUCES DETRIMENTAL EXTERNALITIES (POLLUTION)

The firm's profit-maximizing output, at which its marginal private cost and its marginal private revenue are equal, is 100,000 tons. But if the firm paid all the social costs of its output instead of shifting some of them to others, its marginal cost curve would be the curve labeled "marginal social cost." Then it would pay the firm to reduce its output to 70,000 tons, thereby reducing the pollution it causes.

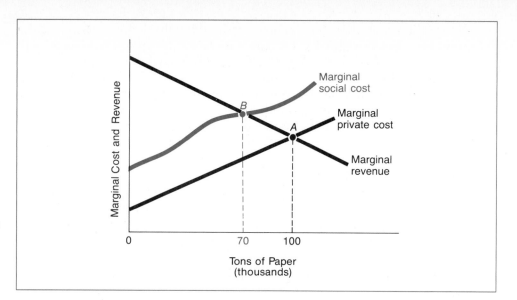

attained with 100,000 tons of output corresponding to the intersection between the marginal cost and marginal revenue curves (point A).

Now suppose that the factory's wastes pollute a nearby waterway, so that its production creates a detrimental externality whose cost the owner does not himself pay. Then marginal social cost must be higher than marginal private cost, as shown in the diagram, and the socially desirable level of output (70,000 tons) is at point B rather than point A.

Notice that if instead of being able to impose the external costs on others the mill's owner were forced to pay them himself, his own private marginal cost curve would correspond to the higher of the two curves shown. His output of the polluting commodity would then fall to 70,000 tons, corresponding to point B, the intersection between the marginal revenue curve and the marginal *social* cost curve. But because the firm does not in fact pay for the pollution damage its output causes, it produces an output (100,000 tons) that is larger than the output it would produce if the cost imposed on the community were instead borne by the firm (70,000 tons).

The same sort of diagram can be used to show that the opposite relationship will hold when the firm's activity produces beneficial externalities. The firm will produce less of its beneficial output than it would if it were rewarded fully for the benefits that its activities yield. Beneficial externalities arise when the activities of firm A create incidental benefits for firm B or individual C (and perhaps for many others as well); or when A's activities *reduce* the costs of others' activity. For example, Firm A's research laboratories, while making its own products better, may also incidentally discover new research techniques which reduce the research costs of other firms in the economy.

But these results can perhaps be seen more clearly with the help of a production possibilities frontier diagram similar to that in Figure 29–1. In Figure 29–3 we see the frontier for two industries: electricity generation, which causes air pollution (a detrimental externality), and tulip growing, which makes an area more attractive (a beneficial externality). We have just seen that detrimental externalities make marginal social cost greater than marginal private cost. Hence, if the electric company charges a price equal to its own marginal (private) cost, that price will be less than the true marginal social cost. Similarly, in tulip growing, a price equal to marginal private cost will be above the true marginal cost to society.

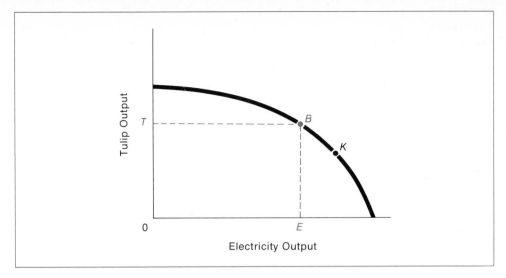

Figure 29–3
EXTERNALITIES, MARKET
EQUILIBRIUM, AND
EFFICIENT RESOURCE
ALLOCATION
Because electricity producers
emit smoke (a detrimental
externality), they do not bear
the true marginal social cost
of their output. So electricity
price will be below marginal
social cost, and electricity
output will be inefficiently
large (point *K*, not point *B*).
The opposite is true of tulip
production. Because they
generate beneficial
externalities, tulips will be
priced above marginal social
cost and tulip output will be
inefficiently small.

We saw earlier in the chapter that an industry that charges a price above marginal cost will reduce quantity demanded through this high price, and so it will produce an output too small for an efficient allocation of resources. The opposite will be true for an industry whose price is below marginal social cost. In terms of Figure 29–3, suppose point *B* again represents the efficient allocation of resources, involving the production of *E* kilowatt hours of electricity and *T* dozen tulips.

Because the polluting electric company charges a price below marginal social cost, it will produce more than *E* kilowatt hours of electricity. Similarly, because tulip growers generate external benefits, and so charge a price above marginal social cost, they will produce less than *T* dozen tulips. The economy will end up with the resource allocation represented by point *K* rather than that represented by point *B*. There will be too much smoky electricity production and too little attractive tulip growing. More generally:

An industry that generates detrimental externalities will have a marginal social cost higher than its marginal private cost. If its price is equal to its own marginal private cost, it will therefore be below the true marginal cost to society. The market mechanism thereby tends to encourage inefficiently large outputs of products that cause detrimental externalities. The opposite is true of products that cause beneficial externalities — private industry will provide inefficiently small quantities of these products.

The Universality of Externalities

Externalities occur throughout the economy. Many are beneficial. A factory that hires unskilled or semiskilled laborers gives them on-the-job training and provides the external benefit of better workers to future employers. Benefits to others are also generated when firms produce useful but unpatentable products, or even patentable products that can be imitated by others to some degree.

Detrimental externalities are also widespread. The emission of air and water pollutants by factories, cars, and airplanes is the source of some of our most pressing environmental problems. The abandonment of buildings causes the quality of a neighborhood to deteriorate and is the source of serious externalities for the city.

Externalities

Externalities lie at the heart of some of society's most pressing problems: the problems of the cities, the environment, research policy, and a variety of other critical issues. For this reason, the concept of externalities is one of our **12 Ideas For Beyond the Final Exam.** It is a subject that will recur again and again in this book as we discuss some of these problems in greater detail.

Government Policy and Externalities

Because of the market's inability to cope with externalities, governments have found it appropriate to support activities that are felt to generate external benefits. Education is subsidized not only because it helps promote equal opportunity for all citizens but also because it is believed to generate beneficial externalities. For example, educated people normally commit fewer crimes than uneducated people, so the more we educate people, the less we will need to spend on crime prevention. Also, academic research that has been provided partly as a byproduct of the educational system often benefits the entire population and has, indeed, been judged to be a major contributor to the nation's economic growth. We have consequently come to believe that if education were offered only by profit-making institutions, the output of these beneficial services would be provided at less than the optimal level.

Similarly, governments have recently begun to impose fines on companies that contribute heavily to air and water pollution. This approach to policy is in fact suggested by the economist's standard analysis of the effects of externalities on resource allocation. The basic problem is that, in the presence of externalities, the price system fails to allocate resources efficiently in the way it usually does. Resources are used up without any price being charged for them, and benefits are supplied without financial compensation to the provider. As a result, the market will produce excessive quantities of polluting outputs and of other outputs which create detrimental externalities because they are, in effect, provided at a bargain price — a price that does not cover their entire marginal social cost. Consequently:

One effective way to deal with externalities may be through the use of taxes and subsidies, making polluters pay for the costs they impose on society, and paying the generators of beneficial externalities for the incidental benefits of their activities (which can be considered as an offset or deduction from the social cost of the activity).

For example, firms that generate beneficial externalities should be given a *subsidy* per unit of their output equal to the difference between their marginal social costs and their marginal private costs. Similarly, those that generate detrimental externalities should be *taxed* so that the firm that creates such externalities will have to pay the entire marginal social cost. In terms of Figure 29–2, after paying the tax, the firm's marginal private cost curve will be shifted up until it coincides with its marginal social cost curve, and so the market price will be set in a manner consistent with an efficient resource allocation.

While there is much to be said for this approach in principle, it often is not easy to implement in practice. Social costs are rarely easy to estimate, partly because they are so widely diffused throughout the community (everyone in the area is affected by pollution) and partly because many of the costs and benefits (effects on health, unpleasantness of living in smog) are not readily assessed in monetary terms. The pros and cons of this approach and the alternative policies available for the control of externalities will be discussed in greater detail in Chapter 34 on environmental problems.

Public Goods

Another area in which the market fails to perform adequately is in the provision of **public goods.** These are commodities which are valuable socially but whose provision, for reasons we will now explain, cannot be financed by private enterprise. Thus, government must pay for public goods if they are to be provided at all. Standard examples range from national defense to the services of lighthouses.

It is easiest to explain the nature of public goods by contrasting them with the sort of commodities called **private goods,** which are at the opposite end of the spectrum. *Private goods are characterized by two important attributes.* One can be called **depletability.** If you eat a steak or use a gallon of gasoline, there is that much less beef or fuel in the world available for others to use. Your consumption depletes the supply available for other people, either temporarily or permanently.

But a pure public good is like the legendary widow's jar of oil, which always remained full no matter how many people used it. Once the snow has been removed from a street, the improved driving conditions are available to every driver who uses that street, whether 10 or 1000 cars pass that way. One passing car does not make the road less snow-free for another. The same is true of the spraying of swamps near a town to kill disease-bearing mosquitoes. The cost of the spraying is the same whether the town contains 10,000 or 20,000 persons. A resident of the town who benefits from this service does not deplete its advantages to others.

The other property that characterizes private goods but not public goods is **excludability,** meaning that anyone who does not pay for the good can be excluded from enjoying its benefits. If you do not buy a ticket, you are excluded from the ball game. If you do not pay for an electric guitar, the storekeeper will not give it to you.

But some goods or services are such that, if they are provided to anyone, they automatically become available to many other persons whom it is difficult, if not impossible, to exclude from the benefits. If a street is cleared of snow, everyone who uses the street benefits, regardless of who paid for the snowplow. If a country provides a strong military establishment, everyone receives its protection, even persons who do not happen to want it.

A public good is defined as a good that lacks depletability. Very often, it also lacks excludability. Notice two important implications.

First, since nonpaying users usually cannot be excluded from enjoying a public good, suppliers of such goods will find it *difficult* or *impossible to collect fees* for the benefits they provide. This is the so-called "free rider" problem. How many people, for example, will *voluntarily* cough up $4000 a year to support our national defense establishment? Yet this is roughly what it costs per American family. Services like national defense and public health, which are not depletable and where excludability is simply impossible, *cannot* be provided by private enterprise because no one will pay for what he can get free. Since

A **public good** is a commodity or service whose benefits are *not depleted* by an additional user and for which it is generally difficult or *impossible to exclude* people from its benefits, even if they are unwilling to pay for them. In contrast, a **private good** is characterized by both excludability and depletability.

A commodity is **depletable** if it is used up when someone consumes it.

A commodity is **excludable** if someone who does not pay for it can be kept from enjoying it.

private firms are not in the business of giving services away, the supply of public goods must be left to government authorities and nonprofit institutions.

The second thing we notice is that, since the supply of a public good is not depleted by an additional user, *the marginal cost of serving an additional user is zero*. With zero marginal cost, the basic principle of optimal resource allocation calls for provision of public goods and services to anyone who wants them *at no charge*. In a word, not only is it often *impossible* to charge a market price for a public good, it is often *undesirable* as well. Any nonzero price would discourage some users from enjoying the public good; but this would be inefficient, since one more person's enjoyment of the good costs society nothing. To summarize:

It is usually *not possible* to charge a price for a pure public good because people cannot be excluded from enjoying its benefits. It may also be *undesirable* to charge a price for it because that would discourage some people from using it even though using it does not deplete its supply. For both these reasons we find government supplying many public goods. Without government intervention, public goods simply would not be provided.

Referring back to our example in Figure 29–1, if hospital linens were a public good and their production were left to private enterprise, the economy would end up at point *A* on the graph, with zero production of hospital linens and far more output of handkerchiefs than is called for by efficient allocation (point *B*). Usually, communities have not been content to let that happen; and today a quite substantial proportion of government expenditure, indeed the bulk of municipal budgets, is devoted to the financing of public goods or to services believed to generate substantial external benefits. National defense, public health, police and fire protection, and research are among the services provided by governments because they offer beneficial externalities or because they are public goods.

The Cost Disease of the Service Sector

Our next problem may or may not be considered a failure of the market mechanism. While private standards of living have increased and material possessions have grown, the community has simultaneously been forced to cope with deterioration in a variety of services, both public and private.

Throughout the world, streets and subways have grown increasingly dirty. Public safety has declined as crimes of violence have become more commonplace in almost every major city. Bus and train service has been reduced. In the middle of the nineteenth century in suburban London, there were twelve mail deliveries per day on weekdays and one on Sundays. We all know what has happened to postal services since then.

There have been parallel cutbacks in the quality of private services. Doctors have become increasingly reluctant to visit patients at home; in many areas, the house call, which thirty years ago was a commonplace event, has now become something that occurs only in a life and death emergency, if even then. Another example, though undoubtedly a matter for less general concern, is what has happened to restaurants. Although they are reluctant to publicize the fact, a great number of restaurants, including some of the most elegant and expensive, serve preprepared, frozen, and reheated meals. They charge high prices for what amount to little more than TV dinners.

There is no single explanation for all these matters. It would be naïve to offer any cut-and-dried hypothesis purporting to account for phenomena as diverse as the rise in crime and violence throughout Western society and the deterioration in postal services. Yet at least one common influence underlies all these problems of deterioration in service quality — an influence that is economic in character and that may be expected to grow more serious with the passage of time. The issue has been called the **cost disease of the personal services.**

Consider these facts. During the inflationary 1970s, virtually all costs in the economy rose; but the costs of services rose even faster than most. During earlier periods, when the nation's price level was nearly constant, service costs nevertheless rose at a significant rate. One typical example will illustrate the point. Between 1945 and 1965, the cost of public education per pupil day rose, on the average, 4 percent a year *more rapidly* than the general price level. This means that every year — even when other prices in the economy were not increasing — the cost of education was rising. These cost differentials were cumulative and compounded so that over the two decades as a whole the cost of education per pupil more than doubled relative to the cost of manufactured goods. By the end of the period, the cost of an education was therefore equivalent to twice as many cars or refrigerators as it was at the beginning. A similar pattern has been followed by the costs of other services, such as health care, libraries, doctor's fees, and theater tickets.

One serious consequence of this phenomenon is that a terrible financial burden has been placed on municipal budgets by the soaring costs of education, health care, and police and fire protection. But what accounts for these ever-increasing costs? Are they attributable to inefficiencies in government management or to political corruption? Perhaps, in part, to both. But there is another reason — one that could not be avoided by any municipal administration no matter what its integrity and efficiency — and one that affects private industry just as severely as it does the public sector.

The problem stems from the basic nature of these services. Most such services require direct contact between those who consume the service and those who provide it. Doctors, teachers, and librarians are all engaged in activities that require direct person-to-person contact. Moreover, the quality of the service deteriorates if less time is provided by doctors, teachers, and librarians to each user of their services.

In contrast, the buyer of an automobile usually has no idea who worked on it, and could not care less how much labor time went into its production. A labor-saving innovation in auto production need not imply a reduction in product quality. As a result, it has proved far easier for technological change to save labor in manufacturing than in providing services. While output per hour of labor in manufacturing and agriculture went up in the period after World War II at an average rate of something like 2 percent a year, the number of teacher hours per pupil actually *increased* because classes became smaller.

These disparate performances in productivity have grave consequences for prices. When wages in manufacturing rise 2 percent, the cost of manufactured products is not affected because increased productivity makes up for the rise in wages. But the nature of services makes it very difficult to introduce labor-saving devices in the service sector. So a 2-percent rise in the wages of teachers or police officers is not offset by higher productivity and must lead to an equivalent rise in municipal budgets. Similarly, a 2-percent rise in the wages of hairdressers must lead beauty salons to raise their prices.

The Cost Disease of the Personal Services

In the long run, wages and salaries throughout the economy tend to go up and down together, for otherwise the activity whose wage rate falls seriously behind will tend to lose its labor force. Auto workers and police officers will see their wages rise at roughly the same rate in the long run. But if productivity on the assembly line advances while productivity in the patrol car does not, then police protection must grow ever more expensive as time goes on.

This phenomenon is another of our **12 Ideas for Beyond the Final Exam.** Because productivity improvements are very difficult for most services, their cost can be expected to rise faster, year in, year out, than the cost of manufactured goods. Over a period of several decades, this difference in the growth rate in costs of the two sectors can add up, making services enormously more expensive compared with manufactured goods.

If services continue to grow ever more expensive in comparison to goods, the implications for life in the future are profound indeed. This analysis portends a world in which the typical home contains luxuries and furnishings that we can hardly imagine; but it is a home surrounded by garbage and perhaps by violence. It portends a future in which the services of doctors, teachers, and police officers are increasingly mass-produced and impersonal, and in which the arts and crafts are increasingly supplied only by amateurs because the cost of professional work in these fields is too high.

If this is the shape of the economy a hundred years from now, it will be significantly different from our own, and some persons will undoubtedly question whether the quality of life has increased commensurately with the increased material prosperity. Some may even ask whether it has increased at all.

Is this future inevitable? Is there anything that can be done to escape it? The answer is that it is by no means inevitable. To see why, we must first recognize that the source of the problem, paradoxically, is the growth in productivity of our economy—or rather, the *unevenness* of that growth. Trash removal costs go up not because garbage collectors become less efficient but because labor in car manufacturing becomes *more* efficient, thus enhancing the sanitation worker's value as a potential employee on the automotive assembly line. His wages must go up to keep him at his job of garbage removal.

But increasing productivity can never make a nation poorer. It can never make it unable to afford things it was able to afford in the past. Increasing productivity means that we can afford more of *all* things—medical care and education as well as TV sets and electric toothbrushes.

The role of services in our future depends on how we order our priorities. If we value services sufficiently, we can have more and better services—at *some* sacrifice in the rate of growth of manufactured goods. Whether that is a good choice for society is not for economists to say. But it is important to recognize that society *does* have a choice, and that if it fails to exercise it, matters are very likely to proceed relentlessly in the direction they are now headed—toward a world in which there is an enormous abundance of material goods and a great scarcity of many of the things that most people now consider primary requisites for a high quality of life.

How does the cost disease relate to the central topic of this chapter—the performance of the market and its implications for the economic role of government? Here the problem is that the market *does* give the appropriate price signals; but these signals are likely to be misunderstood by government and to lead to decisions which do not promote the public interest most effectively.

Health care is an appropriate example. The cost disease itself is capable of causing the costs of health care (say, per patient day) to rise faster than the economy's rate of inflation because medical care cannot be standardized enough to enjoy the productivity gains offered by automation and assembly lines. As a result, if standards of care in public hospitals are not to fall, it is not enough to allow health care budgets to grow at the rate of inflation. Those budgets must actually grow *faster* to prevent quality from declining. For example, when the inflation rate is 4 percent per year, it may be necessary to raise hospitals' budgets by 6 percent annually.

In these circumstances, something may seem amiss to a state legislature that increases the budget of its hospitals by 5 percent per year. Responsible legislators will doubtless be disturbed by the fact that the budget is growing steadily in real terms and yet standards of quality are constantly slipping. If the legislators do not realize that the cost disease is the cause of the problem, they will be expected to look for villains — greedy doctors or hospital administrators who are corrupt or inefficient, and so on. The net result, all too often, is a set of wasteful rules that hamper the freedom of action of hospitals and doctors inappropriately or that tighten hospital budgets below the level that demands and costs would require if they were determined by the market mechanism rather than by government.

In sum, the cost disease is not a case where the market performs badly. But it is a case in which the market *appears* to misbehave by singling out certain sectors for particularly large cost increases. And because the market *seems* to be working badly there, it is likely to lead to reaction by governments which can well be highly detrimental to the public interest.[3]

Allocation of Resources Between Present and Future

When a society invests, more resources are devoted to building capacity to produce consumers' goods in the future. But the inputs that go into building new plant and equipment are unavailable for consumption now. Fuel used to make steel for a factory cannot be used to heat homes or drive cars. Thus, the allocation of inputs between current consumption and investment — that is, their allocation between present and future — determines how fast the economy grows.

In principle, the market mechanism should be as efficient in allocating resources between present and future uses as it is in allocating resources among different outputs at any one time. If future demands for a particular commodity, say, computers for the home, are expected to be higher than they are today, it will pay manufacturers to plan now to build the necessary plant and equipment so they will be ready to turn out the computers when the expanded market materializes. More resources are thereby allocated to future consumption.

The allocation of resources between present and future can be analyzed with the aid of a production possibilities frontier diagram, such as that in Figure 29–1. Suppose the issue is how much labor and capital to devote to

---

[3]Governments have also apparently been induced to intervene in the operation of some private sectors affected by the cost disease. For example, they control the prices of automotive insurance policies which pay for such things as medical care of accident victims and repair of damaged automobiles, both of which are at least somewhat susceptible to the disease.

Figure 29–4

PRODUCTION POSSIBILITIES FRONTIER BETWEEN PRESENT AND FUTURE

With a given quantity of resources, the economy can produce one million cars for immediate use and build no factories for the future (point *A*). Alternatively, at the opposite extreme (point *B*), it can build 10 factories where products will become available in the future, while no cars are produced for current consumption. At points in between on the frontier, such as *C*, the economy will produce a combination of some cars for present consumption and some factories for future use.

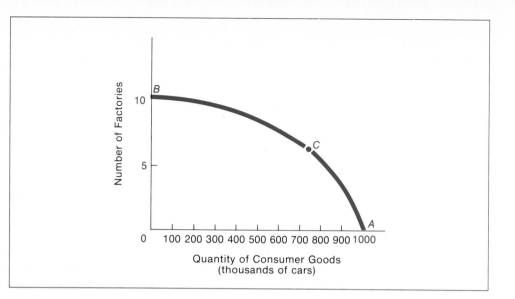

producing consumer goods and how much to devote to construction of factories to produce output in the future. Then, instead of handkerchiefs and linens, the graph will show consumer goods and number of factories on its axes, but otherwise it will be exactly the same as Figure 29–1. Such a graph appears in Figure 29–4.

The profit motive directs the flow of resources between one time period and another just as it handles resource allocation among different industries in a given period. The lure of profits directs resources to those products *and those time periods* in which high prices promise to make output most profitable. But one feature of the process of allocation of resources among different time periods distinguishes it from the process of allocation among industries. This is the special role that the *interest rate* plays in allocation among the periods.

If the receipt of a given amount of money is delayed until some time in the future, the recipient suffers an *opportunity cost* — the interest that the money could have earned if it had been received earlier and invested. For example, if the rate of interest is 9 percent and you can persuade someone who owes you money to make a $100 payment one year earlier than originally planned, you come out $9 ahead. Put the other way, if the rate of interest is 9 percent and the payment of $100 is postponed one year, you lose the opportunity to earn $9. Thus, the rate of interest determines the size of the opportunity cost to a recipient who gets money at some date in the future instead of now. For this reason, as we saw in Chapter 9:

Low interest rates will persuade people to invest more now, since investments yield many of their benefits in the future. Thus, more resources will be devoted to the future if interest rates are low. Similarly, high interest rates make investment, with its benefits in the future, less attractive. And so high interest rates will tend to increase the use of resources for current output at the expense of reduced future outputs.

On the surface, it seems that the price system can allocate resources among different time periods in the way consumers prefer. For the supply of and demand for loans, which determine the interest rate, reflects the public's preferences between present and future. Suppose, for example, that the public suddenly became more interested in future consumption (say, people wanted to save more for their old age). The supply of funds available for borrowing would increase and interest rates would tend to fall. This would stimulate investment and add to the future output of goods at the expense of current consumption.

But several questions have been raised about the effectiveness, in practice, with which the market mechanism allocates resources among different time periods.

One thing that makes economists uneasy is that the rate of interest, which is the price that controls allocation over time, is also used for a variety of other purposes. As we saw in Chapter 14 the interest rate can be used to deal with business fluctuations. And in Chapter 20 we saw that it plays an analogous role in international monetary relations. As a result, governments frequently manipulate interest rates deliberately. In so doing, policymakers seem to give little thought to the effects on the allocation of resources between present and future, and so we may well worry whether the resulting interest rates are the most appropriate ones.

Second, it has been suggested that even in the absence of government manipulation of the interest rate, the market may devote too many resources to immediate consumption. One British economist, A. C. Pigou, argued simply that people suffer from "a defective telescopic faculty"—that they are too shortsighted to give adequate weight to the future. A "bird in hand" point of view leads people to care so much about the present that they sacrifice the legitimate interests of the future. As a result, too much goes into today's consumption and too little into investment for tomorrow.

A third reason why the free market may not invest enough for the future is that investment projects, like the construction of a new factory, are much greater risks to the investor than to the community. Even if a factory falls into someone else's hands through bankruptcy, it will probably go on turning out goods. But the profits will not go to the investor or his heirs. Therefore, the loss to the individual investor will be far greater than the loss to society. For this reason, individual investment for the future may fall short of the amounts that are socially optimal. Investments too risky to be worthwhile to any group of private individuals may nevertheless be advantageous to society as a whole.

Fourth, our economy shortchanges the future when it despoils irreplaceable natural resources, exterminates whole species of plants and animals, floods canyons, "develops" attractive areas into acres of potential slums, and so on. Worst of all, industry, the military, and individuals bequeath a ticking time bomb to the future when they leave behind lethal and slow-acting residues, such as nuclear wastes, which may remain dangerous for hundreds or even thousands of years and whose disposal containers are likely to fall apart long before their contents lose their lethal qualities.

Such actions are essentially *irreversible*. If a factory is not built this year, the deficiency in facilities provided for the future can be remedied by building it next year. But a canyon, once destroyed, can never be replaced. For this reason:

Many economists believe that **irreversible decisions** have a very special significance and must *not* be left entirely in the hands of private firms and individuals.

Recently, however, several writers have questioned the general conclusion that the free market will not tend to invest enough for the future. They have pointed out that the prosperity of our economy has grown fairly steadily from one decade to the next, and that there is every reason to expect future generations to have real incomes and an abundance of consumer goods far greater than our own. Pressures to increase investment for the future then may be like taking from the poor to give to the rich — a sort of backward Robin Hood redistribution of income.

Some Other Sources of Market Failure

We have now completed our survey of the most important imperfections of the market mechanism. But that list is not complete, and it can never be. In this imperfect world nothing ever works out ideally, and by examining anything with a sufficiently powerful microscope one can always detect some more blemishes. However, some of the items we have omitted from our list are also important. Let us therefore conclude with a brief description of three of them.

Imperfect Information

The analysis of the virtues of the market mechanism in Chapter 26 assumed that consumers and producers have all the information they need for their decisions. But in reality things are very different. When buying a house or a second-hand car, or selecting a doctor, consumers are vividly reminded of how little they know about what they are purchasing. The old motto "Let the buyer beware" applies. Obviously, if participants in the market are ill-informed, they will not always make the optimal decisions described in our theoretical models.

Yet, not all economists agree that imperfect information is really a failure of the market mechanism. They point out that information, too, is a commodity that costs money to produce. Neither firms nor consumers have complete information because it would be irrational for them to spend the enormous amounts needed to get it. As always, the optimum is a compromise. One should, ideally, stop buying information at the point where the marginal utility of further information is no greater than its marginal cost. With this amount of information, the business executive or the consumer is able to make what have been referred to as "optimally imperfect" decisions.

Rent Seeking

Rent seeking refers to unproductive activity in the pursuit of economic profit, that is, profit in excess of competitive earnings.

An army of lawyers, expert witnesses, and business executives crowd our courtrooms and pile up enormous costs. Business firms seem to sue each other at the slightest provocation, wasting vast resources and delaying business decisions. Why? Because it is possible to make money by such unproductive activities — by legal battles over profit-making opportunities.

For example, suppose a municipality awards a contract to produce its electricity to Firm A, offering $20 million in profit. It may pay Firm B to spend $5 million in a lawsuit against the municipality and Firm A, hoping the courts will award it the contract (and thus the $20 million profit) instead.

In general, any source of unusual profit, such as a monopoly, is a temptation for firms to waste economic resources in an effort to obtain control of that source of profits. This process, called "rent seeking" by economists (meaning that the firms hope to obtain earnings without contributing to production), has been judged by some observers to be a major source of inefficiency in our economy.

Moral Hazard

Another widely discussed problem for the market mechanism is associated with insurance. Insurance — the provision of protection against risk — is viewed by economists as a useful commodity, like shoes or the provision of information.

At the Frontier: Asymmetric Information, Lemons, and Agents

Have you ever wondered why a six-month-old car sells for so much less than a new one? One explanation is offered by economists, who have recently intensified their study of the effects of imperfect information on markets. The problem is that some small proportion of automobiles are "lemons"; that is, they are constantly subject to mechanical troubles. The new car dealer must sell *all* his cars, and, in any event, he probably knows no more than the buyer whether a particular car is a lemon. The two parties, therefore, have *symmetric* information and a car purchased from a new-car dealer is unlikely to turn out to be a lemon. In the second-hand market, however, information is *asymmetric*. The seller knows whether the car is a lemon, but the buyer does not. Moreover, a seller who wants to get rid of a fairly new car is likely to be doing so only because it is a lemon. Potential buyers realize that. Hence, if some person is forced to sell a good new car because of an unexpected need for cash, she too will be stuck with a low price because she cannot *prove* that her car really works well. The moral is that asymmetric information tends to harm the honest, informed dealer.

Asymmetric information pervades most economic relationships and leads to what are called *principal-agent problems* whose analysis is a major concern of recent economic research. The issue arises from the necessity of delegating many critical tasks to others. Stockholders in a corporation delegate the running of the firm to its management team; U.S. citizens delegate lawmaking to Congress; union members delegate many decisions to the union leadership. In such cases the persons who give away part of their decision-making powers are called the *principals* and those who exercise those powers are called the *agents*, who are, in effect, hired by the principals to do the jobs in question.

Asymmetric information is crucial here. The principals know only imperfectly whether their agents are serving their interests faithfully and efficiently or are instead neglecting or even acting against their interests to pursue selfish interests of their own. Misuse of principals' property, embezzlement, and political corruption are extreme examples of such dereliction of duty by agents and, unfortunately, they seem to occur more and more often. Among other things, economic analysis studies ways of curing or at least alleviating such problems by arranging for the compensation of agents, which bring the agents' interests more closely into line with those of the principals. For example, if the salaries of corporate management depend heavily on company profits or on the market value of company shares, then by promoting the welfare of stockholders managers will make themselves better off. Shareholders, even though they know only imperfectly what management is doing, can have a fair degree of confidence that management will try to serve their interests well.

But it also creates a problem by encouraging the very risks against which it provides protection. For example, if an individual has jewelry which is fully insured against theft, she has little motivation to take steps to protect it against burglars. She may, for example, fail to lock it up in a safe-deposit box, and this failure makes burglary a more attractive and lucrative profession. This problem — the tendency of insurance to encourage the source of risk — is called **moral hazard,** and it makes a free market in insurance hard to operate.

Moral hazard refers to the tendency of insurance to discourage policyholders from protecting themselves from risk.

Market Failure and Government Failure

This chapter has pointed out some of the most noteworthy failures of the invisible hand. We seem forced to the conclusion that a market economy, if left entirely to itself, is likely to produce results which are, at least in some respects, far from ideal. In our discussion we have noted either directly or by implication some of the things government can do to correct these deficiencies. But the fact that government often *can* intervene in the operation of the economy in a constructive way does not always mean that it actually *will* succeed in doing so. The fact is that governments cannot be relied upon to behave ideally, any more than business firms can be expected to do so.

It is apparently hard to make this point in a way that is suitably balanced. Commentators too often stake out one extreme position or the other. Those who think the market mechanism is inherently unfair and biased by the greed of those who run its enterprises seem to think of government as the savior that can cure all economic ills. Those who deplore government intervention are prone to consider the public sector as the home of every sort of inefficiency, graft, and bureaucratic stultification. The truth, as usual, lies in between.

Governments are inherently imperfect, like the humans who compose them. The political process leads to compromises which sometimes bear little resemblance to rational decisions. For example, legislators' versions of the policies suggested by economic analysis are sometimes mere caricatures of the economists' ideas. (For a satirical editorial illustrating this point, see the box at the top of the next page.) Yet, often the problems engendered by an unfettered economy are too serious to be left to the free market. The problems of dealing with inflation, environmental decay, and the provision of public goods are cases in point. In such instances, government intervention is likely to yield substantial benefits to the general public. However, even when it is fairly clear that *some* government action is warranted, it may be difficult or impossible to calculate the *optimal* degree of governmental intervention. There is, then, the danger of intervention so excessive that the society might have been better off without it.

But in other areas the market mechanism is likely to work reasonably well, and the small imperfections that are present do not constitute adequate justification for intervention. In any event, *even where government intervention is appropriate, it is essential to consider market-like instruments as the means to correct the deficiencies in the workings of the market mechanism*. The tax incentives described in our discussion of externalities are an outstanding example of what we have in mind.

Evaluative Comments

This chapter, like Chapter 26, has offered a rather unbalanced assessment of the market mechanism. We spent Chapter 26 extolling the market's virtues and spent this chapter cataloguing its vices. We come out, as in the nursery rhyme, concluding that the market is either very, very good or it is horrid.

There seems to be nothing moderate about the performance of a market system. As a means of achieving efficiency in the production of ordinary consumer goods and of responding to changes in consumer preferences, it is unparalleled. It is, in fact, difficult to overstate the accomplishments of the price system in these areas.

On the other hand, it has proven itself unable to cope with business fluctuations, income inequality, or the consequences of monopoly. It has proved to

The Politics of Economic Policy

In 1978, Alfred Kahn, an economist in the Carter administration, advocated reducing pollution by raising the tax on leaded gasoline and lowering the tax on unleaded gasoline. *The Washington Post*, in an editorial excerpted below, agreed that Kahn's idea was a sound one, but worried about what might emerge from Congress:

GROPPER, William. *The Senate*. (1935). Collection, The Museum of Modern Art, New York. Gift of A. Conger Goodyear.

> If the administration adopts the Kahn plan, recent history offers a pretty clear view of the rest of the story.
>
> Mr. Kahn will draft a one-page bill to raise the tax on the one kind of gas and lower it on the other. But the White House political staff will immediately point out that his draft fails to address profound questions of social equity. What about the poor, who buy leaded gas because it's cheaper? What about young people driving old cars? What about the inhabitants of lower Louisiana, who need their outboard motors to get around the swamps and bayous? There will have to be a rebate formula. It will take into account each family's income, the number and ages of its various automobiles and the distance from its front doorstep to the bus stop. The legislative draftsmen at the Energy Department have had a lot of experience with that kind of formula and eventually the 53-page bill will be sent to Congress. . . .
>
> The real fun will start when it arrives at the Senate Finance Committee. First the committee will add tuition tax credits for families with children in private schools. Then, warming to its work, it will vote import quotas on straw hats from Hong Kong, beef from Argentina and automobiles from Japan. . . . [I]t will then add several obscure but pregnant provisions that seem to refer to the tax treatment of certain oil wells in the Gulf states. When the 268-page bill comes to the Senate floor, the administration will narrowly manage to defeat an amendment to improve business confidence by repealing the capital-gains tax and returning to the gold standard.
>
> When the bill gets back to the House, liberal Democrats will denounce it as an outrage and declare all-out war. They will succeed in getting all references to gasoline taxes and the environment stricken — but not, fortunately, the import quotas or the obscure tax changes for the oil wells. By the time the staff of the Joint Committee on Taxation has straightened out a few technical difficulties, the bill will run to 417 pages and Ralph Nader will be calling on President Carter to veto it. But the feeling at the White House will be that Congress has worked so long and hard on the bill that he has no choice but to sign it. By the time the bill is finally enacted, Mr. Kahn might well wish he had chosen some other instrument of policy.

SOURCE: *The Washington Post*, December 26, 1978. Copyright *The Washington Post*.

be a very poor allocator of resources among outputs that generate external costs and external benefits, and it has shown itself completely incapable of arranging for the provision of public goods. Some of the most urgent problems that plague our society — the deterioration of services in the cities, the despoilation of our atmosphere, the social unrest attributable to poverty — can be ascribed in part to one or another of these shortcomings of the market system.

Most economists conclude from these observations that while the market mechanism is virtually irreplaceable, the public interest nevertheless requires considerable modifications in the way it works. Proposals designed to deal directly with the problems of poverty, monopoly, and resource allocation over time abound in the economic literature. All of them call for the government to intervene in the economy, either by supplying directly those goods and services that, it is believed, private enterprise does not supply in adequate amounts, or by seeking to influence the workings of the economy more indirectly through regulation. Many of these programs have been discussed in earlier chapters; others will be encountered in chapters yet to come.

Summary

1. There are at least seven major imperfections in the workings of the market mechanism: inequality of income distribution, fluctuations in economic activity (inflation and unemployment), monopolistic output restrictions, beneficial and detrimental externalities, inadequate provision of public goods, deteriorating quality and rising costs of services, and finally, misallocation of resources between present and future.

2. Efficient resource allocation is basically a matter of balancing the benefits of producing more of one good against the benefits of devoting the required inputs to the production of some other good.

3. A detrimental externality occurs when an economic activity incidentally does harm to others; a beneficial externality occurs when an economic activity incidentally creates benefits for others.

4. When an activity causes a detrimental externality, the marginal social cost of the activity (including the harm it does to others) must be greater than the marginal private cost to those who carry on the activity. The opposite will be true when a beneficial externality occurs.

5. If manufacture of a product causes detrimental externalities, its price will generally not include all the marginal social cost it causes, since part of the cost will be borne by others. The opposite is true for beneficial externalities.

6. The market will therefore tend to overallocate resources to the production of goods that cause detrimental externalities and underallocate resources to the production of goods that create beneficial externalities. This is one of the **12 Ideas for Beyond the Final Exam.**

7. A public good is defined by economists as a commodity (like clean air) that is not depleted by additional users and from whose use it is difficult to exclude anyone, even those who refuse to pay for it. A private good, in contrast, is characterized by both excludability and depletability.

8. Free-enterprise firms generally will not produce a public good even if it is extremely useful to the community, because they cannot charge money for the use of the good.

9. Because personal services — such as education, medical care, and police protection — are not amenable to labor-saving innovations, they suffer from a cost disease whose symptom is that their costs tend to rise considerably faster than costs in the economy as a whole. The result can be a distortion in the supply of services by government because their rising cost is misinterpreted as mismanagement and waste. This cost disease of the service sector is another of our **12 Ideas for Beyond the Final Exam.**

10. Many observers feel that the market often shortchanges the future, particularly when it makes irreversible decisions that destroy natural resources.

Concepts for Review

Opportunity cost	Public goods	Asymmetric information
Resource misallocation	Private goods	Principals
Production possibilities frontier	Excludability	Agents
Price above or below marginal cost	Depletability	Rent seeking
Externalities (detrimental and beneficial)	Cost disease of the personal services	Moral hazard
Marginal social cost and marginal private cost	Irreversible decisions	

Questions for Discussion

1. Specifically, what is the opportunity cost to society of a pair of shoes? Why may not the price of those shoes adequately represent that opportunity cost?

2. Suppose that because of a new disease that attacks coffee plants, far more labor and other inputs are required to raise a pound of coffee than before. How might that affect the efficient allocation of resources between tea and coffee? Why? How would the prices of coffee and tea react in a free market?

3. Give some examples of goods whose production causes detrimental externalities and some examples of goods that create beneficial externalities.

4. Compare cleaning an office building with cleaning the atmosphere of a city. Which is a public good and which is a private good? Why?

5. Give some other examples of public goods, and discuss in each case why additional users do not deplete them and why it is difficult to exclude people from using them.

6. Think about the goods and services that your local government provides. Which of these are "public goods" as economists use the term?

7. Explain why the services of a lighthouse are sometimes given as an example of a public good.

8. Explain why education is not a very satisfactory example of a public good.

9. In recent decades, college tuition costs have risen faster than the general price level even though the wages of college professors have failed to keep pace with the price level. Can you explain why?

10. A firm holds a patent which is estimated to be worth $20 million. The patent is repeatedly challenged in the courts by a large number of (rent seeking) firms, each hoping to grab away the patent. In what sense may the rent seekers be "competing perfectly" for the patent? If so, how much will end up being spent in the legal battles? (*Hint*: Under perfect competition should firms expect to earn any economic profit?)

30

The action of the stock market must necessarily be puzzling at times since otherwise everyone who studies it only a little bit would be able to make money in it.

B. GRAHAM, D. L. DODD, AND S. COTTLE

Real Firms and Their Financing: Stocks and Bonds

Earlier chapters have provided a theoretical analysis of the decisions of business firms. But a business firm does more than just select inputs, outputs, and prices. In this chapter, we look at some additional features of firms as they exist in reality. In this chapter, we will begin by describing the different types of firms that make up U.S. business. We will encounter small firms operated by individual owners, partnerships, and corporations of all sizes. Then, we will describe the most important ways in which firms acquire the resources they need for investment. In particular, we will look at the markets where stocks and bonds are sold and to which many individuals bring their money, hoping to make that money grow.

The stock market is really something of an enigma. No other economic activity is reported in such detail in so many newspapers and followed with such concern by so many people; yet no activity seems to have been so successful in eluding those who devote themselves to predicting its future. There is no shortage of "experts" who are prepared to evaluate the future of one stock versus that of another. And usually they are paid well for their efforts. But there are real questions about what these experts deliver. For example, Burton G. Malkiel of Yale University reported the following results from a study of leading analysts' predictions of company earnings, on which they based their price forecasts for the companies:

We wrote to nineteen major Wall Street firms . . . among the most respected names in the investment business.

We requested — and received — past earnings predictions on how these firms felt earnings for specific companies would behave over both a one-year and a five-year period. These estimates . . . were . . . compared with actual results to see how well the analysts forecast short-run and long-run earnings changes.

Bluntly stated, the careful estimates of security analysts (based on industry studies, plant visits, etc.) do little, if any, better than those that would be obtained by simple extrapolation of past trends.

For example . . . the analysts' estimates were compared [with] the assumption that every company in the economy would enjoy a growth in earnings of about 4 percent over the next year (approximately the long-run rate of growth of the national income). It turned out that... this naïve forecasting model... would make smaller errors in forecasting long-run earnings growth than... [did] the forecasts of the analysts.

When confronted with the poor record of their five-year growth estimates, the security analysts honestly, if sheepishly, admitted that five years ahead is really too far in advance to make reliable projections. They protested that while long-term projections are admittedly important, they really ought to be judged on their ability to project earnings changes one year ahead.

Believe it or not, it turned out that their one-year forecasts were even worse than their five-year projections.[1]

Later in this chapter we will be in a position to give the explanation many economists offer for this poor performance record.

Firms in the United States

It is customary to divide firms into three groups: *corporations, partnerships,* and *individual proprietorships* (businesses having a single owner). To understand how important corporations are in the economy, consider that annual receipts of corporations amount to more than 87 percent of GNP in the United States. Almost all large American firms are corporations. General Motors by itself sold over $100 billion in 1986, and Exxon and Ford each sold over $50 billion. The sales of these three firms alone amount to considerably more than the GNP of Austria, Belgium, the Netherlands, Sweden, Switzerland, and many, many more countries.

But while economic power resides in the corporations, this form of business organization actually constitutes a *minority* of American business firms, measured in terms of the total number of enterprises. The reason is that most firms are small. Even a large proportion of the corporations are quite small — more than 40 percent of them have total assets (cash and physical property) worth less than $100,000. But by far the greatest number of firms (counting all firms large and small, and including the corner grocery store and shoe repair shop) are proprietorships. For example, about 90 percent of family farms are proprietorships. Of the more than 16 million business firms in the United States, over 12 million are proprietorships, somewhat more than 2 million are corporations, and somewhat more than a million are partnerships. Thus, as is true of the income of individuals:

A very small proportion of American firms accounts for a very large share of U.S. business. Obviously, business is not distributed equally among firms.

This result is brought out strikingly by *Fortune* magazine's annual listing of the largest American firms, their assets, and their volume of business. Taken together, in 1986 the 500 largest industrial corporations — that is, a negligible proportion of America's almost 16 million firms — had about one and three-quarter trillion dollars in sales, amounting to nearly 50 percent of the nation's GNP in that year. Most industries in which these giant firms are found are *oligopolies,* a market form we analyzed in Chapter 28. A few are *monopolies,* the market form discussed in Chapter 27.

At the other end of the spectrum, the nation's small business firms have a disproportionately small share of U.S. business. These small firms have earnings

[1]Burton G. Malkiel, *A Random Walk Down Wall Street* (New York: W. W. Norton & Company, Inc., 1973), pages 140–141.

that are not only relatively low but also very risky — risky in the sense that the average new firm does not last very long (its average life is reported to be less than 7 years). When making economic decisions, the buyer is not the only one who must beware!

Just what are the three basic forms of business organization, and what induces organizers of a firm to choose one form rather than another?

Proprietorships

A **proprietorship** is a business firm owned by a single person.

The **proprietorship** is the form of business organization involving the fewest legal complications. Most small retail firms, farms, and many small factories are run as proprietorships. To start a proprietorship, an individual simply decides to go into business and opens up a new firm or takes over an existing firm. Aside from special regulations, such as health requirements for a restaurant or zoning restrictions that limit business activity to particular geographical areas, the individual does not need anyone's permission to go into business. This is one of the main advantages of the proprietorship form of organization. But probably its main attraction is that the owner can be his or her own boss and the firm's sole decision maker. No partners or stockholders have to be consulted when the proprietor wants to expand or change the company's product line or modify the firm's advertising policy. A proprietorship also has tax advantages, particularly compared with the corporation. The proprietor's income is taxed only once. If the firm were to incorporate, its income would be taxed twice — once as income of the firm (corporate income tax) and again as personal income of the owner.

Unlimited liability is a legal obligation of a firm's owner(s) to pay back company debts with whatever resources he or she owns.

There are, on the other hand, two basic disadvantages of a proprietorship, difficulties that make it almost impossible to organize large-scale enterprises as proprietorships. First, the owner has **unlimited liability** for the debts of the firm. If the company goes out of business leaving unpaid bills, the former owner can be forced to pay them out of personal savings. The owner can be made to sell the family home, private collections of stamps or paintings, or any other personal assets, no matter how unrelated to the business, so that the proceeds can be used to pay off the company's obligations. Often proprietors guard themselves against this danger by signing away all their property to other members of their families or to others whom they feel they can trust. But such transfers are subject to federal and state gift taxes. In any event, there are many tales of tragedy that begin with the signing away of all of one's possessions — King Lear's betrayal by his daughters might well serve as the classic warning to those proprietors who are apt to be too trusting.

A second and equally basic shortcoming of the proprietorship is that it inhibits expansion of the firm by making it difficult to raise money. People outside the company are reluctant to put money into a firm over which they exercise no control. This means that the proprietorship's capital is usually no greater than the amount its owner is willing and able to put into it, plus the amount that banks or other commercial lenders are willing to provide.

SUMMARY

The three main advantages of the individual proprietorship are:

1. It leaves full control in the hands of the owner.
2. It involves little legal complication.
3. It generally subjects its owners to lower taxes.

Its two main disadvantages are:

1. The unlimited liability of the owner for the obligations of the company.
2. The difficulty of increasing the amount of funds that can be raised for the firm.

Partnerships

Measured in terms of the amount of their capital, **partnerships** tend to be larger than proprietorships but smaller than corporations. However, the largest partnerships greatly exceed the smallest corporations in terms of both their financing and their influence. For example, some of the most prestigious law firms and investment banks are partnerships. When you call a law firm and are greeted by "Smith, Jones, Brown, and Pfafufnik; Good Morning," you are almost certainly being treated to a partial listing of the company's current or past senior partners (the partners who own the largest share of the firm or who founded the firm).

A **partnership** is a firm whose ownership is shared by a fixed number of proprietors.

The advantage of the partnership over the proprietorship is that it brings together the funds and expertise of a number of people and permits them to be combined to form a company larger than any one of the owners could have financed or managed alone. If one cannot hope to run a particular type of firm with an inventory of less than $2 million, a person who is not rich may be unable to get into the business without the aid of a partner. A partnership may also bring together a variety of specialists, as often happens in a medical practice. The partnership also offers the advantage of freedom from double taxation, a benefit it shares with the proprietorship.

But the partnership has disadvantages, some of them substantial. Decision making in a partnership may be harder than in any other type of firm. The sole proprietor need consult no one before acting; the corporation appoints officers who are authorized to decide things for the company. But in a partnership it may be necessary for every partner to agree before any steps are taken by the firm, and this is the primary bane of this form of enterprise. A partnership has been compared to two people in a horse costume, each supplying two of the legs, each prepared to go in a different direction, and each unable to move without the other.

Furthermore, in a partnership, as in a proprietorship, the individual partners have unlimited liability, meaning that they can conceivably be in danger of losing their personal possessions to pay off company debts. Finally, the partnership suffers from unique legal complications. A partnership agreement is like a marriage contract entered into solely for the financial advantage of the participants, and so there is likely to be considerable haggling about the terms. And under the law, if a partner dies, or decides to leave the firm, or the others decide to buy that person's share in the enterprise, the partnership may have to be dissolved and haggling about the contract may start all over again.

SUMMARY
The benefits of the partnership to the owners of the firm are:

1. Access to larger quantities of capital.
2. Protection from double taxation.

Its disadvantages are:

1. The need to obtain the agreement of many if not all partners to all major decisions.
2. Unlimited liability of the partners for the obligations of the company.
3. The legal complications, including automatic dissolution of the partnership, when there is *any* change in ownership.

Corporations

A corporation is a firm that has the legal status of a fictional individual. This fictional individual is owned by a number of persons, called its stockholders, and is run by a set of elected officers (usually headed by a president) and a board of directors, whose chairman is often also in a powerful position to influence the affairs of the firm.

Limited liability is a legal obligation of a firm's owners to pay back company debts only with the money they have already invested in the firm.

Most big firms are **corporations,** a form of business organization that has quite a different legal status from that of a proprietorship or a partnership. Because a corporation is an individual in the eyes of the law, its earnings, like those of other individuals, are taxed. This leads to double taxation of the stockholders, who also pay tax on any dividends they receive from the firm.

But this disadvantage is counterbalanced by an important advantage: Any debt of the corporation is regarded as an obligation of that fictitious individual, not as a liability of any stockholder. This means that the stockholders benefit from the protection of limited liability — they can lose no more than the money they have put into the firm. Creditors cannot force them to sell their personal possessions to help repay any outstanding debts incurred by the firm.

Limited liability is the main secret of the success of the corporate form of organization. Thanks to that provision, individuals from every part of the world are willing to put money into firms whose operations they do not understand and whose managements they do not know. A giant firm may produce computers, locomotives, and electrical generators; it may have, as subsidiaries, publishing houses and shoe factories. Few of its stockholders will know or care about all the firm's activities. Yet each investor knows that by providing money to the firm in return for a share of its ownership, no more is risked than the amount of money provided. This has permitted corporations to obtain financing from literally millions of shareholders, each of whom receives in return a claim on the firm's profits, and, at least in principle, a portion of the company's ownership.

As indicated, the profits of a corporation are subject to taxation. Smaller corporations get a tax break, but the larger firms, whose total profits are high, pay a federal tax rate of 34 percent on all *net* earnings over $100,000. In addition, most states levy corporate taxes of their own, pushing the total tax rate above 40 percent. This means that corporate investors are left with about 40 percent less out of each dollar of company earnings than investors in a partnership or a proprietorship. In other words, there is a **double taxation** of payments to the owners. That is, corporate earnings are taxed twice, once when they are earned by the company, and a second time, when they go to the investors in the form of dividends and are subject to the ordinary income tax on the investor's income.

Corporations are directed by a hired group of managers: a chairman of the board of directors, a president, various vice presidents, and so on. These executives are, legally, employees of the owners of the firm who, as we will see, are the stockholders of the corporation. This arrangement has great advantages. It prevents the quarrels and indecision that are often problems for partnerships. On the other hand, since the management is made up of hired personnel it cannot always be trusted to do what is best for the owners. Managers are often accused of looking after their own interests first and, if necessary, sacrificing those of the stockholders (the owners).

Corporations escape one other problem that troubles partnerships. As we saw, if a partner wants to leave the firm, the entire enterprise may have to be reorganized. But in a corporation, any owner who wants to quit just sells her stocks on the stock market, while the corporation goes on exactly as before. In this way, at least in theory, a corporation can continue forever.

SUMMARY
Benefits of the corporate form to the owners:

1. Limited liability.
2. Access to large quantities of capital.
3. Ease of operation with the help of a hired management.
4. "Permanence": the firm is not dissolved or reorganized each time an owner leaves.

Its disadvantages are:

1. Double taxation of payments to the owners.
2. The possibility that hired managers will act in their own interests rather than those of the owners.

It is worth digressing briefly to consider the economic effects of the double taxation of corporate earnings. Does an investor end up earning less by putting money in a corporation than by putting it in a company that is about equally risky but not subject to double taxation? Paradoxically, the answer is that investors, on the average, will *not* lose anything by choosing the corporation. The tax will not and cannot put those who make one type of investment at a disadvantage in comparison with those who choose any other.

How is this possible? How does the effect of the additional tax on corporate stocks disappear before it reaches the stockholder? There are two processes that achieve this act of magic. First, corporations are forced to avoid some investment opportunities that partnerships and proprietorships can afford to take on. Suppose that in 1988 the market rate of return to people who provide money to firms is 9 percent, and a new product is invented that is expected to bring a 12 percent return to a firm that manufactures it. An individual proprietor can afford to produce the new item—borrowing the necessary funds at 9 percent and keeping the 3 percent additional return on the new item for herself. But a large corporation *cannot* afford to produce the new item. For in order to compete for funds, it must also pay investors 9 percent, which means that it will have to earn about 15 percent on its investments since about 40 percent of that money will be siphoned off into taxes.

Thus, double taxation keeps corporate business out of various economic activities that offer a real, but limited, earnings potential. This effect may be unfortunate from the viewpoint of the efficiency of the economy, because it means that many firms are induced to stay out of activities in which it might be useful for them to take part. For instance, corporations may find it too costly to open retail outlets in slum areas or to run trains to isolated rural areas—activities that might be profitable in the absence of the tax.

Second, there is another fail-safe mechanism that protects new investors in corporate stocks from earning a lower return on the average than they would on other securities of equal risk. Suppose two otherwise identical securities, A and

B, each offer a return of $60 per year but A is subject to a 50 percent tax while B is not. *Question:* If the market price of security B is $1000, what will be the market price of A? *Answer:* The price of A will be only $500, exactly half the price of security B. Why? Because since it will bring in only $30 per year after taxes, exactly half of what security A returns, investors will be willing to pay only half as much for it as they are willing to pay for the untaxed security. At those prices investors in either security will earn the same rate of return after payment of taxes.

Double taxation of corporate earnings tends to restrict the activities of corporate firms, keeping them out of relatively low-profit operations. However, double taxation does not mean that the individual investor earns less by putting money into a corporation than by putting it into other businesses.

The Hybrids: Limited Partnerships and Subchapter S Corporations

The law permits some small firms to enjoy both some of the tax benefits of partnerships and some of the limited liability benefits of corporations. The two most frequent uses of such hybrid forms are the **limited partnership** and the **subchapter S corporation.**

A limited partnership is a firm in which some partners are granted limited liability. However, the organization of such a firm is subject to a number of legal restrictions, relating to types and number of investors and the amounts of their investments. These restrictions are intended for the protection of poorly informed investors. At least one of the partners, and any partner who participates in the operation and management of the business, must be designated as a "general partner," whose liability can exceed the amount of money that person has put into the firm. That is, if the firm cannot pay its debts, a general partner can be sued by the company's creditors (that is, the people to whom the firm owes money), in order to collect money from the general partner's privately held funds. The other partners in the firm, who are generally called "limited partners," cannot be sued in this way. As you can imagine, rich people usually avoid becoming general partners in a risky firm because they have a good deal to lose.

A subchapter S corporation is a firm which is relieved of part of the burden of double taxation that is imposed on other corporations. It can have no more than 35 shareholders. Unlike a limited partnership it contains no individuals who run the risks of a general partner. That is, every stockholder in such a firm has the full advantages of limited liability. However, such a corporation does not enjoy all the tax advantages of a partnership. In particular, in some states it is not exempt from corporate taxation. In addition, investors cannot use losses from the S corporation to reduce tax payments on their other income.

Financing Corporate Activity

Our discussion of the earnings of an investor in corporate securities introduces a subject of interest to millions of Americans—*stocks* and *bonds,* the financial instruments that provide funds to the corporate sector of the economy. (Stocks and bonds will be defined later in the chapter.) In fact, as we will see, there are three principal ways in which corporations obtain money: by sale of stocks, by borrowing (which, we will note, includes the sale of bonds), and by

A **limited partnership** is a firm, generally small, which though organized as a partnership, gives some of the partners the legal protection of limited liability.

A **subchapter S corporation** is a small corporation which is permitted to escape part of the burden of double taxation.

"plowback"—keeping some part of company earnings to invest back into the company, rather than paying the money out as income to the firm's owners.

When a corporation needs money to add to its plant or equipment or to finance other types of real investment, it can get it by printing new stocks and new bonds and selling them to people who are looking for something in which to invest their money. What enables the firm to get money in exchange for printed paper? Doesn't the process seem a bit like counterfeiting? If done improperly, there are grounds for the suspicion. But, carried out appropriately, it is a perfectly rational economic process. As long as the funds derived from a new issue of stocks and bonds are used effectively to increase the firm's capacity to produce and earn a profit, then these funds will automatically yield the means for any required repayment and for the payment of appropriate amounts of interest and dividends to the purchasers of the new bonds and stocks. But there have been times when this did not happen. It is alleged that one of the favorite practices of the more notorious nineteenth century manipulators of the market was "watering" of company stocks—the issue of stocks with little or nothing to back them up. The term is derived from the practice of some cattle dealers who would force their animals to drink large quantities of water just before bringing them to be weighed for sale.

Another major source of funds is **plowback** or **retained earnings.** For example, if a company earns $30 million after taxes and decides to pay out only $10 million in dividends and invest the remaining $20 million back into the firm, that $20 million is called plowback.

When business is profitable so that management has the funds to reinvest in the company, it will often prefer plowback to other sources of funding. One reason for this preference is that it is less risky to management. This source of funds does not require prior approval by the Securities and Exchange Commission (SEC), as do other sources.[2] Moreover, plowback does not depend on the availability of eager customers for new company stocks and bonds, for an issue of such new securities turns into a disappointment if there is little demand for them when they are offered to the public. Above all, a plowback decision generally does not lead anyone to reexamine the efficiency of management's operation in the way that a new stock issue invariably does. In these instances, the SEC, potential buyers of the stock, and their professional advisers all scrutinize the company carefully.

A second reason for the attractiveness of plowback is that issuing new stocks and bonds is usually an expensive and lengthy process. The company is required by the SEC to gather masses of data in its prospectus—a document describing the financial condition of the company—before the new issue is approved. Not only is this costly, but the many months of delay that are involved require the firm to wait for the funds when it needs them quickly, and also subject the firm to the risk of a change in stock market conditions (during the period of delay a brisk demand for new stocks and bonds may dwindle or even evaporate).

A final way for a company to obtain money is by borrowing it from banks, insurance companies, or other private firms with money to lend. It may also sometimes borrow from a U.S. government agency either directly or with the agency's help (the agency serves as guarantor in this instance, promising to make sure the loan is repaid). For example, loans may be arranged with the help of the national defense agencies if they want a private firm to undertake

Plowback or **retained earnings** is the portion of a corporation's profits that management decides to keep and invest back into the firm's operations rather than to pay out directly to stockholders in the form of dividends.

---

[2]The Securities and Exchange Commission, established in 1934, protects the interests of people who buy securities. It requires firms that issue stocks and other securities to provide information about their financial condition, and it regulates the issue and trading of securities.

Figure 30–1

Figure 30–1
SOURCES OF NEW
FUNDS, U.S.
CORPORATIONS, 1986
Corporations in the United
States get about 75 percent
of their reinvestment funds
from plowback. About 20
percent of this consists of
money earned by the firms
as profits but not paid out to
stockholders. The remainder
of plowback consists of
depreciation—funds
accumulated for replacement
of plant, equipment, and so
on, as it wears out or
becomes obsolete. New
stocks account for only 9
percent of the total new
funding of corporations.
SOURCE: *Federal Reserve
Bulletin*, January 1987.

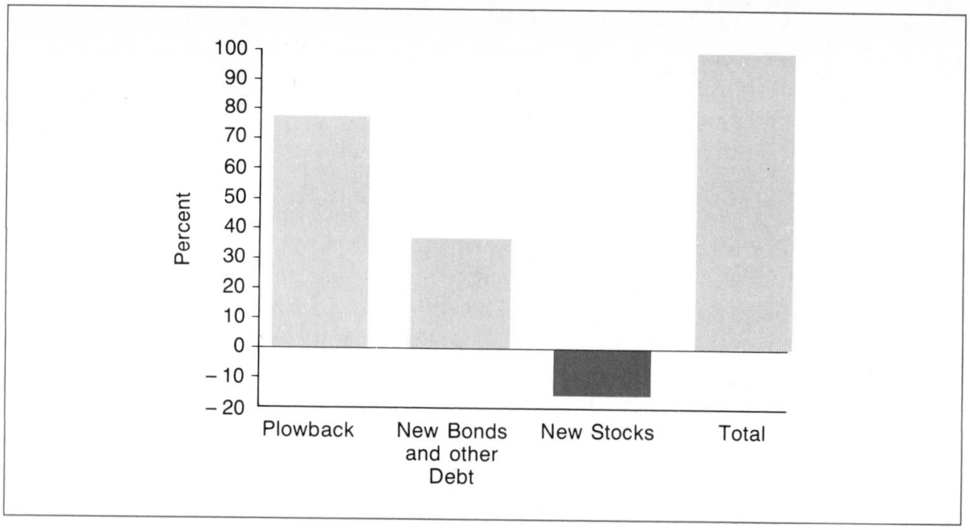

the design and production of an expensive new weapons system. Small business firms, too, are eligible for various forms of assistance in borrowing.

Figure 30–1 (a bar chart) shows the relative importance of each of the different sources of funds to U.S. corporations. It indicates that plowback is by far the most important source of corporate financing, constituting some 78 percent of the total financing to the corporate sector of the economy in 1986. This is followed by issues of new bonds and other forms of borrowing, which supply 37 percent of the total, while new stocks supply very little. In recent years new stocks have actually supplied a *negative* amount of funding, on balance, as corporations reduced the number of their stocks in the hands of the public by buying some of them back.

The Financing of Corporate Activity: Stocks and Bonds

A **common stock** of a corporation is a piece of paper that gives the holder of the stock a share of the ownership of the company.

A **bond** is simply an IOU by a corporation that promises to pay the holder of the piece of paper a fixed sum of money at the specified *maturity* date and some other fixed amount of money (the *coupon* or the *interest payment*) every year up to the date of maturity.

We return now to the other major sources of corporate financing besides plowback and direct borrowing—the corporate securities, like **common stocks** and **bonds.** Stocks represent ownership of part of the corporation. For example, if a company issues 100,000 shares, then a person who owns 1000 shares actually owns 1 percent of the company and is entitled to 1 percent of the company's *dividends*, which are the corporation's annual payments to stockholders. The shareholder's vote counts for 1 percent of the total votes in an election of corporate officers or in a referendum on corporate policy.

Bonds differ from stocks in several ways. First, whereas the purchaser of a corporation's stock *buys* a share of its ownership and receives some control over its affairs, the purchaser of a bond simply *lends* money to the firm. Second, whereas stockholders have no idea how much they will receive for their stocks when they sell them, or how much they will receive in dividends each year while they own them, bondholders know with a high degree of certainty how much money they will be paid if they hold their bonds to maturity. For instance, a bond with a face value of $1000, with an $80 coupon that matures in 1998, will provide to its owner $80 per year every year until 1998, and in addition it will repay the $1000 to the bondholder in 1998. Unless the company goes bankrupt, there is no doubt about this repayment schedule. Third, bondholders have a *legally prior claim* on company earnings, which means that nothing can be paid by the company to its stockholders until interest payments to the company's bondholders have been met. For all these reasons, bonds are considered less risky than stocks.

In reality, however, some of the differences between stocks and bonds are not as clear-cut as have just been described. Two such misconceptions are particularly worth noting. First, the ownership of the company represented by the holding of a few shares of its stock may be more apparent than real. A holder of 0.002 percent of the stocks of General Motors—which is a *very large* investment—exercises no real control over GM's operations. In fact, many economists believe that the ownership of large corporations is so diffuse that no stockholder or stockholder group has any effective control over management. In this view, the management of a corporation is a largely independent decision-making body; as long as it keeps enough cash flowing to stockholders to prevent discontent and rebellion, management can do anything it wants within the law. Looked at in another way, this last conclusion really says that stockholders are merely another class of persons who provide loans to the company. The only real difference between stockholders and bondholders, according to this interpretation, is that stockholders' loans are riskier and therefore entitled to higher payments.

Second, bonds *can* be quite risky to the bondholder. Persons who try to sell their bonds before maturity may find that the market price for bonds happens to be low, so that if they need to raise cash in a hurry, they may have to sell at a substantial loss. Also, bondholders may be exposed to losses from inflation. Whether the $1000 promised the bondholder at the 1998 maturity date represents substantial purchasing power or only a little depends on what happens to the general price level in the meantime. And no one can predict the price level this far in advance with any accuracy.

Bond Prices and Interest Rates

Why is investment in bonds risky? That is, what makes their price go up and down? The main element in the answer is that changes in interest rates cause bond prices to change. There is a straightforward relationship between bond prices and interest rates. Whenever one goes up, the other must go down. For example, suppose that Sears Roebuck had issued some 15-year bonds when interest rates were comparatively low, so that the company had to offer to pay only 6 percent to find buyers for these bonds. People who invested $1000 in new Sears bonds received in return a contract that promised them $60 per year for 15 years plus the return of their $1000 at the end of that period. Suppose further that two years later interest rates in the economy rise so that new 15-year bonds of companies of similar quality pay 12 percent. Now for $1000 one can buy a contract that offers $120 per year. Obviously, no one will any longer pay as much as $1000 for a bond that promises only $60 per year. Consequently, the market price of the two-year-old Sears bonds must fall. There are many bonds in existence now that were issued years ago at interest rates of 6 percent and even less. In today's markets, with interest rates well above 6 percent such bonds sell for a price well below their original value.

When interest rates in the economy rise, there must be a fall in the prices of previously issued bonds with their lower interest earnings. For the same reason, when interest rates in the economy fall, the prices of previously issued bonds must rise.

It follows that as interest rates in the economy change because of changes in monetary policy or other reasons, bond prices fluctuate. That is one reason why investment in bonds can be risky.

Corporate Choice Between Stocks and Bonds

We have seen why a corporation may prefer to finance its real investment, such as construction of factories and equipment, through plowback or retained earnings rather than the issue of new stocks or bonds. But suppose it has decided to do the latter. How does it determine whether bonds or stocks suit its purposes better?

Two considerations are of prime importance. Although issuing bonds generally causes more risk to the firm than issuing stocks, the corporation usually expects to pay more money to stockholders over the long run than to bondholders. In other words, to the firm that issues them, bonds are cheaper but riskier. The decision about which is better for the firm therefore involves a trade-off between the two considerations.

Why are bonds risky to the corporation? When it issues $20 million in new bonds at 10 percent, the company commits itself to pay out $2 million every year for the life of the bond. It is obligated to pay that amount each year, whether that year happens to be one in which business is booming or one in which the firm is losing money. That is a big risk. If the firm is unable to meet its obligation to bondholders in some year, it faces bankruptcy.

The issue of new stocks does not burden the company with any such risk since the company does not promise to pay the stockholders *any* fixed amount. Stockholders simply receive whatever is left of the company's net earnings after payments to bondholders. If nothing is left to pay the new stockholders in some years, legally speaking, that is just their bad luck.

Why, then, do stockholders normally obtain higher average expected payments from the company than bondholders? The answer is obtained by looking at the risk-return trade-off from the investor's point of view. In the case of bonds, the company assumes as much risk as possible by guaranteeing a specified payment to the bondholder. In the case of stocks, however, the company assumes little or no risk, leaving it all to the stockholder.

The situation is reversed for the individual who provides the money: bonds are safer than stocks. Since this is true, no investor will want to buy stocks rather than bonds unless she can expect a sufficiently higher return on the stocks to make up for the added risk. So if a company offers both stocks and bonds, their prices and prospective returns must offer a higher (but riskier) average rate of return to stockholders than to bondholders.

To the firm that issues them, bonds are riskier than stocks because they commit the firm to make a fixed annual payment even in years when it is losing money. For the same reason, stocks are riskier than bonds to the buyers of securities. That is why stockholders expect to be paid more money than bondholders.

Buying Stocks and Bonds

Although stocks and bonds can be purchased through any brokerage firm, not all brokers charge the same fees. Until recent years the charges to small investors were fixed by collusive agreement and did not vary from broker to broker. But in 1975, the SEC ruled this fixed price to be illegal. Since then, bargain brokerage houses have appeared and proliferated. They usually advertise in the financial pages of newspapers, offering investors very little service—no advice, no research, no other frills—other than merely buying or selling what the customer wants them to, at lower fees than those charged by higher-service brokerage firms.

Many investors are not aware of the various ways in which stocks can be purchased (or sold). The following are some of the possibilities: (a) *Round lot* purchases: Purchases of 100 shares or 200 shares or any number of shares in multiples of 100. (b) *Odd lot* purchases: The purchase of some number of shares that is not a multiple of 100. The brokerage fee per dollar of investment is normally higher on an odd lot than on a round lot. (c) A *market order* purchase: This simply tells the broker to buy a specified quantity of stock (either a round lot or an odd lot) at the best price the market currently offers. (d) A *limit order:* An agreement to buy a given amount of stock when its price falls to a specified level. If the investor offers to buy at $18, then shares will be purchased by the broker if and when the market price falls to $18 per share or less.

There are many investment information services that supply subscribers with a variety of information on performance of stocks, bonds, and other securities. These firms offer analyses of particular companies, forecasts, and advice.

Selecting a Portfolio: Diversification

Rational planning by an individual of what stocks, bonds, and other financial investments to hold requires more than just careful examination of the merits and demerits of individual securities. It is important to select a combination of securities that meet one's needs effectively. Such a combination of holdings is called the individual's portfolio of investments. For example, an individual who is saving to send children to college in ten years does not need securities which pay money regularly in the meantime, whereas a retired person who depends on periodic payments wants securities which provide regular and convenient returns.

A far more important consideration in planning a portfolio is selecting combinations of securities with low risk. A portfolio may well be far less risky than any of the individual securities it contains. The secret is **diversification,** not putting all one's eggs in one basket.

If Joe Jones holds only stocks of company A and the company goes bankrupt, then all may be lost. However, if Jones divides his holdings among companies A, B, and C, the portfolio may perform satisfactorily even if company A goes broke. Moreover, suppose company A specializes in producing luxury items, which do well in prosperous periods but very badly during recessions, while company B sells cheap clothing, whose cyclical demand pattern differs greatly from that of company A. If Jones holds stock in both companies, the overall risk is less than if he owned stock in only one of the companies. All other things being equal, a portfolio containing many different types of securities tends to be less risky than a portfolio with fewer types of securities.

Diversification means including a number and variety of stocks, bonds, and other such items in an individual's portfolio. If the individual owns airline stocks, for example, diversification requires the purchase of a stock or bond in a very different industry, such as an electric company.

Following a Portfolio's Performance

Newspapers carry daily information on stock and bond prices. Figure 30–2 is an excerpt from a *Wall Street Journal* stock market report. In the first two columns, before the company name, the report gives the stock's highest and lowest price in the last year. In the highlighted example, the price of Alcoa stock is reported to have ranged between $52 and $32\frac{5}{8}$. Next, after the name of the stock, there

Figure 30–2
EXCERPT FROM A STOCK MARKET PAGE
This table from *The Wall Street Journal* gives the highest and lowest price in the current year; the current dividend rate; the dividend yield; the ratio of stock price to company earnings (P/E ratio); the number of shares sold; the highest, lowest, and final price on the previous day; and the change in price from the day before.
SOURCE: Reprinted by permission of *The Wall Street Journal*, Dow Jones & Company, Inc., 1987.

52 Weeks High	Low	Stock	Div.	Yld %	P-E Ratio	Sales 100s	High	Low	Close	Net Chg.
37½	25¼	AlisC pf		...	...	8	30⅜	30¼	30⅜	− ¼
47¼	35¼	ALLTL	2.04	5.4	15	361	38¼	37	37⅝	− ⅝
52	32⅝	Alcoa	1.20	2.5	225	5260	47⅝	47	47¼	− ¾
24⅝	10½	Amax		...	33	7213	21¼	20⅜	20⅝	− ⅝
37⅜	16½	AmHes		...	14	1102	36	35½	35⅝	...
43⅛	9⅜	ABrck g		...	...	1206	39⅝	37½	38⅜	− 1⅜
53	40⅜	ABrnd s	2.08	4.9	13	2320	42⅞	41½	42⅞	+ ⅝
34⅞	31⅝	ABrd pf	2.75	8.6	...	122	31⅞d	31½	31⅞	+ ¼
28	21⅛	ABldM	.90	3.6	17	17	25	25	25	...
33⅜	23¼	ABusPr	.80	2.8	17	11	29	28⅝	29	+ ⅜
25⅜	20⅛	ACapBd	2.20	9.8	...	66	22½	22⅜	22½	+ ¼
35⅜	29¾	ACapCv	5.82e	18.1	...	24	32¼	31¾	32⅛	+ ⅜
24⅞	14⅝	ACMR	1.00a	6.0	11	71	16¾	16⅜	16¾	− ⅛
7⅞	2⅞	ACentC		...	...	1	3⅛	3⅛	3⅛	...
98½	69⅞	ACyan	2.10	2.5	18	874	86	85¼	85½	+ ¼
49¼	34⅞	ACyan wi		...	...	1	43½	43½	43½	+ ¼
31⅝	24⅝	AElPw	2.26	8.7	10	3071	26¼	25⅝	26⅛	+ ¼
40⅝	26⅞	AExp s	.76	2.3	13	8940	33⅜	32¾	33⅛	+ ⅛
18⅝	10	AFaml s	.22	2.0	8	1341	11	10½	10¾	+ ⅜
46¾	34⅛	AGnCp	1.25	3.5	8	5175	35⅞	34⅞	35⅞	+ ⅝
24	14¼	AGnl wt		...	...	107	14¾	14½	14⅝	− ⅛
54¼	51⅝	AGnl pfA	4.01e	7.6	...	1	52⅞	52⅞	52⅞	...
20	15¼	AHltP n	.22e	1.4	...	308	15¾	15½	15¾	+ ⅛
9⅝	6⅛	AHoist		...	...	32	8⅞	8⅝	8⅝	...
94⅞	71¾	AHome	3.34	4.2	15	1712	80⅜	79¾	80⅜	+ ¾
101½	77⅜	Amrtc s	5.00	6.4	10	1409	78⅞	77¾	78½	+ ½
82	54⅞	AInGr s	.25	.4	13	2171	63½	61⅝	62⅜	+ ¼
20¼	13⅜	AMI	.72	4.1	111	1745	17⅞	17½	17¾	+ ⅛
4¾	2½	AmMot		...	...	10183	4⅜	4⅛	4⅜	+ ⅛
38	22	AMotr pf	2.37	6.4	...	147	36⅞	36¾	36⅞	+ ⅛
42¾	20½	APresd	.50	1.3	21	487	40	39⅝	39⅞	...
79¼	48½	APrsd pf	3.50	4.6	...	110	76	75½	75¾	− ¼
19⅜	11½	ASLFla		...	2	125	14	13¼	13½	− ¼
24⅜	19¾	ASLFl pf	2.19	10.6	...	28	20¾	20¼	20¾	+ ½
12	7⅜	AShip	.40	5.5	...	118	7½d	7	7¼	− ¼
51⅞	36	AmStd	1.80	4.5	8	1634	40⅞	39½	39¾	+ ⅜
71¼	51⅝	AmStor	.84	1.3	18	230	66¾	66	66⅜	+ ⅝
81	63¼	AStr pfA	4.38	6.0	...	120	73	72⅝	72⅝	− ⅝
61	54½	AStr pfB	6.80	12.3	...	4	55½	55½	55½	− ⅜
27⅞	22⅛	AT&T	1.20	4.7	21	10668	25¾	25¼	25⅜	+ ⅛
52½	46½	AT&T pf	3.64	7.2	...	9	50⅝	50⅜	50⅝	...
53	47¼	AT&T pf	3.74	7.4	...	74	50⅝	50⅜	50⅝	...

appears the annual dividend per share ($1.20). Following that is the yield, or the dividend as a percent of the closing price (2.5 percent). The next column reports the *price earnings* (P/E) ratio (225 for Alcoa). This latter figure is the price per share divided by the company's net earnings per share in the previous year, and it is usually taken as a basic measure indicating whether the current price of the stock overvalues or undervalues the company. However, no simple rule enables us to interpret the P/E figures — for example, a very risky firm or a slowly growing firm with a low P/E may be considered overvalued, while a safe, rapidly growing firm with a high P/E may still be a bargain. The next column indicates the number of shares that were traded on the previous day (526,000), an indication of whether that stock is actively traded. Finally, the last four figures indicate yesterday's highest price ($\$47\frac{5}{8}$), its lowest price ($47), the price at which the last transaction of the day took place ($\$47\frac{1}{4}$), and the change in that price from the previous day (down $\frac{3}{4}$).

Figure 30–3, also from *The Wall Street Journal,* gives similar information about bonds. The first thing to notice here is that a given company may have several different bonds — differing in maturity date and coupon (annual interest payment). For example, Citicorp offers five different bonds. The one that is highlighted is labeled Citicp$12\frac{1}{2}$93, meaning that these bonds pay an annual interest of $12\frac{1}{2}$ percent (the coupon) on their face value and that their maturity (redemption) date is 1993. Next, the current yield is reported as 12 percent. This is simply the coupon divided by the price. Since that yield, 12 percent, is lower than the coupon, the bond must be selling at a price above its face value, so that the return per dollar is correspondingly low. The remaining information in the table means the same as that reported for stock prices.

Bonds	Cur Yld	Vol	High	Low	Close	Net Chg.
ChCft 15s99	14.2	7	106	106	106	...
Chryslr $12\frac{3}{4}$s92	11.2	25	$114\frac{1}{4}$	112	$114\frac{1}{4}$	$+ 3\frac{1}{4}$
ChryF $9\frac{3}{8}$s87	9.3	40	$100\frac{1}{2}$	$100\frac{1}{2}$	$100\frac{1}{2}$	$+ \frac{3}{16}$
ChryF zr90	...	16	$74\frac{5}{8}$	74	74	$+ \frac{3}{4}$
ChryF 12s92	11.0	20	$108\frac{5}{8}$	$107\frac{3}{4}$	$108\frac{5}{8}$	...
ChryF 10.6s90	10.2	20	$103\frac{7}{8}$	$103\frac{5}{8}$	$103\frac{7}{8}$	$+ 2\frac{3}{8}$
ChryF $9\frac{3}{4}$s90D	9.6	4	$101\frac{1}{2}$	$101\frac{1}{2}$	$101\frac{1}{2}$	...
ChryF $9\frac{3}{4}$s90F	9.6	38	$101\frac{1}{4}$	$101\frac{1}{4}$	$101\frac{1}{4}$	...
CirclK $8\frac{1}{4}$s05	cv	15	118	$116\frac{1}{2}$	118	$+ 1\frac{1}{2}$
CirclK $7\frac{1}{4}$s06	cv	186	97	$95\frac{3}{4}$	97	...
Citicp 8.45s07	9.8	9	$86\frac{1}{4}$	$84\frac{3}{4}$	$86\frac{1}{4}$	$+ \frac{3}{8}$
Citicp $8\frac{1}{8}$s07	9.9	150	$82\frac{1}{4}$	82	82	...
Citicp 7.05s04†	7.8	15	$90\frac{5}{8}$	$90\frac{5}{8}$	$90\frac{5}{8}$	$- 2\frac{3}{4}$
Citicp 12s90	11.8	12	102	$101\frac{3}{4}$	102	...
Citicp $12\frac{1}{2}$s93	12.0	5	$104\frac{1}{8}$	$104\frac{1}{8}$	$104\frac{1}{8}$	$- 3\frac{1}{8}$
CitSvc zr88	...	46	$87\frac{1}{2}$	$87\frac{3}{8}$	$87\frac{3}{8}$	$- \frac{5}{8}$
CitSvc zr89	...	17	80	80	80	$- \frac{3}{4}$
Claytn 6s07	cv	20	87	85	85	$- 5\frac{1}{2}$
ClevEl $8\frac{3}{4}$s05	10.2	111	$85\frac{5}{8}$	84	$85\frac{5}{8}$	...
ClevEl $9\frac{1}{4}$s09	10.4	10	$89\frac{1}{8}$	$89\frac{1}{8}$	$89\frac{1}{8}$	$+ 2\frac{7}{8}$
ClevEl $8\frac{3}{8}$s11	10.5	20	80	80	80	...
Coastl $11\frac{3}{4}$s06	11.9	53	$98\frac{3}{4}$	$97\frac{7}{8}$	$98\frac{3}{4}$	$+ \frac{7}{8}$
Coastl 8.48s91	9.2	25	$92\frac{7}{8}$	92	92	...
Coleco 11s89	cv	83	100	$99\frac{1}{2}$	$99\frac{3}{4}$	$+ \frac{1}{4}$
Coleco $11\frac{1}{8}$s01	14.8	32	77	75	75	$+ 1$
ColuG 9s94	9.0	8	$99\frac{1}{2}$	$99\frac{1}{2}$	$99\frac{1}{2}$	...
ColuG $8\frac{3}{4}$s96	8.9	3	$94\frac{1}{8}$	$94\frac{1}{8}$	$94\frac{1}{8}$	$- \frac{5}{8}$
ColuG $9\frac{5}{8}$s89	9.6	32	101	$100\frac{1}{2}$	$100\frac{1}{2}$	$- \frac{1}{2}$
ColSo $13\frac{3}{8}$s95	11.1	4	120	120	120	...
CmlCr $7\frac{3}{4}$s92	8.5	23	$91\frac{1}{8}$	$91\frac{1}{8}$	$91\frac{1}{8}$	$- 1\frac{5}{8}$
CmwE $8\frac{3}{4}$s05	9.7	10	90	89	90	$+ 2\frac{1}{2}$
CmwE $9\frac{3}{8}$s04	10.0	15	$95\frac{3}{8}$	$93\frac{3}{4}$	$93\frac{3}{4}$	$- \frac{3}{4}$
CmwE $8\frac{1}{8}$s07D	9.7	20	$83\frac{1}{2}$	$83\frac{1}{2}$	$83\frac{1}{2}$	$+ \frac{1}{2}$
CmwE $8\frac{1}{4}$s07	9.9	10	$83\frac{1}{8}$	$83\frac{1}{8}$	$83\frac{1}{8}$	$+ 1\frac{1}{8}$
CmwE $9\frac{1}{8}$s08	10.0	5	$91\frac{5}{8}$	$91\frac{5}{8}$	$91\frac{5}{8}$	$- \frac{1}{8}$
CmwE $17\frac{1}{2}$s88	15.8	3	111	111	111	$+ \frac{1}{8}$
CmwE 16s90	15.5	1	$103\frac{1}{8}$	$103\frac{1}{8}$	$103\frac{1}{8}$	...
CmwE $14\frac{1}{4}$s92	13.3	10	107	107	107	$+ \frac{1}{8}$
Compq $5\frac{1}{4}$s12	cv	28	124	$121\frac{1}{4}$	122	$- 3$
CmpAsc $5\frac{3}{4}$s12	cv	10	$121\frac{1}{2}$	$121\frac{1}{2}$	$121\frac{1}{2}$	$+ \frac{1}{2}$
Cmpvsn 8s09	cv	20	78	78	78	$- \frac{1}{2}$

Figure 30–3

EXCERPT FROM A BOND PRICE TABLE

This report from *The Wall Street Journal* shows annual payment; the year in which the bond will be redeemed (that is, the year in which the company will repay that debt); the yield (that is, the annual payment per dollar of current market price); and the previous day's highest, lowest, and closing price of the bond, as well as the change in price from the day before.

SOURCE: Reprinted by permission of *The Wall Street Journal*, Dow Jones & Company, 1987.

Stock Exchanges and Their Functions

The *New York Stock Exchange* — the "Big Board" — is the most prestigious stock market. Located at the beginning of Wall Street in New York City, it is "*the* establishment" of the securities industry. Only the best known and most heavily traded securities are dealt with by the New York Stock Exchange, which handles over 2000 stocks. The leading brokerage firms hold "seats" on the Stock Exchange, which enable them to trade directly on the floor of the Exchange. Altogether, the Exchange has over 600 member organizations. Seats are traded on the open market, and in 1987 a seat was purchased for approximately $1,000,000 for the first time. In contrast, as recently as 1983 a seat on the New York Stock Exchange was worth less than $350,000, but a booming stock market changed all that.

Someone who wants to buy a stock on the New York Stock Exchange must use a broker who will deal with a firm that has a seat on the Exchange. Suppose you live in Ohio and want to buy 200 shares of General Motors. The broker you approach may be employed by a firm that holds a seat on the Exchange, or she may work through another firm that holds one. The broker who is to fill your order contacts a person called a "specialist," who works on the floor of the Exchange and who handles GM stock.

The specialist usually owns some GM stock of his own that he will offer for sale to you if no other sellers are available at the moment. Usually, in addition, a number of investors have given to the specialist limit orders offering to sell specified quantities of GM stock at specified prices. There may, for example, be one offer to sell 5000 shares at any price above $55 and another offer to sell 1200 shares at any price above $60. Similarly, the specialist is likely to have a number of limit orders to buy at various specified prices. Your order is brought by the floor broker to the specialist, who determines a price that, in his judgment, more or less balances supply and demand as indicated by his recent sales and purchases and the limit orders in his possession. At this price the specialist will fill your order from one of the limit orders to sell (he must do so whenever possible), or he will fill it from his personal inventory of General Motors stock. The price determination process that has just been described is sometimes called "the auction market" process.

The New York Stock Exchange is not the only exchange on which stocks are traded. While 85 percent of stock market transactions (in dollars) are handled by the Big Board, the *American Stock Exchange*, located a few blocks away, trades many stocks that are heavily demanded but that are not exchanged in quite as large a volume as those handled by the Big Board. About 2.5 percent of the dollar volume of stock trades occurs on the American Stock Exchange. There are also *regional exchanges* — such as the Midwest, Cincinnati, Pacific Coast, Philadelphia, and Boston exchanges — which deal in many of the same stocks that are handled on the New York Stock Exchange. A good portion of the business of regional exchanges is serving large "institutional" customers such as banks, insurance companies, and mutual funds. Their volume amounts to about 12.5 percent of the total stock traded.

In addition to the trading on these organized exchanges, stocks are traded on the so-called *third market*. The third market is not a public market at all. It is not a place where many buyers and sellers meet to make exchanges simultaneously. Rather, the third market is run by a number of firms, each operating more or less independently of the others. When a buyer brings an order to such a firm, the broker simply shops around by telephone, seeking to find someone to match the purchase demand with a corresponding supply offer, or the broker may buy or sell for his own account the stocks supplied or demanded by the order. Thus, in dealing on the third market, each broker does the job that is done by a specialist on one of the exchanges. Obviously, trading on the third market is a much less structured and less organized affair than it is on the exchanges.

With the advent of computers and improved electronic means of communication, there is now talk of arranging what is, in effect, a single national market. It would consist of an electronic network through which every buy or sell order would be announced from coast to coast, as would the price and quantity of every completed transaction. In this way, the market would, indeed, have the opportunity to match all supplies and demands and to produce an equilibrium reflecting the demands of every market participant. There are those who predict that such a national market will be in operation within a few years, and that it will increase the efficiency with which the stock market serves the economy.

Stock Exchanges and Corporate Capital Needs

While corporations often raise the funds they need by selling stocks, they do not normally do so through any of the stock exchanges. When new stocks are offered by a company, the new issue is usually handled by a special type of bank called an *investment bank*. In contrast, the stock markets trade almost exclusively in "secondhand securities" — stocks in the hands of individuals and others who had bought them earlier and who now wish to sell them.

Thus the stock market does not provide funds to corporations that need the financing to expand their productive activities. The markets only provide money to persons who already hold stocks previously issued by the corporations.

Yet stock exchanges have two functions that are of critical importance for the financing of corporations. First, by providing a secondhand market for stocks, they make it much less risky for an individual to invest in a company. Investors know that their money is not locked in—if they need the money, they can always sell their stocks to other investors or to the "specialist" at the price the market currently offers. This reduction in risk makes it far easier for corporations to issue new stocks. Second, the stock market determines the current price of the company's stocks. That, in turn, determines whether it will be hard or easy for a corporation to raise money by selling new stocks. For example, suppose a company initially has one million shares and wants to raise $10 million. If the price is $40 per share, an issue of 250,000 shares can bring in the required funds, leaving the original stockholders with four-fifths of the company's ownership. But if the price of the stock is only $20, then 500,000 new shares will have to be issued, cutting the original stockholders back to two-thirds of the ownership of the company. This is a less attractive proposition.

Some people believe that the price of a company's stock is closely tied to the efficiency with which its productive activities are conducted, the effectiveness with which it matches its product to consumer demands, and the diligence with which it goes after profitable innovation. In this view, those firms that can make effective use of funds because of their efficiency are precisely the corporations whose stock prices will usually be comparatively high. In this way the stock market tends to channel the economy's investment funds to those firms that can make best use of the money. In sum:

If a firm has a promising future, its stock will tend to command a high price on the stock exchanges. The high price of its stock will make it easier for it to raise capital by permitting it to amass a large amount of money through the sale of a comparatively small number of new stocks. Thus, the *stock market helps to allocate the economy's resources to those firms that can make the best use of those resources*.

Are there any rules for a firm to follow when it decides on the trade-off between risk and cost in choosing whether to issue stocks or bonds? There is no general rule, but some principles do hold. For example, new, relatively risky firms find it hard to raise money by issuing stocks because investors want protection from the perils of investing in an unproven company. For similar reasons, very safe companies prefer stock to bond financing because the safety of the firm means that stockholders will not have to be paid much more than bondholders.

The Recent Surge in Takeover Battles

In recent years the stock market and the managements of a number of corporations have been shaken by attempts by "outsiders" to take over firms which they do not currently control. A company is said to have undergone a **takeover** when a group of financiers not currently in control of the firm buys a sufficient amount of company stock to gain control. Often, the new controlling group will simply fire the current management and will substitute a new chairman, president, and other top officers. A company becomes a tempting target for a takeover attempt if the price of its stock is very low in comparison with the value of its plant, equipment, and other assets, or when a company's earnings seem very low compared to their potential level—possibly because the firm's current management is not very competent.

An attempt to acquire the company by a group unfriendly to current management is called a "hostile takeover." Naturally, current management will try to fight it off since the officers of the corporation do not like to lose their high-paying jobs. They can fight back in many ways. For example, they can try to arrange instead for a "friendly takeover" by a group of investors whom the current management likes better. Or the current management may deliberately attempt to sabotage the company—often, by selling some of its most valuable parts in order to make what is left of the firm unattractive to the group attempting the takeovers. Or management may seek to bribe the takeover group to go away by offering a very high price for the stocks that this group already has managed to acquire. Indeed, takeovers are often attempted in the hope that management will be forced to offer such a bribe to those who threaten to take the company over.

It should also be noted that to succeed in taking over a large corporation it is often only necessary to obtain something like 5 or 10 percent of its stock since most stockholders are likely to own a much smaller proportion of the company than that.

In the mid-1980s, when a large number of takeover battles broke out, the issue received a good deal of publicity and set off a heated debate over its pros and cons.

People who argued for few or no legal restrictions on takeover activity pointed out that it is the most effective means to rid companies of incompetent managements and so it helps to keep the economy at peak efficiency. They also pointed out that this activity helps to drive up the price of an undervalued company's stock, bringing it into line with the true economic value of the firm.

Those who advocated strict regulation or inhibition of takeovers argued that stockholders who are innocent bystanders can be badly hurt in the process,

The Colorful Vocabulary of Takeover Battles

Here are some curious terms you are likely to run across in newspaper discussions of takeovers:

Corporate Raiders. People who specialize in seeking out corporations vulnerable to takeover threats.

Golden Parachutes. Contracts with the members of current management giving them large payments and/or other privileges in case they are fired.

Greenmail. The high price that current management pays the attempted takeover group for its shares, to bribe it to give up its attempt.

Junk Bonds. Bonds (IOUs) often issued by a corporate raider to get the money with which to buy enough stocks of the target corporation to achieve control. They are called "junk bonds" because they often have no plant, equipment, or other assets as backing, unlike the more usual corporate bond.

Poison Pill. An action by current management that deliberately reduces the value of the target firm in order to make it less attractive for a takeover attempt. Usually, a poison pill is arranged to take effect automatically, say, when some group acquires 5 percent of the company's shares.

White Knight. A group that undertakes to carry out a friendly takeover at the urging of current management, in order to head off a hostile takeover.

as when management pays a large bribe to the takeover group or sells off a valuable part of the company when it should not be sold. Moreover, those seeking to buy, say, 7 percent of the company's shares will try to do so as secretly as possible, hoping to obtain the stocks cheaply, in the process, in effect, cheating those who sold them the stocks. Opponents of takeovers also point out rightly that the time taken by bright talented people in planning and carrying out the strategies and counter strategies uses up a valuable resource, part of which may be wasteful. That is, on this view, takeover activity absorbs some of the nation's most capable individuals in financial manipulation rather than productive and innovative activity. These critics are wrong, however, when they argue that the billions of dollars that change hands in the takeover process ties up much of the nation's capital wastefully, or that the process somehow "uses up" the economy's credit supply. Little or no *real* capital (machinery, factories, and the like) is used up in the takeover process. It is only a matter of some money and pieces of paper which are legal certificates of ownership being transferred among different persons.

On balance, is takeover activity good or bad for society? You should judge that for yourself.

The Issue of Speculation

Dealings in securities are often viewed with hostility and suspicion because they are thought to be an instrument of **speculation** (see the discussion in Chapter 19, pages 424–25). When something goes wrong in the market, say, when there is a sudden fall in prices, *speculators* are often blamed. The word "speculators" is used by editorial writers as a term of strong disapproval, implying that those who engage in the activity are parasites who produce no benefits for society and often do it considerable harm.

Economists disagree vehemently with this judgment. They say that speculators perform two vital economic functions:

Individuals who engage in **speculation** deliberately invest in risky assets, hoping to obtain a profit from the expected changes in the prices of these assets.

1. They sell *protection from risk* to other people, much as a fire insurance policy sells protection from risk to a home owner.
2. They help to smooth out price fluctuations by purchasing items when they are abundant (and cheap) and holding them and reselling them when they are scarce (and expensive). In that way, they play a vital economic role in helping to alleviate and even prevent shortages.

Some examples from outside the securities markets will make the role of speculators clear. A ticket broker attends a preview of a new musical comedy and suspects that it is likely to be a hit. He decides to speculate by buying a large block of tickets for future performances. In that way he takes over some of the producer's risk, for the producer now has some hard cash and has reduced his inventory of risky tickets. If the show opens and is a flop, the broker will be stuck with the tickets. If it is a hit, he can sell them at a premium, if the law allows (and be denounced as a speculator or a "scalper").

Similarly, speculators enable farmers or producers of metals and other commodities whose future price is uncertain to get rid of their risk. A farmer who has planted a large crop but who fears its price may fall before harvest time can protect himself by signing a *contract for future delivery* at an agreed-upon price at which the speculator will purchase the crop when it comes in. In that case, if the price happens to fall, it is the speculator and not the farmer who will suffer the loss. Of course, if the price happens to rise, the speculator will reap the gain — that is the nature of risk bearing. The speculator who has agreed to buy the crop at the preset price, regardless of market conditions at the time the sale takes place, has, in effect, sold an insurance policy to the farmer. Surely this is a useful function.

The second role of speculators is perhaps even more important; in effect, they accumulate and store goods in periods of abundance and make goods available in periods of scarcity. Suppose the speculator has reason to suspect that next year's crop of a storable commodity will not be nearly as abundant as this year's. He will buy some now, when it is cheap, for resale when it becomes scarce and expensive. In the process, he will smooth out the swing in prices by adding his purchases to the total market demand in the period of low prices (which tends to bring the price up), and bringing in his supplies during the period of high prices (which tends to push the price down).[3]

Thus, the successful speculator will help to relieve matters during periods of extreme shortage. There are cases in which he literally helps to relieve famine by releasing the supplies he has deliberately hoarded for such an occasion. Of course, he is cursed for the high prices he charges on such occasions. But those who curse him do not understand that prices might have been even higher if the speculator's foresight and avid pursuit of profit had not provided for the emergency. On the securities market, famine and severe shortages are not an issue, but the fact remains that successful speculators tend to reduce price fluctuations by increasing demand for stocks when prices are low and contributing to supply when prices are high.

Far from aggravating instability and fluctuations, speculators work as hard as they can to iron out fluctuations, for that is how they make their profits.

Stock Prices as Random Walks

The beginning of this chapter cited evidence that the best professional securities analysts have a forecasting record so miserable that investors may do as well predicting earnings by hunch, superstition, or any purely random process as they would by following professional advice. (See box, page 671). Similarly, it has been said that an investor is well advised to pick stocks by throwing darts at the stock market page — since it is far cheaper to buy a set of darts than to obtain the apparently useless advice of a professional analyst. Indeed, there have been at least two experiments, one by a U.S. senator and one by *Forbes* magazine, in which stocks picked by dart throwing actually outperformed the mutual funds, whose stocks are selected by the experts. Does this mean that analysts are incompetent people who do not know what they are doing? Not at all. Rather, there is overwhelming evidence that their poor forecasting performance is attributable to the fact that the task they have undertaken is basically impossible.

How can this be so? The answer is that to make a good forecast of any variable — GNP, population, or fuel usage — there must be something in the past whose behavior is closely related to the future behavior of the variable whose path we wish to predict. If a 10 percent rise in this year's consumption

[3]For a diagrammatic analysis of this function, see Discussion Question 7 at the end of the chapter.

If NFC Wins, Buy Stocks

The following excerpt from a column in the business section of the *San Francisco Chronicle* suggests some of the gimmicks stock market analysts turn to in a desperate effort to predict stock prices. The column exaggerates matters somewhat, but not all that much.

If you are a 49er football fan and a stock market investor as well—assuming you can afford both sports—you'll do well in 1984 if the Niners win Super Bowl XVIII.

Even if the 49ers don't make it to the Super Bowl but the Detroit Lions or Washington Redskins do and win, the stock market, based on the Standard & Poor's index of 500 stocks, will be up next year.

But if the Miami Dolphins, Los Angeles Raiders, Pittsburgh Steelers or Seattle Seahawks win the Super Bowl gonfalon next month, run for cover. The market will go down in the next 12 months.

Don't laugh. The Super Bowl Stock Market Predictor, as concocted by a distinguished market analyst, has been on the money since the professional football gala started in 1967.

When Robert Stovall, senior vice president and director of investment policy for Dean Witter Reynolds, started tracking the correlation between Super Bowl winners and the stock market in the late 1960s and early 1970s, his work was viewed as just another analytical aberration. No longer.

Stovall's theory is as simple as pumpkin pie. If an American Football Conference team wins the Super Bowl, the market will go down. If a National Football Conference team wins, the market will go up. . . .

If you are not enough of a jock to pay attention to Stovall's theory, how about getting a telescope to check the stars and planets' 1984 movements to predict stock market action?

That's technical analyst Arch Crawford's game. He charts astronomical patterns. He warns about two dates next year that could be disastrous for the market.

On January 18, he says, Neptune goes into Capricorn, a position that "has been associated with most major panics in this country and which occurs approximately every 55 years. . . ."

Another almost foolproof way to make money in next year's stock market is to check the trend in the length of women's skirts.

One theory goes that as women's skirts get shorter the Dow-Jones industrial average also rises. But a counter theory holds that the average goes down as skirts go up. Take your choice. You can only be half wrong.

SOURCE: Donald K. White, "If NFC Wins, Buy Stock," *San Francisco Chronicle*, December 28, 1983.

always produces a 5 percent rise in next year's GNP, this fact can help us predict future GNP on the basis of current observations. But if we want to forecast the future of a variable whose behavior is completely unrelated to the behavior of *any* current variable, there is no objective evidence that can help us make that forecast. Throwing darts or gazing into a crystal ball is no less effective than analysts' calculations.

There is a mass of statistical evidence that the behavior of stock prices is in fact unpredictable. In other words, the behavior of stock prices is essentially

The time path of a variable such as the price of a stock is said to constitute a **random walk** if its magnitude in one period (say, May 2, 1988) is equal to its value in the preceding period (May 1, 1988) plus a completely random number. That is:

Price on May 2, 1988 = Price on May 1, 1988 + Random number

where the random number (positive or negative) might be obtained by a roll of dice or some such procedure.

random; the paths they follow are what statisticians call **random walks.** A random walk is like the path followed by a drunk. All we know about his position after his next step is that it will be given by his current position plus whatever random direction his next haphazard step will carry him. The relevant feature of randomness, for our purposes, is that it is by nature unpredictable, which is just what the word *random* means.

If the evidence that stock prices follow a random walk stands up to research in the future as it has so far, it is easy enough to understand why stock market predictions are as poor as they are. The analysts are trying to forecast behavior that is basically random; in effect, they are trying to predict the unpredictable.

Two questions remain. First, does the evidence that stock prices follow a random walk mean that investment in stocks is a pure gamble and never worthwhile? And, second, how does one explain the random behavior of stock prices?

To answer the first question, it is false to conclude that investment in stocks is generally not worthwhile. The statistical evidence is that, over the long run, stock prices *as a whole* have had a marked upward trend, perhaps reflecting the long-term growth of the economy. Evidence *does* indicate that stock prices are likely to rise if one waits long enough. Thus, the random walk does not proceed in just any direction—rather, it represents a set of erratic movements *around the basic trend in stock prices*.

Moreover, it is not in the *overall* level of stock prices that the most pertinent random walk occurs, but in the performance of one company's stock compared with another's. For this reason professional advice may be able to predict that investment in the stock market is likely to be a good thing over the long haul. But, if the random walk evidence is valid, there is no way professionals can tell us which of the available stocks is most likely to go up—that is, which combination of stocks is best for the investor to buy.

The only appropriate answer to the second question is that no one is sure of the explanation. There are two widely offered hypotheses—each virtually the opposite of the other. The first asserts that stock prices are random because clever professional speculators are able to foresee almost perfectly every influence that is *not* random. For example, suppose a change occurs that makes the probable earnings of some company higher than had previously been expected. Then, according to this view, the professionals will instantly become aware of this change and immediately buy enough to raise the price of the stock accordingly. Then, the only thing for that stock price to do between this year and next is wander randomly, because the professionals cannot predict random movements, and hence cannot force current stock prices to anticipate them.

The other explanation of random behavior of stock prices is at the opposite pole from the view that all nonrandom movements are wiped out by supersmart professionals. This view holds that people who buy and sell stocks have learned that they cannot predict future stock prices. As a result they react to any signal, however irrational and irrelevant it appears. If the president catches cold, stock prices fall. If an astronaut's venture is successful, prices go up. For, according to this view, investors are, in the last analysis, trying to predict not the prospects of the economy or of the company whose shares they buy, but the supply and demand behavior of other investors, which will ultimately determine the course of stock prices. Since all investors are equally in the dark, their groping can only result in the randomness that we observe. The classic statement of this view of stock market behavior was provided by Lord Keynes, a successful professional speculator himself:

Professional investment may be likened to those newspaper competitions in which the competitors have to pick out the six prettiest faces from a hundred photographs, the prize being awarded to the competitor whose choice most nearly corresponds to the average preferences of the competitors as a whole; so that each competitor has to pick not those faces which he himself finds prettiest, but those which he thinks likeliest to catch the fancy of the other competitors, all of whom are looking at the problem from the same point of view. It is not a case of choosing those which, to the best of one's judgment, are really the prettiest, nor even those which average opinion genuinely thinks the prettiest. We have reached the third degree where we devote our intelligences to anticipating what average opinion expects the average opinion to be. And there are some, I believe, who practice the fourth, fifth and higher degrees. [4]

This may help to explain the impressive rise of the stock market from a Dow Jones index of 800 in 1982 to 2700 in 1987 and its 700-point fall in 2 consecutive days in October 1987.

[4] John Maynard Keynes, *The General Theory of Employment, Interest, and Money* (New York: Harcourt Brace Jovanovich, 1936), page 156.

Summary

1. The three basic types of firms are corporations, partnerships, and individual proprietorships. Most U.S. firms are individual proprietorships, but most U.S. manufactured goods are produced by corporations.

2. Individual proprietorships and partnerships have tax advantages over corporations. But corporate investors have greater protection from risk because they have *limited liability* — they cannot be asked to pay more than they have invested in the firm.

3. Higher taxation of corporate earnings tends to limit the things in which corporations can invest and may lead to inefficiency in resource allocation.

4. Corporations finance their activities mostly by plowback (that is, by retaining part of their earnings and putting it back into the company) or by the sale of stocks and bonds.

5. A stock is a share in the ownership of the company. A bond is an IOU by a company for money lent to it by the bondholder. Many observers argue that the purchase of a stock also really amounts to a loan to the company — a loan that is riskier than the purchase of a bond.

6. If interest rates rise, bond prices will fall. In other words, if some bond amounts to a contract to pay 8 percent and the market interest rate goes up to 10 percent, people will no longer be willing to pay the old price for that bond.

7. If stock prices correctly reflect the future prospects of different companies, promising firms are helped to raise money because they are able to sell each stock they issue at favorable prices.

8. Bonds are relatively risky for the firms that issue them, but they are fairly safe for their buyers, because they are a commitment by the firm to pay a fixed annual amount to the bondholder whether or not the company made money that year. But stocks, which do not promise any fixed payment, are relatively safe for the company and risky for their owner.

9. A portfolio is a collection of stocks, bonds, and other assets of a single owner. The greater the number and variety of securities and other assets it contains, the less risky it is.

10. A corporation is said to be taken over when an outside group buys enough stocks to get control of the firm's decisions. Takeovers are a useful way to get rid of incompetent managements and to force other managements to be efficient. However the process is costly and leads to wasteful defensive and offensive activities.

11. Speculation affects stock market prices, but (contrary to what is widely assumed) there is reason to believe that speculation actually *reduces* the frequency and size of price fluctuations. Speculators are also useful to the economy because they undertake risks that others wish to avoid, thereby, in effect, providing others with insurance against risk.

12. Statistical evidence indicates that individual stock prices behave randomly.

Concepts for Review

Proprietorship	Double taxation	Portfolio diversification
Unlimited liability	Limited partnership	Stock exchanges
Partnership	Plowback or retained earnings	Takeovers
Corporation	Common stock	Speculation
Limited liability	Bond	Random walk

Questions for Discussion

1. Why would it be difficult to run AT&T as a partnership or an individual proprietorship?
2. Do you think it is fair to tax a corporation more than a partnership doing the same amount of business? Why or why not?
3. If you hold shares in a corporation and management decides to plow back the company's earnings some year instead of paying dividends, what are the advantages and disadvantages to you?
4. Suppose interest rates are 14 percent in the economy and a safe bond promises to pay $7 a year in interest forever. What do you think the price of the bond will be? Why?
5. Suppose in the economy in the previous example, interest rates suddenly fall to 7 percent. What will happen to the price of the bond that pays $7 per year?
6. If you want to buy a stock, when might it be to your advantage to buy it using a market order? When will it pay to use a limit order?
7. Show in diagrams that if a speculator were to buy when price is high and sell when price is low he would increase price fluctuations. Why would it be in his best interest *not* to do so? (*Hint*: Draw two supply–demand diagrams, one for the high-price period and one for the low-price period. How would the speculator's activities affect these diagrams?)
8. If stock prices really are a random walk, can you nevertheless think of good reasons for getting professional advice before investing?

PART 8

The Government and the Economy

31

Limiting Market Power: Regulation of Industry

Because the market system may not function ideally in monopolistic or oligopolistic industries, governments have frequently intervened in these areas. In the United States, such intervention has followed two basic patterns. Antitrust laws, which will be studied in detail in the next chapter, have sought to prohibit the acquisition of monopoly power and to ban certain monopolistic practices. In addition, some firms have been subjected to **regulation** which constrains their pricing policies and other decisions.

In this chapter, we will describe the functioning of some of the principal regulatory agencies. We will then offer a more detailed account of the reasons for regulation, discuss the evidence on the effectiveness of regulation, consider the reasons why regulatory agencies have devoted a great deal of attention to limitation of price cuts, and examine both some of the criticisms of the regulatory process and some of the suggestions that have been made to improve it. We will also discuss some recent moves toward deregulation; that is, toward reducing the number of regulations and the powers of the regulatory agencies. This deregulation process has now been underway for most of a decade, and we will review the rather heated debate it has fostered. Finally, we will conclude the chapter with a few comments on nationalization of industries. Much of the chapter will deal with regulatory restrictions of *pricing* by the firm under regulatory control. Regulators control a variety of economic activities other than pricing, as we will note, but price-setting rules and their consequences for economic welfare are most easily analyzed with the help of the tools studied in previous chapters of this book.

Regulation of industry is a process established by law which restricts or controls some specified decisions made by the affected firms. Regulation is usually carried out by a special government agency assigned the task of administering and interpreting the law. That agency also acts as a court in enforcing the regulatory laws.

Monopoly, Regulation, and Nationalization

Throughout the Western economies a number of industries are traditionally run as monopolies. These include postal services, electricity generation, transportation, and gas supply. Since there may be little competition to protect the interests of consumers from monopolistic exploitation in these cases, it is generally agreed that some substitute form of protection from excessive prices and restricted outputs should be found.

Most of Western Europe has adopted **nationalization** as its solution, which means that the state owns and operates certain monopolistic industries. In the United States, we are more reluctant to have government involved in the running of businesses. Yet even here it has happened to some degree. Most cities now run their own public transport systems; the post office and much of the passenger railroad system in the United States are run by public corporations; and the Tennessee Valley Authority is a major experiment in electricity supply by a public agency.

In the United States, however, the main instrument of control of privately owned public utilities has been the regulatory agency. Both the federal and the state governments have created a large number of agencies that regulate prices, standards of service, provisions for safety, and a variety of other aspects of the operations of telephone companies, radio and television stations, electric utilities, airlines, trucking companies, and firms in many other industries — all of which remain in private ownership. Many of these industries are not pure monopolies, but include firms that nevertheless are believed to possess so much market power that their regulation is considered to be in the public interest.

Two Puzzles

INDUSTRY OPPOSITION TO DEREGULATION

An observer who knew nothing about regulated industries might expect that deregulation would be welcomed by the firms affected. After all, regulations curb their freedom of decision making in many ways.

Yet many airlines, trucking companies, and bus lines — and their unions — bitterly fought deregulation. Later, we will discuss some reasons for this opposition. But already we may surmise from this observation that regulation may, inadvertently or deliberately, have been serving the interests of some of the regulated firms rather than making life harder for them.

WHY DO REGULATORS SOMETIMES WORRY MORE ABOUT PRICES BEING TOO LOW THAN BEING TOO HIGH?

In a famous passage in *The Wealth of Nations*, Adam Smith tells us:

It always is and must be the interest of the great body of the people to buy whatever they want of those who sell it cheapest. The proposition is so very manifest, that it seems ridiculous to take any pains to prove it; nor could it ever have been called into question had not the interested sophistry of merchants and manufacturers confounded the common sense of mankind.[1]

Since regulation of industry has presumably been instituted to protect "the interest of the great body of the people," it is quite natural to surmise that the time of the regulatory agencies would have been spent mostly on price reductions. One would think that the typical complaint before a regulatory agency would be that a firm with monopoly power was charging excessively high prices, and that a typical decision of the agency would require prices to be reduced.

In fact, this seems to be virtually the reverse of what has happened. The bulk of cases devoted to price regulation have dealt with complaints that prices charged by the regulated firm are *too low!* Often regulators have then required the firms to raise their prices higher than they wanted to. Because the cost of

[1] Adam Smith, *The Wealth of Nations* (New York: Modern Library, Random House, Inc., 1937), page 461.

additional shipments via railroad is sometimes lower than the cost of shipping via barges, regulators have been known to require the low-priced suppliers (railroads) to raise their fees to match the prices charged by their high-cost competitors (barges).

What just reason is there for this curious pattern for a regulatory agency to devote itself primarily to the imposition of *price floors* rather than *price ceilings?* Later in this chapter, we will be able to indicate just how and why this has happened.

What Is Regulated? By Whom?

The regulatory agencies in the United States can be divided, roughly, into two classes: those that limit the market power of regulated firms and those devoted to consumer and worker protection and safety. In a recent count, at least 14 regulatory agencies were concerned with restraining market power and about 30 were involved in issues such as environmental protection and product safety. A primary example of an agency working toward the latter goal is the Food and Drug Administration (FDA), whose tasks are protecting the public from the sale of harmful, impure, infected, or adulterated foods, drugs, and cosmetics, and preventing the mislabeling or bad packaging of any of these products. Similarly, the U.S. Department of Agriculture supervises the packing and grading of meats and poultry going into interstate commerce — tasks it has had since 1906.

The federal government also has become involved in regulating the safety of automobiles and mines and the use of such substances as dangerous pesticides. This job is performed by the Environmental Protection Agency (EPA). An enormous proportion of the nation's economic activity is affected by these sorts of regulations. For instance, the drug industry, agriculture, auto manufacturing, and the chemical and power industries are just some of the businesses affected by health and safety regulation, and virtually every manufacturing industry is affected by environmental regulations.

Equally pervasive are regulations designed to limit market power. The affected industries together provide perhaps 10 percent of the GNP of the United States. Among the principal industries still regulated in this way are telecommunications, railroads, electric utilities, and oil pipelines.

Brief History

Regulation of industry in the United States first began when indignation over abuse of market power by the nation's railroads led to the establishment of the Interstate Commerce Commission (ICC) in 1887. In particular, there was a public outcry over the support the railroads gave John D. Rockefeller, Sr., in the battle of his Standard Oil Company against its rivals. This, along with other abuses by the railroads, invited government intervention. But for several decades afterward there was little attempt to expand regulation to other industries. Then the Federal Power Commission (FPC) was established in 1920 and the Federal Communications Commission (FCC) in 1934; a substantial proportion of the remaining regulatory agencies were also formed during the 1930s as part of Roosevelt's New Deal.

Today, the principal regulatory agencies of the federal government that control prices include the ICC, which regulates railroads, barges, pipelines, and some categories of trucking; the FCC, which regulates broadcasting and telecommunications; the Federal Energy Regulatory Commission (FERC), which regulates interstate transmission of electric power and sales of natural gas; the Securities and Exchange Commission (SEC), which regulates the sale of securities (stocks); and several agencies led by the Federal Reserve System, which control banking operations. The work of these agencies is complemented by a variety of state agencies, which regulate activities that do not enter into interstate commerce.

Economists have long questioned the effectiveness of regulation and the desirability of some of its consequences, but not until the mid-1970s did such questions begin to be raised seriously outside of academic discussions. Recently, several laws were enacted by Congress limiting the powers of the regulatory agencies. Several industries have been "deregulated" — that is, most of the powers of the regulatory agencies over these activities are now being eliminated.

Presidents Ford, Carter, and Reagan all took the position that the economy was overregulated and that this imposed unnecessary costs on consumers. After several years of effort, deregulation began in earnest in the last few years of the Carter administration. In 1978 an act ending regulation of passenger air transportation was passed by Congress, with the regulatory agency going out of existence in 1984. In the period since 1978 regulatory control over truck transportation rates and entry into or exit from the field have been curtailed sharply. Rail transportation activities that are judged to be adequately competitive have been freed from regulatory constraints, while the remaining rail activities have been placed under a less restrictive regulatory regime consistent with ideas emerging from economic analysis (see the discussion of the new rail regulation policies later in this chapter). In telecommunications, AT&T's monopoly has been ended, and the firm itself broken up under the terms of settlement of an antitrust case. AT&T continues to be regulated quite closely, though a loosening of these regulatory rules is under discussion. AT&T's competitors are now largely free of regulation. In sum, substantial deregulation has occurred during the last decade.

Why Regulation?

Economists recognize a number of reasons that sometimes justify the regulation of an industry.

Economies of Scale and Scope

As we learned in Chapter 27, one main reason for regulation of industry is the phenomenon of **natural monopoly**. In some industries it is apparently far cheaper to have production carried out by one firm rather than by a number of different firms. One reason why this may occur is because of economies of large-scale production. An example of such **economies of scale** is a railroad track, which can carry 100 trains a day with total cost hardly higher than when it carries one. Here is a case in which savings are made possible by expanding the volume of an activity — a case of economies of scale. As we saw in Chapter 23, scale economies lead to an average cost curve that goes downhill as output increases (see Figure 31–1). This means that a firm with a large output can cover its costs at a price lower than a firm whose output is smaller. In Figure 31–1 point A represents the larger firm whose AC is $5 while B is the smaller firm with AC = $7.

Another reason why a single large firm may have a cost advantage over a group of small firms is that it is sometimes cheaper to produce *a number of different commodities together* rather than turn them out separately, each by a different

Economies of scale are savings that are acquired through increases in quantities produced.

Figure 31–1
MARGINAL COST PRICING UNDER ECONOMIES OF SCALE
Economies of scale imply that the average cost (AC) curve is declining, and therefore that the marginal cost (MC) curve is below the average cost curve. If, for example, the regulator forces the firm to produce 100 units and charge a price equal to its marginal cost ($3 per unit), then the firm will take in $300 in revenues. But, since its average cost at 100 units is $5 per unit, its total cost will be $500, and the firm will lose money.

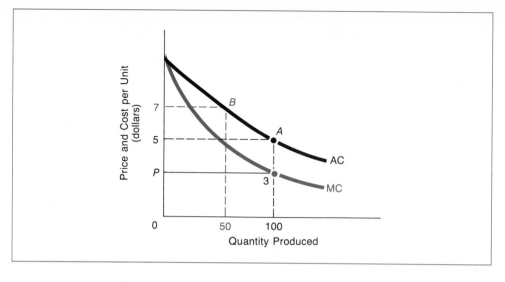

Economies of scope are savings that are acquired through simultaneous production of many different products.

firm. The saving made possible by the simultaneous production of many different products is called **economies of scope.** An example of economies of scope is the manufacture of both cars and trucks by the same producer. The techniques employed in producing both commodities are sufficiently similar to make specialized production by different firms impractical.

In industries where there are great economies of scale *and* scope, society will obviously incur a significant cost penalty if it insists on maintaining a large number of firms. Supply by a number of smaller competing firms will be far more costly and use up far larger quantities of resources than it would if the goods were supplied by a monopoly. Moreover, in the presence of strong economies of scale and economies of scope, society *will not be able to preserve free competition, even if it wants to*. The large, multiproduct firm will have so great a cost advantage over its rivals that the small firms simply will be unable to survive. We say in such a case that free competition is *not sustainable*.

Where monopoly production is cheapest, and where free competition is not sustainable, the industry is a natural monopoly. Because monopoly is cheaper, society may not want to have competition; and if free competition is not sustainable, it will not even have a choice in the matter.

But even if society reconciles itself to monopoly, it will generally not want to let the monopoly firm do whatever it wants to with its market power. Therefore, it will consider either regulation or nationalization of these firms.

"Universal Service" and Rate Averaging
A second reason for regulation is the desire for "universal service," that is, the availability of service at "reasonable prices" even to small communities where the small scale of operation makes costs extremely high. In such cases, regulators have sometimes encouraged a public utility to supply services to some consumers at a financial loss. But a loss on some sales is financially feasible only when the firm is permitted to make up for it by obtaining higher profits on its other sales.

Cross-subsidization means selling one product at a loss, which is balanced by higher profits on another product.

This so-called "rate averaging" of gains and losses, also referred to as **cross-subsidization,** is possible only if the firm is protected from price competition and free entry of new competitors in its more profitable markets. If no such protection is provided by a regulatory agency, potential competitors will sniff out the profit opportunities in the markets where service is supplied at a price well above cost. Many new firms will enter the business and cause prices to be driven down in those markets. This practice is referred to as "cream skimming." The entrants choose to enter only into the profitable markets and skim away the cream of the profits for themselves, leaving the unprofitable markets (the skimmed milk) to the supplier who had attempted to provide universal service. This phenomenon is one reason why regulatory rules, until recently, made it very difficult or impossible for new firms to enter when and where they saw fit.

Airlines and telecommunications are two industries in which these issues have arisen. In both cases, fears have been expressed that without regulation of entry and rates, or the granting of special subsidies, less populous communities would effectively be isolated, losing their airline services and obtaining telephone service only at cripplingly high rates. Many economists question the validity of this argument for regulation, which, they say, calls for hidden subsidy of rural consumers by all other consumers. The airline deregulation act provided for government subsidies to help small communities attract airline service. In fact, what has happened is that this market has been taken over to a considerable extent by specialized "commuter" airlines flying much smaller aircraft than the major airlines, which have withdrawn from many such routes.

"Destructive Competition"

A third reason for regulation is to help prevent **self-destructive competition,** which, for example, economies of scale make possible. In an industry such as railroading, equipment — including roadbeds, tracks, switching facilities, locomotives, and cars — is extremely expensive. Suppose that two railroads, having been built and equipped, are competing for some limited business that happens to be insufficient to use their total facilities to anything near capacity. That is, to meet this level of consumer demand, each railroad may only have to run 40 percent as many trains over the track as can conveniently be scheduled over that route. The management of each road will feel that, with its unused capacity, any business will be worthwhile, provided that it covers more than its short-run marginal costs — fuel, labor, and expenses other than plant and equipment. If the short-run marginal cost of shipping an additional ton of, say, coal is $5, then either railroad will be happy to lure coal-shipping customers away from the other at a price of, say, $7 per ton, even though that price may not cover the entire cost of track and equipment. Each ton of business that pays $7 when marginal cost is $5 will put the railroad $2 ahead of where it would have been without the business. The new business does not add much to the cost of the tracks or locomotives or other equipment, which must be paid for whether that business is acquired or not. Thus, even if the new business only pays for its own marginal cost and a little more, it seems financially desirable.

But the temptation to accept business on such terms will drive both firms' prices down toward their marginal costs, and, in the process, both railroads are likely to go broke. If no customer pays for the track, the roadbed, and the equipment, the railroad simply will be unable to go on. Thus there are those who believe that regulation of rates can be sensible, even in industries subject to competitive pressures, simply to protect the industries from themselves. Without this regulation, self-destructive competition could end up sinking those industries financially, and the public would thereby be deprived of vital services.

Protection Against Misinformation

A final reason for regulation is the danger that consumers will be misinformed or cheated, that the consumers or employees of the firm or the environment will be threatened by unscrupulous sellers, or that even conscientious sellers will be forced to keep up with the questionable practices of less scrupulous rivals. This sort of protection is the province of the second type of regulatory agency described earlier.

SUMMARY

There are four basic reasons for the activities of regulatory agencies:

1. Prevention of excess profits and other undesirable practices in an industry that is considered to be a natural monopoly.
2. The desire for universal service — that is, the desire to provide service at relatively low rates to customers whom it is particularly expensive to serve, and to do so without government subsidy.
3. The desire to prevent self-destructive price competition in multifirm industries with large capital costs and low marginal costs.
4. The desire to protect customers, employees, and the environment from damage resulting from inappropriate behavior by firms.

Why Regulators Sometimes Raise Prices

It has been suggested that regulation sometimes results in prices to consumers higher than they would pay in its absence. One of the most widely publicized examples illustrating the tendency of regulation to push rates upward was the difference in airplane fares between San Francisco and Los Angeles and those between Washington, D.C., and New York City before the airlines were deregulated. The former fare was never regulated by the federal government (since the flight is entirely within the state of California), whereas it did control the interstate flight between New York and Washington, D.C. The distance of the California trip is nearly twice as great as the East Coast trip, and neither is sparsely traveled nor beset by any other noteworthy features that would make for substantial differences in cost per passenger mile. Yet at the time of deregulation, fares were a little over $40 for the long California trip and a little over $50 for the short Washington to New York trip.

Why should regulators ever push for higher prices? (This is the second puzzle with which this chapter began.) The answer is that typically they do so when they want to prevent the demise of existing firms in an industry. We saw earlier that where there are strong economies of scale and scope it simply may be impossible for a number of firms to survive. The largest of the firms in the industry will have such cost advantages over its competitors that it will be able to drive them out of the market while still operating at prices that are profitable. Most observers applaud low prices and price cuts that reflect such cost advantages. However, a firm that wants the market for itself may conceivably engage in price cutting even when such cuts are not justifiable in terms of cost.

The reason such price cutting may not reduce the overall profits of a regulated firm is that regulation often imposes an upper limit on the amount of profit a firm is permitted to earn. To see the connection, consider a regulated firm that produces two commodities, A and B, and which is forced to set each price below its profit-maximizing level in order to limit profits to the allowable ceiling. The firm may be able, without loss of profit, to cut the price of A even below its marginal cost, and make up for any resulting decrease in profit by a sufficient rise in the price of B. In this case, we say that the firm has instituted a **cross subsidy** from the consumers of product B to the consumers of product A. That is, consumers of B are paying an excessive amount for their purchases in order to make up for the deficit in the sale of product A.

Why would any firm want to do this? Suppose A is threatened by competition while B has no competitors on the horizon. Then a cross subsidy from B to A may be a way of preventing the entry of the potential competitors of A or even of driving some current competitors out of the field. The fear by the Department of Justice of such cross subsidy of telephone equipment by the monopoly local telephone companies, which formerly were subsidiaries of AT&T, was one of the elements underlying the decision to break up the Bell Telephone System. After all, one way to prevent a cross subsidy from product B to product A is to require B and A to be produced by two different firms.

But regulation sometimes goes beyond the prevention of cross subsidy. Firms that feel they are hurt by competitive pressures will complain to regulatory commissions that the prices charged by their rivals are "unfairly low." The commission, afraid that unrestrained pricing will reduce the number of firms in the industry, then attempts to "equalize" matters by imposing price floors that permit all the firms in the industry to operate profitably. The ICC once described itself as a "giant handicapper" whose task was presumably to make sure that no firm within its jurisdiction got too far ahead of the others. It did not seem to show a similar concern with whether consumers were winning or losing.

This attitude has produced many strange patterns of resource utilization. For example, there is evidence that for distances of more than, say, 200 miles, railroads have a clear-cut cost advantage over trucks. Yet ICC influence over railroad rates had forced those rates upward sufficiently to make it possible for trucks to "compete" from coast to coast. The resulting waste of resources was probably enormous.

Many economists maintain that this approach to pricing is a perversion of the idea of competition. The virtue of competition is that, where it occurs, firms force one another to supply consumers with products of high quality at *low* prices. Any firm which cannot do this is driven out of business by the market forces. If competition does not do this, it loses its purpose because to the economist it is a means to an end, not an end in itself. An arrangement under which firms are enabled to coexist only by *preventing* them from competing with one another preserves the appearance of competition but destroys its substance.

Marginal Versus Full-Cost Rate Floors

Price floors are used by regulators to prevent "excessive" price reduction, for reasons just discussed. Debate over the proper levels of such floors has raged over hundreds of thousands of pages of records of regulatory hearings and has involved literally hundreds of millions of dollars of expenditures in fees for lawyers, expert witnesses, and research in preparation of the cases. The question has been not whether all floors on the prices of regulated utilities are improper, for virtually everyone agrees that some sort of lower boundary on prices is required in order to prevent cross subsidies, but rather what constitutes the proper formula to set the rate floors. Two alternative criteria have been most widely proposed to determine appropriate floors for prices.

Criterion 1. The price of a commodity should never be less than its *marginal cost.*

Criterion 2. The price should not be less than that commodity's *fully distributed cost* — that is, its "fair share" of the firm's total cost as determined by some accounting calculation.

To calculate the **fully distributed costs** of the various products of the firm, one simply takes the firm's total costs and divides them up in some way among its various products. First, one allocates to each product the costs for which it is obviously directly responsible. For example, a railroad allocates to coal transportation the cost of hauling all cars that were devoted exclusively to carrying coal, plus the cost of operating locomotives on runs in which they carried only coal cars, and so on.

Then, one takes all costs that are incurred *in common* for several or all of the outputs of the company (such as the cost of constructing the roadbed and tracks) and divides them on the basis of some rule of thumb (generally conceded to be arbitrary) among the firm's various products. Usually, the basis of this allocation is some measure of the relative use of the common facilities by the different products. But even "relative use" is an ambiguous term. How does one divide up the cost of the track of a railroad among its shipments of lead, lumber, and gold? If relative use is defined by the weight of the shipments, then the accountants will assign a high proportion of the cost to lead shipments. If prices are then required to exceed full cost, under this definition of "relative use" the railroad will be placed at a disadvantage in competing for lead traffic. If, instead, relative use is defined in terms of bulk, the railroad's lumber business will be harmed; if relative use is defined in terms of market value, it will lose out in competing for gold shipments.

Those who advocate the use of *marginal cost* rather than fully distributed cost as the appropriate basis for any floor on prices argue that **marginal cost** is the relevant measure of the cost that any shipment actually incurs. For, by definition, marginal cost is the difference that an additional shipment makes to the firm's total cost — it is the difference between the cost to the firm if that shipment takes place and the cost to the firm if the shipment is carried by some other means of transportation. The advocates of marginal cost criteria argue that customers of *every* product of the supplier may benefit if the company is permitted to charge a price based on marginal cost, particularly if, as is usual under regulation, there is a legal ceiling on the firm's total profits.

Suppose that a railroad considers taking on some new business whose marginal cost is $7 and whose fully distributed cost is figured at $12. Suppose also that at any price over $10 the railroad will lose the business to truckers. If the railroad charges $9 and gets the business, the price does not cover the fully distributed cost, but it still adds $2 to the company's net earnings for every unit it sells to the new customers. If it was already earning as much profit as the law allows, the company would normally have to reduce its price on other products. Thus every group of customers can gain — the new customers because they get the product more cheaply than it can be supplied by competitors, and the old customers because the prices on their products must be cut in order to satisfy the firm's profit ceiling. Everyone gains except the company's competitors, who will, of course, complain that the price is unfair because it does not cover fully distributed cost. (For an example of an opinion by a regulator defending the use of marginal cost analysis against fully distributed cost, see the boxed insert, opposite.)

Marginal Versus Fully Distributed Cost in Rate Regulation

In the following dissenting opinion, Commissioner Benjamin Hooks of the FCC (who now heads the National Association for the Advancement of Colored People — the NAACP) argues that a fully distributed cost floor is illogical. He says that a marginal (incremental) cost test may cause more work for the regulator, but points out that it is the public interest, not an easy job for regulators, that is important. The rest of the commission disagreed and voted for a fully distributed cost criterion. Since that time, regulatory commissions have begun to move the other way.

The Commission here, over all dictates of common sense, views of Congressional experts, the practices of other regulatory agencies, and the protestations of state regulatory agencies, has adopted a Fully Distributed Cost accounting method that is all but unyielding and defies every proven rule of economic logic. Virtually every economist-observer cited in this proceeding concedes that incremental cost methods are the closest approximation to a free market environment and the courts have ratified the use of marginal cost pricing in the utility field.

I concede that there are imperfections inherent in monitoring marginal costing structures in terms of regulatory administration not present with a simplistic, Fully Distributed Cost basis. However, governmental decisions should not be predicated disproportionately on convenience to the government, but on the broader public interest. What was clearly called for out of this Docket was a system which allows flexibility. . . . Instead we have ordered *rigor mortis*.

SOURCE: FCC Docket 18128, *FCC Reports*, second series, October 1, 1976.

A Problem of Marginal Cost Pricing

Setting price equal to marginal cost is a solution generally favored by most economists, *where it is feasible*. However, a serious problem prevents the use of the principle of marginal cost pricing in many regulated industries and marginal cost pricing in regulated industries is, consequently, not very common in practice. The problem is easily stated:

In many regulated industries, if prices were set equal to marginal cost, the firms would go bankrupt.

This seems a startling conclusion, but its explanation is really quite simple. The conclusion follows inescapably from three simple facts:

Fact 1: In many regulated industries, there are significant economies of large-scale production. As we pointed out earlier, economies of scale are one of the main reasons why certain industries were regulated in the first place.

Fact 2: In an industry with economies of scale, the long-run average cost curve is downward sloping. This means that long-run average cost falls as the quantity produced rises, as illustrated by the AC curve in Figure 31–1. Fact

2 is something we learned back in Chapter 23 (pages 509, 519–20). The reason, to review briefly, is that total costs must double if all input quantities are doubled. But, where there are economies of scale, output will *more* than double if all input quantities are doubled. Since average cost (AC) is simply total cost (TC) divided by quantity (Q), AC = TC/Q must decline when all input quantities are doubled.

Fact 3: If average cost is declining, then marginal cost must be below average cost. This fact follows directly from one of the general rules relating marginal and average data that were explained in the appendix to Chapter 24. Once again, the logic is simple enough to review briefly. If, for example, your average quiz score is 90 percent but the next quiz pulls your average down to 87 percent, then the grade on this most recent test (the marginal grade) must be below both the old and the new average quiz scores. That is, it takes a marginal grade (or cost) that is below the average to pull the average down.

Putting these three facts together, we conclude that in many regulated industries marginal cost (MC) will be below average cost, as depicted in Figure 31–1. Now suppose regulators set the price at the level of marginal cost. Since P = MC, P must be below AC. But P < AC (price per unit less than cost per unit) means that the firm must be losing money, which is the conclusion we set out to demonstrate.

In industries where there are economies of scale, therefore, a regulation that requires P = MC is simply not an acceptable option. What, then, should be done? One possibility is to nationalize the industry, set price equal to marginal cost, and make up for the deficit out of public funds. Nationalization, however, is not very popular in the United States. (More is said about nationalization at the end of the chapter.)

A second option, which is quite popular among regulators, is to (try to) set price equal to *average cost*. In practice, this principle leads to pricing at *fully distributed cost*. But, as explained in the previous section, this method of pricing is neither desirable nor possible to carry out except on the basis of arbitrary decisions.

The problem is that almost no firm produces only a single commodity. Almost every company produces a number of different varieties and qualities of some product, and often they produce thousands of different products, each with its own price. Even General Motors, a fairly specialized firm, produces many makes and sizes of cars and trucks in addition to refrigerators, washing machines, and quite a few other things. In a multiproduct firm we cannot even define AC = TC/Q, since to calculate Q (total output) we would have to add up all the apples and oranges (and all the other different items) the firm produces. But we know that one cannot add up apples and oranges. So, since we cannot calculate AC for a multiproduct firm, it is hardly possible for the regulator to require P = AC for each of the firm's products, though regulators sometimes think they can do so.

The Ramsey Pricing Rule

In recent years economists have been attracted to an imaginative third approach to the problem of pricing in regulated industries that produce a multiplicity of products. This approach derives its name from its discoverer, Frank Ramsey, a brilliant English mathematician who died in 1930 at the age of 26 after making several enduring contributions to both mathematics and economics.

The basic idea of Ramsey's pricing principle can be explained in a fairly straightforward manner. We know that prices must be set *above* marginal costs if a firm with increasing returns to scale is to break even. But how much above? In effect, Ramsey argued as follows: The reason we do not like prices to be above marginal costs is that such high prices distort the choices made by consumers, leading them to buy "too little" of the goods whose prices are set way above MC. Yet, it is necessary to set prices somewhat above marginal costs to allow the firm to survive. Therefore it makes sense to raise prices *most* above marginal cost where consumers will respond the *least* to such price increase; that is, where the *elasticity of demand* is the lowest so that price rises will create the least distortion of demand. This line of argument led Ramsey to formulate the following rule:

Ramsey Pricing Rule: In a multiproduct, regulated firm in which prices must exceed marginal cost in order to permit that firm to break even, the ratios of P to MC should be largest for those of the firm's products whose elasticities of demand are the smallest.

Many economists accept this pricing rule as the correct conclusion on theoretical grounds. It has even been proposed for postal and telephone pricing, and the Interstate Commerce Commission has explicitly decided to adopt the Ramsey principle as its guide for the regulation of railroad rates.

Modified Rail Regulation Policy and Stand-Alone Cost Ceilings

In the regulation of railroads, the Interstate Commerce Commission (ICC) has recently adopted a new approach to regulation explicitly derived from the theory of contestability that we mentioned in Chapter 28 (see pages 628–29). In its decision[2] the ICC recognized the value of the Ramsey pricing rule as a general guideline for policy. (Excerpts from this ICC decision are quoted in the box on page 688.) But the commissioners felt it was not practical to calculate statistically and update constantly all the demand elasticity numbers and marginal cost figures that use of the Ramsey rule requires. Instead the ICC decided to adopt a four-part rule. Its intent is to compel railroads to set the prices they would have set if all of their activities were contestable; that is, as if entry into freight transporation were everywhere sufficiently easy to subject the railroads to a perpetual and constant threat of new competition. The four parts of the new rule are:

1. For those types of freight and routes where competition happens to be substantial and effective, the railroads should be deregulated; that is, let market forces do the job of policing the railroads' behavior.

2. Where competition is inadequate, a floor and a ceiling should be set for each and every railroad price and leave the railroads free to select any level of price they wish within those bounds.

3. The price floor should be the lowest level to which price could fall in the long run under perfectly competitive conditions. This provision, in effect, prohibits the railroad from adopting any price below marginal cost. It is designed to provide adequate and defensible protection to any railroad's rivals against any attempt by the railroad at unfair competitive price cutting.

[2]Interstate Commerce Commission, "Coal Rate Guidelines, Nationwide," Ex Parte No. 347 (Sub-No. 1), Washington, D.C., decided August 3, 1985.

Economic Theory in an ICC Decision

Here are excerpts from the ICC decision described in the text as an embodiment of materials taken directly from economic analysis. Stand-Alone Cost (SAC) is the ceiling imposed on a railroad's prices because no higher prices could be charged in an unregulated competitive market.

... [the] stand-alone cost (SAC) test ... is used to compute the rate a competitor in the market-place would need to charge in serving a captive shipper or a group of shippers who benefit from sharing joint and common costs. A rate level calculated by the SAC methodology represents the theoretical maximum rate that a railroad could levy on shippers without substantial diversion of traffic to a hypothetical competing service. It is, in other words, a simulated competitive price. ...

The theory behind SAC is best explained by the concept of contestable markets. This recently developed economic theory augments the classical economic model of pure competition with a model which focuses on the entry and exit from an industry as a measure of economic efficiency. ... The underlying premise is that a monopolist or oligopolist will behave efficiently and competitively where there is a threat of losing some or all of its markets to a new entrant. In other words, contestable markets have competitive characteristics which preclude monopoly pricing.

SOURCE: Interstate Commerce Commision, "Coal Rate Guidelines, Nationwide," Ex Parte No. 347 (Sub-No. 1), Aug. 3, 1985, p. 10.

4. The price ceiling should be the cost that a *hypothetical* (that is, imaginary) efficient entrant would have to bear to supply each specific service. In other words, in activities where entry is difficult or impossible, the idea is to prohibit the railroads from charging more than they could get away with if entry were instead easy and cheap. The hypothetical cost figure for the efficient entrant is called the **stand-alone cost** of the service. It is the cost that would be required if an efficient entrant were to supply just the service or group of services in question. This provision is intended to protect the interests of railroad customers, guaranteeing them prices no higher than those that might be charged if the markets were effectively contestable.

Most economists who have studied the issue seem to approve of this new approach to rate regulation, although there are still substantial disputes about details of its operation. However, in Congress it has elicited some opposition whose future actions are difficult to judge.

Regulation of Profit and Incentives for Efficiency

Many opponents of regulation maintain that it seriously impairs the efficiency of American industry. Government regulation, these critics argue, interferes with the operation of Adam Smith's invisible hand. One source of inefficiency—the seemingly endless paperwork and complex legal proceedings that impede the firm's ability to respond quickly to changing market conditions—is obvious enough. (Though what to do about this administrative problem is far from obvious.)

But there is another source of inefficiency that may be even more important. It stems from the problem regulators have of trying to prevent the regulated firm from earning excessive profits, while at the same time (a) offering it financial incentives for maximum efficiency of operation, and (b) allowing it enough profit to attract the capital it needs when growing markets justify expansion. From this point of view, it would be ideal if the regulator would just permit the firm to take in that amount of revenue that covers its costs, including the cost of its capital. That is, the firm should earn exactly enough to pay for its ordinary costs plus the normal profit that potential investors could get elsewhere for the same money. Thus, if the prevailing rate of return is 10 percent, the regulated firm should recover its expenditures plus 10 percent on its investment and not a penny more or less.

The trouble with such an arrangement is that it removes all incentive for efficiency, responsiveness to consumer demand, and innovation. For under such an arrangement the firm is in effect *guaranteed* just *one standard rate* of profit, no more and no less. This is so whether its management is totally incompetent or extremely talented and hard working.

Competitive markets do *not* work in this way. While under perfect competition the *average* firm will earn just the opportunity cost of capital, a firm with an especially ingenious and efficient management will do better, and a firm with an incompetent management is likely to go broke. It is the possibility of great rewards and harsh punishments that gives the market mechanism its power to cause firms to strive for high efficiency and productivity growth.

We have strong evidence that where firms are guaranteed a fixed return, no matter how well or how poorly they perform, gross inefficiencies are likely to result. For example, many contracts for purchases of military equipment have offered prices calculated on a *cost-plus* basis, meaning that the supplier was guaranteed that his costs would be covered and that, in addition, he would receive some prespecified amount as a contribution to profit. Studies of the resulting performance of cost-plus arrangements have confirmed that the suppliers' inefficiencies have been enormous.

A regulatory arrangement that in effect guarantees a regulated firm its cost plus a "fair rate of return" on its investment obviously has a good deal in common with a cost-plus contract of an unregulated firm. Fortunately, there are also substantial differences between the two cases and so regulatory profit ceilings need not always have serious effects on the firm's incentives for efficiency. For one thing, when a regulated industry is in financial trouble, as is true of the railroads, there is nothing the regulator can do to guarantee a "fair rate of return." If the current return on capital is 10 percent, but market demand for railroading is only sufficient to give it 3 percent at most, the regulatory agency cannot help matters by any act of magic. Even if it grants higher prices to the railroad (or forces the railroad to raise its prices) the result will be to drive even more business away and therefore cause the firm to earn still lower profits. Thus, the regulated firm will sometimes have to struggle hard to earn even the rate of profit that regulation permits. The regulated firm is not promised any minimum profit rate, unlike the case of an unregulated firm with a cost-plus contract.

There is a second reason why profit regulation does not work in the same way as does a cost-plus arrangement. Curiously, this is a result of the much-criticized delays that characterize many regulatory procedures. In a number of regulated industries, a proposed change in rates is likely to take a minimum of several months before it gets through the regulatory machinery. Where it is bitterly contested, the resulting hearings before the regulatory commission, the appeals to the courts, and so on are likely to last for years. Rate cases lasting ten years are not unknown. This was true, for example, in the case before the FCC referred to in the boxed insert on page 685. This phenomenon, known as **regulatory lag,** is perhaps the main reason that profit regulation has not eliminated all rewards for efficiency and all penalties for inefficiency.

Suppose, for example, the regulatory commission approves a set of prices calculated to yield exactly the "fair rate of return" to the company, say 10 percent. If management then invests successfully in new processes, which reduce its costs sharply, the rate of return under the old prices may rise to, say, 12 percent. If it takes two years for the regulators to review the prices they previously approved, and adjust them to the new cost levels, the company will earn a 2 percent bonus reward for its efficiency during the two years of regulatory lag. Similarly, if management makes a series of bad decisions, which reduces the company's return to 7 percent, the firm may well apply to the regulator for some adjustments in prices to permit it to recoup its losses. If the regulator takes 18 months to act, the firm suffers a penalty for its inefficiency. It may be added that where mismanagement is *clearly* the cause of losses, regulators will be reluctant to permit the regulated firm to make up for such losses by rate adjustments. But in most cases it is difficult to pinpoint responsibility for a firm's losses.

All in all, those who have studied regulated industries have come away deeply concerned about the effects of regulation upon economic efficiency. Although some regulated firms seem to operate very efficiently, others seem to behave in quite the opposite way.

While regulatory lag does permit some penalty for inefficiency and some reward for superior performance by the regulated firm, the arrangement only works in a rough and ready manner. It still leaves the provision of incentives for efficiency as one of the fundamental problems of regulation. How can one prevent regulated firms from earning excessive profits, but also permit them to earn enough to attract the capital they need while still allowing rewards for superior performance and penalties for poor performance?

Modified Regulation with Efficiency Incentives

The problems of regulation just mentioned, along with some other criticisms, have in recent years produced a number of proposals for changes in the regulatory process. Three such proposals are discussed below.

Deregulation Plus Increased Competition

One of the most widely advocated proposals is for regulators to get out of the business of regulating, leaving much more (if not all) of the task of looking after consumer interests to the natural forces of competition. This approach is promising in areas of the economy in which competition can be expected to survive without government intervention — for example, in freight transportation, airlines, and pipelines. As a consequence, a number of economists representing a broad range of political views have been advocating at least some deregulation in these industries. And, as we have seen, deregulation of air travel and freight transportation by truck and rail has largely been completed.

Of course, deregulation will not work in industries where competitors can survive only if government protects them from real competition. Such inherently noncompetitive industries may well be judged to require continued regulatory controls. So there remains the question: Just which regulatory controls will not destroy all incentives for efficiency?

Performance Criteria for Permitted Rate of Return

Some observers have advocated that the legally permitted rate of return not be set at a fixed number, say 10 percent, but that it be varied from firm to firm depending on the firm's record of efficiency and performance. That is, if some measure of quality of performance can be agreed upon (a measure that should take account of cost efficiency as well as product and service quality), then the better the performance score of the regulated firm the more it would be permitted to earn. A firm that performed well in a given year might be permitted 12 percent profits for that year, whereas a firm that did badly might be allowed only 8 percent, and a firm that performed abominably might be permitted only 4 percent.

Such incentives sometimes can be successfully built into the rules that control the operations of the firm. For example, in 1974 such a program was designed for Amtrak, the public corporation that, in effect, then rented passenger transportation service from U.S. railroads (Amtrak now runs its own trains). Under this program, the amount Amtrak paid them depended upon such features as promptness of arrival of trains, infrequency of breakdowns of locomotives, and so on. Thus, the more frequently its trains were on time, the more Amtrak paid to that railroad. The results were dramatic. While over the period 1973 to 1975 the percentage of trains arriving on time increased for railroads as a whole by about 17.5 percentage points from its miserable 60 percent figure in 1973, the railroads that signed incentive contracts increased their on-time arrivals by about 29.5 percentage points from their initial (1973) average of 61 percent.

However, financial incentives cannot easily be built into rate of return formulas that contain no good objective criteria of performance (such as number of minutes behind schedule for a railroad train). Moreover, it is difficult to balance incentives for different aspects of performance. For example, if the formula assigns too high a weight to product quality and too low a weight to low cost, the firm will be encouraged to incur costs that are unjustifiably high from the point of view of public welfare in order to turn out products of slightly higher quality.

Institutionalized Regulatory Lag

It has been proposed that instead of regulatory lag working haphazardly as it does now, regulation should consciously take advantage of the incentive for efficiency made possible by the lag. Under such a program, the regulators would assign product prices to the firms they oversee, decreeing that, *aside from automatic adjustments for inflation*, these prices are unchangeable until the next regulatory review, to occur *at a time selected by the agency*. The regulated firm would be told that the next review will occur, say, sometime between two and six years in the future, depending on what events occur in the economy. But in the meantime, any firm that can manage cost savings by economy or innovation, or that can attract more customers by improving its product without increasing its costs, will be permitted to keep the higher profits that this superior performance elicits. Of course, for the regulated firm there is a catch. If the firm proves able to reduce costs by, say, 30 percent during a period between regulatory reviews, it can, at the next review, expect to have its prices reduced correspondingly. Thus, in order to earn profits, management would constantly be forced to look for ever more economical ways of doing things.

This approach, too, has its problems. For one thing, in a period of inflation, when costs go up no matter how efficient management is, it is not clear just how regulated prices should be adjusted to make up for rises in costs caused by inflation *between* review periods.

Some Effects of Deregulation

The effects of deregulation are still evolving so it is too early to reach final evaluations of its consequences. Yet, several conclusions are becoming clear.

1. *Effects on Prices.* There seems little doubt that deregulation has generally led to lower prices. According to *Business Week:* "Long-distance airline fares, adjusted for inflation, have declined almost 50% in the past seven years [overall, when fares for shorter trips are included they have also fallen, but by a much smaller percentage]. Many trucking rates have skidded down 30% in real terms since 1980. The costs of standard telephones in 1983 have fallen by one third, compared with last year."[3]

2. *Effects on Local Service.* During the debates on deregulation, it was widely feared, even by supporters of deregulation, that smaller and more isolated communities would be deprived of service because the small number of customers would make service unprofitable. It was said that airlines, railroads, and telephone companies would withdraw from such communities once they were no longer forced to stay there by the regulators.

   So far, these worries seem largely groundless. True, the larger airlines have left the smaller communities, as predicted. But they have usually been replaced by smaller commuter airlines that have provided, on the average, more frequent service than their regulated predecessors. Of course, a few communities have been left without service or with service of poorer quality, but other locations have benefited considerably.

3. *Effects on Entry.* As a result of deregulation, older airlines have invaded one another's routes and a number of new airlines have sprung up. Altogether some 14 new airlines and about 10,000 new truck operators have entered the markets since deregulation. Many of them have, however, run into trouble since they opened their doors, and several have had to be sold on an emergency basis. (See boxed insert on page 693.)

4. *Effects on Profits.* Just as deregulation of airlines and trucking went into effect, a severe recession hit the economy. The profits of the older firms in the industry fell sharply and in many cases turned into losses, whether deregulation or recession or both are responsible is very much disputed. Some experienced observers argue that without deregulation, losses would have been even worse, but no one can be sure.

   What was surprising was that deregulation turned out, even during the recession, to be profitable to many new entrants. A number of new airlines, trucking companies, and telephone companies either showed a profit almost at once or showed promise of becoming profitable very soon.

   Indeed, in airlines, trucking, and bus transportation it turned out that the new entrants, instead of suffering from a cost handicap, often had a substantial cost advantage over the older firms. The reason was that the older firms had agreed to union contracts under regulation. The entrants often entered business using a good deal of nonunion labor and paying much lower

---

[3]"Deregulating America," *Business Week,* November 28, 1983, page 80.

Despite Reagan Trend, Regulation Rises in Certain Areas

The following excerpts from a *Wall Street Journal* article describe the recent swing back to government control, especially in matters of public safety.

In the twilight of a Reagan presidency that vastly expanded the deregulation begun by his predecessors, ardent decontrol is fading. Congress and even some agencies are renewing government activism on a broad range of issues — especially those involving safety, the environment and consumer protection.

That doesn't mean a return to the pervasive federal involvement of past years or an end to most economic decontrol. In areas where there is little public pressure, such as telephone service, deregulation is steaming ahead; like Humpty Dumpty, Ma Bell won't be put back together again. "These are eggs that can't be unscrambled," says Missouri Sen. John Danforth, the ranking Republican on the Commerce Committee. Economic reregulation, he adds, "is a dead issue."

Moreover, some areas are buffeted by cross currents. And in flying, despite demands for federal action against service problems, few want to do away with the leeway that has led to cheap air fares.

The Wall Street Journal/NBC News poll shows that 38% of the people still believe there is too much government regulation of the economy, while 32% think there is about the right amount and 23% say there isn't enough. But those results represent a major swing toward regulation from polls taken in 1980, when more than two-thirds believed Washington was overregulating business and damaging the free market.

Transportation safety is perhaps the biggest focus of regulation as the result of worries about midair collisions and the Amtrack-Conrail train crash that killed 16 people early this year.

The trucking industry faces more stringent safety rules amid rising concerns that partial deregulation of the industry in 1980 created pressures that may have led to unsafe practices. Both the department and some lawmakers are considering, for example, eliminating an exemption that permits many big trucks operating solely within certain communities to escape federal safety standards.

Public and congressional frustration over airline flight delays and service, created in part by the frantic mergers since decontrol, is promoting a host of proposed laws and rules. Flight delays last year increased to 417,644 from 333,817 in 1985. While they have declined a bit this year, Congress is expected to pass a bill requiring that passengers be given a record of an airline's on-time performance. And some in Congress may push to expand air-traffic limits to more busy airports.

Many lawmakers are angrily demanding action because they, too, have suffered air-travel problems. "It's time to skewer the airlines," says Republican Rep. Bud Shuster of Pennsylvania. Such talk has airline, railroad and some trucking officials so worried they have formed a coalition, dubbed the Transportation Reform Alliance, to promote continued deregulation.

Even amid airline complaints, there is virtually no support for re-creating the Civil Aeronautics Board, which regulated airlines' routes and rates. The reason is simple: money. The Brookings Institution estimates that since airline deregulation occurred in 1978, it has saved consumers $6 billion a year.

And many passengers are willing to put up with some inconvenience to keep fares low: When asked in the recent Wall Street Journal/NBC News poll whether lower fares or fewer delays and cancellations were more important, 55% of the people cited lower fares; 36% said fewer delays and cancellations, and 9% weren't sure.

SOURCE: Laurie McGinley, "Federal Regulation Rises Anew in Matters That Worry the Public," THE WALL STREET JOURNAL, April 21, 1987.

wages. However, several of these entrants were misled into overexpansion by their initial success and ended up in financial difficulty.

5. ***Effects on the Unions.*** Deregulation has badly hurt unions such as the Teamsters (of the trucking industry) and the Airline Pilots Association. In the new competitive climate, firms have been forced to make sharp cuts in their work forces and to resist wage increases and other costly changes in working conditions. Indeed, there has been strong pressure for retrenchment on all these fronts. It should not be surprising, then, that some of the affected unions have undertaken efforts to get Congress to reimpose regulation.

6. ***Concentration and Mergers.*** Particularly in aviation and rail freight transportation, deregulation was followed by a wave of mergers in which two firms agreed to join together or in which one firm agreed to be bought out by another. This has led to an expansion of the size of the largest companies in the affected industries.

   That this has happened should not be surprising since, as we saw earlier in the chapter, industries with important economies of scale are the most likely targets for regulation. Once freed from regulatory constraints, it was to be expected that firms in such industries would try to take advantage of the opportunity to achieve cost reductions through rapid expansion or by mergers.

   Evaluations of the merger movement have differed sharply. Some have concluded that mergers threaten to increase monopoly power and exploit the public. Others have argued that indirect competitive pressures (for example, barges and trucks are rivals of large railroads) remain strong, and that economies of scale resulting from the mergers will be passed on to the consuming public.

Consequences of Deregulation: General Comments

The preceding list of the effects of deregulation help us to solve the first puzzle with which this chapter started out. That is, we can see now why many airlines, trucking firms, and bus lines, as well as their unions, strongly opposed deregulation even though it offered them more freedom. They realized that regulation protected them from entry and competition. Rather than serving as an instrument to foster competition, regulation had become a means to forestall it. Of course, there were other reasons why regulated firms were unhappy about the offer of increased freedom provided by deregulation, but fear of competition was surely a major reason.

The general consequences of deregulation brought few surprises to economists. Reduced prices, reduced costs, increased pressures upon unions and some rise in mergers were all expected. What *did* come as a surprise was the magnitude of these changes. No one seems to have expected that wages and working hours of pilots employed by the new airlines would differ so sharply from those traditional in the industry. No one seems to have expected that merger activity would be quite so extensive.

The general public seems to have been unpleasantly surprised in another respect. It was to have been anticipated that increased price competition would bring with it some reduction in "frills." To cut costs in order to reduce prices, airlines have had to make meals less elaborate and costly. They have had to limit the number of flights to avoid empty seats, and increased crowding of

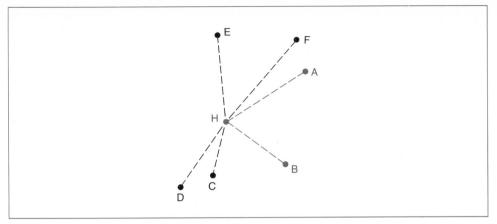

Figure 31–2
A "HUB AND SPOKE"
AIRLINE ROUTING
PATTERN
Passengers do not fly directly
along the sparsely traveled
route from airport A to airport
B. Instead, passengers from
A are flown to hub airport H
and then redistributed to an
airplane flying to airport B.
Deregulation greatly
increased use of this
procedure.

planes is the clear consequence. To fill planes more, many airlines have turned to a "hub and spoke" system (see Figure 31–2). Instead of running a flight directly from a low-demand airport, A, to another low-demand airport, B, the airline flies all passengers from A to the airline's "hub airport," H, where all passengers bound for destination airport B are asked to board the same airplane. This clearly saves money and gives passengers more options as the number of flights between hubs and spokes increases. But it is not as convenient for air passengers as a direct flight from origin to destination.

Critics of deregulation have placed a good deal of emphasis on the reductions of passenger comfort, but economists argue that competition would not bring such results unless passengers as a group prefer the reduction in fares to the greater standards of luxury that preceded them. In 1985, when there was an unusually large number of air accidents, critics even implied that this might be attributable to deregulation as airlines cut expenditures on safety to keep prices low. However, in the following year U.S. commercial airlines achieved an all-time record in terms of passenger safety.

A Word on Nationalization

As we indicated at the beginning of the chapter, in industries in which monopoly or near monopoly offer clear advantages to society over competition, there is an alternative to regulation. This alternative is government ownership and operation of the firms in that industry, or *nationalization*.

In the United States, tradition does not favor such government operation, but the exceptions are growing in number. For example, we have government supply of electricity by the TVA; the U.S. Postal Service; and, more recently, the operation of railroads by the publicly owned agencies Amtrak and Conrail, which may be regarded as an intermediate step in the direction of nationalization, although Conrail is now being returned to private operation. A number of cities operate their own public transport facilities, collect their own garbage, and offer other services that elsewhere are provided by private enterprise.

It is almost an instinctive reaction by people in the United States to consider such public enterprises as being prone to extreme mismanagement and waste. And the near-legendary problems of the Post Office do seem to support this supposition. However, here, too, one should be careful not to jump to conclusions. In recent decades, when railroads were entirely in private hands, that industry had difficulties no less serious than those of the Post Office. It is true that visitors find the nationalized French telephone system a model of chaos and mismanagement. But at the same time, the Swedish telephone system, which is also nationalized, is smooth-working and efficient. And the French government-supplied electricity system has set world standards in its use of the most modern analytic techniques of economics and engineering, and it has adopted innovative pricing policies that promote efficiency.

Despite these accomplishments, no one has yet found a systematic incentive mechanism for efficiency that can do for nationalized industries what the profit motive does for private enterprise. Where the market is unsparing in its rewards for accomplishments and in its penalties for poor performance, one can be quite sure that a firm's inefficiency will not readily be tolerated. But nationalized industries have no such automatic mechanism handing out rewards and penalties dependably and impartially. We have seen, however, that there are analogous problems under regulation; where profits are controlled by the regulator, the rewards for efficiency are also far from automatic. Hence, the relative efficiency of nationalized and regulated private firms is far from clear. (The boxed insert below offers some illustrative evidence.)

Evidence of Inefficiency in Public Enterprise

Since residential garbage collection is a relatively homogeneous task and is carried out both by government and private firms, this service is particularly well suited to comparing the costs of competition, private monopoly, and government monopoly. A study of the relative costs of private and public collection of garbage in about 300 municipalities in the United States found that collection costs were about the same whether the job was done by government or by a group of competing firms.* Competition was expensive because each firm served only scattered customers, and there was much duplication of routes. On the other hand, the costs of both government collection and competitive private collection were some

34 percent higher than the costs of service by a private monopoly collector working under contract to the municipal government. The government services typically had significantly larger crews, higher rates of employee absenteeism, smaller trucks, and less frequent use of incentive systems than did the private collectors.

*E. S. Savas, "Evaluating the Organization of Service Delivery: Solid Waste Collection and Disposal; A Summary." Center for Government Studies, Graduate School of Business, Columbia University, April 1976.

Evidence of Efficiency in Public Enterprise

A recent study compared the costs of 33 private electric utilities and 23 public ones in the United States.* On the basis of a rather sophisticated statistical analysis, the authors concluded that publicly owned electric utilities perform better

*See D. R. Pescatrice and J. M. Trapani III, "The Performance and Objectives of Public and Private Utilities Operating in the United States," *Journal of Public Economics*, vol. 13, 1980, pages 259–76.

than their privately owned regulated counterparts. The costs of the government-owned firms were 24 to 33 percent lower than those of the private firms, a difference similar to that found in other studies of the issue. Thus, at least for the electric utilities they studied, the authors judged that public ownership is a better choice than production by regulated private firms.

By now there have been several dozen studies comparing the efficiency of private unregulated, private regulated, and nationalized firms.[4] While a majority conclude that the costs of unregulated private firms are the lowest, they find considerably more variation in the relative performance of nationalized and private regulated firms. Results seem to vary by type of industry, by country, and by size of enterprise. In sum, it is by no means clear that the regulatory approach always serves the public better than nationalization. In both cases, much seems to depend on the rules employed by the pertinent government agency.

[4]For a good survey of these studies see Yair Aharoni, *The Evolution and Management of State-owned Enterprises*, Ballinger Publishing Company, Cambridge, Mass., 1986, pp. 197–204.

Summary

1. Regulation has two primary purposes: to put brakes on the decisions of industries with monopoly power, and to contribute to public health and safety.
2. Railroads, trucking, telecommunications, and gas and electricity supply are among the industries that are regulated in the United States. In Europe the firms that provide these services are usually owned by the government (they are nationalized).
3. In recent years there has been a major push toward reduction of regulation. So far, air, truck, and rail transportation have been deregulated in whole or in part.
4. Among the major reasons given for regulation are: (a) economies of scale and scope, which make industries into natural monopolies; (b) the danger of self-destructive competition in industries with low (short-run) marginal costs; (c) the desire to provide service to isolated areas where supply is expensive and unprofitable; and (d) the protection of consumers, employees, and the environment.
5. Some economists believe that regulation has had very little effect on regulated industries, but this conclusion is not accepted by everyone.
6. Regulators often reject proposals by regulated firms to cut their prices, and sometimes the regulators even force firms to raise their prices. The purpose of such action is to prevent "unfair competition," and to protect customers of some of the firm's products from being forced to cross-subsidize customers of other products. Many economists disagree with such actions and argue that the result is usually to stifle competition and make all customers pay more than they otherwise would.
7. Economists generally argue that a firm should be permitted to cut its price as long as it covers its marginal cost. However, others (usually non-economists) argue that fully distributed cost is a better criterion. A fully distributed cost criterion, in this sense, usually means that price will be higher than it will be if marginal cost is used as the standard.
8. Regulation is often criticized for providing little or no incentive for efficiency, for tending to push prices upward, and for forcing the regulated parties to engage in an expensive and time-consuming adversary process.
9. Deregulation so far has clearly reduced costs and prices. However, it has also reduced "frills" in service to customers and has been followed by a substantial number of mergers.
10. Nationalized (government-run) industries are frequently suspected of being wasteful and inefficient, but the evidence is not uniform and there are cases in which nationalized firms seem more efficient than similar regulated firms.

Concepts for Review

Nationalization
Price floor
Price ceiling
Natural monopoly
Economies of scale

Economics of scope
Cross-subsidy
Self-destructive competition
Fully distributed cost

Marginal cost pricing
Ramsey Pricing Rule
Regulatory lag
Stand-alone cost

Questions for Discussion

1. Why is an electric company in a city usually considered to be a natural monopoly? What would happen if two competing electric companies were established? How about telephone companies?

2. Suppose a 20 percent cut in the price of freight transportation brings in so much new business that it permits a railroad to cut its passenger fares by 2 percent. In your opinion, is this equitable? Is it a good idea or a bad one?

3. In some regulated industries, prices are prevented from falling by the regulatory agency and as a result many firms open up business in that industry. In your opinion, is this competitive or anticompetitive? Is it a good idea or a bad one?

4. What industries in the United States can be considered nationalized or partly nationalized? What do you think of the quality of their services? Why might this criterion be inadequate as evidence on which to base a judgment of the idea of nationalization?

5. List some industries with regulated rates whose services you have bought. What do you think of the quality of their service?

6. In which if any of the regulated industries mentioned in your previous answer is there competitive rivalry? Why is regulation appropriate in these cases? (Or is it inappropriate in your opinion, and if so, why?)

7. Regulators are much concerned about the prevention of "predatory pricing"—pricing policies designed to destroy competition. The U.S. Court of Appeals has, however, noted that "the term probably does not have a well-defined meaning, but it certainly bears a sinister connotation." How might one go about distinguishing "predatory" from "nonpredatory" pricing? What would you do about it? (Note that no one has yet come up with a final answer to this problem.)

8. Do you think it is fair or unfair for rural users of telephone service to be cross-subsidized by other telephone services?

9. Can you think of a way in which a new rural telephone subscriber contributes a beneficial externality? If so, does it make sense to provide a subsidy to rural subscribers, and who should pay the subsidy?

10. A regulated industry is prohibited from earning profits higher than it now is getting. It begins to sell a new product at a price above its long-run marginal cost. Explain why the prices of other company products will, very likely, have to be reduced.

32

Limiting Market Power: Antitrust Policy

The preceding chapter described the process of regulation, one of the two main instruments used by the U.S. government to offset the undesirable effects that unrestrained monopoly and oligopoly would have on the market mechanism. This chapter analyzes the second of these instruments, *antitrust policy*. **Antitrust policy** is the term used to describe programs designed to control the growth of monopoly and to prevent powerful firms from engaging in practices that are considered "undesirable." Such "undesirable practices" are vaguely defined by a number of federal laws and court decisions. Firms accused of violating the antitrust laws are likely to be sued in court by the federal government, seeking a ruling that both prevents the practice from recurring and punishes the offender by fines or even a prison term.

Antitrust suits are likely to be well-publicized affairs because the accused firms are often the giants of industry. The more spectacular cases in the history of antitrust policy involve such names as Standard Oil, U.S. Steel, the Aluminum Company of America (Alcoa), General Electric, International Business Machines (IBM), and American Telephone and Telegraph (AT&T). The magnitude of an antitrust suit is difficult to envision. After the charges have been filed, it is not unusual for more than five years to elapse before the case even comes up for trial. The parties spend this period preparing their cases: assembling witnesses, gathering evidence, and drawing up numerous documents. With the permission of the courts, the parties may undertake massive searches of one another's files, each side collecting many millions of pages from those files. Dozens of lawyers, scores of witnesses, and hundreds of researchers are likely to participate in the process of preparation. The trial itself is likely to run for years, with each day's proceedings producing a fat volume of transcript. A major case can pour forth literally several thousand volumes of material, and the total cost to the defendant can easily run to *several hundred million* dollars.

What all this means is that when the Department of Justice or the Federal Trade Commission decides to bring suit against a company, it automatically imposes a huge financial penalty upon that company *whether or not* that firm is subsequently found to have violated the law—or even if the case is thrown out of court before it ever comes to trial. That is an awesome power and a great responsibility. What justifies the investment of so much power in a government agency? What are the purposes of the antitrust laws? And how well has the program succeeded? These questions are the main concerns of this chapter. Starting with a little history, we describe how the antitrust program has fared over the nine decades since its inception. We outline the activities that are currently

Two Lingering Antitrust Issues

The Breakup Of The Bell System

In late 1974 the Department of Justice sued AT&T, claiming that the company had engaged in a variety of anticompetitive practices. AT&T was accused of monopolizing the equipment, long-distance, and local calling markets and of using its monopoly power in each market to enhance its position in the other markets. For example, it was claimed that AT&T took deliberate measures to make it difficult for rival suppliers of long-distance services to obtain access to the local telephone network, thus impeding their access to the ultimate consumer.

The suit was settled in 1982 through a voluntary agreement between the Justice department and AT&T under which the latter gave up all the local companies, which were henceforth to be independent and would even compete with AT&T in a number of markets. The divested local companies were required (as soon as the necessary equipment was installed) to offer AT&T and its competitors exactly the same quality of service in reaching the ultimate consumers. While AT&T lost its local companies, it was permitted for the first time to enter a number of fields such as computer applications to communication, for which it considered itself well suited and from which it had until then been excluded by an earlier agreement with the Department of Justice.

While the suit was settled more than six years ago, its consequences are still far from clear. Ancillary negotiations continue, and the industry remains in turmoil.

Resale Price Maintenance

For over 70 years an attempt by a manufacturer to set the price at which retailers must sell one of its products has automatically been considered illegal. In recent years, the Department of Justice has proposed to overturn the universality of this prohibition, letting such issues be decided case by case, depending on the facts involved.

Consumer advocates have long opposed attempts by manufacturers to fix retail prices—called *resale price maintenance*. In the United States, discounting and discount houses flourish as in no other country and provide unique opportunities for bargain shopping. Manufacturers who want to dictate resale prices seek to prevent discounters from carrying their products. The manufacturers claim that discounters cut corners in customer service, offering little help in product selection, installation, and repair. But the discounters make it difficult for full-service retailers to survive. Potential customers go to a full-service department store for product information, then buy the item from a discounter. The final result, it is claimed, can be a decrease in competition, as the full-service retailer is forced out of that business. In such cases, where resale price maintenance is believed to help to preserve competition, the Department of Justice says it should be permitted.

What do you think?

prohibited by law, and then examine the role of monopoly in the economy and the pros and cons of the antitrust program from the viewpoint of economic analysis.

The Public Image of Business at the Time the Antitrust Laws Were Born

The Sherman Antitrust Act, the forerunner of all modern antitrust legislation, was passed in 1890. To understand what brought Congress to attempt to interfere with freedom of business enterprise, we must glance briefly at the character of the most publicized business practices in the United States during the half century following the Civil War. There were, no doubt, many businessmen at that time whose mode of operation was beyond reproach. But these were not the businessmen who made the headlines and who amassed the most spectacular fortunes. The adventures of the more daring breed of entrepreneurs, those who have been described as "the robber barons," compete in lurid detail with the tales of their contemporaries in the Wild West.

One of the most widely publicized cases was that of John D. Rockefeller, Sr., and his Standard Oil Company. About five years after starting in the oil-refining business with an investment of $4000, Rockefeller and his partners formed the Standard Oil Company in 1870. Under its leadership, a number of refineries and other shippers formed a cooperative powerful enough to force the railroads not only to provide discounts to members of the group *and not to its competitors,* but even to give the group "drawbacks" — that is, payments on every shipment of oil refined by a *rival* firm. In 1872 the organization controlled only about 10 percent of the country's refining capacity. Yet only seven years later Standard Oil and its associated companies were producing some 90 percent of the nation's refined oil and had control of all its pipeline capacity.

Then, in 1882, lacking confidence in the trustworthiness of the alliance, and because of legal obstacles to its interstate operations, the group formed the Standard Oil Trust (from which the word "antitrust" was derived). This involved the appointment of a group of nine trustees into whose hands the 40 associated firms placed enough of their stock to give irrevocable control to the trustees. The trust closed down "excessive" and inefficient refinery operations, involving more than half its plants, in an effort to limit output and keep prices at levels that yielded monopoly profits.

While the oil trust was the first to be established in the United States, others soon followed. Successful trusts were formed in sugar, whiskey, lead, cottonseed oil, and linseed oil. In 1892 the Supreme Court of Ohio ordered the dissolution of the Standard Oil Trust, which nevertheless managed to survive as a cooperating set of firms by arranging for the directors of the major refining companies to serve on one another's boards.

Other, more lurid tales of business practices in this period are easy to find: how J. P. Morgan hired an army of toughs to engage literally in pitched battle for a contested section of railroad outside Binghamton, New York; how Philip Armour and his confederates obtained control of meat processing by an understanding with their rivals that each day a different one of them would offer a low bid for the morning shipment of cattle and no one else would ever enter a higher bid. It is easy to go on and on with such stories. But the point is clear:

There was good reason in 1890 for popular distrust of free-swinging business activity. Business practices in the preceding decades had been ridden by scandal.

Business leaders repeatedly indicated their contempt for the public interest. J. P. Morgan announced, "I owe the public nothing," and people long remembered W. H. Vanderbilt's phrase "the public be damned." The population was warned by advocates of control measures that it faced a country "in which the citizen was born to drink the milk furnished by the milk trust, eat the beef of the beef trust, illuminate his home by grace of the oil trust and die and be carried off by the coffin trust."[1] The circumstances were clearly propitious for some legislative action.

The Antitrust Laws

Five acts of Congress constitute the basis of the federal government's antitrust policy. Major provisions of these acts are summarized in Table 32–1. The **Sherman Act**, the first of the U.S. antitrust laws, was passed in 1890, soon after the trust-creating activity reached its peak. The act is brief and very general, containing two main provisions: a prohibition of all contracts, combinations, and conspiracies in restraint of trade (Section 1), and a prohibition of any acts of, or attempts at, monopolization of trade (Section 2). However, the Sherman Act provided no definition of its terms or terminology and no special agency to oversee its enforcement. Thirteen years elapsed after its passage before the antitrust division of the Department of Justice was established under the energetic antitrust proclivities of Theodore Roosevelt.

It was felt by many during Woodrow Wilson's administration that the Sherman Act did not provide adequate protection to the public against restrictive business practices. Consequently, in 1914 Congress passed two supplemental laws, the Clayton Act and the Federal Trade Commission Act.

[1]Matthew Josephson, *The Robber Barons, The Great American Capitalists 1861–1901* (New York: Harcourt Brace Jovanovich, 1934), page 358.

Table 32–1
BASIC ANTITRUST LAWS

NAME	DATE	MAJOR PROVISIONS
Sherman Act	1890	Prohibits "all contracts, combinations and conspiracies in restraint of trade" (Section 1), and monopolization in interstate and foreign trade (Section 2).
Clayton Act	1914	Prohibits price discrimination; contracts in which the seller prevents buyers from purchasing goods from the seller's competitors (tying contracts); and acquisition by one corporation of another's shares if these acts are likely to reduce competition or tend to create monopoly: also prohibits directors of one company from sitting on the board of a competitor's company.
Federal Trade Commission Act	1914	Establishes the FTC as an independent agency with authority to prosecute unfair competition and to prevent false and misleading advertising.
Robinson-Patman Act	1936	Prohibits special discounts and other discriminatory concessions to large purchasers unless based on differences in cost or "offered in good faith to meet an equally low price of a competitor."
Celler-Kefauver Antimerger Act	1950	Prohibits any corporation from acquiring the assets of another where the effect is to reduce competition substantially or to tend to create a monopoly.

The **Clayton Act** deals with certain specific practices thought to be conducive to encroachment of monopoly. It took two steps toward protecting smaller firms from what was considered unfair competition by larger rivals. First, it prohibited **price discrimination,** which it defined as the act, by a seller, of charging different prices to different buyers of the same product. This provision would, for example, have prohibited the railroad rebates that Rockefeller had used to squeeze out his rivals. Second, the Clayton Act prohibited *tying contracts* — arrangements under which a customer who wants to buy some product from a given seller is required as part of the price to agree to buy some other product or products exclusively from that same seller. In addition, the Clayton Act prohibited one firm from purchasing the stock of another if that acquisition tended to reduce competition. While this provision was intended to prevent a firm from buying out its rivals, business found it possible to circumvent the intent of the law by buying a rival's stocks and then merging assets. When this practice was recognized, a new law — the **Celler-Kefauver Antimerger Act** of 1950 — was enacted to prohibit it. Finally, the Clayton Act prohibited *interlocking directorates* between competitors, arrangements under which two companies have in common some of the members of their boards of directors.

> **Price discrimination** occurs when different prices, relative to costs, are charged to different buyers of the same product.

The **Federal Trade Commission Act** created a commission to investigate "unfair" and "predatory" competitive practices and declared illegal all "unfair methods of competition and commerce." But since no definition of "unfairness" was provided by the law, and since, in any event, the Commission's powers were substantially restricted by the courts, the FTC was a rather ineffective agency for the first quarter-century of its existence. In 1938, however, it was given the task of preventing false and deceptive advertising, a task to which it has subsequently devoted a substantial portion of its energies.

In 1936, Congress passed the **Robinson-Patman Act,** which was designed to protect independent sellers — both wholesalers and retailers (primarily in groceries and drugs) — from the "unfair competition" of chain stores and mass distributors. The Robinson-Patman Act was not a natural step in the succession of antitrust laws, since it sought to *restrain* competition by protecting small firms from the competition of larger ones. It was felt that large firms were powerful enough to wrest special financial terms from their suppliers, which gave them an unfair competitive edge over their rivals. Accordingly, the Act prohibited several types of discriminatory arrangements, such as:

1. Special concessions, like promotional allowances by sellers to any favored set of buyers; any such allowances being legal only if available to all buyers on essentially equal terms;

2. Special discounts to favored buyers who purchase the same goods in the same quantities as other buyers who do not get the discount;

3. Lower prices in one geographic area than in another, or prices that are "unreasonably low," if the objective is to eliminate competition;

4. Payment of brokerage fees to a buyer who does not actually use a middleman broker;

5. Discounts for larger purchases, or any other form of discrimination that tends to *reduce* competition or encourage monopoly. This was perhaps the most important provision of the Act, although it did continue to permit price discrimination if it could be justified either by differences in costs or by the necessity of meeting the price charged by a competitor.

The Courts and the Sherman Act

From the earliest days of the Sherman Act, the courts have been rather consistent in their use of Section 1 — the part of the Act that prohibits all contracts, combinations, and conspiracies in restraint of trade. Section 1 has been invoked primarily against price-fixing agreements — that is, agreements under which several ostensibly competing firms coordinate their pricing decisions. The courts have held that such agreements are illegal *per se;* that is, they have held that no excuses or exonerating circumstances can render a price-fixing agreement acceptable to the law.

In the Addyston Pipe case of 1899, six manufacturers of cast-iron pipe argued that the prices they had agreed upon were reasonable and that, had there been no agreement, prices would have been driven to ruinous levels. But Justice William Howard Taft rejected the argument, affirming that *any* price-setting agreement was illegal. This doctrine has been confirmed many times, most notably in the G.E.-Westinghouse case, which was decided in 1961. General Electric, Westinghouse, and several dozen other producers of electrical equipment had gotten together to divide the market up among themselves and to agree on prices. The firms were found guilty of a conspiracy to fix prices and were fined several million dollars. Even more remarkable, officers of the major companies were sentenced to (brief) prison terms.

Cases in which there are no *explicit* price agreements, but in which there are grounds for suspicion that more subtle means have been used to attain the same goals, have proven more difficult for the courts to deal with. For example, a large firm may publish a price list so that all its competitors know in advance what prices it is going to charge. If it also announces in advance that it will reduce its price to equal that of any competitor who attempts to undercut it, this may effectively force rivals to match the published prices. A variety of such types of behavior have been held to facilitate coordination of prices; and some, though not all, of them have been held to be illegal.

Section 2 of the Sherman Act deals with persons "who shall monopolize or attempt to monopolize . . . any part of the trade or commerce among the several states, or with foreign nations." At first the courts proceeded very timidly in dealing with industrial cases under Section 2. For example, in the E. C. Knight case of 1895, the court held that a monopoly of sugar manufacturing was legal on the grounds that manufacturing was not commerce! But the Supreme Court's position toughened markedly in 1911, when it decided to require both the American Tobacco Company and the Standard Oil Company to give up substantial shares of their holdings in other firms. Many of today's leading gasoline suppliers — including Standard Oil of California, Exxon, and Sohio — are offspring of the original Standard Oil Company, spawned by the Court's decision.

At the same time, however, the Court also formulated the troublesome **rule of reason,** which held that trade restraints are not *necessarily* illegal per se. According to this rule, a restraint is against the law only if it is "unreasonable." On that basis, U.S. Steel was exonerated in 1920 even though, when it was formed, it controlled 80 to 95 percent of U.S. output of some steel products. The Court held that mere size does not constitute an offense — that a firm must commit objectionable overt acts before it can be found guilty of violating Section 2 of the Sherman Act. Eastman Kodak and International Harvester, each with very large market shares, were found not guilty on similar grounds. Thus, while the courts held that there were *no* excusable cases of price fixing under Section 1, they ruled that there *were* excusable monopolies under Section 2.

However, a profound departure from this doctrine was enunciated in the decision on the Department of Justice's case against Alcoa. Launched in 1937, the case was settled only eight years later. The Court ruled that Alcoa was guilty *because it controlled some 90 percent of the market,* even though it had not used means to gain this control that would previously have been declared "unreasonable." Thus, the Court's decision took the position that a firm's monopoly power, if sufficiently great, was illegal when *consciously maintained,* even if the firm had done nothing illegal to acquire that power. In other words the Court decided that the legality of the organization of an industry could be determined at least in part from its observable *structure,* for example, from the market share of the largest firm as well as from the *conduct* of any firm in that industry. This feature of the Alcoa decision has so far not been used widely as a precedent for other cases, and some commentators claim it was just an aberration. Others, though, feel that the conclusion about the illegality of monopoly, however acquired, heralded a new phase in the history of antitrust policy.

On Merger Policy

Mergers have long been a subject of suspicion by the antitrust authorities. Particularly when a merger is **horizontal,** it is often feared that because the number of firms in the industry is reduced (that is, concentration is increased), competition will decline.

The Department of Justice and the Federal Trade Commission are both concerned with mergers. They do not wish to impede mergers that seem likely to increase efficiency by improving the coordination of production activities, permitting economies of scale, getting one of the firms out of financial difficulties, or facilitating operations in a variety of other ways. But the antitrust agencies do want to prevent mergers that threaten to reduce competition.

To help firms decide whether a proposed merger will get them into trouble, and for other reasons as well, the Department of Justice issues a set of guidelines which indicate when the Department is (or is not) likely to try to block a merger. For example, the guidelines indicate that the Department generally will not oppose mergers in industries that are very unconcentrated or into which entry is very easy. However, in highly concentrated industries where entry is difficult, the merger of two large firms will usually be opposed. In 1982 the Department issued new guidelines (modified in 1984), easing the criteria which a merger must satisfy if the Department is to refrain from fighting it in the courts. One result of this loosening of the rules has been a much-publicized rise in merger activity (though matters had already been moving in that direction). During 1972–82, companies are reported to have spent $170 billion purchasing other firms in order to merge with them. In 1986, with less government opposition, the amount invested approached $190 billion. The rash of mergers that this expenditure represents has given rise to a good deal of controversy; some observers conclude that it has increased the likelihood of monopoly power, while others believe it has served largely to make the merged firms more efficient. In any event, defenders of the mergers argue that they have not increased the share of big business in the U.S. (see the discussion of concentration in the next section). They point out that in 1986 the percentage of the nation's assets held by the top 200 U.S. corporations was below its level in 1970 and that the share of the labor force employed by those corporations continues to fall.

Though by no means unanimous on the subject, most economists agree that mergers *sometimes* reduce competition, particularly in a market which is

A **merger** occurs when two previously independent firms are combined under a single owner or group of owners. A **horizontal merger** is the merger of two firms producing similar products, as when one toothpaste manufacturing firm purchases another. A **vertical merger** involves the joining of two firms one of which supplies an ingredient of the other's product, as when an auto maker acquires a tire manufacturing firm. A **conglomerate merger** is the union of two unrelated firms, as when a defense industry firm joins a firm that produces phonograph records.

not contestable,[2] so that threats of entry do not prevent the merged firm from raising prices above competitive levels. This danger is particularly acute if the number of firms is sufficiently small to make collusion a real possibility.

On the other hand, where there is reason to believe that the merger will not reduce competition, many economists oppose impediments to merger. They believe that mergers that are not undertaken to reduce competition can have only one purpose—to achieve greater efficiency. For example, the larger firm that results from the merger may enjoy substantial economies of scale not available to smaller firms. Or the two merging companies may learn special skills from one another. Or they may offset one another's risks. Mergers have sometimes proved disappointing and brought little cost saving. But economists who defend freedom to merge when there is no demonstrated threat to competition pose a challenging question: Who can judge better than the firms involved whether their marriage is likely to make their activities more efficient?

Issues in Concentration of Industry

Having reviewed the antitrust laws and their interpretation by the courts, the next logical question is: Do they work? One very rough way to measure the success of antitrust legislation is to look at what has happened to the share of American business in the hands of the largest firms.

First, we can compare the degree of domination by large firms in the U.S. economy with that in other countries. American programs designed to limit monopoly power go back further and involve more powerful government machinery than do comparable programs in virtually any other major free-market economy. Indeed, in some European and Far Eastern countries, monopoly is not really discouraged. Thus, one way to evaluate the effectiveness of an antitrust program is to compare the status of the larger firms in the United States with that of their counterparts abroad.

A second method of evaluation involves observations of firms over a long period of time. Some observers, particularly the Marxists, have predicted that one of the basic tendencies of capitalism is **concentration of industry,** because small firms are increasingly driven out of business, especially during economic crises, and large firms consequently acquire ever-larger shares of the market. One can therefore investigate whether such a tendency has been observed in the United States. If, in fact, concentration has *not* increased, someone who holds these views might be led to surmise that the antitrust program has had a hand in preventing the growth of monopoly. But first we should consider what might have been expected to happen to concentration in the United States in the absence of any countermeasures by government. Is there good reason to expect an inexorable trend toward bigness, as the Marxists suggest?

There are two basic reasons why the larger firms in an industry may triumph over the small. First, larger firms may obtain monopoly power, which they can use to their advantage. They can force sellers of equipment, raw materials, and other inputs to give them better terms than are available to small competitors; and they can also force retailers to give preferences to their products. These are, of course, the sorts of advantages to bigness that the antitrust laws were designed to eliminate.

The second reason why an industry's output may tend to be divided among fewer and larger firms with the passage of time has to do with technology. In some industries, fairly small firms can produce as cheaply or more cheaply than

[2]See Chapter 31, pages 628–29 for a definition and discussion of this concept.

large ones, while in other industries only rather large firms can achieve maximal economy. By and large, the difference in number of firms from one industry to another has tended to correspond to the size of the firm that is least costly. Automobile, steel, and airplane manufacturing are all industries in which tiny companies cannot hope to produce economically and, indeed, these are all industries made up of a relatively few large firms. In clothing production and farming, matters go quite the other way.

Frequently, innovation seems to have increased the plant size that minimizes costs. Such examples as automated processes or assembly lines suggest that new techniques always call for gigantic equipment; but this is not always true. For example, the invention of truck transportation took much of the freight-shipping market away from the giant railroads and gave it to much smaller trucking firms. Technological change also seems to have favored the establishment of small electronics firms. Similarly, the continued development of cheaper and smaller computers is likely to provide a competitive advantage to smaller firms in many other industries. Furthermore:

If innovation provides increased cost advantages to larger firms, the growth of firms will be stimulated. But a fall in the number of firms in the industry need not inevitably result. If demand for the industry's output grows faster than the optimal size of firms, we may end up with a larger number of firms, each of them bigger than before, but each having a smaller share of an expanded market.

For example, suppose in some industry a new process is invented that requires a far larger scale of operation than currently is typical. Specifically, suppose that the least costly plant size becomes twice as large. If demand for the industry's product increases only a little, we can expect a decrease in the number of firms. But if demand for the industry's product happens to triple at the same time, then the optimal number of firms will in fact increase to one and a half times the original number—each firm will be twice as big as before—so that together they serve three times the volume. In such a case, each firm's share of industry output will in fact have declined.

In the twentieth century, technological developments do seem to call for larger firms, which are best adapted to take advantage of the resulting economies. Perhaps this has somewhat outstripped even the rate of growth in output—that is, the growth of GNP. If so, we should expect some fall in the number of firms in a typical industry, somewhat as many Marxists expect. However, as was just noted, not all technological change has worked in this direction. For example, many firms in the electronics industry are relatively small, and there are observers who argue that new techniques will permit smaller firms to supply some telecommunications services without incurring high costs. We must turn to the evidence to judge whether or not American industry has grown more concentrated.

Evidence on Concentration in Industry

There have been many statistical studies of concentration in American industry. One common way of measuring concentration is to calculate the share of the industry's output produced by the four largest firms in an industry, the so-called **concentration ratio.** Of course, there is no reason why the three or five or ten largest firms could not be used for the purpose, but conventionally four firms are used as the standard.

A **concentration ratio** is the percentage of an industry's output produced by its *four* largest firms. It is intended to measure the degree to which the industry is dominated by large firms, that is, how closely it approximates a monopoly.

Table 32-2

1982 CONCENTRATION RATIOS FOR REPRESENTATIVE INDUSTRIES

INDUSTRY	4-FIRM RATIO	INDUSTRY	4-FIRM RATIO
Hard surface floor coverage	99	Ship building and repairing	35
Motor vehicles and car bodies	92	Musical instruments	33
Electric lamps	91	Pharmaceutical preparations	26
Cereal breakfast foods	86	Apparel mens' and boys' suits and coats	25
Rubber tires and inner tubes	66	Brooms and brushes	18
Aircraft	64	Fluid milk	16
Primary aluminum	64	Jewelry-precious metal	16
Phonograph records and pre-recorded tape	61	Boat building and repairing	14
Fabricated metal cars	50	Bottled and canned soft drinks	14
Buttons	37	Bolts, nuts, rivets and washers	13
Dolls	36	Apparel women's and misses' dresses	6
Motors and generators	36		

SOURCE: "Concentration Ratios in Manufacturing," Bureau of Census MC82-5-7, April 1986.

Table 32–2 shows concentration ratios in a number of industries in the United States. We see that concentration varies greatly from industry to industry: automobiles, electric lamps and breakfast cereals are produced by highly concentrated industries, while the jewelry, clothing, and soft drink industries show very little concentration. But only comparisons over time and by geographic area can reveal the most significant implications of these figures. Here, the available evidence suggests that (perhaps simply because the American market is larger) concentration in U.S. industry is somewhat lower than it is in most other industrialized countries. But the differences are not substantial; and, because of other differences that make comparison difficult, the significance of these differences has been questioned.

In the United States there seems to have been little trend in concentration ratios, at least since the beginning of this century. The evidence is that, on the average during this period, concentration ratios remained remarkably constant. It has been estimated that at the turn of the century 32.9 percent of manufactured goods were produced by industries in which the concentration ratio was 50 percent or more (meaning that at least 50 percent of industry output was produced by the four largest firms). By 1963 the figure had risen only to 33.1 percent. And by 1970 it actually fell to 26.3 percent, although it has risen slightly since then. These figures and those for other years are shown in Table 32–3.

More recent data show the share of total manufacturing assets (that is, roughly speaking, the total investments) that are owned by the 200 largest manufacturing corporations. Table 32–4 does suggest that concentration has increased from 54.8 percent to 59.9 percent during the 17 years from 1963 to 1980. But, as the previous table indicates, we have had comparable rises (and comparable falls) in concentration before. Moreover, the asset share held by the largest 200 corporations fell from 40 percent in 1963 to 38.3 percent in 1978 in the broader nonfinancial sector of the economy.

In a frequently quoted statement, M. A. Adelman, a noted authority on the subject, concluded, "Any tendency either way, if it does exist, must be at

Table 32-3

THE TREND IN CONCENTRATION IN MANUFACTURING INDUSTRIES
(SELECTED YEARS)

	(around) 1901	1947	1954	1958	1963	1966	1970	1972
Percent of value added in industries with 4-firm concentration ratios over 50 percent	32.9	24.4	29.9	30.2	33.1	28.6	26.3	29.0

SOURCES: P. W. McCracken and T. G. Moore, "Competition and Market Concentration in the American Economy," Subcommittees on Antitrust and Monopoly, U.S. Senate, March 29, 1973, and F. M. Scherer, *Industrial Market Structure and Economic Performance* (Boston: Houghton Mifflin, 1980), page 68.

Table 32-4

THE TREND IN CONCENTRATION IN MANUFACTURING ASSETS (SELECTED YEARS)

	1963	1967	1972	1974	1975	1976	1977	1978	1979	1980
Percent of assets held by top 200 corporations										
Manufacturing	54.8	56.1	58.3	56.5	56.7	57.5	58.0	58.3	59.0	59.9
Nonfinancial	40.0	39.9	41.0	39.7	39.2	39.5	39.1	38.3	—	—

SOURCES: D. Duke, "Trends in Aggregate Concentration," Working Paper No. 61, Federal Trade Commission, June 1982. The manufacturing sector figures since 1974 are FTC data. The other figures involve the IRS Statistics of Income, *Compustat*, and *Moody's Industrial Manual*, and they are not perfectly comparable with the FTC figures.

the pace of a glacial drift."[3] Or, as a more recent report puts it, "Almost all observers of the industrial scene . . . agree that . . . the evidence fails to support a claim that competition has declined. While concentration has increased in some areas, decreases have occurred elsewhere, leaving the overall structure unaffected."[4]

Concentration in the United States seems to be somewhat lower than it is in most other industrialized economies. Over the course of the twentieth century, concentration in individual U.S. industries has shown no tendency to increase.

Since concentration is intended as a measure of the "bigness" of the firms in an industry, from such information one can perhaps surmise that the antitrust program has been effective to some degree in inhibiting whatever trend toward bigness may in fact exist. But even this very cautious conclusion has been questioned by some observers. In fact, some economists and other observers have expressed the view that these laws have made virtually no difference in the size and the behavior of American business. Whether it is desirable for the antitrust program or for some other program to inhibit concentration or big size of firms is the issue to which we turn next.

[3]M.A. Adelman, "The Measurement of Industrial Concentration," *Review of Economics and Statistics*, vol. 33, November 1951, pages 295-96.
[4]P.W. McCracken and T.G. Moore, "Competition and Market Concentration in the American Economy," Subcommittee on Antitrust and Monopoly, U.S. Senate, March 29, 1973.

The Pros and Cons of Bigness

Why has antitrust become so accepted a part of government policy? Are the effects of bigness or monopoly always undesirable? We *do* know that monopoly power can be abused; the history of the Rockefellers, the Armours, and the Morgans described at the beginning of this chapter confirms that adequately. But even when the giants of business are not so swashbuckling in their operations, unrestrained monopoly and bigness give rise to a number of problems:

1. *Distribution of income.* The flow of wealth to firms with market power — and thus to those who are able to influence prices in their favor — is widely considered to be unfair and socially unacceptable.

2. *Restriction of output.* We learned in Chapter 27 that if an unrestrained monopoly is to maximize its profits, it must restrict its output below the amount that would be provided by an equivalent competitive industry. This means that unregulated monopolized industries are likely to produce smaller outputs than the quantities that serve society's interests.

3. *Lack of inducement for innovation.* It is sometimes argued that firms in industries with little or no competition are under less pressure to introduce new production methods and new products than are firms in industries in which each is constantly trying to beat out the others. Without competition, the management of a firm may choose the quiet life, taking no chances on risky investments in research and development. But a firm that operates in constant fear that its rivals will come up with a better idea, and come up with it first, can afford no such luxury.

So far we have presented only one side of the picture. In fact, bigness in industry need not be advantageous only to the firm. It can also, at least *sometimes*, work to the advantage of the general public. Again, there are several reasons:

1. *Economies of large size.* Probably the most important advantage of bigness is to be found in those industries in which technology dictates that small-scale operation is inefficient. One can hardly imagine the costs if automobiles were produced in little workshops rather than giant factories. The notion of a small firm operating a long-distance railroad does not even make sense, and a multiplicity of firms replicating the same railroad service would clearly be incredibly wasteful.

   On these grounds, most policymakers have never even considered an attempt to eliminate bigness. Their objective, rather, is to curb its potential abuses and to try at the same time to help the public benefit from its advantages. Of course, it does not follow that every industry in which firms happen to be big is one in which big firms are best. There are observers who argue that many firms in fact exceed the size required for cost minimization.

2. *Required scale for innovation.* Some economists have argued that only large firms have the resources and the motivation for really significant innovation. While many inventions are still contributed by individuals, to put a new invention into commercial production is often an expensive, complex venture that can only be carried out on a large scale. And only large firms can afford the funds and bear the risks that such an effort demands. In addition, according to this view, only large firms have the motivation to lay out the funds required for the innovation process, because only large firms will get to keep a considerable share of the benefits. A small company, on the

other hand, will find that its innovative idea is soon likely to be followed by close imitations, which enable competitors to profit from its research outlays.

There have been many studies of the relationship between firm size, competitiveness of the industry, and the level of expenditure on research and development (R and D). While the evidence is far from conclusive, it does indicate that highly competitive industries comprising very small firms tend not to spend a great deal on research. Up to a point, R and D outlays and innovation seem to increase with size of firm and concentration of industry. However, some of the most significant innovations introduced in the twentieth century have been contributed by smaller firms. Examples include the electric light, alternating current, the photocopier, FM radio, and the electronic calculator.

Other Government Programs Related to Bigness

Because the issues raised by bigness and concentration are complex, they would appear to call for a variety of policy measures. Certainly, antitrust programs alone cannot do everything that the public interest requires. For example, in cases where large firms are far more efficient than small ones, it does not seem reasonable to break up industrial giants. In fact, it is often considered most desirable, on grounds of economy, to permit a market to be served by only a single firm — such as a supplier of electricity, local transportation, or local telecommunications services.

Where one firm offers considerable savings in comparison to a multiplicity of suppliers — that is, where the industry is a *natural monopoly* — it is usually agreed that it would not serve the public interest to subdivide the supplying firm into a number of rival companies. Instead, one of two policies is usually adopted. Either the monopoly firm is *nationalized* and run as a government enterprise (telephone service in Sweden and electricity generation in France are good examples). Or, as is typical in the United States, the natural monopoly is left as a private firm but its operations are *regulated* in one of the ways described in the previous chapter.

The possibility of inhibition of innovation by competition is another important issue, which, as we have seen, affects policy toward bigness and concentration. The main instrument government has employed in this area is the **patent** system, which rewards the innovator by the grant of a temporary monopoly. The patent restricts imitation and is designed to offer small-firm innovators the same advantages from their research activities as are enjoyed by innovators in industries that contain no competitors ready to erode profits by imitation. Thus, somewhat ironically, while government prohibits monopolies, it also guarantees monopoly power to protect small firms in competitive industries. Of course, sometimes the protected firms themselves grow big with the help of the protection. Once-small firms like Polaroid and Xerox grew into industrial giants with the help of government protection through the patent laws.

A **patent** is a temporary grant of monopoly rights over an innovation.

Questions have been raised about the effectiveness of patents in inducing expenditure on R and D, and the evidence certainly does not provide overwhelming support for the view that patents constitute a strong stimulus for innovation. Questions have also been raised about the desirability of granting an innovator an unrestricted monopoly for 17 years, as the patent program now does in the United States. Similar issues have been raised about copyright laws, which restrict reproduction of written works.

Finally, government has provided special help to small business in a variety of ways. For example, there are programs designed to make it easier for small firms to raise capital; and special government agencies, such as the Small Business Administration, have been set up for the purpose. There is also some degree of *progressivity* in business taxation, meaning that smaller firms are subject to taxes lower than those paid by larger firms. And special legislation, such as the "fair trade" laws — which, though since repealed, permitted manufacturers to designate and enforce "fair" retail prices for products — are intended, in part, to protect small retailers from the competition of larger rivals.

Issues in Antitrust Policy

In recent years there has been a searching reexamination of government policy toward business. For example, there have been calls for a decrease in the overall power of the regulatory agencies; and the antitrust program is unlikely to be ignored in such a review. Some voices call for abolition of the antitrust laws altogether, while others advocate their strengthening and expansion. But even if one grants the desirability of an antitrust program with teeth in it, there still remain questions about whom or what to bite.

Structure versus Conduct

A major issue is the relative weights that should be assigned to *structure* and *conduct* in deciding which firms it is in the social interest to prosecute. Most people accept the basic notion that socially damaging conduct, such as price fixing or threats of physical violence, should be discouraged; though there is often disagreement over what types of conduct are undesirable.

But many more questions are raised about the use of structural criteria in antitrust policy. Is bigness always undesirable per se? What if the large firm is more efficient and has engaged in no practices that can reasonably be considered to constitute predatory competition? Many economists have reservations about the prosecution of such a firm, fearing that it will only serve to grant protection to inefficient competitors and do so at the expense of consumers. They also point out the danger that successful firms will be singled out for attention under the antitrust laws simply because their success makes them noticeable and their efficiency enables them to outstrip their competitors. The fear is that such an orientation will discourage efficiency and entrepreneurship and reduce competition.

Concentration and Market Power

In this chapter, as in many other discussions of antitrust issues, much was said about concentration. Why should anyone care about concentration ratios? One should care about them if they are a good measure of **market power.** Market power is usually defined as the ability of a firm to raise its price significantly above the competitive price level and to maintain this high price profitably for a considerable period. The question, then, is this: If an industry becomes more concentrated, will the firms necessarily increase their ability to institute a profitable rise in price above the competitive level?

Many economists have concluded that this does not necessarily happen. Specifically, the following three conclusions are now widely accepted:

Market power is the ability of a firm to raise its price significantly above the competitive price level and to maintain this high price profitably for a considerable period.

1. If, after an increase in concentration, an industry still has a very low concentration ratio, then its firms are very unlikely to have any market power either before or after the rise in concentration.

2. If circumstances in the industry are in other respects favorable for successful price collusion (tacit or explicit agreement on price), a rise in concentration will facilitate market power. It will do so by reducing the number of firms which need to be consulted in arriving at an agreement and by decreasing the number of firms which have to be watched to make sure they do not betray the collusive agreement.

3. Where entry into and exit from the industry are easy and costless, that is, where the market is highly *contestable,* then even when concentration increases, market power will not be enhanced because an excessive price will attract new entrants who will soon force the price down.

Price Discrimination

An example of lack of agreement between economists and lawmakers about the sorts of conduct that the law should proscribe concerns the issue of *price discrimination,* which, we learned earlier in the chapter, the law defines as the sale of the same item to two different customers at different prices. To economists, this legal definition is misleading. Suppose, for instance, that one person lives on a mountaintop far from the place where a good is produced, and another customer is located in an area that enjoys easy access to the good in question. Economists would say that it is not discriminatory to charge each a different price for delivered products to the home. *On the contrary, economists hold that in such cases it is discriminatory to charge both customers the same price, because it does not account for the substantial difference in the two delivery costs.*

Even more important than this definitional argument, though, is the issue of the desirability or undesirability of discrimination. The word *discrimination* is what has been called a "persuasive term"—in this case, a word that automatically implies gross misconduct. *But, in fact, price discrimination can sometimes be beneficial to all parties to a transaction.*

Suppose, for example, a commodity is available to the poor only if it is sold at a relatively low price, though one that still more than covers the good's marginal cost (the cost incurred in expanding into the lower-income market). In this case, the contribution from the lower-income market may permit *some* reduction in price to the rich, since the firm might not be able to cover its total cost if it were to charge the rich the *same* low price necessary for entry into the low-income market. The result is that everyone—the poor, the wealthy, and the selling firm—will benefit from this discriminatory pricing.

An example is pricing by doctors, who often charge higher fees to their wealthy patients than to their poor ones. If the reduced fees permit more patients to visit them, the doctors may be able to earn an even better income than they could by charging a uniformly high fee to everyone. Even the fee to the rich may go down in the process because of the doctors' increased earnings from their enlarged pool of poor patients. If this is so, and discrimination leads to lower fees for everyone, again, all parties are made better off—the wealthy patients, the poor ones, and the doctors.

Regulated firms, whose overall earnings are restrained by a regulatory profit ceiling, have often argued that lower fees to some classes of buyers can bring in profits from markets that would not otherwise be served. In such cases, it is asserted, the regulatory profit ceiling forces the firm to charge lower fees than it would have otherwise—to all its customers. Are such acts of discrimination really so unjust?

Summary

1. Antitrust policy refers to programs designed to control the growth of monopoly and to prevent big business from engaging in "undesirable" practices.
2. The Sherman Act is the oldest U.S. antitrust law. It prohibits contracts, combinations, and conspiracies in restraint of trade and also prohibits monopolization.
3. The Clayton Act prohibits price discrimination that tends to reduce competition or create monopoly; it also prohibits competing firms from sharing directors.
4. There are several other important antitrust laws, including the Federal Trade Commission Act, which sets the commission up as an independent antitrust agency, and the Robinson-Patman Act, which generally prohibits discriminatory price discounts.
5. In their early cases, the courts generally held that a large share of market by a single firm was illegal only if the firm had acquired its relatively large share by illegal means; but in the early postwar period the courts seemed to take the view that bigness per se was presumed to be illegal unless such bigness was "thrust upon the firm" by economies of scale, unusual efficiency, or other similar influences.
6. The evidence indicates that there has been no significant increase in the concentration of individual American industries into larger firms during the twentieth century. Evidence as to whether antitrust laws have been effective in preventing monopoly is inconclusive, and observers disagree on the subject.
7. The arguments *against* unregulated monopoly are that it is likely to distribute income unfairly, produce undesirably small quantities of output, and provide inadequate motivation for innovation.
8. Defenders of big business argue that only large firms have funds sufficient for effective research, development, and innovation, and that where economies of scale are available, large firms can serve customers more cheaply than can small ones.
9. Contrary to popular thinking, price discrimination is not necessarily undesirable per se. Discriminatory pricing in some instances can be beneficial to all parties to a transaction.

Concepts for Review

Antitrust policy
Sherman Act
Clayton Act
Price discrimination
Celler-Kefauver Antimerger Act
Federal Trade Commission Act

Robinson-Patman Act
Rule of reason
Structure versus conduct
Vertical merger
Horizontal merger

Conglomerate merger
Concentration of industry
Concentration ratio
Patent
Market power

Questions for Discussion

1. Suppose Sam lives in the central city while Fran's home is far away, so that it requires much more gas to deliver newspapers to Fran than to Sam. Yet the newspaper charges them exactly the same amount. Would the courts consider this to be price discrimination? Would an economist? Would you? Why?
2. A shopkeeper sells his store and signs a contract that restrains him from opening another store in competition with the new owner. The courts have decided that this contract is a *reasonable* restraint of trade. Can you think of any other types of restraint of trade that seem reasonable? Any that seem unreasonable?
3. Which of the following industries do you expect to have high concentration ratios? Automobiles, aircraft manufacture, hardware production, railroads, production of expensive jewelry. Compare your answers with Table 32–2.
4. Why do you think the industries you selected in Question 3 are highly concentrated?
5. Do you think structure or conduct is the more reasonable basis for antitrust regulation? Give reasons for your answer.
6. Do you think it is in the public interest to launch an antitrust suit that costs a billion dollars? What leads you to your conclusion?

33

Taxation, Government Spending, and Resource Allocation

Chapter 29 examined several reasons why the government might want to interfere with the workings of the market mechanism. Some of these interferences involve levying taxes; for example, we noted that taxes may be useful in correcting misallocations of resources caused by externalities. Other interferences involve direct spending by government— provision of national defense is a good example—and this spending, in turn, requires that taxes be levied to raise the necessary revenue. These, then, are the two main reasons for taxes: to improve resource allocation and to raise revenue for what President Reagan termed "legitimate government purposes." Of the two, the revenue-raising function is by far the more important in practice. So this chapter opens with a brief look at the things on which governments in the United States spend money; that is, the reasons why government needs revenue. We then turn to the types of taxes that are used to raise this revenue, their effects on the allocation of resources and the distribution of income, and the principles that distinguish "good" from "bad" taxes.

Government Spending: An Overview

During the 1987 fiscal year, the federal government spent about $1010 billion. This sum is literally beyond comprehension; perhaps the best way to understand it is to note that federal spending amounted to over $4300 for every man, woman, and child in America. Figure 33–1 shows where the money went. About one-third went for *pensions* and *income security* programs, which include both social insurance programs, like social security and unemployment compensation, and programs designed to assist the poor. Over one-quarter went for *national defense*. If we add interest on the national debt, these three functions alone accounted for 74 percent of federal spending. The rest went for health and education (about 14 percent of the budget), and for support of such activities as science, agriculture, housing, and transportation.

Government spending at the state and local levels was over $650 billion. Education claimed the lion's share of state and local government budgets (35 percent), with health and public welfare programs in second place (22 percent).

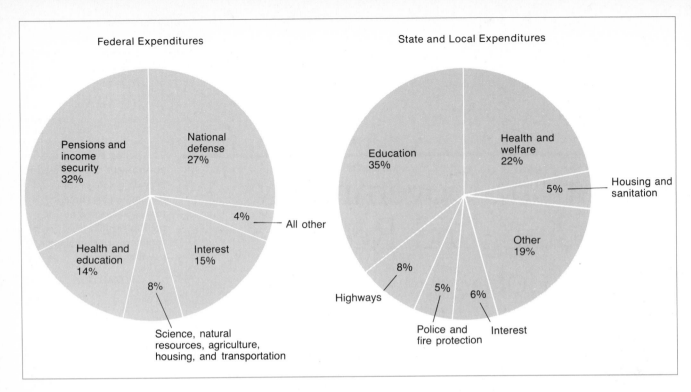

Federal Expenditures

State and Local Expenditures

Figure 33–1
THE ALLOCATION OF
GOVERNMENT
EXPENDITURES
These graphs show how the
government dollar is spent.
The federal government
spends most of its money on
national defense (27 percent)
and on transfer payments to
retirees, the poor, the
unemployed, and veterans
(32 percent). Most of state
and local government
spending goes for education
(35 percent), with health and
welfare expenditures (22
percent) in second place.
SOURCE: Statistical Abstract of
the United States, 1987.

It is interesting to relate these spending programs to the discussion in
Chapter 29 of the reasons for government intervention in the marketplace.
Many income security and welfare programs are designed to *redistribute income:*
from the young to the old (social security), from the nonpoor to the poor (welfare programs), from the employed to the unemployed (unemployment
insurance), and so on. National defense is the classic example of a **public good**.
Some of the other spending programs can be rationalized on the grounds that
they provide **beneficial externalities** (education, support of research), though
critics of "big government" question how strong these externalities really are. A
variety of other public services (the post office, various transportation programs,
and so on) are difficult to rationalize on any of the grounds enumerated in
Chapter 29; but, for one reason or another, governments have not left provision of these services to the free market. We should not lose sight of the fact
that political, not economic, considerations often dictate what services the government will provide.

Taxes in America

To finance this array of goods and services, taxes are required. Sometimes it
seems that the tax collector is everywhere. We have income and payroll taxes
withheld from our paychecks, sales taxes added to our purchases, property taxes
levied on our homes; we pay gasoline taxes, liquor taxes, and so on and on.
According to the old saying, nothing is certain but death and taxes. Americans
have long felt that there are too many taxes and that they are too high.

Yet by international standards, Americans are among the most lightly
taxed people in the industrialized world. Figure 33–2 compares the fraction of
income paid in taxes in the United States with that paid by residents of other
industrialized nations. The tax collector clearly is much gentler here than in

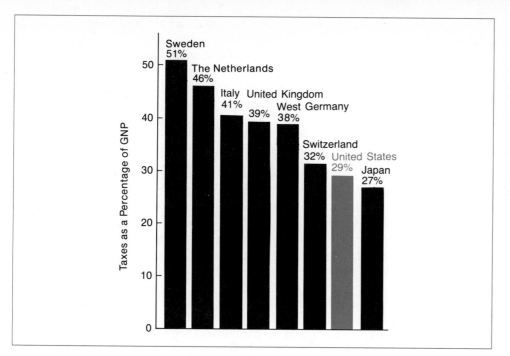

Figure 33–2
THE BURDEN OF
TAXATION IN SELECTED
COUNTRIES, 1984
Americans are lightly taxed in
comparison with the citizens
of other advanced industrial
countries. The Swedes and
the Dutch, for example, pay
far higher taxes than we do.
The Japanese, however, pay
lower taxes.
SOURCE: Statistical Abstract of
the United States, 1987.

Sweden and the Netherlands although Americans do pay more taxes than the Japanese.

Another way to put the burden of taxation into perspective is to study how it has changed over time. Figure 33–3 helps you to do this by charting the behavior of both federal and state and local taxes *as a percentage of GNP* since 1929. The figure shows that the share of federal taxes in GNP has been rather steady for almost 40 years. It climbed from less than 4 percent in 1929 to 20 percent during World War II, fell back to 15 percent in the immediate postwar period, and has generally fluctuated in the 18 to 20 percent range ever since. Although there was some upward trend in the ratio of federal taxes to GNP from 1975 until the Reagan tax cuts of 1981, it simply is not true that the

Figure 33–3
TAXES AS A
PERCENTAGE OF GROSS
NATIONAL PRODUCT
Federal taxes have
accounted for a fairly
constant fraction of GNP
since the 1940s. State and
local taxes, however,
absorbed an ever-increasing
portion from the 1940s until
the early 1970s.
SOURCE: Economic Report of the
President, 1987.

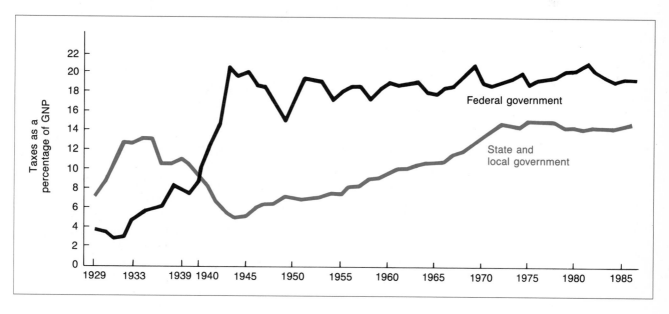

federal government has been thrusting its hand deeper and deeper into our pockets each year.

But the same cannot be said of state and local governments.

The share of GNP taken in taxes by the federal government has not increased since World War II. There was, however, an unmistakable upward trend in the fraction of GNP taken in state and local taxes until about 1972.

This fraction climbed from 5 percent in 1945 to 8.4 percent in 1960, and to 11.7 percent in 1972. In 1986, it was 12.2 percent. This trend has worried many tax reformers who, for reasons to be explained in this chapter, view the federal tax system as far superior to that of the states and localities.

The main reason for the faster growth of state and local taxes than of federal taxes seems to be the differing expenditure patterns of the various levels of government. Apart from national defense, the federal government spends little on purchases of goods and services; but direct provision of public services accounts for the preponderant share of state and local budgets. It seems that citizens demand more and better schools, hospitals, parks, and other public services as the economy gets richer. And—for reasons explained in Chapter 29—these services become more and more expensive each year. The resulting strain on state and local budgets has forced these units of government into tax increases that the federal government has, by and large, managed to avoid.

Progressive, Proportional, and Regressive Taxes

A **progressive tax** is one in which the average tax rate paid by an individual rises as his income rises.

A **proportional tax** is one in which the average tax rate is the same at all income levels.

A **regressive tax** is one in which the average tax rate falls as income rises.

The **average tax rate** is the ratio of taxes to income.

The **marginal tax rate** is the fraction of each *additional* dollar of income that is paid in taxes.

Economists classify taxes as *progressive, proportional,* or *regressive.* Under a **progressive tax,** the fraction of income paid in taxes *rises* as a person's income increases. Under a **proportional tax,** this fraction is constant. And under a **regressive tax,** the fraction of income paid to the tax collector *declines* as income rises. Since the fraction of income paid in taxes is called the **average tax rate,** these definitions can be formulated as they are in the margin.

Often, however, the *average* tax rate is less interesting than the **marginal tax rate,** which is the fraction of each *additional* dollar that must be paid to the tax collector. The reason, as we will see, is that the *marginal* tax rate, not the *average* tax rate, most directly affects economic incentives.

Direct Versus Indirect Taxes

Direct taxes are taxes levied directly on people.

Indirect taxes are taxes levied on specific economic activities.

Another way to classify taxes is to divide them into **direct taxes** and **indirect taxes.** Direct taxes are levied directly on *people.* Primary examples are *income taxes* and *inheritance taxes,* though the notoriously regressive *head tax*—which charges every person the same amount—is also a direct tax. In contrast, indirect taxes are levied on goods and services, such as buying gasoline, using the telephone, owning a home, and so on. It is only a slight distortion of the facts to say that the federal government raises revenues by direct taxes, while the states and localities raise funds via indirect taxes. *Sales taxes* and *property taxes* are the most important indirect taxes in the United States, although many other countries rely heavily on the *value-added tax,* a tax that has never been adopted in the United States.[1] In fact, as a broad generalization, the U.S. government relies more heavily on direct taxation than do the governments of most other countries.

[1]The concept of *value added* was defined and explained in an appendix to Chapter 8. The value-added tax simply taxes each firm on the basis of its value added.

The Federal Tax System

The **personal income tax** is the biggest source of revenue to the federal government. Most people do not realize that the **payroll tax**—a tax levied on wages and salaries up to a certain limit—is the next biggest source. Furthermore, payroll taxes are growing much more rapidly than income taxes. In 1956, payroll tax collections were less than 35 percent of personal income tax collections; by 1976 this figure had reached 68 percent. And by 1986, after the large income tax reductions of the first Reagan administration, payroll taxes amounted to 91 percent of personal income-tax collections. The rest of the federal government's revenues come mostly from the **corporate income tax** and from various excise (sales) taxes. Figure 33–4 shows the breakdown of federal revenues anticipated for the fiscal year 1988 budget. Let us look at these taxes in more detail.

The Federal Personal Income Tax

The tax on individual incomes began with the Sixteenth Amendment to the Constitution in 1913, but was inconsequential until the beginning of World War II. Then the tax was raised substantially to finance the war and has been the major source of federal revenue ever since. The personal income tax has been in the news throughout the 1980s because President Reagan made phased reductions in personal tax rates in 1981–1984 the cornerstone of his economic policy and because the tax code was thoroughly rewritten in 1986.[2]

Many taxpayers actually have little tax to pay when the annual April 15th day of reckoning comes around, because income taxes are *withheld* from payrolls by employers and forwarded to the U.S. Treasury. In fact, many taxpayers are, "overwithheld" during the year and receive a refund check from Uncle Sam in the spring.

It is well known that the personal income tax is *progressive*. Table 33–1 shows that average tax rates do indeed rise as income rises, but that progressivity nearly disappears at very high income levels. In a departure from past

[2]For a detailed discussion of the Reagan tax cuts, see Chapter 12.

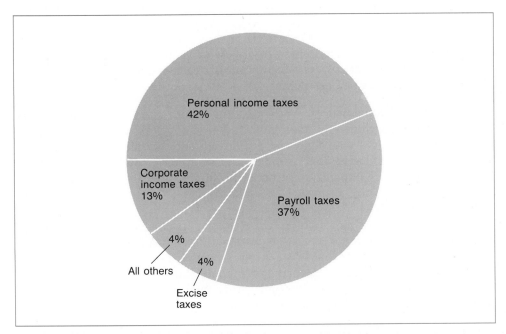

Figure 33–4
SOURCES OF FEDERAL GOVERNMENT REVENUE, FISCAL YEAR 1988 (PROJECTION)
This pie diagram gives the projected shares of each of the major sources of federal revenues for fiscal year 1988 (October 1987 through September 1988). Personal income taxes and payroll taxes clearly account for the majority of federal revenues. SOURCE: Congressional Budget Office.

Table 33–1

FEDERAL PERSONAL INCOME TAX RATES IN 1988*

INCOME	TAX	AVERAGE TAX RATE (percent)	MARGINAL TAX RATE (percent)
$ 5,000	0	0	0
10,000	0	0	0
25,000	1,830	7.3	15
50,000	6,549	13.1	28
100,000	21,314	21.3	33
250,000	68,600	27.4	28
1,000,000	278,000	27.9	28

*For a married couple with two children filing jointly and claiming the standard deduction.

practice, the Tax Reform Act of 1986 made the income tax almost proportional beyond some point — about $200,000 for a family of four. However, few families have such high incomes; so most live under a progressive tax structure.

Marginal tax rates under the new law are shown in the last column of the table. They have at least two notable features. First, they display a curious pattern — rising to a peak of 33 percent and then dropping back to 28 percent. This happens because Congress placed a special tax surcharge on incomes within certain ranges — for a family of four, between about $80,000 and about $200,000. Second, marginal income tax rates in the United States are now far lower than they used to be and much below those prevailing in other advanced countries — especially for high-income families. The 1986 tax reform achieved such low personal tax rates by raising taxes on corporations and by closing numerous **tax loopholes.**

However, some loopholes remain open. Let us see what a few major ones are.

A tax loophole is a special provision in the tax code that reduces taxation below normal rates (perhaps to zero) if certain conditions are met.

Tax exempt status of municipal bonds.   As a way of helping state and local governments and certain public authorities raise funds, Congress has made interest on their bonds exempt from federal income tax. Whether or not this was the intent of Congress, this provision has turned out to be one of the biggest loopholes for the very rich, who invest much of their wealth in tax-free municipal bonds. In fact, this **tax exemption** has long been the principal reason why some millionaires pay no income tax at all.

A particular source of income is tax exempt if income from that source is not taxable.

Tax benefits for homeowners.   Among the sacred cows of our income tax system is the deductibility of payments that homeowners make for mortgage interest and property taxes. These **tax deductions** substantially reduce the taxes homeowners pay and give them preferential treatment compared to renters. The plain intent of Congress is to encourage homeownership. However, since homeowners are, on the average, richer than renters, this loophole also erodes the progressivity of the income tax.

A tax deduction is a sum of money that may be subtracted before the taxpayer computes his or her taxable income.

But why call this a "loophole" when other interest expenses and taxes (such as those paid by shopkeepers, for example) are considered to be legitimate deductions? The answer is that it is a loophole because — unlike shopkeepers — homeowners do *not* have to declare the income they earn by incurring these expenses. This is because the "income" from owning a home accrues not in cash, but in the form of living without paying rent.

Once again, an example will make things clear. Mutt and Jeff are neighbors. Each earns $30,000 a year and lives in a $100,000 house. The difference is that Mutt owns his home while Jeff rents. Most observers would agree that Mutt and Jeff *should* pay the same income tax. Ignoring other deductions and exemptions, let us compare the taxable income of the two men. Mutt has a $70,000 mortgage at a 10 percent interest rate, so he pays about $7000 a year in interest. Suppose he pays an additional $3000 a year in local property taxes. Since both these payments are tax deductible, he pays income tax on only $30,000 − $7000 − $3000 = $20,000 (see Table 33–2). Now consider Jeff, who, we may assume, pays $10,000 in annual rent. (This just covers the bills that his landlord has to pay.) He pays tax on his entire $30,000 income and thus pays far more tax than Mutt.

How could this situation be rectified? One way is to allow renters to deduct their rent bills. Another way would be to disallow the interest and tax deductions of homeowners. Still a third alternative would be to force homeowners to add their "imputed rent" ($10,000 a year in this example) to their income. All of these would give Mutt and Jeff the same taxable income.

We could go on listing more tax loopholes, for, while the Tax Reform Act of 1986 eliminated a number of important tax exemptions and deductions, quite a few remain. But enough has been said to illustrate the main point:

Every tax loophole encourages particular patterns of behavior and favors particular types of people. But since most loopholes are mainly beneficial to the rich, they erode the progressivity of the income tax.

This was an extremely serious problem in the U.S. prior to 1986. Now it is less serious.

The Payroll Tax

The second most important tax in the United States is the payroll tax, whose proceeds are earmarked to be paid into various "trust funds." These funds, in turn, are used to pay social security benefits, unemployment compensation, and other social insurance dividends. The payroll tax is levied at a fixed percentage rate (now about 15 percent) that is divided between employees and employers, each paying roughly half the amount. This means that a firm paying an employee a gross monthly wage of, say, $1000 will deduct $75 ($7\frac{1}{2}$ percent of $1000) from that worker's check, add an additional $75 of its own funds, and send the $150 to the government.

On the face of it, this seems like a *proportional* tax, but it is actually highly *regressive* for two reasons. First, only wages and salaries are subject to the tax.

Table 33–2
OWNING VERSUS RENTING A HOME

ITEM	MUTT (owner)	JEFF (renter)
Income	$30,000	$30,000
Mortgage interest	7,000	—
Property tax	3,000	—
Rent	—	10,000
Taxable income	$20,000	$30,000

People whose incomes come from interest and dividends do not pay. Second, because there are upper limits on social security benefits, earnings above a certain level (which changes each year) are exempted from the tax. In 1987, this level was $43,800 per year. Above this limit, the *marginal tax rate* on earnings is zero.

The Corporate Income Tax

The tax on corporate profits is also considered to be a "direct" tax, because corporations are considered to be fictitious "people" in the eyes of the law.[3] The basic marginal tax rate is now 34 percent, and this rate is paid by all large corporations (firms with smaller profits pay a lower rate). Since the tax applies to *profits*, not to income, all wages, rents, and interest paid by the corporation are deducted before the tax is applied. During the period since World War II, corporate income tax collections have accounted for a declining share of federal revenue—a trend that was accelerated by President Reagan's business tax cuts in 1981. However, the 1986 tax reform act raised corporate taxes.

Excise Taxes

An excise tax is a sales tax on the purchase of a particular good or service. While sales taxation is traditionally the preserve of state and local governments in the United States, the federal government does levy excise taxes on a hodge-podge of miscellaneous goods and services, including cigarettes, alcoholic beverages, gasoline, and tires. These taxes constitute a minor source of federal government revenue, but raising revenue is not their only goal. Some of these taxes are designed to discourage consumption of a good by raising its price.

The Payroll Tax and the Social Security System

In government statistical documents, the payroll tax is euphemistically referred to as "contributions for social insurance," though these "contributions" are far from voluntary. The term signifies the fact that, unlike other taxes, the proceeds from this particular tax are set aside in "trust funds" for use in paying benefits to social security recipients and others.

But the standard notion of a trust fund really does not apply in this case. Some private pension plans are trust funds: You pay in money while you are working, it accumulates at compound interest, and then you withdraw it bit by bit in your retirement years. But the social security system does not operate in this way. Since its early years, the system simply has essentially taken the payroll tax payments of the current working generations and handed them over to the current retired generation. The benefit checks that your grandparents receive each month are not, in any real sense, the dividends on the investments they made while they were working. Instead they are the payroll taxes that you and your parents pay each month.

So far this "pay as you go" system has managed to give every retired generation more in benefits than it contributed in payroll taxes. Social security "contributions" have indeed been a good investment! How has this miracle been achieved? It has relied heavily on growth: both population growth and economic growth. As long as there is continued population growth, there are always more and more young people to tax in order to pay the retirement benefits of senior citizens. Similarly, as long as wages keep increasing, the same payroll tax *rates* will permit the government to pay benefits to each generation that

[3]For a discussion of corporations and other forms of business organization, see Chapter 30.

exceed that generation's contributions, without endangering the solvency of the system. Ten percent of today's average wage is, after all, a good deal more money than 10 percent of the wage your grandfather earned 50 years ago.

Yet the social security trust fund almost ran out of money in the early 1980s. There were two principal reasons why benefits exceeded payroll tax receipts for some years.

The first was, we hope, transitory; but it lasted long enough to become worrisome. Steady growth in real wages, one of the cornerstones of the solvency of the pay-as-you-go system, ceased in the 1970s. Real wages in 1981 were about what they were in 1972. But during this time social security benefits continued to grow rapidly and in 1975 became fully protected from inflation by *indexing*, whereas wages are not.[4] Fortunately, real wages started rising again after 1981.

The second reason poses a much longer-run problem: Population growth has slowed significantly in the United States. Birthrates in this country were very high from the close of World War II until about 1958 (the "postwar baby boom") and have generally been falling since then. As a result, the fraction of the U.S. population that is over 65 has climbed from only 7.5 percent in 1945 to 11.9 percent in 1985, and is certain to go much higher. Projections clearly show that by the time the people born between 1945 and 1958 reach retirement age, the social security system will have to pay benefits to a great many more retired people than it does now.

By the early 1980s, it was abundantly clear that either payroll taxes would have to be raised or social security benefits would have to be lowered if the trust fund was to remain solvent. But since both raising taxes and cutting benefits are politically distasteful, the issue was contentious. After months of deliberation in 1983, a bipartisan presidential commission headed by economist Alan Greenspan made recommendations for benefit reductions and tax increases that Congress speedily enacted. If current projections of population, real wages, and retirement behavior prove reasonably accurate, these reforms should keep the social security system afloat for some years. But, in the long run, social security still faces funding problems which will have to be met by some combination of higher taxes and lower benefits.

The State and Local Tax System

Indirect taxes are the backbone of state and local government revenues, though income taxes are becoming increasingly popular. Sales taxes are the principal source of revenue to the states, while cities and towns rely heavily on property taxes. Figure 33–5 shows the breakdown of state and local government receipts for 1985.

Sales and Excise Taxes

These days, the majority of states and large cities levy a broad-based sales tax on the purchase of most goods and services, with certain specific exemptions. For example, food is exempted from sales tax in many states. Overall sales tax rates are typically in the 5 to 7 percent range. In addition, there are special excise taxes in most states on such things as tobacco products, liquor, gasoline, and luxury items.

---

[4] For a full discussion of indexing, see Chapter 17.

Figure 33–5
SOURCES OF STATE
AND LOCAL REVENUE,
1985
This pie diagram shows the
major sources of revenue to
state and local governments
in the fiscal year 1984–1985.
SOURCE: U.S. Department of
Commerce.

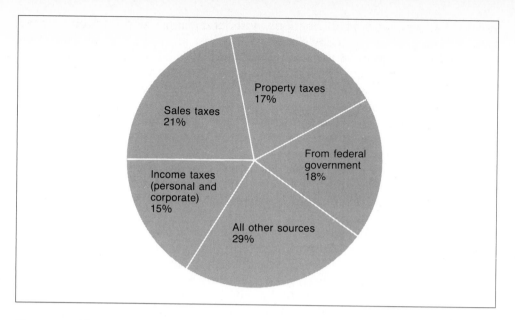

Property Taxes

Municipalities raise revenue by taxing the values of properties, such as houses and office buildings, again with certain exemptions (educational institutions, church property, and so on). The procedure is generally to assign to each taxable property an *assessed value*, which is an estimate of its market value, and then to place a tax rate on the community's total assessed value that yields enough revenue to cover expenditures on local services.

Because properties are *reassessed* much less frequently than market values change, certain inequities arise. For example, one person's house may be assessed at almost 100 percent of its true market value while another's may be assessed at little more than 50 percent of its value. Property taxes generally run about 2 to 4 percent of true market value, though some communities deviate markedly from this norm.

The property tax is among the most controversial in the entire U.S. tax system. Some economists view it as a tax on one particular type of wealth — real estate. In this view, since families with higher incomes generally own much more real estate than do families with low incomes, the property tax is *progressive* relative to income; that is, the ratio of property tax to income rises as we move up the income scale. However, other economists view the property tax as an excise tax on rents; and since expenditures on rent generally account for a larger fraction of the incomes of the poor than of the rich, this makes it seem *regressive* relative to income.

There is also political controversy over the property tax. Because local property tax revenues have been the traditional source of financing for public schools, wealthy communities with much expensive real estate have been able to afford higher-quality schools than have poor communities. The reason is made clear with a simple arithmetical example. Suppose that real estate holdings in a wealthy school district average $150,000 per family, while in a poor district real estate holdings average only $50,000 per family. If both districts levy a 2 percent property tax to pay for their schools, the wealthy community will generate $3000 per family in tax receipts, while the poor one will generate only $1000. In the 1970s, glaring inequalities like this led the supreme courts of many states to declare unconstitutional the financing of public schools by local property tax revenues because it deprives children in poorer districts of an equal opportunity to receive a good education.

State and Local Income Taxes

Although some states and localities have been taxing individual and corporate incomes for many years, only recently have taxes on individual incomes begun to account for a substantial share of state and local revenue. Between 1938 and 1960, only one state enacted a personal income tax. But many more have joined the club since the 1960s, and by now 41 states have income taxes. It seems likely that personal income taxes will be an increasingly important source of state and local revenues in years to come. Experts in public finance generally applaud this trend because, for reasons we will explain at the end of this chapter, they view the personal income tax as among the best ways to raise revenue.

Fiscal Federalism

Figure 33–5 pointed out that grants from the federal government are a major source of revenue to state and local governments. In addition, grants from the states are vital to local governments. This system of transfers from one level of government to the next is referred to as **fiscal federalism** and has a long history.

Aid from this source has come traditionally in the form of *restricted grants*, that is, money given from one level of government to the next on the condition that it be spent for a specific purpose. For example, the U.S. government may grant funds to a state *if* that state will use the money to build highways. Or a state government may give money to a school district for expenditure on a specified program or facility.

Fiscal federalism refers to the system of grants from one level of government to the next.

The Concept of Equity in Taxation

Taxes are judged on two criteria: *equity* (Is the tax fair?) and *efficiency* (Does the tax interfere unduly with the workings of the market economy?). It is curious that economists have been mostly concerned with the latter, while public discussions about tax proposals almost always focus on the former. Let us, therefore, begin our discussion by investigating the concept of equitable taxation.

Horizontal Equity

There are three distinct concepts of tax equity. The first is **horizontal equity,** which simply asserts that equally situated individuals should be taxed equally. Stated in this way, there are few who would quarrel with the principle. But it is often difficult to apply in practice, and violations of horizontal equity can be found throughout the tax code.

Horizontal equity is the notion that equally situated individuals should be taxed equally.

Consider, for example, the personal income tax. Horizontal equity calls for two families with the same income to pay the same tax. But what if one family has eight children and the other has one child? Well, you answer, we must define "equally situated" to include equal family sizes, so only families with the same number of children can be compared on grounds of horizontal equity. But what if one family has unusually high medical expenses, while the other has none? Are they still "equally situated"? By now the point should be clear: Determining when two families are "equally situated" is no simple task. In fact, the U.S. tax code lists hundreds of requirements that must be met before two families are construed to be "equal."

Vertical Equity

The second concept of fair taxation seems to flow naturally from the first. If equals are to be treated equally, it appears that unequals should be treated unequally. This precept is known as **vertical equity.**

Just saying this, of course, does not get us very far. For the most part, vertical equity has been translated into the **ability-to-pay-principle,** according to which those most able to pay should pay the highest taxes. But this still leaves a definitional problem similar to the problem of defining "equally situated": How do we measure ability to pay? The nature of each tax often provides a straightforward answer. In income taxation, we measure ability to pay by income; in property taxation, we measure it by property value; and so on.

A thornier problem arises when we try to translate the notion into concrete terms. Consider the three alternative income-tax plans listed in Table 33–3. Under all three plans, families with higher incomes pay higher income taxes. So all three plans could be said to operate on the ability-to-pay concept of vertical equity. Yet the three have very different distributive consequences. Plan 1 is a progressive tax, like the individual income tax in the United States: The average tax rate is higher for richer families. Plan 2 is a proportional tax: Every family pays 10 percent of its income. Plan 3 is quite regressive: Since tax payments rise more slowly than income, the average tax rate for richer families is lower than that for poorer families.

Which plan comes closest to the ideal notion of vertical equity? Many people find that Plan 3 offends their sense of "fairness," for it makes the distribution of income *after taxes* even more unequal than the distribution *before taxes.* But there is much less agreement over the relative merits of Plan 1 (progressive taxation) and Plan 2 (proportional taxation). Often, in fact, the notion of vertical equity is taken to be synonymous with progressivity. Other things being equal, progressive taxes are seen as "good" taxes in some ethical sense because they make the distribution of income more equal. Conversely, regressive taxes are seen as "bad." On these grounds, advocates of greater equality of incomes support progressive income taxes and oppose sales taxes.

The Benefits Principle

Whereas the principles of horizontal and vertical equity, for all their ambiguities and practical problems, at least do not conflict with one another, the final principle of fair taxation often violates commonly accepted notions of vertical equity. According to the **benefits principle of taxation,** which is often applied when the proceeds from certain taxes are earmarked for specific public services, those who reap the benefits from government services should pay the taxes.

One clear example is gasoline taxes. Receipts from gasoline taxes typically are earmarked for maintenance and construction of roads. Thus, those who use

Table 33–3
THREE ALTERNATIVE INCOME-TAX PLANS

INCOME	PLAN 1		PLAN 2		PLAN 3	
	TAX	AVERAGE TAX RATE	TAX	AVERAGE TAX RATE	TAX	AVERAGE TAX RATE
$ 10,000	$ 300	3%	$ 1,000	10%	$1,000	10%
$ 50,000	8,000	16%	5,000	10%	3,000	6%
$250,000	70,000	28%	25,000	10%	7,500	3%

the roads pay the tax roughly in proportion to the amount they use them. Most people seem to find this system fair.

But in other contexts—such as public schools, hospitals, and libraries—the body politic has been loath to apply the benefits principle because it clashes so dramatically with common notions of fairness. So these services are normally financed out of general tax revenues rather than by direct charges for their use.

The Concept of Efficiency in Taxation

The concept of economic *efficiency* is the central notion of Parts 6 through 8 of this book. The economy is said to be *efficient* if it has used every available opportunity to make someone better off without making someone else worse off. In this sense, taxes almost always introduce *inefficiencies*. That is, if the tax were removed, some people could be made better off without anyone being harmed.

However, a comparison of a world with taxes to a world without taxes is not terribly pertinent. The government does, after all, need to raise revenues to pay for the goods and services it provides. For this reason, when economists discuss the notion of "efficient" taxation, they are usually looking for the taxes that cause the *least* amount of inefficiency.

To explain the concept of efficient taxation, we need to introduce one new term. Economists define the **burden of a tax** as the amount the taxpayer would have to be given to make him just as well off in the presence of the tax as he is in its absence. An example will clarify this notion and also make clear why *the burden of a tax normally exceeds the revenues raised by the tax*.

Suppose the government, in the interest of energy conservation, levies a high tax on the biggest gas-guzzling cars, with progressively lower taxes on smaller cars.[5] For example, a simple tax schedule might be the following:

The **burden of a tax** to an individual is the amount he would have to be given to make him just as well off with the tax as he was without it.

CAR TYPE	TAX
Cadillac	$1000
Chrysler	500
Ford	0

Harry has a taste for big cars and has always bought Cadillacs. (Harry is clearly no pauper.) Once the new tax takes effect, he has three options: He can still buy a Cadillac and pay $1000 in tax, he can switch to a Chrysler and avoid half the tax, or he can switch to a Ford and avoid the entire tax.

If Harry chooses the first option, we have a case in which the burden of the tax is exactly equal to the amount of tax the person pays. Why? Because if Harry's rich uncle gives him $1000, Harry winds up exactly as well off as he was before the tax was enacted. In general:

When a tax induces no change in economic behavior, the burden of the tax can be measured accurately by the revenue collected.

However, this is not what we normally expect to happen. And it is certainly not what the government intends by levying a tax on big cars. Normally, we

[5] A similar tax was enacted in 1977 and became effective in 1984. It collected about $75 million in fiscal year 1987.

expect taxes to induce some people to alter their behavior in ways that reduce or avoid tax payments. So let us look into Harry's other two options.

If he decides to purchase a Chrysler, Harry pays only $500 in tax. But this is an inadequate measure of the burden of the new tax because Harry is greatly chagrined by the fact that he no longer drives a Cadillac. How much money would it take to make Harry just as well off as he was before the tax? Only Harry knows for sure. But we do know that it is more than the $500 tax that he pays. Why? Because, even if someone were to give Harry the $500 needed to pay his tax bill, he would still be less happy than he was before the tax was introduced, owing to his switch from a Cadillac to a Chrysler. Whatever the (unknown) burden of the tax is, the amount by which it exceeds the $500 tax bill is called the **excess burden** of the tax.

Harry's final option makes the importance of understanding excess burden even more clear. If he switches to buying a Ford, Harry will pay no tax. Are we therefore to say he has suffered no burden? Clearly not, for he longs for the Cadillac that he no longer has. The general principle is:

The **excess burden** of a tax to an individual is the amount by which the burden of the tax exceeds the tax that is paid.

Whenever a tax induces people to change their behavior—that is, whenever it "distorts" their choices—the tax has an excess burden. This means that the revenue collected systematically understates the true burden of the tax.

The excess burdens that arise from tax-induced changes in economic behavior are precisely the inefficiencies we referred to at the outset of this discussion. And the basic precept of efficient taxation is to try to devise a tax system that *minimizes* these inefficiencies. In particular:

In comparing two taxes that raise the same total revenue, the one that produces less excess burden is the more efficient.

Notice the proviso that the two taxes being compared must yield the *same* revenue. We are really interested in the *total* burden of each tax. Since:

$$\text{Total burden} = \text{Tax collections} + \text{Excess burden},$$

we can unambiguously state that the tax with less *excess* burden is more efficient only when tax collections are equal. Excess burdens arise when consumers and firms alter their behavior on account of taxation. So this precept of sound tax policy can be restated in a way that sounds consistent with President Reagan's statement at the beginning of this chapter:

In devising a tax system to raise revenue, try to raise any given amount of revenue through taxes that induce the smallest changes in behavior.[6]

Shifting the Burden of Taxation: Tax Incidence

The **incidence of a tax** is an allocation of the burden of the tax to specific individuals or groups.

When economists speak of the **incidence of a tax,** they are referring to who actually bears the burden of the tax. In discussing the tax on gas-guzzling autos, we have adhered so far to what has been called the **flypaper theory of tax**

[6]Sometimes, in contrast to President Reagan's statement, a tax is levied not primarily as a revenue-raiser, but as a way of inducing individuals or firms to alter their behavior. This possibility will be discussed later.

incidence: that the burden of any tax sticks where the government puts it. In this case, the theory holds that the burden stays on Harry. But often things do not work out this way.

Consider, for example, what will happen if the government levies a $1000 tax on luxury cars like Cadillacs. Figure 33–6 shows this tax as a $1000 vertical shift of the supply curve. If the demand curve does not shift, the market equilibrium moves from point A to point B. The quantity of luxury cars declines as Harrys all over America react to the higher price by buying fewer luxury cars. Notice that the price rises from $18,000 to $18,500, an increase of $500. So people who continue buying luxury cars bear a burden of only $500—just half the tax that they pay!

Does this mean that the tax imposes a *negative* excess burden? Certainly not. What it means is that consumers who refrain from buying the taxed commodity have managed to *shift* part of the burden of the tax away from consumers as a whole, including those who continue to buy luxury cars. Who are the victims of this **tax shifting?** In our example, there are two main candidates. First are the automakers, or, more precisely, their stockholders. Stockholders bear the burden to the extent that the tax, by reducing auto sales, cuts into their profits. The other principal candidates are auto workers. To the extent that reduced production leads to layoffs, or to lower wages, the automobile workers bear part of the burden of the tax.

People who have never studied economics almost always believe in the flypaper theory of incidence, which holds that sales taxes are borne by consumers, property taxes are borne by homeowners, and taxes on corporations are borne by stockholders. Perhaps the most important lesson of this chapter is that:

The flypaper theory of incidence is often wrong.

Failure to grasp this basic point has led to all sorts of misguided tax legislation in which Congress, or state legislatures, *thinking* they were placing a tax burden on one group of people, inadvertently placed it squarely on another. Of course, there are cases where the flypaper theory of incidence is roughly correct. So let us consider some specific examples of tax incidence.

> **Tax shifting** occurs when the economic reactions to a tax cause prices and outputs in the economy to change, thereby shifting part of the burden of the tax onto others.

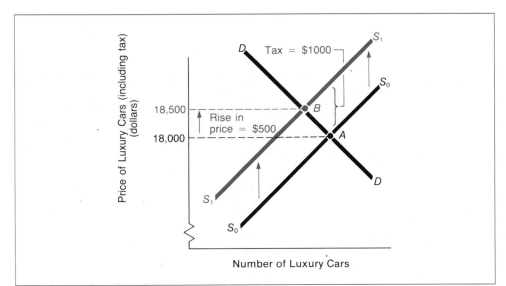

Figure 33–6
THE INCIDENCE OF AN EXCISE TAX
When the government imposes a $1000 tax on luxury cars, the supply curve relating quantity supplied to the price *inclusive of tax* shifts upward from S_0S_0 to S_1S_1. The equilibrium price in this example rises from $18,000 to $18,500, so the burden of the tax is shared equally between car sellers (who receive $500 less) and car buyers (who pay $500 more, including the tax). In general, how the burden is shared depends on the elasticities of demand and supply.

Excess Burden and Mr. Figg

Humorist Russell Baker discussed the problem of excess burden in the newspaper column reproduced below. It seems that every time his mythical Mr. Figg took a step to avoid paying taxes and to satisfy the tax man, he became less and less happy.

New York — The tax man was very cross about Figg. Figg's way of life did not conform to the way of life several governments wanted Figg to pursue. Nothing inflamed the tax man more than insolent and capricious disdain for governmental desires. He summoned Figg to the temple of taxation.

"What's the idea of living in a rental apartment over a delicatessen in the city, Figg?" he inquired. Figg explained that he liked urban life. In that case, said the tax man, he was raising Figg's city sales and income taxes. "If you want them cut, you'll have to move out to the suburbs," he said.

To satisfy his local government, Figg gave up the city and rented a suburban house. The tax man summoned him back to the temple.

"Figg" he said, "you have made me sore wroth with your way of life. Therefore, I am going to soak you for more federal income taxes." And he squeezed Figg until beads of blood popped out along the seams of Figg's wallet.

"Mercy, good tax man" Figg gasped. "Tell me how to live so that I may please my government, and I shall obey."

The tax man told Figg to quit renting and buy a house. The government wanted everyone to accept large mortgage loans from bankers. If Figg complied, it would cut his taxes.

Figg bought a house, which he did not want, in a suburb where he did not want to live, and he invited his friends and relatives to attend a party celebrating his surrender to a way of life that pleased his government.

The tax man was so furious that he showed up at the party with blood-shot eyes. "I have had enough of this, Figg" he declared, "Your government doesn't want you entertaining friends and relatives. This will cost you plenty."

Figg immediately threw out all his friends and relatives, then asked the tax man what sort of people his government wished him to entertain. "Business associates," said the tax man. "Entertain plenty of business associates, and I shall cut your taxes."

To make the tax man and his government happy, Figg began entertaining people he didn't like in the house he didn't want in the suburb where he didn't want to live.

Then was the tax man enraged indeed. "Figg," he thundered, "I will not cut your taxes for entertaining straw bosses, truck drivers and pothole fillers."

"Why not?" said Figg. "These are the people I associate with in my business."

"Which is what?" asked the tax man.

"Earning my pay by the sweat of my brow," said Figg.

"Your government is not going to bribe you for performing salaried labor," said the tax man. "Don't you know, you imbecile, that tax rates on salaried income are higher than on any other kind?"

And he taxed the sweat of Figg's brow at a rate that drew exquisite shrieks of agony from Figg and little cries of joy from Washington, which already had more sweated brows than it needed to sustain the federally approved way of life.

"Get into business, or minerals, or international oil," warned the tax man," or I shall make your taxes as the taxes of 10."

Figg went into business, which he hated, and entertained people he didn't like in the house he didn't want in the suburb where he did not want to live.

At length the tax man summoned Figg for an angry lecture. He demanded to know why Figg had not bought a new plastic factory to replace his old metal and wooden plant. "I hate plastic," said Figg. "Your government is sick and tired of metal, wood and everything else that smacks of the real stuff, Figg," roared the tax man, seizing Figg's purse. "Your depreciation is all used up."

There was nothing for Figg to do but go to plastic and the tax man rewarded him with a brand new depreciation schedule plus an investment credit deduction from the bottom line.

SOURCE: *International Herald Tribune*, April 13, 1977, page 14. © 1977 by The New York Times Company. Reprinted by permission.

The Incidence of Excise Taxes

Excise taxes have already been covered by our automobile example, because Figure 33–6 could represent any commodity that is taxed.[7] The basic finding is that *part* of the burden will fall on consumers of the taxed commodity (including those who stop buying it because of the tax), and part will be shifted to the firms and the workers who produce the commodity.

The amount that is shifted depends on the slopes of the demand and supply curves. We can see intuitively how this works. If consumers are very loyal to the taxed commodity, so that they will continue to buy almost the same quantity no matter what the price, then it is clear that they will be stuck with most of the tax bill because they have left themselves vulnerable to it. Thus we would expect that:

The more inelastic the demand for the product, the larger is the share of the tax that consumers will pay.

Similarly, if suppliers are determined to supply the same amount of the product no matter how low the price, then most of the tax will be borne by suppliers. That is:

The more inelastic the supply curve, the larger is the share of the tax that suppliers will pay.

One extreme case arises when no one stops buying luxury cars when their prices rise. The demand curve becomes vertical, like the demand curve DD in Figure 33–7. Then there can be no tax shifting. The price of a luxury car (inclusive of tax) rises by the full amount of the tax — from $18,000 to $19,000. So consumers bear the entire burden.

The other extreme case arises when the supply curve is totally inelastic (see Figure 33–8). Since the number of luxury cars supplied is the same at any price, the supply curve will not shift when a tax is imposed. Consequently, automakers must bear the full burden of any tax that is placed on their product. Figure 33–8 shows that the tax does not change the market price (including tax), which, of course, means that the price received by sellers must fall by the full amount of the tax.

Demand and supply schedules for most goods and services are not as extreme as those depicted in Figures 33–7 and 33–8, so the burden is shared. Precisely how it is shared depends on the elasticities of the supply and demand curves.

[7]Although we did not use the term "incidence," excise taxes were analyzed in detail in Chapter 22. If you need review, see pages 480–83.

Figure 33–7
AN EXTREME CASE OF
TAX INCIDENCE
If the quantity demanded is
totally insensitive to price
(completely *inelastic*), then
the demand curve will be
vertical. As the diagram
shows, the price inclusive of
tax rises to $19,000, so
buyers bear the entire
burden. Since price exclusive
of tax remains at $18,000,
none of the burden falls on
the sellers.

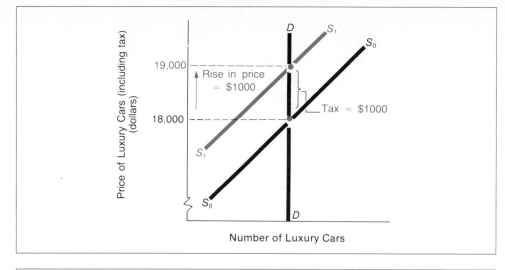

Figure 33–8
ANOTHER EXTREME
CASE OF TAX
INCIDENCE
If the quantity supplied is
totally insensitive to price,
then the supply curve *SS* will
be vertical and will not shift
when a tax is imposed. The
seller will bear the entire
burden because the price he
receives ($17,000) will fall by
the full amount of the tax.

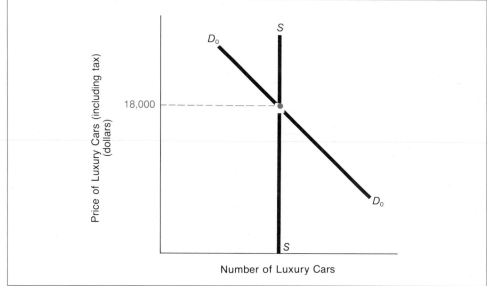

The Incidence of the Payroll Tax

The payroll tax may be thought of as an excise tax on the employment of labor.
As we mentioned earlier, the U.S. payroll tax comes in two parts: Half is levied
on the employees (payroll deductions) and half on employers. A fundamental
point, which people who have never studied economics often fail to grasp
is that:

The incidence of a payroll tax is the same whether it is levied on employers or
on employees.

A simple numerical example can illustrate why this is so. Consider a
employee earning $100 a day with a 15 percent payroll tax that is "shared
equally between the employer and the employee, as under our present law. How
much does it cost the firm to hire this worker? It costs $100 in wages paid to
the worker plus $7.50 in taxes paid to the government, for a total of $107.50 a
day. How much does the worker receive? He gets $100 in wages paid by the
employer less $7.50 deducted and sent to the government, or $92.50 a day.

The difference between wages paid and wages received is $107.50 − $92.50 = $15.

Now suppose Congress tries to "shift" the burden of the tax entirely onto firms, by raising the employer's tax to $15 while lowering the employee's tax to zero. At first, the daily wage is fixed at $100, so firms' total labor costs (including tax) rise to $115 per day and the workers' net income rises to $100 per day. Congress seems to have achieved its goal.

But this is not an equilibrium situation. With the daily wage at $115 for firms and $100 for workers, the quantity of labor *demanded* by firms will be *less* and the quantity of labor *supplied* by workers will be *more* than when the two wages were $107.50 and $92.50. There will therefore be a *surplus of labor* on the market (an excess of quantity supplied over quantity demanded), and this surplus will put downward pressure on wages.

How far will wages have to fall? It is easy to see that a wage of $92.50 will restore equilibrium. If the daily wage is $92.50, labor will cost firms $107.50 per day, just as it did before the tax change. So they will demand the same quantity as they did when the payroll tax was shared. Similarly, workers will receive the same $92.50 net wage as they did previously; so quantity supplied will be the same as it was before the tax change. Thus, in the end, the market will completely frustrate the intent of Congress.

The payroll tax is an excellent example of a case in which Congress, misled by the flypaper theory of incidence, thinks it is "taxing firms" when it raises the employer's share and that it is "taxing workers" when it raises the employee's share. In truth, who is really paying depends on the incidence of the tax. But no difference results from a change in the employee's and the employer's shares.

Who, then, really bears the burden of the payroll tax? Like any excise tax, the incidence of the payroll tax depends on the elasticities of the supply and demand schedules. In the case of labor supply, there is a large body of empirical evidence pointing to the conclusion that the quantity of labor supplied is not very responsive to price for most population groups. The supply curve is almost vertical, like that shown in Figure 33–8. The result is that workers as a group are able to shift little of the burden of the payroll tax.

But employers *can* shift it in most cases. Firms view their share of the payroll tax as an additional cost of using labor. So when payroll taxes go up, firms try to substitute cheaper factors of production (capital) for labor wherever they can. This reduces the quantity of labor demanded, lowering the wage received by workers. And this is how market forces shift part of the tax burden from firms to workers.

To the extent that the supply curve of labor has some positive slope, the quantity of labor supplied will fall when the wage goes down, and in this way workers can shift some of the burden back onto firms. But the firms, in turn, can shift that burden onto consumers by raising their prices. As we know from Part 7, prices in competitive markets generally rise when costs (like labor costs) increase. It is doubtful, therefore, that firms bear much of the burden of the payroll tax. Here, the flypaper theory of incidence could not be further from the truth. Even though the tax is collected by the firm, it is really borne by workers and consumers.

When Taxation Can Improve Efficiency

We have spent much of this chapter discussing the kinds of inefficiencies and excess burdens that arise from taxation. But, before we finish this discussion, two things must be pointed out.

First, economic efficiency is not society's only goal. For example, the tax on gas-guzzling cars causes inefficiencies if it changes people's behavior patterns. But this, presumably, was exactly what the government sought to accomplish. The government wanted to reduce the number of big cars on the road to conserve energy, and it was willing to tolerate some economic inefficiency to accomplish this end. We can, of course, argue whether this was a good idea— whether the conservation achieved was worth the efficiency loss. But the general point is that:

Some taxes that introduce economic inefficiencies are nonetheless good ideas because they help achieve some other goal.

A second, and more fundamental, point is that:

Some taxes that change economic behavior may lead to efficiency *gains*, rather than to efficiency *losses*.

As you might guess, this can happen only when there is an inefficiency in the system prior to the tax. Then an appropriate tax may help set things right. One important example of this phenomenon will occupy much of the next chapter. There we will see that because firms and individuals who despoil clean air and clean water often do so without paying any price, these precious resources are used inefficiently. A corrective tax on pollution can remedy this problem.

Equity, Efficiency, and the Optimal Tax

In a perfect world, the ideal tax would raise the revenues the government needs, reflect society's views on equity in taxation, and it would induce no changes in economic behavior and so would have no excess burden. Unfortunately, there is no such tax.

Sometimes, in fact, the taxes with the smallest excess burdens are the most regressive. For instance, a head tax, which charges every person the same number of dollars, is incredibly regressive. But it is also quite efficient. Since there is no change in economic behavior that will enable anyone to avoid it, there is no reason for anyone to change his or her behavior. As we have noted, the regressive payroll tax also seems to have small excess burdens.

Fortunately, however, there is a tax that, while not ideal, still scores highly on both the equity and efficiency criteria: a comprehensive personal income tax with few loopholes.

While it is true that income taxes can be avoided by earning less income, we have already observed that in reality the supply of labor is changed little by taxation. Investing in relatively safe assets (like government bonds) rather than risky ones (like common stocks) is another possible reaction that would reduce tax bills, since less risky assets pay lower rates of return. But it is not clear that the income tax actually induces such behavior because, while it taxes away some of the profits when investments turn out well, it also offers a tax deduction when investments turn sour. Finally, because an income tax reduces the return on saving, many economists have worried that it would discourage saving and thus retard economic growth.[8] But the empirical evidence does not suggest that this has happened to any great extent.

[8]For this reason, some economists prefer a tax on consumption to a tax on income.

On balance then, while there are still unresolved questions and research is continuing:

Most of the studies that have been conducted to date suggest that a comprehensive personal income tax with no loopholes induces few of the behavioral reactions that would reduce consumer well-being, and thus has a rather small excess burden.

On the equity criterion, we know that personal income taxes can be made as progressive as society deems desirable, though if marginal tax rates on rich people get extremely high, some of the potential efficiency losses might get more serious than they now seem to be. On both grounds, then, many economists—including both liberals and conservatives—view a comprehensive personal income tax as one of the best ways for a government to raise revenue.

The Real Versus the Ideal

That seems to be a cheerful conclusion, because the federal personal income tax is the biggest tax in the U.S. revenue system. Unfortunately, however, our actual tax system did not closely resemble an ideal, comprehensive income tax prior to the 1986 tax reform. In this chapter, we mentioned just a few loopholes (pages 720–21), but there were so many that legal tax avoidance had become a major industry.

We have already noted that loopholes make the income tax less progressive than it seems to be. But they also make it far less *efficient* than it could be. The reason follows directly from our analysis of the incidence of taxation.

When different income-earning activities are taxed at different marginal rates, economic choices are distorted by tax considerations; and this impairs economic efficiency.

Thus a major objective of the Tax Reform Act of 1986 was to enhance both the equity and efficiency of the personal income tax by closing loopholes and lowering tax rates. To a remarkable extent, the effort succeeded—against the political odds. (See the attached box.) By roughly doubling the personal exemption, the new law removed about six million households from the tax rolls. For most of the rest of the population, tax progressivity—as measured by average tax rates—is about the same as it was under the old law. But marginal tax rates are now much lower. Most Americans are in the 15 percent tax bracket, meaning that their taxes rise by only 15 cents for each dollar they earn. Most of the rest, including the very rich, are in the 28 percent tax bracket.

These low tax rates were achieved by shifting some of the tax burden onto corporations and by closing many important tax loopholes. Tax rates on different sources of income were equalized. Many deductions and exemptions were reduced or eliminated. Abusive tax shelters were a particular target of tax reformers, though the details are best left to more advanced courses on taxation.

The United States personal income tax code still falls a good distance short of the economist's ideal. But it is a giant step closer than it was prior to 1986.

Tax Reform: The Possible Dream

The tax reform movement existed long before 1986, but mainly as a glimmer in the eyes of some economists, lawyers, and accountants—and a few farsighted politicians like Senator Bill Bradley (D.-New Jersey). It first received important political momentum when President Reagan ordered the Treasury to produce a proposal for change in 1984.

The Treasury's original plan came remarkably close to advocating the economist's ideal income tax. It featured low tax rates, eliminated almost all tax loopholes, and would have been much simpler to boot. However, it stepped on so many powerful political toes that even the president refused to support it. The Treasury's staff was sent back to the drafting room.

In May 1985, the Treasury issued a revised proposal with the official imprimatur of the White House. Comparing the two documents made it clear that politics, not economics, had dictated the changes. Many of the features that economists had found most attractive in the Treasury's original plan were deleted and a number of special interest groups were protected. Economists disagreed over whether they preferred the revised proposal or existing law. So did members of Congress.

After a six-month political struggle, during which lobbyists worked overtime and tax reform often seemed doomed, a bill finally passed the House of Representatives. In its broad contours, the House bill resembled the White House proposal. Where it differed, it retreated to the safety of current law. Tax reform was fading fast.

When the bill went to the Senate Finance Committee, where several members were openly hostile to tax reform, the lobbyists descended en masse. At first, the committee behaved as expected: Senators took turns adding one gimmick after another to the bill. The news media and many politicians declared tax reform dead.

But a remarkable political turnaround occurred in May 1986. Chairman Bob Packwood (R.-Oregon) shocked everyone by scrapping the committee's work of six months and promoting a radical plan that vigorously attacked loopholes in return for even lower tax rates than the president's proposal. The plan had an uncanny resemblance to a 1982 proposal by Senator Bradley. Within days, the whole committee was on board. Within weeks, the whole Senate followed suit. And within months, comprehensive tax reform was the law of the land. Political pundits were amazed. Tax reformers were delighted.

Summary

1. Spending patterns differ greatly at the various levels of government. The federal government spends money mostly on national defense and income security programs. States and localities spend more on education, health, and public welfare.

2. Taxes in the United States are generally lower than they are in most other industrial countries. While federal taxes as a percentage of gross national product have been quite constant, state and local taxes increased between 1945 and 1972.

3. The federal government raises most of its revenue by direct taxes, such as the personal and corporate income taxes and the payroll tax. Of these, the payroll tax is increasing the most rapidly.

4. Keeping the social security system solvent has been a serious problem since the 1970s, partly because of the decrease in population growth. Recent changes in taxes and benefits should keep the system afloat.

5. State and local governments raise most of their tax revenues by indirect taxes. States rely mainly on sales taxes, while localities are dependent upon

property taxes.

6. There is controversy over whether the property tax is progressive or regressive, and even more controversy over whether local property taxes are an equitable way to finance public education.

7. In our multilevel system of government, the federal government makes various sorts of grants to state and local governments, and states in turn make grants to municipalities and school districts. This system of intergovernmental transfers is called fiscal federalism.

8. There are three concepts of fair, or "equitable," taxation that occasionally conflict. Horizontal equity simply calls for equals to be treated equally. Vertical equity, which calls for unequals to be treated unequally, has often been translated into the ability-to-pay principle—that people who are more able to pay taxes should be taxed more heavily. The benefits principle of tax equity ignores ability to pay and seeks to tax people according to the benefits they receive.

9. The burden of a tax is the amount of money an individual would have to be given to make her as well off with the tax as she was without it. This burden normally exceeds the taxes that are paid, and the difference between the two is called the excess burden of the tax.

10. Excess burden arises when a tax induces some people or firms to change their behavior. Excess burdens represent economic inefficiencies, so the basic principle of efficient taxation is to utilize taxes that have small excess burdens.

11. When people change their behavior on account of a tax, they often shift the burden of the tax onto someone else. This is why the "flypaper theory of incidence"—the belief that the burden of any tax always stays where Congess puts it—is often incorrect.

12. The burden of a sales or excise tax normally is shared between the suppliers and the consumers. The manner in which it is shared depends on the elasticities of supply and demand.

13. The payroll tax is like an excise tax on labor services. Since the supply of labor is much less elastic than the demand for labor, workers bear most of the burden of the payroll tax. This includes both the employer's and the employee's share of the tax.

14. Sometimes, "inefficient" taxes—that is, taxes that cause a good deal of excess burden—are nonetheless desirable because the changes in behavior they induce further some other social goal.

15. When there are inefficiencies in the system for reasons other than the tax system (for example, externalities), taxation can conceivably improve efficiency.

17. The Tax Reform Act of 1986 moved the U.S. income-tax system closer to the ideal by closing loopholes and lowering tax rates.

Concepts for Review

Progressive, proportional, and regressive taxes	Tax loopholes	Benefits principle of taxation
Average and marginal tax rates	Tax Reform Act of 1986	Burden of a tax
Direct and indirect taxes	Social security system	Excess burden
Personal income tax	Property tax	Incidence of a tax
Payroll tax	Fiscal federalism	Flypaper theory of incidence
Corporate income tax	Horizontal and vertical equity	Tax shifting
Excise tax	Ability-to-pay principle	

Questions for Discussion

1. "If the federal government continues to raise taxes as it has been doing, it will ruin the country." Comment.

2. Why have state and local taxes been increasing so much faster than federal taxes? Is this trend likely to continue?

3. Using the adjacent hypothetical income tax table, compute the marginal and average tax rates. Is the tax progressive, proportional, or regressive?

INCOME	TAX
$10,000	$ 1,000
20,000	3,000
30,000	6,000
40,000	10,000

4. Which concept of tax equity, if any, seems to be served by each of the following:
   a. The progressive income tax.
   b. The federal tax on gasoline.
   c. The property tax.
5. Use the example of Mr. Figg (see the boxed insert on page 730) to explain the concepts of efficient taxes and excess burden.
6. Think of some tax that you personally pay. What steps have you taken or could you take to reduce your tax payments? Is there an excess burden on you? Why or why not?
7. Suppose the supply and demand schedules for cigarettes are as follows:

PRICE PER CARTON (dollars)	QUANTITY DEMANDED (millions of cartons per year)	QUANTITY SUPPLIED (millions of cartons per year)
3.00	300	120
3.25	285	150
3.50	270	180
3.75	255	210
4.00	240	240
4.25	225	270
4.50	210	300
4.75	205	330
5.00	190	360

   a. What is the equilibrium price and equilibrium quantity?

   b. Now the government levies a $0.75 per carton excise tax on cigarettes. What is the equilibrium price paid by consumers, price received by producers, and quantity now?
   c. Explain why it makes no difference whether Congress levies the $0.75 tax on the consumer or the producer. (Relate your answer to the discussion of the payroll tax on pages 732–33 of the text.)
   d. Suppose the tax is levied on the producers. How much of the tax are producers able to shift onto consumers? Explain how they manage to do this.
   e. Will there be any excess burden from this tax? Why? Who bears this excess burden?
   f. By how much has cigarette consumption declined on account of the tax? Why might the government be happy about this outcome, despite the excess burden?
8. The country of Taxmania produces only two commodities: bread and mink coats. The poor spend all their income on bread, while the rich purchase both goods. Both demand for and supply of bread are quite inelastic. In the mink coat market, both supply and demand are quite elastic. Which good would be heavily taxed if Taxmanians cared mostly about efficiency? What if they cared mostly about vertical equity?
9. Discuss President Reagan's statement on taxes quoted on the first page of the chapter. Do you agree with the president?

34

Environmental Protection and Resource Conservation

"The picture's pretty bleak, gentlemen . . . The world's climates are changing, the mammals are taking over, and we all have a brain about the size of a walnut."

We learned in Chapter 27 that *externalities* (the incidental benefits or damages imposed upon people not directly involved in an economic activity) can cause the market mechanism to malfunction. The first half of this chapter takes up a particularly important application of the analysis of externalities—the problem of environmental deterioration. In the second half we address the closely related subject of natural resource depletion and the interwoven questions of energy use and environmental decay.

The Economics of Environmental Protection

Environmental problems are by no means new. What *is* new and different is the amount of attention the community is now prepared to give them. Perhaps much of this increased interest can be attributed to rising incomes, which have freed people from the more urgent concerns about food, clothing, and shelter, and thus have allowed them the luxury of concentrating on the next level of needs—the *quality* of their lives.

Economic thought on the environment preceded the outburst of public concern with the subject by nearly half a century. In 1911, a noted British economist, A. C. Pigou, wrote a remarkable book called *The Economics of Welfare,* which offered an explanation of the market economy's poor environmental performance that is still generally accepted by economists today. What is more, that same book outlined an approach to environmental policy that is still favored by most economists and that is beginning to win over lawmakers and bureaucrats as well. Pigou's analysis suggested that a system of charges on emissions can be an effective and efficient means of controlling pollution. In this way, the price mechanism can remedy one of its own shortcomings!

The Environment in Perspective: Is Everything Getting Steadily Worse?

Much of the discussion of environmental problems in the popular press leaves the reader with the impression that matters have been growing steadily worse, and that pollution is largely a product of the profit system and modern industrialization. As we will see, there are environmental problems today that are both enormous and pressing, but in fact pollution is nothing new. Medieval cities were pestholes—the streets and rivers were littered with garbage and the air stank of rotting wastes. At the beginning of the eighteenth century, a German traveler reported that to get a view of London from the tower of St. Paul's, one had to get there very early in the morning "before the air was full of coal smoke." And early in the twentieth century the automobile was hailed as a source of major improvement in the cleanliness of city streets, which until then had fought a losing battle against the proliferation of horse dung.

Since World War II there has been marked progress in solving a number of pollution problems, much of it the result of concerted efforts to protect the environment. The quality of the air has improved in most U.S. cities. In New York City, for example, the concentration of suspended particulates, or soot, in the air has fallen dramatically since World War II. In fact, national pollution standards for suspended particulates, sulfur dioxide, lead, and nitrogen dioxide have now been achieved for most of the United States. Figure 34–1 illustrates the dramatic decline in the Pollution Standards Index, a national measure of air quality representing daily concentrations of the principal air pollutants, for four representative metropolitan areas—Chicago, Philadelphia, St. Louis, and Washington, D.C., between 1976 and 1984.[1] Rapid declines in automobile pollution have played a large role in this improvement in air quality. There has also been progress in Europe. The famous, or rather infamous, "fogs" of London are almost a thing of the past because of the improvement in air quality since 1950. The cleaner air in Britain's capital city has resulted in an astounding 50 percent increase in the numbers of hours of winter sunshine. In short, pollution problems are not a uniquely modern phenomenon, nor is every part of the environment deteriorating relentlessly.

Environmental problems do not occcur exclusively in capitalist economies. For example, in the People's Republic of China, coal soot from factory smokestacks in Peking envelops the city in a thick black haze reminiscent of Pittsburgh in the old days of unbridled industrial activity. And the Soviet Union has all sorts of serious environmental troubles, which it has publicized widely in its own newspapers and magazines.[2] For example, because of smoke in the air, the number of clear daylight hours is 40 percent lower in Leningrad than in Pavlovsk—a town only 20 miles away. The Iset and the Volga rivers are so filled with chemicals that they have actually caught fire! The number of dams, canals, and reservoirs along the waterways leading into the Aral and Caspian seas have caused so much evaporation that both seas have fallen rapidly. In fact, some claim that by the end of the century, the Aral Sea may have deteriorated into a salt marsh.

The preceding discussion is meant to put matters into perspective, not to suggest that all is well with our environment, nor that there is nothing more to

---

[1]The only city in the United States showing an upward trend in the Pollution Standards Index is Anchorage, Alaska, which has a unique carbon monoxide problem related to parked idling cars in the winter. To prevent freezing, cars must be left running, and carbon monoxide builds up.

[2]For an excellent nontechnical discussion, see Marshall Goldman, *The Spoils of Progress* (Cambridge, Mass.: M.I.T. Press, 1972).

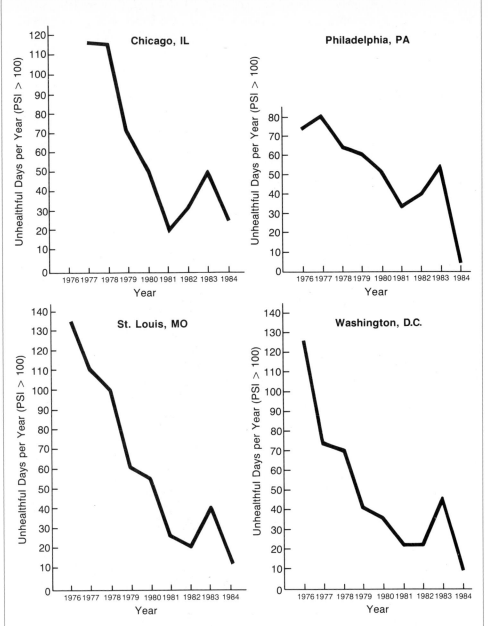

Figure 34–1
POLLUTION TRENDS
FOR FOUR CITIES
SOURCE: U.S. Council on
Environmental Quality,
Environmental Quality 1984, 15th
Annual Report (Washington, D.C.:
U.S. Government Printing Office,
1984), p. 26.

do. Along with the improvements that have been described, our world has been subjected to a number of new pollutants, most of which are far more dangerous than those we have reduced, even though they may be less visible and less malodorous. Despite the improvement mentioned above, severe air quality problems continue to plague a number of major U.S. urban areas. For instance, in 1983 New York City experienced nearly 70 days when the air was deemed "unhealthful," the Denver-Boulder metropolitan area had about 60 such days, and the Los Angeles-Long Beach area logged almost 100 unhealthful days. Carbon monoxide and ozone (smog) are the most pervasive problems in these cities. There is also growing evidence that formerly pristine wilderness areas are increasingly threatened by air pollution.

A variety of highly toxic substances—PCBs (polychlorinated biphenyls), chlorinated hydrocarbons, dioxin, heavy metals, and radioactive materials—are dumped carelessly, left to cause cancer and threaten life and health in other ways. Some of these substances linger in the environment so long that they are likely to constitute a threat for many thousands of years. The accumulation of these and other byproducts of modern technology may well cause damage that is all but irreversible. Ironically, successful cleanup of conventional water pollutants has resulted in the return of fishlife to some previously "dead" waterways. But the fish are nonetheless inedible or nearly so since they are contaminated with high levels of toxic substances. New York State, for example, warns fishermen to eat only one meal per week of fish caught anywhere in the state, and New Jersey advises pregnant women not to consume any fish caught in New Jersey.[3]

While environmental problems are neither new nor confined only to capitalist, industrialized economies, these facts are not legitimate grounds for complacency. The potential damage that we may be inflicting on ourselves and on our surroundings is very real and very substantial.

The Law of Conservation of Matter and Energy

The physical law of conservation of matter and energy tells us there is no way that objects can be made to disappear—at most they can be changed into something else. Oil, for instance, can be transformed into heat (and smoke) or into plastic—but it will never vanish. This means that after a raw material has been used, either it must be used again (recycled) or it becomes a waste product that must somehow be disposed of.

If it is not recycled, any input used in the production process *must* ultimately become a waste product. It may end up on the garbage heap of some municipal dump. It may literally go up in smoke, contributing its bit to the pollution of the atmosphere. It may even be transformed into heat, warming up adjacent waterways and killing aquatic life in the process. But the laws of physics tell us there is nothing we can do to make used inputs disappear altogether from the earth.

Although recycling rates for such commonly used materials as aluminum, paper, and glass appear to be rising in many industrial countries, only one country, The Netherlands, recovers more than half these materials. As we see in Figure 34–2, the United States lags well behind a number of industrial countries in recovery rates for these relatively easily recycled products.

The Edifice Complex

Many people think of industry as the primary villain in environmental damage. But:

While private firms have done their share in harming the environment, private individuals and government have also been prime contributors.

[3]William Drayton, *America's Toxic Protection Gap* (Washington, D.C.: Environmental Safety, July 1984), p. 38; he cites U.S. Environmental Protection Agency, "Summary of the 1983 Regional Environmental Management Reports," August 23, 1983, SW11.

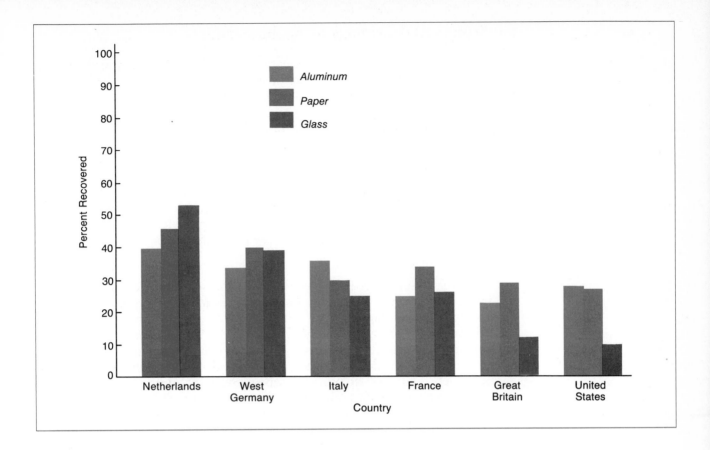

The emissions of private passenger cars play an important role in the air pollution problems of most major cities, and wood-burning stoves are becoming a source of particulate pollution, especially in the mountain states of the West. Wastes from flush toilets and residential washing machines also cause significant harm.

Governments, too, add to the problem. The wastes of municipal treatment plants are a major source of water pollution. Military aircraft leave a long trail of exhaust and make a lot of noise. Obsolete atomic materials and byproducts associated with chemical and nuclear weapons are among the most dangerous of all wastes, and the problem of their disposal is far from over.

There is at least one type of environmental damage that is especially closely associated with governments. The construction of giant dams and reservoirs that flood farmlands and destroy canyons often renders surrounding soil unusable because of seepage of salts into the earth, and it changes the water table (the level of water under the ground) by evaporation and seepage. Often, the drainage of swamps has subsequently altered local ecology irrevocably; the building of canals has diverted the flow of rivers; and the construction of dams has flooded and destroyed irreplaceable areas of natural beauty. The U.S. Army Corps of Engineers, in particular, has been accused of acting on the basis of this so-called *edifice complex*.

But the edifice complex has reached its greatest heights in the communist states. Perhaps the leading advocate of giant earth-moving projects was Stalin, and his pride in enormous hydroelectric installations and huge canals was well publicized in the Soviet press.

Figure 34–2
RELATIVE RECYCLING RATES: ALUMINUM, PAPER, AND GLASS, 1985
This graph indicates that the United States recycles a smaller proportion of the recoverable resources that it uses than these other countries do.
SOURCE: Cynthia Pollock, "Realizing Recycling's Potential," Chapter 6 in Lester R. Brown, *et al., State of the World 1987* (New York: W. W. Norton & Co., 1987), p. 111.

Environmental Damage as an Externality

It is clear that our very existence means that some environmental damage is inevitable. Products of the earth must be used up, and wastes must be generated in the process of creating the means of subsistence.

There is no question of reducing environmental damage to zero. As long as the human race survives, complete elimination of such damage is literally impossible. *It is not even desirable to get as close as possible to zero damage.* Some pollutants in small quantities are quickly dispersed and rendered harmless by natural processes, and it is not worth the opportunity cost to eliminate others whose damage is slight. Use of a large quantity of resources for this purpose may so limit their supply that there will not be materials available for the construction of hospitals, schools, and other things more important to society than the elimination of some pollutants.

The real issue then is not whether pollution should exist at all, but whether environmental damage in an unregulated market economy tends to be more serious and widespread than the public interest can tolerate. This issue immediately raises three key questions. First, why do economists believe that environmental damage is unacceptably severe *in terms of the public interest?* And how do they measure "the public interest"? Second, why does the market mechanism, which is so good at providing about the right number of toasters and trucks, generate too much pollution? What goes wrong with the system? And, third, what can we do about it? We will consider these questions in order.

Economists do not claim any special ability to judge what is good for the public interest. They normally prefer to accept the wishes of the members of the public as adequate indicators of "the public interest." When the economy reflects these wishes as closely as it can, given the resources and technology available, economists conclude that it is working effectively. When it operates in a way that frustrates the desires of the people, they conclude that the economy is functioning improperly. Why, then, do economists believe that the market mechanism generates "too much" pollution?

To answer this, we must deal with the fundamental analysis of A. C. Pigou that we referred to at the beginning of this chapter. In Chapter 29 we discussed some of the failures of the market mechanism and singled out externalities as a primary cause of market failure. An *externality*, it will be recalled, is an incidental consequence of some economic activity that can be either beneficial or detrimental to someone who neither controls the activity nor is intentionally served by it. The emission of pollutants constitutes one of the most clear-cut examples of a detrimental externality. The smoke from a chemical plant affects persons other than the management of the plant or its customers. Because the incidental damage done by the smoke does not enter the financial accounts of the firm that produces the emissions, the owners of the firm have no financial incentive to restrain those emissions, particularly since emission control costs money. Instead, they will find it profitable to produce their chemical product and to emit their smoke as though it caused no external damage to the community.

One way to look at the matter is as a *failure of the pricing system*. Through the smoke externality, the business firm is able to use up some of the community's clean air without paying for the privilege. Just as the firm would undoubtedly use oil and electricity wastefully if they were obtainable at no charge, the firm will also use air wastefully, despoiling it with smoke far beyond the level that the public interest can justify. Rather than being at the (low) socially desirable level, the quantity of smoke will be at whatever (usually high) level is necessary to save as much money as possible for the firm that emits it, because the external damage caused by the smoke costs the firm nothing.

Externalities
Externalities play a crucial role affecting the quality of life. They show why the market mechanism, which is so efficient in supplying consumers' goods, has a much poorer record in terms of its effects on the environment. The problem of pollution illustrates the importance of externalities for public policy and indicates why their analysis is one of our **12 Ideas for Beyond the Final Exam.**

Supply–Demand Analysis of Environmental Problems

Basic supply–demand analysis can be used to explain both how externalities lead to environmental problems and how these problems can be cured. As an illustration, let us deal with the problem of solid wastes—and the damage that the massive generation of garbage is doing to our environment.

In Figure 34–3 we see a demand curve, *DE*, for garbage removal. As usual, this curve has a negative slope, meaning that if the price of garbage removal is set sufficiently high, people will become more sparing in the amount of garbage removal they order. They may more often bring papers, bottles, and cans to recycling centers and public dumps; they may repair broken items rather than throwing them out; and so on. In short, a higher price of garbage removal can be expected to reduce the quantity demanded of garbage removal services.

The graph also shows the supply curve, *SS*, which we can expect to prevail in an ideal market for garbage removal. Garbage disposal is expensive to society—it requires people and trucks to haul it away; garbage dumps occupy valuable land; and the use of fire or other means to get rid of the garbage creates pollution which, as we have seen, has a high real cost to the community. As we saw in our analysis of competitive industries (Chapter 25), the position of the market's supply curve depends on the marginal cost of garbage removal. If suppliers had to pay the full costs of garbage removal, the supply curve would be comparably high (as drawn in the graph) and have a positive slope, meaning that the marginal cost of garbage disposal rises as the quantity rises. We see that, for the community depicted in the graph, the price of garbage removal

Figure 34–3
FREE DUMPING OF POLLUTANTS AS AN INDUCEMENT TO ENVIRONMENTAL DAMAGE
Whether wastes are solid, liquid, or gaseous, they impose costs upon the community. If the emitter is not charged for the damage, it is as though the resulting wastes were removed with zero charges to the polluter (blue removal supply curve *TT*). The polluter is then induced to pollute a great deal (25 million tons in the figure). If the charges to him reflect the true cost to the community (supply curve *SS* of waste removal), it would pay to emit a much smaller amount (10 million tons in the figure).

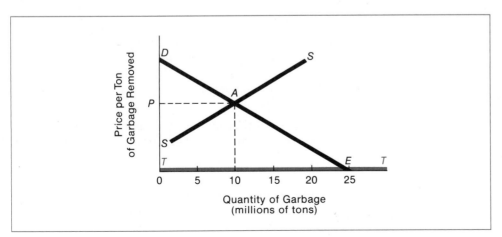

will be P dollars per ton, and at that price 10 million tons will be generated (point A).

But what if the community's government decides to remove garbage "free"? Of course, that means the government is really charging the consumer for the service in the form of taxes, but not in a way that makes each consumer pay for the quantity of garbage that he produces. The result is that the supply curve is no longer SS. Rather it becomes the blue line TT, which lies along the horizontal axis, because any household can increase the garbage it throws away at no cost. Now the intersection of the supply and demand curve is no longer point A. Rather it is point E, at which the price is zero and the quantity of garbage generated is 25 million tons—an amount substantially greater than would be produced if those who made the garbage had to pay the cost of getting rid of it.

Similar problems occur if the community offers the oxygen of its waterways and the purity of its atmosphere without charge to all who choose to utilize them. The amount that will be wasted and otherwise used up is likely to be enormously greater than it would be if users had to pay for the cost of their actions to society. And that, in the view of economists, is one major reason for the severity of our environmental problems. Several conclusions follow:

1. The magnitude of our pollution problem is attributable in large part to the fact that the market lets individuals, firms, and government agencies deplete such resources as oxygen in the water and pure air without financial charge.

2. One way of dealing with pollution problems is to charge those who emit pollution, and who despoil the environment in other ways, a price commensurate with the costs they impose on society.

3. This is another instance in which higher prices—on environmentally damaging activities—can be beneficial to the community.

Basic Approaches to Environmental Policy

In broad terms, three general methods have been proposed for the control of activities that damage the environment.

1. **Voluntary programs,** such as nonmandatory investment in pollution control equipment by firms that decide to act in a manner that meets their social responsibilities, or voluntary separation of solid wastes by consumers who deliver them to collection centers for recycling.

2. **Direct controls,** which either (a) impose legal ceilings on the amount any polluter is permitted to emit or (b) specify how particular activities must be carried on—for example, they may prohibit backyard incinerators, or the use of high-sulfur coal, or require smokestack "scrubbers" to capture emissions of electric-generating installations.

3. **Taxes on emissions,** or the use of other monetary incentives or penalties to make it unattractive financially for emitters of pollutants to continue to pollute as usual.

Each of these methods has its place. If used appropriately, together they can constitute an effective and efficient environmental program. Let us consider each of them in turn.

Voluntarism

We can deal very briefly with voluntary programs, for voluntarism has usually proved to be weak and unreliable. Voluntary programs for the collection and separation of garbage into different and easily recyclable materials have rarely managed to reroute more than a small fraction of a community's wastes from the garbage dump to the recycling plants. Some business people with strong consciences have manifested good intentions and made sincere attempts to improve the practices of their companies. Yet competition has usually prevented them from spending more than token amounts for this purpose. No business, whatever its virtues, can long afford to have the prices of its products undercut by rival suppliers.

As a result, voluntary business programs have often been more helpful to the companies' public relations activities than to the environment. Firms with a real interest in environmental protection have called for legislation that *requires* all firms, including competitors, to undertake the same measures, thereby subjecting all firms in the industry to similar handicaps. Even then, competitive pressures and weak consciences may lead to behavior that is more than a bit questionable, as exemplified by the spurt of dumping of toxic wastes just before new regulations went into effect in November 1980.

Yet voluntary measures do have their place. They are appropriate where alternative measures are not readily available. Where surveillance and, consequently, enforcement is impractical, as in the prevention of littering by campers in isolated areas, there is no choice but an appeal to people's consciences. And in brief but serious emergencies, in which there is no time to plan and enact a systematic program, there may also be no good substitute for voluntary compliance. Several major cities have, for example, experienced episodes in which there were temporary but dangerous concentrations of pollutants and the authorities were forced to appeal to the public to avoid activities that would have aggravated the problem. One can easily cite cases in which the public response to appeals requiring cooperation for short periods was enthusiastic and gratifying. To summarize:

Voluntary programs are not dependable ways to protect the environment. However, in brief, unexpected emergencies or where effective surveillance is impossible, the policymaker may have no other choice. Sometimes in these cases voluntary programs even work.

Direct Controls

Direct controls have been the chief instrument of environmental policy in the United States. The federal government, through the Environmental Protection Agency, formulates standards for air and water quality and requires state and local governments to adopt rules that will assure achievement of those goals. Probably the best known of these are the standards for automobile emissions. Since 1968, new automobiles have been required to pass tests showing that their emissions of a number of pollutants do not exceed specified amounts. In addition, several states have required that used cars also adhere to certain limits on emissions.

As another example, localities may prohibit the use of particularly "dirty" fuels by industry or may require the adoption of certain processes to "cleanse" those fuels or their emissions. Typical of these programs are local ordinances regulating the type and sulfur content of the fuels used by power plants, factories, and other stationary sources of sulfur dioxide pollution. Relocation of such pollution sources outside populated areas, and the required installation of smokestack emissions controls, have also contributed to better air quality.

Taxes on Emissions

Most economists agree that a nearly exclusive reliance on direct controls is a mistake and that, in most cases, financial penalties on polluters can do the same job more dependably, more effectively, and more economically.

The most common suggestion is that firms be permitted to pollute all they want but be forced to pay a tax for the privilege to make them *want* to pollute less. A tax on emissions requires the polluter to install a meter that records his emissions in the same way his electric meter records his use of electricity. At the end of the month the government automatically sends him a bill charging him a stipulated amount for each gallon of wastes (the amount must also vary with the quality of the wastes — a higher tax rate being imposed on wastes that are more dangerous or unpleasant). Thus, the more damage the polluter does the more he must pay.

Such taxes are deliberately designed to *encourage* the use of a glaring loop-hole — the polluter *can* reduce the tax he pays by decreasing the amount he emits. In terms of Figure 34–3, if the tax is used to increase the payment for waste emissions from zero (blue supply line TT) and instead forces the polluter to pay its true cost to society, emissions will automatically be reduced from 25 to 10 million tons.

Businesses do respond to such taxes. One widely publicized example is the Ruhr River basin in West Germany, where emissions taxes have been used for more than three decades. Though the Ruhr is one of the world's most concentrated industrial centers, those of its rivers that are protected by taxes are sufficiently clean to be usable for fishing and other recreational purposes. Firms have also found it profitable to avoid taxes by extracting pollutants from their liquid discharges and recycling them. Almost 70 percent of the industrial acids used in the Ruhr have been recovered in this way.

Emissions Taxes Versus Direct Controls

It is important to see why taxes on emissions may prove more effective and reliable than direct controls. Direct controls essentially rely on the enforcement mechanism of the criminal justice system. Rules are set up that the polluter must obey. If the polluter violates those rules, he must first be caught. Then the regulatory agency must decide whether it has enough evidence to prosecute. Next, it must win its case before the courts. And, finally, the courts must impose a penalty that is more than just a token gesture. If any one of these steps does not occur, then the polluter gets away with his damaging activities.

Enforcement Issues

The enforcement of direct controls requires vigilance and enthusiasm by the regulatory agency, which must assign the resources and persons needed to carry out the task of enforcement. Yet experience indicates that regulatory vigor is far from universal and often evaporates as time passes and public concern recedes. In many cases the resources devoted to enforcement are pitifully small. Under the Reagan administration environmental outlays have, indeed, been cut severely.

The effectiveness of direct controls also depends upon the speed and rigor of the courts. Yet the courts are often slow and lenient. An example is the notorious case of the Reserve Mining Company, which was involved in one of the nation's longest environmental and public health lawsuits. Starting in September 1969, several Minnesota communities, environmentalists, federal agencies, and officials from three states attempted to stop this company from pouring its wastes (which contain asbestos-like fibers believed to cause cancer) into Lake Superior, the source of the communities' drinking water. In 1980, after more than a decade of litigation and 16 judicial decisions, the courts finally ordered Reserve to curb this discharge (which totalled 67,000 tons over nearly a quarter of a century); the company was also ordered to pay $1.84 million to the city of Duluth and three other communities for water filtration systems.

Finally, direct controls can work only if the legal system imposes meaningful penalties on violators. In a few cases, sizable penalties have been levied. For instance, in October 1986 a New Jersey company agreed to pay a $1.25 million fine plus up to $4 million to finance the cleanup of water pollution and groundwater contamination by its perfume plant.[4] But the following are much more typical: "During three years of intense environmental regulation in Connecticut (1971–1974), only 16 of 1469 air pollution violations were referred to the State Attorney General for possible prosecution.... Of the 16 cases... by 1975, the state [environmental] agency had obtained three injunctions and no fines or penalties of any type."[5] One can cite many cases in which large firms have been convicted of polluting and fined less than $5000 — an amount beneath the notice of even a relatively small corporation. Another New Jersey company convicted in 1980 of discharging hydrofluoric acid into a parking lot, where it could seep into the ground and contaminate the groundwater, was fined a mere $2,125.[6] The total of all air pollution fines collected by the U.S. Environmental Protection Agency during the four fiscal years 1977–1980 amounted to only $27 million — less than 1/100th of one percent of estimated compliance costs.[7]

Where more drastic penalties are available, their very magnitude may make the authorities reluctant to impose them. In an extreme case, in which the only legal remedy is to force the closing of an offending plant, the government agency is likely to back down under local pressure to preserve the community's source of jobs and income.

In contrast, pollution taxes are automatic and certain. No one need be caught, prosecuted, convicted, and punished. The tax bills are just sent out automatically by the untiring tax collector. The only sure way for the polluter to work his way out of paying pollution charges is to cut down his emissions.

Efficiency in Clean Up

A second difference between direct controls and taxes is worth noting. Suppose there is a ruling under a program of direct controls that Filth, Inc., must cut its emissions by 50 percent. Then that firm has absolutely no motivation to go one drop further. Why should it cut its emissions by 55 or even 52 percent when the law offers it neither reward nor encouragement for going beyond the selected quota? Under a system of emission taxes, however, the more the firm cuts back on its pollution, the more it saves in tax payments.

---

[4]"Polluter to Pay Up to $5 Million," *New York Times*, October 31, 1986, p. B6.

[5]William Drayton, "Economic Law Enforcement," *Harvard Environmental Law Review* 4, No. 1, 1980, page 2, fn. 3.

[6]"DEP Fines Firm in Dumping," *Newark Star Ledger*, October 2, 1980.

[7]Robert W. Crandall, *Controlling Industrial Pollution* (Washington, D.C.: The Brookings Institution, 1983), p. 107, who cites EPA data.

A third important difference between direct controls and taxes on emissions is the greater efficiency of the latter in the use of resources. It is claimed that the tax approach can do the job far more cheaply, saving labor, fuel, and raw materials, which can instead be used to build schools, hospitals, and housing for low-income groups. Statistical estimates for several pollution control programs suggest that the cost of doing the job through direct controls can easily be twice as high as under the tax alternative.

Why should there be such a difference? The answer is that under direct controls the job of cutting back emissions is apportioned among the various polluters on some principle (usually intended to approximate some standard of fairness) that is selected by the regulators. This rarely assigns the task in accord with ability to carry it out cheaply and efficiently. Suppose it costs firm A only 3 cents a gallon to reduce emissions while firm B must spend 20 cents a gallon to do the same job. If both firms spew out 2000 gallons of pollution a day, a 50 percent reduction in pollution can be achieved by ordering both firms to limit emissions to 1000 gallons a day. This may or may not be fair, but it is certainly not efficient. The social cost will be 1000 times 3 cents, or $30, to firm A and 1000 times 20 cents, or $200, to firm B, a total of $230.

If, instead, a tax of 10 cents a gallon had been imposed, all the work would have been done by firm A—which can do it more cheaply. Firm A would have cut its emissions out altogether, paying the 3 cents a gallon this requires, to avoid the 10 cents a gallon tax. Firm B would go on polluting as before, because it is cheaper to pay the tax than the 20 cents a gallon it costs to control its pollution. In this way, under the tax, *total daily emissions will still be cut by 2000 gallons a day*. But the entire job will be done by the polluter who can do it more cheaply, and the total daily cost of the program will therefore be $60 (3 cents × 2000 gallons) instead of the $230 it would cost under direct controls.

The secret of the efficiency induced by a tax on pollution is straightforward. Only polluters who can reduce emissions cheaply and efficiently can afford to take advantage of the built-in loophole — the opportunity to save on taxes by reducing emissions. The tax approach simply assigns the job to those who can do it most effectively.

Advantages and Disadvantages

Given all these advantages of the tax approach, why would anyone want to use direct controls?

There are three general and important situations in which direct controls have a clear advantage:

1. *Where an emission is so dangerous that it is decided to prohibit it altogether.* Here there is obviously nothing to be gained by installing complicated procedures for the collection of taxes that will never be paid because there will be no emissions for which payment is required.

2. *Where a sudden change in circumstances — for example, a dangerous air quality crisis — calls for prompt and substantial changes in conduct, such as temporary reductions in use of cars or incinerators.* It is difficult and clumsy to change tax rules, and direct controls will usually do a better job here. The mayor of the threatened city can, for example, forbid the use of private passenger cars until the crisis passes.

3. *Where effective and dependable metering devices have not been invented or are prohibitively costly to install and operate*. In such cases there is no way to operate an effective tax program because the amount of wastes the polluter has emitted cannot be determined and so his tax bill cannot be calculated. In that case the only effective option may be to *require* him to use "clean" fuel, or install emissions-purification equipment.

In reality there is often no device analogous to a gas or water meter that can be used to measure pollution emissions cheaply and effectively. For example, to evaluate emissions in waterways, the standard procedure is to take samples, bring them to a laboratory, and subject them to a series of complicated tests that often take weeks to carry out, to determine the chemical contents of the emissions. For a polluter whose emissions are very large, this may be worth doing. But for the emitter who only spews out a few gallons of pollutants a day, the cost of such a complex process is likely to exceed the benefits. Whatever their other inefficiencies, direct controls are still likely to do the job of controlling such sources of pollution more cheaply. On the other side of the argument, however, the widespread adoption of emissions charges and the resulting rise in demand for metering devices may lead to research and development that produces cheaper and more effective meters.

Other Financial Devices to Protect the Environment

The basic idea underlying the emissions-tax approach to environmental protection is that it provides financial incentives that induce the polluter to reduce the damage he does to the environment. But emissions taxes are not the only form of financial inducement that have been proposed. There are at least two others that deserve consideration: *subsidies for reduced emissions* and the requirement of *emissions permits* for polluters, each permit authorizing the emission of a specified quantity of pollutant. Such permits would be offered for sale in limited quantities fixed by the authorities at prices set by demand and supply.

Subsidies
Subsidies are already in use. Their advocates say that financial inducements can be just as effective when they take the form of a reward for good behavior as when they are composed of penalties (taxes) on behavior that is considered harmful. A donkey can be induced to move forward just as surely (and with much less unpleasantness) by dangling a carrot in front of his nose as by applying a stick to his rump. Environmental subsidies usually take one of two forms:

1. Partial payment of the cost of installation of some sort of pollution control equipment.
2. The offer of a fixed reward for every reduction in emissions from some base level, usually some amount that the polluter used to emit in the past.

A subsidy to help defray the cost of control equipment can be effective when the purchaser of the equipment was considering doing it anyhow but did not because of the high cost. This may be the case for a municipality that wants to treat its wastes more thoroughly but has not found a way to afford the cost. It may also be the case in private industry, where collection of the wastes that would otherwise be emitted can yield products that are valuable and reusable but where the equipment required for the process is too costly. But where the polluter gains nothing from such control, a partial subsidy for the purchase of control equipment is unlikely to be effective. It simply reduces the cost of something he does not want to do in any event.

The second type of subsidy — a reward based on quantity of reduced emissions — does indeed have the same sort of incentive effects as a tax for the *individual* polluter. In both cases the more he emits, the worse off he is financially, either because he receives a smaller subsidy payment or because his tax bill is higher. But as far as the *industry* is concerned, there is a world of difference between the effect of a tax and the effect of a subsidy.

A tax discourages the output of commodities whose production causes pollution, whereas a subsidy encourages such output to expand.

Consider the difference between the tax and subsidy approaches in the case of automotive emissions. A tax will increase the cost of operating cars, thereby encouraging the use of public transportation (which produces far lower quantities of emissions per passenger-mile traveled than does the automobile). On the other hand, a subsidy for the installation of emissions-control devices will tend to encourage the use of autos at the expense of public transportation by keeping down the price of cars.

It is a paradox that a subsidy intended to induce an industry to reduce its emissions can actually *increase* the size of the industry's output and consequently *increase* its total emissions.

This paradox is readily illustrated with the help of a standard supply–demand diagram for a competitive industry. We see in Figure 34–4 that a tax on polluting output will raise the costs of the industry and hence raise the price of whatever quantity it supplies. Thus, the supply curve will be shifted upward by a tax to the curve labeled "supply after tax." Similarly, the subsidy will reduce dollar costs to the industry and so will shift the supply curve downward to the curve labeled "supply after subsidy." So, under a tax on emissions, the equilibrium point will move from point E to point T, reducing the output of the polluting product from e to t. But the subsidy, which moves the supply–demand equilibrium point from E to S, will actually increase the output of the polluting industry from e to s!

How does this happen? While the pollution-reduction subsidy will induce each firm to decrease its emissions somewhat, it will also attract new polluting

Figure 34–4
SUPPLY–DEMAND EQUILIBRIUM IN A POLLUTING COMPETITIVE INDUSTRY
A tax on pollution raises costs and so shifts the supply curve upward; that is, a higher price is needed to elicit a given quantity supplied. This causes equilibrium output to fall from e to t and succeeds in its purpose — reducing pollution. But a subsidy to those who decrease their polluting output reduces costs and shifts the supply curve downward. By reducing costs, it attracts more firms into the industry. Paradoxically, output of the polluting product actually must increase from e to s.

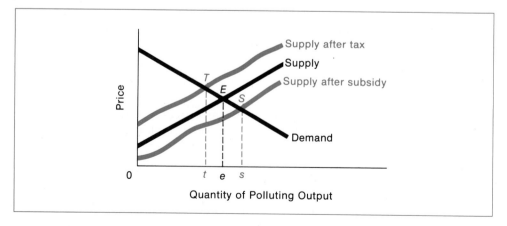

firms into the industry and, as the graph shows, the net result may be that the subsidy will backfire, and instead of reducing pollution, as it is intended to do, it will actually increase it.

The main advantage of subsidies over taxes as a financial inducement to decrease pollution is that subsidies attract less opposition and are therefore more easily adopted through the political process. Obviously, industry always prefers a subsidy to a tax. But the rest of the community may well be worse off if a subsidy is selected instead of an emissions tax.

Emissions Permits

A third type of financial inducement strongly advocated by some economists is the sale of *marketable emissions permits*. Under this arrangement, the environmental agency decides what quantity of emissions per unit of time (say, per month) is tolerable and then issues a batch of permits authorizing (altogether) just that amount of pollution. The permits are offered for sale to the highest bidders. Their price is therefore determined by demand and supply. It will be high if the number of permits offered for sale is small and there is a large amount of industrial activity that must use the permits. Similarly, the price of a permit will be low if many permits are issued but the quantity of pollution for which they are demanded is small.

The emissions permit in many ways works like a tax — it simply makes it too expensive for the polluter to continue emitting as much as he would have without it. In addition, the permit offers two clear advantages over the tax approach. First, it reduces uncertainty about the quantity that will be emitted. Under a tax we cannot be sure about this in advance, since that depends on the extent to which polluters respond to the tax rate that is selected. In the case of permits, the ceiling on emissions is decided in advance by the environmental authorities, who enforce the ceiling simply by issuing permits authorizing a specific total quantity of emissions.

Second, any given tax on emissions will be eroded and therefore made ineffective by inflation. Suppose that in 1970 the legislature adopted a tax of $10 per ton of some type of noxious emission. At that date, when the dollar was worth nearly 3 times as much as it is today, that might have cut emissions considerably. But today, unless a higher level of the tax is adopted, it will hardly deter any industrial polluter any more. In contrast, as long as there is no change in quantity of emissions authorized by license, inflation will obviously have no effect on the amount of pollution. It will simply raise the price of a license along with the prices of other commodities.

A shortcoming of the pollution license idea is its apparent political unattractiveness. Many people react indignantly to the notion of "licenses to pollute." Yet the EPA has introduced some compromise measures which can be regarded as approximations to a market in emissions permits (see the boxed insert on the next page). These programs now seem to be well-established and illustrate how much can be achieved by intelligent compromise in policy making.

Two Cheers for the Market

We have seen in the first part of this chapter that protecting the environment is one task that cannot be left to the free market: because of the important externalities involved, the market will systematically allocate too few resources to the job. However, this market failure does not imply that the price mechanism must be discarded. On the contrary, we have seen that a legislated market

Putting Theory to the Test: EPA's Emissions Trading Program

As indicated in the text, one remedy for pollution long advocated by economists as an alternative to direct controls is the issuance of a limited set of pollution permits which could be sold on a free market. About ten years ago, the Environmental Protection Agency (motivated by theoretical studies suggesting huge savings in pollution control costs and under pressure from approaching pollution standards deadlines) began to experiment with a program of emissions trading, the two principal components of which are the emissions offset program and the "bubble concept," both of which work like a market in emissions permits.

The Emissions Offset Program

In several rulings issued in the mid-1970s, the EPA introduced a new program designed to facilitate economic growth while holding the line on air pollution. This policy allows new factories or other new sources of air pollution to be constructed in areas where pollution standards have not been attained, so long as their emissions are more than offset by reductions in pollution from sources that are already in operation. Firm A can open for business if it can induce firm B (via direct payments or in some other way) to adopt pollution controls which cut down B's emissions by an amount at least equal to A's proposed emissions. This program opens up the possibility that what amounts to a market in pollution permits might spring up, in which current polluters sell some of their permitted emissions levels to potential polluters. The sale price would constitute a tax on emissions which should be effective in discouraging them.

So far few of the offset transactions have worked out quite this way. Instead, most firms have obtained permits to build new plants by internal offsets, that is, by offsetting reductions in pollution from other plants they own (for example, the U.S. Steel Corporation's factory in Birmingham, Alabama, was required by the local pollution board to cut back its emissions before adding new facilities), and in some cases by offsetting reductions in emissions by some government agency (in Pennsylvania state officials worked out a trade-off involving a switch to nonpolluting road-paving materials on the state's highways to offset the pollution from a new Volkswagen auto assembly plant in New Stanton). As certain legal-

Classified advertisement in *The Wall Street Journal*, June 5, 1986, page 32.

ities of the program have been ironed out, interest in the program has grown. One study estimates that since the policy was instituted in 1976, about 2,000 pollution sources have obtained offsets, most of them internal, that is, within a company. However, only one area of the country, the Los Angeles basin in Southern California, seems likely in the near future to come close to approximating a true market in offsets.[*]

The Bubble Concept

This program, begun in 1979, deals with firms already in operation rather than newly established plants or firms, as the offset program does. In other respects, however, the programs are similar. Under the bubble program a firm is permitted to satisfy its mandatory air pollution ceiling in any way it finds most economical. With the old direct controls, each pollution discharge point in a factory or plant was regulated. But under the bubble concept, rather than requiring a firm to reduce emissions from one discharge point by 10 tons, emissions from another discharge point by 10 tons, and emissions from a third discharge point by 20 tons, the firm can divide its required 40-ton reduction among its discharge points in any way it wants (subject to a number of conditions). The entire set of operations by the firm is thus considered to be encased in an imaginary bubble with a single discharge point. The EPA does not care what goes on inside the bubble, that is, whether emissions come from one point or another, as long as emissions from the entire bubble stay within the required limits.

[*]Robert W. Hahn and Gordon L. Hester, "Where Did All the Markets Go? An Analysis of EPA's Emissions Trading Program," Carnegie-Mellon University, December 17, 1986, mimeo.

More recently, firms whose total emissions fall below the required limits are permitted to sell the unused emission rights to other firms whose "bubbles" are not performing so well, or the firm may store these extra rights in an emission reduction "bank" for future use or trade. Through 1986, EPA had approved 42 bubbles for firms emitting suspended particulates, volatile organic compounds (precursors of smog) and sulfur dioxide, seven bubbles had been proposed and 91 were being developed. The total reported cost savings were substantial: a total of $132 million reported by 20 firms. In addition 89 bubbles had been approved under state rules as of the end of 1984. By one estimate, the total potential savings in pollution control costs from all these bubbles (approved, proposed or under development) add up to $650 million,** and EPA's own estimate of these cost savings is $800 million.

** *Ibid.*, pp. 35–36 and 43.

---

solution based on pollution charges may well be the best way to protect the environment. At least in this case, the power of the market mechanism can be harnessed to correct its own failings.

We turn now, in the second half of the chapter, to the case of natural resources, where the market mechanism also plays a crucial role.

The Economics of Energy and Natural Resources

The "energy crisis" of the 1970s and early 1980s, during which prices of oil leaped dramatically first in 1973–74 and then again in 1979–80, had profound effects throughout the world—one of which was a marked change in our attitudes about unlimited stocks of natural resources simply ours for the taking. Indeed, at that time there was near-panic about the prospect of running out of a number of commodities—from coffee and paper products to oil itself. One headline in a leading magazine asked, "Are we running out of *everything?*"

In this part of the chapter, we will try to sort matters out. On the one hand, natural resources have always been scarce, and one may argue with good reason that they have been used wastefully. On the other hand, we are *not* about to run out of the most vital resources, there is reason to be optimistic about the availability of substitutes, and many of the shortages of the 1970s can with some justice be ascribed as much to the folly of government programs and misunderstanding by the general public as to any signs of imminent exhaustion of petroleum and other natural resources.

We start by reviewing the facts and allegations about the available stocks of natural resources and then describe what economic theory tells us will happen in a free market to the prices and usage of finite resources as time passes and the available quantities decline. Then the history of the energy crisis will be examined briefly and, finally, several important policy issues—such as rationing—will be discussed.

A Puzzle: Those Resilient Resource Supplies

It is a plain fact that the earth is endowed with only finite quantities of such vital resources as oil, copper, lead, coal, and many others. This fact has led to a veritable parade of doomsday forecasts about the imminent exhaustion of one resource or another. The boxed insert on page 756 lists a number of bleak prophecies about oil production in the United States, all of which have proved

The Permanent Fuel Crisis

Humanity has a long history of panicking about the imminent exhaustion of natural resources. In the 13th century a large part of Europe's forests was cut down, primarily for use in metalworking (much of it for armor). Wood prices rose, and there was a good deal of talk about depletion of fuel stocks. People have been doing it ever since, as the following cases illustrate.

Past Petroleum Prophecies (and Realities)

DATE	U.S. OIL PRODUCTION RATE (BILLION BARRELS/YEAR)	PROPHECY	REALITY
1866	0.005	Synthetics available if oil production should end (U.S. Revenue Commission).	In next 82 years the U.S. produced 37 billion barrels with no need for synthetics.
1891	0.05	Little or no chance for oil in Kansas or Texas (U.S. Geological Survey).	14 billion barrels produced in these two states since 1891.
1914	0.27	Total future production only 5.7 billion barrels. (Official of U.S. Bureau of Mines).	34 billion barrels produced since 1914 or six times this prediction.
1920	0.45	U.S. needs foreign oil and synthetics: peak domestic production almost reached (Director of U.S. Geological Survey).	1948 U.S. production in excess of U.S. consumption and more than four times 1920 output.
1939	1.3	U.S. oil supplies will last only 13 years (Radio Broadcasts by Interior Department).	New oil found since 1939 exceeds the 13 years' supply known at that time.
1947	1.9	Sufficient oil cannot be found in United States (Chief of Petroleum Division, State Department).	4.3 billion barrels found in 1948, the largest volume in history and twice our consumption.
1949	2.0	End of U.S. oil supply almost in sight (Secretary of the Interior).	Recent industry shows ability to increase U.S. production by more than a million barrels daily in the next 5 years.

SOURCE: William M. Brown, "The Outlook for Future Petroleum Supplies," in Julian L. Simon and Herman Kahn, eds., *The Resourceful Earth: A Response to Global 2000* (Oxford, England: Basil Blackwell Publisher Ltd., 1984), p. 362, who cites Presidential Energy Program, Hearings Before the Subcommittee on Energy and Power of the Committee on Interstate and Foreign Commerce, House of Representatives. First session on the implication of the President's proposals in the Energy Independence Act of 1975, Serial No. 94–20, p. 643. 17, 18, 20, and 21 February, 1975.

far off the mark. And Table 34–1 depicts some equally mysterious estimates of known reserves of four important nonfuel minerals—zinc, nickel, lead, and copper. Reading this table we see that the supplies of each of these minerals actually *grew* between 1960 and 1980 even though mankind had been using them up at a rapid rate. Economic principles, as we will see at the end of this chapter, help a great deal in clearing up these mysteries.

Table 34–1
EXPECTED LIFE (IN YEARS) OF SOME WORLD MINERAL RESERVES, ESTIMATES FOR 1960 AND 1980

	ZINC	NICKEL	LEAD	COPPER
1960	24	43	19	37
1980	42	71	47	59

SOURCE: Bureau of Mines, U.S. Department of the Interior, *The Domestic Supply of Critical Minerals*, 1983, page 21.

Note: We had more years' supply of each of these depletable resources in 1980 than in 1960, despite 20 years of consumption!

The Free Market and Pricing of Depletable Resources

If figures on known reserves behave as peculiarly as those we have just seen, one begins to doubt their ability to indicate whether we are really coming uncomfortably close to running out of certain resources. Is there some other indicator of growing scarcity that seems more reliable? Most economists agree that there is — that *the price of the resource* serves this function well.

As a resource becomes scarcer, we expect its price to rise for several reasons. One is that for most resources the process of depletion is not simply a matter of gradually using up the supply of a homogeneous product, every unit of which is equally available. Rather, the most accessible and highest quality deposits of the resource are generally used up first, then industry turns to less accessible locations and/or deposits of lower purity or quality, and then finally to deposits that are still harder or more costly to extract or of still poorer quality. Oil is a clear example of this. First, Americans relied primarily on the most easily found domestic oil wells. Then they turned to imports from the Middle East with their higher transport costs. At that point it was not yet profitable to embark on the dangerous and extremely costly process of bringing up oil from the floor of the North Sea. We know that the United States still possesses tremendous stocks of petroleum embedded in shale (rock), but so far this has been too difficult and, therefore, too costly to get at.

Increasing scarcity of a resource such as oil is not usually a matter of imminent and total disappearance. Rather, it takes the form of exhaustion of the most accessible and cheapest sources so that new supplies become more costly.

A second reason for rising resource prices is hidden in the operation of the supply–demand mechanism. To see how it works let us consider the simpler (if less realistic) case in which extraction of a resource does not grow increasingly difficult as its reserves dwindle. That is, we envision the earth's supply of a mythical mineral, Zipthon, all of identical quality, which can be extracted and delivered to market with negligible extraction and transportation cost. How quickly will the reserves of Zipthon be used up, and what will happen to its price with the passage of time?

If the market for Zipthon is perfectly competitive, we can provide a remarkably concrete answer about the behavior of prices. The answer, which was discovered by the American economist Harold Hotelling, tells us that as long as the supply of Zipthon lasts, its price must rise at a rate equal to the rate of interest. That is, if in 1988 the price of Zipthon is $100 per ounce and the rate of interest is 10 percent, then its price in 1989 must be $110.

Under perfect competition the price of a depletable resource whose cost of transportation and extraction are negligible must rise at the rate of interest. If the rate of interest is 10 percent, the price of the resource must rise 10 percent every year.

Why is this so? The answer is simple. People who have money tied up in inventories of Zipthon must earn exactly as much per dollar of investment as they would by putting their money into, say, a government bond. For suppose instead that $100 invested in bonds would next year rise in value to $112, while $100 in Zipthon would grow only to $110, and suppose the two were equally risky. What would happen? People who owned Zipthon would obviously find it profitable to sell the Zipthon and put their money into bonds instead.

But as more Zipthon was dumped on the market, it would become increasingly abundant today and increasingly scarce tomorrow. So its expected *future* price would rise while its actual *current* price would fall. This and other associated changes in Zipthon prices and bond prices would continue until there was no further advantage in the one investment as against the other—that is, until both offered the same rate of return per dollar of investment.

The same process, working in reverse, would apply if Zipthon prices were rising faster than the rate of interest. Investors would switch from bonds to Zipthon, and with more Zipthon held for investment rather than released for current consumption, current prices of Zipthon would rise. At the same time the abundance of future stocks would be increased and thus expected future prices would fall.

Following this fundamental principle about the pricing of a scarce resource with fixed extraction costs, let us see what will happen to the price of $100 worth of Zipthon over the course of, say, four years. We have the following pattern of Zipthon prices:

INITIAL DATE	ONE YEAR LATER	TWO YEARS LATER	THREE YEARS LATER	FOUR YEARS LATER
$100	$110	$121	$133.10	$146.41

These prices follow from the fact that $110 is 10 percent higher than $100, $121 is 10 percent higher than $110, and so on. What is to be noted is that because of the compounding effect, the dollar quantity of the price increase is greater and greater each year. Zipthon rises in value by $10 in the first year, $11 in the second year, $12.10 in the third, $13.31 in the fourth, and so on indefinitely. Thus we conclude:

The basic law of pricing of a depletable resource tells us that as its stocks are used up its price in a perfectly competitive market will rise every year by greater and greater dollar amounts.

Notice that we have been able to make these predictions about the price of Zipthon without any knowledge about the supply of Zipthon or consumer demand for it. This is really remarkable. But if we want to go on to determine what will happen to the consumption of Zipthon—the rate at which its inventory will be used up—we do need to know something about supply and demand.

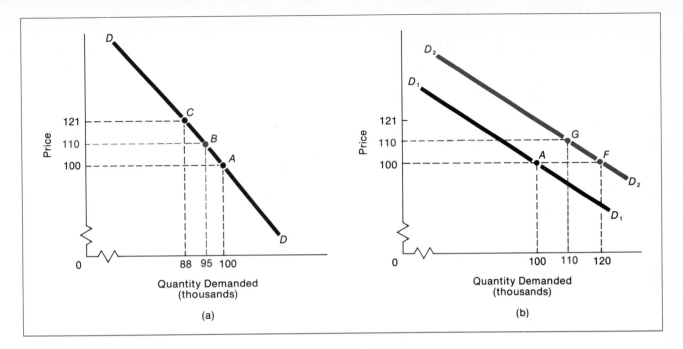

Figure 34–5
CONSUMPTION OVER
TIME OF A DEPLETABLE
RESOURCE
The price of the resource
must rise year after year
(from $100 to $110 to $121,
and so on). If the demand
curve does not shift [part
(a)], quantity demanded will
be reduced every year. Even
if the demand curve does
shift outward [as in part (b)],
the increasing price will keep
any rise in quantity
demanded lower than it
would otherwise have been.

Figure 34–5(a) is a demand curve for Zipthon, *DD*, which shows the amount people want to use up *per year* at various price levels. On the vertical axis we show how the price must rise from year to year in the pattern we have just calculated—from $100 per ton in the initial year to $110 in the next year, and so on. Because of the negative slope of the demand curve it follows that each year consumption of Zipthon will fall. That is, *if there is no shift in the demand curve,* consumption will fall from 100,000 tons initially to 95,000 tons in the next year, and so on.

But in reality such demand curves rarely do stay still. As the economy grows and population and per-capita incomes increase, demand curves can be expected to shift outward. And there is every reason to believe that this has been true of the demands for most scarce resources. Shifts in the demand curve will naturally tend to increase consumption, thereby offsetting at least part of the reduction in quantity demanded that results from rising prices. Nevertheless, it remains true that rising prices do help to cut back consumption growth relative to what it would have been if price had remained constant. In Figure 34–5(b) we depict an outward shift in demand from curve D_1D_1 in the initial period to curve D_2D_2 a year later. If price had remained constant at the initial value, $100 per ton, quantity consumed per year would have risen from 100,000 tons to 120,000 tons. But since, in accord with the basic principle, price must rise to $110, quantity demanded will only increase to 110,000 tons—which is smaller than 120,000 tons. Thus, whether or not the demand curve shifts, we conclude:

The ever-rising prices that accompany increasing scarcity of a depletable resource discourage consumption (encourage conservation). Even if quantity demanded is growing, it will grow less rapidly than if prices were not rising.

Resource Prices in the Twentieth Century

How do the facts match up with this theoretical analysis? As we will see now, their correspondence is very poor indeed. Figure 34–6 shows the behavior of

Figure 34–6
PRICES OF LEAD, ZINC,
AND TIN 1900–1984, IN
1967 CENTS*
Note that these prices have
not been rising steadily even
though all three minerals are
gradually being used up.
SOURCE: *Historical Statistics of
the U.S., Metal Statistics,* 1981
(American Metal Market, Fairchild
Publications), and *Statistical
Abstract of the United States,
1986*. *As deflated by the
producer price index (all
commodities).

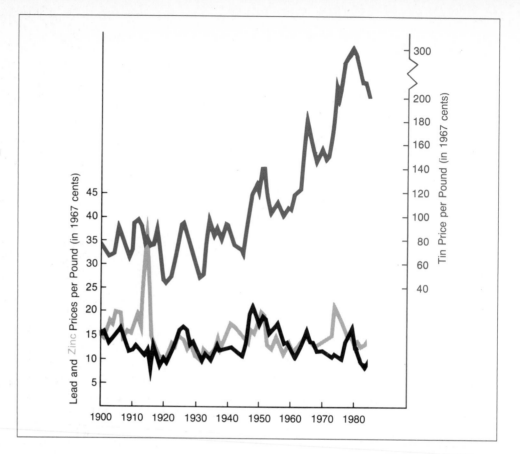

the prices of three critical metals—lead, zinc, and tin—since the beginning of the twentieth century. These figures are all expressed in real terms; that is, they have all been recalculated in terms of dollars of constant purchasing power to eliminate the effects of inflation or deflation.

What we find is that instead of rising steadily, as the theory might have led us to expect, two of them actually remained amazingly constant. Between 1900 and 1940 lead and zinc prices actually rose more slowly than the general price level, while tin prices just about kept pace with general inflation between 1900 and 1945. More recently the price of tin has gone up substantially faster than other prices—in 1980 its relative price was nearly twice as high as it was in 1970. But even during the 1970s, zinc and lead prices rose only slightly faster than prices in general.

Figure 34–7 shows the relative price of crude oil in the United States since 1947. It gives price at the wellhead, that is, at the point of production, with no transportation cost included. The data show that in 1973 the price of oil was actually about 8 percent lower, relative to other prices, than it was in 1948. Only from 1973 to 1981 did it rise faster than prices in general; by 1986 the price of oil had fallen all the way back to its real price in 1973. There are even more peculiar cases. From 1923 (the earliest date for which figures are available) to 1980, the price of magnesium actually fell relative to other prices by nearly 84 percent. (For the oil price story, see the boxed insert on page 764.)

How does one explain this strange behavior of the prices of finite resources, which surely are being used up, even if only gradually? Have the laws of supply and demand somehow broken down? Actually, what these figures indicate is that reality is much more complicated than our simple analytic

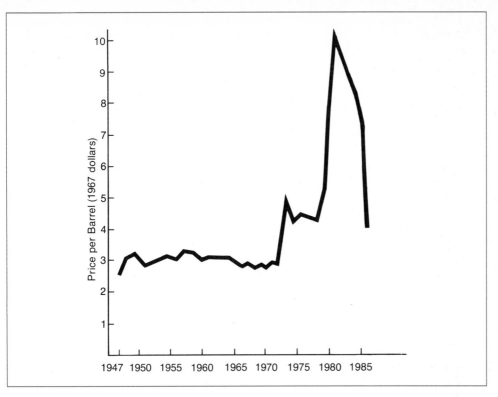

Figure 34–7
PRICE OF DOMESTIC OIL AT THE WELLHEAD, 1947–1986, IN 1967 DOLLARS*
Note the long period of near constancy in real oil prices. SOURCE: *Historical Statistics of the U.S.; Monthly Energy Review; Minerals Year Book; U.S. Energy Information Administration; U.S. Department of Labor, Bureau of Labor Statistics; Statistical Abstract of the United States,* various years; and Dermot Gately, "Lessons from the 1986 Oil Price Collapse," *Brookings Papers on Economic Activity,* 2: 1986, pp. 237–284. *As deflated by the producer price index (all commodities).

model, and that sometimes the complications grow so extreme that prices behave very differently from what the simple theory predicts. While many things can interfere with the price patterns that the theory leads us to expect, we will mention only four:

1. ***Unexpected discoveries of reserves whose existence was previously not suspected.*** If we were to stumble upon a huge and easily accessible reserve of Zipthon, which came as a complete surprise to the market, the price of Zipthon would obviously fall. This is illustrated in Figure 34–8, where we see that people originally believed the available supply curve to be that represented by curve S_1S_1. The discovery of the new Zipthon reserves leads

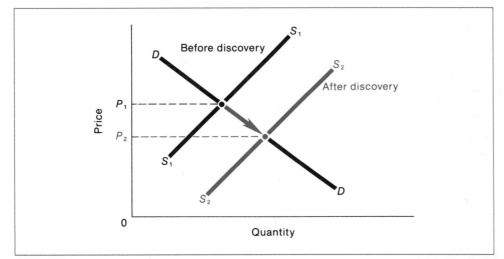

Figure 34–8
PRICE EFFECTS OF A DISCOVERY OF ADDITIONAL RESERVES
A discovery causes a rightward shift in the supply curve of the resource. That is so because the cost to suppliers of any given quantity of the resource is reduced by the discovery, so it will pay them to supply a larger quantity at any given price. This must lead to a price fall (from P_1 to P_2).

them to recognize that the supply is much larger than they had thought (curve S_2S_2). Like any outward shift in a supply curve, this can be expected to cause a fall in price. A clear historical example was the discovery of gold and silver in Central and South America by the Spaniards in the sixteenth century. This led to sharp and substantial drops in the prices of these precious metals in Europe, and was a source of major economic problems for the Tudor monarchs.

2. **The invention of new methods of mining or refining that may significantly reduce extraction costs.** This, too, can lead to a rightward shift in the supply curve as it becomes profitable for suppliers to deliver a larger quantity at any given price. The situation is therefore again represented by a diagram like Figure 34–8. Only it is now a reduction in cost, not a new discovery of reserves, that shifts the supply curve to the right.

3. **A government subsidy.** From the point of view of the supplier, a government subsidy is exactly the same as a reduction in mining or processing costs—either will decrease his cost per ton of supplying the resource. Thus the supply curve will shift to the right (from S_1S_1 to S_2S_2 in Figure 34–8) and the price will fall.

4. **Price controls which hold prices down or decrease them.** A legislature can pass a law prohibiting the sale of the resource at a price higher than P^* (see Figure 34–9). Sometimes this works, though not always, for in many cases an illegal black market emerges, where very high prices are charged more or less secretly. But even where it does work it causes problems. Since the objective is to make the legal ceiling price, P^*, lower than the market equilibrium price, P, at price P^* quantity demanded (five million tons in the figure) will be higher than the free-market level (four million tons). Similarly, we may expect that now quantity supplied (two million tons in the figure) will be less than its free-market level. Thus, as always happens in these cases, the quantity supplied is insufficient to match the quantity demanded—a shortage emerges.

Many economists believe that this is exactly what happened after 1971 when President Nixon decided to experiment with price controls. It was just at

Figure 34–9
CONTROLS ON THE PRICE OF A RESOURCE
By law price is kept to P^*, which is below the equilibrium price, P. This reduces quantity supplied from four to two million tons and raises quantity demanded from four to five million tons. A shortage measured by length AB, or three million tons, is the result.

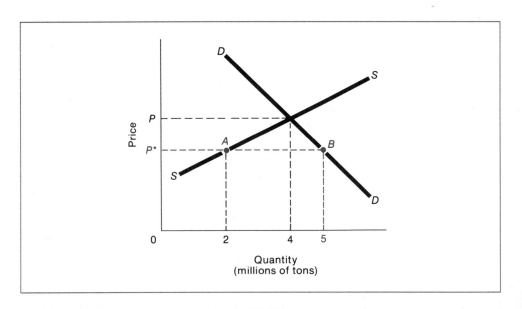

this time that the economy experienced a sudden plague of shortages and we seemed to be "running out of nearly everything." But the shortages apparently were attributable to the controls, not to anything happening to resource supplies or the productive process. And after price controls ended in 1974, most of the "shortages" disappeared.

Each of the examples of minerals whose prices did not rise can be explained by one or more of these factors. For example, both zinc and magnesium have benefited from technological changes that lowered extraction costs. In the case of the latter, the process that turns the mineral into ingots has grown far more efficient than it was in the 1920s. The case of lead is quite different. There, some new mines in Missouri turned out to hold abundant quantities of ore that were much easier to extract and much cheaper to refine than what had been available before. This was apparently enough to keep the price of lead from rising very fast. Obviously, events in reality are more complex than a naïve reading of theoretical models might lead us to believe.

Yet, despite these influences, which have postponed the price rises in depletable resources predicted by the theory, both logic and evidence indicate that in the long run supply and demand must win out. As a resource really becomes scarce and costly to obtain, its free-market price must ultimately rise, and so must its actual price, unless government interferes.

The Free Market and Resource Depletion

Popular views of the process of depletion of a vital resource envision a scenario in which consumption grows year after year and stocks of the item dwindle as a result until, one day, quantity supplied can no longer keep up with quantity demanded. From then on, the nation faces a history of steady shortfalls, with rationing or chaos the inevitable result. Economists pay little attention to such scenarios. Though it seems implausible to anyone who has not studied economics, it is nevertheless true that:

In a free market, quantity demanded can never exceed quantity supplied, even if a finite resource is undergoing rapid depletion. The reason is simple: In any free market, quantity demanded must always equal quantity supplied, for price will automatically adjust to eliminate any difference between them.

In fact, there have been cases of real shortages in the past. For example, twice during the 1970s the quantities of gasoline supplied were, in many parts of the United States, lower than the quantities demanded, and chaos did indeed result. There were long lines of cars at those gas stations that remained open, and huge amounts of petroleum and time were wasted in the process as the cars inched forward (sometimes for hours) toward the gas pumps. During World War II, meat, sugar, and other commodities were in short supply, and there was a period in the 1970s when supplies of paper, copper, and other commodities were inadequate to meet demand. But in every such case there were regulations or laws which prohibited full adjustment of prices. In a sense, then, it was these price regulations, and not any disappearance of resources, that were responsible for the shortages.

In theory, any shortage—any excess of quantity demanded over quantity supplied—must be artificial; that is, must be ascribed to a decision to prevent the price mechanism from doing its job.

The Messy Story of Oil Prices

Oil is, perhaps, the most important energy source in the world, and the history of oil prices provides an important lesson on how different the real world can be from the pure supply–demand model of perfect competition. Yet we will see that even with almost constant government interference and control by a powerful cartel (that is, a monopolistic association of suppliers), the forces of supply and demand continue to play a crucial role in the price of petroleum. Indeed, we will see that the cartel succeeded not *in spite of* the supply–demand mechanism, but *because* it was able to use that mechanism.

Traditionally, the oil industry was virtually controlled by seven large companies, which made price and production decisions, negotiated terms separately with each of the oil-producing countries, and extracted the oil from the ground. Throughout the 1950s, the world market price of oil remained low, enabling oil to drive out many competing energy sources. Both the world's output and energy consumption tripled during this decade, and oil became very nearly the unchallenged source of power. During the 1960s it apparently became increasingly difficult for production to keep up with the burgeoning demand, a sure sign that prices were being kept artificially low.

After some earlier abortive attempts, Iran, Iraq, Kuwait, Saudi Arabia, and Venezuela formed the Organization of Petroleum Exporting Countries (OPEC) in 1960. OPEC was quiet until 1970 when Libya opened an offensive to gain control of its oil resources, and by 1973, partly through extensive expropriation by the OPEC countries, the role of the oil companies had been reduced to that of technical contractors. The OPEC countries now imposed massive price increases; in 1973–74 the real price of crude oil more than tripled. The Arab countries also announced a production cutback of 5 percent, and an embargo of sales to the United States and Holland (as punishment for their support of Israel in October 1973), thus causing an inward shift of the supply curve and a sharp price rise. The public, waiting in mile-long gas lines, had time to ruminate on the new look of world energy: its rising cost and the fact

that a high proportion of the supply to the industrialized world was controlled by powers that did not necessarily wish them well.

For a while thereafter, OPEC price increases became more moderate, roughly keeping pace with world inflation. Then in January 1979, with the fall of the Shah of Iran, oil exports dropped sharply, again shifting the supply curve inward. Predictably, the price of oil shot up, rising from $12 a barrel in the beginning of 1979 to more than $25 at the end of that year and peaking at about $40 a barrel in mid-1980.

But, even in the presence of the cartel, forces of supply and demand beyond its control played a part. In 1981 and 1982, widespread recession in the industrialized world, together with measures to induce conservation, shifted the demand curve for oil inward. The world price dropped, and world oil production between 1979 and 1983 declined about 10 percent. By mid-1981 oil consumption outside the communist countries had fallen to 46 million barrels per day from 49.5 million a year earlier. The price of oil continued on its downward path through 1985 before dropping spectacularly in early 1986 to a level (about $12 a barrel) on a par with its price in 1974. Global oil surpluses are now expected to continue until the end of the decade. But ultimately the fact that oil is a finite resource means that its continued depletion is likely to cause its price to begin to rise once more.

To say that the cause is artificial, of course, does not settle the basic issue—whether freedom of price adjustments is desirable when resource depletion is underway, or whether interference with the pricing process is justified.

There are many economists who believe that this is another of those cases in which the disease—shortages and the resulting dislocations in the economy—is far worse than the cure—deregulation of prices. They hold that the general public is misguided in its clamor against the rising prices that must ultimately accompany depletion of a resource, and that people are mistaken in regarding these price rises as the problem, when in fact they are part of the cure.

It is, of course, easy to understand why no consumer loves a price rise. And it is also easy to understand why many consumers ascribe any such price rise to a plot—to a conspiracy by greedy suppliers who somehow deliberately arrange shortages in order to force prices upward. Sometimes, this view is even correct. For example, the members of OPEC have openly and frankly undertaken to influence the flow of oil in order to increase the price they receive for it. But it is important to recognize from the principles of supply and demand that when a resource grows scarce its price will tend to rise automatically, even without any conspiracies or plots.

On the Virtues of Rising Prices

Rising prices help control the process of resource depletion in three basic ways:

1. They discourage consumption and waste and provide an inducement for conservation.

2. They stimulate more efficient use of the resource by industry, providing incentives for the employment of processes that are more sparing in their use of the resource or that use substitute resources.

3. They encourage innovation—the discovery of other, more abundant resources that can do the job and of new techniques that permit these other resources to be used economically.

Let us examine each of these a bit more carefully.

It used to be said that consumer demand for oil was highly *inelastic*—that prices would never make a significant dent in consumption of petroleum—but events seem to have proved otherwise. When fuel prices rose people began to insulate their homes, keep home temperatures lower, take fewer shopping trips, and buy smaller automobiles. All of this had striking results. Between 1960 and 1973, U.S. demand for oil increased by over 75 percent, but between 1973 and 1985, demand actually declined by about 10 percent.[8]

In part, the reduced demand was initially attributable to recession in the United States; but, particularly as the recession ended, observers have concluded that reactions to rising prices also played a substantial role. As a matter of fact, energy consumption as a percent of real GNP has fallen steadily since 1973.

Moreover, in the long run, we can expect even more demand adjustment—that is, the *long-run* demand curve for oil is probably more elastic than the *short-run* curve. As the nation's fleet of cars wears out they will all gradually be replaced by vehicles that economize on fuel. New homes will be built more

[8]Dermot Gateley, "Lessons From the 1986 Oil Price Collapse," *Brookings Papers on Economic Activity* 2: 1986, pp. 269–70.

snugly to save on heat, and they will be located closer to the workplace to save on fuel in transportation.

The second way in which a price increase helps to conserve a scarce resource is through its effect on industrial usage. Like a final consumer, a business firm can economize on its use of a resource. It can use more fuel-efficient means of transportation and more insulation. It can locate its new plants in ways that reduce the need for transportation. And it can substitute labor and other inputs for scarce resources. The use of a pick and shovel involves the employment of more labor to save the fuel that might have been used by a bulldozer. Farmers who gather manure save the fuel necessary to produce chemical fertilizers.

Finally, rising prices help to slow the disappearance of a resource by stimulating the production of substitutes and even by inducing more production of the resource itself. The last statement is paradoxical: If a resource is finite, how can more be produced? Certainly it can be extracted and sold faster, but that only hastens the process of depletion. How can we get *more* of a *finite* resource? Of course, we cannot. But rising prices will make it feasible to use repositories of the resource that otherwise would have been considered too inaccessible and simply not worth the effort. It has recently proved profitable, for example, to reopen old oil wells using expensive procedures to force out substantial amounts of petroleum which had been abandoned because they did not flow out unaided. Similarly, the extraction of oil from shale has long been talked about, but only higher prices will make it feasible.

And higher prices of the vanishing resource also stimulate research and development which lead to the emergence of substitute products. It is high oil prices that will transform solar energy, wind energy, and biomass energy from romantic notions, which cynics can deride as impractical, into effective sources of energy which may some day make substantial contributions to the economy.

A final word on the price mechanism and resource conservation is in order. One often hears about the rape of our natural resources by greedy owners who rush to exchange them for profits without any thought for the needs of the future. But the price mechanism has built-in incentives to prevent this from happening. We have seen how a resource's price can be expected to rise automatically as its stocks dwindle. Obviously, when the price rise is sufficiently rapid it becomes more profitable to leave more of it underground for future extraction rather than to sell it now at today's lower prices. That, indeed, is one of the things some of the OPEC countries have done and one of the reasons oil prices rose so rapidly. One may legitimately object to this for many reasons, but surely *not* on the grounds that oil supplies are being squandered by excessive and irresponsible rates of extraction.

Freedom of pricing of a dwindling resource induces conservation by consumers and by industry; it encourages the introduction of substitute products; and it induces moderation in rates of extraction by owners of the sources.

Growing Reserves of Exhaustible Resources: Our Puzzle Revisited

We began the second half of this chapter with a brief look at some pessimistic views about future resource supplies, including an estimate made in 1960 that by 1985 we would have only 18 years of nickel reserves and 12 years of copper reserves, and would have run out of zinc and lead. Yet in Table 34–1 page 757) we saw, strangely enough, that between 1960 and 1980 the reserves of all of these finite resources actually increased!

This paradox has a straightforward economic explanation: rising reserves are a tribute to the success of exploration activity that took place in the meantime. Minerals are not discovered by accident. They are discovered by difficult and costly work requiring the services of geologists and engineers and the use of extremely expensive machinery. Exploration requires an enormous expenditure which industry does not find worth making when reserves are high and when mineral prices are low.

Consequently, over the course of the twentieth century proven reserves have not changed very much. Every time some mineral's known reserves fell, particularly if its price therefore tended to rise, exploration increased until the decline was offset. The law of supply and demand worked. Falling reserves or rising prices of a mineral caused an upsurge in exploration, just as we expect from supply–demand analysis. In the 1970s, for example, the rising price of oil led to very substantial increases in oil exploration, which helped to build up reserves. While, to protect ourselves from OPEC, it may not be wise for us to *consume* more oil from American sources, it certainly does seem prudent for us to increase our reserves through exploration. Increased profitability of exploration is perhaps the most effective way to get that done.

Summary

1. Pollution is as old as human history; and contrary to some popular notions, some forms of pollution were actually decreasing even before government programs were initiated to protect the environment.

2. Both planned and market economies suffer from substantial environmental problems.

3. The production of commodities *must* cause waste disposal problems unless everything is recycled, but even recycling processes cause pollution (and use up energy).

4. Industrial activity causes environmental damage, but so does the activity of private individuals (as when they drive cars that emit pollutants). Government agencies also damage the environment (as when military airplanes emit noise and exhaust, or a hydroelectric project floods large areas).

5. Pollution is an externality—when a factory emits smoke, it dirties laundry and may damage the health of persons who neither work for the smoking factory nor buy its products. Hence, pollution control cannot be left to the free market. This is another of our **12 Ideas for Beyond the Final Exam.**

6. Pollution can be controlled by voluntary programs, direct controls, taxes on emissions, or other monetary incentives for the reduction of emissions.

7. Most economists believe that the tax approach is the most efficient and effective way to control detrimental externalities.

8. The quantity demanded of a scarce resource can exceed the quantity supplied only if something prevents the market mechanism from operating freely.

9. As a resource grows scarce on a free market, its price will rise, inducing increased conservation by consumers, increased exploration for new reserves, and increased substitution of other items that can serve the same purpose.

10. In fact, in the twentieth century the relative prices of many resources have remained roughly constant, largely because of the discovery of new reserves and because of cost-saving innovations.

11. The price mechanism and rationing are the only known alternatives to chaos in the allocation of scarce resources.

12. In the 1970s, OPEC succeeded in raising the relative price of petroleum, but the rise in price led to a substantial decline in world demand as well as to an increase in production in countries outside OPEC.

13. Known reserves for depletable scarce resources have not tended to fall with the passage of time because as the price of the resource rises with increasing scarcity, increased exploration for new reserves becomes profitable.

Concepts for Review

Externality
Direct controls
Pollution charges (taxes on emissions)
Subsidies for reduced emissions
Emissions permits

Known reserves
Organization of Petroleum Exporting Countries (OPEC)
Rationing
Paradox of growing reserves of finite resources

Questions for Discussion

1. What sorts of pollution problems would you expect in a small African village? In a city in India? In communist China? In New York City?

2. Suppose you are assigned the task of drafting a law to impose a tax on the emission of smoke. What provisions would you put into the law?
   a. How would you decide the size of the tax?
   b. What would you do about smoke emitted by a municipal electricity plant?
   c. Would you use the same tax rate in densely and sparsely settled areas?
   What information will you need to collect before determining what you would do about each of the preceding provisions?

3. Production of commodity X creates 10 pounds of emissions for every unit of X produced. The demand and supply curves for X are described by the following table:

PRICE (DOLLARS)	10	9	8	7	6	5
Quantity demanded	80	85	90	95	100	105
Quantity supplied	100	95	90	85	80	75

   What is the equilibrium price and quantity, and how much pollution will be emitted?

4. If the price of X to consumers is $9, and the government imposes a tax of $2 per unit, show that because suppliers get only $7 they will produce only 85 units of output, not the 95 units of output they would produce if they received the full $9 per unit.

5. Show that, with this tax, the equilibrium price is $9 and the equilibrium quantity demanded is 85. How much pollution will now be emitted?

6. Compare your answers to Questions 3 and 5 and show how large a reduction in pollution emissions occurs because of the $2 tax on the polluting output.

7. Discuss some valid and some invalid objections against letting rising prices eliminate shortages of supplies of scarce resources.

8. Describe what must be done by a government agency that is given the job of rationing a scarce resource.

9. Some observers believe that a program of rationing may work fairly satisfactorily for a few months or for one or two years, particularly during an emergency period when patriotic spirit is strong. However, they believe that over longer periods and when there is no upsurge of patriotism it is likely to prove far less satisfactory. Do you agree or disagree? Why?

10. Why may a rise in the price of fuel lead to more conservation after several years have passed than it does in the months following the price increase? What does you answer imply about the relative size of the long-run elasticity of demand for fuel and its short-run elasticity?

PART 9

The Distribution of Income

35

I'm especially grateful, as I have no other marketable skills.

JOHNNY CARSON,
ON SIGNING A NEW NBC
CONTRACT FOR AN
ESTIMATED $5 MILLION
A YEAR.

Pricing the Factors of Production

Parts 6, 7, and 8 have been devoted to examining the things the free-market system does well and the things it does poorly. We mentioned in Chapter 29 that the market mechanism cannot be counted on to distribute income in accord with ethical notions of "fairness" or "justice," and we listed this failing as one of the market's shortcomings. But there is much more to be said about how income is distributed in a market economy and about how governments interfere with and alter this distribution process. These are the subjects of Part 9.

The broad outlines of how the market mechanism distributes income are familiar to all of us. Each person owns some **factors of production** — the inputs used in the production process. Many of us have only our own labor; but some of us also have funds that we can lend, land that we can rent, or natural resources that we can sell. These factors are sold on markets at prices determined by supply and demand. So the distribution of income in a market economy is determined by the level of employment of the factors of production and by their prices. For example, if wages are rather high and are fairly equal among workers, and if unemployment is low, then few people will be poor. But if wages are low and unequal and unemployment is high, then many people will be poor.

For purposes of discussion, the factors of production may be grouped into five broad categories: land, labor, capital, exhaustible natural resources, and a rather mysterious input called **entrepreneurship.** Exhaustible natural resources were studied in Chapter 34. In this chapter, we will study the payments made for the use of three other factors: the interest paid to capital, the rent of land, and the profits earned by entrepreneurs.

Since this chapter focuses on the *theories* of interest, rents, and profits, it may be useful first to have a brief look at how much these factors earn in *reality*. According to U.S. data for 1986, interest payments accounted for about 9.5 percent of national income, land rents for less than 1 percent, corporate profits for about 8.3 percent, and earnings of other proprietors for about 8.5 percent. In total, the returns to all the factors of production dealt with in this chapter amounted to about one-quarter of national income. Where did the rest of it go? The answer is that almost three-quarters of national income was composed of

Entrepreneurship is the act of starting new firms, introducing new products and technological innovations, and, in general, taking the risks that are necessary in seeking out business opportunities.

employee compensation—wages and salaries. The huge share of labor in national income is one of the reasons why the next chapter is devoted entirely to this subject.

The distribution of income is perhaps the one area in economics in which any one individual's interests almost inevitably conflict with someone else's. By definition, if a larger share of the total income is distributed to me, a smaller share will be left for you. It is also a topic about which emotions run high and the facts or the logic of the issues are often ignored. In this chapter we will encounter examples of serious misunderstandings about the facts: misapprehensions about the true magnitudes of interest rates and profits, people's unwillingness to face up to the consequences of rent controls, and so forth.

The Principle of Marginal Productivity

By now it will not surprise you to learn that factor prices are analyzed in terms of supply and demand. The supply sides of the markets for the various factors differ enormously from one another, which is why each factor market must be considered separately. But one basic principle, the **principle of marginal productivity,** has been used to explain the demand for every input. Before restating the principle, it will be useful to recall two concepts that were introduced in Chapter 23: **marginal physical product** (MPP) and **marginal revenue product** (MRP).[1]

Table 35–1, which repeats Table 23–6 (page 514), helps us review these two concepts by recalling the example of Farmer Pfister who had to decide how much fertilizer to apply to his fixed plot of land. The marginal *physical* product (MPP) column tells us how many additional bushels of corn each additional ton of fertilizer yields. For example, according to the table, the fourth ton increases the crop by 300 bushels. The marginal *revenue* product (MRP) column tells us how many dollars this marginal physical product is worth. In the example in the table, corn is assumed always to sell at $2 per bushel, so the marginal revenue product of the fourth ton of fertilizer is $2 per bushel times 300 bushels, or $600. We can now state the marginal productivity principle formally:

The marginal productivity principle states that when factor markets are competitive it always pays a profit-maximizing firm to hire that quantity of any input at which the marginal revenue product is equal to the price of the input.

[1]To review these concepts see Chapter 23, pages 502 and 514.

The **marginal physical product** (MPP) of an input is the increase in output that results from a one-unit increase in the use of the input, holding the amounts of all other inputs constant.

The **marginal revenue product** (MRP) of an input is the additional sales revenue that a firm obtains by selling the marginal physical product of that input.

Table 35–1
MARGINAL PHYSICAL PRODUCTS AND MARGINAL REVENUE PRODUCTS OF FARMER PFISTER'S FERTILIZER

TONS OF FERTILIZER	MARGINAL PHYSICAL PRODUCT (bushels)	MARGINAL REVENUE PRODUCT (dollars)
1	250	500
2	300	600
3	350	700
4	300	600
5	250	500
6	150	300
7	50	100
8	0	0
9	−50	−100

The basic logic behind the principle is both simple and powerful. If the input's marginal revenue product is, for example, greater than its price, it will pay the firm to hire more of it because an additional unit of input brings the firm an addition to revenue (via the output it contributes) that exceeds its cost. Consequently, if MRP > input price, then the firm should expand the quantity of the input it purchases up to the level at which diminishing returns reduce the MRP to the level of the input's price. By similar reasoning, if MRP is less than price, then the firm is using too much of the input. Let us use Table 35–1 to demonstrate how the marginal productivity principle works.

Suppose the firm were using four tons of fertilizer at a cost of $350 per ton. Since the table tells us that a fifth ton has a marginal revenue product of $500, the firm could obviously add $150 to its profit by buying a fifth ton. Only when the firm has used so much fertilizer that (because of diminishing returns) the MRP of still another ton is less than $350 does it pay to stop expanding the use of fertilizer. In this example, five tons is the optimal amount to use.

One corollary of the principle of marginal productivity is obvious: The quantity of the input demanded depends on its price. The lower the price of fertilizer, the more it pays a firm to hire. In the example of the previous paragraph, it pays the firm to use five tons when the price of fertilizer is $350 per ton. But if fertilizer were more expensive, say $550 per ton, that price would exceed the value of the marginal product of the fifth ton. It would, therefore, pay the firm to stop after the fourth ton. Thus, *marginal productivity analysis shows that the quantity demanded of an input normally will decline as the price of the input rises*. The "law" of demand applies to inputs just as it applies to consumer goods.

The Derived Demand Curve for an Input

We can, in fact, be much more specific than this, for the marginal productivity principle tells us precisely how the demand curve for any input is derived from its marginal revenue product (MRP) curve.

Figure 35–1 presents graphically the MRP schedule from Table 35–1. Recall that, according to the marginal productivity principle, the quantity

Figure 35–1
A MARGINAL REVENUE PRODUCT SCHEDULE
This diagram depicts the data in Table 35–1, which show how the marginal revenue product (MRP) of fertilizer first rises and then declines as more and more fertilizer is used. Since the optimal purchase rule is to keep applying fertilizer until MRP is reduced to the price of fertilizer, the *downward sloping portion* of the MRP curve is Farmer Pfister's demand curve for fertilizer.

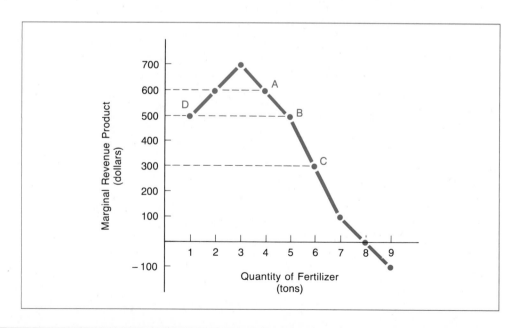

demanded of the input is determined by setting MRP equal to the input's price. Figure 35–1 considers three different possible prices for a ton of fertilizer: $600, $500, and $300. At a price of $600 per ton, we see that the quantity demanded is four tons (point A) because at that point MRP = price. Similarly, if the price of fertilizer drops to $500 per ton, quantity demanded rises to five tons (point B). Finally, should the price fall all the way to $300 per ton, the quantity demanded would be six tons (point C). Points A, B, and C are therefore three points on the demand curve for fertilizer. Thus:

The demand curve for any input is the downward-sloping portion of its marginal revenue product curve.

Note that we restrict ourselves to the *downward-sloping* portion of the MRP curve. The logic of the marginal productivity principle dictates this. For example, if the price of fertilizer is $500 per ton, as shown in Figure 35–1, there are two input quantities for which MRP is $500: one ton (point D) and five tons (point B). But point D cannot be the optimal stopping point because the MRP of a second ton ($600) is greater than the cost of the second ton ($350). The marginal productivity principle applies only in the range where returns are diminishing.

The demand for fertilizer (or for any other input) is called a **derived demand** because it is derived from the underlying demand for the final product (corn in this case). For example, suppose that a surge in demand drove the price of corn to $4 per bushel. Then, at each level of fertilizer usage, the marginal revenue product would be twice as large as when corn fetched $2 per bushel. This is shown in Figure 35–2 as an *upward shift* of the (derived) demand curve for fertilizer, from $D_0 D_0$ to $D_1 D_1$.[2] We conclude that, in general:

An outward shift in the demand curve for any commodity causes an outward shift of the derived demand curve for all factors utilized in the production of that commodity.

Conversely, an inward shift in the demand curve for a commodity leads to inward shifts in the demand curves for factors used in producing that commodity.

This completes our discussion of the marginal productivity principle as a general explanation of the *demand* for any and all inputs. Now we will deal with the main factors of production individually and see how their earnings are determined by the interaction of demand *and* supply. We begin with *interest payments*, the return on loans of money.

The Issue of Usury Laws: Are Interest Rates Too High?

The rate of interest is the price at which funds can be rented (borrowed). And, like other factor prices, the rate of interest is determined by supply and demand. However, this is one area in which many people have been dissatisfied with the outcome of the market process. Fears that interest rates, if left unregulated, would climb to exorbitant levels have made usury laws quite popular in many times and places. Until recently in the U.S., for example, usury laws have set maximum rates on consumer loans, home mortgages, and the like.

---

[2]To make the diagram easier to read, the (irrelevant) upward-sloping portion of each curve has been omitted.

Figure 35–2

A SHIFT IN THE DEMAND CURVE FOR FERTILIZER
If the price of corn goes up, the marginal *revenue* product curve shifts upward — from $D_0 D_0$ to $D_1 D_1$ in the diagram — even though the marginal *physical* product curve has not changed. In this sense a greater demand for corn leads to a greater *derived* demand for fertilizer.

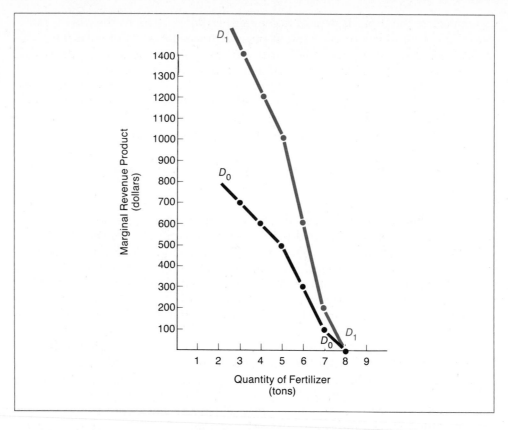

However, usury laws, when they are effective, interfere with the operation of supply and demand and are often harmful to economic efficiency.[3]

Whether a usury ceiling will or will not be effective depends on what the equilibrium rate of interest would have been in a free market. For example, a ceiling of 18 percent annual interest on consumer loans is quite irrelevant if the free-market equilibrium is 15 percent, but it can have important effects if the free-market rate is 25 percent. To see why this is so, we turn to the market determination of interest rates through the forces of supply and demand. But, first, it is necessary to define a few pertinent terms.

Investment, Capital, and Interest

There are many ways in which funds are loaned (meaning that they are rented to users): home mortgages, corporation or government bonds, consumer credit, and so on. On the demand side of these credit markets are borrowers — people or institutions that, for one reason or another, wish to spend more than they currently have.

In business, loans are used primarily to finance investment. To the business executive who "rents" (borrows) funds in order to finance an **investment** and pays interest in return, the funds really represent an intermediate step toward the acquisition of the machines, buildings, inventories, and other forms of physical **capital** that the firm will purchase.

Though the words "investment" and "capital" are often used interchangeably in everyday parlance, it is important to keep the distinction in mind. The

Investment is the *flow* of resources into the production of new capital. It is the labor, steel, and other inputs devoted to the *construction* of factories, warehouses, railroads, and other pieces of capital during some period of time.

Capital refers to an inventory (*a stock*) of plant, equipment, and other productive resources held by a business firm, an individual, or some other organization.

[3]For example, we learned in Chapter 6 that usury laws caused particularly severe problems for housing during periods of rapid inflation and hence many of them were abolished.

relation between investment and capital has an analogy in the filling of a bathtub: The accumulated water in the tub is analogous to the *stock* of capital, while the flow of water from the tap (which adds to the tub's water) is like the *flow* of investment. Just as the tap must be turned on in order for more water to accumulate, the capital stock increases only when there is investment. If investment ceases, the capital stock stops growing. Notice that when investment is *zero,* the capital stock *remains constant;* it does not fall to zero any more than a bathtub suddenly becomes empty when you shut the tap.

The process of building up capital by investing and then using this capital in production can be divided into five steps, which are listed below and summed up in Figure 35–3.

Step 1. The firm decides to enlarge its stock of capital.

Step 2. It raises the funds with which to finance its expansion.

Step 3. It uses these funds to hire the inputs, which are put to work building factories, warehouses, and the like. This step is the act of *investment.*

Step 4. After the investment is completed, the firm ends up with a larger stock of *capital.*

Step 5. The capital is used (along with other inputs) either to expand production or to reduce costs. At this point the firm starts earning *returns* on its investment.

Interest is the payment for the use of funds employed in the production of capital; it is measured as a percent per year of the value of the funds tied up in the capital.

Notice that what the investor puts into the investment process is *money,* either his own or funds that he has borrowed from others. The funds are then transformed, in a series of steps, into a physical input suitable for use in production. If the funds are borrowed, the investor will someday return them to the lender with some payment for their use. This payment is called **interest,** and it is calculated as a percentage per year of the amount borrowed. For example, if the *interest rate* is 12 percent per year and $1000 is borrowed, the annual interest payment is $120.

The marginal productivity principle governs the quantity of funds demanded just as it governs the quantity of fertilizer demanded:

Firms will demand the quantity of borrowed funds that makes the marginal revenue product of the investment financed by the funds just equal to the interest payment charged for borrowing.

There is one noteworthy feature of capital that distinguishes it from other inputs, like fertilizer, for example. The fertilizer applied by Farmer Pfister is

Figure 35–3
THE INVESTMENT PRODUCTION PROCESS
The investor (1) decides to increase the capital stock, (2) raises funds, (3) uses the funds to buy inputs that produce capital stock like machinery and factory buildings (this step is called *investment*): (4) now holds more capital than before, and (5) uses this capital and other inputs to produce goods and services.

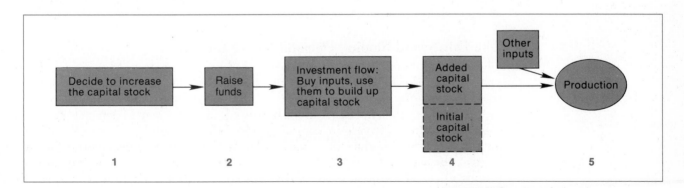

used once and then it is gone; but a blast furnace, which is part of a steel company's capital, normally lasts many years. The furnace is a *durable* good; and because it is durable it contributes not only to today's production, but also to future production. This fact makes calculating the marginal revenue product more complex for a capital good than for other inputs.

To determine whether the MRP of a capital good is greater than the cost of financing it (that is, to decide whether an investment is profitable), we need a way to compare money values received at different times. To make such comparisons, economists and business people use a calculation procedure called **discounting.** Discounting is explained in detail in the Appendix to this chapter, but it is not important that you master this technique in an introductory course. There are really only two important points to learn:

1. A sum of money received at a future date is worth less than a sum of money received today.

2. This difference in values between money today and money in the future is greater when the rate of interest is higher.

It is not difficult to understand why this is so. Consider what you could do with a dollar that you received today rather than a year from today. If the annual rate of interest were 10 percent, you could lend it out (for example, by putting it in a bank account), and receive $1.10 in a year's time — your original $1 plus 10 cents interest. For this reason, money received today is worth more than the same number of dollars received later. Specifically, at a rate of interest of 10 percent per year, $1.10 to be received a year from today is equivalent to $1 of today's money. This illustrates the first of our two points.

Now suppose the annual rate of interest was 15 percent instead. In this case $1 invested today would grow to $1.15 (rather than $1.10) in a year's time, which means that $1.15 received a year from today would be equivalent to $1 received today, and so $1.10 one year in the future must now be worth less than $1 today. This illustrates the second point.

The Market Determination of Interest Rates

Let us now return to the way in which interest rates are determined in the market. We are concerned about the level of interest rates because they play a crucial role in determining the economy's level of investment, that is, in selecting the amount of current consumption that consumers will forgo in order to use the resources to build machines and factories that can increase the output of consumers' goods in the future. For that reason, the interest rate is crucial in determining the allocation of society's resources between present and future — an issue that we discussed in Chapter 29 (pages 643–46).

The Downward-Sloping Demand Curve for Funds

The two attributes of discounting discussed on this page are all we need to explain why the quantity of funds demanded declines when the interest rate rises, that is, why the demand curve for funds has a negative slope.

Remember that the demand for borrowed funds is a *derived demand,* derived from the desire to invest in capital goods. But part, and perhaps all, of the marginal revenue product of a machine or a factory is received in the future. Hence, the value of the MRP *in terms of today's money* shrinks as the rate of interest rises. The consequence of this shrinkage is that a machine that appears to be a good investment when the rate of interest is 10 percent may look like a terrible investment when the rate of interest is 15 percent.

Here is a simple example that is easy to work out. Suppose a particular machine costs $1000 and its MRP is $1140, all of which is received one year from today. Should the machine be bought? If the rate of interest is 10 percent, $1000 in today's money is worth the same as $1100 in money a year from today. Since the machine will return $1140, the machine is worth more than its $1000 price. It is therefore a good investment. But what if the rate of interest were 15 percent instead? Then the $1000 that it takes to buy the machine would grow to $1150 after a year. Since this sum ($1150) is more than the machine will yield ($1140), it would be unwise for the firm to purchase the machine. While this example is quite contrived, the basic principle is valid:

As the rate of interest on borrowing rises, more and more investments that previously looked profitable start to look unprofitable. The demand for borrowing for investment purposes, therefore, is lower at higher rates of interest.

An example of a derived demand schedule for borrowing is given in Figure 35–4. Its negative slope illustrates the conclusion we have just stated:

The higher the interest rate, the less people and firms will want to borrow to finance their investments.

The Supply of Funds

Similar principles apply on the supply side of the market for funds—where the *lenders* are consumers, banks, and other types of business firms. Funds lent out are usually returned to the owner (with interest) only over a period of time. Loans will look better to lenders when they bear higher interest rates, so it is natural to think of the supply schedule for loans as being upward sloping—at higher rates of interest, lenders supply more funds. Such a supply schedule is

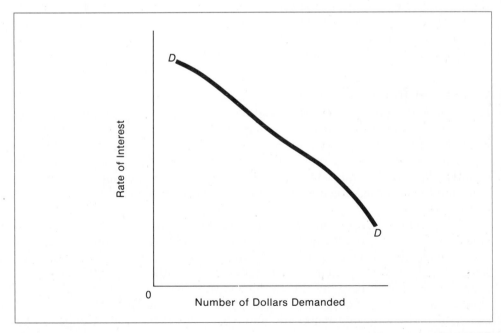

Figure 35–4
THE DERIVED DEMAND CURVE FOR LOANS
The rate of interest is the cost of a loan to the borrower. The lower the rate of interest, the more it will pay a business firm to borrow in order to finance new plant and equipment. That is why this demand curve has a negative slope.

Figure 35–5

EQUILIBRIUM IN THE MARKET FOR LOANS

Here the free-market interest rate is 12 percent. At this interest rate, the quantity of loans supplied is equal to the quantity demanded. However, if an interest-rate ceiling is imposed, say, at 8 percent, the quantity of funds supplied (point A) will be smaller than the quantity demanded (point B).

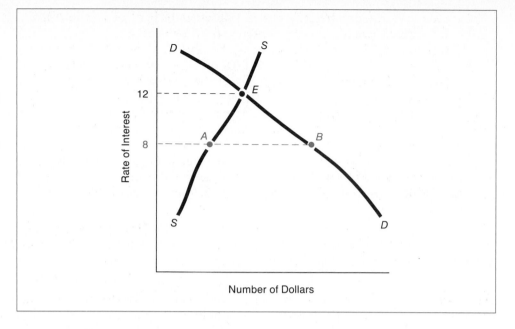

Rate of Interest

Number of Dollars

shown by the curve SS in Figure 35–5, where we also reproduce the demand curve, DD, from Figure 35–4.

It is interesting to note, incidentally, that some lenders may have supply curves that do not slope uphill to the right like curve SS. Suppose, for example, that Jones is saving to buy a $10,000 boat in three years, and that if he lends money out at interest in the interim, at current interest rates he must save $3000 a year to reach his goal. If interest rates were higher, he could save less than $3000 each year and still reach his $10,000 goal. (The higher interest payments would, of course, contribute the difference.) So his saving (and lending) might decline. But this argument applies only to savers, like Jones, with a fixed accumulation goal.

Generally, we do expect that the quantity of loans supplied will rise when the interest reward rises, so the supply curve will have a positive slope, like SS in Figure 35–5. The equilibrium rate of interest is, as always, at point E, where quantity supplied and quantity demanded are equal. We conclude that the equilibrium interest rate on loans is 12 percent.

Ceilings on Interest Rates

Let us now assume that the preceding diagram refers to the supply of loans by banks to consumers. Consider what happens if there is a usury law that prohibits interest of more than 8 percent per annum on consumer loans. At this interest rate, the quantity supplied (point A in Figure 35–5) falls short of the quantity demanded (point B). This means that many applicants for consumer loans are being turned down even though the banks consider them to be credit worthy.

Who generally gains and who loses from this usury law? The gainers are easiest to identify: those lucky consumers who are able to get loans at 8 percent even though they would have been willing to pay 12 percent. The law represents a windfall gain for them. The losers come on both the supply side and the demand side. First, there are the consumers who would have been willing and able to get credit at 12 percent but who are not lucky enough to get it at 8 percent. Then there are the banks (or, more accurately, bank stockholders) who could have made profitable loans at rates of up to 12 percent if there were no interest-rate ceiling.

This analysis helps explain the political popularity of usury laws. Few people sympathize with bank stockholders; indeed, it is the feeling that banks are "gouging" their borrowers that provides much of the impetus for usury laws. The consumers who get loans at lower rates will, naturally, be quite pleased with the result of the law. The others, who would like to borrow at 8 percent but cannot because quantity supplied is less than quantity demanded, are quite likely to blame the bank for refusing to lend, rather than blaming the government for outlawing mutually beneficial transactions.

This analysis has little good to say about usury ceilings, and economists generally oppose them. However, as is the case for minimum wage laws (see the next chapter), interest-rate ceilings can play a constructive role when there is a monopoly over credit. If there is a monopoly lender, the analysis of Chapter 27 leads us to expect him to restrict his "output" (the volume of loans) by raising his "price" (the interest rate). Under such circumstances, an interest rate ceiling may conceivably make sense.[4] But *may* is not *will*. Most economists believe that, except for isolated instances, the credit market is far closer to the competitive model than it is to the monopoly model, so that usury ceilings will harm the general public even if they contribute to the popularity of the politicians who enact them.

The Determination of Rent: Simple Version

In analyzing interest, the special feature is that both the demand curve and the supply curve depend on the evaluation of flows of money received at different dates. In contrast, in the market for land — the second main factor of production — the special feature occurs on the supply side: land is one factor of production whose quantity supplied is (roughly) the same at every possible price. Indeed, the classical economists used this notion as the working definition of land. And the definition seems to fit, at least approximately. Although people may accumulate landfill, clear land, drain its swamps, fertilize it, build on it, or convert it from one use (a farm) to another (a housing development), it is difficult to change the total supply of land very much by human effort.

What does that fact tell us about the determination of land rents? Figure 35–6 helps to provide an answer. The vertical supply curve SS represents the fact that no matter what the level of rents there are still 1000 acres of land in a small hamlet called Littletown. The demand curve DD is a typical marginal revenue product curve, predicated on the notion that the use of land, like everything else, is subject to diminishing returns. The free-market price is determined, as usual, by the intersection of the supply and demand curves. In this example, each acre of land in Littletown rents for $2000 per year. The interesting feature of this diagram is that, because quantity supplied is rigidly fixed at 1000 acres whatever the price:

The market level of rent is entirely determined by the demand side of the market.

If, for example, the relocation of a major university in Littletown attracts more people who want to live there, the DD curve will shift outward, as depicted in

[4]As we will see in the appendix to the next chapter, in such a case a usury ceiling might actually increase the volume of loans.

Figure 35–6

DETERMINATION OF
LAND RENT IN
LITTLETOWN

The supply curve of land, *SS*, is vertical, meaning that 1000 acres are available in Littletown regardless of the level of rent. The demand curve for land slopes downward for the usual reasons. Equilibrium is established at point *E*, where the annual rental rate is $2000 per acre.

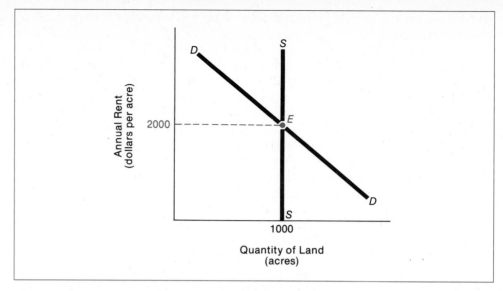

Figure 35–7. Equilibrium in the market will shift from point *E* to point *A*; there will still be only 1000 acres of land, but now each acre will command a rent of $2500 per acre. The landlords will collect more rent, though they themselves have done nothing productive.

The same process also works in reverse, however. Should the university shut its doors and the demand for land decline as a result, the landlords will suffer even though they in no way have contributed to the decline in the demand for land. (To see this, simply reverse the logic of Figure 35–7. The demand curve begins at $D_1 D_1$ and shifts to $D_0 D_0$.)

The Rent of Land: Some Complications

If every parcel of land were of identical quality, this would be all there is to the theory of land rent. But, of course, plots of land do differ—in quality of soil, in topography, in access to sun and water, in proximity to marketplaces, and in other ways. The classical economists realized this, of course, and took it into

Figure 35–7
A SHIFT IN DEMAND
WITH A VERTICAL
SUPPLY CURVE

Now imagine that something happens to increase the demand for land—that is, to shift the demand curve from $D_0 D_0$ to $D_1 D_1$. Quantity supplied cannot change, but the rental rate can, and does. In this example, the annual rental for an acre of land increases from $2000 to $2500. Land that is just on the borderline of being used is called *marginal land*.

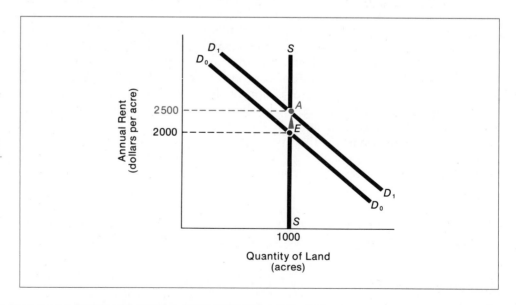

account in their analysis of rent determination — a remarkable piece of economic logic formulated late in the eighteenth century and still considered valid today.

The basic notion is that capital invested on any piece of land must yield the same return as capital invested on any other piece that is actually used. Why? If it were not so, capitalists would bid against one another for the more profitable pieces of land until the rents of these parcels were driven up to a point where their advantages over other parcels had been eliminated.

Suppose that on one piece of land a given crop is produced for $160,000 per year in labor, fertilizer, fuel, and other nonland costs, while the same crop is produced for $120,000 on a second piece of land. The rent on the second parcel must be *exactly* $40,000 per year higher than the rent on the first, because otherwise production on one plot would be cheaper than on the other. If, for example, the rent difference were only $30,000 per year, it would be $10,000 cheaper to produce on the second plot of land. No one would want to rent the first plot and every grower would instead bid for the second plot. Obviously, rent on the first plot would be forced down by a lack of customers, and rent on the second would be driven up by eager bidders. These pressures would come to an end only when the rent difference reached $40,000, so that both plots became equally profitable.

At any given time, there are some pieces of land of such low quality that it does not pay to use them at all — remote deserts are a prime example. Any land that is exactly on the borderline of being used is called **marginal land.** By this definition, marginal land earns no rent because if any rent were charged for it, there would be no takers.

Land that is just on the borderline of being used is called **marginal land.**

We now combine these two observations — that the difference between the costs of producing on any two pieces of land must equal the difference between their rents, and that zero rent is charged on marginal land — to conclude that:

Rent on any piece of land will equal the difference between the cost of producing the output on that land and the cost of producing it on marginal land.

That is, competition for the superior plots of land will permit the landlords to charge prices that capture the full advantages of their superior parcels.

A useful feature of this analysis is that it helps us to understand more completely the effects of an outward shift in the demand curve for land. Suppose there is an increase in the demand for land because of a rise in population. Naturally, rents will rise. But we can be more specific than this. In response to an outward shift in the demand curve, two things will happen:

1. *It will now pay to employ some land whose use was formerly unprofitable.* The land that was previously on the zero-rent margin will no longer be on the borderline, and some land that is so poor that it was formerly not even worth considering will now just reach the borderline of profitability. The settling of the American West illustrates this process quite forcefully. Land that once could not be given away is now quite valuable.

2. *People will begin more intensive use of the land that was already in use.* Farmers will use more labor and fertilizer to squeeze larger crops out of their acreage, as has happened in recent decades. Urban real estate on which two-story buildings previously made most sense will now be used for high-rise buildings.

Rents will be increased in a predictable way by those two developments. Since the land that is marginal *after* the change must be inferior to the land that was marginal previously, rents must rise by the difference in yields between the old and new marginal lands. Table 35–2 illustrates this point. We deal with three pieces of land: A, a very productive piece; B, a piece that was initially marginal; and C, a piece that is inferior to B but nevertheless becomes marginal when the upward shift in the demand curve for land occurs.

The crop costs $80,000 more when produced on B than on A, and $12,000 more when produced on C than on B. Suppose, initially, that demand for the crop is so low that C is unused and B is just on the margin between being used and left idle. Since B is marginal, it will yield no rent. We know that the rent on A will be equal to the $80,000 cost advantage of A over B. Now suppose demand for the crop increases enough so that plot C is just brought into use. Plot C is now marginal land, and B acquires a rent of $12,000, the cost advantage of B over C. Plot A's rent now must rise from $80,000 to $92,000, the size of its cost advantage over C, the new marginal land.

But there is a second factor pushing up land rents — the increased intensity of use of land that was already in cultivation. As farmers apply more fertilizer and labor to their land, the marginal productivity of land increases just as factory workers become more productive when they are given better equipment. Once again, the landowner is able to capture this increase in productivity in the form of higher rents. (If you do not understand why, refer back to Figure 35–7 and remember that the demand curves are marginal revenue product curves.) Thus, we can summarize the classical theory of rent as follows: As the use of land increases, landlords receive higher payments from two sources:

1. Increased demand leads the community to employ land previously not good enough to use; the advantage of previously used land over the new marginal land increases, and rents go up correspondingly.

2. Land is used more intensively; the marginal revenue product of land rises, thus increasing the ability of the producer who uses the land to pay rent.

As late as the end of the nineteenth century, this analysis still exerted a powerful influence beyond technical economic writings. An American journalist, Henry George, was nearly elected mayor of New York in 1886, running on the platform that all government should be financed by "a single tax"—a tax

Table 35–2
NONRENT COSTS AND RENT ON THREE PIECES OF LAND

TYPE OF LAND	NONLAND COST OF PRODUCING A GIVEN CROP	TOTAL RENT	
		Before	After
A. A tract that was better than marginal before and after	$120,000	$80,000	$92,000
B. A tract that was marginal before but is not anymore	200,000	0	12,000
C. A tract that was previously not worth using but is now marginal	212,000	0	0

on landlords who, he said, are the only ones who earn incomes while contributing nothing to the productive process and who reap the fruits of economic growth without contributing to economic progress.

Generalization:
What Determines Lee Iacocca's Salary?

Land is not the only scarce input whose supply is fixed, at least in the short run. Toward the beginning of this century some economists realized that the economic analysis of rent can be applied to inputs other than land. As we will see, this extension yielded some noteworthy insights.

Consider as an example the earnings of Lee Iacocca, Chairman of the Board of Chrysler Corporation. Such business executives seem to have little in common with plots of land in downtown Chicago. Yet, to an economist, the same analysis—the theory of rent—explains the incomes of these two factors of production. To understand why, we first note that there is only one Lee Iacocca (or so he would like his stockholders to believe). That is, he is a scarce input whose supply is fixed just like the supply of land. Because he is in fixed supply, the price of his services must be determined in a way that is similar to the determination of land rents. Hence, economists have arrived at a more general definition of **economic rent** as *any payment made to a factor above the amount necessary to keep that factor in its present employment*.

To understand the concept of economic rent, it is useful to divide the payment for any input into two parts. The first part is simply the minimum payment needed to acquire the input: the cost of producing a ball bearing or the compensation for the unpleasantness, hard work, and loss of leisure involved in performing labor. The second part of the payment is a bonus that does not go to every input, but only to those that are of particularly high quality. Payments to workers with exceptional natural skills are a good example. These bonuses are like the extra payment for a better piece of land, and so are called *economic rents*.

Notice that only the first part of the factor payment is essential to induce the owner to supply the input. If a worker is not paid at least this first part, he will not supply his labor. But the additional payment—the economic rent—is pure gravy. The skillful worker is happy to have it as an extra. But it is not a deciding consideration in the choice of whether or not to work.

A moment's thought shows how this general notion of rent applies both to land and to Lee Iacocca. The total quantity of land available for use is the same whether rent is high, low, or zero; no payments to landlords are necessary to induce land to be supplied to the market. So, by definition, the payments to landholders for their land are entirely economic rent—payments that are not necessary to induce the provision of the land to the economy. Lee Iacocca is (almost) similar to land in this respect. He has executive talents that are somewhat unique and cannot be reproduced. What determines the income of such a factor? Since the quantity supplied of such a unique, nonreproducible factor is absolutely fixed, and therefore unresponsive to price, the analysis of rent determination summarized in Figure 35–6 applies. *The position of the demand curve determines the price*.

Figure 35–8 summarizes the "Lee Iacocca market." Vertical supply curve *SS* represents the fact that no matter what wage he is paid there is only one Lee Iacocca. Demand curve *DD* is a marginal productivity curve of sorts, but not quite the kind we encountered earlier in the chapter. Since the question,

Economic rent is said to be earned whenever a factor of production receives a reward that exceeds the minimum amount necessary to keep the factor in its present employment.

Figure 35–8
HYPOTHETICAL MARKET FOR LEE IACOCCA'S SERVICES
At an annual wage of $35 million or more, no one is willing to bid for his time. At a somewhat lower wage, $20 million, two thirds of his time will be demanded (point G). Only at an annual wage no higher than $12 million will all of Iacocca's available time be demanded (point E).

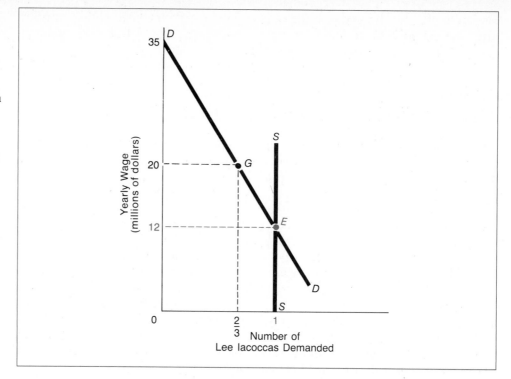

"What would be the value of a second unit of Lee Iacocca?" is nonsensical, the demand curve is constructed by considering only the *portion* of his time demanded at various wage levels. The curve indicates that at an annual salary of $35 million, no employer can afford even a little bit of Lee Iacocca. At a lower salary of, say, $20 million per year, however, there are enough profitable uses to absorb two-thirds of his time. At $12 million per year, Iacocca's full time is demanded; and at lower wage rates, the demand for Iacocca's time exceeds the amount of it that is for sale.[5]

Equilibrium is at point E in the diagram, where the supply of and demand for his time are equal. His annual salary here is $12 million. Now we can ask: How much of Lee Iacocca's salary is economic rent? According to the economic definition of rent, his entire $12 million salary is rent. Since, according to the vertical supply schedule, Iacocca's financial reward is unnecessary to get him to supply his services, every penny he earns is rent.

This is why we said that top executives like Iacocca are *almost* good examples of pure rent. For, in fact, if his salary were low enough, Iacocca might well prefer to stay home rather than work. Suppose, for example, that $50,000 per year is the lowest salary at which Iacocca will offer even one minute of his services, and that his labor supply then increases with his wage up to an annual salary of $300,000, at which point he is willing to work full time. Then, while his equilibrium salary will still be $12 million per year, not all of it will be rent, because some of it, at least $50,000, is required to get him to supply any services at all.

This same analysis applies to any factor of production whose supply curve is not horizontal, as in Figure 35–9. There we see that at any price above $5

---

[5]These numbers are not entirely hypothetical. The press reports that over the past three years Mr. Iacocca earned $37.5 million.

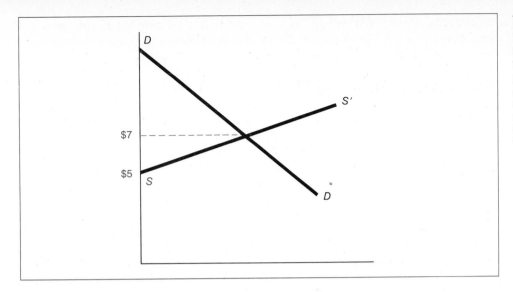

Figure 35–9
RENT WHEN THE
SUPPLY CURVE IS NOT
VERTICAL
Some of the input would be
supplied (point *S*) at a price
of $5 (or a bit more), but the
equilibrium price is $7 so
some units of input must be
earning a rent of $2.

suppliers are willing to provide some units of the input; that is, at any price above point S quantity supplied is greater than zero. Yet the supply–demand equilibrium point yields a price of $7—well above the minimum price at which some input supply would be forthcoming. The difference must constitute a rent to the input suppliers, who get paid more than the minimum amount required to induce them to work.

Almost all employees earn some rent. What sorts of factors earn no rent? Those that can be exactly reproduced by a number of producers at constant cost. No supplier of ball bearings will ever receive any rent on a ball bearing, at least in the long run, because any desired number of them can be produced at (roughly) constant costs—say 50 cents each. If one supplier tried to charge a price above 50 cents, someone else would undercut him and take his customers away. Hence the competitive price will include no rent.

Rent Controls: The Misplaced Analogy

Why is the analysis of economic rent important? Because only economic rent can be taxed away without reducing the quantity of the input supplied. And here common English gets in the way of sound reasoning. Many people feel that the *rent* that they pay to their landlord is economic rent. After all, their apartments will still be there if they pay $500 per month, or $300, or $100. This view, while true in the short run, is quite myopic.

Like the ball-bearing producer, the owner of a building cannot expect to earn *economic* rent because there are too many other potential owners whose costs of construction are roughly the same as his own. If he tried to charge a price that included some economic rent—that is, a price that exceeded his production costs plus the opportunity cost of his capital—other builders would undercut him. Thus, far from being in perfectly *inelastic* (vertical) supply, like raw land, buildings come rather close to being in perfectly *elastic* (horizontal) supply, like ball bearings. As we have learned from the theory of rent, this means that builders and owners of buildings cannot collect economic rent in the long run.

Since apartment owners collect very little economic rent, the payments that tenants make in a free market must be just enough to keep those apartments on the market. (This is the definition of zero economic rent.) If rent controls push these prices down, the apartments will start disappearing from the market.[6]

Issue: Are Profits Too High or Too Low?

This completes our analysis of rent. We turn next to business profits, a subject whose discussion seems to elicit more passion than logic. With the exception of some economists, almost no one thinks that the rate of profit is at about the right level. Critics on the left point accusingly at the billion-dollar profits of some giant corporations and argue that they are unconscionably high. They call for much stiffer profits taxes. On the other hand, the Chambers of Commerce, National Association of Manufacturers, and other business groups complain that regulations and "ruinous" competition keep profits too low, and they are constantly petitioning Congress for tax relief.

The public has many misconceptions about the nature of the U.S. economy, but probably none is more severe than the popular view of the amount of profit that American corporations earn. We suggest to you the following experiment. Ask five of your friends who have never had an economics course what fraction of the nation's income they imagine is accounted for by profits. While the correct answer varies from year to year, in 1986 about 17 percent of GNP (before-tax) was business profits. A comparable percent of the prices you pay represents before-tax profit. Most people think this figure is much, much higher. (See the boxed insert at top of page 787).

As you have no doubt noticed by now, economists are reluctant to brand factor prices as "too low" or "too high" in some moral or ethical sense. Rather, they are likely to ask, first, What is the market equilibrium price? And then they will ask whether there are any good reasons to interfere with the market solution. This analysis, however, is not so easy to apply to the case of profits, since it is hard to use supply and demand analysis when you do not know what factor of production earns profit.

In both a bookkeeping and an economic sense, *profits are the residual*. They are what remains from the selling price after all other factors have been paid.

But what factor of production receives this reward? What factor's marginal productivity constitutes the profit rate?

What Accounts for Profits?

Economic profit, it will be recalled from Chapter 25, is the amount a firm earns *over and above* the payments for all other inputs, including the interest payments for the capital it uses and the opportunity cost of any capital provided by the owners of the firm. The profit rate and the interest rate are closely related. In an imaginary (and uninteresting) world in which everything was certain and unchanging, capitalists who invested money in firms would simply earn the market rate of interest on their funds. Profits beyond this level would be competed away. Profits below this level could not persist, because capitalists

---

[6]None of this is meant to imply that temporary rent controls in certain locations cannot have salutary effects in the short run. In the short run, the supply of apartments and houses really is fixed, and large shifts in demand would hand windfall gains to landlord — gains that are true economic rents. Controls that eliminate such windfalls should not cause serious problems. But knowing when the "short run" fades into the "long run" can be a tricky matter. "Temporary" rent control laws have a way of becoming rather permanent.

Public Opinion on Profits

Most Americans think corporate profits are much higher than they actually are. A recent public opinion poll, for example, found that the average citizen thought that corporate profits *after tax* amounted to 32 percent of sales for the typical manufacturing company. The actual profit rate at the time was only 3.8 percent! Interestingly, when a previous poll asked how much profit was "reasonable," the response was 26 cents on every dollar of sales — over six times as large as profits actually were.

SOURCE: "Public Attitudes Toward Corporate Profits," Opinion Research Corporation, *Public Opinion Index*, Princeton, N.J., June 1986.

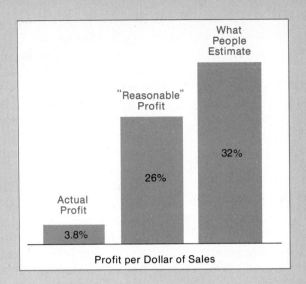

Profit per Dollar of Sales

would withdraw their funds from the firms and deposit them in banks. Capitalists in such a world would be mere moneylenders.

But the real world is not at all like this. Some capitalists are much more than moneylenders, and the amounts they earn often exceed the interest rate by a considerable margin. These activist capitalists who seek out or even create earnings opportunities are called **entrepreneurs.** They are the ones who are responsible for the constant change that characterizes business firms and who prevent the operations of the firms from stagnating. Since they are always trying to do something new, it is difficult to provide a general description of their activities. However, we can list three primary ways in which entrepreneurs are able to drive profits above the level of interest rates.

Exercise of Monopoly Power

If the entrepreneur can establish a monopoly over some or all of his products, even for a short while, he can use the monopoly power of his firm to earn monopoly profits. The nature of these monopoly earnings was analyzed in Chapter 27.

Risk Bearing

The entrepreneur may engage in risky activities. For example, when a firm prospects for oil it will drill an exploratory shaft hoping to find a pool of petroleum at the bottom. But a high proportion of such attempts produce only dry holes, and the cost of the operation is wasted. Of course, if the investor is lucky and does find oil, he may be rewarded handsomely. The income he obtains is a payment for bearing risk.

Obviously, a few lucky individuals make out well in this process, while most suffer heavy losses. How well can we expect risk takers to do on the average? If, on the average, one exploratory drilling out of ten pays off, do we expect its return to be exactly ten times as high as the interest rate, so that the *average* firm will earn exactly the normal rate of interest? The answer is that the payoff will be *more* than ten times the interest rate if investors dislike gambling; that is, if they prefer to avoid risk. Why? Because investors who dislike risk will be unwilling to put their money into a business in which nine firms out of ten lose out unless there is some compensation for the financial peril to which they expose themselves.

In reality, however, there is no certainty that things always work out this way. Some people love to gamble, and these people tend to be overoptimistic about their chances of coming out ahead. They may plunge into projects to a degree unjustified by the odds. If there are enough such gamblers, the average payoff to risky undertakings may end up below the interest rate. The successful investor will still make a good profit, just like the lucky winner in Las Vegas. But the average participant will have to pay for the privilege of bearing risk.

Returns to Innovation

The third major source of profits is perhaps the most important of all from the point of view of social welfare. The entrepreneur who is first to market a desirable new product, or to employ a new cost-saving machine, or to innovate in some other way will receive a special profit as his reward. **Innovation** is different from **invention.** Invention is the act of generating a new idea; innovation is the next step, the act of putting the new idea into practical use. Business people are rarely inventors, but they are often innovators.

Invention is the act of generating a new idea. **Innovation,** the next step, is the act of putting the new idea into practical use.

When an entrepreneur innovates, even if his new product or his new process is not protected by patents, he will be one step ahead of his competitors. He will be able to capture much of the market either by offering customers a better product or by supplying the product more cheaply. In either case he will temporarily find himself with some monopoly power left by the weakening of his competitors, and monopoly profit will be the reward for his initiative.

However, this monopoly profit, the reward for innovation, will only be temporary. As soon as the success of the idea has demonstrated itself to the world, other firms will find ways of imitating it. Even if they cannot turn out precisely the same product or use precisely the same process, they will have to find ways to supply close substitutes if they are to survive. In this way, new ideas are spread through the economy. And in the process the special profits of the innovator are brought to an end. The innovator can only resume earning special profits by finding still another promising idea.

Entrepreneurs are forced to keep searching for new ideas, to keep instituting innovations, and to keep imitating those that they have not been the first to put into operation. This process is at the heart of the growth of the capitalist system. It is one of the secrets of its extraordinary dynamism.

The Issue of Profits Taxation

So profits in excess of the market rate of interest can be considered as the return on entrepreneurial talent. But this is not really very helpful, since no one can say exactly what entrepreneurial talent is. Certainly we cannot measure it; nor can we teach it in a college course (though business schools try!). Therefore, we do not know how the observed profit rate relates to the minimum reward necessary to attract entrepreneurial talent into the market—a relationship which is crucial for the contentious issue of profits taxation.

Consider the windfall profits tax on oil companies as an example. If oil company profit rates are well above this minimum, they contain a large element of economic rent. In that case, we could tax away these excess profits (rents) without fear of reducing oil production. On the other hand, if the profits being earned by oil companies do not contain much economic rent, then the windfall profits tax might seriously curtail exploration and production of oil.

This example illustrates the general problem of deciding how heavily profits should be taxed. Critics of big business who call for high, if not confiscatory, profits taxes believe that profits are mostly economic rent. But if they are wrong, if most of the observed profits are necessary to attract people into entrepreneurial roles, then a high profits tax can be dangerous. It can threaten the very lifeblood of the capitalist system. Business lobbying groups predictably claim that this is the case. Unfortunately, neither group has offered much evidence for its conclusion.

Criticisms of Marginal Productivity Theory

The theory of factor pricing described in this chapter is another example of supply–demand analysis. Its special feature is its heavy reliance on the principle of marginal productivity to derive the shape and position of the demand curve. For this reason, the analysis is often rather misleadingly called *the marginal productivity theory of distribution*.

Over the years this analysis has been subject to attack on many grounds. One frequent accusation, which is largely (but not entirely) groundless, is the assertion that marginal productivity theory is merely an attempt to justify the distribution of income which the capitalist system yields—that it is a piece of pro-capitalist propaganda. According to this argument, when marginal productivity theory claims that each factor is paid exactly its marginal revenue product, this is only a sneaky way of asserting that each factor is paid exactly what it deserves. These critics claim that the theory legitimizes the gross inequities of the systems—the poverty of many and the great wealth of the few.

The argument is straightforward but wrong. Payments are made not to *factors of production* but to the people who happen to own them. If an acre of land earns $2000 because that is its marginal revenue product, this does not mean the payment is *deserved* by the landlord, who may even have acquired it by fraud.

Second, an input's marginal revenue product (MRP) does not depend only on "how hard it works" but also on how much of it happens to be employed—for, according to the "law" of diminishing returns, the more that is employed the lower its MRP. Thus, that factor's MRP is not and cannot legitimately be interpreted as a measure of the intensity of its "productive effort." In any event, what an input deserves may be taken to depend on more than what it does in the factory. A worker may be held to deserve funds because he is sick, because he has many children, and for many reasons other than his productivity.

On these and other grounds, no economist today claims that marginal productivity analysis shows that distribution under capitalism is either just or unjust. It is simply wrong to claim that marginal productivity theory is pro-capitalist propaganda.[7] The marginal productivity principle is just as relevant to organizing production in a socialist society as it is in a capitalist one.

Others have attacked marginal productivity theory for using rather complicated reasoning to tell us very little about the really urgent problems of income distribution. In this view, it is all very well to say that everything depends on supply and demand and to express this in terms of many complicated equations (as is done in more advanced books and articles). But these equations do not tell us what to do about such serious distribution problems as malnutrition among Indians in Latin America or poverty among minority groups in the United States.

[6]For more on this criticism of marginal productivity theory, see Chapter 41, especially pages 920–22.

Though it does exaggerate somewhat, there is certainly truth to this criticism. We have seen in this chapter that the theory does provide some insights on real policy matters, though not as many as we would like. In Chapters 37 and 38 we will see that economists do have things to say about the problems of poverty and underdevelopment. But much of this does not flow from marginal productivity analysis.

Perhaps, in the end, what should be said for marginal productivity theory is that it is the best model we have at the moment, that it offers us *some* valuable insights into the way the economy works, and that until a more powerful model is found we are better off hanging on to what we have.

Summary

1. A profit-maximizing firm purchases the quantity of any input at which the price of the input equals its marginal revenue product.
2. Interest rates are determined by the supply of and demand for funds. The demand for funds is a derived demand, since these funds are used to finance business investment. Thus the demand for funds depends on the marginal productivity of capital.
3. A dollar obtainable sooner is worth more than a dollar obtainable later because of the interest that can be earned in the interim.
4. Increased demand for a good that needs land to produce it will drive up the prices of land either because inferior land will be brought into use or because land will be used more intensively.
5. Rent controls do not significantly affect the supply of land, but they do tend to reduce the supply of buildings.
6. Economic rent is any payment to the supplier of a factor of production that is greater than the minimum amount needed to induce the desired quantity of the factor to be supplied.
7. Factors of production that are unique in quality and difficult or impossible to reproduce will tend to be paid relatively high economic rents because of their scarcity.
8. Factors of production that are easy to produce at a constant cost and that are provided by many suppliers will earn little or no economic rent.
9. Economic profits over and above the cost of capital are earned (a) by exercise of monopoly power, (b) as a payment for bearing risk, and (c) as the earnings of successful innovation.
10. The desirability of increased taxation of profits depends on its effects on the supply of entrepreneurial talent. If most profits are economic rents, then higher profits taxes will have few detrimental effects. But if most profits are necessary to attract entrepreneurs into the market, then higher profits taxes can threaten the capitalist system.

Concepts for Review

Factors of production	Usury law	Marginal land
Entrepreneurship	Investment	Economic rent
Marginal productivity principle	Capital	Entrepreneurs
Marginal physical product	Interest	Risk bearing
Marginal revenue product	Discounting	Invention versus innovation
Derived demand		

Questions for Discussion

1. A profit-maximizing firm expands its purchase of any input up to the point where diminishing returns has reduced the marginal revenue product so that it equals the input price. Why does it not pay the firm to "quit while it is ahead," buying so small a quantity of the input that diminishing returns do not set in?

2. Which of the following inputs do you think include a relatively large economic rent in their earnings?
   a. Nails.
   b. Coal.
   c. A champion racehorse.
   Use supply–demand analysis to explain your answer.

3. Three machines are employed in an isolated area. They each produce 1000 units of output per month, the first requiring $17,000 in raw materials, the second $21,000, and the third $23,000. What would you expect to be the monthly charge for the first and second machines if the services of the third machine can be hired at a price of $9000 a month? What parts of the charges for the first two machines are economic rent?

4. Economists conclude that a tax on the profits of firms will be shifted in part to consumers of the products of those firms, in the form of higher product prices. However, they believe that a tax on the rent of land usually cannot be shifted. What explains the difference?

5. Many economists argue that a tax on apartment houses is likely to reduce the supply of apartments but that a tax on all land, including the land on which apartment houses stand, will not reduce the supply of apartments. Can you explain the difference? What is the relation of this answer to the answer to Question 4?

6. Distinguish between investment and capital.

7. If you have a contract under which you will be paid $10,000 two years from now, why do you become richer if the rate of interest falls?

8. What is the difference between interest and profit? Who earns interest, in return for what contribution to production? Who earns economic profit, in return for what contribution to production?

9. Do you know any entrepreneurs? How do they earn a living? How do they differ from managers?

10. Explain the difference between an invention and an innovation. Give an example of each.

11. "Marginal productivity does not determine how much a worker will earn—it only determines how many workers will be hired at a given wage. Therefore, marginal productivity analysis is a theory of demand for labor, not a theory of distribution." What, then, do you think determines wages? Does marginal productivity affect their level? If so, how?

12. Comment on the Johnny Carson quotation at the beginning of the chapter in terms of the concept of economic rent.

Appendix
Discounting and Present Value*

Frequently, in business and economic problems, it is necessary to compare sums of money received (or paid) at different dates. Consider, for example, the purchase of a machine that costs $11,000 and will yield a marginal revenue product of $14,520 two years from today. If the machine can be financed by a two-year loan bearing 10 percent interest, it will cost the firm $1100 in interest at the end of each year, plus $11,000 in principal repayment at the end of the second year (see the table below). Is the machine a good investment?

COSTS AND BENEFITS OF INVESTING IN A MACHINE

	End of Year 1	End of Year 2
Benefits		
Marginal revenue product of the machine	0	$14,520
Costs		
Interest	$1100	1100
Repayment of principal on loan	0	11,000
Total	1100	12,100

*The authors are grateful to Professor J. S. Hanson of Willamette University for correcting an error in an earlier edition.

The total costs of owning the machine over the two-year period ($1100 + $12,100 = 13,200) are less than the total benefits ($14,520). But this is clearly an invalid comparison, because the $14,520 in future benefits are not worth $14,520 in terms of today's money. Adding up dollars received (or paid) at different dates is a bit like adding apples and oranges. The process that has been invented for making these magnitudes comparable is called **discounting,** or **computing the present value** of a future sum of money.

To illustrate the concept of present value, let us ask how much $1 received a year from today is worth *in terms of today's money.* If the rate of interest is 10 percent, the answer is about 91 cents. Why? Because if we invest 91 cents today at 10 percent interest, it will grow to 91 cents plus 9.1 cents in interest = 100.1 cents in a year. Similar considerations apply to any rate of interest. In general:

If the rate of interest is i, the present value of $1 to be received in a year is: $\dfrac{\$1}{(1 + i)}$.

This is so, because in a year $\frac{\$1}{(1 + i)}$ will grow to $\frac{\$1}{(1 + i)}(1 + i) = \$1$.

What about money to be received two years from today? Using the same reasoning, $1 invested today will grow to $\$1 \times (1.1) = \$1.10$ after one year and to $\$1 \times (1.1) \times (1.1) = \$1 \times (1.1)^2 = \$1.21$ after two years. Consequently, the present value of $1 to be received two years from today is:

$$\frac{\$1}{(1.1)^2} = \frac{\$1}{1.21} = 82.64 \text{ cents}.$$

A similar analysis applies to money received three years from today, four years from today, and so on.

The general formula for the present value of $1 to be received N years from today when the rate of interest is i is: $\frac{\$1}{(1 + i)^N}$.

The present value formula highlights the two variables that determine the present value of any future flow of money: the rate of interest (i) and how long you have to wait before you get it (N).

Let us now apply this analysis to our example. The present value of the revenue is easy to calculate since it all comes two years from today.

Since the rate of interest is assumed to be 10 percent ($i = 0.1$) we have:

$$\text{Present value of revenues} = \frac{\$14,520}{(1.1)^2}$$

$$= \frac{\$14,520}{1.21}$$

$$= \$12,000.$$

The present value of the costs is a bit trickier in this example since costs occur at two different dates.

The present value of the first interest payment is $\$1100/(1 + i) = \$1100/1.1 = \$1000$. And the present value of the final payment of interest plus principal is:

$$\frac{\$12,100}{(1 + i)^2} = \frac{\$12,100}{(1.1)^2} = \frac{\$12,100}{1.21} = \$10,000.$$

Now that we have expressed each sum in terms of its present value, it is permissible to add them up. So the present value of all costs is:

Present value of costs
$$= \$1000 + \$10,000 = \$11,000.$$

Comparison of this to the $12,000 present value of the revenues clearly shows that the machine is really a good investment. This same calculation procedure is applicable to all investment decisions.

Summary

To determine whether a loss or a gain will result from a decision whose costs and returns will come at several different periods of time, the figures represented by these gains and losses must all be discounted to obtain their present value. For this, one uses the present value formula for X dollars receivable N years from now:

$$\text{Present value} = \frac{X}{(1 + i)^N}.$$

One then adds together the present values of all the returns and all the costs. If the sum of the present values of the returns is greater than the sum of the present values of the costs, then the decision to invest will promise a net gain.

Concepts for Review

Discounting
Present value

Questions for Discussion

1. Compute the present value of $1000 to be received in four years if the rate of interest is 15 percent.
2. A government bond pays $100 in interest each year for three years and also returns the principal of $1000 in the third year. How much is it worth in terms of today's money if the rate of interest is 10 percent? If the rate of interest is 15 percent?

36

Masters are always and every
where in a sort of tacit, but
constant and uniform
combination, not to raise
the wages of labour...

ADAM SMITH

Labor: The Crucial Input

Labor is by far the most important factor of production. As noted in the previous chapter, the earnings of labor amount to about 75 percent of national income. Wages and employment are important because they represent the primary source of income to the vast majority of Americans and because they are related to a variety of important social and political issues.

The chapter is divided into two main parts. In the first part we deal with the determination of wages and employment in *competitive labor markets;* that is, labor markets in which there are many buyers and many sellers, none of whom is large enough to have any appreciable influence on wages. We consider why some types of workers are paid far more than others and explore a number of important issues, including the effects of education on wages and of minimum wage legislation.

In the second part of the chapter we consider labor markets that are monopolized on the selling side by trade unions. First, the development of the labor movement in America is summarized. Then we consider alternative goals for a union and how these goals might be pursued. Finally, we turn to situations in which a single seller of labor (a union) confronts a single buyer of labor (a monopsony firm), and examine some of the analytical and practical difficulties that arise under collective bargaining.

Issue: The Minimum Wage and Unemployment

Unemployment among teen-agers is always higher than it is in the labor force as a whole, and among black teen-agers it is significantly higher still. Figure 36–1 shows the record. It indicates that whenever unemployment rates went down in the economy as a whole, they almost always decreased for both black and white teen-agers. However, young workers, and especially young black workers, have always suffered more from unemployment than the average worker. When things are generally bad, things are much, much worse for them. Despite social and legislative pressures against race discrimination, efforts to improve the quality of education available to children in the ghettos, and many

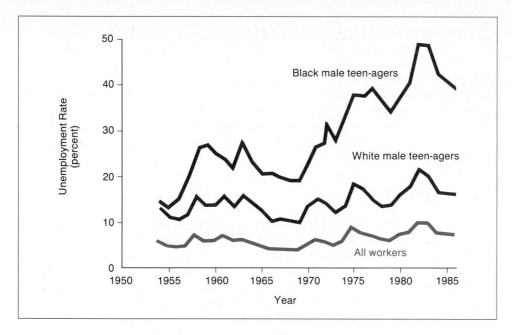

Figure 36–1
THE TEEN-AGE
UNEMPLOYMENT
PROBLEM
Teen-age unemployment
rates have consistently been
much higher than the overall
unemployment rate, and
black teen-agers have fared
worse than white teen-agers.
For the most part the three
employment rates have
moved up and down
together, as can be seen in
this chart.
SOURCE: U.S. Department of
Labor, Bureau of Labor Statistics.

related programs, there has been no improvement in black teen-age unemployment in recent years.

Many economists feel less surprised than other concerned persons about the intractability of the problem. They maintain that despite all the legislation that has been adopted to improve the position of black people, there is a law on the books, which, though apparently designed to protect low-skilled workers, is actually an impediment to any attempt to improve job opportunities for blacks. As long as this law remains effective, the young, the inexperienced, and those with educational disadvantages will continue to find themselves handicapped on the job market, and attempts to eliminate their more serious unemployment problems will stand little chance of success.

What is the law? None other than the **minimum wage law.** Later in this chapter we will explain the grounds on which many observers believe that this law has such pernicious — and presumably unintended — effects.

Competitive Labor Markets

The minimum wage law interferes with the operation of a free labor market. But to understand how, we must first understand how the labor market would operate in its absence. We approach this in three steps. First we consider the determinants of the supply of labor, then the determinants of demand, and finally the market equilibrium, in which both wages and employment levels are established.

The Supply of Labor

The economic analysis of labor supply is based on the following simple observation: Given the fixed amount of time in a week, a person's decision to *supply labor* to firms is simultaneously a decision to *demand leisure* time for oneself. Assuming that after necessary time for eating and sleeping is deducted a worker has 90 usable hours in a week, a decision to spend 40 of those hours working is simultaneously a decision to demand 50 of them for other purposes.

This suggests that we can analyze the *supply* of this particular input—labor—with the same tools we used in Chapter 21 to analyze the *demand* for commodities. In this case, the commodity is leisure. A consumer "buys" her own leisure time, just as she buys bananas, or back scratchers, or pizzas. In Chapter 21 we observed that any price change has two distinct effects on quantity demanded: an income effect and a substitution effect. Let us review these two effects and see how they operate in the context of the demand for leisure (that is, the supply of labor).

1. ***Income effect.*** Higher wages make consumers richer. We expect this increased wealth to raise the demand for most goods, leisure included.

The income effect of higher wages probably leads most workers to want to work less.

2. ***Substitution effect.*** Consumers "purchase" their own leisure time by giving up their hourly wage, so the wage rate is the "price" (the opportunity cost) of leisure. When the wage rate rises, leisure becomes more expensive relative to other commodities that consumers might buy. Thus, we expect a wage increase to induce them to buy *less* leisure time and *more* goods.

The substitution effect of higher wages probably leads most workers to want to work more.

Putting these two effects together, we are led to conclude that some workers may react to an increase in their wage rate by working more, while others may react by working less. Still others will have little or no discretion over their hours of work. In terms of the market as a whole, therefore, higher wages could lead to either a larger or a smaller quantity of labor supplied.

Statistical studies of this issue in the United States have reached the conclusions that (a) the response of labor supply to wage changes is not very strong for most workers; (b) for low-wage workers the substitution effect seems clearly dominant, so they work more when wages rise; and (c) for high-wage workers the income effect just about offsets the substitution effect, so they do not work

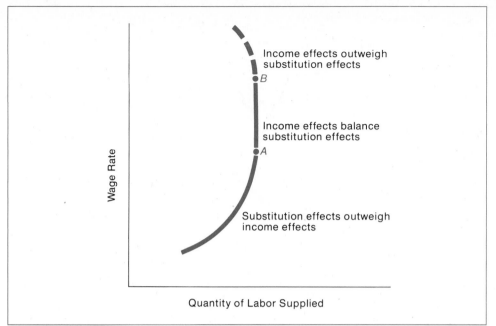

Figure 36–2
A TYPICAL LABOR
SUPPLY SCHEDULE
The labor supply schedule
depicted here has a positive
slope up to point A, as
substitution effects outweigh
income effects. At higher
wages, however, income
effects become just as
important as substitution
effects, and the curve
becomes roughly vertical. At
still higher wages (above
point B), income effects
might overwhelm substitution
effects.

more when wages rise. Figure 36–2 depicts these approximate "facts." It shows labor supply rising (slightly) as wages rise up to point A. Thereafter, labor supply is roughly constant as wages rise.

It is even possible that when wages are raised sufficiently high, further increases in wages will lead workers to purchase more leisure and therefore to work less. The supply curve of labor is then said to be "backward bending," as illustrated by the broken portion of the curve above point B.

Does the theory of labor supply apply to college students? A study of the hours of work performed by students at Princeton University found that it does.[1] Estimated substitution effects of higher wages on the labor supply of Princeton students were positive and income effects were negative, just as the theory predicts. Apparently, substitution effects outweighed income effects by a slim margin, so that higher wages attracted a somewhat greater supply of labor. Specifically, a 10-percent rise in wages was estimated to increase the hours of work of the Princeton student body by about 3 percent.

An Application: The Labor Supply Paradox

Income-substitution effect analysis plays an even more important role in explaining the striking historical trends in labor supply. Throughout the twentieth century, wages have generally been rising, both in number of dollars paid per hour and in the quantity of goods those dollars can buy, as is clearly shown by the data depicted in Figure 36–3. Yet labor has asked for and received *reductions* in the length of the workday and workweek. At the beginning of the century, a workweek of $5\frac{1}{2}$ days and a workday of 10 or more hours (with virtually no vacations) was standard, making a workweek of 50 to 60 hours. Since then, labor hours have generally declined. Today the standard workweek is down to 35 to 40 hours. It has been estimated that since 1870 the number of hours an average American worker works per year has declined about 45 percent! Where

---

[1]Mary P. Hurley, "An Investigation of Employment among Princeton Undergraduates During the Academic Year," Senior thesis submitted to the Department of Economics, May 1975.

Figure 36–3
TRENDS IN REAL WAGES AND HOURS WORKED

This graph shows how real wages (measured in dollars of 1967 purchasing power) have been rising throughout the twentieth century in the United States, while hours worked per week have been declining, despite the higher rewards for each hour of work. The sharp drop in hours during the 1930s reflects the high unemployment of the Great Depression, and the sharp rise in hours in the 1940s reflects the unusual circumstances of World War II. Note that real wages have actually fallen since about 1970.

SOURCE: Compiled by the authors from data in *Historical Statistics of the United States* and *Economic Report of the President*. Data on both weekly hours and hourly earnings pertain to the entire economy for the 1947–1986 period, but only to the manufacturing sector for earlier years because of the unavailability of economy-wide data.

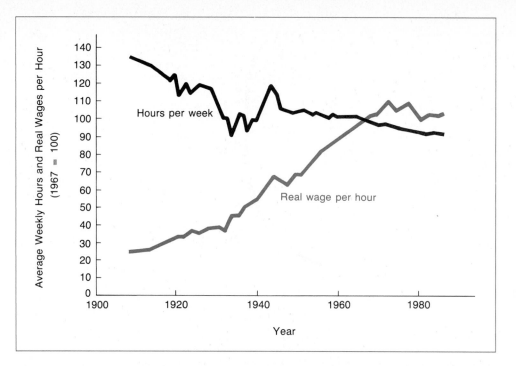

has the common-sense view of the matter gone wrong? Why, as hourly wages have risen, have workers not sold more of the hours they have available instead of pressing for a shorter and shorter workweek?

Part of the answer becomes clear when one recalls that any wage increase sets in motion *both* a substitution effect *and* an income effect. If only the substitution effect operated, then rising wages would indeed cause people to work longer hours because the high price of leisure makes leisure less attractive. But this reasoning leaves out the income effect. As higher wages make workers richer, they will want to buy more of most commodities, including vacations and other leisure-time activities. Thus the income effect of increasing wages induces workers to work fewer hours.

It is the strong income effect of rising wages that may account for the fact that labor supply has responded in the "wrong" direction, with workers working ever-shorter hours despite their rising real wages. If so, the long-run supply curve of labor is indeed backward bending.

The Demand for Labor and the Determination of Wages

There is not much to be said about the demand for labor that has not already been said about the demand for other inputs. Like any factor of production, labor has a marginal revenue product curve from which a downward-sloping demand curve for labor can be derived. This demand curve is shown in Figure 36–4 as curve *DD*. The figure also includes a supply curve, labeled *SS*, much like the one depicted in Figure 36–2.

If there are no interferences with the operation of a free market in labor (such as minimum wages or unions—which we will consider later), equilibrium will be at point *E*, where the supply and demand curves intersect. In this example, 500,000 workers will be employed at a wage of $300 per week.

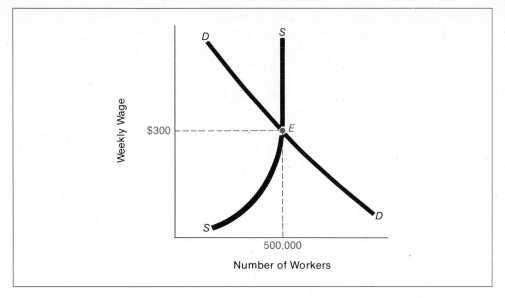

Figure 36–4
EQUILIBRIUM IN A
COMPETITIVE LABOR
MARKET
In a competitive labor market,
equilibrium will be
established at the wage that
equates the quantity supplied
with the quantity demanded.
In this example, equilibrium is
at point *E*, where demand
curve *DD* crosses supply
curve *SS*. The equilibrium
wage is $300 per week and
equilibrium employment is
500,000 workers.

Why Wages Differ

But, of course, there is not one labor market but many—each with its own supply and demand curves and its own equilibrium wage. We all know that certain groups in our society (the young, the black, the uneducated) earn relatively low wages, and that some of our most severe social ills (poverty, crime, drug addiction) are related to this fact. But why are some wages so low while others are so high?

Supply-and-demand analysis at once tells us everything and nothing about this question. It implies that wages are relatively high in markets where demand is great and supply is small [see Figure 36–5(a)], while wages are comparatively low in markets where demand is weak and supply is high [see Figure 36–5(b)].

Figure 36–5
WAGE DIFFERENTIALS
(a) The market depicted here
has a high equilibrium wage,
because demand is high
relative to supply. This can
occur if qualified workers are
scarce, or if productivity on
the job is high or if the
demand for the product is
great. (b) By contrast, the
equilibrium wage w_2, is low
here, where supply is high
relative to demand. This can
result from an abundant
supply of qualified workers,
or low productivity, or weak
demand for the product.

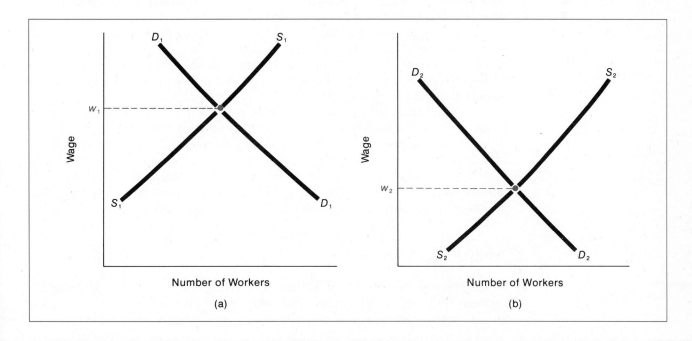

This can hardly be considered startling news. But to make the analysis useful, we need to breathe some life into the supply and demand curves.

We begin our discussion on the demand side. Why is the demand for labor greater in some markets than in others? The marginal productivity principle teaches us that there are two types of influences to be considered. Since a worker's marginal revenue product depends both on his *marginal physical product* and on the *price of the product* that he produces, variables that influence either of these will influence his wage.

The determinants of the prices of commodities were discussed at some length in earlier chapters, and there is no need to repeat the analysis here. It is sufficient to remember that because the demand for labor is a *derived demand,* anything that raises or lowers the demand for a particular product will tend to raise or lower the wages of the workers that produce that product.

A worker's marginal physical product depends on several things, including of course, his own *abilities* and *degree of effort* on the job. But sometimes these characteristics are less important than the *other factors of production* that he has to work with. Workers in American industry are more productive than workers in many other countries because they have generous supplies of machinery, natural resources, and technical know-how to work with. As a consequence, they earn high wages.

Turning next to differences in the supply of labor to different areas, industries, or occupations, it is clear that the *size of the available working population* relative to the magnitude of industrial activity in a given area is of major importance. This helps explain why wages rose so high in sparsely populated Alaska when the Alaska pipeline created many new jobs, and why wages have been and remain so low in Appalachia, where industry is dormant.

Second, it is clear that the *nonmonetary attractiveness* of any job will also influence the supply of workers to it. (The monetary attractiveness is the wage itself, which governs movements *along* the supply curve.) Jobs that people find pleasant and satisfying—such as teaching—will attract a large supply of labor, and will consequently pay a low wage. In contrast, a premium will have to be paid to attract workers to jobs that are onerous, disagreeable, or dangerous—such as washing the windows of skyscrapers.

Finally, the amount of ability and training needed to enter a particular job or profession is relevant to its supply of labor. Brain surgeons and professional football quarterbacks earn generous incomes because there are few people as highly skilled as they, and because it is time consuming and expensive to acquire these skills even for those who have the ability.

In addition to all of the above, it is important to recognize that adjustments in the labor market are slow in comparison with those in the markets for other inputs and commodities. Workers, for example, will be reluctant to move from low-wage geographic areas to high-wage areas; so wage differentials often persist longer than price differentials. In the labor markets, long-run equilibrium takes a long time to attain, particularly where substantial retraining and relocation is required to eliminate differences in wages among jobs.

Ability and Earnings

In considering the effects of ability on earnings, it is useful to distinguish between skills that can be duplicated easily and skills that cannot. If Jones has an ability that Smith cannot acquire, even if he undergoes extensive training, then the wages that Jones earns will contain an element of *economic rent*, just as in the case of Lee Iacocca.[2]

The salaries of professional athletes provide particularly clear examples of how economic rents can lead to huge wage differentials. Virtually anyone with moderate athletic ability can be taught to toss a basketball at a hoop. But in most cases, no amount of training will teach the player to shoot a basketball like Larry Bird. Bird's high salary is a reward for his unique ability.

But many of the abilities that the market rewards generously—such as the skills of doctors and lawyers—clearly are duplicable. Here the theory of rent does not apply, and we need a different explanation of the high wages that these skilled professionals earn. Once again, however, part of our analysis from Chapter 35 finds an immediate application because the acquisition of skills, through formal education and other forms of training has much in common with business investment decisions. Why? Because the decision to undertake more education in the hope of increasing future earnings involves a sacrifice of *current* income for the sake of *future* gain—precisely the hallmark of an investment decision.

Investment in Human Capital

That education is an investment is a concept familiar to most college students. You made a conscious decision to go to college rather than to enter the labor market, and you are probably acutely aware that this decision is now costing you money—lots of money. Your tuition payments may be only a minor part of the total cost of going to college. Think of a high school friend who chose not to go to college and is now working. The salary that he or she is earning could, perhaps, have been yours. You are deliberately giving up this possible income in order to acquire more education.

In this sense, your education can be thought of as an *investment* in yourself—a *human investment*. Like a firm that devotes some of its money to building a plant that will yield profits at some future date, you are investing in your own future, hoping that your college education will help you earn more than your high-school-educated friend or enable you to find a more pleasant or prestigious job when you graduate. Economists call activities like going to college **investments in human capital** because such activities give the human being many of the attributes of a capital investment.

Doctors and lawyers earn such high salaries partly because of their many years of training. That is, part of their wages can be construed as a *return on their (educational) investments*, rather than as economic rent. Unlike the case of Larry Bird, there are a number of people who conceivably *could* become surgeons if they found the job sufficiently attractive to endure the long years of training that are required. Few, however, are willing to make such a large investment of their own time, money, and energy. Consequently, the few who do become surgeons earn very generous incomes.

Economists have devoted quite a bit of attention to the acquisition of skills through human investment. There is an entire branch of economic theory—called **human capital theory**—which analyzes an individual's decisions about education, training, and so on in exactly the same way as we analyzed a firm's decision to buy a machine or build a factory in the previous chapter. Though educational decisions can be influenced by love of learning, desire for prestige,

[2]See the previous chapter, pages 783–85.

and a variety of other preferences and emotions, human capital theorists find it useful to analyze a schooling decision as if it were made purely as a business plan. The optimal length of education, from this point of view, is to stay in school until the marginal revenue (in the form of increased future income) of an additional year of schooling is exactly equal to the marginal cost.

One implication of human capital theory is that college graduates should earn enough more than high school graduates to compensate them for their extra investments in schooling. Do they? Will your college investment pay off? Many generations of college students have supposed that it would, and for years studies of the incomes earned by college students indicated that they were right. These studies showed that the income differentials earned by college graduates provided a good "return" on the tuition payments and sacrificed earnings that they "invested" while in school.

Human capital theory stresses that jobs that require more education *must* pay higher wages if they are to attract enough workers, because people insist on a financial return on their human investments. But the theory does not address the other side of the question: What is it about more-educated people that makes firms willing to pay them higher wages? Put differently, the theory explains why the quantity of educated people *supplied* is limited but does not explain why the quantity *demanded* is substantial even at high wages.

Most human capital theorists complete their analyses by assuming that students in high schools and colleges are acquiring particular skills that are productive in the marketplace. In this view, educational institutions are factories that take less-productive workers as their raw materials, apply doses of training and produce more-productive workers as outputs. It is a view of what happens in schools that makes educators happy and accords well with common sense. However, a number of social scientists doubt that this is how schooling raises earning power.

Education and Earnings: Dissenting Views

Just why is it that jobs with stiffer educational requirements typically offer higher wages? The common-sense view that educating people makes them more productive is not universally accepted.

Education as a Sorting Mechanism

One alternative view denies that the educational process teaches students anything directly relevant to their subsequent performance on jobs. On this view, people differ in ability when they enter the school system and differ in more or less the same way when they leave. What the educational system does, according to this theory, is to *sort* individuals by ability. Skills like intelligence and self-discipline that lead to success in schools, it is argued, are closely related to the skills that lead to success in jobs. As a result, more able individuals stay in school longer and perform better. Prospective employers know this, and consequently seek to hire those whom the school system has suggested will be the most productive workers.

The Radical View of Education[3]

Many radical economists question whether the educational system really sorts people according to ability. The rich, they note, are better situated to buy the

[3]Radical economics is considered in greater depth in Chapter 41, especially pages 919–25.

best education and to keep their children in school regardless of ability. Thus, education may be one of the instruments by which a more privileged family passes its economic position on to its heirs while making it appear that there is a legitimate reason for firms to give them higher earnings. As radicals see it, education sorts people according to their social class, not according to their ability.

Radicals also hold a different idea about what happens inside schools to make workers more "productive." In this view, instead of serving primarily as instruments for the acquisition of knowledge and improved ability to think, what schools do primarily is teach people discipline — how to show up five days a week at 9 A.M., how to speak in turn and respectfully, and so on. These characteristics, radicals claim, are what business firms prefer and what causes them to seek more-educated workers. They also suggest that the schools teach docility and acceptance of the capitalist status quo, and that this, too, makes schooling attractive to business.

The Dual Labor Market Theory

A third view of the linkages among education, ability, and earnings is part of a much broader theory of how the labor market operates — the theory of **dual labor markets.** Proponents of this theory suggest that there are two very different types of labor markets, with relatively little mobility between them.

The "primary labor market" is where most of the economy's "good jobs" are — jobs like computer programming, business management, and skilled crafts that are interesting and offer considerable possibilities for career advancement. The educational system helps decide which individuals get assigned to the primary labor market and, for those who make it, greater educational achievement does indeed offer financial rewards.

The privileged workers who wind up in the primary labor market are offered opportunities for additional training on the job; they augment their skills by experience and by learning from their fellow workers; and they progress in successive steps to more responsible, better paying positions. Where jobs in the primary labor market are concerned, dual labor market theorists agree with human capital theorists that education really is productive. But they agree with the radicals that admission to the primary labor market depends in part on social position, and that firms probably care more about steady work habits and punctuality than about reading, writing, and arithmetic.

Everything is quite different in the "secondary labor market" — where we find all the "bad jobs." Jobs like domestic service and fast-food service, which are often the only ones ghetto residents can find, offer low rates of pay, few fringe benefits, and virtually no training to improve the workers' skills. They are dead-end jobs with little or no hope for promotion or advancement. As a result, lateness, absenteeism, and thievery are expected as a matter of course, so that workers in the secondary labor market tend to develop the bad work habits that confirm the prejudices of those who assigned them to inferior jobs in the first place.

In the secondary labor market, increased education leads neither to higher wages nor to increased protection from unemployment — benefits that increased schooling generally offers elsewhere in the labor market. For this reason, workers in the secondary market have little incentive to invest in education.

In sum, we have a well-established fact — that people with more education generally earn higher wages — but very little agreement on the theory that accounts for this fact.

The Effects of Minimum Wage Legislation

As we have observed, the "labor market" is really composed of many submarkets for labor of different types, each with its own supply and demand curves. To understand the possible effects of minimum wage legislation, it suffices to consider two such markets, which we call for convenience "skilled" and "unskilled" labor and portray in the two parts of Figure 36–6. As drawn, the demand curve for skilled workers is higher than that for unskilled workers. The reason is obvious: Skilled workers have higher productivity. Conversely, we have drawn the supply curve of skilled workers farther to the left than the supply curve of unskilled workers to reflect the greater scarcity of skilled workers. The consequence, as we can see in Figure 36–6, is that the equilibrium wage is much higher for skilled workers. In the example, the equilibrium wages are $8 per hour for skilled workers and $2.50 per hour for unskilled workers.

Now suppose the government, seeking to protect unskilled workers, imposes a legal minimum wage of $3.50 per hour (the blue line in both parts of Figure 36–6). Turning first to part (a), we see that the minimum wage has no effect in the markets for skilled workers like carpenters and electricians. Since their wages are well above $3.50 per hour, a law prohibiting the payment of wage rates below $3.50 cannot possibly matter.

But the effects of the minimum wage may be pronounced in the markets for unskilled labor — and presumably quite different from those that Congress intended. Figure 36–6(b) indicates that at the $3.50 minimum wage, firms want to employ only 30 million unskilled workers (point A) whereas employment of unskilled workers would have been 43 million (point E) in a free market. Although the 30 million unskilled workers lucky enough to retain their jobs do indeed earn a higher wage ($3.50 instead of $2.50 per hour) in this hypothetical example, 13 million of their compatriots earn no wage at all because they have been laid off. The job-losers will clearly be those workers with the lowest productivity, since the minimum wage effectively bans the employment of workers whose marginal revenue product is less than $3.50 per hour.

Figure 36–6
POSSIBLE EFFECTS OF MINIMUM WAGE LEGISLATION
(a) Imposing a minimum wage of $3.50 per hour does not affect the market for skilled labor because the equilibrium wage there ($8 per hour) is well above the legal minimum. (b) However, the minimum-wage legislation does have important effects in the market for unskilled labor. There the equilibrium wage ($2.50 per hour) is below the minimum, so the minimum wage makes the quantity supplied (45 million workers) exceed the quantity demanded (30 million workers). The result is unemployment of unskilled labor.

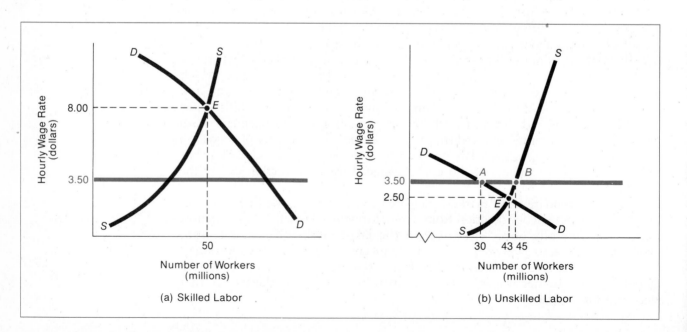

(a) Skilled Labor

(b) Unskilled Labor

Although the minimum wage does lead to higher wages for those unskilled workers who retain their jobs, it also restricts employment opportunities for unskilled workers.

In addition, minimum wages may have particularly pernicious effects on those who are the victims of discrimination. Because of the minimum wage, as Figure 36–6(b) shows, employers of unskilled labor have more applicants than job openings. Consequently, they will be able to pick and choose among the available applicants and may, for example, discriminate against blacks who have been prevented by past discrimination from acquiring the skills required for admission to the higher-paid portion of the labor force.

For these reasons, many economists feel that the teen-age unemployment problem, and especially the black teen-age unemployment problem, will be very difficult to solve as long as the minimum wage remains effective. Obviously, the minimum wage is not the only culprit; the data strongly suggest that there is more to the story. Yet it is hard to dismiss the analytic conclusion that forced overpricing of unskilled labor contributes to unemployment.

Unions and Collective Bargaining

Our analysis of competitive labor markets has ignored one rather important fact: The supply of labor is not at all competitive in many labor markets; instead it is controlled by a labor monopoly, a union.

While important, unions in America are not nearly so important as is popularly supposed. For example, most people who are not acquainted with the data are astonished to learn that only about 17 percent of American workers belong to unions. This percentage is much higher than it was before the New Deal, when unions were quite unimportant in this country, but lower than it was in the heyday of unionism in the mid-1950s, when the figure was just over 25 percent (see Figure 36–7). This percentage has been falling fairly steadily since then, and the decline has recently accelerated.

Unions seem much more prevalent than this to the public because they are such large, and therefore newsworthy, institutions. The giant Teamsters union, for example, has almost 2 million members. The second largest union is now the National Education Association, with 1.7 million members—evidence of the decreasing importance of manufacturing and the growth of the services in the nation's employment. Because of their size, the actions of these unions are reported daily in the media. By contrast, unless you are a student of labor statistics, you will hardly ever hear anything about the more than 90 million workers in America who do not belong to unions.

Unionization is also much less prevalent in America than it is in most other industrialized countries. For example, about 50 percent of British workers and about 80 percent of Swedish workers belong to unions. The differences are quite striking and doubtless have something to do with our tradition of "rugged individualism."

The Development of Unionism in America

While its roots can be traced back earlier, serious unionism in America is only about 100 years old. Large-scale unions in this country began with the Knights

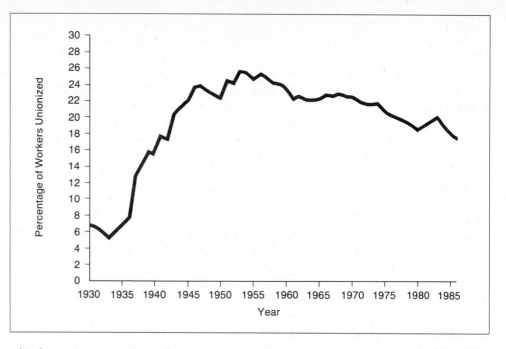

Figure 36–7

UNIONIZATION IN THE UNITED STATES, 1930–1986

In 1930, unions had enrolled just under 7 percent of the U.S. labor force and by 1933 this figure had slipped to barely above 5 percent. Unionization took off with the New Deal, reaching almost 16 percent of the labor force by 1939. It then drifted irregularly upward to a peak of about 25 to 26 percent of all workers in the mid-1950s, from which it has since fallen more or less steadily to about 17.5 percent in 1986.
SOURCE: U.S. Department of Labor, *Employment and Earnings,* Jan. 1981.

of Labor — a very politically motivated workers' organization that was quite different from the unions of today. Toward the end of the nineteenth century, membership in the Knights of Labor approached 750,000 workers; but it failed to achieve higher wages or better working conditions for its members, and the organization declined rapidly. Today American unions are noteworthy for their basically nonpolitical stance, in contrast to the highly politicized unions of many European countries.

The American labor movement as we know it today began to take shape in 1881 with the founding of the American Federation of Labor by Samuel Gompers, who headed the AFL for nearly 50 years and did more to shape the American labor movement than any other person. At that time, working conditions were incredibly bad by today's standards. And unscrupulous labor practices fostered the growth of unions (see the box on page 807).

Gompers believed strongly that unions should be nonpolitical organizations seeking to get *more* for their members: more pay, better working conditions, longer vacations, and so on. He also believed that unions should be organized along craft lines — carpenters in one union, plumbers in another — rather than trying to include all types of workers in a given industry. Finally, he was a staunch advocate of free collective bargaining without government interference.

The AFL grew rather steadily from about 1900 until the 1920s, went into decline during the Roaring Twenties, but then grew rapidly thanks to the favorable attitudes and legislation of the Roosevelt administration in the 1930s. The Norris-La Guardia Act of 1932 sharply limited the power of the federal courts to interfere in labor disputes. In 1938 the Fair Labor Standards Act abolished child labor, imposed a minimum wage on most activities whose products entered into interstate commerce, and wrote extra pay for overtime work into law.

Even more important, the National Labor Relations Act (Wagner Act) in 1935 guaranteed workers the right to form unions and to choose the union that would represent them in collective bargaining. It also set up the National Labor Relations Board (NLRB) to protect labor from "unfair labor practices" by

The Way It Was

The calamitous Triangle Shirtwaist Factory fire of 1911, in which 146 women and girls lost their lives, was a landmark in American labor history. It galvanized public opinion behind the movement to improve conditions, hours, and wages in the sweatshops. Pauline Newman went to work in the Triangle Shirtwaist Factory at the age of eight, shortly after coming to the Lower East Side. Many of her friends lost their lives in the fire. She went on to become an organizer and later an executive of the newly formed International Ladies Garment Workers' Union, and served as its educational director until she was almost 90 years of age. [*]

The Triangle Factory, now part of New York University.

We started work at seven-thirty in the morning, and during the busy season we worked until nine in the evening. They didn't pay you any overtime and they didn't give you anything for supper money. Sometimes they'd give you a little apple pie if you had to work very late. That was all. Very generous. . . .

We had a corner on the floor that resembled a kindergarten — we were given little scissors to cut the threads off. It wasn't heavy work, but it was monotonous.

Well, of course, there were laws on the books, but no one bothered to enforce them. The employers were always tipped off if there was going to be an inspection. "Quick," they'd say, "into the boxes!" And we children would climb into the big boxes the finished shirts were stored in. Then some shirts were piled on top of us, and when the inspector came — no children. The factory always got an okay from the inspector, and I suppose someone at City Hall got a little something, too.

The employers didn't recognize anyone working for them as a human being. You were not allowed to sing. . . . We weren't allowed to talk to each other. . . . If you went to the toilet and you were there longer than the floor lady thought you should be, you would be laid off for half a day and sent home. And, of course, that meant no pay. You were not allowed to have your lunch on the fire escape in the summertime. The door was locked to keep us in. That's why so many people were trapped when the fire broke out. . . .

The employers had a sign in the elevator that said: "If you don't come in on Sunday, don't come in on Monday." You were expected to work every day if they needed you and the pay was the same whether you worked extra or not.

Conditions were dreadful in those days. We didn't have anything. . . . There was no welfare, no pension, no unemployment insurance. There was nothing. . . . There was so much feeling against unions then. The judges, when one of our girls came before him, said to her: "You're not striking against your employer, you know, young lady. You're striking against God," and sentenced her to two weeks.

I wasn't at the Triangle Shirtwaist Factory when the fire broke out, but a lot of my friends were. . . . The thing that bothered me was the employers got a lawyer. How anyone could have *defended* them! — because I'm quite sure that the fire was planned for insurance purposes. And no one is going to convince me otherwise. And when they testified that the door to the fire escape was open, it was a lie! It was never open. Locked all the time. One hundred and forty-six people sacrificed, and the judge fined Blank and Harris seventy-five dollars!

[*]This introduction and the following narrative are excerpted from the book *American Mosaic: The Immigrant Experience in the Words of Those Who Lived It*, by Joan Morrison and Charlotte Fox Zabusky, copyright 1980 by Joan Morrison and Charlotte Fox Zabusky. Reprinted by permission of the publisher, E. P. Dutton, Inc.

employers. Today the NLRB oversees elections in business firms to determine which union will represent the workers. It can also force employers to take back workers whom it considers to have been fired unjustly.

By no coincidence, in the year of the Wagner Act, John L. Lewis founded the Congress of Industrial Organizations (CIO), a federation of many **industrial unions** that at first rivaled the AFL for leadership of the U.S. labor movement.

It was felt by those who advocated industrial unions that many specialized **craft unions** (which often quarreled among themselves) were not likely to be very powerful in their dealings with large employers. Despite their differences, the AFL, with its craft unions, and the CIO, with its industrial unions, eventually merged in 1955.

The favorable public attitude toward unions soured somewhat after World War II, perhaps because of the rash of strikes that took place in 1946 (see Figure 36–11 on page 814). One result of these strikes was the **Taft-Hartley Act** of 1947, which specified and outlawed certain "unfair labor practices" by unions. Specifically, the act:

1. Severely limited the extent of the **closed shop,** under which only union members can be hired.
2. Permitted state governments, at their discretion, to ban the **union shop,** an arrangement that requires employees to join the union. These so-called right-to-work laws have been adopted by several states.
3. Provided for court injunctions to delay strikes that threaten the national interest for an 80-day "cooling-off" period.

Today, the character of American unionism is still somewhat unsettled. Unions are struggling very hard to make inroads into labor markets that by tradition have not been unionized — such as the agricultural and white-collar office markets. Notable successes have been achieved in organizing teachers and many government employees. But at the same time union membership as a percent of the labor force is on the decline, largely because the manufacturing sector — the traditional home of unions — is employing a smaller fraction of the nation's labor force.

U.S. labor unions are very different from those in Europe and Japan. Unlike Japanese unions, there is great antagonism between American unions and management. The century-long tradition of hostile labor–management relations in this country impedes current attempts to emulate the Japanese model of labor–management cooperation. U.S. labor still feels that employers are all too likely to adopt unfair practices unless they are restrained by powerful unions. Yet despite all this, U.S. unions are strongly committed to capitalism and rarely espouse socialism — unlike their European counterparts.

Unions as a Labor Monopoly

Unions require that we alter our economic analysis of the labor market in much the same way that monopolies required us to alter our analysis of the goods market (see Chapter 27). You will recall that in a monopolized product market the firm selects the point on its demand curve that maximizes its profits. Much the same idea applies to unions, which are, after all, monopoly sellers of labor. They too face a demand curve — derived this time from the marginal productivity schedules of firms — and can choose the point on it that suits them best.

An **industrial union** represents all types of workers in a single industry, such as auto manufacturing or coal mining.

A **craft union** represents a particular type of skilled worker, such as newspaper typographers or electricians, regardless of what industry they work in.

A **closed shop** is an arrangement that permits only union members to be hired.

A **union shop** is an arrangement under which nonunion workers may be hired, but then must join the union within a specified period of time.

The problem for the economist trying to analyze union behavior—and perhaps also for the union leader trying to select a course of action—is how to decide which point on the demand curve is "best." Unlike the case of the business firm, there is no obvious goal analogous to profit-maximization that clearly delineates what the union should do. Instead there are a number of *alternative* goals that sound plausible. In part, the reason is that union members themselves differ in their objectives, particularly in the tradeoff between higher wages and job security. If older workers are protected from being fired by **seniority rules** which require those who have held jobs longest to be the last to be dismissed, these older workers may give greater priority to high wages than younger workers do. What policy union leaders will pursue may depend on the relative power of the different groups of members in a union's election of its leaders.

Seniority rules are rules which give special job-related advantages to workers who have held their jobs longest. In particular this usually requires that workers most recently hired be the first to be fired when a firm cuts employment.

Alternative Union Goals

The different implications of alternative union goals can be illustrated with the aid of Figure 36–8, which depicts a demand curve for labor, labeled *DD*. The union leadership must decide which point on the curve is best. One possibility is to treat the size of the union as fixed and force employers to pay the highest wage they will pay and still employ all the union members. If, for example, the union has 4000 members, this would be point A, with a wage of $12 per hour. But this is a high-risk strategy for a union. Firms forced to pay such high wages will be at a competitive disadvantage compared with firms that have nonunion labor, and they may even be forced to shut down.

Alternatively, union leaders may be interested in increasing the size of their unions. As an extreme case of this, they might try to make employment as large as possible without pushing the wage below the competitive level. If the competitive wage were $6 per hour in the absence of the union, this strategy would correspond to selecting point C, with employment for 8000 workers. In this case the existence of the union has no effect on wages or on employment.

An intermediate strategy that has often been suggested is that the union maximize the total income of all workers. This would dictate choosing point B,

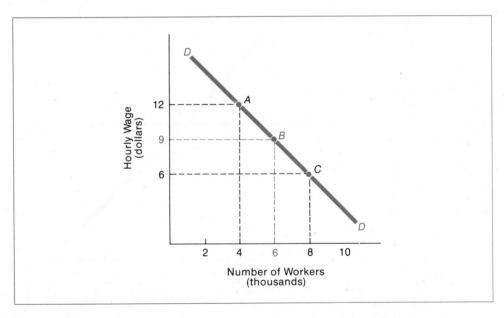

Figure 36–8
ALTERNATIVE GOALS FOR A UNION
Line *DD* is the demand curve for labor in a market that becomes unionized. Point *C* is the equilibrium point before the union, when wages were $6 per hour. If the union wants to push wages higher, it normally will have to sacrifice some jobs. Points *A* and *B* show two of its many alternatives.

with a wage of $9 per hour and jobs for 6000 workers. Other possible strategies can also be imagined, but these suffice to make the basic point clear.

Unions, as monopoly sellers of labor, have the power to push wages above the competitive levels. However, since the demand curve for labor is downward sloping, such increases in wages normally can be achieved only by reducing the number of jobs. Just as the monopolist must limit his output to push up his price, so the union must restrict employment to push up the wage.

This can be seen clearly by comparing points B and A with point C (the competitive solution). If it selects point B, the union raises wages by $3 per hour, but at the cost of 2000 jobs. If it goes all the way to point A, wages are raised to twice the competitive level, but employment is cut in half.

What do unions actually try to do? There are probably as many different choices as there are unions. Some seem to pursue a maximum-employment goal much like point C, raising wages very little. Others seem to push for the highest possible wages, much like point A. Most probably select an intermediate route. This implies, of course, that the effects of unionization on wage rates and employment will differ markedly among industries.

Alternative Union Strategies

How would a union that has decided to push wages above the competitive level accomplish this task? Two principal ways are illustrated in Figure 36–9, where we suppose that point U on demand curve DD is the union's choice, and point C is the competitive equilibrium.

In Figure 36–9(a), we suppose that the union pursues its goal by *restricting supply*. By keeping out some workers who would like to enter the industry or occupation, it shifts the supply curve of labor inward from $S_0 S_0$ to $S_1 S_1$. This sort of behavior is often encountered in craft unions, which may require a long period of apprenticeship. Such unions sometimes offer only a small number of new memberships each year, largely to replace members who have died or

Figure 36–9
TWO UNION STRATEGIES
The two parts indicate two alternative ways for the union to move from point C to point U. In part (a), it keeps some workers out of the industry, thereby moving the supply curve to the left from $S_0 S_0$ to $S_1 S_1$. As a consequence, wages rise. In part (b), it fixes a high wage (W) and provides labor only at this wage. Therefore, firms reduce employment. The effects are the same under both strategies.

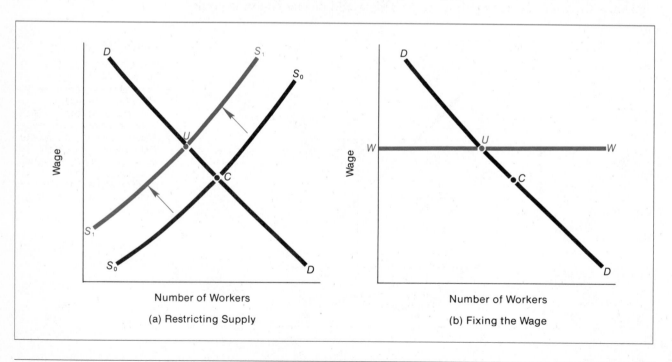

(a) Restricting Supply

(b) Fixing the Wage

retired. Membership in such a union is very valuable and is sometimes offered primarily to children of current members.

In Figure 36–9(b), instead of restricting supply, the union simply *sets a high wage rate*, W in the example. In this case, it is the employers who will restrict entry into the job, because with wages so high they will not want to employ many workers. This second strategy is more typically employed by industrial unions like the United Automobile Workers or the United Mine Workers. As the figure makes clear, the two wage-raising strategies achieve the same result (point U in either case) by what turns out to be the same means. Wages are raised only by reducing employment in either case.

In some exceptional cases, however, a union may be able to achieve wage gains without sacrificing employment. To do this, the union must be able to exercise effective control over the demand curve for labor. Figure 36–10 illustrates such a possibility. Union actions push the demand curve outward from $D_0 D_0$ to $D_1 D_1$, simultaneously raising both wages and employment. Typically, this is difficult to do. One way to do it is by *featherbedding* — forcing management to employ more workers than they really need.[4] Quite the opposite technique is to institute a campaign to raise worker productivity, which some unions seem to have been able to do. Alternatively, the union can try to raise the demand for the company's product either by flexing its political muscle (for example, by obtaining legislation to reduce foreign competition) or by appealing to the public to buy union products.

Have Unions Really Raised Wages?

The theory of unions as monopoly sellers of labor certainly suggests that unions have some ability to raise wages, but it also shows that they may be hesitant to

[4]The best-known example of featherbedding involved the railroad unions, which for years forced management to keep "firemen" in the cabs of diesel engines, in which there were no burning fires. Similarly, the musicians' union in New York City forces Broadway producers who use certain theaters to employ a minimum number of musicians — whether or not they actually play music. Of course, it is not only labor that has tried to create an artificial demand for its services. Lawyers, doctors, and business firms, among others, have sought ways to induce consumers to buy more of their products and services. EXERCISE: Can you think of ways in which they have done this?

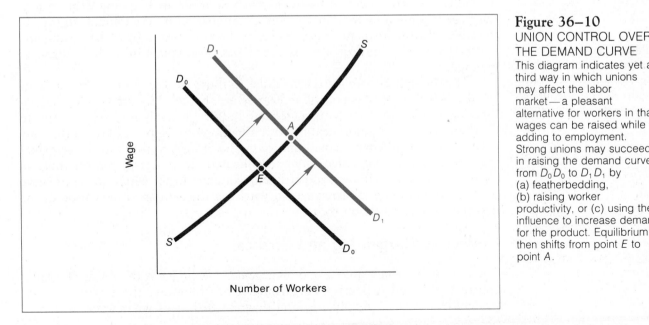

Figure 36–10
UNION CONTROL OVER THE DEMAND CURVE
This diagram indicates yet a third way in which unions may affect the labor market — a pleasant alternative for workers in that wages can be raised while adding to employment. Strong unions may succeed in raising the demand curve from $D_0 D_0$ to $D_1 D_1$ by (a) featherbedding, (b) raising worker productivity, or (c) using their influence to increase demand for the product. Equilibrium then shifts from point E to point A.

use this ability for fear of reducing employment. To what extent do union members actually earn higher wages than nonmembers?

The consensus that has emerged from economic research on this question would probably surprise most people. It seems that most union members earn wages 10 to 20 percent above those of nonmembers who are otherwise identical (in skill, geographical location, and so on). While certainly not negligible, this can hardly be considered a huge differential.

This 20 percent differential does not mean, however, that unions have raised wages no more than 20 percent. Some observers believe that union activity has also raised wages of nonunion workers by forcing nonunion employers to compete harder for their workers. If so, the differential between union and nonunion workers will be less than the amount by which unions raised wages overall.

Monopsony and Bilateral Monopoly

While the analysis we have just presented has its applications, it oversimplifies matters in several important respects. For one thing, it envisions a market situation in which one powerful union is dealing with many powerless employers: The labor market is assumed to be monopolized on the selling side but competitive on the buying side. There are industries that more or less fit this model. The giant Teamsters' union negotiates with a trucking industry that comprises thousands of firms, most of them quite small and powerless. Similarly, most of the unions within the construction industry are much larger than the firms with which they bargain.

But there are many cases that simply do not fit the model. The "Big Three" automakers do not stand idly by while the UAW picks its favorite point on the demand curve for auto workers. Nor does the Steelworkers' union sit across the bargaining table from representatives of a perfectly competitive industry. In these and other industries, while the union certainly has a good deal of monopoly power over labor supply, the firms also have some **monopsony** power over labor demand. Just as a monopoly union on the selling side of the labor market does not passively sell labor at the going wage, a monopsony firm on the buying side does not passively purchase labor at the going wage, nor at the wage suggested by the labor union. Analysts find it very difficult to predict the wage and employment decisions that will emerge when both the buying and selling side of a market are monopolized—a situation called **bilateral monopoly.**

The difficulties here are quite similar to those we encountered in considering the behavior of oligopolistic industries in Chapter 28. Just as one oligopolist, in planning his strategy, is acutely aware that his rivals are likely to react to anything he does, a union dealing with a monopsony employer knows that any move it makes will elicit a countermove by the firm. And this knowledge makes the first decision that much more complicated. In practice, the outcome of bilateral monopoly will depend partly on economic logic, partly on the relative power of the union and management, partly on the skill and preparation of the negotiators, and partly on luck.

Collective Bargaining and Strikes

The process by which unions and management settle upon the terms of a labor contract is called **collective bargaining.** Unfortunately, there is nothing as straightforward as a supply–demand diagram to tell us what wage level will

Monopsony refers to a market situation in which there is only one buyer.

Bilateral monopoly is a market situation in which there is both a monopoly on the selling side and a monopsony on the buying side.

Unions Under Pressure

The organized labor movement lost 2.7 million members among employed wage and salary workers between 1980 and 1984. This was a particularly sharp drop in the number of union members compared with the experience between the end of World War II and 1980, a period of generally rising union membership. Because this decline took place while the nation's workforce grew, the proportion of employed wage and salary workers who were union members declined during the period, continuing a trend that began in the late 1950s.

The change in the number and proportion of union members took place while changes in the American economy were having a particularly severe impact on employment in goods-producing industries and in transportation, where many union members worked. Competition from imports was growing and government deregulation of the transportation industry in 1980 increased competition from nonunion firms. The "smokestack" industries, the traditional source of union strength, were stagnant or declining, while the less-organized service-producing industries had vigorous employment gains. During the recession

of 1981–1982, unemployment hit hardest in industries where unions were strong but, to date, the recovery has been most vigorous in industries and occupations that typically have low levels of unionization.

SOURCE: Larry T. Adams, "Changing Employment Patterns of Organized Workers," *Monthly Labor Review*, February 1985, p. 25.

emerge from a collective bargaining session. Furthermore, actual collective bargaining sessions range over many more issues than wages. For example, fringe benefits—such as pensions, health and life insurance, paid holidays, and the like—may be just as important as wages to both labor and management. Wage premiums for overtime work and seniority privileges will also be negotiated. Work conditions, such as the speed with which the assembly line should move, are often crucial issues. Many labor contracts specify in great detail the rights of labor and management to set work conditions—and also provide elaborate procedures for resolving grievances and disputes. This list could go on and on. The final contract that emerges from collective bargaining may well run to many pages of fine print.

With the issues so varied and complex, and with the stakes so high, it is no wonder that both labor and management employ skilled professionals who specialize in preparing for and carrying out these negotiations, and that each side enters a collective bargaining session armed with reams of evidence supporting its positions.

The bargaining in these sessions is often heated, with outcomes riding as much on personalities and the skills of the negotiators as on cool-headed logic and economic facts. Negotiations may last well into the night, with each side seeming to try to wear the other out. Each side may threaten the other with grave consequences if it does not accept its own terms. Unions, for their part, generally threaten to strike or to carry out a work slow-down. Firms counter with the threat that they would rather face a strike than give in, or may even close the plant without a strike. (This is called a "lock-out.")

Mediation and Arbitration

Where the public interest is seriously affected, or when the union and firm reach an impasse, government agencies may well send in a **mediator,** whose job is to try to speed up the negotiation process. This impartial observer will sit down with both sides separately to discuss their problems, and will try to persuade each side to yield a bit to the other. At some stage, when an agreement looks possible, he may call them back together for another bargaining session in his presence.

A mediator, however, has no power to force a settlement. His success hinges on his ability to smooth ruffled feathers and to find common ground for agreement. Sometimes, in cases where unions and firms simply cannot agree, and where neither wants a strike, differences are finally settled by **arbitration**—the appointment of an impartial individual empowered to settle the issues that negotiation could not resolve. In fact, in some vital sectors where a strike is too injurious to the public interest, the labor contract or the law may stipulate that there must be *compulsory arbitration* if the two parties cannot agree. However, both labor and management are normally reluctant to accept this procedure.

Strikes

Most collective bargaining situations do not lead to strikes. But the right to strike, and to take a strike, remain fundamentally important for the bargaining process. Imagine, for example, a firm bargaining with a union that was prohibited from striking. It seems likely that the union's bargaining position would be quite weak. On the other hand, a firm that always capitulated rather than suffer a strike would be virtually at the mercy of the union. So strikes, or more precisely, the possibility of strikes, serve an important economic purpose.

Fortunately, however, the incidence of strikes is not nearly so common as many people believe. Figure 36–11 reports the percentage of worker-days of labor lost as a result of strikes in the United States from 1930 to 1986. Despite the headline-grabbing nature of major national strikes, the total amount of

Figure 36–11

TIME LOST BECAUSE OF STRIKES, 1930–1986
The fraction of total work time lost to work stoppages varies greatly from year to year, but is never very large. In most years, it is between one-tenth and one-quarter of 1 percent. The worst year for strikes was 1946, and it is probably no coincidence that the Taft-Hartley law was enacted in the following year.
SOURCE: U.S. Department of Labor, Bureau of Labor, *Monthly Labor Review,* April 1987 (and previous issues).

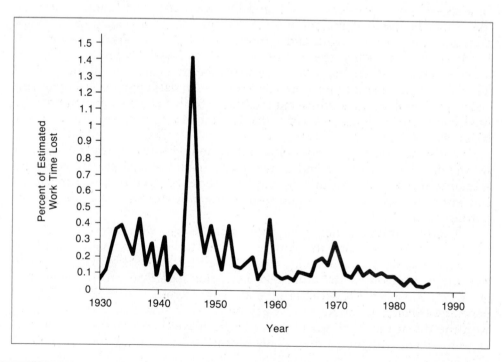

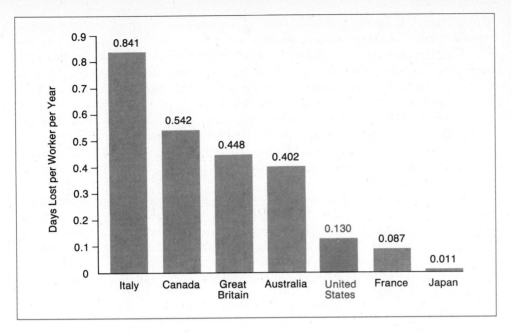

Figure 36–12
THE INCIDENCE OF
STRIKES IN INDUSTRIAL
COUNTRIES
Although strikes in the United
States are much less
common than they are in Italy
or Canada, they are much
more common here than in
Japan or France. (*Note:* Data
are averages for the five-year
period 1981–85.)
SOURCE: U.S. Department of
Labor, unpublished data.

work time lost to strikes is truly trivial — far less, for example, than the time lost to coffee breaks! Compared with other nations, America suffers more from strikes than, say Germany or Japan, but has many fewer strikes than such countries as Italy and Canada (see Figure 36–12).

Collective Bargaining in the Public Sector

We have argued that strikes serve an important function in private-sector bargaining, as a way of dividing the fruits of economic activity between big labor and big business. But does the same rationale for strikes apply to the public sector, where strikes or work stoppages until recently were becoming increasingly common among mail carriers, police, fire fighters, air-traffic controllers, and so on?

It is not clear that it does. In most private-sector strikes, labor and management are inflicting harm upon one another in a kind of battle of "survival of the fittest." Consumers normally suffer only mild inconveniences. When General Motors is on strike, many potential car buyers will be disappointed, but they can turn to Ford or Chrysler, not to mention imports. Similarly, when other private products disappear from the shelves because of strikes, the consumer can easily replace them with close substitutes. Thus, in many cases we can think of consumers as being relatively innocent and unharmed spectators when large unions and large private firms slug it out.

But public-sector bargaining is different. Here, management does not represent the interests of capital against those of labor; rather, it represents the public. And there is no pool of profits to be divided between the union and the stockholders. Instead, what management agrees to give to the union comes out of the pockets of the taxpayers.

Finally, it is quite clear that the public is not just a spectator in such strikes, but is the primary victim. When police or fire-protection services are reduced, when mail delivery ceases, when public schools or airports shut down, consumers cannot find substitutes for these services. In a very real sense, then, strikes in the public sector are strikes against citizens, not strikes against management. They pit representatives of a particular group of workers against representatives of taxpayers as a whole.

For these reasons, the right of public employees to strike has traditionally been much more severely limited than that of private-sector workers. In some states, public-sector strikes are simply outlawed, although this ban has proved hard to enforce. This system seemed logical and worked tolerably well when unionization in the public sector was rather rare. The public was protected, but the public-sector workers were not. In recent years, many public-sector employees have come to feel that they need and deserve a voice in the determination of their work conditions and that they have no choice but to organize and, sometimes, to strike.

However, as more and more government employees organized, America's system of labor relations for public employees started showing signs of strain. Illegal strikes or "job actions," for example, became increasingly common. This atmosphere changed abruptly when the air-traffic controllers went on strike in 1981 and President Reagan simply fired them all. Because the President was able to stick to his decision, public-sector unions seem to have become far more cautious.

Summary

1. The supply of labor is determined by free choices made by individuals. Because of conflicting income and substitution effects, the quantity of labor supplied may rise or fall as a result of an increase in wages.

2. Historical data show that hours of work per week have fallen as wages have risen, suggesting that income effects may be dominant.

3. The demand curve for labor, like the demand curve for any factor of production, is derived from the marginal revenue product curve. It slopes downward because of the "law" of diminishing marginal returns.

4. In a free market, the wage rate and the level of employment are determined by the interaction of supply and demand. Workers in great demand or short supply will command high wages and, conversely, low wages will be assigned to workers in abundant supply or with skills that are not in great demand.

5. Some valuable skills are virtually impossible to duplicate. People who possess such skills will earn economic rents as part of their wages.

6. But most skills can be acquired by means of "investment in human capital," such as education. The financial rate of return on college education, while still positive, is not as high as it was in the 1960s.

7. Human capital theory assumes that people make educational decisions in much the same way as businesses make investment decisions, and tacitly assumes that people learn things in schools that increase their productivity on jobs.

8. Other theories of the effects of education on earnings deny that schooling actually raises productivity. One view is that the educational system primarily sorts people according to their abilities. Another view holds that schools sort people according to their social class and teach them mainly discipline and obedience.

9. According to the theory of dual labor markets, there are two distinct types of labor markets, with very little mobility between them. The primary labor market contains the "good" jobs, where wages are high, prospects for advancement are good, and higher education pays off. The secondary labor market contains the "bad" jobs, with low wages, little opportunity for promotion, and little return to education.

10. One reason that teen-agers, especially black teen-agers, suffer from such high unemployment rates is, apparently, that minimum wage laws prevent the employment of low-productivity workers.

11. About 20 percent of all American workers belong to unions, which can be thought of as monopoly sellers of labor. Compared with many other industrialized countries, the union movement in America is younger, less widespread, and less political.

12. Analysis of union behavior is complicated by the fact that a union can have many goals. For the most part, unions probably force wages to be higher and employment to be lower than they would be in a competitive labor market. However, there are exceptions.

13. Collective bargaining agreements between labor and management are complex documents covering much more than employment and wage rates.

14. Strikes play an important role in collective bargaining as a way of dividing the fruits of economic activity between big business and big labor. Fortunately, strikes are not nearly so common as is often supposed.

15. Strikes in the public sector, however, take on a different character because the adversaries are no longer "labor" versus "capital" but rather "labor" versus the "public interest." For this reason, the rights of public employees to strike have been curtailed.

Concepts for Review

Minimum wage law
Income and substitution effects
Backward-bending supply curve
Economic rent
Investment in human capital
Human capital theory

Dual labor markets
Union
Industrial and craft unions
Taft-Hartley Act (1947)
Closed shop
Union shop

Monopsony
Bilateral monopoly
Collective bargaining
Mediation
Arbitration
Public-sector bargaining

Questions for Discussion

1. Colleges are known to pay rather low wages for student labor. Can this be explained by the operation of supply and demand in the local labor markets? Is the concept of monopsony of any use? How might things differ if students formed a union?

2. College professors are highly skilled (or at least highly educated!) labor. Yet their wages are not very high. Is this a refutation of the marginal productivity theory?

3. The following table shows the number of pizzas that can be produced by a large pizza parlor employing various numbers of pizza chefs.

NUMBER OF CHEFS	NUMBER OF PIZZAS PER DAY
1	100
2	160
3	205
4	230
5	250
6	230

a. Find the marginal physical product schedule of chefs.

b. Assuming a price of $3 per pizza, find the marginal revenue product schedule.

c. If chefs are paid $50 per day, how many will this pizza parlor employ? How would your answer change if chefs' wages rose to $70 per day?

d. Suppose the price of pizza rises from $3 to $4. Show what happens to the derived demand curve for chefs.

4. Discuss the concept of the financial rate of return to a college education. If this return is less than the return on a bank account, does that mean you should quit college? Why might you wish to stay in school anyway? Are there circumstances under which it might be rational not to go to college, even when the financial returns to college are very high?

5. It seems to be a well-established fact that workers with more years of education typically receive higher wages. What are some possible reasons for this?

6. Explain why many economists blame the minimum wage law for much of the employment problems of youth.

7. Approximately what fraction of the American labor force belongs to unions? (Try asking this question of a person who has never studied economics.) Why do you think this fraction is so low?

8. What are some reasonable goals for a union? Use the tools of supply and demand to explain how a union might pursue its goals, whatever they are. Consider a union that has been in the news recently. What was it trying to accomplish?

9. "Strikes are simply intolerable and should be outlawed." Comment.

10. "Public employees should have the same right to strike as private employees." Comment.

Appendix
The Effects of Unions and Minimum Wages Under Monopsony

We have argued in this chapter that if a union or a minimum wage law raises wages, it must necessarily reduce employment. In this appendix we examine a possible exception to this rule.

When there is a monopsony on the buying side of the labor market, a union or a minimum wage law might succeed in raising wages without reducing employment. It might even be able to increase employment.

The Hiring Decisions of a Monopsonist

To establish these results, we begin by considering the hiring decision of a single firm operating in a labor market that is competitive on the supply side. (Later we will bring unions into the picture.) In such a market structure, there is a competitive *supply* curve for labor as usual, but there is a rather different sort of *demand* curve. In Figure 36–13, the supply curve is labeled *SS* and the firm's marginal revenue product (MRP) schedule is labeled *RR*. In this context, however, the MRP schedule is *not* the demand curve. The diagram has one additional curve, which will be explained presently.

How many workers will the monopsonist wish to hire? Table 36–1 helps us answer this

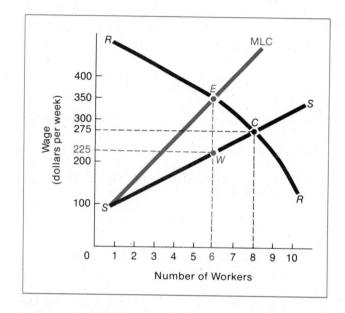

Figure 36–13
LABOR MARKET EQUILIBRIUM UNDER MONOPSONY
Under monopsony, labor market equilibrium occurs at the employment level that equates marginal labor cost (curve MLC in the diagram) to the marginal revenue product (curve *RR*). In this case, equilibrium is at point *E*, where six workers are employed. The corresponding wage is $225 per week. By contrast, if this were a competitive market, equilibrium would be at point *C*, with a wage of $275 and employment of eight workers.

Table 36–1
LABOR COSTS AND MARGINAL REVENUE PRODUCT OF A MONOPSONIST

(1) NUMBER OF WORKERS	(2) WAGE RATE	(3) TOTAL LABOR COST	(4) MARGINAL LABOR COST	(5) MARGINAL REVENUE PRODUCT
1	$100	$ 100	$100	$475
2	125	250	150	450
3	150	450	200	425
4	175	700	250	400
5	200	1000	300	375
6	225	1350	350	350
7	250	1750	400	325
8	275	2200	450	275
9	300	2700	500	225
10	325	3250	550	150

question by displaying the monopsonist's cost and revenue calculations. What does he gain by hiring an additional worker? He gains that worker's marginal revenue product, which is given in column 5 of the table. What does he lose? Not just the wage he pays to the new worker. Because he is the only employer, and because the labor supply schedule is upward-sloping, he can attract an additional worker only by *raising the wage rate*. And this higher wage must be paid to *all his employees*, not just the new one. For this reason, the cost of hiring an additional worker—what we call **marginal labor costs**—exceeds the wage rate. By how much? Table 36–1 provides the answer. The first two columns are just the labor supply schedule, curve SS of Figure 36–13. By multiplying the wage rate by the number of workers, we can compute the *total labor cost*, which is shown in column 3. For example, the total labor cost of hiring five workers is five times the weekly wage of $200, or $1000. From these data, *marginal labor costs* are computed in the usual way—as the changes in successive total labor costs—and the results are displayed in column 4. This is the information the monopsonist wants, for it tells him that the first worker costs him $100, the next $150, and so on. The numbers in column 4 are displayed on the graph by the blue curve labeled MLC (marginal labor cost).

What employment level maximizes the monopsonist's profits? The usual marginal analysis applies. As he hires more workers, his profits rise if the marginal revenue product exceeds the marginal labor cost. For example, when he expands from one worker to two, he receives $450 more in revenue and pays out only an additional $150 to labor; so profits rise by $300. This continues up to the point where marginal labor costs and the marginal revenue product are equal—at six workers in the example. Pushing beyond this point would reduce profits. For example, hiring the seventh worker would cost $400 and bring in only $325 in increased revenues—clearly a losing proposition. We therefore conclude:

A monopsonist maximizes profits by hiring workers up to the point where marginal labor costs are equal to the marginal revenue product.

In the example, it is optimal for the firm to hire six workers, and it does this by offering a wage of $225 per week. This solution is shown in Figure 36–13 by points E and W. Point E is the

equilibrium of the firm, where marginal labor costs and marginal revenue product are equal. To find the corresponding wage rate, we move vertically downward from E until we reach the supply curve at point W.

Let us compare this result with what would have emerged in a competitive labor market. As we know, equilibrium would be established where the supply curve of labor intersects the marginal revenue product curve because the marginal revenue product curve *is* the demand curve of a competitive industry. Figure 36–13 shows that this competitive equilibrium (point C) would have been at a wage of $275 and employment of eight workers.[5] In contrast, the monopsonist hires fewer workers (only six) and pays each a lower wage (only $225 per week). This finding is quite a general result:

As long as the supply curve of labor is upward sloping and the marginal revenue product schedule is downward sloping, a monopsonist will hire fewer workers and pay lower wages than would a competitive industry.

Unions Under Monopsony

Where monopsony firms exist, their workers are very likely to be unionized. Let us therefore consider what would happen if the workers organized into a union and demanded a wage of no less than $250 per week. This action would change the supply curve, and hence the MLC curve, that the monopsonist faces in a straightforward way. No labor could be hired at wages below $250 per week. At that wage, the monopsonist could attract up to seven workers (see column 2 of Table 36–1). At higher wages, he could attract still more labor according to the supply curve. Thus, his new effective supply curve would be *horizontal* at the wage of $250 up to the employment level of seven workers, and then would follow the old supply curve. This is given numerically in column 2 of Table 36–2 and is shown graphically by the kinked supply curve SWS in Figure 36–14.

From this information, we can compute the revised marginal labor cost (MLC) schedule just as we did before. Column 3 in Table 36–2 gives us

---

[5]This conclusion can also be seen in Table 36–1 where, in a competitive market, columns 1 and 2 give the supply curve, while columns 1 and 5 give the demand curve. Quantity supplied equals quantity demanded when the wage is $275.

Table 36–2
LABOR COSTS AND MARGINAL REVENUE PRODUCT OF A MONOPSONIST FACING A UNION

(1) NUMBER OF WORKERS	(2) WAGE RATE	(3) TOTAL LABOR COST	(4) MARGINAL LABOR COST	(5) MARGINAL REVENUE PRODUCT
1	$250	$ 250	$250	$475
2	250	500	250	450
3	250	750	250	425
4	250	1000	250	400
5	250	1250	250	375
6	250	1500	250	350
7	250	1750	250	325
8	275	2200	450	275
9	300	2700	500	225
10	325	3250	550	150

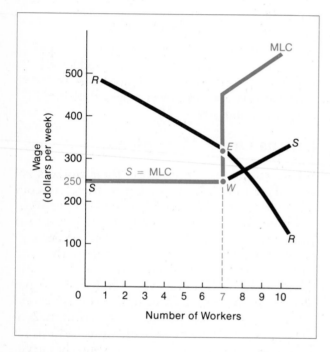

Figure 36–14
THE EFFECTS OF A UNION UNDER MONOPSONY

A union can change the character of the MLC schedule facing a monopsonist. In this example, MLC is horizontal up to seven workers, and then jumps as indicated by the heavy blue line. Consequently, equilibrium employment is determined by point E, where seven workers are employed at a wage of $250. Comparing this with Figure 36–13, we see that the union can raise both wages and employment.

total labor costs at each employment level, and column 4 shows the corresponding marginal cost. The heavy blue curve labeled MLC in Figure 36–14 depicts this information graphically. Notice that the marginal labor cost schedule has become *horizontal* up to the point where seven workers are

hired. This is a result of the union's behavior, which tells the monopsonist that he must pay the *same* wage per worker whether he hires one or seven employees. Beyond seven workers, the schedule returns to its previous level since the union minimum is irrelevant.

The condition for profit maximization is unchanged, so the monopsonist seeks the employment level at which marginal labor costs and marginal revenue product are equal. Since MLC jumps abruptly from $250 for the seventh worker to $450 for the eighth, this cannot be achieved exactly. But Table 36–2 makes it quite clear that it is now profitable to employ the seventh worker (marginal labor cost equals $250, marginal revenue product equals $325), but unprofitable to employ the eighth (marginal labor cost equals $450, marginal revenue product equals $275). Points E and W in Figure 36–14 show, once again, the monopsonist's equilibrium point and the wage he must pay.

Comparing Figures 36–13 and 36–14 (or Tables 36–1 and 36–2), we see that the union has raised wages from $225 to $250 per week, and at the same time has *increased* employment from six to seven workers. As was claimed, the union can raise both wages and employment in the presence of monopsony.

Minimum Wage Laws Under Monopsony

Virtually the same kind of result as the one just discussed *can* be achieved by a minimum wage law under monopsony. That is, *if* the government selects the right minimum wage, it might succeed in raising both wages and employment.

Refer back to Figure 36–13, in which we depicted the equilibrium wage ($225 per week) and employment level (six workers) in a monopsonized labor market with no minimum wage. Just like our union, a minimum wage law creates a horizontal supply curve at the minimum wage. The effects will be just the same as the effects of the union. In both cases, the differences between wages and marginal labor costs are eliminated. As an exercise, use Figure 36–13 to convince yourself that a minimum wage can succeed in raising *both* wages *and* employment by imposing a horizontal supply curve of labor at a wage between $225 and $350 per week. (*Hint:* What will be the monopsonist's MLC under the minimum wage?)

We caution you against reading strong policy conclusions into this finding, however. Examples of actual monopsony (one buyer) in labor markets are quite hard to find. Certainly the types of service establishments that tend to hire the lowest-paid workers—restaurants and snack bars, amusement parks, car washes, and so on—have no monopsony power whatever. While minimum wage laws *can* conceivably raise employment, few economists believe that they actually have this pleasant effect except in some exceptional cases.

Summary

1. A profit-maximizing monopsonist hires labor up to the point where the marginal revenue product equals the marginal labor cost.
2. Because marginal labor cost exceeds the wage rate, this results in less employment and lower wages than would emerge from a competitive labor market.
3. By eliminating the difference between marginal labor costs and wages, it is possible that a union could raise both wages and employment under monopsony.
4. For the same reason, a minimum wage law can conceivably raise wages without sacrificing jobs if the employer is a monopsonist.

Concept for Review

Marginal labor costs

Questions for Discussion

1. Consider the pizza chef example of Question 3 on page 000 and suppose that pizzas sell for $3 each. Let the supply curve of chefs be as follows:

NUMBER OF CHEFS	WAGE PER DAY
1	$40
2	50
3	60
4	70
5	80
6	90

   a. How many chefs will be employed, and at what wage, if the market is competitive?
   b. How many chefs will be employed, and at what wage, if the market has a monopsony pizza parlor? (*Hint:* First figure out the schedule of marginal labor cost.)
   c. Compare your answers to a. and b. What do you conclude?
   d. Now suppose that a union is organized to fight the monopsonist. If it insists on a wage of $70 per day, what will the monopsonist do?
2. Given what you have learned about minimum wage laws in the chapter and in the appendix, do you think they are a good or a bad idea?

37

Poverty, Inequality, and Discrimination

The white man knows how
to make everything, but he
does not know how to
distribute it.

SITTING BULL

The last two chapters analyzed the principles by which factor prices—wages, rentals, and interest rates—are determined in a market economy. One reason for concern with this issue is that these factor payments determine the *incomes* of the people to whom the factors belong. The study of factor pricing is, therefore, an indirect way to learn about the *distribution of income* among individuals.

In this chapter we turn to the problem of income distribution more directly. Specifically, we seek answers to the following questions: How much income inequality is there in the United States, and why? How can society decide rationally on how much equality it wants? And, once this decision is made, what policies are available to pursue this goal? In trying to answer these questions, we must necessarily consider the related problems of poverty and discrimination, and so these issues, too, receive attention in this chapter.

We will also offer a full explanation of one of the **12 Ideas for Beyond the Final Exam:** *the fundamental trade-off between economic equality and economic efficiency*. Taking it for granted that equality and efficiency are both important social goals, we shall learn why policies that promote greater income equality (or less poverty or less discrimination) often threaten to interfere with economic efficiency. In this chapter we explain *why* this is so and *what* can be done about it.

The Politics and Economics of Inequality

It is apparent that the trade-off between equality and efficiency is not widely understood. Social reformers often argue that society should adopt even the most outlandish programs to reduce discrimination or increase income equality or eradicate poverty, regardless of the potential side effects these policies might have. Defenders of the status quo, for their part, often seem so obsessed with these undesirable side effects—whether real or imagined—that they ignore the benefits of redistribution or of antidiscrimination programs.

Drawing by Mulligan; © 1978 The New Yorker Magazine, Inc.

The continuing debate over supply-side economics is a good illustration.[1] Many of the tax incentives advocated by supply siders, such as reducing or eliminating taxes on interest, dividends, and capital gains, clearly would be of greatest benefit to the wealthy. The poor, after all, do not own much corporate stock. On the other hand, these measures are designed to increase the incentives to save and invest; and, if they are successful, the whole nation will benefit from the resulting increase in investment and productivity. The more zealous advocates of supply-side initiatives trumpet the hoped-for gains in productivity and show little appreciation of the harmful effects on income equality. Some of their opponents vocally decry the widening of income differentials and show little concern for increasing the nation's productivity. Each side claims to have a monopoly on virtue. Neither has.

Economists try not to paint these issues in black and white. They prefer to phrase things in terms of trade-offs — to reap gains on one front, you often must make sacrifices on another. A policy is not necessarily ill conceived simply because it has some undesirable side effects, *if* it makes an important enough contribution to one of society's basic goals. But, on the other hand, some policies have such severe side effects that they deserve to be rejected, even if they serve a laudable goal.

Admitting that there is a trade-off between equality and efficiency — that while supply-side tax cuts may help solve the productivity problem, they may also increase inequality — may not be the best way to win votes. But it does face the facts. And in that way it helps us make the inherently political decisions about what should be done. If we are to understand these complex issues, a good place to start is, as always, with the facts.

The Facts: Poverty

In 1962, Michael Harrington published a little book called *The Other America*, which was to have a profound effect on American society. The "other Americans" of whom Harrington wrote were the poor who lived in the land of plenty. Ill clothed in the richest country on earth, inadequately nourished in a nation where obesity was a problem, infirm in a country with some of the world's

---

[1]This debate was considered in greater detail in Chapter 12.

highest health standards, these people lived an almost unknown existence in their dilapidated hovels, according to Harrington. And, to make matters worse, their inadequate nutrition, lack of education, and generally demoralized state often condemned the children of the "other Americans" to repeat the lives of their parents. There was, Harrington argued, a "cycle of poverty" that could be broken only by government action.

The work of Harrington and others touched the hearts of many Americans who, it seemed, really had no idea of the abominable living conditions of some of their countrymen. Within a few years, the growing outrage over the plight of the poor had crystallized into a "War on Poverty," which was declared by President Lyndon Johnson in 1964. An official definition of poverty was adopted: The poor were those families with an income below $3000 in 1964.

This dividing line between the poor and nonpoor was called the **poverty line**, and a goal was established: to get all Americans above the poverty line by the nation's bicentennial in 1976. The definition of the poverty line was subsequently modified to account for differences in family size and other considerations, and it is now also adjusted each year to reflect changes in the cost of living. In 1986, the poverty line for a family of four was about $11,200 and about 13.6 percent of all Americans remained in poverty by official definitions.

Who are the poor? Relative to their proportions in the overall population, they are more likely to be black than white, young than old, and female than male. They are less educated and in worse health than the population as a whole, and tend to live in bigger families. Indeed, nearly 40 percent of the poor are children.

Substantial progress toward eliminating poverty was made in the decade from 1963 to 1973; the percentage of people living below the poverty line dropped from 20 percent to 11 percent (see Figure 37–1). But thereafter a series of recessions and a slowdown in the growth of social welfare programs reversed the trend. By 1984, the poverty rate was back to what it had been in 1967.

The **poverty line** is an amount of income below which a family is considered "poor."

Figure 37–1
PROGRESS IN THE WAR ON POVERTY
This figure charts the declines in the number and percentage of Americans classified as "poor" by official definitions. While substantial progress has been made in the War on Poverty, more than 13 percent of Americans remain below the poverty line. The broken line shows one of the experimental measures of poverty that includes noncash benefits.
SOURCE: For 1959–1986, U.S. Bureau of the Census. For 1955–1958, estimates kindly provided by Gordon M. Fisher.

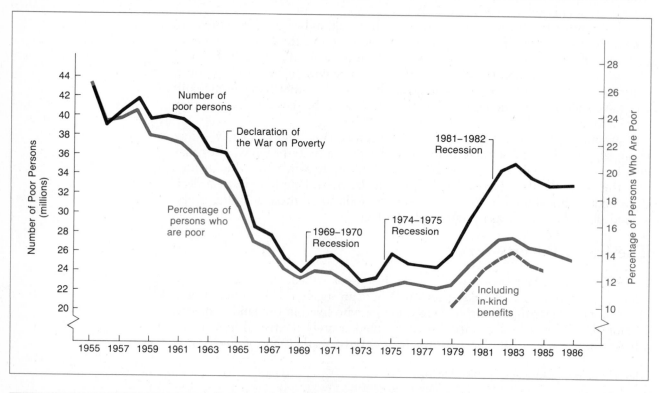

The rise in poverty since the late 1970s worries many people. But some critics argue that the official data badly overstate the poverty population; some even go so far as to claim that poverty would be considered a thing of the past if the official definition (based on cash income) were amended to include the many goods that the poor are given in kind: public education, public housing, health care, food, and the like.

These criticisms prompted the Census Bureau to develop several experimental measures of poverty which include the value of goods given in kind. If these new measures are accepted as valid, fewer people are classified as poor, but the basic trend in recent years is the same: Poverty has risen sharply since 1979. (See again Figure 37–1.)

This debate raises the fundamental question of how to define "the poor." Continuing economic growth will eventually pull almost everyone above any arbitrarily established poverty line. Does this event mark the end of poverty? Some would say, "Yes." But others would insist that the biblical injunction is right: "The poor ye have always with you."

There are two ways to define poverty. The more optimistic definition uses an *absolute concept of poverty:* If you fall short of a certain minimum standard of living, you are poor; once you pass this standard, you are no longer poor. The second definition is based on a *relative concept of poverty:* The poor are those who fall too far behind the average income.

Each definition has its pros and cons. The basic problem with the absolute poverty concept is that it is arbitrary. Who sets the line? Most of the people of Bangladesh would be delighted to live a bit below the U.S. poverty line, and they would consider themselves quite prosperous. Similarly, the standard of living that we now call "poor" would probably not have been considered so in America in 1780, and certainly not in Europe during the Middle Ages. (See the boxed insert on page 826.) Different times and different places apparently call for different poverty lines.

The fact that the concept of poverty is culturally, not physiologically, determined suggests that it must be a relative concept. For example, one suggestion is to define the poverty line as one-half of the national average income. In this way, the poverty line would automatically rise as the nation grows richer.

Once we start moving away from an absolute concept of poverty toward a relative concept, the sharp distinction between the poor and the nonpoor starts to evaporate. Instead, we begin to think of a parade of people from the poorest soul to the richest millionaire. The "poverty problem," then, seems to be that disparities in income are "too large" in some sense. The poor are so poor because the rich are so rich. If we follow this line of thought far enough, we are led away from the narrow problem of *poverty* toward the broader problem of *inequality of income.*

The Facts: Inequality

Nothing in the market mechanism prevents large differences in incomes. On the contrary, it tends to breed inequality, for the basic source of the great efficiency of the market mechanism is its system of rewards and penalties. The market is generous to those who are successful in operating efficient enterprises that are responsive to consumer demands, and it is ruthless in penalizing those who are unable or unwilling to satisfy consumer demands efficiently. Its financial punishment of those who try and fail can be particularly severe. At times it

Life in a Slum and in a Castle

There is little doubt that the unfortunate souls who inhabit America's worst urban slums are "poor" by any reasonable definition. Yet there are striking parallels between the standard of living of these people and that of the powerful but vermin-covered barons of the Middle Ages, as the following two passages show. Together these passages graphically point out the need for a relative concept of poverty.

A Twentieth Century Slum

We were living in deplorable conditions. We would cook a pot of oatmeal in the morning, then reheat it up on the radiator in the afternoon. . . . Whenever the sewer would back up, all that filth would come up under our floor and run around all over the floor. . . . One time this went on for four days. My wife had to keep the kids up on the bed. All that stuff floating around through the apartment until they got the Roto-Rooter man there.

In the wintertime . . . we go to bed with all our clothes on. . . .

When it's real cold, we close off the two bedrooms completely and burn the oven and then we all sleep in here together. . . .

One of my babies has been in the hospital twice for lead poisoning. She'd pick plaster and paint and stuff off the walls. . . .

SOURCE: Herb Goro, *The Block* (New York: Random House, 1970), pages 82–86.

A Medieval Castle

The knight's castle was extremely simple and must have been most uncomfortable. There were usually two rooms: the hall and the chamber. In the hall the knight did his business. . . . The chamber was the private room of the lord and his family. There he entertained guests of high rank. At night the lord, his lady, and their children slept in beds, while their personal servants slept on the chamber floor. . . . The castles were cold and drafty. The windows were covered by boards, or open. If the castle was of wood—as most were before the thirteenth century—the knight could not have a fire. In a stone castle one could have fire, but as chimneys did not appear until the late twelfth century, the smoke must have been almost unbearable. It seems likely that if one of us were offered the choice between spending a winter night with the lord or his serf, he would choose the comparatively tight mud hut with the nice warm pigs on the floor.

SOURCE: Sydney Painter, *A History of the Middle Ages 284–1500* (New York: Alfred A. Knopf, 1953), page 122.

even brings down the great and powerful. Robert Morris, once perhaps the wealthiest resident of the American colonies, ended up in debtors' prison. In recent years, the newspapers have carried periodic stories about the bankruptcy proceedings of the Hunt brothers of Texas, once one of America's richest families.

Most people have a pretty good idea that the income distribution is quite spread out—that the gulf between the rich and the poor is wide. But few have any concept of where they stand in the distribution. In the next paragraph, you will find some statistics on the 1986 income distribution in the United States. But before looking at these, try the following experiment. First, write down what you think your family's income before tax was in 1986. (If you do not know, take a guess.) Next, try to guess what percentage of American families had incomes *lower* than this. Finally, if we divide America into three broad income classes — rich, middle class, and poor — to which group do you think your family belongs?

Now that you have written down answers to these three questions, look at the income distribution data for 1986 in Table 37–1. If you are like most college students, these figures will contain a few surprises for you. First, if we adopt the tentative definition that the lowest 20 percent are the "poor," the highest 20 percent are the "rich," and the middle 60 percent are the "middle class," many fewer of you belong to the celebrated "middle class" than thought so. In fact, the cut-off point that defined membership in the "rich" class in 1986 was only about $50,000 before taxes, an income level exceeded by the parents of many college students. (Your parents may be shocked to learn that they are rich!)

Next, use Table 37–1 to estimate the fraction of U.S. families that have incomes lower than your family's. (The caption to Table 37–1 has instructions to help you do this.) Most students who come from households of moderate prosperity have an instinctive feeling that they stand somewhere near the middle of the income distribution; so they estimate about half, or perhaps a little more. In fact, if your parents earn about $82,000 a year, about 95 percent of American families are poorer than yours!

This exercise has perhaps brought us down to earth. America is not nearly so rich as Madison Avenue would like us to believe. Let us now look past the average level of income and see how the pie is divided. Table 37–2 shows the shares of income accruing to each fifth of the population in 1986 and several earlier years. In a perfectly equal society, all the numbers in this table would be "20 percent" since each fifth of the population would receive one-fifth of the

Table 37–1
DISTRIBUTION OF FAMILY INCOME IN THE UNITED STATES IN 1986

INCOME RANGE (dollars)	PERCENTAGE OF ALL FAMILIES IN THIS RANGE	PERCENTAGE OF FAMILIES IN THIS AND LOWER RANGES
Under 2500	1.8	1.8
2500 to 4999	2.8	4.6
5000 to 7499	3.7	8.3
7500 to 9999	4.1	12.4
10,000 to 12,499	4.9	17.3
12,500 to 14,999	4.8	22.1
15,000 to 19,999	9.7	31.8
20,000 to 24,999	9.8	41.6
25,000 to 34,999	18.1	59.7
35,000 to 49,999	19.6	79.3
50,000 and over	20.7	100.0

SOURCE: U.S. Bureau of the Census.

If your family's income falls close to one of the end points of the ranges indicated here, you can approximate the fraction of families with income *lower* than yours by just looking at the last column.

  If your family's income falls within one of the ranges, you can interpolate the answer. *Example:* Your family's income was $45,000. This is two-thirds of the way from $35,000 to $50,000, so your family was richer than roughly $(\frac{2}{3}) \times 19.6$ percent = 13.1 percent of the families in this class. Adding this to the percentage of families in lower classes (59.7 percent in this case) gives the answer — about 72.8 percent of all families earned less than yours.

Table 37–2
INCOME SHARES IN SELECTED YEARS

INCOME GROUP	1986	1980	1970	1960	1950
Lowest fifth	4.6	5.1	5.5	4.9	4.5
Second fifth	10.8	11.6	12.0	12.0	12.0
Middle fifth	16.8	17.5	17.4	17.6	17.4
Fourth fifth	24.0	24.3	23.5	23.6	23.5
Highest fifth	43.7	41.6	41.6	42.0	43.6

SOURCE: U.S. Bureau of the Census.

income. In fact, as the table shows, this is certainly not the case. In 1986, for example, the poorest fifth of all families had less than 5 percent of the total income, while the richest fifth had more than 43 percent — $9\frac{1}{2}$ times as much.

Depicting Income Distributions: The Lorenz Curve

Statisticians and economists use a convenient tool to portray data like these graphically. The device, called a **Lorenz curve,** is shown in Figure 37–2. To construct a Lorenz curve, we first draw a square whose vertical and horizontal dimensions both represent 100 percent. Then we record the percentage of families (or persons) on the horizontal axis and the percentage of income that these families (or persons) receive on the vertical axis, using all the data that we have. For example, point C in Figure 37–2 depicts the fact (known from Table 37–2) that the bottom 60 percent (the three lowest fifths) of American families in 1986 received 32 percent of the total income. Similarly, points A, B, and D represent the other information contained in Table 37–2. We can list four important properties of a Lorenz curve.

1. It begins at the origin because zero families naturally have zero income.
2. It always ends at the upper-right corner of the square, since 100 percent of the nation's families must necessarily receive all the nation's income.

Figure 37–2
A LORENZ CURVE FOR THE UNITED STATES
This Lorenz curve for the United States is based on the 1986 distribution of income given in Table 37–2. The percentage of families is measured along the horizontal axis, and the percentage of income that these families receive is measured along the vertical axis. Thus, for example, point C indicates that the bottom 60 percent of American families received 32 percent of the total income in 1986.

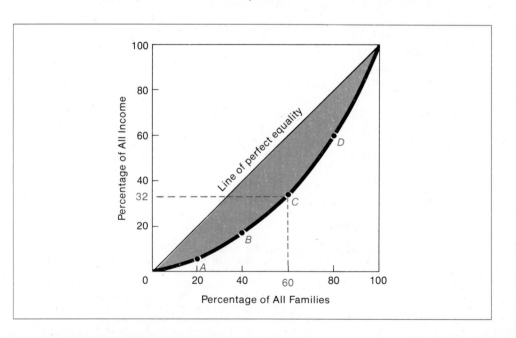

3. If income were distributed equally, the Lorenz curve would be a straight line connecting these two points (the thin solid line in Figure 37–2). This is because, with everybody equal, the bottom 20 percent of the families would receive 20 percent of the income, the bottom 40 percent would receive 40 percent, and so on.

4. In a real economy, with significant income differences, the Lorenz curve will "sag" downward from this line of perfect equality. It is easy to see why this is so. If there is any inequality at all, the poorest 20 percent of families must get less than 20 percent of the income. This corresponds to a point below the equality line, such as point A. Similarly, the bottom 40 percent of families must receive less than 40 percent of the income (point B), and so on.

In fact, the size of the area between the line of perfect equality and the Lorenz curve (the shaded area in Figure 37–2) is often used as a handy measure of inequality. The larger this area, the more unequal is the income distribution. For U.S. family incomes, this so-called area of inequality usually fills up about 40 percent of the total area underneath the equality line.

Standing by itself, the Lorenz curve tells us little. To interpret it, we must know what it looked like in earlier years or what it looks like in other countries. The historical data in Table 37–2 show that *the U.S. Lorenz curve has not moved much in the last 36 years*. To some, this remarkable stability in the income distribution is deplorable. To others, it suggests some immutable law of the capitalist system. In fact, neither view is correct.

The apparent long-run stability in the income distribution is the result of a standoff between certain demographic forces that were pushing the Lorenz curve outward, such as more young and old people and more families headed by women, and other forces that were pulling it inward, such as government antipoverty programs. Notice, moreover, that the distribution of income has grown substantially more unequal since 1980: The lowest fifth now gets a smaller share and the highest fifth a larger one than they did then.

Comparing the United States with other countries is much harder, since no two countries use precisely the same definition of income distribution. More than a decade ago, the Organization for Economic Cooperation and Development (OECD) made a heroic effort to standardize the income distribution data of its member countries so they could be compared.[2] In this analysis, Japan stood out as the industrialized country with the most equal income distribution, with Australia, West Germany, the Netherlands, and Sweden bunched rather closely in second place. France and the United States seemed to have the most inequality.

Before extrapolating from these findings, it should be pointed out that only 12 industrial countries were compared. Israel, which is often thought to have the most equal income distribution in the noncommunist world, is not in the OECD. Nor are any of the less developed countries, which are generally found to have much more inequality than the developed ones. The conclusion seems to be that:

The United States has rather more income inequality than most other developed countries.

[2]Malcolm Sawyer, "Income Distribution in OECD Countries," *OECD Occasional Studies*, July 1976, pages 3–36.

Some Reasons for Unequal Incomes

Let us now begin to formulate a list of the *causes* of income inequality. Here are some that come to mind.

1. *Differences in ability.* Everyone knows that people have different capabilities. Some can run faster, ski better, do calculations more quickly, type more accurately, and so on. Hence it should not be surprising that some people are more adept at earning income. Precisely what sort of ability is relevant to earning income is a matter of intense debate among economists, sociologists, and psychologists. The kind of talents that make for success in school seem to have some effect, but hardly an overwhelming one. The same is true of innate intelligence ("IQ"). It is clear that some types of inventiveness are richly rewarded by the market, and the same is true of that elusive characteristic called "entrepreneurial ability." Also, it is obvious that poor health impairs earning ability.

2. *Differences in intensity of work.* Some people work longer hours than others, or labor more intensely when they are on the job. This results in certain income differences that are largely voluntary.

3. *Risk taking.* Most people who have acquired large sums of money have done so by taking risks — by investing their money in some uncertain venture. Those who gamble and succeed become wealthy. Those who try and fail go broke. Most others prefer not to take such chances and wind up somewhere in between. This is another way in which income differences arise voluntarily.

4. *Compensating wage differentials.* Some jobs are more arduous than others, or more dangerous, or more unpleasant for other reasons. To induce people to take these jobs, some sort of financial incentive normally must be offered. For example, factory workers who work the night shift normally receive higher wages than those who work during the day.

5. *Schooling and other types of training.* In Chapter 36 we spoke of schooling and other types of training as "investments in human capital." We meant by this that workers can sacrifice *current* income in order to improve their skills so that their *future* incomes will be higher. When this is done, income differentials naturally rise. Consider a high school friend who did not go on to college. Even if you are working at a part-time job, your annual earnings are probably much below his or hers. Once you graduate from college, however, the statistics suggest that your earnings will quickly overtake your friend's earnings.

   It is generally agreed that differences in schooling are an important cause of income differentials. This particular cause has both voluntary and involuntary aspects. Young men or young women who *choose* not to go to college have made voluntary decisions that affect their incomes. But many never get the choice: Their parents simply cannot afford to send them. For them, the resulting income differential is not voluntary.

6. *Work experience.* It is well known to most people and well documented by scholarly research that more experienced workers earn higher wages.

7. *Inherited wealth.* Not all income is derived from work. Some is the return on invested wealth, and part of this wealth is inherited. While this cause of inequality does not apply to many people, a great number of America's super-rich got that way through inheritance.

And financial wealth is not the only type of capital that can be inherited; so can human capital. In part this happens naturally through genetics: Parents of high ability tend to have children of high ability, although the link is an imperfect one. But it also happens partly for economic reasons: Well-to-do parents send their children to the best schools, thereby transforming their own *financial* wealth into *human* wealth for their children. This type of inheritance may be much more important than the financial type.

8. **Luck.** No observer of our society can fail to notice the role of chance. Some of the rich and some of the poor got there largely by good or bad fortune. A farmer digging for water discovers oil instead. An investor strikes it rich on the stock market. A student trains herself for a high-paying occupation only to find that the opportunity has disappeared while she was in college. A construction worker is unemployed for a whole year because of a recession that he had no part in creating. The list could go on and on. Many large income differentials arise purely by chance.

The Facts: Discrimination

Some of the factors we have just listed lead to income differentials that are widely accepted as "just." For example, few quarrel with the idea that it is fair for people who work longer hours to receive higher incomes. Other factors on our list ignite heated debates. For example, some people view income differentials that arise purely by chance as perfectly acceptable. Others find these same differentials intolerable. However, almost no one is willing to condone income inequalities that arise strictly because of discrimination.

The facts about discrimination are not easy to come by. **Economic discrimination** is defined to occur when equivalent factors of production receive different payments for equal contributions to output. But this definition is hard to apply in practice because we cannot always tell when two factors of production are "equivalent."

Probably no one would call it "discrimination" if a woman with only a high school diploma receives a lower salary than a man with a college degree (though one might legitimately ask whether discrimination helps to explain the difference in their educational attainments). Even if they have the same education, the man may have 10 more years of work experience than the woman. If they receive different wages for this reason, are we to call that "discrimination"?

Ideally, we would compare men and women whose *productivities* are equal. In this case, if women receive lower wages than men, we would clearly call it discrimination. But discrimination normally takes much more subtle forms than paying unequal wages for equal work. For instance, employers can simply keep women relegated to inferior jobs, thus justifying the lower salaries they pay them.

One clearly *incorrect* way to measure discrimination is to compare the typical incomes of different groups. Table 37–3 displays such data for white men, white women, black men, and black women in 1986. Virtually everyone agrees that the amount of discrimination is less than these differentials suggest, but far greater than zero. Precisely how much is a topic of continuing economic research. Several studies suggest that about half of the observed wage differential between black and white men, and at least half of the differential between white women and white men, is caused by discrimination in the labor market (though more might be due to discrimination in education, and so on). Other

Economic discrimination is defined to occur when equivalent factors of production receive different payments for equal contributions to output.

Table 37–3

MEDIAN INCOMES IN 1986

POPULATION GROUP*	MEDIAN INCOME	PERCENTAGE OF WHITE MALE INCOME
White males	$18,060	100
Black males	10,822	60
White females	7,760	43
Black females	6,566	36

*Persons 15 years old and over.
SOURCE: U.S. Bureau of the Census.

studies have reached somewhat different conclusions. While no one denies the existence of discrimination, its quantitative importance is a matter of ongoing controversy and research.

The Economic Theory of Discrimination*

Let us see what economic theory tells us about discrimination. In particular, consider the following two questions:

1. Must the existence of *prejudice*, which we define as arising when one group dislikes associating with another group, always lead to *discrimination* (unequal pay for equal work)?

2. Are there "natural" economic forces that tend either to erode or to exacerbate discrimination over time?

As we shall see now, the analysis we have provided in previous chapters sheds light on both these issues.

Discrimination by Employers

Most attention seems to focus on discrimination by employers, so let us start there. What happens if, for instance, some firms refuse to hire blacks? Figure 37–3 will help us find the answer. Part (a) pertains to firms that discriminate; part (b) pertains to firms that do not. There are supply and demand curves for labor in each part, based on the analysis of Chapter 36. We suppose the two demand curves to be identical. However, the supply curve in part (b) must be farther to the right than the supply curve in part (a) because whites *and* blacks can work in part (b) whereas only whites can work in part (a). The result is that wages will be lower in part (b) than in part (a). Since all the blacks are forced into part (b), we conclude that there is discrimination against blacks.

But now consider the situation from the point of view of the *employers*. Firms in part (a) of Figure 37–3 are paying more for labor; they are paying for the privilege of discriminating against blacks. The nondiscriminatory firms in part (b) have a cost advantage. As we learned in earlier chapters, if there is effective competition, these nondiscriminatory firms will tend to capture more and more of the market. The discriminators will gradually be driven out of business. If, on the other hand, many of the firms in part (a) have protected

*This section may be omitted in shorter courses.

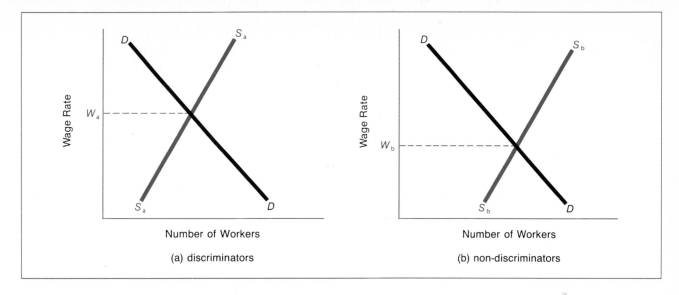

(a) discriminators

(b) non-discriminators

monopolies, they will be able to remain in business. But they will pay for the privilege of discriminating by earning lower monopoly profits than they otherwise could (because they pay higher wages than they have to).

Discrimination by Fellow Workers

Thus competitive forces will tend to reduce discrimination over time if employers are the source of discrimination. Such optimistic conclusions cannot necessarily be reached, however, if it is workers who are prejudiced. Consider what happens if, for example, men do not like to have women as their supervisors. If men do not give their full cooperation, female supervisors will be less effective than male supervisors and hence will earn lower wages. Here prejudice does lead to discrimination, even in the long run.

Statistical Discrimination

A final type of discrimination, called **statistical discrimination,** may be the most stubborn of all and can exist even when there is no prejudice. Here is an important example. It is, of course, a fact that only women can have babies. It is also a fact that many, though certainly not all, working women who have babies quit their jobs (at least for a while) to care for their newborns. Employers know this. What they cannot know, however, is *which* women of child-bearing age are likely to drop out of the labor force for this reason.

Suppose three candidates apply for a job that requires a long-term commitment. Susan plans to quit after a few years to raise a family. Jane does not plan to have any children. Jack is a man. If he knew all the facts, the employer would prefer either Jane or Jack to Susan, but would be indifferent between Jane and Jack. But the employer cannot tell Susan and Jane apart. He therefore presumes that both Jane and Susan, being young women, are more likely than Jack to quit to raise a family; so he hires Jack, even though Jane is just as good a prospect. Jane is discriminated against.[3]

In terms of the two questions with which we begin this section, we conclude that different types of *discrimination* lead to different answers. Prejudice

Figure 37–3
WAGE DISCRIMINATION
Part (a) depicts supply and demand curves for labor among discriminatory firms; part (b) shows the same for nondiscriminatory firms. Since only whites can work in part (a), while both races can work in part (b), the supply curve in part (b) is farther to the right than the supply curve in part (a). Consequently, the wage rate in part (b), W_b, winds up below the wage rate in part (a) W_a. Workers in part (b) are discriminated against.

Statistical discrimination is said to occur when the productivity of a particular worker is estimated to be low just because that worker belongs to a particular group (such as women).

[3]Lest it be thought that this example justifies discrimination against women, it should be pointed out that women generally have less absenteeism and job turnover for nonpregnancy health reasons than men do.

often but not always leads to economic discrimination. And discrimination may occur even in the absence of prejudice. Finally, the forces of competition tend to erode some, but not all, of the inequities caused by discrimination. Most observers feel that much more must be done to combat the effects of discrimination; the market will not do the job by itself.

The Optimal Amount of Inequality

We have seen that substantial income inequality exists in America, and we have noted some reasons for it. Let us now ask a question that is loaded with value judgments, but to which economic analysis has something to contribute nonetheless: *How much inequality is the ideal amount?* We shall not, of course, be able to give a numerical answer to this question. No one can do that. Our objective is rather to see the type of analysis that is relevant to answering the question. We begin in a simple setting in which the answer is easily obtained. Then we shall see how the real world differs from this simple model.

Consider a world in which there are two people, Smith and Jones, and suppose we want to divide $100 between them in the way that yields the most *total utility*. Suppose further that Smith and Jones are alike in their ability to enjoy money; technically, we say that their *marginal utility* schedules are identical.[4] This identical marginal utility schedule is depicted in Figure 37–4 below. We can prove the following result: *The optimal distribution of income is to give $50 to Smith and $50 to Jones,* which is point E in Figure 37–4.

To prove it, we show that if the income distribution is unequal, we can improve things by moving closer to equality. So suppose that Smith has $75 (point S in the figure) and Jones has $25 (point J). Then, as we can see, because of the law of diminishing marginal utility, Smith's *marginal utility* (which is s) must be *less* than Jones's (which is j). If we take $1 away from Smith, Smith *loses* the low marginal utility, s, of a dollar to him. Then, when

[4]If you need to refresh your memory about marginal utility, see Chapter 21, especially pages 459–62.

Figure 37–4
THE OPTIMAL DISTRIBUTION OF INCOME
If Smith and Jones have the identical marginal utility schedule (curve *MU*), then the optimal way to distribute $100 between them is to give $50 to each (point *E*). If income is not distributed this way, then their marginal utilities will be unequal, so that a redistribution of income can make society better off. This is illustrated by points *J* and *S*, representing an income distribution in which Jones gets $25 (and hence has marginal utility *j*), while Smith gets $75 (and hence has marginal utility *s*).

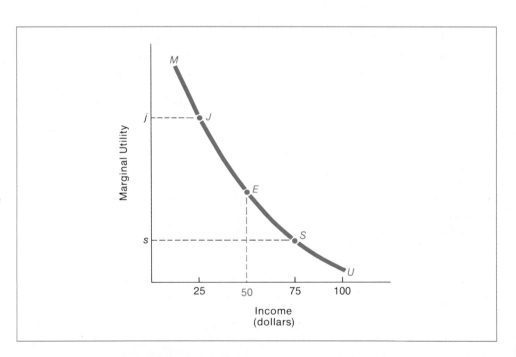

we give it to Jones, Jones *gains* the high marginal utility, j, that a dollar gives him. On balance, society's total utility rises by $j - s$ because Jones's gain exceeds Smith's loss. Therefore, a distribution with Smith getting only $74 is better than one in which he gets $75. Since the same argument can be used to show that a $73-$27 distribution is better than $74-$26, and so on, we have established our result that a $50-$50 distribution — point E — is best.

Now in this argument there is nothing special about the fact that we assumed only two people or that exactly $100 was available. Any number of people and dollars would do as well. What really *is* crucial is our assumption that the same amount of money would be available no matter how we chose to distribute it. Thus we have proved the following general result:

To maximize total utility, the best way to distribute any *fixed* amount of money among people with identical marginal utility schedules is to divide it equally.

The Trade-Off Between Equality and Efficiency

If we seek to apply this analysis to the real world, two major difficulties arise. First, people are different and have different marginal utility schedules. Thus *some* inequality can probably be justified.[5] The second problem is much more formidable.

The total amount of income in society is *not* independent of how we try to distribute it.

To see this in an extreme form, ask yourself the following question: What would happen if we tried to achieve perfect equality by putting a 100 percent income tax on all workers and then dividing the tax receipts equally among the population? No one would have any incentive to work, to invest, to take risks, or to do anything else to earn money, because the rewards for all such activities would disappear. The gross national product (GNP) would fall drastically. While the example is extreme, the same principle applies to more moderate policies to equalize incomes; indeed, it is the basic idea behind supply-side economics.[6]

The Trade-Off Between Equality and Efficiency
Policies that redistribute income reduce the rewards of high-income earners while raising the rewards of low-income earners. Hence, they reduce the incentive to earn high income. This gives rise to a trade-off that is one of the most fundamental in all of economics, and one of our **12 Ideas for Beyond the Final Exam.**
Measures taken to increase the amount of economic equality will often reduce economic efficiency — that is, lower the gross national product. In trying to divide the pie more equally, we may inadvertently reduce its size.

Because of this trade-off, the result that equal incomes are always optimal does not apply to the real world. On the contrary:

The optimal distribution of income will always involve *some* inequality.

[5]It can be shown that if we know that people differ, but cannot tell who has the higher marginal utility schedule, then the best way to distribute income is still in equal shares.
[6]For a full discussion of supply-side economics, see pages 234–43.

But this does not mean that attempts to reduce inequality are always misguided. What we should learn from this analysis are two things:

1. There are better and worse ways to promote equality. In pursuing further income equality (or fighting poverty), we should seek policies that do the least possible harm to incentives.
2. Equality is bought at a price. Thus, like any commodity, we must decide rationally how much to purchase. We will probably want to spend some of our potential income on equality, but not all of it.

Figure 37–5 on this page illustrates both these lessons. The curve *abcde* represents possible combinations of GNP and income equality that are obtainable under the present system of taxes and transfers. If, for example, point *c* is the current position of the economy, raising taxes on the rich to finance more transfers to the poor might move us downward to the right, toward point *d*. Equality increases, but GNP falls as the rich react to higher marginal tax rates by producing less. Similarly, reducing both taxes and social welfare programs might move us upward to the left, toward point *b*. Notice that, to the left of point *b*, GNP falls as inequality rises. This might be because very poorly-paid workers are less productive due to inadequate investments in human capital, poor nutrition, or just a general sense of disaffection. The curve *ABCDE* represents possible combinations of GNP and equality under some new, more efficient, redistributive policy. It is more efficient in the sense that, for any desired level of equality, we can get more GNP with the policy represented by *ABCDE* than with the policy represented by *abcde*.

The first lesson is obvious: We should stick to the higher of the two curves. If we find ourselves at any point on curve *abcde*, we can always improve things by moving up to the corresponding point on curve *ABCDE*, that is, by changing policies. By picking the most efficient redistributive policy, we can have more equality *and* more GNP. In the rest of this chapter, we discuss alternative policies and try to indicate which ones do the least harm to incentives.

The second lesson is that neither point *B* nor point *E* would normally be society's optimal choice. At point *B* we are seeking the highest possible GNP

Figure 37–5
THE TRADE-OFF BETWEEN EQUALITY AND EFFICIENCY
This diagram represents the fundamental trade-off between equality and efficiency. If the economy is initially at point *c*, then movements toward greater equality (to the right) normally can be achieved only by reducing economic efficiency, and thus reducing the gross national product. The movements from points *C* and *c* toward points *D* and *d* represent two alternative policies for equalizing the income distribution. The policy that leads to *D* is preferred since it is more efficient.

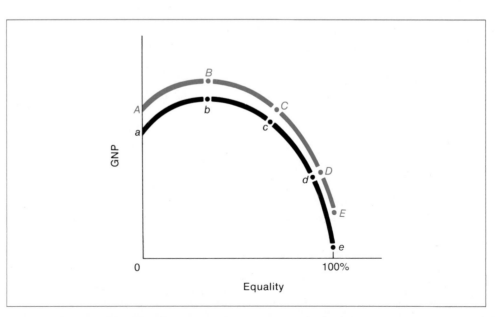

with utter disregard for whatever inequality might accompany it. At point *E* we are forcing complete equality, even if work incentives vanish and a minuscule GNP is the result.

It is astonishing how much confusion is caused by a failure to understand these two lessons. Proponents of measures that further economic equality often feel obligated to deny that their programs will have any harmful effects on incentives. At times these vehement denials are so patently unrealistic that they undermine the very case that the egalitarians are trying to defend. Conservatives who oppose these policies also undercut the strength of their case by making outlandish claims about the efficiency losses that are likely to arise from greater equality. Neither side, it seems, is willing or able to acknowledge the basic trade-off between equality and efficiency depicted in Figure 37–5. And so the debate generates more heat than light. Since these debates are sure to continue for the next 10 or 20 years, and probably for the rest of your lives, we hope that some understanding of this trade-off stays with you well **Beyond the Final Exam.**

But just understanding the terms of the trade-off will not tell you what to do. By looking at Figure 37–5, we know that the optimal amount of equality lies between points *B* and *E*, but we do not know what it actually is. Is it something like point *D*, with more equality and less GNP than we now have? Or is it a movement back toward point *B*? Everyone will have a different answer to this question, because it is basically one of value judgment. Just how much is more equality worth to you?

The late Arthur Okun, a former chairman of the Council of Economic Advisers, put the issue graphically. Imagine that money is liquid, and that you have a bucket that you can use to transport money from the rich to the poor. The problem, however, is that the bucket is leaky. As you move the money, some gets lost. Will you use the bucket if only 1 cent is lost for each $1 you move? Probably everyone would say yes. But what if each $1 taken from the rich results in only 10 cents for the poor? Only the most extreme egalitarians will still say yes. Now try the hard questions. What if 20 to 40 cents is lost for each $1 that you move? If you can answer questions like these, you can decide how far down the hill from point *B* you think society should travel, for you will have expressed your value judgments in quantitative terms.

Policies to Combat Poverty

Let us take it for granted that the nation has a commitment to reduce the amount of poverty. What are some policies that can promote this goal? Which of these does the least harm to incentives, and hence is most efficient?

The traditional approach to poverty fighting in the United States has utilized a variety of programs collectively known as *public assistance*. The best known, and most controversial, of these is **Aid to Families with Dependent Children (AFDC).** This program provides money to families in which there are children but no breadwinner, perhaps because there is no father and the children are too young to permit the mother to work. In 1986, about 11 million people received benefits from AFDC, and the average monthly grant was about $115 per person. In total, some $15 billion was spent.

AFDC has been attacked as a classic example of an inefficient redistributive program. Why? One reason is that it provides no incentive for the mother to earn income. After a four-month grace period, welfare payments are reduced by $1 for each $1 that the family earns as wages. Thus, if a member of the family gets a job, the family is subjected to a 100 percent tax rate. It is little wonder that many welfare recipients do not look very hard for work.

A second criticism is that AFDC provides an incentive for families to break up. As originally conceived, welfare was not to be paid to a family with a father who could work, even if he was unemployed. So if this father earned very little, or if he had no job, the children would get more income if he left them. Some fathers did. About half the states have now started a special AFDC-UF program (the "UF" stands for unemployed father) so that benefits can be paid to families with an unemployed father.

A third problem is geographical disparities in benefits. It is widely thought (though not conclusively proven) that many poor families migrated from the South to northern cities because of the more generous welfare benefits available there. This placed an enormous financial burden on these cities. Finally, the tedious case-by-case approach of AFDC, with its cumbersome bureaucracy and mountains of detailed regulations, seems to frustrate all parties concerned.

Another welfare program that burgeoned before President Reagan cut it back is **Food Stamps,** under which poor families are sold stamps which they can exchange for food. The dollar amount of the stamps they receive, and how much they pay for them, depends on the family's income. The more income the family earns, the more it must pay for the stamps. About 21 million people now receive Food Stamps, and federal spending on the program is about $13 billion per year.

In addition, many of the poor are provided with a number of important goods and services, either at no charge or at prices that are well below market levels. Medical care under the Medicaid (as opposed to Medicare) program[7] and subsidized public housing are two notable examples. These programs significantly enhance the living standards of the poor. However, most of them offer benefits that decline as family income rises. Taken as a whole, all the antipoverty programs may actually put a poor family in a position where it is *worse* off if its earnings *rise* — an effective tax rate well over 100 percent. When this occurs, there is a powerful incentive not to work.

The Negative Income Tax

These problems, and others like them, have contributed to the "welfare mess" and have led to frequent calls to scrap the whole system and replace it with a simple structure designed to get income into the hands of the poor without providing such adverse incentives. The solution suggested most frequently by economists is the so-called **negative income tax (NIT).**

The name "negative income tax" derives from its similarity to the regular (positive) income tax. Let us illustrate how NIT would work. To describe a particular NIT plan, we require two numbers: a minimum income level below which no family is allowed to fall (the "guarantee"), and a rate at which benefits are "taxed away" as income rises. Consider a plan with a $6000 guaranteed income (for a family of four) and a 50 percent tax rate. A family with no earnings would then receive a $6000 payment (a "negative tax") from the government. A family earning $2000 would have the basic benefit reduced by 50 percent of its earnings. Thus, since half its earnings is $1000, it would receive $5000 from the government plus the $2000 earned income for a total income of $7000 (see Table 37–4).

---

[7]The *Medicaid* program pays for the health care of low-income people, whereas *Medicare* is available to all elderly people, regardless of income.

Table 37-4

ILLUSTRATION OF A NEGATIVE INCOME TAX PLAN

EARNINGS	BENEFITS PAID	TOTAL INCOME
$ 0	$6000	$ 6000
2000	5000	7000
4000	4000	8000
6000	3000	9000
8000	2000	10000
10000	1000	11000
12000	0	12000

Notice in Table 37-4 that, with a 50 percent tax rate, the increase in total income as earnings rise is always half of the increase in earnings. There is *always some* incentive to work under an NIT system. Notice also that there is a "break-even" level of income at which benefits cease. In this case, the break-even level is $12,000. This is not another number that policymakers can arbitrarily select in the way they select the guarantee level and the tax rate. Rather, it is dictated by the choice of the guarantee level and the tax rate. In our example, $6000 is the maximum possible benefit and benefits are reduced by 50 cents for each $1 of earnings. Hence benefits will be reduced to zero when 50 percent of earnings is equal to $6000 — which occurs when earnings are $12,000. The general relation is:

$$\text{Guarantee} = \text{Tax rate} \times \text{Break-even level}.$$

The fact that the break-even level is completely determined by the guarantee and the tax rate creates an annoying problem. If we are truly to make a dent in the poverty population through an NIT system, the guarantee will have to come fairly close to the poverty line. But then, if we are to keep the tax rate moderate, the break-even level will have to be much above the poverty line. This means that families who are not considered "poor" (though they are certainly not rich) will also receive benefits. For example, a low tax rate of $33\frac{1}{3}$ percent means that some benefits are paid to families whose income is as high as three times the guarantee level.

But if we raise the tax rate to bring the guarantee and the break-even level closer together, the incentive to work shrinks, and with it the principal rationale for the NIT in the first place. So the NIT is no magic cure-all. Difficult choices must still be made.

The Negative Income Tax and Work Incentives

For people now covered by welfare programs, the NIT would increase the incentive to work. However, we have just seen that it is virtually inevitable that a number of families who are now too well-off to collect welfare would become eligible for NIT payments. For these people, the NIT imposes work disincentives, both because it provides them with more income and because it subjects them to the relatively high NIT tax rate, which reduces their aftertax wage rate.[8]

[8]For a review of income and substitution effects in labor supply analysis, refer to Chapter 36, pages 796–98.

These possible disincentive effects have worried both social reformers and legislators, so in the late 1960s the government initiated a series of social experiments to estimate the effect of the NIT on the supply of labor. Families from a number of American cities were offered negative income tax payments in return for allowing social scientists to monitor their behavior. A matched set of "control" families, who were not given NIT payments, was also observed. The idea was to measure how the behavior of the families receiving NIT payments differed from that of the families that did not receive them. The experiments lasted about a decade and showed clearly that the net effects of the NIT on labor supply were small — but certainly not zero. Members of families receiving benefits did work slightly less than the others. But the fears of those who predicted that NIT payments would induce widespread withdrawals from the labor force were unfounded.

Economists believe that it is more efficient to redistribute income through an NIT system than through the existing welfare system because the NIT provides better work incentives. In terms of Figure 37–5, the NIT is curve *ABCDE* while the present system is curve *abcde*. If this view is correct, then by replacing the current welfare system with NIT, we can have more equality *and* more efficiency at the same time. But this does not mean that equalization would become costless. The curve *ABCDE* still slopes downward — by increasing equality, we still diminish the GNP.

The Personal Income Tax

If we take the broader view that society's objective is not just to eliminate poverty but to reduce income disparities, then the fact that many nonpoor families would receive benefits from the NIT is perhaps not a serious drawback. After all, unless the plan is outlandishly generous, these families will still be below the average income. Still, in popular discussions the NIT is largely thought of as an antipoverty program, not as a tool for general income equalization.

By contrast, the federal personal income tax *is* thought to be a means of promoting equality. Indeed, it is probably given more credit for this than it actually deserves. The reason is that the income tax is widely known to be *progressive*.[9] The fact that the tax is progressive means that incomes *after* tax are distributed more equally than incomes *before* tax because the rich turn over a larger share of their incomes to the tax collector. This is illustrated by the two Lorenz curves in Figure 37–6. These curves, however, are not drawn accurately to scale. If they were, they would lie almost on top of each other because research suggests that the degree of equalization attributable to the tax is rather modest.

Death Duties and Other Taxes

Taxes on inheritances and estates levied by both the state and the federal governments are another equalizing feature of our tax system. And in this case they seem clearly aimed at limiting the incomes of the rich, or at least at limiting their ability to transfer this largesse from one generation to the next. But the amount of money involved is too small to make much difference to the overall distribution of income. In 1988, total receipts from estate and gift taxes by all levels of government are well under 1 percent of total tax revenues.

---

[9]For definitions of progressive, proportional, and regressive taxes, see Chapter 33, page 718.

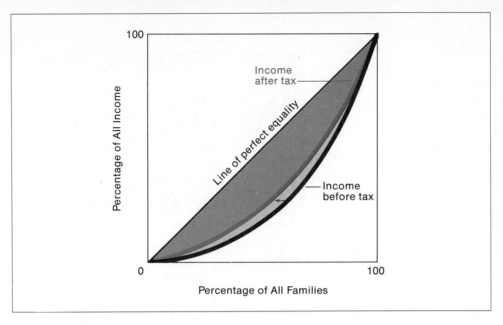

Figure 37–6
THE EFFECT OF
PROGRESSIVE INCOME
TAXATION ON THE
LORENZ CURVE
Since a progressive income
tax takes proportionately
more income from the rich
than from the poor, it reduces
income inequality.
Graphically, this means that
society's Lorenz curve shifts
in the manner shown here.
The magnitude of the shift
however, is exaggerated to
make the graph more
readable. In reality, the
income tax has only a small
effect on the Lorenz curve.

There are many other taxes in the U.S. system, and most experts agree that the remaining taxes as a group — including sales taxes, payroll taxes, and property taxes — are decidedly regressive. On balance, the evidence seems to suggest that:

The tax system as a whole is only slightly progressive.

Policies to Combat Discrimination

The policies that we have considered so far for combating poverty or reducing income inequality are all based on taxes and transfer payments — on moving dollars from one set of hands to another. This has not been the approach used to fight discrimination. Instead, governments have decided to make it *illegal* to discriminate.

Perhaps the major milestone in the war against discrimination was the **Civil Rights Act of 1964,** which outlawed many forms of discrimination and established the **Equal Employment Opportunities Commission (EEOC).** When you read a want ad in which a company asserts it is "an equal opportunity employer," the firm is proclaiming its compliance with this and related legislation.

Originally, it was thought that the problem could best be attacked by outlawing discrimination in rates of pay and in hiring standards — and by devoting resources to enforcement of these provisions. While progress toward the elimination of discrimination according to race and sex undoubtedly was made between 1964 and the early 1970s, many people felt the pace was too slow. One reason was that discrimination in the labor market proved to be more subtle than was first thought. Officials rarely could find proof that unequal pay was being given for equal work, because determining when work was "equal" turned out to be a formidable task.

So, in the early 1970s, a new wrinkle was added. Firms and other organizations with suspiciously small representation of blacks or women in their work forces were required not just to end discriminatory practices, but also to demonstrate that they were taking **affirmative action** to remedy this imbalance. That

Affirmative action refers to active efforts to locate and hire members of minority groups.

The Supreme Court on Affirmative Action

The legal issues surrounding affirmative action programs are many and complex. Several landmark cases have been decided by the Supreme Court. Here is a brief rundown.

In *Regents of the University of California vs. Bakke* (1978), a slim 5–4 majority of the Court ruled that the affirmative action plan at the medical school of the University of California at Davis discriminated against whites. But it stated that better conceived admissions plans favoring blacks might be legal nonetheless. This decision puzzled more people than it englightened.

A year later, the Court handed down a clearer verdict in *United Steelworkers vs. Weber* when it upheld a voluntary plan that gave blacks preference for admission to a special training program in a steel plant. Without giving blanket approval to all affirmative action plans, *Weber* clearly validated reasonable plans, even if based on numerical quotas.

In *Fullilove vs. Klutznick* in 1980, the Court extended this view beyond the workplace by upholding a federal law that set aside 10 percent of public-works funds for minority businesses.

But in *Firefighters Local vs. Stotts* (1984), the Court, with more conservative members, ruled that layoffs of firefighters must follow seniority rules unless there are particular black employees who can prove they were victims of racial bias.

Nonetheless, two important verdicts in 1986 — *Firefighters vs. City of Cleveland* and *Local 28 vs. Equal Employment Opportunity Commission* — upheld affirmative action as a remedy for past job discrimination against minority groups, even when particular victims of discrimination could not be identified.

---

is, they had to *prove* that they were making efforts to locate members of minority groups and females and to hire them if they proved to be qualified.

This new approach to fighting discrimination was highly controversial and remains so to this day. (See the boxed insert above.) Critics claim that affirmative action really means hiring quotas and compulsory hiring of unqualified workers simply because they are black or female. Proponents counter that without affirmative action discriminatory employers would simply claim they could not find qualified minority or female employees. The difficulty revolves around the impossibility of deciding on *purely objective criteria* who is "qualified" and who is not. What one person sees as government coercion to hire an unqualified applicant to fill a quota, another sees as a discriminatory employer being forced to mend his ways. Nothing in this book — or anywhere else — will teach you which view is correct in any particular instance.

Lately, some people have concluded that affirmative action will never put appreciable numbers of women into "men's jobs" and have sought to combat sex discrimination by setting wage rates according to some standard of **comparable worth.** The argument, which has sparked acrimonious debate in recent years, runs as follows. Women are frequently discriminated against by relegating them to low-paying occupations while men get the better-paid jobs. To remedy the resulting wage disparities, the government should use job evaluations to decide which men's and women's jobs are "comparable," and then insist that employers pay equal wages to jobs judged to be of comparable worth.

Critics of comparable worth scoff at the idea that the government can decide the relative values of different jobs on objective criteria. The forces of

Comparable worth refers to pay standards that assign equal wages to jobs judged "comparable."

supply and demand described in Chapter 36, they argue, are the only sensible way to set relative wages. Otherwise some occupations will have severe shortages while others are beseiged by a surplus of applicants.

The controverises over affirmative action and comparable worth are excellent examples of the trade-off between equality and efficiency. Without a doubt, giving more high-paying jobs to members of minority groups and to women would move society's Lorenz curve in the direction of greater equality. Supporters of affirmative action and comparable worth seek this result. But if affirmative action disrupts industry and requires firms to replace "qualified" white males by other "less qualified" workers, the nation's productivity may fall. And if comparable worth creates chronic surpluses in some occupations and shortages in others, economic efficiency may suffer. Opponents of affirmative action are greatly troubled by these potential losses. How far should affirmative action or comparable worth be pushed? Good questions, but ones without good answers.

Postscript on the Distribution of Income

Now that we have completed our analysis of the distribution of income, it may be useful to see how it all relates to our central theme: What does the market do well, and what does it do poorly?

We have learned that a market economy uses the marginal productivity principle to assign an income to each individual. In so doing, the market attaches high prices to scarce factors and low prices to abundant ones, and therefore guides firms to make *efficient* use of society's resources. This is one of the market's great strengths. However, by attaching high prices to some factors and low prices to others, the market mechanism often creates a distribution of income that is quite unequal; some people wind up fabulously rich while others wind up miserably poor. For this reason, the market has been widely criticized for centuries for doing a rather poor job of distributing income in accord with commonly held notions of *fairness* and *equity*.

On balance, most observers feel that the criticism is justified: The market mechanism is extraordinarily good at promoting efficiency but rather bad at promoting equality. As we said at the outset, the market has both virtues and vices.

Summary

1. The War on Poverty was declared in 1964 and by 1974 the fraction of families considered poor by official definitions had dropped substantially. However, the poverty population has risen since the late 1970s.

2. The difficulty in agreeing on a sharp dividing line between the poor and the nonpoor leads one to broaden the problem of poverty into the problem of inequality in incomes.

3. In the United States today, the richest 20 percent of families receive over 43 percent of the income, while the poorest 20 percent of families receive under 5 percent. These numbers have changed little over the past 35 years and represent somewhat more inequality here than in many other advanced industrial nations.

4. Individual incomes differ for many reasons. Discrimination and differences in native ability, in the desire to work hard and to take risks, in schooling and experience, and in inherited wealth all account for income disparities. All of these factors, however, explain only part of the inequality that we observe. A portion of the rest is due simply to good or bad luck, and the balance is unexplained.

5. Prejudice against a minority group may lead to discrimination in rates of pay, or to segregation in the workplace, or to both. However, discrimination may also arise even when there is no prejudice (this is called statistical discrimination).

6. There is a trade-off between the goals of reducing inequality and enhancing economic efficiency: Policies that help on the equality front normally harm efficiency, and vice versa. This is one of the **12 Ideas for Beyond the Final Exam.**

7. Because of this trade-off, there is an optimal degree of inequality for any society. Society finds this optimum in the same way that a consumer decides how much to buy of different commodities: The trade-off tells us how costly it is to "purchase" more equality, and preferences then determine how much should be "bought." However, since people differ in their value judgments about the importance of equality, there will inevitably be disagreement over the ideal amount of equality.

8. There may, however, be some hope of reaching agreement over the policies to use in pursuit of whatever goal for equality is selected. This is because more efficient redistributive policies let us buy any amount of equality at a lower price in terms of lost output. Economists claim, for example, that a negative income tax is preferable to our current welfare system on these grounds.

9. Even the negative income tax, though, is no panacea. Its primary virtue lies in the way it preserves incentives to work. But if this is done by keeping the tax rate low, then either the minimum guaranteed level of income will have to be low or many nonpoor families will become eligible to receive benefits.

10. The goal of income equality is also pursued through the tax system, especially through the progressive federal income tax and death duties. But other taxes are typically regressive, so the tax system as a whole is only slightly progressive.

11. The problem of economic discrimination has been attacked by making it illegal, not through the tax and transfer system. But simply declaring discrimination to be illegal is much easier than actually ending discrimination. The trade-off between equality and efficiency applies once again: Strict enforcement of affirmative action or standards of comparable worth will certainly reduce discrimination and increase income equality, but it may do so at a serious cost in terms of economic efficiency.

Concepts for Review

Poverty line	Optimal amount of inequality	Negative income tax (NIT)
Absolute and relative concepts of poverty	Trade-off between equality and efficiency	Civil Rights Act
Lorenz curve	Aid to Families with Dependent Children (AFDC)	Equal Employment Opportunities Commission (EEOC)
Economic discrimination		Affirmative action
Statistical discrimination	Food stamps	Comparable worth

Questions for Discussion

1. Discuss the "leaky bucket" analogy (page 837) with your classmates. What maximum amount of income would you personally allow to leak from the bucket in transferring money from the rich to the poor? Explain why people differ in their answers to this question.

2. Continuing the leaky bucket example, explain why economists believe that replacing the present welfare system with a negative income tax would help reduce the leak.

3. Suppose you were to design a negative income tax system for the United States. Pick a guaranteed income level and a tax rate that seem reasonable to you. What break-even level of income is implied by these choices? For the plan you have just devised, construct a corresponding version of Table 37–4 (page 839).

4. Following is a complete list of the distribution of income in Disneyland. From these data, construct a Lorenz curve for Disneyland.

NAME	INCOME
Donald Duck	$100,000
Mickey Mouse	172,000
Minnie Mouse	68,000
Pluto	44,000
Ticket taker	16,000

How different is this from the Lorenz curve for the United States (Figure 37–2 on page 828)?

5. Suppose the War on Poverty were starting anew and you were part of a presidential commission assigned the task of defining the poor. Would you choose an absolute or a relative concept of poverty? Why? What would be your specific definition of poverty?

6. Discuss the concept of the "optimal amount of inequality." What are some of the practical problems in determining how much inequality really is optimal?

7. Do you think wages for government employees should be set by standards of comparable worth?

PART **10**

Alternative Economic Systems

38

The development of
capitalist production . . .
compels [the capitalist]
to keep constantly
extending his capital . . .
by means of progressive
accumulation. . . . Fanatically
bent on making value
expand itself, he . . . forces
the development of the
productive powers of society,
and creates those material
conditions, which alone can
form the real basis of a
higher form of society.

KARL MARX

Growth in Developed and Developing Countries

In this chapter we discuss the factors that determine the rate at which an economy grows and examine the desirability of rapid growth. We begin by considering how growth can be measured and go on to examine the effects of population growth on prospects for rising per capita incomes. Next, we examine the views of those who have argued that in wealthier countries economic growth is a mixed blessing that may do more harm than good. Then, in the second part of the chapter, we turn to the special problems of the less developed countries (LDCs) and look at the measures that have been proposed to increase their rates of growth. We show that although in the 1970s standards of living in some of the LDCs began to rise significantly, their rapid population growth and their vulnerability to such external shocks as periods of drought, a rise in oil prices, an accumulation of debts, and other similar perils more recently held back the economic growth of many of the LDCs. Indeed, as we saw in Chapter 7, real per capita incomes in some LDCs have been falling further and further behind that of the industrial countries. Next, we examine the problems that impede growth in the LDCs, including scarcity of capital, lack of education, and unemployment. While doing this we consider what the LDCs can do to help themselves and what the rest of the world can do to help them.

Growth in General

How to Measure Growth: Total Output or Output per Capita?

Adam Smith, like many of his successors, took it for granted that expansion of productive capacity is inherently desirable. But he also took it for granted, apparently without examining the matter very closely, that growth in the size of population is to be wished for. His reason was that a larger population provides a larger work force, and a larger work force makes a larger national output possible. Few economists since Smith's time have argued in this way. Nowadays we usually measure a nation's prosperity not in terms of its total output but in terms of its output *per person*. India has a GNP more than twice as large as Sweden's. But with a population more than 90 times as large as Sweden's, India remains a poor country while Sweden is highly prosperous. The point is that:

If the objective of growth is the material welfare *of the individuals* who make up a country, then the proper measure of the success of a program of economic development is how much it adds to output per person. The relevant index is not total output. It is total/output *divided by total population* that is, **output per capita.**

From this point of view, the appropriate objective of growth is not, as the old cliché puts it, "the greatest good for the *greatest number*" — it is the greatest good *per person* in the economy. Per capita figures tell this story well. To make the appropriate comparison of well-being in Sweden and India, we note that per capita GNP in Sweden is more than $12,000 a year, whereas in India, even after a generous adjustment to correct for lower prices in that country, the figure is about $900 a year.

Only where the objective of the government is grandeur or military strength may the number of inhabitants alone seem an appropriate part of its goal. A small country like Finland, for instance, cannot hope to overwhelm a giant neighbor like the Soviet Union, even if Finland has a much higher per capita GNP than the Soviet Union.[1] But where the goal of the government is not national power but the elimination of poverty, illiteracy, and inadequate medical care, sheer increase in population becomes a questionable pursuit.

On Growth in Population: Is Less Really More?

In 1798, the Reverend Thomas R. Malthus (who was to become England's first professor of political economy) published *An Essay on the Principle of Population*. This book was to have a profound effect on people's attitudes toward population growth. Malthus argued that sexual drives and other influences induce people to reproduce themselves as rapidly as their means permit. Unfortunately, he said, when the number of humans increases, the production of food and other consumption goods generally cannot keep up.

The problem is the noted *law of diminishing returns* to additional labor used with a fixed supply of land, a relationship we encountered before (in Chapter 23). This states that if we use more and more labor to cultivate a fixed stock of land, we will eventually reach a point at which each additional laborer will contribute less additional output than the previous laborer. Ultimately, as the labor force increases, output per worker will decline.

Malthus and his followers concluded that the tendency of humankind to reproduce itself must constantly exert pressure on the economy to keep living standards from rising. Wages will gravitate toward some minimal subsistence level — the lowest income on which people are willing to marry and raise a

---

[1] Even where military power is the primary objective, a large but impoverished population may not be a very effective means to that end. China has long had an enormous population, but in the modern era its military presence is certainly quite recent.

family. If wages are above subsistence, the population can and will grow. Thus, a wage that is above subsistence will set forces into motion that will drive wages down toward subsistence because of diminishing returns.

Sometimes, according to Malthus, the population will grow beyond the capability of the economy to support it. Then the number of people will be brought back into line by means that are far more unpleasant than a decrease in wages — by starvation and disease or by wars that produce the required number of casualties.

Later in the nineteenth century and during the first half of the twentieth century, the gloomy Malthusian vision seemed to lose credibility. New technology and improved agricultural practices generally enabled the output of food and other agricultural products to increase faster than the population (at least in the wealthier industrialized nations). In addition, it turned out that as living standards rose, people became less anxious to reproduce, and so the expansion of population slowed substantially. Figure 38–1 illustrates this trend in Germany over a period considerably longer than a century. All in all, it began to look as though population growth constituted no significant threat — it was something with which human technological skills and ingenuity could cope.

More recently, however, there has been renewed concern over population. With improvements in medicine — notably, improved hygiene in hospitals, the use of such public health measures as swamp drainage, and the discovery of antibiotics — death rates have plunged in the developing countries, especially for infants. At the same time, birth control programs in most of these countries have, at least until quite recently, not been very successful. As a result, the populations of developing countries have continued to expand dramatically, eating up a good proportion of any output increases obtained through their governments' economic development programs.

It has been widely concluded that significant improvement in living standards in the developing areas is impossible without a substantial reduction in their population growth. But the "neo-Malthusians" go further than this, arguing that a rapid approach to birthrates so low that populations cease expanding — that is, to *zero population growth* — is virtually a matter of life and death even for the most prosperous nations. It is illuminating to consider the logic of their argument.

Figure 38–1
GERMAN BIRTHRATES, 1850–1985
This chart shows that birthrates in Germany have generally been declining since 1850.
SOURCE: Statistisches Bundesamt, *Statistisches Jahrbuch* (Weisbaden, Germany).

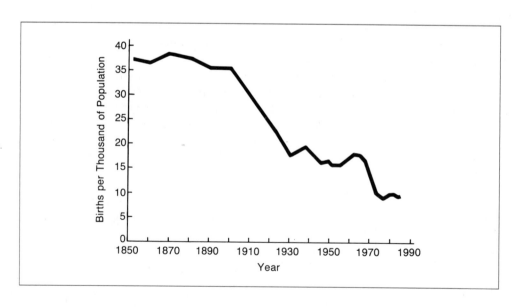

The Crowded Planet:
Exponential Population Growth

Malthus used an argument that has caught many imaginations ever since:

Population, when unchecked, increases in a geometrical ratio. Subsistence increases only in an arithmetical ratio. A slight acquaintance with numbers will shew the immensity of the first power in comparison of the second.[2]

In modern discussions, such a "geometric" growth pattern is referred to as **exponential growth,** or "compounded growth" or "snowballing." Exponential growth is growth at a constant *percentage rate*. For example, at a 10 percent growth rate, a population of 100 persons will increase by 10 persons a year; but a population of a million persons will increase by 100,000 persons a year. Thus, although the *rate* of growth is the same for large and small populations, the *numbers* are dramatically different. The bigger the population, the more it will add annually. And each year's growth implies still faster growth in the following year. It is like a snowball rolling downhill, accumulating more snow the bigger it gets, thus expanding faster and faster all the time.

If the population doubles (grows 100 percent) in 35 years, it will quadruple (grow another 100 percent) in 70 years, increase 8-fold in 105 years, 16-fold in 140 years, and so on indefinitely. The doubling sequence 2, 4, 8, 16, 32, 64, and so on, is the basic pattern of exponential growth. Figure 38–2 shows how astronomical such a growth sequence is. Projecting the world's population 175 years into the future on the assumption that population will grow exponentially at about its current rate, it shows that by the year 2160 the population will have reached about 92 billion—almost 20 times as many people as there are today.

> Exponential growth is growth at a constant percentage rate.

[2]Malthus, *An Essay on the Principle of Population,* (London, 1798), page 20.

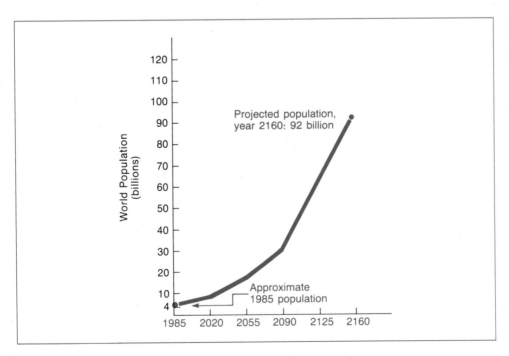

Figure 38–2
PROJECTED GROWTH OF THE WORLD'S POPULATION IN 175 YEARS AT CURRENT RATE OF GROWTH
This figure shows the sensational acceleration of population growth *if* population expands exponentially.

It turns out that in describing the consequences of exponential growth, Malthus was conservative. He did not begin to spell out the wonders and the horrors that his premise implied. Consider some calculations by one leading authority on population (who derived his conclusions simply by carrying through the arithmetic of exponential growth rates):

- *If population were to grow at today's rates for another 600–700 years, every square foot of the surface of the earth would contain a human being;*

- *If it were to expand at the same rate for 1200 years, the combined weight of the human population would exceed that of the earth itself;*

- *If that growth rate were to go on for 6000 years (a very short period of time in terms of biological history), the globe would constitute a sphere whose diameter was growing with the speed of light.*[3]

And none of this is conjecture. It is *sure* to come about *if* the present (exponential) rate of growth of the earth's population continues unabated.

Of course, none of this can really happen. Our finite earth just does not have room for that sort of expansion. The fate of humanity is not determined by the rules of arithmetic — it depends on the course of nature and on the behavior of the human race. It is true that if the number of humans continues to swell until it presses upon the earth's capacity, the process will ultimately be brought to a halt in a Malthusian apocalypse. Disease, famine, and war must finally put a stop to the expansion process.

But there is a better alternative. People can choose to stop raising large families. There is no inevitability about the family of six or ten children. As we have just noted, there has in fact been a decline in the rate of expansion in the wealthier societies — so much so that in the United States in the last few years the rate of reproduction has reached what can ultimately give us zero population growth (see Figure 38–3). Even in the developing nations, as we will see later in this chapter, the birthrate has recently been declining.

A more balanced view of the matter recognizes the serious difficulties that rapid population growth can lead to, and suggests that its encouragement will

[3]Ansley J. Coale, "Man and His Environment," *Science,* vol. 179 (October 9, 1970), pages 132–36. Copyright 1970 by the American Association for the Advancement of Science.

Figure 38–3

ANNUAL PERCENTAGE GROWTH RATE OF THE U.S. POPULATION

Note how rapidly the rate has fallen in recent years. It has just about returned to the low level of the Great Depression. (The years after 1986 are a projection.)
SOURCE: U.S. Bureau of the Census, *Current Population Reports*, Series P-25.

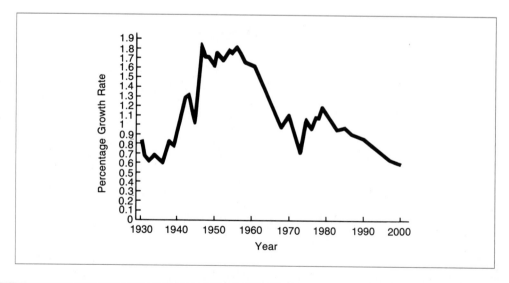

not serve the interests of society. Yet, it does *not* imply that a great catastrophe is at hand or that the appropriate reaction is panic.

Requirements for Increased Growth

What can be done to increase the growth rate of an economy? Unfortunately, no one has a handy list of sure-fire recipes.

Growth can be attributed to a number of factors that no one knows how to explain: (1) *inventiveness,* which produces the new technology and other innovations that have contributed so much to economic expansion; (2) *entrepreneurship,* the leadership that recognizes no obstacles and undertakes the daring industrial ventures needed to move the economy ahead; and (3) *the work ethic* that leads a work force to high levels of productivity. No one really knows what features of economic organization and social psychology actually lead a community to adopt these goals, as Great Britain is said to have done at the beginning of the nineteenth century, as the United States is reputed to have done in the first half of the twentieth century, and as Japan is apparently doing today. We do know, however, that:

Growth requires two things that people can influence directly:

1. A large expenditure on *capital equipment:* factories, machinery, transportation, and telecommunications equipment.
2. The devotion of considerable effort to research and development from which innovations are derived.

Both these types of expenditures help to increase the economy's ability to *supply* goods, which brings us back to the analysis of Parts 2–4. There we stressed that the level (and, consequently, the growth) of national income is determined by the interaction of *aggregate supply and aggregate demand.* It is the need for capital equipment in any growth process that provides a vital link between aggregate demand and aggregate supply, for an economy acquires a larger capital stock by investing. Recall that aggregate demand is the sum of consumption, investment, government spending, and net exports $Y = C + I + G + X - IM$. But I is the only part of Y that creates more capital for the future. Such investment can be carried out either by the private sector of the economy or by government. In free market economies government investment is, of course, a much smaller share of the total than it is in centrally directed economies.

The *composition* of aggregate demand is a major determinant of the rate of economic growth. If a larger fraction of total spending goes toward investment rather than toward consumption, government purchases, or net exports, the capital stock will grow faster and the aggregate supply schedule will shift more quickly to the right.

Accumulating Capital by Sacrificing Consumption: The Case of Soviet Russia

The importance of the *composition* of demand stands out sharply if we turn away from the United States and consider a *centrally planned* economy, such as the Soviet Union.

When the Soviet Union undertook to expand its industrial output very rapidly, it was clear from the earliest stage of planning that a tremendous amount of capital equipment would be required to carry out the expansion. Not only did the Russians have to build modern factories and acquire sophisticated machinery, they also needed a **social infrastructure**—a transportation network to bring raw materials to the factories and take finished products to the markets, an efficient telecommunications system, and schools in which to train the population sufficiently to be an effective labor force. All this and much more was needed, and all of it required labor, raw material, and fuel for its construction.

Obviously, such a use of resources has its *opportunity cost*. Fuel and steel that are employed to build a train become unavailable for the production of refrigerators and washing machines. The real price of accumulating plant, equipment, and infrastructure is paid in the form of consumer goods that must be given up in order to build that capital equipment. In other words:

Through saving, the public gives up some consumption, which is the price it must pay for the accumulation of plant, equipment, and infrastructure. Without this sacrifice, growth generally cannot occur.

This is the hard lesson that the inhabitants of the Soviet Union have been living with for over half a century. Ever since the Russian Revolution in 1917, the Soviet leadership has been determined to promote rapid economic growth and has imposed on the general public whatever sacrifices of current consumption were deemed necessary for the purpose. Only in the most recent decades has an increase in the supply of consumer goods been assigned any priority. Yet, even now, investment in the U.S.S.R. is still about one-third of GNP, while in the United States the figure is less than half that amount. As a result, Soviet living standards have been rising very slowly, particularly because the demands of the military forces have joined those of the growth planners in competing for the resources that might otherwise go into consumption.

The reason for this harsh trade-off is clear enough. If the economy is producing at its full potential, then real output Y cannot be increased further. Since $Y = C + I + G + X - IM$, a decision to devote more resources to the production of heavy machinery (which is in I) or armaments (which are in G) is simultaneously a decision to forgo some consumption or to import more. Where resources are already fully employed, it is simply not possible to have both more guns *and* more butter.

The Payoff to Growth: Higher Consumption in the Future

We may seem to be painting a rather grim picture of growth, and indeed, the process has often been harsh in the U.S.S.R. and in other nations that have enforced a high rate of economic growth. But it is also true that if the growth process is successful, the sacrifice of consumption that it requires is only a temporary loss. Consumers give up goods and services now in order to make possible the construction of productive capacity that will permit them to consume even more goods and services at a later date. After all, from the consumers' point of view, that is what growth is all about. It is not an end in itself, but a means to an end—a standard of living higher than they could have attained without the process of economic expansion.

At least in a consumer-oriented economy, the decision to save in order to promote economic growth is simply an *exchange between present and future consumption*. Consumers sacrifice consumption now in order to be able to increase consumption in the future by more than they gave up in the past.

Of course, the payoff may never come if something goes wrong. An earthquake may destroy factories and roads, or a government with military ambitions may divert the increased productive capacity into the manufacture of armaments. So there is a risk in the decision to give up consumption now for increased consumption later. The growth process is a gamble — it means trading in a relatively sure thing (present consumption) for a risky future return (increased future consumption).

But betting on the future is not necessarily foolhardy. Economies would remain stagnant if people were unwilling to take chances. And some of the risk of investment plans can be reduced if decision makers understand fully the terms of the trade-off.

Growth Without Sacrificing Consumption: Something for Nothing?

Of course, some growth can be achieved without much sacrifice of present consumption. For at least one of the main engines of growth can be powered with relatively small increases in the nation's stock of factories, equipment, and infrastructure. Research and development can teach society new and more efficient ways of using the nation's productive resources. Thus, *innovation* — the process of putting inventions into operation — can permit an economy to get more output from the same inputs rather than by *expansion* of capital stock.

Everyone knows that this has in fact occurred. From the invention of the steam engine to that of the modern computer, our economy has benefited from a stream of inventions — some sensational, some more routine — which together have increased enormously the productivity of the nation's resources. Estimates of the relative contributions of innovation and accumulation to the growth process differ. A number of analysts attribute considerably more than half of the economic growth of the United States to research and invention. But whatever the correct figure, it is certainly large.

Another way of describing this conclusion is to say that while a substantial proportion of growth is **embodied** in increased quantities of plant, equipment, and infrastructure, a very large proportion of the economy's growth is **disembodied.** That is, it is attributable to better ideas — to improved methods of finding and using the same quantities of resources.

Embodied growth has two serious costs that disembodied growth avoids. First, embodied growth necessarily speeds up the use of society's depletable resources: its iron ore, its petroleum supplies, and its stocks of other minerals and fuels. Second, the resources that are used up in a process of embodied growth must ultimately end up on society's garbage heap. The physical laws of conservation of matter and energy tell us that no raw material can ever disappear. It can be transformed into smoke or solid waste, but unless it is recycled *entirely* (something that is both beyond the capability of our technology and impractical for other reasons), the greater the quantity of resources used in the productive process, the greater the quantity of wastes that must ultimately result.

Economist Kenneth Boulding has likened our planet to a spaceship hurtling through the solar system but constrained by terrestrial littering laws to keep its garbage on board. In spaceship Earth, we can transform waste materials into other forms—as by melting old bottles for reuse or converting them into energy, or by burning combustible garbage for heat—but we cannot simply toss them overboard.

So far, we have enjoyed substantial success in our efforts to achieve growth in output without commensurate increases in our use of resources. One statistical analysis, for example, attributes only about half of the growth in the United States to increased use of physical inputs. The remainder must be ascribed to improvements in technology as well as to increased education and skill of the labor force.[4]

One final remark on disembodied growth is in order. Economists are fond of pointing out that there is no such thing as a free lunch. Except in rare instances, improvements in technology are not "manna from heaven." They result, instead, from the work of scientists and technicians in government and industrial laboratories, from the labor of inventors in their basements or garages, and from the effort of management specialists studying the organization of factories and assembly lines. This means that labor (along with other resources) is diverted from other activities into the production of knowledge. *In a fully employed economy, the opportunity costs of investing in the discovery of new knowledge are the consumption of and physical investment in goods that would otherwise have been produced.* So even here, we cannot get something for nothing.

Is More Growth Really Better?

A number of writers have raised questions about the desirability of faster economic growth as an end in itself, at least in the wealthier industrialized countries. Yet faster growth does mean more wealth, and to most people the desirability of wealth is beyond question. "I've been rich and I've been poor—and I can tell you, rich is better," a noted stage personality is said to have told an interviewer, and most people seem to have the same attitude about the economy as a whole. To those who hold this belief, a healthy economy is one that is capable of turning out vast quantities of shoes, food, cars, and TV sets. An economy whose capacity to provide all these things is not expanding is said to have succumbed to the disease of *stagnation.*

Economists from Adam Smith to Karl Marx saw great virtue in economic growth. Marx argued that capitalism, at least in its earlier historical stages, was a vital form of economic organization by which society got out of the rut in which the medieval stage of history had trapped it. As we saw in the opening quotation of this chapter, Marx believed that "the development of the productive powers of society . . . alone can form the real basis of a higher form of society. . . ." Marx went on to tell us that only where such great productive powers have been unleashed can one have "a society in which the full and free development of every individual forms the ruling principle."[5] In other words, only a wealthy economy can afford to give all individuals the opportunity for full personal satisfaction through the use of their special abilities in their jobs and through increased leisure activities.

Yet the desirability of further economic growth for a society that is already wealthy has been questioned on grounds that undoubtedly have a good deal of

[4]Edward F. Denison, *Accounting for United States Economic Growth 1929–1969* (Washington, D.C.: The Brookings Institution, 1974). More recently, however, there has been a decline in the rate of growth in output relative to input quantities used. See E. F. Denison, *Accounting for Slower Economic Growth* (Washington, D.C.: The Brookings Institution, 1979), page 62. This slowdown was discussed in Chapter 7.
[5]Marx, *Capital,* vol. I (Chicago: Charles H. Kerr Publishing Co., 1906), page 649.

validity. It is pointed out that the sheer increase in quantity of products has imposed an enormous cost on society in the form of pollution, crowding, proliferation of wastes that need disposal, and some claim it has had very unfortunate psychological and social effects. It is said that industry has transformed the satisfying and creative tasks of the artisan into the mechanical and dehumanizing routine of the assembly line. It has dotted our roadsides with junkyards, filled our air with smoke, and poisoned our food with dangerous chemicals. The question is whether the outpouring of frozen foods, talking dolls, CB radios, and headache remedies is worth its high cost to society. As one well-known economist put it:

The continued pursuit of economic growth by Western societies is more likely on balance to reduce rather than increase social welfare. . . . Technological innovations may offer to add to men's material opportunities. But by increasing the risks of their obsolescence it adds also to their anxiety. Swifter means of communications have the paradoxical effect of isolating people; increased mobility has led to more hours commuting; increased automobilization to increased separation; more television to less communication. In consequence, people know less of their neighbors than ever before in history.[6]

Virtually every economist agrees that these concerns are valid, though many question whether economic growth is their major cause. Nevertheless, they all emphasize that pollution of air and water, noise and congestion, and the mechanization of the work process are very real and very serious problems. There is every reason for society to undertake programs that grapple with these problems. Chapter 34, which dealt with problems of the environment, examined these issues more closely and described some policies to deal with them.

Despite the costs of growth in terms of human and environmental damage, there is strong evidence that if the economy's total output were kept at its present level, the community would pay a high price over and above the loss of additional goods and services.

First, it is not easy to carry out a decision to prevent further economic growth. Mandatory controls are abhorrent to most Americans. We cannot *order* people to stop inventing means to expand productivity. Nor does it make any sense to order every firm and industry to freeze its output level, since changing tastes and needs require some industries to expand their outputs at the same time that others are contracting. But who is to decide which should grow and which should contract, and how shall such decisions be made? *The achievement of zero economic growth may very well require government intervention on a scale that becomes expensive and even repressive.*

Second, without continued growth it will be no easy matter to finance effective programs of environmental protection. To improve the purity of our air and water and to clean up urban neighborhoods, tens of billions of dollars must be made available every year. Continued growth would enable the required resources to be provided without any reduction in the availability of consumer goods. But without such growth, we may actually be forced to cut back on our programs to protect the environment. Society could thus end up with less goods and a worse environment.

Finally, zero economic growth may seriously hamper efforts to eliminate poverty both within our economy and throughout the world. Much of the

[6]E. J. Mishan, *The Costs of Economic Growth* (New York: Frederick A. Praeger Publishers, 1967), pages 171, 175.

earth's population today lives in a state of extreme want. And though wealthier nations have been reluctant to provide more than token amounts of help to the **less developed countries (LDCs),** less wealth means there would be even less to share. So perhaps the only hope for improved living standards in the impoverished countries of Africa, Asia, and Latin America lies in continued increases in output.

Problems of the Less Developed Countries

Living in the LDCs

Three quarters of the world's population lives in areas whose average per capita GNP is about $1,500 or less per year, evaluated (as well as it is possible to do) in terms of today's prices in the United States. Table 38–1 shows that there are countries in which annual per capita GNP is under $300. Even after adjustment for differences in measurement of GNP in the United States and the poorer countries, this probably comes to an annual GNP figure under $1000.

To us, residents of an economy that offers an average GNP nearly 15 times as high as this, such a figure is not only likely to seem incredible, it is all but incomprehensible. Few of us can *really* imagine what life would be like if our family income were reduced to, say, $2000 per year. It is even hard to envision survival on such amounts. It must be emphasized that these figures do *not* represent the living standards of a small group of outcasts from their own societies. Rather, they are *typical* of perhaps a majority of those who live in Asia, Africa, and Latin America.

What can life be like in such circumstances? No brief description can really bridge the gulf between our range of experience and theirs. Yet it can offer us a glimpse into a way of life that few of us will want to share.

Inhabitants of many of the less developed countries live with their large families in one-room shanties or apartments, their water supplies are scanty, polluted, and often miles from home, their only source of energy is that of man and beast, and their sparse harvests are wrung from miserable soil in good years,

Table 38–1
PER CAPITA GNP IN DEVELOPED AND LESS DEVELOPED COUNTRIES, 1983

	(measured in U.S. dollars)
Developed Countries	
United States	$14,080
West Germany	11,400
Sweden	12,440
Less Developed Countries	
Bolivia	$480
China	300
Egypt	690
Ethiopia	120
Haiti	290
India	260

SOURCE: Population Reference Bureau, 1986.

with starvation threatened perhaps every five years when the rains do not come and the crops fail.[7] With no surplus in production, no food can be put into reserves, and the old, the infirm, and the very young are likely to perish.

The life of a man in an LDC is hard enough, with its low nutritional level, its lack of equipment to help him in his work, and its frequency of debilitating diseases. But his life is luxurious compared with that of his wife. She is usually married by the age of 14, bears 8 or 10 children, and by 35 is often a toothless old crone. If (as is true of some 80 percent of the population) she inhabits a rural area, she may have to trudge miles every day to fetch water for the family. She sews all the family's clothes by hand and cooks its meals. There is not enough money for preground flour, so part of the woman's daily work is to pound the grain by hand for food for the family—perhaps an additional two hours of hard labor. She also tends the gardens that produce food for the family, although, except in Moslem countries where women are sequestered, she is also expected to put in a full day in the fields during the six months of the agricultural season.

Another duty of the woman in an LDC is to bring produce, wood, or whatever she has to trade to market a couple of times a week, and she must often walk as many as 10 miles each way with bundles as heavy as she can carry on her back or on her head. She has no respite in the raising of her children, since they are likely not to have a school to attend when they are well or a hospital to go to when they are sick. It is no wonder that she ages so much faster than a woman in our society.

Table 38–2 gives the percentage of infant deaths for each 1000 live births and the average life expectancy of a newborn child in some countries ranging from the most underdeveloped to the most affluent. The contrasts are dramatic. In Bolivia, 119 babies die of every 1000 that are born, while the comparable figure in Sweden is only six. In many countries people survive only until their

[7]It has been estimated that in some famine years in the 1970s, half a million people died as a result in Bangladesh; 200,000 in Ethiopia; 100,000–250,000 in the Sahelian zone of Africa; and more than 800,000 in just three of the states of India (*The New York Times*, October 27, 1976).

Table 38–2
INFANT MORTALITY AND LIFE EXPECTANCY IN DEVELOPED AND LESS DEVELOPED COUNTRIES, 1981–85

	INFANT MORTALITY (deaths per 1000 live births)	LIFE EXPECTANCY AT BIRTH (years)
Developed Countries		
United States	10.5	75
West Germany	9.6	74
Sweden	6.4	77
Less Developed Countries		
Bolivia	119	51
China	50	64
Egypt	100	58
Ethiopia	168	41
Haiti	108	53
India	110	53

SOURCE: Population Reference Bureau, 1986.

40s or 50s, while in Scandinavia they live to be 77. There is little question about the quality of life in less developed lands.

Most of the inhabitants of many LDCs are shockingly poor. Malnutrition and disease are widespread. The sheer process of living and surviving taxes the people to the utmost and makes them old before their time.

Recent Trends

Do recent trends offer hope of improvement? Here there is both good news and bad. The good news is perhaps the most remarkable. In the decade of the 1970s, real GNP in the LDCs grew, on average, more than 5 percent a year. (See Table 38–3 for examples.) Even more important, income per capita grew at an annual rate greater than $2\frac{1}{2}$ percent. The world recession of the early 1980s hit some LDCs very hard and enmeshed them in a serious debt burden (see pages 862–63). Nevertheless, for some of the LDCs the long-term outlook continues to be promising. This means that:

Despite population increases, some LDCs have succeeded in breaking out of the stagnation trap. If growth continues as it has recently, an average family in the successful developing areas can look forward to a doubling of its living standards in less than 30 years. Or put another way, standards of living will be increasing faster than they did in the United States in the nineteenth century!

Clearly, the experience of the 1970s offered hope for a major reduction in absolute poverty in at least some LDCs.

While there was good news in the 1970s, the beginning of the 1980s was not so favorable. Aside from their debt problems, which will be discussed a bit later, there are several developments that can be considered either as merely unfortunate or as thoroughly ominous for the LDCs.

First, while the percentage rates of growth of per capita incomes in the LDCs have been impressive, the industrialized countries, with their initially

Table 38–3
AVERAGE ANNUAL GROWTH RATES OF REAL GROSS DOMESTIC PRODUCT IN DEVELOPED AND LESS DEVELOPED COUNTRIES, APPROXIMATELY 1970–1983

	1970–1975 (percent)	1975–1980 (percent)	1980–83 (percent)
Developed Countries			
United States	2.8	3.7	0.7
Italy	3.1	3.6	−0.5
Sweden	2.8	1.3	1.0
Less Developed Countries			
Colombia	6.0	5.6	1.3
Haiti	3.8	5.3	−2.3
Pakistan	4.5	6.7	5.5
Zimbabwe	6.8	1.5	5.0
Zambia	2.9	−0.6	0.1
Sri Lanka	3.3	5.6	5.2
Uganda	0.1	−4.0	6.6

SOURCE: United Nations, *Statistical Yearbook*, 1983–84.

high incomes, have not exactly been standing still. Indeed, largely because their population growth has been slower, the percentage growth rate in per capita incomes has been higher in the developed countries. But even if the *percentage* increases in their per capita incomes had been very similar, *absolute* incomes would have continued to rise more quickly in the richer lands. Where per capita income is $100 a year, a $2\frac{1}{2}$ percent growth rate translates into a $2.50 annual improvement; however, where per capita income is $5000 a year, the same $2\frac{1}{2}$ percent rate of growth adds $125 a year to the income of the average person. As a result:

The purchasing power of the average family in an LDC is falling further behind that of a typical family in a wealthy economy.

Second, many critics, notably those on the left, emphasize that the $2\frac{1}{2}$ percent growth rate has been accompanied by a worsening distribution of income in some of the LDCs. The rise in population has worsened the living standards of people on marginal lands with inadequate rain (about 40 percent of Indian farmers and a large proportion of Africans). Partly as a result, there have been entire economies among the less developed countries that have been falling behind the rest of the world. Add the massive explosion of urban unemployment, and one gets several hundred million people who are no better off and possibly worse off.

Third, a continuing problem within the LDCs is the relatively high growth rate of their populations.

While net population growth has fallen almost to zero in the United States and some countries of Western Europe, the population explosion continues in some of the LDCs, particularly in Africa.

Table 38–4 tells the story. For the sample of LDCs shown, the annual growth rate of population continues perhaps ten times as high as it is in the industrialized countries. Clearly, the more closely the growth in population

Table 38–4
BIRTHRATE MINUS DEATH RATE IN DEVELOPED AND LESS DEVELOPED COUNTRIES, 1981–85 (ESTIMATED)

	(births minus deaths as percent of population)
Developed Countries	
United States	0.7
West Germany	−0.2
Sweden	0.0
Less Developed Countries	
Bolivia	2.8
China	1.0
Egypt	3.2
Ethiopia	2.1
Haiti	2.3
India	2.3

SOURCE: Population Reference Bureau, 1986.

approximates the growth in national income, the more slowly standards of living will rise, since there will be that many more persons among whom the additional product must be divided.

Fourth, the relatively high growth rate in per capita incomes has not been uniform throughout the LDCs. In some countries, such as Sri Lanka, Ghana, Chad, and Cuba, growth rates have been extremely low. In some cases, as in Uganda and Nigeria, real per capita incomes actually seem to have fallen. Yet in others, notably the Ivory Coast, Singapore, South Korea, and Taiwan, growth has been so spectacular that some of them are no longer considered LDCs, despite oil shocks, increasing restrictions against their exports, and lack of mineral resources.

Finally, the LDCs have shown themselves highly vulnerable to such events as the oil crisis in 1979 and the high real interest rates of the 1980s. Much as the fall in Iranian exports and rise in oil prices affected the industrialized economies, it undoubtedly damaged the LDCs even more, leading to enormous deficits and foreign debts for the countries least able to afford them. (See the boxed insert on pages 862–63.) In other words, the new growth trends in the LDCs may be quite fragile, and their continuation cannot simply be taken for granted.

It is ironic that the leveling-off of oil prices at the beginning of the 1980s not only left many oil-importing LDCs with their crippling debts, but caused similar problems for some of the oil exporters. As a result, Mexico and Venezuela joined Brazil in the group of countries whose economies are severely constrained by huge indebtedness to the rest of the world.

Impediments to Development in the LDCs

No one has produced a definitive list of causes of the poverty of the LDCs, just as no one can pretend to have produced a foolproof prescription for its cure. Yet there is general agreement on the main conditions contributing to the economic problems of LDCs. These include lack of physical capital, rapid growth of populations, lack of education, unemployment, and social and political impediments to business activity. Let us consider each of these.

Scarcity of Physical Capital

The LDCs are obviously handicapped by their lack of modern factories and machinery. In addition, they lack infrastructure—good roads, railroads, port facilities, and so on. But capital is not easy to acquire. If it is to be provided by the populations of the LDCs themselves, they must save the required resources—that is, as we saw earlier in this chapter, they must give up consumption in order to free the resources needed to build plants, equipment, and roads. That is fairly easy in a rich community, where substantial saving still leaves the public well off in terms of current consumption. But in an LDC, where malnutrition is a constant threat, the bulk of the inhabitants cannot save except at enormous sacrifice to their families. Moreover, in many of the LDCs, tradition imputes little virtue to investment in business, so that even the wealthy are not terribly anxious to put their savings into productive equipment. Thus:

Because of poverty, which makes saving difficult, if not impossible, and because of traditions that do not encourage investment, the LDCs' growth rates of domestically financed capital are lower than those in the developed countries.

One way to help matters is to obtain the funds for investment from abroad. There is a long tradition of foreign investment in developing countries. For example, throughout the first half of the nineteenth century the United States almost constantly drew capital from abroad, though the amounts involved were only a small proportion of U.S. GNP. In recent decades a considerable share of the resources going to the LDCs from abroad has come from foreign governments as part of their aid programs. While some of the resources provided in this way have been used wastefully, informed observers generally agree that the waste incurred under these programs has not been spectacularly great, and they conclude that these capital transfers from the rich countries to the poor have at least worked in the right direction.

Capital can also be transferred to an LDC when a private firm chooses to invest money in such a country to build a factory or to explore for oil in order to increase its own profits. This too seems to have been helpful to the LDCs. In earlier days, it sometimes gave an unacceptable degree of political influence to the foreign firms, particularly when the LDC was a colony of an industrial country. In recent years this difficulty may have become rarer. Nowadays, it is more often the outside firm that is afraid of the government of the LDC rather than vice versa, with foreign proprietors frequently fearful of rigid control by the government of the LDC in which it invests. Sometimes it even fears outright expropriation — that the government will simply take over its property in the LDC with, or even without, compensation because of the hostile attitudes that residents of many LDCs hold toward large foreign companies.

It is difficult for a resident of an industrialized country like the United States to realize how much hatred and resentment is felt in less developed countries toward the "northern imperialist powers." This resentment is focused in particular on **multinational corporations** — companies like IBM, Royal Dutch Shell, Volkswagen, and Unilever — which have their headquarters in an industrialized country and their operations in a variety of less developed countries. Multinationals may first process their own raw materials in one country, ship them to another to make them into parts, and assemble them in still a third. Some of these corporations, among them the oil companies, specialize in the extraction and/or marketing of raw materials, while others, like IBM and Volkswagen, specialize in manufacturing. Many LDCs regard these and other giant foreign corporations as instruments of imperialist exploitation, not as firms which happen to carry on their activities wherever the dictates of efficiency require, contributing benefits to each of the countries in which they operate.

It is true that foreign firms hope to make more money out of an LDC than they put into it, but that is only natural, since otherwise their investment would not have been expected to be profitable, and the funds would therefore not have been invested in the first place. But there are usually *mutual* gains from trade. Investment will be useful to the LDCs if in the process of earning these profits foreign firms build factories, infrastructure, and provide jobs that leave the community wealthier than it would otherwise have been. The evidence is that this is in fact what foreign private investment has typically accomplished in recent decades.

A problem with foreign business investment that is more serious is the danger that foreign firms will fail to train native personnel in the skills necessary to run the factories built by those companies. Often the firm brings with them their own managers, engineers, and technicians, and the work force from the LDCs is kept in menial jobs in which on-the-job training is minimal. In

The Continuing Debt Crisis of the Developing Countries

Although there had been previous isolated cracks in the international debt terrain, it was not until 1982 that the problem erupted in dramatic proportions. In August of that year, Mexico announced that it was unable to meet its debt obligations to foreign creditors, although it was taking steps to rectify the situation. In response, the U.S. government mounted a rescue operation, involving the creditor banks, the International Monetary Fund (IMF), and other creditor governments. The package included a strict program of adjustment for the Mexican economy and a rescheduling of much of the debt. Nervous banks began to cut back lending to other countries that appeared to be heavily indebted, with Brazil the most obvious target. As long as the banks had been willing to continue lending, the debtor countries had had the foreign exchange necessary to continue servicing their accumulated debt, i.e., making scheduled payments of interest and amortization of principal. As the banks cut back, the debtors found debt-service obligations increasingly difficult to meet. One by one, Brazil, Argentina, and many other debtor countries found it necessary to seek debt relief from their creditors, while implementing programs of economic adjustment monitored by the IMF.

The following is from a U.S. government report:

The debt problem threatens to undermine growth in much of Latin America, particularly Mexico, Brazil, Argentina, and Venezuela, and African countries such as Nigeria. It was caused by overborrowing and overspending during the 1970s when prosperity and growth seemed easy to

recent years the LDCs have begun to deal with this problem by restricting immigration of foreign personnel, giving them work permits only for limited periods and requiring at least some minimum employment of native personnel in key positions.

Another danger posed by foreign investment is that it may prevent future financial independence. Profits are a major source of the funds used for investment. If foreign investment takes over the LDCs' most profitable industries, then newly formed capital—new plants and equipment—will also be owned predominantly by foreigners.

Population Growth

Population growth is often described as the primary villain in the LDCs. We have already noted that their populations grow far more rapidly than those in the wealthier countries. And though the growth rate has recently been declining in many of the less developed countries, overall, the population of the LDCs is expanding at a rate that will double in less than 30 years, requiring a doubling of housing, schools, hospitals, and so on—a heavy real cost for an LDC.

The growth in population has been stimulated by improvements in medical care, which have reduced death rates spectacularly. Today, in some areas, sustain; by the high oil prices of the 1970s, which hurt the oil-importing LDCs; by the fall in oil prices in the early 1980s, which hurt the oil-exporting LDCs; and by high interest rates, which hurt them all.

The debt crisis is forcing widespread adoption of austerity policies—reducing already low consumption levels so that less has to be imported and more goods are left over for export. It prevents any ambitious investment programs for the same reason, thus impeding future growth. It is indeed a major problem for the LDCs and, incidentally, for the large banks in the industrialized countries to whom the money is owed and who fear the loss of their loans.

SOURCE: From the *Economic Report of the President,* February 1984, page 71.

According to *The Wall Street Journal:*

The international debt crisis that erupted in 1982 is flaring up again, and it holds new risks for U.S. banks and debtor countries alike....

Brazil a week and a half ago...announced it was suspending payments on about $67 billion of foreign debt and freezing about $15 billion of short-term credits and money-market deposits lent by foreign banks.

Like other Third World nations, from Ecuador and Argentina to the Philippines, Brazil hopes to win a "restructuring" of its debt and possibly get new financing as well. That for example, was what Mexico was able to negotiate last fall, in a deal expected to be concluded later this month....

In the Mexican and other past negotiations, [the] Federal Reserve Board Chairman...has succeeded in holding the international debt structure together by getting the creditor banks to agree to new terms and new financings.

But this time [the Chairman] may be losing some of his tight control of the situation. Deep schisms have developed among creditors. New York's Citicorp has differed with other big money-center banks, insisting that the terms in restructurings be as strict as possible.* More and more regional banks are refusing to lend money to sickly debtors...

For their part, some of the debtors, realizing their economies can't readily support current levels of debt, have become bolder. Peru has gone so far as to essentially default on its $14 billion of debt by limiting interest payments to a fraction of its scant export earnings....

*Author's Note: Citicorp has since declared a substantial portion of these debts to be uncollectable, as have other banks.

SOURCE: Charles F. McCoy and Peter Truell, *The Wall Street Journal,* March 3, 1987, page 1.

death rates (ratio of deaths to population) are only one-quarter or one-fifth as high as birthrates. While formerly it was not unusual for half a nation's children to die before the age of 20, today in many countries this is true of only some 4 percent of those populations. This dramatic decline can be attributed primarily to inexpensive public health measures—reduction in intestinal diseases through purer water supplies, reduction in the incidence of malaria by the draining of swamps, insecticide spraying of the breeding grounds of infectious mosquitoes, eradication of smallpox by vaccination, and so forth. The more expensive treatment of illness, using modern medical techniques and miracle drugs, seems to have contributed far less.

But not all LDCs suffer from serious population problems. India, Indonesia, and Egypt are frequently cited examples of population pressures. On the other hand, many African countries and parts of Latin America still have populations so small that they are denied economies of larger scale communication and transportation. The economy of a sparsely settled country whose electric power and telecommunication lines must traverse great unpopulated areas is under a costly handicap.

Governments in a number of LDCs have been struggling to find workable ways to cut population growth. Programs set up to distribute contraceptives and propaganda against large families have achieved modest success; but in some countries with particularly severe population problems the governments have been dissatisfied with the results of these voluntary efforts. In India, a program making use of compulsory sterilization aroused the anger of the public and finally led to the downfall of the government.

Ironically enough, it was communist China which, along with Singapore, decided to employ strong financial incentives for the purpose. In China, government support is provided for a first child. For a second, the support is withdrawn and some financial penalties imposed; and for a third child, the penalties are really prohibitive for most people. Observers come away impressed with its initial impact in the cities. Everywhere in Chinese urban areas one meets people who say they are determined to have only one child. However, reports indicate that in rural areas the program has been considerably less effective.

Educational and Technical Training

Everyone knows that educational levels in the LDCs are much lower than they are in the wealthier countries. There are fewer graduates of elementary schools, far fewer graduates of high schools, and enormously fewer college graduates. The percentage of the population that is literate is much lower than in industrialized nations. The issue is how much of a handicap this constitutes for economic growth.

If, by "education," we refer to general learning rather than technical (trade) schooling, the evidence is that it makes considerably less difference for economic growth than is often believed. For example, the number of jobs that clearly require secondary (high school) education rarely seems to exceed 10 percent of the labor force. Various studies that have investigated whether there is a statistical relationship between the economic growth of an economy and its typical educational level have failed to turn up any significant correlation between the two. Other suggestive evidence can easily be cited. For example, in 1840 when Great Britain ruled the markets of the world, only 59 percent of the British adult population was literate, while in the United States, Scandinavia, and Germany, then all relatively undeveloped countries, the figure was about 80 percent.

All of this is not meant to imply that education is worthless. On the contrary, it obviously offers many benefits in and of itself, which need not be discussed here. But it does suggest that if a government invests in education *purely as a means to stimulate economic growth*, only a very limited outlay is justifiable on these grounds.

Matters are quite different when we turn to technical training. There is clearly a high payoff to the training of electricians, machinists, draftsmen, construction workers, and the like. While the number of persons involved need not be very high in proportion to the population, the role played by such specialists is crucial. However, the LDCs would find it a very heavy drain upon their scarce foreign currency to send young people abroad to learn these skills in the numbers called for by the needs of the economy. One of the main inhibitions to adequate training in these areas is that in many countries such skills are held in low esteem and considered inferior to training in the liberal arts. Consequently, technical education is often handicapped by low budgets, low teacher salaries — which discourage good people from entering the field — and the prejudice of potential students against such fields.

Training in improved farming methods also has a great deal to contribute. In many of the LDCs, agricultural methods produce yields far lower than the best of the known techniques can offer. As one leading observer, Nobel Prize-winner Sir W. Arthur Lewis, has remarked:

If this gap could be closed, the economies of these countries would be unrecognizable. Indeed . . . no impact can be made on mass living standards without revolutionizing agricultural performance.[8]

There seem to be no easy ways to provide the necessary education to the farmers who cannot spare the time to attend schools, and training their children also involves a number of critical obstacles. Religious beliefs often lead parents to object to schooling of their children, particularly of girls; in areas where literacy is low (where the problem is generally most serious), truly literate and knowledgeable teachers are almost impossible to find in any substantial numbers; and children who do complete schooling have a tendency to leave the farms and move to the cities.

Programs to provide help to the peasants on their own farms have had only limited success. Indeed, lack of training is only part of the problem. Many other things are needed to make modern farming methods possible — farms larger than the five acres that are typical in a number of countries are required to permit the use of modern machinery where it is appropriate. Roads and storage facilities must be built. Credit must be made available to farmers. Financial arrangements must be changed so the farmer need no longer give up half his crop to landlords and tax collectors whom he can surely regard as little more than parasites and who undermine his incentives for improved productivity.

Unemployment

One of the most noteworthy features of the growth of the LDCs has been an increase in unemployment as population shifted out of agriculture into the cities. Increased schooling has stimulated the migration out of the rural areas, as has unionization, which has often produced a huge gap between urban and rural wages. Government investment policies have also favored construction of schools, hospitals, and other facilities in the cities, and as a result, large numbers of migrants have entered the cities to swell the ranks of the unemployed. The unemployment rate among young urban workers has been particularly high; indeed, rates as high as 50 percent are not unheard of.

These figures are compounded by the phenomenon of **disguised unemployment.** For example, ten persons may do a job for which only six are needed. The statistics would show no unemployment among the ten workers, even though four of them really contribute nothing to output. Some observers believe that this is such a widespread problem in rural areas that even a substantial reverse migration of the urban unemployed back to the farms would add very little to production, at least in some of the LDCs.

An important consequence of all this is that in many LDCs unemployment may not be accompanied by any substantial reduction in output, in contrast to the situation in industrialized economies. But this does not mean that unemployment in the LDCs is not a serious problem. What it does mean is that it may sometimes be desirable for those economies to avoid the use of labor-saving equipment, partly because it will result in better use of an abundant resource and partly because it will contribute to the solution of a serious social problem. Thus, increased jobs are desirable perhaps primarily because they sop up unemployed labor. This is in contrast to the usual situation in the developed countries in which increased employment is desirable perhaps primarily because it increases income and output.

[8]W. A. Lewis, *Development Economics, An Outline* (Morristown, N.J.: General Learning Press, 1974), page 25.

Social Impediments to Entrepreneurship

As we saw earlier in this chapter, one of the magic ingredients of economic growth is **entrepreneurship.** It is clear that the LDCs need entrepreneurs if their economies are to grow rapidly. But in many of these economies, there are serious inhibitions to entrepreneurship. Traditional social values often accord relatively low status to business activity. Indeed, those traditional values even prevent businesses from seeking ways to attract and please their customers and their work force. In addition, high positions in business in many LDCs are often determined by family connections and inheritance, not by ability.

In the LDCs, growth will be inhibited until customs can be modified to increase the social status of economic activity, to make it respectable for private business people and managers of public enterprises to do their best to attract business and increase productivity, and to assign responsibility on the basis of ability rather than family connections.

Government Inhibition of Business Activity

In addition to social impediments to business, the political situation in the LDCs often is detrimental to business success. Business is not helped by unstable governments or by the uncertainty that accompanies such an environment, especially if there is a high likelihood of revolution. Foreign investment will be discouraged where there is fear of expropriation or of unstable currencies that may fall in value and wipe out hard-earned profits. And native business people may live in fear of nationalization or even imprisonment—possibilities that are not likely to encourage investment.

In addition, in the normal course of events, governments in the LDCs are often inclined to interfere with business activity in a variety of ways that seem relatively innocuous—but whose effects can be deadly. Price controls are often imposed at levels that make the controlled activity totally unprofitable and cause it to wither. Licenses and other direct controls are frequently administered by incompetent bureaucrats, who tie up business activity in red tape. As a matter of prestige of the currency, exchange rates are often set so high that exports from the LDC cannot compete on the world market. The governments sometimes expropriate and seek to operate foreign firms before they have trained native personnel to run them. In short:

Poorly conceived economic policies can impede business activity and hence economic growth in the LDCs. But, then, it must be admitted that the LDCs have no monopoly on foolish economic policies!

Help from Industrialized Economies

We have just seen that the two primary needs of the LDCs are technical skills and capital resources. Happily, these are precisely the things that the more prosperous nations are in a position to offer. We have the trained teachers, classrooms, laboratories, and equipment necessary to provide an education of the highest quality to students from the LDCs. However, there is a danger here that has received a great deal of attention, the so-called **brain drain.** This refers to the temptation for students from LDCs to try to stay in the countries where they have studied and enjoy the higher living standard, rather than to return home where their abilities are needed so badly.

There are several ways to deal with this. For example, one can require students to return to their homelands for at least some given number of years after completion of the educational program, or offer higher wages for trained persons in the LDCs to make returning more attractive. Yet the problem is there, and the large number of doctors, teachers, and other skilled personnel from LDCs who are seeking jobs in the developed countries suggests that it is not negligible.

A second major contribution that the wealthier countries can make to the LDCs is to offer them trained technicians and technical advice from their own populations. Such counseling and personnel can be very helpful as a temporary measure, but in the long run they can prove detrimental if provision for the training of local personnel for the ultimate replacement of the foreign technicians and advisers is not built into the program.

Third, the world can help the LDCs through research. One of the hardest problems for the developing world is what to do in the rural areas that suffer from inadequate rainfall, where several hundred million people live in both Asia and Africa. These people are badly in need of new dry-farming techniques. Until some are discovered, their poverty will increase as their numbers grow. An international research organization devoted to food production in problem areas in the LDCs would have much to contribute.

Fourth, the developed countries can help by encouraging freedom of trade and investment. This will help those LDCs whose exports are now being held back by barriers to trade. Exports of sugar, meat, cotton, and other agricultural products are inhibited by industrialized countries' tariffs and other restrictions. LDCs would also benefit substantially from a lifting of tariffs and quotas upon the export of processed or manufactured goods. Such restrictive measures make it difficult for LDCs to export anything but raw materials and impedes their industrialization and modernization. All in all, increased freedom of trade is a matter of highest priority for the LDCs.[9]

A last, and very important, type of assistance from the developed to the less developed countries takes the form of money or physical resources provided either as loans made on favorable terms or as outright grants (gifts).

Loans and Grants by the United States and Others

Since World War II a number of countries have provided capital to the LDCs. An international organization, the International Bank for Reconstruction and Development (the **World Bank**), was created largely for this purpose. It has 144 member countries, each providing an amount of capital related to its wealth; for instance, the United States has contributed approximately one-third of the total. The Bank makes loans that finance its bonds and has acted as guarantor of repayment to encourage some private lending. Since its inception the Bank has approved loans totalling $131.5 billion to 104 countries, mostly for infrastructure, dams, communications, and transportation. In addition, it provided technical assistance and planning advice.

United States' loans and grants have exceeded the total given by all other countries and international agencies, with U.S. interest and repayment terms generally far more generous than those of other governments. However, the

---

[9]Not everyone agrees with this conclusion. There are those who have argued that participation of LDCs in international trade is bad for them because it weakens their capacity to develop as self-reliant, mature economies. It is held that new manufacturing industries in the LDCs will not take off without protection from foreign competition; that development of raw material exports creates a politically powerful vested interest that inhibits manufacturing; and that foreign participation in trade and production of exports inhibits domestic investment and the development of local entrepreneurship.

In this view, LDCs are therefore held back by international trade and they would do better to integrate regionally and develop their own home markets without foreigners, who also bring unsuitable habits, tastes, and technology, and impart a crippling inferiority complex to the natives.

bulk of the assistance provided by the United States has gone to a small number of countries, such as India, Pakistan, South Korea, and Turkey.

During the 1960s, our expenditures on aid ran to more than $3 billion per year. In the past decade, expenditures on foreign aid have become less popular politically, and the amounts provided consequently have gone down sharply and steadily from about half a percent of U.S. GNP in 1965 to under 0.3 percent of GNP in 1984–85.

France, Great Britain, West Germany, and other industrialized noncommunist countries now provide about $29 billion per year, which is about 0.4 percent of their GNP. The Soviet Union has also become a major source of assistance to the LDCs, now providing, along with its associated countries, about $3.4 billion, or 0.23 percent of their GNP. While the Soviet funds have obviously been distributed in a way intended to maximize its political advantage, it can hardly be claimed that the U.S. foreign aid program has been entirely free of political considerations.

Many economists have advocated greater generosity in our assistance to LDCs. It is argued that an effective aid program that really helps the growth of LDCs will also serve our own interests. By making those countries more stable economically and politically, we can contribute to our own economic tranquility. By increasing the LDCs' power to buy and sell, we contribute to the prosperity of the entire world.

Can LDCs Break Away from Poverty?

It is easy to jump to the conclusion that the economic problems of the LDCs are staggering and that the prospects of their ever catching up with the industrialized countries are negligible. Yet a number of LDCs and former LDCs have made enormous progress. The African countries Kenya, Cameroon, and the Ivory Coast increased their GNPs during the 1970s at a rate of about 5 to 6 percent a year, which is considerably faster than their population growth. In the Americas, Costa Rica's performance has been comparable. Even more striking is the expansion of output in a number of places in the Far East — particularly Hong Kong, Taiwan, South Korea, and Singapore, where prosperity is unprecedented and economic activity is expanding at an astonishing rate. Here per capita GNPs have been growing at a rate of 6.5 percent a year and more.

But the most impressive case is that of Japan. Many of your professors will remember clearly when U.S. business feared the flood of goods produced by cheap Japanese labor, and when the label "made in Japan" suggested inexpensive and shoddy merchandise. From one of the world's impoverished countries, Japan has risen to one of the world's richest. Its goods are now feared by American manufacturers not because they are produced and sold so cheaply, but because their quality is so high. Japanese cars and sophisticated electronic equipment find a ready market in the United States. And as a result, per capita income in Japan has surpassed that in Great Britain. A less developed country need not lag behind forever.

Summary

1. If growth is evaluated in terms of its effect upon the well-being of individuals, a country's economic growth should be measured in terms of *per capita* income, not in terms of GNP or some other index of total output of the economy.

2. A rapidly rising population poses a threat to growth of per capita incomes.

3. On our finite planet, exponential growth (growth at a constant percentage rate) is, in general, impossible except for relatively brief periods.

4. Increases in growth depend heavily on entrepreneurship, accumulation of capital equipment, and research and development.
5. Saving is necessary for the accumulation of resources with which to produce factories, machinery, and other capital equipment. Thus, saving is a critical requisite for growth, particularly in less developed countries.
6. Many observers argue that even if continued growth does not lead to catastrophically rapid depletion of resources (as some have predicted), its desirability is nevertheless questionable because it produces pollution, overcrowding, and many other undesirable consequences.
7. Those who favor growth argue that without it there is no chance of ridding the world of poverty.
8. Standards of living in many LDCs are extremely low; per capita incomes that are equivalent to $1500 a year are not uncommon. Life expectancy is low and daily living is very difficult, particularly for women.
9. GNP and per capita incomes in the LDCs grew considerably in the 1970s, though in many cases they slowed in the 1980s.
10. Nevertheless, the gap between family incomes in the less developed and the industrialized countries has continued to widen.
11. In many LDCs, population continues to grow much faster than that in the industrialized countries.
12. Growth in the LDCs is impeded by shortages of capital caused by poverty, traditions that do not encourage investment, rapid population growth, poor education, unemployment, lack of entrepreneurship, and government impediments to business.
13. Industrialized countries can help the LDCs by providing capital through loans and grants, by offering training and education to people from those lands, and by encouraging freedom of trade with the LDCs.
14. In the post-World War II period many countries, including the United States and the Soviet Union, have provided large amounts of money to the LDCs in the form of loans and grants.
15. Several international organizations, most notably the World Bank, have been organized to provide economic assistance to the LDCs.

Concepts for Review

Output per capita
Exponential growth
Social infrastructure
Exchange between present and
    future consumption

Embodied growth
Disembodied growth
Less developed countries (LDCs)
Growth rate in GNP vs. per capita income
Multinational corporations

Disguised unemployment
Entrepreneurship
Brain drain
World Bank

Questions for Discussion

1. Which do you think has the higher total GNP, Pakistan or Luxembourg? Which has the higher per capita GNP? In which do you think people are better off economically?
2. Suppose population grows at a constant exponential rate and doubles every 10 years. How many times will it have grown in 30 years? How many years does it require to expand to 16 times its initial level?
3. Can you think of any innovations that permit growth without proportionate increases in use of inputs?
4. Name as many undesirable consequences of growth as you can think of.
5. Are the undesirable consequences of growth more likely to be considered serious in a less developed country or in an industrialized country? Why?
6. To many families living in less developed countries, an income equivalent to $2000 per year is considered a high standard of living. Can you make up a budget for a U.S. family of four earning $2000 a year?
7. Explain how it is possible for the per capita income of an LDC to grow at a faster rate than that in the United States and yet for the difference between the incomes of average families in both countries to increase. Can you give a numerical example showing how this happens?

8. Discuss the advantages and disadvantages to an LDC of a U.S. manufacturing company investing in that country.

9. If you were economic adviser to the president of an LDC, what might you suggest that he or she do to encourage increases in saving and investment?

10. No one knows what encourages or discourages the supply of entrepreneurs. Do you have any ideas about policies that may be capable of stimulating entrepreneurship?

11. Name some countries in which entrepreneurship seems to be abundant these days and some countries in which it seems to be scarce. What is your impression about what is happening to the supply of entrepreneurs in the United States?

12. Discuss what you have read in the newspapers and heard from other sources about the Japanese "growth miracle." What does it portend for the future of the Japanese economy? For that of the United States?

39

The Economics of Karl Marx

What is certain is that I am not a Marxist.

KARL MARX TO HIS
SON-IN-LAW.[*]

For more than a century radical and reformist groups throughout the world have drawn inspiration from the writings of Karl Marx. Nations with governments claiming to be run on Marxist principles include the Soviet Union, the People's Republic of China, Cuba, and at least a dozen other countries in Eastern Europe, Asia, Africa, and Latin America, containing among them more than one-third of the world's population.

In this chapter we summarize the major ideas in Marx's economic theories. And one of the main conclusions we draw is that his work contains very little that is helpful to a communist economy. This judgment is made not because the Marxian analysis is poor in quality or short of ideas. On the contrary, even some very conservative economists have acknowledged the originality and importance of at least some of Marx's analyses. Rather, we find that his ideas are not particularly helpful to a central planner because Marx chose to devote almost all his attention to the *capitalist* economy, seeking to explain the principles of its evolution, its strengths, and its weaknesses. Hence, he left wide open the questions about how a communist economy should be run.

It is a mistake to think that Marx despised every feature of capitalism. It is true that he believed its accomplishments exacted a very high cost in human misery and exploitation. And he also believed that it was rapidly outliving its usefulness and its historical role. But he was a profound admirer of its early vigor and enormous accomplishments, which, in his phrase, rescued humanity from the "universal mediocrity" that feudalism had imposed on the economy.

[*]Quoted in a letter from Friedrich Engels to Eduard Bernstein in November 1882. Much of the material in this chapter conflicts very strongly with popular (mis)conceptions about what Marx really said. It is, perhaps, important to emphasize that this chapter's contents are based on years of research and study of Marx's published and (until recently) unpublished writings, his letters, and many, many other documents. In Marx's lifetime, the process of misinterpreting what he had plainly written, by people who had not read him carefully, had already began. Marx's son-in-law was a "Marxist" of this sort—which is what led Marx to make the statement quoted here.

Except for Marx's use of the word *bourgeoisie*, the following passage from the *Communist Manifesto* (1848) might have been penned by a publicist for the Chamber of Commerce:

> *The bourgeoisie . . . has accomplished wonders far surpassing Egyptian pyramids, Roman aqueducts, and Gothic cathedrals . . . The bourgeoisie cannot exist without constantly revolutionizing the instruments of production . . . The bourgeoisie, during its rule of scarce one hundred years, has created more massive and more colossal productive forces than have all preceding generations together.*[1]

The Marxian Framework: Historical Materialism

To Marx, a historical perspective was essential to understand the capitalist system, or any other form of economic organization. All economic systems evolve from others that are very different, and they can each be expected to be replaced by some other form of economic organization. Thus, to understand how a particular economy works we must keep in mind the predecessor from which it evolved and the process by which it grew. Marx frequently criticized the classical economists for their nonhistorical viewpoint, their treatment of all other economic forms as more or less mini-capitalist systems, and their tacit assumption that capitalism will prevail throughout all time. He said, with some scorn, that to these economists "there has been history, but there is no longer any."

What determines the evolutionary direction of a society? According to Marx the primary influence is economic—the current state of technology and the method of organizing production. At each stage of history, these factors determine which group will be in charge of the economy and which groups will be subjugated. In the feudal economy, for instance, the manor lords were in control of the economy while the serfs were under their domination. Under the free-enterprise economy, the medieval lord has been replaced by the modern capitalist and the serf by the free laborer—in reality a propertyless proletarian who "has nothing to sell but his hands." But the relationship between the serf and his lord was, of course, very different from that between the free laborer and the capitalist. Technology, which is primarily responsible for this difference, affected the productivity of the two economies, which in turn changed the course of the economy's growth and the character of the struggle between the dominant and dominated groups.

By saying that economic conditions determine the direction of the evolutionary process, Marx did *not* mean that people care only about their financial well-being. Unlike a number of later historians and modern (non-Marxist) economists who have analyzed everything in human activity—from crime and marriage to the provisions of the U.S. Constitution—in terms of the narrow economic interests of those involved, Marxian analysts have always recognized that history is affected by altruism, passion, prejudice, social pressures, and a wide variety of other noneconomic influences. Nevertheless, these Marxists are quick to point out that such influences are themselves strongly affected by the nature of the economic system. This analysis of social evolution is the basis of Marx's theory of **historical materialism.**

Marx's **historical materialism** asserts that we cannot understand any economy without recognizing its place in history. It asserts also that while historical events are influenced primarily (though not exclusively) by economic conditions, the form of this influence is often very indirect and subtle—filtering through current social customs, political organizations, and so forth. Historical materialism does *not* assert that people follow only their monetary self-interest.

[1]Karl Marx, *Communist Manifesto, Collected Works*, vol. 6 (New York: International Publishers, 1976), pages 487–89.

Biographical Note: Karl Marx (1818–1883)

Karl Marx was born in Trier, Germany, the son of a successful Jewish lawyer who later converted to Christianity. Marx's acquaintances considered him brilliant, but he was also stubborn and quarrelsome. Throughout his life he broke with one associate after another, the only exception being Friedrich Engels, his lifelong friend, collaborator, and benefactor.

Marx studied at the universities of Bonn and Berlin, hoping first to become a poet. After a resounding failure at poetry, he entered a circle of young philosophers in Berlin, all devoted followers of Hegel, whose ideas about the crucial role of history in understanding current events, art, and science had recently swept German universities. The young Hegelians, however, were radical in their opposition to Hegel's religious views, and this attitude may have influenced Marx's later attacks against religion. Marx received his doctorate of philosophy at the age of 23, meanwhile having married ("above his station") Jenny von Westphalen, the daughter of his father's closest friend. Jenny's family opposed the marriage, and, as it turned out, their concerns were justified, since Marx was never able to support her. Much of their lives was spent in great poverty, and the deaths of three of their six children were probably the result of privation.

After a brief stint as a newspaper editor, Marx's troubles with the authorities propelled him first out of Germany and then Paris and Belgium. It was in Paris that Marx first met Engels, and in Brussels they together wrote the *Communist Manifesto*, a revolutionary pamphlet that was the only writing of Marx's to achieve wide circulation during his lifetime. After the demise of the revolutions that shook all of Europe in 1848, but in which Marx played little part, he fled finally to London where he spent the rest of his life. There Marx helped form revolutionary groups, and

otherwise spent most of his time cloistered in the British Museum studying the history of economic thought and writing *Das Kapital*. Aside from some meager earnings as correspondent for *The New York Tribune*, a job he held for about ten years, Marx lived entirely on money given to him by Engels (who, although an anticapitalist, nevertheless owned factories in Manchester and Germany) and by other admirers.

Marx was never very successful in organizing revolutionary groups, and he finally engineered the breakup of The First International, the revolutionary organization that he helped found and develop but which seemed about to fall into the hands of opponent radicals. Marx finished writing volume I of *Capital* and saw it published in 1867. He had previously written most of volumes II and III, but never completed them in the 15 years that remained to him. It was left to Engels to edit and publish these volumes after Marx's death. Marx died in 1883, two years after the death of his wife, Jenny, and only several months after the unexpected death of his eldest daughter, Jenny Longuet.

Throughout his life Marx attracted and fascinated many people by his brilliance and through the force of his personality and ideas. And though most of his associates eventually became estranged from Marx the man, almost all retained their allegiance to his ideas.

To underline the distinction between the Marxian view of the process of change and the view that people are motivated only by their own economic interests, one need only look at the fact that revolutionary fervor among lower-income groups often accelerates rather than wanes when their economic conditions improve. The reason, according to some Marxian economists, is that increased income and leisure finally afford the poorest members of the economy the time to think about their miserable condition and the material strength and means to do something about it. Thus, economic conditions are indeed an important determinant of the timing of revolutionary unrest, but unrest does not necessarily peak at the moment in history when the lowest classes have the most to gain from it.

On the Nature of Communist Society

Among the many thousands of pages Marx wrote and published, and among those published by others after his death, there are scarcely a dozen dealing with the nature of the economy under socialism (which Marx never distinguished clearly from communism). Marx did tell us that socialism must come, and that it must begin with "the dictatorship of the proletariat," though this concept, too, is left somewhat fuzzy. There is no doubt, however, about his ideology. He clearly and repeatedly stated that this "higher form of society" will be dedicated to "the full and free development of every individual," with work transformed into a stimulating and pleasant activity and the deadening effects of extreme specialization brought to an end.

Perhaps Marx's most famous passage on the nature of socialism appears in one of his last economic writings, in which he envisions the post-capitalist society passing through two stages. In the first, there is already "common ownership of production." But this early socialist society is "still stamped with the birth marks of the old society from whose womb it emerges." In this stage, the income of the individual is exactly equivalent to the amount of labor he contributes.

> He receives a certificate from society that he has furnished such and such an amount of labour . . . and with this certificate he draws from the social stock of means of consumption as much as costs the same amount of labour. The same amount of labour which he has given to society in one form he receives back in another. [However,] . . . in a higher phase of communist society, after the enslaving subordination of the individual to the division of labour, and with it also the antithesis between mental and physical labour has vanished; after labour has become not only a means of life but itself life's prime want; after the productive forces have also increased with the all-around development of the invididual, and all the springs of cooperative wealth flow more abundantly — only then can the narrow horizon of bourgeois right be crossed in its entirety and society inscribe on its banner: From each according to his ability, to each according to his needs![2]

About the only other concrete attribute of a communist society described in Marx's writing is the abolition of the division of labor, which, claimed Marx, transforms workers from creative, satisfied humans into discontented, alienated near-machines. According to Marx and Engels:

> In communist society, where nobody has one exclusive sphere of activity but each can become accomplished in any branch he wishes, society regulates the general production and thus makes it possible for me to do one thing today and another tomorrow, to hunt in the morning, fish in the afternoon, rear cattle in the evening, criticise

---

[2]Karl Marx, *Critique of the Gotha Programme* (Moscow: Progress Publishers, 1971), pages 17–18.

after dinner, just as I have a mind, without ever becoming hunter, fisherman, cowboy or critic.[3]

Certainly these are fascinating notions, but they tell us nothing about the coordination of production, the planning of new plant and equipment, the arrangements for industrial research, the devising of a monetary policy (if money is to be used), and the many other issues that must be settled in designing any (even a communist) economy.

It seems clear that Marx did not intend to provide detailed guidance to the leaders of communist societies. Rather, his work was devoted to a painstaking analysis and critique of capitalism.

Commodities, Productive Labor, and Capital

One of the reasons it is hard to understand Marx is that he often employed words to mean things other than what they mean in ordinary usage. (Marx was, after all, an economist!) Since Marx considered it so important to distinguish capitalism from all other economic systems, he defined his basic economic terms and concepts in a way intended to emphasize their role in a free-enterprise economy.

A *commodity* for Marx is therefore not simply any good or service that consumers consider useful — which is how modern economists would define the term. Thus, when a primitive stoneworker trades some of his handiwork (say, arrowheads) for the meat that has been brought in by a hunter, neither the meat nor the arrowheads are "commodities" in Marxian terminology. Meat and arrowheads become commodities only when they are processed or produced by commercial firms, not because they are any more useful than the meat and arrowheads traded by the stoneworker and the hunter, but because they are produced as means to earn *profits*.

Commodity production is therefore just another element serving the one central purpose of the capitalist system — the accumulation of wealth, which in turn is the engine for the continuing expansion of the economy.

Analogously, Marx called labor under capitalism "productive" only when it turns out commodities, that is, when its outputs are offered for sale as part of the normal process of profit making and accumulation. Two pieces of work may appear perfectly identical, yet one can be productive and the other unproductive in Marx's view. Thus, a baker on the staff of the White House who makes a cake for a diplomatic dinner is engaged in "unproductive activity" (as are the diplomats!). The cake has no part in the capitalistic economy and does not differ in any way from the work of a baker in the court of a medieval prince. But another baker who makes an identical cake for a commercial bakery is "productive" because, to his employer, he is producing not cake but profit. *Capital* also was defined by Marx in a way that differs from that of modern economists, who employ it to mean plant, equipment, and other produced means of production. To Marx, capital meant a social process rather than a set of physical objects. The term can include the hiring of labor power, the construction of machinery, the production of commodities, the exchange of products for money, and the reinvestment of that money in another round of the

---

[3]Karl Marx and Friedrich Engels, *The German Ideology, Collected Works*, vol. 5 (New York: International Publishers, 1976), page 47.

profit-generating process. *Capitalism* is the all-embracing term that includes every one of the steps of this mechanism. With such a broad definition, it is no wonder that Marx chose the word "capital" as the title to his most important book.

Marx's Value Theory: Surplus as the Source of Accumulation

Perhaps the single most confusing thing about Marx's book *Capital* is its use of the term *exchange value*. To classical economists, this term was a synonym for *price*, and much of their work was intended to explain how market prices are determined—why a particular pair of shoes sells for a price twice as high as a certain hat, for example. But to Marx, the revolutionary, this was not an important issue. Rather, his central purpose, as we shall see, was to explain the accumulation process. And for this it was convenient to use a totally different concept of value.

Central to Marx's value analysis is something he regarded as a puzzle of fundamental importance—one whose solution he claimed had escaped his predecessors. Accumulation, the engine of economic growth, is financed out of profits, and profits appear to come from the sale of commodities. But how, he asked, can that possibly be? If two people exchange two goods of equal value, they may both be better off, for each may prefer the goods he gets to the goods he gives up. But in such a process neither party can gain *financially* since each has given as much value as he has received. It is true that one party in the exchange can profit at the expense of the other if he delivers less value than he receives, but the other party must then lose as much as the first one gains. The mystery, then, is this: How can the economy as a whole pour forth the profits needed for accumulation if the exchange process on which accumulation is based is fundamentally incapable of yielding net gains to the group of parties involved?

Marx's proposed solution starts off with a definition: The *value* of a commodity is precisely equal to the labor time necessary for its production. Note that Marx clearly stated that this is a *definition,* not a deduction: "[A good] which is not the product of labour cannot have a value; in other words, it cannot be *defined* . . . as the social expression of a certain quantity of labour."[4]

Ricardo and other predecessors of Marx had already proposed something that *sounded* very similar but really was not. They had argued that, in certain circumstances, pure competition tends to drive relative market prices of different goods very close to the relative amounts of labor needed to produce them. Notice that this can be *deduced* from economic theory if most production costs are labor costs, since under perfect competition, as we saw in Chapter 22, price tends to equal marginal cost. But Marx spurned this theory and criticized Ricardo severely for it, saying that in fact prices usually differ substantially from each good's labor content. Though Ricardo considered such deviations to be exceptions to a generally accurate rule, Marx said they happen so often that Ricardo's "rule becomes the exception and the exception the rule."

By divorcing the concepts of price and value, Marx freed himself to play with the word *value*. He could now define value and labor time to be the same thing, even though he believed that prices differ systematically from the labor time required in the production process.

---

[4]Karl Marx, *Theories of Surplus Value*, vol. III (Moscow: Progress Publishers, 1963), page 520. Italics added.

Why did he adopt this apparently curious definition? Because, in his view, it helps to explain where profits really come from and, concurrently, how wealth is accumulated. For this purpose he formulated one more concept, the value of labor power, about which he wrote:

> The *value of labour-power is determined, as in the case of every other commodity, by the labour-time necessary for the production, and consequently also the reproduction, of this special article. . . . The value of labour-power is the value of the means of subsistence necessary for the maintenance of the labourer.* [5]

In defining the *value of labor power* as a *minimum* subsistence level for the worker, Marx did not mean that *wages* are in fact always set at that subsistence level. Just as the price of a commodity is not generally equal to its (Marxian) value, the wage for an hour of labor need not be equal to the value of that much labor power. In fact, Marx argued vigorously that the level of wages is determined by the outcome of a constant struggle between workers and capitalists, and that one of the main purposes of union activity is to force wages above bare subsistence.

The value analysis gave Marx his solution to his puzzle about the origin of profits. Suppose that the average worker needs to labor for five hours to produce a day's subsistence but that the standard workday is eight hours. Then, in one workday, labor power, which has a value of five hours, is transformed into a product that carries a value of eight hours. The difference, which Marx called **surplus value,** is the portion of output that does not have to be consumed by the worker for his survival and that instead can be accumulated and used by the capitalist to expand his property and to make the economy grow.

According to Marx, profits and accumulation are possible only because the value of labor power — the amount of labor needed to produce a worker's daily subsistence — is no more than a fraction of a workday. The remainder of the worker's day goes into the production of surplus value, which can be accumulated by the capitalist.

The Ethics of Surplus Value

Over the years, many people have concluded that Marx's aim was to establish that capitalism is immoral and that profits amount to robbery of the worker who really deserves the surplus he earns. Marx explicitly and repeatedly denied that this was his opinion; in fact, his anger was aroused by others who did hold such views. Marx made clear, right at the point in *Capital* where he defined the value of labor power, that:

> It is a very cheap sort of sentimentality which declares this method of determining the value of labour-power, a method prescribed by the very nature of the case, to be a brutal method. [6]

But if it was not Marx's goal to show that surplus value is robbery, then what was the purpose of the value theory? Engels stated that the purpose of Marx's analysis, the very analysis on which he based his revolutionary demands,

[5]Karl Marx, *Capital*, vol. 1 (Chicago: Charles H. Kerr Publishing Company, 1906), pages 189–96.
[6]*Ibid.*, page 192.

was to demonstrate "the inevitable collapse of the capitalist mode of production." Later in this chapter we will see how the value theory could, in Marx's view, help explain the "laws of motion of capitalism." It was these laws that he interpreted as calling for precisely the sort of revolutionary change he was advocating—the replacement of capitalism by a communist society.

There is also a second issue that the theory of surplus value was intended to deal with. In providing himself the answer to the question of how profits can be produced by an exchange economy, Marx believed he had also shown that profits (as well as rents and interest payments) are *produced by workers*. Put the other way, Marx believed he had shown that profit is *not* produced by the capitalist, that interest is *not* produced by the moneylender, and that rent is *not* produced by the landlord.

In saying this, Marx never denied that land and produced means of production contribute to the output of the economy. Nor did he ever argue that labor is the only useful means of production:

> [When he does his work, the laborer] is constantly helped by natural forces. We see, then, that labour is not the only source of material wealth, of use-values produced by labour. . . . labour is its father and the earth its mother.[7]

But while *land* (or natural resources generally) contributes to production, it does not necessarily follow that the *landlord*, the person who happens to own the land, contributes anything. A given output can be produced just as well if the land is publicly owned and there is no landlord to collect income from the production process. It was Marx's contention, therefore, that labor is the only *human* (he called it "social") input that contributes to production. True, a capitalist may sometimes help in the production process by organizing and planning it, but then, according to Marx, he is merely serving as a (part-time) laborer. In sum:

Marx emphasized that labor is not the only useful factor of production. However, he did argue that it is the only useful factor of production contributed by *human society*. In this sense he considered it necessary to define all value and, therefore, all surplus value (profit, interest, and rent) as something that is produced by labor.

The Marxian Analysis of Pricing and Profit

If in Marxian economics, price and value are generally *unequal*, then how are prices determined? The answer is that they are determined in exactly the same way as proposed by the classical economists, such as Adam Smith and David Ricardo. Marx repeatedly stated that he had no new analysis of pricing to offer. But he did maintain that he had an important new insight into the relationship between price and value, which underlies the relationship between surplus values and profits.

Having asserted that only labor is capable of producing surplus value, Marx concluded that the surplus value produced by any industry will be roughly proportional to the amount of labor time it uses. This means that such service industries as restaurants and theaters—whose inputs contain a very high proportion of labor—can be expected to yield a great deal of surplus value while other sorts of industries, such as public utilities—which use enormous amounts

[7]*Ibid.*, page 50.

of equipment but relatively little labor—will end up producing comparatively small amounts of surplus value. If each industry kept all the surplus value it generated, it would follow that a theater would be far more profitable than an electric utility company. But the competitive mechanism permits no such imbalance in the *profitability* of different industries.

Where differences in profitability do occur, investors rush to withdraw their funds from the less profitable businesses and transfer them to those industries whose earnings are high. This means that the industries that are initially more profitable expand, and that their increased production then forces down their prices and hence their profits. At the same time, the industries that are initially *less* profitable will have to reduce production levels as their capital exits, which will then raise the prices of their products and hence their profit rates. Competition will always tend to eliminate differences in profit rates among industries in this way. For as long as one industry is significantly more profitable than another, funds will flow into the more profitable industry and out of the industry in which profits are low. This mechanism, which had already been described in detail by Smith and Ricardo, was adopted by Marx without reservation.

Thus, regardless of how much surplus value is produced by any one industry, competition will force prices and outputs to adjust in ways that redistribute the goods and services that make up this surplus value, and every capitalist will end up with an equal rate of return. He called this type of sharing "capitalist communism."

According to Marx, then, prices under capitalism are set so as to redistribute the *surplus value* produced by the entire economy. All capitalists end up receiving an equal rate of return on their investments. And in order for this to happen, the price of each commodity must be equal to its cost of production, including the opportunity cost of capital (the standard rate of profit on each capitalist's investment). Price must cover the wages of labor, the cost of raw materials, and the opportunity cost of capital.

As we learned in Chapter 25, this analysis of the way prices will be set under perfect competition is precisely the view taken by modern economists. It is also exactly the same as the one Adam Smith outlined nearly a century before Marx. Marx knew this very well, and said so repeatedly:

> *The price of production includes the average profit. . . . It is, as a matter of fact, the same thing which Adam Smith calls natural price, Ricardo price of production, or cost of production.*[8]

In Marxian theory, commodity prices are equal to long-run average costs of production, including a competitive return to capital. This is the pricing rule that appears in both classical and modern competitive analyses. Marx recognized that there was nothing new in this pricing result.

The Purpose of the Marxian Price–Value Analysis

If Marx knew that his pricing analysis got him to exactly the same point at which the classical economists had all arrived much earlier, why did he make so much of his discussion of price? Why did he get back to Smith's pricing principle in such a roundabout manner, that is, by starting with the *unequal production* of surplus value by different industries and its *redistribution* through the price

---

[8]Marx, *Capital*, vol. 3 (Chicago: Charles H. Kerr Publishing Company, 1909), page 73.

mechanism? Marx explains that prices and the resulting distribution of profits are merely an "outward disguise," that they show simply how the economy *appears* to work, whereas through his value analysis, "the actual state of things is here revealed for the first time."

The fact that profits are paid to capitalists in proportion to the amount they invest, and that landlords are paid rent in proportion to the amount of land they provide, makes it *appear* as though two inanimate things, money and land, had actually produced the surplus value received by owners.

> *It is an enchanted, perverted, topsy-turvey world, in which Mister Capital and Mistress Land carry on their goblin tricks as social characters and at the same time as mere things. . . . These are the forms of the illusion . . .* proclaiming the natural necessity and eternal justification of [*the ruling classes'*] sources of *revenue*.[9]

Marx said that value analysis taught us that labor time, not inanimate land and equipment, produces surplus value. Land and equipment do, of course, play a role in the production of goods, but labor is the only factor that human society contributes to the production of surplus value. And it is surplus value that constitutes the resources that enable both the economy's production and the capitalists' wealth to grow.

While Marx's value analysis does *not* claim to give us any new model of price determination, it does claim to give us a new insight into the source of surplus value by stripping away "the forms of illusion" created by the manner in which prices redistribute labor's products.

Alienation

From the time Marx began to write about economics in 1843 until about 1858 (roughly a decade before *Capital* was published), he devoted a significant portion of his writing to a phenomenon he called **alienation.** Very little on the subject was published by him during his lifetime. Thus we do not know whether Marx really considered it important and would have included it in the portions of *Capital* published after his death, or whether he purposely did not publish it because he changed his mind and decided it was a false direction.

It was not until the middle of the twentieth century, when the Soviet Union began to publish some of Marx's accumulated notes and manuscripts, that the materials on alienation became available to the public. But once the idea was made public, it attracted a great deal of attention among Marxist scholars, particularly among those who specialized in political science and sociology. And while the concept of alienation seems to hold less appeal for economists, it is useful for helping us reconstruct some of what Marx was after.

Actually, alienation seems to refer to at least two different concepts. The first, which has most intrigued noneconomists, describes the psychological state of workers in relation to the capitalist production process. According to Marx, capitalism, by replacing artisanship with mass-production techniques, by putting workers on assembly lines where their functions are reduced to repetitive detail rather than concern with the quality of the whole product, and by treating workers (or, rather, their labor power) as mere commodities that are bought and sold as part of the profit-making process, causes workers to lose any sense of satisfaction from their labor and any means for identifying with their

[9]*Ibid.*, pages 966–67.

output. In short, modern workers are *alienated* from the production process in ways that the medieval artisans were not.

What . . . constitutes the alienation of labour? First . . . that in his work . . . he does not . . . feel content but unhappy, does not develop freely his physical and mental energy but mortifies his body and ruins his mind. . . . Lastly, the external [alien] character of labour for the worker appears in the fact that it is not his own, but someone else's . . . that in it he belongs, not to himself, but to another.[10]

The second concept of alienation, which has more relevance to our present discussion, describes the connection between the accumulation process and the produced means of production that are made available to the economy. According to Marx, such items as plant and equipment are as much the product of labor as are any other commodities. However, in industrial economies, the worker's job depends on the availability of factories and machinery. Thus, after he has labored to make these particular products, the worker must confront them again, this time as domineering, alien objects that hold the power to determine whether he will remain employed. The very items that the worker has made with his own hands become the means by which capitalists can control him.

Aside from the domination to which the worker is subjected by the alienated products of his own making, this form of alienation is significant because it has an inherent tendency to escalate. Accumulation, by its very nature, builds up the economy's stock of productive equipment. As this happens, workers become increasingly dependent on more and more equipment in order to remain employed. And as time passes, their dependence on the alienated products of their labor continues to grow proportionally with the economy.

In the early stages of capitalism, workers could easily find employment on their own in industries that utilized relatively few machines. But as capitalism matures, workers more and more are forced into automated factories with all the frustration and alienation that attends such work places. Here we have the seeds of the class antagonism that Marx predicted would contribute to the demise of capitalism. In other words, here we have a law of motion of capitalism.

If this interpretation of alienation is valid (and it is not entirely clear from Marx's unfinished writing on the subject), it is a problem that lies at the heart of the dynamics of capitalism as Marx saw them. The very mechanism that produces surplus value and capital accumulation must aggravate alienation, and through it, we are told, capitalism does indeed sow the seeds of its own destruction.

Thus, Marx felt that a revolution spurred by worker alienation might be one way that capitalism would die. Another would be through a spasmodic business cycle.

Marxian Crisis Theory

Marx wrote at a time when many leading economists believed that general overproduction is impossible because "supply creates its own demand." This view, dating back to Adam Smith, is now called *Say's Law* after the French economist J. B. Say, who publicized it early in the nineteenth century. The argument states that anybody who earns income from the production process

[10]Karl Marx, *Economic and Philosophical Manuscripts of 1844, Collected Works*, vol. 3, pages 273–74.

must be doing so in order either to spend it on consumer goods or to invest it in a way that earns more money. In the latter case, there is an implicit or explicit demand for more production goods, such as plant and equipment. Thus, in either case, every penny earned in the production process is quickly spent so that the effective demand for any economy's output is always exactly equal to the amount it costs to produce the output. In this way, argued the classical predecessors of Marx, there can never be a general insufficiency of the demand needed to sell an economy's output. True, there can be overproduction of individual items. Industry may miscalculate and produce too many yo-yos at a time when the public would rather buy Frisbees, but such errors are quickly corrected when toy manufacturers notice unsold yo-yo inventories beginning to pile up.

However, not every economist in the early nineteenth century believed that general overproduction was impossible. There were some, including the conservative Thomas Robert Malthus and a number of early socialists, who believed that the threat of depression was very real; and the harsh facts of economic reality certainly supported them. Unfortunately, though, their analysis was confused and unsystematic, and no match for the powerful logic of the followers of Adam Smith and J. B. Say. Among those who argued that economic crises were a real danger, a recurrent theme was that the economy tends not to give consumers enough purchasing power to buy all the available output. This idea provided the basis for the **underconsumption models** set forth by writers at both ends of the political spectrum. Malthus implied that the remedy is to provide more money to the idle rich. He felt that if those who demanded goods without producing them had more money to spend, they would increase the demand without adding to the supply. The early socialists, on the other hand, argued that the proper way to deal with the problem is to pay more money to workers because their poverty forces them to spend everything they earn, whereas large portions of capitalists' profits, because they are not spent on consumption, reduce the effective demand.

Marx rejected both arguments — those that claimed overproduction is impossible as well as those that have been called the "naïve underconsumption" theories. Marx's grounds for rejection were remarkably compatible with modern ideas on the subject. He believed that general overproduction would result if those who sell inputs and receive income from the production of products decided not to use their money *at once* to demand goods or if they decided to hold on to the money itself instead of spending it. But even the capitalists' saving is *not* a deduction from demand if they use their money to buy new factories and machines instead of consumer goods.

Having established that business fluctuations can be a real problem for a profit economy and that the reasons are more complex than those offered by the naïve underconsumption model, Marx went on to propose a variety of crisis analyses of his own. Implicit in his argument was the view that there is not necessarily only one model to explain all business fluctuations. Accordingly, his analyses varied widely.

For example, one of his models emphasized the delay between the time the building of a large project, such as a railroad, produces income for construction workers (thus creating demand) and the later time when the products of such projects begin to be available (thus creating supply). At this later time, the former construction workers of a completed railroad no longer are earning the income with which to demand the goods the railroad carries.

Another of Marx's cycle models stressed the way accumulation leads to competition for workers, which in turn bids up wages and cuts into profits, causing trouble for business firms. A third model indicated that problems can arise when the timing of outputs by industries that make producers' goods does not match the needs of the industries that make consumers' goods. And still another model was a more plausible version of the underconsumption analysis.

In fact, the Marxian models covered such a wide range of cyclical relationships that there is hardly a modern theory of the business cycle that cannot find some antecedent in Marx's writings. And for this reason Marx must be considered the father of all modern cycle analyses. Yet the Marxian models were never fully worked out. Marx discussed them only briefly and unsystematically, and none ever went beyond a mere outline or hint of the full mechanism underlying the analysis.

Will the Business Cycle Kill Capitalism?

One issue in particular that has given rise to considerable speculation is Marx's views about the future of business cycles. Did he see them as growing increasingly more severe? Did he predict that capitalism would inevitably collapse in one gigantic crisis? The answers are unclear because Marx never thoroughly discussed the specific ways in which capitalism would collapse. To be sure, there are several colorful passages that paint a dramatic picture of its ruin, but these can hardly have been meant to constitute serious analysis. Here is an example from the first volume of *Capital*:

> Along with the constantly diminishing number of magnates of capital, who usurp and monopolise all advantages . . . grows the mass of misery, oppression, slavery, degradation, exploitation; but with this too grows the revolt of the working class, a class always increasing in numbers, and disciplined, united, organised by the very mechanism of capitalist production itself. The monopoly of capital becomes a fetter upon the mode of production, which has sprung up and flourished along with, and under it. Centralisation of means of the production and socialisation of labour at last reach a point where they become incompatible with their capitalist integument. This integument is burst asunder. The knell of capitalist private property sounds. The expropriators are expropriated.[11]

In the *Communist Manifesto* (1848) Marx and Engels mention "the commercial crises that by their periodic return put on its trial, each time more threateningly, the existence of the entire bourgeois society." And they do say that the process of recovery paves "the way for more extensive and destructive crises."

However, the *Communist Manifesto* appeared two decades before *Capital*, Marx's mature work, and we are not told how he felt about the subject at this later time. There is, though, one place in which a much older Engels specifically states that crises of increasing severity are *not* inevitable under capitalism. In 1884, writing about trends he had recently been observing (this was one year after the death of Marx and nearly 40 years after the *Communist Manifesto*), Engels said, "The period of general prosperity preceding the crisis still fails to appear. If it should fail altogether, then chronic stagnation would necessarily become the normal condition of modern industry, with only insignificant fluctuations."[12] In short, Marx was convinced that capitalism must fall. But just how that fall will occur, from what causes and in what stages, is never made clear in his writings.

[11]Marx, *Capital*, vol. 1, pages 836–37.
[12]Preface to the first German edition (1884) of *Poverty of the Philosophy* (London: Martin Lawrence Ltd., N.D.), page 18fn.

Conclusion

The writings of Marx are stamped by brilliance and originality. Parts of the writings are long-winded and dull (in fact, Marx told Engels he did this deliberately to make his work "weightier"), but they contain many sparkling and powerful passages. Many of Marx's ideas are still highly illuminating, even to non-Marxists, and in areas such as business-cycle analysis, almost all modern thinking stems from his, either directly or indirectly. In short, he contributed enormously to current thought within the discipline of economics as well as in politics throughout the world.

Summary

1. Marx agreed that capitalism had been extraordinarily productive and had contributed to general economic advancement, but he also believed that it had outlived its usefulness and had become a drag upon further progress.
2. Marx deliberately offered almost no guidance for the running of socialist economies.
3. Historical materialism, Marx's basic philosophy, asserts that one can understand a society only from a study of its history, and that this history is determined primarily by economic conditions.
4. To Marx, the central task of the capitalist is accumulation of profits, which are then invested in ways that expand the output of the economy.
5. The purpose of Marx's value theory was to show that labor is the source of the profits accumulated by capitalists.
6. Marx denied that the objective of his value analysis was to show that capitalism robs the workers and that they deserve all the economy's output. Rather, he wished to show how the process of accumulation increases the unhappiness of workers and undermines the capitalist economy.
7. Marx is considered the father of modern analyses of business cycles because most of today's theories have their roots in Marx's writings.

Concepts for Review

Historical materialism
Marxian "commodity"
Marxian "value"

Value of labor power
Surplus value
Marxian price–value analysis

Alienation
Underconsumption models
Marx's business-cycle analysis

Questions for Discussion

1. Given how little Marx said about the actual running of a socialist (or communist) society, do you think that the economies of the Soviet Union and China are consistent or inconsistent with Marx's views, or that the two have nothing to do with each other or with Marx's intentions?
2. Do you think that, if Marxian theory is valid, labor deserves 100 percent of the national output? Why do you think Marx and Engels disagreed with this conclusion?
3. In the Middle Ages, according to Marx, the nobility were the exploiters while the serfs were the exploited. What did the medieval nobles "do for a living," and how, in Marx's view, does the answer to this question explain why GNP did not grow during the Middle Ages as it does under current economic systems?
4. In your opinion, what do you think Marx would have considered the most likely causes of the end of capitalism?
5. Some economists have suggested that many human decisions, including marriage, family size, and even suicide, can be explained to a considerable extent by the narrow economic self-interest of the decision maker. Would Marx have agreed?

40

Comparative Economic Systems: What Are the Choices?

Every generation regards as natural the institutions to which it is accustomed.

R. H. TAWNEY

The words of the British historian and economist R. H. Tawney are worth heeding as we near the end of this book, which has been geared closely to the particular circumstances of the contemporary United States. Our current economic institutions are not eternal. Economic systems are not static; they grow, adapt, and evolve. Even in the relatively stable environment of the United States, the economy of the 1980s is far different from the economy of the 1880s, and by the year 2080 our economy will have changed even more.

Tawney's remark can be applied across geographical space as well as through time. The world today has a great diversity of economic systems, and this diversity seems likely to prevail in the future. There are, in fact, many ways to organize an economy other than the mixed capitalistic structure that we have focused on in this book. And no one form of economic organization is likely to be the right one for all countries for all time.

In this chapter we examine some of these *alternative economic systems* and consider how a society might choose an appropriate form of economic organization. The first parts of the chapter sketch out the elements of the two major choices that must be made by every society: Should economic activity be organized through *markets*, or by government *plan*? And should industry be *privately* or *publicly* owned? As we shall see, there are arguments on both sides of each question; and, as you might expect, different countries in different times have made different choices.

In the last sections of the chapter, we therefore turn to some of the actual choices that have been made in the contemporary world. We examine, in turn, the economic structures of Sweden, France, Yugoslavia, the Soviet Union, and the People's Republic of China, looking in each case for similarities and differences among countries, and for areas in which one system has either succeeded admirably or failed miserably. Does the United States have much to learn from the experiences of these other countries? Read this chapter, and then decide.

Will They Bury Us?

In 1958, Soviet Premier Nikita Khrushchev made his boastful pledge about "burying" the United States economically. His optimistic mood was probably colored both by Russia's successful launching of an earth satellite and by the outstanding performance of the Soviet economy that year: real growth of almost 11 percent over 1957. With the United States simultaneously slipping into a severe recession, the ratio of Soviet GNP to American GNP jumped from 39 percent in 1957 to 44 percent in 1958 (see the accompanying chart).

No sensible statistician would extrapolate the performance of one year far into the future. But Khrushchev was a flamboyant political leader, not a sensible statistician. By 1965, the ratio was still stalled at 44 percent and, perhaps by coincidence, Khrushchev had been ousted and was living the quiet life. As the chart shows, the Soviet/U.S. GNP ratio resumed its upward climb in the late 1960s, and by 1975 had reached 53 percent — owing in part to another serious recession in the United States. But the ratio had slipped back to 47 percent by 1985.

It may be helpful to put these figures into historical perspective. According to one estimate, Russian and American GNPs were about equal on the eve of our Civil War. But, czarist Russia did not do well compared with capitalist America, and by 1913 Russian GNP had dwindled to only 39 percent of American GNP. With the enormous human and economic losses of World War I, the Russian Revolution, and the ensuing civil war, Soviet GNP fell still further — to only about 27 percent of U.S. GNP at the start of the First Five Year Plan (1928).

Then came the beginnings of rapid economic growth in the U.S.S.R. and the Great Depression in the United States. Soviet GNP climbed swiftly to 42 percent of the U.S. level at the start of World War II, only to fall back to 29 percent after the wartime devastation. From that point, it

The Challenge to Modern Capitalism

The question of choosing among economic systems is far from academic. Indeed, it has been of vital concern to people throughout the world for centuries, and it remains an issue today. For example, 30 years ago former Russian leader Nikita Khrushchev made his famous promise to Americans that "we will bury you." This was not a military threat nor a prediction that capitalism would perish under the weight of its own garbage; rather it was a pledge that the great productivity and growth of the Soviet economy would enable it to surpass the productive capacity of the U.S. economy. So far, the Russians have not redeemed this pledge. (See the boxed insert above.) But the economic competition between these two giant nations has captured the attention of the world for decades.

Many of the observers of this competition have a keen interest in its outcome. Nations of the Third World have watched attentively, wondering which economic system might be best for them. During the years since Khrushchev's declaration, a number of these nations seem to have made a choice. But many others are still teetering on the brink of indecision. Should they try to emulate the U.S. system of free markets, as, to a degree, Taiwan and Brazil have done? Should they follow the route of "democratic socialism" that is favored by many Western European nations, a route approximately traveled by Israel and India?

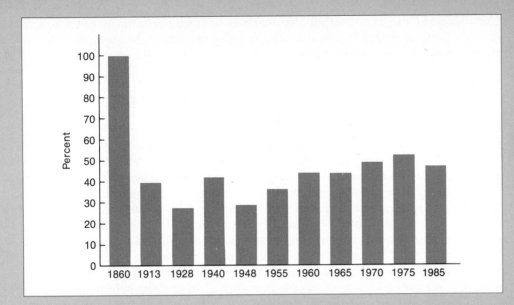

RATIO OF RUSSIAN
REAL GNP TO U.S.
REAL GNP
SOURCE: Herbert Block, "Soviet
Economic Power Growth—
Achievements under Handicaps,"
*Soviet Economy in a New
Perspective. A Compendium of
Papers Submitted to the Joint
Economic Committee*, Congress
of the United States. 94th
Congress, 2nd Session, October
1976. Updated to 1985 by the
authors.

climbed rather steadily and was still rising when Khrushchev made his famous boast.

What of the future? It is anyone's guess. A prudent long-run estimate for the U.S. growth rate might be 3 percent a year. As for the Soviet Union, only a decade ago experts were projecting a long-term annual growth rate of 5 to $5\frac{1}{2}$ percent. However, the poor performance of the Soviet economy in recent years has led these estimates to be scaled down to 2 to 3 percent, or even lower.

If the Soviet economy does manage to grow 5 percent per year while ours grows 3 percent per year, Russia will indeed "bury" us with a larger GNP by around the year 2025. (Remember, though, that Russia's population is about 20 percent larger than ours.) On the other hand, if current projections prove correct and the Russian economy grows no faster than our own, the burial will never take place.

Should they enter the Soviet sphere and opt for a communist system with rigid state planning, as North Korea and Vietnam seem to have done? Or, finally, should they choose a more revolutionary brand of communism, following the model of Cuba?

The choices are many. And they are of the utmost importance because a nation's economic structure has a profound influence not only over its material well-being, but also over its political system, the individual rights of its citizens, its relations with other countries, and so on.

And the Third World is not the only place where the contest among alternative economic systems is going on. During the past decade, several countries in Western Europe—including France, Spain, and Italy—flirted with communism in a serious way. On the other side of the Iron Curtain, several nations have been introducing elements of capitalism. Yugoslavia and Hungary, in particular, rely heavily on markets and the price system to guide their "communist" economies, and China is moving rapidly in that direction. There are even signs of change in the Soviet Union under the leadership of Mikhail Gorbachev.

Naturally, noneconomic factors play major roles in any debate over the future of a nation's economic system. Internal political considerations, for example, are probably far more important than economic analyses. Yet, to a considerable extent, the proof of the pudding will be in the eating.

Demonstrated success of either free markets or state planning in solving economic problems probably will do more to sway the undecided nations than all the ideological incantations in the world.

Economic Systems: Two Important Distinctions

Economic systems can be distinguished along many lines, but two seem most important. The first is, *How is economic activity coordinated—by the market or by the plan?* The question does not, of course, demand an "either, or" answer. Rather the choice extends over a range running from laissez faire to rigid central planning, with many, many gradations in between. Society must decide to what extent it wants decisions made by individual businesses and consumers, each acting in their own self-interest, to determine their economic destiny, and to what extent it wants to persuade these businesses and consumers to act more "in the national interest." It is worth stressing that most types of planning involve some degree of *coercion*. But this term is not necessarily pejorative; all societies, for example, coerce people not to steal from their neighbors.

The second crucial distinction among economic systems concerns the question: *Who owns the means of production;* specifically, are they privately owned by individuals or publicly owned by the state? Again, there is a wide range of choice and, to our knowledge, there are no examples of nations at either the **capitalist** extreme where all property is privately owned or at the **socialist** extreme where no private property whatever is permitted.

Capitalism is a method of economic organization in which private individuals own the means of production, either directly or indirectly through corporations.

Socialism is a method of economic organization in which the state owns the means of production.

For example, while most industries are privately owned in the United States, owners face restrictions on what they can do with their capital. Owners of automobile companies must comply with environmental and safety regulations. Owners of private communication and transportation companies often have both their prices and the conditions of their services regulated by the government. And in communist Russia, where no one can own a factory, anyone who can afford it can own a car or hold a bank account. There is also a small "capitalist" sector in which peasant farmers sell what they grow on their small private plots of land.

There is a tendency to merge the two distinctions between economic systems and think of capitalist economies as those that have both a great deal of privately owned property *and* rely heavily on free markets. By the same token, socialist economies typically are thought of as heavily planned. However:

While there is an undeniable association between the degree of socialism in a country and the degree to which it plans its economy, it would be a mistake to regard these two features as equivalent.

Modern Yugoslavia, for example, provides an important instance of a country in which the means of production are socially owned but economic activity is organized mainly by markets. Closer to home, there is a great deal of state ownership in the market economies of Western Europe. On the other hand, Germany under Hitler provided an example of a capitalist economy with rigid central planning.

We are not suggesting that capitalist economies are typically as heavily planned as socialist ones. In fact, socialist states normally have more economic planning. However, in thinking about a society's *choice* among economic systems, it is best to keep the two distinctions separate.

The Market or the Plan? Some Issues

The choice between **planning** and reliance on **free markets** requires an understanding of just what the market accomplishes and where its strengths and weaknesses lie. Since these issues have been the focal point of much of this book, our review can be rather concise here.

What goods to produce and how much of each. In a market economy, consumers, by registering their dollar votes, determine which goods and services shall be provided and in what quantities. Items that are not wanted, or that are overproduced, will fall in price, while items that are in short supply will rise in price. These price movements act as *signals* to profit-seeking firms, which then produce larger amounts of the goods whose prices rise and less of the goods whose prices fall. This mechanism is called **consumer sovereignty.**

Of course, the doctrine of consumer sovereignty is not absolute, even in market economies. Governments interfere with the price mechanism in many ways—taxing some goods and services while subsidizing others. These interferences certainly alter the bill of goods that the economy produces. We have also learned that in the presence of **externalities** the price system may send out false signals, leading to inappropriate levels of output for certain commodities.

How to produce each good. In a market economy, firms decide on the production technique, guided once again by the price system. Inputs that are in short supply will be assigned high prices by the market. This will encourage producers to use them sparingly. Other inputs whose supply is more abundant will be priced lower, which will encourage firms to use them.

Once again, the same two qualifications apply: Government taxes and subsidies alter relative prices, and externalities may make the price system malfunction. But on the whole, the market system has yet to meet its match as an engine of productive efficiency.

How income is distributed. The price system, by setting the levels of wages, interest rates, and profits, determines the distribution of income among individuals in a market economy. As we have stressed (especially in Chapter 37), there is no reason to expect the resulting income distribution to be "good" from an ethical point of view. And, in fact, the evidence shows that capitalist market economies produce a considerable degree of inequality.

This is certainly one of capitalism's weak points, though there are many ways for the government to alter the distribution of income without destroying either free markets or private property (for example, through progressive income taxation or a negative income tax, both of which were discussed in Chapter 37). It is also noteworthy that some planned economies have rather unequal income distributions.

Economic growth. The rate of economic growth depends fundamentally upon how much society decides to save and invest. In a free-market economy, these decisions are left to private firms and individuals who determine how much of their current income they will consume today and how much they will invest for the future. Once again, however, government policies can influence these choices by, for example, making investment more or less attractive through tax policy.

Business fluctuations. As we explained in Parts 2 through 5, a market economy is subject to business fluctuations—periods of boom and bust, inflation and unemployment. This holds not only in capitalist market economies like the United States, but also in socialist market economies like Yugoslavia.

> **Consumer sovereignty** means that consumer preferences determine what goods shall be produced, and in what amounts.

Interestingly, the highly planned but mostly capitalist economy of France showed little evidence of business cycle problems from 1958 until the mid-1970s. Thus, it seems that the business cycle, which Marx dubbed one of the fundamental flaws of *capitalism*, is really a problem for *market* economies, be they capitalist or socialist.

Let us now go over this list again, seeing how each question is resolved in a planned economy, and comparing this with a market economy.

What to produce and how much. Under central planning, the bill of goods that society will produce is not normally selected by consumer sovereignty. Instead, the planners decide. Depending on their particular beliefs and on the political structure of the country, their decisions may or may not be strongly influenced by consumers' desires.

Whether this is a strength or weakness of central planning depends upon your point of view. On the one hand, there is the danger that society's resources will be devoted to producing items that nobody wants. In Soviet Russia, for example, there are clearly fewer cars and more copies of Marx's *Capital* than consumers want to buy. On the other hand, consumer sovereignty can lead to some bizarre products, the kinds of things that social reformers find offensive: designer jeans, fast-food chains, low-quality television programming, and so on. But, on balance, most adherents to traditional Western values will find more to like than to dislike under consumer sovereignty. After all, who knows what is good for consumers better than consumers themselves?

How to produce. Planned economies can allow plant managers to choose a production technique, or they can let central planners do it instead. Under Soviet-style planning, plant managers have traditionally had little discretion, and this has led to such monumental inefficiencies as production curtailments due to lack of materials, poor quality, and high production costs — inefficiencies that Soviet leader Gorbachev is now seeking to reduce. But no incentive system has yet been designed that can match the profit motive of competitive firms for keeping costs down.

How income is distributed. The distribution of income is always influenced by government to some extent. Even in basically market economies like ours, the government taxes different people at different rates and pays transfer payments to others, seeking thereby to mitigate the inequality that capitalism and free markets tend to generate. Governments in planned economies do the same things, and more. For instance, they may try to tamper directly with the income distribution by having the planners, rather than the market, set relative wage rates. This, however, leads to troubles similar to those mentioned in the previous paragraph. Thus, even in the Soviet Union relative wages are established more or less by supply and demand.

Economic growth. In general, planned economies have more direct control over their growth rates than do unplanned ones because the state can determine the volume of investment. They therefore can, if they choose to, engineer very high growth rates — an option they often have exercised. Whether such rapid growth is a good idea, however, is another question. In Stalin's Russia and Mao's China, for example, this goal was achieved at enormous cost — some of it paid for by sacrificing current consumption, some by sacrificing personal freedom, and some by bloodshed. Furthermore, the U.S.S.R. has not been very successful in achieving its growth goals recently, while some of the fastest growth rates in the postwar world have been achieved by market economies like Japan, Taiwan, and Hong Kong.

Business fluctuations. We explained in Chapter 9 that business fluctuations are not much of a problem for highly planned economies. This is because total spending in such economies is controlled tightly by the planners and is not permitted to get far out of line with the economy's capacity to produce. As we shall see later in this chapter, the U.S.S.R. has many serious economic problems, but the business cycle is not one of them.

The Market or the Plan? The Scoreboard

As we look back over this list, what do we find? Concerning *what to produce*, adherents to Western values probably will give a clear edge to the market, though conceding the need to curb some of its more flagrant abuses. But, of course, much of the world does not prize individualism as dearly as we in the West do.

As to *productive efficiency*, the market mechanism is clearly superior. But when we consider the *distribution of income*, we find that all societies have decided to plan; they differ only in degree.

High growth, it seems, can be achieved with or without planning, though planned systems may have an easier time of it. Here an advanced nation will pause to question whether faster is always better, and often will conclude that it is not. But among the less developed countries, the goal of rapid development is typically of paramount importance. Many of these countries also lack the savings and the financial markets needed to channel funds into their most productive uses. If so, they may have little choice but to plan.

Finally, in managing *business fluctuations*, there is no question that planned economies can do much better. The results of our scoreboard are clearly mixed. Do we, therefore, score the contest a tie? Certainly not. What we do conclude is the following:

Different countries — with their different political systems, value judgments, traditions, and aspirations — will score the contest differently. Some will find the market more attractive, while others will opt for the plan. Most will divide their economies into two sectors — leaving some decisions to the market mechanism and others to conscious planning.

Capitalism or Socialism?

Although the choice between capitalism and socialism seems to excite more ideological fervor, it may be much less important than the choice between the market and the plan.

If it could design an appropriate incentive structure, a socialist market economy could do just as well as a capitalist market economy in terms of producing the right set of goods in the most efficient way. However, we have emphasized the word "if" to underscore the fact that designing such an incentive system may be quite difficult under socialism.

Lacking the profit motive, a socialist society must provide incentives, either material or otherwise, for its plant managers to perform well. This has proved difficult enough. But a still deeper problem caused by the absence of the profit motive is the need to maintain inventiveness, innovation, and risk-taking in a system in which large accumulations of personal wealth are impossible. Socialist systems are noticeably low on "high rollers."

Income distribution under socialism seems naturally more equal than under capitalism simply because the profits of industry do not go to a small group of stockholders but instead are dispersed among the workers or among the populace as a whole. However, if supply and demand rules the labor market, a socialist nation may have as much inequality in the distribution of labor income as a capitalist economy does—and for the same reasons: to attract workers into risky, or highly skilled, or difficult occupations. Indeed, students of the Soviet economy have concluded that wage differentials in the U.S.S.R. are comparable to those in the United States.

The capitalist-socialist cleavage is much more important in regard to the issue of economic growth. To oversimplify, under capitalism it is the capitalists who determine the growth rate, while under socialism it is the state. Still, government incentives can prod capitalists to invest more; and instances of both fast and slow growth can be found under both systems.

Finally, the persistence of business fluctuations in a country depends much more on whether its economy is planned or unplanned than on whether its industries are publicly or privately owned.

Socialism, Planning, and Freedom

There is, however, a *noneconomic* criterion that is of the utmost importance in choosing between capitalism and socialism, or between the market and the plan: *individual freedom*.

Planning must by necessity involve some degree of coercion; if it does not, then the plan may amount to little more than wishful thinking. In the extreme case of a command economy (Soviet Russia, Nazi Germany), the abridgement of personal freedom is painfully obvious. Less rigid forms of planning involve commensurately smaller infringements of individual rights, infringements that most people find tolerable.

Even within a basic framework of free markets, some activities may be banned—such as prostitution and selling liquor to minors. Other economic activities may be compelled by law; safety devices in automobiles and labeling requirements on foods and drugs are two examples. Each of these can be considered a type of planning, and each limits the freedom of some people. Yet most of these restrictions command broad public support in the United States.

Taxation is a still more subtle form of coercion. Most people do not view taxes as seriously impairing their personal freedom because, even though tax laws may make them pay for the privilege, they remain free to choose the courses of action that suit them best. Indeed, this is one major reason why most economists favor taxes over quotas and outright prohibitions in many instances. It is true, however, that taxation can be a potent tool for changing individual behavior. As Chief Justice John Marshall pointed out with characteristic perspicacity, "The power to tax involves the power to destroy."

Individual freedom is also involved in the choice between capitalism and socialism. After all, under socialism there are many more restrictions on what a person can do with his or her wealth than there are under capitalism. On the other hand, the poorest people in a capitalist society may find little solace in their "freedom" to go homeless and hungry.

Once again, it would be a mistake to paint the issue in black and white. Under rigid authoritarian planning, the restrictions on individual liberties are so severe that they are probably intolerable to most people with Western values. But more moderate and relaxed forms of planning—such as the French system discussed later in this chapter—seem compatible with personal freedoms.

Similarly, a doctrinaire brand of socialism that bans all private property (even the clothes on your back?) would entail a major loss of liberty. But a country with a large socialized sector can be basically free; the French, for example, do not feel notably less free than do Americans. And citizens of some countries with largely capitalist economies, such as South Korea or Taiwan, do not enjoy much political freedom.

The real question is not *whether* we want to allow elements of socialism or planning to abridge our personal freedoms, but by *how much*.

Just as your freedom to extend your arm is limited by the proximity of your neighbor's chin, the freedom to build a factory need not extend to building it in the midst of a residential neighborhood. Just as freedom of speech does not justify yelling "Fire!" in a crowded movie theater when there is no fire, freedom of enterprise does not imply the right to monopolize trade.

Different societies have struck the balance between the market and the plan and between socialism and capitalism in different places. What follow in the rest of this chapter are rather brief descriptions of some of the alternative economic systems actually in existence today. We start with Sweden, where public ownership of the means of production is only slightly more common than it is in the United States, and work our way toward the "communist" economies of Russia and the People's Republic of China, where state socialism is the dominant form of economic organization.

Sweden's Welfare State

The Swedish economy has been characterized as a happy marriage between capitalism and socialism. But, in fact, at least as we have defined the terms, Sweden is almost as capitalistic as the United States: More than 90 percent of Swedish industry is privately owned. A more accurate statement is that:

Sweden has a capitalist market economy very much like our own, but with more extensive government interference to promote two social goals of overriding importance: full employment and an equal distribution of well being.

Full Employment Policy

Sweden has one of the longest and most active traditions of Keynesian macroeconomic management in the world—a tradition that even predates Keynes's *General Theory of Employment, Interest, and Money* (1936). In addition to using the standard tools of monetary and fiscal policy more vigorously than we do in the United States, and inventing a few novel tools of their own, the Swedes limit unemployment by intervening directly in the labor market. For example, the Swedish government offers subsidies to private firms that maintain employment when production falls, allows early retirement for workers who lose their jobs, sponsors retraining programs, and, when necessary, hires workers directly into government jobs. As a result of all this, unemployment does not rise much even when GNP falls.

Judging by the results, the Swedish full employment policy seems to have borne fruit. Figure 40–1 compares the unemployment rates in Sweden and in the United States from 1960 to 1986. It is clear not only that the average rate of unemployment has been kept quite low (generally below 3 percent), but also

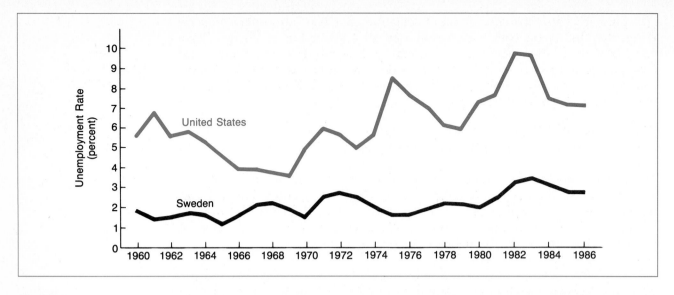

Figure 40–1
UNEMPLOYMENT IN
SWEDEN AND THE
UNITED STATES
As this figure indicates,
Sweden's unemployment rate
has been consistently lower
than our own, and its
fluctuations have also been
less severe.
SOURCE: U.S. Bureau of Labor
Statistics, *Statistical Abstract of
Sweden,* and International Labour
Office.

The term **welfare state**
refers to a variety of
government programs
aimed at assisting the
poor and unfortunate and
protecting individuals
from the rigors of the
marketplace.

that the fluctuations have been restrained. However, the Swedes have not been able to avoid recessions, and industrial production in Sweden has increased rather little in the last decade. In addition, as our discussion of the trade-off between inflation and unemployment suggests, the Swedes have paid the price for their low unemployment by making sacrifices on the inflation front (see Figure 40–2). Their inflation rate has typically been higher than ours.

Income Distribution Policy

Sweden, as is well known, has one of the world's most comprehensive **welfare states,** with social programs that extend, quite literally, from the cradle to the grave. There are financial allowances for children, municipal day care centers, free education at all levels, a national health service, extensive benefits for the unemployed, retirement pensions that are far more generous than our own social security system, and many more social welfare programs.

Naturally, the heavy burden of financing these programs leads to commensurately high taxes, and in recent years some of the disadvantages of a comprehensive welfare state have become more apparent. Critics argue, for example, that the steeply progressive Swedish income tax is destroying incentives to work.

Nonetheless, Sweden's social welfare programs have been effective in accomplishing their goals. It is really difficult to find the telltale signs of poverty, such as slums and shabby clothing, in Sweden. And it is widely agreed that Sweden has one of the most equal income distributions anywhere — a feat it has managed to accomplish while also becoming one of the richest nations in the world. Yet, here too there are problems. Absenteeism has been rising, demands for greater worker control over industry are being heard, and class antagonisms have arisen in this "classless" society.

Sweden and the United States

In many ways, the Swedish and American economic systems seem similar, and the apparent success of Swedish economic policy has raised the question of whether their principles can be applied here. Yet some fundamental differences exist, differences that may make it impossible to import Swedish economic policy to America.

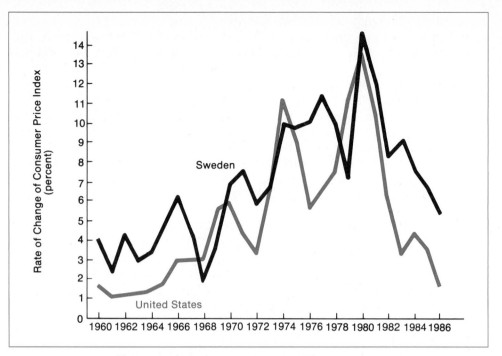

Figure 40–2
INFLATION IN SWEDEN
AND THE UNITED
STATES
As might be expected,
Sweden has paid the price
for lower unemployment by
having more inflation than the
United States. This figure
shows that inflation in
Sweden has normally been
higher than inflation in the
United States.
SOURCE: Organization for
Economic Cooperation and
Development.

First, Sweden is a small country whose labor unions and industries are both highly concentrated. This facilitates "consensus building" and also makes coordination easy to accomplish without formal planning. Second, Sweden is an ethnically homogeneous country. So the racial and ethnic antagonisms that underlie some of America's worst social problems are absent. Third, the Swedes care much more about full employment and much less about inflation than Americans do. They are proud of their strong record on employment and less concerned with their inability to maintain price stability. Americans might react differently to this same record.

France: Planning by Consensus

The basically capitalist economy of France has developed a unique method of organizing economic activity that one expert has called "the most elaborate and detailed planning system among the advanced Western nations."[1]

The system is called **indicative planning**, a name meant to suggest planning by voluntary compliance and agreement rather than by government coercion.

Under the French system, a national economic plan is hammered out and agreed to by representatives of government, industry, and labor, along with other technical experts. The aim is to achieve a good degree of *coordination* of economic activity without the need for *coercion* simply by passing both information and ideas back and forth among all the parties.

For example, if it turned out that the production plan of the automobile industry required the use of more steel than the steel industry was expecting to sell, the participants in the plan could sit down and reconcile the differences. Was one forecast too optimistic or too pessimistic? Would government actions (such as tariffs and import quotas) render these two forecasts consistent or

Indicative planning means government *guidance*, rather than direct *control*, of economic activity.

[1]Gregory Grossman, *Economic Systems,* Second Edition (Englewood Cliffs, N.J.: Prentice Hall, 1974), page 87.

inconsistent? Through negotiations like these, French planners hope that individual industries can discover potential shortages and surpluses before they arise, and thereby adjust their own plans to conform with a broad overall plan for the nation.

They further hope that *participation* in the plan will lead to *voluntary compliance*. Often this is so. But when it fails, the French government does not hesitate to use a wide variety of tools — including taxes, subsidies, and price controls — to persuade businesses to abide by the plan. It has been said that "French planning may be indicative, but it is not permissive or passive."[2]

The government exercises particularly strong control over both the volume and direction of investment spending: It directly controls about half of national investment and strongly influences the rest by regulating access to the credit market.

How well has the system performed? Until recently, very well indeed. Prior to the worldwide recessions of the mid-1970s and early 1980s, the French record was one of full employment and rapid growth (see Figure 40–3). Of course, this does not prove that indicative planning has been the key to France's success. West Germany, for example, grew even faster without planning. But it does suggest that something has gone right.

Indicative Planning for the United States?

Many countries envied the French growth record in the 1950s and 1960s, and some tried to emulate it. Can indicative planning be practiced successfully in the United States? There are several reasons to think that it would not work as well here. First, the U.S. government controls a much smaller fraction of total investment than does the French government, and the comprehensive controls that the French government exercises over the credit market run counter to American financial practice.

A second difference is that the United States does not have the French tradition of a close marriage between government and industry. The "old boy" network is particularly strong in France, and many of the government officials and industrialists who work together on the plan are old friends from their days as students at France's elite *écoles*. State intervention in business has long been the norm in France; here it would be a major departure.

[2]Egon Neuberger and William Duffy, *Comparative Economic Systems* (Boston: Allyn and Bacon, 1976), page 235.

Figure 40–3
FRENCH ECONOMIC GROWTH SINCE 1958
This chart of real gross national product in France shows a remarkable absence of business fluctuations. Only the severe world wide recession of 1974–1975 broke the upward march of real GNP in France. But growth slowed to a crawl in the 1980s.
SOURCE: Organization for Economic Cooperation and Development.

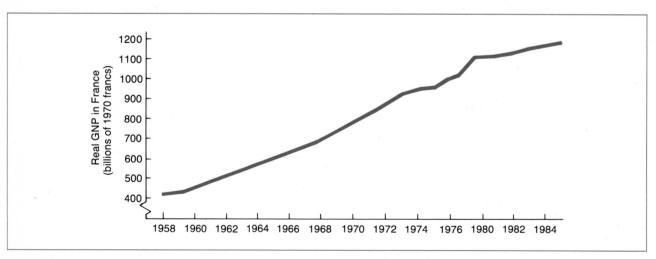

Third, planning along French lines would run afoul of America's antitrust laws. With firms sharing common forecasts and production plans, and with the government parceling out investment allotments to industries that then divide them among their constituent firms, collusion among firms is almost inevitable. This sort of cozy arrangement is widely accepted in France, where government tolerance of and even support for monopolies and cartels is traditional. But it runs counter to deeply held beliefs about American capitalism.

Workers' Management in Yugoslavia

Yugoslavia was forced by events to become the clearest illustration in the contemporary world of the fact that "socialism" need not be synonymous with "planning." A serious political rift between Tito and Stalin in the 1940s kept Yugoslavia out of the Soviet economic sphere and forced the Yugoslavs to go it alone.

Searching for a way out of their economic plight, the Yugoslavs embarked on a great economic experiment by passing the *Law on Worker Management of Enterprises* in 1950. This law and subsequent legislation gave to the workers of each firm the authority to make most of the decisions that are normally reserved for management. The world has watched this experiment with great interest. In recent years, there has been talk that nations as far apart ideologically as Great Britain and China may have something to learn from the Yugoslav system, and experiments with **workers' management** have been made in the United States and Canada.

Under a system of **workers' management,** the employees of an enterprise make most of the decisions normally reserved for management.

While Yugoslav industry is almost wholly socialistic, enterprises are *not* run by state-appointed managers following a national plan. Instead, Yugoslav managers are chosen by the workers and are expected to seek high profits.

While firms in Yugoslavia are subject to more regulations than firms in the United States, each Yugoslav firm can decide within limits *what* to produce, *how much* to produce, and by *what technique* to produce. Though there are a number of price controls, taxes, and subsidies, most commodity prices are established in free markets, and consumer sovereignty calls the tune. Firms flourish if they produce what consumers want and produce it efficiently. After paying for its nonlabor inputs, each enterprise can decide how much of its net income to invest in expansion and how much to pay out in wages to its workers.

Under workers' management, Yugoslavia has achieved a good record of growth in total output, but a number of problems have surfaced.

For one, like other market economies, Yugoslavia is subject to the ups and downs that we call the *business cycle*. This country has had periodic bouts with stagnation, and seems plagued with both chronically high inflation and unemployment. The persistent inflation has led to greater reliance on price controls—a movement away from free markets that has been motivated not by ideology, but by desperation.

Income distribution has posed another problem. Since what is called *wages* in Yugoslavia include a share of what is called *profits* in a capitalist system, equal work in different firms is not rewarded equally. Instead, workers in the most efficient enterprises earn a bonus, and the resulting wage disparities among different firms and different regions in the country have caused social frictions.

Related to this are the twin problems of inadequate labor mobility and sluggish employment growth. In a capitalist system, the most efficient firms would expand, hiring more workers, and thus driving down their marginal productivity. Under Yugoslavia's system of worker control, this may not happen because workers in a highly profitable firm care more about maximizing *profits per worker* than about *total* profits. Since profits per worker may well *fall* if more labor is allowed to join the enterprise, new employment opportunities may not arise very often.

While there is virtually no central planning of the Soviet variety, we would not want to leave the impression that the Yugoslav economy is totally unmanaged. This is not the case. But what planning there is, is of the French *indicative* style. As in France, the government exercises its control, often rigorously, through the credit market. There it influences both the overall volume of credit for investment purposes and the allocation of these funds among regions and industries.

The Soviet Economy: Historical Background

In November 1917, a determined group of Bolsheviks led by V. I. Lenin overthrew the democratic provisional government that Kerensky had established after the fall of the Czar just eight months earlier, and Russia became the first country in the world to establish a communist government. There is a great irony here in that this first triumph of communism contradicted one of the central tenets of Marxian theory. Marx had prophesied that socialism would be the inevitable outgrowth of a decaying, advanced capitalist system. Instead, it came first to a land that had barely emerged from feudalism.

The Russian Revolution both surprised and dismayed the Western world, the more so since Lenin was an outspoken apostle of worldwide communist revolution. Outside support for the anticommunists helped prolong a bloody civil war between "Red" and "White" Russians, a war that Lenin's army finally won. The Soviet system of state planning as we know it today emerged from the dire circumstances of a wartime economy.

When the war was won, a pragmatic Lenin reacted to the chaotic legacy of the war by permitting substantial amounts of both capitalist ownership and market organization under his New Economic Policy (NEP). The NEP was a great success, especially among the peasants who were hostile to the Communist regime, and it helped rebuild the badly battered Russian economy. After Lenin's death, there was both a fierce struggle for power within the Communist party and a vigorous policy debate over basic economic strategy. Joseph Stalin won both contests and ruthlessly set the Soviet Union on a course that it followed for decades.

Stalin's strategy called for single-minded application of Soviet resources to the goal of rapid *industrial* development with emphasis on *heavy* industry, particularly *armaments*.

To achieve such rapid growth and industrialization, it was necessary to limit consumption severely; so the Russian consumer was asked — or rather forced — to make sacrifices. To feed the urban laborers needed for industrial expansion, Russia's backward agricultural peasants were forced — at extremely high human and economic costs — onto collective farms where they were required to sell their food at low prices and to work for pitifully low wages.

The events of the early Stalinist years left their mark on Soviet economic life. To this day, the Russian economy is characterized by:

- A high degree of centralization, with basic economic goals set by planners, particularly by the leaders of the Communist party. Lower levels of the hierarchy are expected to follow orders, though the methods of guaranteeing compliance are far less Draconian than in Stalin's day.

- A stress on growth, industrialization, and military power, with corresponding downgrading of consumption. While the Soviet GNP grew rapidly from 1928 until recently, the Russian consumer shared few of the fruits of this growth.

- Continuing problems in the agricultural sector, where productivity is very low and the rural peasants remain quite poor.

- A planning system based on quantity targets and quotas, which makes little use of the price system.

In surveying almost 50 years of Soviet economic development, one expert commented that "the surprising thing about the Soviet planning system is not how much it changed since its inception, but how little."[3] However, as this book is being written, Secretary Gorbachev is trying to shake up the rigid Soviet planning process and introduce elements of incentives and markets. How well he will succeed remains to be seen.

Central Planning in the Command Economy

The structure of the Russian economic system is in many ways similar to the hierarchy of a giant corporation.

At the top may be a single strongman or a ruling clique. The political leadership plays the role of chairman of the board, setting overall policy objectives, but has much more absolute authority than that of the chairman of any corporation.

Given the overall goals and priorities established by the top echelons of the Communist party, the State Planning Commission (*Gosplan*, in Russian) has responsibility for the preparation of the national economic plans (discussed below). Beneath the Gosplan are a number of ministries, which direct each industrial sector, and the various regional authorities. These bureaus oversee the day-to-day management of the individual industries or regions within their purview.

Several other layers of the hierarchy intervene as we move down the organizational pyramid. Finally, we reach the level of the enterprise. Enterprise managers in the U.S.S.R. have less authority than do their counterparts in the United States. They are expected to carry out directives handed down from above, fill their quotas, and send information back up the hierarchical ladder. They are bureaucrats rather than entrepreneurs. This is one of the main things that Gorbachev is seeking to change.

Communications within the hierarchy are predominantly vertical. Orders flow down from top to bottom, while data flow up from bottom to top. Since the data requirements are so immense, and the number of layers within the bureaucracy so large, the problems of accurate data transmission and processing

---

[3]Neuberger and Duffy, *Comparative Economic Systems*, page 168.

are monumental.[4] A detailed study of the operation of a large Soviet enterprise in the 1960s found that compliance with the plan required 44 *million* characters of information be passed up to the next highest level in a single year, and that this was only about 12 to 15 percent of the total information gathered by the enterprise. This situation led one Soviet cyberneticist, in one of those wild extrapolations, to observe that preservation of the same planning apparatus until 1980 would require the employment of every Russian adult.[5] As far as we know, the prophecy was not fulfilled.

Markets and Prices in Soviet Economic Life

Although central planning is certainly dominant in Soviet economic life, the Russians do rely on the market mechanism for some purposes.

For instance, *given* the production target for each consumer good as set down in the plan, Soviet planners try to set prices to ration the quantity demanded down to the available quantity supplied. The result is that consumer prices often are set far above production costs, with the difference made up by the so-called *turnover tax*, the main source of government revenue. But the planners often do not succeed in equating the quantities supplied and demanded, and any visitor to the Soviet Union is struck by the frequency with which long lines appear in front of stores. Conversely, large stocks of unwanted goods sit waiting for customers at other establishments. Consumers do exercise free choice among the available goods, but they are certainly not sovereign.

The price system is used even more extensively in the labor market. Given the plan for industrial output, Soviet planners try to set wages to attract workers to the right industries and the right regions. With some exceptions, Soviet workers now have considerable freedom to work where they please—a far cry from the situation in Stalin's day. Partly as a result of the strong desire to direct labor to the areas assigned top priority by the plan, wage differentials among Soviet blue-collar workers are large. According to most observers, they are at least as large as those in the United States, and they lead to considerable inequality in the distribution of labor income. Of course, income from property is negligible in the U.S.S.R. and the gap between blue-collar and white-collar incomes is far smaller than in the United States. So the overall distribution of income is much more equal than ours.

The Five-Year and One-Year Plans

Russia's celebrated Five-Year Plans lay down the basic strategies and growth targets for Soviet economic development, but in many ways they are not as important as the less well known One-Year Plans.

Both of these documents are the responsibility of the Gosplan.

The **Five-Year Plans** set the nation's basic strategy for resource allocation: How much for investment? How much for consumption? How much for military procurement and for scientific research? They also provide guidelines for the distribution of these totals among the various industries (Will there be more

[4]Giant corporations have a similar problem of handling and transmitting data. However, not even the largest corporation approaches the size and scope of the Soviet economy.
[5]Neuberger and Duffy, *Comparative Economic Systems*, pages 179–80.

The Visible Absence of the Invisible Hand

Since we live in a consumer-oriented society, it is hard to imagine what everyday life is like in a society where the consumer is not king. No one disputes the fact that the consumer has not yet ascended to the throne in the Soviet Union. In the following excerpt from an article in TIME magazine, we get a glimpse of the problems that plague the Russian consumer.

The workingman, and particularly the working woman, . . . spends an inordinate amount of time tracking down scarce consumer goods. . . . Although the capital is by far the best-supplied city in the Soviet Union, TIME Moscow Bureau Chief Marsh Clark reports that "soap, toothpaste, perfumes, detergents, toilet paper, hairpins, and matches are either of inferior quality or not available at all. The soaps don't clean, the mint-flavored toothpaste is harsh and repugnant, and the perfumes smell like overripe raspberries." The shortages are so common that people join any queue they see, then ask what it is for. In Moscow recently, Clark spotted a crowd jostling about a man selling something at a table. As the eager buyers got nearer, they saw that the choice item on sale was an English-language textbook entitled *Animal Physiology*.

Along with shortages, there are bizarre examples of superabundance. Because of poorly coordinated planning and lack of inventory control, goods may suddenly appear in disproportionate profusion. Tiny commissaries on collective farms that carry only the barest necessities may suddenly receive shipments of silk neckties or Italian vermouth. A decade ago there was a glut of condoms, which Russians casually used as bottle caps and garters; today, there is a rubber shortage, and prophylactics can scarcely be found in Moscow. . . .

Letters and editorials in the Soviet press often complain about the inferior quality of Soviet-made merchandise. . . . According to Moscow's *Literary Gazette*, the seal of quality, which indicates that an item conforms to international standards, was awarded in 1974 to only .6% of all Soviet footwear and less than 1% of clothes. *Krokodil* [a Soviet humor magazine] recently published a satirical sketch about a couple seeking to buy furniture. The sofas were all big, clumsy and "of a shade combining the colors of a country backroad in autumn and of a World War I dreadnought destroyer." The author recommended against buying these dreadnought sofas because "one mustn't scare the children with furniture."

SOURCE: "Inside Russia: A Nation of Parallel Lives," TIME, March 8, 1976, pages 7–8. Copyright 1976 TIME Inc. All rights reserved. Reprinted by permission from TIME.

cars or more refrigerators?), and they may include specific large construction projects, such as hydroelectric power plants.

Much attention is paid, both in the West and in the U.S.S.R., to the numerical goals posted by these plans. Table 40–1 lists a few of the goals and actual achievements in the Tenth Five-Year Plan (1976–1980) and the Eleventh Five-Year Plan (1981–1985). It is clear that the goals set out in recent plans have not been attained. And it appears unlikely that the Soviet economy will meet the ambitious goals of the Twelfth Five-Year Plan (1986–1990).

Table 40–1
THE TENTH AND ELEVENTH SOVIET FIVE-YEAR PLANS

| ITEM | TENTH FIVE-YEAR PLAN (1976–1980) | | ELEVENTH FIVE-YEAR PLAN (1981–1985) | |
	TARGET GROWTH RATE (percent per year)	ACTUAL GROWTH RATE (percent per year)	TARGET GROWTH RATE (percent per year)	ACTUAL GROWTH RATE (percent per year)
GNP	5.0	2.3	4.0	2.0
Industrial output	6.5	2.6	4.9	2.0
Agricultrual output	5.0	1.0	5.0	2.0

SOURCE: Central Intelligence Agency, *Handbook of Economic Statistics*, 1986.

The Five-Year Plans are not detailed enough to serve as blueprints for action. This job is left to the **One-Year Plans**—enormous sets of documents covering almost every facet of Soviet economic life. In fact, One-Year Plans are so detailed and complex that any one of them is normally not completed until well into the year to which it applies. Sometimes these plans are never completed.

The planning procedure starts with a set of broad national goals (and some rather specific ones) handed down from the political leadership to the Gosplan. The planners then attempt to translate these goals—which are partly reflections of the current Five-Year Plan—into a set of specific directives for subordinate ministries and agencies. As the plan is passed down from one level of the hierarchy to the next, the lower level is constantly supplying the higher level with both data and suggestions for changes—changes in specific tactics, not in basic goals (which are never questioned).

One perennial problem of Soviet planning is that enterprises strive to obtain low production quotas that they will find easy to meet and surpass, because their success is measured by their ability to meet the quotas. To this end, they may deliberately mislead their superiors and understate their productive capacity.

The process of give-and-take up and down the hierarchy eventually leads to a complete One-Year Plan that, the planners hope, is *internally consistent.* Consistency, however, is not often achieved. To see why, let us briefly consider one of the major problems of Soviet planning—achieving what they call **material balance.** This phrase means nothing more than equating quantity supplied and quantity demanded for each type of input—a manageable task for a market economy, but an overwhelming one for Soviet planners.

To take a simple example, suppose three industries (called A, B, and C) use ball bearings. The output targets for industries A, B, and C will then imply a corresponding need for inputs of ball bearings. This quantity (the quantity of ball bearings demanded) must, then, be equal to the output target of the ball-bearing industry (the quantity of ball bearings supplied). This seems simple enough. But the complications become apparent once it is realized that the ball-bearing industry needs inputs, too, and that some of these inputs may be the outputs of industries A, B, and C. So if, for example, the production of ball bearings is to be increased, more steel and machinery may be required; and these additional outputs will require more ball bearings as inputs; and so on and so on.

To see the complexity of the task facing Soviet planners, try your hand at the following simple problem. Suppose there are only three goods—ball bearings, steel, and automobiles—and that the national plan calls for individual consumers to get no ball bearings, $\frac{1}{2}$ unit of steel, and 1 unit of automobiles. How much must each of the three industries produce to achieve material balance?

To try to answer this, you must know the input requirements of each industry. Suppose the inputs required *per unit of output* of each industry are as follows:

OUTPUT	NECESSARY INPUTS
Ball bearings (one unit)	$\frac{1}{2}$ unit of steel *plus* $\frac{1}{4}$ unit of automobiles
Steel (one unit)	$\frac{1}{4}$ unit of ball bearings *plus* $\frac{1}{4}$ unit of steel *plus* $\frac{1}{4}$ unit of automobiles
Automobiles (one unit)	$\frac{1}{3}$ unit of ball bearings *plus* $\frac{1}{2}$ unit of steel *plus* $\frac{1}{6}$ unit of automobiles

Use trial and error to figure out the necessary production levels for each industry. It will not take long to convince yourself that the problem is quite difficult.[6]

The mathematical technique devised to cope with problems like this is called *input–output analysis*,[7] and the preceding little problem is easily solved using this method. But the Russian planners face a problem of this character with, literally, tens of thousands of commodities. Not even the most sophisticated high-speed computer is capable of carrying out the necessary calculations — even if all the data were available. So a perfectly correct solution to the problem of material balance is impossible.

What, then, do the Russians do? In practice, input–output analysis is of little use in formulating One-Year Plans. Trial and error is the only viable approach, and planners seek to avoid as many material imbalances as they can in the time allotted to them. They concentrate particularly on avoiding bottlenecks in industries that are accorded highest priority by the political leadership. If necessary, Soviet planners will redirect scarce inputs to the high-priority sectors to make sure that production is not interrupted. Thus Soviet spacecraft factories are unlikely to close down for lack of steel, but factories producing toasters are quite likely to.

Performance and Problems of Soviet Planning

Most observers rate the Soviet performance as good on growth, at least until recent years, but poor on economic efficiency.

Rigorous economic planning quickly brought the backward Soviet economy of the 1920s into the modern age. Postwar economic growth averaged

---

[6]The answer is: 2 units of ball bearings, 4 units of steel, and 3 units of automobiles.
[7]Input–output analysis was discussed in Chapter 26, pages 585–87.

about 7 percent in the 1950s and somewhat more than 5 percent in the 1960s. However, like the Western economies, the Soviet economy has experienced a growth retardation in recent years. The Soviet growth rate slipped into the $2\frac{1}{2}$ to $3\frac{1}{2}$ percent range — about the same as the U.S. growth rate — during the 1970s and seems to have been only about 2 percent per year in the 1980s.

There are several reasons for this slowdown in Soviet economic growth. For one thing, part of the rapid early growth was achieved by borrowing advanced technology from the West; this obviously could not last forever.

For another, the Soviet Union (like the United States) achieved part of its industrial growth through the migration of peasants to the cities — which also could not last forever.

A third factor was the increasing outcry of the Soviet citizenry for more and better consumer goods. Only in recent years has the regime been willing to accommodate these demands, which required cutting back on investment.

Finally, the plain fact is that the Russian economic mechanism does not function smoothly and seems to be growing increasingly arthritic. The rigorous system of central planning that worked in Stalin's day, when the economic goals were simple and well defined, seems ill-suited to the more sophisticated modern Soviet economy, with its complex and diverse goals. Greater flexibility is perhaps the central goal of Gorbachev's reform proposals.

Both Western and Soviet observers agree that Russia's economic problems are manifold:

- Concern with quotas and targets *stifles innovation,* despite rewards for plant managers who innovate. Innovation carries risks, and Russian managers worry about not fulfilling their plan. They also realize that a brilliant production performance this year will bring with it a tougher quota next year.

- We have already mentioned the tremendous *burden of information transmission.* The result is that planners are often misinformed and make correspondingly incorrect decisions. The fact that firms seeking easy quotas have an incentive to falsify information compounds this problem.

- The system of production targets based on physical quantities rather than on profits or sales often leads to *huge stockpiles of unwanted and inferior goods and equally huge waiting lines for other goods.* For example, since automobile factories generally have quotas stated in terms of cars, there is an almost legendary shortage of spare parts in the Soviet Union. Manufacturers simply do not want to produce things that do not help fulfill their quotas. Similarly, a manufacturer ordered to produce 10,000 pairs of shoes, but faced with a shortage of leather, may produce 10,000 pairs of children's shoes. Selling them is not his concern.

- Because government policy has generally led to shortages of most consumer goods, managers of enterprises producing these goods have been able to turn out *low-quality merchandise,* knowing that eager consumers will buy up almost anything. (See the boxed insert on page 901.)

- Worries about the future unavailability of materials have led some Soviet enterprises to maintain *inventories of crucial materials at levels that would be considered ludicrous in the United States,* and sometimes even to hide this fact from the authorities.

- The Soviet Union has never been able to develop a satisfactory agricultural system. Their agricultural productivity is a small fraction of ours.

Widely publicized reforms in 1965, following suggestions made by the Soviet economist E. Liberman (and hence dubbed "Libermanism"), attempted to deal with some of these problems by introducing the profit motive into Soviet enterprise. With managerial bonuses based on *sales* or *profits*, it was hoped that some of the adverse incentives of the quantity-oriented planning system could be avoided. The reforms scored some measure of success, but were too limited to change the basic character of Soviet industry. For many enterprises, the quantity of output remains the most important indicator of success. Furthermore, the profit motive may not produce desirable results when market prices indicate neither production costs nor values to consumers.

The current Gorbachev initiatives hold out greater hope for success since they are personally backed by the powerful Soviet leader. His goals are to streamline Soviet industry, increase its efficiency, and improve product quality by giving managers more freedom to make their own production plans, to choose their own suppliers, and to respond to what they perceive as market forces. In the West, this is an old and commonplace idea. In the Soviet Union, it is considered radical and revolutionary.

The reform proposals were announced in June 1987 and immediately provoked objections from hardliners and political foes of Premier Gorbachev. No one at this point can predict to what extent they will be adopted, much less how well they will work in practice.

China Under Mao: Revolutionary Communism

A brief look at the economy of the People's Republic of China is an excellent way to conclude this chapter because the Chinese have spent much of the last 40 years groping to find an economic model that suits them. In the process, they have vividly confronted the fundamental questions of this chapter — socialism or capitalism? market or plan? — and have come up with different answers at different times.

Immediately after the communist takeover in 1949, the Chinese economy was patterned on the Russian model and developed with Russian economic aid and technical expertise. In particular, China's was very much a command economy, perhaps even more so than the Soviet economy. Also, China's emphasis on rapid economic growth, particularly industrial growth, was similar to Russia's. Finally China, like Russia, accorded high priority to the goal of economic self-sufficiency. Until the mid-1970s, China's foreign trade was negligible.

But there were also important differences stemming in part from ideology and in part from the fact that the Soviet model was not quite suitable to China. Probably the most important of these differences was the decision by Mao Tse-tung *not* to rely on **material incentives** to motivate the work force. Mao and the Chinese leadership looked with disdain at this "bourgeois" practice and preferred to motivate Chinese workers by exhortation, patriotism, and, where necessary, force.

Russian communism bent socialist doctrine to accommodate human nature. But Chinese communism for many years seemed determined to bend human nature to accommodate Maoist doctrine — to create "the new man in the new China," an effort that has now been abandoned.

A second, less important difference is that Chinese planning has always been less centralized than Russian planning. Local and industrial authorities have more power and discretion than they do in the U.S.S.R. This decentralization probably was dictated by China's immense size and economic backwardness in 1949. Without modern communications (and perhaps even *with* it), there was no way for planners in Beijing to hope to control economic activity in the outlying provinces.

Chinese economic growth under the communist regime has proceeded in fits and starts.

The immediate problem after the Maoist takeover was to lift China from the devastation of World War II and to establish communist institutions and values in a vast and semiliterate country. With Soviet assistance, the plan was apparently successful at first. But then the Soviet model ran into problems, and Mao changed course.

China's next step, the **Great Leap Forward** (1958–1960), turned out to be a giant step backward. Why did the Great Leap Forward fail so miserably? First, the Great Leap's production goals were unrealistically ambitious from the start. Second, because the ideologically pure "Reds" were in Mao's favor while the technocratic "experts" were not, the means selected for carrying out the Great Leap were more romantic than rational. China's vast economic structure was supposed to be decentralized, though tightly controlled by the communist party; massive applications of brute labor were supposed to make up for China's shortages of machinery and advanced technology; and material incentives were deemphasized.

In retrospect, the Great Leap Forward seems to have achieved several things—most of them not very good for China. First, China's national income fell substantially (see Figure 40–4), particularly in the agricultural sector. It took years to make up for the losses of 1959–1962. Second, the ideological excesses of the period accelerated the growing schism between Russia and China. Third, it persuaded the Chinese leadership to throw out the "Reds" and bring back the "experts," signaling a return to rational economic calculation.

In large measure, China's Five-Year Plan covering 1961 to 1965 moved this giant nation back toward the Soviet model, though some elements of

Figure 40–4
REAL NATIONAL INCOME IN THE PEOPLE'S REPUBLIC OF CHINA
While Chinese economic statistics are notoriously inaccurate, the official data are portrayed here. The Great Leap Forward and the Cultural Revolution stand out as major blemishes on the record of Chinese economic growth. Growth has been particularly rapid since 1976. SOURCE: Gregory C. Chow, "Money and Price Level Determination in China," *Journal of Comparative Economics,* September 1987. Updated by authors.

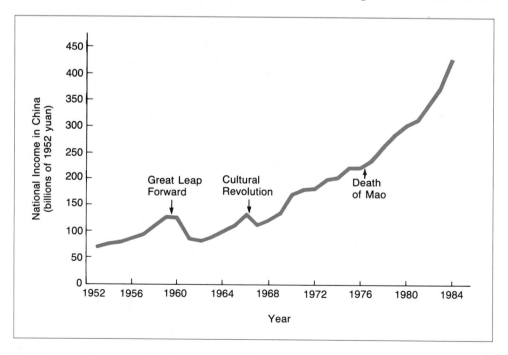

decentralization from the Great Leap were retained. One departure both from Soviet practice and from China's first Five-Year Plan (1953–1957), however, was the greater emphasis on agricultural development—no doubt a wise decision given China's resources. As a result, economic growth resumed.

Then, inexplicably, Mao changed China's course once again with the **Great Proletarian Cultural Revolution** (1966–1968). The "Reds" were in and the "experts" were out as never before. The infamous Red Guards (later assisted by the army) were sent out to purge rightist elements from Chinese society, organize revolutionary cadres, and spread the teachings of Chairman Mao. If anyone worried about economic productivity in this environment, it did not show. By the summer of 1967, both the Chinese economy and other elements of Chinese society were in utter disarray. Output fell again, but recovered more quickly than it had from the Great Leap (see Figure 40–4).

Things began to change in the 1970s. The period until Mao's death in 1976 was one of consolidation and economic growth. The Chinese revolutionary fever receded and, once again, the "experts" were rehabilitated. There was a restoration of material incentives and rational economic calculation—both of which had been considered reactionary during the Cultural Revolution. In general, there was less politics and ideology and more economic growth.

China Since Mao

Since the death of Mao, the Chinese economic system has once again been changing rapidly. The leaders who succeeded Mao have shown themselves to be far less interested in doctrine and far more interested in results.

The opening of China to the West began with President Richard Nixon's visit there in 1972; it proceeded slowly at first, but in a torrent after Mao's death. The technicians and scientists who fell into disgrace in the Cultural Revolution were rehabilitated and put into positions of influence. In a startling reversal of roles, it was Mao and the revolutionaries whose wisdom was questioned.

Late in the 1970s, the Chinese began a series of reforms which amounted to stepping away from the Soviet model and adopting important features of the market economy in its place.

China, long closed to the West, began to welcome Western tourism, trade, and technology. Chinese managers, engineers, and economists came to the United States and other Western nations to study modern business techniques.

Perhaps most important, material incentives were restored, and the Chinese showed themselves willing to experiment with a wide variety of different models of economic organization. The Yugoslav system of worker management was studied carefully. Even small-scale capitalism was allowed back on the Chinese mainland.

These trends accelerated in the early 1980s, as market forces were allowed to supplement central planning more and more. Farmers were given land to do with as they please—once they paid a fixed amount of produce to the state. Markets, and even limited amounts of local entrepreneurship, were allowed to flourish in the form of private shops and other small businesses. Foreign companies were invited to set up operations in China, and the Chinese seem eager to learn the ways of Western business. Late in 1984, the Chinese government announced its intention to allow more market elements into its economy.

Given China's volatile past, no one really knows how far these trends will go. At this writing, there is some resistance within the Chinese bureaucracy to any further liberalization, and China remains a firmly communist and largely planned economy outside of agriculture.

Summary

1. Economic systems differ in the amount of planning they do and in the extent to which they permit private ownership of property. However, socialism (state ownership of the means of production) need not go hand in hand with central planning, and capitalism need not rely on free markets. The two choices are distinct, at least conceptually.

2. Free markets seem to do a good job of selecting the bill of goods and services to be produced and at choosing the most efficient techniques for producing these goods and services. Planned systems have difficulties with both these choices.

3. Market economies, however, do not guarantee an equitable distribution of income and are often plagued by business fluctuations. In these two areas, planning seems to have clear advantages.

4. A major problem for socialism is how to motivate management to achieve maximal efficiency and to maintain inventiveness in the absence of the profit motive.

5. Individual freedom is a noneconomic goal that is of major importance in the choice among economic systems. Any elements of planning or of socialism will infringe upon the personal freedoms of some individuals. Yet complete freedom does not exist anywhere, and certain limitations on individual freedom command wide popular support.

6. The Swedish economy is almost entirely capitalistic, and there is little planning. The chief departures from the U.S. economic system are in the comprehensive ways the Swedish government intervenes to maintain full employment and in its extensive "welfare state."

7. Much more planning is done in France, which also has a rather larger socialist sector than does Sweden. But French planning differs from coercive Soviet-style planning in that it is "indicative," that is, it relies on consensus-building and on voluntary compliance.

8. Yugoslavia has a unique type of economic system called workers' management in which the managers of a firm are actually employed by the workers, who make all major decisions for themselves. While it is almost entirely socialist, the Yugoslav economy relies mainly on free markets and does little planning.

9. Since the days of Stalin, the Soviet Union has followed a rather rigid system of central planning in which heavy industry and armaments are emphasized and consumer needs are deemphasized.

10. Russia's planning system is bureaucratic and hierarchical; it has encountered monumental difficulties in transmitting accurate information. Goals and methods are set forth in Five-Year Plans and in even more detailed One-Year Plans.

11. While Soviet consumers are free to spend their money on what they please, there is no consumer sovereignty. Instead, it is the planners, not the consumers, who decide what will be produced. The labor market, however, operates much like it does in America — using wage rates to equate supply and demand.

12. With central planning replacing the price system, even tasks that are rather simple for a market economy can become inordinately complex. The Soviet Union's difficulties in achieving material balance — that is, in equating supply and demand for the various inputs — illustrate this complexity.

13. The Chinese economic system has changed several times since the Communist takeover in 1949, passing through several periods of intense revolutionary fervor and little economic progress. Planning there appears now to be similar to that in Russia, although somewhat less centralized.

14. Over the last decade, the Chinese have introduced important aspects of the market economy — and even bits of capitalism — into their economic system. In 1987, the Russians began speaking of taking similar steps.

Concepts for Review

Capitalism	Welfare state	Material balance
Socialism	Indicative planning	Material incentives
Planning	Workers' management	Great Leap Forward
Free markets	Soviet Five-Year and One-Year Plans	Great Proletarian Culture Revolution
Consumer sovereignty		

Questions for Discussion

1. Explain why the choice between capitalism and socialism is not the same as the choice between markets and central planning. Cite an example of a socialist market economy and of a planned capitalist economy.

2. If you were the leader of a small, developing country, what are some of the factors that would weigh heavily in your choice of an economic system?

3. Which type of economic system generally has the most trouble achieving each of the following goals? In each case, explain why.
   a. An equal distribution of income
   b. Adequate incentives for industrial managers
   c. Eliminating business fluctuations
   d. Balancing supply and demand for inputs

4. What are some of the advantages and disadvantages of the system of workers' management of industry as it is practiced in Yugoslavia?

5. "Both the goals and the techniques of Soviet economic planning have changed dramatically since Stalin's day." Comment.

6. If you were a Russian plant manager, what are some of the things you might do to make your life easier and more successful? (Use your imagination. Russian plant managers do!)

7. At the beginning of the chapter, we posed the question, "Does America have much to learn from the experiences of these other countries?" Given what you now know about Sweden, France, Yugoslavia, the U.S.S.R., and the People's Republic of China, what do you think?

41

Let a hundred flowers
blossom . . . Let a hundred
schools of thought contend.

MAO TSE-TUNG

Dissenting Opinions: Conservative, Moderate, and Radical

The principles that have been expounded in this book represent the mainstream view of modern economics. While they command the assent of a large majority of American economists, there are dissenters. And these dissenters are not all fanatics and polemicists. Many of them are serious thinkers who are disturbed in one way or another by some aspects of either the modern American economy or the state of economic science, or both.

The dissent comes from both the left and the right of the mainstream of economics. On the right are the *libertarians,* who, while they agree with the portrayal of the virtues of the capitalist market economy given in this book, would no doubt insist that we have vastly overstated its vices and limited the realm of the market much too severely. To libertarians, the market rather than the state is the ultimate guarantor of freedom, and, consequently, they argue that the realm of the market should be expanded at the expense of the state. These are economic Jeffersonians who believe "that government is best that governs least."

Toward the left, the celebrated liberal economist and author John Kenneth Galbraith has been arguing for more than thirty years that most of the economics profession has been using the wrong model of the economy and, as a predictable result, has been generating policy prescriptions that look more and more absurd. Still farther to the left, a group of *radical economists,* claiming to be the intellectual heirs of Marx, attracted increasing numbers of adherents during the 1960s and 1970s. These critics claim that mainstream economists not only are asking all the wrong questions and seeking answers in all the wrong ways, but are little more than apologists for the interests of the capitalist ruling class.

The reader who has come this far will no doubt realize that the authors of this book generally ascribe to the mainstream view. But since that perspective has had a sufficiently long airing in this book, we believe it is useful now to take a brief look at the views of the dissenters. For one thing, history may yet prove that at least some of the dissenters have it right after all! In any event, it is certain that each of the critiques carries valuable lessons for mainstream economic analysis. Indeed, as we shall see, parts of each dissenting view have already been integrated into the body of standard economic analysis.

The Libertarian Credo

Libertarianism is really a philosophy rather than a system of economic thought. Libertarians prize individual freedom above all other social goals—way above them. They are willing to tolerate restrictions on individual freedom in only a very few cases; so few, in fact, that most observers find the more extreme variants of libertarian doctrine totally outlandish. Would you, for example, permit unhappy 10-year-olds to run away from home *legally,* provided only that they could support themselves? Would you sell city streets and highways to private businesses to operate for a profit? Would you permit drug companies to sell anything they want, without labeling requirements (but with legal liability for any harm done by their products)? There are libertarians who would advocate all of these measures, and many, many more.[1]

On economic matters, libertarians are usually associated with the political right wing as staunch defenders of laissez faire. But in issues concerning civil rights, legislation of morality, and protection of citizens against government coercion, their views coincide more with the political left wing. There can be no question that they fervently support civil liberties. As one outspoken libertarian put it:

> *The central idea of libertarianism is that people should be permitted to run their own lives as they wish. We totally reject the idea that people must be forcibly protected from themselves. A libertarian society would have no laws against drugs, gambling, pornography—and no compulsory seat belts in cars. We also reject the idea that people have an enforceable claim on others, for anything more than being left alone.*[2]

The Libertarian Economics of Milton Friedman

The hallmark of libertarian economics is a belief—we might call it a *devout* belief—in the ability of free markets not only to do the tasks normally assigned to them by economists (efficient production of goods, utilization of scarce resources, and so on), but to do *almost everything*.

There is no question that the leading apostle of libertarian economics is Milton Friedman. So unquestioned is his preeminence that the libertarian school is often referred to by economists as the "Chicago School," a name acquired during the many years that Friedman taught at the University of Chicago.[3] While he is a sufficiently brilliant technical economist to have earned the Nobel Prize, he is also an irrepressible public advocate of his libertarian views. In fact, it is in this latter role (frequently voiced in newspaper and magazine articles) that Friedman has received the most notice, or notoriety.

Libertarianism is a school of thought that emphasizes the importance of individual freedom.

[1]See, for example, David Friedman, *The Machinery of Freedom* (New York: Harper & Row, 1973), where each of these is advocated.
[2]*Ibid.,* page xiii.
[3]He is now retired and a resident scholar at the Hoover Institution in Stanford, California. In fairness, we should note that the University of Chicago has had several other great libertarian economists on its faculty.

We might as well treat Friedman as the spokesman for all libertarian economists, for that is more or less what he is. According to Friedman:

The kind of economic organization that provides economic freedom directly, namely, competitive capitalism, also promotes political freedom because it separates economic power from political power and in this way enables the one to offset the other.

Historical evidence speaks with one voice on the relation between political freedom and a free market. I know of no example in time or place of a society that has been marked by a large measure of political freedom, and that has not also used something comparable to a free market to organize the bulk of economic activity.[4]

We have spent many pages in this book detailing the appropriate role of government in a modern mixed capitalist society (see especially Chapters 26 and 29). Friedman would make this role much smaller, limiting it essentially to the following three tasks.

1. ***The government as umpire.*** Friedman is surely no anarchist, although some libertarians are. He recognizes that any society needs laws, and that legislation and enforcement of the law are proper roles for government in a free society. The government must, for example, enforce private contracts and adjudicate disputes.[5]

2. ***Control of natural monopoly.*** As we have noted in earlier chapters (see especially Chapters 27 and 31), some industries have such strong economies of large-scale production that it is inevitable, for technical reasons, that only one firm can survive. Local telephone service, for example, probably comes close to fitting this model. Some have suggested (though others have disputed the claim) that the postal service also is a good example. In such cases, *competitive* capitalism is simply impossible, so society has only three choices:

   - Allow an unregulated private monopoly to exist.
   - Make the industry a public monopoly (as in the case of the U.S. Postal Service).
   - Allow private monopoly to exist, but regulate it carefully "in the public interest" (as we do, for example, with local telephone companies).

   To Friedman, "all three are bad, so we must choose among evils." While Friedman is willing to decide which of the three alternatives is least bad on a case-by-case basis, he is skeptical that the choice typically made in America (regulated monopoly) is the best one.

3. ***Externalities.*** For reasons we have elaborated at some length in this book (see especially Chapters 29 and 34), the government must intervene to promote or protect the public welfare wherever there are beneficial or detrimental externalities. If it does not, the competitive price system will send out false signals and, as a result, will misallocate resources.

[4]Reprinted from *Capitalism and Freedom* by Milton Friedman by permission of the University of Chicago Press (Chicago: University of Chicago Press, 1962), page 9.
[5]More extreme libertarians will suggest that even police protection could be a private enterprise. See, for example, Robert Nozick, *Anarchy, State, and Utopia* (New York: Basic Books, 1974), in which the state *arises from* a private system of police protection.

Friedman accepts this analysis but cautions against applying it too freely. The externalities argument, he notes, often is just an excuse for allocating to the public sector something that could be done better by the private sector. And even in such cases as the control of pollution, where government intervention in the market can *in principle* improve the allocation of resources, the government may not have the knowledge it needs to correct the externality.

. . . the very factors that produce the market failure also make it difficult for government to achieve a satisfactory solution. Generally, it is no easier for government to identify the specific persons who are hurt and benefited than for market participants, no easier for government to assess the amount of harm or benefit to each. Attempts to use government to correct market failure have often simply substituted government failure for market failure. . . . The imperfect market may . . . do as well or better than the imperfect government.[6]

Beyond this short list, Friedman believes, there is little else for government to do in a free society.

Libertarian Economics and Public Policy

We began this discussion of libertarianism by giving some examples of rather extreme policy proposals made by some libertarians (though not necessarily by Milton Friedman). Yet some of Friedman's suggestions, which many people considered absurd when they were first made, have since been incorporated into the mainstream of economic thought or have become the law of the land, or both.

For example, Friedman's was one of the first voices arguing that the system of fixed exchange rates among currencies was potentially dangerous and should be replaced by a system of floating rates, set not by governments but by supply and demand. We now have such a system. Friedman was also among the earliest advocates of the all-volunteer army. This piece of "insanity" became fact in 1973. His proposal for a negative income tax as a means to help poor people (see Chapter 37) is now supported by many economists—be they of the left, the center, or the right—as well as by three of our last four presidents (though often in disguised form). The hostility toward the many government regulatory agencies that is now so much in vogue was present in Friedman's speeches and writings long before it became fashionable.

Yet there are many, many other issues about which the majority of economists and society as a whole continue to believe that Friedman is wrong. (See the boxed insert on page 914). His voice continues to be one of dissent, and one that is every bit as radical as those on the far left. But that voice is irrepressible. As a *Wall Street Journal* columnist put it:

Mr. Friedman, it appears, has grown convinced that his ideas can be made to work here on earth just as marvelously as they already do in heaven.[7]

---

[6]Milton and Rose Friedman, *Free to Choose* (New York: Harcourt Brace Jovanovich, Inc., 1979), pages 214–18.

[7]Alfred L. Malabre, Jr., "The Milton Friedman Show," *The Wall Street Journal,* January 11, 1980. Reprinted by permission of *The Wall Street Journal* © Dow Jones & Company, Inc., 1978. All rights reserved.

An Application of Libertarian Economics: The Licensing of Doctors

Your family doctor has a license to practice medicine in your state. He or she probably displays it prominently on the office wall. You probably would be worried if your doctor did not have one. Yet libertarians like Professor Friedman think that licensing of doctors is a bad idea. He explains why in this excerpt from his celebrated book *Capitalism and Freedom*.[*]

Offhand, the question, "Ought we to let incompetent physicians practice?" seems to admit of only a negative answer. But I want to urge that second thought may give pause.

Licensure is the key to the control that the medical profession can exercise over the number of physicians. . . . The American Medical Association is perhaps the strongest trade union in the United States. The essence of the power of a trade union is its power to restrict the number who may engage in a particular occupation.

How can it do this? The essential control is at the stage of admission to medical school. The Council on Medical Education and Hospitals of the American Medical Association approves medical schools. In almost every state in the United States, a person must be licensed to practice medicine, and to get the license, he must be a graduate of an approved school.

Control over admission to medical school and later licensure enables the profession to limit entry in two ways. The obvious one is simply by turning down many applicants. The less obvious, but probably far more important one, is by establishig standards for admission and licensure that make entry so difficult as to discourage young people from ever trying to get admission.

To avoid misunderstanding, let me emphasize that I am not saying that individual members of the medical profession . . . deliberately go out of their way to limit entry in order to raise their own incomes . . . the rationalization for restriction is that the members of the medical profession want to raise what they regard as the standards of "quality" of the profession. . . .

It is easy to demonstrate that quality is only a rationalization and not the underlying reason for restriction. The power of the . . . American Medical Association has been used to limit numbers in ways that cannot possibly have any connection whatsoever with quality. The simplest example is their recommendation . . . that citizenship be made a requirement for the practice of medicine. I find it inconceivable to see how this is relevant to medical performance.

It is clear that licensure has been at the core of the restriction of entry and that this involves a heavy social cost. . . . Does licensure have the good effects that it is said to have?

It is by no means clear that it does raise the standards of competence in the actual practice of the profession. . . . The rise of the professions of osteopathy and of chiropractic is not unrelated to the restriction of entry into medicine. . . . These alternatives may well be of lower quality than medical practice would have been without the restrictions on entry into medicine.

More generally, if the number of physicians is less than it otherwise would be, and if they are fully occupied, as they generally are, this means that there is a smaller total of medical practice by trained physicians.

When these effects are taken into account, I am myself persuaded that licensure has reduced both the quantity and quality of medical practice. . . . I conclude that licensure should be eliminated as a requirement for the practice of medicine.

SOURCE: *Capitalism and Freedom* by Milton Friedman by permission of the University of Chicago Press (Chicago: University of Chicago Press, 1962), pages 149–59.

[*]For further discussion of this issue, see Discussion Question 3 at the end of this chapter (page 926).

John Kenneth Galbraith: The Economist as Iconoclast

Milton Friedman is barely over 5 feet tall; John Kenneth Galbraith is about $6\frac{1}{2}$ feet tall. There the similarity ends. Friedman's reverence for the market is countered by Galbraith's irreverence about almost everything. Friedman's proposals for laissez faire are opposed by Galbraith's proposals to control almost everything.

John Kenneth Galbraith is a phenomenon in modern economics. This perpetual maverick, who has been blasting (often in ascerbic tones) what he calls "the conventional wisdom" for thirty years, was a member of the Department of Economics at Harvard University—the bastion of the "establishment"—until his retirement in 1975. Without a doubt the most widely read economist in the world, he is perhaps more highly regarded outside the profession than within it. Yet his fellow economists elected him president of the prestigious American Economic Association in 1972. In addition to his achievements in economics, he has been an adviser to presidents, the U.S. ambassador to India, leader of the Americans for Democratic Action, novelist, and TV personality.

Galbraith began to move away from his successful career as a mainstream economist—which included a stint as a price-controller during World War II—with the publication of his book *American Capitalism* in 1952. There he argued that economists, in focusing on the interplay between supply and demand in impersonal markets, ignored the pervasiveness of **economic power,** and thereby blinded themselves to some of the most important things that were going on in the economy. He added further wrinkles to his developing view of the modern capitalist economy in his best-selling book *The Affluent Society* (1958) in which he argued that modern corporations, far from being the servants of consumer sovereignty they are supposed to be, actually *create* demand for their products through advertising.

> A buyer or seller is said to have **economic power** if, by his own actions, he can influence the market price.

These and other strands of Galbraithean thought were brought together in *The New Industrial State* (1967), which remains perhaps the most comprehensive statement of his views of modern capitalist enterprise. The book was, and is, quite controversial.

The Galbraithean Critique of Conventional Economic Theory

Galbraith maintains that conventional economists have squirreled themselves away in a dream world of their own creation, a world that has less and less to do with the real modern economy. In this hypothetical framework:

The best society is the one that best serves the economic needs of the individual. Wants are original with the individual; the more of these that are supplied the greater the general good. Generally speaking, the wants to be supplied are effectively translated by the market to firms maximizing profits therein. If firms maximize profits they respond to the market and ultimately to the sovereign choices of the consumer.[8]

The crucial omission from this picture, in Galbraith's view, is *power*, especially the power of the giant corporation, but also the power of big labor, government bureaucracies, and so on. Rather than being controlled by the market, he believes, the modern corporation controls, or even supplants, the market.

[8]J. K. Galbraith, "A Review of a Review," *The Public Interest*, Fall 1967, page 117.

By ignoring these phenomena, Galbraith claims, economists have been led into increasingly ridiculous policy positions. For example, the theory of monopoly (outlined in Chapter 27) stresses the *inefficiency* caused by its *restriction of output* in order to raise prices. Yet, as Galbraith sees the world, it is precisely the giant corporations that are *most efficient* and who produce *excessive amounts* of output. They do this by advertising campaigns that create the demand for the goods they are so adept at supplying.

As another example, the focus on markets has led the vast majority of economists to oppose wage and price controls and therefore to accept the disagreeable trade-off between inflation and unemployment (see Chapter 17). Galbraith's is one of the few voices that refuses to accept this trade-off, putting his faith instead in a *permanent* system of wage–price controls.

What does the Galbraithean model of our economy look like? In the first place, according to Galbraith, our economy involves a great deal of *planning*.

In place of the market system, we must now assume that for approximately half of all economic output, there is a power or planning system... I cannot think that the power of the modern corporation, the purposes for which it is used or the associated power of the modern union would seem implausible or even very novel were they not in conflict with the vested doctrine.[9]

This *planning system* is run by *technocrats:* managers, engineers, accountants, lawyers, cyberneticists, even economists! The kinds of work they do, and the kind of hierarchical structures they create, are more or less similar in corporations, nonprofit institutions, government bureaus, and even (to a limited extent) labor unions. The nature of their work is also basically the same under capitalism as it is under socialism, in market economies, or in planned economies. It is dictated not by ideology, but by the overwhelming complexity of modern technology. "The enemy of the market is not ideology but the engineer."[10]

These technocrats, whom Galbraith calls the **technostructure,** manipulate consumer demand through advertising. They also manipulate costs to a considerable degree, or else render them quite predictable through long-term contracts with labor unions and suppliers of other inputs (which are also giant corporations). And since the industrial giants can finance their own investment through retained earnings, they need not rely on the capital market. Thus, the market is bypassed.

The firm must take every feasible step to see that what it decides to produce is wanted by the consumer at a remunerative price. And it must see that the labor, materials, and equipment that it needs will be available at a cost consistent with the price it will receive. It must exercise control over what is sold. It must exercise control over what is supplied. It must replace the market with planning.[11]

The technocrats are guided by their own self-interest, not by the interests of their stockholders. In particular, they are certainly *not* interested in maximizing profits.

Instead, their primary interest is growth and expansion.

[9]J. K. Galbraith, "Power and the Useful Economist," *American Economic Review*, March 1973, page 4.
[10]J. K. Galbraith, *The New Industrial State* (Boston: Houghton Mifflin, 1967), page 33.
[11]*Ibid.*, page 24.

If the technostructure . . . maximizes profits, it maximizes them . . . for the owners. If it maximizes growth, it maximizes opportunity for . . . advancement, promotion and pecuniary return for itself. That people should so pursue their own interest is not implausible. [12]

The Galbraithean Critique of the American Economy

What are the results of this system for organizing economic activity? Not very good, according to Galbraith. First, American society is deluged with a dazzling array of private consumption goods of dubious merit:

What is called a high standard of living consists, in considerable measure, in arrangements for avoiding muscular energy, increasing sensual pleasure and for enhancing caloric intake above any conceivable nutritional requirement. [13]

Second, the nature of the system of want-creation effected by the planning system dictates that the outputs of the giant corporations will be produced in abundance while the outputs of what might be considered "competitive" industries (home building, for example) will remain puny:

That the present system should lead to an excessive output of automobiles, an improbable effort to cover the economically developed sections of the planet with asphalt, a lunar preoccupation with moon exploration, a fantastically expensive and potentially suicidal investment in missiles, submarines, bombers, and aircraft carriers, is as one would expect. These are the industries with power. [14]

Third, there is a shocking disparity between the abundant supplies of private consumption goods and the pitiful supplies of public consumption goods. The reason? Madison Avenue does not whet consumers' appetites for public goods. "The engines of mass communication, in their highest state of development, assail the eyes and ears of the community on behalf of more beer but not of more schools." [15]

Fourth, and finally, the system shows a shocking disregard for the environment, or what may be termed more generally "the quality of life":

The family which takes its mauve and cerise, air-conditioned, power-steered, and power-braked automobile out for a tour passes through cities that are badly paved, made hideous by litter, blighted buildings, billboards, and posts for wires that should long since have been put underground. They pass on to a countryside that has been rendered largely invisible by commercial art. . . . They picnic on exquisitely packaged food from a portable icebox by a polluted stream and . . . spend the night at a park which is a menace to the public health and morals. Just before dozing off on an air mattress, beneath a nylon tent, amid the stench of decaying refuse, they may reflect vaguely on the curious unevenness of their blessings. Is this, indeed, the American genius? [16]

---

[12]Galbraith, "A Review of a Review," page 113.
[13]Galbraith, as quoted by R. M. Solow, "The New Industrial State or Son of Affluence," page 107.
[14]Galbraith, "Power and the Useful Economist," page 7.
[15]J. K. Galbraith, *The Affluent Society* (Boston: Houghton Mifflin Company, 1958), page 205.
[16]*Ibid.*, pages 199–200.

A Critique of the Critique

The typical mainstream economist's reaction to Galbraith is to ignore him. However, on occasion, the Galbraithean challenge has been met head-on.

Undoubtedly, the best of these occasions was when a prominent mainstream economist, Professor Robert Solow of M.I.T., published a scathing review of *The New Industrial State* in 1967. Solow's basic contentions were, first, that while the Galbraithean view of the economy no doubt contains some important insights (for example, modern economics pays too little attention to the giant corporation), the things that Galbraith appeals to as "facts" are really not facts at all; and second, that the Galbraithean model as a whole lacks structure and coherence. Our guess is that Solow's review of Galbraith represents the views of many economists. And since Solow is one of the few economists who can match Galbraith's wit and verbal dexterity, their debate is both lively and informative.

Has the modern corporation really preempted the market mechanism? Solow thinks not:

It is unlikely that the economic system can usefully be described either as General Motors writ larger or as the family farm writ everywhere . . . it will behave like neither extreme. . . . Galbraith's story that the industrial firm has "planned" itself into complete insulation from the vagaries of the market is an exaggeration, so much an exaggeration that it smacks of the put-on.[17]

Has advertising really robbed the consumer of his sovereignty and made him a puppet of the corporation? Solow finds the claim vaguely implausible and wants to see evidence:

Professor Galbraith offers none; perhaps that is why he states his conclusion so confidently and so often. . . . I should think a case could be made that much advertising serves only to cancel other advertising.

If Hertz and Avis were each to reduce their advertising expenditures by half . . . what would happen to the total car rental business? Galbraith presumably believes it would shrink. People would walk more, and spend their money instead on the still-advertised deodorants. But suppose . . . that all advertising were reduced . . . Galbraith believes that in the absence of persuasion . . . total consumer spending would fall. Pending some evidence, I am not inclined to take this popular doctrine very seriously.[18]

Is the model of profit maximization, so beloved by mainstream economists, really irrelevant to modern forms of business organization? While recognizing that profit maximization cannot be a *literal* description of corporate behavior ("Most large corporations are free enough from competitive pressure to afford a donation to the Community Chest"), Solow suggests that it is still a workable *approximation*. There is, for example, an *opportunity* cost of funds even when those funds are generated by internal financing. Furthermore, managements that stray too far from profit maximization in the pursuit of other goals, thereby depressing the value of their common stock, may—and lately do—find their jobs threatened by a takeover bid.

---

[17]Robert M. Solow, "The New Industrial State or Son of Affluence," *The Public Interest*, no. 9 (Fall 1967), pages 103–104. Copyright © 1967 by National Affairs, Inc.
[18]*Ibid.*, page 105.

Are the outputs of the system really that bad? As Solow notes, it is hard to disagree with Galbraith's disparaging remarks about chrome-plated automobiles, pungent deodorants, and ostentatiously useless gadgets "without appearing boorish." Yet these are not the wasteful expenditures of the idle rich. It must be remembered that the median family income in the United States is not excessively high — it is currently about $30,000 per year. And by definition, fully *half* of American families earn less than this. Are they squandering their money on frivolities, or are these the things that the American people really want?

His [Galbraith's] attitudes toward ordinary consumption remind one of the Duchess who, upon acquiring a full appreciation of sex, asked the Duke if it were perhaps too good for the common people.[19]

In sum, Solow views *The New Industrial State* as strong on style and wit, but weak on substance: "A book for the dinner table not for the desk."

Not surprisingly, Galbraith was unmoved by this and other attacks, viewing them as the predictable reactions of conventional economists who see their vested interests threatened:

Neoclassical economics is not without its instinct for survival. It rightly sees the unmanaged consumer, the ultimate sovereignty of the citizen and the maximization of profits and resulting subordination of the firm to the market as the three legs of a tripod on which it stands. These are what exclude the role of power in the system. All three propositions tax the capacity for belief.[20]

The Radical Economics of the Left

The newest of the three major challenges to mainstream economics comes from the far left. Spawned by the student movement of the 1960s, radical economics is highly critical both of contemporary capitalism as practiced in America (and elsewhere) and of contemporary economic analysis as practiced by most economists. Radical economics has grown and matured. Its views are no longer circulated in leaflets handed out on street corners. They appear in scholarly journals and even in testimony before Congress. While the movement is too diverse to define concisely, it behooves us to take a close look at some of what the radicals have been saying.

Radical economists view themselves as the inheritors of Marxism, both of its intellectual traditions and its political activism.

Like Marx, radical economists stress the pervasive importance of the *mode of production*, including not only its influence on economic activity, but also its effects on personal attitudes and social institutions. They write much about the *class struggle* and leave no doubt about where they line up. Like Marx, they seek to uncover the inner *contradictions* in modern capitalism, contradictions that, they believe, will contribute to its ultimate demise. And, also like Marx, their writings are replete with stinging criticisms of both contemporary economic analysis and contemporary economic institutions.

There is also much of Galbraith in the writings of the radical economists: They share his emphasis on power rather than on markets, his critique of the

---

[19]*Ibid.*, page 108.
[20]Galbraith, "Power and the Useful Economist," page 5.

giant corporation, his belief that consumers are manipulated by producers, and his dismay over the outputs of the industrial system. But Galbraith is surely no radical economist, and the radical economists are not Galbraithean. They find his propensity to turn to the government to solve problems hopelessly naïve. In their view, the government is part and parcel of the corporate state—a contributor to the problem, not an instrument toward a solution.

The Shortcomings of Mainstream Economics: Point and Counterpoint

In brief, radical economists hold that mainstream economists are asking all the wrong questions and using the wrong set of tools (economic models) to provide the answers. Let us examine their complaints one by one.[21]

Narrowness of Focus

Radicals argue that economists typically narrow their field of inquiry so much that they are incapable of addressing the important questions.

For one thing, in contrast to Marx's teachings, modern economics is *ahistorical*. It is very much based on the here and now, with scant attention paid to the origins of the current system or the directions in which it may be headed. Perhaps as a consequence of this narrow scope, mainstream economics *accepts institutions as given and (tacitly) as immutable*. Little attention is paid to how institutions change.

Amplifying the attack, the radicals chide conventional economists for their preoccupation with analysis of *marginal* changes, using the celebrated tools of marginal analysis that we have described in earlier chapters. This, they argue, makes economics incapable of dealing with the really big issues: the institution of private property, poverty and discrimination, unemployment, and alienation. For example, Professor John Gurley of Stanford University, who converted from conventional to radical economics many years ago, scoffed at a prominent economist who expressed the belief that reducing unemployment would do more good things for the distribution of income than any measure he could imagine.

Well, any radical economist can imagine a direct measure that would do even better things—expropriation of the capitalist class and turning over of ownership of capital goods and land to all the people. That, of course, sounds wild—unimaginable—to anyone who does not question the existing system.[22]

The consequence of this disciplinary narrowness, radicals contend, is that economists become, whether deliberately or unwittingly, apologists for the present system, supporters of the propertied class, and defenders of the status quo.

[21]Another attempt to draw up a list of key tenets of the radicals, similar in spirit to what we do here, appears in Assar Lindbeck's *The Political Economy of the New Left: An Outsider's View,* Second Edition (New York: Harper & Row, 1977).

[22]J. G. Gurley, "The State of Political Economics," *American Economic Review,* May 1971, page 59.

Most economists are prepared to plead guilty to the charge of disciplinary narrowness. As Yale's Nobel prize winner, James Tobin, put it:

Most contemporary economists feel ill at ease with respect to big topics — national economic organization, interpretation of economic history, relations of economic and political power, origins and functions of economic institutions. The terrain is unsuitable for our tools. We find it hard even to frame meaningful questions, much less to answer them. [23]

But mainstream economists tend to view their inadequacy in this area as a misdemeanor, not a felony. They point out, in their defense, that a narrow focus is imperative if progress in analysis is to be made. And they are quite proud of the achievements of economic science compared with those of the more diffuse social sciences, such as sociology and political science. They counter that radicals try to paint with such broad strokes that everything becomes necessarily superficial and imprecise. And they argue that the radicals, with their very clear political biases, are hardly in a position to question the objectivity of other economists.

Acceptance of Tastes and Motivation as Given

Just as they do with institutions, conventional economists accept the tastes of consumers and the motivations of workers and managers as given and unchangeable: "just human nature."

Radicals, on the other hand, agree with Galbraith that the consumer is manipulated; and they go on to widen the charge. Not only is the consumer bombarded by Madison Avenue, he is brainwashed in the school system, influenced by politicans, and subtly molded by other social institutions.

These institutions, furthermore, are set up for the convenience of the ruling (capitalist) class.

Economics . . . takes preferences as being exogenously determined and then shifts the burden of studying their formation and change onto "other disciplines." The New Left rejects this compartmentalization and takes the Marxian view . . . that new needs are created by the same process by which their means of satisfaction are produced. [24]

This argument is broadened further by the assertion that the need for material incentives to motivate both workers and managers is culturally acquired rather than innate, a product of capitalism rather than a cause of it.

Naturally, mainstream economists do not really believe that tastes are God-given. Everyone realizes that they are acquired and influenced by many things. The question is: What are we to do about this? Lacking a theory of taste formation, basic economic analysis proceeds on the assumption that consumer tastes are to be respected *regardless* of how they got to be what they are. If we forsake this principle, we find ourselves on some dangerous ground: If consumers do not know what's good for them, who does? Still, most economists would willingly concede that more research on taste formation is desirable; and

[23] J. Tobin, book review of Lindbeck's *The Political Economy of the New Left*, *Journal of Economic Literature*, December 1972, page 1216.
[24] S. Hymer and F. Roosevelt, "Comment," *Quarterly Journal of Economics*, November 1972, page 649.

some have worked on this. The radicals have no doubt pushed the profession in a healthy direction.

Obsession with Efficiency Rather Than Equality

Earlier in this book we described in some detail the fundamental trade-off between efficiency and equality. All mainstream economists appreciate and understand this principle, and a great many—in their role as private citizens—advocate greater equality. However, radicals are quite right to complain that:

The preponderant majority of economic analysis and research is concerned with efficiency, not with equality.

Many conventional economists agree with this criticism. But radical economists do not ask simply for a change in emphasis; they also want a change in the economist's tool kit. The marginal productivity theory of income distribution, they argue, is irrelevant. They maintain that to understand the distribution of income in contemporary America, we must first understand the distribution of *power*, which is largely determined by who controls the means of production.

According to marginal productivity theory, workers receive the marginal product of labor and capitalists receive the marginal product of capital. This conservative theory tries to justify the present distribution of income. Critics claim that it explains nothing, is unrealistic and refers to nothing measurable, and confuses the product of capital with the product of the capitalist.

According to radical theory, workers produce the whole product but capitalists expropriate part of it in profits (by means of their control of all the resources and productive facilities).[25]

As a radical economist sees it, the shares of national income going to workers and to property owners are largely determined by the relative power of the two groups.[26]

Here the conventional and the radical economists part company. The conventional economist wants to know just how this "power" is measured. Are there statistical studies showing that "power" influences the distribution of income? In short, mainstream economics treats this approach to distribution theory as rhetoric, not as science.

Myopic Concentration on Quantity Rather Than Quality

Much like Galbraith, the radical left is critical of mainstream economists' preoccupation with policies designed to increase the gross national product. They argue that a great deal of this output is no more than junk, and using society's resources to produce such things is patently irrational. They also point to the spoliation of the environment caused by modern industrial production, though at least some radicals concede that conventional economics has some solutions to these problems (see Chapter 34). And they echo Galbraith's dismay that a system that is so good at producing private consumer goods should be so pathetically bad at feeding the hungry, housing and clothing the poor, and providing public services of all kinds.

[25]E. K. Hunt and Howard J. Sherman, *Economics: An Introduction to Traditional and Radical Views*, Second Edition (New York: Harper & Row, 1975), pages 249–50.
[26]Gurley, "The State of Political Economics," page 59.

Radicals add one further element to Galbraith's indictment. In addition to ruining the quality of the environment, capitalist production ruins human beings.

It makes them aggressive, competitive, even dehumanized, by forcing them into a rat race for material gain. In Marxian terms, workers have little voice in determining the nature of their productive activities and so become *alienated* from their work rather than being proud of their accomplishments. (See Chapter 39, especially pages 880–81).

The answers that conventional economists have to most of these charges have already been noted in connection with our discussion of Galbraith (refer back to pages 918–19). The new charges are those of alienation and the dehumanizing effects of capitalism. We think it is safe to say that conventional economists have never known what to make of the notion of alienation. They scratch their heads about it, but that is about all. If this is an important way in which capitalism has damaged the quality of life, then conventional economics surely has been blind to it. Like "power," however, no one has yet figured out a way to measure alienation. As to the alleged dehumanization of the labor force, this seems to be a side effect of modern industrial activity — whether that activity is conducted under capitalism or under socialism.

Naïve Conception of the State

Radical economists maintain that both mainstream economists and Galbraith hold a naïve and sentimental view of the state. In this view, government is available to set things right when the market system fails (as in the case of externalities, for example), and in so doing, government decisions are dictated by the broad public interest. By contrast:

The State, in the radical view, operates ultimately to serve the interest of the controlling class in a class society. Since the "capitalist" class fundamentally controls capitalist societies, the state functions in capitalist societies to serve that class. It does so either directly, by providing services only to members of that class, or indirectly, and probably more frequently, by helping preserve and support the system of basic institutions which support and maintain the power of that class. [27]

This *subservience of the state to the capitalists* manifests itself in several ways. First, since capitalists are driven by competition to accumulate capital continually and to expand production, more and bigger markets are necessary on which to sell this bountiful output. As a result, capitalist nations turn to *imperialist ventures* to secure new markets. Second, in order to maintain domestic demand at high levels, the military-industrial complex promotes a *war economy*, which, if not actually at war, is continually spending inordinate sums on armaments. Third, even reforms that appear to be pro-labor, such as social welfare programs, unemployment insurance, and the like, are really intended to *"buy off"* the working class so that they will not rise up in revolt, as they imply Marx had predicted. In this view, for example, the New Deal was not motivated by a desire to help the working class, but rather by a desire to forestall the coming revolution.

Mainstream economists admit to a certain political naïvete. Yet most economists are unimpressed by the radicals' view of the state. Without denying

[27]D. M. Gordon, *Theories of Poverty and Underemployment* (Lexington, Mass.: D. C. Heath & Company, 1972), page 61.

that corporations often curry political favor, and often succeed, mainstream economists wonder how the radical model can explain progressive income taxation, inheritance taxes, antitrust legislation, equal opportunity laws, affirmative action regulations, and many, many more acts that the preponderance of the wealthy opposed bitterly at the time they were enacted. Furthermore, they point out, the policy prescriptions that conventional economists offer to improve the functioning of markets are intended as just that — as prescriptions for improvement, not as predictions about what government will actually do. Economists are not *that* naïve.

The Radical Critique of the American Economy

Much of the radical criticism of modern industrial capitalism has already been mentioned in connection with its criticism of modern economics. Radicals dislike the great disparities in income and wealth that the system produces; they despise the discrimination against blacks and women that, they argue, capitalism promotes; they blame the system for alienating its labor force and dehumanizing people in other ways (as in the schools); they cite the irrational use of resources to produce too much private junk and too few public services; they abhor what they see as its imperialist and militaristic tendencies; and they claim that the system is unable to cope with the problem of macroeconomic instability.

Taken as a whole, this is a powerful indictment. But almost all these problems have been raised many times before by nonradical economists.

What distinguishes the radical attack from the attitudes of liberal reformers is that the radicals have a unified view of it all.

Liberals see each of these . . . problems as separate and distinct. The problems, they believe, are the results of past mistakes, inabilities, and ineptitudes or the results of random cases of individual perversity . . . liberals generally favor government-sponsored reforms designed to mitigate the many evils of capitalism. These reforms never threaten the two most important features of capitalism: private ownership of the means of production, and the free market.

Radicals, however, see each of the . . . problems . . . as the direct consequences of private ownership of capital and the process of social decision making within the impersonal cash nexus of the market. The problems cannot be solved until their underlying causes are eliminated, but this means a fundamental, radical economic reorganization.[28]

What Is the Radical Alternative?

What would the radicals put in place of our system of market capitalism? There are many answers, but none commands anything like universal support.

Few radicals prefer a system of rigid state planning along Soviet lines. Most see oppression by bureaucrats of the Soviet type as little better than (and little different from) oppression by capitalists, and they deplore the losses of human rights that accompany totalitarianism. Some advocate a system of market socialism, along Yugoslav lines. But this runs counter to the argument that the institution of markets is one of the root causes of America's difficulties. Others

[28]Hunt and Sherman, *Economics,* page 186.

see the Israeli kibbutz system, perhaps the purest form of communism ever practiced, as a model.

In fact, the radicals' hostile attitude both toward markets *and* central planning has put them in an awkward position. As one thoughtful critic put it:

It may be possible to make a strong case against either markets or administrative systems, but if we are against both we are in trouble; there is hardly a third method for allocating resources and coordinating economic decisions, if we eliminate physical force.[29]

If both the market and the plan are discarded, how is the economy to be organized? The radical viewpoint is perhaps vague, but two characteristics stand out quite clearly. First, radicals want a *decentralized* system, not one in which power is concentrated (either in the hands of capitalists or of commissars). Second, they want a *participatory* system in which workers have some real control over what they do and how they do it, not one in which orders only flow from the top down. These changes, radicals believe, would make workers both happier and more productive.

[29]Lindbeck, *The Political Economy of the New Left: An Outsider's View*, page 32.

Summary

1. Mainstream economic analysis is not without its dissenters — conservative, moderate, and radical.
2. The libertarian philosophy translates, in economic matters, to a defense of laissez faire and to a devout belief in the workings of markets. This is because libertarians see free markets as the best guarantor of individual freedom.
3. Libertarian economists like Milton Friedman would limit government to three basic roles: enforcement of the law, regulation of natural monopolies, and control of externalities. Some libertarians would give government even less scope than this.
4. John Kenneth Galbraith has argued for years that conventional economic analysis has accorded insufficient attention to large and powerful organizations like the modern corporation. In his view, this omission has made modern economics largely irrelevant to modern society.
5. According to Galbraith, large corporations have the power to control, or even supplant, market forces by creating the demand for their products through advertising and by manipulating their own costs. This "planning system" is run by technocrats, who are more interested in growth and expansion than in maximizing profits.
6. Because the modern corporation controls the market, rather than vice versa, the U.S. economy, according to Galbraith, turns out tons of consumer baubles of dubious merit but underproduces crucial goods like housing, keeps the public sector starved, and despoils the environment.
7. Mainstream economists feel that Galbraith overstates his case and substitutes assertion for fact. They doubt that the corporation can avoid the discipline of the market entirely, and they are skeptical of the view that the consumer is a puppet of Madison Avenue.
8. Radical economists are the economic and political heirs of Marx, though their analysis of twentieth century capitalism bears the unmistakable stamp of Galbraith. However, they disdain Galbraith's "liberal" view of the state and view the goverment as an instrument of the capitalist class.
9. Radicals criticize mainstream economists for having an unduly narrow focus; for accepting consumer tastes and human nature as "givens" rather than treating them as the results of the economic system; for stressing efficiency rather than equality as an economic goal; and for concentrating on increasing the quantity of output rather than the quality of life.
10. While their critique of both economic theory and the modern economy is quite clear and forceful, radicals are much less clear about what type of system should be put in its place.

Concepts for Review

Libertarianism
Economic power
Technostructure
Radical economics

Manipulation of the consumer
Alienation
Liberal versus radical views of the state

Questions for Discussion

1. What might a libertarian think of:
   a. laws prohibiting smoking cigarettes in public places?
   b. laws prohibiting smoking marijuana in private?
   c. compulsory seat belts in cars?
   d. speed limits on highways?
   e. censorship?
2. Explain why a libertarian would support the all-volunteer army. Explain why many who are not libertarians would also support it. How are the concepts of *supply and demand* and *opportunity cost* relevant?
3. Friedman believes that the medical profession has kept doctors' fees high by making it difficult to get into medical school (see page 914). Explain his argument with a supply and demand diagram. What are the costs and benefits to society of licensing doctors? How would you go about deciding whether the benefits exceed the costs, or vice versa?
4. Friedman has advocated replacing the current system of public schools by a "voucher" plan in which the parents of each school-age child would get a voucher worth, say, $3000. These educational vouchers could be spent only on education, but could be spent in any accredited school, public or private, of the parents' choosing.[30] What do you think of this idea? How might your own elementary and secondary schooling have differed if this plan had been in effect?
5. Galbraith says that about 50 percent of the American economy is in the "planning system" rather than in the competitive market. What are some industries that seem to fall under both headings?
6. According to Galbraith, modern economic analysis rests on three assumptions: consumer sovereignty, profit maximization, and the subordination of the firm to the market. Explain what he means.
7. Discuss the divergent views of the role of the state in the economy held by (a) libertarians, (b) Galbraith, and (c) radical economists. Which do you find most appealing?
8. Discuss the radical critique of conventional economics, point by point. Where do you find room for improvement in mainstream economics?
9. Radicals blame the American economic system for inequality, alienation and dehumanization, irrational use of resources, militarism, and macroeconomic instability. In your view, which of these are valid criticisms? Do you think these criticisms are indictments of private ownership of capital, of a market system, or of industrial systems in general?

[30]For a full discussion of the proposal, see Milton and Rose Friedman, *Free to Choose*, Chapter 6.

Glossary

Numbers in parentheses indicate pages in the text where the terms are discussed.

Ability-to-pay principle The idea that persons with greater ability to pay taxes should pay higher taxes. (726)

Absolute advantage Of one country over another in the production of a particular good is said to occur if it can produce that good using smaller quantities of resources than can the other country. (384)

Abstraction Ignoring many details in order to focus on the most important factors in a problem. (10)

Affirmative action Active efforts to locate and hire members of minority groups. (841)

Aggregate demand The total amount that all consumers, business firms, and government agencies are willing to spend on final goods and services. (139)

Aggregate demand curve Graphic presentation of the quantity of national product that is demanded at each possible value of the price level. (77, 174)

Aggregate saving The difference between disposable income and consumer expenditure. (155)

Aggregate supply The total amount that all business firms are willing to produce. (198)

Aggregate supply curve A graph that shows, for each possible price level, the quantity of goods and services that all the nation's businesses are willing to produce, holding all other determinants of aggregate quantity supplied constant. (77, 198)

Aggregation Combining many individual markets into one overall market. Economic aggregates are the focus of macroeconomics. (75)

Aid to Families with Dependent Children (AFDC) Major transfer program that pays cash benefits to poor families with dependent children. (837)

Allocation of resources The decision on how to divide up the economy's scarce input resources among the different outputs produced in the economy and among the different firms or other organizations that produce those outputs. (37)

Antitrust policy Programs designed to control the growth of monopoly and to prevent powerful firms from engaging in practices considered "undesirable," as defined by certain federal laws and court decisions. (699)

Appreciation Of a nation's currency is said to occur when exchange rates change so that a unit of its own currency can buy more units of foreign currency. (408)

Arbitration Process in which an outsider is authorized to dictate the terms of a settlement of a labor-management dispute if a voluntary agreement cannot be reached. (814)

Asset An item that an individual or a firm owns. (258)

Automatic stabilizer An arrangement that automatically supports aggregate demand when it would otherwise sag and holds down aggregate demand when it would otherwise surge ahead; thus reduces the sensitivity of the economy to shifts in demand. (309)

Autonomous increase in consumption An increase in consumer spending without any increase in incomes. Represented graphically as a shift of the entire consumption function. (190)

Average cost curve Shows, for each output, the cost per unit, that is, total cost divided by output. (505)

Average physical product (APP) Total physical product (TPP) divided by the total quantity of input used. (501)

Average revenue (AR) Total revenue (TR) divided by quantity. (536)

Balance sheet An account statement listing the values of all assets on the left-hand side and of all liabilities and net worth on the right-hand side. (258)

Barter A system of exchange in which people directly trade one good for another, without using money as an intermediate step. (250)

Benefits principle of taxation The idea that people who derive benefits from a service should pay the taxes that finance it. (726)

Bilateral monopoly Market situation in which there is both a monopoly on the selling side and a monopoly on the buying side. (812)

Bond A corporation's promise to pay the holder a fixed sum of money at the specified *maturity* date and some other fixed amount of money (the *coupon* or *interest payment*) every year up to the date of maturity. (660)

Brain drain Occurs when the educated natives of a less developed country emigrate to wealthier nations. (866)

Budget deficit Amount by which the government's expenditures exceed its receipts during a specified period of time, usually one year. (322)

Budget line Represents graphically all the possible combinations of two commodities that a household can purchase, given the prices of the commodities and some fixed amount of money at its disposal. (470)

Burden of a tax The amount of money an individual would have to be given to make him just as well off with the tax as he was without it. (727)

Capital Inventory (stock) of plant, equipment, and other productive resources held by a business firm, an individual, or some other organization. (774)

Capitalism Method of economic organization in which private individuals own the means of production, either directly or indirectly through corporations. (887)

Capital gain An increase in the market value of a piece of property that occurs between the time it is bought and the time it is sold. (235)

Capital good An item that is used to produce other goods and services in the future, rather than being consumed today. (42)

Capital loss A decrease in the market value of a piece of property that occurs between the time it is bought and the time it is sold. (235)

Cartel Group of sellers of a product who have joined together to control its production, sale, and price in the hope of obtaining the advantages of monopoly. (619)

Central bank A bank for banks. The central bank of the United States is the Federal Reserve System. (269)

Closed economy An economy that does not trade with other nations in either goods or services. (435)

Closed shop An arrangement that permits only union members to be hired. (808)

Collective bargaining Negotiations between union representatives of an industry's labor force and the employers of those workers. (812)

Commodity money An object used as a medium of exchange but which also has substantial value in alternative (nonmonetary) uses. (251)

Common stock A piece of paper that gives the stockholder a share in ownership of the company. (660)

Comparable worth A pay standard that assigns equal wages to jobs judged "comparable." (842)

Comparative advantage Of one country over another in the production of a particular good relative to other goods it can produce is said to occur if it produces that good least inefficiently compared with the other country. (385)

Complements Refers to two goods if an increase in the price of one reduces the quality demanded of the other, all other things remaining constant. (491)

Concentration of industry The share of the industry's total output (in money terms) supplied by some given number (usually four) of its largest firms. (706)

Concentration ratio Percentage of an industry's output produced by its *four* largest firms. It is intended to measure the degree to which the industry is dominated by large firms, that is, how closely it approximates a monopoly. (707)

Consumer expenditure (consumption) Symbolized by the letter C; the total amount spent by consumers on newly produced goods and services (excluding purchases of new homes, which are considered investment goods). (139)

Consumer Price Index The most popular index number for the price level. Its weights are based on the spending patterns of a typical urban household. (113)

Consumer sovereignty Consumer preferences determine what goods shall be produced, and in what amounts. (887)

Consumption function Relationship between total consumer expenditure and total disposable income in the economy, holding all other determinants of consumer spending constant. (147)

Consumption good An item which is available for immediate use by households and which satisfies wants of members of households without contributing directly to future production by the economy. (42)

Corporation A firm with the legal status of a fictional individual. It is owned by stockholders and run by elected officers and a board of directors, whose chairman often influences the firm's affairs. (656)

Correlation A relationship between two variables such that they tend to go up or down together. Correlation need not imply causation. (14)

Cost disease of personal services Tendency of the cost of services such as auto repair and legal counsel to rise faster than the economy's overall inflation rate because it is difficult to increase productivity (output per person hours) in these services. (641)

Craft union Represents a particular type of skilled worker regardless of the industry. (808)

Cross elasticity of demand For product X to a change in the price of another product, Y, is the ratio of the percentage change in quantity demanded of product X to the percentage change in the price of product Y that brings about the change in quantity demanded. (491)

Cross-subsidization Selling one product at a loss, which is balanced by higher profits on another product. (680)

Crowding in Occurs when government spending, by raising real GNP, induces increases in private investment spending. (335)

Crowding out Occurs when deficit spending by the government forces private investment spending to contract. (335)

Cyclical unemployment The portion of unemployment that is attributable to a decline in the economy's total production. Cyclical unemployment rises during recessions and falls as prosperity is restored. (96)

Deficit, balance of payments Amount by which the quantity supplied of a country's currency (per year) exceeds the quantity demanded. Such deficits arise when the exchange rate is artificially high. (416)

Deflating (by a price index) Dividing some nominal magnitude by a price index in order to express that magnitude in dollars of constant purchasing power. (114)

Deflation A sustained decrease in the general price level. (81)

Demand, law of States that a lower price generally increases the amount of a commodity that people in a market are willing to buy. Thus, for most goods, demand curves have a negative slope. (479)

Demand curve A graph showing how the quantity demanded of a certain product during a specified period of time changes as the price of the product changes, holding all other determinants of quantity demanded constant. (53)

Demand schedule A table showing how the quantity demanded of a

certain product during a given period of time changes as the price of the product changes, holding all other determinants of quantity demanded constant. (53)

Deposit creation Process by which the banking system turns a dollar of reserves into several dollars of deposits. (259)

Deposit insurance A system that guarantees that most depositors will not lose money even if their bank goes bankrupt. Most deposits are insured against loss by the Federal Deposit Insurance Corporation (FDIC) or the Federal Savings and Loan Insurance Corporation (FSLIC). (257)

Depreciation (of capital goods) The value of the portion of the nation's capital equipment that is used up within the year. It indicates how much output is needed just to keep the economy's capital stock intact. (160)

Depreciation (of a currency) Is said to occur when exchange rates change so that a unit of its own currency can buy fewer units of foreign currency. (408)

Depreciation allowances Tax deductions that businesses may claim when they spend money on investment goods. (167)

Devaluation Reduction in the official value of a currency. (409)

Direct taxes Taxes levied directly on the people. (718)

Discount rate The interest rate the Fed charges on loans it makes to banks. (276)

Discounting Process of determining the present worth of a quantity of money receivable or payable at some future date. (791)

Discouraged worker An unemployed person who gives up looking for work and is therefore no longer counted as part of the labor force. (94)

Discrimination, economic Occurs when equivalent factors of production receive different payments for equal contributions to output. (831)

Discrimination, statistical Occurs when the productivity of a particular worker is estimated to be low just because that worker belongs to a particular group. (833)

Disguised unemployment Occurs when tasks are carried out by a number of persons larger than the number that can complete them most efficiently. (865)

Disposable income A measure of income derived by subtracting personal income taxes from personal income. (140)

Diversification Including a number and variety of stocks, bonds, and other such items in an individual's portfolio of investments. (663)

Division of labor Breaking up a task into smaller, more specialized tasks so that each worker can become more skilled in the particular job. Division of labor creates efficiency and increases productivity. (44)

Dual labor market theory Asserts that workers generally work in one of two types of jobs—those which offer opportunities for acquisition of skills and promotions, and "dead end jobs" which offer little scope for improvement. (803)

Dumping Selling goods in a foreign market at lower prices than those charged in the home market. (402)

Econometric model A set of mathematical equations that embody the economist's model of the economy. (310)

Economic growth A condition in which an economy is able to produce more goods and services for each consumer. (42)

Economic model A simplified, small-scale version of some aspect of the economy. Economic models are often expressed in equations, graphs, or words. (14)

Economic power A buyer or seller is said to have economic power if, by his own actions, he can influence the market price. (915)

Economic profit Net earnings minus the firm's opportunity cost of capital. (571)

Economic profit, total Of a firm or an industry, is the total revenue it derives from the sale of its products minus the total cost of its inputs, including the opportunity cost of any inputs supplied by the proprietors. (535)

Economic rent Said to be earned whenever a factor of production receives a reward that exceeds the minimum amount necessary to keep the factor in its present employment. (783)

Economies of scale Savings acquired through increases in quantities produced. (519, 679)

Economies of scope Savings acquired through simultaneous production of many different products. (680)

Efficiency The absence of waste, achieved primarily by gains in productivity resulting from specialization, division of labor, and a system of exchange. (43)

Efficient allocation of resources One that takes advantage of every opportunity to make some individuals better off in their own estimation while not worsening the lot of anyone else. (577)

Elasticity of demand, price Ratio of the *percentage* change in quantity demanded to the *percentage* change in price that brings about the change in quantity demanded. (483)

Employment Act of 1946 Act in which Congress declared the achievement of full employment to be a goal of national policy. (96)

Entrepreneurship The act of starting new firms, introducing new products and technological innovations, and, in general, taking the risks necessary in seeking out business opportunities. (770)

Equation of exchange States that the money value of GNP transactions must be equal to the product of the average stock of money times velocity (M x V = P x Y). (291)

Equilibrium A situation in which there are no inherent forces that produce change. Changes away from an equilibrium position occur only as a result of "outside events" that disturb the status quo. (57, 169)

Equilibrium level of GNP (on the demand side) Level of GNP which makes aggregate demand equal to production. (169)

Equilibrium price Price at which quantity demanded and quantity supplied are equal. This common quantity is called the equilibrium quantity. (175)

Excess burden of a tax The amount by which the burden of the tax exceeds the tax that is paid. (728)

Excess capacity theorem Asserts that monopolistic competitive firms will tend to produce outputs lower than those that minimize average costs, that is, that they will tend to produce less than their capacity. (616)

Excess reserves Reserves held in excess of the legal minimum. (259)

Exchange A mechanism by which workers can trade the various products resulting from specialization and the division of labor. (45)

Exchange controls Laws restricting the exchange of one nation's currency for that of another. (423)

Exchange rate States the price, in terms of one currency, at which another currency can be bought. (408)

Exchange rates, fixed Rates set by government decisions and maintained by government actions. (415)

Exchange rates, floating Rates determined in free markets by the law of supply and demand. (409)

Excise tax Sales tax on a specific commodity. (481)

Expected rate of inflation Forecasted rate of price change. Also, the difference between the nominal interest rate and the real interest rate. (105)

Expediture schedule Illustration of the relationship between national income (GNP) and total spending. (170)

Exponential growth Growth at a constant percentage rate. (849)

Export subsidy Payment by the government to exporters to permit them to reduce the selling price of their goods so they can compete more effectively in foreign markets. (394)

Externality, beneficial Result of an activity that causes incidental benefits to others with no corresponding compensation provided to or paid by those who generate the externality. (634)

Externality, detrimental Result of an activity that causes damages to others with no corresponding compensation provided to or paid by those who generate the externality. (634)

Federal Open Market Committee (FOMC) Chief policymaking committee of the Federal Reserve System. (271)

Federal Reserve System The central bank of the United States. (269)

Fiat money Money decreed as such by the government. It has little value as a commodity, but it maintains its value as a medium of exchange because people believe the issuer will back it and limit its production. (252)

Final goods and services Those that are purchased by their ultimate users. (79)

Fiscal federalism The system of grants from one level of government to the next. (725)

Fiscal policy The government's plan for spending and taxation, designed to direct aggregate demand in a desired direction. (221)

Fixed cost Cost of the indivisible inputs which the firm needs to produce any output at all. The total cost of these inputs does not change when output changes. (506)

Food Stamps Transfer program under which poor families receive coupons which they can exchange for food. (838)

A 45° line A ray through the origin with a slope of + 1. It marks off points where the variables measured on each axis have equal values, assuming that both variables are measured in the same units. (23)

Fractional reserve banking A system under which bankers keep in their vaults as reserves only a fraction of the funds they hold on deposit. (256)

Frictional unemployment Unemployment resulting from the normal workings of the labor market. Includes people who are temporarily between jobs because they are moving or changing occupations, or for similar reasons. (95)

Game theory Analyzes the behavior of competing firms mathematically, treating this as analogous to the strategies of rival players in a competitive game. (622)

Gold-exchange system (Bretton Woods system) International monetary system that prevailed from 1944 to 1971. Under this system, the United States fixed the value of the dollar in terms of gold, and other countries fixed the values of their currencies in terms of the dollar. (421)

Gold standard System in which exchange rates are set in terms of gold and pegged by buying or selling gold as necessary. (420)

Government purchases Symbolized by the Letter G, all the goods and services purchased by all levels of government. Transfer payments, such as social security and unemployment benefits, are not included. (139)

Gross national product (GNP) The sum of the money values of all final goods and services produced by the economy during a specified period, usually one year. (78, 158)

Gross national product, nominal Calculated by valuing all outputs at current prices. (79)

Gross national product, real The sum of the real values of all final goods and services produced by the economy during a specified period, using the prices that prevailed in some agreed-upon year (currently 1982). (79)

Gross national product deflator Price index obtained by dividing nominal GNP by real GNP. (114)

Growth, disembodied Refers to increases in an economy's output which can occur without being accompanied by (embodied in) additional capital stock. (853)

Growth, embodied Refers to increases in an economy's output which are made possible by increased or improved plant, equipment, or other forms of capital. (853)

High-employment budget Hypothetical budget the United States *would have* if the economy were operating near full employment. (328)

Historical materialism Marx's theory that we cannot understand an economy without recognizing its place in history. Also, while historical events are influenced primarily (though not exclusively) by economic conditions, the form of this influence is often indirect and subtle, filtering through current social customs, political organizations, and similar structures. (872)

Horizontal equity The notion that equally situated persons should be taxed equally. (725)

Human capital theory Interprets education as an investment in a human being's earning power, just as an improvement in a factory is an investment in the factory's earning capacity. (801)

Incidence of a tax An allocation of the burden of the tax to specific individuals or groups. (728)

Income effect A portion of the change in quantity of a good demanded when its price changes. A rise in price cuts the consumer's purchasing power (real income), which leads to a change in the quantity demanded of that commodity. That change is the income effect. (465)

Income-expenditure diagram (45° line diagram) A plotting of total real expenditures (on the vertical axis) against real income (on the horizontal axis). The 45° line marks off points where income and expenditure are equal. (173)

Incomes policy Variety of measures to curb inflation *without* reducing aggregate demand. (369)

Increasing costs, principle of As the production of a good expands, the opportunity cost of producing another such unit generally increases. (39)

Indexing Provisions in a law or contract whereby monetary payments are automatically adjusted whenever a specified price index changes; sometimes called *escalator clauses*. (374)

Index number A number indicating the percentage change in some variable (such as the price level) between the base period and some other period. Typically, the value of the index number in the base period is arbitrarily set to 100. (112)

Indicative planning Government guidance rather than direct control of economic activity. (895)

Indifference curve Line connecting all combinations of commodities that are equally desirable to the consumer. (471)

Indirect taxes Taxes levied on specific economic activities. (718)

Induced increase in consumption An increase in consumer spending that stems from an increase in consumer incomes. Represented graphically as a movement along a fixed consumption function. (190)

Induced investment Investment which rises when GNP rises and falls when GNP falls. (171)

Industrial union Represents all types of workers in a single industry. (808)

Inferior good A commodity whose quantity demanded falls when the purchaser's real income rises, all other things remaining equal. (465)

Inflation A sustained increase in the general price level. (77)

Inflation, creeping An inflation that proceeds for a long time at a moderate and fairly steady pace. (109)

Inflation, galloping An inflation that proceeds at an exceptionally high rate, perhaps for only a relatively brief period. This type of inflation is generally characterized by accelerating inflation rates, so that the inflation rate is higher this month than last month. (109)

Inflation accounting Adjusting standard accounting procedures for the fact that inflation lowers the purchasing power of money. (326)

Inflationary gap The amount by which equilibrium real GNP exceeds the full-employment level of GNP. (176)

Innovation The act of putting a new idea into practical use. (788)

Input Any item which a firm uses in its production process. (501)

Interest Payment for the use of funds employed in the production of capital; measured as a percent per year of the value of the funds tied up in the capital. (775)

Intermediate good One that is bought for resale or for use in producing another good. (79)

International Monetary Fund (IMF) International organization set up originally to police and manage the gold-exchange system. (421)

Invention The act of generating a new idea. (788)

Investment Flow of resources into the production of new capital. (774)

Investment, gross private domestic Sum of business investment expenditures on plant and equipment, residential construction expenditures, and inventory change. (158)

Investment schedule Table or curve showing how investment spending depends on GNP. (171)

Investment spending Symbolized by the letter *I*, the sum of the expenditures of business firms on new plant and equipment, plus the expenditures of households on new homes. Financial investments and resales of existing physical assets are not included. (139)

J curve A curve that shows the typical pattern of response of net exports to a change in currency values. (440)

Jawboning Informal pressures on firms and unions to slow down the rates at which prices and wages are rising. (369)

Labor force The number of people seeking jobs. (94)

Labor productivity A measure of total output divided by the amount of labor used to produce it. It is a measure of output per unit of labor employed. (120)

Laissez faire A program of minimal interference with the workings of the market system. (582)

Leading indicator A variable that, experience has shown, normally turns down before recessions start and turns up before expansions begin. (311)

Less developed countries (LDCs) Countries whose share of output composed of agricultural products, mining, and the like is relatively high, which engage in relatively little industrial high-technology activity, and whose per capita incomes are generally comparatively low. (856)

Liability An item that an individual or a firm owes; collectively, liabilities are known as *debts*. (258)

Liability, limited Legal obligation of a firm's owners to pay back company debts only with the money they have already invested in the firm. (656)

Liability, unlimited Legal obligation of a firm's owners to repay company debts with whatever resources they own. (654)

Libertarianism School of thought that emphasizes the importance of individual freedom. (911)

Limited partnership A firm, generally small, which though organized as a partnership, gives some of the partners the legal protection of limited liability. (658)

Liquidity, of an asset The ease with which it can be converted into cash. (255)

Long run Period of time long enough for all the firm's commitments to come to an end. (511)

Loophole, tax Special provision in the tax code that reduces taxation below normal rates (perhaps to zero) if certain conditions are met. (720)

Lorenz curve Graph depicting the distribution of income. (828)

M1 The narrowly defined money supply, which is the sum of all coins and paper money in circulation, plus certain checkable deposit balances at banks and savings institutions. (254)

M2 The broadly defined money supply, which is the sum of all coins and paper money in circulation, plus all types of checking account balances, most forms of savings account balances, shares in money market mutual funds, and a few other minor items. (255)

Macroeconomics The study of the behavior of economies. (75)

Marginal cost, long-run *Addition* to the supplier's total cost resulting from the supply of the output *including whatever additional plant and equipment* is needed in the long run to provide that output. Inclusion of this marginal capital cost (of the necessary additions to plant and equipment) is the crucial distinction between *long-run* and *short-run* marginal cost. (684)

Marginal cost curve Shows, for each output, the increase in the firm's total cost required if it increases its output by an additional unit. (505)

Marginal land Land that is just on the borderline of being used. (781)

Marginal physical product (MPP) Increase in total output that results from a one-unit increase in the input, holding the amounts of all other inputs constant. (502, 771)

Marginal profit The addition to total profit resulting from one more unit of output. (540)

Marginal propensity to consume (MPC) Ratio of the change in consumption to the change in disposable income that produces the change in consumption. On a graph, it appears as the slope of the consumption function. (148)

Marginal propensity to save (MPS) Graphically, the slope of the saving function, which indicates how much more consumers will save if disposable income rises by $1 billion. (156)

Marginal returns, law of diminishing To an input, X, asserts that if the quantities of all other inputs are held constant, the employment of additional quantities of X by a firm or an industry will eventually yield smaller and smaller (marginal) increases in output. (504)

Marginal revenue (MR) The addition to total revenue resulting from the addition of one unit to total output. (537)

Marginal revenue product (MRP) Additional revenue earned from increased sales of an input when an additional unit of the input is used. (514, 771)

Marginal social cost (MSC) The sum of *marginal private cost (MPC)*, which is the share of marginal cost caused by an activity that is paid for by the persons who carry out the activity, and *incidental cost*, which is the share borne by others. (635)

Marginal utility, law of diminishing Asserts that additional units of a commodity are worth less and less to a consumer in money terms. As the individual's consumption increases, the marginal utility of each additional unit declines. (460)

Market The set of all sale and purchase transactions that affect the price of some commodity. (557)

Market demand curve Shows how the total quantity demanded of some product during a specified period of time changes as the price of the product changes, other things being constant. (478)

Market power The ability of a firm to raise its price significantly above the competitive price level and to maintain this high price profitably for a considerable period. (712)

Market system A form of organization of the economy in which decisions on resource allocation are left to the independent decisions of individual producers and consumers acting in their own best interests without central direction. (46)

Maximin criterion Selecting the strategy that yields the maximum payoff, on the assumption that your opponent does as much damage to you as he can. (625)

Mediation Process in which an outsider is brought into a labor management negotiation in the hope that this person can lead the two sides to a voluntary agreement through persuasion. (814)

Merger The combining of two previously independent firms under a single owner or group of owners. A **horizontal merger** involves two firms producing similar products. A **vertical merger** involves two firms one of which supplies an ingredient of the other's product. A **conglomerate merger** is the union of two unrelated firms. (705)

Microeconomics The study of the behavior of individual decision-making units, such as farmers or consumers. (74)

Minimum-wage law Requires all employees (with some specified exceptions) to be paid at least some fixed given dollar amount per hour. Congress has increased this minimum wage several times in the past. (795)

Monetarism Mode of analysis that uses the equation of exchange to organize macroeconomic data. (295)

Monetary policy Actions that the Federal Reserve System takes to change the equilibrium of the money market; that is, to alter the money supply, move interest rates, or both. (281)

Monetizing the deficit The effect of the central bank's purchasing the bonds the government issues. (332)

Money Medium of exchange; that is, the standard object used in exchanging goods and services. (251)

Money fixed asset Asset with a face value fixed in terms of dollars, such as money, government bonds, and corporate bonds. (150)

Monopolistic competition Competition among firms each of which has products that are somewhat different from those of its rivals. (612)

Monopoly, pure Industry in which there is only one supplier of a product for which there are no close substitutes, and in which it is difficult or impossible for another firm to coexist. (598)

Monopsony Market situation in which there is only one buyer. (812)

Moral hazard Tendency of insurance to encourage risk taking. (647)

Moral suasion Informal requests and warnings designed to persuade banks to limit their borrowings from the Fed. (277)

Multinational corporations Corporations whose production activities occur in a number of different countries. (861)

The multiplier The ratio of the change in equilibrium GNP (Y) divided by the original change in spending that causes the change in GNP. (184)

National debt Federal government's total indebtedness, which has resulted from previous deficits. (322)

National income The sum of the incomes of all individuals in the economy earned in the forms of wages, interest, rents, and profits. It excludes transfer payments and is calculated before any deductions are taken for income taxes. (140)

National income accounting Bookkeeping and measurement system for national economic data. (157)

Nationalization Government ownership and operation of a business firm. (695)

National product The total production of a nation's economy. (75)

Natural monopoly Industry in which advantages of large-scale production make it possible for a single firm to produce the entire output of the market at lower average cost than a number of firms each producing a smaller quantity. (599)

Natural rate of unemployment The unemployment rate when the economy is at "full employment." (356)

Near moneys Liquid assets that are close substitutes for money. (255)

Negative income tax Transfer program under which families with income below a certain threshold (the "breakeven level") would receive cash benefits from the government; these benefits would decline as income rose. (838)

Net exports Exports minus imports. (139)

Net national product (NNP) Gross national product minus depreciation. (160)

Net worth The value of all assets minus the value of all liabilities. (258)

Oligopoly Market dominated by a few sellers, at least several of which are large enough relative to the total market to be able to influence the market price. (617)

Open-market operations The Fed's purchase or sale of government securities through transactions in the open market. (272)

Open economy An economy that trades with other nations in goods and services. (432)

Opportunity cost The foregone value of the next best alternative that is not chosen. (36)

Origin The lower left-hand corner of a graph where the two axes meet. In two-variable diagrams, both variables equal zero at the origin. (19)

Output The good or service that a firm produces. (501)

Paradox of thrift The fact that an effort by a nation to save more may simply reduce national income and fail to raise total savings. (192)

Partnership A firm whose ownership is shared by a fixed number of proprietors. (655)

Patent A temporary grant of monopoly rights over an innovation. (711)

Perfectly contestable market One in which entry and exit are costless and unimpeded. (629)

Personal income A measure of income derived by subtracting corporate profits, retained earnings, and payroll taxes from national income, then adding in transfer payments. Personal income measures the income that actually accrues to individuals. (163)

Phillips curve Graph depicting the rate of unemployment on the horizontal axis and either the rate of inflation or the rate of change of money wages on the vertical axis; normally downward sloping, indicating that higher inflation rates are associated with lower unemployment rates. (351)

Phillips curve, vertical (long run) Shows the menu of inflation/unemployment choices available to society in the long run; a vertical straight line at the natural rate of unemployment. (356)

Potential gross national product The real GNP the economy would produce if its labor and other resources were fully employed. (99)

Poverty line Amount of income below which a family is considered "poor." (824)

Price ceiling Legal maximum price that can be charged. (64)

Price discrimination Charging different prices to different buyers of the same product. (703)

Price floor Legal minimum price that can be charged. (66)

Price leadership One firm sets the price for the industry and the others follow. (620)

Price war A situation in which each competing firm is determined to sell at a price that is lower than the price of its rivals, usually regardless of whether that price covers the pertinent cost. (621)

Private good Commodity or service whose benefits are depleted by an additional user and for which people are excluded from its benefits. (639)

Production function The *maximum* amount of product that can be obtained from any specified *combination* of inputs, given the current state of knowledge. (515)

Production indifference curve (sometimes called an *isoquant*), a curve in a graph showing quantities of *inputs* on its axes. Each indifference curve indicates *all* combinations of input quantities capable of producing *a given* quantity of output. (526)

Production possibilities frontier A graphical presentation of the different combinations of various goods that a producer can turn out, given the available resources and existing technology. (38)

Productivity The amount of output produced by a unit of input. (201)

Profit sharing A system of compensating labor in which workers receive both a fixed base wage and a share of the company's profits. (373)

Progressive tax One in which the average tax rate paid by an individual rises as his income rises. (718)

Property tax Tax on assessed value of real property. (724)

Proportional tax One in which the average tax rate is the same at all income levels. (718)

Proprietorship Business firm owned by a single person. (654)

Public good Commodity or service whose benefits are *not depleted* by an additional user and for which it is generally difficult or *impossible to exclude* people from its benefits, even if they are unwilling to pay for it. (639)

Purchasing power The purchasing power of a given sum of money is the volume of goods and services it will buy. (100)

Purchasing-power parity theory (of exchange rates) Theory that the exchange rate between any two national currencies adjusts to reflect differences in the price levels of the two nations. (411)

Quantity demanded The number of units consumers want to buy. (52)

Quantity supplied The number of units sellers want to sell. (54)

Quantity theory of money A simple theory of aggregate demand based on the idea that velocity is constant, so that norminal GNP is proportional to the money stock. (291)

Quota Specifies the maximum amount of a good that is permitted into the country from abroad per unit of time. (394)

Random walk The time path of a variable, such as the price of a stock, when its magnitude in one period equals its value in the preceding period plus a completely random number. (672)

Rate of interest, nominal The percentage by which the money the borrower pays back exceeds the money that he borrowed, making no adjustment for any fall in the purchasing power of this money that results from inflation. (105)

Rate of interest, real The percentage increase in purchasing power that the borrower pays to the lender for the privilege of borrowing. It indicates the increased ability to purchase goods and services that the lender earns. (105)

Rational decision A decision that best serves the objective of the decision maker, whatever the objective may be. The term "rational" connotes neither approval nor disapproval of the objective. (36)

Rational expectations Forecasts which, while not necessarily correct, are the best that can be made given the available data. If expectations are rational, forecasting errors are pure random numbers. (363)

Ray through the origin (or ray) A straight line emanating from the origin, or zero point on a graph. (23)

Recession A period during which the total output of the economy declines. (78)

Recessionary gap The amount by which the equilibrium level of real GNP falls short of potential GNP. (176)

Regressive tax One in which the average tax rate falls as income rises. (718)

Relative price The price of an item in terms of some other item rather than in terms of dollars. (102)

Regulation of industry A process established by law which restricts or controls some specified decisions made by the affected firms. (676)

Rent seeking Unproductive activity in the pursuit of profit. (646)

Required reserves The minimum amount of reserves (in cash or the equivalent) required by law. Required reserves are usually proportional to the volume of deposits. (258)

Resources The instruments provided by nature or by people that are used to create the goods and services people want. (35)

Research and Development (R and D) The activity of business firms in which systematic efforts are undertaken to invent new or improved products or productive techniques and to make them ready to market or for use in production processes. (127)

Retained earnings (plowback) The portion of a corporation's profits that management decides to keep and reinvest in the firm's operations rather than pay out directly to stockholders in the form of dividends. (659)

Revaluation Increase in the official value of a currency. (409)

Run on a bank An event that occurs when many depositors withdraw cash from their accounts almost simultaneously. (249)

Sales maximizing firm One whose objective is to sell as much of its outputs as possible (measured in terms of the revenue they bring in) rather than to maximize the company's product. (621)

Saving function The schedule relating total consumer saving to disposable income in the economy, holding other determinants of saving constant. (156)

Saving schedule Table or curve showing how saving depends on GNP. (173)

Scatter diagram Graph showing the relationship between two variables. Each year is represented by a point in the diagram. The coordinates of each year's point show the value of the two variables in that year. (145)

Self-correcting mechanism The economy's way of curing inflationary or recessionary gaps automatically via inflation or deflation. (327)

Seniority rules Rules which give special job-related advantages to workers who have held their jobs longest. (809)

Service industry One that does not turn out physical products. (128)

Shortage An excess of quantity demanded over quantity supplied. When a shortage exists, buyers cannot purchase the quantities they want. (57)

Short run A shorter period of time than the long run so that some, but not all, of the firm's commitments will have ended. (511)

Slope of a budget line Amount of one commodity the market requires an individual to give up in order to obtain one additional unit of another commodity without any change in the amount of money spent. (473)

Slope of a curved line At any particular point, the slope of the straight line that is tangent to the curved line at that point. (21)

Slope of an indifference curve Referred to as the marginal rate of substitution between the commodities involved, represents the maximum amount of one commodity the consumer is willing to give up in exchange for one more unit of another commodity. (473)

Slope of a straight line The ratio of the vertical change to the corresponding horizontal change as we move to the right along the line. The ratio of the "rise" over the "run." (20)

Socialism Method of economic organization in which the state owns the means of production. (887)

Specialization The process whereby a worker becomes more skilled at a particular job. Specialization enables division of labor and the consequent increase in productivity. (382)

Speculation Investment in risky assets in the hope of obtaining a profit from unexpected changes in the prices of these assets. (669)

Stabilization policy The name given to government programs designed to prevent or shorten recessions and to counteract inflation (that is, to stabilize prices). (88)

Stagflation Inflation that occurs while

the economy is growing slowly ("stagnating") or having a recession. (86)

Store of value An item used to store wealth from one point in time to another. (251)

Structural unemployment Refers to workers who have lost their jobs because they have been displaced by automation, because their skills are no longer in demand, or for similar reasons. (95)

Subchapter S corporation A small corporation which is permitted to escape part of the burden of double taxation. (658)

Substitutes Refers to two goods if an increase in the price of one raises the quantity demanded of the other, all other things remaining constant. (491)

Substitution effect Change in quantity demanded of a good resulting from a change in its relative price, exclusive of whatever change in quantity demanded may be attributable to the associated change in real income. (465)

Sunk cost A cost to which a firm is precommited for some limited period, either because the firm has signed a contract to make the payments or because the firm has already paid for some durable item and cannot get its money back except by using that item to produce output for some period of time. (511)

Supply curve A graph showing how the quantity supplied of some product during a specified period of time changes as the price of that product changes, holding all other determinants of quantity supplied constant. (55)

Supply-demand diagram Diagram showing both a supply curve and a demand curve. (56)

Supply schedule A table showing how the quantity supplied of some product during a specified period of time changes as the price of that product changes, holding all other determinants of quantity supplied constant. (55)

Surplus An excess of quantity supplied over quantity demanded. When there is a surplus, sellers cannot sell the quantities they want to supply. (57)

Surplus, balance of payment Amount by which the quantity demanded of a country's currency (per year) exceeds the quantity supplied. Such surpluses arise when the exchange rate is artifically low. (416)

Tariff Tax on imports. (394)

Tax-based incomes policy An incomes policy that uses the tax system to provide incentives favoring noninflationary behavior. (373)

Tax deduction A sum of money that may be subtracted before the taxpayer computes his or her taxable income. (720)

Tax rate, average Ratio of taxes to income. (718)

Tax rate, marginal Fraction of each *additional* dollar of income that is paid in taxes. (718)

Tax shifting Occurs when the economic reactions to a tax cause prices and outputs in the economy to change, thereby shifting part of the burden of the tax onto others. (729)

Technostructure Professionals who, according to Galbraith, run most of the important economic institutions, including corporations, government bureaus, and large unions. (916)

Theory A deliberate simplification of relationships whose purpose is to explain how those relationships work. (13)

Time series graph A type of two-variable diagram that depicts the change in a variable over time. The horizontal axis always represents time. (25)

Total cost curve Shows, for each possible quantity of output, the total amount which the firm must spend for its inputs to produce that amount of output plus any opportunity cost incurred in the process. (505)

Total physical product (TPP) curve A curve that shows what happens to the quantity of a firm's output as one changes the quantity of one of the firm's inputs while holding the quantities of all other inputs unchanged. (501)

Trade adjustment assistance Provides special unemployment benefits, loans, retraining programs, and other aid to workers and firms that are harmed by foreign competition. (399)

Transfer payments Sums of money that certain individuals receive as outright grants from the government rather than as payments for services rendered to employers. (141)

Unemployment insurance Government program under which some, but not all, employed workers receive transfer payments. (97)

Unemployment rate The number of unemployed people, expressed as a percentage of the labor force. (94)

Union shop An arrangement under which nonunion workers may be hired but then must join the union within a specified period of time. (808)

Unit of account The standard unit for quoting prices. (251)

Usury law Establishes a maximum permissible interest rate for a particular type of loan. Loans at rates above the usury ceiling are illegal. (106)

Utility, marginal Of a commodity to a consumer (measured in money terms) is the maximum amount of money he or she is willing to pay for *one more unit* of it. (460)

Utility, total Of a quantity of goods to a consumer (measured in money terms) is the maximum amount of money he or she is willing to give in exchange for it. (459)

Value added The value added by a company is its revenue from selling a product minus the amount paid for goods and services purchased from other firms. (161)

Variable An object, such as price, whose magnitude is measured by a number. (18)

Variable cost Any cost that is not a fixed cost. (506)

Velocity Number of times per year that an "average dollar" is spent on goods and services; the ratio of nominal GNP to the number of dollars in the money stock. (291)

Vertical equity The notion that differently situated persons should be taxed differently in a way that society deems fair. (726)

Wage-price controls Legal restrictions on the ability of industry and labor to raise wages and prices. (371)

Wage-price freeze An outright ban on wage or price increases. (373)

Wage-price guideposts Numerical standards for permissible wage and price increases. (370)

Wage rate, real The wage rate adjusted for inflation. It indicates the volume of goods and services that money wages will buy. (100)

Welfare state A variety of government programs aimed at assisting the poor and protecting individuals from the rigors of the marketplace. (894)

Workers' management System under which employees of an enterprise make most of the decisions normally reserved for management. (897)

Index

C D E F G H I J   9 0 1 2 3 4 5 6

SELECTED U.S. MACROECONOMIC DATA, QUARTERLY 1978–1987

Year	Gross National Product	Personal Consumption Expenditure	Gross Private Domestic Investment	Government Purchases	Net Exports	Gross National Product	Personal Consumption Expenditure	Gross Private Domestic Investment	Government Purchases	Net Exports	Potential GNP*
	(in billions of dollars)					(in billions of 1982 dollars)					
1978:1	2111.4	1332.6	379.7	405.6	−6.6	3020.5	1923.0	544.0	592.5	−39.0	3071.1
1978:2	2230.3	1391.1	420.2	417.6	1.3	3115.9	1960.8	584.6	601.3	−30.7	3093.4
1978:3	2289.5	1424.6	424.7	433.4	6.8	3142.6	1970.3	583.3	611.5	−22.4	3115.9
1978:4	2367.6	1465.7	442.7	444.2	15.0	3181.6	1989.7	595.8	611.1	−15.1	3138.5
1979:1	2420.5	1501.8	446.9	449.2	22.7	3181.7	1997.5	582.2	606.7	−4.8	3161.3
1979:2	2474.5	1537.6	463.2	458.6	15.2	3178.7	1994.1	590.1	606.9	−12.4	3184.3
1979:3	2546.1	1590.0	461.5	472.8	21.8	3207.4	2007.9	575.7	611.3	12.5	3207.4
1979:4	2591.5	1637.5	447.8	490.7	15.4	3201.3	2018.0	552.9	611.7	18.7	3228.3
1980:1	2673.0	1682.2	461.0	509.1	20.7	3233.4	2015.4	556.7	617.8	43.5	3249.4
1980:2	2672.2	1688.9	425.0	528.2	30.1	3157.0	1974.1	499.2	625.1	58.6	3270.6
1980:3	2734.0	1749.3	405.4	532.6	46.8	3159.1	1996.3	467.7	621.1	74.1	3291.9
1980:4	2848.6	1810.0	456.4	551.4	30.8	3199.2	2015.6	513.5	617.9	52.2	3313.4
1981:1	2978.8	1862.9	506.9	570.1	38.9	3261.1	2022.9	552.3	626.3	59.7	3335.0
1981:2	3017.7	1896.4	515.3	577.0	29.0	3250.2	2022.4	551.2	626.4	50.2	3356.7
1981:3	3099.6	1940.9	535.9	591.9	30.9	3264.6	2031.5	560.7	630.2	42.1	3378.6
1981:4	3114.4	1960.2	504.0	613.3	36.9	3219.0	2020.0	517.9	635.9	45.3	3400.6
1982:1	3112.6	1996.3	459.5	622.1	34.7	3170.4	2031.2	464.2	634.6	40.4	3422.8
1982:2	3159.5	2023.8	467.8	625.7	42.1	3179.9	2041.0	467.5	629.7	41.7	3445.1
1982:3	3179.4	2065.6	452.2	647.1	14.5	3154.5	2051.8	448.6	642.5	11.7	3467.6
1982:4	3212.5	2117.0	409.6	671.8	14.1	3159.3	2078.7	408.8	660.1	11.7	3490.2
1983:1	3265.8	2146.6	428.3	668.1	22.8	3186.6	2094.2	427.1	649.2	16.1	3513.0
1983:2	3367.4	2213.0	481.3	675.2	−2.1	3258.3	2135.1	486.9	650.9	−14.6	3535.9
1983:3	3443.9	2262.8	519.7	680.7	−19.3	3306.4	2163.0	524.8	653.6	−35.0	3558.9
1983:4	3545.8	2315.8	579.8	676.1	−25.8	3365.1	2191.9	577.2	642.2	−46.2	3582.1
1984:1	3674.9	2361.1	663.0	696.5	−45.7	3451.7	2212.1	655.2	653.0	−68.6	3605.5
1984:2	3754.2	2417.0	664.2	735.8	−62.8	3498.0	2246.7	658.4	680.2	−87.3	3629.0
1984:3	3807.9	2450.3	670.3	746.6	−59.3	3520.6	2257.3	664.2	684.5	−85.5	3652.7
1984:4	3851.8	2493.4	661.8	764.5	−67.9	3535.2	2281.1	655.7	693.2	−94.8	3676.5
1985:1	3921.1	2549.9	638.6	784.1	−51.5	3568.7	2314.1	632.1	703.4	−81.0	3700.5
1985:2	3973.6	2602.0	648.4	800.5	−77.3	3587.1	2337.0	645.7	712.1	−107.7	3724.6
1985:3	4042.0	2665.4	628.6	832.8	−84.7	3623.0	2376.1	623.2	738.6	−114.9	3748.9
1985:4	4104.4	2700.1	650.8	857.0	−103.5	3650.9	2383.2	643.3	753.7	−129.3	3773.3
1986:1	4174.4	2737.9	683.4	846.9	−93.8	3698.8	2409.7	674.4	737.6	−123.0	3797.9
1986:2	4211.6	2765.8	679.4	867.2	−100.8	3704.7	2434.3	665.6	751.6	−146.8	3822.7
1986:3	4265.9	2837.1	660.8	878.5	−110.5	3718.0	2477.5	645.0	757.2	−161.6	3847.7
1986:4	4288.1	2858.6	660.2	886.3	−116.9	3731.5	2480.5	631.0	771.8	−151.8	3872.8
1987:1	4377.7	2893.8	699.9	896.2	−112.2	3772.2	2475.9	671.8	759.6	−135.2	3898.1
1987:2	4447.7	2947.3	700.9	918.2	−118.6	3793.7	2489.0	670.5	767.5	−133.3	3923.5

*From Robert J. Gordon, *Macroeconomics*, fourth edition (Boston: Little, Brown, 1987), Table B-1. Reprinted by permission. Updated by authors.
SOURCES: U.S. Department of Commerce, Bureau of Labor Statistics, Federal Reserve System, and Professor R. J. Gordon.